PIMLICO

786

THAT SWEET ENEMY

'War, diplomacy and politics, treaties, revolutions and rebellions naturally enough crowd the pages of this magnificent book, which teems with life and incident.' *New Statesman*

'Absolutely wonderful – revelatory.' Nick Ross, *Guardian*

'Robert and Isabelle Tombs have startling and insightful things to say about the lives of exiles, sports, food, literature and cross-pollination in countless other fields... and even those who think they know everything about either country will relish it.' *Times Literary Supplement*

'Crisply written, fact-packed, caricature-illustrated, a hugely entertaining history of the relationship between Britain and France... Robert and Isabelle Tombs... successfully demonstrate how the relationship between Britain and France has shaped the modern world.' *Glasgow Herald*

'An exemplary incarnation of entente cordiale or adversarial co-existence... The *War and Peace* of Franco-British relations.' Andy Martin, *Independent*

'Superbly researched, beautifully written... scholarly and hugely readable.' Andrew Roberts, *Sunday Times*

'Deftly written and meticulously researched... It is striking to learn just how long ago national stereotypes were formed and for how long they have endured... Packed with detail and anecdote.' John Thornhill, *Financial Times*

'A book combining wit and scholarship... For all the brickbats, as Mr and Mrs Tombs delightfully demonstrate, there is a deep undercurrent of affection... *That Sweet Enemy* captures the strange, enduring ambivalence at the heart of the relationship.' Ben Macintyre, *The Times*

'Well-written and thoroughly researched... A satisfying and intelligent book, packed with information and provoking in its assertions and conclusions' Simon Heffer, *Daily Telegraph*

'Lucid and compelling... From Louis XIV and the struggle for continental hegemony, through the American, French and Industrial Revolutions, to the two World Wars and the new struggle for continental hegemony embodied in the development of European unity, Robert and Isabelle Tombs have produced a major work of historical analysis, written in a deceptively accessible style.' Judith Flanders, *Spectator*

'A model of lucid and dispassionate exposition... Even handed and judicious... Rich in detail... Fascinating.' Allan Massie, *Literary Review*

'A well-written, aptly-illustrated, and interesting book... full of fascination.' *BBC History Magazine*

'Monumental... The canvas is vast and the bones of contention innumerable... The detail and erudition are impressive and many clichés and misconceptions are laid to rest.' *Tablet*

THAT SWEET ENEMY

The French and the British from the
Sun King to the Present

ROBERT and ISABELLE TOMBS

PIMLICO

Published by Pimlico 2007

4 6 8 10 9 7 5

First published in Great Britain in 2006 by
William Heinemann

Pimlico edition 2007

Pimlico
Random House, 20 Vauxhall Bridge Road,
London SW1V 2SA

www.randomhouse.co.uk

Addresses for companies within The Random House Group Limited can be found at:
www.randomhouse.co.uk

Maps and diagrams copyright © ML Design, 2006

The Random House Group Limited Reg. No. 954009

A CIP catalogue record for this book
is available from the British Library

ISBN 9781845951085

The Random House Group Limited makes every effort to ensure that the papers used in its books are made from trees that have been legally sourced from well-managed and credibly certified forests. Our paper procurement policy can be found at: www.randomhouse.co.uk/paper.htm

Printed and bound in Great Britain by
Mackays of Chatham plc, Chatham, Kent

To our late fathers, Denis and Joseph: once comrades in arms
without knowing it.

To our mothers, Kathleen and Yvonne,
who ignore the Channel.

Having this day my horse, my hand, my lance
Guided so well, that I obtained the prize,
Both by the judgment of the English eyes,
And of some sent from that sweet enemy, France;
Horsemen my skill in horsemanship advance,
Town folk my strength; a daintier judge applies
His praise to sleight, which from good use doth rise;
Some lucky wits impute it but to chance;
Others, because from both sides I do take
My blood from them that do excel in this,
Think Nature me a man at arms did make.
How far they shoot awry! the true cause is,
    Stella looked on, and from her heavenly face
    Sent forth her beams, which made so fair a race.

Sir Philip Sidney, *Astrophel and Stella*, Sonnet XLI, 1591

Contents

List of Illustrations

List of Maps

List of Figures

Acknowledgements

Documents from the Royal Archives are quoted by gracious permission of Her Majesty the Queen.

The generosity of the Leverhulme Trust made possible an indispensable year's sabbatical leave, which colleagues in the History Faculty and St John's College, Cambridge, kindly supported.

One of the great pleasures of writing this book has been the number not only of friends, colleagues and acquaintances, but of people we have never met, who have given generously of their advice, knowledge and time. Our greatest thanks go to those who have been willing to read and comment in detail on substantial extracts: David A. Bell, Steven Englund, M.R.D. Foot, Iain Hamilton, Robin Harris, Dick Holt, John Keiger, Charles-Edouard Levillain, John Morrill, Helen Parr (who also allowed us a preview of her recent book), Simon Prince, Jean-Louis Six, John Ranelagh, Dennis Showalter, and three fellows of St John's, Sylvana Tomaselli, Bee Wilson and John Harris.

We are particularly grateful to present and former students, mostly from Cambridge, who have kindly allowed us to refer to their unpublished work – namely Katy Caie, Philippe Chalon, Marion Lenoir, Katie Watt and David Young de la Marck – or who have provided items of expert information, including Edward Castleton, Emmanuelle Hériard-Dubreuil, Sarah Howard, Katsura Miyahara, Siau Yin Goh and Kiva Silver. Special thanks to Katrina Gulliver for assembling the bibliography.

Working in the college of Wordsworth, Castlereagh, Wilberforce, Palmerston and Matthew Prior (and more obscurely, of James Dawson, hanged, drawn and quartered for participation in the 1745 rebellion), where a French queen was betrothed and the D-Day landings were partly planned, has been a constant and pleasant reminder of how dense is the web of cross-Channel connections. Fellows, graduate students and undergraduates in a variety of disciplines have been on tap – sometimes without realizing it – to provide instant expertise across the dining table, in particular Victoria Argyle, Jack Goody, Susie Grant, John Iliffe, Joe McDermott, Richard Nolan, Mary

Sarotte, Simon Szreter, George Watson and Marcus Werner. We often felt that nowhere but in Cambridge could this book have been prepared so easily, and for that, generations of librarians deserve our gratitude.

Many others – scholars, participants in events, occasionally both – have patiently answered questions, allowed us previews of forthcoming work, checked snippets of text, or kindly supplied (even volunteered!) information. They include Martin Alexander, Christopher Andrew, Lucy Ash, Simon Atkinson, Stéphane Audoin-Rouzeau, Christina de Bellaigue, Tom Bartlett, Annette Becker, Jeremy Black, Tim Blanning, Roy Bridge, Tony Bohannon (grandson of a Communard refugee), Florence Bourillon, Simon Burrows, Betty Bury (who showed us papers belonging to the late Patrick Bury), Yvonne Bussy (a tireless voluntary press service, and Isabelle's mother), Corinne Chabert, June Charman, Chris Clark, Jonathan Conlin, Martyn Cornick, Martin Daunton, Philip Dine, Jack Douay, David Dutton, Graham Floater, Joëlle Garriaud-Maylam, Caroline Gomez, Björn Hagelin, David Heley, Rachel Hammersley, Jacques Herry (formerly of Leclerc's 2e Division Blindée), Boyd Hilton, John Horne, Hubertus Jahn, Keith Jeffery, Colin Jones, Jean-Marc Largeaud, John Leigh, Renaud Morieux, Patrick Minford, Bill Philpott, Patrice Porcheron, Jean de Préneuf, Munro Price, Emma Rothschild, Guy Rowlands, George St Andrews, Meg Sanders, Ruth Scurr, Jim Secord, Brendan Simms, Hew Strachan, Kirk Swinehart, Francis Tombs and Paul Vallet. Cécile, Bruno, Juliette and Charles kept us in touch with views from the école, the lycée, and the fac. Henry Woudhuysen casually suggested the title. Nicholas Garland generously permitted us to reproduce one of his cartoons.

To these and all others who gave help and encouragement we are sincerely grateful. We have benefited enormously from their help. All opinions expressed, and errors unspotted, are entirely ours.

We owe much to Bill Hamilton, Ravi Mirchandani, Caroline Knight and Amanda Russell for their unflagging encouragement and professional dynamism.

Chapters 13 and 14 were written by Robert Tombs, and the opinions expressed in them are his. No information in them was supplied by Isabelle Tombs through her employment at HM Foreign and Commonwealth Office.

Unless otherwise stated, all translations from French are ours.

Introduction

This is the story of an intense and troubled relationship: one of the most intense, most troubled, and most significant of modern times. When our story begins, the French and the British had already had a long and eventful history, and it was already the stuff of legend. The Norman Conquest began a close but fraught connection with the Continent, in which princes and nobles fought for power, wealth and glory throughout the islands and on the mainland, and laid early foundations of national pride, resentment and identity. The struggle peaked in the Hundred Years War (conventionally dated 1328–1453). Legends of cruelty and heroism were created on both sides: the Black Prince, the burghers of Calais, King Harry and the bowmen of Agincourt, the siege of Orleans, and above all the martyred Maid, Jeanne/Joan, burnt by the English in 1431. Her famous injunction to 'bouter les Anglais hors de France' ('kick the English out of France') was fulfilled in 1453 when the English crown lost its prized possession of Bordeaux (though it still bought the wine). Yet English rule came and went in parts of what is now French territory – Calais, Dunkirk, Corsica – for a long time yet. English and British monarchs continued to describe themselves as kings of France until Napoleon insisted they stop in 1802. Suspicions that they coveted bits of France lingered at least until the First World War. Even now, certain reefs in the Channel can arouse strong feelings. The Scots and the Irish, of course, had a very different relationship, acting on the risky principle that my enemy's enemy is my friend. The Franco-Scottish 'Auld Alliance' (first concluded in 1295) had a late and deadly flowering in the sixteenth century, in the reign of the half-French Mary, Queen of Scots. Though religious differences complicated matters, later French encouragement of Scottish and Irish resistance to English domination is a recurring element in the first part of this book.

For two centuries after the end of the Hundred Years War, Anglo–French relations mattered less for both sides. The internal and external conflicts caused by the religious turmoil of the Reformation created a new ideological and political world in which France and the British Isles acquired new enemies – variously Spain, Austria and the Dutch Republic. France and the islands were equally racked by bloody religious wars. After the peaceful restoration of Charles II in 1660, French culture gave the tone to London and its court. The three Stuart kingdoms, relatively small and with a newly reinstalled and financially weak monarchy, seemed likely to become satellites of the mighty France of Louis XIV, especially as they shared an enemy, the Dutch Republic. Events, however, took a different and momentous turn in 1688, creating a new era in British and French history, and indeed in that of the world. There our story will begin.

But already we have to pause a moment. We are going to talk about 'the French' and 'the British'. The idea of 'the French' seems to pose no problem. They know who they are, and so does everyone else. Yet the boundaries of France, and even the meanings of 'Frenchness', are not eternal. That Strasbourg is a French city, and that Brussels and Geneva are not; that Corsicans speak French rather than English; that the French are seen as urbane yet close to the soil, as rebellious and yet respectful of authority; that rugby has as many devotees in Lourdes as in Wigan; that *steack-frites* is the evocative national dish – all these characteristics, as we shall see in the following pages, owe much to contact with the peoples we will often refer to as 'the British'. This collective appellation is more of a problem. Some historians believe that the very idea of 'the British' was invented in order to fight the French. What were called 'The Three Kingdoms' (England and Wales, Scotland and Ireland) became in stages 'The United Kingdom' as a direct result of war with France. The fact that vast areas of 'British' territory in North America and most of the United Kingdom across the Irish Sea are not now British are also outcomes linked directly or indirectly with the French struggle. What then is the correct term for the lands and peoples north of the Channel? Some writers have suggested 'the Atlantic archipelago' or, rather coyly, 'these islands'. Contemporaries had a variety of terms, including using 'English' for everyone – a practice the French generally followed, and often still do. For practical reasons, and because we agree with a recent American historian that 'it is not always possible to choose the right adjective [because] there is not always a right adjective to choose',[1] we often use 'British' and 'French', without forgetting that in 1700, 1800, 1900 and 2000 both entities had different boundaries and included different peoples – including many who would have preferred not to belong. Yet this very complication is one sign of how formative the Franco–British relationship was.

This book is not a parallel or a comparative history of France and Britain. It covers only what arises from or affects their mutual contact. That is a great deal: wars, alliances, hatred, coexistence, envy, admiration, emulation – even, sometimes, love. Our account contains all the great historical events that we believe must be there. But we have also included things that we found intriguing, illuminating, or just funny – for this is a story of people, not just of states. We do not always agree, and have included some of our disagreements. We would be delighted if you, in reading this book, were sometimes as surprised, amused, exasperated and moved as we were in writing it.

PART I: STRUGGLE

On Guy Fawkes Day, 1688, Europe invaded England, in the shape of 20,000 Dutch, German, Danish, French, Swedish, Finnish (in bearskins,) Polish, Greek and Swiss troops. They came in 500 ships – a fleet more than twice the size of the Spanish Armada that had failed to invade a century before, to the day. It would be the biggest seaborne invasion in European waters until D-Day. Landing at Torbay, the Dutch were shocked by the filthiness of the country but were amused to be welcomed with apples and cider and shouts of 'God Bless You!' They marched slowly but inexorably on London in what was to be the most transforming invasion – part conquest, part liberation – since 1066. The invaders' aim was to pull the Three Kingdoms of England, Ireland and Scotland into a European struggle to stem the spreading dominance of France. The improbable outcome of this struggle was to transform the weak, turbulent islands from 'European laughing stock to global great power'.[1] 'Britain' came into being, not only through the creation of the United Kingdom of Scotland and England in 1707, but by making the very concept of 'Britishness' meaningful to its inhabitants. The main cause and consequence of this transformation has been called 'the second hundred years war' – a Franco-British duel through six great wars between 1689 and 1815, which scorched the whole planet and left the two main participants utterly changed. France would find its dominance of Europe unexpectedly challenged and undermined, its role outside the Continent stubbornly countered and then destroyed, and eventually its state and society revolutionized. Little England was no more: the next three centuries would see unremitting efforts to 'punch above its weight', and make its will prevail in Europe and the wider world.

CHAPTER I

Britain Joins Europe

England is worth conquering, and whenever there is a probability of getting
it, it will surely be attempted. When the people are . . . weak, cowardly,
without discipline, poor, discontented, they are easily subdued; and this is
our condition . . . nothing can be added to render them an easy prey to a
foreigner unless a sense of their misery and hate of them that cause it make
them look on any invader as a deliverer.

ALGERNON SIDNEY, political writer [1]

A Nation which hath stood its ground, and kept its privileges and freedoms
for Hundreds of Years, is in less than a Third of a Century quite undone;
hath lavishly spent above 160 Millions in that time, made Hecatombs of
British Lives, stockjobb'd (*or cannonaded*) away its Trade, perverted and
then jested away its Honour, Law, and Justice.

Political pamphlet, 1719 [2]

In a Europe devastated by more than a century of ferocious religious conflicts, culminating in a Thirty Years War (1618–48) that had killed millions, France, emerging from its own internal conflicts in the 1650s, became the pre-eminent power by reason of its population, armed force, wealth and cultural influence. The embodiment of that power was Louis XIV, who acceded to the throne at the age of four in 1643 and reigned for seventy-two years. Of the fifty-four years when he effectively ruled, thirty-three were years of war. His life was dedicated to ensuring that the king dominated France – culturally and politically – and that France dominated Europe. This was a time when war and predation were normal conditions. The *métier de roi* – the king's job – was to direct these conflicts, burnishing his *gloire* and that of his dynasty and realm, whose prosperity and security were the prizes of his strength and cunning.

Louis XIV dominated Europe less by force of intellect or character – he was hard-working rather than brilliant – than by the length of his reign and his tireless devotion to promoting an image of majesty. Artists, writers, architects, musicians and priests were enrolled, to create (as Louis himself wrote) 'an extremely useful impression of magnificence, power, wealth and grandeur'. Versailles, practically complete by 1688, provided a setting that impressed all Europe. It has long been believed – and Louis's own comments lend support – that his motivation was a reckless thirst for glory. This is not wholly false, but *la gloire* must be understood to include over-tones of 'renown', even 'duty'. Unlike some British historians, French historians argue that France under Louis was following no grand strategy, whether to seize the Spanish Empire or to gain territory up to what would later be claimed as France's 'natural frontiers' – the Pyrenees, the Alps and the Rhine. He and his entourage certainly believed in his right as Europe's greatest monarch to aggrandize his kingdom and dynasty, and to equal or surpass the great men of history – he was hailed as an 'Augustus', a 'new Constantine' or 'new Charlemagne'. These vague and potentially unlimited ambitions, manifested in imperious words and belligerent acts, rallied most of Europe against him. That Britain was dragged into this maelstrom was Louis's part in British history. That, against the odds, Britain came to lead the coalition against Louis was its part in his. His personal support of the Stuarts – part chivalry, part piety, part *Realpolitik* – caused durable bitterness within and between the Three Kingdoms, and made conflict with France inevitable.

THE SUN KING

Louis XIV by H. Rigaud.

It is up to you to become the most glorious king there has ever been.
CARDINAL MAZARIN to Louis XIV[3]

Louis XIV was the curse and pest of Europe . . . this high-heeled,
periwigged dandy, strutting amid the bows and scrapes of mistresses
and confessors . . . disturbed and harried mankind during more than
fifty years of arrogant pomp.
WINSTON CHURCHILL[4]

By the early 1680s Louis and his ministers could contemplate Europe with satisfaction.

> France . . . is naturally fortified against foreign attack, being almost
> surrounded by seas, by high mountains, or by very deep rivers. She
> produces an abundance of the things needed for man . . . She has
> an unusual perfection as a state . . . and her inhabitants are almost
> infinite in number, robust and generous, born for war, frank and
> disciplined.[5]

The largest population in Europe – 20 million and rising – made France a giant among pygmies. Spain had only 8.5 million; the countless city states, bishoprics and principalities of Germany totalled 12 million, but with a mosaic of vulnerable micro-states on France's eastern marchlands; the United Provinces of the Netherlands, nearly 2 million; the Scandinavian kingdoms, between 2 and 3 million combined. Well down the pecking order came the 'Three Kingdoms', with a total population of 8 million and falling, and reckoned by the French foreign ministry to constitute Europe's sixth-ranking power, their government revenues one-fifth those of France, their armies a quarter the size of Sweden's.

France's natural strength was consolidated by hard labour. In the 1670s the great minister Colbert had built a larger navy than the Dutch or the English. The army, over 200,000 strong, dwarfed all others. The engineer Marshal Vauban built a vast ring of fortresses, which made the kingdom a protected space and, as can be seen from the many still standing, the most fortified country in the world, able to fight nearly all its wars on foreign soil. Nature and labour were seemingly confirmed by Divine Providence, which favoured France in war and diplomacy, bountifully creating a power vacuum into which Louis had stepped. The old Habsburg enemy, which had once ruled both the Spanish and the Holy Roman empires, was now divided between Madrid and Vienna. Spain, though its colonies were temptingly rich, was in decline. The Empire, fragmented and ravaged by war and religious conflict, was assailed by the Turks, who in 1683 were besieging Vienna. Louis seemed to represent the future: absolute royal authority, professional administration, and religious uniformity. French officials and pamphleteers became accustomed to describing any state that opposed them as 'arrogant' and 'pretentious', so rightful did their superiority appear.

The Three Kingdoms, after the restoration of their Euro-Scottish dynasty the Stuarts in 1660, had gravitated towards the Bourbon sun. They had not fully emerged from their own share of the religious and military cataclysm that had sundered Europe, and which had cost Charles I his head and 250,000 of his English and Scottish subjects, and an incalculable number of Irish, their lives.[6] The return of Charles II from French exile had been popular at first, after the Puritan republic of 'Fanatics' (as their enemies commonly called them). Charles and his brother James, Duke of York, worked to consolidate their restoration by moving towards a modern absolutist regime, bypassing the archaic nuisance of Parliament. This needed French support, including grants of money, sometimes delivered personally to Charles by his valet.[7] The French were concerned by England's budding commercial and naval success, and wanted an ally on the British thrones. Charles's senior mistress, Louise de Penancouët de Kéroualle, Duchess of Portsmouth, was a useful agent of influence: the French expatriate writer Saint-Evremond suggested that 'the silk ribbon round her waist holds France and England together'. Charles did not need such pleasurable inducements: his 'mental map of Europe had its centre not in England at all, but France'.[8] He helped to start Louis's aggressive war in 1672 against the Dutch, England's national enemy. But this war, far from cementing an Anglo-French alliance, seemed sudden proof that the real threat came from France. The French army was alarmingly successful, while their navy was believed to have deliberately shirked battle so that the British and Dutch would destroy each other. French sailors reportedly 'bragged that after they had Holland, they hoped to have England'.[9] English opinion felt they had been duped into serving Louis's aggressive designs, with the connivance of a francophile court. As one MP put it, 'Our main business is to keep France out of England.'[10] Charles assured Louis that he was 'standing up for the interests of France against his whole kingdom'.[11] Astonishingly, Louis revealed the details of his dealings with Charles to the parliamentary opposition – which he was also bribing. His strategy (he acted similarly in Holland) was to stir the embers of the Civil War in order to keep the Three Kingdoms weak.

Many at home and abroad assumed that the Stuarts' power depended on the support of Versailles. Ironically, given his eventual fate, James II of England and VII of Scotland (who succeeded Charles in 1685) moved somewhat out of the French orbit, realizing that Louis would sacrifice the Stuarts if it suited him. Although he appointed a French crony, the Marquis de Blanquefort, alias Earl of Feversham (whose brother commanded the French army in 1688) to command his new mercenary army, raised for internal use, and sent an Irish Catholic with a French title, the Marquis d'Albeville, to represent him at the crucial post of The Hague, he did not intend to become wholly dependent, like his brother, on France. His strategy was to avoid expensive European wars while using sea power to counter the French in North America, consolidating his possessions there into a vast private domain – New York already belonged to him – and using the income to become independent of his parliaments. Those of Scotland and Ireland could be ignored, and that of England subverted.

Religion was crucial. The struggle that had convulsed Europe since Luther and Calvin was tilting towards a victory for Catholicism, and hence, so many thought, for monarchs. Louis XIV considered Catholicism the pillar of his power, as well as the source of divine favour. Pressure on France's remaining 1.5 million Protestants mounted during the 1680s, ending the relative tolerance that had previously caused English religious Dissenters (Presbyterians, Quakers, Baptists) to praise France in contrast to the persecution they suffered in England. Soldiers were billeted on Protestant families to make life unbearable – the infamous *dragonnades*. In October 1685, Louis, the 'New Constantine', proclaimed victory over the dwindling 'Huguenots' (the insulting nickname for Protestants) by revoking the 1598 Edict of Nantes, which had supposedly recognized their religious, civil and political rights in perpetuity. He declared that the 'so-called reformed religion' no longer existed in his realm. Hence, there could be no public or private Protestant worship, and no marriage or inheritance. All schools and churches were to be demolished. This was the most popular act of his reign, producing 'explosions of joy' among his Catholic subjects, including the court writers La Bruyère, La Fontaine and Racine. Crowds demolished Protestant churches and desecrated cemeteries. There was some armed resistance. The minister of war Louvois ordered: 'take very few prisoners . . . spare the women no more than the men'.[12] Protestant refugees flooded into Holland and Britain, bringing harrowing stories of persecution. At the behest of the French ambassador, one of the most influential published accounts was seized and burnt by the English government.

This trauma across the Channel darkened the first months of James's reign, when in February 1685 he became the Catholic king of Europe's largest remaining Protestant realm. Like several other circumspect northern princes, Charles and James had moved towards Catholicism, partly for personal and family reasons – the influence of their French mother – but also because they shared the universal view that Catholicism buttressed royal authority. Charles's position was mainly political, but James was genuinely Catholic. In either case, their combination of religious and secular power was stigmatized by their opponents as 'Popery'. It was all the more alarming in the light of the persecution in France, which James approved of. The choice, as one peer put it, was 'whether I will be a slave and a Papist, or a Protestant and a free man'.[13] Rebellions against James broke out in Scotland and in the West Country, where Charles I's illegitimate Protestant son the Duke of Monmouth proclaimed himself king. The risings were quickly and harshly suppressed. A woman was burned at the stake for harbouring a traitor, and some 300 men were hanged, drawn and quartered: the execution grounds were awash with body fluids. James's aim was to legalize Catholicism in his kingdoms. He tried to both charm and bully Anglicans into an alliance with Catholics against the turbulent Dissenters, even meeting every MP individually. When this failed, he switched desperately to an opposite strategy: to create an alliance of Catholics and Dissenters against the Anglican establishment by offering toleration to both. He dared not end the exclusion of Catholics from Parliament, but instead took steps to pack the House of Commons with Dissenters. He sacked two-thirds of Anglican JPs and Lords Lieutenant and appointed a disproportionate number of Dissenters and Catholics to positions of military and political power: Catholics included a Secretary of State, the acting Lord Lieutenant of Ireland, the Lord Chancellor, and the commander of the fleet. A Jesuit, Father Edward Petre, joined the Privy Council. James intended Catholicism to attain equality with the 'established' church, with its own bishops, parishes, tithes and colleges. This meant displacing Anglicans: for example Magdalen College, Oxford, was ordered to elect a Catholic president, and when its Fellows refused they were all expelled.[14] Mass was publicly celebrated at the Chapel Royal, and a papal nuncio received. Some hoped and many feared that in the fullness of time the whole country would, like France, be brought back to Catholicism. James's strategy became suddenly more credible when in June 1688 a male heir, who took precedence over his Anglican half-sisters Mary and Anne, was born and baptized a Catholic. The rumour spread that the baby was not genuine, but had been smuggled into the queen's bedroom in a warming-pan.

It is often assumed that James's ambitions were limited, that popular fears of 'Popery' were bigotry and hysteria, or that even if he was seeking absolute power, he could never have succeeded. But some authoritative recent accounts conclude on the contrary that his bold aims were 'not only perfectly feasible but close to being attained'.[15] That seemed the way Europe was going. Denmark and Sweden had been the latest to lose their representative assemblies. James's policies threatened Britain with another bout of religious mayhem and civil war. It would be doubly threatening if he had French support: 'Our jealousies of Popery, or an arbitrary government, are not from a few inconsiderable Papists here, but from the ill example we have from France.'[16]

That Louis XIV was on the march as the self-appointed champion of Catholicism alarmed his Protestant neighbours. It also worried Catholic princes, including the most Catholic of all, Pope Innocent XI, whose ecclesiastical authority within France had been flouted. He was so angry at Louis's cooperation with the Turks that he excommunicated him in 1687. Louis was accused by Protestant and Catholic opponents alike of aiming at 'universal monarchy'. This implied hegemonic religious and secular authority, made credible by French hints of Louis's ambition to be elected Holy Roman Emperor. British Protestants were happy to ally with Catholic states that opposed him. Louis's defenders, including some recent historians, have dismissed these fears as paranoia. His ambitions, they argue, were essentially defensive, asserting his dynastic rights and rounding out France's frontiers.

This 'defensive' perspective, of course, depended on which side of Vauban's grim new ramparts you were standing. The French policy of using dubious legal claims backed by armed force to secure every strategic 'gate' to their territory – including Lille (detached from the Spanish Netherlands), Metz, Strasbourg (formerly a free city of the Empire) and Franche-Comté – meant that their neighbours were increasingly vulnerable: 'gates' allow access both ways. In recent years, Savoy, the Spanish Netherlands, several German states, Tripoli, Algiers and Genoa had all suffered French aggression. It was no secret that France coveted the Spanish Netherlands (most of modern Belgium), Lorraine and the Rhine frontier. In petty matters the French aimed not merely to dominate but to humiliate. The nominally independent Duke of Savoy was forbidden to go on holiday to Venice, and the Duke of Mecklenburg, another independent ruler, was imprisoned when visiting Paris as a tourist. Among the peace conditions offered to Holland in 1672 – and rejected – was the demand that every year a Dutch delegation should bring Louis a gold medal humbly thanking him for giving them peace. The French government behaved as a law unto itself, using (as a modern French specialist puts it) 'sometimes threats to intimidate a neighbour, sometimes violence to impose French will'.[17] It was impossible to say where its future ambitions might lead.

One of the minor victims of Louis's imperiousness had been the independent principality of Orange, a small Protestant enclave in Languedoc, which in 1682 was occupied, with the usual accompaniment of looting and rape, by Louis's dragoons, experts in low-intensity anti-Protestant operations. Protestants in England were alarmed and outraged. So was the young prince of the little state, Guillaume d'Orange, as Louis had intended. When his envoy went to complain, Louis's minister threatened him with the Bastille. The idea – and it proved a very bad one – was to punish Guillaume for being a nuisance to France in his other persona, Willem III van Oranje. His family, Counts of Nassau in Germany and Princes of Orange in France, derived their prominence from the strange office of *stadhouder* (or stadholder) of the Dutch Republic, partly elective and partly hereditary, and always resented by the republican oligarchy. A stadholder was appointed in emergencies by the provinces of the Republic to direct the government and command the armed forces. The house of Orange–Nassau had provided stadholders for several provinces since Willem I ('the Silent') had led the struggle against Spain that had created the Republic in 1579. There had been no stadholder from 1650 until 1672. In that year, Louis, abetted by Charles II, had invaded the Republic, and the young Willem III had been appointed stadholder for life to command the resistance. The French had only been halted when the Dutch flooded the approaches to Amsterdam. Bourgeois trading interests, especially in Amsterdam, had subsequently made a deal with

The second hundred years' war: phase 1, 1688–1745

Legend:
- Territory gained by France
- Land battle
- Naval Battle
- Holy Roman Empire in 1721
- Major national borders
- Marlborough's march into Germany

RUSSIA

Moscow
Kiev

POLAND
Warsaw

PRUSSIA
Königsberg
Berlin
BRANDENBURG

HANOVER

GERMANY
Prague
Vienna
AUSTRIA
Oettingen
Blenheim
PALATINATE
Bern

HUNGARY
Buda
Belgrade

OTTOMAN EMPIRE

Black Sea
Aegean Sea
Ionian Sea
Adriatic Sea
Tyrrhenian Sea
Mediterranean Sea
North Sea
Baltic Sea

Rome
Sicily
Sardinia
Corsica
Cyprus
Crete

GREAT BRITAIN
Edinburgh
Prestonpans
Culloden
Derby
London
Beachy Head
Dunkirk
Amsterdam
Utrecht
Brussels
Ramillies
Oudenaarde
Lille
Malplaquet
La Hague
LORRAINE
Calais
Paris

IRELAND
Glenfinnan
Derry
Enniskillen
Boyne
Aughrim
Limerick
Dublin
Bantry Bay

Portsmouth
Torbay
St Ost
Brest
Saint-Malo
Cancale
Rochefort
Quiberon Bay

FRANCE
Lyons
ORANGE
Marseilles
Toulon

Atlantic Ocean
Bay of Biscay

SPAIN
Madrid

PORTUGAL
Lisbon

GIBRALTAR
Minorca
Port Mahon

0 100 200 300 400 500 miles
0 200 400 600 800 kilometres

France, one of their largest markets. Charles II had married his brother James's eldest daughter Mary to Willem (a grandson of Charles I) in 1677 in the hope of influencing him out of another conflict with France; but the marriage worked the opposite way too – it gave Willem a legitimate voice in the foreign policy of Britain.

By 1687 Louis would no longer demean himself by conciliating Dutch 'cheese mongers' and 'herring fishers', especially as buying their produce was draining French gold. Trading agreements were disdainfully cancelled, threatening the Dutch, not least their pro-French mercantile oligarchy, with ruin. When they protested, 100 Dutch ships were seized in French ports. The very existence of the Republic was again threatened. It was clear that a major war was looming between France and Holland, which would probably involve much of Europe. The Dutch response was desperate, risky and decisive: the biggest enterprise in their history.[18] They had to stop Britain and its navy – Europe's largest by the 1680s – from again joining with the French, and if possible to bring that navy, and whatever other resources of men and money could be raised, to their side. Their fears seemed confirmed when James signed a naval agreement with France in April 1688. Willem arranged to be invited by domestic opponents of James to intervene by force in English politics. The habitually quarrelsome Dutch provinces and cities agreed to provide money, men and ships for Willem to invade England and force James to 'be useful to [his] friends and allies, and especially to this state'.[19] Louis's Catholic enemies, the Pope, the Emperor and the king of Spain, tacitly approved, on condition that British Catholics were not harmed. The Dutch blandly maintained that they were only planning a punitive raid against the Barbary pirates, but the French ambassador solemnly warned on 9 September 1688 that any act against James II would be regarded by Louis as 'an act of war against his own crown'.[20] This made things worse, as it finally convinced the Dutch that there really was a Franco-British alliance.

France's failure to take action to prevent the Dutch invasion of England is of fateful historic importance, and yet it remains mysterious. One reason is James's estrangement from Louis. He might have had French military and naval help had he been willing to accept satellite status. But he was reluctant to depend on Louis. One might detect unease in his remark to the French ambassador that 'he was so confident of [Louis's] friendship that he would never be jealous of his greatness and he would like him to conquer all of Germany'.[21] Another reason is that Louis, at this crucial moment, had his attention drawn to seemingly more important events far away to the south-east, which were permanently redrawing the map of Europe. The Holy Roman Empire, his enemy, had begun to win its long war with the Turks. As recently as 1683 (to the ill-concealed delight of the French) the Ottoman army had been besieging Vienna: this raised the thrilling possibility that the Habsburgs would lose the Imperial crown, enabling Louis to become the 'protector' of central Europe, and perhaps Emperor too. But the Turks were thrown back, and in 1686 the Imperial army took Buda, 'the bastion of Islam'. Protestants and Catholics alike celebrated throughout Germany – but not in France. The Venetians attacked the Turkish province of Greece (incidentally wrecking the Parthenon by blowing up the gunpowder stored inside); and Christian armies fanned out into the Balkans. In Istanbul, the disgraced sultan was deposed. The huge Turkish fortress Belgrade fell on 6 September 1688, and the Turks forever ceased to be a threat. This stunning victory meant that Imperial forces would be free to move west, to defend the spongy statelets along the Rhine. The French, determined to forestall them, decided to strengthen their military position in Germany and encourage the Turks to keep fighting. One of Louis's marshals explained that

> The Court was quite undecided which gambit would be best to take; to support James about to be attacked or to prevent the Turks from making peace . . . which the next moment would bring down on us all the forces of the Emperor . . . M. de Louvois [the powerful minister of war] decided upon the second gambit . . . nothing was more important for us than to make a diversion to keep the Turks in the war.[22]

So the French fleet concentrated in the Mediterranean, and troops were sent, not to attack the Dutch and defend the Stuarts, but to mount 'a great offensive of intimidation' in the Rhineland.[23] On Louis's direct orders, troops began systematic devastation of the Palatinate as a warning to potential enemies and to create a scorched-earth barrier against attack. Heidelberg, Mannheim, Spire, Worms and other towns were sacked and burnt. The result persuaded the Turks to keep fighting, but created outrage in Germany and a general rallying of Europe against France.

Both Louis and James and their advisers were fatally slow to appreciate the seriousness of the threat Willem posed. They assumed the English navy could stave off any invasion.[24] The French calculated that even if there were an invasion of England (their ambassador did not think one imminent) it would cause violence and chaos that would long keep Willem occupied. It is even possible that Louis was willing to tempt the Dutch into this dangerous trap, simultaneously punishing James for his hostile actions in North America. James did eventually ask the French to bring a fleet to Brest in case of emergency, but they did nothing effective to help him. According to a French agent of the governor of the Spanish Netherlands, the French, having sent their ships to the Mediterranean and troops to the Rhine, 'were not in a position to give much help', but they told London that they were refusing it until James toed the line and signed an alliance with France.²⁵ So James had the worst of all worlds: hints of future French support spurred his Dutch and English enemies into action, but the support never materialized.

Louis and James were right that an invasion of England was highly dangerous. Willem was taking a 'stupendous gamble', the very rumour of which provoked a run on the Amsterdam stock exchange. The fleet, seen off by cheering, praying and weeping crowds, was vulnerable to naval attack and stormy winter weather, and it sailed 'in defiance of all common sense and professional experience'.²⁶ At its second attempt to beat the weather, it was blown down the Channel to Torbay by winds that kept James's navy stuck in the Thames estuary. The landing was followed by several days of nervous fence-sitting by the English nobility, and no response at all in Scotland. But soon there were armed meetings and declarations in the Midlands and North. Nottingham declared that 'We count it rebellion to resist a king that governs by law, but . . . to resist [a tyrant], we justly esteem it no rebellion, but a necessary defence.'²⁷ Riots against James and Popery broke out, most seriously in London, where Catholic embassies and their chapels were attacked. Disturbances persisted for weeks. It was rumoured that Irish Catholic troops had burned down Birmingham and were massacring Protestants. This disorder radicalized the situation. What had begun as a military *pronunciamento* turned into a 'Glorious Revolution' in December when James, after a nervous breakdown that caused his army commanders to abandon him, sent his wife and son to France, threw the Great Seal of the kingdom into the Thames, and – firmly escorted to the coast by the Dutch – sought asylum from Louis XIV.

The Sun King's enemies breathed a sigh of relief. An Italian Protestant wrote, 'the Dutch by this enterprise have greatly contributed to the public welfare and liberty of Europe'.²⁸ Willem marched his troops into London, tactfully placing English and Scottish regiments of the Dutch army in the van. He threatened to return to Holland unless given the crown, and the so-called Convention Parliament invited him to ascend the 'vacant' throne as William III, with his wife as Queen Mary II. In return, he accepted a Declaration of Rights. This, which became the Bill of Rights, restricted the powers of the Crown and entrenched those of Parliament. William believed that he had a providential mission to save European freedom from French 'universal monarchy', and he had invaded in order to recruit Britain into the struggle. For this overriding purpose, he wanted the greatest unity he could achieve in his new kingdom. Otherwise, the French expectation that he would be engulfed by another British civil war might come true. If native co-operation meant accepting the permanent involvement of Parliament in political life, so be it. He would have to manage as he did with the States General in Holland. The crucial question was financing the war. For a start, William presented a bill for £663,752 for his invasion. The English Parliament would only agree – unlike under previous monarchs – to vote short-term financial and military powers to the Crown. The consent of the House of Commons was now required every year, and so parliament became 'an institution, rather than an event'.[29] Warfare, not ideology, transformed English politics.

WILLIAM OF ORANGE

William III.

I see that this people is not created for me, neither am I for this people.[30]

William III was to prove one of the ablest, most important, least loved and most forgotten of British monarchs. He undoubtedly changed British history: perhaps that is the reason – the British cherish those who symbolize continuity. He was half Stuart through his mother, and English was his rusty maternal tongue. His succession to the British crowns had always been a possibility. Physically sickly, he was given a careful education and brought up to expect high responsibilities early. In 1672, in his early twenties, he was commanding Dutch forces against Louis XIV's invasion. Despite long experience, the 'stadholder-king' never became an outstanding soldier, but tireless determination made him a formidable politician and diplomat. His unpopularity came from his dour and taciturn nature and his understandable preference for competent and trustworthy Dutch troops and advisers. But its main cause was the unprecedented ordeal of war he imposed on Britain.

Many who had welcomed William's intervention found his accession to the throne deeply troubling, for it flouted the principle of hereditary monarchy by divine right. Charles I had been beheaded, but his son had succeeded him; whereas James and his son were still alive, and had simply been replaced. Did this mean that Parliament, or the people, or armed force, could impose and dismiss monarchs as they wished? Did it mean the end of legitimate government founded on secure legal principle and divine sanction? What about Scotland and Ireland, which were separate kingdoms? Might it not open the gates to endless conflict, reigniting the nightmarish civil wars of the 1640s and 50s? So within weeks the consensus against James gave way to a spectrum of quarrelling factions, from Divine-Right 'Tory' loyalists to disappointed radicals. Even a century later the meaning of 1688, given new point by the French revolution, could still cause profound disagreement. The pro-Stuart 'Jacobite' opposition to the new monarch and his successors would persist for half a century in England, for longer in Scotland, and longer still in Ireland. Much blood would be shed; and the 'rage of party' would last and leave scars that could still ooze three centuries later.

Yet 1688, only vaguely remembered by the British people, was the beginning of a new era. Never again would a monarch rule as the Stuarts had tried to do. Parliament, and the principles of representation and consent, became permanent foundations of the State; indeed, Parliament acquired an effective sovereignty that in theory it still possesses. Censorship laws lapsed. Greater religious toleration was supported by William in the hope of increasing unity for the coming war and soothing his Catholic allies Spain and the Empire. The result, in the words of the philosopher-politician John Locke (an opponent of the Stuarts who now returned from exile), was that toleration 'has now at last been established by law in our country.

Not perhaps so wide in scope as might be wished for . . . Still, it is something to have progressed so far.'[31] The danger of an absolutist state based on religious uniformity, whether Anglican, Puritan or Catholic, was no more.[32] This was a milestone in the evolution of English political and cultural identity, with its emphasis on moderation, compromise and the middle way, and its increasing conviction that Britain – more precisely England – was different.

Yet the domestic story of 1688 is not the whole story; not even the main story. In Craig Rose's words, 'the most revolutionary aspect of the revolution [was] a radical reorientation of England's foreign policy'.[33] The political settlement and the State structures that emerged in Great Britain – and, with tragically different results, in Ireland – were not a consequence of domestic choices alone. William was ready to make concessions in Ireland as in Scotland and England. Catholic Ireland could possibly have reached 'an accommodation with William III [and] some form of political and religious independence'.[34] In that case, the history of the islands would have been very different. But the French belatedly decided to support a Stuart counter-revolution with ships, men and money, igniting the British civil war they had expected and hoped for. In March 1689, a French naval squadron, money, arms and 8,000 troops arrived at Kinsale and Bantry Bay. Louis sent James with them, rather than let him wallow in self-pity at the palace-in-exile at Saint-Germain. The English and Scottish parliaments agreed to William's demand to declare war on France. The 'second hundred years war' began.

Ireland was James's springboard to reconquer Great Britain, for his pro-Catholic policy in the 1680s had won support among its Catholic nobility, and he was cheered in Dublin. But the battle was not to be simply an Irish or even a British one: Ireland became as much a European battleground as Flanders or the Rhineland, and the future of the Three Kingdoms depended on external forces. James knew his best hope was to gather Irish troops and cross over to Scotland, where he also had formidable support. The Dutch invasion had ignited a revolution in Scotland more extreme and violent than in England. The Edinburgh parliament declared squarely that James had 'forfaulted' the crown – no mealy-mouthed talk of 'vacancy' – and the Lowland Presbyterians embarked on an unceremonious and often violent demolition of the Episcopalian church, ejecting clergy and bishops and purging the universities. William had little choice but to accept Presbyterianism (which was anyway close to his own Calvinist views) as the new Church of Scotland. But this mainly urban, Lowland initiative alienated the Episcopalian or Catholic loyalties of the patriarchal, largely feudal, society of the Highlands, and the Episcopalian clergy and lairds turned to King James as the only way of protecting themselves against Presbyterian

extremism. A tiny army of Jacobite highlanders under Viscount Dundee –
a hard-bitten mercenary, later romanticized as 'Bonnie Dundee' – won a
brief pyrrhic victory over a Scots–Dutch force at Killiecrankie in July 1689,
at which Dundee was killed. This inspired the last major Latin epic written
in Scotland.[35] Further advance was stopped short in August by a
Presbyterian force at Dunkeld. The clans were given an ultimatum to submit
to William's authority: one clan that missed the deadline was the
Macdonalds of Glencoe, so thirty-eight of them were massacred by
Campbell soldiers in February 1692. Scottish Jacobitism was far from dead,
however, as the future would show.

James had missed the chance of uniting with Dundee because he was
delayed in Ireland besieging Derry and Eniskillen. The siege of Derry
(subsequently renamed Londonderry), that legend of Ulster Protestantism,
began when thirteen apprentices shut its gates against James's troops.
Derry's resistance from April to July 1689 against its French-led besiegers
was 'the turning-point of the British war of succession'.[36] The Comte
d'Avaux, an experienced diplomat sent by Louis as James's minder, abandoned the idea of invading Scotland, deciding to prolong the struggle in
Ireland. The golden rule of French policy in Ireland or Scotland, whether
under the Bourbons, the revolutionaries of the 1790s, or Napoleon, was
to mount the noisiest diversion by creating the greatest mayhem at the
least cost to themselves. The results were gratifying. William III had to
divert first-class troops from Flanders and then come over himself, enabling
the French to win a crushing victory at Fleurus in the Spanish Netherlands
on 21 June 1690.

Much depended on the outcome when the rival kings met at the River
Boyne, on the road north from Dublin, on 1 July. The largest and most
famous battle in Irish history, it was also the most European battle ever
fought in these islands, the offshoot of a war also being fought in Flanders,
Catalonia and the Rhineland. The Williamite army was principally Dutch,
Danish and Huguenot, eked out with unreliable English rookies, many of
whom fell sick and 'died like rotten sheep'.[37] The core of the Jacobite army
of 20–30,000 men were 7,000 French, German and Walloon troops in French
service. Both armies were commanded by actual or former soldiers of Louis
XIV – the Williamites by a Marshal of France, Friedrich von Schomberg
(only one of whose staff officers spoke English); the Jacobites by the Comte
de Lauzun.[38] As he reconnoitred the field, William's shoulder was grazed
by a cannonball, which tore his coat and shirt ('It's well it came no nearer,'was
his typically laconic comment). Rumour spread that he had been killed.
When it reached France, there was spontaneous drinking and dancing in the
streets; a crowd at Versailles forced its way into the palace courtyard and lit
a bonfire under Louis's window. The Boyne was not devastating – each side

lost a few hundred men (including Marshal Schomberg, who led the Huguenot attack with the cry 'Allons, messieurs, voici vos persécuteurs!') – but it was decisive. The Williamites pushed across the river, and the Jacobite retreat became a rout, which French officers subsequently blamed on their Irish infantry.

Everything could have changed on 10 July, when the French navy won its greatest victory over the Anglo-Dutch fleet at 'Cap Bézeviers' – Beachy Head. This was a confused action in which the British failed to support the Dutch, and so had to send an abject apology to the States General, with the offer to pay for the repair of their ships and compensate the families of the men killed.[39] Louis was delighted that 'I now find myself master of the Channel after having defeated the English who prided themselves for several centuries on being its masters', and Te Deums were sung.[40] The victory not only enabled the French to maintain communications with Ireland, but also raised the possibility that they could isolate William there and even invade England in his absence. But, to the fury of Louis, his admirals would not attempt anything so aggressive. The fleet had sustained damage and many of the crews were sick. The French navy was stronger on paper than at sea, and its commanders seem to have had no strategy at all. James's lieutenant in Ireland, the Earl of Tyrconnel, was to say that 'the want of a squadron of French men of war in St George's Channel has been our ruine . . . [William] could have sent hither neither forces nor provisions, and [his] army would have starved'.[41] William soon returned to the Netherlands, and James left hastily for France to seek reinforcements and to urge an invasion of England. But after the Boyne Louis was less ready than ever to risk a major commitment of troops to Ireland – indeed Lauzun's brigade was fetched home. As for England, the French confined themselves to setting fire to Teignmouth. When in 1692 the French did decide to mount an invasion, it was too late.

James's departure from Ireland was regarded by generations of embittered Jacobites as desertion. His army fled to the western ports, supplied by the French navy. The following year, a new commander, the Marquis de Saint-Ruth, fetched from slaughtering Protestant rebels in the south of France, decided to force a decision, destroying the bridges behind his army and digging in at Aughrim, near Galway. In July 1691 a bloody battle was fought. Saint-Ruth was decapitated by a cannonball, and the Jacobites crumbled and fled, losing 7,000 men to the Williamite army commanded by the Dutch general Baron van Ginckel (created Earl of Athlone) and later by the Huguenot Marquis de Ruvigny (created Earl of Galway). Although Limerick, under the Marquis de Boisseleau, sustained a short siege, most Irish leaders were now as eager to accept terms as the Dutch were to offer them. A Treaty of Limerick, offering pardons and religious liberty, was signed with Ginckel in October 1691. A French relief squadron appeared three weeks too late. The French sought to withdraw their soldiers and as many Irish recruits as they could muster to fight on the Continent. The treaty allowed 15,000 Irish soldiers – the famous 'Wild Geese' – to sail for France, where they paraded before James II and served France under his banner, confident of a quick and victorious return. William, eager to calm Ireland down and concentrate on Europe, was happy with a moderate treaty. However, a continuing Jacobite guerrilla war in parts of the country, fed by the hope of another French-backed invasion, made the Treaty of Limerick a dead letter, and led the Irish parliament to pass laws aimed at breaking the economic and social power of the Catholic aristocracy. These 'penal laws' were to poison Irish–British relations for generations.

EXILES: HUGUENOTS AND JACOBITES

The revocation of the Edict of Nantes brought some 40–50,000 Huguenots to the British Isles, and the Glorious Revolution caused almost as many Jacobites to leave for Europe, especially France. Many of these were soldiers or sailors. About 25,000 troops, mainly Irish, followed James to France. Marshal Vauban estimated that about 20,000 Protestant soldiers and sailors left France. Refugees and their descendants fought on opposite sides for generations, sometimes face to face. Jean-Louis Ligonier became commander in-chief of the British army in 1757. Irish and Scottish Jacobites were to provide two Marshals of France and eighteen generals, and acquire a near monopoly of command in French colonies – like their countrymen in those of Britain. Jacobites settled at the exiled Stuart court at Saint-Germain (west of Paris), in western seaports, and in Paris itself. Irish Catholics acquired prominent positions in shipping, slave-trading, and wines and spirits, practically creating cognac, the high-quality brandy distilled for export to London and Dublin.[42] London had the largest settlement of Huguenots, concentrated in Spitalfields and Soho. Some became shareholders or directors of the new Bank of England. The famous Spitalfields silk industry used new techniques from Tours and Lyons. Refugees made important contributions to every branch of craft and fashion, notably as gold- and silversmiths, clockmakers, gunsmiths, cabinet-makers, printers, translators, publishers, engravers, sculptors, and hatters – cardinals in Rome had their red hats made by Huguenot refugees in Wandsworth.[43]

Britain at the Heart of Europe, 1688–1748

This war is for the defence and protection of the laws libertys customs and
religion as well papist as protestant from the barbarous and avaricious
tiranny and invasion of the French king.

SIR RICHARD COCKS, 1695[44]

We took this war in hand to assert the liberties of Europe, and, to
encourage us to carry it on, we have the examples, ancient and modern, of
nations that have resisted great monarchies, and who have worked out their
freedom by patience, wisdom and courage.

CHARLES DAVENANT, 1695[45]

The wars on which the Three Kingdoms had brusquely embarked – the
Nine Years War (also known as the War of the League of Augsburg)
and then, after a brief lull, the War of the Spanish Succession – were the
most sustained intervention they had ever made in European politics. British
troops ventured further into Europe than they ever did again until 1945. The
cost and suffering revived support for the Stuarts. Yet the link the Glorious
Revolution had created – and which Louis XIV continually confirmed –
between resistance to France and resistance to the Stuarts meant that the war
'against popery and slavery' and 'for the liberties of Europe' could not easily
be abandoned. France – for whom the conflict with Britain was only one
aspect of the struggle, though an increasingly important one – also suffered
grievously. In 1688 Louis had expected fighting to last a few months, but it
persisted for nearly twenty-five years. By the end, all the combatants were
exhausted, and Louis was not alone, as he approached death, in being
convinced that war was a divine punishment on him, his dynasty and France.

Both wars became wars of attrition. Huge armies (not seen again until
Napoleon's day) were long to assemble, hard to move and hard to feed; they
had to disperse with the approach of winter. Movement was further
constrained by long defence lines, anticipating the trenches of 1914–18, and
numerous fortresses, especially in Flanders, so that a year's campaigning
might focus on besieging one or two fortresses, or simply occupying territory to seize food and cash. Large areas were deliberately ravaged to make
them incapable of sustaining an enemy army. Battles were sometimes
hideously bloody, but were rarely decisive, and so rulers and generals often
tried to avoid them. Little of the gruelling fighting in Flanders, the
Rhineland, and Spain remains, therefore, in national memories. From the
Nine Years War – the first and most obscure of various conflicts that have
been suggested as the 'real first world war' – only a few vaguely familiar
names from memorial plaques or regimental colours remain. They fail to

evoke the intense horror of the huge close-range killing matches. For the French, the names of a few naval swashbucklers who singed the king of England's wig, such as Jean Bart, still adorn warships, streets and bars. In retrospect, the most decisive and important campaign was William III's victory in Ireland, because it confirmed the Anglo–Dutch union as the political, financial and military core of the anti-French alliance.

Belatedly, the French made a serious effort to try to reverse the Glorious Revolution in the first of many attempts to invade that would continue until the climax under Napoleon. In 1692, 30,000 French and Irish troops, nominally commanded by James II, assembled in Normandy. But in May the French navy met an Anglo–Dutch fleet nearly twice their size off Barfleur, at the battle of La Hougue (for the British La Hogue). The French fought with skill and courage, and withdrew successfully under cover of night and fog. But winds and geography took a hand: most of the fleet was caught on the wrong side of the Cherbourg peninsula, with no fortified base in which to take refuge. At Saint-Vaast harbour, there was hand-to-hand fighting as the British attacked in boats – one British sailor unhorsed a French cavalryman at the water's edge with his boathook. Despite volleys of musketry fired by King James's troops from the shore, a dozen French ships of the line and nearly all the invasion transports were burned.[46] The British planned a tit-for-tat counter-invasion, including Irish Protestant troops, aiming to raise a Protestant revolt in France, but the navy decided it was not feasible. With mutual invasion abandoned, the Irish troops were marched off to fight on opposite sides of the Rhine and in Flanders. Plots and betrayals on both sides continued, but neither could land a serious body blow. This set a pattern for the next 100 years.

The war was costing a great deal of money, in addition to the disruption of maritime trade on both sides. The British were paying for troops in the Low Countries; the French were fighting simultaneously on four fronts. The British raised taxes and found new means of borrowing, but not without pain or resistance. Many taxpayers, whose grievances were expressed by the 'Country party', felt that they were being fleeced to benefit a self-serving clique of William's Dutch entourage and the ruling Whig 'junto', and to enrich the 'monied men' of the City of London, 'enabled to deck their Wives in Velvet . . . while poor Country Gentlemen are hardly able to afford their Wives a Gown of Lindsey Woolsey'.[47] Resentment was all the greater among those 'Tories' who doubted William's right to rule, or who felt that he was pushing Britain into a war that had gone far beyond its true interests.[*]

---

[*] 'Whigs' were those, often wealthy nobles, who had opposed the Stuarts, welcomed the Glorious Revolution, and supported William and his Protestant successors. 'Tories', often smaller gentry, retained at least some loyalty to the Stuarts, were pillars of the Anglican establishment, and resented the Whig oligarchy and its expensive policies.

Without being fully Jacobite, it was possible to see a negotiated return of James or his son as desirable, or just inevitable: William and Mary (who died of smallpox in 1694) had no children, and Anne, the next Protestant heir, had only one surviving son, who was to die in 1700. In these circumstances, not only disaffected Tories in the shires but leading soldiers such as John Churchill, government ministers, and even William and Princess Anne themselves were maintaining more or less discreet contacts with the exile court at Saint-Germain. James's handicaps in this subtle and duplicitous game were his own personality, increasingly intransigent and devout (he spent much time at the monastery of La Trappe), and the fact that he and his family were puppets of Louis XIV. Few Tories would contemplate a Catholic monarch imposed by France.

France was suffering severely from the effects of war. In 1693–4 it was hit by famine. Though not caused by the war, it was aggravated by the army's consumption of food and by the disruption of seaborne grain imports from the Baltic. Perhaps 10 per cent of the population – some 2 million people – died. Yet, brutally, an effect of starvation was to force hungry men into France's unconquerable armies: during the whole war, the French did not lose a major land battle. The absolutism of the monarchy (which had not summoned the Estates General since 1614) deprived the discontented of a political voice.

By 1696, both sides were nearing exhaustion. Moreover, both were aware that a long-expected geopolitical crisis was looming: the succession to the throne of Spain. Carlos II had been physically weak since childhood, and had never been expected to survive long or produce an heir – a prophecy that the lavish ministrations of his doctors helped to make self-fulfilling. By the mid-1690s, he was clearly nearing his end. The leading claimants to the succession were a French prince (Louis's grandson) and an Austrian archduke. This meant that not only Iberian Spain itself, but also its possessions in Italy, the Netherlands and the Americas could swing either into the Bourbon or into the Habsburg camp. The hazards of births and deaths might even unite the whole into a single Franco-Spanish or Austro-Spanish monarchy. This would make a further, even more far-reaching European war inevitable. It was necessary either to prevent it or to prepare for it.

The Nine Years War, now a stalemate, was wound up in 1697 by the Treaty of Rijswijk, principally negotiated between the French and the Anglo-Dutch – a sign of the new importance of Britain in European affairs. Territorially, there were few changes. Politically, Louis recognized William and Mary as monarchs and promised to give no further help to the exiled Stuarts. James's Irish troops in France were disbanded, leaving thousands destitute. Jacobites were outraged, but in fact, recognition of William was a façade. The Stuarts remained at Saint-Germain, the Jacobite diaspora remained active, and the Irish troops were incorporated into the French army. France celebrated, with firework displays and the slogan 'Louis XIV Gives Peace to Europe'.[48] But at court the treaty was viewed as a defeat, especially after so many glorious victories and triumphant Te Deums. Marshal Vauban thought it 'infamous'.[49] Louis's own conclusion was that 'I sacrificed the advantages I gained in the war . . . to [the needs] of public tranquillity.'[50] In any case, it was all to be fought over again in another war that has been proposed as 'the real first world war', the War of the Spanish Succession.

William and Louis, the would-be arbiters of Europe, first tried to prevent this further war by agreeing to carve up the Spanish domains. However, the ailing Carlos was determined not to see his empire divided, so in October 1700 he bequeathed the whole to the sixteen-year-old Duc d'Anjou, Louis's grandson, and thereupon died. William wrote that 'if this Will takes effect, England and the Republic are in the greatest danger of being completely lost'.[51] France would dominate the Low Countries, the Mediterranean and the Americas. Louis and his ministers, after intense discussion, concluded that 'it was the will of Heaven', not only that Anjou should be king of Spain, but that he should remain in line of succession to the throne of France too. After this 'bold, brash, arrogant challenge'[52] they acted fast, perhaps in the belief that the British and Dutch were too weak to respond. In December 1700, Philippe d'Anjou, now Felipe V of Spain, left Versailles clutching instructions for kingship written for him by Louis. French soldiers and advisers followed him to Madrid, seemingly to make Spain and its empire a French protectorate. French troops surrounded the 'barrier fortresses' in Spanish Flanders – held under treaty by the Dutch to protect the Republic's security – and took their garrisons prisoner. Louis was ready for war to secure an immense dynastic triumph for the House of Bourbon.

The Spanish succession affected all of southern and western Europe, raising more than ever the spectre of French 'universal monarchy'. William feared that the fruits of his twenty-eight years of struggle had been lost 'in a single day without firing a shot',[53] because Tories in Britain and Republicans in Holland preferred to make a deal with Louis. After Rijswijk, to William's chagrin, a parsimonious and anti-military parliament had reduced the British army to 7,000 men. However, the French now seriously mishandled the situation, combining provocation with delay, and giving their opponents both cause and time to prepare resistance. The most flagrant example was that when James II died in September 1701, Louis, against the advice of his ministers, publicly recognized his son as James III and VIII, breaching the Treaty of Rijswijk. The British immediately severed diplomatic relations. William's sudden death, after a fall from his horse, in March 1702 did not halt the march to war as Queen Anne ascended the throne. In May Britain declared war, leading as before a coalition that included the Dutch, the Empire, Denmark, Brandenburg and several smaller states.

In some obvious ways this was to be a continuation of the Nine Years War, focusing mainly on the Low Countries and the upper Rhine, with other fronts in Spain and Italy. But a great difference was that Spanish America was now at stake, with significant implications for British trade and prosperity, and so there was also fighting across the Atlantic. Another difference was that during the Nine Years War the French had won all the battles but had not managed to win the war. This time, the Allies won the great battles but could not knock out France. These huge and bloody contests, the most terrible of the whole century – Blenheim, Ramillies, Oudenarde, Malplaquet – were associated with the unsettling brilliance of John Churchill, Duke of Marlborough.

Blenheim (the anglicized name of the Bavarian village of Blindheim) was fought on 13 August 1704, when Marlborough, to save the Holy Roman Empire from probable defeat, marched into southern Germany. He moved far and fast, yet managed to keep his army in a state to fight. This was made possible by his painstaking organization of supply, and his ability to pay cash for food and fodder, with wagons of money provided by the City of London. At Blenheim, for the first time in at least half a century, a French army was destroyed: half its men were killed, wounded, prisoners or dispersed; its artillery, its regimental colours and its commander were captured. In an afternoon, France lost its position in Germany and its military superiority over the Continent.[54] In Versailles no one knew what had happened: dispatches remained unanswered. News trickled through in scribbled letters from captured officers to their families; but for some days no one dared to tell Louis. According to Voltaire, it was left to the Marquise de Maintenon, his morganatic wife, to break the news 'that he was no longer invincible'.[55] Two years later, in the Low Countries, Marlborough won the no less crushing victory of Ramillies, which excluded France from the Spanish Netherlands, and then Oudenarde, which led to the fall of the great fortress of Lille and began to open the way for a march on Paris. Malplaquet in 1709, where the death-toll was comparable with the terrible first day of the Somme in 1916, shocked all the combatants, and increased suspicion of Marlborough's strategy.

MALBROUCK S'EN VA-T-EN GUERRE

Marlborough . . . was the most fatal man for the greatness of France that
had been seen for several centuries . . . He had . . . that calmness of
courage in the midst of tumult . . . that the English call a 'cool head'.
VOLTAIRE[56]

Until the advent of Napoleon no commander wielded such widespread
power in Europe. Upon his person centred the union of nearly twenty
confederate states. He held the Grand Alliance together no less by his
diplomacy than by his victories. He rode into action with the combinations
of three-quarters of Europe in his hand.
WINSTON CHURCHILL[57]

John Churchill, Earl and later Duke of Marlborough, is not just England's
most brilliant general, he is England's *only* brilliant general. His greatest successors – as well as being mostly from Scotland or Ireland – exude dour, dutiful
and taciturn competence, even the greatest of them, Wellington, epitome of
the stiff upper lip. Marlborough was quite different: a courtier first, a soldier
and politician second, a handsome charmer always. His breathtaking ambition
and bland duplicity – he abandoned James II and then when serving William
intrigued with the Jacobites (which brought him a spell in the Tower) – did
not prevent him from being generally liked. Though he had gained some military experience alongside the French in Flanders, his successes came less from
professional expertise than from boldness of conception, ruthless offensive-
ness, efficiency of preparation, tactical inventiveness, and rapidity of reaction.
He led a British army (of mainly German soldiers) deeper into the Continent
than ever. He was victorious in four of the biggest battles of the century.
However, the expense and carnage of these battles (in which about a quarter
of all combatants were casualties) caused alarm at home and in Holland.
Marlborough, whose avarice was almost as legendary as his prowess, was accused
of corruption and prolonging the war out of self-interest. In particular, his
wish to invade France itself, and march on Paris, was prevented. Whether this
would have brought disaster or decisive victory can never be known.

He became the most famous Englishman of his time, and a legendary figure
in France. The still well-known song 'Malbrouck s'en va-t-en guerre' (the
tune is roughly that of 'For He's a Jolly Good Fellow') testifies to this, as did
the use of his name – sometimes rendered as Malbougre – to frighten naughty
children. The son of a Dorset squire, he became the wealthiest British subject
ever; a duke, a prince of the Holy Roman Empire, and the owner of the
greatest palace of the age, Blenheim, for which his heirs still deliver each year

to the monarch, as rent for the royal manor of Woodstock, a fleur-de-lys banner symbolizing his victories.

A war of such intensity was bound to have domestic consequences. Revolts broke out in Scotland and in the Protestant Cevennes, in south-central France. Both were encouraged and subsidized by the other side, but not effectively supported. The most important consequence of the conflict for Britain was the Act of Union between England and Scotland in 1707. Scots had to chose between facing a dangerous world as the junior but privileged partner of England, or as a minor and expendable auxiliary of a European coalition. With the choice influenced by English threats to treat Scotland as a foreign country, and by bribes from London, the Scottish parliament chose union.

As in the previous war, France was grievously hit by famine. A sudden steep drop in the temperature in 1708–9 – long remembered as *le grand hiver* – destroyed seedlings, buds, vines and trees. The following year's harvest was inevitably disastrous. Hunger led to disease. Rising food prices caused a general economic slump. The city of Lyons went bankrupt. Taxes were unpaid; wine and salt duties uncollected. This halted the French war machine. Starving people rioted, attacking markets, convents and chateaux. Louis took the unprecedented step of appealing directly to his subjects. His letter, read in every church, assured them that 'my tenderness for my peoples is no less lively than for my own children', but insisted that the Allies had made impossible demands exposing France to invasion and dishonour, and so even greater efforts must be made. With more or less good grace, courtiers sent even more of their silverware to the mint, and a new tax was levied. This convinced many foreigners that France would fight on, and that its absolute monarchy was more resilient in war than a tumultuous parliamentary system like Britain's.

For if the House of Commons was an effective means of national mobilization, it was also effective at expressing discontent. Taxation, financial instability, disruption of trade, and the feeling that true British interests were being ignored increased criticism of the Whig ministers and Marlborough by Tories and crypto-Jacobites. This mattered when Queen Anne too changed her position. A new Tory ministry, led by Robert Harley, later Earl of Oxford, and Henry St John, later Viscount Bolingbroke, began secret peace negotiations. The first disavowable contacts were made in 1711 through a London-based French Catholic priest, François Gaultier, and an enterprising Cambridge poet, pamphleteer and diplomat Matthew Prior, who had previously run an effective spy network at the exiled Stuart court. Harley survived being stabbed on 8 March 1711 at a cabinet meeting by a shady

French 'refugee' – a unique event even in Franco-British history. 'Matt' Prior was one of the most unusual of many highly unusual Franco-British go-betweens. Queen Anne disliked using someone of 'very meane extraction' as an envoy – his rise had begun when as a child he was discovered reading Latin behind the bar of his uncle's London pub. But he was too useful to neglect, and his central role caused the subsequent agreement to be known as 'Matt's peace'. Secret negotiations took place at his London house. In Paris he was welcomed literally with open arms, having a torrid affair with a libertine aristocratic nun, Claudine de Tencin, described as 'the beautiful and wicked canoness', later one of the century's foremost women intellectuals, and mother of the philosopher d'Alembert. Marlborough was dismissed, and his army ordered to take no further offensive action – a decision of which the French were informed before the Allies. London's insistence on peace saved France from probable invasion, and permitted Louis to die undefeated.

The Treaty of Utrecht was signed in April 1713. It ended a period of extreme instability in European affairs, marked by religious conflict, territorial changes, unstable monarchical succession and protracted wars. Since 1688, nearly 2 million soldiers had been killed. The danger of French hegemony had receded. The union of the crowns of France and Spain was forbidden by the treaty, although Felipe kept the Spanish crown, and Spain later became France's main ally in future wars with Britain. The Spanish Netherlands were ceded to Austria, safeguarding Holland. Britain had clearly become one of the dominant powers. France again recognized its Protestant succession and this time expelled the Stuarts. Britain gained large tracts of North America, Gibraltar, Minorca and a hopefully lucrative trading concession – the *asiento* (permission to supply slaves and send one annual trading ship to Spanish South America). France demolished the fortifications and harbour of that nest of privateers Dunkirk, and accepted a resident British 'Commissary and Inquiror' to ensure they were not rebuilt – a perennial source of ill feeling.

The political wind shifted in both France and Britain, confirming that Utrecht was a watershed. The death of Queen Anne in 1714 was followed by the peaceful succession of her Protestant cousin, Elector Georg of Hanover, as George I. He regarded the Tories as crypto-Jacobite enemies. Harley and Prior were arrested, and Bolingbroke fled to France, where he became for a time chief adviser to the Stuart Pretender and gained an inflated reputation as a political thinker. In September 1715, Louis XIV died, unmourned by his long-suffering people: he had turned France, it was said, into a vast poorhouse. That Louis XV succeeded his grandfather at the age of two guaranteed a long period of caution under the regency of his cousin the Duc d'Orléans; doubly cautious as the king of Spain had a possible claim to the French throne whatever treaties might say. With both France and Britain headed by potentially vulnerable rulers, it was sensible to avoid conflict and agree not to encourage each other's rivals. This rapprochement came too late to head off an abortive Jacobite rebellion led by the Earl of Mar in 1715, but it did thereafter lead to a period of peace and even alliance for twenty years. This began in 1716, under the auspices of the Regent's adviser Cardinal Dubois, who arranged a casual encounter with the soldier and politician Lord Stanhope when buying books at The Hague. Stanhope's vision of an Anglo-French alliance was a brave attempt to entrench peace. The entente continued under Cardinal Fleury and Sir Robert Walpole in the 1720s, but with less ambitious aims. Walpole wished to keep out of Continental wars, while Fleury was delaying a more ambitious policy until France recovered her strength.

This Franco-British 'alliance' was certainly of benefit to Europe. Their desire to avoid war spread to their allies, clients and neighbours. But this 'new European order', as Lucien Bély calls it, was shaken by the grinding tectonic plates in eastern Europe, as Russia and Prussia grew increasingly aggressive, and Sweden, Poland, Turkey and even the Empire faltered. Every political accident, especially those caused by disputed monarchical succession, provided a pretext for predation. Fleury knew that good relations with Britain were unpopular at court and in the army. France was still the European giant. Its monarchy seemed more powerful and stable than that of Britain, subject to perennial party quarrels and disputed succession. France was able to muster its strength faster and without public dissent. Its foreign trade was increasing rapidly while Britain's was stagnant; and its navy was growing. Fleury broke off the entente as soon as he felt France was strong enough: in 1731 London was informed that the two countries' interests were too far apart for them 'to deliberate together upon the affairs of Europe'.[58] By the late 1730s France was again, as the king of Prussia declared, the 'arbiter of Europe', and fears of its hegemonic ambitions, and its support for Stuart counter-revolution, revived.

Walpole was determined to keep out of the War of the Polish Succession (1733–5): 'Madam,' he famously told the queen, 'there are 50,000 men slain this year in Europe, and not one Englishman.'[59] But friction over trade and colonies was less easy to avoid. Clashes in Spanish America between illegally trading British merchant ships and Spanish 'coastguards' – in effect, licensed pirates – began the 'War of Jenkins's Ear' in 1739, after a British sea captain had an ear sliced off to teach him respect for Spanish orders. France, as an ally of Spain, was resigned to being drawn in. However, the situation was transformed when in 1740 Prussia took advantage of a dispute between rival pretenders to the Austrian throne to invade the province of Silesia – hence the War of Austrian Succession. Britain and France at first became involved in this free-for-all only as 'auxiliaries', lending troops to their respective allies Austria and Bavaria. So although the battle of Dettingen (1743) was the last time a British king, George II, commanded an army in battle – against the French, of course – he was acting as Elector of Hanover and his British regiments fought under the Hanoverian flag, provoking patriotic grumbling. The war soon turned into the depressingly familiar and forgettable series of campaigns in central Europe, the Low Countries and Italy. When it eventually ended in 1748, the only significant change was that Prussia kept Silesia.

However, for France and Britain other issues emerged, and turned the Silesian quarrel into another Franco-British duel. The conflict between them was more clearly than ever extending beyond Europe. The most important British operation of the war was in North America: the seaborne capture in June 1745 of the fortress of Louisbourg, commanding the mouth of the River St Lawrence, though this was eventually exchanged at the peace table for Madras, captured by the French. In Europe, the French won a notable victory over the British at Fontenoy. Finally, and most importantly, the war made possible the last and most formidable Jacobite rebellion, the 'Forty Five', France's best chance of reversing 1688.

FONTENOY, 11 MAY 1745

Fontenoy: the greatest Franco–Irish victory over the British.

Tirez les premiers, messieurs les Anglais!
COMTE D'ANTERROCHES, commander of Garde Française

Cuimhnigi ar Luimneach agus feall na Sasanach!
(Remember Limerick and English treachery!)
War cry of the Irish Brigade

Fontenoy (now in Belgium) is largely forgotten in England, just as Blenheim is rarely emphasized in France. British, Dutch and German troops under the Duke of Cumberland were beaten by the French commanded by Marshal Maurice of Saxony. It stands out from the interminable account of eighteenth-century carnage for three reasons. It was the last time a French king symbolically led his army in battle. This made Louis XV for a time 'le Bien Aimé', and, judged Napoleon, gave the Bourbon monarchy a new lease of life. It was also the proudest victory of the Jacobite Irish over the British, 'the greatest of Irish battle honours' commemorated into the twentieth century in Ireland and among Irish Americans.[60] And the invitation to the English to fire first is one of the most famous French battlefield stories.

The Irish 'Wild Geese' were a notable presence in the French army, though, as theoretically the British army in exile, they carried the Cross of St George on their colours, wore red coats, and used English as their language of command. All armies employed foreign troops from poorer regions of Europe that had a surplus of males: Swiss, Germans, Scots, Irish and Croats were all reputed soldiers. The Irish were distinctive in being, like the Huguenots in the British army, also political and religious exiles. Jacobites were present in many parts of Europe, including Spain, Austria and Russia. In France they were most numerous and fulfilled a special role, as an invasion and counter-revolutionary force in waiting. Irish nobles whose estates had been confiscated found honourable careers serving the kings of France. Charles O'Brien, Viscount Clare, became a Marshal of France, and as governor of Languedoc had a heavy hand with rebellious Protestants. Many families served for generations, and several (such as the Dillons, Shees, Clarkes, Lallys and MacMahons) became members of the French nobility. Fontenoy was the high noon of the Irish Brigade: its six regiments found themselves face to face with British – including Protestant Irish and Scottish – units and saved the day for France. On the British side, the Black Watch, their advance supposedly led by their chaplain Adam Ferguson (later professor at Edinburgh and a leading figure of the Scottish Enlightenment), also created a heroic and specifically 'British' legend. James Campbell was reported to have killed nine men with his broadsword before having his arm shot off by a cannonball. That the regiment, raised for police duties in Scotland, had been lured abroad by a trick, and had mutinied, could be forgotten.[61]

It was the encounter of the Garde Française and the Foot Guards that produced the famous invitation to fire first. As a gallant gesture, it encapsulates the idea of eighteenth-century war as *la guerre en dentelle* (war in lace) – a succinct reference to elaborate uniforms, to aristocratic style, and to the fallacious supposition that it was not very lethal. The story also suggests courtesy between French and English gentlemen, who, after many hard-fought battles, had developed, if not affection, then respect. However, there is no less a suggestion that this courtesy was a kind of taunt. Muskets were inaccurate, and the killing range of their bullets short. The first volley, when the muskets had been carefully loaded in advance, was the most effective, and could even be decisive. The side that fired first, at longer range, wasted that advantage and made itself vulnerable. The side that held its fire could come close while the enemy was reloading and fire a more deadly volley. So the apparent courtesy is also a grim, and mutually understood, joke – a characteristic French mixture of gallantry and levity.

France and the Young Chevalier, 1744–6

Although the King is in no way involved in the project the young Prince
Charles Edward has . . . had the boldness and resolution to execute, it is . . .
always politic to profit from every occasion to embarrass the enemy.
MARSHAL DE NOAILLES, 1745[62]

Had they thrown in ten thousand men in time . . . France would soon have
seen all the western world her own.
Old England newspaper, October 1745[63]

Scotland after the Act of Union was not a contented country. Acrimony between Episcopalians and Presbyterians broadly reflected both the cultural difference between Highlands and Lowlands and the political divide between Jacobites and Whigs. Wars with France had increased taxation. Customs and Excise were unwanted consequences of Union. Smuggling and other lawless activity multiplied. Valuable trade with the Continent, and especially with France, was disrupted by privateering and naval action. The unwillingness of Scots to accept hardship for the sake of British monarchs was shown luridly in 1736, when Captain Porteus, of the Edinburgh city guard, was lynched after he fired on an unruly crowd at the execution of a smuggler, and several days of rioting ensued.

Contenders for power had to decide whether to scramble for new opportunities in the wider British polity, or look to the other potential patrons – the exiled Stuarts and the French. Among the first who looked to London were the ambitious and talented Dalrymples, politicians, soldiers and diplomats, who helped govern Scotland for James II and then for William. Thereafter, they helped to govern Britain for the Hanoverians. John Dalrymple, 2nd Earl of Stair, was a successful and 'insolent'[64] ambassador in Paris, where he managed the post-Utrecht rapprochement and kept a wary eye on the Jacobites. Also aligned with the Hanoverians were some great clans, notably the Campbells, and city corporations such as that of Glasgow. Least willing to compromise were Episcopalian lairds, backed by a disestablished clergy. The feudal authority of the clans, their warrior values and Gaelic culture, were incompatible with the egalitarian Presbyterianism and commercialism of the Lowland towns. Episcopalians always formed the great majority of active Scottish Jacobites.[65]

Discontent could only become politically formidable through the Stuarts and the French. Rarely did either show much ability or daring. Abortive conspiracies, cancelled invasions and failed rebellions were their hallmark. During the Franco-British rapprochement after Utrecht, the Stuarts had to move their once brilliant court from the splendours of Saint-Germain to independent Lorraine, then to papal Avignon, to Spain and finally to Italy. Their cause waned. One conspiracy was even betrayed to London by the French government. Yet they retained sympathy in France, as well as being potentially useful. The French provided funds and arranged marriages to maintain a supply of Pretenders. The War of Austrian Succession revived Stuart prospects. Even before it was officially declared, Versailles made plans for invasion – 'an enterprise on which depends the fate not only of England, but even the whole of Europe'.[66] A royal proclamation was drawn up in advance assuring 'la nation anglaise' (sic) that the French were not coming as enemies, but at the invitation of 'good and faithful Englishmen', to 'throw off the foreign yoke' and restore their rightful king.[67]

The first plan was for a surprise attack on London. But the British were warned. François de Bussy, their most highly placed agent in France, sold them the details for £2,000. The illegitimate son of a minor courtier and a noble lady, his mother's connections enabled him to enjoy a successful diplomatic career, but his pedigree ruled out promotion to ambassador. Resentment may have played a part in his treason, but money was the immediate motive when Lord Waldegrave recruited him in Vienna. His lavish spending aroused suspicions, but he was never exposed, and was even posted to London in the 1760s. His tip-off led to hasty naval defence measures. These, and bad weather, aborted the plan as the French invasion force approached the Kentish coast in March 1744.

Prince Charles Edward Stuart, grandson of James II, aged twenty-five, charming, ruthless, and querulous when drunk (which was fairly often), resolved to force the French to try again. He was encouraged by adventurous

Irish and Scottish advisers, prominent among them Anthony Walsh (known by the French as 'Gouelsch') of Saint-Malo, the ringleader of a wealthy Irish lobby of shipowners and slave-traders, who offered ships and money. Their patriotism was whetted by the prospect of distracting the British navy to allow a clear run for their privateers. Walsh was also promised a peerage. In June 1745, Charles and a few followers sailed in two warships provided by Walsh, without Versailles knowing what was afoot. A parting letter to Louis in Charles's big childish hand justified his escapade and promised that 'if [Your Majesty] makes me succeed, you will find in me a faithful ally'.[68] After a brush with an English warship, he reached the Western Isles, then raised the Stuart standard at Glenfinnan, on the mainland, on 19 August.[69] He assured wary sympathizers that rebellion could succeed, because substantial French help was imminent. As Lord George Murray, who became his military commander, later observed, 'certainly 4,500 Scots had never thought of putting a king upon an English throne by themselves'.[70] Charles's promises, eloquent appeals to honour and self-interest, and feudal compulsion by his aristocratic supporters, assembled a small army of around 1,800 men, which rose to a peak of 5,000 by the end of the year.[71]

Louis and his advisers pondered.[72] It was not evidently worth their while to make a major effort to restore the Stuarts, whose promised gratitude might never materialize. A Catholic restoration would revive old fears among France's Protestant allies in Germany, including Prussia. Was restoration possible anyway, especially in all three kingdoms? The Jacobites were quarrelsome, unreliable, indiscreet and grossly over-optimistic: 'one must not believe that the whole Nation is easily and quickly giving up the principles of the 1688 revolution which the majority still regard today as the base and foundation of their liberties'. On the other hand, it was a tempting opportunity to create a diversion, forcing London to recall troops from Flanders and ships for home defence, and panicking the City of London. If prolonged civil strife ensued, Britain would be neutralized and its Continental allies left unsupported. So it was worth sending arms, money and even troops. But where? Cautious voices advised against another attempt to invade England: there would be no chance of success unless major forces were committed, which was risky and would weaken France on the Continent. One (well-paid) pessimist was Bussy, who declared that a landing near London would be doomed. The safest option was Ireland, where there would be widespread support and the Spanish navy could join with the French. But bolder voices, favoured by Louis XV, prevailed. Prince Charles has long been condemned for misleading his followers with promises of French aid. But he was right in thinking that they would not stand aside. The Marquis d'Eguilles was sent to Scotland as Louis's envoy. French ships ferried in money and supplies. Encouraged by the news of the startling Jacobite victory at Prestonpans on 21 September, the royal council agreed on 14 October to land an army in England with the aim of restoring the Stuarts. On 24 October this was formalized in the Treaty of Fontainebleau, though it was not guaranteed how much of the British Isles would be restored to Stuart rule. Money and troops were requested from Spain, Sweden, the Papacy, Genoa and Switzerland.

British ministers had known that invasion was in the offing. Few were frightened by Charles's escapade in Scotland, even after his victory at Prestonpans. Nor did they take seriously the notion of a Jacobite revolt in England. But they were fearful of a French landing in a country denuded of troops: 'London is theirs as soon as they can march to it', in the view of Field-Marshal Wade.[73] The government, 'obsessed with their role as Good Europeans',[74] were reluctant to withdraw forces from the 'struggle for European liberties' on the Continent. In September they at last ordered the Duke of Cumberland and much of his army back from the Low Countries. But it would take weeks to arrive. Charles urged his reluctant followers to march into England. He wanted to trigger a Jacobite rising there, to make certain the French would invade. He promised his men that French troops would land early in December – news he had received from his brother in Paris. D'Eguilles confirmed that the French were minded to invade, but only if the Jacobite rising spread to England. So in November the Scots marched south.

French preparations were advancing briskly in November and early December. Walsh had been commissioned to procure ships. The Duc de Richelieu, one of France's leading generals, was appointed commander – proof of the importance of the enterprise. Men and artillery assembled at Dunkirk, Calais and Boulogne. Voltaire, France's principal expert on Britain, was commissioned to draft a propaganda leaflet explaining that Louis XV was only invading to 'help' both a worthy prince and 'the healthiest elements' of the English nation, in order to 'pacify England and Europe' and 'unite two nations' – the English and the French – 'who ought to respect each other'.[75] As a first token of this help, 1,000 men under a Scottish officer in the French army, Lord John Drummond, landed at Montrose on 7 December. They were principally the Royal Écossais regiment, reinforced with Scots soldiers from units of the Irish Brigade (but no Irish, it was decided – the Scots detested them). D'Eguilles was offering bets that the French had already landed in England or would arrive within days.[76] Meanwhile, in Paris, officers were saying their farewells and promising to celebrate Christmas, or at least New Year, with Prince Charles in London.

But Charles's army, which had arrived almost without opposition at Derby, had turned back north on 5 December. Charles considered his Scots as expendable in a daring gamble to bring out the English Jacobites, bring in the French, and restore his family to St James's Palace. But the Scottish commanders and their men naturally had different priorities – they wanted to live to fight another day, in Scotland, where a guerrilla war, with French aid, could defend their homes. By now they realized that the Prince's assurances that English Jacobites would join them – optimists had predicted a mass enrolment of students from that home of lost causes, Oxford – were illusory. The Scots did not know that the Hanoverian troops facing them had just been ordered south to defend London (where there was widespread panic and a run on the Bank of England), that men were being diverted to defend the English coast, that beacons had been set up to signal a French landing, and that horses and cattle were being driven off to deprive invaders of transport and food.

Subsequent debate as to whether the retreat north was necessary prudence or fatal loss of nerve misses the vital point: the decisive events took place not at Derby, but at Dunkirk. Launching an invasion proved more complicated than anyone expected. Some 300 vessels had to be requisitioned from all along the Channel coast, which took time and could not be kept secret. There were insufficient officers and cannon, which Richelieu claimed prevented him from ordering embarkation early in December when he arrived to take command. Then came both bad weather and bad news – of the Jacobite retreat from Derby. British naval units and privateers sailed inshore to ravage assembling invasion convoys, causing Richelieu increasing misgivings. But then came favourable weather from 20 to 24 December: southerly winds which could have blown at least part of the invasion force from Calais and Boulogne to Kent while keeping the British navy out of action. This, in retrospect, was their best chance. Not for the first or last time, a French commander poised to invade hesitated to take the supreme risk. Richelieu missed his chance.[77]

When he held a council of war on 5 January to plan another attempt, it was black comedy. Having shifted operations from Dunkirk to Boulogne, the French discovered that the tides would allow only a few ships at a time to leave harbour, which meant that the British would pick them off as they emerged. They would have to shift again to Calais and Ostend. The final attempts, on 13 January and 6–8 February, were cancelled because the British navy was out in force. By then, everyone was simply going through the motions to save face. Voltaire wrote to console his friend Richelieu: 'whatever happens [you] will have the honour of having undertaken the most glorious expedition in the world . . . Either I shall attend you soon or I shall go and pay court to you in London. I shall see you crowning a king and making [Louis XV] again the arbiter of Europe.' But he added significantly,

'All this would have been done if one had been able to leave on the 25th [December]. On such things hang the fates of empires!'[78]

On this philosophical note, the fate of the Jacobite rebellion was sealed. All that was left were its death throes. The Scots commanders wanted to retreat into the far north, but Charles refused, for familiar reasons:

> What opinion will the French and Spaniards then have of us, or
> what encouragement will it be to the former to make the descent for
> which they have been so long preparing, or the latter to send us any
> more succours?[79]

Almost as these words were uttered, Richelieu gave up and returned to Paris, and his troops marched back to Flanders. French diplomats hinted that they might abandon the Jacobites if the British price were right.[80] Meanwhile, they managed to get a ship through to Aberdeen with a few dismounted cavalrymen, but other attempts, and ships carrying money to maintain Charles's army, were intercepted. This precipitated the final drama, because with no money to pay his hungry and deserting soldiers, Charles insisted on a last stand at Culloden on 16 April 1746. D'Eguilles preferred not to witness the massacre: 'I retired in haste to Inverness, there to burn all my papers and think over the means for preserving for your Majesty that portion of the [Franco-Scottish] troops which might survive the action.'[81] The French had always worried that Scottish or Irish officers in their service who had been sent to Scotland might be executed for treason if or when the enterprise failed. Drummond's troops surrendered at Culloden and were given quarter, but their future, and that of d'Eguilles, looked grim. Strong representations – backed up by the arrest, effectively as hostages, of all British subjects in France without passports – were needed to secure their eventual release. France's final gesture was to send ships to rescue Charles. He owed his legendary escape to Skye to Flora MacDonald, but from there to France to the courage of French sailors. The rest of the Jacobite army, given no quarter, were hunted down. Versailles pressed for clemency, and the British conceded that they would pardon all except those previously involved in the 1715 rising.

The '45, a disaster for the Jacobite cause, was far from profitless for France. A small investment of arms, men and money (less than 5 million livres) had forced British, Dutch and German troops to be hastily shipped to Britain, weakening the Allies in Flanders. So, as Charles's little army was trudging to its doom, the French were capturing Brussels (which netted 20 million livres), and they went on to threaten Holland.[82] Tying up the British navy had allowed French privateers to land a rich haul of prizes. The British had also been unable to reinforce North America. British vulnerability had been made visible to all Europe. The French were in a somewhat stronger position to negotiate the Peace of Aix-la-Chapelle in 1748, ending the War of the Austrian Succession.

These compensations cannot mask the historic failure of France's best-ever opportunity to reverse the Glorious Revolution and undermine Britain's power inside and outside Europe. If tides and weather, as so often, played a part, there was also an intellectual obstacle. France's rulers had no agreed view of their interests and priorities. Some saw the Low Countries as the focus, others Germany, or the Mediterranean, or even Canada. So they could not work out what to do about Britain. The first difficulty, as the clear-minded Noailles pointed out, was that if France restored the Stuarts, they might well be forced by Parliament and people to adopt an anti-French policy: so why bother? Should Versailles instead aim to break up the Three Kingdoms, and make Scotland or Ireland a French protectorate? Some Jacobites advocated this as a panacea for France's global problems, but sustaining such a presence in the British Isles would have required open-ended military, naval and financial commitments. And how would other European states react to such a change in the balance of power?

So in 1745 Versailles dithered, and effectively settled for exploiting the Jacobites as a diversion. Richelieu and Walsh were left struggling to slip a few regiments across the Channel in fishing boats and privateers, while the French navy, splendidly aloof in Brest, was concentrating on quite another enterprise: preparing a fleet of seventy ships and 3,500 soldiers to cross the Atlantic and try to recapture Louisbourg: they put cod before conquest. Here is a poignant epilogue to the '45: this fleet sailed two months after Culloden, it was ravaged by sickness, its commander died, his successor tried to commit suicide, and 2,300 men perished from scurvy off the Canadian coast – more than were killed at Culloden. What if they had been sent to Ireland or Scotland instead?

SYMBOLS

Both countries' patriotic symbols emerged from their 'hundred years war'. There is little evidence for the common French claim that 'God Save the King' was originally written by Jean-Baptiste Lully for Louis XIV as 'Dieu protège le Roi', though it does seem to have emerged from earlier words and music. In its modern form it was arranged by Thomas Arne and performed in September 1745 at the Drury Lane theatre to raise morale at the worst of the Jacobite crisis. James Thomson's 'Rule Britannia' was written in 1740, and David Garrick's 'Hearts of Oak' in 1759, the 'Year of Victories' in the

Seven Years War. The 'Marseillaise' was composed in its present form at Strasbourg in 1792 by a young officer, Rouget de Lisle, but its most famous phrases – including the stirring refrain 'Aux Armes, Citoyens! Formez vos bataillons' – were taken from verses that appeared during the explosion of anti-English writings published during the Seven Years War. The 'sang impur' which was to 'abreuver nos sillons' was not originally that of the Austrians and Prussians in 1792, but from that 'perjured race' the English, in 1757.[83] That the colours of the two national flags are basically the same is probably not a coincidence. The Union Flag was of course progressively put together from the banners of St George, St Andrew and St Patrick as the struggle with France brought about a consolidation of the three kingdoms into one. The Tricolour, invented by La Fayette in 1789, was probably inspired in part by the red, white and blue of the American flag, which had developed from the British.

The End of the Beginning

In the sixty years between the Glorious Revolution and the Peace of Aix-la-Chapelle, the Three Kingdoms had been transformed by their participation in, and ultimately leadership of, a coalition against the French superpower. Britain had become a great power, whose armies had, at times, won great victories, and whose navy could claim, with occasional lapses, to rule the waves. It had created systems for raising money to fund these expensive ambitions. Trade and colonies fed, and were expanded by, this new power, and were soon to revolutionize the whole economy. The political system of Crown, Parliament and Church, and the union of two of the Three Kingdoms, had solidified. Political culture, and in the long run a sense of national identity – officially defined three centuries later as 'concepts of rights and duties, toleration, fair play, freedom of speech and of the press etc.'[84] – are largely developments of these years, in plain contrast to the extremism, violence and instability of previous history.

At the time of Aix-la-Chapelle, France remained, in spite of the blood and treasure expended by and against her, the dominant Continental state. Prussia was friendly, Spain was ruled by a Bourbon, and Austria had become less of a threat. Voltaire told Frederick II of Prussia that France was like 'a very rich man surrounded by people who, little by little, come to ruin. He buys up their property cheaply.'[85] France had absorbed Roussillon, Franche-Comté, Alsace and half of Flanders; it would soon take Lorraine and Corsica. Being so much bigger and stronger, the French monarchy had not needed to change its fundamental institutions. Seen from Versailles, Britain was a growing threat, increasingly involving the world beyond Europe. But it was not the sole, or even the main, preoccupation. For most Frenchmen, Austria and the Holy Roman Empire were the hereditary enemy. Holland and, early on, Spain were almost as hateful. Realization that something significant had happened to Britain aroused both interest and disapproval. Marc Fumaroli writes that there had been since 1688 a 'metaphysical dimension' in the quarrel between France and Britain.[86] But it needed another century to reach its climax.

ON HIS MOST CHRISTIAN MAJESTY'S SERVICE

The end of the war and the return of diplomatic relations with Britain brought Louis XV a very personal satisfaction, and his mistress Madame de Pompadour considerable relief. The secretary of the British embassy explained on 26 April 1749:

> His Majesty it seems has an utter aversion to his Mistresses bearing Children . . . this your Royal Highness will allow is a Circumstance of a very delicate nature, for a Lady to manage with any dexterity, especially as His Majesty is thought to have a great affection for her Person; in spite of all her Care and precautions, she was not long since alarm'd, with terrible apprehensions of her being pregnant, and His Majesty was said to be much disconcerted about it . . . I had a Commission given me about the same time . . . to procure from England, as it is not a manufacture of this Country, 300 or more, of those preventive machines, made use of by the Gallant tho' prudent young Gentlemen of this age; I was desired for fear of search or seizure as Counterband, to have them directed for H.M.C.M., and I expect them with great impatience, tho' my merchant was startled at the quantity, and begg'd a few days extraordinary to provide them; I am almost tempted to ask an exclusive priviledge for the importing of them into France, and think it would be a very genteel way of raising a fortune.[87]

The jocular term *redingote anglaise* – 'English riding coat' – was used later in the century (among others, by Casanova), and was succeeded in the nineteenth by *capote anglaise* (with a similar literal meaning), which remains in common use.

MONEY:
Waging War with Gold

The Wars of these times are rather to be Waged with gold than with Iron.
WILLIAM PATERSON, founder of the Bank of England[88]

He who has the longest purse will wear the longest sword.
The Monitor, 6 September 1765[89]

Between 1688 and 1815 Britain stood up to France – a country with twice its territory, twice its Gross National Product even in 1788, and three times its population – in six of the twelve greatest wars in history. To understand how this was possible we have to understand money. Both Britain and France were wealthy countries, with a much higher Gross Domestic Product per capita than many Third World countries today. Both spent an unprecedented amount of money on their mutual conflict. But from the early 1700s onwards, Britain managed when necessary to outspend France, devoting as much as five times the proportion of its GNP to war as its enemy.[90] It could thus sustain its own armed forces (especially the navy), also counteracting French strength by hiring foreign troops (often half the manpower of 'British' armies) and subsidizing allies.

Pitt's resort to the Bank of England epitomizes the relationship by which British world power was financed.

Military Expenditure

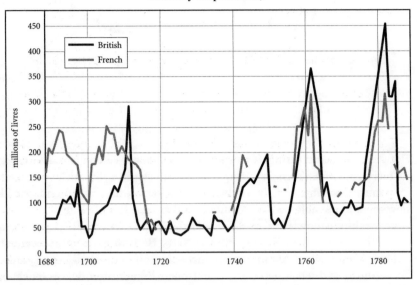

Although British peacetime expenditure was generally lower, it was always able to outspend France at times of greatest effort (Sargent and Velde (1995) p. 486).

The total cost to Britain of the 'hundred years war' was well over £2,000 million, in eighteenth-century prices.[91] To put such sums in perspective, the total annual national income of England in the 1680s has been estimated at £60 million, and the Gross National Income of Great Britain in the 1810s as £300 million.* The annual revenue of the British Crown, £4 million in the 1680s, had risen to £8 million by 1760; and to £16 million by 1795. The revenue of the French Crown was similarly ratcheted up: in 1726, it was 181 million *livres* (£7.9 million), and in 1788, 471 million (£20 million). Both countries were spending around three-quarters of state revenue directly or indirectly on war. Astonished observers at home and abroad repeatedly warned that the financial strain, and particularly the growth in debt, was unsustainable and would lead to disaster. It did: in both

* There is no easy way of translating eighteenth-century into twenty-first-century prices, as commodities move at different rates, and patterns of consumption change. To have a feel for eighteenth-century prices in modern terms therefore means multiplying them by a range of figures: from 50 (roughly the increase in the sterling price of gold since the early eighteenth century) to 300–400 (for basic commodities), up to 500–1,000 (for rents and incomes). Exchange rates were stable. The pound sterling – 20 shillings (20s), each of 12 pence (12d) – was worth approximately 23 *livres tournois* from the late 1720s until the collapse of the French currency early in the revolution. The metric *franc germinal* (of 1795) returned to near the pre-revolutionary rate: 24 to the pound, which was maintained until the First World War.

America and France (which defaulted on its public debt six times in seventy years) it provoked revolution.

Britain: 'Breaking windows with guineas'[92]

Revenue is the chief occupation of the State. Nay, more, it is the State.
EDMUND BURKE[93]

Britain fought France from 1689 to 1815 by raising taxes by 1,600 per cent and increasing borrowing by 24,000 per cent.[94] Taxes rose fast. During the Nine Years War they doubled, and by the end of the War of the Spanish Succession in 1713, tax as a proportion of national income had nearly tripled since 1688.[95] Over the whole period of the 'hundred years war', taxation rose five times faster than economic growth. Tax was always a source of furious debate, periodic riot, and constant evasion, especially through smuggling. As Burke put it, 'To tax and to please, no more than to love and to be wise, is not given to men.' Yet political problems within Britain itself were manageable. The historic result was not mass revolt (though riots were not infrequent) but rather total dependence of the Crown on Parliament. Parliamentary consent and supervision legitimized taxation. England was a single political, legal and administrative unit, so no regional or corporate tax privileges existed, unlike in most of Europe. Consequently, it was broadly accepted that taxes were fair and honest. When wars seemed to be a response to the French or Spanish threat, or when they seemed to be in the national interest – defending or expanding colonial possessions and trade – their cost was accepted as necessary and even beneficial, and the level of compliance was 'remarkable', especially by comparison with France and other states.[96]

Up to 1713 the main source of revenue was land tax, which reached 20 per cent of income. This was subsequently overtaken by a range of excise duties – on drink, tobacco, tea, glass, legal documents, hair powder, playing cards, even bachelors – collected by a professional bureaucracy with sweeping powers. These duties were far from popular. The wit Sidney Smith famously denounced a system which meant that 'the dying Englishman, pouring his medicine, which has paid 7 per cent, into a spoon which has paid 15 per cent, flings himself back upon his chintz bed, which has paid 22 per cent, and expires in the arms of an apothecary who has paid a licence of a hundred pounds'. Yet indirect taxation was relatively stealthy. Moreover, Parliament was equitable and prudent enough to put a large part of the burden on the relatively wealthy. It did not tax food (though it did beer – the biggest single yielder), and it spared the Celtic fringe. Growth in the economy, especially in overseas trade and manufactured goods, made customs and excise more bearable and easier to collect. A national system of poor relief, by far the most extensive in Europe, cushioned the most vulnerable. Despite the baroque stories of exploitation and incompetence that colour popular views of the eighteenth century, the reality is that taxpayers were relatively law-abiding, the revenue system efficient, and state administration cheap and 'remarkably uncorrupt'.[97]

Tax revenue, however, could never meet wartime surges in expenditure: governments had to borrow to meet roughly three-quarters of the cost.[98] The public debt went from £3 million in the 1680s to £100 million in 1760, £300 million in 1796, and £745 million by 1815. By 1715 half of tax revenue went to paying the interest, and by 1815, 60 per cent. This required a more sophisticated financial system than ever before, by which short-term liabilities – in effect, IOUs from government departments – were replaced by long-term, low-interest bonds. During the 1690s, ministers, MPs, and businessmen studied Dutch and Venetian methods. Experiments, and mistakes, were made with lotteries and life annuities, appealing to the public's taste for a flutter and a nest-egg. In 1694, William Paterson, a 'persistent Scot',[99] and an Englishman, Michael Godfrey, had their plans for a Bank of England (modelled on the Bank of Amsterdam) approved by Parliament: an event of truly historic importance. Immediately, in 1695, the Bank proved its worth by saving the government from a collapse of its credit, and enabled it to keep paying for the war until peace came two years later. Not only did it lend the government money, it also became the mainstay and regulator of England's whole financial structure. Financing war against France transformed the City, through the sale of permanent, interest-bearing government bonds. Parliamentary control was the indispensable underpinning of credit. It made default unlikely (not least because many MPs were bondholders), and it voted the taxation necessary to cover regular interest payments. As confidence grew, the rate of interest the government had to pay fell from 14 per cent in 1693 to 3 per cent in 1731.[100] Though there were crises and scares throughout the period, Britain, in the Duke of Newcastle's words, would never default 'as long as land lasts and beer is drunk'.[101] The combination of the House of Commons and the City of London was to create a world power.

In spite of endless pessimistic predictions, Britain was not bled dry by the effort: on the contrary. Investment in tax-free government stock, which could be freely traded, provided a secure means of saving. The growth of government borrowing, and the financial institutions servicing it, stimulated financial modernization. The City grew into the world's financial centre, and three centuries later remained the bedrock of the British economy, described in 2005 as the greatest concentration of brain and computing power on the planet. The wars against France and its main ally Spain permitted Britain to gain the lion's share of Europe's trade with the outside world, for which the City provided credit and insurance. This trade became the dynamo of the Industrial Revolution (below, page 145). After Waterloo the British had by far the highest per capita income in Europe, some 30 per cent higher than the French. As with the United States in the twentieth century, war paid.

BLOWING BUBBLES

[Law] pretended he will set France higher than ever she was before,
and put her in a condition to give the law to all Europe; that he can
ruin the trade and credit of England and Holland whenever he pleases;
that he can break our bank whenever he has a mind, and our
East India Company.

EARL OF STAIR, British ambassador, 1719[102]

John Law of Lauriston was a professional gambler and an economic visionary. Faro and Lansquenet were his specialities – simple games requiring memory, mental arithmetic and nerve. Forced to flee from London in 1701 after a questionable duel, he travelled the Continent and settled in Paris, where his card-playing prowess opened aristocratic doors. He convinced the Regent that he had a 'system' to solve France's debt problem. The recent wars had burdened France and Britain with unprecedented liabilities. Louis XIV had left 600 million *livres* in short-term debts, and 2 billion in long term; and the treasury was bare. It was generally believed that these debts would cause disaster, and make it impossible to wage war. Whichever country could reduce them would gain a political and strategic advantage. Law's suggestion was more subtle than the usual French expedients of locking up creditors and refusing to pay, which though effective made future loans problematic. Instead, in 1716 he founded a bank able to emit paper currency like the Bank of England – the Banque Générale – and in 1717 an overseas trading company – the Compagnie d'Occident – whose mouth-watering prospects would induce Crown creditors to exchange their bonds for shares, thus privatizing the public debt and stimulating the whole economy. He also organized an unprecedented effort to entice skilled British workers to France.

Success depended on producing a tempting rise in the Compagnie's share price, which duly occurred, and fed off itself as the public scrambled to buy. The government allowed Law to take over the Compagnie des Indes, awarded his bank the right to collect taxes, and enforced the use of its currency notes. In short, Law now headed a huge privatized agency monopolizing State finance and overseas trade. He became one of the greatest men in France, controller-general of finance, and owner of several estates and property in Paris, including one-third of the opulent Place Vendôme, where he lived. A new word, *millionnaire*, was coined to describe the leading profiteers from his 'system'.

In England, Law's exploits aroused envy and alarm: France seemed to be reducing its debts, and would be able to start another war while Britain languished. So Law's scheme was copied. The South Sea Company, set up to benefit from the concessions won in the Treaty of Utrecht to supply slaves and goods to South America, began in 1719 to encourage state creditors to exchange government debt for shares. In London, as in Paris, the scheme worked wonderfully, the share price rose by 700 per cent in six months, and 85 per cent of the public debt was privatized.

The Paris and London companies were both competing for the same international speculative capital. Their trading prospects were equally inadequate to support their paper value. Things began to unravel early in 1720, when sensible Dutch investors began to sell. Law struggled to keep his share price rising, falsifying profit forecasts, printing more money, and buying back shares. This postponed disaster, but made it all the more spectacular when it came in the summer. Furious mobs of dowagers and ex-millionaires stormed Law's offices in the Rue Quincampoix. He narrowly escaped as his carriage was smashed to pieces. Simultaneously, the South Sea Company's shares crashed in London amid general panic. Suicides rose 40 per cent. The Chancellor of the Exchequer was sent to the Tower of London, and Law's business partners to the Bastille.

The consequences of the crashes were both less and more than might appear. Finance and the economy were not devastated in either country. Sir Robert Walpole in England and the Regent in France were able, in very different ways, to restore financial calm. Both governments had greatly reduced their debts at the expense of gullible investors – one reason why ministers protected Law and permitted him to escape from France. His family subsequently became members of the French nobility. In both countries, the financial establishment went back to business. But there was a crucial difference: in London the Bank of England emerged strengthened, as it took over and salvaged the South Sea Company. This was the City's first 'big bang', and regulation was introduced to make investment safer. Consequently, English public finance became 'more honest, as well as more efficient, than that of any other country in Europe'.[103] But in France, the idea of a state bank was discredited for generations, paper money was rejected, and financial modernization halted. It seemed obvious that an absolutist monarchy would always cheat. Silver and gold became perennially short, as people hoarded coins:

France became literally a country of hidden treasure, even into the twentieth century. The crash ruined the French credit market 'for at least a century'.[104] The Crown resumed the crude old methods of absolutism, repudiating hundreds of millions of *livres* of debts. The dominance of the *financiers* (a hybrid species of businessman, civil servant and courtier, who purchased their offices) and their complex and cumbersome methods was restored. France's military effort was handicapped, as was its economic growth. The monarchy itself was in the long run undermined. So John Law occupies a special place in Franco-British history.

France: The Insolvent Landlord

How is it that, of two landowners, one having 10,000 a year in income, and the other more than 40,000, the former, who has more debts, can raise more cash?

HENRI-LEONARD BERTIN, controller-general of finance, 1759[105]

French officials such as Bertin and independent commentators too were 'stupefied' and 'obsessed' by British financial power.[106] They considered it a conjuring trick by which wealth was produced on paper without any real backing, such as land or gold. They hoped to find a way of exposing the deception, and bringing the whole structure of British power tumbling down.

French state finance was marked by complexity and inequality.[107] The tax system, an accretion of personal and property taxes and duties, was riddled with the entrenched historical privileges of provinces and corporations. Taxes were badly assessed, with no regard for ability to pay, and were impossible to collect in full. Evasion was blatant by rich and poor alike. France's richest individual, the Duc d'Orléans, announced that he 'always arrange[d] things' with the relevant official.[108] Prosperous tenant farmers pretended to be labourers. Thousands of the poor fought a guerrilla war with revenue men to smuggle duty-free salt. The system was so complex, according to the banker and royal minister Necker, that only one or two men in each generation understood it. Consequently, despite the myth of a nation groaning under the burden, France was under-taxed: when the revolution broke out in 1789, levels were one-third those in Britain. But mistrust of a system seen as unjust and unaccountable meant that raising rates or improving efficiency was always politically fraught. Open political conflict over taxation began in the 1750s, owing to the costs of the Seven Years War, and continued spasmodically until the fall of the monarchy.

Crown revenues were managed by the *financiers*, who collected taxes on behalf of the Crown (as farmers-general and receivers-general), managed budgets (as treasurers of various ministries and regions) and provided loans. Their profits came from commission, from investing money belonging to the State in private business activities, and by making high-interest advances to the Crown on the security of future tax revenue. This often amounted to lending the king his own money. When the Crown was desperate for gold and silver in wartime, their position was strong. Afterwards, ministers traditionally tried to redress the balance by arresting large creditors, accusing them of fraud, imposing huge fines backed up by the galleys and the pillory, or simply by repudiating or writing down what they owed, as they did 1759, 1760 and 1770. This meant that future loans carried a sizeable risk premium. The French Crown in the 1780s had to pay double the interest paid by the British[109] – in other words, could raise only half the amount of money for an equivalent cost.

The opacity of the system was a source of power for insiders who could navigate the labyrinth, find sources of credit and make themselves indispensable. Financial dynasties such as that of the four Pâris brothers, who rose from humble origins, or the Crozat family, were admired and resented. Proof of their opulence and ambition is still visible in their great chateaux with huge English-style parks, and their Paris mansions. The Elysée Palace was built by Antoine Crozat for one of his daughters. They were patrons of music, literature and science. Crozat built up one of the world's greatest private art collections – over 400 paintings and 19,000 drawings. There were few comparable profiteers in eighteenth-century Britain.

The *financiers* had to be powerful at court as the friends, paymasters and even fathers-in-law of princes, courtiers and politicians. Crozat married one of his granddaughters to the Comte (later Duc) de Choiseul, Louis XV's ablest minister, who in turn arranged a series of marriages between French and Habsburg *financiers*. A succession of Louis XV's mistresses had their expenses generously paid by the Pâris brothers. In 1745, they provided the king with a new lover: a woman of intelligence and refinement who could get inside the king's head as well as his bed. Jeanne-Antoinette Poisson was the daughter of one of the Pâris' junior employees and god-daughter of one of the brothers – perhaps, indeed, his own illegitimate child.[110] She was married off to one of their gentlemanly hangers-on to provide respectability, educated, dressed and, aged twenty-four, carefully introduced to the king at a masked ball. He took the bait, and she became the Marquise de Pompadour, her estate and title bought with Pâris money. She was the lynchpin of a financial-military-sexual complex that dominated politics for nineteen years, including the period of the Seven Years War. Her principal successor as royal mistress, the Comtesse du Barry, had connections with contractors to the navy. To put it mildly, such a system was not easy to reform: too many important people profited. It took the revolution, which guillotined twenty-eight of the great *financiers*, to change it.[111]

Moreover, it worked, in a way. Contracting out revenue collection (for example to the notorious farmers-general or to local authorities) saved Versailles a huge administrative burden, and the many privileged bodies (the Church, the provinces, the cities and the *financiers* themselves) could be politely forced to provide loans and extra contributions. However, global wars created unprecedented demands. In 1759 and 1770 traditional remedies were applied: defaulting on payments and forcibly reducing interest. But the need for money forced the Crown to look beyond domestic sources to the bankers of Amsterdam, Geneva, Germany and even (clandestinely) London. These could not be bullied in the usual way, and to default on such debts would be disastrous. Given France's record, lenders demanded a sizeable risk premium. Even then, the prudent treasurers of the wealthy German cities avoided French loans 'like the plague', though they eagerly bought British bonds. So Versailles – whether by necessity or ineptitude is unclear – was reduced to very expensive expedients. It sold life annuities – presumably it was attracted by the idea of the debt automatically dying out. But astute Genevan bankers invested hundreds of millions in the names of carefully selected girls as young as four, who were given special medical supervision. France was still paying out vast sums during the revolution, and – had the system not collapsed – would have paid 400–500 per cent in total interest well into the nineteenth century.[112]

By the 1780s, the Bourbon monarchy had reached a financial impasse. It had to pay more for its loans than Britain because it did not inspire trust, and yet it had lost the authority and self-confidence to default on them. Indeed, Louis XVI on his accession had vowed not to do so. The budget was in deficit, largely because of interest payments on war debt. The Crown could not raise taxes without arousing angry political resistance. The implications were urgent and fundamental.[113] Who was responsible for state debt? Should it be repudiated (devasting lenders) or honoured (burdening taxpayers)? Would repudiation strengthen or weaken France in relation to Britain? Would it cause civil and foreign conflict? Did a solution require despotic authority or greater accountability, perhaps with elected assemblies on British or American lines? Who had the right to raise taxes? Who represented the nation? The cost of the struggle against Britain thus created formidable political and ideological problems, which as we shall see in Chapter 4, ended in revolution. In the words of one politician, 'We only made the revolution to become masters of taxation.'[114]

CHAPTER 2

Thinking, Pleasing, Seeing

The art of pleasing seems to be that of the French, and the art of thinking
seems to be yours.

VOLTAIRE[1]

There is hardly a French cook that is not better bred than most
Englishmen of quality, and that cannot present himself with more ease,
and a better address.

EARL OF CHESTERFIELD[2]

The Peace of Utrecht (1713) inaugurated eighty years of cross-Channel scrutiny. Never before or since have the French and British shown such intense interest in each other's ways of thinking and behaving, and never has the outcome – an intellectual revolution – been so important. This interest was new on the French side. In the seventeenth century, especially after the Stuart Restoration, Britain had been a cultural dependency of France: literature, the stage, art and fashion had been imported or imitated from Versailles. Louis XIV once asked his ambassador whether England had any writers or men of learning.[3]

Scientific thought acted as the 'spearhead . . . of English hegemony'.[4] Bacon and Newton offered a new way of understanding the universe: by observation and reason. Power and politics also changed the perspective. British victories, and the success of the Glorious Revolution in creating the basis for them, suddenly made Britain a subject of envy, interest and even admiration. The bloodbath of the Civil War had given birth to civil peace, however fragile. 'Science, knowledge, reason, freedom and liberty all became linked in a manner that suggested that the very formation of Britain was a result of the Enlightenment.'[5] Seventeenth-century English political and philosophical writings, above all those of John Locke, came to dominate European philosophy in the early eighteenth century: ideas that seemed to express, and be sustained by, a political system that was proving its worth. Locke's *Essay on Human Understanding* (translated in part in 1688 and in full in 1700 as *Un Essai sur l'entendement humain*) was probably Europe's most widely read work of philosophy, arguing that all knowledge was a product of sensory experience, not predetermined by original sin or innate truths. English writing would influence French thinking on politics, religion and philosophy, and also provide models for 'tactics, literary genres and styles', for example the satire of Swift and the verse polemics of Pope.[6]

At another level, Addison's daily *Spectator* (1711–14), influenced by the writings of the Earl of Shaftesbury, consciously promoted a culture of 'politeness' – a sociable, equable, moderate manner of thinking, behaving and even feeling – that was intended to efface the religious hatred and violent faction of the previous century. The *Spectator*'s novel mixture of news, moral exhortation, literature, fashion and conversation had an immense influence. Back numbers were republished in book form and in translation. A sample of private libraries in the Paris region in mid-century shows the *Spectator* to have been the most popular piece of literary prose, and the fifth most widely owned work of any description.[7] It made English life and letters the model of modernity for a Continental readership, as well as inspiring imitators such as Marivaux's *Le Spectateur Français*.

The flotsam and jetsam of conflict – the Huguenots in Britain, the Jacobites in France, displaced soldiers, fugitive politicians, aristocratic exiles

– acted as go-betweens. Huguenots did not cease to be French, to purvey French ideas and fashions, and to translate and publish in both languages, including French editions of Locke, Pope, Swift and Defoe. Jacobites established Irish, Scottish, and English presences in French trade,[8] culture and government, and not least introduced freemasonry, which by the end of the century had become an important channel for cultural and political innovation, with 50–100,000 members, including perhaps one in ten of all French writers.[9] Many now forgotten exiled writers helped to shape Franco-British perceptions. None did more to create a sense of what Englishness and Frenchness meant than Paul de Rapin, seigneur de Thoyras (1661–1725), who wrote the first major history of England up to his own day, and Anthony Hamilton (1646–1719), who created an enduring ideal of French masculinity.

PORTRAYING THE OTHER: RAPIN AND HAMILTON

Rapin was a minor Protestant noble from Languedoc who landed with William of Orange and fought in Ireland in 1689. While recovering from a wound at Limerick he developed an interest in history, and after the war ended began a ten-volume *Histoire d'Angleterre* (1723–7) which dominated the rest of his life. He was the first historian to compose a coherent saga of the whole of English history to his own day, including the Saxons, Alfred the Great, Magna Carta, the history of parliament and the struggle against the Stuarts, culminating in the Glorious Revolution. Rapin was, in short, the pioneer Whig historian, for whom English history was a long and ultimately successful struggle for freedom. Freedom was a deep-seated national characteristic, inherited from Germanic ancestors: 'The English have been at all times extremely jealous of their liberties.'[10] Written in French, Rapin's history was widely read on the Continent, for it told those secrets of English success that Europeans were eager to discover, and its themes were echoed in the works of Voltaire and Montesquieu. It was also translated into English and became the standard work during the first half of the century. Although eventually overshadowed by the Scottish historian David Hume's *History of England* (1754–62), it shaped popular English understanding of the great events and meanings of their own history and hence their own identity.

Anthony ('Antoine') Hamilton was a Catholic who followed the opposite trajectory to Rapin, fighting in Ireland for James II, and then joining the exile court at Saint-Germain. A soldier, courtier and relative of the earls of Abercorn, he settled comfortably into the French nobility, writing a French admired for its 'purity', elegance and wit. His masterpiece, the *Mémoires de la vie du comte de Gramont* (1713), is a picaresque, semi-fictitious history of his brother-in-law's youthful adventures in France and Restoration England. His Gramont is a soldier, lover, gambler, courtier, joker and wit; willing to cheat those who deserve it, but generous with his winnings; loved by his companions and inferiors; irreverent to his superiors; and always ready to get in and out of scrapes. In short, Hamilton created in Gramont an archetype of French gallantry, not pious or correct, but funny, carefree, fearless and sexy. His popularity extended across the Channel: Horace Walpole published the *Mémoires* in England in 1772 and had a room in his neo-Gothic house at Strawberry Hill decorated with illustrations of Hamilton's characters. The book, according to the nineteenth-century critic Sainte-Beuve, became 'the breviary of the young French nobility'. Hamilton was the literary godfather of generations of swashbuckling fictional heroes.

Voyages of Intellectual Discovery

An English man is full of taughts, French all in miens, compliments, sweet words.
VOLTAIRE'S NOTEBOOK, 1720s[11]

Don't you see that these three gentlemen are just back from London? They must, for some months anyway, parade gravity, put on the air and aspect of thinkers.
Mercure de France, 1766[12]

Henry St John, Viscount Bolingbroke, the first illustrious and involuntary cross-Channel traveller of the 1700s, was a Tory thinker, an influential political exile, and one of the few English politicians more respected in France than in England. Escaping impeachment, he found compensations in exile. Regarded as both a friend of France and a fount of British political wisdom, pensioned by Versailles and married to a wealthy widow, the Marquise de La Villette (at whose chateau at La Source, on the Loire, he created one of the first of France's many English gardens), he became a magnet for both exiled and native intellectuals. He was a member of the exclusive Club de l'Entresol, the first French society devoted to free political discussion, and the first to use the Anglicism 'club'. It assembled the tiny elite of Parisian radical thinkers in the 1720s until it was banned for its presumption. He befriended and influenced the two men who did most to make England a model for French reformers: Voltaire and Montesquieu. He introduced into France, especially through his *Idea of a Patriot King*, translated into French in 1750, a new vocabulary of *le patriotisme* – the first appearance of the word in France[13] – which made it possible to speak of political loyalties and duties other than those of mere obedience to a divinely appointed monarch. Thus a Tory ex-minister, opposing a Whig government, introduced ideas that later served a French revolution.

One of Bolingbroke's admirers was the rising poet François Marie Arouet, self-styled 'de Voltaire'. Their association decided Voltaire, aged thirty-two, to make a trip to England in 1726. An incident in Paris (there are several versions) precipitated that visit and gave it heightened significance. The Chevalier de Rohan-Chabot, scion of a great courtier family, demanded that the commoner Voltaire give up his seat at the theatre. An exchange of sarcasms ensued, and Rohan sent his servants to give Voltaire a public thrashing. Voltaire's demand for satisfaction led to a spell in the Bastille, followed by banishment from Paris, and he left for London in a frame of mind easily imaginable. London he saw by contrast as a place where thinkers were free, honoured and eventually (as in his own case) prosperous. He made contacts with the literary and theatrical worlds, as well as with political and court circles. He wrote to a friend in 1726 that in England 'the Arts are all honoured and rewarded . . . there are differences in conditions but none between men save merit . . . one can think freely and nobly without being restrained by servile fear'.[14] The grandiose spectacle of Newton being buried 'like a king' in Westminster Abbey in 1727 confirmed his admiration, even if everyday life in London was testing.

Voltaire decided to write his first political prose work to describe this 'nation of philosophers'.[15] He read industriously, including Rapin, Locke, Bolingbroke, the *Spectator*, Defoe and Swift. The outcome was *Letters concerning the English Nation*, in French the *Lettres philosophiques* or *Lettres anglaises*, the only French classic first published in English. Voltaire even implied, falsely, that he had written it in English – chosen for its 'liberty' and 'energy'.[16] The book, mostly written in 1728 and augmented in 1732 after his return to France, took the form of twenty-five letters to a friend, as if merely chatty traveller's jottings. Short, punchy, accessible and seemingly artless, they are far from being a guidebook or traveller's diary, however. They contain nothing about the sights, smells, bad food, drunkenness, rough pastimes and eccentricities of England – the staples of a growing French literature. (He did note, however, that the clergy drank – though 'without scandal'.) Rather, he writes about English ideas: tolerance, liberty and (a novelty for the French) literature and thought, because, he says, it is a place where 'people commonly think'. The contrast with an oppressive and stultified France is obvious, which does not prevent Voltaire from constantly pointing it out. The tone, as in his later masterpiece *Candide*, was of a tongue-in-cheek innocence that made his studied insolence all the more funny – and provocative.

Beginning surprisingly with four letters on the Quakers (he had learned English from Quaker teachers) permits Voltaire to note that an Englishman 'chooses his own road to heaven'. A simplified section on Parliament, which he misunderstood and never attended, refers sonorously to 'the majesty of the English people'. In England, he claimed, commerce was honoured, and even young noblemen practised it; for it created liberty, wealth and the greatness of the State. At the Stock Exchange men of all religions traded peacefully, and only bankrupts were treated as 'infidels'. England was open to new and foreign customs, such as Lady Mary Wortley Montagu's introduction of inoculation from Turkey. There are letters on the ideas of Bacon ('the father of experimental philosophy') and Locke, and several on Newton, hailed as the 'destroyer of the Cartesian system'. A paradoxical effect of this attack was to confirm the status of Cartesianism as the quintessence of French thought.

One of the most striking letters was 'On tragedy'. Alongside Dryden, Otway and Addison, his favourite, Voltaire discussed Shakespeare – a subject that would gnaw at him throughout his life. As a sample, he provided a polished translation – the first into French – of Hamlet's soliloquy, an attempt to civilize Shakespeare which leaves him sans eyes, sans teeth, sans everything:

> Demeure; il faut choisir, passer à l'instant
> De la vie à la mort, ou de l'être au néant
> Dieux cruels! s'il en est, éclairez mon courage.
> Faut-il vieillir courbé sous la main qui m'outrage,
> Supporter ou finir mon malheur et mon sort?
> Qui suis-je? qui m'arrête? et qu'est-ce que la mort?

Voltaire pronounced 'a curse on literal translators', so in that spirit here is our own attempt to give the flavour of his 'To be or not to be':

> Remain; to choose one must, and in a moment pass
> From life to death, from being to nothingness.
> Cruel gods! if such there be, enlighten my resource
> Must I grow old bowed down by insult's force,
> Endure, or end my pain and my life's breath?
> Who am I? Who restrains me? What is death?

Voltaire formulated what became the standard French judgement: Shakespeare embodied untutored genius, crude and untamed. He therefore epitomized Englishness itself.

The *Lettres*, 'one of the major texts of Enlightenment philosophy',[17] gave not a mere impression of England, let alone an accurate description, but an ideological vision, and a message: England is now superior to ancient Greece and Rome, embodying reason and liberty, and hence enjoying peace, prosperity, power and cultural vigour. This implicit disparagement of France would inevitably cause an outcry. So after his semi-clandestine return to France in 1729, Voltaire delayed completing the manuscript, finally publishing it in English in London in 1733 and in French in both London and France in 1734. The outcry duly came: the authorities seized copies and searched his Paris lodgings for proof of authorship and complicity in the publication. Voltaire went on the run as the Bastille again beckoned. His career as celebrity dissident began. However comfortably protected by aristocratic friends and by his subsequent wealth and fame, he remained in a semi-fugitive state for much of his life, preferring to live within easy reach of a frontier and receiving a constant stream of admiring visitors, including several hundred British. The *Lettres* were condemned to be torn up and burnt as contrary to religious orthodoxy, morality and respect for authority. On two of those counts they were gloriously guilty.

Persecution was no bar to commercial success. On the contrary. The *Lettres* were Voltaire's first and one of his greatest triumphs, comparable with his later *Candide*. They went through at least thirty-five editions: an authoritative estimate of 20,000 copies sold in France in the 1730s is remarkable in the light of a recent suggestion that the total number of really serious readers was only about 3–5,000.[18] According to the philosopher Condorcet, the *Lettres* began 'a revolution'. They made anglophilia not merely fashionable, but essential to an enlightened outlook. One unconvinced Frenchman summed up Voltaire's 'miracle': 'the surprising metamorphosis of the English . . . This people which had always been known as the most proud, the most jealous . . . the most ferocious . . . is according to M. Voltaire the most generous, magnanimous . . . model of perfection.'[19] By the 1740s, there were sixteen periodicals in France dealing principally with English literature and thought.[20] The book also launched Voltaire's reputation in Britain, where as a historian, essayist and campaigner for liberty, even more than as a poet and critic, he was to become one of the century's most celebrated, if controversial, authors.

Another epoch-making voyager arrived in England late in 1729, about the time Voltaire left. Although they had common acquaintances (notably Bolingbroke and the Earl of Chesterfield) and may have briefly coincided in London, they seem not to have met. Perhaps not surprisingly. Charles-Louis de Secondat, Baron de Montesquieu,[21] hereditary president of the Bordeaux *parlement*, was a vastly more respectable and weighty figure than the subversive Arouet 'de Voltaire'. Despite his daringly satirical *Lettres persanes* (1721), which had brought him European notoriety, he was far from being, like Voltaire, a semi-refugee. He was a pillar of the established order, conveyed to British shores from Holland in the ambassador's yacht. Yet the explosive effect of his writings was at least as great as, and far more durable than, all Voltaire's squibs.

Montesquieu's voyage to London was part of an intellectual project to which, having grown tired of the provincial bench, he devoted the later part of his life. His interest in England may have stemmed from his involvement in the claret trade – he owned some of the best vineyards of Graves and Médoc. His interest grew through contact with Jacobite exiles, Bolingbroke and British freemasons, and it focused on the increasingly fashionable subject of England's post-1688 political system. So he made London the culminating point of a studious grand tour of Italy, Germany and Holland, made with his friend Lord Waldegrave, that lasted from 1728 to 1731. It was a good time to visit. The *détente* between the two countries meant that Montesquieu's friendships with Jacobite exiles such as the Stuart Duke of Berwick (governor of Bordeaux) and Irish poets and priests were now no bar to friendship with Whig peers such as Chesterfield and Waldegrave (a fellow freemason in Paris). They presented him to George II, with whose queen he engaged in French political gossip. He was elected a Fellow of the Royal Society, became familiar with literary and political circles, frequented Huguenot intellectuals; and whereas Voltaire had attended the theatre, Montesquieu attended Parliament.

This exposure to English life was seminal. Montesquieu arrived a sceptic, sharing typical French reservations: the English were excessively turbulent, they held extreme opinions, their culture was eccentric, their science dubious, and above all their political system incoherent and on the verge of collapse. This changed. He found a few of the natives friendly and civilized, and, like Voltaire, appreciated the relative freedom and openness of society. He noted in his journal, 'England is at present the country in the world where there is the greatest freedom. I do not make an exception for any republic.' On the other hand, 'money is more important than honour or virtue and the people are coarse, insociable and, worst of all, corrupt' [22]

His stay in London, which lasted until 1731, contributed crucially to the most influential political book of the eighteenth century, and one of the most important of modern times, *L'Esprit des lois*. He began it in about 1734, aware of the interest in things English aroused by Voltaire's *Lettres* but at the same time made cautious by the condemnation Voltaire had incurred. He took more than ten years over the book, mostly at his castle at La Brède. Material was sent by friends at the Royal Society. To escape French censors, *L'Esprit* was printed and published in Geneva in 1748. Several hundred early copies were destined for Britain, where they were expected to have an eager readership, though Montesquieu prudently dropped the idea of dedicating it to the Prince of Wales – France and Britain had, after all, again been at war.

L'Esprit des lois examined the relation between a country's laws and its constitution, civil society and physical circumstances. It proceeded by studying the historical origins of laws – in the English case, seen as a Germanic inheritance. In making history and law central to political theory, Montesquieu 'set the tone and form' of modern political thought.[23] He discussed two crucial examples, ancient Rome and modern England, but unlike other writers, not least Voltaire, he was not suggesting that they provided ready models for France to imitate. Each nation was unique, and so had to draw on its own circumstances and experiences. Reformers must be prudent, and respect existing institutions, which had deep roots and complex causes – a view eloquently developed in Edmund Burke's 1790 attack on the French revolution (see below, p. 198). But tolerance and the ability to correct and improve its own workings were essential to all societies, and here Montesquieu identified England's advantage:

> The government of England is wiser, because it has a body that constantly scrutinizes it, and constantly scrutinizes itself. Whatever its mistakes, they do not last long . . . A free government, one that is always agitated, could not maintain itself, were it not open to corrections through its own laws.[24]

While he agreed with Voltaire that the English system was superior to those of Greece and Rome, he did not share Voltaire's provocative optimism. The influence of Bolingbroke, Locke and English republican writers, and opposition attacks on the growing power of the Crown and its patronage, as well as the seeming instability of the party system and of parliamentary power, caused him to warn of the precariousness of political freedom. This concern engendered the most famous and enduring feature of his analysis, the idea of the separation of powers. In Book 10, Chapter 6, 'De la Constitution d'Angleterre', he defined the freedom of states by the relationship between three powers, legislative, executive and judicial. If all are in the same hands, the State is a despotism; if one of them is independent, it is a 'moderate' state; if all are separate, it is a free state. The mingled reflections of a disaffected Tory and a hereditary French judge 'dignified and rationalized' what had begun as a party political slogan, 'linked it to a theory of liberty, and handed it to posterity'[25] – above all as the keystone of the future American constitution and all those influenced by it.

Montesquieu was cautious about the future. England was in theory free, but the practice was less certain. If, or when, the executive corrupted Parliament, freedom would be at an end. The survival of freedom would depend on the 'general spirit' of the nation – what we would call its political culture – and on the 'spirit of liberty' of 'ordinary people'. While tending towards pessimism, Montesquieu believed that 'in Europe the last gasp of liberty would come from an Englishman'.[26]

Montesquieu's vast learning, power of argument and brilliance of style gave his book unequalled weight as the fundamental handbook of political freedom across Europe; and moreover gave it some protection from authorities who detested its message but were incapable of rebutting it. Critics at the Sorbonne backed down. *L'Esprit* was soon freely published in France, selling thirteen editions in eighteen months. Though it was placed on the papal index of forbidden books, even Catholic criticisms were minor. Many opponents could not suppress grudging admiration. This was literally a new political language for France: the very words *constitution* and *exécutif* were anglicisms. Montesquieu was a loyal Frenchman, but he hailed England as the modern world's ark of freedom. He was a faithful subject, but his work gave ammunition to those who attacked the Bourbon monarchy as a 'despotism'.

Not the least offshoot of Montesquieu's pessimistic analysis of the precariousness of political systems was Edward Gibbon's *The Decline and Fall of the Roman Empire* (1776–88), one of the greatest English historical and literary works by one of the most francocentric of English thinkers, and which David Hume advised him to write in French. Gibbon, familiar with French historiography and philosophy, drew on Montesquieu in his account of Rome's political decline into despotism. He also paralleled the latter's secular analysis of history. His account of the greatest of historical epics is not only independent of divine Providence – revolutionary enough – but it depicts Rome's decline as caused by the very rise of Christianity.

Intellectual traffic was not, therefore, one way. The second half of the century, despite the disruption and resentment caused by successive wars, was a time of deep and fruitful dialogue, in which thoughtful disagreement was as important as emulation. Though visions of modernity came from Britain, France, notwithstanding the capricious workings of censorship and repression, remained Europe's cultural arena. Thus, for example, Ephraim Chambers in London had the brilliant idea of publishing a *Cyclopaedia, or Universal Dictionary of Arts and Sciences*, in 1728. In the late 1740s a group of French publishers with masonic connections copied the idea, and commissioned Denis Diderot (in prison for his writings) and Jean d'Alembert to direct it. Their *Encyclopédie* dwarfed Chambers's model. This mighty product of the French republic of letters, though it depended on a core of writers, finally involved 20,000 people.[27] It began to appear in 1751, and over the next twenty years placed a permanent French imprint on Enlightenment culture. Britain, however innovative its cultural life, lacked the infrastructure – libraries, academies, monasteries, universities – for scholarly work on such a scale.

Cross-Channel exchanges inspired two giants of the Scottish

Enlightenment, David Hume and his friend Adam Smith. Hume's early philosophical work, a non-religious explanation of morality, was influenced by the writings of the seventeenth-century French Jesuit Malebranche. His *History of England* (1754–62), the first presentation of history as politics, complicated and unpredictable, consciously aimed to supersede the cautious chronicle of Rapin and the racy, unreliable narratives of Voltaire. The francophile Hume returned to Paris in 1763, immediately after the Seven Years War, as secretary to the British ambassador. His religious scepticism made him fashionable, and his affability made *le bon David* a great social success, attracting the almost obligatory (though in his case probably unwelcome) attention of the *philosophe* groupie the Comtesse de Boufflers. He greatly regretted the termination of his diplomatic post, and was tempted to live in Paris rather than London, where 'Scotsmen are hated'.[28] As we shall see, he did return to London, and took Jean-Jacques Rousseau with him – a sad mistake.

The visit of Adam Smith from 1764 to 1766 is comparable in intellectual consequence only with that of Montesquieu in the other direction. Smith's visit, his only ever excursion into the great world, was planned during the Seven Years War – one example among many of how cultural relations sidestepped wars. Hume at the embassy paved the way. Smith was known in France as the author of the *Theory of Moral Sentiments* (1759), just published in French. Hume assured him that – despite or because of its being banned – the Marquise de Pompadour, the king's mistress, and the Duchesse de Choiseul, the chief minister's wife, had read it. Smith's *Theory* explained morality as a product of nature, 'when she formed man for society'. He had drawn on French thought: his student notes refer to Montesquieu; his title echoed Levesque de Pouilly's *Théorie des sentiments agréables* (1747); and his ideas were partly a response to Jean-Jacques Rousseau's *Discours sur l'origine et les fondements de l'inégalité parmi les hommes* (1755). Travelling as tutor to the young Duke of Buccleuch, Smith visited Paris, Toulouse and much of the south, met Voltaire several times, and carried out research on French taxation and trade, partly to diagnose the weaknesses that had caused France's defeat in the Seven Years War. Despite his bad French and what at least one Parisian lady considered extreme ugliness, Smith made his mark in the more intellectual salons. He had many discussions with advocates of economic freedom, principally members of the Physiocratic school, Dupont de Nemours, François Quesnay and the intellectual civil servant and future minister Anne Robert Turgot. Many considered Smith the Physiocrats' disciple, though in fact he was sceptical of 'men of system'. These researches and exchanges – 'the most exciting passage in Smith's intellectual development'[29] – helped to shape his *Inquiry into the Nature* and *Causes of the Wealth of Nations* (1776), not least in that he rejected the central Physiocrat doctrine that agriculture was the sole basis of wealth. He also concluded from his French observations that economic enterprise could survive even incompetent government, and hence that social and economic improvement did not need state direction, but only the rule of law and security for persons and property.

The revolutionary thrust of Smith's mighty work – the wittiest, if not the only witty, economic treatise – was to make economic freedom the foundation of a peaceful and non-oppressive society. This fulfilled the central Enlightenment ambition of discovering 'natural laws' of human behaviour – in this case 'the obvious and simple system of natural liberty'. The individual instinct for self-betterment would serve the general good 'in the natural course of things', as if by 'an invisible hand'. 'It is not from the benevolence of the butcher, the brewer, or the baker, that we expect our dinner, but from their regard to their own interest.' So economic freedom was not only right, it was also efficient. Oppression and slavery were not only wrong, but also impractical. Even well-meaning state interference was self-defeating: 'It retards, instead of accelerating, the progress of the society towards real wealth and greatness.' As all benefited from the labours of all, the only requirement was that 'every man [should be] left to pursue his own interest his own way'.[30]

Smith had synthesized important themes of French and British thought. His ideas were taken up by early leaders of the French revolution for a diversity of reasons, and continued to be debated. Yet, as the intellectual historian Claude Nicolet has remarked, Smith's ideas and those of the Scottish Enlightenment generally, 'the birth-certificate of modernity', have not taken root in French political culture.[31] Smith's vision was of a constantly changing world without certainty or superior authority. This conflicted with French absolutist traditions of economic control (commonly ascribed to Louis XIV's minister Colbert), Catholic paternalism, republican patriotism, and later the Bonapartist emphasis on state-directed modernization. It also aroused fears of social upheaval during the long aftermath of the revolution. Hence French distaste for what a recent prime minister, Edouard Balladur, described as 'the law of the jungle'. Above all, it was the French revolution that repudiated the modern emphasis on individual liberty in favour of an idealized vision of the citizenship of the ancient world. Republicans condemned Britain ('Carthage') as a selfish commercial society, and praised France ('Rome') for upholding nobler values. Two centuries later, this arguably still marks France off from the Anglophone world. French rejection of the European Constitution in 2005 was in large part a continuation of 'the old quarrel between the heirs of Colbert and of Adam Smith'.[32]

Travellers' Tales

It is certain that the English are the people of Europe who travel the most
. . . Their island is for them a sort of prison.

ABBE LE BLANC, 1751[33]

You are not sent abroad to converse with your own countrymen:
among them, in general, you will get little knowledge, no languages, and I
am sure, no manners . . . Their pleasures of the table end in beastly drunkenness, low riot, broken windows, and very often (as they well deserve)
broken bones.

LORD CHESTERFIELD, 1749[34]

The greatest advantage a sensible Englishman derives from seeing foreign
countries is the knowledge he thereby acquires of the incomparable superiority of his own.

JOHN ANDREWS, 1783[35]

The six decades between Voltaire's hurried arrival in London and the beginning of the French revolution saw significant numbers of Europeans travelling for pleasure and from curiosity. This was an aspect of Enlightenment cosmopolitanism, as religious hatreds abated; a form of consumption associated with spreading wealth; an aspect of cultural exchange, in parallel with reading foreign literature; and not least one element in the formation of a sense of national identity through comparing one's own with foreign ways. Travelling increased everywhere, but cross-Channel travelling, especially by the British, increased most. A surge followed every war, for though war was not an absolute bar, especially for the bold or the well connected, Channel storms were risk enough without the added danger of privateers. Peace – in the 1720s, the early 50s, the mid-60s, the 80s, and in 1802 – saw a rush to visit the former enemy.

Ambivalent feelings spiced the experience. For the French, British victories increased, if not their admiration, at least their desire to understand how perfidious Albion pulled it off. Their reactions often suggest the impoverished aristocrat, innately superior and disdainful of upstart vulgarity. The British resembled the *nouveau riche*, eager to show off their money and modernity and shocked by dirt and smells. Both sides were quick to take offence, and eager for reassurance. Yet despite wars and religious and political differences, reactions were rarely one-dimensional: admiration and criticism went together, and personal relationships crossed national and ideological boundaries.

There were broad differences between French and British tourists.[36]

There are no reliable statistics. Contemporary comments on 'vast numbers' refer to dozens, not thousands. Several historians accept an annual figure of 12,000 British visiting the Continent in the late 1760s, rising to over 40,000 in the mid-1780s. This suggests that 5 per cent of the population might have travelled abroad, mostly to or through France. This is an impressive figure if true; but French police records suggest that it was an exaggeration – unless the authorities overlooked most visitors.[37] Whatever the true total, the British were certainly the most noticeable and numerous element. French observers perceived this as a consequence of the awfulness of British life and the superiority of their own. France had everything, so why bother travelling? Still, the French were said to be the most numerous foreign visitors to London. More of the British were young, dispatched before or after university on a supposedly educational 'grand tour'. More were women – French women rarely travelled abroad. And the British were more varied: from grandees to people of 'the middling sort' hungry for a taste of sophistication:

> we went out of England, a very awkward, regular, good English
> family! but half a year in France, and a winter passed in the warmer
> climate of Italy, have ripen'd our minds to every refinement of ease,
> dissipation and pleasure.[38]

This satirical fiction resembles Hester Thrale's summary of her family's real experience: 'We left Paris – where we have spent a Month of extreme Expence, some Pleasure and some Profit; for we have seen many People & many Things; and Queeny has picked up a little French & a good deal of Dancing.'[39] Enjoyment was a larger part of British motivation than of French; for even when education was on the agenda, fun was never far behind. Whereas, proverbially, no Frenchman ever visits England for pleasure. Those of higher rank were often on an intellectual mission, and the list of philosophical visitors is almost a roll call of the Enlightenment, including, as well as Voltaire and Montesquieu, Helvetius, Buffon, Rousseau, Prévost, Holbach, Raynal and Necker. Those of lower rank went to make rather than spend money. 'On either side of the Channel there was a career to be made from being a foreigner',[40] by cashing in on fashionable stereotypes. The career of Frenchness undoubtedly offered more openings: London had French musicians, dancing-masters, teachers, artists, dressmakers, wigmakers and servants – described by one French observer as unskilled, insolent and immoral.[41] Paris imported bankers and jockeys, whose reputation was no better.

Books about travelling, real and imagined, catered for vicarious tourism among those who were intellectually rather than geographically mobile. As well as providing amusing or shocking anecdotes and practical information, they were full of political and social commentary. The supposedly factual overlapped with the fictional. *Gulliver's Travels* inspired not only Voltaire in *Candide*, but many humbler authors who produced guidebooks brimming with what they hoped was corrosive Swiftean satire.[42] Existing books were plagiarized by writers who had never set foot in the places they breezily described. Even when they had, their ignorance of the language hampered direct knowledge. This was a weakness of the French (who expected foreigners to speak their language) more than of the British. Thus, Pierre-Jean Grosley had difficulty with 'Sakespear'/'Sakhspear'; Madame Du Bocage enjoyed the pleasure gardens of 'Faxhall' (Vauxhall) and 'Renelash' (Ranelagh). One guidebook provided helpful phonetic versions of English phrases, such as the ingenious *il te rince* for *it rains*.[43] (This kind of pleasantry is still enjoyed by the French, who know that anglophones express gratitude by saying '*Saint-Cloud Paris-Match*'.) Literary convention, plagiarism and outright propaganda caused themes and stereotypes to recur, which in turn shaped tourists' expectations. Whether personal experience fitted expectations was therefore a staple of published travel writing and private letters and diaries.

The two travel books that long dominated the French market were Le Blanc's *Lettres d'un François*, first published in 1745, and Grosley's three-volume *Londres*, of 1770. Grosley's book was based on a six-week visit to London in 1765. He did not speak English – 'no man of sense meddles with foreign languages after forty' – so he depended for information on his cook and the family with whom he lodged. He could only understand a little of the insults ('French dog', 'French b.') he claimed to have been subjected to at every street corner. A happier memory was of 'unbridled' and 'unconstrained' English bosoms, which 'in their growth and development . . . enjoy all the benefits of liberty'.[44] Le Blanc, frequently re-edited and plagiarized, was one of the best-sellers of the eighteenth century, and, after Voltaire, the most widely read book on Britain.[45] He was tirelessly supercilious in his efforts to set his compatriots straight and cut the British down to size: 'In France people think both too well and too ill of the English; they are neither what they say themselves to be, nor what we suppose them to be.'[46] In short, England was foggy, and its people uncivilized, crude, dull and getting worse. However, because of the damp, the countryside was fertile, and so fruit and vegetables were better and more varied than in France – the main attraction Le Blanc could discern.

LE BLANC'S ENGLAND

Abbé Jean-Bernard Le Blanc visited England during 1737–8, not for the seven years his publisher claimed. He was an acquaintance of Voltaire and of Hume, whose work he helped introduce into France and some of which he translated. His *Lettres* appeared during the War of Austrian Succession. He has been described as a 'moderate anglophile',[47] which shows how very moderate anglophilia could be.

It is to the fogs with which their island is almost always covered that the English owe the richness of their pastures and the melancholy of their temperament.

In Paris, footmen and chambermaids often ape their masters in their dress. In London it is quite the opposite; it is the masters who dress like their servants and duchesses who copy their chambermaids – an almost inconceivable absurdity.

Frenchmen enjoy the company of women, Englishmen fear it
. . . Our women who love the perfume of amber are little like the women of this country, who relish the scent of the stable
. . . It is more graceful for women to speak of hairstyles and ribbons, the play and the opera, than of saddles and horses
. . . She who has not the timidity of her sex more often replaces it by vice than by virtue.

England is without contradiction the country with most eccentrics in the world; the English regard eccentricity if not as a virtue, as least as a merit . . . They criticize us for being all the same. Reasonable people are enemies of eccentricity – a fault as rare in France as it is common in England.

Humour [is] a ridiculous extravagance of conversation . . . joking combined with eccentricity.

They relieve boredom with alcohol . . . getting rid of the women and covering the table with mugs, bottles and glasses, even tobacco and pipes . . . I never witnessed the elegant orgies of the Gentlemen of Cambridge and Oxford. I was not brave enough to pursue my research to such extremes.

Nothing is so rare among the English as gentle wit and gaiety of mood . . . They do not know how to enjoy life so well as the French.

Though not all the book is negative – it was regarded by contemporaries as a dispassionate description – its tenor can be gauged from some of the chapter headings: 'the lack of progress of English eloquence'; 'English bad taste in buildings'; 'the pernicious opinions of Hobbes'; 'the dangerous abuse of the Press'; 'cruelty in Shakespeare'; 'on the English taste for violent exercise'; 'on highwaymen and the negligence of the English police'; 'the excessive English interest in politics' etc.

Two of the most popular of many English guidebooks date, like that of Grosley, from the post-war tourist boom of the 1760s. Philip Thicknesse's *Observations on the Customs and Manners of the French Nation* (1766) and John Millard's anonymously published *Gentleman's Guide in his Tour through France* (n.d.) were respectively by an army and a naval officer, which perhaps assured readers of their intrepid ability to cope with whatever France could throw at them. The *Gentleman's Guide* aimed at severe and impersonal practicality, concentrating on routes, addresses, prices and practical advice: from the number and types of shirts to take to warnings to be 'extremely cautious in your amours (if any you propose!)'. Indeed, the need for caution when dealing with the French was a leitmotif. Otherwise, the author's personality rarely intrudes (he prefers English women and dislikes rich monks), other than to exhort his readers to spend as little as possible 'in the Country of our natural enemy', and concluding that if one avoided the 'follies, vices and fopperies of that vain, superficial people' one could live for eighteen months on £150.[48] Thicknesse, comparatively francophile (despite being sometimes 'miserable for want of tea'), was concerned to rebut Tobias Smollett's 'injustice' in drawing 'so vile a portrait' of the French in his controversial *Travels through France and Italy* (1766). Smollett's error, he asserted, had been to mix with the common people rather than 'people of fashion'. Thicknesse was no keener on 'low-bred rich people' from Britain making a 'trip' across the Channel, where they made a spectacle of themselves and spoilt things for the discerning traveller, such as the author and readers of *Observations*. He was happy to make a spectacle of himself, however, travelling with his family, guitar and a good supply of opium in the eighteenth-century equivalent of a camper-van, with a liveried monkey riding postillion.[49]

Thus informed and perhaps emboldened, the traveller could set off. Most went via Calais or Boulogne and Dover, the shortest sea crossings. Individual fares were twelve *livres* (half a guinea) for masters, six for servants. A private boat at three to five guineas could take a whole family plus carriage and horses. This short crossing, however, meant longer and much more expensive road journeys to and from Paris. Via Dieppe and Brighthelmstone (Brighton) was therefore cheaper. But the hazards of a longer crossing must have been a deterrent for all but the intrepid or hard up. Although in ideal weather the Calais–Dover crossing could be done in three hours on the mail packet, unfavourable winds meant days of delay, and unexpected storms could involve being blown hither and thither for a day or more, wet, seasick, and miserable, landing miles from anywhere, and often in highly dangerous conditions. The writer Madame Du Bocage in 1750 was blown off course to Deal: 'The captain took me into his arms to help me into the boat, which the waves constantly drove from the vessel, so that a slip which he made upon the ladder obliged him to let go: by good luck, instead of falling into the water, I found myself alone upon this skiff in the midst of the rowers, at the mercy of the waves, and trembling with fear.'[50] Passengers were at the mercy not only of the elements, but of sailors, boatmen, porters and customs men, all demanding tips.

By the last decades of the century, tourism between London and Paris was as well organized as it could be in the days before steam. An all-in ticket could be bought at the stagecoach office in the Rue Notre Dame des Victoires for 120 *livres*, including coach, boat, board and lodging, luggage and customs fees. Doing it on the cheap, via Dieppe and Brighton, came to only about forty livres. Coaches between London and Dover left hourly, and cost a guinea (half-price on top), and took sixteen or seventeen hours. Thrifty French visitors were advised not to try walking: it would take several days and so cost more in accommodation. From Calais to Paris was a bigger expedition: three days, with the charges for post-horses and postillions alone about £10. Large inns ran their own coaches, or hired out carriages. Those planning a longer stay often brought their own carriage or bought one second-hand (about 20 guineas), which they would trade in on their return. Some travellers preferred public stagecoaches – 'like Noah's ark' – doubtless for economy, but also because it enabled the gregarious to mingle with the natives; in England, there was usually silence, in France, general conversation.

The seaports were reputed – for good and ill – for their inns. The choleric Scot Tobias Smollett damned Dover in 1766 as 'a den of thieves', whose people 'live by piracy in time of war; and by smuggling and fleecing strangers in time of peace'.[51] Dover had a French inn managed in the 1780s by 'honest sieur Mariée' from Calais, which cost 5 shillings for bed and board. The unfortunate Grosley, however, had to fetch his own beefsteak from the kitchen, and was woken at 3 a.m. and told to vacate his room. Yet he noted that in most inns 'an English lord is as well served as in his own house, and with a cleanliness much to be wished for in most of the best houses in France'.[52] Dunkirk had the English-owned White Hart. Calais had several that catered for British tourists: most famous was the new Hôtel d'Angleterre (with its own theatre and carriage hire), said to be the finest hotel in Europe.

Once on the road, accommodation was chancier in France. Inn-keepers and postillions were surly and demanding – possibly a symptom of widespread anglophobia, which Thicknesse thought was concealed by the good manners of the upper classes, but betrayed 'upon most occasions' by ordinary people. Fleas and bedbugs were endemic – 'I never shall get over the dirt of this country,' exclaimed the francophile Horace Walpole.[53] Food, however, was sometimes a pleasant surprise. Tourism raised prices and made it prudent to agree on the bill beforehand: 'The multitudes of English in this country has made travelling as dear as in England'[54] – especially as they were all assumed to be *milords* laden with guineas. French roads were reputed safer, thanks to the iron hand of the *maréchaussée*, the mounted police. English highwaymen gave French visitors a particular *frisson*. They were a downside of English liberty and misplaced humanity – merely hanging delinquents rather than breaking them on the wheel. Guide books advised carrying two purses – one for the robber – and travelling on Sundays, the highwaymen's day off.

Travellers' writings display interesting consistencies. It became commonplace for French visitors to praise the unparalleled beauty of the English countryside, 'like a vast and magnificent garden', and to marvel at the prosperity of rural people, the men dressed in broadcloth, the women like shepherdesses in a novel. From this, political conclusions could be drawn about the merits of a free peasantry and equal taxation. Almost all were impressed by the Dover road (although Smollett considered it 'the worst in England', with 'not a drop of tolerable malt liquor to be had'), and by the coaches, for competition meant lower prices, unlike in France where the hire of post-horses was a state monopoly. They were even more impressed by there being a footpath and occasional seats – a sign of the republican egalitarianism of England where 'laws are not made only by people in carriages'.[55] British visitors had mixed impressions of northern France. Some found the inns and people dirty, the towns dingy and gothic churches old-fashioned – though Amiens cathedral was generally admired (and the nearby Bull's Head provided a decent cup of tea). Others praised the variety of the countryside, marvelled at the profusion of game (hunting being a noble monopoly), and loved the food. First-timers were amazed at the differences that twenty miles could make: 'Monks could be seen in all the streets . . . with their feet bare or in sandals . . . The carriages, carts, horses and even dogs were different, so that the scene altogether was particularly striking.'[56] After the hardships of the Seven Years War, many remarked on the poverty that commonly featured in British stereotypes of France, blamed on royal, noble and ecclesiastical rapacity. Both Thicknesse and Hester Thrale were struck by the prevalence of deformity, though the latter blamed it on young girls being forced to wear corsets.

The hazards of travel recall those met with in third-world countries today: accidents (common with horse-drawn transport), arguments over prices and bills, harassment by crowds of would-be guides and porters, over-indulgence in cheap alcohol, occasional crime and intestinal disorders. British doctors were preferred – the French 'talk such old-fashioned nonsense, even the best of them'. Lady Spencer in 1767 suffered the ordeal of being 'forced to submit to the manners of the place and . . . squirted with clysters almost incessantly' and having 'the whole circle of men [told] how often I have a motion'.[57] Travellers were alerted to such dangers by the *Gentleman's Guide*. Excretion was, and long remained, a matter of the utmost concern to British visitors. The water in Paris caused 'fluxions' – a fearsome problem, for 'no place in the delicate or polite world is so ill provided with Conveniences', part of the explanation for the 'beastly custom' among the French, unanimously deplored by the British, of 'dropping their daizy' in the street.[58]

Paris and London, as now, were the main destinations. Here there was considerable agreement not only among compatriots, but even between the two nationalities. Paris was grander, London more modern. Paris had monuments; London had shops. Paris had aristocratic salons; London had public pleasure gardens. Lord Dalrymple (the British ambassador's brother) wrote in 1715, 'I have not been long enough here, to know, whether London or Paris is the most diverting town. The people here are more gay, the ladies less handsome, and much more painted, love galantry [*sic*] more than pleasure, and coquetry more than solid love'[59] – a succinct statement of views long common on both sides of the Channel.

Smollett was ashamed that French travellers passed through the grimy wastes of Southwark before they found themselves amid the splendours of London and Westminister. This, he thought, damaged British prestige. He need not have worried: the French were not much impressed by London and Westminster either. St Paul's was at least big, and the best sight in London. The buildings of state – St James's, the Houses of Parliament – were embarrassingly inadequate. Even the temples of Mammon lacked splendour. As for the Thames, which could have provided a magnificent panorama, it had been fenced off to prevent what the French knew to be the English penchant for suicide (all that fog, beer and melancholy), or else was hidden behind warehouses. It was therefore necessary to go downstream to Greenwich, to admire the naval hospital (at last, a monument!) and gasp at the bustle of the port of London. This French visitors understood: the sea, trade and the navy were the foundations of British greatness. London's pavements were scarcely less memorable an expression of Englishness: the life and limb of mere walkers was protected against the high and mighty on wheels. The astronomer La Condamine is said to have exclaimed: 'God be praised! A country where they look after pedestrians.'[60] Street lights ('like a ball-room') and piped water were marvelled at – the latter, claimed Grosley, introduced by a French refugee.[61] The French increasingly admired London parks as the fashionable taste for Nature spread. St James's was 'nature in the raw', with deer and cows. Ladies and their maids, dressed simply in straw hats and white aprons, 'walked like nymphs'. Some French visitors found the parks too open to the plebs. One of the commonest observations concerned the free-and-easy mixing of British society. Some were amused: 'It is worth your while to come to England, were it only to see an election and a cock match. There is a celestial spirit of anarchy and confusion.'[62] Masters and servants, the French found, dressed alike; entertainments seemed open to all; and people of quality appeared happy to mingle with their inferiors:

> Nothing is more common than to see in a tavern or café, Milords and Artisans sitting at the same table, talking familiarly about the public news and the affairs of the government. It is the same in the promenades, balls and plays.[63]

In both cities, visitors were recognizable by their clothes, and many hastened to disguise themselves as natives. British gentlemen – apparently more than ladies – with social ambitions had to kit themselves out: coats, breeches, wigs and hats were one of the largest items of tourist expenditure. Mixing with French society was the object of the visit, and correct style was essential. It would take four or five days for a tailor to run up the necessary. Until then, nothing more ambitious than sightseeing was permissible. Lord Chesterfield in 1750 instructed his son:

> When you come to Paris, you must take care to be extremely well dressed . . . Get the best French tailor to make your clothes . . . and then wear them, button them or unbutton them, as the genteelest people you see do. Let your man learn of the best *friseur* to do your hair well, for that is a very material part of your dress.[64]

Wearing native clothes might not work. Thicknesse warned that 'an Englishman's beef and pudding face' might look silly under a smart little French hat.[65] The two nations looked, stood and moved differently. French ladies and gentlemen were schooled by dancing masters into what Chesterfield praised as 'an habitual genteel carriage'.

Typical British mockery of French foppishness, signified by umbrellas, muffs, elaborate wigs, coiffured dogs, and underfed people.

The French feared being insulted in the London streets – a theme of generations of travel books. It is impossible to know to what extent the prevalence of these stories is evidence of English francophobia or of French anglophobia.[66] Frenchmen dressed more elaborately, and so class resentment as well as xenophobia was a potential cause of hostility. Muffs and umbrellas were foppish giveaways, the motifs of many cartoons. Only one Englishman was known to carry an umbrella in mid-century, James Hanway, philanthropic founder of the Marine Society. His was a splendid tent-like accessory, covered in pale green silk and lined with straw-coloured satin decorated with small fruits and flowers. He seems to have been a tolerated eccentric. Less so were later British umbrella carriers, the fashionable francophile 'macaronis', who raised certain suspicions: 'BRITONS, for shame! Be male and female still. Banish this foreign vice.' Such associations may have stung the Iron Duke into reprimanding several young guards officers on a rainy battlefield in 1813: 'Lord Wellington does not approve of the use of umbrellas during the enemy's firing, and will not allow gentlemen's sons to make themselves ridiculous in the eyes of the army.'[67]

Both cities had districts where visitors felt more at home. The British could find hotels, English bankers, coffee houses, bread and butter and a cup of tea in the vicinity of the embassy near Saint-Germain-des-Prés. The French equivalents were in the lowlier atmosphere of Leicester Fields and Soho. In both cities, travellers staying for some time were recommended on grounds of cost, propriety and society to take lodgings in a respectable private house, or to rent rooms. They should engage a local servant, and, at least in Paris, find a hairdresser for the daily curl and powder necessary for both sexes. In both cities one could order take-away food; but there were also many eating-houses. The Paris restaurant was in its infancy, and English-style establishments such as Beauvillier's Grande Taverne de Londres set the trend.[68] In London, boarding-house meals seem timeless: soup, steak or lamb chops and potatoes. However, the Canon in Jermyn Street and the Sept Etoiles in Eagle Street served French food for a shilling.[69] French visitors were advised to steer clear of the wine, expensive and often ersatz; thirsty visitors should stick to porter, which had 'a gentle purgative effect'[70] – helpful in coping with English cuisine. On this, French opinions differed. Some found the ingredients better and more varied than at home, but the meat was revoltingly under-cooked, and the flavour of coal smoke discernible. The water in Paris (drawn from the sewage-rich Seine) had a more drastic laxative effect, but the food was superior. Thicknesse declared that one could dine better in Paris for seventeen pence than in London for seventeen shillings – a combination of indulgence and economy that has beguiled British tourists for three centuries.

There was no denying the superiority of Paris when it came to monu-ments. British taste favoured the modern: baroque and neo-classical buildings such as the Louvre, the Invalides and the towering new churches of Saint-Sulpice (completed 1736), Saint-Roch (completed 1760), and Sainte-Geneviève (1757–90). Guidebooks listed largely the same sites as they do today: Notre Dame, the Luxembourg, the Louvre, the Place Vendôme and the Place des Victoires ('See it'). Other attractions have not survived France's history – the Tuileries and 'an odd Kind of stone building', the Bastille (exterior visits only). The Gobelins tapestry works were a special attraction because managed by a British Jacobite.

Indeed, tourist attitudes to the Jacobite and Catholic presence suggest that, at least from mid-century onwards, the British were less bigoted than historians have suggested. Guidebooks pointed out that the bodies of 'our King James II' and his daughter could be seen at the Val de Grâce monastery, their coffins unburied and symbolically awaiting return. The nearby English Benedictine monastery was a place to visit, for the monks were 'very civil to their countrymen' and would happily act as guides if treated to refreshments and perhaps given a small present. Dr Johnson and Mrs Thrale spent a notable part of their trip visiting monks and nuns, and Johnson arranged a visit to Pembroke College, Oxford, for one of his monastic acquaintances.

A teenage visitor who in 1789 described Paris as an 'ill-built, dirty, stinking town' was missing the point. Whatever its other odours, Paris simply reeked with class. Italy was still the centre of the arts; but Paris was the arbiter of taste. Although neighbouring palaces – Marly, Saint-Cloud, Fontainebleau and of course 'second to nothing of the Kind in Europe, I mean VERSAILLES'[71] – were the centres of court and government, where royals could be gawped at as they ate, prayed or even dressed, they were not the principal attraction. The British wanted to acquire Parisian gloss. They signed up for fencing and dancing lessons, bought furnishings and sat for portraits. Acquiring style was the aim:

> to be well-bred without ceremony, easy without negligence, steady and intrepid with modesty, genteel without affectation, insinuating without meanness, cheerful without being noisy, frank without indiscretion, and secret without mysteriousness; to know the proper time and place for whatever you say or do.[72]

In France, salons organized by and around women were the centres of cultural activity, and were open to the well connected or the famously talented. The successful 'blue-stocking circle' in London could not compete for elegance or prestige. Parisian patronesses – nearly all of the nobility, but not necessarily of the court, and not necessarily conventionally respectable – had European reputations. British intellectuals, including Horace Walpole, David Hume and Edward Gibbon, were among the star guests. Among the most intellectually acute patronesses were the Marquise de Tencin, the blind Marquise du Deffand (a close friend of Walpole) and Madame Geoffrin, on good enough terms with Hume to call him 'mon gros drôle' and 'mon aimable coquin'. Salons gave French culture a characteristic sociability, organized round conversation. Critics said it deprived it of depth: style was more important than substance. Walpole remarked that 'everyone sings, reads their own works . . . without hesitation or capacity'.[73] As everyone realized, it made women, and contact between men and women, central to cultural life:

> at Paris, where both women and men are judges and critics . . . conversations that both form and improve the taste and whet the judgment are surely preferable to the conversations of our mixed companies here; which, if they happen to rise above brag and whist, infallibly stop short of everything either pleasing or instructive. I take the reason of this to be that (as women generally give the *ton* to the conversation) our English women are not nearly so well informed and cultivated as the French.[74]

MRS THRALE AND MADAME DU BOCAGE

Two prominent travel writers and women of letters were Marie-Anne Du Bocage (1710–1802), author of *Lettres sur l'Angleterre, la Hollande et l'Italie* (1764) and Hester Thrale (1741–1821), author of *Observations and Reflections Made in the Course of a Journey through France, Italy and Germany* (1789). Du Bocage had visited England in 1750, wrote poetry inspired by Milton and Pope, and frequented the Chesterfields and Lady Mary Wortley Montagu. She became fond of tea and even of 'the simple cookery of the English, of which we have so bad an opinion (their substantial meat, their plum-pudding, their fish)'. Thrale, accompanied by her family and its formidable adjunct Samuel Johnson, first visited Paris in 1775. They paid the usual courtesy visits to Madame Du Bocage and were invited to dinner (at which their hostess showed her liking for English cuisine by serving 'an English Pudding made after the Receipt of the Duchess of Queensbury'). But the encounter was not a success: Du Bocage was not greatly impressed with her guests, and they were discomfited by the footman putting sugar in their cups with his fingers, and horrified when, faced with an old teapot that would not pour, the footman and then madame solved the problem by blowing down the spout to dislodge whatever was causing the blockage. This confirmed Thrale's impression that the French were an 'indelicate' people, who moreover ate rotten meat and hawked and spat with abandon.[75]

London attracted fewer French visitors, partly because fewer travelled. Those who did realized that London represented something new. Coffee houses, clubs, theatres, concerts, pleasure gardens, spectacles of all kinds constituted a commercialized and hence relatively open social and cultural scene.[76] Many deplored this as vulgar and disquieting: one risked rubbing shoulders with the undesirable, people in the streets lacked deference, and they might even insult well-dressed foreigners. Yet the attraction of such public spaces, and of private spaces that were independent of the authorities and the official social hierarchy, can be seen in France after 1760 in the advance of freemasonry, the popularity of clubs and cafés, and finally, in the social and commercial success of the Palais Royal, France's first *centre commercial*.

Few places were visited outside the capital cities and the major routes. French visitors sometimes ventured to Oxford or Cambridge, and many British travelled on to Italy. Few were as intrepid as Arthur Young, who crossed France on horseback in the 1780s: decent roads, food and accommodation for visitors were sparse. Fashionable interest did grow in wild romantic nature, epitomized by Scotland, the Pyrenees or the Alps. Pioneers included Lawrence Sterne, who reached Bagnères-de-Bigorre in 1762, despite the Seven Years War. In the summer of 1770, Henry Temple MP (father of Lord Palmerston) spent six weeks in the Alps with the painter William Pars, who displayed his works the following year at the Royal Academy. By then, about a dozen Englishmen visited the glaciers each season.[77]

Men, and sometimes women, of letters also visited out-of-the-way intellectual celebrities. There was a stream of British visitors to Voltaire (including Oliver Goldsmith, Gibbon, the radical politician John Wilkes and Adam Smith) and to the less gregarious Rousseau (including James Boswell, who expressed his admiration for the latter by seducing his long-suffering 'housekeeper', Thérèse Levasseur, as a sort of souvenir). Private hospitality when off the beaten track was essential, and for this, personal or academic contacts or freemasonry were invaluable. Constant correspondence kept this European intellectual network together.

Two towering intellectual figures made spectacularly unsuccessful cross-Channel visits despite efforts to smooth their journeys: Jean-Jacques Rousseau and Samuel Johnson. Rousseau, pursued by both the French

Rousseau by Ramsay: Rousseau thought this portrait so unflattering that he suspected a conspiracy to ridicule him.

authorities and importunate admirers, was persuaded by a well-meaning David Hume to accompany him to England in January 1766. Things started badly when Horace Walpole, as a joke, circulated a spoof letter supposedly from Frederick the Great: 'My dear Jean-Jacques . . . the French have issued a warrant for your arrest; so come to me . . . Your good friend, Frederick.' For the hyper-sensitive and paranoid Rousseau, this was the first sign that Hume and his coterie were conspiring to humiliate and discredit him. His suspicions persisted, despite his being fêted in London, offered a royal pension at Hume's request (which he loftily refused and then changed his mind), and taken by David Garrick to a gala performance at Drury Lane attended by the king and queen, who 'looked more at Rousseau than at the players'. Rousseau was so eager to be seen that he almost fell out of his box.[78] When Hume had Rousseau's portrait painted by Allan Ramsay, the result so displeased the sitter that he decided that making him look ugly was a further move in the plot. A wealthy admirer, Richard Davenport, offered him the use of Wootton Hall in Staffordshire, only a few miles from intellectually ambitious Lichfield. There he retreated with Thérèse (escorted from Switzerland by the assiduous Boswell, who claimed to have had sex with her thirteen times en route). They spent several happy months at Wootton, where Rousseau continued writing his *Confessions*. The generous 'Mr Ross Hall' was popular with the locals, and was made much of by aristocratic ladies and the local intelligentsia. From Lichfield came Dr Erasmus Darwin (future leader of what might be called the 'Midlands Enlightenment'), who was thrilled to find Rousseau meditating in a cave. It was too good to last. Rousseau accused first Hume and then Davenport of plotting against him, and fled, writing to the Lord Chancellor to demand a bodyguard to protect him from assassination.[79] Finally, he locked himself in the cabin of a ferry from Dover and returned to France in May 1767. Hume, at first bemused and then angered, perhaps unwisely decided to publish their correspondence, to the morbid fascination of literary Europe.

Dr Johnson's visit to France eight years later could hardly have been as extravagantly disastrous, but it was disappointing. He had long wished to go, but only in 1775, at the age of sixty-six, thanks to his wealthy friends the Thrales, did he do so. Unable to speak French, though he could read it, he fell back on Latin, by now an archaic eccentricity. This prevented sparkling conversation, and his failing hearing and eyesight made things worse. He did converse with the writer Fréron, who planned to translate one of his books, and met his young son, later a leading Jacobin Terrorist. He spent much time in libraries and with English monks, or unenthusiastically sight-seeing. According to one contemporary, he made an absurd spectacle with his ordinary brown London suit and dark stockings, so he bought white silk stockings (*de rigueur* for all but peasants), a wig and a hat – this at the time when Benjamin Franklin was cleverly playing on his own similar (and wigless) appearance to create an image of rustic wisdom. Unlike Franklin, who became a social celebrity, Johnson was ill at ease. He only visited the Court as a tourist, and expressed his regret that France, unlike Britain, had no 'tavern life . . . where people meet all upon a footing, without any care or anxiety'.[80] He turned this into a general conclusion about French society, reiterating in his notes and subsequent letters that 'In France there is no middle rank.'

This was far from being a drawback for those who went to learn noble manners. Many young gentlemen – among them sixteen-year-old Arthur Wellesley, the future Duke of Wellington – went to the Royal Academy of Equitation at Angers or other military academies in the Loire valley, where the purest French was reputedly spoken, to learn the language, and perfect elegant styles of horsemanship, fencing and dancing:

> your dancing-master is at this time the man in all Europe of the
> greatest importance to you. You must dance well, in order to sit, stand,
> and walk well; and you must do all these well in order to please.[81]

Wellesley retained excellent French and a life-long respect for France. Impecunious young Captain Horatio Nelson made do with a boarding-house in Saint-Omer when trying to learn French in 1783. William Pitt, twenty-four-year-old ex-Chancellor of the Exchequer, did the same with two university friends in Rheims that same year – though when he went to see the sights at Fontainebleau he was treated as a celebrity, meeting the royal family and ministers. Though Pitt never returned to France, he retained a few words of French and the realization that if the French had no political rights, they enjoyed much social freedom. Some of that freedom was enticingly risky: gambling and gallantry. To be willing to play and lose at such English imports as 'wisk' (whist) and 'creps' (dice) were necessary for admission to high aristocratic and court circles. This had been John Law's entrée early in the century, and had ended with him gambling with the wealth of the whole country. As for gallantry, young men hoped to be initiated by experienced women, not only or even mainly sexually, but in the manners of elegant flirtation. No doubt the advice of fathers and mothers conflicted here. Lord Elgin's mother urged him 'for God sake keep free of mistresses, for besides the immorality . . . they always turn out the most expensive petts in the world both of health and purse'. But even she countenanced polite gallantry: 'love is quite a la mode en francois, you may railly the pretty-girls as far as is consistent with spirit & good humour that they may not call you le ensencible' (*sic*).[82] Chesterfield wanted his son put more thoroughly through his paces: 'A propos, are you in love with Madame de Berkenrode still . . . ? *Un arrangement honnête sied bien à un galant homme.* In that case I recommend to you the utmost discretion and the profoundest silence.'[83] Discretion was not always the rule, especially with women of lower rank: showing off with famous dancers from the opera, for example, was much of the fun. Press comments were usually disapproving, though occasionally expressing pride at this further extension of British conquest. There was a price: gambling losses and venereal disease often left scars that never healed.[84]

From the middle of the century, new and less frivolous interests developed among travellers to Britain. Wealth had always meant power; but now it had new sources, and Britain had an astonishing ability to create it. Perceptive observers realized that something unprecedented was happening, and they visited places and learned lessons that would never have occurred to Voltaire or Montesquieu. Every traveller complained about coal smoke, but one of the first to realize that coal was the foundation of a new kind of economy was an inspector of manufactures, Ticquet, in 1738. He reported on new iron-making techniques using coal in the Midlands, and noted the high living standards of the workers. Over the next half-century, the French, more than any other nation, sent a succession of official and semi-official observers – several of them frankly spies – to discover methods, acquire machinery and recruit workers. They aimed both at economic advantage and at military applications. The Marquis de Blosset, at the embassy, acted as head of intelligence, providing contacts, money and papers, and lending the embassy chaplain, Fr MacDermot, as an interpreter. In the 1760s Gabriel Jars, a mining inspector, was sent to investigate mining techniques and discover whether iron could really be smelted with coal and 'what the English call "coucke"'. He was also to report on a perennial question: 'why industry is pushed ahead very much further than in France, and whether this difference arises, as there is every reason to think, because the English are not hindered by regulations'. Bonaventure Joseph Le Turc, a professional spy who combined a taste for excitement with patriotism and self-advancement, in the 1780s smuggled out a range of dismantled textile machinery and samples of manufactured goods from stockings to chamber pots, some of which he intended to copy. His great success, following a commission from the navy minister Marshal de Castries – the navy was persistently involved in espionage – was in bringing back techniques for mass-producing pulley blocks (see below, page 260). He was protected by being given diplomatic status, and was rewarded with a decoration and a pension, but was ruined by the revolution.[85]

These efforts were very successful at one level. The great innovations of the Industrial Revolution – spinning jennies, blast furnaces, steam engines

– were brought to France within a few years of their invention. A succession of British businessmen and workers responded readily to French approaches. Some had particular reasons – the Holkers were Jacobites, and the Birmingham hardware manufacturer Michael Alcock had run off to France with one of his young female employees – but for most it was simply business. Most of it was legal, and what was not was rarely repressed, even in wartime. The export of a new type of cannon to France for testing was done with official permission in the 1770s. Yet some activities sailed close to the wind, and required concealment, bribery or string-pulling. The most blatant was an agreement by the brilliant and grasping Wilkinson brothers to build the navy a cannon factory near Brest using recently patented techniques in 1777–8, just in time for the American war. The French realized that William Wilkinson – 'activated solely by that spirit of gain which is all too common in that nation' – had to be brought over before hostilities began, else 'he would not be able to come here without being . . . held guilty of felony'. The great engineers Matthew Boulton and James Watt connived in acts that 'amounted to a gross lack of patriotism, even treason'.[86] At a time when techniques could only be taught face to face, skilled workers also had to be recruited, and although some in the early days were Catholics or Jacobites, high wages and a wish to get on were usually sufficient motives – a foreman might get a £40 golden hello. The numbers were small – a few dozen businessmen and a few hundred workers over the century – but the impact in shaping French industrial development was significant. Alcock set out to make Saint-Etienne 'Birmingham in France', and development at Le Creusot was initiated by Wilkinson. Both towns became important industrial centres in the nineteenth century.

In the short term, however, the results were disappointing: iron, steel, coke and glass works all failed expensively and humiliatingly. French agents rarely understood the full complexity of industrial processes. France lacked the infrastructure of roads and canals; it was short of vital raw materials, especially different varieties of coal, ore and clay; it lacked skilled labour and a network of workshops able to make tools and parts and repair machinery. Imported British workers were often men who could not succeed at home, insubordinate, obstreperous and drunk. Le Turc's blockmakers discovered the joys of cheap wine and were managing five bottles a day.[87] In short, as a later generation might have put it, 'Failed In London Try Honfleur'. Yet this was also one symptom of a broader cultural difference. The intense nineteen-year-old François de La Rochefoucauld came across it when in 1784 he studied modern agriculture in Norfolk and Suffolk, and realized that more was involved than just planting turnips. He was amazed by the confidence of ordinary farmers – mere peasants! – who could talk knowledgeably and enthusiastically about their methods, meet in clubs to exchange ideas, mix with gentlemen on equal terms when fox-hunting, and even spontaneously invite a duke's son like himself to lunch. This was a different world from the Normandy he knew. Another 1780s traveller found the English 'determined to rise above their station'. The liberal economist and businessman Dupont de Nemours was irritated by imported English workers – 'haughty, quarrelsome, risk-takers and greedy'. But all this showed independence, self-confidence and a remarkable readiness to face change.[88] Contemporaries could not fully grasp what would only retrospectively be dubbed 'la révolution industrielle' by a French economist in the 1820s. But some did diagnose economic dynamism as being part of a deeper political and cultural revolution, seen as characteristically British:[89] freedom of enterprise and of information; security of persons and property; a less hierarchical society; more rational and equal taxation; and social gregariousness. In short, liberty, equality, fraternity. Whereas Voltaire and Montesquieu had admired a society that was good for intellectuals, that same society was now seen as being good for farmers, manufacturers, and even workers.

No one was more eager to spread this message than the self-appointed apostle of agricultural modernization, Arthur Young, an agronomist whose accounts of his travels gave him European celebrity. He explored France in the 1780s, and found little to praise. Poverty, archaism and oppression dogged his every step. It is easy to dismiss some of Young's triumphant comparisons – and those of his French disciples such as La Rochefoucauld – as rose-tinted and one-sided. Certainly, poor regions such as Brittany compared badly in terms of productivity with Norfolk; but so did much of Britain. And of course, there were losers as well as gainers from modernization. But we should not redress the balance too far by imagining eighteenth-century England as a Hogarthian hell of gin, gibbets, prostitutes and starving poachers. By the standards of the Continent, ordinary English people were less poor, freer, more equal, and had vastly more political say. The reiteration of that comparison spread the idea that France's political and social systems – absolutism and vestiges of feudalism – were holding it back. Young warned that the Old Regime was on the edge of the abyss. Ironically – seeing that he became a fierce critic of the French revolution – the translation of his *Travels* became official propaganda for the revolutionary regime, which bought 20,000 copies for distribution to every region of France.

Fashionable Feelings: The Age of Pamela and Julie

> The vapours of the bogs of Albion have engendered a philosophical
> epidemic, which kills genius, agitates minds and produces anti-national taste.
>
> RIGOLEY DE JUVIGNY, 1772[90]

> Our women, our horses, and dogs . . . are sure to be admired through
> all parts of France.
>
> *The Gentleman's Guide in his Tour through France (c. 1765)*

The prevailing cultural wind had always blown from France. In many
areas of fashion and manners, this remained so. At the Drury Lane
theatre, for example, plays with a French theme, including many adapted
from Molière, were a staple of the repertoire.[91] The eighteenth century saw
a shift: the new and the challenging came from Britain, and France came to
represent majestic conservatism. From the 1740s, Britain came to be seen
as a source not only of novelties in science, philosophy and politics, but also
of new ways of feeling, and therefore of behaving and appearing. This was
reflected powerfully back, above all in the works of Jean-Jacques Rousseau,
to Britain.

Origins of these new ways of feeling could be traced back almost indefinitely. The idea of the English as a tempestuous and melancholy race
because of their island situation and weather was expressed in a famous
memoir by an ambassador, the Duc de Sully, early in the seventeenth
century. Spleen and suicide were seen as the characteristic English distem-
pers, induced by fog, beef and beer, which 'give rise to a chyle, whose
vicious heaviness can transmit none but bilious and melancholy juices to
the brain'.[92] The unwitting alchemist who convinced the French that this
might have positive aspects, namely emotional depth, was Samuel
Richardson, in his hugely admired (and scarcely less mocked) novel *Pamela,
or Virtue Rewarded* (1740–41). This story of the trials and tribulations of
a girl who defends her virginity and is rewarded by marriage, became an
international craze, translated and copied all over Europe. That Richardson
was a self-taught printer, the son of a joiner from Derby, added to the
sense that this was something fresh, 'sentimental' (a new word, and a term
of praise), a source of true emotion, and an authentic exploration of human
virtue and vice. Immediately translated by the anglophile Abbé Prévost
(who found asylum in London in the 1730s after absconding from the
abbey of Saint-Germain-des-Prés), *Paméla* became one of the most popular
novels of the century. Richardson's darker and even longer *Clarissa*
(1748–9), which dealt with desire, sexual violence and remorse, translated
as *Clarisse Harlowe* (1752), had a stunning impact, deeply influencing

Rousseau and the *philosophes*. Rousseau wrote in 1758 that 'no one has ever written in any language a novel that equals or even approaches it'. 'O Richardson!' exclaimed Diderot in 1761, 'were I forced to sell all my books, you would remain to me on the same shelf as Moses, Homer, Euripides and Sophocles.'[93]

The popularity of English novels among French readers at this time has never been equalled. A study of the contents of 500 private libraries belonging to nobles, clergy and professional men in and near Paris in the middle decades of the century shows that three-quarters of the fiction consisted of translations from English, albeit abbreviated, gallicized and purged of anything 'inappropriate'. Three of the four most widely owned novels were *Paméla*, *Tom Jones* and *Clarisse Harlowe*. Other novels by Richardson and Fielding, novels featuring English plots, and *Oronoko* (presumably a translation or adaptation of Afra Behn's older work) were all among the most popular twenty works of fiction. The Marquis de Sade, when in the Bastille for his sexual delinquencies, had Richardson, Fielding and Smollett to keep him amused.[94] English novelists, male and female, led France and Europe in what Roy Porter has called 'the enlightened voyage into the self'.[95]

Richardson's influence on French writers such as Laclos, Marivaux, Restif de La Bretonne and Sade was evident in style, subject and even the names of characters. But his impact on Rousseau was infinitely more important. As with Bolingbroke and Montesquieu, the pupil far excelled the master. Rousseau's great novel of love, separation and virtue, *Julie, ou la Nouvelle Héloïse* (1761) – although Jane Austen and her family laughed at it later – marked a new era in European cultural history. The cultivation and expression of elevated, sincere emotion – endlessly analysed, talked about and relived – became the aim of art, indeed of life. The natural purity of the mountains now assailed the corrupt cities of the plains.

British poetry too became popular for the first time in France, not least because it was seen as possessing characteristics of sentiment, naturalness, moral elevation and affecting melancholy. Thomas Gray's *Elegy Written in a Country Churchyard* (1751) is the sole example widely known today, but it was only part of a wider vogue for introspection, nocturnes, death and rural elegies, including James Thompson's *The Seasons* (1726–30) and Edward Young's funereal *Night Thoughts* (1742–5). Translated into French in the 1760s and 70s, they spawned *Saisons*, *Nuits*, *Jardins*, *Poèmes champêtres* and *Idylles* galore in the 1770s and 80s. James Macpherson published *Fingal, an Ancient Epic Poem* in 1761, purportedly a translation of the ancient bard Ossian, which had huge success in France, making Scotland at least as much as Rousseau's native Switzerland the source of pure mountain hot air. Shakespeare too gained hugely in stature (see below, page 108).

Literary influence was not confined to works by British authors. British characters and settings (sometimes as a place of liberty for star-crossed lovers, or as a place where fortunes could be made) were important features in dozens of novels. Abbé Prévost pioneered the trend for English settings in the 1730s with *Le Philosophe anglais, ou Histoire de M. Cleveland, fils de Cromwell*. In Rousseau's *Julie* one of the leading characters is the virtuous, passionate and melancholy Milord Edouard Bomston, and the frustrated hero Saint-Prieux goes off round the world with (the real life) Admiral Anson. The fashion took off in the 1760s in a stream of novels with characters named Fanni, Jenny, Sidnei, Wuillaume, Nency and Betsi, and populated by numerous milords, miladys and sirs (including a 'sir W. Shittleheaded'). Even approximate authenticity was not indispensable: the main characters in one popular 'English' novel are called Warthei, Hinsei and Zulmie.[96] What mattered was the image of England as the home of 'sensibility', freedom and exotic novelty – tea drinking, horse racing, boxing. Horace Walpole, who wanted the French to stay French, lamented their taste – 'could one believe that when they read our authors, Richardson and Mr Hume should be their favourites?' and he 'blushed' at Garrick's 'insufferable nonsense about Shakespeare'.[97]

Gardens were the most elaborate expression of fashionable sensibility. The 'English garden', designed to look picturesquely natural, owed much to the imagined landscape paintings of Claude Le Lorrain, always popular in Britain. To possess an English garden, a place where the sensitive spirit could be refreshed by nature and simultaneously shown off to one's friends, became an expensive Continental craze, inspiring several treatises and serious attention in the *Encyclopédie*. Its more ambitious examples became 'total art . . . embracing philosophy, literature, architecture, sculpture, painting, sport and music'.[98] The trendsetter was the Marquis de Girardin at his magnificent chateau of Ermenonville, north of Paris. The garden was planned in 1763 and finished in 1773; Scottish gardeners did the lawns. Girardin, a devotee of Rousseau, had discovered his ideal of nature near Dudley, at the Leasowes, house of the minor poet and country squire William Shenstone, the author of, among other things, an influential essay on 'landskip gardening'. Built in the 1740s and 50s in a hilly landscape, Shenstone's garden contained woods, lakes, rills and rustic bridges, as well as a temple of Pan, a 'ruined priory', and a hermitage. Although less famous than Kew or Stowe, it became a model for connoisseurs, including Rousseau, who criticized Stowe as overdone.[99] In 1777 Girardin wrote a book on the composition of landscapes in which he rejected the geometrical style of the traditional French garden, and praised the Leasowes.[100] Cross-Channel celebrity seems to have caused Shenstone misgivings:

Trembling I view the Gaul's illusive art
That steals my lov'd rusticity away.[101]

On a grand scale, Ermenonville emulated his topographical features and constructions designed to evoke philosophical, literary and aesthetic reactions: a dolmen, a waterfall, an altar to dreaming, a grotto of the Naiads, and a Temple of Modern Philosophy, purposely unfinished, inscribed with the names of contemporary thinkers. At the foot of an obelisk, Girardin inscribed in English:

> To William Shenstone
> In his verses he displayed
> His mind natural
> At Leasowes he lay'd
> Arcadian greens rural.[102]

Girardin acquired the ultimate feature in 1778: Jean-Jacques Rousseau himself, who briefly pottered about the garden, died and was buried on a lake island. Ermenonville became the shrine to this saint of nature and sensibility, visited by pilgrims from across the European world, including Marie-Antoinette, various monarchs, Benjamin Franklin, Mirabeau, Danton, Robespierre and Napoleon. The Leasowes had a less illustrious fate: engulfed by the Black Country, it is now part golf course, part slightly sad municipal park.

Not to be outdone in fashion, the Duc de Chartres commissioned in 1773 a lavish *jardin à l'anglaise* for his house at Monceau, on the northern edge of Paris, part of it now one of the city's prettiest parks. His intention – or that of the artist Carmontelle who designed it – was to surpass the English, whose unimaginative monochrome lawns he thought insufficiently amusing for Parisian taste. Every fashionable feature was packed into a space that the busy metropolitan could walk round between social engagements: Chinese gate, Dutch windmill, minaret (with camel and turbaned attendant), coloured pavilions, winter garden, pyramid, grotto, medieval tower, ruined temple, vineyard with statue of Bacchus, gothic building (housing a chemistry laboratory), white marble dairy, lake, rustic bridge, flock of sheep with rustic shepherd, island with pillars, etc. Some thought this excessive, not least the duke's financial advisers. The austere Scot, Thomas Blaikie – 'the Capability Brown of France' – pronounced it 'a confusion', and was commissioned to tone it down. Blaikie also designed a garden for the Comte d'Artois's little *folie*, 'Bagatelle'. The result made Blaikie's name: 'disordered like a *coquette en negligée* whose dress apparently put together in a haphazard way is really a work of art; but art so realistically disguised that Nature herself would be taken in by it'.[103] Marie-Antoinette took him to show her round Ermenonville.

She built her own garden at the Petit Trianon at Versailles, with its famous, or notorious, 'hamlet', including sheep, cows and dairy, in the later 1770s. The last, and biggest, English garden of the Old Regime, begun in 1785, was that of the *financier* the Marquis de Laborde, at Méréville, which included a memorial to Captain Cook. Work was still going on when Laborde was arrested and guillotined in 1794. Even this was not the end: revolution and

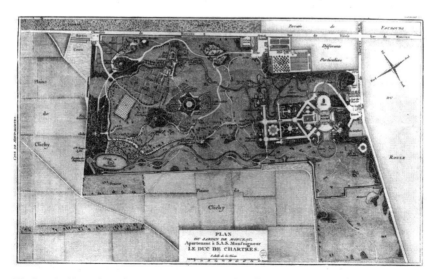

The Duc de Chartres's garden was to contain every fashionable feature and outdo all its rivals.

war notwithstanding, the Empress Josephine stocked her lavish garden at La Malmaison with 19,515 francs' worth of English plants and seeds.[104]

While English visitors to Paris, as we have seen, hastily dressed up in French styles, some of the French elite began from the 1760s onwards to wear English clothes in France – an affectation that persisted for over two centuries. Until then, French fashions had dominated in both countries, and continued to do so for highly formal occasions – with French milliners (at least milliners with French names) supplying the London market, and dressed dolls imported as patterns of the latest Paris styles. But English clothing styles for men and women reflected different cultural trends: informality, naturalness, sport and the country. They were influenced too by the relatively classless sober style of London, and by children's clothes. So for men, stronger, rougher materials (wool and even leather rather than silk), less embroidery and lace, shorter and less voluminous cut, plainer colours, shorter wigs or natural hair, boots, hats ('à la jockei') and coats suitable for riding, such as the *redingote* (from 'riding coat') and *frac* (from 'frock', a loose overcoat). For women, lighter materials (Indian muslin rather than brocaded silk), paler colours for summers out of doors; suppler yet tighter shapes, with fewer layers and less ornamentation; riding clothes; much less make-up; and most startling of all, their own hair and hats (including in straw) for the sun. The hat was originally a rural accessory which upper-class French women did not wear in town because of their huge artificial hairpieces. As the *Courrier de la Mode* put it in 1768, English fashion was 'more picturesque and less stiff . . . every day we move towards beautiful simplicity'.

All this stood for activity, youth ('from 15 to 50'[105]), informality and freedom. It was rebellious. It was also sexy. So it caused outrage. Men and women looked alike, lamented some, all dressed in 'the colour of London soot'. The writer Fougeret de Montbrun attacked those who had the 'indecency' and 'dirtiness' to 'show themselves shamelessly in the most respectable places, wrapped in an ugly great jacket, mudsplashed to the shoulders, their hair pulled up by a comb under the hat'. Other writers condemned noblemen who 'without embroidery, without braid, with a thick cane, a thick cravat, want absolutely to pass as London bourgeois', and regretted that 'people want to be English at any cost, and this pretention wipes out our national spirit . . . our fashions, our customs, to become like our neighbours whom we hate'. Lord Chesterfield agreed about the inferiority of British dress and behaviour: 'with the manners of footmen and grooms, they assume their dress too; for you must have observed them in the streets here, in dirty blue frocks, with oaken sticks in their hands, and their hair greasy and unpowdered, tucked up under their hats of an enormous size'.[106] Louis XVI, though he introduced English water closets to Versailles, was irritated by English fashions, and 'anglomaniacs' risked disfavour. He remarked to the

Marquis de Conflans (who was 'wearing a plain *frac* with hair cut like a jockey, without powder or pommade') that he 'looked like a locksmith', and told the Duc de Lauzun that if one was so fond of the English one should go and live among them.[107] Some compromise was reached: the *habit à la française* and the *habit à l'anglaise* coexisted and the informal frock-coat was produced in both its plain English form and in a more decorative French version.[108] Marie-Antoinette, a revolutionary at least in fashion, launched the *chemise de la reine*, a muslin dress combining English, Indian, Rousseau-esque and neo-classical influences, first launched in England by the Duchess of Devonshire. A portrait of the queen thus dressed, painted by Elizabeth Vigée-Lebrun, had to be withdrawn from the 1783 *salon* as too indecorous. Versions of this style, after the queen's demise, came to typify the society of the late Republic and Napoleonic empire.[109]

THE SINCEREST FORM OF FLATTERY

Louis XVI's brother, the Comte d'Artois (later Charles X), overdoing the English country-gentleman look: note the jockey cap.

Engravings by Hubert Bourguignon, known as Gravelot, helped to spread English fashions in France. Son of a Parisian tailor, he stayed for almost twenty years in England – among other things he gave lessons to Gainsborough and produced illustrations for *Pamela*. Returning to France in 1744, 'he introduced . . . the taste for innocent looking straw hats, plain gowns and white stuffs'.[110] From 1760, magazines blossomed with a cross-Channel exchange of engravings: *The Fashionable Magazine or Lady's and Gentleman's Monthly Recorder of New Fashions, being a compleat Universal Repository of Taste, Elegance and Novelty for Both Sexes* appeared in London, including illustrations that reappeared several months later in *Le Magasin des Modes Nouvelles Françaises et Anglaises*.[111]

'Chapeau à l'anglaise': though ladies' hats were an English import, here it is greatly elaborated for urban French taste.

'Anglomania' was both emulation of and rivalry with the English. The arch-anglomaniac was the Duc de Chartres, heir to the duchy of Orléans. The d'Orléans were the junior branch of the royal family, eager to seek popularity by distancing themselves from their Bourbon cousins and from the stuffiness of Versailles. Anglomania made them appear modern, open, and, however vaguely, linked with liberty. It was also smart and fun. In the 1770s Chartres, along with cronies such as the Comte d'Artois (Louis XVI's wild youngest brother), Lauzun, Conflans and Fitz-James, set up a horse-racing and gambling coterie, with imported mounts and jockeys. They hoped to create a 'French Newmarket' at Sablons, just west of Paris, where the first French horse races had taken place in 1766. Courtiers deplored their mingling with raffish English hangers-on 'of base extraction' whom they took along to Versailles to dine, 'their elbows on the table and in the most free and easy manner'.[112] They ran highly publicized races in the presence of Marie-Antoinette, who, if she detested English politics, could not resist the tyranny of fashion, and had English middle-class friends, the Swinburnes.

Clothes, carriages, horses, dogs, portraits, furnishings, food and drink ('le plumpouding', 'le ponche', etc.), gardeners, jockeys, friends and mistresses were imported from Britain during the 1770s and 80s. The American war, in which several anglomaniacs participated, was hardly even an interlude. As hostilities loomed, Chartres got permission to bring over eight horses and twenty hounds to tide him over. No less prized a filly was Grace Dalrymple Elliott, a blonde Scottish adventuress painted by Gainsborough (and the subject of a recent film by Eric Rohmer). She was the mistress of Artois and then of Chartres, with whom she remained friends. The most extraordinary import, however, was Pamela.

THE OTHER PAMELA

At Easter 1780, at the height of the American war, a horse dealer brought the Duc de Chartres 'the prettiest mare and the prettiest little girl in England'.[113] The latter had been sent by his English friend and agent, Nathanial Parker Forth, who had been asked to search the London foundling hospital for a pretty brunette of about six, who 'must absolutely not have too big a nose or know a word of French'. Chartres wanted a playmate for his daughters so that they could grow up speaking English. Anne ('Nancy') Sims, from Christchurch in Hampshire, was probably born in Newfoundland, the illegitimate daughter of Mary Sims or Syms, whose father was in the salt cod trade. Fashionably renamed Pamela, 'the little angel' was an immediate success, and was brought up as an adored member of his highly unconventional household by Chartres and a

former mistress (now governess to his children), the Comtesse de Genlis.[114]
She, an intelligent self-taught bohemian, was, as one might expect, a devotee
of Richardson and a disciple of Rousseau, whose *Emile* provided her with ideas
to apply to the Orléans children and Pamela. Indeed, the vogue for Rousseau
had made the adoption of children for pedagogical experiments alarmingly fashionable. In 1785 she took Pamela on a long-anticipated trip to England. They
made a pilgrimage to Richardson's garden, where Madame sat with her flesh-
and-blood Pamela on the very bench where the original *Pamela* had been written.
Pamela's adventures were far from over. Fleeing the revolution in 1792, she
married Lord Edward Fitzgerald, radical scion of Ireland's grandest family, en
route. He became one of the leaders of the United Irishmen and was killed by
the British. Pamela sought refuge in England, then Hamburg, briefly married
the American consul there, and seems to have lived subsequently with a number
of men. The childhood playmate who became Duc d'Orléans, and then in 1830
King Louis-Philippe, kept her at a distance, but paid for her funeral in 1831.
In 1880 her remains were reburied in England by her descendants.

Partly to defray the costs of his extravagant hobbies, and partly as another sign of modern-mindedness, the Duc d'Orléans (as Chartres became in 1785) developed the family's Parisian seat, the Palais Royal, into a commercial enterprise inspired by London pleasure gardens such as Vauxhall. 'So,' sneered Louis XVI, 'you've become a shopkeeper.' After a shaky start, the Palais Royal gardens, surrounded by galleries of coffee houses, the new 'restaurants', clubs of varying levels of respectability, and shops crammed with English goods and advertisements, became the lodestone of Paris fashion and dissipation. 'They call it the capital of Paris . . . a little town of luxury enclosed within a greater.'[115] Protected by the Orléans royal privilege, it also became a centre of political discussion and pamphleteering. For the duke, this success brought profit and popularity as a defender of freedom. It was from the garden of the Palais Royal that the attack on the Bastille was launched on 14 July 1789.

By then, English manners and fashions had become familiar. Copying British styles did not, of course, necessarily mean liking British ideas or people. The Seven Years War and the American war had hardened resentments, and a determination that if Britain was to be copied, it was with the intention of overtaking it. Fashionable anglomania had little in common with the sort of political interest that Voltaire and Montesquieu had shown. Nevertheless, many observers were struck by its visibility, even in wartime. An American envoy was astonished to see shops all over Paris advertising 'English Goods just imported'.[116] A diplomat returning from Turkey in 1782 wrote:

I had not been to Paris for fifteen years: in arriving, I thought I was in London. In the streets I met only English carriages, containing women wearing elegant hats, a fashion from England; English-style cabriolets driven by young gentlemen in riding-coats with double, triple or quadruple collars turned down like capes, with little round hats; horsemen dressed and mounted in English style; pedestrians in the same accoutrement . . . shops stocked with all sorts of English merchandise and entitled *Magasins Anglois*, with English punch advertised outside innumerable cafés.[117]

Young Antoine Santerre (who later presided over the execution of Louis XVI) made one of the biggest and quickest fortunes in Paris by brewing pale ale. Anglomania was no longer confined to the aristocracy: 'a financier's son . . . a business clerk, wears the long narrow coat, the hat well down on his head . . . Nevertheless, none of them has ever seen England, neither do they understand one word of English.'[118] As anglomania raged in Paris, 'Macaronis' remained the cynosure of fashonable London and a gift to cartoonists, wearing, despite their name, largely French-inspired fashions –

The Englishman who copies dress, hairstyle and deportment from 'Monkey Land' – where everyone copied each other.

MY LORD TIP-TOE.
Juſt arrived from Monkey Land.

which for men included umbrellas, muffs, tall hairpieces and tight breeches – and displaying profound admiration for all things French. In large cities, it was asserted, 'everything is à la Française'.[119] The interior of the Prince of Wales's new Carlton House was largely decorated and furnished by French artists, showing his 'close identification with the style and splendour of the Bourbon court'.[120] Amusingly, when the Duc d'Orléans at last obtained Louis XVI's permission to visit London in 1783 (he had taken a house in the new Portland Place), he was praised in the London press for his sober and un-affected (English-style) dress, in contrast with the (French-style) foppery of the Prince of Wales.

A French cartoon, presumably for an English public, satirizing not only French fashions, but also the contrast between the rich and the poor children in clogs.

The *FRENCH LADY*   of di *PROMENAIDE*

Soutiens, Jasmin, je succombe,   *Que si ma coëffure tombe,*
Et prends bien garde, Kiquin.   *Tu auras ton compte demain.*

Love, Hate and Ambivalence

A Frenchman who, with a fund of virtue, learning and good sense, has the manners and good-breeding of his country, is the perfection of human nature.
EARL OF CHESTERFIELD, 1747[121]

We are the only nation in the universe the English do not despise. Instead, they pay us the honour of hating us as heartily as possible.
FOUGERET DE MONTBRUN, *Préservative contre l'anglomanie,* 1759[122]

All I object to is their quitting their own agreeable style, to take up the worst of ours. Heaven knows, we are unpleasing enough.
HORACE WALPOLE, 1765[123]

Several recent books have stressed the importance of conflict between Britain and France in shaping the two national identities. Popular xenophobia was said by some contemporary writers to be stronger in Britain than in France, and many modern historians have accepted this. If the British were indeed more vocal and extreme about the French, the obvious reason is that they were more vocal and extreme about everything: there was no French equivalent of Gillray until after the fall of the Bastille, that deterrent to impertinence. In Britain, francophobia expressed fear of absolutism and resentment of snobbery. When London artisans jeered at 'French dogs' in the street, their victims were as likely to be overdressed Englishmen. Francophobia waxed and waned with the seriousness of the French threat, and it seems to have subsided after mid-century, until revived in an entirely different form in the 1790s. In France state-sponsored anglophobia was virulent from the time of the Seven Years War, and it remained a staple of conservative political discourse. French desire for revenge which, as we shall see, marked the 1770s and 80s, combined with a wishful belief that Britain was in decline, meant that its political and social systems were frequently denounced. On both sides of the Channel, polemicists regarded themselves as representing superior values.

Religion was important. French champions of Catholicism stigmatized the British as 'heretics' and 'sectarians', turbulent and violent, as evidenced by their ultimate political crime, the regicide of Charles I. British defenders of Protestantism attacked the Bourbon monarchy as the enemy of religious and political liberty, and the manipulator of superstition – the strategy summed up as 'Popery'. However, religion was not the basic cause of cross-Channel polarization. The British were always more afraid of Versailles than of Rome. Moreover, Catholics and Protestants were themselves bitterly divided. French Jansenists, followers of a devout but unorthodox tendency within Catholicism, saw their enemies as the Jesuits, the church hierarchy and the Crown, not Protestants; and they looked to England as a model of religious liberty. Anglicans and Scottish Episcopalians, faced with troublesome Dissenters, could for their part see merits in French Catholicism. One Tory Archbishop of Canterbury early in the century advocated unity between the established Anglican and Gallican (i.e. French Catholic) churches, if the latter would finally sever its tenuous links with Rome. Fear of Popery diminished in Britain after the defeat of the Jacobite threat in 1745, and religion ceased to be 'an important factor' in British foreign policy.[124] In France, although Catholic conservatism revived during the Seven Years War, the rising theme of anglo-phobia was not Protestantism but commercialism. Britain was denounced as 'Carthage' – materialistic, insatiable and duplicitous.

It would be wrong to assume that cross-Channel rivalry created two nations united in their hostility to 'the Other'. In Britain, the struggle 'opened up internal tensions' – political, ethnic and religious – 'as often as it resolved them'.[125] In France too, attitudes towards England reflected internal differences. Anglophilia always implied a certain dissidence from, and even outright criticism of, religious and political absolutism. Anglophobia meant support for royal and ecclesiastical power and resistance to social change. Fashionable anglomania in the 1780s began as elite alienation from the 'sad and barren' political and cultural establishment of Versailles – a trend that also included a vogue for Italian and German music.[126]

Antagonism, therefore, is not the sole key to Franco-British relations. If each nation helped to form the other's sense of itself, it was also through self-criticism, discussion, admiration and emulation. Both sides eagerly read, applauded, disagreed with, copied and responded to each other in a constant exchange. Both were tending towards the view that they were the joint leaders of civilization, even if they were trying to lead it in different directions. Wars did not poison personal relations. Remarkably, officers of the armed forces wore their uniforms when visiting the 'enemy' country – guidebooks advised it – as it guaranteed a polite reception and permitted them to dine at the messes of their opposite numbers. Reactions to two well-known books on France – Smollett's *Travels through France and Italy* (1766) and Sterne's *Sentimental Journey* (1768) – reveal the mood of the British reading classes well. Smollett's curmudgeonly criticisms – construed as xenophobic, although his grumpiness was universal – were regarded as in poor taste. Sterne's simpering charm met the mood of the moment. Gentle monks, wise innkeepers, coy nuns, pretty chambermaids and flirtatious ladies all won his heart, and composed just the picture of France the British sought: good food, good manners and a hint of erotic adventure.

A central theme – or rather, variations on a theme – emerged from this century of dialogue: that Britain stood for freedom, and France for order. Or, especially during the second half of the century, that Britain stood for nature, and France for civilization – in Garrick's pithy summing up, France meant stiff stays and fruit out of season. This was so pervasive an idea that it shaped experience, and so in a sense became true. It accommodated a range of positive and negative interpretations: for it is striking how admirers and critics agreed about the essence of what they judged so differently. Hence, British freedom, or naturalness, could explain violent crowds, drunken boorishness, coarseness of taste and dullness of conversation. But it also accounted for Newton, Locke, Shakespeare, political participation, tolerance, relative social equality, liberty of speech and writing, openness to change, prosperity, sincerity, sensitivity and kindness. It could explain extremes of both good humour and melancholy; the affecting beauty of Pamela and the cloddishness of 'Jack Rosbif'. The connexion with the political system seemed obvious: 'It is not surprising that a people that is ceaselessly told that it is free, that it is only subordinate to the laws, is proud and insolent.'[127]

French order and civilization similarly encapsulated ecclesiastical and royal oppression, downtrodden peasants, persecuted Protestants, censorship, effete repressed culture, the foppish 'effeminacy' and strutting conformism of Versailles. Many on both sides of the Channel felt the French were too polite, too contrived and too enslaved to convention and fashion: the manners of the dancing master, or (as they were often caricatured) the imitativeness of the monkey. But this also explained their elegance, urbanity, wit, cultural sophistication, intelligence, fashion, gaiety, manners, hospitality, safe highways, and the courtesy of ordinary people. France's calm, order and authority attracted many British visitors who basked in the deference of the lower orders, the gradations of distinction, and the non-commercial cultural world of the salons. Lord Ferrers paid an undeniably sincere tribute to this ideal when, condemned to death in 1760 for the murder of his steward, he defied the egalitarianism of the sentence by turning out to be hanged in his embroidered white silk *habit à la française*.

DRAWING A LESSON

If one could sum up a vast range of language and imagery, it would be that the British either admired or laughed at the French, and the French either envied or sneered at the British. The British admired French superiority and mocked French (and French-style) pretentiousness, foppishness and the careful pose taught by the dancing master. The French envied British liberty and wealth, and disdained British crudeness and lack of *savoir-faire*.

One of many cartoons showing the French and British as opposites – clothes, mannerisms, diets, body shapes, even dogs. Gillray, typically, mocks both.

Drunkenness has long been seen by the French as a characteristic English vice.

GARRICK'S FRENCH DANCERS

Although eighteenth-century wars impinged surprisingly little on other activities, 1755 was not the best moment for Franco–British cultural exchanges. In December, the actor-manager David Garrick brought over a troupe of 'French' dancers (led in fact by a Swiss, Noverre, renowned at Versailles) to perform at Drury Lane. This led to several nights of uproarious, exciting and sometimes bloody rioting between the noble patrons in the boxes, who insisted that the dancers should perform, and the more plebeian occupants of the pit and gallery, who were determined that they should not. As a French newspaper reported,

> All the My Lords leaped into the Pit, some with staves others sword in hand, and descended upon a group of demonstrators . . . the English Ladies, far from being affrighted by the horrible scuffle . . . pointed out to them the people to be knocked out . . . The ballet begins, the stage is covered with several bushels of peas mixed with tacks. The *milords* sweep the stage with their hats, more peas are thrown; the *milords* jump once more into the Pit, the doors of which are forced open by a troop of butchers . . . hitting right and left at the demonstrators.

Magistrates and troops tried to stop the trouble in the theatre and the surrounding streets, where Garrick's house had its windows smashed.

This event is often cited as proof of brutal English xenophobia. It was widely reported in France, causing the Marquis d'Argenson to note in his journal, 'What a nasty people, as ferocious as they pretend to be philosophical.' Given that fighting had already started in North America and the press was reporting French preparations for an invasion of Britain, some francophobia is not surprising. Moreover, the interruptions were at least partly fomented by out-of-work actors, the managers of rival theatres, and Huguenot exiles. There were paid toughs on both sides. What is truly remarkable is that the *milords* in the audience were so eager to defend the French dancers, and that the King and Queen attended the first night (he was reported to have 'laughed very heartily' at the tumult). Francophilia and francophobia have always had class connotations. There were no hard feelings: Noverre returned for a less turbulent season a few years later and his brother (who had almost killed a rioter) made a career as a dancing master in Norwich.[128]

'Philia' and 'phobia' are misleading suffixes if they are assumed always to signify polarized attitudes. In the paintings and caricatures of Hogarth, Gillray and Rowlandson, British and French are *both* mocked, just as in the writings of Voltaire or Montesquieu both societies are praised and criticized. French guidebooks warned their readers that they might be robbed by highwaymen, jostled by the London mob, and snubbed by haughty *milords*; but also led them to expect efficient transport, comfortable beds, pavements, and clean, well-lit streets. English travellers were on the lookout for lazy monks, officious bureaucrats, and famished peasants; but also for good food, universal courtesy, intellectual sparkle and metropolitan polish. Whether they liked what they found – accident aside – was largely a matter of prejudice, in the sense that some deplored what others admired. Samuel Foote's popular farces *The Englishman in Paris* and *The Englishman Returned from Paris* amused 1760s audiences by caricaturing familiar prejudices, and also the suddenness with which they could change. His typical English 'hero', Squire Buck, arrives in Paris annoyed that streets are called Rues, gets into a fight with a Frenchman who 'turn'd up his nose and called me une Bête', and complains that 'the Men are all Puppies, mincing and dancing, and chattering, and grinning; the Women are a parcel of painted Dolls; their food's fit for Hogs'. By the time he returns to London, he speaks an elegant Franglais and proclaims that 'the French are the first People of the Universe; that in the Arts of living they do or ought to give Laws to the whole World, and that whosoever would either eat, drink, dress, dance, fight, sing or even sneeze, *avec Elégance*, must go to Paris to learn it'.[129]

Central to social perceptions were the contrasting role and behaviour of women, artlessly summed up by one travel writer: 'I should prefer a French woman for a mistress, but an English woman for a wife.'[130] In both countries women were prominent, in comparison with some other parts of Europe, in economic activity and cultural life. In England, more women were famous as writers, and in France, more as patrons through their salons, even if this might mean being 'self-effacing facilitators'.[131] Much discussed was what this showed about the two societies. It was a common complaint of French visitors that Englishwomen, though often beautiful, athletic and virtuous, lacked charm, confidence, conversation and flirtatiousness; in short, were *froides*. Here again, the 'nature'/'civilization' contrast appears. Many agreed that France was more civilized because more sociable, and that women were the creators of that sociability, and the bearers of that civilization. 'Lively, cheerful, witty, facetious, their disposition fits them naturally for company; the communicativeness of their temper, and the engagingness of their behaviour, beget reciprocal harmony, and circulate a spirit of pleasure that is the principal delight and merit of conversation.'[132] But many British visitors found French women alluringly (and/or shockingly) bold. Some were titillated, others repelled, by the sophisticated artificiality of fashion. Smollett as usual was 'Disgusted of Dumbarton':

> fashion in France prescribes to all ladies . . . the *fard*, or *white*, with which their necks and shoulders are plaistered [and] the *rouge*, which is daubed on their faces, from the chin up to the eyes . . . [This] renders the aspect really frightful . . . their heads are covered with a vast load of false hair . . . compleately whitened.[133]

One English visitor was delighted when visiting Versailles to see the naturally 'lovely appearance' of two English women 'who without patch, paint or powder rivall'd all the French dolls.'[134] But young Lord Nuneham was 'fonder of rouge well put on than ever . . . to me the finest pale face, the finest shape ill dressed is nothing'.[135]

British culture appeared more masculine, more physical, and arguably more brutal – again, the antithesis of a civilized and ordered society. Several aspects were repeatedly noted by French observers. The English theatre was violent. Garrick noted in his journal that 'the French can't bear Murder upon ye Stage but rack Criminals for small thefts'.[136] This was missing the point (and the core of French objections to Shakespeare): that the theatre should be a protected civilized space. The French were also shocked by the popularity of boxing and the frequency of street fights, and even more by the willingness of gentlemen to watch and even take part. Chivalrous duelling between gentlemen was one thing; the brawling of gentlemen with the plebs quite another. In London, wearing swords went out of fashion in the 1720s, and duels became increasingly frowned upon by the 1770s; what is more, ordinary passers by intervened to stop them.[137] If this was seen in Britain as an advance in civilized values, by French standards it was a decline. Sport was another manifestation of indecorous physicality: that a nobleman could play cricket with his servants was even more incomprehensible than that an adult should wish to play games at all. This kind of egalitarianism was utterly different from the familiarity of the French with domestic servants – a familiarity so sensationally subverted by Beaumarchais's *Figaro*. Instead of bowing and curtseying, the British kissed or shook hands ('taking one's man by the arm and shaking enough to dislocate the shoulder'). Marie-Antoinette was dumbfounded when the British ambassador shook hands with one of her ladies. This habit, revealingly, became more French when it became more formal. In food too – always a crucial topic – the British were a 'bleeding dish' nation, disgustingly close to nature for the French, who were a civilized 'sauce nation', where food was transformed and disguised.[138]

In both Britain and France, fears that 'effeminacy' was corrupting male 'republican' virtues led Patriots to denounce the cultural and social mores of a degenerate aristocracy. Its hallmarks were the influence of women, excessive interest in feminine matters such as fashion, and a consequent lack of interest in public affairs: 'what we might gain in Delicacy and Refinement, we might lose in Manliness of Behaviour and Liberty of Discourse; the two Pillars of which the Edifice of our national character is mainly supported'.[139] Questions of fashion, sociability and the place of the sexes were given serious moral and political importance. Some British commentators suspected a Bourbon plot to undermine the nation. Silly though this was, it was in some form widely held.[140] The equivalent view in France was that the importation of cruder and more egalitarian British styles was undermining traditional French values, which conservatives hoped did indeed promote contented apolitical loyalism. As one song, entitled 'Caractère de la Nation Française', defined it

> As in the old days
> Loyal, frank and courteous
> Respecting our laws
> Adoring our lovelies
> Loyal to our kings
> Always in love, always faithful subjects.[141]

The writer Louis-Sébastien Mercier, despairing in the 1780s that 'we shall never adopt anything from the English save their dress', sarcastically urged his compatriots to return to French styles: 'wear your lace . . . stick a little hat under your arm' because 'wearing other people's clothes will not provide . . . brains and character'.[142]

Two stock figures that represented and summed up these perceptions of difference are the French dancing-master and the English jockey. The former inculcated order, urbanity, elegance, self-control and tradition – in short, *les bienséances* (the proprieties). But critics dismissed this 'politeness' as mere external show. The jockey was a symbol of daring, physical prowess and modernity, but equally, said critics, of coarse manners and rustic pastimes. The anglophile La Rochefoucauld, amid his notes on farming practices, felt it worth recording that in England 'both sexes dance equally badly, without the least grace or step or rhythm; they make no study of dancing as we do. The women hold themselves badly . . . The men dance with their knees bent . . . in short they present a most unpleasing appearance.'[143] Hester Thrale, on the other hand, mocked French incompetence at horse racing.[144] Mercier deplored jockeys as 'libertines in the bud . . . I should need Solomon's pen to give a true description of the harm that jockeys, and riding coats, and public betting . . . have done.'[145] Of the many uses of 'dancing master' as a term of abuse, the most famous is Samuel

Johnson's dismissal of Lord Chesterfield's *Letters* as teaching 'the morals of a whore and the manners of a dancing master'. The second half at least of the judgement was perfectly true.

Philip Dormer Stanhope, 4th Earl of Chesterfield, was a lucid admirer of French civilization, and his mid-century letters to his half-French son on manners and society constitute, according to the leading French cultural historian Marc Fumaroli, the 'moral testament of French Europe'.[146] Their antithesis is *Emile, ou de l'éducation* (1761), a novel by the Genevan Jean-Jacques Rousseau. This epoch-making manifesto about 'nature' and liberty was deeply influenced by Locke and by Defoe's *Robinson Crusoe*. So fundamental is the conflict between civilization and nature, Fumaroli believes, that 'the century, and not only the century, the history of Europe, turn on the hinges' of Chesterfield and Rousseau.[147]

Both are about educating a young man. For Chesterfield, the human brute had to be civilized. Social success and power could only be gained by mastering *les bienséances*, and by constant self-control to create the appearance of relaxed naturalness: 'Take particular care that the motions of your hands and arms be easy and graceful.' For Chesterfield, the hallmark of success was to pass as French – 'to make the French say, *qu'on diroit que c'est un François*'. As Rousseau put it, 'The man of the world consists wholly of his mask . . . What he is means nothing to him, what he appears to be means everything.' For Rousseau, natural instinct had to be preserved from distortion and corruption, and sincerity and individual self-expression cultivated. 'Everything is good as it leaves the hands of the Creator: everything degenerates in the hands of man . . . He wants nothing as nature has made it, not even man; he has to be trained like a circus horse, twisted like a tree in his garden.' Emile would 'follow nature', breast-fed, unswaddled, growing up in solitude, and learning by experience, with only one book – *Robinson Crusoe*, Rousseau's model.[148]

Dancing was important for both. Rousseau regarded dancing as good in itself, whereas Chesterfield considered it 'ridiculous, though at the same time really important' as training. Both refer to the same famous dancing master, M. Marcel. 'Apply yourself now to Marcel's lectures,' instructs Chesterfield; 'desire him to teach you every genteel attitude that the human body can be put into.' But Rousseau declares that 'If I were a dancing master, I would not do all Marcel's monkey tricks . . . I would take [my student] to the foot of a rock . . . to tread the steep paths lightly . . . I would make him copy a mountain goat rather than a ballet dancer.'[149]

Where Chesterfield and Rousseau meet is in their desire to dominate. Chesterfield subjected his unfortunate son to 400 letters of intimidating advice over thirty years. Rousseau, in spite of his praise of freedom and nature, makes Emile's upbringing wholly contrived and regulated by a wise, all-seeing and ruthlessly benevolent tutor – an idealization of himself. Rousseau won the debate: when Chesterfield's letters were published in 1774, they were attacked as both old-fashioned and immoral: true 'politeness' must be sincere and natural.

The contest between nature and *les bienséances* echoed across Europe – certainly as far as 1760s Lichfield. Thomas Day, one of the local devotees of Rousseau, picked an eleven-year-old girl from Shrewsbury orphanage to train as a model wife, renaming her 'Sabrina Sidney', and subjecting her to a course of reading, lectures, a trip to France, and training in Spartan fortitude. But she showed little sign of 'ability that should, one day, be responsible for the education of youths, who were to emulate the Gracchi'. He gave up, and decided to seek a wife by more conventional means. In effect abandoning Rousseau for Chesterfield, he tried to make himself more eligible by going to France for a year in 1771 to learn 'the military gait, the fashionable bow, minuets and cotillions'. He even had his knock-knees painfully splinted into elegant straightness. Alas, Staffordshire was cruelly provincial, and on his return his 'studied bow on entrance, the suddenly recollected *assomption* of attitude, prompted the risible instead of the admiring sensation'.[150] But all was not lost: eventually he married an heiress.

Towards the end of the century, many thought France was moving in a British direction, or at least in the direction of 'liberty' and 'nature'. The *parlements* were claiming to represent the nation. Commerce was expanding. The salons were giving way to more public and male-dominated cafés, clubs and lodges, as political debate pushed aside pleasurable 'effeminate' conversation. Eventually, the French revolutionaries, following Rousseau, were to banish women from politics, ostracize 'aristocrats' of all classes, and assert the values of 'nature' over those of a corrupt civilization. The British found themselves on the other side. If they never quite mastered *les bienséances* as Chesterfield prescribed, Britain nevertheless became the citadel of eighteenth-century politeness against stern republican virtue.

THE FRENCH AND
SHAKESPEARE: The Age of Voltaire

Shakespear has quite a good imagination, thinks naturally, and expresses
himself with finesse; but these good qualities are overshadowed by the
rubbish he mixes into his plays.

First recorded French comment on Shakespeare, 1704[151]

Shakespeare has been a weathervane for French attitudes to English culture.
Since Voltaire had introduced him to a large readership in the *Lettres
philosophiques* (1734), he was regarded as the quintessence of English genius
– 'a powerful, fruitful genius, natural and sublime, without a spark of good
taste or the least knowledge of the rules . . . the English poetic genius dies if
forced and pruned like a shrub in the gardens of Marly'. From the beginning,
the English 'genius' was explicitly seen as the antithesis of the French. Hence,
to judge Shakespeare was also to judge French culture. So Voltaire, while
praising Shakespeare's primitive virtues, also underlines his primitive vices:
vigorous but lacking in *les bienséances*; original but unsophisticated; profound
but incoherent; with moments of sublime poetry spoiled by squalid lower-
class characters, crude horseplay, gratuitous violence and generally *des sottises*.
His successes had damaged the English stage by ingraining bad habits, thought
Voltaire; and besides, the English language was probably now in decline.

No doubt Voltaire regarded his own plays on Shakespearean themes, such
as his popular *Mort de César* (1733) and *Zaïre* (1732), inspired by *Othello*,
as more successful than their models, and sufficient to rejuvenate the French
theatre by a moderate transfusion of Shakespearean vigour. He wrote in
1750, 'T'is true we have too much of words, if you have too much of action,
and perhaps the perfection of the Art should consist in a due mixture of
the french taste and english energy.' He always considered French literature
superior, and hence preferred Addison to Shakespeare, because Addison
wrote like a Frenchman, with elegance, polish and correctness. Voltaire's
judgements, accepted in France, were widely shared in England, proof of
the continuing prestige of French classicism – including his own plays,
sixteen of which were produced in London. On *both* sides of the Channel
Shakespeare was censored and cleansed, even by his great champions Samuel
Johnson and David Garrick. His vocabulary was made more poetical, his
plots more comprehensible and his endings more cheerful.

The vogue Voltaire initiated soon far outran his condescending approval.
A later generation of writers and *philosophes* admired Shakespeare precisely
because he ignored the classical conventions: 'the genius of poetry has an
independent spirit, too jealous of its liberty to suffer being confined by that

multitude of Rules'.[152] The francophile yet patriotic Garrick (son of a Huguenot) performed extracts from Shakespeare in Paris salons in the 1750s and 60s, while also reintroducing him to the British stage as the national bard, the champion of English drama.

Exalting Shakespeare slighted the classical tradition of Corneille and Racine, of which Voltaire himself was the leading contemporary exponent. He decided to cut his posthumous rival down to size. Vanity and political expediency animated his hostility, which had begun in the 1740s, when he had described *Hamlet* as 'a coarse and barbarous piece which would not be tolerated by the lowest populace of France or Italy'.[153] But more was at stake than vanity. French classical drama was philosophical (turning on moral dilemmas), Shakespeare's was psychological (exploring the development of character – hence the impact of Garrick's 'pantomime', using facial expressions and bodily movements, rather than merely declaiming the verses). French drama was based on poetic description of unseen events, Shakespeare on their staging (including distasteful ones such as fights and killings). The former was concentrated and ordered (observing the unities of time, place and action), the latter diffuse, complex, even incoherent. The former was moral and usually optimistic, the latter amoral and frequently pessimistic. The former appealed to an educated elite, the latter to a diverse audience. For Voltaire, the former was simply a higher form of art created by a more advanced civilization; the latter, whatever its power, was infantile and crude: 'It is certainly more difficult to write well than to put on stage murders, gallows, witches and ghosts.'[154] Voltaire is rather like the patrician music critic who deigns to recognize merit in the songs of the Beatles, but is horrified when people start saying that Paul Macartney is better than Schubert. Or, in this case, better than Voltaire. He lamented that, 'I had wanted to liven up the theatre a little by including more action, but now everything is action and pantomime . . . goodbye to fine verse, goodbye to heartfelt sentiments, goodbye to everything.' He repented to a friend, 'The worst of the calamity is that it was I who first mentioned this Shakespear [and] showed the French the few pearls I had found in his enormous dung-heap.'[155]

The Seven Years War created an anglophobe climate, just as British cultural influences seemed to be challenging France's ascendancy. In 1761 Voltaire (claiming to be fighting for 'la patrie') published an appeal 'to all the nations of Europe'. This was his declaration of war on English culture.[156] Shakespeare now became 'the village clown', 'the barbarous mountebank', 'the drunken savage'. He gave a deadpan summary of the plot of *Hamlet*, with paraphrases of some of the speeches, making it sound absurd, crude and stupid. Its success he explained by the lack of distinction of English society, in which violence, comedy and the grotesque on stage was an entertainment for 'porters, sailors, cabbies, shop-boys, butchers, and clerks', who set public standards which 'revolt people of taste throughout Europe'.

Garrick raised the stakes by organizing a patriotic Shakespearean jubilee in 1769, and they rose again in 1776 when Pierre Le Tourneur began publishing a translation of Shakespeare's complete works, in twenty volumes. His version was intended to be read, not performed, and so aimed at greater fidelity than stage conventions would allow. Nevertheless, 'mean and vulgar' language was ennobled. In *Othello*, the 'black ram . . . tupping your white ewe' became 'a black vulture' and 'a young white dove'. The merely commonplace was poeticized: a dog also became a 'vulture', a cricket an 'insect of the hearth', and so on. Le Tourneur's edition was amazingly successful, with members of the royal family and leading politicians (including the anglophobe Duc de Choiseul) among its subscribers – a remarkable sign of Shakespeare's reputation and the prestige of English culture even when the two countries were on the brink of war. In a preface addressed to the king, Le Tourneur declared that 'no man of genius has ever penetrated the human heart so deeply' or created characters 'entirely resembling those of nature'. Voltaire was furious that 'this impudent imbecile' should insult France by hailing Shakespeare as 'the only model of true tragedy . . . trampling under foot the crowns of Racine and Corneille'. He wrote a letter to the French Academy denouncing Shakespeare's obscene language and 'infamous turpitude', which some 'dared to oppose to the majesty of our theatre'.[157] This was read to the Academy by d'Alembert in August 1776, in the frowning presence of the ambassador Lord Stormont and the no less formidable Elizabeth Montagu. She had written a stinging rebuttal of Voltaire's earlier attacks, an *Essay on the Writings and Genius of Shakespeare, compared with the Greek and French Dramatic Poets* – one of many retorts that thundered back across the Channel.

The French literary world split in a contest between 'genius' and 'taste'. In Montagu's words, 'genius, powerful genius only, (wild nature's vigour working at the root!) could have produced such strong and original beauties'.[158] Genius won – though not untamed. As in England, Shakespeare was house-trained. Jean-François Ducis, who knew little English and worked from translations, made him 'bearable' for French audiences, slashing indecorous action and disturbing plots, and adding ballet.[159] His unabashed reworkings – *Hamlet* and *Roméo et Juliette* were the most popular – drew thousands of spectators in the 1770s and 80s. Remarkably, the first performance of *Le Roi Lear* (in a Ducis adaptation, with a happy ending) was performed at the Court of Versailles in 1783 – while France and Britain were still at war. The best was yet to come: in September 1793, with the two countries again at war and the revolutionary Terror at its height, a musical version of *Roméo et Juliette* was successfully produced in Paris.

CHAPTER 3

The Sceptre of the World

However chimerical the aim of Universal Monarchy, that of universal influence through wealth would cease to be a chimera if one nation managed to take control of all the commerce of America.

MARSHAL DE NOAILLES, 1755[1]

We must be merchants while we are soldiers . . . our trade depends on a proper exertion of our maritime strength; . . . trade and maritime force depend upon each other; and . . . the riches that are the true resources of this country depend upon its commerce.

LORD HOLDERNESS, secretary of state, 1757[2]

The discovery of the New World has transformed the political system of Europe. Once, land forces made the destiny of states, but since a century ago Neptune's trident has become the sceptre of the world.

French foreign ministry report, 1779[3]

The contest begun in 1688 spread from Europe into the Americas, Asia, Africa and the Pacific. The spur was commerce. France and Britain hugely expanded their foreign trade over the century, transforming their domestic economies. The most dynamic element of this trade was outside Europe. Is this then the simple answer: that the 'second hundred years war' was fought for profit? French commentators at the time, and many historians since – especially but not only French historians – have blamed the insatiable greed of the nation of shopkeepers, harnessing the power of the State to their grand ambition of pillaging the world. The hapless French, according to this view, wishing only to trade peaceably with non-European peoples, were constantly being savaged by the ravening British bulldog. This is a grave accusation, but it turns the story on its head: it was the conflict between the two states in Europe that transformed commercial competition into imperial war.

Everyone knew that trade was power. As early as 1714, a French report warned that 'our industry and shipping will be eclipsed and England will become formidable by an increase of population, work and wealth'.[4] Trade increased tax revenue and underpinned the ability to borrow. It built up the merchant fleet and the number of sailors to man the navy in time of war. The British merchant fleet increased from 340,000 tons in 1686 to nearly 2.5 million in 1815; the French, though much smaller, became the world's second-largest. Half the ocean-going ships of both countries were employed in colonial trade.[5] Both were always aware of the stakes, and of how unstable was the balance of power. George III noted at the height of the American War of Independence that 'if we lose our Sugar Islands it will be impossible to raise money to continue the war'. At the end of the century, a British minister was stating the obvious when he recalled that 'Great Britain can at no time propose to maintain an extensive and complicated war but by destroying the colonial resources of our enemies and adding proportionately to our own commercial resources, which are, and must ever be, the sole basis of our maritime strength.'[6]

Interests on both sides – financiers, the great seaports, some manufacturers, the chartered trading companies – supported 'patriotic' expansion. In Britain, imperial wars were more popular than Continental expeditions. But if easy victory was popular, long wars were politically perilous. For every interest served, another was harmed. Both the British and French East India Companies found that their military burdens could easily absorb all their profits. In any case, neither Versailles nor Whitehall was driven by commercial lobbies or public opinion: their priorities were security, prestige and power.

As Britain eventually emerged as the greatest imperial state, largely at France's expense, it was natural to explain the process as premeditated despoliation. Yet it was France that regularly took the initiative – for example raiding New York in the 1690s – in order to divert British forces from Europe.[7] It was France and Spain (France's main ally, linked by a Bourbon 'family compact') that planned and prepared for war by naval building in the 1740s, 1750s, 1770s and 1780s. All Britain's peacetime alliances were defensive. British statesmen saw their actions, however bellicose they might become, as motivated by fear of France. Jeremy Black concludes that 'No British government sought unprovoked war for the sake of seizing new territories.'[8] Imperial conquest leading to permanent occupation and government took place only when France and Britain were direct antagonists, and where each was desperate to restrain or exclude the other: in North America, the Caribbean and India. Neither side yet sized up neutral Asian states. Neither turned on the softer targets of the Portuguese, Dutch or Spanish empires. Some colonial expeditions did turn into huge looting sprees, such as the capture of Manila and Havana at the end of the Seven Years War. But these tempting prizes – Spanish, not French – only came after Spain had voluntarily entered the war on France's side.

Neither Britain nor France had a clear world strategy, or even (at least before the revolution) the aim of destroying the other's power. To do so would turn the rest of Europe against the victor. But each was convinced that the other did have such a strategy. Because France was 'naturally' the dominant European power, Britain was alarmed by any hint of 'universal monarchy'. France was sensitive to the 'arrogance' and 'pretension' of Britain in undermining that established dominance, especially through overseas trade.

Their conflict had profound and long-term consequences all round the world because the eighteenth century was a period of global political instability in which for various reasons the authority and power of established European and non-European empires were weakening. In Mughal India, the French and British were partly drawn, and partly pushed themselves, into local power struggles, in which strategic, political and economic interests interacted.[9] Britain's final victory over France, in the context of this global crisis, brought it a predominance that would previously have been inconceivable. It is hard to exaggerate the importance of these years, which clear-sighted contemporaries were fully aware of. As one French historian points out, they decided the shape of the West and the world balance of power well into the twentieth century.[10]

Sugar and Slaves

The labours of the colonists settled in these long-scorned islands are the sole basis of the African trade, extend the fisheries and cultivation of North America, provide advantageous outlets for the manufactures of Asia, double and perhaps triple the activity of the whole of Europe. They can be regarded as the principal cause of the rapid movement that stirs the Universe.

ABBE RAYNAL, 1770[11]

Sugar was the succulent sap of both empires. No commodity in history, except bullion and oil, can compare in geopolitical consequence. One of the first products of mass consumption to be brought from the tropics, it was the most valuable commodity imported into Europe in the eighteenth century. As Adam Smith noted, its profitability was 'much greater than any cultivation that is known'. The sugar planters of the Caribbean were the richest group in the world. Demand kept rising: Britain imported 25,000 tons in 1715, and over 100,000 by 1780, as per capita consumption rose from 4lb per head to 20lb. Sugar went into tea, which became simultaneously the national drink, and into alcoholic drinks. Treacle sweetened bread and porridge. Jams and puddings became national symbols. This increased demand for neglected agricultural products, especially fruit and berries, and helped to nourish the expanding urban population.

Sugar was differently important for France. Because the French (being poorer and having wine) consumed less of it, most of their production, which outstripped that of the British colonies, was re-exported across Europe and the Middle East. The French possessed Saint-Domingue (now Haiti). It was the most valuable territory in the world. With ideal soil and geography, by 1743 it produced more and cheaper sugar than all the British islands combined, with coffee, cotton and indigo as bonuses. Its trade in the 1780s equalled that of the entire United States. In addition, France possessed Martinique, Guadeloupe and other islands. French maritime and economic dynamism before the revolution was fuelled by sugar. While domestic exports increased fourfold between 1716 and 1789, colonial trade increased tenfold, and by the 1780s Caribbean products accounted for 40 per cent of total French exports.[12]

Sugar was the hub of wider commerce. It buttressed other major trades such as rum and tea. It drew imports into the Caribbean: linen from Ireland, Scotland and Brittany, fish from Newfoundland, timber from New England, luxury goods from England and France (including 40 per cent of the wines of the Bordelais). Duties on sugar accounted for a large slice of state income – over one-eighth of the hugely expanded British revenue at the height of the Napoleonic wars.[13]

Sugar meant slaves. Here, France and Britain were accomplices and rivals. Some 6 million people, plus the huge number who died in the process, were shipped from Africa – one of the largest enforced movement of people in history. Though every European country was involved, the British became the largest shippers, carrying about 3.6 million people, and the French, because of Saint-Domingue, the largest buyers. African rulers provided slaves in return for vast quantities of cotton cloth from India and Lancashire, woollens from Normandy and Yorkshire, enough guns from Birmingham and Charleville to equip several armies, rum from North America, brandy from western France, and cowrie shells from the Pacific. The main slaving ports were Liverpool and Nantes, which over the century outdistanced London, Bordeaux, Bristol and Le Havre, though most ports shared in the trade. Liverpool's advantage was that it was safely distant from privateers in the Channel. Liverpool and Nantes astounded contemporaries with their opulence. Nantes was 'fuller of motion, life and activity than any place I have been at in France'. These ports drew on their hinterlands for goods to trade. Hence, western France was the centre of French manufacturing. Similarly, by 1780 one-third of Manchester's cloth exports went to Africa.[14] This was the notorious triangular trade: carrying manufactured goods to Africa to exchange for slaves, sold in the Caribbean to purchase sugar for Europe.

Criticism of the trade was muted. John Locke denounced slavery as vile and indefensible, but he owned shares in a slaving company. So did King's College, Cambridge, philanthropic Dissenters, American Quakers and French religious orders. The Jesuits were major slave owners, and the failure of their Caribbean business ventures precipitated their expulsion from France. At the other end of the scale, Ursuline nuns owned 'but three boiling pans in one shed and nineteen old negroes'.[15] Naval heroes, French, British and American, were keen supporters and participants. Many arguments were used to soothe pricking consciences. Slavery had always existed; it was condoned by religion and history. Africans were 'suited to live in servitude', asserted the mayor of Nantes.[16] The slaves themselves were generally captives in war or condemned criminals, who faced death or enslavement anyway: their lot in the Americas would be no worse, and it might save their lives and even, argued pious slavers, their souls. In any case, the trade was economically too important to risk. Not to engage in it would merely hand a dangerous advantage to the enemy. And of course in spite of risks it was profitable for the metropolises, the colonies and the African rulers. So it became routine, with slave ships called *Charming Sally* and *Aimable Cécile*, *Reformation* (a Quaker ship) and, in the early years of the French revolution, *Egalité*. One Scottish-run slaving post off Sierra Leone had a golf course.[17] Laws were passed in France and Britain to give slight protection to slaves, but there was little serious criticism of the trade until the 1760s. It reached its peak in the 1780s.

These sources of wealth and power were not left in peace for long. Even the golf course was ravaged by the French in 1779. In the Caribbean, war had been endemic since the fifteenth century. The Franco-British struggle, in parallel with their European conflict, began in earnest in the 1680s. The Caribbean was a focus of every subsequent war. Tens of thousands of troops were repeatedly sacrificed to tropical diseases: both British and French officers resigned and men deserted when ordered there. But the islands had to be kept at any cost. The French were prepared to sign away Canada to regain Guadeloupe and Martinique in 1763, and the British to abandon Philadelphia to defend Jamaica in 1778.

The Wealth of the Indies

India will some day be the biggest prize for the European powers.
French foreign ministry report, 1777[18]

Trade in the high-value products of Asia had long tempted Europeans. To silk and spices was now added a booming demand for light and colourful cotton, of which India was the unrivalled producer; also for Chinese and Indian tea, coffee, indigo and Indian saltpetre – vital for the mass production of gunpowder. The profits from these trades – several hundred per cent – had already helped the British to finance the early wars against Louis XIV. A few thousand Europeans from several nations were established in trading posts, especially Madras and Pondicherry on the Coromandel coast and Calcutta and Chandernagore in Bengal. By mid-century, the French and British were the largest traders, with the Dutch next. Their respective East India Companies were simultaneously rivals and partners, with a shared interest in ensuring that money-making was not disrupted by war. The French controller-general of finance, Silhouette, stated in 1752 that 'we only want some outposts to protect our commerce; no victories, no conquests, only plenty of merchandise and some augmentation of dividends'.[19] Future enemies traded energetically with each other and intermarried. Jean-François Dupleix, the governor-general of the French establishments, had many British friends and business partners, and Robert Clive made large loans to the French.[20] There were many enterprising and footloose adventurers untroubled by national allegiancies. One was the Frenchman Claude Martin, who eventually joined the British and commanded a force of French deserters. Among other exploits, he was tough enough to operate successfully on his own bladder stones with a long piece of steel wire, reflective enough to report on the procedure to the Medical Society of London, and financially successful enough to found a school, La Martinière, in Lucknow, which remains one of India's most prestigious.[21]

Repeated attempts were made to preserve local neutrality, and hence trading profits, but from the 1740s this became ever more difficult. Contemporaries and subsequent historians have identified culprits, not usually the same ones; but given the widening global conflict between France and Britain, conflict in India would become inevitable. Furthermore, the weakening of the Mughal empire by Persian and Afghan invasions led to struggles among local rulers, which tempted the French and British to join in. Serious battles were fought on Indian soil and in Indian waters during the 1740s as part of the War of Austrian Succession. The poorly fortified British post at Madras was taken by the French, who bloodily repulsed Admiral Boscawen's attempt to seize Pondicherry. The 1748 Treaty of Aix-la-Chapelle restored the *status quo ante*. However, the French soldier Charles Bussy thought that 'neutrality between the two nations [in India] is a pipe-dream'.[22] Dupleix, who had recruited several thousand Indian troops, entered into local political struggles to extend French power, make money, and halt the British. 'That nation, which is said to be the one in Europe that thinks best' – a clear jab at Voltaire – 'does not think that making its neighbours jealous should halt its plans. It goes ahead regardless. Why should we not do the same?'[23] The governor of Madras, Thomas Saunders, feared that the French 'aim at nothing else than to exclude us from the trade of the coast and by degrees from that of India'.[24] The East India Company followed Dupleix into Indian politics, raising troops and seeking allies. In the unlikely figure of Robert Clive, clerk turned soldier, it found an audacious and effective commander. With a few hundred men he caused serious embarrassment to Dupleix and his allies. Dupleix's political ambitions cost the Compagnie des Indes too much money, and in 1754 he was recalled to France. Perhaps he derived some consolation from the fact that (in the words of his recent biographer) 'for ten years his exploits made arrogant England bend the knee'.[25] What he had done was to change the rules of the game: from peaceful trade to armed force, territorial expansion and tax collection. Clive and the British followed suit.

'A few acres of snow'

> The two countries are at war over a few acres of snow in Canada, and they're spending more on this war than the whole of Canada is worth.
> VOLTAIRE, *Candide*, 1759

Compared with the fortunes of the islands, and the easy money that could be made in India, North America – especially the further north one went – was a less dazzling prospect. Though there had been a French presence since the 1500s, and British settlements since the early 1600s, even basic facts were little known in Europe. Frederick the Great confused North and South America, George III mistook the Mississippi for the Ganges, and a British secretary of state regarded the interior of the Continent as 'a complete desert and useless'.[26] The cod fishery off Terre Neuve (Newfoundland) was important both economically and for employing several thousand seamen – an essential reserve for the national navies. Otherwise, the far north generated a modestly profitable fur trade, which largely passed via the Protestant merchants of La Rochelle, preferred by Versailles so that heretics should bear the risks of a trade threatened by other heretics. The colony of Nouvelle France, spread along the River St Lawrence, never broke even. It was subsidized because of its strategic importance: it menaced the British colonies further south. For the best part of a century, since the Comte de Frontenac had brought the European war to America by trying to sack New York and Boston in the 1690s, settlers and their native allies had been involved in sporadic and vicious warfare. There was a scalp market in Quebec. Indians friendly with the British risked being 'boiled and eaten'.[27] The British colonies, whose inhabitants multiplied from 265,000 in 1700 to 2.3 million in 1770, were hugely more valuable than New France. The southern colonies exported plantation crops, especially tobacco. Those in the north supplied the Caribbean islands, exported strategically important timber for ship-building, and built ships themselves. Above all, as a prosperous and expanding economy largely confined to the primary sector, they constituted a buoyant market for British manufactured goods.

Versailles and London agreed on the growing importance of North America in the general scheme of power politics. The War of Austrian Succession had made France stronger. The Duke of Newcastle, the long-serving secretary of state, aimed to contain French power both by a 'system' of alliances on the Continent and by strengthening the defences of the colonies, building a fortified naval base at Halifax, and sending cannon to Virginia.[28] The French resumed a strategy they had followed sporadically for more than half a century: trying to link New France with their colony Louisiana via the Ohio valley. Their plan was to place a military barrier to British westward encroachment. If they failed to hem in the British colonists, they feared that it would only be a matter of time before they dominated all of North America, and then the whole of the Americas.[29] In 1749, only a year after peace was signed at Aix-la-Chapelle, the governor of Nouvelle France, the Marquis de La Galissonnière, began sending detachments, mobilizing native allies, massacring the allies of the British, raiding settlements near the disputed frontiers, arresting or killing British traders, and building forts. French troops rather optimistically left lead plaques at various prominent spots engraved with their claims to 'the River Oyo [*sic*] and all its tributaries and all the lands on both sides up to the sources of the said rivers as previous kings of France have enjoyed or ought to have enjoyed and are upheld by force of arms and by the treaties of Ryswick, Utrecht and Aix la Chapelle'.[30]

In short, both sides believed that a confrontation was unavoidable in America as part of the global rivalry of the two empires. The French believed that the British were preparing for 'the execution of their vast plans for the whole of America'.[31] The British believed, in the words of a meeting of colonial representatives in 1754, that the French intended an attack to bring 'the whole continent to [its] rule [in] a unified French plan [for] universal monarchy'.[32] So both made pre-emptive and incompatible territorial claims, and the French and the Spanish expanded their navies.

The Seven Years War, 1756–63

The English, Sire, are the oldest, most dangerous and most formidable
enemies of France, a haughty nation, jealous of Your Majesty's greatness
and power, pretending to dispute with you the first rank in Europe, to
equal your power on land, and dominate entirely at sea . . . They desire
peace only as a means of augmenting their power and their commerce . . .
but there is no war so dangerous and damaging as such a peace . . . which
will soon enable them to lay down the law to all of Europe.
MARSHAL DE NOAILLES, February 1755[33]

It is a question of remaining the first Power or becoming the second.
DUC DE CHOISEUL, 1760[34]

It has become a commonplace, following Winston Churchill, to call the Seven Years War the true 'first world war'. In a sense it is the *only* world war – the only global conflict involving all the great European powers that began outside Europe, was fought primarily for extra-European aims, and whose consequences were greatest beyond Europe.

The first direct clash took place in the disputed Ohio valley in May 1754, when George Washington murdered a party of peaceful French emissaries. So at least it was reported in France. French attempts to secure the valley by force seem in retrospect reckless, even suicidal. Britain normally had command of the seas, making French reinforcement of their colonies difficult in case of hostilities. The thirteen British colonies had over 1,000,000 inhabitants, against 75,000 in Canada and 6,000 in Louisiana. Yet French soldiers and colonial administrators were confident they could nip British expansion in the bud. New France, governed by the Navy Ministry, was, unlike the British colonies, tightly controlled and militarized. All able-bodied men from sixteen to sixty were incorporated into a militia 16,000 strong.

The Seven Years War

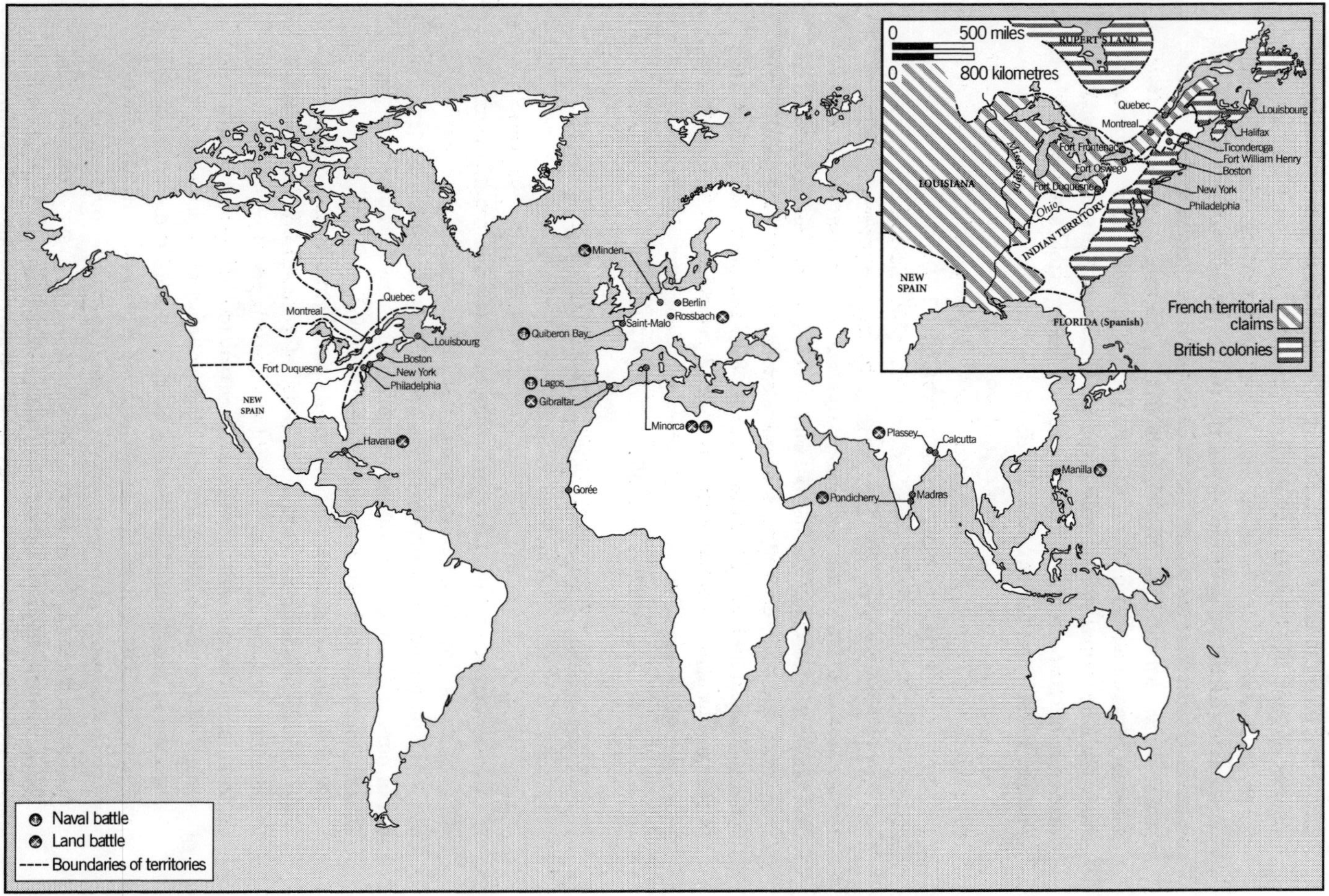

Naval battle
Land battle
Boundaries of territories

French territorial claims
British colonies

500 miles
800 kilometres

RUPERT'S LAND
Quebec
Montreal
Louisbourg
Halifax
Ticonderoga
Fort William Henry
Boston
New York
Philadelphia
Fort Niagara
Fort Duquesne
Ohio
INDIAN TERRITORIES
FLORIDA (Spanish)
Mississippi
LOUISIANA
NEW SPAIN

Manila
Calcutta
Plassey
Madras
Pondicherry

Berlin
Rossbach
Saint-Malo
Minden
Quiberon Bay
Lagos
Gibraltar
Minorca
Gorée

Quebec
Montreal
Louisbourg
Boston
New York
Philadelphia
Fort Duquesne
NEW SPAIN
Havana

The French had more native allies – a key advantage – for although the various nations tried to play off the Europeans against each other, many were accustomed to, or had been cowed by, the French, who also posed less of a territorial threat than the land-hungry British. Hurons, Abenaki and Algonquins were under the influence of French missionaries, who accompanied their expeditions. So the French were rightly confident of their superior striking ability. Once they had penned the British into the coastal strip, the large population would become a burden rather than a benefit to Britain, while the need to defend a vulnerable land border would distract the British from meddling in Europe.[35]

Early in 1755 Versailles and London began to square up. For the first time, both sent large regular forces to North America. The French sent a squadron of warships and troopships to reinforce Nouvelle France. Admiral Boscawen sailed to the mouth of the St Lawrence to intercept it, and although most of the French ships slipped through in the June fog, two were captured. France broke off diplomatic relations. Meanwhile, a force of British regular troops under General Braddock had been sent to the Ohio to take Fort Duquesne, and on 9 July 1755 it was ambushed and slaughtered by an Indian and French force. The following month, the British began to seize all French shipping. The two countries were still formally at peace. Neither side was yet ready for war.

PERFIDIOUS ALBION

The English lie at mid-point between men and beasts. All the difference I can see between the English and the Savages of Africa is that the latter spare the fair sex.
ROBERT-MARTIN LESUIRE, *Les sauvages de l'Europe* (1760)[36]

The idea that perfidiousness – at first meaning religious waywardness and later duplicity and hypocrisy – is a characteristic trait of the English remains part of the popular French stereotype, though now semi-jocular. The phrase was coined by Louis XIV's apologist Bishop Bossuet. The beginnings of the Seven Years War gave it new force. Several events marked opinion deeply.

The incident that made the 22-year-old George Washington briefly notorious took place in the no-man's-land of the Ohio forests on 28 May 1754. His force of about 100 Virginian militiamen and native allies met a French patrol of some 35 men. The French were killed or captured, and their commander, Ensign de Jumonville, was brained by a Seneca chief. The inexperienced Washington stood helplessly by; but when he was captured shortly after, he signed a paper admitting responsibility for the murder. When the news reached France, Jumonville was hailed as a martyr to English savagery:

> The bloodthirsty Englishman yells to the skies
> And barbarous joy gleams out from his eyes.[37]

The incident reappeared in propaganda as late as the 1930s.

Altogether more serious were attacks on French ships in peacetime. Even today this is recorded indignantly by French textbooks as 'piracy', while it has entirely disappeared from British memories. According to French accounts, Admiral Boscawen's ships hailed the French with shouts of 'Peace' before opening fire – 'an ignominious way for Britain to begin the war', accuses a recent American historian.[38] The French emphasized their indignation:

> The insult just made by the English to the King's flag, and the attack
> on His Majesty's ships, are acts of the utmost violence and most
> odious bad faith . . . There can be no compensation in affairs of
> honour as there might be for affairs of interest.[39]

They were not unsuspecting innocents, however. Versailles knew that sending reinforcements to Canada might provoke naval interception; but they were willing to take a calculated risk, with the intention of using any British attack for propaganda purposes in Europe. They largely succeeded, as most of their forces arrived, and the British indeed felt they had suffered a propaganda defeat. The subsequent round-up by Admiral Hawke of some 300 French merchant ships and 7,000 crewmen proved far more effective. Recent French historians suggest that this 'extreme example of blatant defiance of international law' made naval defeat inevitable by imprisoning a quarter of France's experienced seamen.[40] British history chooses to forget this inglorious master-stroke. At the time, French fury – the historian Gibbon, forced to cross France in disguise, found 'it had rendered that polite nation somewhat peevish and difficult'[41] – made it a turning-point in attitudes towards Britain.

The third perfidious act – again, not prominent in British histories – was *le grand dérangement*, the wholesale deportation of the population of the strategically important Acadia, renamed Nova Scotia. The 7–8,000 Acadians were removed from their homes, which were either burned or handed over to British settlers. They were then allowed to make their way back to France or dispersed to other colonies: the 'Cajuns' of Louisiana are their best-known descendants. A British view is that 'this ulcer needed to be excised', as the Acadians, although British subjects, refused to take an oath of allegiance, and, stirred up by La Galissonnière and a politicized and bigoted clergy, formed a 'fifth column'.[42]

But francophone histories regard it as comparable with twentieth-century 'genocide' and 'ethnic cleansing'.[43] In 2003, a Canadian royal proclamation 'acknowledged' Acadian sufferings.

These incidents helped to make the Seven Years War a struggle not simply of monarchs but of nations. Official anglophobia rejected the favourable view of England expressed by intellectuals for a generation. Now England, dominated by 'common people', was labelled 'Carthage', the faithless merchant state of 'pirates', 'assassins', 'usurpers', 'perjurers', 'vultures', 'brigands' and 'homicidal monsters'.[44] It would have to be destroyed by the 'Rome' of France, representing European civilization. These themes were revived during the revolution, and as late as the Second World War, the collaborationist Radio Paris was promising that 'England, like Carthage, will be razed'.[45]

Meanwhile, negotations in Europe produced the 'diplomatic revolution' or 'renversement des alliances' of 1756. Austria and France agreed that as their arch rivals were now respectively Prussia and Britain, they had better be allies rather than enemies. With Louis XV's mistress Madame de Pompadour an enthusiastic go-between, a first Treaty of Versailles was signed between Bourbons and Habsburgs on 1 May 1756, and a second on 1 May 1757. Meanwhile, Britain and Prussia had signed a Convention of Westminster in January 1756. Thus, the struggle that began on the Ohio became another great European war, simultaneously of Britain against France and of Prussia versus the Rest – France, Austria, Sweden and eventually Russia. France's aims were clear: 'to play the leading role in Europe that is appropriate to her seniority, dignity and grandeur, and to bring down any power that attempted to raise itself above her.'[46]

France was in an excellent position as leader of the stronger alliance, and the war began well. The French mustered troops for an invasion – a feint that forced most British troops and ships to stay at home, making them vulnerable elsewhere. In April 1756, the Toulon fleet under La Galissonnière (back from Canada) and 15,000 troops under Marshal de Richelieu attacked the vulnerable British naval base of Minorca. A weak British squadron under Admiral Byng did little to stop them and withdrew to Gibraltar. The British garrison at Port Mahon surrendered in June. The French reported being greeted as liberators. The victory caused rejoicing in France, marked by the creation of a new egg sauce, *la mahonnaise*. Byng – 'a scandal to the navy', said Boscawen – was court-martialled and shot.

In India, where the French had reinforced their troops, the British East India Company had vainly tried to negotiate a neutrality agreement. The first dramatic event was in June 1756, when France's ally the Nawab of Bengal captured the British post at Calcutta. A number of British prisoners were locked in a small cell – the notorious 'Black Hole of Calcutta' – where many died. In south India, the Jacobite General Lally promised to 'exterminate all the English in India'.[47] As in other eighteenth-century colonial wars, French Protestants fought for Britain against Irish Catholics fighting for France.

In America, the French captured Fort Oswego in New York colony in August 1756. The French commander, the Marquis de Montcalm, was horrified when his native auxiliaries scalped several dozen wounded soldiers and civilians. France's Delaware allies were raiding deep into Pennsylvania. The bulwark of the northern frontier, Fort William Henry (named after the two royal princes), surrendered in August 1757 to a French and Indian force drawn from thirty nations. Montcalm gave the garrison honourable terms, but his allies, who fought for plunder, trophies, and captives (for adoption, ritual torture, or occasionally cannibalism), felt cheated of their reward, and seized or scalped several hundred, mainly provincial militia and camp followers. This further poisoned relations between the British and French in America, and was immortalized in James Fenimore Cooper's *The Last of the Mohicans* (1826). Though too ambivalent or even sympathetic about its characters to count as a work of propaganda, the novel did create a memorable story of frontier savagery and French treachery that matched French condemnation of *la perfide Albion*. Fenimore Cooper depicts a suave but ruthless Montcalm, a personification of European courtly values, permitting the massacre for reasons of expediency: 'generous sentiments, high courtesy and chivalrous courage [lost] their influence . . . when it became necessary to prove how much principle is superior to policy'. In reality, Montcalm hastened to stop the killing, and subsequently ransomed as many prisoners as he could – at 130 *livres* and thirty bottles of brandy per head. Several captives chose to stay with the Indian families that had adopted them. Montcalm's attempt to placate the British without alienating the Indians proved unsuccessful on both counts. Indian support, vital for the defence of Nouvelle France, dwindled. The biggest human tragedy, however, was that smallpox, caught from prisoners and infected scalps, ravaged the Great Lakes region.[48]

In Europe events also favoured the French. They and the Austrians marched into Germany. The British, desperate to draw the French away from Hanover and help the hard-pressed Prussians, sent a large invasion fleet in September 1757 to seize the Atlantic naval base at Rochefort. The expedition was an expensive damp squib (see below, page 134). The same month, the French forced the Duke of Cumberland to capitulate with his Hanoverian army. Hanover was overrun, while Prussia was invaded by the Russians, Austrians, French and Swedes. As after the Minorca defeat, there was a public demand that heads should roll. It looked as though French assertions that British power was a façade were proving true. Lord Chesterfield was

> sure we are undone . . . at home, by our increasing debt and
> expenses; abroad by our ill-luck and incapacity. The King of
> Prussia, the only ally we had in the world, is now, I fear, hors
> de combat. Hanover I look upon to be, by this time, in the same
> situation with Saxony; the fatal consequence of which is too
> obvious. The French are masters to do as they please in America.
> *We are no longer a nation. I never saw so dreadful a prospect.*[49]

In France, plays and songs celebrated victory and mocked *les Anglois* as cowardly buffoons. One theatrical triumph was *La Mahonaise*, celebrating the capture of Minorca, in which the scheming, mean and utterly un-sexy Englishman Faithless loses not only the island but the gorgeous Picolette, who is swept off her feet by the dashing, brave and honest Marquis de Francheville.[50] The British envoy to Prussia reported that 'The English 'til now were envied and hated upon the Continent. At present they are despised . . . as triflers incapable of acting for themselves or of assisting their allies.'[51]

The situation was transformed on 5 November 1757 by the Prussians. Far from being hors de combat, they routed the French at Rossbach. This humiliation caused a sensation throughout Europe. The Prussians then turned on the Austrians and defeated them at Leuthen. French hopes of a rapid victory on the Continent, which would have enabled them to concentrate their forces against Britain, vanished. King Frederick II of Prussia became a British national hero, and enjoyed that rare distinction of having pubs named after him (though most would change their names in 1914). The war was now to become a long and bloody slugging match, giving Britain a second chance.

ENCOURAGING THE OTHERS

Voltaire's novel *Candide* (1759), the century's greatest international best-seller, describes its hero arriving at Portsmouth to see 'a rather stout man kneeling blindfold on the deck of one of the naval ships. Four soldiers . . . each fired three shots into his skull, as calmly as you please.' Candide is told that 'in this country it is considered a good thing to kill an admiral from time to time *pour encourager les autres*'.[52] The loss of Minorca had caused rioting, and Admiral Byng was an obvious scapegoat. It has been suggested that he was the victim of his homosexuality and 'macaroni' tastes – 'effeminate' French-style fashions and manners, supposedly undermining British martial valour.

Ironically, Voltaire contributed to Byng's death by sending him a secret letter congratulating him on his conduct, which was intercepted. Even more ironically, Byng's execution does seem to have encouraged the others: according to the naval historian N. A. M. Rodger it had a 'profound effect'. He suggests that Byng really had shied away from a superior enemy: admirals and captains on the quarter deck were particularly exposed to death and injury.[53] Whatever the truth about Byng's action – his subordinates disagreed – the public outcry brought down two successive governments. This was a dangerous time to fail. The commander of the Rochefort expedition was court-martialled. The king's own son, the Duke of Cumberland, victor of Culloden, was disgraced after his capitulation, and replaced by the veteran Huguenot Sir John Ligonier. After the Battle of Minden – a great British victory – Lord George Sackville was charged with cowardice. His disgrace was inscribed in the orderbook of every regiment, so that all should know that 'neither high birth nor great employments can shelter offences of such a nature'.

Candide, on witnessing Byng's execution, flees England in horror – a horror ostentatiously shared by Voltaire's countrymen at this new example of English savagery. But they themselves were soon to execute a commander to encourage the others. He too won the sympathy of Voltaire. He was General Thomas Arthur, Comte de Lally, diehard Jacobite grandson of Sir Gerald O'Lally (who had followed James II to France in 1689), former ADC of Bonny Prince Charlie, and a veteran of Dettingen and Fontenoy. After surrendering Pondicherry to the British in January 1761, he was allowed to return to France on parole to defend his honour. Imprisoned in the Bastille, and found guilty of treason, he was bound, gagged and beheaded in May 1766 – another sacrifice to patriotic disappointment.

This national war changed both France and Britain. Economic disruption, food shortages, taxation, and demands for manpower produced violent dissent. In Britain, the loss of Minorca provoked riots in June and July 1756 in regions where war had disrupted trade and made workers idle, or where men had been impressed into the navy. The riots combined distrust of government with scapegoating of Byng, a symbolic 'aristocrat' who 'lolls at ease on his soft couch, and is supported by a court interest'. Ministers were similarly attacked, especially the francophile Duke of Newcastle (nicknamed 'Chateauneuf'), notorious for his profligate spending on French art, servants, food and wine.[54] The most serious food riots of the century began in August 1756, drawing on existing discontent with land enclosure and the game laws. By December, there had been 140 riots in thirty counties, mostly against what people saw as unjust and unpatriotic profiteering. Economic grievances aggravated by the war were combined with an attack on an elite seen to be failing in its duty to the nation: popular patriotism was turbulent and demanding. At least twenty people were killed, 200 prosecuted, and four hanged during the food riots, yet in every case the government was forced to make concessions.

Organized 'patriotism' appealed to the idealism and interest of assertive commercial and artisan groups, most powerful in the turbulent and relatively democratic politics of the City of London, Westminster, Middlesex and America. The war saw the foundation or extension of organizations such as the Laudable Society of Anti-Gallicans, the Society of Arts, the Marine Society and the Troop Society, and some that combined patriotic and philanthropic causes, such as Captain Coram's London foundling hospital. The patriotic societies published propaganda, awarded prizes for services to the nation, and recruited paupers and boys for the armed forces. This was an opportunity for men and some women from outside the elite to participate in political life, display their patriotism and promote both the national interest and their own. If the societies often enjoyed royal and noble patronage, they could also be violently critical of what they diagnosed as unpatriotic, aristocratic vices.[55]

In France, the war created a comparable amalgam of ideological stresses and material grievances over food prices and taxes. The most important ideological conflicts were religious: the harsh though sporadic persecution of Protestants, and the running conflict between the Jansenist current of dissenting Catholicism and the official Church hierarchy backed by the Crown. Catholic orthodoxy as a pillar of royal authority was supported by the 'devout' (*dévot*) faction at court. Jansenism had become the core of political as well as religious dissent, representing the liberties of the nation against the Crown. It was influential within the *parlements* (law courts), which were the sole forum of licit political debate. Royal edicts to increase taxes gave the *parlements* a new cause of opposition. These tensions were dramatically manifested early in the war by the act of an unstable former servant, Robert-François Damiens, who committed the sacrilege of stabbing Louis XV (not very seriously) at Versailles on 5 January 1757. He declared that he had not intended to kill the king but to 'prompt him to restore all things to order and tranquillity in his states', and spare the 'misery of the people'.[56] The horrific spectacle of his execution (with burning sulphur, red-hot shears, boiling pitch, and horses to tear the limbs from his living trunk) was powerless to exorcize sullen discontent and alarming rumours of plots. The *dévots* – not implausibly – accused the *parlements* and the Jansenists of stirring up dissidence. The Jansenists accused the *dévots*' allies the Jesuits of having planned Damiens's attack – regicide being one of their supposed specialities. Spies eavesdropped on conversations sympathizing with Damiens and criticizing the king and the authorities. Hostile placards appeared on Parisian walls. Speech crimes could bring disaster to the loose-tongued: prison, the galleys, torture, and in aggravated cases the noose or the wheel. Louis XV, reported a British agent, was deeply despondent, contemplating abdication, and having to be propped up by Pompadour – who herself narrowly avoided being dismissed from court as a pious gesture by the king, who habitually turned devout when frightened.

France's alliance with Catholic Austria and subsequently with Spain against Britain and Prussia was widely perceived on both sides as having a religious dimension. The well-placed Marquis d'Argenson saw it as 'a general crusade of the Catholic party against the Protestant in Europe'.[57] In Louis XV's words, it was the 'only way . . . to maintain the Catholic religion'.[58] The British government proclaimed the cause was 'liberty and religion'.[59] By now, this was for the British no more than conventional phraseology – they had, after all, previously been allies of Catholic Austria for sixty years, and showed little solidarity with their new Protestant ally, Prussia. In France religion was more serious. French Protestants saw the war as an opportunity to gain greater toleration. Some, especially those within reach of the south-western coast, hoped to link up with a British invasion.[60] The Catholic majority, whether orthodox or Jansenist, saw Protestants as potential or actual traitors. A consequence of British coastal raids was disarmament of Protestants, a further wave of *dragonnades*, arrests, the demolition of clandestine chapels, sectarian murders and military attacks on religious assemblies. However, the most notorious single event in this, the last major religious persecution until the revolution, was the Calas case, in which an elderly Protestant shopkeeper was wrongly convicted in 1761 of murdering his Catholic son, and broken on the wheel.

Voltaire bravely championed Calas, but the *philosophes* were on the defensive. Anglophilia could now be seen as treason, and seditious writers 'of whatever rank or condition' were threatened with the death penalty. The message was reiterated in a satirical pamphlet and a satirical play, which, because they were officially sponsored, were viewed by the *philosophes* as unveiled threats. The pamphlet *Nouveau Mémoire pour servir à l'histoire des Cacouacs* (1757) was a Swiftian fable about a strange people who considered themselves superior, worshipped foreign ideas and had no loyalty to their native land. The play *Les Philosophes* (1760) presented at the Comédie Française with the support of the court, attacked them as uncritical admirers of foreign ways, unpatriotic and irreligious. Abbé Morellet, who answered back, landed in the Bastille. Helvetius's *De l'Esprit* was condemned and burnt in 1758; and he warned his friend David Hume that he could not write to him too often 'without being suspected'. Diderot's *Encyclopédie* was banned in 1759. A pro-*philosophe* newsletter lamented that 'The light that was starting to spread will soon be out; barbarity and superstition will soon have regained their power.'[61] Voltaire played the patriotic card. His attitude was complex and often duplicitous. As a cosmopolitan philosopher, he genuinely detested the war as ending a golden age for Europe. As a sceptic he mocked it as absurd, even publicly celebrating the fall of Quebec, to him an unwanted liability. But he believed in France's cultural primacy, and as a man of the world he cultivated those in power. So in 1761 he entered the lists in a characteristic manner, with a pseudonymous but transparent attack on British culture known as his 'Appeal to All the Nations of Europe' (see above, page 109).

The most serious challenge to the French Crown came from within the legal establishment, which resisted the huge rises in war taxation.[62] It had already honed its weapons and found outspoken leaders during the Jansenist conflict in the early 1750s. When an edict of July 1756 doubled the *vingtième* tax, resistance appeared in the Assembly of Clergy, provincial Estates (elite representative bodies existing in certain provinces), and the law courts. This was the beginning of an insoluble political struggle that would fatally undermine Bourbon absolutism. The Paris *parlement* refused its consent to tax increases in 1756, warning that the result would be an 'inexpressible series of injustices' and 'extreme misery'.[63] By 1759 the Crown was nearly bankrupt, and had to suspend naval building. Another edict of 1760 added a further 50 per cent to the *vingtième* and also doubled the *capitation* (poll tax). Various *parlements* defied royal orders – even when uttered directly by Louis himself: 'I am your master . . . I ought to punish you . . . I want to be obeyed.' Royal governors who marched into sessions with troops to dictate edicts to court clerks were no more successful. *Parlementaires* illegally published their protests. Ministers realized that news of this defiance would 'spread in a week to the cafés of London and the newspapers of Holland', and increase the difficulty of raising international loans. It became steadily clearer that this was an ideological challenge to the authority of the Crown. The finance minister condemned as 'Anglican principles' demands to vote taxes and supervise expenditure. *Parlementaires* publicly used dangerous language, talking of legislative sovereignty, 'liberty', 'despotism', the rights of the 'nation' and its 'citizens', and even, fatefully, demanding a meeting of the Estates General, the representative body of the realm that had not met since 1614. The chief minister Choiseul and the king changed tactics after 1760 and tried persuasion, urging the *parlements* to let 'our enemies see that we are in a condition to resist them'; but they soon reverted to repression.

Both Britain and France, if shuddering with unrest, still managed to fight across the globe for seven years. Their governments were able to gather and expend blood and treasure. These exertions were associated at the time and since with two great 'patriot' ministers, both called to power as things went wrong, William Pitt, subsequently created Earl of Chatham, and Etienne-François de Choiseul-Stainville, created Duc de Choiseul. Pitt was appointed a secretary of state briefly in 1756, aged forty-eight, and again in uneasy coalition with the veteran Duke of Newcastle, from June 1757 to October 1761. Choiseul was appointed minister of foreign affairs in November 1758, aged thirty-nine, and remained in office until 1770. Both were to have profound effects on the history of both countries.

Pitt and Choiseul

His ambition . . . is not wealth, for he despises it, and is incorruptible, but power . . . An extreme Republican in a moderate Monarchy, he wishes above all to be patriotic, or at least appear it, to be the favourite of the people . . . Mr Pitt, insolent to his sovereign, in France would end his days imprisoned in Mont Saint-Michel; . . . in Russia, would have made a revolution, or had his tongue torn out and perished under the knout; . . . in England, he obtained a great and lucrative office . . . Woe to States which in times of crisis have such ministers.

French foreign ministry report, October 1763[64]

After dinner was presented . . . to the duc de Choiseul . . . a little volatile being, whose countenance and manner had nothing to frighten me for my country. I saw him but for three seconds, which is as much as he allows to any body or thing.

HORACE WALPOLE, October 1765[65]

In their different worlds, Pitt and Choiseul harnessed the novel forces of 'patriotism'. In Britain, this meant appearing to come from outside the supposedly corrupt ruling elite, and to represent the interests of the nation. Pitt was an outsider, if less than he seemed. The grandson of 'Diamond Pitt', who had grown rich in India, he gloried in the sarcastic label 'the Great Commoner'. A political maverick, he depended on swaying the House of Commons by the power of his bombastic, rambling but sometimes brilliant oratory. His heedlessly destructive and implacable ambition made him a man whom it was safer to have inside than outside the tent. He was an early example of a coldly professional politician; yet he cared little for his supporters inside or outside the Palace of Westminster and sat for a rotten borough. In the international sphere patriotism meant opposing continental involvement (seen as the selfish interest of the Hanoverian court) and supporting a 'blue water' policy of imperial conquest and trade. Pitt famously promised the House in 1757 that he 'would not now send a drop of our blood to the Elbe, to be lost in that ocean of gore'.[66] His actions belied his words – the 'now', of course, is the hallmark of the professional – but he was blessed with the gift of being able to 'deny his own words with an unembarass'd countenance'.[67] He managed to make 'patriotism' an instrument of government rather than of opposition, enjoying the support of the relatively democratic and fully plutocratic world of the City of London, of Tories in the shires, and of many on the fringes of the political nation. He was thus the channel by which public opinion could act on governments, and governments influence public opinion: 'that Genius [who] first raised the abject Spirits of the Nation and . . . conducted them to Glory and Conquest'.[68] His great contributions were to justify increased involvement in Germany, which he and other patriots had long opposed; to persuade Parliament to vote unprecedented sums of money for the war; and (even if this was often exaggerated) to communicate a feeling of boldness and determination. Choiseul considered him a 'charlatan' and a 'demagogue', but learned from him the need to engage with public opinion.

Choiseul was more of an insider: a cosmopolitan, pedigree-conscious nobleman from the still independent Duchy of Lorraine, one of those hereditary all-purpose soldiers, diplomats, administrators and courtiers that every European monarch employed. Yet his family was not one of the great metropolitan dynasties that dominated the court by right. He, like Pitt, had to make his way by ruthless use of his talents and opportunities. Fashionable, amusingly impertinent, charming when necessary, a Don Juan, vain, indiscreet, a spendthrift, a patron and connoisseur (he had an English garden and an opulent collection of paintings), he claimed to

> detest work, I love pleasure as if I were twenty years old, I am little concerned with money . . . I have a very fine and comfortable house in Paris, my wife is very clever and, amazingly, does not cuckold me, my family and circle are infinitely agreeable . . . people say I have had passable mistresses.

Despite this dilettante pose (which deceived Walpole) he was no lightweight. He even proved an effective administrator: 'I have always made others work more than I work myself. One should not bury oneself in papers.'[69] He depended on those who provided the king with essential services – the great *financiers* and the ambitious women. Madame de Pompadour, to whom he had been useful, was his patroness. She raised him from the diplomatic corps to the foreign ministry: enemies called him 'her little monkey'. His wife was the granddaughter of Antoine Crozat, one of the richest and most powerful of the State *financiers*, and an early patron of Pompadour. So both Pitt and Choiseul were connected with the new wealth derived from imperialism and war. Choiseul supported the Austrian alliance because he hoped it would free France to fight the British upstart overseas, and in general he seems to have had a clearer view of international strategy than Pitt, whose supposed global vision was an invention of his admirers – and his enemies. Choiseul hated and feared Pitt as the evil genius of British power: 'This minister is greedy for glory.' He suspected that, 'drunk with success', he had adopted the 'vast project' of stripping France of all its colonies.[70]

The obvious differences between the two men reflect the gulf between two systems of power. Pitt was a parliamentarian, one of the most compelling there has ever been. Choiseul was a courtier in a country where all political careers began and ended at court. Pitt acted mainly in public; Choiseul in private. Pitt orated, Choiseul chatted. Pitt hectored, Choiseul charmed. As his most recent biographer puts it, in France, there was no need to seduce a nation, only to please one man, or one woman.[71] For that reason, Pitt became more of a legend in his own lifetime and for two centuries thereafter. He was given credit for the work of others and aided by events, and people began to take him at his own estimation: 'I am sure I can save this country, and nobody else can.' He was the prototype of those great war leaders – his son William Pitt the Younger, David Lloyd George and Winston Churchill – who by mastery of parliamentary oratory and through its resonance in the country gave utterance and inspiration to a nation in peril. Like them, he found his apotheosis in war, and lost direction in peace. He was, without doubt, a more seriously flawed personality and more of a fake than they. Yet, within Britain and in France and Prussia, the belief grew that his willpower and inspiration underpinned Britain's greatest-ever victory. Edmund Burke best expressed the ambivalence of insiders, calling him 'that great artificer of fraud . . . Oh! but this does not derogate from his great, splendid side.'[72]

Despite being a courtier, Choiseul believed that, like Pitt, he must harness new political forces in the struggle. He wrote to the king, 'Make no mistake, patriotic virtue is degenerating year by year in France . . . One of my objects . . . is to reestablish the interest and love of the Fatherland in French hearts; I would like us to put the interest of our villages, our provinces, our kingdom before our own interest.'[73] He commissioned patriotic and anglophobe propaganda, set up a newspaper to put the government's line, and himself drafted pamphlets arguing his policies to a public well beyond Versailles. He made conciliatory moves to the *parlements* in the hope of winning their financial support for war. He (along with Pompadour) maintained contacts with the *philosophes*, even while permitting attacks on their anglophilia. And later he did nothing to oppose the expulsion of the Jesuits in 1764 by the Paris *parlement*, using as a pretext the collapse of the their West Indies sugar business, ruined by British naval action. The Jesuits were the hate-figures of Gallicans, Jansenists, *philosophes* and *parlementaires* – in short, of France's 'patriot' party – and Choiseul hoped their expulsion would win him popular support, and prevent criticism of the peace terms he had negotiated.

Choiseul's internal policy has been interpreted by his many admirers as an attempt to modernize the monarchy and link it with progressive forces. One even calls this 'the birth of the Left'.[74] No such nativity was intended. Although Choiseul had read his Montesquieu and Voltaire, as he liked to show, his aim was certainly not to favour representative government in France. He despised parliamentary politics except in so far as, under a demagogue like Pitt, they could stimulate warlike patriotism. His aim was to do the same in France, but under the banner of an absolute monarchy. Central themes of his propaganda were the loyalty and happiness of the French under strong, paternal rule, and the superiority of that system over Britain's corrupt, faction-ridden and ultimately doomed parliamentary regime.

Choiseul's propaganda had one remarkable triumph. In November 1761 he discreetly engineered an 'offer' of money by the Estates of Languedoc to build a warship for the battered navy. This inspired a wave of patriotic enthusiasm, as the provinces and great corporations of the realm each vied to pay for their own ship, with the lesser guilds and trades (such as the roofers and *maîtres-limonadiers*) clubbing together. Patriotism was also good policy. *Dons gratuits* (free gifts) to the Crown were the way for privileged bodies to purchase their advantages, and so much the better if they could serve local interests too. The canny Bretons made sure that the battleship Bretagne was built with oak from Breton forests, sails woven in Rennes and ironwork forged at Paimpont.[75] Soon sixteen line-of-battle ships had been pledged, whose names would proclaim the civic virtue of their donors: the 'Languedoc', the 'Ville de Paris', the 'Diligent' (sponsored by the post-masters), the 'Zealous' (by the tax collectors), the 'Useful' (a hopeful public-relations effort by the farmers-general), and (fashionably though with some effrontery) the 'Citizen', by the court bankers and military *financiers*. Choiseul thus boosted morale at a depressing time, but the propaganda was risky. The donors – many of them opponents of tax increases – were asserting their patriotic 'citizenship', voluntarily subscribing money for spending of which they approved. The contrast with the Crown's attempts to impose tax increases was glaring. But however magnanimous these gestures seemed to those making them, the amount of money they produced was a drop in the ocean. The struggle over taxes, patriotism and citizenship was only beginning. The Seven Years War opened the era of revolution.

We have seen the by now familiar gambit of both France and Britain: forcing the other to commit forces to Europe, hence weakening it further afield. Britain enjoyed the immense advantage of having Frederick the Great of Prussia as an ally. As both Austria and Russia wanted to bring Prussia down, he had no option but to fight desperately; and as he was the greatest military leader of his day, Britain's investment of money and men to support him paid a large dividend. Austria and France proved to be a less successful combination, each pursuing different aims, and each suspecting the other, with reason, of trying to pass on the main burden of war.

Pitt, reluctant to send forces to sink into 'that ocean of gore' in Germany, pressed for a landing in France, which would appeal to the 'patriot' preference for seaborne operations and mollify the Prussians by forcing the French to keep thousands of troops guarding their coasts. In fact, the French coasts were scarcely defended, as their cannon had been taken for the navy. The governor of Brittany, the Duc d'Aiguillon, lamented that 'not one battery in the province is armed . . . there is not a pound of gunpower on the coast, not a single cannonball'.[76] A large invasion fleet of eighty-two ships, carrying 10,000 troops, sailed from Spithead on 7 September 1757. In the words of a classic French history, 'this was certainly more than was necessary to be sure of success'.[77] The target was the naval base of Rochefort. The fleet nosed around off the estuary for ten days, demolished a small fort on the Ile de Ré, and then the commanders decided that a landing on the mainland was too risky and they sailed home, losing a ship on the way to a Dunkirk privateer. Though arguably justified on grounds of military prudence, this fiasco caused disappointment and recrimination comparable with that following the fall of Minorca. Pitt's reputation suffered. However, he persisted with this strategy, urged on by the Prussians, who must have realized this was the only help they would get. Careful preparations were made, including the building of special landing craft. The target was the privateering port of Saint-Malo, 'which had always gloriously provoked English anger',[78] and on 5 June 1758 16,000 troops were landed at Cancale, nine miles east. The state of the roads and the impassable *bocage* country of hedges and banks – like that which caused serious trouble to tanks in 1944 – made it impossible to move siege artillery to Saint-Malo. Meeting no resistance on land or sea, the invaders re-embarked after four days on French soil, burning ships and 'destroying everything in their path'. Both sides seemed satisfied. The mayor of Saint-Malo reported that 'in burning our ships, the enemy has only inflamed our zeal', and asked as a reward that his town should be given duty-free status.[79]

Two months later, Cherbourg was attacked. Its small garrison (containing many 'cripples, beggars and children') had fled, and thirty-five ships were captured and the harbour destroyed during a week's occupation. The victors re-embarked with a substantial sum of money, over 10,000 cattle, sheep and horses, and 'a prodigious quantity' of poultry.[80] So far, the British had met no significant resistance, but the landings were causing increasing outrage among the Bretons, who were clamouring to take up arms. When the British made a second attempt to capture Saint-Malo in September, it became clear how dangerous invasions were for the invaders. They landed 4,000 men safely, but for practical reasons took an inland route towards Saint-Malo, losing touch with the fleet. A French force of some 10,000 regulars, coast-guards and militia, led by d'Aiguillon, came hurrying to meet them. The British retreated to the sea at Saint-Cast, where most re-embarked. However, the French arrived on 11 September as the Guards were still on the beach, and despite courageous efforts by Admiral Howe and naval boat crews to take them off, some 750 – far more according to the French – were killed or captured. 'At last we've thrashed the English . . . For a loss of 300 men, we have made them leave 1,000 –1,200 to manure the beach.'[81] D'Aiguillon politely invited captured officers to dinner, but he was not in a forgiving mood after recent depredations: when the British drank the health of the king of France, 'I did not return the compliment.'[82] A hundred years later, a victory column was erected on the dunes. But both sides could celebrate victory. The British had carried out the biggest landings in France since the Hundred Years War without the French navy daring to leave port. They had destroyed a lot of troublesome privateers, and paraded twenty-two captured cannon triumphantly through Hyde Park. The French, for their part, were delighted to have 'thrown them into the sea'. Voltaire, in one of his patriotic moods, wrote, 'I greatly doubt that they've killed 3,000 English near Saint-Malo; but I admit I wish they had. It's not humane; but can one pity pirates?'[83]

Whether the landings had diverted more British forces than French remains debatable. Arguably Versaillles was more worried that ships and men might be sent to Flanders or Germany than by the fate of Breton fishing boats and poultry. However, the raids did have one serious, utterly unpredictable, consequence. D'Aiguillon raised local taxes to improve Brittany's feeble defences and roads. This caused a confrontation with the *parlement* at Rennes, which accused him of acting illegally. The cause was taken up by the whole dissident legal establishment, and it led eventually to what is generally called a coup d'état by the chancellor, Maupeou, in 1771 – one of the milestones towards revolution in 1789.

The British gave up raiding France. Pitt insisted on diversionary attacks in West Africa and the Caribbean instead. But he, like everyone, now realized that the decisive point was Germany. If the French won there, they could turn against Britain; but while the French army was engaged, Britain could risk sending most of its own army across the Atlantic: in 1759 there were thirty-two battalions of redcoats in America, and only six in Germany; while of France's 395 battalions, only twelve were in Canada and four in India.[84] Keeping a land war going in Germany was costing both sides more and more money. We have seen the difficulties the French had in trying to raise taxes. The British too felt the strain: in 1758, there was a crisis of confidence in the City as the government delayed paying its bills and the Bank of England warned that a collapse of credit was looming. The Duke of Newcastle calmed fears by raising the interest on government loans, though he himself worried that 'we are engaged in Expenses infinitely above our strength'.[85] Yet by the end of 1758, the war seemed slowly to be going Britain's way. The situation in Germany was stable, if costly. Trade was flourishing, while that of France was being wrecked by attacks in Africa, India and the West Indies, where rich Guadeloupe was captured. In North America, after a series of failures, 45,000 men were preparing to invade New France.

Years of Victory, 1757–63

Come, cheer up, my lads! 'tis to glory we steer,
To add something new to this wonderful year,
'Tis to honour we call you, not press you like slaves,
For who are so free as the Sons of the Waves?
'Hearts of Oak', DAVID GARRICK, 1759[86]

Can we easily leave the remains of such a year as this? It is still all gold . . .
We have not had more conquest than fine weather: one would think we had
plundered East and West Indies of sunshine. Our bells are worn threadbare
with ringing for victories.
HORACE WALPOLE, 21 October 1759[87]

The war had begun in North America, which was to be its greatest prize. Events there were at last taking a decisive turn. One might ask – as some contemporaries did – why it had taken so long. The struggle was less one-sided than it might seem. The French could field 25,000 regular troops and militia, most used to fighting in American conditions. They had many Indian allies, a potent advantage. Distance, 'those hellish forests', mountains, bad weather, the absence of roads (requiring movement by boat) and shortage of supplies made moving large forces arduous and dangerous, and made it hard for the British to employ their numerical advantage. For all these reasons, French officers regarded New France as impregnable.

On the British side, the colonial militias were unreliable and far less hardy than their French counterparts. Friction between British generals and colonial governments was constant. London, and especially Pitt, did not help by formulating unrealistic plans, giving orders too late, and sacking commanders when things went wrong. Pitt was, however, willing to spend vast sums in America as in Europe. His assumption of the costs of the campaign smoothed many difficulties with the colonists and fuelled an economic boom, as barrels of gold and silver arrived from London. British commanders and troops learned forest warfare. Lord Howe adapted tactics and equipment to local conditions: coat-tails were cut off, pipeclay and starch forgotten, and moccasins and tomahawks adopted. Officers had to eat stew out of a common pot. Scottish highland units, including men who thirteen years earlier had fought for Bonny Prince Charlie, began to create a new military legend under the Union Flag. Some were happy to fight the French to punish their 'treacherous promises in 1745'.[88] Irregulars such as Robert Rogers's Rangers became famous, or notorious, for adopting the ruthless practices of frontier war. Yet disaster could still strike. In July 1758, an attack on Fort Carillon, at Ticonderoga, which commanded the Lake Champlain route from New York to Montreal, began with Howe being killed in a skirmish, and then the incompetent General Abercromby, fearing the approach of French reinforcements, attempted to rush the defences with his regular troops. Two thousand men were shot down in suicidal attacks, and the army streamed back in disorder. Montcalm thought at first it was a ruse; he then decided it was a miracle, and erected a cross with a pious inscription. But there was no simultaneous miracle 600 miles to the north-west, where New France's fate was sealed by a daring seaborne attack on the fortified naval base of Louisbourg, which commanded the approach to the St Lawrence, and made French reinforcement and supply impossible. It would only be a matter of time before the competent and methodical General Jeffery Amherst, who replaced Abercromby, converged on Quebec and Montreal. In retaliation for the massacre of Fort William Henry, Amherst shipped off the Louisbourg garrison as prisoners, and the 8,000 civilian inhabitants were deported to France, their homes being taken by settlers from New England.

In India, naval strength had swung the conflict decisively against the French. Already in June 1757, by a mixture of boldness and trickery, Clive had defeated France's ally the Nawab of Bengal at Plassey, which gave the British control of one of India's richest provinces. In the south, the French were defeated at Wandewash in 1759 – the Irish Colonel Coote overcoming France's Irish troops led by the Irish General Lally.

The usual logic dictated that France must now go for checkmate: an invasion of Britain. Since the end of 1758 troops, ships and barges had been assembling in the Channel ports, and attempts were made to enlist Russian and Swedish support. The French plan was to land diversionary expeditions in Ireland and Scotland, where some hoped to fan the embers of Jacobitism; then to sail down the North Sea to cover the main crossing to Essex from Ostend. This aimed at a knockout blow on London, causing the collapse of government and the financial system. English land defences were negligible, especially as Pitt, blithely sceptical of the threat, was still dispatching troops abroad. The militia would not hold up French regulars, even if drilling them did help Captain Edward Gibbon to understand the tactics of the Roman legions. Once landed, the French could certainly reach London. Large sums were spent on landing craft. The problem was to assemble a fleet strong enough to escort the troopships.

As the invasion force waited, 1759, Britain's great 'Year of Victories', began – even though all the victories were risky, and some even partly accidental. The first, and unexpected, British and Hanoverian victory was on 1 August, at Minden, in north-western Germany, when a seemingly unstoppable French advance was reversed. What warmed British hearts was that a mere six battalions of British infantry – marching forward intrepidly, though seemingly by mistake – threw back repeated assaults from superior forces of French infantry and cavalry, commanded by the Stuart Duc de Fitzjames. The French lost 7–10,000 men to the British–Hanoverian 2,700. At the end of the day the French army, its confidence shattered, was in humiliating retreat. The threat to north-west Germany was removed for another year, and the French could not withdraw more troops to invade Britain. The only blot was that mentioned earlier – General Sackville had failed to attack with his cavalry.

The most famous victory was the capture of Quebec on 13 September, which made General James Wolfe the posthumous hero of a saga once known to every British schoolboy. Wolfe's small army had been carried 300 difficult miles up the St Lawrence in 170 ships – a feat the French thought impossible, and which owed much to the skills of the yet unknown Lieutenant James Cook. But it stuck before the city's formidable natural and man-made defences, whose numerous garrison included even a unit of students (nicknamed the 'Royal Syntax'). Montcalm had only to hold out until the approach of winter forced the British to sail away till next spring. Various attempts by Wolfe to find a way of attacking the city, perched high above the river, came to nothing. The British were reduced to trying to provoke an attack by waving their hats, and more grimly by ravaging the surrounding country, which produced the usual massacres and scalpings. The young Wolfe was to attain a halo of patriotic martyrdom as a brilliant and humane soldier – he was reputed to have refused to kill a wounded Jacobite at Culloden. In fact he had a vicious streak and a highly neurotic personality, which proved an effective combination in the circumstances. As George II famously remarked, if Wolfe was mad, he hoped he would bite some of the other generals. With only a week before winter would have forced a retreat, and convinced that he was both terminally ill and facing disgrace, Wolfe came up with a death-or-glory plan to lead an amphibious night attack up the steep cliffs overlooking the St Lawrence west of Quebec. The French were taken by surprise – 'the enemy hasn't got wings', said Montcalm. Without waiting for outlying detachments, Montcalm led his available 5,000 men out of the city to throw back the 4,500 British before they could dig in. His mixture of French regulars, Canadian militia and native auxiliaries was unsuited to the open field of the Plaine d'Abraham, and they were quickly routed by the devastating tactic perfected by Wolfe: mass volleys at point blank range. Quebec fell. If Wolfe's gamble had failed, everything would have had to be put off for another year, with unpredictable political consequences: it is not impossible that a compromise peace would have saved part of Nouvelle France. And if the French had still been there, the British colonies would not have been so soon tempted by independence.

DEAD HEROES

Neither Wolfe nor Montcalm had been keen on a posting to the American backwoods, away from the real soldiering in Germany. Both had welcomed the opportunity to fight a proper battle at last at Quebec. Wolfe was hit by two bullets from irregular sharpshooters on the flank of the attack, and he died as the battle was ending. Montcalm was struck by grapeshot from a cannon the sailors had managed to haul up the cliffs, and he died the next morning. Deeply shamed by Indian treatment of prisoners, Montcalm had struggled to impose European standards on a frontier war: the resulting desertion by native allies weakened him badly. Wolfe had been less scrupulous about the occasional massacre and even paid cash for scalps. The capture of Quebec caused jubilation in America and Britain, with fireworks and bonfires, illuminations, toasts, feasts, concerts and sermons. One Boston preacher predicted a great imperial and Protestant future, 'great cities arising on every hill . . . great fleets . . . happy fields and villages'.[89] Wolfe's victory was not conclusive. Quebec was almost recaptured by the French the following spring. But as a symbol it was unforgettable. The painting of Wolfe's death by the American artist Benjamin West celebrated not only the sacrifice of the young general, but also the unity of the Empire, personified by the American ranger, the Scottish highlander, and the faithful Mohawk warrior – none of whom was actually present. Several French artists tried to emulate or plagiarize West, here Louis-Joseph Watteau. Both paintings became icons: Wolfe symbolized the youthful daring of a rising empire, Montcalm (the Marquis de Montcalm-Gozon de Saint-Véran, in full) the stoical chivalry of a beleaguered aristocracy. There was some truth in the contrast. The French armed forces were dominated by the nobility and court. Among 151 French generals there were eight princes, eleven dukes, thirty-eight marquises, forty-four counts, six barons and fourteen chevaliers.[90] It is unthinkable that a thirty-two-year-old untitled son of a marine officer like Wolfe could have commanded a French army, even in the colonies. Yet Wolfe and Montcalm, like most regular officers, had more in common with each

Dead heroes: rival attempts to create an iconic image, with similar heroic poses, lamentations, and participants.

other than with their respective colonial compatriots. When West's picture was shown in 1770, it attracted more spectators and probably made more money than any British painting in history.[91] But the unity it celebrated was already collapsing.

The French could still turn everything round by invading Britain. To prevent this, the British fleet under Admiral Hawke were managing for the first time ever to stay at sea for weeks on end, managing to keep healthy by strict cleanliness and taking fresh provisions from supply ships. This closed the main French western ports, with serious economic and strategic consequences, and kept the main fleet bottled up in Brest. The British Mediterranean fleet was similarly blockading Toulon. However, it was impossible to stay indefinitely, largely owing to weather. The French could wait for any interruption in the British screen to break out. In August, the French fleet escaped from Toulon to reinforce the veteran Vice-Admiral Marshal de Conflans at Brest, but it was caught and savaged off Lagos in Portugal. Arguably, the French should now have cancelled their invasion plans. But an invasion was their only hope, and Conflans, who believed the credibility of the navy was at stake, was ordered by Versailles to undertake what was, in the opinion of a sympathetic American historian, 'little better than a suicide mission'.[92] When gales blew Hawke off his station, Conflans sailed on 14 November with twenty-one ships of the line to pick up d'Aiguillon's 20,000 troops in Quiberon Bay and sail for Scotland, and thence to Ostend. But Hawke came plunging back through a gale with twenty-three ships of the line and sighted the French on 20 November. Conflans raced for shelter amid the rocks and shoals of Quiberon Bay, not thinking 'the enemy would dare to follow me' in such weather.[93] But Hawke did, trusting in his men and his weather-beaten ships. Two French battleships were cannonaded into surrender with huge casualties, and three were sunk by the sea billowing in through their gunports as inexperienced crews struggled to fire broadsides. Only a handful of survivors were picked up by British boats. Nightfall halted the battle, and permitted eight French ships to escape. Next morning, the rest, including Conflans's flagship, ran themselves aground and were set on fire, or escaped into the Vilaine estuary, where eleven were trapped and their captains dismissed in disgrace. The British had lost about 300 men to the French 2,500, mainly Breton conscripts.

The battle, called Quiberon Bay by the victors and Les Cardinaux by the vanquished, was one of the most audacious in naval history. In Hawke's own words, it was 'akin to a Miracle that half our ships was not ashore in the pursuite of the Enemy, upon their own coast, which wee were unacquainted with'.[94] Had that happened, Britain would have been open to invasion, and history might have taken a different turn. As it was, Quiberon Bay became 'the graveyard of the French navy', and the end of France's last hope of defeating Britain. 'What is in store for this unhappy country!' wrote a French officer. 'God help us! I have wept for it and am weeping still!'[95] The British made themselves at home on France's offshore islands, planting vegetables, playing cricket, and cocking a snook at Versailles.

The following year, French resistance in Canada was mopped up. Captain Vauquelin, commanding the only French frigate left on the St Lawrence, dropped anchor, nailed his colours to the mast, fought till his ammunition ran out, and threw his sword into the river rather than surrender it. Equally defiant, 700 French soldiers escaped by a seven-month march to Nouvelle Orléans. French settlers, economically desperate and angry at their seeming abandonment, gave up the struggle, swore allegiance to King George, and started trading with the British. The British responded by guaranteeing freedom of religion. This beginning of reconciliation, notes one French historian, marked the end of Nouvelle France.

The 'Year of Victories' ended, but the war was far from over. If Britain had triumphed overseas, France had hopes of winning on the Continent, and it planned to commit 300,000 men to the war in Germany.[96] Prussia – also beset by Austria and Russia – was desperate, and demanded more men and above all more money from Britain. Moreover, Spain was preparing to join France. Pitt demanded a pre-emptive strike to seize its treasure fleet from South America, and he resigned in October 1761 when his colleagues demurred. Spain declared war in January 1762. Unpredictably, the death of the tsarina Elizabeth that same month transformed the situation in Germany, for her successor Peter III at once made peace with Prussia. Spain proved to be a soft target for the British. Fired up by the prospect of huge sums of prize money, navy and army enthusiastically attacked two of the richest colonial cities, Havana and Manila, and took both. Disease proved the most dangerous enemy: nearly one-third of the troops diverted from North America died in Cuba. Manila was taken by a scratch force gathered in India, including French prisoners. The attackers had the advantage of surprise, as news of the outbreak of war had not reached the Spanish defenders. The loot from both cities was stupendous. After the government had taken its cut, the lion's share went to the commanders, with a few pounds each for ordinary soldiers and sailors. In India, General Lally failed to take Madras in the biggest and most expensive expedition the French ever mounted in India: it bankrupted the Compagnie des Indes. Then, with his troops deserting after a five-month siege, Lally surrendered Pondicherry. Pigot, the British governor of Madras, who was of Huguenot origin, ravaged Pondicherry in reprisal for damage done to Madras. 'The dazzling white palace of Dupleix, like the dreams of its builder, sank in the dust and ruin of unsuccessful war.'[97] The French and Spanish dreamt of reversing their defeats by yet another plan to invade England late in 1762, but naval weakness forced its rapid abandonment.

It was obvious now, after the death of a million soldiers, that neither side had anything more to fight for. The new king, George III, who had acceded in 1760, and his close adviser and former tutor the Earl of Bute, a donnish Scot, were eager for peace. They wanted to cut loose from European conflicts, being indifferent to the future of Hanover – 'that horrid Electorate', the king called it[98] – and heedless of the interests of the bloody but unbowed Prussians. The main issues for Britain lay outside Europe. Yet contrary to contemporary French belief, still tenaciously held by French historians, the British had no plan for world domination or for destroying the French empire. Pitt even thought of giving back Quebec. The British feared alarming other European powers by excessive gains. The Duke of Bedford, their principal peace negotiator, opposed asking the French to 'let us cut their throats', and thought

> We have too much already, more than we know what to do with, and I very much fear, that if we retain the greater part of our conquests out of Europe we shall be in danger of over-colonizing and undoing ourselves by them, as the Spaniards have done.[99]

Some colonies would therefore be returned to France and Spain: but which? Britain's priority now was defence. It preferred to keep Canada, thus ending the conflict in North America, rather than the French sugar islands of Guadeloupe and Martinique. Choiseul seemed to have abandoned the colonial game by offering Louisiana to Spain, but his secret intention was to induce the Spanish to agree to a quick peace and then build up its navy for a new war against Britain in five years' time. Choiseul wanted the return of the sugar islands and he was adamant in keeping fishing rights off Newfoundland. He told the royal council that the fisheries were worth more than all French possessions in North America.[100] The reason was that this 'nursery' provided one quarter of all French seamen, and so was indispensable to his plans for a maritime war of revenge. Britain kept several smaller islands (Grenada, St Vincent, Tobago) and regained its naval base at Minorca. Havana and Manila were returned to Spain, in return for Florida. In West Africa and India, the French trading posts were returned, but they were demilitarized. 'Pondicherry is only a pile of ruins, wells are filled in and trees cut down . . . and the Chandernagore settlement is almost in the same state.'[101]

The French monarchy, as contemporaries realized, had been weakened. Defeat had exposed Louis XV as a nonentity, apparently allowing himself to be dominated by the Austrophile Pompadour and her cronies. The raising of a statue of Louis in Paris in 1763 provoked open derision. The war had intensified traditional resentment of Austria, blamed for France's defeats, a resentment that a generation later brought down retribution on the uncomprehending head of Queen Marie-Antoinette, 'l'Autrichienne' chosen by Choiseul to embody the alliance. The war made anglophobia a staple of French patriotism. Although fashionable 'anglomania' persisted on a superficial level, the idea of England as a model was undermined, both by patriotic resentment and by the post-war conflicts that shook the British political system.

The greatest consequence of the Seven Years War was economic. The Industrial Revolution was beginning. The causes and extent of this transformation have long been debated. Recent research links it firmly with the expansion of British overseas trade, as well as with the financial power of the City, both products of the struggle against France: 'Britain's economic progress cannot be separated from the establishment of its military hegemony.'[102] Its ability to win, and keep, dynamic overseas trade, financed by the City and protected by the navy, was its unique advantage over the rest of Europe, and the Seven Years War increased that advantage. As everyone at the time knew, trade helped pay for war, and war extended trade. Trade encouraged investment, raised wages, broadened consumption and spurred new technologies and skills. Much of the new manufacturing output was exported, increasingly outside Europe. In some industries, such as Black Country hardware or Yorkshire woollens, up to 70 per cent went abroad. Had Britain lost the war – as was repeatedly possible – its economic, as well as its political, history would have been different. 'Power and plenty came together; indeed power led to plenty . . . and without the control of the seas the growth of the economy would have been limited and some other European power possibly become dominant.'[103]

The Treaty of Paris (1763) could be seen as conciliatory: Britain had returned several conquests without compensation. The French were relieved, and some in Britain grumbled. It remained none the less 'the most favourable peace treaty in European history',[104] Britain's greatest-ever victory, and France's greatest-ever defeat. It confirmed Britain as a global power. But could it remain one? Britain's triumph proved temporary, as we shall see; yet France's defeat turned out to be permanent: Britain, not France, would dominate the next century. Yet hindsight is doubly misleading if it makes history seem obvious and inevitable. The Seven Years War appears now as a watershed, but only because it was eventually confirmed through another fifty years of conflict: 1763 was only the halfway stage. France continued to challenge Britain's new hegemony outside Europe, both politically and commercially. It had no choice.

Taking Possession of the Globe

Regions Caesar never knew
Thy posterity shall sway
Where his eagles never flew
None invincible as they.

WILLIAM COWPER, 'Boadicea'

North America was lost – the French never seriously attempted to regain territory there – but that was all the more reason to press on elsewhere. Choiseul immediately established a new colony in Guiana in 1763–4. It was a horrific failure, with 10,000 colonists quickly dying of disease and hunger. British predominance in India, as some realized, potentially shifted the world balance of power, with implications for Europe. This could not be allowed. Versailles was invincibly sure that Britain could not be as strong as it looked. Its victory was ascribed to the devilish talents of Pitt and the financial trickery of the City. It could be resisted.

This is why the following decades saw an intense period of maritime exploration, which made those involved European celebrities. It centred on the Pacific Ocean, where geographers expected to find new territories, even

Louis XVI giving orders to La Pérouse: showing the king's interest in global exploration, and also the poise and elegance of courtly decorum.

a new southern continent 'adapted to the product of Commodities usefull in Commerce', and a north-west passage joining the Atlantic to the Pacific. Strategic points, such as the Malouines/Falkland Islands, were coveted. France wanted to compensate for defeat; Britain, to consolidate victory. Exploration became a characteristic expression of eighteenth-century culture. It combined intense scientific curiosity – in mathematics, astronomy, cartography, mechanics, philosophy, biology and anthropology – with national prestige and an unashamed thirst for profit. And it followed the typical Franco-British pattern of competition and cooperation, jealousy and admiration. 'Geographers from the two countries continued to correspond, and British and French explorers would meet and part amicably enough; but beneath the exchange of mutual compliments national rivalries ran deep and strong.'[105]

From the 1740s, the French ministry of marine and the intellectual establishment had cooperated in a succession of well-funded expeditions, which reached the Polynesian islands, Australia, Tasmania and New Zealand. An astronomical event – the transit of Venus across the sun in 1769 – was the occasion for the first French circumnavigation of the world, by a large expedition under Louis-Antoine de Bougainville, a former musketeer who had been Montcalm's ADC in Canada. His orders were to observe the transit (a means to calculate the distance from the earth to the sun) and search for the southern continent. This stimulated the Admiralty, never before interested in such esoteric matters, to send out a scientific expedition in a converted collier renamed *Endeavour*, commanded by Lieutenant James Cook, a junior officer with a reputation for navigation. It was kitted out from the ample private fortune of an enthusiastic naturalist and Fellow of the Royal Society, Joseph Banks: 'they have all sorts of machines for catching and preserving insects; all kinds of nets, trawls, drags and hooks', and even 'a curious contrivance' for seeing underwater.[106] Like Bougainville, Cook also had orders to seek the southern continent, and contact local peoples to 'gain their consent for possession to be taken of convenient situations'. The President of the Royal Society urged him to 'patience and forbearance' towards peoples who were 'the natural [and] legal possessors . . . the work of the same omnipotent Author', and perhaps more 'entitled to his favour' than 'the most polished European'. Louis XVI gave like instructions. French and British expeditions aimed to bring the unknown into the European intellectual, political and economic realm. They followed similar itineraries and had similar experiences with Polynesian societies – mutual astonishment, admiration, misunderstanding, tension, violence and awkward reconciliation. Across Europe their reports had avid readers. Both expeditions brought a Polynesian back to Europe, who was similarly fêted by fashionable French and British society. Reports of peoples that were unspoilt, noble and seemingly unfettered by convention fascinated a Europe that idolized Rousseau. 'Farewell, happy and wise people,' wrote Bougainville in his internationally best-selling account in 1771. 'Remain always as you are now. I will always remember you with delight, and as long as I live will celebrate the happy island of Cythera, it is the true Utopia.'[107] Cythera was the island of Venus, and it was not only the intellect of the explorers and their readers that was stimulated. Polynesian hospitality, curiosity, propitiation and trade extended to uninhibited sex. Both British and French left venereal and other diseases – something that Cook tried vainly to prevent. This was not the only dark side to the discovery. The Europeans unknowingly envenomed local power struggles and infringed religious rules.

The voyages were the focus of another field of rivalry: in navigation and time-keeping, most testing in the expanses of the Pacific. The inability to compute longitude caused recurrent navigational disasters. Solving the problem – for which a huge prize of £20,000 had been offered by Parliament in 1714 – required either unfeasibly precise astronomical observation and complex mathematics, or a way of comparing with incredible accuracy local time with that of a known place – for example, Greenwich. A Yorkshire carpenter turned clockmaker, John Harrison, devoted most of his life and his extraordinary ingenuity to making a series of chronometers that by 1760 managed to keep time indefinitely in the harshest sea-going conditions. English and French clockmakers, notably Pierre Le Roy, vied with each other in the 1760s to 80s – including by plagiarism and espionage – to equal or surpass Harrison. The French Academy of Sciences offered its own prize. George III and Louis XVI – both amateur clockmakers – were keenly interested in what were by far the most sophisticated manufactured objects in existence. Examples still work 250 years later. The king ensured that Harrison, in the teeth of obstruction from the astronomers, got his prize – 'By God, Harrison, I'll see you righted!' Le Roy, whose own chronometer was successfully tested in 1769, proclaimed this a patriotic triumph, vindicating 'the reputation of our Arts among Foreigners, especially those of a nation that has always been our competitor and rival'.[108] Copies of Harrison's latest model were tested by Cook on his second and third voyages in the 1770s, and their worth was proved in accurate navigation and mapping. French manufacturing was less technically advanced, and it was the British who from the 1780s managed to make chronometers in quantity and at a reasonable price.

Cook answered Europe's big questions about the Pacific, and his journals, soon published in French – and read by Louis XVI and Marie-Antoinette – made him famous. He charted New Zealand and the east coast of Australia, of which he claimed possession, and established that no other southern continent existed except Antarctica. In the words of one of his officers, 'The Grand Bounds of the four Quarters of the Globe are known.'[109] He was killed on his third voyage, in a clash with Hawaiian islanders in February 1779 – shocking proof that contact between even the most 'enlightened' Europeans and 'noble savages' could not be innocent. The news was received across Europe as a tragedy, including in France, despite the two countries being again at war. The court banker, Jean-Joseph de Laborde, deeply involved in French overseas trade and exploration, built a great monument at his chateau inscribed 'Cook, receive this tribute from a son of France'.[110]

France's victory in the American War of Independence (as we shall see in the next chapter) revived its ambitions of global hegemony. The navy continued to expand, with the goal of breaking British power in India. Meanwhile, peaceful expeditions were dispatched, combining scientific research with military reconnaissance. Work was also pursued in conserving forests, establishing botanical gardens and introducing new plants. Here the British felt 'twenty years behind' and struggled to catch up.[111] In 1785, French balloonists made the first Channel crossing. That same year came the culminating effort. An expedition of two ships was planned under the command of Jean-François de Galaup, Comte de La Pérouse, an admirer of Cook. Louis XVI was closely involved in the planning. The expedition included botanists, an engineer, a geographer, an astronomer, a geologist, a clockmaker and several draughtsmen. They carried seeds, gifts, and more than 1,000 shrubs. La Pérouse was personally instructed by the king to avoid violence and conquest, but to seek sites for trading posts, carry out discreet espionage and affirm France's ascendancy over the British. After an accident off Alaska and a clash with Samoans, they reached Botany Bay in January 1788 to check what the British were up to – and found that a fleet of eleven British ships under Captain Arthur Phillip had arrived just before them to establish a penal colony. The French sailed away, and were never seen again. A lonely memorial at Botany Bay, still visited by passing French naval crews, symbolizes the disappearance not just of the expedition, but of France's maritime dreams, which the turmoil of the French revolution the following year snuffed out. Louis XVI, that vicarious explorer, asked on the way to the guillotine if there was any news of La Pérouse.

In a phrase used by several French historians, France thus 'missed her rendezvous with the ocean'. To Pierre Chaunu, this became an essential part of Frenchness:

> Our sedentary peasant mentality means that we cannot endure the hiatus of the sea. To board a boat, to cross the sea, is an uprooting, a rupture. In so far as we have intensely interiorized France . . . we cannot really take an interest in the overseas . . . The French . . . have their piece of land . . . and they need nothing else to imagine the universe.[112]

If this is true, the corsairs, the merchant-venturers, the woodsmen of the Great Lakes and the oceanic explorers became decreasingly part of the nation's self-image. France's greatest heroes were not overseas adventurers, but those who had united France, rounded out its territory and fortified its frontiers.[113] In contrast, the British came to see themselves as having a global destiny. Despite occasional defeats, Britannia ruled the waves and London was the crossroads of the world. However bumbling and unplanned their acts, and however unforeseen the consequences, they liked to think of themselves as a people of seafarers, traders, explorers, conquerors and, increasingly, rulers. Whereas the million people who emigrated from France largely ceased to be French, the British – Scots and Irish in the lead – become a diaspora nation, scattered across the globe but linked to 'home'. Europe, with its 'oceans of gore', was now regarded even by the House of Hanover as a place to be wary of. Blenheim and Minden were outshone in memory by Plassey and Quebec.

LANGUAGE: THE CHALLENGE TO FRENCH ASCENDANCY

The English have corrupted the mind of my kingdom; let us not expose the new generation to the danger of being perverted by their language.
LOUIS XV[114]

Talk of war with a Briton, he'll boldly advance,
That one English soldier will beat ten of France;
Would we alter the boast from the sword to the pen,
Our odds are still greater, still greater our men . . .
First Shakespeare and Milton, like Gods in the fight,
Have put their whole drama and epick to flight . . .
And Johnson, well-arm'd like a hero of yore,
Has beat forty French, and will beat forty more!
DAVID GARRICK, 'On Johnson's Dictionary', 1756[115]

The time of the Seven Years War seems as good a point as any to mark the time at which the English language was set to become the first world language, despite the predominance of French in Europe. Voltaire was right: the language of Shakespeare was not superior to the language of Racine. But languages are spread not by literature or even by fashion, but by power and money.

French only became established as the language of diplomacy in the early eighteenth century. The Treaty of Utrecht (1713) was in French. The older practice of using Latin persisted a little longer, and governments in Spain, Germany and Italy still for a time used their own languages. But during the first decades of the century, French became increasingly the medium for international exchanges for both its prestige and its convenience – not least because the British were competent only in French. This practice would last broadly until the First World War. Bérenger and Meyer have pointed out that the hegemony of the French language was established just as the hegemony of the French state was about to decline.[116] David Hume predicted complacently just after the Seven Years War, 'Let the French, therefore, triumph in the present diffusion of their tongue . . . Our solid, and increasing establishments in America . . . promise a superior stability to the English language.'[117] However, in very few parts of the world is the subsequent spread of English due to direct American influence. It was the defeat of France, the consequent expansion of the British empire, and corresponding British domination of international commerce and communications that would ensure that English became the practical medium of communication for much of the world.

French was long unrivalled as the language of the cultural and social elites. When Corneille was given an English translation of his play *Le Cid*, he regarded it as a curiosity, kept on the shelf with another exotic translation, into Turkish. France was by far the biggest exporter of books between 1680 and 1760.[118] Saint-Evremond, a habitué of the Stuart court, learned no English during his forty years in London – a feat almost matched by the long-serving twentieth-century ambassador Paul Cambon. At Versailles in the 1740s, according to one story, no one could be found able to translate an English document except a musketeer from Calais.[119] Louis XV opposed its being taught more widely. In Britain, knowing French remained part of approved general culture well into the twentieth century. The travel writer Grosley even thought that England was returning to French, as under the Normans, and there was indeed a fashionable tendency to gallicize vocabulary and spelling (older forms – 'honor', 'center' – survived or were readopted in America).[120] Learning French was an important aspect of the 'grand tour'. Most British intellectuals could at least attempt salon conversation, even if (as in the case of David Hume and Adam Smith) it was a struggle. Anthony Hamilton and William Beckford gained renown as French authors. In the mid nineteenth century, young women wishing to be governesses commonly trained by teaching in schools in France, because 'French acquired in France' was in high demand in upper-class English families.[121]

French interest in English increased during the eighteenth century for both fashionable and ideological reasons. Voltaire played as important a role in propagating English in France as he did in universalizing French in Europe. He was probably right in claiming to be the first member of the French Academy to learn English, though he was soon followed by Montesquieu.

Voltaire's intimate patron the Marquise du Châtelet learned it well enough to translate Newton, and also to bicker in Franglais with Voltaire. As English was not taught in schools, Irish and Scottish Jacobites gave private tuition, and many language textbooks were published.[122] The *encyclopédiste* Denis Diderot managed to learn with a Latin–English dictionary. Only in the 1770s and 80s did English become widely fashionable, along with other aspects of 'anglomania'. For ladies, it was replacing Italian as an elegant cultural attainment. M. Pissot began publishing cheap editions of English classics, as 'the English language has so spread in France in recent years'.[123] A satirical writer in the 1770s mocked those who could 'mangle a few words': 'O di dou miss, kis mi'.[124] At court, the Comte de Provence (the future Louis XVIII) decided to learn English – which would prove infinitely more useful than he could have imagined during his long exile during the revolution. Louis XVI, who both resented and was fascinated by England, taught himself English against the wishes of his mother, who considered it the language of sedition.[125] He translated passages from Milton and his version of Horace Walpole's history of Richard III was published posthumously. He studied the history of the Stuarts while himself awaiting the guillotine. It became fashionable – including by the king – to use anglicized turns of phrase or words: *site* for *situation*; *prononcer* for *exprimer*. This annoyed purists, especially when such terms had social or political implications: *tolérance, budget, vote, opposition, club, pétition, constitution, législature, convention, jury, pamphlet*.

Inevitably, comparisons were made between the two languages. Some *philosophes* praised English – though Voltaire twisted his earlier praise into sarcasm:

> The genius of the English language [lies in] its naturalness, which
> does not shun either the basest or most monstrous ideas; in its
> energy, which other nations might take for harshness; in its daring,
> which minds less accustomed to foreign usage would consider
> gibberish.[126]

Rousseau's influence led to some shifts in values. Graceful French conversation began to be criticized as over-refined, loquacious, insincere and 'effeminate'.[127] What had previously been criticized as English bluntness and taciturnity could be interpreted as sincerity and naturalness. There were deliberate moves to simplify both languages. Samuel Johnson laboured in his *Dictionary* (1755) to rein in the 'Gallick structure and phraseology' so fashionable among the social elite. The poet Christopher Smart hoped that 'the ENGLISH TONGUE' would become the 'language of the WEST'.[128]

A resounding international vindication of French came in 1783, when the Royal Academy of Sciences in Berlin held a competition on the theme 'What has made the French language universal? Why does it merit this prerogative? Is it likely to keep it?' Essays could only be submitted in Latin, German, or of course French. The international competitors broadly agreed on the unique attractions of French, its popularity, the greatness of its literature, and its durable primacy. The joint winner, Antoine Rivarol – 'the man with the best hairstyle of his day' – judged German too guttural, Spanish too solemn, and Italian insufficiently virile. As for English, apart from the unpleasantness of those who spoke it, it was too close to barbarism, too peripheral to Europe, its literature lacked taste, its grammar was 'bizarre' and its pronunciation inferior. French, as well as literary greatness, had a unique 'genius': other languages might be more poetical or musical, but French was unique in its politeness, logic, clarity, and hence 'probity'. Moreover, it was sustained by French intellectual leadership, and crowned by its recent liberation of America, which had eclipsed both English literature and English power. Rivarol's brilliant summary of what was already widely accepted helped to fix certain notions about the inherent virtues of the language: in his most famous phrase, 'If it is not clear, it is not French.'[129] For Marc Fumaroli, this precision of meaning is very different from what he calls the 'flabby transparency' (*transparence molle*) of twentieth-century global English, able only to convey approximate meaning without style, which makes it incapable of providing a civilized global language for the twenty-first century.[130] Its role is indeed very different from that of French in its heyday, associated with power and high culture. French has been a badge of distinction; English, 'a passport to self improvement'.[131]

CHAPTER 4

The Revenger's Tragedy

It seems to me impossible to be French without wishing ill to England, but this sentiment, so just and so reciprocal, increases every day that one is obliged to live among the English. That is at least what I feel, and I would like to live long enough to see descending on them all the evils that their constitution prepares at home and their insolence deserves abroad.

DUC DE CHATELET, ambassador in London, 1769[1]

The strains of the Seven Years War plunged France and Britain into turmoil. Monarchs and ministers were reviled. Opponents demanded a greater voice. The language of 'patriotism', citizenship, representation and rights infused political debate, and made conflict over taxation increasingly dangerous. American colonists rebelled. Political instability threatened Britain. Something approaching a royal coup d'état convulsed France, but could not suppress political tensions. What doomed both the British empire and the Bourbon monarchy was the determination of France's rulers to overturn the outcome of the Seven Years War, which they considered both outrageous and precarious.

Choiseul Plans Revenge

> I am completely astounded that England, which is a very tiny bit of
> Europe, is dominant . . . One might reply that it is a fact; I must concur;
> but as it is impossible, I shall continue to hope that what is
> incomprehensible will not be eternal.
>
> DUC DE CHOISEUL, 1767[2]

Choiseul, a 'virulent and impenitent anglophobe',[3] saw the Treaty of Paris as merely a truce. When ambassador in Vienna early in the Seven Years War, his impatience with the Austrian alliance was due to his conviction that it was forcing France 'to neglect the sea war and America, which was the real war'.[4] This nobleman from Lorraine could grasp the importance of 'a few acres of snow' because of their European consequences. If he could break Britain's control of its colonies and take over their trade for France, his ability to influence the affairs of Europe would increase, and Britain's meddling diminish. France's prestige and security in the face of growing Prussian and Russian power would be strengthened. He wrote to the king that

> England is the declared enemy of your power and your State: she
> always will be. Her commercial greed, her haughty tone in negotia-
> tions, her jealousy of your power . . . must make you foresee that it
> will take centuries to make lasting peace with this State, which aims
> at supremacy in the four corners of the earth . . . We must employ
> the genius and all the power of the nation against the English.[5]

That he reacted to crushing defeat by planning another war is testimony to the self-confidence and determination of this seemingly frivolous courtier, who prepared as heavy a blow against Britain as any statesman in history.

He believed that Britain had overreached itself – a commonplace in French political circles, and shared by many in Britain. Public debt, high taxes, trade upheavals, political factionalism and ethnic discontents encouraged the wishful thought that British power was built on sand. The most notorious spokesman of public grievances was the clever, unscrupulous, lecherous and charming political adventurer, John Wilkes – the biggest 'scoundrel' whose last refuge was, in Samuel Johnson's famous phrase, Patriotism. In 1763 Wilkes fled to France to escape a charge of seditious libel and blasphemy, and stayed five years until forced to flee his creditors. A francophobic anti-papist Patriot might seem an unlikely refugee in France, and more unlikely still as a social celebrity. But a famous enemy of the British government could be sure of finding friends, and his campaign for 'liberty' struck a chord among opponents of the French crown too. *Mouchoirs à la Wilkes* – kerchiefs printed with his address to the electors of Middlesex plus a picture of the 'patriotic hero', pen in hand – became a fashion item. The British government tried unsuccessfully to silence him by paying an agent (who assiduously practised pistol shooting in his garden) to go over and try to kill him in a duel.[6]

Choiseul was contemptuous of Wilkes and his ineffective persecutors – 'a government so weak that it dares not punish one of the dregs of its people who insults and taunts it'. He read reports of riots in London with 'real pleasure': 'The English will never kill each other sufficiently to satisfy us.'[7] It all showed that France had nothing to fear. Its political system and physical strength were inherently superior. That 'the Poor of Tours' petitioned that 'the whole people is at the end of its tether' did not ruffle Versailles.[8] 'What can Britain do beside a power that can raise a hundred and sixty thousand seamen and two hundred and fifty thousand soldiers?[9] All that was needed was to act: 'Only let a clever minister rise in France, and England will fall immediately into its original condition of mediocrity.[10] And there was no cleverer minister than Choiseul.

The French identified as Britain's vulnerable point the theatre of her greatest triumph: America. Choiseul told the king as early as 1765 that 'only a revolution in America . . . will return England to the state of weakness in which Europe will no longer have to fear her.[11] If the colonies contributed nothing to the British state, the cost of the Empire would be crushing. But if Britain tried to tax them, 'they will easily break away . . . without the slightest fear of punishment, for England would not be able to sustain a war against them'.[12] Events fortified these hopes: the American Duties Act (1764) and the Stamp Act (1765) caused mayhem in New England.

If Choiseul's strategy was to wait on developments in America, he was far from passive. He sent agents to gather political and military intelligence in London and America, where an attempt – unsuccessful for the time being – was made to suborn the patriotic imperialist Benjamin Franklin. A key agent in London was the baby-faced Chevalier d'Eon de Beaumont, a cavalry officer later famous as a cross-dressing hermaphrodite. For the moment, he was merely a diplomat and spy – an agent of the *secret du roi*, the king's private diplomatic and espionage service. Successive ambassadors joined the planning for war. 'Whoever is born French,' wrote the Comte de Guines, ambassador in 1773, 'must see with extreme pain that there exists a nation that has always markedly prevailed over his own . . . This evil, though ancient, is not irremediable.'[13] Guines was another colourful figure, famous for his flute-playing and his taste for tight breeches (his valet when preparing his outfit was reputed to ask whether he planned to sit down that day). He helped with espionage and plotted to make a stock-market killing when the crisis broke. Captain de la Rozière surveyed the Sussex and Kent coasts, permitting detailed disembarkation plans to be finalized with the Comte de Broglie, head of the *secret du roi*. These were presented to the king in 1765. By 1766, strategic plans had been drawn up in Versailles and Madrid.[14] But d'Eon quarrelled with his government over money, and began to 'play the Wilkes' by publicly attacking Versailles. This made him a political hero in England and an improbable student of seventeenth-century English republican writings, some of which he translated. The real danger was his threat to provoke a premature war by publishing the embassy's invasion plans. This horribly embarrassed the French government, which tried unsuccessfully to poison and then kidnap him from Vauxhall gardens – making him even more of a celebrity.[15]

Choiseul pursued his campaign to fan patriotic zeal. Pierre Belloy's government-sponsored play, *Le Siège de Calais* (1765), was 'the first French Tragedy that has given the Nation the pleasure of seeing itself'.[16] It drew enthusiastic audiences in Paris and the provinces. In garrison towns, officers staged amateur productions. The plot, loosely based on the English siege of Calais in 1347, featured the 'proud', 'cruel', 'arrogant' 'ambitious' English against the noble altruistic French, 'an immense family' indomitable in defeat, who shame the English into seeing the error of their ways. The play ends with a stirring appeal in the name of Humanity and Europe. Though dedicated to the king, the idea of monarchy the play presented would have seemed daring even in England: kingship was 'vain without the approval of the Subjects'; 'the free and proud People . . . make for themselves . . . just and supreme law'.[17] Such ideas, the essence of Patriotism, were precisely what the absolutist monarchy would spend the rest of its existence trying to deny.

Preparation for revenge was far-reaching. The Austrian alliance had to be consolidated to keep Europe quiet when France acted overseas. Spain, needed for her navy, had to be tempted into the adventure and built up into an effective auxiliary. Envoys were sent to the Mughals in Delhi, the powerful Maratha federation, and other Indian warlords, notably Haider Ali of Mysore. Bases in the Mediterranean, the Caribbean and the Indian Ocean had to be prepared. Money had to be raised for naval and military modernization. All this needed formidable political support and control of the State machinery. So friends at court had to ensure that Louis XV heard helpful opinions and was surrounded by reliable people. Choiseul was in his element in this world of antechambers, bedchambers and nepotism. His ally was still Madame de Pompadour. She was now more the king's friend than his lover, but ever present, and ambitious to be more than just a purveyor of amusements.

Choiseul's priority was the navy, which, he told the king, 'will be the salvation of the realm or its downfall'. During the war, it had been 'not only crushed, but disgraced'.[18] Ninety-three ships had been lost (compared to one lost by Britain), leaving only forty battered survivors. Choiseul handed over foreign affairs to his cousin, took over the ministry of the navy, and set out to learn about the sea. He aimed at a navy of ninety ships of the line and forty-five frigates, and promised the king to reach sixty-four ships of the line

The Duc de Choiseul: 'A little volatile being', but a deadly enemy of the British empire.

in four years. The seventeen mighty ships, a million *livres* apiece, patriotically pledged during the war, were coming off the stocks. Large strategic reserves of timber and masts were accumulated. By 1765 Choiseul informed the king he had 'almost doubled' the force ready for sea, with sixty-two ships of the line and twenty-three frigates. Spies were recruited at Portsmouth and Plymouth; others went to the English Black Country to discover techniques of coke-smelting for casting cannon. Dockyards were improved or built, including in the West Indies. Plans were made for a harbour at Cherbourg to support operations in the Channel. Ile de France (Mauritius) was strengthened as a springboard for operations in India. Corsica was occupied in 1769, largely to deprive the British of a possible base overlooking Toulon. The British public admired the resistance led by the Enlightenment hero Pasquale Paoli. Sympathizers gave arms and money, but Whitehall was unwilling to fight for Corsica. It took 25,000 French troops months to crush the Patriots and chase Paoli into honoured exile in England. Nabuleone di Buonaparte was born that very year, 'as my fatherland was dying'. He was thus a French rather than a Genoese – or even conceivably a British – subject.

Choiseul would not be in power to taste the revenge he had planned. His need for money inevitably produced resistance from the *parlements*, which he tried to conciliate. But this offended conservatives at court, who accused him of weakening royal authority – he was even accused of poisoning the dauphin. It was at court that his fate was sealed, as with all Bourbon ministers. His self-assurance, greed for power and glory, contempt for his opponents, and recklessness with the fortunes of the kingdom, had made many enemies. The death of Pompadour in 1764 weakened his hold over the king, and he failed to have her replaced by one of his own followers – his sister had been in the running. He did not trouble to hide his disdain for the new incumbent – 'Well, my girl, how's business?' He got rid of her by having the royal bedchamber spied on and bringing Louis a humiliating report of his own sexual inadequacies purportedly based on her gossip. Such petty triumphs were short-lived. In 1769 a more formidable operator, the gorgeous, funny, featherbrained Jeanne Bécu, the successful call-girl 'Mademoiselle Ange', found ways of reviving the flagging royal libido and was created Comtesse du Barry for her pains. Choiseul, motivated by jealousy and snobbery, tried to dispose of her too, so she became the channel by which Choiseul's enemies dripped poison into the royal ear. They accused Choiseul of increasing his own power by conniving with the *parlements*: 'Miss Angel' persistently reminded her lover what had happened to Charles I. Realizing he was in danger, Choiseul arranged several Bourbon–Hapsburg marriages to cement the alliance with Austria, most importantly in 1770 that of the future Louis XVI with the Archduchess Marie-Antoinette, whom he had spotted while she was still a child.

His downfall came over the Falkland Islands, when the rival claims of Britain and Spain clashed in 1770. Choiseul at first urged caution on an over-confident Spain. He knew that they were not yet ready to take on the British navy, and he may have given up hope of an immediate American rebellion. The king, however, feared that Choiseul might gamble on war to maintain his power, and indeed the latter's plans remain enigmatic.[19] As was the Bourbon way, the king dismissed him without ceremony, giving him twenty-four hours to quit Versailles for his country estate. Choiseul lived until 1785 but never returned to power, in spite of lobbying by Marie-Antoinette. Property speculation and the sale of some of his paintings (now in the Louvre, the Hermitage and the Wallace Collection) occupied his spare time and partly defrayed his lordly extravagance. He became the focus of what was arguably France's first opposition party, public, patriotic and vocal.

His fall marked a brief change of direction and a period of violent political conflict. His successors calmed relations with Britain so as to be free to crack down on domestic opposition and turn their attention to problems in eastern Europe. In 1771 the chancellor, Maupeou, tried to snuff out opposition by abolishing the *parlements*. Whether this was short-sighted obscurantism or a bold and salutary reform has divided historians ever since. But the sudden death of Louis XV in May 1774 – once 'the Well Beloved', now the generally detested – brought a reversal of policy. The young Louis XVI dismissed Maupeou and reinstated the *parlements*. Like George III, he aimed to be a 'patriot king', both leader and servant of the nation, a healer of wounds, and an example of virtue (both kings broke with tradition by remaining faithful to their wives). Louis seemed much more likely to succeed than George, whose realm was about to explode.

Taking the Great out of Britain: the Second War for America, 1776–83

The 'Great' will be soon be gone from Britain . . . in a few years she will fall to the second or third rank of European powers without hope of ever rising again.

French foreign ministry report, 1777[20]

The great power that once held France in check is now fallen utterly and for ever, all influence and force lost . . . a second-class power, comparable with Sweden and Denmark.

JOSEPH II, Holy Roman Emperor[21]

In the years after their shared imperial triumph in 1763, the American colonists and the home government fell out, as the French had expected. At stake were what the American leader Samuel Adams called 'our British privileges'.²² The two greatest issues were control of vast territories gained through the defeat of the French, and management of the colossal war debt, which was straining the world financial system. It was necessary to raise taxes, but also difficult to do so. An inevitable post-war cut-back in government spending began a devastating economic slump. So taxpayers' protests in Britain and America were radicalized by bankruptcy, unemployment and hunger.

The problem of land speculation and settler encroachment on native land was fundamental and insoluble. British officials feared a bloody and expensive Indian war. Many had good relations with Indian nations, now British subjects. The Northern Indian Superintendent, Sir William Johnson, was an adopted member of the Mohawk tribe, spoke their language, and lived with a Mohawk princess, Gon wa tsi ja yenni (usually known as Molly Brant or 'the Indian Lady Johnson'). Their son became an officer in the British army. Their house, Johnson Hall, was the centre of a genuine British–Indian society.²³ In October 1763 a Royal Proclamation forbade further European settlement beyond the Appalachians and the Mississippi. To colonists, this meant that the fruits of victory over the French were being withheld.

Ministers in London wanted lightly taxed colonists to contribute to their own past and future defence costs. But colonists considered the Navigation Acts, which gave Britain a monopoly of American trade, to be a sufficient contribution. Riots, mass resignations of officials and above all a boycott of British imports convinced businessmen and politicians in Britain that the government had been too high-handed. William Pitt, out of power, and leading Whigs such as Edmund Burke eloquently defended the colonists. The Stamp Act of 1765 was repealed the following year, amid patriotic rejoicing and fireworks on both sides of the Atlantic. But joy was short-lived. The underlying problems of taxation, trade regulation, debt and land ignited further conflicts of ideology and of interest.²⁴ Public tranquillity was never re-established, especially in the biggest ports, Boston, New York and Philadelphia. This led to confrontation when in 1773 the port of Boston was closed as a punishment for disorder. A Continental Congress, representing all the colonies, met in Philadelphia in September 1774. Fighting broke out between militia and troops in Massachusetts in April 1775.

What was seen as a British civil war created dissension on both sides of the Atlantic, with the political opposition accusing the government of plotting to undermine liberty throughout the Empire. Ill-gotten wealth extorted from India was, they suspected, being deliberately used to corrupt the political system. The Quebec Act (1774), which recognized the Catholic Church in the conquered French colony but did not set up an elected assembly – 'popery and slavery' – seemed proof of absolutist tendencies. Leading Whigs such as Lord Rockingham, Lord Shelburne and Edmund Burke denounced the use of force in America. In Rockingham's words, 'If an arbitrary Military Force is to govern one part of this large Empire . . . it will not be long before the whole . . . will be brought under a similar Thraldom.'[25] Such views inspired the most famous ever Commons motion, in April 1780, that 'The influence of the Crown has increased, is increasing, and ought to be diminished.' The resistance of the colonists, culminating in the Declaration of Independence on 4 July 1776, had many supporters in Britain. The strongest of them were Dissenters – particularly English 'rational dissenters' and Ulster Presbyterians – who sympathized with the rebels on religious and political grounds. One of them, John Horne Tooke, opened a subscription for the 'widows, orphans and aged parents of our beloved American fellow subjects . . . FAITHFUL to the character of Englishmen . . . inhumanly Murdered by the KING'S troops'.[26] Those who supported the government were broadly speaking all who believed that the rebellion undermined the rule of law, and threatened the existence of an empire without which Britain would be no match for France. This view was so strongly held in Scotland that English opponents denounced the conflict as 'a Scotch war'. In Ireland, Catholics felt little sympathy with 'Puritan' rebels, and many were eager to demonstrate their loyalty to the Crown.

In France too, attempts to resolve post-war financial problems led to simultaneous popular and political resistance. Turgot, the controller-general of finances, was a *philosophe* in power, a physiocrat economist, dogmatic and self-righteous – though admittedly often right. Physiocrats believed that economic freedom would increase national wealth and government revenue. Turgot deregulated the grain trade, but at a time of bad harvests, which created popular panic. Rioting in the countryside spread to Paris and Versailles, where crowds besieged the palace itself. Emergency measures had to be taken to procure grain, and the 'flour war' was ended by force. Turgot's 'Six Edicts' (1776), aiming to suppress financial privileges and reform taxation, aroused angry opposition from vested interests, including courtiers and the *parlements*. This French counterpart of the British troubles in North America was a more direct threat to the centres of power – the king himself saw the crowds of hungry peasants. But for that very reason it was easier to suppress: 25,000 troops were on hand for the 'flour war', whereas Britain had only 3,500 in Massachusetts. Moreover, the French State was again ready to brush its financial problems under the carpet by increasing its debts.

It even undertook large increases in military spending from the mid-1770s. 'Providence has marked out this moment for the humiliation of England', thought the new foreign minister, the Comte de Vergennes.[27] A gala performance of *The Siege of Calais* was arranged to stimulate patriotic fervour. William Wilkinson was hastily recruited to build a cannon foundry. Cod-fishermen off Newfoundland were ordered back to port to man warships. The British knew what was going on. They had an efficient spy network in France, supervised by the ambassador, Lord Stormont. When Benjamin Franklin, whose disillusioned imperialism had evolved into American patriotism, set up a makeshift embassy in a house in a Paris suburb, the British soon penetrated it.

One man tediously preached caution: Turgot. He sympathized with the American cause more than his opportunistic colleagues. He believed that American independence – indeed that of all colonies – was inevitable eventually. France's interest, he argued, was to let the Anglo-American conflict drag on. Intervention might even reconcile the two sides and turn them against her. Above all, France could not afford war. 'The king knows the State of his finances': war would be 'the greatest of misfortunes, since it would make essential reforms impossible for a long time, if not for ever . . . If we use our strength prematurely, we risk making our weakness permanent.'[28] He refused to increase the navy budget from 30 million to 62 million *livres*. On 12 May 1776 he was dismissed. Now, money was no object. The navy began to prepare at Brest and Toulon.

Turgot's dismissal is regarded as one of the turning-points in French history: the end of the Old Regime's best chance of reforming itself, and a fatal step towards its downfall. Turgot's warning that the first cannon shot would mean revolution may be apocryphal, but fundamentally it was true. His voice, as head of the State finances, was surprisingly feeble. As one insider noted, 'the habit of ministers is to regard a controller-general as a mere money gatherer, to execute and not to block their political plans'.[29] This could serve as the epitaph of the Bourbon monarchy.

Vergennes, a career diplomat, resumed Choiseul's policy of restoring France's preeminence at Britain's expense:

> the separation of her northern American colonies; her shrunken and
> diminished trade, her more encumbered finances, will proportion-
> ately reduce her power and make her less worrisome and less proud.
> She will be unable to kindle and feed the fire of division and
> discord among the great States of Europe.[30]

Vergennes detested the political ideas of the rebels; but ideology was not the issue. He would support Patriots in Boston as 'our friends' against Britain, as he simultaneously suppressed Patriots in Geneva as 'agents of England'.[31] But he was careful. Britain might try to foment a war on the Continent. So other states must not feel themselves threatened by French ambitions. 'We shall be feared less if we content ourselves with cutting off our enemy's arms than if we insist on running him through the heart.'[32] Best of all would be to fight as long as possible by proxy, giving discreet help to the rebels, and simultaneously encouraging opposition to Britain in India. As the king put it, 'the more they fight, the more they destroy themselves'.[33]

ENTER FIGARO

The famous quarrel between America and England will soon divide the world and change the system of Europe [. . .] You will only maintain the peace you desire, Sire, by thwarting peace between England and America at all costs, and preventing the complete triumph of either.'
PIERRE AUGUSTIN CARON DE BEAUMARCHAIS to Louis XVI, February 1776[34]

Pierre Caron, alias Caron de Beaumarchais, was a watchmaker, royal harp teacher, magistrate, entrepreneur, suspected murderer, would-be courtier and playwright. He was also an agent of the *secret du roi*, and factotum to the Duc de Choiseul, the Almaviva to his Figaro. *The Barber of Seville* was performed in 1775 – his first great literary success.

That summer he was sent to London as a secret agent to sort out the long-running problem of the Chevalier d'Eon, now earning a living as a female fencing instructor for ladies, and still threatening to publish secret documents unless paid 318,000 *livres* 26 *sous*. Louis XVI, to end the embarrassment, wanted d'Eon to return to France and live as a woman, wearing exclusively women's clothes. Beaumarchais made contact: 'the wench is mad about me . . . who the devil would have thought that the king's service would require me to pay court to a captain of dragoons?'[35] He persuaded d'Eon to hand over the compromising papers in return for a pension of 12,000 *livres* a year, payment of his London debts, a dress allowance of 2,000 *écus*, and royal permission to wear the Cross of St Louis with female clothes ('only in the provinces'). Beaumarchais also contacted Wilkes and other pro-American politicians. He himself had no sympathy for democratic ideas in France, but became their enthusiastic supporter in America. He wrote to the king and Vergennes urging the dispatch of money and weapons to the rebels: 'this meagre aid they are asking for . . . will assure us the fruits of a great victory without the dangers'.[36] In May 1776, Vergennes authorized him to float a company 'at your own risk' to supply arms: 'it is important that the operation should have in the eyes of the British government and even the Americans the character of a private speculation of which we know nothing'.[37] The government advanced 2 million *livres*, the Spanish another million, and the farmers-general a fourth. Beaumarchais set up Roderigue Hortalez et

Compagnie in Paris and bought weapons from government arsenals. The Americans immediately ordered 30,000 muskets, 30,000 uniforms, 2,000 barrels of gunpower, cannon, shot and 4,000 tents, to be paid for in tobacco. By March 1777, Beaumarchais had dispatched nine vital shiploads, only one of which was intercepted.[38] Soon he had his own miniature navy. But he never made much profit.

After the war, he returned to the theatre, writing *The Marriage of Figaro*. Its insolent mockery of the nobility by a clever upstart caught the post-war mood. The fashionable court set loved it and had it staged in April 1784, despite the vehement objections of Louis XVI, who famously said that allowing its performance would be like demolishing the Bastille.

London, hoping to limit the war, ignored French gun-running. But Versailles allowed American privateers to seek shelter in French ports, and this caused a diplomatic crisis. In June 1777, the British navy was ordered to stop and search French ships heading for America. Britain seized 158 French merchant vessels and their crews[39] – an act, echoing 1755, to deprive France of seamen. In December 1777 came the sensational news of the surrender of General Burgoyne's force at Saratoga, causing a stock-market collapse in London. A popular French song praised 'The Successes of the Insurgents':

> To finish the job one day
> Send your children to dance
> On the ruins of England.[40]

The king and Vergennes did not want the Americans to win before France had time to encumber them with help. They believed (on Beaumarchais's assurance) that the British had decided to grant American independence and recoup their losses by attacking French and Spanish colonies, perhaps in alliance with the former rebels.[41] Vergennes decided to provoke war 'without [France] being materially the aggressor'.[42] The foreign ministry predicted that 'the year 1778 will decide the fate of England and the predominance of France.'[43] American privateers were again given port facilities, and in February this was made official when the French navy gave a nine-gun salute to the American flag carried by the notorious privateer John Paul Jones in Quiberon Bay. In March Versailles informed London that France had signed treaties with the Americans, recognizing their independence. Both sides withdrew their ambassadors, and the British 'Commissary and Inquiror' at Dunkirk was expelled amid patriotic jubilation. On 20 March, Benjamin Franklin was officially presented at court as the American envoy. The assembled ladies, prelates and nobles were thrilled by his New World candour: brown suit, heavy shoes, glasses and no wig (which was taken to be a Puritan statement, but apparently it had been blown overboard on the crossing). Still the British would not be provoked into declaring war.

First blood came at last on 17 June 1778 off Roscoff, when the frigates *Belle Poule* and *Arethusa* fought. Both sides celebrated a glorious victory – a difference of opinion still reflected in each country's histories. Though the *Belle Poule* was severely damaged and forced to seek shelter with a fifth of her crew dead, her captain became a national hero: Isaac-Jean-Timothée Chadeau de La Clochéterie was a third-generation naval officer whose father had died in combat against Admiral Anson thirty years earlier. His 'courage, if not lunacy'[44] finally triggered hostilities, though it took another three weeks to declare war formally. At Versailles, women wore the 'Belle Poule' hairstyle, with hair combed and lacquered into the form of a hull.

The war was popular. Admirers of English liberty saw the colonists as its true defenders. Conservatives welcomed the chance of demonstrating the inferiority of what Beaumarchais termed Britain's 'mixed and turbulent . . . royal-aristo-democracy'. Traders hoped for customers. All looked forward to France's resuming (in the words of one newspaper) 'her empire, her preponderance . . . the place she should never have forfeited among the first powers of Europe'.[45] A popular song hoped that 'You will knock down the rostrum/Of these merchants, so-called statesmen/Petty politicians of the Commons.'[46]

REVOLUTIONARY ARISTOCRATS

> We stepped out gaily on a carpet of flowers, little imagining
> the abyss beneath.
> COMTE DE SEGUR[47]

Marie Joseph Motier, Marquis de La Fayette, is the most famous of a cohort of young French nobles who sought glory and revenge by aiding the Americans. The Duc de Lauzun, one of Marie-Antoinette's favourites, commanded his own Legion. The young Comte de Ségur, son of a minister of war, Baron de Montesquieu, grandson of the philosopher, Comtes Théodore, Charles and Alexandre de Lameth, the Prince de Broglie and the Vicomte de Noailles all offered their services. The Swedish Count Fersen (later famous as Marie-Antoinette's would-be rescuer and assumed lover) wangled a position too.

Several of them only took ship in the spring of 1782, dawdled at the Azores (establishing 'amiable relations' with young Portuguese nuns), narrowly escaped from the British navy and landed when the fighting was nearly over. La Fayette's role was far more prominent. An ancestor was a Marshal of France during the first Hundred Years War, and his father had been killed at Minden. He was eager for adventure, glory and vengeance – 'to harm England is to serve (dare I say avenge) my country'.[48] He slipped out of France in 1777 without royal permission, having bought his own ship, and offered Washington his help. Washington was eager for French aid, and La Fayette offered to use his social influence to that end. At first relations between the twenty-year-old marquis and his American allies were edgy – as between the French and the Americans generally – but La Fayette idealized America, its natives and colonists. French officers were irritated 'to see on so many occasions the Marquis de La Fayette lower himself to copy the manners and habits of American democrats'.[49] He worshipped Washington, who repaid him with paternal affection.

La Fayette returned to France a hero, and remains a symbol of Franco-American friendship. He, and other noblemen who had served in America, especially the Lameth brothers, later took leading parts in the political opposition to the absolute monarchy and in the early phase of the revolution.

La Fayette and his black servant: the double irony of a patriotic aristocrat helping a slave-owning republic.

French intervention burst on a bitterly divided Britain, and changed perceptions of the war and its reality. On one hand it created a widespread sense of foreboding, redoubling criticism of the government for leading the country into such peril. There were riots, hangings in effigy, attacks on ministers' houses, and agitation in Ireland. On the other hand, many opponents rallied to what now seemed a patriotic struggle, and a mortal danger that reduced the American rebellion to a sideshow.[50] A Dissenting congregation in Cambridgeshire, which had prayed for 'an end to this bloody and unnatural war' against the Americans, now prayed for divine aid 'against the French'. Similarly, Ulster volunteers toasted 'Speedy peace with America, and war with France'.[51]

French strategy was to wage a limited war: to force the British to keep forces, especially ships, at home by threatening invasion, and then to attack isolated outposts in India, the West Indies and especially North America, disrupting trade, causing panic and undermining the British ability to fight. So in early spring 1778, before war began, they had sent the Toulon fleet to America. This time, it all worked. There was no Continental war to divide French forces. The British, especially the navy, were weak and ill-prepared: they had not kept up with French and Spanish naval expansion, and had delayed mobilization for fear of being provocative. They decided to withdraw most of their forces from North America to defend the vital West Indies.

Events in North America, however, were not progressing anything like as well as the French had expected. The rebels were on their last legs, and the British too were looking for a compromise. France risked missing its revenge. Spain, the necessary ally in a naval war, now decisively influenced French plans. The Spanish government had suffered its own colonial tax revolts since the Seven Years War and disliked aiding rebellion. They would only contemplate a short war with major rewards – Gibraltar and Minorca – and would then happily abandon the Americans. Only an invasion of England could achieve this. Vergennes proposed a limited landing in Ireland to stir up the 'fanatically democratic' Presbyterians. An Irish veteran of the 1745 invasion, General Wall, drafted plans. But the Spanish insisted on a decisive landing in England. Otherwise, warned the French ambassador, they would only contribute their worst ships, commanded by their 'most ignorant and unpleasant officers'.[52] Wall's plans were filed and came in useful in 1796. Vergennes, seemingly drawing on the Comte de Guines's plans, agreed to land 20,000 men on the Isle of Wight and at Portsmouth to destroy the naval base and end British dominance of the Channel. Attacks could then be made on Bristol, Liverpool, Dublin and the main supply base for the army in America, Cork, where there were 50,000 barrels of salt beef to be looted. Portsmouth might even become a French Gibraltar, crippling Britain and making France dominant in Europe. The French daydreamed

The American War of Independence

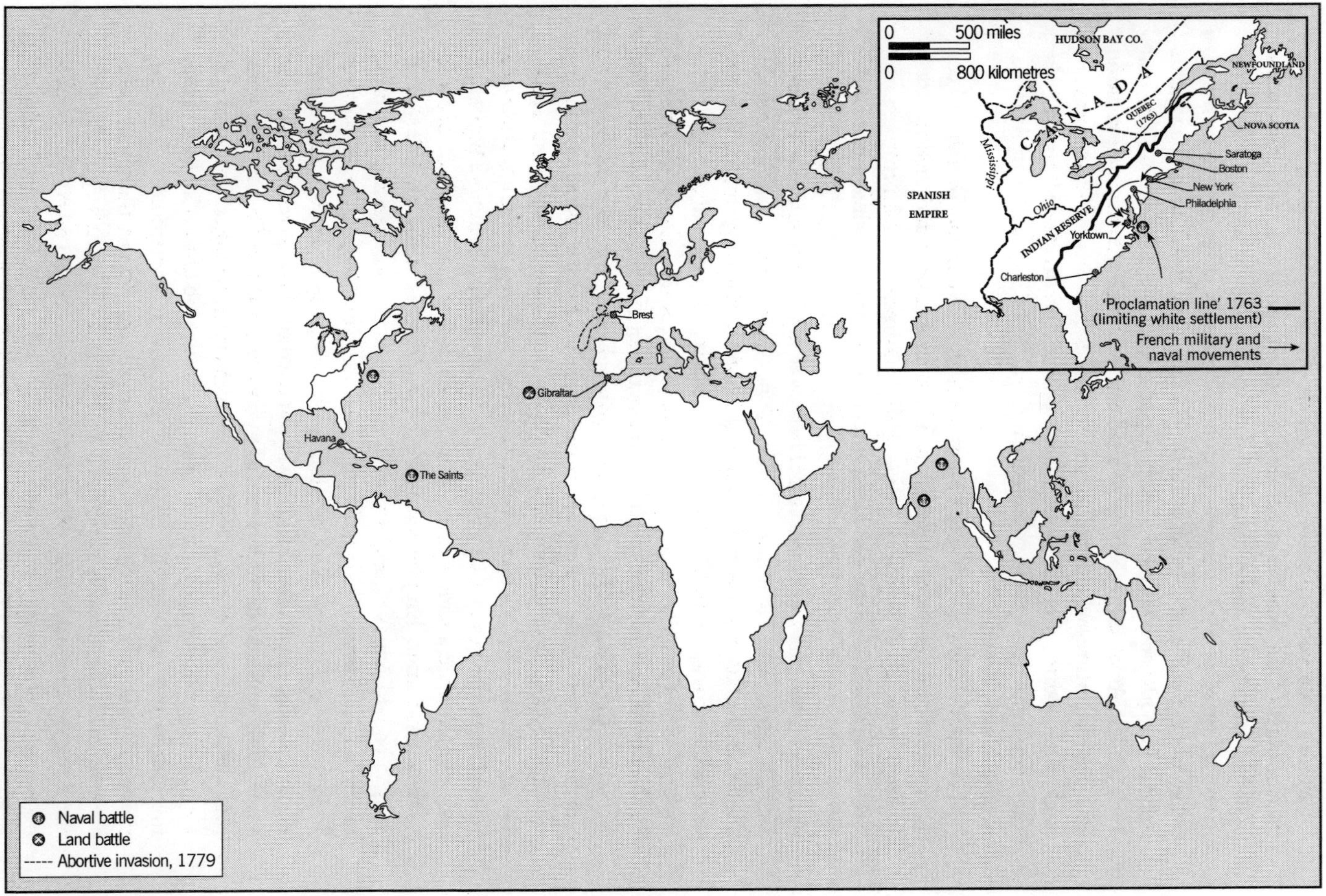

0 500 miles
0 800 kilometres
HUDSON BAY CO.
NEWFOUNDLAND
CANADA
QUEBEC (1763)
NOVA SCOTIA
Mississippi
Ohio
INDIAN RESERVE
SPANISH EMPIRE
Saratoga
Boston
New York
Philadelphia
Yorktown
Charleston
'Proclamation line' 1763 (limiting white settlement)
French military and naval movements
Brest
Gibraltar
Havana
The Saints
Naval battle
Land battle
Abortive invasion, 1779

longingly: 'The Bank of England is destroyed; its fake currency shrinks to its real currency, at least nine-tenths less; its credit lost; its resources annihilated; and general terror.'[53]

In the spring of 1779, 30,000 troops made ready to sail from Le Havre and Saint-Malo. La Fayette, back from America in a state of high excitement, dreamed of 'planting the first French flag in the midst of that insolent nation ... The thought of seeing England humiliated and crushed makes me tremble with joy.' D'Eon was eager to gird up his loins and volunteer for the navy: 'I might wear skirts in peace time, but in wartime, impossible.'[54] Instructions were issued for dealing with the natives:

The Englishman is puffed up when he is prosperous, but easily depressed by adversity ... Money will all the more readily induce them to sell us their wares, since profit-making is the main interest of this nation.[55]

Courtiers and their ladies converged on Normandy to share in the glory, and officers' billets became outstations of Versailles. Young René de Chateaubriand all his life recalled the sight of the dashing Duc de Lauzun on an Arab horse – 'one of those men in whom a world was ending'.[56]

Across the Channel, camps were set up at Coxheath near Maidstone and Warley near Brentwood to defend the capital. As in France, they became the focus of fashionable society, and the subject of plays, cartoons and musical comedies. Coaches from London catered for visitors. Dr Johnson went. So did the king and queen, who stayed with a local Catholic peer – a remarkable gesture of patriotic unity. The Duchess of Devonshire and her friends, dressed in fetching versions of military uniform, appeared daily on horseback and pitched camp with several rug-bedecked marquees composing entertaining rooms, sleeping quarters, kitchens and a servants' hall.[57] The troops' equipment was less impressive: they had no wagons or stores. Combining patriotism with self-promotion, citizens pleaded for permission to command their own corps of volunteers. Major Holroyd was allowed to recruit Sussex smugglers 'lately out of business'. Their regimental song went: 'No Spaniard nor Frenchman our women need fear/While Holroyd's Dragoons in their cause will appear.'[58] But most such requests were turned down, including one from a Mr Wentworth, who wished to form a unit from imprisoned debtors, bearing François I's famous motto, 'All is lost save honour.'[59] Only when manpower shortages grew severe did the government allow private recruiting, especially in the Scottish Highlands.

In July 1779, excited Parisians saw soldiers practising with cork life-jackets in the Seine. Rumours anticipated Vergennes's appointment as Viceroy of England, with George III interned at the Château de Chambord. In August,

Beaumarchais claimed that 'all the London café patrons are bandying the question whither they should retreat in the event of a Descent. The concensus is in favour of Scotland.'[60] A run on the Bank of England was predicted. A firm of London merchants wrote to Ireland that 'this Kingdom' had been thrown into 'a Consternation never before experienced'. Bumbling preparations began to remove livestock, vehicles and grain from threatened areas. An optimistic military planner hoped that all male civilians would make 'a Stand against the enemy', with 'women and boys blocking roads and driving off cattle'. The *Morning Post and Daily Advertiser* encouraged its readers:

> Tho' *Monsieur* and *Don* should combine,
> What have true *British* Heroes to fear?
> What are Frogs, and soup-meagre and wine,
> To beef, and plum-pudding, and beer?[61]

Experts on both sides considered British land defences feeble, while the combined Franco-Spanish fleet – 104 ships – would greatly outnumber the British. Five hundred transports were waiting to embark the army in Normandy. 'Never, at any moment in history . . . was the French navy so near the goal it had so often contemplated, a landing in England: the Channel was open, the enemy was skulking in port.'[62]

Not for the first or last time, England was saved by its enemies' ineptitude and the forces of nature. The French fleet arrived to rendezvous with its allies off the Spanish coast on 10 June 1779. It then sailed around for six weeks waiting. When the Spanish finally arrived, the two fleets had to practise manoeuvres; they could not read each others' signals: 'The number of mediocre captains is even greater than last time.' Food and water dwindled. Smallpox, scurvy and cholera broke out, 'a terrible plague that disarms our ships'. 'Men had been taken on who were unfit . . . water had been drawn from tainted springs. We set out with no sorrel and no lemon. Catastrophe is inevitable.'[63] On 15 August, the Allies arrived off the Cornish coast. The British fleet, its commanders quarrelling, retreated up the Channel. The Allies, aware that time was running out, switched their target to Falmouth, with the intention of occupying Cornwall as a bridgehead. The French commander Admiral d'Orvilliers then missed his chance of making history. He decided he could not risk a landing before defeating the British fleet: but this was keeping ingloriously but sensibly out of reach. After sailing forlornly up and down in worsening weather, d'Orvilliers returned to Brest in mid-September, with 8,000 sailors sick and dying – worse losses than in any naval battle. So many corpses had been thrown into the sea that the people of Cornwall and Devon were said to be refusing to eat fish. It was 'the worst strategic French mistake of the war'.[64] Indeed, of the century. Wrote Marie-Antoinette, 'The public is much annoyed that M. d'Orvilliers, with forces so far superior to those of the English, was unable to join battle with them . . . It will have cost a great deal' – 100 million *livres*! – 'and accomplished nothing, and as yet I see no indication that peace can be treated this winter.'[65]

So the struggle would continue, and become worldwide. The navy minister, Sartine, secured huge increases in his budget, which rose from a peacetime level of about 20 million *livres* to 35 million in 1776, 100 million in 1778, 169 million in 1780, and 200 million by 1782.[66] The French discovered that the Spanish fleet had to be repaired and remasted from their own precious stocks of timber.[67] At least they could import timber from the Baltic, and indispensable masts and other naval materials could be safely carried in Dutch ships or floated via Holland's canals, out of reach of British cruisers; whereas the British had lost vital supplies from North America. The British army and navy were diverted from decisive action in America: they had to defend Britain against another possible invasion, relieve Gibraltar, resist France and her Indian allies in the subcontinent, and guard the West Indies. With Spain and later Holland in the war, the British navy was outnumbered: to its ninety-four ships of the line, the Allies opposed 137.[68] Control of the sea was lost, and 'the consequences were to be felt throughout the world'.[69]

Britain mobilized its people and resources to a degree beyond that in any previous war. The navy increased from a peacetime strength of 16,000 men to 100,000 by 1782; by then, 250,000 men were in the regular army or the militia, plus 60,000 Irish volunteers. Taxes rose by 30 per cent, and by the end of the war absorbed 23 per cent of national income – more than in any previous war or in any other belligerent country. The struggle enhanced the sense of 'Britishness' in Great Britain and Ireland. The army in America celebrated the feast-days of 'our brother saints', Andrew, David, George and Patrick. This the government encouraged. Unlike in previous wars against France, there was no longer any danger of a Jacobite 'fifth column'. The wearing of Scottish Highland dress was not merely legalized, but large orders for tartans to clothe new Highland regiments were placed. Greater autonomy was given to the Irish parliament. The Catholic Relief Act (1778) reduced legal disabilities against Catholics, whose recruitment into the army was welcomed.

This caused a radical pro-American backlash among Protestants, who accused the government of flirting with 'popery' to undermine liberty. Starting in Scotland, it culminated in London with the most destructive outburst of political violence in modern British history: more property was wrecked than in the whole of the French revolution.[70] On 6 June 1780 Lord George Gordon, backed by a crowd of 50,000, presented a protest to Parliament. Ministers and the archbishop of Canterbury were mobbed. Nearly a week of uncontrollable rioting followed in the capital and some provincial towns, in which radical associations were involved. The legend of the 'Gordon riots' – drunken anarchy and primeval savagery – is overdrawn. The rioters consistently targeted Catholic institutions, pro-government politicians and symbols of authority, including finally Newgate prison and the Bank of England. Working-class Catholics were mainly left alone.[71] The effects were to deter opposition politicians from further encouragement of mass action, discourage reform proposals, increase official suspicion of Dissenters, and make Catholics seem less dangerous.

We know little about the immediate effects of the war effort on France; historians have been preoccupied with the longer-term consequences that culminated in the revolution of 1789. The war must have affected the French people far less than the British. The number of troops engaged was far smaller than in earlier wars, for there was no fighting on the Continent. Naval conscription struck the maritime population of Brittany, Normandy and Provence: sailors tried to avoid the call-up, for service in unhealthy naval ships was grim. The sick from the 1779 fleet filled the hospitals for miles inland. As always in wars against England, commerce was disrupted by naval action and privateering. The government decided to pay for the war by loans, not by a combination of borrowing and increasing taxes as in Britain. In the short term, this caused an economic boom. A popular song proclaimed:

> The Briton sees enraged
> Our exploits and his debts
> But we have lots of cash
> Just look at all our *fêtes*.[72]

The war affected the French elite in a way that Simon Schama has described as 'profoundly subversive and irreversible'.[73] This was not obvious at the time: how could glorious revenge be dangerous? As usual the authorities commissioned patriotic paintings and statues. However, the conflict popularized the new kind of patriotism already visible during the Seven Years War, and now embodied by the Americans. This was different from old traditions of service to the king. One indication was the lionizing of La Fayette on his return in 1779. At first he was placed under house arrest for going to war without royal permission. But he was cheered in the Parisian theatres, and soon the king invited him to the royal hunt, and Marie-Antoinette, previously contemptuous, had him appointed commander of the royal dragoons at the age of twenty-two. Benjamin Franklin was no less a star. His rugged simplicity, brilliantly acted, recalled the imagery of Rousseau and Greuze. His *Poor Richard's Almanach* became a best-seller as *La Science du Bonhomme Richard*, and his fashionable electrical experiments seemed to show that genius lurked within his 'ostentatiously unostentatious' exterior.[74] The Court joined in and even led the adulation; but both La Fayette and Franklin embodied cultures and values that implicitly passed judgement on the frivolous routine of Versailles.

The French government realized that it would have to commit not only ships, arms and money but also troops to rescue the American rebels. The British were strongly established in New York and were making progress in the southern colonies. The Crown had strong support from colonial loyalists, not least German and Scottish settlers (among the latter Flora MacDonald, thirty years after her intrepid rescue of Bonny Prince Charlie). More Americans were fighting as Loyalists than in Washington's army. Thousands of Shawnees, Creeks, Mohawks, Cherokees and other nations sided with the Crown against the land-hungry settlers. African slaves leaving rebel masters were offered freedom, and Loyalist African military units were formed. As many as 100,000 seized the chance – 'the first mass escape in the history of American slavery' – including many belonging to George Washington.[75] A leading Pennsylvania politician feared that high taxes were making colonists ready to 'renew their connexion with Great Britain'. Wrote one congressman in 1780, 'we are pretty near the end of our tether'.[76] Washington implored French help. An American historian judges that 'without money and supplies from France, the survival of the United States would have been unlikely, and without French military and naval help the expulsion of the British from all their American positions would have been almost impossible'.[77]

In July 1780, seventeen warships, thirty transports and 5,000 troops slipped into Newport, Rhode Island – fewer than had been sent to Ireland in 1689, but a huge logistical and financial effort none the less. The soldiers came from all parts of France, though as usual more recruits came from the military and patriotic eastern provinces – comparable with the role the Scottish Highlands were beginning to play for Britain. The sailors were mainly Normans and Bretons, as the maritime conscription system dictated, who had learned to hate the English over generations of wars, raids, and privateering. They were commanded by the Comte de Rochambeau, whose job the previous year had been to spearhead the invasion of England. He was a capable professional, who 'talked only of feats of arms . . . without an idea outside his profession'. The French did not expect much of the Americans. Rochambeau had been told to 'conceal his grievances, his fears, and accept silently the incompetence of the people with whom he will have to combine operations'. Even so they were taken aback by the state of Washington's forces, wracked by desertion and mutiny despite harsh punishments. The French naval commander reported that 'the continent is in desperate straits. They want peace.' Rochambeau appealed to Vergennes for 'troops, ships and money, but do not count on these people nor on their resources, they have neither money nor credit, their forces only exist momen-tarily'.[78] But Vergennes was reluctant to send more troops when the Americans themselves were giving up.

French soldiers and ships remained cooped up in Newport, preparing for a British attack and largely dependent for news on loyalist newspapers from New York. They killed time by grumbling, gambling and quarrelling. Their relations with the Americans were polite but wary. They knew that many Americans regarded Frenchmen with suspicion, and the troops were kept in camp to prevent friction between French 'gallantry and *légèreté*' and American 'austerity and rusticity'. To avert accidental conflict, sentries were instructed, if there was no answer to their challenge 'Qui vive?', to shout 'Ou is dair?'[79] Officers were trusted to mingle with Americans, who were surprised to find that they were not weedy and 'effeminate' as national stereotypes suggested. The burghers of Newport seemed flattered that noblemen were ready to risk their lives in their cause. Montesquieu, benefiting from his grandfather's renown, was lionized. In return, when George Washington visited the French camp in March 1781, he was idolized by officers getting their first exposure to republican virtue. The unfortunate Jumonville incident of 1755 was forgotten.

Only weeks after Rochambeau's arrival it seemed the British were winning. France was desperately short of money, despite raising loans on exorbitant terms in Geneva and Amsterdam. The country was haemorrhaging cash. Coins were short everywhere, as over 100 million *livres* were sent to America and India. Sartine secretly issued 21 million *livres* in IOUs to keep the navy going, which led to his sacking in October. Jacques Necker, a Genevan banker and France's latest finance minister, resigned the following May when he was refused control over expenditure – the first time a minister of the French crown had ever presumed to walk out. British intelligence reported this opti-mistically as 'a fatal stab to the credit of France, and to the independence of America'.[80] French, Americans and Spanish were all making unofficial peace approaches to London. The French expected Britain to retain the territories it held, namely New York, the Carolinas, Georgia and most of Maine. As the British war minister Lord George Germain saw it:

> so very contemptible now is the rebel force in all parts, and so vast
> is our superiority, that no resistance on their part is to be appre-
> hended . . . and it is a pleasing . . . reflection . . . that the American
> levies in the King's service are more in number than the whole of
> the enlisted troops in the service of the Congress.

Lord North, the prime minister, assured Parliament that there was the prospect of 'a just and an honourable peace'.[81]

Vergennes decided on a final throw of the dice. He persuaded the king that honour was at stake. The Americans were sent the equipment and money (barrels of hard cash sent by fast frigate) for one last campaign; and in March 1781 twenty ships of the line sailed to the West Indies under Admiral the Comte de Grasse. The British Admiral Rodney, brilliant but crooked, was too preoccupied with capturing West Indian booty to intercept him: arguably, North America was lost in the Caribbean. So Grasse could move north to support Rochambeau, or evacuate him if things did not improve. Expectations in Versailles were not high: 'it is not in North America that we may expect to strike the decisive blow'.[82] In June 1781, Rochambeau's 5,000 men at last stirred from Rhode Island and joined Washington's hopeless siege of New York.

The British situation was not as strong as it looked. Troops were withdrawn to defend the West Indies. The king's army could still win battles, but the rebels could replace their losses more easily. As one general put it, 'the enemy's plan should be to lose a battle with you every week until you are reduced to nothing'. This is what happened with General Cornwallis's intrepid or foolhardy sweep from South Carolina to Virginia in the summer of 1781, aiming to destroy the core of American resistance. It reduced his own force from 4,000 to 1,400 men, so he withdrew to Yorktown, on the Chesapeake Bay, to be picked up by the navy.

In August 1781, Washington and Rochambeau, at the latter's insistence,[83] moved south against Cornwallis, in response to a summons from Grasse. As always in this war, control of the sea was decisive, and Grasse had sent a message that he was taking his fleet and troop reinforcements from the West Indies to the Chesapeake. He sailed into Chesapeake Bay and landed 3,000 more French troops. Admiral Graves came south from New York with his fleet, arriving at the mouth of the Chesapeake on 5 September, just after Grasse. Though outnumbered, he attacked the French and achieved a draw, leaving both fleets damaged. But the French were still there, cutting off Cornwallis's army. Graves has often been criticized for not forcing his way into the Chesapeake to help Cornwallis's force to escape. But his own ships might have been trapped. Piers Mackesy sums up the dangers:

> important though the loss of Cornwallis's army was to prove, the
> loss of the fleet would have been a worse disaster . . . The Leeward
> Islands and Jamaica would have fallen. New York would have been
> assaulted or starved. India could not have been defended. And if the
> French had permitted it, Nova Scotia and Canada would have
> passed to American rule.[84]

Graves withdrew to New York for repairs. Plans were made to return for Cornwallis, who was expected to hold out for several weeks.

But Rochambeau and Washington were ferried down the Chesapeake in

Grasse's ships, and on 6 October besieged Yorktown. This was the French army's only significant combat in America. They were well equipped with tools and heavy artillery, and the attack was professionally and vigorously pressed forward: it was Rochambeau's fifteenth siege. La Fayette, commanding an American brigade, incensed his compatriots by offering American help when they were having difficulty in taking one of the English strongpoints. By 16 October, Cornwallis had just over 3,000 fit men against 7,800 French, 5,800 of Washington's army, and 3,000 Virginia militia. He had run out of artillery ammunition, and had no way of resisting the imminent final assault. On 19 October 1781 his men marched out to lay down their arms, with a band playing 'The World Turned Upside Down'. It was France's greatest naval and military victory over Britain, and it made history.

Cornwallis, pleading sickness, sent his Irish second-in-comand, General O'Hara, to make the surrender. O'Hara tried to hand his sword to Rochambeau, who politely refused it, rather than to Washington. This was surely deliberate. The British and Americans now loathed each other, and there were many mutual accusations of atrocities, often justified. The French instinctively sympathized with the British, and wished to preserve the 'usages of European nations at war'.[85] This became a source of discord between the Allies. Some of the French had been shocked by their first sight of the 'implacable, bloody and ravenous' behaviour of American soldiers near New York. They considered the Americans' demeanour after Yorktown unchivalrous, and their mistreatment

The surrender of Yorktown: the British detested surrendering to the Americans, and would have preferred to surrender to the French, shown here on the left under their white banner.

of British prisoners criminal. The Americans resented French fraternization with the captured British – Rochambeau, for example, lent money to Cornwallis, who later paid glowing tribute to his generosity. The French retorted 'that good upbringing and courtesy bind men together, and that, since we had reason to believe that the Americans did not like us, they should not be surprised at our preferences for the English'.[86] Prisoners of war on parole in Brittany were treated with similar kindness.

SAVING CAPTAIN ASGILL

One of the Yorktown prisoners, nineteen-year-old Charles Asgill, was chosen by lot to be executed in retaliation for the hanging of a rebel officer by loyalists. In desperation, his mother wrote a pleading letter to Vergennes on 18 July 1782, and he showed it to Louis and Marie-Antoinette. Asgill's youth won him much sympathy, and the king and queen told Vergennes to intervene. He sent a courteous but unambiguous letter to Washington. Writing 'as a Man of sensibility and as a tender father', but also 'with the knowledge and consent of His Majesty', he reminded Washington that the prisoners had been captured with the aid of the French army, and stated that 'the goodness of their Majesties' Hearts induces them to desire that the inquietudes of an unfortunate Mother may be calmed'.[87] Though there were grumblings in the Congress about 'obsequiousness' to France, the Americans had no option but to release Asgill (who lived to be a general). The whole Asgill family went to Versailles to express their gratitude to the king and queen in person. The British and the French regarded themselves as inhabiting the same world of chivalry and 'sensibility'. Americans, it seemed, did not.

News of Yorktown, carried by the Duc de Lauzun, reached Versailles in November 1781. The court was more interested in the recent birth of a royal heir, and Lauzun was the first of many to resent indifference at home to their distant victory. In both countries Yorktown's importance was psychological more than material – it was a tiny battle compared with Spain's simultaneous siege of Gibraltar. But how much more significant. La Fayette wrote to Vergennes, 'after this attempt, what English general will undertake the conquest of America?'[88] Lord North took the news like 'a ball in the breast', throwing up his arms and exclaiming 'Oh God! It is all over.' This was the universal reaction, at least for the moment. Coming after French successes in India, the Mediterranean and the Caribbean, with the Allied navies able to strike across the globe, and with the financial burden of war ever increasing, it was a recipe for despair.

Vergennes reacted more soberly: 'one would be wrong to think that it means an immediate peace; it is not in the English character to give up so easily'.[89] He knew that time was not on his side. News of Yorktown in fact saved the Allied war effort from collapse.[90] The battle of the Saints – Les Saintes – on 9–10 April 1782, one of the most important naval battles of the century, was sudden proof that the scales had tilted away from France. After Yorktown, Grasse sailed to the West Indies, taking St Kitts, Nevis, Montserrat and other islands. The great prize was Jamaica, whose loss it was hoped would force the British to give in, and against which Grasse led his fleet. So vital were the sugar islands that the main British fleet sailed to stop him in the only great battle the Royal Navy has ever fought outside European waters, and the last time until late 1944 that its main force went so far from home. Rodney and Hood smashed through the French fleet, capturing five ships of the line, including the flagship *Ville de Paris* – one of Choiseul's patriotic vessels – and its admiral. Rodney boasted to London, 'You may now despise all your enemies.' The new French navy minister, Marshal the Marquis de Castries, greeted the news as 'a grim disaster'.[91] The government persuaded the *parlements* to agree to an emergency tax increase – the last such increase the Old Regime would ever be given. Like Yorktown, the Saints had a psychological impact. As Vergennes saw it,

the English have to some degree regenerated their navy while ours has been used up. Construction has not been at all equivalent to consumption; the supply of good sailors is exhausted and the officers show a lassitude which contrasts in a disadvantageous way with the energy that not only the sailors but the entire English nation eagerly manifest.[92]

Vergennes was not wholly wrong. Rodney joined the select band of heroes whose surname became a boys' Christian name. For many in Britain, the war could now be seen as at least a moral victory. In the words of the vicar of Hanbury, Staffordshire,

To future ages it will appear to be an incredible Thing . . . that these Kingdoms shd. Maintain . . . a glorious, but unequal, Conflict for several Years, with the most formidable & unprovoked Confederacy . . . viz. France, Spain, the United Provinces of the Netherlands, & the 13 revolted Colonies of North-America.[93]

It was time, to everyone's relief, for the usual duplicitous game of diplomatic musical chairs. Lord North was succeeded by the erratic, devious and confusedly high-minded Irish magnate Lord Shelburne, a francophile as well as a sympathizer with the Americans. He offered generous terms to the latter in the hope of salvaging trading and political relations. He also talked of Franco-British partnership in Europe. He abandoned Loyalists and Britain's Indian allies to the Americans and to political expediency – a betrayal attacked in the House of Lords as 'shameful and unpardonable'.[94] But Albion was far from being uniquely perfidious. The Americans, conscious of their weakness, suspected the French of wanting a deal with Britain to partition America – fears the British confirmed by showing them captured French documents. The French all along had the corresponding fear of an Anglo-American deal by which the British would recoup their losses by seizing French and Spanish possessions. The Americans indeed secretly urged the British to retake Florida from their own ally. The Spanish were interested in Gibraltar: if they secured it by force or concession, or if they gave up hope – as they had to after the failure of their four-year siege in 1783 – they too would seek peace. Shelburne was willing to exchange Gibraltar for Puerto Rico, but was prevented by a parliamentary outcry. All combatants were in desperate financial straits. Moreover, a new danger threatened: Russia was taking advantage of the situation to threaten Turkey, one of France's traditional allies. So peace beckoned, and Shelburne signed preliminary terms with the Americans in January 1783, who thus betrayed their French ally by making a separate peace.

On the other side of the world, the Anglo-French struggle continued. France's allies, principally the Marathas and Haider Ali, the ruler of Mysore, with help from French troops and ships, had come within sight of destroying the British position in India in 1779–80. French strategists believed that as the United States must sooner or later dominate the Americas, India had become the great prize, and this was France's chance to win some of it. As in America, ultimately everything depended on sea power. French activity was reinvigorated by the arrival in 1782 of Admiral Suffren, one of the most remarkable of the many French naval heroes ignored by British history but immortalized in French street names and school textbooks. Pierre-André de Suffren de Saint-Tropez was a fat, scruffy, irascible and Rabelaisian southerner who, unlike most French commanders, had been long at sea – he had joined the Knights of Malta in his teens. Throughout 1782 and the first half of 1783 he fought a series of engagements with Admiral Hughes's British squadron off south-eastern India. They are unique in naval history for the intensity and balance of the fighting. But the French had no overall strategy and, despite Dutch and Danish help, they had insufficient forces either at sea or on land to defeat the British decisively. News arrived in June 1783 that an armistice had been concluded five months earlier.[95]

In September 1783, the Treaty of Versailles was signed. The police proclaimed the good news in the Paris cafés. There was jubilation in France.

The war had lasted eight years, from the first shots in New England to the last in southern India. The French had taken dazzling revenge. Britain had been humbled and reduced: a quarter of the nation had broken away. 'With America largely lost; British India wasted by war, famine, and corruption; Ireland restive; and the British West Indies in economic difficulties . . . the British empire faced an uncertain future.'[96] Even the indomitable George III had moments of despair. The First Lord of the Admiralty, Lord Sandwich, expected that 'we shall never again figure as a leading power in Europe, but think ourselves happy if we can drag on for some years a contemptible existence as a commercial state'.[97] The *Norfolk Chronicle* feared that 'Great Britain seems hastening to a revolution or a dissolution'.[98]

These were not foolish predictions. Parliamentary government, already shaken by the American revolt, was soon in crisis. Shelburne was overthrown by the Commons in February 1783 for being unpleasant, dishonest, too generous to Britain's enemies and indifferent to the Loyalists. Shortly afterwards a coalition government was formed by the wealthy, dissolute, francophile populist Charles James Fox and the discredited loser of the war, Lord North. This was greeted with widespread revulsion as a piece of corrupt politicking. George III considered abdicating and retiring to Hanover. But in December 1783, in a bold, or reckless, act which combined principle, personal vindictiveness, and an unexpectedly shrewd calculation of political opinion, the king forced the coalition out of office and appointed the strait-laced reformer William Pitt, aged twenty-four, as prime minister. This might have caused constitutional crisis, abdication, even revolution. Instead it became a royal triumph when in 1784 Pitt smashed the Fox–North party in a general election and set out to clean up the financial system and reduce the debt burden. Time-servers, moralists, tax-payers and modernizers rallied to Pitt's reforms. George III, helped by his deserved reputation for dullness and domestic virtue, came to embody the Patriot King, guardian of the constitution. In France, these strange contortions confirmed views that Westminster politics were no model for France. Louis XVI, a close observer of British politics, wished George well. He faced similar problems himself.

For France, the fruits of victory contained little juice. Prestige was brilliantly restored, but material gains were 'derisory'.[99] The Allies, including America, were more weakened by victory than Britain by defeat. Holland had been humiliated, its hold on its colonies shaken, and its internal stability undermined. Spain – as its rulers had feared – was to find an independent America as dangerous as Britain, and its days as a major colonial power were numbered. Not only could things have been worse for Britain – the West Indies, India, Canada and Gibraltar might also have been lost – but commercial relations with the United States were re-established with remarkable speed.

American trade was crucial. The French had seen it as the means to equal or overtake British financial power. But the gains never appeared: the vision of Choiseul and Vergennes was 'the pipe-dream of armchair strategists who confused diplomatic intrigue with commercial conquest'.[100] British businessmen knew the market, could supply the world's cheapest manufactured goods, and offered unmatchable credit. American demand for British goods became 'the most dynamic factor during the long boom of 1783–1801 and beyond',[101] and fuelled the Industrial Revolution. Franco–American relations, often cool even when they were allies, became increasingly distant, and French exports to the United States collapsed after the war. As Turgot had warned, France had made its financial weakness permanent.

French intervention prevented the British from keeping more of America. Did France do Britain an unintended favour in forcing a clean break? Otherwise, like South America, the northern continent would probably have become a patchwork of colonies and independent states. How much worse transatlantic tension would have been if Britain had ruled not only Canada and the West Indies, but New York, South Carolina, Georgia and large areas of the West. Even if Britain had managed to suppress the rebellion and recover all the colonies – compromising over taxation and self-government – the resentment between 'Patriots' and 'Loyalists' would doubtless have festered, as many British politicians and soldiers realized. London would also have met in extreme form the problem it largely failed to solve in South Africa and Australia: how to restrain attacks on and dispossession of native peoples. It would have faced the formidable problem of slavery: with the movement for abolition emerging in Britain from the 1780s onwards, friction with slave-holding American colonies would have been inevitable. If open conflict could miraculously have been avoided, would not the centre of imperial power have moved, as Adam Smith predicted and Benjamin Franklin hoped, from London to New York? If Britain's defeat was not without consolations, France's victory triggered the greatest cataclysm in her history.

The Biter Bit, 1783–90

The war . . . that abyss of so much money, the greatest cause of our financial disorder and of the evils with which France is now assailed . . .
Gentlemen of the Third Estate, who wanted that war? You yourselves, who
. . . saw in imagination the whole English navy swallowed up, and drank in
long draughts, in advance, the pleasure of vengeance.
'Avis salutaire au Tiers Etat', 1789[102]

The war . . . favoured the coming of the revolution in three ways: it filled
the nation with ideas of revolt and liberty, it undermined the army's loyalty
to the old order, and it led to the collapse of the old financial system.
ANTOINE BARNAVE, revolutionary leader[103]

The American war, which contemporaries estimated cost 100,000 dead, also, because of its global extent, cost a vast amount of money. The British spent £80 million, and ended the war with a national debt of £250 million, requiring £9.5 million per year in interest – more than half the total tax revenue. The French spent about 1.3 billion *livres* (£56 million) – they could not be precise because of the complexity of their financial system. French government debt had reached at least 2–3 billion *livres* (£187 million), which required 165 million *livres* (£7.2 million) in interest – 50 per cent of state revenue. The French hoped that Britain's greater burden would be crushing. But the British government, helped by the City and its superior record as a debtor, could borrow more cheaply. Hence, while the French debt was only 62 per cent of the British, its interest payments were 75 per cent. France, with its larger population and GDP, should have been better able to bear its smaller burden. But for reasons noted earlier, it was unable to raise taxes. So state expenditure exceeded revenue by over 100 million *livres* per year.[104]

France's financial burden was worsened because ministers contemplated yet another war with Britain. Vergennes preferred to consolidate his victory peacefully, confirming France as the world's predominant power through diplomatic influence and expanding trade. He hoped the chastened and diminished British might submit. But he feared, quite wrongly, that 'proud and haughty' Britain might seek revenge, and so even his peaceful policy required an expensive navy. Others, led by Marshal de Castries, went much further. Castries believed Vergennes had made peace too soon in 1783, missing a decisive victory. France must prepare for another war to wrest global power from Britain once and for all: 'More than two centuries of experience have taught that the power that rules the waves can dominate the Continent.' India, the key to world power, was the prize. He refused to allow his enormous budget to be supervised by the controller-general – 'a powerful navy is a good investment'.[105]

The British had a shrewd suspicion of these plans, and the embassy reported in February 1786 that 'France is at this moment straining every nerve to put her navy on the most formidable footing'.[106] The combined strength of the French and allied Spanish and Dutch navies was rapidly drawing further ahead of the British. In 1786 work started on a fabulously expensive naval base at Cherbourg, to support a Channel fleet opposite Portsmouth. The works were visited by Louis XVI – the only time since his coronation he had ventured more than a few miles from Versailles. Louis shared the public fascination with ships and the sea, encouraged by France's recent victories. It was now, as we saw earlier, that expeditions were sent into the Pacific. Interested eyes were also cast on Egypt and Indo-China.

William Pitt managed Britain's financial problem by ostentatious economies (especially cutting Crown employees), setting up a Sinking Fund to reduce the debt, and increasing parliamentary scrutiny by the Accounts Committee, thus creating an impression of prudence and responsibility. (He was habitually careless with money, but only with his own, not that of the State.) Vergennes too tried to control expenditure by creating a *conseil des finances* and reforming tax collection, but was defeated by Castries and his ally the war minister, Marshal the Marquis de Ségur. Both were military aristocrats who saw attempts to control their spending as 'dangerous economies' and 'a war to the death between the bureaucrats and people like us'.[107] So the government, under Charles de Calonne, controller-general from 1783, tried the opposite tack: to spend and borrow even more. The British ambassador reported that 'there appears at present no disposition whatever to economy'.[108] This was not quite as mad as it sounds. France was, compared with Britain, lightly taxed. Calonne believed that lack of confidence in government was the problem, and that he could remedy it by behaving confidently himself, 'like an adroit steward to a bankrupt debauchee'.[109] In France, he declared, 'resources are increased by the very act of expenditure'.[110] He could seize the opportunity created by victory to encourage trade and economic growth. So new loans were raised – over 650 million *livres* between 1783 and 1787. Money was spent on the court – 'useful splendour', thought Calonne – including the refurbishment and purchase of palaces. The unpopular Wall of the Farmers-General was built round Paris to increase excise revenue. Castries kept laying down more battleships. Money was spent on industrial schemes which, it was optimistically assumed, would quickly enable France to catch up with Britain in 'the industrial combat'. Loans, subsidies, and investments by courtiers and the Crown's financial officers went into sugar refineries, a planned freight service using hot-air balloons, waterworks, coalmines, arms factories and overseas trading companies. Le Creusot became the biggest plant in France, a showcase of British-style industry, with blast-furnaces, steam engines, glassworks and railways. As we have seen, some of the greatest names in Franco-British economic history were involved, including Wilkinson, Watt, Boulton, Wendel and Perier. But although in 1785 with Wilkinson's help Ignace de Wendel produced the first coke-blast iron on the Continent there, Le Creusot soon became a white elephant, lacking a developed economic and technical environment to sustain it.

Calonne, an unctuous and self-assured hybrid of John Law and John Maynard Keynes, has divided contemporaries and historians: a reckless, slippery charlatan, or the monarchy's last great statesman? Certainly 'the most creative and the most destructive force in politics'.[111] Doubts surfaced in 1785, when the Paris *parlement* had to be commanded in person by the king to register a new loan – the last the unreformed monarchy got away with. The British embassy – who thought the French ministers insane – were hoping that inevitable financial disaster would oblige them to keep the peace.

In 1786 Britain and France, on the latter's insistence, signed a trade treaty, known in Britain as the Eden Treaty after its chief negotiator, William Eden. The intentions of Vergennes and Calonne were to forestall confict (every Frenchman knew that the way to an Englishman's heart was through his pocket), to facilitate the import of technology, and to increase tax revenue by increasing trade volume and decreasing the flood of contraband. The treaty raised an outcry from domestic manufacturers on both sides of the Channel, most damagingly in France, where it unfortunately coincided with an economic recession. Before the treaty, legal trade was about 23 million *livres* each way; by 1787, legal French exports had increased to 38 million, but British to 51 million.[112] Many French manufacturers were ruined. Workers rioted. 'Buy French' campaigns were organized, and in Rouen and Lyons balls were held to which only those wearing French-made *modes patriotiques* were admitted. The mayor of Lyons, France's second city, banned advertisements for British goods. Even the government's own intendant for commerce condemned 'that fatal treaty with England, the death warrant for French manufacturers'.[113] Guilds, chambers of commerce and the press all denounced the betrayal of French interests and the creation of 200,000 unemployed. There could have been no worse time for the scandalous 'diamond necklace affair', an elaborate confidence trick played on the court jeweller and Marie-Antoinette, the main consequence of which was to besmirch the queen with slanderous charges of adultery and fraud.

Calonne's bubble burst in 1787, when bad harvests reduced revenue, wartime taxes lapsed, and the State and many of its major financial officers, badly overstretched, became insolvent. In February the treasurer-general of the navy, Claude Baudard de Sainte-James, one of the most opulent and envied of the Parisian plutocracy, had to beg the king to confine him in the Bastille so that he could unravel his accounts with thick stone walls between himself and his creditors. Over the next few weeks four more leading state *financiers* failed, including the treasurer-general of the army.[114] Prominent courtiers and royal personages burnt their fingers. But Calonne was a cool customer. As his schemes unravelled he pulled out the blueprints for root and branch fiscal reform that had been discussed and shelved for years. They amounted to remodelling government as well as finance: new provincial assemblies of landowners would administer a new universal land tax. This would bypass the *parlements*, end fiscal privileges and of course greatly increase the Crown's revenue. An Assembly of Notables was convened to rubber-stamp his plans and give them political legitimacy.

The 144 Notables gathered at Versailles in February 1787, just as Baudard was going bankrupt. Although chosen to be pliable – princes, dukes, bishops, judges, officials – they showed that they no longer feared the Crown, and were unwilling to buy 'a used cabriolet' from Calonne.[115] They refused to authorize open-ended changes in taxation. They demanded more information and an equivalent of Pitt's Public Accounts Committee. La Fayette made the fateful demand for the summoning of the Estates General for the first time since 1614. Calonne tried public blackmail. The clergy had to read from the pulpit his attack on the Notables: 'Some people will pay more . . . But who? Only those who have not paid enough in the past.'[116] The consequence of this fiasco was that the Assembly was prorogued and the king was forced to dismiss Calonne – the first such defeat of a monarch for over a century. Calonne's successor, Archbishop Loménie de Brienne, tried to force through a stamp tax – many recalled the prelude to the American revolt – and the land tax. The government painted an absurdly rosy picture of 'order restored to the finances . . . a formidable navy, the army regenerated . . . abuse eliminated, a new port built on the English Channel to ensure the glory of the French flag, laws reformed, public education perfected'.[117] The reality was that the Paris *parlement* had been forced to accept the royal tax decree and then exiled. The government was facing determined resistance both to tax increases and (the obvious alternative) to a default on its debt: this dilemma was the dominating political issue. With breathtaking aplomb, Calonne appeared in London and was soon briefing Pitt on France's financial weakness and its consequent inability to go to war over Holland.

With friends like these, the monarchy had little need of enemies. Alas, it had those too. It was forced to slash foreign affairs spending by 40 per cent, and the army had less money than at any time since the death of Louis XIV. The other powers took advantage. The most serious consequence came in the Netherlands. France needed the Dutch for their navy and Indian Ocean bases, and for loans from the Amsterdam banks. Castries – 'this old Bitch' as one British diplomat called him – was actively promoting a Franco-Dutch campaign to 'chase the British out of India', in alliance with powerful Indian rulers, and finally reduce British power to the level of 'Denmark or Sweden'.

For Castries, 'France's greatest interest is to maintain the alliance with Holland, and that of England is to break it'.[118] But the cost to the Dutch of being France's ally in the American war had caused financial and political turmoil. The Patriot party – opponents of the stadholder William of Orange – presumed on French support to go on the political offensive. Britain's enterprising envoy Sir James Harris financed and organized the rival Orangist party. When the Patriots arrested the Princess of Orange (who was the king of Prussia's sister), Britain and Prussia decided to act. Prussian troops marched into Holland on 13 September 1787. Versailles and Whitehall were both clear that their global ambitions were in the balance. British warships made ready in case France intervened. Ségur and Castries wanted to pick up the gauntlet. An intervention force under Rochambeau began to assemble on the northern frontier. La Fayette hoped to command a corps of volunteers. Could another war with England have solved, or at least postponed, the crisis of the monarchy? Castries urged Louis XVI to

> present the idea of glory to Frenchmen, and you will effect . . . the
> most useful diversion from the present turmoil. Give the appearance
> of necessity to taxation, and the mood will calm and perhaps you
> will see government recapture a part of what it is ready to lose.[119]

But, as Calonne informed Pitt, the French government had no money. So it accepted humiliation, abandoning its Dutch allies and its own global and Continental ambitions. Ségur and Castries resigned: 'We have lost everything.'[120]

Thus, disillusionment came only five years after the great American revenge. Louis and his ministers lacked the money to maintain the honour of France. But that very failure made it unthinkable that they would be allowed to raise taxes without fundamental political concessions: 'all classes of the population, from the galleries of Versailles to the cafés of the Palais Royal,' said Ségur, 'spoke out against the negligence of the ministers'.[121] This loss of confidence, even contempt, affected groups whose loyalty was indispensable: the nobility, the army, the ruling elite itself. Army officers had been discontented since the failures of the Seven Years War, and now cuts in the army budget and new restrictions on promotions further angered them. The highest circles of the established system questioned its practices and principles, using the language of Patriotism, increasingly familiar since the 1760s. Their spokesman turned out to be the suddenly popular Duc d'Orléans, the royal anglomaniac, hereditary troublemaker for his Bourbon cousins and the richest man in France (who privately estimated that tax reform would cost him 200,000 *livres* a year). In an unprecedented scene, he stood up in the Paris *parlement* on 19 November 1787 and told Louis XVI that his tax increases were illegal, to which the astonished king could only mumble the stock absolutist answer that they were legal because he said so. D'Orléans was arrested and exiled to his estates. There followed months of conflict between the Crown and the *parlements*. An attempt in May 1788 to suppress opposition by force led to insurrection in several provinces. In Rennes, Grenoble, Toulouse and Besançon noble army officers neglected to suppress popular riots, even resigning their commissions. In Paris and the provinces, soldiers joined in the demonstrations.

Money had caused the problem and it decided the outcome. The Crown had spent in advance 240 million *livres* of the 1788 tax receipts, and so needed to borrow an equivalent amount in order to meet its 1788 obligations, including interest payments on its war debt. Political disorder and uncertainty, and rumours of default and even civil war, discouraged lenders. Hailstorms in July 1788 destroyed crops and reduced tax receipts. By August, the treasury was effectively empty: cash payments were suspended; government stocks collapsed; and there was a run on the banks. Brienne, desperate to revive government credit, was forced to summon the Estates General for 1 May 1789. He then resigned and advised the king to recall Necker, widely believed to be a financial genius – the first time in history that a dismissed minister had been recalled. Necker postponed all reforms until the Estates General met. The absolute monarchy thus effectively abolished itself, and appealed to its subjects to solve its problems.

How very different was the home life of George III. His recovery from a spell of madness in April 1789 was greeted with genuine rejoicing. It ended a constitutional crisis that had threatened to bring the detested Prince of Wales to power as regent, along with his discredited crony Fox. Why this apotheosis of the defeated Hanoverian, when the victorious Bourbon teetered on the edge of the abyss? Both kings tried to reign as patriots. George was certainly more resolute and experienced, and had the accidental advantage of not being isolated in a British equivalent of Versailles (which British monarchs had lacked the money and the nerve to build). He had an outstanding minister in Pitt, whose priggish high-mindedness was better suited to austerity than Calonne's viscosity or Necker's trickiness. More fundamentally, Britain had functioning political institutions, while France was trying to improvise new ones in the teeth of a crisis. Finally, it came down to money. Britain could raise more tax and had solid credit; the French monarchy was insolvent. Shelves have been filled with books about why the Bourbons failed to reform their financial system. But had it not had to pay for the struggle with Britain, that unreformed system would have been no more inadequate than those of its neighbours. The Bourbon monarchy was the victim of its own revenge, and of its determination to prepare for yet another war. A 'fundamental misreading' of British intentions 'warped' its foreign and domestic policy.[122] On the edge of bankruptcy, it was still building battleships.

Its slide down the precipice is one of the great stories of history: voters drafting lists of complaints (*cahiers de doléances*); political clubs burgeoning; the economic situation deteriorating, with bad harvests in the summer of 1789. Most important of all was the self-assertiveness of the Third Estate, the Commons, when the Estates General met in Versailles in May 1789. On 17 June, with support from some of the clergy and nobles, it declared itself a 'National Assembly'. Three days later it openly defied the Crown in the famous Tennis Court Oath. Violent popular discontent shook Paris: attacks on Calonne's customs wall, riots, seizure of grain and a search for weapons culminated in the storming of the Bastille on 14 July 1789. One of the few prisoners in the notorious fortress was a long-bearded Major White, who demanded to be taken to a lawyer and soon showed further symptoms of insanity. Even luckier was Lord Massareene, who, after eighteen years' incarceration for debt, escaped from La Force prison in the confusion.

'Patriots' (otherwise called the 'National Party') played a leading role during these months. Prominent were nobles such as d'Orléans and many military men, who had vehemently expressed their anger with the government in the *cahiers* of the Second Estate.[123] Leading patriots were the American connection (the Lameth brothers, Noailles, Ségur, La Rochefoucauld-Liancourt, Lauzun), members of former Jacobite families Dillon and Lally-Tollendal, and above all La Fayette, made vice-president of the National Assembly and commander of the Paris militia. Many of their ideas – including the very term *patriote*, and La Fayette's idea of adopting red, white and blue as the national colours – were influenced by British and American practices. In return their efforts were greeted with enthusiasm by British and American sympathizers. La Fayette discussed his drafts for a Declaration of the Rights of Man with the American ambassador Thomas Jefferson. Lord Lansdowne (who as Lord Shelburne had negotiated peace in 1783) and his progressive intellectual circle, which included Samuel Romilly, young Jeremy Bentham, leading radical Dissenters such as Richard Price and Joseph Priestley, and exiled Genevan revolutionaries, were generous with advice to fledgling French politicians. Lansdowne paid a young Genevan exile, Dumont, to act as research assistant, speech-writer and publicist for the rising political star the Comte de Mirabeau. Romilly wrote a summary of House of Commons procedures for the guidance of the new National Assembly.[124]

Many in Britain assumed that the French, a century after the Glorious Revolution, would adopt a perfected version of the British constitution. The embassy secretary Hailes thought they had developed a taste not only for British goods but for British ideas: 'The intercourse of the French with the Americans . . . has brought them nearer to the English than they had ever been before. The almost unrestrained introduction of our daily publications [has] attracted the attention of the people more towards the freedom and advantages of our constitution.'[125] The ambassador, the Duke of Dorset, was one of many who assumed that the revolution was over. Two days after the storming of the Bastille he reported that 'the greatest Revolution that we know anything of has been affected with . . . the loss of very few lives: from this moment we may consider France as a free country; the King a very limited monarch, and the Nobility as reduced to a level with the rest of the Nation.'[126]

There was also great relief that the threat from France had vanished. The embassy reported that

the Army is without discipline and almost without soldiers. The Treasury is without money and nearly without credit . . . It is certainly possible that from this chaos some creation may result; but I am satisfied that it must be long before France [can be] a subject of uneasiness to other nations.[127]

Dorset's private reactions combined the common Protestant obsession with nuns with his own notorious libidinousness: 'the people continue to pillage everywhere, and they have violated two nunneries and fu-k [sic] all the nuns, I think there is something jolly in that idea'.[128] British tourists continued to circulate, and to write home with their excited and usually positive impressions. They commonly found that their nationality assured a friendly reception:

Englishmen say they, [are] our friends. We also shall be free now . . . The industry of the French is astonishing. This added to their happy climate and fruitful soil and enjoying as they soon will do the blessing of Liberty must make them a very happy and glorious people.[129]

But France and Britain were not converging. Tensions emerged as early as the summer of 1789. The obvious reason is that 'for the Frenchman of 1789, the Englishman is the enemy'.[130] The *cahiers de doléances*, especially from ports and textile towns, demanded action to stem English imports. There were persistent rumours that the British were fomenting revolutionary violence – Dorset was worried about reports that he had been 'distributing great sums of money for the purpose of cherishing and augmenting the discontents'.[131] There was lasting recrimination over the failure of Britain to supply grain. Even those who admired the British system were not arguing for friendship.

Throughout the debates in the Constituent Assembly and in the press, the British example was constantly referred to. No other country, even the United States, was so present in minds and speeches. But leading Patriots no longer considered it a model. The American rebellion and subsequent turmoil in Britain had tarnished the image of parliament. Abbé Sieyès, the leading ideologist of the National Assembly, dismissed the British constitution in his seminal pamplet of 1789, *Qu'est-ce que le Tiers état?* as 'much more the product of chance and circumstance than of enlightenment', and he called on the French to supersede Britain as 'an example to the nations'. When Mirabeau, prompted by the Lansdowne circle, proposed adopting House of Commons procedures, there were shouts of 'We want nothing that is English, we have no need to imitate anybody.'[132]

Some French politicians, especially those from outside the cosmopolitan nobility, seized on the idea of starting afresh, and creating a superior system that would be specifically French, with no external inspiration except ancient Greece and Rome. This marked a great ideological divide from the British and American revolutions of 1649, 1688 and 1776. Maximilien de Robespierre declared that 'The representatives of the French nation . . . were not delegated to copy slavishly an institution born in times of ignorance.[133] They would design new rational institutions to express the 'general will' of the nation. The horse-trading and corruption of British politics were spurned, and appeals to tradition and precedent rejected. Others were interested in learning from England, but it was not the England of George III that inspired them, but that of Oliver Cromwell. The earliest French republicans thought the Commonwealth of the 1650s provided the best modern example of a working democracy, and they pored eagerly over its histories and political tracts with the aim of producing a better version. The young orator Camille Desmoulins declared that 'We shall go beyond these English, who are so proud of their constitution and who worked at our servitude.'[134] The constitutional monarchists were the most anglophile. One of their leading members, Mounier, deplored the changing climate: 'Not a year ago we spoke enviously of the liberty of the English . . . and now while we are still exerting ourselves in the midst of anarchy to obtain liberty . . . we dare to look with contempt upon the constitution of England.' He urged the National Assembly to 'consult the lessons of experience and not disdain the examples of history'.[135] The Protestant minister Rabaut Saint-Etienne scotched that idea succinctly: 'history is not our law'. British institutions, long admired, now became divisive shibboleths. Those who favoured the 'separation of powers', 'lords' and 'commons', or a royal prerogative were identified with resistance to the revolution. British reformers who had hoped to be at the centre of exciting developments in both countries found themselves and their French friends marginalized. Mirabeau cut his connections with Lansdowne's circle. 'While the English viewed Lansdowne and the Dissenters as the secret emissaries of the French Revolution which had in fact rejected them, the French denounced them as the apologists of a political establishment which was in the process of disowning them.'[136]

CRICKET: THE TOUR OF 89[137]

What is human life but a game of cricket – beauty the bat and
man the ball.

THE DUKE OF DORSET

The ambassador, the finest all-rounder of his day, thought that cricket might calm tensions in Paris and demonstrate his own, and Britain's, goodwill. He contacted a cricketing chum, the Earl of Tankerville, who agreed to bring a side consisting of himself, William Bedster (once his butler and a well-known Surrey batsman, now running a Chelsea pub), Edward 'Lumpy' Stevens (the Earl's gardener and a formidable bowler) and various well-known veteran players. The ambassador himself would make up the numbers. They planned to arrive early in August 1789. However, Paris had become so volatile that the embassy was at risk, and Dorset left Paris and intercepted the team as they were about to embark at Dover. At least the duke was able to see the first day of the Kent–Surrey match, in which 'Lumpy' played. Revolution thus prevented the first real attempt to introduce the French to the spirit of fair play. Marie-Antoinette was said to have kept Dorset's bat as a souvenir.

CHAPTER 5

Ideas and Bayonets

A revolution is an idea plus bayonets.

NAPOLEON BONAPARTE

The revolution was made, not to make France free, but to make her formidable.

EDMUND BURKE[1]

The revolution, seen at first as bringing France and Britain together, in fact signalled a new parting of the ways. But the meaning of their opposition was now reversed: Britain, hitherto the byword for change and modernity, came to symbolize stability and tradition. France, formerly the epitome of monarchical power and social hierarchy, represented rejection of the past, democracy and upheaval. The revolution, at first assumed to weaken France, soon made it stronger, and the combination of war with revolution threatened to reverse, and could actually have reversed, the results of 100 years of struggle between France and Britain. France expanded further than under Louis XIV, while Britain's hold on Ireland, the Caribbean and India was shaken.

Blissful Dawn

Oh! pleasant exercise of hope and joy!
For mighty were the auxiliars which then stood
Upon our side, we who were strong in love!
Bliss was it in that dawn to be alive,
But to be young was very heaven! – Oh! times,
In which the meagre, stale, forbidding ways
Of custom, law, and statute, took at once
The attraction of a country in romance! . . .
Not in Utopia, subterranean fields,
Or some secreted island, Heaven knows where!
But in the very world, which is the world
Of all of us, – the place where in the end
We find our happiness, or not at all!
WILLIAM WORDSWORTH[2]

I defy the ablest Heads in England to have planned, or its whole Wealth
to have purchased, a Situation so fatal to its Rival, as that to which France
is now reduced by her own intestine Commotions.
LORD CARMARTHEN, Foreign Secretary, 1789[3]

Reactions in Britain and Ireland to the sensational news of 1789 were overwhelmingly favourable. London theatres re-enacted the events. Bastille Day almost began as a British celebration, for the House of Commons proposed a 'day of thanksgiving for the French Revolution', which was rejected by the Lords by only 13 votes to 6. Reformers hoped that France would provide a healthy example to Britain: that its recent emancipation of Jews and Protestants would spur the abolition of religious discrimination, and its constitutional debates revive flagging parliamentary reform. Many foresaw France moving closer to Britain, following in the footsteps of the 'Glorious Revolution', whose centenary had just been celebrated. Events were also a source of patriotic *Schadenfreude*. Lord Carmarthen felt that British diplomats would be 'strutting about Europe with an Air of Consideration unknown to us for some Time'. War with France, so close a few months earlier, was now remote. Wordsworth, who most famously expressed the euphoria, was an undergraduate at St John's College, Cambridge, in 1789 more concerned with his examinations and job prospects than with the revolutionary dawn; but he did develop a genuine enthusiasm during a visit in 1791–2, stimulated by a love affair with a girl from Blois, and friendship with a Patriot officer.[4]

The greatest enthusiasts were religious Dissenters and the opposition Whigs, led by Charles James Fox: 'How much the greatest event it is that ever happened in the world! and how much the best!' Fox and his followers were not very knowledgeable or concerned about what was really happening in France, but they were obsessed with the mythical threat to liberty posed by George III and a conspiratorial 'junto'. So they saw the defeat of the Bourbons as another blow against 'despotism', like the American Revolution. A friend of aristocratic French reformists, Fox assumed that the latter would take control. He persistently sought French 'Whigs' – even in such unlikely figures as the Jacobin terrorists Robespierre and Saint-Just. The Whig line was that the French revolution, whatever its horrors, was more sinned against than sinning, and that its victory over Austria, Prussia and later Britain (under a leader, William Pitt, whom they demonized) would be a victory for progress. Fox continued to blame the domestic and foreign opponents of the revolution for all that went wrong, and urged negotiation and peace with France from a mixture of sympathy, stubbornness, defeatism and fear.

The leading pro-revolution intellectuals were 'rational Dissenters', many of them from the Unitarian tendency of Presbyterianism. They denied the doctrine of the Trinity and the divinity of Christ. This undermined the basic assumption of the religious, political and social order: that Church and State were divinely ordained. Prominent Unitarian ministers such as Dr Richard Price and Dr Joseph Priestley (also a renowned scientist), political sympathizers such as the Duke of Richmond, the Marquis of Lansdowne and the Duke of Grafton, and young enthusiasts such as Samuel Taylor Coleridge, interpreted the revolution as a Providential blow against Popery and state religion. In Priestley's notorious phrase (which won him the nickname 'Gunpowder Joe'), 'a train of gunpowder [was] being laid to the Church establishment'. For years Priestley, as assiduous an analyst of the prophecies of Daniel, Isaiah and Revelations as of atmospheric gases, had been expecting 'the downfall of Church and State together . . . some very calamitous, but finally glorious events'. Now it had happened: 'The French Revolution is of God,' pronounced a Baptist minister in radical Norwich. 'No power exists or can exist, by which it can be overthrown.' However great the turmoil and suffering, it would destroy the Whore of Rome and the Beast of the Apocalypse, and usher in the Second Coming and the Kingdom of God on earth. Many millenarian pamphlets appeared with titles such as *A Prophecy of the French Revolution and the Downfall of Antichrist*. 'The Saints of the Most High', predicted Priestley reassuringly, 'shall take the Kingdom and possess it for ever.' The sinners, victims of the revolution, were consigned by 'the discipline of a wise and kind Providence' to the same theological dustbin as those engulfed by Noah's flood or incinerated in Sodom and Gomorrah.[5] The intellectual certainty, moral invincibility and millenarian expectancy of these 'miserable bigots', as Edmund Burke called them, shaped the British version of revolutionary ideology.

Such expectations touched a range of intellectual opinion. In Cambridge, endemic religious radicalism led the intense undergraduate Coleridge to burn the words 'Liberty' and 'Equality' with gunpowder on to the smooth lawns of St John's and Trinity, and more sedately caused the Vice-Chancellor's Latin prize to be given in 1790 to an essay praising the revolution as 'likely to prove advantageous to this country'.[6] However, the wider conflict was over the next few years played out in Cambridge on a lilliputian scale. William Frend, a Unitarian fellow of Jesus, not only declared that the execution of 'Louis Capet' was 'no business of ours', but also roped in the 'men in black' of the Anglican church and their 'superstitious' sacraments, implicitly compared with 'the orgies of Bacchus'. This caused him to be deprived of his fellowship for blasphemy, causing demonstrations amid which Coleridge narrowly escaped being sent down. The chaplain of Trinity more cautiously identified the Austrians and Prussians as the Beast of the Apocalypse. Religious and social radicals such as William Godwin, Mary Wollstonecraft and William Blake shared this millenarian perspective. Blake, influenced by the Swedenborgian New Jerusalem sect, believed that 'the Beast and the Whore rule without control', and that 'the English Crusade against France [was due] to State Religion'. A radical underworld, sometimes highly eccentric even by the generous standards of the time, combined visionary religion and political conspiracy.[7]

The French revolution appealed to those on the margins of the British political system: self-educated small businessmen, professional men and skilled artisans in old cities such as Norwich, Bristol, Leicester and Newcastle and in rising industrial centres such as Birmingham, Belfast, Sheffield and Manchester. Dissenting congregations provided organization and audiences. The foremost spokesman of this community was the picaresque Thomas Paine, once corsetmaker, sometime Quaker, excise man, privateer, journalist, and a famous defender of, and participant in, the American Revolution. A network of societies spread the word. Some dated from the Seven Years War and the American Revolution (the Societies for Constitutional Information, Friends of the Constitution, Patriotic Societies). Others were new, most famously the London Corresponding Society, founded in January 1792 by a cobbler, Thomas Hardy. Fraternal relations were established between political societies such as the Jacobin Club in Paris and the Society for Commemorating the Revolution, presided over by the Whig Earl Stanhope, at whose annual dinner in November 1791 Jérôme Pétion, who had recently escorted Louis XVI and his family back to Paris as prisoners after an attempted escape, was guest of honour.

One fraternal gesture had durable consequences. Richard Price, who as well as being a Unitarian minister was a leading writer on political economy, spoke 'On the Love of our Country' to the Society for Commemorating the Revolution on 4 November 1789. His address was subsequently read out in the French Constituent Assembly. At home it caused a sensation by stating that 'most' governments were 'usurpations on the rights of men', that established churches were 'priestcraft and tyranny', and that 'love of country' should be purged of 'prejudices' and 'does not imply any . . . particular preference of its laws and constitution'. He ended with a stirring declaration that the French revolution had 'kindled into a blaze that lays despotism in ashes, and warms and illuminates EUROPE!'[8] Price ignited a great war of ideas, for his words elicited Edmund Burke's 'thundering'[9] *Reflections on the Revolution in France*, published a year later in November 1790. This is the most important English book ever written about France, and one of the most important ever written about Britain, because, as Derek Beales has remarked, 'everything in the book is about France, and everything in the book is about Britain'.[10]

REFLECTING ON REVOLUTION

No Monarchy limited or unlimited, nor any of the old Republics, can possibly be safe as long as this strange, nameless, wild, enthusiastic thing is established in the Centre of Europe.

EDMUND BURKE, June 1791[11]

Hardly had we conquered a fraction of our liberty than the English let loose the orator Burke against France: his insulting writings and salaried quibbles flooded our provinces.

BERTRAND BARERE, speech in the Convention, 1794[12]

Edmund Burke, born in Dublin in 1729, is, if not Britain's greatest political thinker, surely its greatest thinking politician. He was a critic of Crown patronage, a supporter of Catholic emancipation in Ireland and of American independence, the scourge of corruption and oppression in India, a friend of Charles James Fox and a correspondent of Thomas Paine and Richard Price, and his attack on the French revolution owed part of its impact, and much of the vituperation it aroused, to his seeming apostasy. He split the Whig opposition and broke with his friends, reducing Fox to tears in the House of Commons.[13] Burke has been criticized as an enemy of the Enlightenment, a counter-revolutionary ideologue, a prophet of Romanticism, a xenophobe, a harbinger of Fascism, even the spiritual father of the American Neocons. In fact, he was defending what he saw as the Enlightened 'Commonwealth of Europe': tolerant, pluralist, hierarchical, propertied, commercial, practical, and cosmopolitan – the Enlightenment of Locke, Hume, Smith, Gibbon and Montesquieu, whose *Esprit des lois* Burke described as the most important book since the Bible. He did not gloat at the downfall of France, and was one of the first to warn, in November 1789, of the dangers of 'the total political extinction of a great civilized Nation situated in the heart of our Western System'.[14] He condemned revolution as a regression into chaos and violence, driven by precisely the same psychological naivety and theoretical arrogance that he denounced in imperialism.[15] He defended the middle ground, the 'third option', between the 'despotism of the monarch' and the 'despotism of the multitude'.[16]

'Smelling out a rat': Burke, champion of American and Indian liberty, was accused of now siding with authority – hence the crown and the crucifix.

Burke tried to define the differences between the (justified) Glorious Revolution and the (unjustified) French Revolution, against those who took them as jointly demonstrating the absolute right of a people to overthrow its rulers. He had also to defend existing social and political systems that he admitted to be imperfect against those who demanded theoretical perfection – what he had earlier mocked as 'the fairy land of philosophy'. The heart of his argument is that sentiment, experience and real life outweigh abstract theory. Interestingly, his disagreement with Price on how human beings understand the world – through experience or through metaphysics – went back thirty years. The events of 1789 made that philosophical difference a matter of life and death in the face of what he later called the revolution's 'homicide philanthropy'.

Burke asserted that the justification of a political system was not its theoretical basis – 'the nakedness and solitude of metaphysical abstraction' – but its practical ability to 'provide for human wants'. These constituted the 'real' rights of man, such as 'justice' and 'the fruits of their industry'. Political stability, which the people of England regarded as 'among their rights, not among their wrongs', was indispensable. This did not rule out careful reform or, in extreme cases, the punishment of 'real' tyrants. But societies and states could not be set up or pulled down on 'abstract principles', in reality the ideas of an arrogant few. 'I cannot conceive how any man can have brought himself to that pitch of presumption to consider his country as nothing but *carte blanche*, upon which he may scribble whatever he pleases.'[17] Such people 'have no respect for the wisdom of others; but they pay it off by a very full measure of confidence in their own'. Political systems were made by human beings in different cultures and circumstances, not ordained by universal laws of nature. Their functioning relied on willing acceptance and loyalty, 'prejudices' which 'the longer they have lasted . . . the more we cherish them'. Individual reason was fallible, and so individuals should 'avail themselves of the general bank and capital of nations, and of ages'. In the English case, this 'capital' of liberties went back to Magna Carta, and was an 'inheritance' not dependent on any abstract theory of rights. Societies and states were, like the Common Law, the result of generations of accumulated decisions and experience, 'the wisdom of unlettered men'. This inheritance was the true contract between government and governed, a permanent 'partnership' of the living, the dead and the yet unborn. Unless it were willingly accepted that none had the right to 'separate and tear asunder' this partnership, government could depend only on force. He predicted that such would be the fate of France until finally 'some popular general [is] the master of your assembly, the master of your whole republic'.

Unlike his opponents, who interpreted events in France (to which they often paid scant attention) according to their domestic political and theological concerns, Burke followed the development of the revolution closely. He realized it was something new, a 'dreadful energy' that could not be explained as the rational redress of real grievances. It came from the ideological impulse to create what Burke called 'despotic democracy', which rejected all restraint on its own power; and also from a utopian vision of total change as expressed by a prominent member of the National Assembly, the Calvinist minister Rabaut de Saint-Etienne: 'everything must be destroyed, yes everything; for everything must be recreated'. For Burke, political wisdom was both to 'preserve' and 'improve', because to destroy historic structures was also to destroy modern society.[18]

Reflections had an immediate impact: 7,000 copies were sold in a week in England, and 13,000 in a year in France[19] – a high proportion of the reading public. It provoked a spate of criticism, often accusing Burke of siding with absolutism and Popery (hence the symbols in Gillray's cartoon). Fox called it 'Cursed Stuff', and the Prince of Wales 'a Farrago of Nonsense'. The most influential rebuttals were Paine's *Rights of Man* (1791) and Mary Wollstonecraft's *Vindication of the Rights of Men* (1790) and *Vindication of the Rights of Woman* (1792). Wollstonecraft paraphrased Rousseau (above 106): 'Nature, or, to speak with strict propriety, God, has made all things right; but man had sought out many inventions to mar the work.' She asserted that God-given reason was the only source of legitimate authority, rejecting the claims of tradition (the English constitution was 'a heterogenous mass . . . settled in the dark days of ignorance'). She condemned property, politeness, 'effeminacy' and commerce as sources of oppression and immorality, and called for a moral revolution. Paine's *Rights of Man* was sly, rambling, naïve, and a huge publishing success. He did not try to engage with Burke, but simply to dismiss him; Burke did not bother to reply. For Paine, everything in France was going wonderfully: the revolution was simply 'a renovation of the natural order of things . . . combining moral with political happiness and national prosperity'.[20]

Burke's polemic was regarded by many moderates, including his friends, as absurdly extreme and alarmist. Pitt famously judged the *Reflections* to be 'Rhapsodies in which there is much to admire and nothing to agree with.' Pitt never accepted that the revolution was intrinsically wrong, and is said to have thought privately that Paine would be right 'if everybody had sense to act as they ought'.[21] Yet Burke largely prevailed in the war of ideas. None of his opponents would attempt a systematic defence of the French revolution as it developed after 1792: with civil war, economic collapse, the Terror, external aggression, war with Britain, attacks on Christianity and Bonaparte's coup d'état, which fulfilled Burke's prediction concerning 'some popular general'. Paine's confidence that 'they order these things better in France', and that 'a thousand years hence' the French would look back on the revolution 'with contemplative pride'[22] gave way to attempts to blame all problems on foreign interference. Wollstonecraft, horrified by the 'barbarity and misery', wished 'I had never heard of the cruelties . . . practised here'.[23] Paine, fleeing prosecution in England, was feted in France, became a citizen, a member of the National Convention, an official propagandist, and an amateur adviser on plans to invade England. But he backed the wrong faction, was arrested during the Terror, imprisoned, and narrowly escaped the guillotine. He understandably reverted to the safer field of homespun theology in *The Age of Reason* (1794), and wrote nothing further on the revolution. Yet if Burke won the battle of ideas, endowing the British system with 'historic pedigrees of incalculable legitimising force',[24] he died in 1797 fearing that Pitt's search for coexistence with the revolution would eventually allow it to triumph.

Burke's conception of a political community as a complex and restraining accretion of agreements, rights, duties and sentiments was his alternative to the universalist 'despotic democracy' shaped by republican idealization of Sparta and Rome. Though usually described as conservative, Burke's vision was an indispensable ingredient of what the philosopher Benjamin Constant was to call 'the liberty of the moderns', based on individual political and economic freedoms. Burke differed from French counter-revolutionary theorists, who called for theocracy and the iron rod of authority as the only cure for revolution. Reflecting on the French revolution redefined British and European political ideas, for Burke's 'third option' made him a godfather both of conservatism, through his praise of tradition and loyalty, and of liberalism, through his acceptance that change was necessary for survival.

The main popular response to the revolution in Britain was not radicalism. Radical societies had dozens or at most a few hundred core members (probably the largest provincial group, the Sheffield Society for Constitutional Information, had about 600 active members in 1792).[25] More significant was Loyalism, which mobilized British society as the revolution mobilized that of France. There were eventually some 2,000 loyalist societies, such as the Association for the Preservation of Liberty and Property against Republicans and Levellers, founded in November 1792. Loyalists argued that rich and poor alike stood to lose from a French-inspired upheaval. But Loyalism did not mean unqualified support for Pitt's government. It often sympathized with popular grievances, particularly over food shortages; and it did not guarantee unflinching support for a long and hopeless war. At the sedate end of the spectrum of its activities were loyal addresses to George III bearing thousands of signatures, and sermons, poems, pamphlets and newspapers. Less sedate were popular festivities – marches, bonfires with Tom Paine as Guy Fawkes, fireworks, ox-roasting, and drinking, often subsidized by local gentry. Intimidating radicals was an important aspect of Loyalist activity: burning them in effigy, ejecting them from pubs and friendly societies, boycotting and sacking them, and privately prosecuting writers and publishers. At the extreme end of the spectrum was violent disorder. The most notorious example was the 'Priestley riots' in Birmingham, which stifled radicalism in one of its strongholds.

On 14 July 1791, a dinner held to celebrate Bastille Day by some ninety reformers at a hotel in Birmingham led to three days of rioting across the town and in surrounding villages – the biggest popular tumult of the revolutionary period.[26] The main targets were Dissenting chapels and the houses of men attending the Bastille dinner; then, the houses of leading members of the local Dissenting patriciate – bankers, ministers, magistrates, and large manufacturers – some with dubious business connections with France (see above, page 83); and finally, those of members of the Lunar Society, the core of the Midlands Enlightenment. Its members included Matthew Boulton, Birmingham's leading industrialist, James Watt, Britain's leading engineer (they were Anglicans, so their houses were spared) and Joseph Priestley, Fellow of the Royal Society, renowned experimenter with air and electricity and a Unitarian fundamentalist who believed that the revolution heralded the overthrow of the Antichrist and the Second Coming – 'It cannot, I think, be more than twenty years.'[27] Although he prudently stayed away from the dinner, perhaps warned off by threatening graffiti, his house was gutted and his scientific instruments and papers were destroyed. In all, one Baptist and three Unitarian chapels and at least twenty-seven houses were looted, vandalized or pulled down in the ritual of English popular protest, their owners terrified and humiliated but not physically hurt. One victim was 'hauled to a tavern . . . forced to shake a hundred hard and black hands', and buy the crowd 329 gallons of beer. Why did the owners of those hard, black hands – Birmingham and Black Country harness-makers, metal-workers, carpenters, glaziers, button-makers, colliers and bricklayers – turn on genteel francophiles in the name of 'Church and King'? The Dissenters were the local plutocracy: the ten men who suffered most property damage were all extremely rich. They were traditionally unpopular as killjoy Puritans the West Midlands had seen recurrent riots against them throughout the century, formerly under the Jacobite banner. Dissenters' demands for religious and political reform – never widely popular – crowned by their public enthusiasm for the increasingly menacing French revolution, seemed to threaten the traditional ideal of a united, harmonious and stable society. This patriotic ideal of unity had powerful appeal to skilled tradesmen; the alternative seemed to be 'a cruel universe in which exploitation of the many by the few ran rampant'.[28]

Priestley moved away to London, succeeding Richard Price as minister to a Unitarian congregation. He was made a French citizen and elected to the Legislative Assembly, though he declined to serve on the grounds that he could not speak French. Despite the Terror, he continued to see the revolution as 'opening a new era in the world and presenting a near view of the millennium', and he 'read with . . . enthusiasm the admirable Report of *Robespierre* on the subject of *morals* and *religion*, and I rejoice to find by it, that so great and happy a change has taken place in the sentiments of the leading men of France'.[29] He eventually retreated to America.

Loyalists and radicals alike were stimulated by events on the Continent. Growing violence turned many decisively against the revolution. A new level of horror was reached on 2–6 September 1792, when revolutionaries, threatened by invading armies and fearing a plot by their imprisoned enemies, began to massacre the inmates of the Paris gaols. Princesses, prostitutes, bishops, beggars, officers, ex-ministers, vagrant children and *financiers* by the hundred were dragged into the street and cut down by patriotic tribunals acting as judge, jury and executioner. The killings were particularly shocking as they contradicted the conventional image of the French people as lighthearted, gentle and deferential.

The unexpected success of French forces in turning back Prussian and Austrian invaders on 20 September 1792 at Valmy in eastern France caused surprise and, to sympathizers, relief. Charles James Fox, though upset by the September Massacres, wrote of Valmy that 'no public event, not excepting Saratoga and York Town, ever happened that gave me so much delight'.[30] Other French victories in the Austrian Netherlands caused jubilation among British sympathizers, who had been collecting clothes, blankets, boots and ammunition for the hard-pressed French armies. Now they planted Trees of Liberty, roasted oxen, rang church bells and illuminated their windows. Clearly, revolutionary France would not, after all, be powerless.

The British, and particularly the English, reaction to the French revolution has long been a subject of debate. Left-wing historians saw the radical response, including the multiplication of political societies, as a sign that England too might have had its revolution, or at least might have pursued a more democratic path. Recent scholars, however, generally concur that earlier historians 'severely overestimated' popular sympathy for the revolution. Rather, 'one of the most significant impacts . . . was the enormous boost it gave to popular conservatism'.[31] Many famous early enthusiasts eventually changed their minds under the pressure of events, including the poets Wordsworth, Coleridge and Robert Burns. Charles Maurice de Talleyrand-Périgord, the ex-bishop turned diplomat who was serving the first of what would be several spells as envoy to Britain over the next forty years, reported in 1792 that

the mass of the nation . . . attached to its constitution by ancient prejudices, habit, comparison of its lot with other states, and prosperity, does not imagine that anything would be gained from a revolution of which the history of England makes it fear the dangers. The country is solely occupied with questions of material prosperity.'[32]

Only when the strains of war damaged that prosperity was there serious unrest.

CANNIBALS AND HEROES

Gillray drew and etched 'Un petit souper' quickly, and it was published, with bright, elementary colouring, a fortnight after the first news of the September Massacres reached London. An eyewitness account of the massacres by a diplomat, Colonel Munro, was later echoed by the two great British image-makers of the revolution, Thomas Carlyle, in his *History of the French Revolution* (1837) and Charles Dickens, in *A Tale of Two Cities* (1859).

The execution of Louis XVI on 18 January 1793, some four months after the September Massacres, had a comparably negative effect on British opinion, not least because it recalled the execution of Charles I. Louis drew the same parallel. Obsessed with the lessons of British history, he read Hume's *History of England* and Clarendon's *History of the Rebellion* during his last months. Perhaps he reflected on Hume's dictum that in historical events a 'great measure of accident . . . commonly concurs with a small ingredient of wisdom and foresight'.[33] He was accompanied to his death by Abbé Edgworth, a priest of Irish Jacobite descent, to whom was ascribed the memorable but apocryphal farewell at the steps of the guillotine: 'Son of St Louis, climb up to heaven.'

Gillray's hanging bishop, monks and judge, the profaned crucifix and the burning church – this was not a time for anti-Popery – illustrate the image's subtitle, sarcasm aimed at the revolution's British sympathizers: 'Religion, Justice, Loyalty & all the Bugbears of Unenlightened Minds, Farewell!' France had declared war on Britain twelve days before this print appeared. The central figure of the *sans-culotte* (always taken literally by Gillray) is linked to pre-revolutionary francophobe imagery. The long bagged hair and the fiddle had long been symbols of French frivolity, now transmuted into capricious political cruelty. The message was that French vices had been worsened, not cured, by revolution. As Lord Auckland put it, 'all the ferocity of barbarism had been engrafted on the corruption of a polished society'.[34]

'Polished society' was even more harshly criticized by the revolutionaries themselves, who extended ideas of patriotism and virtue partly imported from

The zenith of French glory.

England.[35] They intended to create a new morality and culture as well as a new political system, spurning the aristocratic French style so admired by the likes of Chesterfield (see above, page 106). Maximilien Robespierre declaimed in 1794, at the height of the revolutionary Terror:

> We will substitute . . . morality for egoism, probity for honour . . . the empire of reason for the tyranny of fashion . . . good people for good company, merit for intrigue, genius for cleverness, truth for brilliance, delight in goodness for satiety in voluptuousness, the greatness of man for the pettiness of great men, a magnanimous, powerful and happy people for an agreeable, frivolous and wretched people, that is to say, all the virtues and all the miracles of the Republic for all the vices and all the absurdities of monarchy.[36]

Plain clothes and natural hair combed casually forward – a development of the fashionable English look of the 1780s – became associated with radical chic. For women, the simplicity of the English look took on pseudo-Greek tones, with eventually far more revealing effect. In fashion, as in politics, revolutionary France took the English style to new extremes.

Jour de gloire

> Unquestionably, there never was a time in the history of this country, when, from the situation of Europe, we might more reasonably expect fifteen years of peace than at the present moment.
>
> WILLIAM PITT in the House of Commons, 17 February 1792[37]

> It will be a crusade for universal liberty . . . Each soldier will say to his enemy: Brother, I am not going to cut your throat, I am going to free you from the yoke you labour under; I am going to show you the road to happiness.
>
> BRISSOT DE WARVILLE in the Jacobin Club[38]

War was neither desired nor expected on either side of the Channel in the first years of the revolution. It seemed that France would settle down as a constitutional monarchy less likely to threaten its neighbours. War was not caused by the wish of Europe's monarchs to reinstate Bourbon absolutism, which they feared. Nor did they march on France to suppress the horrors of revolution – most of which, it is worth recalling, had not yet happened, for they were the consequences, not the causes, of war. The main

Continental powers were on the verge of another bout of predatory conflict in eastern Europe and the Balkans, the details of which need not detain us. Revolutionary France might even be a useful ally. Its internal politics were its own affair.

The impulse towards war came from within France, as its factions, for quite different reasons, came to see war as a solution to political difficulties. Foremost were the 'Brissotins', followers of Brissot de Warville, who wanted war to make the king and his ministers seem unpatriotic, to bring about a republic, and to put themselves into power. 'War is necessary to France,' Brissot told the Assembly, 'for her honour, external security, internal tranquillity, to restore our finances and public credit, to put an end to terror, treason and anarchy.'[39] The Austrians reluctantly, and the Prussians eagerly, took up the challenge, and declarations, threats and ultimatums flew back and forth. The French National Assembly voted on 20 April 1792 to declare war, with only seven votes against. Both sides expected an easy victory. The Austrians and Prussians assumed that professional troops would rout the revolutionary rabble and be home by the autumn. The Brissotins imagined revolutionary patriotism sweeping aside tottering monarchies: 'Louis XIV, with 400,000 slaves, knew how to defy all the powers of Europe; can we, with our millions of free men, fear them?'[40]

The British government was bent on 'the most scrupulous neutrality in the French business', in the words of the new foreign secretary, Lord Grenville. He thought Austro-Prussian threats against the French 'ill-conceived and undignified'. Britain had its own problems with Spain in North America and with Russia in the Near East. The experienced William Eden (now Lord Auckland) admitted that while 'abstractedly considered' he detested the revolution, in practice a 'disjointed and inefficient' government in France suited Britain well. Similarly, the Brissotins, who had no liking for Britain – abstractedly considered – had enough enemies. In October 1792 Brissot complimented 'the power which has respected our revolution and its emblems most scrupulously'. A Foreign Office official thought that, protected by its 'salt-water entrenchment', British involvement in a Continental war was 'as unlikely a contingency as can well be foreseen'.[41]

The war with Austria and Prussia began badly for the French. Their commanders, the heroes of the American war La Fayette and Rochambeau, considered their troops unfit to fight. When the enemy appeared, they retreated, provoking accusations of treason. These early reverses radicalized the revolution far more suddenly and violently than the Brissotins could have imagined. The Duke of Brunswick, commander of the Austro-Prussian forces, issued a Manifesto threatening to punish Paris if the royal family were harmed. In response, arms were distributed to the people. But they used them to attack the Tuileries palace on 10 August 1792 and overthrew the monarchy. The British ambassador left, but London remained 'extremely neutral'.[42] Enemy troops advanced on the capital. Verdun, the last fortress in their path, surrendered on 2 September. Several 'virgins of Verdun' were later guillotined for welcoming the invader. Amid rumours of treason and conspiracy, the September Massacres took place (see above, page 202), followed by the epoch-making French resistance at Valmy. Grenville congratulated himself that 'we had the wit to keep ourselves out of the glorious enterprize . . . of sharing the spoils in the division of France [and] crushing all democratic principles all over the world'. He insisted that 'this country and Holland ought to remain quiet as long as it is possible'.[43]

What changed the situation was an unexpected threat to the bulwark of British security, the Low Countries. On 6 November 1792 the French routed the Austrians at Jemmapes and occupied Brussels. This astonishing change from peril to triumph, with reports that French troops were being greeted as liberators, encouraged the new National Convention to heights of daring, as rival factions vied to demonstrate their patriotism and cautious voices were drowned. 'Revolution . . . donned warrior's garb to challenge the world.'[44] On 19 November the Convention unanimously decreed 'fraternity and assistance' to all peoples struggling for liberty. Soon invasion was being justified not simply as assistance, but as an assertion of revolutionary France's universal rights. Georges Danton declared that 'just as it is our duty to give freedom to other peoples . . . we also have the right to tell them "you will have no more kings"'. 'We cannot be calm,' wrote Brissot, 'until Europe, all Europe, is in flames.' And he asserted that 'The French Republic's only border should be the Rhine.'[45]

Pitt's government also felt confident. At first, French victories and the approach of war had given a worrying boost to the radicals. But a surge of loyalist activity from November 1792 buoyed up the government's spirits, as did the break-up of the Foxite opposition, precipitated by Burke. As Grenville put it to Auckland, ambassador at The Hague, 'Nothing can exceed the good dispositions of this country in the present moment. The change within the last three weeks is little less than miraculous. God grant that it may last long enough to enable us to act with that vigour which can alone preserve us . . . it will enable us to talk to France in the tone which British Ministers ought to use . . . and to crush the seditious disposition here.'[46] Frantic semi-official diplomacy continued almost until the outbreak of war, but could not bridge the widening abyss. In a Note dated 31 December 1792, Grenville stated that 'England never will consent that France shall arrogate the power of annulling at her pleasure, and under the pretence of a . . . natural right, of which she makes herself the only judge, the political system of Europe.'[47]

It was the French who declared war on Britain and Holland on 1 February 1793, eleven days after Louis XVI was guillotined in a gesture of defiance to monarchist Europe. Paine drafted a call to the British people to rise in revolt, which was smuggled into England by French fishing boats and American travellers. Pitt's statement to the House of Commons placed the struggle on an elevated plane: 'a free, brave, loyal and happy people' were fighting for 'the tranquillity of this country, the security of its allies, the good order of every European Government, and the happiness of the whole of the human race'.[48] Britain's entry into the war created the 'First Coalition', essentially a London–Vienna axis.

Should Pitt and his colleagues have done more to avoid war, as critics then and later accused? Was personality – 'Pitt's icy reserve and Grenville's haughty arrogance' as one French historian puts it[49] – a barrier to an understanding with the French, by which they would have kept out of Holland in return for British recognition of the French Republic and assurances of neutrality? This is to misunderstand the dynamism of revolutionary politics, as Fox and his colleagues, who urged negotiation and appeasement, constantly did. François Furet explains that 'the revolutionary war had no definite aim because it sprang from deep within the revolution itself . . . That is why even French victories could at best result only in truces; to look for peace was . . . suspect.'[50] This, another French historian has recently argued, created something new in history: total war.[51]

As in many long wars, both sides expected a quick victory. French agents, who spent much time drinking and reading newspapers at the White Bear in Piccadilly, reported that Britain was on the verge of revolution. Evidence came from fraternal messages from radical societies such as the Stoke Newington branch of the Friends of the People, or an address from 'several patriotic societies' proclaiming, 'Frenchmen, you are already free, but the Britons are preparing to free themselves. When we look for our enemies, we find them amongst the members of that voracious aristocracy that is rending the heart of our society.'[52] That the French took this seriously is an example of blissful, but culpable, ignorance: no attempt was made to sound out wider opinion in the country, or even to talk to the founder of the London Corresponding Society, whose shop was just down the street from the White Bear.[53] The British government had more reason to believe that France was in a state of chaos, dissension and near bankruptcy. But its error was to suppose that this would stop the French from fighting: their ability to do so, at immense cost in suffering, was to astonish the world.

War changed the nature of the revolution, and the revolution changed the nature of war. France's leaders – especially now that they were regicides – were literally fighting for their lives: against the foreign invader, against the royalists within, and even against each other, as failure or weakness could mean death. Their followers risked the loss of newly gained rights, freedoms, property and position. The dangers were magnified by an omnipresent fear of foreign and internal conspiracies – not always imaginary – planning murder, famine and massacres. As the 'Marseillaise' emphasizes, failure meant that the bloody flag of tyranny would fly, ferocious enemy soldiers would rampage through the countryside, and the wives and children of patriots would be massacred. 'They tear out the entrails of pregnant women and slit the throats of old men.'[54]

First, volunteers were raised. Then 300,000 men were drafted. Local communities, with quotas to fill, sent the halt and the lame or those causing trouble on both sides of the political fence (priests, nobles, and republican militants). Deserters had their property confiscated or had soldiers billeted on their families. There was a rush to get married to avoid the draft: elderly widows had never been in such demand. On 23 August 1793 the Convention decreed a *levée en masse*, total mobilization:

> The young men will go to battle; married men will forge arms and transport provisions; women will make tents and clothing and serve in the hospitals; children will shred linen; old men will have themselves carried to public places to arouse the courage of the warriors and preach hatred of kings and the unity of the Republic.

The result, though less than hoped, was still a vast horde – chaotic, disorganized, filthy, ragged, unequipped, and armed often with pitchforks, pikes and shotguns hastily fitted with bayonets. Hungry, and tormented by epidemics of scabies and venereal disease, thousands (sometimes whole units) deserted or flocked into fetid hospitals that killed far more than the Austrians could. Yet large numbers still remained to fight, and even to win: by 1794 France had 800,000 men under arms.[55] The legend of the barefoot citizen soldier triumphing over the foreign invader by combining enthusiastic bayonet charges with revolutionary zeal inspired, and to some extent still inspires, republican patriotism. Superior numbers were a crucial part of the explanation: the bigger army practically always won, and it was usually the French. In Britain, the perceptive realized that this was a 'new invention': a formidable 'military democracy' mobilized by 'popular tyranny' and 'waging war with their whole substance'.[56]

War pushed France into a vortex of terror from 1791 to 1794. The *levée en masse* caused unprecedented riots across the country. Bands of deserters turned to brigandage. All over western France, in what was known as the Vendée uprising, there was open revolt, and towns were invaded by angry peasants. The cost of war, met by printing more money as taxes were withheld, caused galloping inflation; the official printing house literally caved in under the weight of new notes. Bad harvests, trade disruption and hoarding raised the price of corn by 25–50 per cent in 1791, causing more rioting. The government responded by economic controls and requisitions backed by terror. Black-marketeering and military defeats were blamed on treachery, and led to purges of those considered lukewarm or unreliable. A succession of generals fled to the enemy. As the Austrians and Prussians advanced again on Paris, the formerly dominant Girondin faction was driven out of the National Convention by the Paris crowd in June 1793, and their leader Brissot was accused of being a British agent. Power was concentrated in the hands of the Convention and its executive committees, most crucially the Committee of Public Safety, dominated from the summer of 1793 by Maximilien Robespierre. Repression of real or suspected opponents ignited more violent resistance. The Federalist civil war broke out between the Paris regime and the cities of the south, Lyons, Bordeaux, Toulon and Marseilles, led by the ousted Girondins. The revolution's enemies hoped that this presaged collapse. But accounts of the republic's demise proved premature, and in June 1794 it won a crushing victory over the Austrians at Fleurus.

The impact of war on Britain was vastly less traumatic, and remarkable for that very reason. In comparison with France, England, Wales and Scotland had low levels of political and social conflict. The rowdy enthusiasm of Loyalism palely reflects that of the Jacobin clubs and the *sans-culottes*. Official days of fasting and thanksgiving, and more flamboyant celebrations of victory, helped to buttress support. Most accepted the arguments of anti-revolutionary propagandists such as Hannah More that rich and poor alike would lose from a French victory. The churches, including most Dissenters, now supported the message, to which the actions of the French – the Terror, attacks on religion, and external aggression – gave substance.

Even so, support for the war fluctuated seriously, with strong pressure on the government to make peace in 1796–7 and 1800–1802, especially from manufacturing interests. Though people lit bonfires to celebrate the naval victory of Camperdown in 1797, they burned Pitt in effigy on them. This was partly because of continuing ideological division over the revolution itself; partly because of confusion over Britain's war aims; but mostly because of the seeming impossibility of winning. There were waves of riots and strikes, serious war-weariness, a few revolutionary conspiracies, and alarming naval mutinies. But most unrest in Great Britain was of a non-revolutionary kind, provoked by food shortages, recruitment and economic disruption. Recent research shows that disturbances were generally handled with sense and even sensitivity by relatively efficient and confident central and local authorities. Acts to repress sedition were little used. Generous administration of the Poor Law in times of economic strain and for the families of men in the armed forces was an essential factor: spending on poor relief was far higher than in any other country. The economy and overseas trade remained generally buoyant. The country accepted huge increases in taxation, including an income tax in 1799. The government was careful to place the main burden on the better-off. Paper money was introduced, while a low rate of inflation was maintained. Compulsory militia service caused riots, but volunteer units proved a great success. All in all, the ordeal of war revealed a society mostly accepting that its system of government was legitimate and its independence worth defending. Ireland was a different story, as we shall see.[57]

National hatred was an inevitable product of the conflict. As in past wars, there was the usual asymmetry: France was Britain's great enemy; but Britain was only one of France's enemies. Austria, the treacherous former ally, the invader and the homeland of the detested Marie-Antoinette, was the target of the most visceral French loathing during 1789–93. When popular resistance flared up in the 'liberated' Low Countries, Germany and Italy from 1795 onwards, the revolutionaries tended to dismiss their peoples as treacherous, fanatical, cowardly and generally inferior. Yet Britain was soon raised to the highest eminence of hatred. This drew on existing anglophobia accumulated earlier in the century, particularly at the time of the Seven Years War. As conflict persisted, 'England' was identified as the most stubborn enemy, with 'venal and shopkeeping London' the heart of the anti-revolutionary struggle. The republicans knew as well as the Bourbons that British control of the oceans weighed in Continental power politics, and that France could not dominate Europe without destroying Britain. 'Carthage' – vampire, tyrant of the seas, 'perfidious' enemy and bearer of a corrupting commercial civilization – contrasted with 'Rome', bearer of universal order, philosophy and selfless values. 'A people of Soldiers must vanquish a people of Merchants.'[58]

As early as the summer of 1789, rumours of British plots had disturbed the short-lived euphoria. Fear of conspiracy heated the murderous factionalism of the 1790s. Politicians accused their enemies of being Pitt's agents. The Jacobin Club itself was said to be full of French-speaking Englishmen taking notes. One speaker in the National Convention asserted that

> Paris is full of Englishmen . . . they come here to insult us with
> their openly counter-revolutionary clothes. By their jeers they
> provoke any Frenchman who fails to adopt English manners and
> customs. They flaunt their luxury at the same time that they spy
> on us and betray us.[59]

It is easy to see why Britain became the chief suspect. For a century it had financed anti-French alliances. Many French revolutionaries and ex-revolutionaries did have British links, not least Mirabeau, General Dumouriez (a genuine traitor), Danton, Brissot and the ferocious Marat. Jean-Paul Marat had practised fraudulently as a doctor in England, had been wrongly suspected of theft from the Ashmolean Museum in Oxford, had been greatly influenced by Wilkes and earlier English republicanism, and his earliest political writings were written and published in England.[60] The British government really did have agents, it did forge French currency, and it did use money to influence politics. Pitt's machinations – 'rivers of gold' flowing from the slave cabins of the West Indies via the hovels of the Vendée to 'the seraglio of Constantinople' – were a necessary excuse for factionalism, revolts, shortages, defeats, and inflation. 'Of all the Powers of Europe, England is undeniably that which has plotted most actively not only against the liberty of France, but even against the existence of its inhabitants.'[61] Robespierre produced the ultimate conspiracy theory in 1793: the British had plotted the whole revolution, abetted by the Duc d'Orléans, in order to weaken France, put the Duke of York on the throne, seize 'the three great objects of its . . . jealousy' (Dunkirk, Toulon, and the French colonies) – and then reconquer America.[62] Pitt was officially declared an 'enemy of the human race'.

At first, the 'English' people were regarded differently from 'the infamous Pitt' and 'the imbecile George'. They were thought not to want to fight France, and so they would sooner or later overthrow Pitt or at least

The great Jean-Louis David, the revolutionary regime's all-purpose artist, turns his hand to caricature *à la* Gillray.

demand peace, if only because 'they are losing valuable trade, and they love their wealth more than they hate us'.[63] The Committee of Public Safety was urged to appeal to British opinion by expressing its 'esteem for that brave and generous nation'; and by holding out the prospect of 'the two most powerful and enlightened nations in Europe, no longer the playthings of politicians' passions, assuring the peace of Europe and nurturing the arts useful to humanity'.[64] But as war continued, reality dawned:

> We have deluded ourselves about the true character of the English people. Superstitiously attached to their Constitution and their Religion, they have never liked, and can never like, French princi-ples. If they applauded our revolution, it was rather due to an old hatred of our Kings than to any love for a Republican System. Used for several centuries to a mixed government, they have rarely felt the direct blows of despotism. Their benefits are numerous; their civil rights are assured by wise laws; and their political rights, cleverly combined with those of the aristocracy and the King, give them a deceptive importance that contents them.[65]

The English people were doubly guilty because they opposed the revolution freely: 'they reject liberty because we embrace it; they draw closer to the pope because we have renounced him . . . they will never forgive us for having dethroned the son of Mary . . . Never were Rome and Carthage more deter-mined to destroy each other.' A tidy-minded foreign ministry official drew up a table of the Republic's policy towards its many enemies: while the smaller states were to be 'intimidated and contained', Russia 'watched', Holland 'ruined', and Prussia 'fought and defeated', Austria and England, at the top of the list, were to be 'exterminated'.[66] Robespierre himself ended all ambiguity early in 1794: 'Why should I distinguish between a people that makes itself the accomplice of the crimes of its government and that perfidious govern-ment? . . . There is something more contemptible than a tyrant and that is a slave.'[67]

Anglophobia in the Convention accelerated. British goods were embar-goed. British subjects were ordered to be arrested. As the Terror reached its peak in the summer of 1794, Bertrand Barère, a spokesman for the Committee of Public Safety, demanded the killing of all British and Hanoverian prisoners of war:

> a feeling of esteem used to attach us to the inhabitants of England . . . we invoked its liberty, we believed in its philanthropy, we envied its constitution. This dangerous error was spread by the perfidious English themselves, along with their fashions and their books . . .

There must be an immense ocean between Dover and Calais; young republicans must suck hatred of the English name with their mothers' milk . . . If, being more enlightened than the soldiers of other governments, the Englishman comes to murder liberty on the Continent, he is the more guilty: generosity towards him is a crime against humanity . . . Every calamity that besets the Revolution and strikes the people, stems from the system of horrors organized in London . . . whose Machiavellianism has indirectly killed more than a million Frenchmen . . . The civilized savages of Great Britain are foreign to Europe, foreign to humanity: they must disappear . . . Let the English slaves perish and Europe will be free.[68]

The Convention responded with 'the liveliest enthusiasm', and decreed that 'No English or Hanoverian prisoners will be taken.' It seems that some prisoners were indeed killed after the French victory at Fleurus a month later; and the crew of a captured merchantman were executed. However, Robespierre complained that the decree was not being generally obeyed, and it was soon a dead letter.[69]

EXILES: THE REVOLUTION

Let us hope that the victorious troops of liberty will lay down their arms only when there are no more tyrants or slaves . . . we shall see the formation of a close union between the French republic and the English, Scotch and Irish nations.

British 'Club of the Friends of the Rights of Man', Paris, 1792[70]

If by birth a Frenchman I
'Tis with thee my loyalties lie,
In my breast an English heart
Hails thy virtuous energy
In the fight 'gainst tyranny.

Verses by a French exile in England, 1798[71]

The revolution attracted the curious and the committed, radical exiles and refugees. A British club met regularly in Paris at White's Hotel or the Hôtel d'Angleterre. On 28 November 1792 it sent a fraternal address to the Convention, like those sent by similar groups in Britain: 'You have taken up arms solely to make reason and truth triumph. It doubtless appertained to the French nation to enfranchise Europe.'[72] However, the extension of war to Britain broke up the club, as many of its members went home. Some stayed to join in the revolutionary struggle, including Mary Wollstonecraft, Helen Maria Williams, and inevitably Thomas Paine. They were close to the ascendant Girondin faction, and when this was overthrown Williams and Paine were imprisoned by the Jacobins, who replaced revolutionary internationalism with xenophobic suspicion. Some 250 British subjects were arrested in 1793, including remaining members of the eighteen Irish and British religious houses, and several descendants of Irish Jacobites serving in the army. Some were guillotined, among them Martin Glynn, superior of the Irish seminary in Bordeaux, Generals Ward and O'Moran, and a boy, Thomas Delany, accused of spying.[73] Two Irish seminarians were reprieved to serve in the French navy. There were some British Jacobins. Two Scots, John Oswald and William Maxwell, were among those guarding Louis to the scaffold, and Oswald and his sons were later killed – reportedly by their own men – when fighting against rebels in the Vendée. After the end of the Terror in 1794, the most significant presence was that of Irish radicals, including the leader of the United Irishmen, Theobald Wolfe Tone, who arrived in 1796.

Exile in Britain was a much bigger phenomenon. The earliest and most noted arrivals were members of the royal family and great nobles. The king's brother, the Comte d'Artois, arrived immediately after the fall of the Bastille. As the revolution radicalized, several deputies of the Constituent Assembly followed. The revolutionary wars began the largest influx, with steady arrivals from the early months of 1792. By the end of the year, hundreds of refugees were arriving daily along a stretch of coast from Dover to Southampton. Beaumarchais arrived in this period, though he was later expelled for buying arms. Escaping became increasingly difficult and expensive, and many refugees arrived penniless. Probably half the total were clergy, including thirty bishops. The Anglican church raised funds for their support: 'the difference is wide in doctrine [but] those venerable exiles [are] endeared to us by patient suffering for conscience' sake'. Oxford University Press printed large numbers of Latin bibles and Catholic breviaries free of charge. The government gave Winchester Castle as a temporary monastery, and provided a solid ration including a pound of meat and four pints of beer a day.[74] Political antagonisms were not forgotten: 'Even Noailles has taken refuge in England, the last country in which he ought to have shown his face. Lafayette and he, Noailles, were treated in England with a generosity and frankness that no foreigners ever before or since experienced, and yet they went, warm with our civilities, in the most treacherous manner, as if they had come here merely as spies, to attack us in America.'[75] The war inevitably caused friction. Fear of republican agents led to the resented Aliens Act (1792) which placed exiles under surveillance. The British government was lobbied by bitterly opposing factions among the refugees, and it refused to commit itself to a Bourbon restoration. Enterprises involving exiles repeatedly went wrong, especially the disastrous landing at Quiberon Bay in 1795 (see below, page 221). After the end of the Jacobin dictatorship, and especially during the 1800s once Bonaparte was in power, most went home.

The refugees needed financial help. The main fundraiser was John Eardley Wilmot, a lawyer and former MP, who in November 1792 formed a committee, including Burke, which collected over £400,000. After Quiberon Bay, a women's committee was set up to help widows and children. Between 1794 and 1799, the government gave more than £1 million. Much of the money was managed by the Bishop of Saint-Pol de Léon and the Duc d'Harcourt. Burke was very active, among other things in founding a school for French boys under an exiled priest. If some former courtiers for a time went 'from château to château, very fêted everywhere', most exiles soon had to earn a living. The Comtesse de Guéry ran a London café famous for its ice cream. A former Benedictine monk used his library to open a bookshop.[76] Erard founded his great piano-making business. Refugees worked as seamstresses, dancing or fencing masters, tutors or governesses. Several schools were founded, including the Jesuit school at Stonyhurst. Auguste Charles Pugin, who arrived in 1792, produced engravings for the publisher Ackerman. Marc Brunel, who arrived in 1799, designed machinery for the navy. Both married Englishwomen, and their sons created some of the greatest monuments of nineteenth-century Britain.

Soho maintained its position as the centre of exile life, particularly attracting those of intellectual bent and little money, such as the writer René de Chateaubriand. Two bookshops became meeting places, and the French House in Lisle Street offered French meals for two or three shillings. Marylebone attracted the aristocracy and princes of the blood, including the Comte d'Artois, the Duc de Berry and the Prince de Condé, who colonized Portman and Manchester squares. A meeting place was the Rose of Normandy, in Marylebone High Street, and for less convivial assemblies, the French Chapel Royal. Poorer exiles lived in large numbers across the river in the slums of Southwark.

These years saw the closest-ever contact of the French elite with Britain and its ways, far greater that that of the Free French during the Second World War, the only comparable episode. Though numbers fluctuated, the total has been estimated at 60–80,000, among them France's next three kings and several future prime ministers. Chateaubriand, France's first great Romantic writer, declared that his years in exile had made him

English in manners, in taste and, up to a point, in thought; because, if, as has been claimed, Lord Byron took some inspiration from René in his Childe Harold, it is also true that eight years of living in Britain . . . and a long habit of speaking, writing and even thinking in English, had necessarily influenced the development and expression of my ideas.[77]

On a less exalted note, a French schoolboy wrote, 'J'aime John Bull, j'aime les beef-steaks et comme dit Lord Byron, j'love a porter beer as well as any.'[78] We may safely conclude that 'the years of the Emigration softened the animosity which had existed between the two populations and promoted lasting links between the two nations in the nineteenth century'.[79] However, if Chateaubriand on his return to France found it difficult to get used to 'the dirt of our houses . . . our uncleanliness, our noise, our familiarity, the indiscretion of our chatter', he soon found that 'our characteristic sociability . . . our absence of pride and prejudice, our inattention to wealth and name' convinced him that 'Paris is the only place to live.'[80]

Internal Injuries

France . . . is, I am convinced, weakness itself if you can get to
grapple with her internally.
EDMUND BURKE, 1793[81]

The coup of 9 Thermidor (27 July 1794) overthrew the Jacobin dictatorship, executed Robespierre and his entourage, set up a governing Directory, and ran down the Terror. Pitt, who never accepted Burke's idea of an ideological crusade, was prepared to negotiate with a stable Republican regime, which the Directory might have become. But instead war continued and intensified. The British would not accept French possession of conquered territories, especially in the Low Countries; and Pitt's moderate-sounding war aims – 'security, with just a mixture of indemnification'[82] – were unthinkable for the French. With the war going well, they would not give up the conquests on which the prestige of the Republic and its political and economic stability depended. Realpolitik laced with ideology was enough to cause each to inflict long-term damage on the other by fomenting civil war. There was nothing new in this. French aid to Jacobites had been a feature of previous conflicts, and if Britain had failed to aid Protestant rebels in France, it had been largely due to lack of opportunity. In the 1790s, opportunity abounded. Both sides exaggerated the vulnerability of the other, portrayed as staggering towards a collapse that internal revolt would hasten. Both discerned ideological allies and popular unrest among the enemy, and the idea of exploiting these was energetically, if not always wisely, encouraged by exiles in both Paris and London. The consequence was that both sides ended up helping Catholic peasants abroad, and slaughtering them at home.

The struggle to mobilize France for war in 1793 had met violent resistance, as we have observed. Rural communities were forced to provide large

Revolutionary and Napoleonic Europe, 1795–1815

numbers of men to defend a distant republic whose acts had often disappointed popular feeling and at worst – especially in religious policy – had outraged it. Over the spring of 1793, two-thirds of France saw disturbances. The most serious were in the west. Devotion to the Church, ethnic difference, disputes over land sales, mass conscription, and not least distance from the war zones (hence sparseness of government troops) were a recipe for wholesale insurrection, which became known as 'the Vendée'. It began in April 1793, when rebels seized towns and butchered republican officials. The following month the Girondin faction was expelled from the National Convention, and this, as we have seen, precipitated revolt in Bordeaux, Lyons, Marseilles and Toulon. The south too felt its separateness from Paris; it had suffered economically from the war; and ancient hatred between Catholics and Protestants bedevilled local politics. The expulsion of the Girondins was the last straw. In west and south, rebel leaders looked for external aid.

Across the Atlantic, the Caribbean was as always the great strategic and economic prize. This time, ideology and politics changed everything. Revolution in France led to a conflict for power in the sugar islands between the planter oligarchy and the free mixed-race and freed-slave 'middle class', often themselves slave owners. In 1791 the conflict spread to the huge slave population of Saint-Domingue, and it would eventually cost 200,000 lives. When war broke out with Britain, the French encouraged revolts against British rule, especially in islands recently taken from France such as Grenada, and then, in 1793 and 1794, they proclaimed the liberation of slaves in the hope of winning the support of the vast African majority, and thus preserving control over Saint-Domingue and striking a blow at Britain. By 1795, all the islands hung in the balance, and with them trade, finances, and ability to finance the war.

Britain and Ireland were in a far less incendiary state in 1793 than France or the Caribbean. Before 1790 there was no nationalist movement in Ireland. Political concessions during the American war had opened prospects of economic growth, greater autonomy and reasonable coexistence with Britain. Imperial connections brought commercial benefits. Full Catholic emancipation seemed in the offing. In short, there was 'a general mood of confidence'.[83] War with France gave further reason for conciliating Catholics in order to bolster Irish unity in the face of what one Catholic bishop called 'the diabolical spirit of the Jacobins'.[84] Hence, a militia was established in which Catholics and Protestants served together, and in 1793 Catholic gentlemen were given the vote.

Optimism was misplaced. As in Great Britain, Presbyterians in Ireland – 'a stiff, proud, discontented people' – were drawn to the democratic and anti-Catholic aspects of France's revolution. Belfast paraded on Bastille Day, and small Ulster towns celebrated French victories: 'They were all on the

Americans' side during the American war. Now they are all on the French side.'[85] In Belfast, a group of Presbyterian businessmen set up the Society of United Irishmen in October 1791, which also attracted members of the Catholic gentry, many of whom had links with France through education or military service. Like its counterparts in Britain, the society made fraternal contacts with French revolutionaries. However, it was not a revolutionary society. Its aim was political reform, which it now expected to accelerate. But events in France stimulated a rawer kind of militancy: that of the Defenders, a Catholic secret society born of land hunger and sectarian violence in rural south Ulster in the 1780s. In response to Defenderism, Protestants created the Orange Order in 1790. Wartime hardships aggravated sectarian violence, and Defenderism began to spread across rural Ireland in the millenarian belief that 'the French Defenders will uphold the cause, the Irish Defenders will pull down the British laws'.[86] 'The great majority of the people [are] in favour of the French,' noted a contemporary, even 'in mountains where you could not conceive that any news could reach'.[87]

The British government was chary of French politics. They mistrusted the royalist émigré leaders, whom they found excessively reactionary, quarrelsome, anti-English and unreliable. Neither Bourbons nor Hanoverians forgot that they had been enemies. The foreign secretary Grenville had 'an extremely bad opinion of any scheme the success of which is in the smallest degree to depend on the exertions, or prudence, or means of the French Aristocrates'.[88] However, the Federalists in Marseilles and Toulon asked for British and Spanish aid in July 1793 – a strategic windfall. Admiral Hood's Mediterranean fleet sailed into Toulon, the great Mediterranean naval base, in August. The government was not committed to the Bourbons, for a weakened Republic might offer favourable peace terms. Events in Toulon somewhat forced their hand, for the rebels – royalists and anti-Jacobin republicans – proclaimed the young son of Louis XVI, imprisoned in Paris, as Louis XVII. This, said Pitt, was not 'in all respects as we would wish'. The British kept republican officials and institutions in Toulon in place, and London published a declaration to the French people stating that they would not seek to impose a regime on France, even though they considered that a constitutional (not absolute) monarchy was the best alternative. But Louis XVII's little kingdom could not survive a determined land attack, in which the young Napoleon Bonaparte first made his name. Hood evacuated the port after four months' presence, taking away or burning thirteen French ships of the line and eight frigates – a blow comparable with Trafalgar. It was compounded by the torching of Toulon's huge stocks of shipbuilding timber, which put the dockyard out of action for years. The Federalists fled on British ships or into the hills. The Republic taught another of its lessons: mass executions (in Lyons, some by cannon-fire), and the symbolic obliteration of the rebel cities, which were renamed 'Freedtown', 'Nameless Town', and 'Mountain Port'. The loss of Toulon increased Corsica's importance as a naval base. Under their old leader Pasquale Paoli, the Corsicans asked to join the British empire on the same basis as Ireland, with George III as king of Corsica. This plucky wartime experiment in Enlightenment nation-building – with a parliamentary constitution, trial by jury, religious toleration, and *habeas corpus* – was realized in 1795. Despite good will on both sides there were predictable disagreements. But the outcome was determined by strategy, not politics. Finding the island too hard to defend, the British withdrew at the end of 1796, taking with them 12,000 refugees. Corsica was reoccupied by the French.[89]

In August 1793 the Vendée rebels similarly asked Britain for aid: arms, troops, money and a Bourbon prince to lead them. The government were willing to send money, arms and French *émigré* troops – though not a Bourbon – if the rebels could capture a harbour. They marched north in October to take the port of Granville. This sudden expedition, known as '*la virée de Galerne*', turned into catastrophe: Granville held out, and the rebels, accompanied by their families, suffered horrific losses during their long retreat – 60–70,000 were slaughtered. When British ships arrived, there were no rebels. Aware of British involvement, the Republic reacted ferociously to the Vendéen threat, ordering 'extermination' of the rebels, complete destruction of the countryside, deportation of surviving women and children (one suggestion was to Madagascar), and resettlement with Republican colonists. At Nantes, there were mass executions, including several thousand by drowning. In the countryside, General Turreau's 'hell columns' set out to exterminate opposition by rape, torture, massacre, devastation and famine: 'Burn the mills . . . demolish the ovens . . . If you find peasants or women . . . shoot them, all support our enemies, all are spies.' Wrote one soldier to his father, 'We shoot them every day in batches of 1,500.'[90] Some towns were still uninhabited in 1800.

In spite or because of these reprisals, guerrilla war continued in the west, and 'White Terror' – revenge killings of republican officials and militants – in the south. After the fall of the Jacobin dictatorship in July 1794 an attempt was made to pacify the west: General Lazare Hoche, the regional commander, offered amnesties and cash bounties for disarmament. A peace treaty was signed with the rebel leaders. But in 1795 the British and the royalist leaders reignited the revolt as part of an ambitious plan to defeat the Republic by combining seaborne landings in the west, resistance in the south, and Allied invasion from the east, facilitated as usual by 'Pitt's gold' spread among French generals. On 25 June 1795, 4,500 French royalists enrolled in the British army landed on the Quiberon peninsula to link up with local guerrillas, the Chouans, and secure the area for later British reinforcements. The

Republican authorities sounded the alarm: 'the English (may the very name of that perfidious and ambitious nation make you tremble with horror and indignation) have just vomited onto the coast . . . the wickedest scoundrels who have ever infected their country's soil'.[91] The invaders lost the advantage of surprise by quarrelling and dithering. The royalist gentlemen-soldiers found their Chouan allies uncouth and incomprehensible, 'like Indians'. Hoche used the respite to seal off the peninsula. Amid bad weather which forced British warships out to sea, he overran the landing zone, trapped 9,000 royalists and captured 10 million *livres*' worth of forged money, 20,000 muskets, 150,000 pairs of boots, sides of 'best Irish salt beef' on which his victorious troops feasted, and coffee, a luxury most had never tasted. It was, reported Hoche, 'like the port of Amsterdam'.[92] Over 700 royalists were shot on the spot, many of them ex-officers of the Bourbon navy. This stunned the émigré community in London. Although the British navy had striven under fire to rescue 2,000 French from the beaches, there were inevitable recriminations, even accusations that London had planned the disaster to weaken France.

Neither the royalists nor the British gave up. Despite bad weather and French gunboats, money, weapons and encouragement continued to trickle into western France. This helped to keep resistance alive, even after the original leaders were captured and killed. New plans were drawn up for mass uprisings supported by British troops. In the south, money channelled through Switzerland similarly maintained royalist resistance, which now often took the form of assassination of hundreds of Republican officials and Jacobins. Far more money, reaching to Paris itself, paid for royalist political organizations and propaganda, which threatened to overthrow the Republic. But its beleaguered rulers held on to power through a series of coups between 1795 and 1799, backed by the army. Thus, Britain unwittingly paved the way for the eventual dictatorship of General Bonaparte.

After the Quiberon invasion, the French decided to retaliate, outraged by British incitement of what they saw as savage banditry. Hoche became the driving force behind a plan to invade Britain. He combined Republican zeal with ambition, seeing a chance to end the war at a stroke and establish himself as France's leading general – a primacy he was disputing with Bonaparte. He planned to land criminals in England to cause maximum disorder and violence. More important was a landing in Ireland, 'England's Vendée'. This was being urged by the United Irishmen, whose main intermediaries were the Protestant Dubliner Theobald Wolfe Tone, and Lord Edward Fitzgerald, Jacobin son of the Duke of Leinster. They were alarmed when the French suggested that the Irish might like a Stuart (the elderly Cardinal Duke of York) as ruler – Ireland had changed in five years, let alone in fifty. The United Irishmen had become a republican nationalist movement, principally because of the hardening political situation. Pitt's government failed to bring in Catholic political emancipation – one of several reform measures postponed indefinitely because of the fraught international situation and George III's opposition. The United Irishmen, banned in 1794 for contacts with France, concluded an alliance with the Defenders for a nationwide uprising. The leaders trusted in a French invasion to bring them to power, and to restore order before there could be a peasant revolt against landlords and a sectarian bloodbath.

In December 1796 15,000 men under Hoche sailed from Brest, with another 15,000 ready to follow. As the British had found in Brittany the year before, communication and coordination posed insurmountable problems. Hoche slipped past the Royal Navy under cover of bad weather, but his ships were scattered. The main force – minus Hoche, the only man who knew the plans – reached Bantry Bay in a snowstorm, and found no Irish revolutionaries; indeed, no Irishmen at all. So they went home. This was sensible, even inevitable. But it was another lost opportunity for France to win the Hundred Years War, and for the revolution to knock out its principal enemy. Ireland had few regular troops, and the United Irishmen now had the will and capacity to raise a major insurrection. The panic caused by Hoche's other idea – to land a band of criminals – shows how vulnerable a war-weary Great Britain was too. In February 1797, 1,400 men, some taken from the prisons of western France, and wearing uniforms captured at Quiberon, set off to burn Bristol under the command of an elderly American pirate named William Tate. Winds forced them to Fishguard, in Pembrokeshire, where, famished, they spent their time scouring the countryside for food. They quickly surrendered, tradition has it after spotting a group of Welsh women in red cloaks whom they took for 'a Ridgment of Soldiers . . . and the Lord took from our Enemies the Spirit of War and to him be the Prais'. This fiasco was the last invasion of Great Britain, for which in 1853 Queen Victoria awarded the Pembrokeshire Yeomanry the battle honour 'Fishguard'.[93] Yet it was enough to cause alarm in London and a run on the Bank of England, forcing the government to end the convertibility of paper money into gold. The French had aimed at causing a financial panic like this for half a century, and they managed it with a few hundred bedraggled gaolbirds. They were convinced that it would ruin British credit. Unexpectedly, the paper currency turned out to be economically beneficial.

More serious blows to British self-confidence were the naval mutinies of 1797, when Britain was without allies and dependent on its fleet. In April 1797 the Channel Fleet refused to put to sea, though the mutineers repeatedly promised to do so if there were any movement by the French. After negotiations and major concessions, a settlement was reached with the sailors, and celebrated at Portsmouth with a banquet of mutineers, admirals and civic dignitaries. This encouraged mutineers in the North Sea Fleet at the Nore and Yarmouth, who made further demands. The government now contemplated coercion, while offering to pardon men returning to duty. Much of the public turned against the mutineers, for fear of French invasion. Letters from families urged submission, and suspected mutineers on shore were beaten up. Open conflict threatened, and sailors fought among themselves. On 14 June, the mutiny ended. Over thirty men were hanged, and over 300 received lesser sentences, including flogging and transportation. Contemporaries and later historians have assumed that civilian democratic and anti-war groups influenced the mutineers; moreover, a proportion of sailors were Irish, including suspected republicans drafted into the navy as a precautionary measure. Yet the evidence for political motivation is negligible, and there is substantial evidence to the contrary, including the ostentatiously loyal acts and declarations of most of the mutineers. The mutinies seem essentially to have been large-scale instances of the traditional collective bargaining tolerated in the navy, which included petitions to the Admiralty and Parliament. But discontent was made less controllable by huge wartime expansion, from 16,000 men to 114,000; by inflation reducing the value of sailors' pay; and by the rigours of blockade duty. Though patriotism and loyalism prevailed in the fleet as on shore, discontented minorities remained.[94]

Though Hoche had missed his chance in 1796, the Bantry Bay expedition had terrible consequences. The Dublin government ordered General Lake to disarm Ulster, the main stronghold of the United Irishmen. Wrote one officer, 'I look upon Ulster to be a La Vendée . . . It will not be brought into subjection but by the means adopted by the republicans [in France] – namely spreading devastation through the most disaffected parts.' Murder, torture, and looting showed that this was meant literally – 'every crime, every cruelty that could be committed by Cossacks or Calmucks has been transacted here,' protested General Abercromby, who resigned his command.[95] The United Irish leadership was being rounded up, so they set off rebellion in May 1798, mainly in north-eastern and south-eastern Ireland. The rebels were convinced that this would bring France to their aid. The outcome was horribly similar to the Vendée: a civil war in which religion, socioeconomic grievance and politics engendered genocidal fear, hatred and horrific violence – the outcome the United Irish leaders had hoped French intervention would prevent. The largely Catholic militia and the Protestant yeomanry, with some Scottish and English support, were ordered by Lake to 'take no prisoners', and they duly imitated the savagery of Turreau's hell columns. After a few small battles, most famously Vinegar Hill on 21 June, and many punitive expeditions and vicious skirmishes, the rebellion was stamped out amid massacre, rape, plunder and arson. As Wolfe Tone saw it, 'to their immortal disgrace and infamy the militia and yeomanry of Ireland concur with the English to rivet their country's chains and their own'. They did this to defend Irish property against a revolution of the Irish poor. The Irish elites looked to either France or Britain to maintain the social order. Even if the rebellion and a French invasion had succeeded, argues Brendan Simms, the outcome would have been 'not the end of an old trauma for Catholic Ireland, but the beginning of a new one'. Social, political and religious divisions meant that the rebellion contained opposing revolutionary and counter-revolutionary elements, united only by hostility to Britain. If the British had been defeated, these divisions would have emerged, as on the Continent, with the likely outcome 'a murderous bourgeois secular satellite state, subservient to the needs of French foreign policy', at war with the Catholic church and the Irish peasantry.[96]

When it was too late, in August 1798, 1,000 French soldiers arrived unannounced in the remote north-west of Ireland under General Humbert (who had crushed France's own rebels at Quiberon three years earlier). Jubilant Mayo peasants rallied to the French, but soon little love was lost between them. Humbert and his men, veterans of the real Vendée, found their Irish allies too much like their own peasant enemies – superstitious, dirty and indisciplined – and they executed a few as a sharp lesson. Humbert marched far inland in the hope of restarting the rebellion. He routed Lake's militia, but was met by a large Anglo-Irish force at Ballinamuck on 8 September – the last French battle in these islands. Humbert's 4,000 Irish volunteers, firmly placed in front by the French, were slaughtered, and many of the survivors massacred. The French surrendered and were well treated. Humbert and his officers regaled their British counterparts in Dublin with anecdotes about Irish stupidity. The United Irish leaders were dead, in gaol, awaiting the gallows, or in exile. Prisoners were conscripted into the British and Prussian armed forces, or transported to labour in New South Wales or Prussian coalmines. The lucky ones reached America – missionaries preaching vengeance against England. Others reached France, where they served succeeding regimes: republican, Bonapartist and finally the restored Bourbon. Some lived on in France until the 1860s.

Both sides had done each other permanent damage in these 'internal grapplings'. Neither was devoid of sincerity. Grenville, Burke, William Windham (the Secretary at War) and the controlling agent in Swizerland, Wickham, were sincerely royalist and keen not to abandon their French allies. Hoche and Lazare Carnot, the Jacobin war minister, to name only two, felt similarly genuine concern for Irish liberty. But other priorities, whether military events or embryonic peace negotiations, would cause plans to be postponed, or ships, troops, arms and money diverted to other destinations. Even when seaborne operations were pursued, they were at the mercy of weather and enemy action. Communications and coordination with guerrillas, conspirators and agents were tenuous. British and French ships arrived early, or late, or in the wrong place. In Provence, the Vendée, Ulster and Leinster it was not only material assistance, but the expectation of help that counted. Both British and French were more impressive in their promises than in their delivery. The great 1798 Irish rebellion happened between Hoche's failure and Humbert's failure, but in the firm belief that the French would eventually come. The price was paid by those who started, or got caught up in, rebellion. Knowledge that the enemy was involved increased the ferocity of repression. A modern estimate of the number killed in Ireland in 1798 is 10,000.[97] The total loss of population in the civil war in Western France alone – in combat, from massacres, epidemics, and privation – was 250,000 or more.[98] In both countries, senior commanders representing the central government tried to curtail the violence and offered amnesties, but too late.

Livid emotional and political scars remained. The west and south of France were hotbeds of violence until 1815 and later. Strong support for the Right – Catholic and anti-Republican – lasted well into the twentieth century, constituting one of the deep divides in the ideological and political struggle that has been called 'the Franco–French War'. The consequences for Ireland and Britain were greater still. Optimism and progress were replaced by fear and hatred. The Ulster Presbyterians, who had been the bedrock of the United Irishmen, moved over to the other side of a sectarian divide. A direct consequence of the mess – in which some British politicians and soldiers were horrified by the incompetence and brutality of the Anglo-Irish authorities – was the Act of Union of 1800. This aimed vainly to control and pacify Ireland by abolishing its parliament and government and bringing it into the United Kingdom, and so strengthening the whole against France. As one official argued, 'the French will never cease to intrigue in this kingdom [Ireland]' and 'as we wish to check the ambition of that desperate, and unprincipled power . . . we should be favourable to the principle of union'.[99] But union made the 'Irish question' a perennial issue in British politics, especially as the *quid pro quo* of full Catholic political rights was postponed. As Marianne Eliott sums it up, 'An entire world separated the nineteenth century from those years when Ireland had seemed to be moving towards a gradual resolution of her problems. The French revolution itself may simply have reacted upon the underlying tensions, but it is unlkely that the upheavals which consumed any chance of lasting solutions would have occurred without it.'[100]

From Unwinnable War to Uneasy Peace

The great object . . . was defence in a war waged against most of the
nations of Europe, but against us with particular malignity . . . I had hopes
of our being able to put together the scattered fragments of that great and
venerable edifice [the French monarchy] in the stead of that mad system
which threated the destruction of Europe . . . This, it is true, has been
found unattainable.

WILLIAM PITT in the Commons, November 1801[101]

When war began in 1793, an ideological gulf had already opened between
France and Britain. Yet the cause of the war was conventional and
familiar: control of the Low Countries. It was not, and is not, possible to
make a clear distinction between ideology and realpolitik. This ambivalence
about the nature, causes and aims of war affected contemporaries, and has
divided historians. Pitt was a realist, ready to treat with any French government that was stable and would renounce a policy of revolutionary conquest.
But was any republican regime stable, and could any give up its conquests?
For France to stigmatize Britain as the new Carthage to be destroyed was
both an extreme ideological view and a realistic assessment of Britain's colonial and commerical dominance. French support for revolutions abroad was
an ideological crusade. But it was also an instrument of power, ruthlessly
used. The Republic soon made clear that it would only support revolution
in unfriendly countries, and only help those who could help themselves, as
the Irish discovered to their cost. Even if liberated, the 'sister republics'
found themselves paying for French armies on their soil, fighting France's
wars, and being treated as cultural and political satellites.

French strategy was mainly continental. The collapse of its navy and the
loss of valuable colonies eclipsed its overseas power and trade. Gains in
European territory, treasure and natural resources compensated. Paris heard
the news of the conclusion of a peace treaty with Holland when the French
negotiator rushed into the Committee of Public Safety, threw down a handful
of golden guilders, and proclaimed 'I have brought you a hundred million
of these.' This was one of endless such infusions from the Low Countries,
Germany, and Italy. Belgian towns were still paying off the costs in the 1920s.
Bonaparte rose to power on loot. His famous proclamation to his threadbare Army of Italy defined a whole system: 'Soldiers, you are naked and
hungry; the government . . . can give you nothing . . . I am leading you into
the most fertile plains on earth. Rich provinces and cities will be in your
power; you will find there honour, glory and wealth.' During the first few
months, official booty alone amounted to over 45 million francs in cash and
12 million in bullion – several times the previous annual tax burden.

Bonaparte became the paymaster of the Republic.[102] War had become both self-sustaining and indispensable.

British strategy was subject to diverging assumptions about the war. The least ideological view, consistently represented by Pitt's friend and colleague Henry Dundas, was that in this war, like any other, Britain should advance its own interests and security, and prepare for a negotiated settlement. So it should seize strategic and economic assets in the Caribbean and the Indian Ocean, which would finance the war and ensure an advantageous peace. Dundas argued that 'a compleat success in the West Indies is essential . . . No success in other quarters will palliate a neglect there . . . By success in the West Indies alone you can be enabled to dictate the terms of peace.[103] The greatest military effort was made there, using and losing through disease the core of the army. It kept the sugar trade flowing and supported the huge cost of the war. The opposite view, trumpeted by Burke and consistently urged by Pitt's other most influential colleague, his cousin and foreign secretary Grenville, was that this was no conventional war. The revolution itself had to be defeated, for no secure peace was possible with an unstable 'military democracy' that used subversion and aggression for its own survival and expansion. So the war should concentrate on France itself, by invasions, by aiding internal resistance, by building coalitions of European powers, and if necessary returning colonial conquests to sweeten a Bourbon restoration. In Grenville's view, 'the Jacobin principle has remained unshaken . . . and so it will be, as I believe . . . till the principle itself be attacked and subdued in its citadel at Paris'.[104] Pitt was in the middle, more concerned with the social, political and economic costs of war. British strategy has been criticized as incoherent, with effort being spread too widely; or alternatively defended as the inevitable consequence of stretched commitments, uncertain allies and the changing fortunes of war. Emphasis on maritime or continental strategy alternated, as circumstances dictated. Britain could not defeat France alone, and so had to fit her actions to her allies. But they – most importantly Austrians and Russians – had their own interests, which might better be served by agreement with France. Moreover, they mistrusted Britain. The 'Carthage' image was not for French consumption alone.

In brief, the story of the War of the First Coalition (1793–7) is that of the French armies rolling up opposition on the Continent. Austria and Britain were forced out of the Low Countries; Austria and Spain made peace; and Holland (valuable for its fleet and its wealth) declared war on Britain. The Quiberon invasion, as we have seen, failed in 1795. But Britain seized the Cape of Good Hope, sent powerful forces into the Caribbean, and, in December, made the first peace feelers to France, which came to nothing, and were renewed with no more success in 1796. During 1796 and 1797 Britain's position in Europe worsened: Spain changed sides, and the Royal

Navy left the Mediterranean, abandoning Corsica. Hoche had his near miss at Bantry Bay, the Bank of England suspended its gold payments, and parts of the fleet mutinied. Another attempt was made to negotiate with France, and contemptuously rejected after the coup of Fructidor (4 September 1797) foiled British plans for a royalist takeover in Paris. Austria, Britain's main ally, cut its losses after Bonaparte's advance through Italy and made a deal with France in the Treaty of Campo Formio in October. Within a few months the Republic consisted of a vast block of territory from Holland via the Rhineland and Switzerland to northern Italy. Bonaparte began to assemble an 'Army of England' for his first invasion attempt – the second of four increasingly elaborate projects between 1794 and 1805. Yet things were not as bad for Britain as this bald summary suggests. Control of the oceans, and of colonial trade, was kept, and affirmed by a series of naval victories – most notably over the Spanish in February 1797 at Cape St Vincent and the Dutch in October at Camperdown (won by the recently mutinous Nore fleet), which were occasions of state-sponsored but genuinely popular rejoicings.

In May 1798 Bonaparte tried to break the stalemate. He postponed invasion of England. 'Truly to overthrow England,' he told the Directors, 'we must occupy Egypt.'[105] Using plans drawn up in the 1770s, he sailed with an army in 280 ships from Toulon, seized Malta on the way, and in July defeated a Turkish army at the battle of the Pyramids, making the grandiose proclamation: 'Soldiers, forty centuries are watching you.' This incursion was a historic turning-point in the relationship between the Muslim world and the West. Napoleon intended to capture trade with the Levant, and compensate for the loss of France's sugar islands and British colonial conquests. It opened the possibility of controlling North African food production, greatly increasing France's war-making power. Bonaparte also intended, as the British feared, to make Egypt his base for a land attack on India. Admiral Nelson, in hot pursuit, attacked the French fleet anchored in Aboukir Bay on 1 August 1798 in the Battle of the Nile. Admiral Dupetit-Thouars, his legs smashed by a cannonball, had himself propped up inside a barrel to encourage his men to keep fighting as the British methodically worked their way down the paralysed French line, destroying it ship by ship. It was one of the most complete victories in naval history: eleven out of thirteen battleships were destroyed or captured. Bonaparte and his army were thus cut off in Egypt, but they remained a threat to Turkey and India. A consequence was that the British in India, to pre-empt a French attack, defeated France's abandoned ally Tipu Sultan, the ruler of Mysore, 'a victim', in Pitt's words, 'to his attachment to France'.

Nelson's victory encouraged Austria, Russia and Turkey to risk joining Britain in a Second Coalition in 1798. Pitt, though worried by war weariness, financial strains and food shortages in Britain, agreed to one final effort in 1799 to overthrow the tottering French Republic. This time success seemed certain. The French had vast territories to defend with dwindling manpower. Revolts broke out in all the conquered territories and inside France, with both the West and the South again up in arms; while France's allies in Ireland and Naples were bloodily crushed. British troops prepared another invasion to link up with the Vendée rebels, and the navy mopped up remaining French colonies. The Russians and Austrians were advancing through Italy, Switzerland and Germany. British and Russian troops landed in Holland and captured the Dutch fleet.

This was indeed the final crisis of the Republic, but not in the way the British expected. Bonaparte slipped out of Egypt in a fast corvette, telling a friend, 'If I am lucky enough to get back to France, the reign of the chattering classes is over.'[106] He reached Provence on 9 October 1799. A month later he had seized power in the coup d'état of Brumaire, telling his troops that the politicians were in British pay. He at once offered peace terms, which were promptly rejected by Grenville. The British thought that Bonaparte, on the verge of defeat, was trying to gain time and divide the Coalition: 'the whole game is in our hands now, and it wants little more than *patience* to play it *well, to the end*'.[107] The final push was set for the summer of 1800, when the Allies would march into France from Germany and Italy, and the British army would land in Brittany. But as First Consul, Bonaparte showed himself to be more than just another general. He ended the western rising by force and concession, leaving the British with nowhere to land. He then struck a devastating blow where no one expected it, in Italy, narrowly defeating the Austrians at Marengo on 14 June. Hopes of a Coalition victory vanished in a day. Bonaparte sent a letter to the Austrian Emperor, supposedly written on the field of Marengo 'surrounded by 15,000 corpses', offering peace and blaming the war solely on the greed and selfishness of England – a version that many in Europe found plausible.

It was Britain that faced defeat now. Austria and Russia sought peace. Bonaparte aimed to win over the Russians, telling their envoy that 'we are called to change the face of the world'. He was preparing an alliance with Spain to attack Ireland, Portugal and India. Prussia occupied Hanover, the last British foothold in Europe. Russia, Denmark and Sweden were forming an 'Armed Neutrality' and excluding British ships from the Baltic. Gold reserves were dwindling and bread prices rose to three times their 1798 level. Oxford students were rationed. Others less fortunate starved. A wave of riots tied down a large part of the army. Demands for peace became deafening. Pitt, on the edge of a breakdown, resigned in March 1801 when the king refused to extend equal political rights to Catholics following union of Britain and Ireland. Succeeded by a lesser though competent figure, Henry Addington, Pitt supported the new government's search for peace, which he considered inevitable.

The British now lived their recurring nightmare: a dominant France preparing a Continental attack on British seapower. This had to be pre-empted by what Dundas called 'a shake at the naval strength of the enemy'. He hoped that 'one brilliant act of British enterprise would intervene to check and soften the uniformity of calamity and defeat'.[108] Fortunately for Britain there were two. In March 1801 General Abercromby forced a landing in Egypt and went on to defeat the larger French army – a remarkable success for the despised British. Grenville's brother wrote, 'we appear to have broken that magical invincibility *sur terre* of the great nation'.[109] In April Nelson, at the first battle of Copenhagen, destroyed the Danish fleet, threatened to bombard the city, and forced Denmark to withdraw from the 'Armed Neutrality', whose other members prudently did likewise. Tsar Paul was assassinated, and Russian rapprochement with France halted.

So a compromise peace could be signed at Amiens in March 1802. No agreement in British history, except that of Munich in 1938, has been so vilified and so welcome. As with Hitler at Munich, the hope was that Napoleon would be satisfied with his gains. Britain agreed to return its maritime acquisitions, including the Cape and Malta, whose inhabitants had requested British aid to expel the French. France in effect gave nothing in return. 'We are going fast down the gulf-stream,' wrote Windham, 'and shall never stop, I fear, till, with the rest of Europe, we fall under the universal empire of the great Republic.'[110] Even those who made the treaty regarded it as a sad necessity, precarious and, as the king said, 'experimental'. Peace was publicly supported by most of the naval and military commanders, including Cornwallis, St Vincent and Nelson, who saw no prospect of victory and feared for the morale and discipline of their men. Pitt, as usual, provided calm conviction:

> We have survived the violence of the revolutionary fever. We have seen Jacobinism deprived of its fascination, stripped of the name and pretext of liberty, capable only of destroying, not of building . . . I trust this important lesson will not be thrown away on the world . . . I will venture to predict that [Bonaparte] will not select this country for the first object of his attack; and if we are true to ourselves, we have little to fear from that attack, let it come when it will.[111]

The public was overjoyed. Food prices fell and rioting subsided. When the French envoy General Lauriston (a descendent of John Law) arrived in London with ratification of the preliminary agreement, a jubilant crowd pulled his carriage through the streets. The government itself illuminated public buildings. One critic of the peace admitted 'the real enthusiasm and frantic joy . . . in the faces of every person I met, whether farmer, labourer or manufacturer'. The London Corresponding Society wrote an adulatory letter to Bonaparte declaring their devotion to France and thanking him that 'peace reigns on earth, and this is the work of Frenchmen'. Charles James Fox owned that 'the Triumph of the French government over the English does in fact afford me a degree of pleasure which it is very difficult to disguise.'[112] The French people rejoiced too. When the British ambassador arrived in Calais, he was greeted by cheering crowds, a band playing 'God Save the King', and a delegation of market women with a present of fish. He noted on the road to Paris the 'misery and poverty' of the peasants.[113] More than a century of Franco-British struggle thus ended with Britain intact but France victorious, with her power in Europe established to an extent that Louis XIV had never attained.

THE FIRST KISS THIS TEN YEARS!

> Lords, lawyers, statesmen, squires of low degree,
> Men known, and men unknown, sick, lame, and blind,
> Post forward all, like creatures of one kind,
> With first-fruit offerings crowd to bend the knee,
> In France, before the new-born Majesty.
> WILLIAM WORDSWORTH, 'Calais, August, 1802'

The peace boosted Bonaparte's reputation in Britain. Gillray's un-martial Britannia, quivering to be seduced, is Charles James Fox in drag. He was one of many political personalities (including eighty-two MPs and thirty-one peers) who went to see the charismatic dictator. Many were impressed. Fox, however, found him rather a dull fellow, which by Fox's exacting standards of amusement (wit, wine, women, horses and cards) he undoubtedly was. Though Bonaparte was a gambler, it was for infinitely higher stakes. Fox considered him 'considerably intoxicated by success' and realized, as did many visitors of all political persuasions, that France had become a dangerously powerful military dictatorship.

Ordinary tourists streamed across the Channel, as after previous wars. All wanted to see what post-revolutionary France was like. They noticed ruined churches and chateaux, and lots of soldiers. Some thought French manners had become 'abrupt and familiar'. The eighteen-year-old Lord Aberdeen, in military uniform, was 'hissed', and he found French people, though generally 'obliging', as gloomy as the 'Scotch'. Many visitors – according to French cartoonists – made straight for the new *restaurants*. A few sought out compatriots who had stayed on in France during the war. One was a Mr Thompson,

The first Kiss this Ten Years! — or — the meeting of Britannia & Citizen François

who looked after the elephant in the zoo. More famous was Tom Paine, who had kept busy writing propaganda and drawing up invasion plans. But after a tiff with Bonaparte, his hope of becoming head of a British Republic had evaporated, and he was drowning his sorrows in Paris. The end of the blockade allowed him to slip safely away to America, to fantasize in peace about an invasion of England. Artists, including Turner, made for the Louvre, crammed with captured booty. Some 3,000 French visitors travelled to Britain, though as usual with more practical concerns. Some came to report on British industrial progress, and were astonished at the changes. One French agent renewed pre-war contacts with John Wilkinson and James Watt. Others went for private business reasons, such as the famous balloonist and pioneer parachutist, André-Jacques Garneri, who planned to give displays; and Madame Tussaud, who brought waxworks of Napoleon and Josephine, and a collection of revolutionary horrors – including Robespierre's death mask, a guillotine, and a waxwork of Marat stabbed in his bath.[114]

CULTURE WARS

Britain owes a considerable part of its 'national heritage' directly to the French revolution and Napoleon. Revolutions are a godsend to the art world: 'bliss indeed was it to be a collector in that dawn, but to be a dealer was very heaven'.[115] Men with money and others keen to help them spend it – one of the shrewdest a young Scottish law student named William Buchanan – developed a sudden passion for art. In 1792 the Duc d'Orléans sold his family's collection of 400 pictures, considered the world's greatest in private hands, including multiple works attributed to Leonardo, Michelangelo, Raphael, Titian, Rembrandt, Correggio, Tintoretto, Veronese, Rubens, Velasquez and many others. They went for 1.2 million *livres* (£52,000) to the banker Laborde (the admirer of Captain Cook) – a 'panic price'. Laborde shipped the pictures to England – a suspicious act, which may have contributed to his subsequent arrest and execution. World events did not encourage buyers, and the whole was eventually bought cheaply for £43,000 by a syndicate led by the Duke of Bridgewater, who kept the best for themselves and almost covered their costs by selling off the rest. Lesser French collections were also sold in London, including that of the émigré ex-minister Calonne. Lord Yarmouth bought works in Paris for the royal collection and started what later became the Wallace Collection. Furniture, sculpture and porcelain (including an incomplete Sèvres service for Louis XVI, which was planned to take twenty years to make) also crossed the Channel, and some

Marble metope: The French revolution and the Napoleonic Wars brought a flood of art treasures to Britain.

of the finest is now at Windsor Castle. In 1796, Bonaparte rampaged through Italy levying huge contributions in cash and in hundreds of named works of art. Princely families were forced to sell their collections to pay the French. Most of what was not taken for the Louvre came to London, especially paintings, as Bonaparte was mainly interested in sculpture. The same happened on a smaller scale in Spain and Germany.[116] In both France and Britain, the public display of works, including those privately owned, became a demonstration of individual patriotism and of national prestige.

The treasure hunt extended beyond Europe. Napoleon's 1798 Egyptian invasion was cultural as well as military, with 160 scientists and artists forming an Institute under his patronage to carry out 'a veritable conquest . . . in the name of the arts'.[117] The Rosetta stone, the key to understanding Egyptian hieroglyphics, was their greatest archaeological find. When the French army surrendered, they were allowed to keep their notes and specimens of insects and animals, but not manuscripts or antiquities. General Menou tried to keep the Rosetta stone, but it was seized amid the jeers of French troops by a British detachment commanded by a keen antiquarian colonel, who took it to the British Museum. British and French scholars competed subsequently to decipher it. The French consoled themselves by publishing a multi-volume *Description de l'Egypte* (1809–22), and in the 1830s obtained the Luxor obelisk, now in the Place de la Concorde. Meanwhile, the British had beaten the French to Assyrian antiquities.

The greatest cultural tussle took place in Greece. The French ambassador appointed in 1783, the Comte de Choiseul-Gouffier, was an avid collector, and he instructed his agent, the artist Fauvel, to 'Take away everything you can. Miss no opportunity to pillage Athens and its territory of all that is pillageable.'[118] Covetous eyes had long been cast on the statues, external panels and internal frieze of the Parthenon itself. Though seriously damaged by wars and vandalism, and increasingly dilapidated by illegal sale of fragments of sculpture to tourists, this was not yet 'pillageable' on a large scale, though Fauvel managed to acquire fallen pieces, now in the Louvre. War provided a new opportunity. The Ottoman empire needed British help against the French, and the young ambassador Lord Elgin attained an unprecedented position of favour. He and his agents were given permission to enter the Acropolis to make drawings and casts, to excavate, and to 'take away any sculptures or inscriptions'. The original intention was not to remove pieces from the building, but this gradually began, with the negligent acquiescence of the Turkish authorities. Elgin, using his own initiative and money, was spurred on by the accelerating damage being done to the sculptures, and by knowing that the French were after them too. He decided to remove as much as he could. Appropriately, he used equipment, including a huge cart, made by Choiseul-Gouffier for that very purpose. He was not a connoisseur: his attitude was similar to that of Napoleon – that this was a question of national (and personal) prestige. In August 1801 his chaplain reported that 'these admirable specimens . . . which have repeatedly been refused to the gold and influence of France in the zenith of her power' were on board ship. By June 1802, Lady Elgin was confident that 'We yesterday got down the last thing we want from the Acropolis so now we may boldly bid defiance to our enemies.'[119] The end of the Franco–Turkish war and the return of French diplomatic influence came just too late. Much that had not been removed was subsequently defaced or stolen by swarms of souvenir hunters. Elgin, travelling home through France, was arrested and interned when war resumed in 1803, and was treated with some rigour. He believed that Napoleon was trying to force him to cede his collection to France. The finest part was still in Athens, and French agents – now allies of Turkey – were determined to get hold of it. They succeeded with some small pieces, which they dispatched overland to the Louvre, where they remain; but the huge marbles could only be moved by sea, where the French were powerless. Another reversal of alliances enabled Elgin to ship over fifty heavy cases of marbles during 1810 and 1811. These included the best of the Parthenon sculptures. The one intact panel secured by the French was captured at sea by the Royal Navy, and is now also in the British Museum. Elgin was violently denounced for vandalism and theft, most famously by Byron, lover of Greece and admirer of Napoleon. Elgin's marriage collapsed and the family was ruined for two generations by the huge expenses he had incurred, which an ungrateful nation refused to defray. To escape his creditors, he spent his last years in France.

CHAPTER 6

Changing the Face of the World

I am destined to change the face of the world; at least, I believe so.

NAPOLEON BONAPARTE, 1804[1]

We must recollect . . . what it is we have at stake, what it is we have
to contend for. It is for our property, it is for our liberty, it is for our
independence, nay for our existence as a nation; it is for our character,
it is for our very name as Englishmen; it is for everything dear and valuable
to man on this side of the grave.

WILLIAM PITT in the Commons, 22 July 1803[2]

Napoleonic Visions

I wanted to rule the world – who wouldn't have in my place?
CHARLES MAURICE DE TALLEYRAND[4]

NAPOLEON BONAPARTE, 1815[3]

One single man was alive in Europe then; all other beings tried to fill
their lungs with the air he had breathed.
ALFRED DE MUSSET

What a pity the man wasn't lazy.
CHARLES MAURICE DE TALLEYRAND[4]

Napoleon Bonaparte is the last Frenchman to have transformed British and world history. He forced Britain into its greatest sustained effort in war, which would leave it the major global power for more than a century. His reign marked the apogee of the period in which France came close to becoming the hegemonic power of the European continent, and, potentially, of the planet. His admirers compared him to Alexander, Caesar and Charlemagne. We might prefer comparisons with more recent pretenders to world power, Hitler and Stalin, at least in that his rise from obscurity, deeds, misdeeds, and rejection of limit testify to an exceptional and flawed personality. But he was much more intelligent and creative than they, and vastly more competent, the army being a better school for dictators than beer-hall rallies and party committees. Though ruthless, a bully, and a 'walking laboratory of complexes and neuroses',[5] he was far less cruel, and was capable of love, friendship, and forgiveness. He was too arrogant to be vain, and too disdainful to be vindictive – or so he liked to appear. But he was sensitive to criticism or mockery, blamed others for his failures, and had in full measure the Great Man's self-righteousness and finally self-pity.[6]

His ideas were the commonplaces of the late eighteenth century, and more precisely, of a radical, authoritarian interpretation of the Enlightenment. He had imbibed the fashionable culture of his youth. For a time he worshipped Rousseau; he had a shot at an English-style gothic novel about the Earl of Essex; he adored Macpherson's kitsch pseudo-bardic Ossian, and commissioned a huge, hallucinatory *Dream of Ossian* from Ingres for his never-occupied Roman palace. Like many *philosophes*, he idolized the philosopher-soldier-king Frederick the Great. He admired Abbé Raynal's best-selling attack on European (and especially British) imperialism – 'Englishmen, you have abused your victory. This is the moment for justice or for vengeance.'[7] He liked to parade his intellectual interests – literally, for he had a mobile campaign library mounted on a gun carriage. Improving mankind by sweeping away the dross of the past was his platitudinous aim.

But far from being in the grip of an ideology, he had no precise object, other than his own ever-widening power, in pursuit of what he believed was his historic destiny. He could act in a pragmatic and opportunist manner, with a mind 'blunt, chancy, and wild'.[8] But he had no fulfilment, and nowhere to stop. Deep down, he was aimless.

The Corsican patriotism of the young Nabuleone di Buonaparte and his detestation of the French – invaders who, in his words, were 'spewed up on our coasts, drowning the throne of freedom in a tide of blood' in 1769, the year he was born – were increased by his miserable experience from the ages of nine to fourteen at a military college at Brienne, in bleak Champagne, where he was lonely, aggressive, mocked and snubbed.[9] This privilege of noble status, with a scholarship, was won by his father's collaboration with the French, and, according to rumour, his mother's horizontal collaboration with the French governor. His ambition to be a Corsican leader was squashed by political quarrels on the island in the 1790s which forced the Buonapartes, vilified as traitors, to seek refuge in Toulon, weeks before it called in the British in 1793. Napoleon found himself committed to the urban elite against the peasant masses, to Jacobinism against counter-revolution, and to France against England: 'since one must take sides, one might as well choose the side which is victorious, the side which devastates, loots and burns . . . It is better to eat than be eaten.'[10] His Corsican background may explain why his vision was never truly francocentric. France and the French were the expendable resources of European, Mediterranean and global ambitions. The axis of his Empire ran from Italy, via the Rhone and Rhine, to the Low Countries and north-western Germany, based on cities, often surrounded by a hostile countryside. It has often been pointed out – including by Napoleon himself – that this was Charlemagne's Europe, as if to confer legitimacy on a collection of conquests. Recently, Napoleon has been hailed as a prophet of the European Union: 'there is not enough sameness among the nations of Europe'.[11] But this overlooks his maritime and imperial ambitions in the Middle East, the Americas, India and the Pacific.

There is a famous story that he led his fellow pupils at Brienne in a great snowball battle, thus demonstrating precocious military leadership. In fact, he was rather a swot, quiet and good at maths. Though he certainly possessed the qualities of a great general – accurately summing up his strengths as 'will, character, application and daring' – his early career as an artillery officer showed lack of interest in professional minutiae. He was rarely a military innovator, but an effective user of other people's ideas.[12] The army was his instrument, not his passion. He was always a political soldier, and he tried to apply military methods to politics, society and economics: authority, regulation, efficiency and discipline were his watchwords. He was useless in normal politics, unable to organize and lead without overt coercion.[13] He believed that, after the catastrophe of the revolution, Europe welcomed the imposition of law and order: 'the world begged me to govern it'.[14] Much of it did. But there was a high price: as well as being run like an army, Europe became a vast recruiting ground for an endless war. Enforcing conscription was the primary task of the Empire, and the main reason for extending its efficient bureaucracy.

Napoleon realized that the horrors of the 1790s had discredited democracy. But they had certainly not eradicated the revolution: its abolition of feudal privilege, sale of Church lands, guarantee of equality under the law, and rational administration created powerful economic and political interests that feared a return to anything like the Old Regime. Napoleon offered a seductive deal: both the ending and the consolidation of the revolution. 'My policy is to govern men as most of them want to be governed. That, I think, is the way to recognize popular sovereignty.'[15] His regime would be a meritocratic amalgamation of the old and new, rejecting the extremes of revolution and counter-revolution, and happy to offer careers to former revolutionaries and former royalists, with few questions asked. Though political rights were suppressed, individual liberties (especially those of property) were mostly respected. The empire was not a reign of terror: it held only about 2,500 political prisoners – vastly fewer than the Jacobin Republic. It demanded only obedience. Its strongest supporters, both in France and in the satellite states, were those who had done well out of the revolution: land buyers, certain business interests, career soldiers, professional administrators, ideological enemies of the old order, and religious minorities. Its strongest opponents were those for whom modernized government meant taxes, impoverishment, dispossession, sacrilege and above all the conscription of hundreds of thousands of men – the new serfs of the revolution.

The question of life and death for so many was why Napoleon never brought about the promised and longed-for peace. Critics have always blamed 'the Corsican ogre' personally: parvenu vanity and the intoxication of being hailed as one of the Great Men of history led him into insatiable aggrandizement, dethroning monarchs, crowning his relatives, proclaiming himself the heir of Charlemagne, remaking Europe and bringing kings, pope and princes to heel. Some of his closest collaborators, such as the ex-bishop Talleyrand and the ex-Terrorist Fouché, eventually concluded that he was out of control. Admirers of Napoleon – and he himself – claimed that he was forced into war to defend the revolution, above all against 'the English merchant aristocracy',[16] avid for profit and willing to pay the forces of reaction to destroy the revolution and restore the iniquities of the Old Regime. 'All my wars came from England.' So a key to unlocking the Napoleonic period is his relationship with Britain. Who was the aggressor? What was the source of their deadly struggle?

Napoleon had a complex relationship with an imaginary Britain he never knew. Corsican patriots had hoped for British protection. One of Napoleon's pieces of juvenile fiction is a Corsican adventure with an English hero. He studied British history, and furthermore learnt that of his own island from James Boswell's *Account of Corsica*. He even considered a career in the Royal Navy (his military college considered that he would make 'an excellent sailor', presumably because of his brains and lack of social graces). But he did not learn any English until St Helena. He thought in the anglophobe (and occasionally anglophile) clichés built up over a century of rivalry. England and France together could 'rule the world'; but otherwise the 'tyrant of the seas' had to be destroyed for the good of all. England was Carthage, a nation of shopkeepers (a phrase he picked up from Adam Smith), whose insatiable greed aimed to monopolize the globe. But its power, built on bluff and paper credit, was a house of cards. He enlivened these clichés with a venom of his own, but could also express conventional admiration for the 'enlightened' English people. François Crouzet points out that little of Napoleon's own time and energy was focused directly on the struggle against Britain.[17] After his final defeat in 1815 he hoped to settle in England as a country gentleman. These wavering notions give no insight into his actions.

Every would-be controller of Europe since the eighteenth century has sooner or later had to deal with the peripheral powers, Russia and Britain: to coexist, to exclude or to conquer. Russia, because of its vast territory and population. Britain, because of its ability to mobilize the world against the Continent. Napoleon tried to strike a deal with Russia; never with Britain. The time of decision, from which there was no turning back, was 1801 to 1803, the period of peace. The Treaty of Amiens (March 1802) – the sixth Franco-British peace since 1688 – is conventionally dismissed as a transparent subterfuge to allow the combatants to draw breath for the next bout. This is misleading, and it obscures responsibility for the renewal of war. Most of Europe – and most Frenchmen and Britons – had greeted peace with relief. France's primacy from the Baltic to the Mediterranean was accepted. Austria had dropped out of the contest. Russia was willing to make a deal. Prussia and Bavaria were junior partners. The smaller states were satellites. Britain was ready to bow out of Europe for the foreseeable future, even abandoning the Low Countries, bloodily defended as a vital interest for centuries. Indian outposts and the strategic Cape of Good Hope were being handed back to France and its satellite Holland. In short, as Bonaparte realized, France had won.

He could have stopped there. Instead, he issued 'a ceaseless, implacable river of orders'.[18] He forced through a 'massive territorial revolution'[19] in Germany and remodelled Italy (with himself as president of the new Italian Republic). Instead of relaxing his grip on Switzerland and Holland, as the

Lonely and good at maths: the boy who would conquer Europe.

British thought he had agreed, new constitutions were imposed on both, confirming them as French dependencies. The aim seemed to be to exclude British influence and trade, and increase France's political and military power: peace was breaking out, yet the satellite states were being militarized. French actions overseas were equally disquieting. An expedition was sent to reconquer Saint-Domingue, independent under the former slave Toussaint Louverture, with whom the British were about to conclude a treaty. He was captured and brought to France, where he died after ill-treatment. Slavery was again legalized. The intention to re-invade Egypt was openly announced, for 'some unfathomable reason that made sense only to the First Consul'.[20] A small expedition was sent to India, with orders to prepare for a future conflict by building alliances with local rulers and recruiting Indian troops (there were seven generals and many NCOs in the party). Louisiana was regained from Spain. Territory ('Napoleonland', of course) was claimed in Australia. A naval building programme was ordered, with compulsory Spanish participation. Bonaparte further increased tension by a gratuitously aggressive and blustering style, which he ordered his diplomats to emulate. He insisted that the British government prevent criticism and satire aimed at him and his family in the press – a matter he took extremely seriously. As a sop, a leading émigré journalist, Jean-Gabriel Peltier, was prosecuted in London for criminal libel of the First Consul, and the judge directed the jury to convict him.[21] This proved, thought the pugnacious journalist William Cobbett, that the British were 'a beaten and a conquered people'.

Both sides did want to keep the peace, but they had a totally different understanding of what this required. The British thought it meant negotiating towards an acceptable general settlement. Bonaparte thought it meant insisting on the letter of the treaty while constantly manoeuvring to gain more – 'he could not stop himself from cheating'.[22] Gradually, the British decided that they would not allow this to continue. They had two sticking points: removing French troops from Holland, and keeping Malta, whose great fortified harbour was the key to the Mediterranean, out of French hands. These were sensitive strategic matters – the former for the security of Britain, the latter for that of Egypt and hence India – but they also became important as a test of intentions. Bonaparte had a two-hour talk with the ambassador Lord Whitworth on 21 February 1803, in which he 'frequently [flew] from one subject to another', and gave 'very few opportunities for saying a word'. The gist was that he did not want another war because he had already won, but that he would make no concessions. Pitt read this as meaning that 'we must soon accept avowedly to receive the law from him, or to encounter war'.[23]

As a warning that they were serious, the British announced limited defensive measures. Napoleon accused them of preparing to renew the conflict, and on 13 March 1803 he publicly threatened Whitworth at a reception at the Tuileries: 'The English want war, but if they are the first to draw the sword, I shall be the last to sheath it.'[24] Whitworth thought that this was not a serious threat, and that Bonaparte was just being boorish. But both sides were raising the stakes, and, dangerously, both had some reason to hope the other was bluffing. Whitworth reported that Bonaparte did not want war yet, and that everywhere there was 'gloomy discontent and despondency'. He also noted that British visitors, 'who disgrace the name and character of Englishmen', were assuring the French that London's warnings were mere bluster. The French ambassador in London was conveying a similar message.[25] Finally, in April 1803 London presented an ultimatum: it would accept recent French acts in Italy and Switzerland if Bonaparte withdrew his troops from Holland and agreed to a temporary British presence in Malta. Talleyrand tried to drag out discussions, but without conceding the British demands, and so Whitworth left Paris on 12 May. Britain declared war on the 18th, and that same day there were naval skirmishes off Brest.

The French blamed the British, accusing them of breaking the treaty over Malta. Many historians (especially French ones) still take that line. Recent studies agree that the responsibility was Bonaparte's, because he had a choice: he was not being threatened and he could have opted for peace. Had he done so, Europe could have had 'at least a decade or two' of calm.[26] His motives remain an enigma. The arrogance of 'new born Majesty' – he was still only thirty-three? Ambitions of world empire? The impatience of 'the last Enlightened Despot' to modernize Europe? Obsessive anglophobia? All have been suggested. His defenders argue that he knew that a frustrated and insatiable Britain was bound to renew the war, and that he was merely preparing for the inevitable. Thus historians still chew over the polemics of the 1800s. Did Bonaparte not know that Britain had slashed military and naval spending, stood down the militia, laid off dockyard workers and discharged half its army and navy?[27] War came because his behaviour in 1803 exemplified a pattern followed to the end of his career: every advantage gained was a step towards the next escalation. He was the ultimate embodiment of eighteenth-century power politics, which the revolution had torn free of conventional restraints. He had literally no conception of a peaceful settlement. Whatever was going on in that capacious brain, the result is plain: 'Just as 1939 was Hitler's war . . . so all the wars after 1802 were Bonaparte's wars.'[28]

Earth's Best Hopes? British Resistance, 1803–5

If for Greece, Egypt, India, Africa,
Aught good were destined, thou wouldst step between.
England! all nations in this charge agree:
But worse, more ignorant in love and hate,
Far – far more abject is thine Enemy:
Therefore the wise pray for thee, though the freight
Of thy offences be a heavy weight:
Oh grief that Earth's best hopes rest all with Thee!
WILLIAM WORDSWORTH, October 1803

The Channel is a ditch that will be crossed when someone has the boldness to try it.
NAPOLEON BONAPARTE, November 1803[29]

England has saved herself by her exertions, and will, as I trust, save Europe by her example.
WILLIAM PITT at the Guildhall, 9 November 1805, three days after the news of Trafalgar[30]

Britain's declaration of war appalled ordinary people on both sides of the Channel, who foresaw years more of hunger, taxation, conscription and impressment. In Britain, seamen sought jobs in coalmines and quarries.

Landsmen grumbled and sometimes rioted when ballots for militia service were ordered. In France, boys took the traditional desperate remedies of self-mutilation or flight. Many realized that both countries faced a deadly war of attrition. The prime minister, Addington, privately – and accurately – reckoned on another twelve years: Britain would remain on the defensive and control the seas; Napoleon would have to try to invade and would fail; and then Britain could create a new anti-French coalition – the usual scenario.[31] British ministers were remarkably confident that France would crack first.

In neither country would the ordeal reignite the troubles of the 1790s. France was quiescent and well policed, and propaganda blamed the war on Britain. The military and bureaucratic machine did not require the turbulent enthusiasm of the 1790s. In Britain, opponents of war no longer pursued the mirage of revolution. French aggression, particularly the violation of Rousseau's republican Switzerland, and atrocities carried out in Egypt, broke the spell, except for beleaguered radicals, celestial millenarians and palpitating power-worshippers. Wordsworth's doleful conclusion that England, with all its faults, was the best hope led him to join the militia.

The renewal of war led to Napoleon being proclaimed Emperor of the French in 1804 in order to strengthen the regime. The new Caesar decided to follow the example of Julius and invade England, and was delighted when Roman coins were found near his camp. His was to be the most formidable of the many invasions France prepared.[32] It was paid for by new taxes and the sale of Louisiana to the United States – the money coming in instalments through Barings of London, who were able to lend it to the British en route. Napoleon concentrated 165,000 men in six camps and seven harbours from Etaples to Antwerp, with the main force at Boulogne. Any point from Sussex to Suffolk was in striking distance. Before war broke out he had started building 2,500 gunboats and specially designed landing-craft for the beaches: 'money is not a problem'.[33] Boatyards as far inland as Paris and Strasbourg were busy. Donations flooded in from a people eager to defeat the national enemy, and sponsor a boat carrying their name – a ramped gunboat for 110 men and two horses cost around 20,000 francs. Napoleon was characteristically attentive to detail. Magazines, barracks and hospitals were built. Guide-interpreters were recruited, many of them Irish. Former galley slaves were summoned to give advice on rowing at sea, and Napoleon, after having his Guard practise on the Seine, drew up a drill book: 'paddle firm', 'ship oars', 'beach'. The troops rehearsed embarkation. There were morale-building ceremonies, for example a mass distribution of the Légion d'Honneur by the new emperor himself, on his birthday, 15 August 1804, with 60,000 men present. The effect was somewhat spoilt when British warships close to shore chased some French boats aground. The heavily armed landing-craft proved barely seaworthy. In July 1804 he overruled his

'The Coffin Expedition': many of Napoleon's naval officers feared precisely this.

admirals' warnings and ordered embarkation practice in heavy weather. Thirty boats sank or were driven ashore. Exaggerated reports of the number drowned caused jubilation in England, but Napoleon was unabashed, and remained determined to invade before his coronation. The geographical problems that had hampered Richelieu sixty years before were worked on by Napoleon's engineers. His main base, Boulogne – 'the worst port in the Channel' – became mud at low tide, leaving the boats high and dry. After months of building and practising, they managed to get only 100 boats to sea each high tide. So the boats had to be moored a mile offshore, exposed to the weather and the British, and laboriously protected by forts and horse artillery galloping along the strand.

Napoleon was never deterred by physical barriers – mountains, deserts, storms, heat, cold, distance. He saw crossing the Channel as essentially the same as crossing a wide river. He could actually see into England, 'the houses and the bustle', hence his famous remark about the 'ditch'. He insisted it was possible, though risky, to cross without battleship cover in the small craft – a swarm of 'flies with terrible stings'.[34] He assured the Prussian ambassador that 'foggy weather and some luck will make me master of London, of parliament and of the Bank of England'.[35] There was no need for the balloons, tunnels or submarines that enthusiasts suggested. Napoleon disliked gadgets. The American inventor Fulton, whose mini-submarine was turned down by the French, went to hawk his 'catamarans' (torpedoes) to the British, who used them to attack the French invasion barges.

Experience proved that at least seven days of favourable weather would be needed to assemble the invasion fleet and get across,[36] not the single night during which Napoleon had originally hoped to attack by stealth. So in May 1804 he accepted that a covering force of big ships was desirable. As with every earlier scheme, this required a concentration of the navy to win temporary local superiority over a scattered British fleet. Napoleon thought up a series of rapidly changing schemes, all supposing considerable incompetence on the British side and an accumulation of luck on his. He finally decided that Admiral de Villeneuve's Toulon fleet should escape from the Mediterranean, sail to meet other ships in the Caribbean, and then, assuming the British would be chasing them all over the Atlantic, speed back to rendezvous with the Spanish and the Brest fleets, 'come up the Channel and appear before Boulogne', and escort the army triumphantly to England. As always, the French assumed that if they could only land they would trample over any defence forces and take London quickly. Perhaps they were right. Yet the stakes were higher than in the past, when (as in 1745 or even 1779) the defencelessness of England meant that the French could consider an invasion with quite small forces. Now it meant gambling the best part of the army in a highly risky adventure, which Napoleon would have to command in person: 'If you send [another general] and he succeeds, he will be greater and more powerful than you.'[37] But failure would destroy Napoleon and his regime, and leave France open to invasion from the east.

As with earlier projected invasions, there seems to have been no clear plan for Britain. Did Napoleon, as Pitt said, threaten 'our existence as a nation', 'our character', 'our very name as Englishmen'? In literal terms, no: it was the smaller states on France's borders – Switzerland, the Low Countries, Piedmont – that faced oblivion. England's immediate danger was of a bloodbath, of which later events in Calabria, Spain and Russia suggest the possible extent. A hardened French army primed with anglophobe propaganda and with no means of retreat would have been opposed by a horde of largely amateur soldiers and a whole society determined to resist. All French invasion plans promised a quick military knock-out, but raised the problem of what to do afterwards. Napoleon asserted that 'a declaration of democratic principles' would create 'a disunion sufficient to paralyse the rest of the nation'; he would be 'a liberator, a new William of Orange'. Once London was taken, 'a powerful political party would be created against the oligarchy'.[38] British resistance and the credit of the City would collapse, and Napoleon would dictate peace from Windsor Castle. But one of Napoleon's more astute marshals warned that 'victory will have no result unless you intend to imitate William the Conqueror'.[39] In other words, the conquest would have to be made permanent. This would have required extended occupation, the break-up of the United Kingdom, destruction of its naval power, annexation of colonies, diversion of trade, a huge indemnity, the consequent implosion of the Industrial Revolution and impoverishment of the rapidly growing population. Ireland might have become a favoured satellite, like Poland, administered by a Patriot junta under the authority of an imperial marshal or relative, and graciously allowed to lavish its blood and treasure on Napoleon's cause. There would have been plenty of confiscated land to reward imperial dukes and princes. 'England was . . . bound to become a mere appendix of France,' Napoleon later reflected, 'one of our islands, just like Oléron or Corsica.'[40]

The palpable danger – on clear days French troops could be seen drilling, and panicky residents deserted Eastbourne and Colchester – caused a surge of activity unparalleled until 1914 and 1940. People were resolute, but not necessarily confident. Diaries show that some had nightmares about invasion, and rumours that the French had landed were frequent. Neighbours gathered 'at their doors in the evening to talk over the rebellion of '45, when the rebels reached Derby, and even listened at intervals to fancy they heard the French . . . cannon'. Coast-watching, beacon-building and spy-hunting multiplied.[41] By 1804, 380,000 men had joined the Volunteers in the 'greatest popular movement of the Hanoverian age'.[42] It was largely a spontaneous local phenomenon, not something the government, doubting the capacities of volunteer units, had planned. But Pitt, returning to office, wanted to go along with the popular tide and demonstrate the breadth of support for national defence. Citizens had a right to bear arms, and this was taken as a sign of trust by the government. In some localities, every able-bodied man was drilling, some armed only with pikes. A Levy en Masse Act was passed, a clear sign of French influence, at least in terminology. But there was a fundamental difference: Britain was unique in relying largely on volunteers; there was never conscription into the regular army. Mass volunteering is certainly a proof of patriotic solidarity. But it was above all *local* patriotism, and was not wholly disinterested. In volunteer units, which were remarkably egalitarian and independent, men remained civilians in uniform, commanded by their neighbours, able to go home when they had had enough, and vocal in defence of their rights and their pay. The regular army was shunned by respectable English workers: between June and December 1803, recruiting sergeants scouring the country could induce only 3,481 men to enlist.[43] That so much manpower was engaged in home defence meant that the regular army was always far shorter of men than the French.

Still, the outcome is astonishing. By 1805, about 800,000 men were doing some form of armed service – 20 per cent of the active male population. This is comparable with the 'total wars' of the twentieth century, and was a far higher proportion than in any other country – the government calculated that France had only 7 per cent.[44] Organization depended on the 'old regime' system of amateur local government: lords lieutenant (at least one of whom relied on his wife as secretary), justices of the peace, parsons and parish officers. The system began to buckle under the strain, but its achievement testifies to the strength and initiative of local communities, which remained the bedrock of British governance until the 1930s. This low-key mobilization is often considered an archaic sign of weakness compared with the mass propaganda and compulsion of France's 'total war' effort. It would be better seen as the deliberately 'anti-total' precursor of the way liberal states would fight in the twentieth century.

NO COMMON WAR

No common war we wage – our *native land*
Is menac'd by a murderous, ruthless band;
The Throne and Altar by their Chief o'erturned,
And at his feet one half the prostrate world!
'Plunder, and Rape, and Death's' the hostile cry,
'Fire to your towns – to Britons slavery!'
 Britons, strike home! Avenge your Country's cause,
 Protect your KING, your LIBERTIES, and LAWS![45]

Certain themes were staples of a huge British propaganda campaign. The constitution protected the rights of rich and poor alike, whereas a Napoleonic conquest would deprive the poor of everything: roast beef and even bread and cheese would be replaced by black bread and *soupe-maigre*. French law and language would be imposed. The revolution, even under Napoleon, was an enemy of Christianity. Invasion would bring pillage and rape – a reiterated fear: 'He promises to enrich his soldiers with our property: To glut their lust with our wives and daughters.'[46] Given the conduct of French armies in Hanover and Italy, this was, if lurid, scarcely fanciful. Napoleon's own deeds in Egypt were emphasized: the massacre of 2,000 Turkish prisoners, and the poisoning of some of his own plague-stricken troops. Alarm was balanced by confidence: history presaged victory, as at Agincourt and Blenheim. *Henry V* played to excited audiences in London. Songs and cartoons portrayed Napoleon as both sinister and absurd, drawing on conventional francophobe mockery.

 Across the Channel, a similar diet of songs, cartoons, poems and exhortations prepared for the effort of invasion. Amiens erected a triumphal arch proclaiming 'The Road to England'. Napoleon had victory medals struck inscribed 'made in London'. History here conjured up Joan of Arc and William

A central theme of wartime propaganda against Republican and Napoleonic France was that ordinary people had as much to lose as the ruling elite.

the Conqueror – the Bayeux tapestry was displayed in Paris. Invasion would be easy – 'It's only a step from Calais to Dover.' The English would be busy drinking tea. 'The whole of Europe charges you, in the name of outraged humanity, with the punishment of that perfidious nation. You will wreak vengeance on England, in the heart of London.'[47]

British planners, under the Duke of York, consulted the records of the 1588 defence against the Armada and produced a thorough scheme. A flotilla of small craft would intercept the invasion fleet. What the French nick-named 'Bulldogs', the famous Martello towers (copied from an original the navy had found tough opposition at Mortella in Corsica), were planned to cause havoc on the beaches. Massive new fortifications were begun at Dover, including the Grand Shaft, a triple circular staircase down which troops could rush to the beaches. The Royal Military Canal, mostly dug by the summer of 1805, cut off the Romney Marshes. Warning would be given both by traditional beacons and a more sophisticated telegraph system connecting Plymouth, Portsmouth, Deal, Yarmouth and London. If the French broke inland, the horde of volunteers was to slow them down, while the country was 'driven' of animals, vehicles and supplies, and roads broken up by civilian pioneers. Non-combatants would be evacuated, taking with them 'a change of linen, and one blanket for each person, wrapped up in the coverlid of your bed, and . . . all the food in your possession'.[48] Mobile forces would harass the invaders day and night. Meanwhile, 113,000 men would be hurrying from all over the country in wagons and carriages as well as on foot to ten rendezvous points north and west of London, the largest being Stilton and Northampton. Defence lines were planned south of London. Dams were built ready to flood the Lea Valley. Coal and flour stocks were gathered for a siege, and Pickfords were engaged to transport them. Plans were made to carry the Bank of England's gold reserves to Worcester. If the worst came to the worst, the fight would carry on north of the capital. One small incident shows how primed the country was. In August 1805 someone mistakenly lit a warning beacon in Yorkshire: before the error was realized, the Rotherham Volunteers had mustered, gathered their wagons, and marched twenty miles towards the coast.[49]

In March 1805 the French began to move. Villeneuve's fleet successfully escaped from Toulon and feinted towards the Caribbean, with Nelson in pursuit as Napoleon had planned. They then raced back to rendezvous with their Spanish allies prior to sailing up the Channel to escort the invasion fleet. Napoleon, keyed up with excitement, went to Boulogne: 'The English don't know what they're in for.' The troops, after much practice, could supposedly embark in an hour and a half. On 26 July he tried to embue Villeneuve with his own determination: 'I count on your zeal, your patriotism, your hatred for that power that has been oppressing us for forty generations . . . Your very arrival, without a doubt, makes us masters of England.'[50] The French and Spanish could have assembled a numerically superior fleet in the Channel in the second week of August, to cover Napoleon's invasion. But this required not only good luck and weather, but also that the Allied fleets and the whole infrastructure should display the same speed and efficiency as the British. Villeneuve was first delayed in Spain by a shortage of supplies, and then lost his advantage in numbers as the British squadrons mustered. Besides, he was convinced, probably rightly, that 'whatever I do I cannot expect to succeed . . . We manoeuvre badly, our ships are slow, our rigging crude and worn out', while the British were 'manoeuvrable, skilful, enterprising and full of confidence'. Napoleon was furious at Villeneuve's hesitation when 'the destiny of the world' was in the balance: all France needed were 'two or three admirals ready to die'. On 22 August he wrote to Villeneuve, 'England is ours. We are all ready, everything is embarked. Get here within 48 hours and it's all over.'[51]

Continental politics intervened. Russia, followed by Austria, was thinking of renewing the war in a 'third coalition' with Britain. If Napoleon's army

J.M.W. Turner, 'The Battle of Trafalgar': the climax, though not the end, of more than a century of maritime conflict.

met serious resistance in England, they would certainly attack, though if he could take London quickly no Continental power would dare to challenge him. He quietly halted further troop movements towards the Channel, and on 23 August summarized the situation to Talleyrand:

> The more I think about the European situation, the more I see that decisive action is urgent . . . If [Villeneuve] follows his orders, joins the Brest fleet and comes into the Channel, there is still time: I am master of England. But if my admirals hesitate . . . my only course is to wait for winter and cross in the boats – a risky operation. In that case, I deal with the most urgent first; I break camp and, on 1st Vendémiaire I'm in Germany with 200,000 men.[52]

Two days later he learned that Villeneuve had retreated to Cadiz: the invasion was off. Napoleon stayed in Boulogne until early September to conceal his change of plan. The Army of England, renamed the Grande Armée, was marching 'to fight England in Germany' as Napoleon put it, where it would win its most brilliant victories far from the White Cliffs. At Ulm, on 17 October 1805, free from the vagaries of winds, tides and admirals, he surrounded an Austrian army and forced its bemused commander to surrender. He entered Vienna, and attended the first night of *Fidelio* in the imperial box at the opera.

Four days after Ulm, Villeneuve and his Spanish allies, ordered back to the Mediterranean by Napoleon, were caught by the prowling Nelson off Cape Trafalgar. It was a one-sided battle, with two-thirds of the Franco-Spanish fleet of thirty-three ships of the line being captured or destroyed by the twenty-nine British at a cost of only 448 British lives – and Nelson's own. His death at the moment of victory – similar to that of Wolfe at Quebec, and also painted by Benjamin West – created a model hero for the age, combining audacity, vulnerability and pathos. Nelson did not save England from imminent invasion: Napoleon was in Vienna. Feelings of salvation, however, inspired a grateful nation, and (though perhaps few of the participants know it) it still celebrates annually at the Last Night of the Proms.* As Admiral St Vincent put it drily, 'I do not say the French will not come. I only say they will not come by sea.' Yet Napoleon returned to planning a surprise crossing in 1807 and again in 1811, and he developed Antwerp as a great arsenal and base, which provoked a disastrous British attack in 1809. So Britain continued to prepare for invasion: most of the new defences of the south coast – including seventy-four Martello towers and the massive fortifications of Dover – were built after Trafalgar, and many of the defences of the Thames estuary and London were still being built at the time of Waterloo.[53]

Five weeks after Trafalgar, on 2 December, came Austerlitz. Napoleon with 73,000 men surrounded a combined Russo-Austrian army of 85,000, led by its two emperors, and killed, wounded or captured a third of them. It was his most complete victory and the most intimidating proof of French military dominance. The War of the Third Coalition was over as soon as it had begun.

There was a British casualty of Austerlitz. Pitt, ill for some time, largely owing to overwork and stress treated with port, died on 23 January 1806 at the age of forty-seven, having been prime minister for nearly eighteen years. Austerlitz, the 'overthrow of all his hopes and labours for the rescue of Europe', as his private secretary put it, hastened his death. He had formulated a comprehensive plan for the future of the Continent: 'Roll up the map of Europe', he is supposed to have said on hearing of Austerlitz. 'It will not be wanted these ten years.' The great French diplomat and historian Albert Sorel called Pitt 'the one great opponent the French Revolution and Napoleon encountered'.[54] Yet although he inherited some of his father's prestige, he was not a natural war leader. Many have thought him not even a good one. His ambitions were for political and financial reform, which war caused him to abandon. He tended, when faced with difficult wartime decisions, to reflect, procrastinate, and seek more information. He disliked

---

* Sir Henry Wood's *Fantasia on British Sea Songs* was first performed to commemorate the centenary of Trafalgar in 1905.

upsetting close colleagues, and this too led to evasiveness and delay. 'He was one of the most eloquent luminous blunderers with which any people was ever afflicted . . . At the close of every brilliant display [of oratory] an expedition failed or a Kingdom fell, and by the time his Style had gained the summit of perfection Europe was degraded to the lowest abyss of Misery.'[55] Not only in France, but also in Britain, 'the shyest man alive' was accused of diabolical conspiracies and lust for power. But his strengths outweighed his weaknesses. He was hard to cast as a fanatic or warmonger: he delayed war in 1792, favoured negotiation, and supported peace in 1802. Although prone to ups and downs, he had fundamental self-confidence. He was honest and selfless – he had no life outside politics – and inspired loyalty, even reverence, among his colleagues. And he expressed all this in compelling oratory founded on reason and conscience. In short, he was pretty well the opposite of Napoleon.

Were he and Wordsworth right in thinking that Britain, with all its faults, represented 'Earth's best hopes' and, eventually, Europe's salvation? We shall leave the value judgements until later. But after 1805 it was the sole barrier against French world hegemony.

RELICS OF WHAT MIGHT HAVE BEEN

The Colonne de la Grande Armée, three miles from the centre of Boulogne on the road to Calais, commemorates a non-invasion. The marble column, fifty-three metres high, was begun as early as November 1804 amid the main camp of the Army of England, but – like many Napoleonic monuments – was finished only after the 1830 revolution brought many of his followers back to power. Badly damaged during the Second World War, it was restored by a subscription from members of the Légion d'Honneur. The top of the column affords a fine view of the cliffs of Dover.

The Royal Military Depot, Weedon, Northamptonshire, was begun in 1803. The site is on an ancient route through the heart of England, not far from the battlefields of Bosworth, Naseby and Edge Hill and close to what is now the Watford Gap service station on the M1 motorway. There Watling Street adjoins the Grand Junction Canal – the ancient Roman road meeting the modern link with the Black Country arms industry. A branch of the canal leads through portcullised guardhouses to a fortified arms depot, whose ranks of vast red-brick warehouses dwarf the cottages and pubs of the village. Weedon stored arms for 200,000 men, cannon, and 1,000 tons of gunpowder to sustain resistance if London fell. A small Royal Pavilion was built for George III and his family, proof of determination to fight on.[56] Weedon remained an ordnance depot for more than 150 years. The pavilion was demolished in 1972, the rest sold off in the 1980s as miscellaneous warehousing. The buildings, which have the functional elegance of their time, are now entirely anonymous. Closed to the public and 'awaiting development', Weedon's oblivion is the perfect non-memorial to a world historic event that never happened.

Could it have happened? Napoleon's 1805 plan had huge flaws, rooted in his deafness to professional advice, systematic underestimation of the enemy, and stubborn refusal to comprehend that sailing ships could not be manoeuvred like cavalry regiments. The naval historian N.A.M. Rodger comments witheringly that Napoleon 'was unwilling to believe that Ganteaume [commander of the Brest fleet] could only sail . . . on a wind which would make it impossible for Villeneuve to come to him, or either of them to get up Channel. He was unwilling to believe that any wind which would move the battleships would be too much for the landing craft.'[57] Had Villeneuve risked everything, he would probably have met an earlier Trafalgar in the Channel. Even if he had somehow reached Boulogne, it is unsure that Napoleon could have got his army successfully across: many French sailors feared half the boats would founder, and British defences were formidable. So Villeneuve's fears may have prevented a swift end to Napoleon's career. The rational conclusion is that Napoleon's plan was near impossible. Yet he was certainly ready to take the gamble. In his own words, 'If we control the crossing for twelve hours, England is dead.'[58] Can we be completely sure he was wrong?

The Whale and the Elephant

The fates seem to have decided to prove to us that, if they have
granted us hegemony of the land, they have made our rivals the
rulers of the waves.

NAPOLEON BONAPARTE[59]

Napoleon could not reverse Trafalgar and the British had no answer to Austerlitz. Never before had each country managed such complete dominance in its respective sphere, with an aura of invincibility that was itself a potent weapon. In earlier wars, as we have seen, British armies fought with success in Germany and the Low Countries. As recently as 1779–81, the French navy had simultaneously threatened Britain and protected America. Yet the 1805 stalemate was the logical culmination of a century of conflict, and to examine it more closely sheds light not only on the Napoleonic wars but on the entire Franco-British struggle.

Fighting for the DUNGHILL — or — Jack Tar settling BUONAPARTE.

Gillray's view of the global war between sea-power and land-power.

THE WHALE

> We are a small spot in the ocean without territorial consequence, and our
> own power and dignity as well as the safety of Europe, rests on our being
> the paramount commercial and naval power of the world.
>
> HENRY DUNDAS, Secretary of State for War[60]

The Royal Navy had become by 1805 one of the most effective instruments
of war there has ever been. During the whole period of the revolutionary
and Napoleonic wars it lost only ten ships (including one line-of-battle ship)
to enemy action, against 377 enemy ships (including 139 line-of-battle ships)
it captured or destroyed. So many captured vessels were incorporated into
the Royal Navy – 245, including eighty-three battleships – that French naval
historians have commented that Napoleon's toiling shipyards were largely
serving the Admiralty.[61] The Royal Navy ceased to have rivals. This was not
a matter of course. Only towards the end of the contest did British sea power
become overwhelming, the consequence of 'the largest, longest, most
complex and expensive project ever undertaken by the British state and
society', and which left few aspects of national life unaffected.[62]

Unless Britain could dominate the surrounding sea it would be wide open
to invasion. Geography gave certain advantages. England has better harbours

in the Channel, able to shelter a fleet, while the French had no base adequate for an invasion fleet and no safe retreat from a battle or a storm – until the invention of reinforced concrete and steam dredging. On the other hand, France has easier access to the Atlantic, from Brest, and hence both to Ireland and beyond. Both sides worked to improve on nature. Britain forced the closure of Dunkirk and fought to keep the French away from the great harbours of the Low Countries. France has two coasts and hence a navy divided between Brest and Toulon. Admittedly, this cut both ways, for the British had to keep watch on the Toulon fleet to stop it breaking loose and taking them by surprise. The acquisition of Gibraltar in 1713 'overturned' the strategic position by hampering the junction of the French fleets.[63] Britain's precarious occupation of Minorca, brief acquisition of Corsica, and later possession of Malta – the spark to the final Anglo-French war – were all efforts to gain a Mediterranean fulcrum. The tussles for strategic harbours in North America, the West Indies and the Indian Ocean were essential steps to supremacy. Sailing fleets in distant seas required roomy, deep and sheltered anchorages, stores of spars, rope, sails and ammunition, and a large hinterland for fresh food and water. As France and her allies lost them, they lost the very possibility of naval action.

The supreme command of each navy differed fundamentally. French navy ministers were generally legally trained administrators. The Admiralty was at least partly controlled by naval officers, and there were also many in Parliament. French naval officers – and French historians – have stressed the superiority of the British system, even if perhaps exaggerating the efficacy of the Board of Admiralty. Nevertheless, the Admiralty did contrast with the general laxity of eighteenth-century administrations. As one job-seeker was firmly reminded, 'Capacity is so little necessary for most employments that you seem to forget that there's one where it is absolutely so – viz. the Admiralty.'[64] The French navy suffered from being controlled by landsmen. The worst example is Napoleon's disastrous invasion strategy of 1805. His hectoring of Villeneuve before Trafalgar caused him to accept a doomed battle and later take his own life. Some French fleets were ordered into action with practically no training, and carrying a high proportion of landsmen or river boatmen. There was less danger of the British navy being given impossible missions. 'War at sea was too serious a business to be left to politicians.'[65]

The word 'strategy' did not yet exist, and naval operations were not based on general theory or staff planning. But there were ground rules, and innovations. Most of the British navy always remained in European waters to defend the islands from invasion, and control the routes connecting Europe with the rest of the world. Only the West Indies were important enough to bring the main fleets to fight across the ocean, and then only once: the battle of the Saints in 1782. In the 1740s, Admirals Anson and Hawke pioneered a Western Squadron based at Plymouth to dominate the Atlantic approaches by long patrols at sea, and this finally proved a decisive instrument of European and world power.[66] Blockades of French ports were gradually tightened. These methods required the British to remain constantly at sea – Admiral Collingwood did not set foot on shore for eight years. This depended on better health and better food for the crews. By the Napoleonic period, unrelenting blockade of French ports was so effective that it permanently reshaped the French economy. The French, between rare fleet offensives, usually to cover invasion attempts, resorted to the *guerre de course*, attacks on merchant shipping. As well as providing some of France's most famous naval heroes, this inflicted damage on British trade. But it could not defeat Britain, which lost only 2 per cent of its merchant fleet during the Napoleonic wars. The French themselves suffered far more: in 1803 they had 1,500 merchant ships, but by 1812 only 179 – compared with Britain's 24,000.[67]

Both navies grew in each successive war: against Louis XIV the British navy had about 170 ships and 40,000 men; against Napoleon it had over 900 ships and 130,000 men. After the Glorious Revolution, the British always had more ships than the French. The French, like the British on land, needed allies: usually the Spanish (the other main colonial rivals of Britain), at times the Dutch, and occasionally smaller maritime powers such as the Danes and the Americans. In the 1780s, thanks to Choiseul, the allies had more ships than the British. The French kept building, and reached their maximum strength as late as 1796, when, with their allies, they considerably outnumbered the British. Moreover, the British navy was necessarily dispersed, protecting colonies and merchant shipping, blockading French ports, and guarding against a French attack, which increased wear and tear. The French could remain in port and choose their moment. As wooden ships needed frequent maintenance, the British needed more ships to ensure a margin of safety: roughly a quarter of the fleet was in dock around the turn of the century. After Trafalgar, Napoleon conscripted satellite countries into a naval race and tried to counteract the blockade of France's ports by developing Antwerp, Genoa and Venice. Producing poor-quality ships in quantity could not threaten British dominance, though it proves that Napoleon's global ambitions were no less than those of Choiseul and Castries.

A navy required elaborate and expensive organization. The Royal Navy was 'the largest industrial unit of its day in the western world, and by far the most expensive and demanding of all the administrative responsibilities of the State'.[68] Most basically, vast quantities of seasoned timber were required. Although both sides had to struggle to secure it, the French were generally less successful, making this a 'congenital weakness'.[69] A medium-sized battleship of 1,900 tons required 3,000 tons of raw timber – the equivalent of 3–4,000 mature trees.[70] The British navy in 1790 was built from well over half a million trees. Mature oaks of certain sizes and shapes (preferably from Sussex and Burgundy respectively) were needed for structural parts; elm for planking; conifers of a certain age and type for masts and spars; varieties of tree that would resist rot and worm, and which would not shatter too badly under cannon-fire – for wood splinters were the principal killer. Teak, otherwise excellent, produced deadly splinters. Britain and France maintained a large domestic supply of oak – Admiral Collingwood always carried a pocketful of acorns for planting in suitable spots, and some of his oak woods still survive. But special needs had to be met from the Baltic, the Mediterranean, North America, Asia and eventually Australasia (where a landing party were eaten by Maori in 1809 while loading kauri). Capturing or destroying enemy supplies was an important task. When Hood burned the mature timber stocks at Toulon in 1793 it was a 'gigantic catastrophe' for the French.[71] The Pope's willingness to sell oak from central Italy to the British was one reason for his confrontation with Napoleon; and an important reason for French annexation of Dalmatia was its forests of mountain oak, including large quantities already cut for the Royal Navy. Most precious were great conifers for masts. Pyrenean fir – hauled down vertiginous paths cut by galley slaves – was too dry, and broke. A French officer complained that the British could hoist more sail and risk getting closer to shore than the French, 'intimidated by the quality of our masts'.[72] Baltic pine was better but the supply was vulnerable; and British development of Canadian pine eventually gave great advantage. Each side used diplomacy, money and force to secure its own supplies and deny those of the enemy. The British bid up prices of Baltic timber and paid in cash. A French agent admitted that 'of all European consumers, the English admiralty is the richest, the safest, the fairest', thus ensuring preferential supply.[73] Navies were gargantuan consumers: of hemp (ten tons for an average battleship), tar, linen (Aberdeen had a huge sail-making industry, later converted to linoleum), copper (which founded the wealth of Swansea), iron, and specialized food and drink, which had to be of guaranteed quality and capable of long storage. Failures here would be literally deadly, and spoilage had been practically eliminated by the Admiralty by the 1750s.[74] A system of naval dockyards, supplemented in Britain by private yards, and a highly skilled workforce laboured constantly to keep the fleets up to strength.

It is often said that French ships were better designed and built. This is broadly a myth. At certain periods the French built more powerful ships. Some were faster, but more fragile and leakier – the British commonly rebuilt and strengthened captured vessels. British ships were built sturdily for long voyages, storms, battles and blockades. They were ahead in important innovations. Copper-bottoming – 'they are sheathed in copper and we in oysters' said a French officer[75] – prevented rapid destruction by tropical shipworms and increased speeds by at least 20 per cent – a decisive tactical advantage.

Bored iron cannon and large-calibre carronades increased firepower. Sustained espionage – abetted by unscrupulous British businessmen, including some of the most famous (see above, pages 83 4) – helped them learn crucial techniques, but they lacked the industrial infrastructure to exploit them. For example, the Wilkinson brothers legally provided coppering techniques in the 1780s, but the French could not make them work, and had to reuse old copper sheets, handled by convict labour because of the toxic dust. The Royal Navy pioneered mechanized mass production. Probably the world's first assembly line made ships' biscuits. Early machine tools made millions of light, low-friction pulley blocks for rigging, which saved manpower, weight and wear. It took the French, despite successful espionage, nearly forty years to copy them. By then the Royal Navy had moved on. Four years after the French naval engineer Marc Brunel arrived in Britain, his designs for block-making machines were accepted by the Admiralty. By 1806, forty steam-powered machines were operating. Only a developed and innovative society could manage this level of technology and organization. By the end of the century most states were dropping out of the race, the vestiges of their fleets rotting.

The costs of navies were immense, and when necessary Britain was willing and able to spend much more – about three times as much as the French at the height of the Seven Years War. During the wars against Louis XIV, the British navy cost £1.8 million per year; against Napoleon, over £15 million per year. Navies cost more than armies. A battleship was the most complex artefact in existence, and it needed constant maintenance. Over her lifetime, HMS *Victory* cost nearly £400,000 – the annual budget of a small state.[76] A modest naval squadron had more artillery than both sides at Austerlitz. Naval budgets had profound political consequences. From 1763 to 1783 the French navy built 700,000 tons of new ships, absorbing one-third of state spending, whereas the British slashed annual spending in the 1760s from £7 million to £1.8 million.[77] The consequence was American independence. The French continued to build rapidly until 1792: the strain contributed to the French revolution.

It was manpower, however, that most severely limited size and effectiveness. No country could afford a large standing navy, and all required a rapid influx of men in wartime. Given the skill and toughness demanded, they needed experienced seafarers to form the nucleus of crews. Warships needed big crews: 1,000 men for a line-of-battle ship, compared with twenty or thirty for an average merchant ship. So a navy required a large merchant marine to supply a pool of sailors, most of whom would be enlisted during a major war. This, as much as economic and financial considerations, is why rival states were so concerned to protect and increase their oceanic trade and fisheries. Access to the Newfoundland cod fishery, which employed 10,000 French sailors, was a contentious issue from the 1600s until the Entente

Cordiale of 1904. The triangular trade based on slaves and sugar was also seen as a strategic interest: from the 1720s to the 1780s, the French share grew faster. Trade share and naval power were intimately connected: to lose one was to lose the other. France's inability in the 1780s to become the main trading partner of its protégé the United States was an irremediable geo-political failure. The pool of seamen available always numerically favoured the British. The French had some 50,000 seamen (about the same as Holland), the British 100,000. Yet the islands needed more sailors, and certainly had no surplus. For example, the coal trade from Newcastle to London (in which James Cook began his career) was an important source of men for the navy, but it was also vital to the economy. So the navy in wartime fought the merchant marine and privateers for men: the demand was two or three times the supply. Foreign sailors filled the gaps. Hence the Impress Service – the notorious 'Press Gangs' – were more often victims than perpetrators of violence. They were regularly attacked by mobs, and even imprisoned by local magistrates where there was a strong ship-owning interest, Liverpool being notorious. However, the often praised French system of maritime conscription was even less effective, and naval service was dreaded there.[78]

Both sides (Britain more efficiently) seized enemy merchant ships and sailors at the start of every war – or even before, accused the indignant French. Two years into the Seven Years War the British had captured some 20,000 Frenchmen. By 1800 nearly all France's pre-war sea-going population were dead or prisoners.[79] To the anger of the French (and their historians), the British kept sailors imprisoned rather than exchanging them, and, they alleged, in deliberately unhealthy conditions. However, the French navy itself was bad at protecting its precious sailors' health, and the century was marked by a succession of sanitary disasters. The British, owing to greater sea-going experience, practised stringent hygiene, and improved nutrition and treatment. Fresh food was regularly issued to prevent scurvy, and lemon juice rations were introduced in the 1790s. French ships were notoriously filthy, and they lagged far behind in nutrition.

Quality of manpower was decisive, because the British rarely had numerical superiority in battle: Jervis was greatly outnumbered at Cape St Vincent; at the Nile, numbers were about equal, and at Trafalgar the Franco-Spanish were more numerous. A French naval historian has suggested that the officers of the two eighteenth-century navies were 'among the most remarkable intellectual and political elites that Europe has ever produced'.[80] However, there was great difference in their effectiveness. The British officer corps was relatively meritocratic and highly experienced, often first going to sea in childhood. It produced a succession of outstanding commanders. From Anson to Nelson, they were capable of administering a fleet, navigating round the world, hauling on a rope and leading a boarding party. As a whole,

French officers were less competent. Under the Bourbons they were excessively exclusive, with a high proportion of Provençal and Breton nobility (having wonderful names like Coëtnempren de Kersaint and Du Couédic de Kergoualen) and ridden by snobbery, faction and insubordination: 'in the navy, they all hate each other', concluded one navy minister.[81] Some of the best commanders, including Grasse and Suffren, started early in the navy of the Knights of Malta. But many blue-blooded French officers were elderly yet inexperienced, negligent and incompetent, as shown by the frequency of accidents. One notorious captain rammed and severely damaged two of his own side in two successive days in April 1782, including the flagship – his fourteenth collision in a year. The resulting loss of speed – for Grasse considered that 'the honour of the flag' would not permit abandoning the damaged ships – brought on the disastrous battle of the Saints.[82] Officer cadets, the Garde-Marine, were trained in the classroom. If their theoretical knowledge was superior to that of British midshipmen, they gained little sea-going experience. They learned dancing, but not swimming. The revolution changed the system, but for the worse. Of 1,600 officers, 1,200 resigned or were expelled, and they were never adequately replaced.

Good crews were made by practice. British sailors spent far more time at sea, and were able to train as ships' companies and as squadrons. Popular traditions about appalling conditions in the British navy are largely mythical. Warships were safer, cleaner and less uncomfortable than merchant ships. Food and drink were good and plentiful – about 5,000 calories a day, including a pound of bread, a pound of meat and a gallon of beer. Discipline was tough, but excessive harshness was frowned upon by the Admiralty. Brutal officers and petty officers were beaten up on shore, met with nasty accidents, or were even sued by their men. As N.A.M. Rodger remarks, the navy's successes are hard to explain if it was 'a sort of floating concentration camp'.[83] Many seamen were volunteers, and good officers had loyal crews who followed them from ship to ship. There was widespread desertion, but largely because of high wartime pay offered by merchant masters and privateers. The navy, however, offered prize money. A witticism attributed to the famous corsair Surcouf remains proverbial in France. A British naval officer supposedly reproached him for fighting for money, unlike the British who fought for honour: 'Each of us fights,' he replied, 'for what he lacks most.' The story is highly improbable, for British sailors of all ranks were avid prize-seekers. The profit made some officers very rich, and was an incentive for all ranks to be alert, enterprising and aggressive, although it sometimes distracted them from less lucrative duties. 'You can't think how keen our men are,' wrote Boscawen in 1756; 'the hope of prize money makes them happy, a signal for a sail brings them all on deck'.[84]

From mid-century – with 1776–82 an interlude – British confidence grew and that of the French waned. The latter became justifiably frightened of the Channel, and repeatedly backed away from invading Britain. Aggression became an imperative of British naval culture and policy, as the execution of Admiral Byng in 1757 for 'failing to do his utmost to destroy the enemy' (which carried a mandatory death sentence) made unmistakable. British admirals took risks to win crushing victories. In 1759 Hawke pursued the French fleet among the rocks of Quiberon Bay. At the battle of the Saints, in 1782, for the first time (perhaps accidentally, perhaps inspired by a new *Essay on Naval Tactics*) the British drove through the enemy battle line rather than sailing in parallel. This, which demanded calculated risk and skill, became the approved tactic. In 1798 Nelson sailed between the anchored French fleet and the shore at Aboukir Bay in 'the first battle of annihilation' the French navy had ever experienced.[85] Tactics were based on forcing close action, firing fast and inflicting maximum damage, which demanded discipline, practice and confidence. The adoption in the 1780s of the large-calibre short-range carronade reinforced this method. Stress was laid on gunnery practice, for speed of firing was decisive. There was much experimentation with firing mechanisms and gun-laying systems. The effective firepower of the British by the 1790s has been reckoned as two or three times that of the French. The French in the late 1770s adopted the opposite course of keeping a distance and firing high at masts and rigging – a defensive ploy to permit escape. They justified this by stressing the importance of completing the mission, rather than getting involved in messy battles, which, said the famous Admiral d'Estaing, 'produce much more noise than profit'.

The outcome is shown by the grisly and unambiguous evidence of casualties: on average about six times as many men were killed on the French side. At Trafalgar, where many of the French and Spanish crews were barely trained, more than ten times as many were killed or drowned. The French *Redoutable*, engaged by the larger *Victory* and two other ships, had 571 of her 643 crew killed or wounded. Of 15,000 Frenchmen engaged, only 4,000 escaped.[86] French and Spanish sailors often abandoned their guns and lay down as British ships with fully loaded broadsides came within 'pistol shot' – sometimes as close as twenty feet. The prospect of being boarded was equally intimidating, as the Royal Navy were 'by far the most formidable close-quarter fighters of any army or navy'.[87] French officers and men increasingly gave up the unequal contest: three-quarters of all losses under the Republic and even more under the Empire were surrenders. The only major French naval success after 1789 was won by the army, when during the terrible winter of 1795 a cavalry force captured the Dutch fleet trapped in the ice.

> Suppose there should arise in Europe a people endowed with energy, with
>   genius, with resources, with government; a people which combined the
> virtues of austerity with a national militia and which added to them a fixed
> plan of aggrandizement; knowing how to make war at small cost and subsist
> on its victories . . . We should see that people subdue its neighbours . . .
> Among men like these let there arise . . . some vast genius. He will . . . put
> himself at the head of the machine and give the impulse of its movement.
>
> GEN. COMTE DE GUIBERT, 1772[88]

French land power is the mirror image of British sea power. France had a
large advantage in men, being during nearly all the eighteenth century the
most populous state in Europe, and it could only be resisted by coalitions.
Napoleon's notorious quip on the numbers killed in one battle – 'One Paris
night will replace that lot' – shows an indifference to manpower losses that
was not confined to him.[89] France had built up arsenals and barracks, which
enabled it to maintain a large standing army. Frontier adjustments and elaborate fortifications made invasion of its heartland almost unthinkable, and
nearly all its wars were fought on foreign soil. The army, the principal service
of the State, enjoyed prestige, and its officer corps, though it included courtly
nonentities, always had men of outstanding ability too. The British army, in
contrast, was always second to the navy, was regarded with ideological suspicion, and was always rapidly run down in peacetime. The need to rebuild
almost from scratch at the start of every war – worse even than the fluctuating fortunes of the French navy – was its greatest handicap. It was never
in the forefront of technical advances, and its officers were amateurish. It
looked abroad for guidance, not least to France, where some of its most
famous commanders were trained. French Protestants provided expertise
during the first half of the century, most notably Jean-Louis (later Sir John
and Earl) Ligonier, commander-in-chief in 1757 and one of the architects
of the Seven Years War. When Arthur Wellesley was at the Angers academy
in 1786, there were more than 100 other British pupils. In the 1800s the
British were happy to take advice from the émigré General Dumouriez in
planning defence against invasion.

The Seven Years War, however, was a disaster for the French army, too
complacent in its pre-eminence. Defeat led to reflection, debate and reform
during the 1770s, encouraged by Choiseul. The artillery was standardized
and redesigned by Gribeauval, who created lighter, more mobile cannons
able to manoeuvre on the battlefield in batteries and fire faster. Tactical
experiments, switching infantry from columns for movement into lines for
combat, were carried out and embodied in the 1788 drill book. Guibert, a

brilliant example of that quintessentially French phenomenon, the intellectual soldier, developed the idea of forming an army into autonomous divisions to permit rapid movement and flexible manoeuvre. It was, however, the revolution, and then the Empire, that gave these ideas their true significance, and created the conditions that enabled the French army to conquer Europe. Traditional military tactics, based on long, slowly moving lines of men, required not just discipline but passivity: soldiers, and even most officers, were not paid to think. The new ideas required initiative and motivation at junior levels. The revolution made this conceivable, and it brought forward officers, including reformist nobles such as Guibert's friend Dumouriez, and soldier-politicians such as the Jacobin minister of war Lazare Carnot, who were eager to put the ideas into practice. It also promoted a generation of young officers who had been brought up on these theories – including Bonaparte, who had studied them with characteristic intensity.[90]

The revolution drew deeply on manpower reserves. The levies of the 1790s, impelled by emergency, ideological fervour and brute compulsion, produced an armed horde larger than any rival. Their way of fighting reflected their strengths and weaknesses. Undrilled soldiers went forward as skirmishers to take pot-shots at the immobile enemy. Unskilled masses with bayonets were crowded into columns, crude approximations of Guibert's idea, and, at the cost of heavy losses – 20 per cent casualties was routine – trampled over an outnumbered enemy. Eighteenth-century armies, expensive and highly drilled, tended to avoid battle except in certain circumstances, and did not try to annihilate a beaten enemy. But the revolutionary armies sought to drown the enemy in blood: they were exhorted to 'fall in masses, like the ancient Gauls', and 'annihilate, exterminate, destroy the enemy once and for all'.[91] A lethal process of natural selection eliminated incompetent and half-hearted officers, including such famous names as La Fayette. Dozens of generals were guillotined, but the Bourbon army bequeathed reserves of ambitious and ruthless commanders, drawn from its junior officers, NCOs and soldiers.

Under Napoleon, this raw material was honed, much of the work being done while training to invade England. The Empire, unlike its enemies, was harnessed for war under a single directing mind. What survived of the revolutionary army was given a new ethos. Napoleon created an 'army of honour'.[92] Its officers and long-service conscripts, including non-Frenchmen, owed their first loyalties to the Emperor and to their unit, sustained by medals for all ranks and meritocratic promotion. The French professed distaste for the ferocious corporal punishments practised in other armies, such as the flogging that was routine in the British.

Napoleon despised innovation for its own sake – rockets, balloons etc.

– but he was a systematizer and an exhaustive planner. The changes originated by Gribeauval and Guibert were practised and applied. The divisional system, to which Napoleon added the *corps d'armée* (composed of several divisions), provided armies of several hundred thousand men with articulations enabling them to disperse over hundreds of miles to forage and march and then come together to execute a complex plan on the battlefield. Napoleon increased the number of cannon, organized them into mobile batteries, and threw them into the thick of the action. The French coordinated skirmishers, fast-moving columns, mobile artillery and cavalry, outclassing passive linear formations, especially when made up of poorly trained or intimidated troops. Napoleon's strategy was not to seize territory or strategic positions, as in earlier warfare, but to smash the enemy army. The results were devastating: from 1805 to 1809 at Ulm, Austerlitz, Jena-Auerstadt, Friedland, Aspern-Essling and Wagram, Austrian, Prussian and Russian armies were crushed. The British were hardly in the running.

France's military effort after 1792 depended on exploiting the wealth, labour and blood of as much of Europe as it could seize. As expanding overseas trade increased both revenue and manpower for the British navy, so Continental conquest did for the French army. This meant quartering armies on foreign soil and at foreign expense, levying huge indemnities, conscripting foreign troops, and requisitioning food, drink, clothing and money. Let us consider one small example. In November 1793 the French Army of the Moselle occupied the tiny duchy of Zweibrücken. All oats, hay, straw, brandy, leather and weapons, 3,000 pairs of shoes and 500 pairs of boots were immediately demanded; the following day, all horses, cattle, sheep and harness; within forty-eight hours all copper, lead, iron and church bells; all cloth was to be made into uniforms by the inhabitants at their expense; and all the booty was to be taken away in requisitioned carts, along with 2 million *livres* in cash. After Napoleon's victories in 1805–9, Austria was forced to pay 125 million francs, and Saxony 25 million. Prussia, the worst treated, was stripped of wealth equal to over sixteen years' taxation. The effects of this impoverishment were such that in Berlin 75 per cent of newborn babies died, and the suicide rate rose sharply. Portugal was to pay 100 million francs, but was saved by the Peninsular War.[93] The French Republic and Empire usually made a profit from war, as Guibert had foretold.

Between 1794 and 1812, the French swept the Continent. Britain, with its lesser population and small, poorly trained army, was powerless. Throughout the century, the Franco-British struggle was also, usually, a Franco-Austrian struggle. During the previous two centuries, France and Austria had been at war with each other for more years, and had fought more battles, than any other states.[94] Britain's ascent, and even survival, depended on France being embroiled in Continental wars. Austria had been France's enemy since 1792. Its willingness to accept defeat, by abandoning its Netherlands provinces, dissolving the Holy Roman Empire in 1806 and marrying the Habsburg archduchess Marie-Louise to Napoleon in 1810, cut Britain adrift. Napoleon's diplomacy was helped by universal jealousy of Britain's ever-growing seapower and wealth. Britain, many believed, was using European wars as an opportunity to monopolize global trade. In 1807 Napoleon met Tsar Alexander I on a raft in the River Niemann and signed the Treaty of Tilsit, sharing out Europe between them. Their first exchange of courtesies was 'I hate the English as much as you do.' 'Then peace between us is made.'

So Britain was excluded from most of Europe. It had only six diplomatic outposts on the whole Continent. France, in contrast, had lost all its major colonies and overseas bases, and the fleets of its potential allies had also been dealt with, most ruthlessly by the attack on Copenhagen in 1807. The war went on. Britain still strengthened its home defences. France tirelessly built more ships. However, there was a crucial difference between military and naval power. Prolonged land warfare destroyed men, and the most combative armies became increasingly reliant on fresh recruits. Prolonged naval warfare ruined ships, so without endless spending and maintenance, navies literally rotted away. But it killed far fewer men, and sea-service and combat improved the effectiveness of crews. So as war continued, the superiority of the French army decreased, while that of the British navy increased.

For the time being there was stalemate. In 1809, as French power reached its zenith, Westminster was more preoccupied with the doings of the Duke of York's mistress. Schroeder comments that not only could Napoleon not bring the British down, he could not even gain their full attention. The two nations needed more effective ways of hurting each other.

The Continental System versus the Cavalry of St George

I want to conquer the sea by the power of the land.
NAPOLEON BONAPARTE[95]

Another year! – another deadly blow!
Another mighty Empire overthrown!
And We are left, or shall be left, alone;
The last that dare to struggle with the Foe.
WILLIAM WORDSWORTH, 'November 1806'

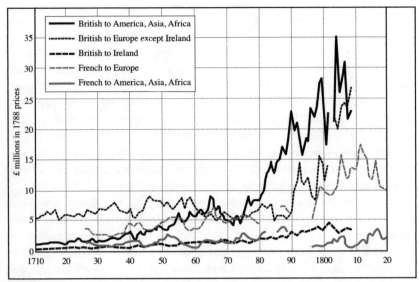

Foreign trade (Prados de la Escosura (2004), p. 59)

In November 1806, having demolished the Prussian army at Jena and occupied its capital, Napoleon turned against the British economy. The Berlin Decree of 21 November 1806 prohibited all trade with Britain, declared all British subjects on the Continent prisoners of war, and ordered the seizure of all merchandise from Britain or its colonies. This would turn the tables on 'Carthage', which, to the rage of the French and the jealousy of most of Europe, had been doing well out of the war.

Since 1790, Britain's overseas trade had expanded by nearly 60 per cent, and colonial re-exports, mainly sugar and coffee, by 187 per cent. The merchant navy had increased from 1.4 to 1.8 million tons.[96] Its population was growing quickly. Domestic demand was strong. Agriculture had a larger acreage under the plough than at any time between the Middle Ages and 1940. The war did not halt the Industrial Revolution, and Britain was widening its economic lead over the Continent. The City had received a flood of capital seeking security, and rival financial centres, notably Amsterdam and Frankfurt, have never recovered. A bigger Stock Exchange was built. Moreover, as the huge expansion of the Port of London showed, large sums were earned from shipping and related activities such as insurance, of which the war gave Britain increasing dominance.

Britain's gain had been France's loss. France too had been an important and successful colonial trader until the 1790s. What changed this were the revolution and its wars, which disrupted the domestic economy and wrecked overseas trade. To raise money for war, the French were forced into a succession of destructive expedients at home and in conquered territories

– confiscation, hyper-inflation and extortion. The biggest single loss came from the slave rebellion in Saint-Domingue, but the sugar trade, like the rest, would have been lost anyway to the Royal Navy, whose blockade blighted the economies of the richest industrial and agricultural regions: Normandy, the Bordelais and the Rhône valley. Shipping, manufacturing and services were all devastated. The ports, including Bordeaux, Nantes, Le Havre and Marseilles, lost employment, investments and population. Many did not recover until well into the nineteenth century; some never really did. Traders turned against the revolution and Napoleon and, even more than in Lancashire and Yorkshire, pleaded for peace. We shall look later at the long-term effects on the French economy, society, and culture.

The maritime and commercial war had one great positive consequence: the abolition of the slave trade. An unprecedented campaign against slavery had grown up in Britain since the 1770s, and to a much lesser extent in France. The revolution and subsequent wars had halted prospects for abolition in Britain, and accelerated them in France. But Napoleon re-established slavery in law, and attempted to do so by force in the Caribbean. British abolitionists seized the opportunity, supported by the government, to ban most of the trade in 1806 as an act of war: to deprive the enemy of new slaves. Once this was accepted, the true motives of the abolitionists, which were religious and humanitarian, extended this in 1807 to a total ban on the trade.[97] A wish to show that Britain was 'the morning star that enlightened Europe, and whose boast and glory was to grant liberty and life' was also important, for it justified victory.[98]

The British state could pay lavishly for war by taxing the generally buoyant domestic and trading economy. Britain fought the Republic and Napoleon – as it had the Bourbons – by turning money into military power. As in the past, it had begun by raising loans in the City. Pitt realized in 1797 that credit was at last reaching its limit, and that this war would have to be paid for increasingly from taxation. The ability of British governments to tax as well as borrow had astonished friends and enemies alike: it seemed always to be reaching the bounds of the possible. But Pitt, followed by Addington, went further. In 1799, for the first time, he imposed a tax on incomes. It was just and politic, said Pitt, that in a war defending property, property should pay. Most of the extra revenue raised after 1803 came from the income tax – £142 million. By 1814, the government was spending six times its pre-war budget – £100 million a year. This undeniably caused financial, economic and political tensions palpable until the 1840s. That it was possible without political revolt or economic disaster shows the general acceptance of the need to defeat Napoleon. It also shows the strength of the economy: government spending peaked at only 16 per cent of national income, compared with 50 per cent of GDP during the First World War.[99]

Money bought allies. The anti-French Coalition powers mistrusted each other and haggled about money. Whitehall did not wish to hand out taxpayers' money to governments that seemed unreliable and likely to use it on aggressive schemes of their own. So money was only sparingly provided in emergencies. Austria, for example, in 1795, 1797 and 1799 was only offered loans to be repaid after the war. But Austria, Prussia and Russia, viciously jealous of each other, were also outraged at what they saw as British plans to scoop up world trade while they did the fighting, and they demanded more. Pitt, thanks to the income tax, could loosen the purse-strings, and pay anyone who would join the fight, with no suggestion of repayment, at a generous rate of roughly £1 per soldier per month – still vastly less than British armies cost.[100]

As early as 1803, Napoleon promised his Council of State that they would 'consolidate on the Continent': he would 'form a complete coastal system and England will end up weeping tears of blood'.[101] In 1806 and 1807 his land blockade was extended to Russia, Scandinavia, Prussia, Austria, Holland, Italy, Spain and Portugal. The British government retaliated with Orders in Council in November 1807 extending its own existing blockade by forbidding any ship from any country to trade with Napoleonic Europe unless it first passed through a British port and paid a 25 per cent duty. Napoleon then decreed the confiscation of every ship that obeyed these orders.

Napoleon planned to mobilize the Continent against the islands, which meant ultimate French political and economic control of Europe, including allies and neutrals. He counted on British unpopularity making his plan acceptable. It involved restructuring the whole Continental market, turning it away from the hostile ocean. The future lay along the Rhine, through Switzerland, into northern Italy, rich territories from Antwerp to Milan that had now become parts of 'France'. With British imports excluded, French industries would have privileged access to all parts of Europe in a one-way Common Market. Prospects for jobs and profits in favoured regions and industries won support for Napoleon which lasted throughout his reign, and even afterwards. Other regions suffered, including Catalonia, Holland and Scandinavia, but they were as likely to blame Britain as Napoleon. This war was fought from the crow's-nests of British blockaders and privateers, and in the offices of 27,000 French customs officials from Hamburg to Trieste. The British hoped to provoke Europe to rebel against France; the French, to force Europe to help defeat Britain. George Canning, foreign secretary, admitted 'we must not hide the fact from ourselves – we are hated throughout Europe'.[102] In 1808 British exports slumped, and Napoleon proclaimed victory:

England, punished in the very source of her cruel policies, sees her merchandise rejected by the whole of Europe, and her ships loaded with useless riches, wandering on the vast seas which they once

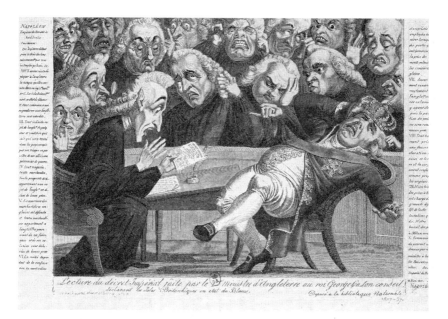

A French vision of the British government struck with terror at the Berlin Decree.

purported to rule, seeking in vain from the Sound to the Hellespont a port open to receive them.[103]

Europe's ports remained more open than he expected, however. Consumers had an insatiable appetite for tobacco, cotton cloth, sugar, coffee, tea, chocolate, spices and manufactures, and once prohibition raised the black-market price, merchants and smugglers rushed to supply them. The French discovery of beet sugar (of which, two centuries later, they remain the largest producers) made no difference. In 1809, British exports bounced back. Huge entrepots for smuggling were set up on Heligoland, seized by Britain in 1807 to supply north Germany and Holland, and in Gibraltar, Malta, Sicily and Salonica to supply Spain, Italy and Austria. Goods landed at Salonica travelled by mule train through Serbia and Hungary to Vienna and on to southern Germany, Switzerland and even France. 'Sometimes goods one bought in Calais, coming from England seven leagues away, had done a detour equivalent to twice round the globe.'[104] Hundreds of thousands of smugglers were busy. Respectable merchants and bankers took part, and a Cologne company offered insurance cover. Solid citizens speculated on the prices of smuggled goods as on stocks and shares. High-ranking French officers sold immunity – French troops even escorted smugglers and fired on their own customs men.[105] Napoleon decided to make an example. Frankfurt, one of the main contraband trading centres, was surrounded by troops in November

1810. Millions of francs' worth of suspect goods were confiscated or publicly burnt, devastating Frankfurt's economy. Other cities saw similar bonfires of precious contraband. The repercussions were grave, though a run of bad harvests may have been equally to blame by raising food prices and bringing down workers' living standards. The British economy staggered for a couple of years. A banking crisis hit London. The textile industries of the north were badly hit, and in 1811–12 the first outbreaks of machine-breaking – 'Luddism' – took place in the east Midlands. Demonstrators raised barricades in London. Corn had to be imported from France, which Napoleon allowed because it would earn gold.

But the exports Napoleon laboured to exclude from France and northern Europe flowed increasingly into the Mediterranean, North and South America and Iberia. The Continental System had not ruined Britain, but it did damage the Continent. All over Germany, Italy and in France itself confidence collapsed, loans went unpaid and banking houses failed. Resentment of French rule grew. The slump affected industry in Paris, where 40 per cent were unemployed. Napoleon gave up trying to eliminate British trade from Europe. Rather, he decided to take the business over. Licences for trade to and from Britain were given to French ships and merchants, but not to those of any ally or satellite. The desperate Bordeaux wine growers were able again to export to England. French troops in Poland wore English boots, and greatcoats woven in Yorkshire. Napoleon's plan was to become the monopoly purveyor of British and colonial goods to the Continent, with prices on a level with the black market, and the profits filling his war chest. Thus, the Continental System became an attempt to enrich France as much as impoverish Britain, with the costs being borne by the rest of Europe.

The only way Napoleon could make this work was by extending his grip over more of Europe's coastline and inland communications. More of Switzerland was annexed to control Alpine passes. So in 1809 was more of central Italy, to close the papal port of Ancona. That same year Trieste and Dalmatia were annexed from Austria. In 1810, Napoleon's brother was made to abdicate the Dutch crown, and Holland became part of France, as beyond it did the Frisian coast and the Hanseatic ports of Hamburg, Bremen and Lübeck. Spain and Portugal were ordered to heel. Pressure was put on Russia, whose elites were smarting from the loss of grain and timber exports to Britain, and whose state finances were tottering. This would eventually contribute to hostilities between Napoleon and Russia. On the other hand, Britain's sea blockade caused the United States to enter the war in July 1812 and attempt ineffectually to conquer Canada.

During these years both Britain and France experienced serious economic and social strain. Though the Continental System was probably never capable of ruining the British economy, it did damage manufacturing industries. A peace campaign had widespread support. It drew on economic distress; on a belief, strongest among Dissenters (many of them businessmen) that the war was futile, immoral and unendurable; and on a lingering sympathy for the French among some of the Whig opposition and writers swooning over Napoleon's 'genius'. The prime minister, Spencer Perceval, was assassinated in the lobby of the House of Commons in May 1812 by a deranged bankrupt businessman. In France, political disagreement could only be expressed in hushed tones among the elite, but respectful warnings to Napoleon by advisers trying to restrain his constant aggressiveness were ignored. The corrupt, sycophantic but intelligent arch-survivor Talleyrand had resigned (or been sacked) in 1807 – an early straw in the wind. Food riots broke out, especially in areas stripped to supply Paris, which Napoleon intended to keep happy.

Britain was spending a lot of money abroad: on importing timber, iron, hemp, etc., and on paying for armies, especially once war broke out in Portugal and Spain. There were also spiralling subsidies to allies: £66 million in all, £20 million in 1814–15 alone. By 1814–15, the transfer of funds abroad for war expenses was running at about £16 million per year, out of a total budget of £100 million. Funds had to be exported either in paper (banknotes, bills of exchange representing commercial debt, or 'federal paper' to be redeemed after the war) or in coin or bullion. All caused balance-of-payments problems, as paper depreciated and coinage and bullion reserves ran short. In emergency, the king authorized the illegal export of golden guineas to feed Wellington's army in the Peninsula, which was costing some £10 million per year, much of it in hard cash. The Treasury used the Rothschild network to run a secret and complex system both to bring in and to pay out a variety of financial assets, including collecting French coins to finance Wellington's eventual invasion of France. These unprecedented transfers were sustainable

'Past – Present – Future', Napoleon's hope: to create a Continental blockade to reduce Albion from wealth to poverty.

because Britain's foreign earnings from goods and services almost balanced the outgoings, and made it possible to import South American bullion and coin – silver Mexican *pesos* were a major international currency. Britain had built up large overseas credits, which – as during the twentieth-century world wars – were partly liquidated. Large shipments of cash from the East India Company, raised by trade and heavy taxation, played a vital role, and had long-term effects on Indian society. The final burst of spending was financed by selling British government bonds abroad – often in the very countries that then received the cash raised, and whose citizens were keener to lend to Britain than to their own governments.[106] Napoleon's belief that the City of London was a house of cards was a fatal illusion.

When by 1813 the other Great Powers reluctantly concluded that Napoleon was insatiable and would have to be defeated, they needed British money to do it, and 'the English covered Germany with blood and gold'.[107] Money and weapons flooded on to the Continent: £10 million and 1 million muskets were distributed in a year to thirty countries, and Russia, Prussia and Austria were enabled to field 700,000 men.[108] Britain now used the leverage this gave. All money for Portugal and Spain passed through Wellington, making him effectively supreme commander in the Peninsula. Spain and Portugal were induced to stop the slave trade. The foreign secretary, Robert Stewart, Viscount Castlereagh, went permanently to Allied headquarters in 1814 to distribute money. He used the influence this gave him to resuscitate Pitt's 1805 'outline for the restoration of Europe', which included re-establishing the rule of law, providing for the 'internal happiness' of states, and concluding a treaty to guarantee future collective security.[109]

What would previously have seemed incredible had been done: £1,500 million was spent on finally defeating France. This left a national debt of £733 million, equal to over forty times pre-war state income, or £37 for every person in Britain – the total annual earnings of a London labourer. This long accumulated financial burden was proportionately several times that left by the First World War.[110] The British government closed the subsidy and loan accounts of the Napoleonic wars in 1906[111] – eight years before the Cavalry of St George saddled up for another charge.

CAPTIVES

Unprecedented numbers of French and British men – and some women – came into contact with each other as captives and captors. In 1803, some 500 British subjects still in France after the Treaty of Amiens were detained in what seemed to them an act of vindictive illegality. A further 16,000 prisoners were subsequently taken, mainly merchant seamen and men of the Royal Navy or Marines whose blockading ships had been driven ashore. They formed a fraction of the multitude from across Europe captured by the French – some 500,000 in all. About 250,000 soldiers and naval and merchant seamen were prisoners in Britain at some time during the whole revolutionary and Napoleonic period.[112] The ordeal of the prisoners on both sides has been largely forgotten, except, perhaps, through the beautiful models of ships (and less beautiful guillotines) carved for sale by French prisoners from wood and meat-bones. But at the time and over succeeding generations, bitter accounts of cruelty left a shadow of mutual recrimination, and even hatred, especially in Brittany, where many French sailors originated.

Prisoners' fates were grim. Routinely robbed and ill-treated, they faced a long captivity: nine years or more in some cases. Systems of prisoner exchange broke down after 1803, and the more 'total' nature of this struggle left ordinary prisoners with little protection, apart from some humanitarian efforts. The large numbers, and economic hardship within the captor countries, made treatment at best spartan. Crowded conditions inevitably meant disease. The British and French treated each other better than most. The British were the only nationality given 'Class I' status, seemingly because far more French prisoners were taken by Britain, and Paris feared reprisals. The annual death rate for both French and British prisoners was probably a little under 10 per cent.

French history books still condemn *les pontons* (the hulks) as 'floating coffins' into which French prisoners were crowded. In fact, most were held on land, in specially constructed prisons such as Dartmoor and the large temporary camp at Norman Cross, near Peterborough. British prisoners suffered too, not least from the long journeys they were forced to make on foot, though their lot was less bad than that of the wretched Austrians, Prussians and Russians. Ordinary soldiers and sailors were imprisoned in fortresses in northern and eastern France. Obedience to captors was officially encouraged. In a 'Bridge over the River Meuse' episode, British sailors struggled to repair a broken bridge near their camp so that Napoleon could cross – a dutiful act that was approved on both sides. According to legend, an appreciative Emperor passed his snuffbox round the deferential British tars, and graciously ordered their release.

Ordinary prisoners on both sides were allowed to take jobs. Officers were given parole and limited freedom. Several thousand French officers were scattered round some twenty small inland towns. The British were mainly concentrated in the fortress town of Verdun, where senior officers and wealthy civilian internees and their families led comfortable lives. Gambling, drinking, duelling, horse racing and sex provided something of a home from home. Shops and schools were established and Paris fashions could be obtained. Parole was a problem for the minority who wanted to escape. Although honourable military conventions had weakened, this one still applied, at least on the British side. Military authorities punished, and even handed back, British officers who escaped while on parole. Would-be escapers had to have their parole withdrawn for minor misdemeanours before they could make a break – even though this might mean having to escape from a cell. There are many piquant escape stories. One young officer, leaving large unpaid bills in Verdun, escaped in a carriage hiding under his French girlfriend's skirts, to the horror of his superiors, who considered he had let the side down. Two of the French invaders who landed at Fishguard in 1797 were similarly helped in tunnelling out of ramshackle Pembroke prison by amorous local girls, whom they later married – one couple returning after the war to run a pub in Merthyr Tydfil. The French worried less about parole, and 674 officers escaped, most aided by English criminal gangs – helping escapers was only a minor offence, so the risk was small.[113]

Most escapes from France were hard, anticipating exploits familiar from the Second World War: forging documents, making disguises, climbing and tunnelling. The notorious hilltop fortress of Bitche outdid Colditz as a punishment prison for the unruly, many being confined in underground bunkers cut into the rock. Unprotected by any equivalent of the Geneva Conventions, escapers risked galley slavery, and ringleaders death. The physical toughness normal in pre-industrial society meant that journeys of hundreds of miles on foot in winter weather and with little food were undertaken to reach either the Channel or Austria. Escapers were often mistaken for army deserters, which won them the sympathy and even the assistance of French peasants. They were helped even more by people in the Low Countries and Germany hostile to French rule. At least one informal escape network existed near Bruges, run by an innkeeper's wife. The most irrepressible escapers were Royal Navy midshipmen, whose boyish recklessness and sea-going experience – including ropemaking and navigation – made them almost impossible to hold. One case may stand for many. In November 1808 Midshipman Boys and four friends wove a forty-five-foot cord to cross by night successive ramparts and moats of the fortress of Valenciennes. They then dug under a massive gate with their penknives. Escaping pursuit, resisting attack by brigands and evading arrest by gendarmes, they were recognized as British by friendly Flemings. They spent months being hidden by them while they tried to steal a boat, and finally they bought a passage home with a smuggler in May 1809.[114]

From the Tagus to the Berezina, 1807–12

The English declare that they will no longer respect neutrals at sea;
I will no longer recognize them on land.
NAPOLEON BONAPARTE, 1807[115]

Any nation of Europe that starts up with a determination to oppose . . .
the common enemy . . . becomes instantly our essential ally.
GEORGE CANNING, foreign secretary, 1808[116]

After his reconciliation with Tsar Alexander I at Tilsit, Napoleon domi-nated the Continent. This gave him the freedom to deal with 'Carthage' by more direct means than merely Continental blockade. Ideas included invasion of Sicily (Britain's only remaining Mediterranean ally); partition of the Ottoman empire; Franco-Spanish attacks on Gibraltar, Egypt, the Cape and the East Indies; and a joint Franco-Russian attack on India: 'An army of fifty thousand men – Russians, Frenchmen, perhaps even Austrians – marching by way of Constantinople into Asia . . . would make England tremble and bring her down on her knees.'[117] Spain was as usual a neces-sary auxiliary because of its naval and colonial strength. Its Bourbon rulers were eager to placate Napoleon. Their first task was to help invade Britain's impudent ally Portugal, which was ignoring the Berlin Decree. In July 1807 Portugal was ordered to close its ports to British ships, arrest all British subjects, confiscate all British merchandise, and declare war on Britain. French troops moved via Spain to invade Portugal. As they reached Lisbon, the whole royal family, the treasury, and much of the ruling elite embarked under British naval escort for their colony of Brazil. Napoleon confiscated their property, levied a large indemnity and imposed a new government.

His Spanish Bourbon allies had proved untrustworthy and factious, so he decided to get rid of them too. As elsewhere in Europe, he believed that a modernizing French administration would be welcomed by those who mattered: 'Every reflecting person in Spain despises the government . . . As to the rabble, a few cannon shots will quickly disperse them.' He calculated that a takeover would cost only 12,000 French soldiers' lives, a worthwhile price for Spain, with the bullion of the Americas and a large if neglected navy. The royal family were summoned to Bayonne to hand over their throne to Napoleon, who gave it to his brother Joseph. In May 1808 'the rabble' of Madrid did indeed show their anger at the removal of the royal family, and hundreds were shot down or summarily executed – the event immortalized in Goya's famous painting. But they were not so easily 'dispersed'. The uprising combined elements of social, religious and national revolt that proved impossible to suppress, and it encouraged anti-French resistance in Portugal too. Over the next five years this was to reduce the whole of the Iberian peninsula to bloody chaos and ruin. It would prove, in Napoleon's famous phrase, an 'ulcer' draining French strength. It was not, as is often said, a sideshow: more than twice as many soldiers would die there as in the invasion of Russia in 1812.[118]

Napoleon's problem was Britain's opportunity. London immediately responded to requests for help from the Portuguese and the Spanish, sending a naval squadron to snatch from the coast of Denmark a Spanish army sent to fight for Napoleon, and landing men, arms and money at Lisbon and Gibraltar. Britain could thus return to the Continent, exploit its seapower round the coast of the peninsula, make best use of its small army in cooperation with the Spanish and the Portuguese, impress the Continental great powers, establish itself as the defender of freedom, and break the blockade of its exports. The British government was not counting on quick victory. Its aim was to perpetuate turmoil in Europe until the tide turned against Napoleon:

> Our interest is that till there can be a final settlement that shall last, every thing should remain as unsettled as possible; that no usurper should feel sure of acknowledgement; no people confident in their new masters; no kingdom sure of its existence; no spoliator sure of his spoil; and even the plundered not acquiescent in their loss. All this touches not us: but in the midst of all this it is our business to shew what England, as England, is: . . . whenever the true balance of the world comes to be adjusted . . . it is only through us alone that they can look for secure and effectual tranquillity.[119]

British and French had fought each other in Spain in earlier wars, but this was to be a far bigger affair. There was an immediate British success: the French occupying force in Portugal surrendered. However, Napoleon – as he would show throughout the war – would make no concession in the Peninsula, which had become for him a matter of prestige. He came in person with 130,000 troops from Germany to stamp on opposition. The British commander, the bold and headstrong Sir John Moore, marched his 40,000 men into northern Spain to threaten French communications, hoping to distract them from immediate seizure of Madrid and Lisbon. When Napoleon realized that instead of taking to the boats the British were advancing into Castile, he turned north to capture them, making his troops link arms to march through blinding snowstorms. Moore, realizing that 'the bubble had burst', fled through the sleet and mud of the Galician mountains towards the port of Corunna (La Coruña). Both armies suffered terribly. French cavalry rode through exhausted British stragglers, 'slashing among them as a schoolboy does among thistles'.[120] Civilians suffered worse. Supply broke down, so troops pillaged the wretched inhabitants. French, Spanish and British accounts agree that British discipline broke down – a recurring phenomenon – with mass drunkenness, looting, rape and even murder. The fleeing troops destroyed what they could not take to deny it to the French:

The English have burnt . . . a large warehouse of corn and flour
. . . we have found in the town more than 200 horses they killed last
night; all the time, people are bringing in Englishmen found in the
cellars or dead drunk in the attics . . . they destroy everything,
especially ovens and mills; they loot, burn, and mistreat the locals
who, when they dare, take their revenge and are willingly bringing
us English stragglers.[121]

Concluded a Spanish general, 'the French themselves could not have found agents better calculated to whip up hate of the British than the army commanded by General Sir John Moore.'[122] They reached Corunna on 12 January 1809, four days ahead of the French. After a rearguard action in which Moore was killed, the army sailed away, with 20 per cent of its men missing and a vast quantity of equipment lost, including by the huge explosion of 4,000 barrels of gunpowder. On the face of it, this was a political and military disaster. Only later was it clear that Moore's foray had bought time by diverting Napoleon's triumphant sweep through the Peninsula. Moore became a posthumous hero, the rushed retreat transmuted by Charles Wolfe into clipped pathos:

Not a drum was heard, not a funeral note,
As his corpse to the rampart we hurried;
Not a soldier discharged his farewell shot
O'er the grave where our hero lay buried.

Slowly and sadly we laid him down,
From the field of his fame fresh and gory;
We carved not a line, and we raised not a stone –
But we left him alone with his glory.

The war remained as atrocious throughout as it had begun. Spanish and Portuguese rebels turned to *la guerrilla* (a word that now became current in other languages). The French responded with burnings, massacres and summary executions, which were met in turn with killing and torture of prisoners: early on, a witness saw a French officer nailed upside down to a barn door with a fire lit under his head. Reprisals and counter-reprisals multiplied. The Spanish revolt was stoked by domestic hatred between conservatives and liberals, Catholics and anticlericals (some, but not all, supporters of the French – the hated *afrancesados*), and by the raw loathing of the poor for their masters. Many guerrilla bands were, or became, mere brigands, reinforced by deserters from every army, preying on rich and poor alike and increasingly detested. Both countries suffered famine, sometimes deliberately caused, in which hundreds of thousands died. All the armies – French, British, Spanish, Portuguese – became terrifying bands of predators, in part because the poverty of the country and bad communications meant that supply arrangements constantly failed, so soldiers and peasants fought each other for food. Some ashamed British thought their own men were worse than the French – certainly, ferocious drunkenness was a British speciality. But French brutality was a systematic counter-insurgency policy; and besides, there were far more of them.

The British and French had in common a growing detestation of the Spanish. The British saw them as treacherous, vain, and feckless, unwilling to help in their own liberation and denying their British allies the aid and supplies they were due. The French saw them as cruel, superstitious and perverse: they 'rejected everything coming from us – even benefits'.[123] Both British and French saw themselves as culturally and politically superior. Many British felt ashamed to be defending a reactionary despotism. British Protestants and French anticlericals despised Spanish Catholicism and indulged in sacrilegious horseplay and vandalism. Both treated the civilian population as fair game, and each other with relative respect, even with a friendliness that infuriated their respective Iberian allies. One Ensign Wheatley put it bluntly: 'I hate a Spaniard more than a Frenchman.'[124] This did not mean that they did not despise each other, at least at first. The British did not expect the speed, hardiness and ingenuity of the French armies. Many of the French – certainly Napoleon – despised Wellington and his men, and made serious blunders by underestimating them. Yet personal contact revealed remarkable lack of animus. The British adopted the revolutionary 'Ça ira' as a marching tune. The single combat to which cavalry officers often challenged each other displayed an archaic chivalrousness. There are many reports of men being ordered not to kill courageous opponents. Sentries did not fire at each other; there are stories that they took it in turns to stand guard. Outposts sometimes asked the other side to move further away to avoid trouble: 'Retirez-vous, Monsieur l'Officier-là.'[125] They certainly gave each other warnings of imminent attacks – a practice that Wellington commended as sensibly humane. He might not have approved of the widespread commerce in food, tobacco and especially drink that went on: one rifle company clubbed together to buy French brandy, but their emissary got so drunk that the French had to send for his comrades to carry him back. Fraternization was common among all ranks. Letters and newspapers were delivered, drinks exchanged and the curious met to chat. The straying greyhounds of one British officer were politely returned, as was half of an escaped French bullock. It became accepted that prisoners and the wounded should be reasonably treated, and sources of food and water in no-man's-land shared.[126] Some of the stories must be apocryphal, but they formed part of subsequent national folklore. Thus it was possible for a young British officer, examining the enemy through his telescope, to reflect that 'the French people are our common enemy, yet I like them as a nation and I really am of the opinion every Englishman does the same in his heart'.[127]

The pattern of the Peninsular War was that the French were by far the strongest military force – in 1812, they had 250,000 men to 60,000 British. But some three-quarters of their strength was tied down attempting to hold all of Spain against the Spanish armies and guerrilla bands. Napoleon, for political reasons, would not allow his subordinates to abandon territory. The British, based in Portugal, commanded from 1808 by General Sir Arthur Wellesley (whose victories successively made him viscount, marquess and duke of Wellington), could therefore periodically invade Spain; but the French would then concentrate enough of their forces to throw them back. This would give a breathing space to the hard-pressed Spanish, in Wellesley's words 'exposing [France's] whole fabric in Spain to great risk'.[128] In short, the French could defeat each of their enemies separately, but not all of them simultaneously.

In 1810, Napoleon decided to finish the war by invading Portugal and defeating the British. The traditional Portuguese defence was a 'scorched earth' strategy, and this was again implemented under Wellington's thorough direction. He had secretly constructed a twenty-nine-mile belt of fortifications covering Lisbon, the Lines of Torres Vedras. He planned that even if the French could cross the devastated wastes of central Portugal, they would be halted and forced to retreat. So it was. Marshal Masséna fought his way across the Portuguese 'desert' – 'not a soul to be seen anywhere, everything abandoned' – was astounded to come up against Wellington's 'lines', and, after hanging on as long as he could, trudged back, having lost 25,000 men, more than half to disease and starvation. Wellington admired this French fortitude, which he was sure the British could not match. The main cost was born by the Portuguese. Ordered to abandon their homes, with everything they could not carry destroyed, the victims of looting and worse by British and French, those who managed to reach the shelter of the Allied lines spent the winter with scanty food and shelter. Those who had refused to flee were attacked by the famished French, who pillaged, murdered and tortured en masse to extort hidden food supplies. French depredations were succeeded by those of the pursuing British, even though some soldiers, shocked at the plight of the Portuguese, gave them some meagre rations. 'Thousands must have died,' wrote one British soldier, 'and thousands more must perish, for there is no help at hand: rich and poor are all reduced to the same state.'[129] Perhaps 50–80,000 Portuguese died.

The fate of the Peninsula was decided beyond the Elbe. The Franco-Russian alliance proved illusory, as Russia refused, in Napoleon's words, to 'act as my second in my duel with England'.[130] The Continental System required economic and political subservience, which the Russians, for reasons of pride, ideology and interest, would not long concede. In December 1810 Russia left the System. Napoleon, deciding to strike the first blow, summoned his allies, satellites and former enemies for a great invasion. He also withdrew troops from Spain. In June 1812 over 600,000 men and 200,000 horses, the largest army ever yet assembled in Europe, invaded Russia. Meanwhile, Wellington had again marched into Spain, and on 22 July won a complete victory against an over-confident Marshal Marmont at Salamanca, proving to all except Napoleon that the man he dismissed as the 'sepoy general' had ability. This was the first time that a British army had proved that it could successfully attack a major French army, and the first time since 1799 that a French army in Europe had been trounced.[131] Meanwhile Napoleon, his army decimated in the summer heat, could not induce the Russians to make peace, and was forced to retreat from the ruins of Moscow when winter set in. The Russian Marshal Kutuzov, sharing the general Continental suspicion of Britain, decided to let some French escape, pointedly telling a British observer that he was 'by no means sure that the total destruction of the Emperor Napoleon and his army would be a benefit to the world'. Nevertheless, Napoleon's army lost 370,000 dead and 200,000 prisoners, only half of whom survived.[132] Even amid this catastrophe, the French in Spain were able to chase Wellington back into Portugal.

Now came the culmination of the European war, and with it the Franco-British struggle at its core. Napoleon proclaimed that he was defending Europe from Russian barbarism and English corruption, but admitted privately that 'if I left Europe to its own devices it would throw itself into England's arms'.[133] Austria and Prussia changed sides and joined Russia. Britain provided money and weapons. France's twenty-year dominance had relied on the divisions of its enemies, most of whom had at some time tried to be its friends, or at least its accomplices, in a free-for-all from which ideology and principle had been absent. In 1813–14, in the face of Napoleon's limitless aggression, the European states began to cooperate and plan a durable peace. Castlereagh, the foreign minister, intended to show that Britain was not – or no longer – the irresponsible Carthaginian predator happy to leave the Continent in flames while it gathered in colonial spoils. He created a partnership among the coalition, intended to continue after the war. He negotiated the Treaty of Chaumont (1814) – 'a British triumph, but not a triumph over foes or even over rivals' – in which Britain promised to pay for another year of war if necessary, and the Allies pledged themselves to maintain peace for twenty years. It was a practical vision of a Europe of independent sovereign states, equal in rights, status and security.[134] Pitt's 'map of Europe' had been unrolled.

Napoleon, to the dismay of his ministers and generals, refused all Allied offers for a negotiated peace. His intransigence helped Castlereagh to keep the coalition together and this sealed France's fate. The Allies had to fight their way to Paris: 1813–14 would be the bloodiest period of the whole war, costing some 900,000 lives – comparable with the worst months of 1914–18.

Castlereagh: Britain's greatest European? Despite his dashing aristocratic elegance, he came from a recently ennobled Ulster Presbyterian family. This was not untypical of the socially mobile elite that governed Britain during the Napoleonic wars. His Austrian counterpart Prince Metternich regarded his no-nonsense style as rather common.

Invasion, 1813–14

It is a very common error among those unacquainted with military affairs
to believe that there are no limits to military success. After having driven
the French from the frontiers of Portugal . . . it is generally expected that
we shall invade France, and . . . be in Paris in a month.

DUKE OF WELLINGTON[135]

A man like me has little regard for the death of a million men.

NAPOLEON BONAPARTE, 1813[136]

The Russians, Prussians and Austrians were halted by Napoleon in
Germany in May 1813 and forced to sign an armistice. Wellington
marched with calculated boldness into northern Spain, threatening French
communications. At Vitoria on 21 June, the French were routed and their
possession of Spain effectively ended. This was the British soldiers' dream
victory: they captured not only all King Joseph Bonaparte's artillery, but his
whole baggage train. Pursuit was delayed if not forgotten as loot beckoned:
millions of pesos in cash, jewellery and works of art lay around for the taking.
Several hundred officers' mistresses were captured. The king's silver
chamber pot was taken by the 14th Light Dragoons, and is still used by their
successors to drink champagne in the mess. Wellington pressed on towards
the Pyrenees, but cautiously in case Napoleon made peace with the eastern
allies and turned on the British. On 9 September they besieged and captured
San Sebastian, the closest port to the French frontier, with the usual bloody
assault followed by the usual orgy of looting, drunkenness and rape.
Wellington crossed the River Bidassoa, the French frontier, on 7 October
1813, eleven days before the huge battle of Leipzig – 'the Battle of the
Nations' – forced Napoleon to abandon Germany.

The militarily decisive campaign was in the north-east, where throughout
January, February and March 1814 Napoleon conducted a brilliant, futile
defence against the invaders, who nevertheless reached Paris at the end of
March. But France's political future was decided by Wellington's advance –
the only major British invasion since the first Hundred Years War. He out-
manoeuvred Marshal Soult: part of his army crossed the passes of the
western Pyrenees, the rest followed the weakly guarded coast towards
Bayonne. Wellington was determined not to arouse popular resistance. He
held his Spanish troops back following early incidents of looting and rape,
as he believed that they would seek vengeance for French atrocities in Spain.
He threatened his own men, who had a dreadful reputation, with summary
floggings and hangings for misbehaviour. The people of south-western
France were tired of the war and of Napoleon. Official warnings that the

'furious' British were coming, 'their steps marked by arson, devastation, murder and carnage', fell flat. The locals found the British less ready to loot than their own troops: 'the English, laden with guineas, pay for everything in cash'; 'The contrast between the enemy's conduct and that of our troops is having a deplorable effect.' Wellington ordered band concerts, dances and parades to win hearts and minds. 'The conduct of the English is extremely perfidious; they use every means to seduce the population and alas are succeeding only too well.' French commanders were disgusted by the 'state of stupor' among the population: 'populous villages surrender at the approach of three or four enemy horsemen'.[137] Ensign Wheatley was delighted that 'the lasses are up with the sun', picturesquely all dressed the same, unlike in England, 'skipping along the road with milk and butter, singing and laughing as unconcernedly as if all was peace and tranquillity', but 'very shy of Englishmen'.[138] Towns cheered the British as liberators. Farmers, officials, merchants and shopkeepers were equally friendly. One land-owner, delighted at getting a good price for his cattle, 'made us dance with his daughters, produced some of his best chateau margot [sic], sang half a dozen of his best songs, slobbered over us with his embraces, and was put to bed crying drunk'.[139] Lost or wounded soldiers were given shelter. Lord Fitzroy Somerset was hidden from French cavalry in a hiding hole previously used by priests fleeing the Jacobins; forty years later, as Lord Raglan, he commanded a British army as France's ally in the Crimea.

Wellington left a division to besiege Bayonne, forced Soult's army north-east towards Toulouse, and, urged by royalists, sent a force marching north across the barren Landes to Bordeaux. They were greeted on 12 March as liberators in a city that had ancient commercial links with Britain that it was desperate to re-establish, and which equated the Bourbon monarchy with peace. The mayor, Comte Lynch (of a Jacobite family from Galway), raised the royalist white standard. When the Bourbon Duc d'Angoulême arrived, exclaiming, 'No more wars! No more conscription! No more oppressive taxes!' he was cheered and a Te Deum sung in the cathedral. Two delegates hastened to England to pay homage to their new – or old – king, Louis XVIII. This was welcome news to the British government, which thought that a Bourbon restoration would give the best chance of a stable and peaceful France, but did not wish to impose it. The Russians and Austrians still favoured a Bonaparte, an Orléans, or even the slippery French Marshal Bernadotte, now adopted as Crown Prince of Sweden. But when the news from Bordeaux reached Allied headquarters, now at Dijon, all agreed that the Bourbons should be backed. Castlereagh and the Austrian chancellor Metternich drank a toast to Louis XVIII – and to mayor Lynch.[140] Soult, still battling on, was 'ashamed . . . that a town of 100,000 souls . . . could get away with refusing to be defended and should greet a few thousand

Englishmen with acclamation'. He met the same problem at equally royalist Toulouse: the defence works he ordered nearly caused a riot, as 'practically the whole city is against being defended'.[141] But defend it he did, and the battle of Toulouse on 10 April was the last real battle in the south, costing 4,500 Allied casualties and 2,700 French. Napoleon had already abdicated on 6 April. Soult marched away unpursued. The British were greeted by the mayor, the city guard, a band and a crowd of citizens all wearing the Bourbon white cockade, who gave them a banquet.

Louis XVIII and the Prince Regent, well-upholstered symbols of peace and plenty, entered London together amid joyful crowds who hauled their carriage through the streets: the Bourbons signified peace for Britain too. A popular song ran: 'England no more your foe, will bring you aid/ When France shall welcome home the White Cockade.' Louis declared that 'it is to your Royal Highness's councils, to this great country, and to the constancy of its people that I shall always ascribe, under Providence, the restoration of our House to the Throne of our Ancestors'. All over Britain people celebrated: 'Bells Ringing Guns Firing and Tom Paines Quaking'. At Yarmouth, 8,000 people feasted on roast beef, plum pudding and beer at a table three-quarters of a mile long. Wellington congratulated his army for 'their conciliating conduct towards the inhabitants of the country which, in almost equal degree with their discipline and gallantry in the field, have produced the fortunate circumstances that now hold forth to the world the prospect of genuine and permanent peace'. Ensign Wheatley did his bit for concili-ation, finding Bordeaux 'magnificent in the extreme. Every necessity of life is dogcheap' – good claret 3d a bottle – 'the people civil and kind [and] the Gascon ladies not inferior to the Parisians in vivacity . . . giggling when they meet anyone, [they] run as if to entice a pursuit. This is gaieté!!!'[142]

LE CIMETIÈRE DES ANGLAIS

Faint traces can still be found of the British invasion: Soult's earthworks on the slopes of the Pyrenees; occasional rusty cannonballs in the undergrowth; a war memorial in St Andrew's church, Biarritz; soldiers' lonely graves in Basque and Gascon churchyards – and a *cimetière des Anglais*, along an over-grown track through a steep oak wood at the end of a torpid suburban street on the northern fringe of Bayonne.

By mid-April 1814 the war seemed over. On 10 April the news arrived that the Allies had entered Paris and Napoleon had abdicated. But Vauban's towering citadel at Bayonne held out, defended by 13,000 men, while a bored and cold British, Portuguese and Spanish army of 28,000 waited in the wet outside. 'We have now been piquetting for two months before this infernal fortress endeav-

The Cimetière des Anglais, Bayonne: the last clash on French soil.

ouring to starve them out, while we are in want of food ourselves. For nothing but herrings and brandy are come-attable. Our tents are pitched by a large swamp and the French pour in cannon shot and shells every ten minutes among us.' News shouted across the lines informed the defenders of the emperor's abdication, or so the British thought. It is unclear whether the commander, General Thouvenot, decided on a final defiant gesture – a *baroud d'honneur* – or whether, uninformed or sceptical of news from outside, he aimed simply to push back the siege lines. A deserter warned the British of an attack, but not many took it seriously. During the moonless night of 14 April, 3,000 men erupted into the British positions on the wooded hills north of the town, killing one of the British commanding generals and capturing the other.

> I heard a pop, then another. I was on the point of again falling off, when more than five hundred reports burst upon our ears, a thunder of cannon followed . . . The air filled with stars and shells like a Vauxhall exhibition . . . every bush and hedge was spangled with flashing stars from the musketry, and the fields covered with blue lights shot from Bayonne to shew the men on the ramparts . . . where to direct their guns.

A confused and vicious mêlée in the dark ensued: 'not a soul could be seen. Now and then a voice in the hedge would say "'Français ou Anglais?'" and a thrust through the bush was the answer.' At daybreak, the attackers withdrew and called a truce. 'The French poured out from the town and a singular scene ensued – they picking up their dead and we ours. I . . . had a long chat with some French Officers who gave me some snuff. And as the French soldiers passed us with their dead comrades, we reflected on the miserable trade of war.'[143] There had been about 900 French and 600 Allied casualties. What to the French was a gallant gesture (commemorated in Bayonne's Rue du 14 Avril and a grandiose imperial eagle monument erected in 1907) was to the British a futile waste of lives. There was no further fighting, and an official armistice was signed on 27 April.

The tiny *cimetière des Anglais* contains the graves of officers of the 3rd Foot Guards, a small obelisk and the cannon-shattered tree trunk that originally marked the spot. Embellished in the nineteenth century by their families and members of the local British community, it became a patriotic shrine, visited by vacationing royalty. But money ran out in the 1970s and it is now owned and maintained by Bayonne town council. The Bordeaux British Legion and their French counterparts, Le Souvenir Français, leave an annual wreath of poppies.[144] It is safe to say that few of the myriad British holiday-makers nearby know or care that here was the last Franco-British battle on French soil.

The End of the Hundred Years War, 1815

Britain has no greater obligation to any mortal on earth than to
this ruffian [Bonaparte]. For through the events that he has brought
about, England's greatness, prosperity, and wealth have risen high. She is
the mistress of the sea and neither in this dominion nor in world trade
has she now a single rival to fear.
GENERAL VON GNEISENAU[145]

The epic, of course, has a famous postscript. Napoleon soon tired of his little realm on the island of Elba, where spies reported he was putting on weight. He sailed with 900 men and landed near Cannes on 1 March 1815. He was acclaimed by the army and a large minority – perhaps one in three – of the country, especially the bureaucracy, workers suffering from the post-war slump, and those who feared losing what they had gained since 1789: rights, jobs and property. Louis XVIII fled to Belgium. France, like a battered wife, wanted to believe that this time Napoleon had changed. British radicals were even more gullible: 'He is now a new man.'[146] Professing peaceful intentions, Napoleon prepared for a general war. As so often, he had no clear plan. Only one thing could have saved him: if Britain had been unwilling or unable to bear the cost of defeating him. But it promised another £9 million, and nearly a million Allied soldiers marched – far more than were actually needed. There was little chance that the Allies would give up. They had learnt that there was no point in negotiating with him. His police minister, Fouché, predicted that he would win two battles and lose the third. He did win – or partially win – two battles, at Ligny against the Prussians, and at Quatre Bras against Wellington's Anglo-Dutch army. The third was Waterloo.

The most famous battle in modern history was fought on 18 June on sloping, rain-soaked fields astride the main road south from Brussels. Wellington's men held a defensive line which Napoleon's larger army had to smash through quickly, before Blücher's Prussians could arrive and give the Allies overwhelming superiority. Both sides were therefore fighting in their characteristic fashion; and – partly because of French haste – there was no subtlety: 'hard pounding, this, gentlemen; let us see who can pound the longest'. The battle became an archetype of the French attacking column against the British defensive line: the tactics of the revolution against those of the old regime, unleashed enthusiasm against disciplined stoicism, *la furie française* against *le flegme britannique*. This style of fighting influenced each nation's self-image, its conceptions of masculinity and courage. The two commanders seemed to sum up, even caricature, these opposites: 'On one side precision, foresight, geometry, prudence, stubborn sang-froid,' wrote Victor Hugo. 'On the other, intuition, guesswork, the unorthodox, superhuman instinct.'[147] The determination on both sides, and the restricted battlefield, created an intense concentration of violence. The French failed to break through. The Prussians arrived. The British advanced. Napoleon returned to Paris and, after briefly trying to rally resistance, abdicated again on 22 June. The rational importance of Waterloo is that by cutting short Napoleon's adventure it kept 'the problems of victory and peace manageable', without throwing every agreement back into the melting pot; and, as principally a British victory, it gave Wellington and Castlereagh the influence to 'settle France and Europe down as quickly as possible'.[148] Linda Colley comments that 'Waterloo made the world safe for gentlemen again'.[149] So it did: also for workers, peasants, women and children.

Meanwhile, the Congress of Vienna, where sovereigns and statesmen met to decide the future of Europe, continued in session. How much had changed since 1688, when the Three Kingdoms had been hustled into European affairs as a minor auxiliary against Louis XIV! Now the United Kingdom was predominant in Europe, it was the sole global power, and it had become the prototype of economic transformation. France, still formidable, was no longer menacing. Though it took nearly another century for it to become entirely clear, the Franco-British war was over, and with it, the series of world wars it had spawned.

ECHOES OF WATERLOO

Waterloo! Waterloo! Waterloo! drear plain!
Cockpit of woods, of hills, of valleys
In which pale death stirred the dark battalions.
On one side was Europe, on the other France.
Bloody clash! and God forsook the heroes;
Victory, you deserted them, and the spell broke.
O Waterloo! I weep and there I halt, alas!
For these last soldiers of this last war
Were great; had vanquished all the earth,
Had put down twenty kings, crossed Alps and Rhine,
And their souls sang in the brazen bugles!
VICTOR HUGO, 'L'Expiation'

The memory of defeat went deeper than the memory of victory. Which is not to say that this victory did not fill the British cup: how much less would have been the effect if Napoleon had surrendered to the Russians somewhere in Bavaria, with Britain merely paymaster-general. Wellington, commander, proconsul, ambassador, prime minister and national hero, would celebrate the day with selected old comrades at Apsley House (known as 'No. 1 London') for the rest of his life, amid the plaudits of Europe. Streets, stations, pubs and the workaday paraphernalia of British memory immortalize the day. One can point out that after the poetry of victory comes the prose of politics; that all political careers, especially those of heroes, end in failure; that Britain faced the usual post-war problems of slump, unemployment, poverty and dissension – well summed up in the sarcasm of the name 'Peterloo', given to the cavalry charge against an inoffensive crowd in Manchester's St Peter's Fields in 1819. But however one darkens the shadows, Waterloo was a permanent source of pride – usually vicarious, though the Prince Regent convinced himself after a good dinner that he had actually been there – and a confirmation that Britain, the British people, the British system, had triumphed. The playing fields of Eton produced invincible generals; the slums and hovels of Britain and Ireland produced invincible ruffians: as Wellington put it, 'I don't know what they do to the enemy but by God they frighten me!' Winning the last battle, after losing so many, was reassuring. Yet Waterloo was not what most deeply stirred, and perhaps even now stirs, the British patriotic fibre. Struggles for survival when the 'snug little Island, a right little, tight little Island'[150] was threatened and alone – the Armada, Trafalgar, Dunkirk, the Battle of Britain – outweigh Waterloo.

Which is why the memory of defeat went deeper, enriching what Jean-Marc Largeaud calls a 'culture of defeat' unique to France.[151] The British often say that they themselves are the people who celebrate defeats. Not so: narrow escapes, yes; even slaughter. Defeat, never. The French, after Waterloo, did and do, if discreetly. Dwelling on 'glorious defeat' was a lesson in sacrifice and proof that France had survived and would rise again. Was it just coincidence that General de Gaulle, that most historically conscious of statesmen, made his first broadcast to the French people on the anniversary of Waterloo? Memories of Waterloo did not minimize the disaster: they laid on the tragedy, the doomed but defiant heroism. They also emphasized, quite wrongly, how near victory had been. Napoleon, who dwelt endlessly on the battle and said he should have died there, blamed his subordinates for blunders and treason, and drew up a list of reasons why Wellington should have lost. Victor Hugo, the bard of Waterloo, invented a hidden sunken lane into which the French cavalry fell just as they were about to conquer. Finally, there were the Prussians, turning up unsportingly to turn the tide – and serving as a way of denying that it was the British who had beaten them. Moral victory – seedbed of future hope – was claimed by the French.

All this is summed up in the famous *mot de Cambronne*, or rather his two *mots*, alternative expressions of heroic defiance. General Cambronne, one of Napoleon's companions on Elba, commanded a brigade of the Imperial Guard, which, late in the battle, formed a square to cover the retreat. They were surrounded and suffering useless casualties, so a British general shouted to Cambronne to surrender. His reply: 'The Guard dies, it does not surrender!' Or (in Hugo's more famous version): 'Merde!' And, Hugo tells us, the Guard died, but Cambronne, for mocking fate, for 'completing Leonidas with Rabelais', was the true victor of Waterloo.[152] Myth is more potent than prosaic truth: there is little evidence that Cambronne said either of his *mots*. The poetic version may have been a journalistic invention. He rejoined the army under Louis XVIII, who made him a viscount.[153]

The French celebrate their defeats, but they are not keen on others doing so. When the British government – naïvely? – proposed a ceremony to mark the 150th anniversary of Waterloo, the French response was frosty, especially as Britain, whose application to join the Common Market de Gaulle had recently vetoed, envisaged a 'European' celebration. The French ambassador to Belgium was not amused by 'festivities organized . . . by the descendants of the soldiers of Wellington and William of Orange'. So the ceremonies were scaled down, to the satisfaction of *Le Monde*: 'they are almost having to apologize for having won'.[154]

Part I: Conclusions and Disagreements
The Second Hundred Years War:
Whose Victory? Whose Defeat?

Between 1689 and 1815 incalculable suffering was caused by the Franco-British struggle, not the sole cause but the fuel for fifty-six years of multinational conflict. Estimates of direct military deaths are difficult, but the total for all the combatants runs into millions – probably approaching 6 million, equal to the total population of England in the 1750s. Two-thirds of these died between 1792 and 1815, when 1.4 million French and over 200,000 British lost their lives – comparable in proportion with the First World War. Roughly one-third of French boys born between 1790 and 1795 were killed or wounded.[1] The maimed soldier reduced to beggary was a familiar sight in both countries. To these must be added civilian death, anguish, hunger, disease, family breakdown and economic disruption, including the enormous 'collateral damage' done to people on every continent dragged into the conflict or made to help pay for it. What Kipling bluntly called the 'Puppets that we made or broke to bar the other's path – Necessary, outpost-folk, hirelings of our wrath' included Indian states and armies, German mercenaries, slave soldiers, Iroquois warriors, Spanish sailors and Portuguese guerrillas. Almost forgotten in the background: famished peasants from Bengal to Portugal, dead babies, enslaved Africans, raped women and their unwanted offspring. In discussing the outcomes, this should never be forgotten. It was not only blood, to quote Kipling again, that was 'the price of admiralty'.

The idea that 1689–1815 constituted a 'second hundred years war' is an arresting one.[2] Was it a single struggle? In important ways, clearly not. Conflict was not always about the same territories, interests or ideas. Conflict was not unremitting, nor was there blank enmity. Mutual admiration and emulation are as characteristic as hatred. Never, before or since, have the two societies found each other so fascinating. Knowing that the other had dangerously attractive qualities gave the rivalry extra intensity. At least until the 1760s, Britain represented liberty and modernity in Europe – relative religious freedom, representative government, political tumult, social fluidity and 'commercial society'. Thereafter – at least in the eyes of its many enemies – it stood for conquest and economic exploitation, and even the Bourbons, during the American war of independence, became defenders of freedom. The French revolution, caused above all by the financial and ideological strains of global war, transformed the nature and meaning of the Franco-British antagonism: France now embodied change, while Britain stood for stability and tradition.

It is commonly stated that in both France and Britain their conflict was crucial in creating national identity.[3] Patriots in both countries were imbued with a sense of unique and contrasting destiny. Several British and American historians have emphasized that conflict with France created a new sense of Britishness, contrasting in religion, manners and politics with the Popery, frogs' legs and absolutism across the Channel. This is true to some extent, for example in promoting greater solidarity between Scots and English, and in spreading a range of symbols and stereotypes. But there was no serious attempt to create a single British identity at the expense of English, Scottish, Welsh or Irish. French historians have paid less attention to British influences in the making of their own national identity, although François Furet notes that 'like other European peoples, and perhaps *par excellence* among them, the French were accustomed to define themselves in relation to an enemy.'[4] But which enemy? As we have noted, there was asymmetry across the Channel. France was Britain's great enemy from the 1670s; but Britain was only one of the pack of lesser breeds snarling at France's heels. Imperial Austria was the detested 'natural enemy', and only from the 1750s did perfidious Albion come to the fore. Ideologically alien, the core of hostile alliances and the model of a coarse commercial society, Britain before, during and after the revolution was the foil – the 'anti-France' – both to royalist and republican patriotism.

The creation of identities was only part of the story, for the long struggle simultaneously created divisions. Both sides underwent revolutions and civil wars. The French repeatedly opened up ideological and ethnic divisions among their island enemies, some of which never closed. A British nation previously seen as spanning the Atlantic broke apart, and British-Irish relations were permanently embittered. France underwent not merely a violent political revolution and civil war, but a traumatic cultural transformation. In the last phase of the struggle, many in France saw Britain as an ally and a model; many in Britain saw France as an example and Napoleon as a hero. In both countries, the political divisions of the nineteenth century owed much to the ideological and economic consequences of their long struggle.

What above all gives unity to this century-long struggle is that it became the first-ever contest for global power, and thus it began a new era in world history. Britain, for geopolitical and ideological reasons, opposed the domination of the Continent by France, the only state whose geographical position and size threatened its home security and its interests in the Low Countries, Germany, the Mediterranean, and on the oceans. Several Continental states also feared France, but all were at times coerced into acquiescence or tempted into complicity. But France could not coerce or tempt Britain, whose intractable opposition was dangerous because of its naval and financial strength, which enabled it to interfere everywhere and with disproportionate effect. Bourbon France tried to project power over-seas to oppose British colonial and commercial expansion and claim its own share. From the 1750s onwards, France even had at crucial moments to reverse its priorities by making European politics subordinate to the global struggle, culminating in Napoleon's impossible effort to dominate the sea by conquering the land. The link between European and world power made the Franco-British struggle very difficult to compromise. Only for a few months, in 1803, did it seem that stalemate had been reached, with Britain abandoning the Continent, and France the oceans – a solution unpalatable to both.

Though geography and economics provide the raw material for the struggle, neither the course of the conflict nor its outcome were predeter-mined. Beliefs, fears, ambitions, prejudices, calculations and choices began, continued and ended it. If any one of France's invasion attempts had succeeded, the story might have finished very differently.

These descriptive comments are as much as a French and a British author can be expected to agree on. What follows shows how we disagree.

Origins

IT: Taking the 'hundred years war' as a whole, its taproot is British aggres-sion. The commercial and financial interests linked to the City of London supported the 'Patriotic' cause and colonial aggrandizement in Asia and the Americas, and this made conflict inevitable. As three recent historians put it, 'In England the throne was surrounded by merchants and bankers . . . England spoke the language of account books, France that of the warrior thirsty for honour and supremacy.'[5] British aggressiveness was expressed through the notorious francophobia (indeed general xenophobia) of British culture, what a leading French historian calls a mixture of 'paranoia' and 'anti-Catholic hysteria' that was 'deep-rooted, constant, intense and influ-ential'.[6] It was noted by many contemporaries and is stressed even by British historians such as Linda Colley and Paul Langford. This culture made colo-nial aggression and even Continental war against France acceptable and popular. France, even under Louis XIV, was essentially on the defensive, concerned with the consolidation of its frontiers, satisfied with its position of diplomatic and cultural primacy in Europe, and determined only to resist an aggressive British monopoly of colonial trade – a stand supported by other countries. It was British money that repeatedly fomented coalitions against France, culminating in the revolutionary and Napoleonic wars. French continental hegemony was 'the consequence and not the cause'[7] of wars fomented by Britain.

RT: It is true that the hoariest clichés about Britain survive. They rest on assumptions about 'the rise of capitalism', rather than on empirical research. Foreign policy was not in fact determined by commerce. Even under Pitt the Elder (the politician closest to City interests and Patriotism) decisions were made by a small royal and official elite concerned with diplomatic influence and above all security. Moreover, public opinion was overwhelmingly hostile to Continental wars. British statesmen saw France as a threat, not as a soft target to be despoiled of its colonies. In India and North America, it was the French who repeatedly took the offensive. Religious prejudice played no part in British policy: it was willing to ally with a variety of sovereignties and systems, from Calvinist republicanism to papal theocracy. As for British or English xenophobia, facile assertions about its uniqueness are meaningless in the absence of comparison with other countries, and have been implicitly disproved by recent research on France. British francophobia was an expression, however crude, of opposition to despotism, religious oppression and extreme social privilege. French anglophobia was at least as virulent, and often more sinister. The real origin of the conflict is that France, by far the most bellicose state in Europe for 250 years, sought to impose a European, and eventually a global, hegemony. As for coalitions, British money made them possible, especially at the end of the period; but all the gold in the City could not create them. It was French aggression that did that.

Culture

IT: The eighteenth century, the century of Enlightenment, was the French century. Its tendency was towards the voluntary unity of European intellectual life in a 'republic of letters' extending from Philadelphia to St Petersburg, communicating in French, and aiming at the rational improvement and modernization of society. The British victory over France had a fundamental effect on European culture, going far beyond the substitution of Shakespeare for Racine and the gradual ascendancy of English. The contest, argues Marc Fumaroli, was 'metaphysical': would the Enlightenment swing towards the commerce-driven 'empiricism and utilitarianism of rapacious England', or the 'classical, Christian and aristocratic presuppositions' embodied by France – 'beauty and truth loved for themselves'?[8] Britain laboured to divide Europe politically and intellectually, and prepared the ground for the warring cultures of the age of nationalism. Only now, after two centuries of conflict and fragmentation, is Europe attempting to rebuild and protect its common culture – still against 'Anglo–Saxon' invasion.

RT: This surely gives too exclusive an importance to the Anglo-French quarrel. Resistance to French cultural hegemony appeared independently in the 'Romantic' rediscovery of native cultures, especially in Germany. As for vulgarizing culture through commerce, British historians such as Roy Porter have proudly pleaded guilty: the Enlightenment came largely from that very source, and it is what made the modern world. The 'classical, Christian and aristocratic' French culture was regarded as stuffy and outmoded even at Paris and Versailles.[9] I'm happy to agree that something precious was lost when the Old Regime was destroyed. Let's forget the censorship and persecution, and agree with Talleyrand that 'those who were not alive around 1780 have not known the pleasure of living' – an upper-class *douceur de vivre* of tolerant hedonism and cultivated intelligence rarely equalled in history. But it was Robespierre who wrecked that, not George III. By the way, it is amusing that French intellectuals who condemn 'Anglo-Saxon' cultural predominance today tend to praise that of France in the past.

Politics

IT: British apologists claimed to stand for liberty: it was easy, because true, to point out that they stood for oppression in Ireland and India. One might excuse their opposition to Louis XIV – though he sought no quarrel with Britain – but the culmination of the Franco-British struggle is Britain's war against the revolution. However one criticizes Jacobin excesses (any worse than those of the English in Ireland and India?), the revolution stood and still stands for a new universal concept of human rights, equality, the end of privilege, and democracy – in short, modern politics. France had the support of leading intellectuals and the most progressive elements in every country – even Britain – and the revolution still remains an inspiration everywhere. The French proclaimed democracy in 1789. Britain, formerly a model for Europe, rallied to king and church. Loyalists smashed Joseph Priestley's scientific instruments – what a symbol! From 1793 to 1815, Britain fought against the revolution: it became the ally of absolutism, aristocracy, the Spanish inquisition, serfdom, fanatical peasants, the ghetto. Its own domestic politics became increasingly reactionary. It crushed United Irishmen and English radicals with as little compunction as Nelson allowing the massacre of Neapolitan patriots to please Emma Hamilton's royal cronies. Napoleon gave ordinary soldiers medals and promotion; Wellington flogged his and called them scum. Thanks to Britain, organizer and paymaster of counter-revolution, Europe rebuilt its Bastilles.

RT: British critics of the revolution – Burke and Wordsworth are good examples – were conscious of their own country's misdeeds (though one might note that oppression in Ireland and India was directly connected with the French threat), and those of the Bourbon monarchy. But they believed the remedy was worse than the disease. Your selective and idealized version of the revolution stresses the rhetoric and overlooks the reality – a trick practised by the revolutionaries themselves, as François Furet observes.[10] The revolution was not attacked by a reactionary coalition led by Britain: it was a nationalist dictatorship that attacked and subjugated its neighbours. It was a 'despotic democracy' that exterminated opposition, as peasants in the Vendée knew. If 'modern politics' is to be credited to the revolution, the balance sheet must show not only today's placid welfare-state democracy, but movements inspired by the mystique of violent revolution, including Communism and Fascism. If Britain found itself the ally of the Inquisition, the French revolution adopted the methods of the Inquisition; if Britain was the ally of serf owners, Napoleon imposed a military serfdom all over Europe. Napoleon indeed gave his soldiers medals, and then led them to the slaughter without turning a hair. Wellington called his scum, but was sparing of their lives and wept after Waterloo. Britain defended the sovereignty of European states, warts and all, against unfettered force; but it used its influence to encourage liberalism and suppress the slave trade. If some of Europe's thinkers supported the French cause, its people rejected it. Britain's victory over Napoleon gave them what they most wanted: peace, security, and stability. This really was 'earth's best hope'.

The Economy

IT: Britain's victory was made possible by, and was the instrument of, a predatory, expanding, globalizing capitalism, whose full effects would be seen in the century after Waterloo. This is what British domination most importantly created, the basis, for good or ill, of modern world organization. The 'Industrial Revolution', overheated by war, damaged the social fabric and the environment, leaving permanent physical and cultural scars. The French economy, more agricultural, and changing more gradually, did less harm to its own society, and French victory would have enabled more balanced and healthier economic development for the world.

RT: France was no less predatory in the eighteenth century: its leading role in the slave trade shows that. It is true that the struggle with France catalysed the Industrial Revolution, and that French victory would probably have slowed economic, and hence social, change. Some aspects of the Industrial Revolution were damaging – though it introduced the system that gives most human beings their livelihood. And one should not idealize pre-industrial agricultural society, which, as still in many parts of the world, meant un-remitting toil, poverty and early death.

Europe

IT: Many historians, both British and French, accept that France, especially after 1789, had a European vision that foreshadowed the European project of today – one reason why the French took a leading role in it from the start. Napoleon removed boundaries, ended discrimination, extended a modern legal code and an administrative system over western Europe – much of which survived him – and abolished archaic and oppressive political units, paving the way for Italian and German unification in the nineteenth century and for integration in the late twentieth. Progressive elites all over Europe welcomed this, and after Waterloo it was these defeated allies of France who spearheaded liberal and democratic movements from Portugal to Poland. Byron mocked Wellington as '"saviour of the nations" – not yet saved, and "Europe's liberator" – still enslaved'. Dominique de Villepin points out that 'history has vindicated [Napoleon's] vision of a "great European family" of the future,' and this is echoed even by a conservative English historian, Andrew Roberts: 'although Wellington won the battle, it is Napoleon's dream that is coming true'.[11]

RT: The analogy with contemporary Europe is not flattering. Napoleon's Europe was an alliance of self-interested elites who despised popular wishes, silenced opposition, and had no clear purpose other than power, advantage and the aggrandizement of the system that provided them: 'we would have settled our interests among ourselves without asking the peoples'.[12] The liberating rhetoric of the revolution soon became a cloak for conquest and exploitation; besides, 'No one loves armed missionaries', as even Robespierre realized. To treat Napoleon's St Helena propaganda as truth is disingenuous. That some of the European elites served France because it was in their interest is not surprising: every occupier finds collaborators, including idealists. As Paul Schroeder argues, what contribution Napoleon made to Europe's future was unintended, and negative: he carried power politics to such an intolerable extreme that Europe had to find another form of international relations. This could only happen when he had been overthrown.[13] More important to Europe's future, and the condition of its unprecedented nineteenth-century peace and prosperity, was the agreement among the victors of Waterloo, led by Castlereagh, to maintain peace. The sincerest tribute was paid unwittingly by Napoleon himself: 'Castlereagh had the Continent at his mercy . . . And he made peace as if he had been defeated. The imbecile!'[14]

The World

IT: Britain's defeat of France meant domination of the globe. Britain came to rule 20 per cent of the world's population, transforming their economic lives and affecting their cultures, and it had a major impact on the other 80 per cent. The most obvious sign is that English became the language of the Empire, and, gradually, the second language of Europe, and hence, the first world language – a process consolidated by the succeeding ascendancy of America. Was this to the world's benefit? Had France been victorious, it would not have become the great colonial power; indeed, its nineteenth-century imperialism was largely a defensive response to that of Britain. Moreover, because France had not the same economic greed and demographic pressures, its relationship with the indigenous peoples of North America and India was one of coexistence, not displacement or genocide, and this would have been so in the nineteenth century. It might have been a more humane and civilized world.

RT: British global dominance, with all its consequences, happened. We cannot say what would otherwise have happened – though there were certainly worse possibilities, above all global anarchy. Nor can we say what France would have been like had Louis XIV, Louis XV, Robespierre or Napoleon triumphed. Had France defeated Britain, French ideology, society, the economy, and even population growth would have been very different. A victorious France's conduct in the world is therefore unpredictable – but surely not, on its record, less aggressive or imperialistic. Imagining different outcomes is amusing, but pure fantasy: a 'French century', French as the world language, the Code Civil universalized, a 'Pax Gallicana' with royal governors or Napoleonic prefects ruling 'Bengale' and 'Nouvelle Zélande' – culminating, perhaps, in a great Franco-American war in the twentieth century? Such fantasies at least remind us that no outcome was predetermined. Would French victory have meant a more humane and civilized world? Perhaps. But if so – given that France consistently stood for greater centralization, power, regulation and uniformity – also a less free and less creative one.

What we can agree is that 1815 set the course of world history. India was now largely under British domination, providing a base for Asian hegemony. The Spanish and Portuguese empires were in turmoil, and the metropolitan countries would never recover. The United States, having had Washington burnt in 1814 by British troops fresh from the Peninsula, painted the Executive Mansion white to cover the scorch marks and kept out of Europe's quarrels for 100 years. Britain's victory came from its ability to call on global resources, mobilizing the world against the Continent, and not until the twentieth century would another Continental power, Germany, attempt to challenge the outcome. Global resources had revolutionized power relations, as the French knew. Napoleon never imagined that he had been defeated on the playing fields of Eton, but he did say that Waterloo had been lost on the plains of Plassey, in India, half a century before. He could conscript and tax Poles, Germans and Italians. But Britain, through the world clearing-house of London, could harness the labours of Bengali peasants, Gujerati weavers, Chinese tea-planters, African slaves, American settlers and Mexican miners. It could profit from the spending of consumers on every continent to finance not only its own ships and regiments, but Portuguese, Spanish, Russian, Italian, Austrian and German armies too. Perhaps whales will always dominate elephants in the end. Defeat after a century of struggle, concludes François Crouzet, left France 'a weak, poor, backward, wretched and unhappy country'.[15]

INTERLUDE: THE VIEW FROM ST HELENA

October 1815–May 1821

England is alone responsible for all the miseries by which Europe has . . .
been assailed.

NAPOLEON BONAPARTE, 1816[1]

Destiny took nails, a hammer, chains,
Seized pale and alive the thief of thunder,
And gleefully nailed him to the ancient rock,
Where the vulture England tears at his heart.

VICTOR HUGO

Quel roman pourtant que ma vie!
[My life – what a story!]

NAPOLEON BONAPARTE

Waterloo did not end Napoleon's struggle against perfidious Albion. His
first thought was to escape to the United States, recently at war with Britain.
But the elephant surrendered to the whale: he was trapped by the Royal
Navy. He declared that he would pay a great compliment to 'the most
powerful, the most constant, the most generous of my enemies' by settling
in England. He envisaged life as a country gentleman – and, no doubt, as a
huge political celebrity. Although the object of popular and official detestation, 'Buonaparte', 'the Corsican ogre', was also the subject of avid curiosity,
admiration and even sympathy, increased by his Hundred Days exploit. This
was not confined to the Whig opposition and dissident intellectuals.[2]
Wellington, like many military men, was passionately interested in him (as
would be Winston Churchill). His carriage, displayed in several towns, and
a collection of memorabilia shown in London, attracted hundreds of thousands. When the warship carrying him reached Torbay, it was surrounded
by crowds, and sympathizers tried to use habeas corpus to keep him in
Britain. But the Allies were in no mood to trifle, and he was dispatched to
St Helena, far in the South Atlantic – Wellington's idea, not least because
he feared the Bourbons or the Prussians were thinking of shooting him.
From there it would be impossible to escape. But not impossible to be rescued.
Bonapartist exiles in America wanted to set up a 'Napoleonic Confederation'
including Mexico and south-western areas of North America. The
swashbuckling British ex-Admiral Cochrane planned to snatch him from the

island and make him emperor of newly independent South America. So, unlike on Elba, 'General Bonaparte' was not a prince, but a prisoner, reduced to gardening, dictating his memoirs, and negligently rogering the wives of his entourage. He also formed a touching friendship with the teenage Betsy Balcombe, the only English person he ever really knew.

Napoleon, and sympathizers then and since, have condemned his treatment as the monstrous persecution of a great man. It gave him the opportunity, eagerly grasped, of reinventing himself. The Corsican ogre became the European martyr: Prometheus suffering from the weather, and confined to the damp and gloomy Longwood House. The island's governor, Sir Hudson Lowe, was cast as tormentor, and features as the villain in practically every succeeding account. He had been chosen as a man who could get on with his prisoner: a fighting soldier who spoke Corsican, having served in the Anglo-Corsican Kingdom and commanded (not very tactful, this) a Corsican unit that had fought Napoleon in Egypt. But Napoleon was not in the mood for fireside reminiscences in patois about the good old days. He and his entourage were soon at loggerheads with Lowe. Every breach of imperial etiquette or restriction on movement was denounced as vindictive humiliation, and treasured as a means of rehabilitation: 'Every day strips me of my tyrant's skin.' Lowe ruefully noted that his prisoner created an imaginary Napoleon, an imaginary Europe, and even an imaginary St Helena.

Suffering was not enough. On St Helena, as J. Christopher Herold nicely puts it, the flesh was made word.[3] Napoleon's flood of rumination was transcribed by his entourage for profitable publication after his death in 1821. The first book to appear, Las Cases's *Mémorial de Sainte-Hélène* (1823), was the greatest European best-seller of its time. This and later publications, including a Last Testament, portrayed Napoleon as a peace-loving philanthropist who had served France and its people, defended the revolution, aimed to liberate all nations, and planned a glorious future. 'I wished to found a European system, a European code of laws, a European judiciary . . . There would be but one people in Europe.' His idealism had been frustrated above all by the insatiable hatred and jealousy of Britain – a theme passionately debated ever since. Yet the future was his: 'Outside the ideas and principles . . . which I made triumph I see nothing but slavery and confusion for France and Europe alike.' Even 'you British' would 'weep for your victory at Waterloo'.[4]

St Helena made Napoleon the most important political propagandist in modern French history. It confirmed the admiration of many of the elite for the 'successor of Caesar and Alexander', who also personified the Romantic fantasy of the restless, doomed hero. Victor Hugo, after a period of royalism, surrendered to hero-worship and fictionalized his conversion in Marius, of *Les Misérables*. The patriotic liberal Adolphe Thiers wrote a monumental

History of the Consulate and Empire (1845–62), which fortified the Napoleonic version not by unalloyed praise, but by measured criticism outweighed by admiration: 'he lost our greatness, but left us glory, which is moral greatness, and in time restores material greatness'.[5] The St Helena message fed a spontaneous grass-roots mythology, strongest in France but not confined to it, spread by former soldiers and officials nostalgic for the glory days, and propagated by astute populists such as the songwriter Béranger:

> The hero went down in defeat
> And he whom a Pope had crowned
> Died far on a desert isle.
> For long none thought it true;
> They said: he will return.
> By sea he is coming again.
> The foreigner he'll bring low.
> But we found it was not so,
> How bitter was my pain.

For decades, all over Europe, political dissidence had a Bonapartist tinge. In Britain, critics of the post-war order, most famously Byron, Shelley and Hazlitt, indulged in hero-worship of Napoleon, the genius who had defied the world. Byron bought his carriage and followed his footsteps round Europe. Young Benjamin Disraeli wrote a verse drama about him. Reports of his escape, sightings, stories that he was returning to liberate France with armies of Americans or Turks, and stubborn refusal to believe in his death were common as late as 1848, even after his body was returned by the British in 1840 and buried with pomp in the Invalides. This 'cult of Napoleon' brought his nephew to power in 1848 as president and then as Emperor Napoleon III. He bought Longwood House in 1858 and it is still conserved as a distant shrine by the French state. Hardy pilgrims take away a handful of soil, some spring water, and a leaf from the willow that shaded the emperor's original grave.

Napoleon remains an ambivalent presence in French political culture. After de Gaulle he is France's favourite hero.[6] The modern French state is largely his design. Yet no Paris street bears the imperial name. (The British have one in St Helena.) The very centrality and attractiveness of the Napoleonic legacy causes intellectual embarrassment, and a tendency to avoid the subject.[7] Several recent writers, however, have turned again to Napoleon. In 2002 France's flamboyant foreign minister, Dominique de Villepin (subsequently prime minister), published a fervently nationalistic history of the Hundred Days, lauding Napoleon as a genius like Caesar or Alexander, raised above banal morality by 'exaltation', 'imagination', and 'passion'. Although

J.M.W. Turner 'The Exile and the Rock Limpet': the sunset of power. But Napoleon managed to turn his exile into an effective propaganda weapon.

Waterloo sealed the historic victory of 'England over France', in defeat France discovered 'another nobility'. For Villepin, the sacrifice of the Garde at Waterloo inspired 'the spirit of resistance' incarnated later in another genius, de Gaulle. This still nourishes 'the French dream . . . the idea we have of ourselves': 'an authoritative State, contempt for parties and compromise, a shared taste for action, obsession with . . . the grandeur of France . . . refusal to bow to the inevitable, and dignity in defeat'.[8]

PART II: COEXISTENCE

For the first time since the Norman Conquest, three generations have gone by without the armies of England and France meeting in battle array. The last of the veterans of Toulouse and of Waterloo have passed away . . . there is no man living who has fired a shot in warfare between the French and English nations . . . and for the first time the manhood of the two peoples have never seen mourning garb worn by their women.

J.E.C. BODLEY, France (1898)[1]

The summer of 1815 began the period during which not only were Britain and France at peace, but there was no prospect of war. All over Europe, most people were heartily relieved: Franco-British peace meant European peace. The Congress of Vienna – in which France took part – established a system for maintaining peace by negotiation between governments, and some statesmen dreamt of permanent European institutions. Tsar Alexander I attempted to give Christian sanction to the bargaining by proposing a 'Holy Alliance'. Described by Castlereagh with stereotypical British pragmatism as 'a piece of sublime mysticism and nonsense', and by democrats and nationalists as a cloak for oppression, it was nevertheless proof of a new desire to inject idealism into international politics. Those who like identifying precursors might see this, rather than Napoleonic imperialism, as the beginning of European integration, and a forerunner of the United Nations to boot. Britain and France had to get used to the idea of peaceful coexistence. They managed fairly easily to work as neighbours, traders, tourists, and even on occasion allies. Friendship, however, proved more difficult.

CHAPTER 7

Plucking the Fruits of Peace

Legitimate monarchy re-entered Paris behind those red uniforms which
had just deepened their dye with Frenchmen's blood.

RENÉ DE CHATEAUBRIAND[1]

To abolish absolute power in the political sphere and the intellectual sphere
. . . that is the role of England in the development of our civilization.

FRANÇOIS GUIZOT, Sorbonne lectures on European civilization, 1828[2]

The realities of power were unmistakable after Napoleon's 'Hundred Days'. The Allied armies occupied northern and eastern France, levied a war indemnity of 700 million francs (on top of the 500 million the occupation cost), and trimmed strategic fortresses from France's frontiers. Castlereagh's four-power Treaty of Chaumont remained in force to prevent any revival of French aggression, and the Admiralty continued discreetly spying on French naval bases: better to be safe than sorry. The Bourbon Restoration – Britain's preferred solution to the French problem – would be overthrown in 1830, as would its successor, the July Monarchy, in 1848. But the story is not wholly one of futility. The historian Pierre Rosanvallon has suggested that two histories of France can be told.[3] One, the 'Jacobin' history, emphasizes conflict: a succession of revolutions and wars lasting at least until the 1870s. The other, the 'English' history – rarely told – is about reform and continuity. From this viewpoint, the Restoration marks the beginning of constitutional government closely copied from Westminster, with the speaker of the House of Commons offering the new French parliament advice on procedure. France had greater intellectual, political and cultural freedom than it had known under the Old Regime, the Republic or Napoleon. Influential voices, such as that of Guizot, argued that the two countries had become partners. Unlike the older idea that they were the two great rivals dividing the world between them, they were now seen as the two great liberal states whose mission was to defend and propagate freedom. Many people on both sides remained unconvinced.

Our Friends the Enemy

Every whore in Paris cries
'Long live our friends the enemy!'
Song by PIERRE-JEAN DE BÉRANGER [1]

In general, the English, whatever their rank, showed themselves as they are always and everywhere: arrogant and haughty.
Souvenirs of a Parisian Doctor[4]

I cannot tell what made me dislike France so *very* much; one reason I think was that I had raised my expectations too high.
MARY BROWNE, aged fifteen[5]

As always, peace meant tourism, which replaced privateering as the main earner for the Channel ports. The British presence, 'massive and unrivalled' – about 14,000 in 1815, 70–80 per cent of all visitors – swamped the foreign potentates, politicians and adventurers who came to France to enjoy what their armies had won, so much so that all foreigners were assumed to be British.[6] 'English' hotels and English-speaking waiters emerged after long hibernation. We might expect big differences: not only were the British the victors, but France had torn itself apart, and destroyed much of what the British had previously admired. Visitors picked up macabre first-hand stories of the Terror. They noted the ruined churches, the uncultivated fields, and the frequency of beggars, including children who had picked up some English from the soldiers: 'How do you do. Give me a penny, papa. I hope you're very well.'[7] France was now a place in which the British had privileges. Pauline Bonaparte had moved out of her palace in the Faubourg Saint-Honoré; Castlereagh moved in, succeeded by Wellington and every British ambassador since. The dais of Pauline's bed acquired a plush throne for visiting monarchs.[8] Sir Walter Scott, who had a wonderful time, described Paris as a frozen lake over whose perilous depths one could now skate without fear. The British no longer needed to show particular tact, or the old sense of cultural inferiority. Those who hurried to the Louvre knew that their government was about to dispose of much of its contents. If French cartoonists can be believed, they no longer felt they had to conceal their Britishness under French fashions. Whereas Lord Chesterfield had considered it the ultimate accolade to be taken for a Frenchman, the British ambassadress Lady Granville was furious when French acquaintances whispered that 'one would never suspect she was English'.[9]

Yet it is striking how much had *not* changed, at least in perceptions. Writers described the same attractions of Paris with the same breathless excitement, and sometimes disapproval, as fifty years earlier. Carriages in Paris still threatened life and limb – despite the revolution. The British still found the French 'forward' and talkative ('they never say they do not know a thing'). The French still found the British stiff and inarticulate. Wellington's laconic sarcasm perplexed French acquaintances: when asked by one lady why he had taken so long to cross the Adour, he replied, 'Il y avait de l'eau, Madame.' British adolescents like Mary Browne were again seeking French tutors to learn genteel dancing, drawing, writing and music, as if Robespierre had never lived. But Mary, a sharp critic, found her teachers hopeless (though cheap), and discovered only one old woman whose 'French politeness . . . was at all like what I expected'.[10] Perhaps the revolution had made a difference after all. But only a temporary one: Paris and France would pursue a successful counter-revolution in manners, and restore their position as the world centre of fashion, pleasure, and elegance.

The British were eager to let bygones be bygones – easy for the winner. The generally untroubled relations the army had established with the population helped.[11] Wellington, who did not believe the French people were to blame for Napoleon's Hundred Days, was commander-in-chief of the Allied armies of occupation. He remained determined to minimize friction, and was tough on troublemakers. Except in the case of his own indiscreet *repos du guerrier* with Napoleon's ex-mistress the singer Grassini, thought insulting to French propriety and sensibilities, he was sensitive to symbols. He told one of his officers – who had bought the battlefield of Agincourt – to stop excavations there; he resisted London's instructions to take back British flags captured at Fontenoy in 1745; and he stopped the Prussians blowing up the Pont de Jéna by placing a British sentry on it.[12] Many British sympathized with their former antagonists. Ordinary redcoats were eager collectors of Napoleonic memorabilia and, reported a French official, 'spoke of [him] with enthusiasm'.[13] Sergeant Wheeler had little time for the king he had helped restore: 'His pottle belly Majesty . . . who blubbered like a big girl . . . an old bloated poltroon, the Sir John Falstaff of France.'[14] When Marshall Ney, one of the heroes of Waterloo, was executed by the Bourbon government, it was reported to have caused universal displeasure in the British army. One of Napoleon's other generals avoided a firing squad thanks to three Englishmen who aided his escape.

One issue on which Wellington's attempt to find a compromise failed, however, was that of the treasures of the Louvre. During the summer of 1815, British riflemen occupied the palace to enforce the return of works of art gloriously conquered/shamefully looted in Italy, Spain, Germany and the Low Countries. The Republic had begun systematic spoliation, justified by 'its power and the superiority of its culture', and Napoleon had systematized the policy. The stupendous haul included 2,000 paintings (among them fifteen Raphaels, seventy-five Rubenses, and dozens of Rembrandts, Leonardos, Titians and Van Dycks); 8,000 ancient manuscripts; hundreds of classical statues; and the Byzantine horses of St Mark from Venice – the greatest accumulation of European art there has ever been. Their removal humiliated Louis XVIII and angered Parisians, who grumbled that Wellington himself had been in the Louvre 'on a ladder' taking down paintings, and 'perched all morning on the monument' supervising the removal of the Venetian horses.[15] It was one consequence of Napoleon's 'Hundred Days' and the increased severity with which France was now treated. Probably most French contemporaries, and many since, regarded this as shockingly vindictive, as did British sympathizers. The British government took the lead, intending to diminish French 'vanity' and prevent Paris from being 'in future the centre of the arts', the cultural dimension of Napoleon's ambition to make it the centre of Europe. The Allies agreed. An international petition of artists urged the return of works to Rome, 'the capital of the arts for all peoples'.[16] The Pope sent the sculptor Antonio Canova (expenses paid by Britain) to recover works belonging to the Church. The

French concealed as much as they could: half the Italian pictures are still in French museums. Meanwhile, to the victors the spoils: in 1816 the Greek antiquities controversially collected by the Earl of Elgin were placed in the British Museum.

What the French thought of the British was largely a function of their political loyalties: to call the invaders 'the Allies' or to call them 'the Enemy' was an unambiguous shibboleth. Supporters of the Restoration, from Louis XVIII down, felt a mixture of resentment and respect. 'It is possible not to like the English,' decided the poet Lamartine, 'but it is impossible not to esteem them.' The Bourbons and many of their advisers had been refugees in Britain. A noticeable sprinkling of the elite had British wives (from the last prime minister of the Restoration, Polignac, to the first President of the Second Republic, that same Lamartine). Others had mistresses, notoriously the ageing royal roué the Duc de Bourbon, whose devotion to the notorious Sophie Dawes (alias Baronne de Feuchères) owed much to her professional skills in 'strangulatory manipulations'.[17] The main British representatives in France, Castlereagh and Wellington, were francophiles, at least in the sense that they sincerely respected the restored Bourbon monarchy and were committed to its success. The American envoy in London was impressed to find that at dinner at Castlereagh's everyone was speaking French (though in fact Castlereagh's own French was not good). British visitors to the French court were equally impressed by Louis XVIII's addressing them in (rather better) English.

The many opponents of the Bourbons (who included former Republicans, Bonapartists, and many Parisian workers) blamed Britain for political and economic ills. 'Hatred for the English is growing daily,' a police agent reported late in 1815. 'They are regarded as the destroyers of French industry.' Despite official friendship, a British Admiralty yacht, flying the British ensign, sent to pick up the secretary to the admiralty and his family at Boulogne, was impounded by zealous – or patriotic – customs officers, and despite apoplectic protests detained for a month. Ordinary travellers frequently complained of ill-treatment by customs officials. British tourists beat a hasty retreat from the Tuileries gardens after being surrounded by a hostile crowd.[18] British officers in Paris had to be ready to fight duels with their demobilized former adversaries, who systematically picked quarrels. The British were certainly the main targets of cartoonists. Probably this was partly because Russians and Prussians were too risky as subjects, partly because mocking the British was an indirect way of mocking the Bourbons, and partly because British visitors were far more numerous and happily bought satirical cartoons of themselves. Nevertheless such cartoons indicate a lively spirit of anglophobia. Rossini's fashionable opera *Il Viaggio a Reims* (1825), commissioned to celebrate the coronation of Charles X, had an English character, 'Lord Sidney', as romantic hero. But in many literary works – including by

Vigny, Stendhal, Nerval and Balzac – the English characters (unlike in eighteenth-century literature) were villains: nearly all the thirty-one English characters in Balzac's novels are bad.[19] The popular (and frequently prosecuted) songwriter Béranger, France's first great *chansonnier*, produced catchy lines that could sound friendly but in context are bitterly sarcastic.

THE BRITISH IN PARIS

The image – or rather images – of the British now became well-established and would last throughout the century, if not longer. If they echo eighteenth-century prejudices, we can even now recognize them as concretely 'British' in a way that rather abstract earlier symbols were not. Both British and French were struck by physical differences between them. The British were indeed taller and plumper. The candid Mary Browne noted that though old women were fat, most French women were 'as flat as boards' – something that fashion encouraged. Some English women, lamented one Henry Mathews, copied them by 'compress[ing] their beautiful bosoms as flatly as possible, and destroy[ing] every vestige of those charms for which, of all other women, they are perhaps the most indebted to nature'.[20] French cartoonists made the British absurd in

Even after a generation of revolution and war, the French still saw themselves as embodying elegance and grace in contrast to British clumsiness, stiffness and lack of taste.

The English, like the French, perceived a strong contrast between the two nations' manners – though they interpreted it rather differently. The umbrella had by now become a badge of Englishness, not Frenchness.

body, dress and behaviour. Men and women are outsized: sometimes fat (in the 'John Bull' manner) but often angular. Their fashions are eccentric and exaggerated. English girls may be shown as pretty, but are insipid, gawky and charmless. As the patriotic General Lamarque put it, 'hundreds of English women lanky as poplars . . . are spoiling the gentle, gracious landscape with their abrupt manners and purposeful stalk'.[21] Men, if not in absurd uniforms (Highlanders in kilts clearly inspired much curiosity) are coarsely dressed, for travelling, and hence are not fashionable, civilized or elegant. Their gestures and bearing lack ease and naturalness. With their gaping and their guidebooks, they are always provincial. The title of one series of caricatures, *Le Suprême Bon Ton* (roughly 'the height of class'), mocks British manners, the anglomaniac fads they inspired, and their hopeless inability to be truly smart.

Lady Granville, wife of the ambassador appointed in 1824, was sensitive to this. She both resented and feared *les élégantes* who would judge you on whether you had 'six curls or five on the side of your head'. Although she thought there was 'not so much mind as would fill a pea shell' among the 'exquisite set', 'their effect upon me is to crush me with a sense of my inferiority whilst I am absolutely gasping with the sense of my superiority . . . they have an aplomb, a language, a dress *de convenance*, which it is as impossible for me to reach as it would be for one of them to think five minutes like a deep-thinking, deep feeling Englishwoman'.[22]

Troupes Anglaises.

LE BAGAGE DE CAMPAGNE.

E. Delacroix, 'Campaign Baggage': the redcoats got on quite well with French civilians – and perhaps introduced them to steak and chips.

FAST FOOD A L'ANGLAISE

One of France's great nineteenth-century gourmets, the novelist Alexandre Dumas, remembered 'having seen, after the 1815 campaign, when the English remained for two or three years in Paris, the birth of *le bifteck* in France'. Dumas advised serving the steak with potatoes 'cut into little square sticks the length of a finger' and fried.[23] France's national dish, *le steack-frites* – which the philosopher Roland Barthes defined as 'the alimentary sign of Frenchness'[24] – was thus imported from England, thanks to Wellington's army.

Above all, the British were famous for spending money, and so they received at least a venal welcome, though not necessarily a good bargain. 'English' shops and services developed. The Irish writer Lady Morgan related that she tried to buy some French sweets for her grand-daughter and was told that the shop stocked only plum-cake, mince pies, apple dumplings and other 'english pastry'.[25] At Mrs Harriet Dunn's establishment near the Palais Royal an English-speaking waiter (from Dunkirk) served roast beef and mutton washed down with porter brewed in Paris. The Great Nelson Hotel served bacon, eggs and tea for breakfast. Galignani's English bookshop (still in existence) began to publish an English newspaper, the *Register*. Paris was the destination of more visitors than ever, and some intended a long stay, for splendid houses could be rented cheaply from Napoleon's dispossessed aristocracy, and a grand style maintained on far less money than in London. Moreover, the origins and respectability of foreigners were less scrutinized. British visitors could be received at court, especially after the 1830 revolution – 'a favour they could never dream of in England, where all they know of His Britannic Majesty is what they read in the newspapers'.[26] As the novelist Thackeray put it snootily, 'foreigners become great personages as long as they have lots of money'. All this was an attraction for *nouveaux riches*, noble families in straitened circumstances, and those who – sometimes spectacularly – had kicked over the traces. These famously included the *ménage a trois* of Lord and Lady Blessington and the Comte d'Orsay (the leading dandy in both Paris and London); the Marquis de Custine and his English lover Edward Sainte-Barbe; and the wealthy, cultivated but notoriously dissipated Hertford family.

Parisian social life became more like that of London. Although salons remained, fashion increasingly centred on commercial public entertainments such as panoramas, arcades, theatres, cafés, restaurants (of which the Café Anglais long remained one of the most celebrated), and pleasure gardens modelled on, and sometimes named after, London originals such as Vauxhall and Ranelagh. The main tourist centre in the 1820s was still the Palais Royal, given over to eating, gambling, shopping ('very dear . . . the people seem to make quite a favour of selling you anything') and sex – 'scenes such as no Englishman can conceive . . . of frightful and unimaginable sensuality'. It also had Paris's first – if not only – public lavatories, which made a handsome profit.[27] British entrepreneurs helped to pioneer a new and eventually more attractive social centre along 'the Boulevard', for example Robinson's new Tivoli gardens, with romantic grottos, scenery inspired by the novels of Scott, a roller-coaster and a dance floor. Horse-racing was imported on a more elaborate scale than in the 1770s. Chantilly, a royal domain, set up a course. The 'derby de Chantilly', run over the same distance as its Epsom model, became the great spring social event, attracting 30,000 spectators by the mid-1830s. Horse-racing provided the pretext for the fashionable and raffish 'Jockey-Club'. The gentleman's club was a post-war British import alien to the French tradition of the salon, organized by women. It is one sign of the development of 'separate spheres' for the sexes that began in the eighteenth century. The English Jockey and Pigeon Shooting Club was founded in 1825 by two English racing enthusiasts, Thomas Bryon and 'Lord' Henry Seymour, an illegitimate offspring of the Hertfords and a flamboyant social figure in Paris. It quickly became the home of the anglomaniac 'dandy', and it established premises on the Boulevard des Italiens, the axis of the new social scene. Seymour resigned, finding the club insufficiently obsessed with racing, and was succeeded by Anne-Édouard Denormandie, winner of the first-ever French steeplechase and so anglomaniac that he sometimes pretended to be English. The Club, apolitical and cosmopolitan, attracted fashionable young men, often from *nouveau-riche* families. Its immediate success symbolized rejection of Republican 'virtue' and Napoleonic discipline and a return to aristocratic indulgence, including gambling and the new amusements of 'the Boulevard', not least the ballerinas of the Opera – club members were allowed to use the stage door. The Jockey-Club linked the upper class with the world of commercial entertainment, and this was the attraction of Boulevard society throughout the nineteenth century.[28] In this the Club played a prominent and often scandalous part. Now more sedate, it is closer to its original purpose of promoting horse-racing.

PAU: BRITAIN IN BEARN

Pau is a pretty town of 25,000 inhabitants, a prefecture, with a court, a lycée, a college, a public library etc . . . But there is a small detail unmentioned in the geographical data . . . Pau is obviously and unambiguously part of England.

FRENCH SATIRIST, 1876[29]

It was not only Paris that drew the British. The seaports had long been a refuge for debtors and those facing other forms of social ruin. Invalids tried the Pyrenean hot springs. Despite discovering that the local alcohol was 'poisoned with aniseed', colonies of visitors and long-term residents settled in the southern provinces for health, economy and enjoyment. The Riviera (still all Italian until 1860) attracted winter residents. Pau owed its strange destiny to a series of accidents. Some British had been interned there in 1803. In 1814 it welcomed Wellington with cries of 'Vive le libérateur!' and dancing in the streets.[30] Such memories encouraged British visitors to return in the following decades, as perhaps did the fact that only three people had been guillotined there during the Terror. British – noticeably Scottish – visitors started coming in hundreds in the 1820s and 30s, attracted by the bracing climate and romantic view of the Pyrenees. All strangers were assumed to be *Anglès*. The town was transformed: 'Twenty years ago, not a single house in Pau had a carpet; there were no carriages for hire. There was only one private carriage in the town; there was no sign of what we now call *le comfort*, and not a single street had a pavement. Today, the houses in part are furnished according to English needs and habits.'[31] In 1841, a Mrs Ellis pioneered a durably popular literary genre with *Summer and Winter in the Pyrenees*, which enlarged on the beauties of the landscape and the quaintness of the inhabitants, unsophisticated, incompetent, but honest and warm-hearted. The town's fortune was made by a medical treatise by Dr Alexander Taylor the following year. Taylor, having opened a practice there, discovered that the life expectancy of the locals was unusually high, and attributed this to the climate, particularly favourable to those with lung complaints. Families started bringing their consumptive members. They found that the surrounding countryside provided stimulus for watercolourists, and the nearby mountains a challenge for the athletic. British climbers rushed in where locals feared to tread. A French observer was 'frozen in horror' in the 1830s to see a 'fairly old' Englishman and his teenage daughter climbing down a waterfall, expecting at every moment to see them 'rolling into the abyss'.[32] The first guidebook, Packe's *Guide to the Pyrenees*, was published in 1862, and the first French guidebook – by another Englishman – three years later.

The Pau Hunt was the only genuine fox-hunting pack on the Continent. Foxes were few, however, and the expedient of bringing captive (and sometimes rather tame) quarry along in boxes made the British rather shamefaced. They had no shame, however, about excluding French members until the end of the century, when a few aristocratic cavalry officers were finally allowed to join. So widely did the hunt's fame spread – giving Pau an advantage over the foxless Riviera – that Americans came, and in 1879 the New York newspaper magnate Gordon Bennett became Master. *L'équitation* became one of the town's great attractions, shrewdly encouraged by the tourist lobby. Pau became, and remains, the capital of French steeplechasing, and also a centre of polo. In 1856, three Scots founded the Pau golf club, another sporting first for the Continent. There was also cricket, skating, croquet, an English Club, and English shops and churches. The local cuisine was English. Russians, Germans, Americans and Italians followed in British footsteps. Mountain resorts, spas, and the seaside resorts of Biarritz and Saint-Jean-de-Luz flourished as its offshoots.

Disaster struck in the 1850s and 60s. A mixture of jealousy and honesty produced damaging allegations. The sewers stank. Tourists were fleeced. It was as much fun as 'a Presbyterian town in Scotland', and bored consumptives spent their days smoking and playing billiards at the Club. In 1864, a Dr Madden demonstrated that the winter climate was the same as Birmingham, and more likely to kill than cure. Pau fought back: not only by denial and prevarication, but by improving its infrastructure (the railway, luxury hotels, a 'winter palace', a theatre, an opera house, banks, clinics) and promoting itself as 'the hub of the sporting world'. So distinguished visitors continued to come: the Prince of Wales, President Grant, Mrs Lincoln – proof of the increasing prominence of Americans, who by the early twentieth century had taken over from the British. By 1913 the secretary of the English Club was an Irish-American oilman.

Pau pioneered tourism as an industry. Britain was the first society rich enough to create the demand and set the pattern. Others – even the French within their own country – followed in British footsteps to the mountains, the country, and the seaside. The Pau golf club still flourishes; the English Club still stands; the Pau Hunt still meets; and in 2003, Ryanair carried 80,000 passengers from London to Pau.[33]

Romantic Encounters

There reigned in every spirit an effervescence of which we have no idea today. We were intoxicated by Shakespeare, Goethe, Byron and Walter Scott . . . we toured the galleries with gestures of frenetic admiration that would make the present generation laugh.

THÉOPHILE GAUTIER, 1855[34]

French people too crossed the Channel, though fewer in number and often with a more serious purpose: to observe and often write about society, the political system or the new economy, or to experience cultural novelty. Like their eighteenth-century predecessors, they tended to be 'struck by the immense prosperity . . . in all classes . . . the people so clean . . . beautiful children so well turned out', and to express aesthetic disappointment with London.[35] Now they often went further, expressing alarm, even horror, at the city's size, smoke, crowds, wealth and poverty. What were new in the nineteenth century were pilgrimages to the sources of Romanticism. This cultural revolution was in part a development of the eighteenth-century cults of nature and sensibility, in part a rejection of other eighteenth-century tendencies towards uniformity, rationalism and materialism. Romanticism was marked by a more acute interest in the past, in nature, in mysticism, in cultural diversity and in individual self-expression. Especially in Germany and Britain, it also signified rejection of French cultural dominance and political ideas. In France – where the Romantic current had been dammed by the neo-classical universalism of the Republic and the Empire – it manifested an interest in older French traditions, and an unprecedented admiration for northern Europe.

The vogue for modern British culture brought pilgrims across the Channel. Many made their way north to the land of Scott and Ossian. 'Today,' said a French guidebook to 'romantic Scotland' in 1826, 'Italy with its beautiful sky and monuments, hardly attracts more leisure travellers, painters and poets than poor Scotland with its mists and druidic stones.' The writer Charles Nodier was overwhelmed: 'Who could communicate with cold ink and sterile words the astonishing emotions that one believed one no longer had the strength to feel!' Scotland made some reflect on the very nature of Romanticism: 'The romantic, in terms of landscape, is it not the *attractiveness of wild nature?* . . . the ruins, the rocks [and] the solitude are lovely and evoke melancholy, and that is what we term a romantic place.'[36]

British history offered keys to France's past and future: 'Sixty years ago France entered on the path opened by England.'[37] Sir Walter Scott won enormous popularity with his vivid historical chronicles, which brought the past to life and made British and French history part of a single epic. One could speak more freely about the death of Charles I than that of Louis XVI, but convey the same messages about revolution and terror. Similarly, Paul Delaroche produced emotive and popular paintings of British episodes, including the famous *Death of Lady Jane Grey*. Victor Hugo wrote a play, *Cromwell*, in 1827. France seemed to be following a parallel historic path: revolution, rule by a military dictator, and restoration of a limited monarchy. 'The English Revolution has . . . borne a double fruit: its authors founded Constitutional Monarchy in England; and in America their descendants founded the Republic of the United States.'[38] France must follow. History became central to political debate. Augustin Thierry discerned a fundamental shared pattern (which Disraeli would later take up as 'the two nations'). English society stemmed from the Norman Conquest, when the Saxons were dispossessed and ruled by a foreign aristocracy. Similarly, said Thierry, the Gauls had been conquered by a Frankish aristocracy, and subsequent history (including the revolution) was the continuing struggle between them. French historians wrote about Britain's revolutions with the intensity of people who had lived through their own. François Guizot aimed to explain how, from a similar starting point, Britain had developed free institutions and France had not. This was a question that brought crowds to his lectures at the Sorbonne, not merely to defy the government (which for seven years banned him from lecturing) but to hear why France, under the Bourbons, the Republic and Napoleon, had been trapped by oppressive systems.

During the 1820s, every area of French cultural novelty was saturated with British themes. The exoticism of Byron, the epics of Scott, and lurid episodes from Shakespeare were transmuted into paintings, opera and music (such as Rossini's *Otello*, a Parisian success in 1821, and Berlioz's Byronic *Harold in Italy*). Artists crossed the Channel in both directions in search of subjects, customers and contact with other artists. London crowds, avid for Napoleana, flocked to see David's huge Coronation painting. But French Romantics were tired of such 'tedious grand paintings',[39] glossy neoclassicism turned into propaganda. This was the very opposite of the individual creativity they aspired to. The London art world, in 'a country flowing with gold', as Eugène Delacroix hopefully put it, meant freedom from stultifying official patronage. The work of Turner, Constable, Richard Parkes Bonington and Sir Thomas Lawrence in more personal, more realistic and less political genres – landscapes, portraits, animals – and in a more spontaneous and relaxed style offered liberation. The young Bonington introduced French artists, especially his friend Delacroix, to the rapid execution and brightness of watercolour (previously regarded as an inferior female and English genre). According to the novelist Théophile Gautier, 'the revolution in painting proceeded from Bonington just as the literary revolution proceeded from Shakespeare'. Constable made a similar impact when he exhibited *The Hay Wain* at the official Salon in 1824 – 'the first time, perhaps,' said the French artist Paul Huet, 'that one saw a luxuriant, verdant nature.' Lawrence aroused controversy with his relaxed and touching (some said mawkish) portraits. Delacroix, the most anglophile of painters, produced in the 1820s a series of dramatic, colourful and stylistically uninhibited works influenced by Bonington, Constable and Turner as well as by the Italian Renaissance. They established him both in London, where his works were acclaimed, and in Paris, where they aroused controversy, as the leader of French Romantic painting. His sadistic *Death of Sardanapalus* (1827), drawn from Byron, brought a warning that he would lose government patronage if he continued in this shocking style. French critics were worried by an 'Anglo-French school' that they saw as unintellectual, sensational, trivial, crude in execution and market-driven, compared with French classicism that was idealistic, inspiring, controlled and perfected. This was precisely the debate that would be heard concerning drama; indeed one leading critic referred to British painting as 'Shakespearean' – not meant as a compliment.

THE FRENCH AND SHAKESPEARE: THE ROMANTICS

Shakespeare is the great glory of England . . . Above Newton there are Copernicus and Galileo; above Bacon there are Descartes and Kant; above Cromwell there are Danton and Bonaparte; above Shakespeare there is no one.

VICTOR HUGO[40]

When in 1822 a British company played *Othello*, notorious for sex and violence, in Paris for the first time in English, the audience booed and pelted 'Wellington's lieutenant' off the stage. When another company tried again in 1827 with *Hamlet*, *Romeo and Juliet*, *Othello*, *Richard III*, *Macbeth* and *King Lear* at the Odéon, it was a triumph. The young Romantics, many of whom had been to see plays in London, acclaimed Shakespeare as the prophet of their own rebellion, 'the interpreter of my life'.[41] Hugo, Vigny, Gautier, Dumas and Delacroix turned out for the first performance of *Hamlet*, always Shakespeare's most famous play in France, on 11 September 1827. 'It's an invasion,' Delacroix wrote jubilantly to Hugo, 'the undermining of all dramatic law and order . . . It behoves the Academy to declare all imports of the kind absolutely incompatible with public decency.'[42] The twenty-four-year-old Hector Berlioz, a rebel against the musical conventions of the Conservatory, was so overwhelmed that he fell madly in love with the company's Ophelia/Juliet, the Irish actress Harriet Smithson.

Victor Hugo, brilliant and pugnacious, the rising leader of literary Romanticism, appointed himself Shakespeare's spokesman. He later recalled that, aged twenty-three, he 'like everybody, had never read him and had laughed at him'. During a lull in the interminable coronation ceremony of Charles X at Rheims in 1825, a friend passed him a copy of *King John*, bought for 6 sous in a junkshop, and they spent the evening deciphering it.[43] Two years later Hugo wrote *Cromwell*, whose preface was the manifesto of French Romanticism, his own declaration of war on 'absurd pseudo-Aristotelian' classical conventions, and at the same time an encomium to 'the leading poet of all time', Shakespeare, 'that god of the theatre'.

Hugo's challenge to the intellectual establishment went far beyond that of Voltaire a century earlier. Voltaire had patronized 'Gilles' Shakespeare as a bumpkin with flecks of genius, but inferior to the French masters. But Hugo saw Shakespeare's supposed defects as signs of superiority: 'The giant oak has a twisted shape, knotted branches, dark leaves, and hard, rough bark. That is what makes it the oak.' He hailed him as 'the Drama itself', for he combined 'the grotesque and the sublime, the terrible and the ridiculous, tragedy and comedy'. Shakespeare was not Voltaire's archaic primitive but the founder of modernism – 'the torrent that has burst its banks'. It was French classicism that was archaic, and Hugo cast himself as Shakespeare's heir who would drag French drama into the nineteenth century.[44]

His *Hernani*, described by critics as an amalgam of Spanish romanticism and Shakespeare (it had hints of *Romeo and Juliet*), opened at the Théâtre Français in March 1830 and started a famous literary battle. Every night defenders of the classical tradition came to jeer and blow whistles. Hugo's friends (he issued wads of free tickets) came to cheer and heckle the hecklers. What the critics hated was what Voltaire had condemned in Shakespeare: irregular versification, unpoetic language, ignoble characters and violent events: a woman calling her lover 'my lion' (which the actress insisted on changing to 'my lord'); bandits on stage; disrespectful words addressed to a monarch; a noblewoman portrayed 'without dignity or modesty'; and naturalistic dialogue – 'What time is it? Nearly midnight.' As one of Hugo's friends observed, what critics wanted were phrases like 'The day will soon attain its last repose.' At issue, as during the previous century, were different conceptions of drama, and of art. In Hugo's words, the classicists wanted art to rectify nature, to ennoble, to discriminate, but he believed it should 'paint life'.[45] Yet Hugo, though he orchestrated the clamour, had not defeated classical decorum, and many of the Romantics, despite their revolutionary aspirations, in practice respected traditional standards, changing Shakespeare's endings and poeticizing his language. In French versions of *Othello*, it took 100 years before Desdemona's handkerchief could be called a 'mouchoir', and another 100 years before it could be described as 'spotted with strawberries'.[46]

Three decades after *Hernani*, Hugo wrote a long preface to the first unabridged French translation of Shakespeare. It was by his son François-Victor, who had begun it in 1853 at the age of twenty-four, knowing no English. This great work, much of which remained the standard version for 140 years, had special significance because it was done in exile, on British soil, and was dedicated 'To England'. Victor could not resist pointing out that in London 'one looks for a statue of Shakespeare, one finds a statue of Wellington', and making the tart comment that Shakespeare's gift to mankind made England seem less selfish – 'It reduces England's resemblance to Carthage.'[47] Shakespeare was duly grateful: his ghost dictated to Hugo (a fanatical spiritualist) a whole new play – in French, as the Bard had finally realized that 'the English language is inferior'.[48]

King Cotton, Queen Silk

Their material civilization is so far ahead of all neighbouring states today that in observing it one foresees in a sense the future of Europe . . . It is an appalling prospect.
ASTOLPHE DE CUSTINE, 1830[49]

The English . . . can forge iron, harness steam, twist matter in every way, invent frighteningly powerful machines: . . . but real art will always escape them; . . . despite their stupendous material advances, they are only polished barbarians.
THEOPHILE GAUTIER, 1856[50]

Peace brought the hope of prosperity. Haltingly, a measure of prosperity came. But the revolution, war and postwar trading conditions shaped the two countries in very different ways, and had permanent effects not only on their economies, but on their societies and cultures too. They had grown much further apart economically than they had been when the Eden Treaty was signed in 1786. Then, both had been dynamic maritime traders and growing manufacturers. The revolution, and the ensuing wars, had profound economic consequences for France. First, the number of small and medium landowners had greatly increased and agricultural productivity had fallen: by 1815 there were about 5 million landowners, a formidable lobby whose power grew after 1830 as the electorate widened. Second, though this is difficult to measure, an instinctive wariness seems to have developed that discouraged economic risk. Investors, with memories of inflation and disruption, preferred to buy land, bricks and mortar, even government bonds. Governments, with memories of popular violence, wanted to avoid economic upheavals and discontents. Third, the colonial trade that had powered France's eighteenth-century growth had gone; the British blockade had strangled the flourishing ports and their hinterlands. Not until the boom of the 1840s did French exports regain their level of the 1780s. Fourth, war had largely cut France off from British technology, which despite legal restrictions it had previously imported. So the French economy could not compete directly with the British, whose products, especially textiles, flooded Europe after 1815. Most Frenchmen did not wish to: they agreed that Britain was courting social and political disaster with its smoky towns and bloated industrial labour force. The French, by choice and by necessity, developed a different kind of economy and society. There was overwhelming support for protection, with quotas and subsidies imposed as early as 1816. The import of cotton cloth was prohibited, and iron carried a 120 per cent tariff. Consequently, France imported and exported relatively few manufactured goods, and deliberately slowed down economic change.[51]

Despite wartime and post-war fluctuations, the British economy continued to grow. It had fundamental advantages: cheap water-borne transport, and vast coal reserves that generated cheap steam-power and smelted cheap iron. It enjoyed unchallenged freedom of the seas. Its manufactured goods, above all cotton, found worldwide markets, inside and outside its empire. Its ships carried them; the City of London financed the trade and lent to developing countries. These conditions made the British economy unlike any other, and it diverged sharply from the French. For at least a century it concentrated heavily on mass production of cheap goods for distant markets: still in 1914 cotton textiles, especially to India, were its largest export item. The British manufacturing labour force overtook the agricultural by 1840; in France, not until the 1950s. France remained, in comparison with Britain, a country of land-owning peasants, self-employed craftsmen, and small towns and villages. In 1850, three out of four Frenchmen lived in districts whose main centre of population had fewer than 2,000 inhabitants. Only three towns, Paris, Lyons and Marseilles, had more than 100,000 people. Small-scale craft production remained, protected by stringent quotas and tariff barriers. There were some free-traders, many linked to the wine exporting trade, and one spokesman, the economist Bastiat, sarcastically called for all shutters to be kept closed to protect French candle-makers from 'unfair' competition from sunshine. But workers, employers, and politicians of all parties were unconvinced. Fear of British competition was a potent source of anglophobia. They used the chilling argument that the 1786 treaty had helped cause the revolution. Protection worked. Hand-weaving actually increased: by 1860, France had 200,000 hand looms, while Britain had only 3,000. Iron was smelted in charcoal furnaces. Machinery was powered by water. In Paris, the main manufacturing city, there were 100,000 firms in 1870 – but nearly two-thirds of them employed only one worker, or the *patron* worked alone. Thanks to state subsidies to protect it against competition from steam, France had the world's largest sailing fleet in 1900.[52]

Unable to compete with Britain in overseas markets for mass-produced products, and with a domestic market dominated by a large peasant population that consumed little, French manufacturers went up-market, supplying luxury goods to the rich consumers of the Continent, America and above all Britain. Their selling-points were fashion, quality and exclusivity, rather than cheapness and technology. The two pillars of French manufacturing exports throughout the nineteenth century were elaborate silks from Lyons and what were called *articles de Paris* – fashion items such as clothes, shoes, jewellery, and perfume. In agriculture too, exports depended on luxury products – wine and brandy. Traditional production reached peaks of sophistication. Peasants worked part-time in specialized industries such as lace-glove- and clock-making. The mighty Lyons silk industry employed more than 300,000 people in the 1860s, in a complex system of domestic outwork spread over a radius of 100 miles from the city. The profits of the luxury industries sustained French trade and provided the money for large overseas investments. Parisian craftsmen (though not women) were well paid. However, much of the economy, and especially much of agriculture, remained unproductive and poor, and overall incomes and wage levels did not keep pace with those in Britain, or, eventually, with other European countries. In the 1890s, Lancashire cotton workers were paid twice as much as those in the Vosges or Normandy, but their unit labour costs were still 30 per cent lower.

Comparing their products with others at the London Great Exhibition of 1851 convinced the French that they could outdo their rivals in design and taste. They concentrated on lavishness, in styles associated with the aristocratic past. But they also kept an eye on cost, successfully providing the middle class with affordable luxury.[53] These economic patterns therefore also shaped perceptions, confirming stereotypes that both French and British accepted.

The French were artistic, sophisticated and natural possessors of *le goût*, just as in the days of Pompadour. The British were down-to-earth, crude and materialistic, able to run banks, build ships or railway engines, and churn out cheap standard products, but not to create beauty, or 'even a hat that a Paris shop-girl would wear'. France seemed to cherish eternal values: cultural elitism, the spartan virtues of peasant life, and the ethics of craftsmanship.

The consequences were deep and durable. Both economies had difficulty in adapting to technological and manufacturing modernization in the late nineteenth and twentieth centuries, when they fell behind Germany and the United States. Both were relatively poor at educating their workforces, the British relying on semi-skilled factory labour, the French on inherited agricultural skills and craft apprenticeship. The effects are still evident. In France, support for the protective and regulatory role of the State; suspicion of globalization and economic liberalism; the political clout of agriculture; the importance for the export trade of quality, prestige and fashion (seen in determination to protect valuable brand names and extend *appellations contrôlées*). In Britain, greater acceptance of free trade and competition; the breadth of global commerce; the importance of the City; and the chronic weakness of mass education and technical training.

However, the most profound and long-term – and also mysterious – socio-economic contrast between the two countries was demographic. France had been by far the most populous country in Europe until matched by Russia towards the end of the eighteenth century. Britain had been a relative pygmy. But in the early 1890s the United Kingdom's population overtook that of France, despite a high level of British emigration to North America and Australasia, while French emigration was negligible. By 1900 the French population was stagnant, and in the 1930s it actually fell. Patriots despaired. The French stopped having babies by choice: they used various kinds of contraception within marriage. The birthrate began to fall during the revolutionary and Napoleonic period. Many attempts have been made to explain why. The answer must be a complex one. Partly the revolution's weakening of traditional pressures to have large families. Partly, perhaps, uncertainty about the future. Certainly after 1789 the chance of social ascent, with the consequent need for saving and education – many lower-middle class families wanted only one son. Where Britain enters the picture (in addition to its part in causing the revolution) is in the global consequences of the Napoleonic struggles and Britain's post-war economic ascendancy. France became more static and more inward-looking. The French had never been keen on colonial emigration, but after Waterloo, the world overseas was even more uninviting. Yet the falling birthrate was not simply a consequence of lack of opportunity: many jobs, especially in the newer industrial sectors, were taken by immigrants – Belgian, German, Italian, even British. Having few children was a fundamental part of the way the French chose to live in the post-revolutionary and post-Napoleonic world. France shrank: as François Crouzet points out, had its population grown at the same rate as Britain's, it would have had 100 million people by 1914.[54]

NAVVIES AND 'KNOBSTICKS'

The export of machinery and the emigration of skilled workers from Britain was in theory illegal until 1825. Nevertheless, thousands of workers and managers helped to bring the 'Industrial Revolution' to France. Technicians and entrepreneurs set up businesses. James Jackson brought over steel-making techniques that the French had been trying to acquire by espionage and bribery since the days of the Duc de Choiseul. Technical skills had to be taught face to face, so skilled workers were tempted to France by big cash payments. This caused jealousy among local workers. Language difficulties, arrogance, offers from rival firms, lots of cash, and being far from home made the British tricky to handle. The Lorraine ironmaster François de Wendel had sent his English foreman back in 1824 to recruit more workers, but found he could not manage the men on his own: 'your absence me nuit beaucoup [causes me great problems] je paye your worckmans and they do not worck the carpentar is an ivrogne [drunkard], one can not employe him. I believe it is better for you to kom and to remaine her.'[55]

The largest group of British workers were navvies, employed by British contractors such as the famous Thomas Brassey to build France's first railways, using substantially British capital. Despite early scepticism regarding the value of rail transport, and violent opposition from coachmen and boatmen, the government – aware of the possibility of war with Britain – wanted a strategic link between the Channel and the Mediterranean. Brassey's first contract was for the Paris–Rouen section, begun in 1841, which also served the tourist trade. He recruited 5,000 British navvies as the core of the workforce, and the same number of Frenchmen. An Anglo-French railway lingua franca grew up, later used across Europe. Some words became naturalized: *rail, tunnel, tender, wagon, ballast*. The British, hardened and experienced, were paid twice the French rate, and were used on the toughest and most dangerous work – though they found that French law gave them more protection in case of accidents. They were a turbulent lot, who spent much of their wages on alcoholic binges. When laid off during the hard winter of 1842–3, many ended up relying on soup kitchens in Rouen. About 1,000 went to work on new Paris fortifications (begun after a crisis in 1840 that brought France and Britain to the brink of conflict). Large numbers continued to work on railway building until financial crisis in 1846 halted work for several years. By that time, Brassey had been involved in building three-quarters of French lines. Economic rivalry and nationalist propaganda meant that relations between British and French were often bad. French workers attacked railways and bridges, and the nationalist press crowed when a British-built viaduct collapsed in June 1846. The nickname 'knobsticks' given to British workers in Paris suggests that they were less than conciliatory. The 1848 revolution, which came in a period of high unemployment, saw riots against British workers, of whom there were some 4,000 in Normandy alone. Some were chased on to boats at Le Havre, and others, frightened by the hostility against them, made for the Channel ports. Yet some British workers did settle in France and marry French women, and others were working again on railway building in the 1850s.

Fog and Misery

Can France and Britain communicate only by gunshots? No indeed; the two nations must see, know and speak to each other . . . So let us risk sea-sickness.
VICTOR-ANTOINE HENNEQUIN, *Voyage philosophique* (1836)[56]

Nothing can distract the imagination from the depression the climate creates, and the most intrepid curiosity will not resist the pitiless monotony that presides over everyday life in this temple of boredom.
ASTOLPHE DE CUSTINE, *Courses en Angleterre et en Ecosse* (1830)[57]

The French rarely leave their country, and when they venture out, they travel too hastily . . . Our stay-at-home habits leave a big gap in our education. Hence our numerous prejudices and our difficult relations with other nations.
FRANCIS WEY, *Les Anglais chez eux* (1854)[58]

More French people visited Britain by choice in the decades after Waterloo than ever before, though they were, as always, only a fraction of the number of British visiting France. Paul Gerbod, using official records, estimates 1,450 in 1815; 3,700 in 1835; and 4,290 in 1847. Travel was becoming easier, quicker and cheaper. Paddle steamers crossed the Channel from 1816, and in ten years replaced sail. If this did not prevent seasickness, at least it reduced its duration. Trains to Rouen and steamboats down the Seine further speeded the journey. The trip from Paris to London could be done in twenty hours, and the cheapest ticket was 31.75 francs – about a week's wages for a skilled worker.[59] Custine was incensed that 'not a soul wanted to understand my English . . . it is not enough to say the words to them, one actually has to pronounce them in a certain way that suits them'.[60] The linguistically challenged could frequent French-speaking establishments concentrated round Leicester Square. There were French hotels, most famously the Brunet, and restaurants such as the Véry (named after a famous Palais Royal establishment). Some thought that although they were more expensive than English eating-houses they were not much better. As in the eighteenth century, many people came to earn a living in the world's biggest and most dynamic city, including language teachers, chambermaids, cooks, jewellers, hairdressers, cobblers and wine merchants. Many, according to the feminist writer Flora Tristan, were bogus asylum-seekers. There were over 7,000 French in London by mid-century, enough to form a recognizable colony. A Société de Bienfaisance (welfare society) was set up in 1842. Attempts were made to set up a Society of French Teachers.[61] Writers came over to observe and to comment, for the benefit of the great majority who derived their impressions of Britain from the printed page.

Even those who went in person usually knew in advance what to expect and how to react. Often badly, because anglophobia was 'the most basic form of patriotic discourse'.[62] Well-known advantages might be grudgingly acknowledged: the rich countryside, the excellent public transport, the cleanliness, even of lavatories (excessive, some thought). Intellectuals admired – or at least envied – the wealth and beauty of Oxford and Cambridge, which some thought wasted on English philistines. But broadly speaking, nineteenth-century French visitors did not like England or the English. The only near-enthusiasts were liberal economists and engineers. Charles Dupin, after wandering the islands in 1816 visiting everything from naval dockyards to hospitals, published six volumes of admiring observations, and helped to pioneer technical education in France. Others had mixed feelings. Romantics admired the Lake District, but were horrified by London and Manchester. Conservatives approved of Britain's victory over Jacobinism, but deplored its coarse manners, Protestantism and parliamentary government, and abominated its treatment of Catholic Ireland. Liberals admired the House of Commons and approved of the relative absence of policemen and soldiers, while regretting the weak coffee, the banal conversation, and the weather. Bonapartists, republicans and the few socialists, however, loathed and resented everything. Britain was the root of every evil, the vision of a future they feared, and above all the victorious enemy out to humiliate them. One writer claimed to have thrashed his cabby for taking him from Waterloo Station via Waterloo Bridge and Waterloo Square to the Waterloo Hotel.

A common first reaction was that Britain was outlandish, 'the Japan of Europe'.[63] 'It's strange,' pronounced King Louis-Philippe, 'it's nothing at all like France' – too tidy, too clean, and too quiet.[64] Fog, as the cultural historian Alain Corbin has pointed out, became a universal cliché, although the climate of southern England is no foggier that of northern France. Different, however, was urban smog, which became a symbol both of depression and of modernity. Food, in contrast to many approving eighteenth-century comments, was found not merely bad but revealing of character. Particularly disliked was the widespread use of pepper and curry – which had just begun its progress towards becoming the English national dish. 'There are links between their severe climate, their cold personality, and their over-spiced dishes,' pronounced one socialist.[65] It was symptomatic of the lack of that quintessentially French quality, *le goût*, as obvious in greasy turtle soup, curried stew, boiled vegetables and English puddings as in architecture and women's fashions. Women, indeed, became as much a symbol of England as fog or cabbage: from this period dates the still common stereotype of the unfeminine, inelegant Englishwoman. Instead of 'taste', the English only had 'comfort' – a word untranslatable into French ('fortunately', sniffed Custine).

Both fascinating and frightening was the Industrial Revolution. The Midlands and the North were now on the circuit for serious tourists. The reaction was overwhelmingly negative. The size, the crowds and the smoke of English cities inspired mythological hyperbole: the Black Country, strewn with coal and slag, was 'the plain of the Cyclops'; Manchester was 'the styx of this new hell'; while if 'the inhabitants [of Birmingham] go to hell they won't find anything new', thought Custine. The economist Adolphe Blanqui (coiner of the term *révolution industrielle*) felt horrified admiration for the scale of industry and the power it represented. Inspecting Black Country foundries, 'for the first time I began to understand English industry'. He recalled the 'fifteen thousand muskets a month' they had produced for use against France, and 'admiration turns to tears and thoughts of vengeance' at the realization of how 'a great empire succumbed to the efforts of a few million islanders'. Though one anglophobe reluctantly admitted that ordinary people were better dressed in England than France, and a Lyons businessman who had lived in America thought that 'the poor seem less poor than elsewhere', these were unusual views.[66] Many visitors stressed the poverty of the urban masses, the pallor and dirt of miners and factory workers, and what they saw as the widening gulf between wealth and poverty. Britain was in a pathological state, and heading for disaster.

One of the most hostile and ideologically charged caricatures was Flora Tristan's widely read *Promenades dans Londres* (1840). Her picture of London is of a foggy, gas-lit hell of poverty, oppression, hypocrisy and crime, full of prostitutes, beggars and thieves. 'Melancholy is in the very air you breathe [creating] an irresistible desire to end one's life by suicide . . . the Englishman is under the spell of his climate and behaves like a brute.' To these old clichés, Tristan, a pioneer feminist and socialist, added the anglophobe nationalism of the French Left. English liberty was a sham: 'a handful of aristocrats . . . bishops, landowners and sinecurists' was able to 'torture and starve a nation of twenty-six million men' because 'the school, the Church and the press' created 'ignorance and fear' which caused 'the English people, plunged into abjection, to await slow and convulsive death by starvation'. This was a lesson and warning to the French 'proletariat'. Such loathing was a problem for French politicians aiming at a closer relationship with Britain.

Ally or 'Anti-France'?

The July Monarchy . . . British liberty in French society, realized
all our ideas.
CHARLES DE RÉMUSAT[67]

If France overcomes, the world will be governed by the twenty-four letters
of the alphabet; if England prevails, it will be tyrannized by the ten figures
of arithmetic. Thinking or counting; those are the alternative futures.
VICTOR HUGO[68]

Between the Frenchman and the Englishman God has created an antipathy
that will not be drowned out by floods of verbosity from the English
milords . . . Let England, confined to her island, remain clearly what God
made her: the natural enemy of all the peoples of the Continent.
La Réforme (leading republican newspaper), 1847[69]

After the July Revolution of 1830, France was ruled, perhaps for the only time in its history, by a party of political anglophiles. Their predecessors, Charles X and his 'ultra-royalist' supporters, had been far less so. They had begun a more assertive foreign policy for which they hoped to obtain the assistance of Britain's other great rival, Russia. Their invasion of Spain in 1823 and their capture of Algiers in 1830 were welcomed in France as acts of defiance against Britain. At best reluctant converts to parliamentary government – the king remarked that 'he would rather chop wood than be king of England' – they attempted what amounted to a coup d'état in July 1830, and popular resistance in Paris toppled the regime. The British ambassador, Castlereagh's pleasure-loving brother Lord Stewart, is said to have reported that 'these fools are in serious trouble and they think everything is going wonderfully'.[70] There was little regret in Britain when Charles X took refuge once again at Holyrood.

The 'Three Glorious Days' of July 1830, interpreted as the French version of the 'Glorious Revolution' of 1688, brought to power an intellectually outstanding and often high-minded liberal elite whose political model was Britain, and who hoped that the two countries would become partners as the progressive powers of Europe. The new king, the clever and voluble Louis-Philippe, formerly the Duc d'Orléans and a hereditary anglophile, peppered his letters and conversation with English, had been an exile in Britain and America, and had hoped to marry into the British royal family (eventually he practically did). He is regarded by his recent biographer as having been at one time effectively a British agent. In 1804 he had written, 'I left my country so early that I have hardly any French habits, and I can truthfully say that I am attached to England not only by gratitude, but also by taste and inclination . . . The security of Europe and the world, the future happiness and independence of the human race, depend on the safety and independence of England.'[71] The chief political personalities of the new regime were the austere Calvinist François Guizot, translator of Gibbon and Shakespeare and the leading historian of English liberty, and the bouncy young journalist-politician Adolphe Thiers, famous for predicting before the revolution that the Bourbons would end like the Stuarts. In the new regime's cultural firmament sparkled Victor Hugo, the worshipper of Shakespeare; Eugène Delacroix, the disciple of Bonington; Alexis de Tocqueville, the analyst of American democracy; Benjamin Constant, the Scottish-educated political philosopher and proponent of 'modern' liberty; and many distinguished commentators on British history and politics. In Britain, many of the governing Whigs – especially the 'Foxite' group, Lords Grey, Clarendon, Lansdowne, and Fox's nephew Lord Holland – were eager to respond. They had deplored the long struggle against France. They saw 1830 as a revival of the hopes of 1789, and a belated vindication of their francophile opinions and tastes. Guizot, when ambassador in London, was a welcome guest at Holland House, where his host 'belonged almost as much to the Continent and France as to England . . . we talked at length of great French writers and orators, La Bruyère, Pascal, Madame de Sévigné, Bossuet, Fénelon'. Holland called for a 'cordial understanding' between France and Britain to resist the reactionary states in Europe – a phrase that would have a distinguished future.[72]

The 1830 revolution briefly aroused fears of a repetition of the wars of the 1790s, but Louis-Philippe followed a determinedly cautious path – 'peace at any price', in the notorious phrase coined by one of his ministers. Although revolution in Belgium, and its separation from Holland, caused a French army to intervene at the request of the Belgians, the government ignored pleas to annex Belgium, refused the throne for Louis-Philippe's son, and resisted nationalist pressure to have the French troops at least blow up the Allied war memorial as they marched through Waterloo. The Belgian crisis was settled between the veteran ambassador Talleyrand and the new foreign secretary Viscount Palmerston, and guaranteed by the Treaty of London (1839), mainly remembered now because it took Britain into war in 1914 as an ally of France. The new King of the Belgians, Leopold of Saxe-Coburg – who was to be the son-in-law of Louis-Philippe and the cousin-in-law of Queen Victoria – became a zealous intermediary between the two countries. In Spain too, Anglo-French difficulties were sorted out by negotiation between Talleyrand and Palmerston, and in 1834 the two countries became allies in a Quadruple Alliance including Spain and Portugal designed to support liberal governments in the Peninsula.

The July Monarchy was a system of compromises; some said of contradictions. A conservative government that emerged from a popular revolt, it had a very regal monarch who put on a 'bourgeois' act, sending his sons to school in Paris and famously strolling about carrying an umbrella. Such compromises were not necessarily disadvantageous: what the elderly La Fayette defined in 1830 as 'a popular throne surrounded by republican institutions' would prove a winning combination in much of Europe, including Britain. But one contradiction proved impossible to manage: that between the regime's pacific and anglophile instincts, and its inescapable need to create a patriotic image. Many of those who had fought the Bourbon troops during the 'Three Glorious Days' of 1830 – including former soldiers of Napoleon – believed they had fought not only the internal system established in 1815, but also the external system commonly called the Holy Alliance, which they detested as humiliating, oppressive and reactionary. General Lamarque, who had fought Wellington, and (as well as disliking 'lanky' English women) was the most vocal nationalist spokesman, proclaimed in parliament that 'the cannon of Paris has silenced the cannon of Waterloo!' France must now resume the struggle. In an enduring left-wing fantasy, oppressed peoples from Ireland to Poland would rally to the French liberators, who, 'half by persuasion, half by force', would create a French-dominated European Republic.

For these left-wing patriots, Britain was the malignant obstacle to their utopia. It was the spider in the post-Waterloo web of worldwide oppression and corruption, and at the same time it embodied a model of the future (liberal, reformist, commercial) that rivalled their own revolutionary vision (democratic, authoritarian, military). It was necessary to emphasize how awful England was – 'a big shop on a big island', a 'cancer' – in case it proved more seductive than their own Spartan ideal. Flora Tristan, whose lurid depiction we have seen, was one of many who insisted that the English were both exploited and exploiting, a corrupted nation motivated by greed, obeying a ruthless aristocratic caste bent on imposing new forms of industrial slavery on the world, and using their power to force unwilling peoples to accept their goods, their machines, and their immigrant workers. In language echoing Jacobin propaganda of the 1790s, the English people as a whole were seen as the universal enemy – 'social vampires', not even a genuine 'nation', but merely 'a race destined to perish.'[73] England, according to the great Republican historian Jules Michelet, was 'the anti-France', the political, moral and cultural negation of the 'leading nation in the universe'.[74] Even moderates agreed that the two countries were engaged in a struggle to shape the future of the planet through ideological, commercial and colonial competition. The anglophobe world view (which ramified into anti-americanism and anti-semitism) explained everything. The ills of French workers stemmed from economic competition from Britain. Political oppression in France was a consequence of France's rulers obeying their British masters. Even resistance to French colonialism was ascribed to British machinations. So Britain's power had to be broken, by war if necessary. Such views were held by a minority, but they were a noisy minority who reached a wide audience. Attempts by the July Monarchy to seek *entente* with Britain therefore led to accusations of national betrayal, cowardice, and corruption – in short of being no better than the deposed Bourbons. The 'Legitimist' supporters of those same Bourbons were eager to join in these accusations against a regime they detested, and to denounce a Britain they too regarded as the embodiment of much that was evil in the modern world. It was the Legitimist press (though it could as easily have been the Left) that stigmatized the July Monarchy as an 'anti-national' creation, 'an English government ruling France'.[75]

So the July Monarchy had somehow to prove itself patriotic as well as pacific. This was not just tactics. Liberals were patriots too, and many were veterans of the Empire and even the Republic. Moreover, they believed that patriotic pride was necessary to hold the nation together at a time of political and social turmoil. The Monarchy proclaimed itself 'the sole legitimate heir of all the proud memories of France' – royal, republican and Napoleonic.[76] This cult of memory had the advantage of focusing emotion on the past. It was the July Monarchy, not Napoleon, that completed the Arc de Triomphe, adding the stirring sculpture by Rude of the republican Volunteers of 1792, one of the great icons of French patriotism. Louis-Philippe constantly recalled that he had fought under the Tricolour at Jemmapes in 1792. Present-day adventures were carried out safely away from Europe, namely the conquest of Algeria (in which the British uneasily acquiesced), where the king's dashing sons played prominent roles.

The climax of the strategy of patriotic symbolism masking peaceful diplomacy came in 1840. The new prime minister, Adolphe Thiers, eager to demonstrate both his patriotism and his good relations with Britain, requested London (which was willing, though privately supercilious) to hand over Napoleon's body, buried at St Helena, for ceremonial enshrinement in Paris. 'If England gives us what we are asking, her reconciliation with France will be sealed; the past fifty years will be wiped out; the effect in France will

The return of Napoleon's remains from St Helena were intended to improve Franco-British relations, but patriotic fervour aggravated the worst crisis since Waterloo.

be huge.'[77] This scheme proved too clever for the regime's own good: 'Napoleon's ashes are still smouldering,' complained Lamartine, 'and they're blowing on the sparks.' When the emperor's remains reached France, they produced probably the greatest peacetime patriotic demonstration in France's history, with crowds of several hundred thousand gathering in Paris.

Even before this, when the 'ashes' were still sailing back from the South Atlantic, the patriotic and political excitement had got out of hand. The emperor's nephew, Louis-Napoleon Bonaparte, attempted a coup d'état. Strikes and riots broke out in Paris. An assassination attempt was made on the king. The most dangerous international crisis since 1815 began in July, and raised spectres of a neo-Napoleonic war. The French supported territorial expansion into Syria by their protégé, the pasha of Egypt, Muhammad Ali. Britain and Russia, unwilling to see France rebuild its power in the Near East and probably destroy the Ottoman empire in the process, ordered the Egyptians to withdraw, and Austria and Prussia supported them. For the French this was a provocative revival of the alliance of 1814. What might seem a trivial and distant issue (though it caused lasting upheaval in the Levant) aroused intense emotion in France. Even level-headed liberals such as Tocqueville wanted France to assert itself: 'no government, indeed no dynasty, would not be exposing itself to destruction if it tried to persuade this country to stand idly by'. To back down would devastate national pride – 'often puerile and boastful but still . . . the strongest link holding this nation together' – and condemn France to a political and moral decline 'more fatal than the loss of twenty battles'.[78] As the British navy dominated the eastern Mediterranean, Thiers tried to bluff the Allies into concessions by threatening to invade Italy and Germany – a milestone in francophobe German nationalism which inspired, among other things, the composition of 'Deutschland über alles'. Within France, patriots clamoured for war. The poet Heinrich Heine, who lived in Paris, noted 'a joyful warlike enthusiasm . . . the unanimous cry is "War on perfidious Albion"'.

In Austria, Prussia and Britain, there were many, including Queen Victoria, the prime minister Lord Melbourne and several cabinet ministers, who pressed the foreign minister Lord Palmerston to give the French government a face-saving way out. 'Letters from [francophiles in] London', according to Palmerston, were encouraging Thiers to hold firm. But hints from Louis-Philippe and his ambassador Guizot indicated that Thiers would not be allowed to go too far. Palmerston regarded the French attitude as posturing that deserved a rebuff to deter further mischief. He informed Thiers 'in the most friendly and inoffensive manner possible, that if France . . . begins a war, she will to a certainty lose her ships, colonies and commerce . . . and that Mehemet Ali will just be chucked into the Nile'.[79] Thiers's bluff having been called, Louis-Philippe dismissed him in October 1840. Guizot, known to favour peace, was recalled from London to form a government.

So 1840, the year Thiers had hoped would seal Franco–British reconciliation, intensified anglophobia and ended with what Lamartine, in the course of a tumultuous parliamentary debate, called 'the Waterloo of French diplomacy'.[80] 'What a profound and perhaps irremediable evil Lord Palmerston has done to the two countries and to the entire world!' was Tocqueville's verdict.[81] But a senior French diplomat concluded, 'Let's be fair . . . Palmerston has very strong arguments on his side.'[82] The blame can certainly be divided several ways. Palmerston's share is that he refused to let the French off the hook when their manoeuvres went wrong. He ascribed the crisis to

> a spirit of bitter hostility towards England growing up among
> Frenchmen of all classes and all parties; and sooner or later this
> must lead to conflict . . . I do not blame the French for disliking
> us. Their vanity prompts them to be the first nation in the world;
> and yet at every turn they find that we outstrip them in everything.
> It is a misfortune to Europe that the national character of a great
> and powerful people . . . should be as it is.[83]

In France, anglophobe pique in the early 1840s, shamefully, caused the government to refuse to cooperate with Britain in its long campaign to stop the African slave trade: as the mercenary British could not really be interested in protecting Africans, they thought, it must be a pretext to interfere with French commerce. Guizot and Louis-Philippe tried to repair the relationship, but their effort was politically damaging. As Louis-Philippe predicted, he was execrated as 'the foreigners' king'.

CHAPTER 8

The War That Never Was

The policy of France is like an infection clinging to the walls of
the dwelling and breaking out in every successive occupant who comes
within their influence.

LORD PALMERSTON[1]

We know that France and Britain were never to fight each other again. That was not how it seemed at the time. The Napoleonic wars cast a long shadow. The mid-century decades were marked by a succession of crises, war scares and preparations for war on both sides. But they only fought as allies, against Russia and China; and they even considered intervening jointly in the American Civil War. But mutual suspicion meant that they were unable to exert a stabilizing effect on Europe in the 1860s, which ended in the disastrous Franco-German war of 1870. That is why their bickering mattered. Not for the last time, they failed to establish a relationship of trust that might have preserved Europe from some of its future disasters.

A Beautiful Dream: The First *Entente Cordiale*, 1841–6

Perhaps the 'intimate and permanent union' of England and France was a dream, but it was a beautiful dream. The idea of these two great peoples . . . enveloping the universe within their vast embrace and forcing it to remain in repose and peace, that idea was great.
ALEXIS DE TOCQUEVILLE to the chamber of deputies, 1843.[2]

The difficulty of destroying English illusions, suspicions and misconceptions about our interests after forty years of contact with them . . . is greatly weakening my confidence that I can establish between Paris and London that cordial and sincere accord which is, I believe, the real interest of both countries and the veritable *alcazar* of European peace.
LOUIS-PHILIPPE to Guizot.[3]

For Louis-Philippe and Guizot, war and revolution were all-consuming destroyers. Both men's fathers – one a prince, one a provincial solicitor – had died on the guillotine, victims of 'the savage beast', in Louis-Philippe's words, that liked to 'dip its muzzle in blood'.[4] Both had known flight and exile. They saw their mission as making France a bulwark of liberty and peace. They hoped that this would gain the respect of other states, especially Britain, and hence please moderate patriots at home. Palmerston, popular spokesman of patriotic liberalism and scourge of Continental conservatism, fell from office following a Tory victory in 1841. The new foreign secretary Lord Aberdeen wished Louis-Philippe well. He and Guizot maintained personal relations, bypassing diplomatic channels. Aberdeen was supported by the Queen and influential Whigs such as Lansdowne, eager to 'smooth the ruffled feathers'. Victoria and Albert visited Louis-Philippe at his castle at Eu in Normandy in 1843, the first visit to France by a reigning British sovereign since Henry VIII,[5] and the first personal gesture of solidarity towards the 'citizen king' by any European monarch. Louis-Philippe was put on his best behaviour by his daughter the Queen of the Belgians: 'Victoria *never* talks politics . . . it is the *paterfamilias* rather than the king she wants to see . . . Dear father must therefore be natural, paternal, patriarchal, unaffected, as usual.'[6] It worked, and the queen duly warmed to the Orléans family, so fecund, domestic and affectionate – so 'Victorian'. The king used the words 'cordiale entente' in his 1843 speech from the throne. He planned a return visit to Windsor in 1844 (his wife wrote to ask Victoria to make sure he did not over-eat or go riding) and inaugurated annual royal and ministerial meetings. He took Victor Hugo into his confidence:

> I'll be welcomed there: I speak English. And the English are grateful to me for knowing them well enough not to hate them, for everyone begins by hating the English . . . But I respect them and I show it. Between ourselves, the only worry is too warm a welcome . . . Popularity there would mean unpopularity here . . . But I mustn't be badly received either: badly received there, mocked here.[7]

The visit went well, and Guizot was jubilant: 'The effects are excellent, excellent in England, excellent here . . . Lively and joyous pride at the welcome he received in England and the spectacle given to Europe. Lively satisfaction at the consolidation of peace . . . We could ask for nothing more from England.'[8] There are few moments in history in which a French head of government could have written such words.

Just as things were going so right, they went suddenly very wrong. George Pritchard, a Methodist missionary, had just returned from the South Seas with a story of French brutality and insult. He had been successfully preaching the gospel in Tahiti, becoming an adviser to Queen Pomare and honorary British consul. In 1842, Admiral Dupetit-Thouars, commander of the French Pacific squadron and a nephew of the legless hero of the Nile (see above, page 229), declared Tahiti a protectorate. He had acted without authorization, but his act conformed with France's policy of acquiring bases in distant oceans as stepping stones to colonial expansion. Patriotic opinion, especially on the Left, favoured this as a means of spreading French civilization and combating Britain. Dupetit-Thouars deposed Pomare in November 1843, declared Tahiti a French possession, and arrested and deported Pritchard. His arrival in England caused much embarrassment to Aberdeen and Guizot. 'It would be deplorable,' wrote the former, if 'you and I, two Ministers of Peace, should be condemned to quarrel about a set of naked savages at the other end of the world.'[9] The press and evangelical philanthropists were angry. Lord Shaftesbury was wrung with 'grief and indignation' at the fate of a 'peaceable and helpless people', a 'Christian model', and moreover 'English in laws and Constitution', who had been 'inundated with bloodshed, devastation, profligacy, and crime', while England did nothing – 'a disgusting and cowardly attitude'.[10] Guizot tried to ignore the whole affair, but eventually offered financial compensation to Pritchard. Even Aberdeen thought this 'rather slender'; but the French parliamentary opposition and press took quite the opposite view: the injured party was France, whose noble efforts to civilize Tahiti had been hampered, and by an Englishman and a creeping Methodist to boot. That the government should actually pay him compensation was an outrage, and proof that 'Lord Guizot' was an abject puppet: 'Nous avons pour ministre un Englishmann bâtard/ Très-humble serviteur du révérend Pritchard', ran one lampoon.[11] *Pritchardiste* became the opposition label for Guizot's supporters for the rest of his time in power. A public subscription bought Dupetit-Thouars a magnificent sword of honour, to which Louis-Philippe's sailor son the Prince de Joinville (who had escorted Napoleon's remains back to France) contributed.

If Tahiti was an embarrassment, Spain was to be a tragi-comedy. No one had forgotten the 'Spanish ulcer' that had weakened Napoleon and devastated the Peninsula. A generation later, Spain was still in turmoil, and France and Britain were supporting rival parties. Though commercial interests had some importance, prestige and security outweighed them. Palmerston, apt to assume the worst, feared that France would take over in Madrid, the Spanish would again revolt, and Britain would be drawn into another peninsular war – or else by appeasement would encourage the French to yet more threatening adventures in Belgium and elsewhere. Court and army factions ruled in Madrid, and as Queen Isabella and her sister were adolescents, providing them with husbands was a way of gaining important political influence. Aberdeen and Guizot thought they had made a deal. Not for the first or last time, the British were happy with the sense that they had a broad agreement, while the French concentrated on the small print. The agreement was to marry the queen to one of her cousins, probably the Duke of Cadiz, and later (once she had had an heir, the British assumed) marry her sister to Louis-Philippe's youngest son, the Duc de Montpensier. But Cadiz – nicknamed 'Paquita' – was, as one historian puts it, 'not a very seductive stallion', and it was widely doubted that he would father an heir – though Louis-Philippe promised breezily that 'an operation would set all to rights'. If Cadiz failed to perform, the Spanish crown would pass in time to Louis-Philippe's eventual grandson – an outcome the French were quietly anticipating. The pro-British party began to think that a Saxe-Coburg prince

Palmerston: this patriotic liberal had little patience with French ambitions.

(another relative of Queen Victoria) might make a more productive sire than Paquita. To forestall this, the pro-French party pushed ahead with the original two weddings on the same day, 10 October 1846. Guizot congratulated himself on having done 'a great and fine thing.'[12] The French knew London would be annoyed, but they underestimated the anger that seized not only hard-liners like Palmerston and his ambassador (who wanted to rent a mob to riot in Madrid), but France's best friend Aberdeen, and life-long francophiles such as Lansdowne (who fumed about 'rottenness', 'duplicity' and 'treachery'). Queen Victoria wrote what Palmerston called 'a tickler' to her former friend Louis-Philippe.

Why did the *entente cordiale* go so wrong? It is common to blame Palmerston: even a present-day French scholar describes him as 'having for the French that hatred and contempt that only the English are capable of'.[13] But Palmerston was sincere in his desire to support the spread of liberal government; and besides, the Pritchard affair and the Spanish marriages row began when he was out of office. Douglas Johnson identifies the real problem:

for the British, the *entente* was a means of restraining France; for the French, it was a means of restraining Britain.[14] Even the most pacific French politician wanted France to be treated as an equal partner: 1815 must be consigned to the past. They wanted colonies, economic concessions and influence over smaller western European states, especially Greece, Belgium and Spain. But no British politician, however emollient, was going to behave as if the Napoleonic wars had never happened, and certainly not as if France had won. There was such bitterness against Britain and the 'Pritchardists' in France that Louis-Philippe and his ministers dared not be too conciliatory. 'Give us this day our daily platitude' was said by his enemies to be the king's morning prayer – *platitude* in French here meaning not a commonplace saying, but an act of self-abasement. Even Guizot, routinely mocked as 'Sir Guizot', the hypocritical Protestant in the pockets of the English, nourished 'an ongoing desire for revenge, a rancour which lurked just below the surface'.[15] In his own words, 'one had to choose between a great success or a great failure, between defeat and a costly victory'. Vengeance was sweet: 'In 1840, over the miserable question of Egypt, England won a victory in Europe. In 1846, over the great question of Spain, she is beaten and alone.'[16] French diplomats argued, and French historians maintain, that France was within its rights over the Spanish marriages, and the British were hypocritical 'bad losers'. The rights and wrongs need not detain us: it had become politically vital to be seen to defeat Britain. But it did not work: critics decried Guizot's 'victory' as a mere dynastic intrigue, irrelevant to France's true honour and interest.

We may think, with olympian hindsight, that the marriage of the Queen of Spain, Pritchard's compensation, or even Egypt's claims to Beirut were not worth all the fuss. But statesmen, journalists and voters are inevitably the prisoners of their history. Each side saw the other as a global rival, and they were right. France had not given up the struggle after Waterloo: indeed, it never has. The most progressive and high-minded elements in both countries, including great liberal thinkers such as Tocqueville and J.S. Mill, were convinced of their respective nation's right and duty as the vanguards of progress to shape the future of the planet. Britain, because of its past victories, its technological mastery, and its self-proclaimed moral rectitude, buttressed by Evangelical philanthropy. France, because of its boasted cultural primacy and its universalist ideological claims, not least those stemming from the 1789 Declaration of the Rights of Man. Consequently, influential figures in both countries still saw the world in terms of Franco-British rivalry. The two countries became the exponents of a new liberal imperialism.[17]

No one could know that this rivalry would never again lead to a Franco-British war. So the Spanish quarrel, like a butterfly's wings in Tokyo setting off a storm in New York, had disproportionate results. The Prince de Joinville had published a pamphlet discussing how French steamships might attack

British commerce and raid its coasts. A surprise invasion using a 'steam bridge' for the French army was something both Wellington and Palmerston considered frighteningly feasible.[18] The government announced a large tax increase to pay for naval reinforcements and home defences. This caused protests and violent demonstrations. To calm the discontent, London began to shift some of the burden to the colonies, who were instructed to pay more and raise their own defence forces. This in turn created a storm of discontent and even rebellion throughout the Empire, which marked the beginning of the historic transformation of the colonies into self-governing states.[19] In Europe, the effects were even greater. The Franco-British split encouraged the Austrians and Russians to crack down on dissidence. They invaded the independent city of Cracow, encouraged conservative Catholic cantons in a civil war in Switzerland, and menaced nationalists in Italy. 'Since the Spanish marriages,' accused Lamartine, 'France, in betrayal of its nature and of centuries of tradition . . . has been Austrian in Piedmont, Russian in Cracow, French nowhere, counter-revolutionary everywhere!' This sudden wave of instability began the collapse of the entire fragile European system.

The July Monarchy was one of the first casualties of the 'year of revolutions' of 1848 that tumbled governments across Europe. Historians cannot say exactly why revolutions happen. The great economic depression that starved much of western Europe and devastated its economy in the late 1840s obviously played a part, creating masses of hungry unemployed workers and bankrupt businessmen. But why revolution in France, and not in Belgium, Holland or Britain? France, of course, was one of those states that had been destabilized by the revolution and the Napoleonic wars, and which were less able to weather serious social and political unrest. The fraught relationship with Britain also counted in two ways. First, Louis-Philippe and Guizot were attacked as 'Pritchardists' who did not defend French interests and pride, and this alienated even former supporters. Second, they themselves believed, not without reason, that they were beset by reckless chauvinists. This made them determined to retain their grip on power by refusing political change. 'You want reform and you won't have it!' the king told one of his ministers, 'it will bring . . . war! And I won't destroy my peace policy.'[20]

As crowds surged towards the Tuileries palace on 24 February 1848, the king and his family fled towards the Channel. Resentment over the Spanish marriages had not cooled. Louis-Philippe's daughter was sure that 'Father's dignity will not permit him to seek asylum on any point of English territory.' But with revolution spreading across Europe there was nowhere else to go. The British vice-consul at Le Havre smuggled him, disguised in dark glasses and a cap, his whiskers shaved off, on to a British ferry, with a false British passport. The last French king left his kingdom as Bill Smith, the consul's uncle: 'my dear Uncle talked so loud and so much that I had the greatest difficulty to make him keep silent'.[21] Guizot escaped to Yorkshire. Queen Victoria – pronouncing primly that events showed 'a great moral' – was less than welcoming. The government rather gracelessly lent the refugees Claremont House, south of London, where they were severely poisoned by lead from the water pipes. Palmerston assured the new Republic in Paris that the exiles would not be allowed to plot. Louis-Philippe ended his days in a bath chair at St Leonard's-on-Sea.

'God bless the narrow sea': From Revolution to Empire, 1848–52

God bless the narrow sea which keeps her off,
And keeps our Britain, whole within herself . . .
I wish [it] were a whole Atlantic broad.
ALFRED TENNYSON, 'The Princess' (1850)

A revolution in France was frightening and exciting, opening vistas of blood, liberation, and war. Revolts broke out across Europe as the news from Paris spread. Polish, Italian and German exiles in Paris and London rejoiced, drafted proclamations and bought guns. Statesmen and monarchs trembled. The king of Prussia predicted that he would end on the guillotine, and an Austrian minister was hanged on a Vienna lamp-post, in French revolutionary style. Even Queen Victoria worried: 'what will soon become of us God alone knows'.[22] Alphonse de Lamartine, a conservative turned republican and one of France's greatest lyric poets, was proclaimed head of the provisional republican government. This was not on the strength of his verses, but because of his recent best-selling *History of the Girondins*, which praised the revolution and established his popular credentials. There was widespread relief inside and outside France, for throughout the July Monarchy he had bravely attacked the ambient nationalism. 'I do not believe it is a good thing ceaselessly to deify war,' he had dared to tell Parliament in 1840, 'to encourage that impetuous rush of French blood that we are told is eager to flow after twenty-five years of truce: as if peace, the happiness and glory of the world, could be a national shame.'[23] This was the man to reassure Europe that the Second Republic did not intend to imitate the First. His colleagues in government included champions of bellicose left-wing nationalism. But in power, facing chaos and bankruptcy, they drew back from the revolutionary Armageddon they had often demanded under Louis-Philippe. 'We love Poland, we love Italy, we love all oppressed peoples,' declared Lamartine, 'but we love France above all.'[24]

In Britain there was no regret for Louis-Philippe, whose fall, said one paper, 'will be welcomed with contented laughter by perhaps three-fourths of mankind'.[25] There were many enthusiasts for the new republic. In Oxford, a young fellow of Exeter College, J.A. Froude, hired a brass band to play the 'Marseillaise' under the vice-chancellor's windows. Radicals, Chartists*, Irish nationalists and political exiles were galvanized by the news. Some heard it in the middle of a political meeting in London: 'Frenchmen, Germans, Poles, Magyars sprang to their feet, embraced, shouted and gesticulated in the wildest enthusiasm . . . great was the clinking of glasses that night in and around Soho and Leicester Square.'[26]

In the more sober atmosphere of Whitehall, resentment over the Spanish marriages remained so acute that expressions of good will were readily dispatched to the new regime. 'We desire friendship and extended commercial intercourse with France,' wrote Palmerston. 'We will engage the rest of Europe from meddling . . . The French rulers must engage to prevent France from assailing any part of the rest of Europe: upon such a basis our relations with France may be . . . more friendly than they have been . . . with Louis Philippe and Guizot.'[27] Problems concerning British workers chased out of France were dealt with calmly. Unlike in 1789, the French government was eager to accept advice, realizing that British protection would make Russian or Austrian attack impossible: 'When France and England agree together to secure the peace of Europe,' wrote Lamartine, 'no power can with impunity disturb it.'[28] He even wrote to the aged Duke of Wellington assuring him that he wanted France to adopt a British-style constitution. He and the ambassador, former Tory MP Lord Normanby, met daily. Lamartine's great virtue, thought Normanby, was that he was the only republican who actually liked Britain; he even had an English wife. Via the embassy, Lamartine informed and consulted London sometimes several times a day about the Republic's external and even internal policies, such as appointments and the electoral system. The hated francophobe Palmerston, who could have played John Bull in any pantomime, and the languorous poet Lamartine, who could have played a stage Frenchman with equal ease, stood joint watch at the cradle of France's first real democracy.

Delegations of Chartists and Irish nationalists hastened to Paris in the weeks following the revolution to convey congratulations and solicit support. Chartists (who had a strong Irish element drawn from immigrants in England) held numerous public meetings hailing the revolution: 'France has the Republic; England shall have the Charter.' Some radical Chartist leaders felt strong affinities with France: Feargus O'Connor was the son of a United Irishman who had become a general under Napoleon, Bronterre O'Brien

---

* Britain's most important democratic movement, with a large working-class membership, which campaigned for a 'People's Charter' of democratic rights.

was writing a biography of Robespierre, and G.J. Harney was an admirer of Marat. The British authorities were sensitive about French contacts with Irish radicals, especially as Ireland was in the agonizing grip of famine and rural unrest. Normanby was incensed by a speech made by the leader of one delegation, William Smith O'Brien, who recalled the Franco-Irish alliance at the battle of Fontenoy. Lamartine responded by telling the delegates of 'Young Ireland', the radical wing of Irish nationalism, that 'we are at peace, and we wish to remain at peace, not with such or such a part of Great Britain, but with Great Britain as a whole'. Palmerston approved this as 'most honourable and gentlemanlike', and Punch portrayed it as the Irish being doused with cold water.[29] France quickly began to figure less prominently in the speeches, and the hopes, of Irish leaders.

Lamartine, besieged by radicals and nationalists, set out the Republic's foreign policy in a carefully phrased Manifesto (2 March) trying to please domestic opinion while placating foreign governments. He ensured that this was clearly understood by Normanby, who received advance notice of the contents:

> War . . . is not now the principle of the French Republic, as it was the fatal and glorious necessity of the republic of 1792 . . . The world and ourselves are desirous of advancing to fraternity and peace . . . The treaties of 1815 have no longer any lawful existence in the eyes of the French republic; nevertheless . . . those treaties are facts . . . The Republic . . . will not pursue secret or incendiary propagandism; [but] will exercise the only honourable proselytism, that of esteem and sympathy.[30]

Lamartine even condemned the July Monarchy over the Spanish marriages, 'an obstacle to our liberal alliances'. Palmerston concluded, 'evaporate the gaseous parts, and scum off the dross, and you would find the remains to be peace and good-fellowship with other Governments'.[31] Yet there was duplicity here. Lamartine, like all republicans, wanted to throw off the treaties of 1815, regain territory lost by Napoleon, and encourage national movements looking to France for leadership. He and his successor Jules Bastide (formerly editor of the bellicose *National*) were active in secretly aiding revolutionaries in Italy, Belgium, Poland, Hungary and Germany. But the biggest dog did not bark: anglophobia stayed muzzled. If we wish to identify a turning-point in Franco-British relations, this is one: the anglophiles of the July Monarchy had seriously considered war with Britain; the anglophobes of the Republic ruled it out. They sought good relations to prevent another anti-French coalition. They were aided by the widespread revulsion caused in Britain by the brutal crushing of national liberation movements in Hungary and Italy in 1848–9 by the Russians and Austrians.

Palmerston even contemplated encouraging the French to end Austrian rule in northern Italy by military force. He joined with them in protecting Hungarian refugees, and he refused to apologize when the Austrian General Haynau was beaten up by London workers.

During the spring and summer of 1848, attention was fixed on internal politics in both Britain and France. The Chartists held a succession of meetings across industrial Britain, culminating in a mass rally in London on 10 April and the presentation of a huge petition to parliament demanding the Charter. The government – advised by Wellington, and learning lessons from events in France – had marshalled large numbers of volunteer special constables armed only with truncheons. This famous day became the subject of conflicting myths. That it passed off without violence, and that Parliament shrugged off the petition, persuaded observers across Europe that Britain was not going to join in 'the year of revolutions'. There had been no chance that it ever would. The ruling classes were far less divided than in France. Efficient steps were taken to keep order. The argument that Britain did not need revolution was easy to make: *The Scotsman* stated that 'the revolution in France arose out of the people not being even allowed to *ask* for less than we already possess'.[32] Britain's empire, as noted earlier, was less stolid – and had fewer rights. There were disturbances in Canada (where parliament was burned down), Australia, Ceylon, the Cape and many smaller colonies, often openly appealing to the French example.[33] Ireland was as always the most ambitious, but without French support an uprising by 'Young Ireland' came to nothing.

The tide of revolution turned in France too, and more bloodily. A huge armed insurrection in June 1848, motivated by the political and social disappointments of unemployed Parisian workers, was crushed by the army under General Cavaignac, one of the few truly republican generals, who became the new head of government. Louis-Philippe commented from England that 'republics are lucky: they can shoot people'. Cavaignac told Normanby that 'he was sure that in London and everywhere else much satisfaction would be felt'.[34] For the time being, revolution in France was over, and it ceased to be an inspiration to radicals in Britain.

The real beneficiary was someone who had recently begun to attract notice in Britain, Louis-Napoleon Bonaparte, Napoleon's nephew. The emperor's only son – 'Napoleon II', 'The Eaglet' – had died young in Austria. Louis-Napoleon was his political heir. Until 1848 his career had been a bad joke. He made absurd attempts in 1836 and 1840 to seize power, was imprisoned, escaped, and lived as a man-about-town in London. After the revolution, he returned to France and found himself a political celebrity. When he announced his candidature to be the first elected president of the republic, it soon became clear that he would win by a landslide; and in December 1848 he duly did. The Napoleonic legend, fashioned on St Helena to portray the emperor as a selfless philanthropist, enabled him to declare that 'my name is a programme in itself'. He had created an image of concern for social problems. The political alternatives – republican, royalist, socialist – had all made themselves unpopular. He attracted support for different, even contradictory, reasons: he would both prevent further revolution and stop royalist counter-revolution; he would both help the poor and restore business confidence; he would both make France great and keep the peace. However, the new constitution allowed presidents to serve for only one four-year term, which was not enough for a Bonaparte. To stay in power he carried out a coup d'état on 2 December 1851, which involved brief fighting in Paris and a major insurrection in the provinces. A plebiscite gave him overwhelming popular support; but it was never forgotten that he had shed French blood and transported thousands to penal colonies.

THE PRINCE-PRESIDENT'S FIRST LADY

'Miss Harriet Howard', born Elizabeth Harryett in 1823, the daughter of a Brighton publican, was a beautiful, intelligent and accomplished courtesan, one of several English women who, notwithstanding the frumpish stereotype, became famous in France for louche glamour. No English woman – except perhaps Queen Victoria – played such an important role in French politics. She had begun her career as the mistress of the champion jockey, Jem Mason. She met Louis-Napoleon in London and astutely picked a winner. As well as providing comforts to the pretender, she also invested vital cash in his political career when he was still a despised outsider. Unlike the hero of Dumas's *La Dame aux camélias*, Louis-Napoleon was not ashamed of profiting from his lover's immoral earnings. Yet however lucrative Miss Howard's charms, it seems implausible that she could have made herself rich enough to give him several hundred thousand francs. Might she have provided a channel for secret donors? When Louis-Napoleon became 'Prince-President', he often held secret meetings with political allies at her house conveniently close to the Elysée. But when she appeared at the Tuileries palace as his unofficial consort after his 1851 coup d'état, Parisian society was scandalized. She quickly had to make way for a suitable wife and mother for the dynasty when the president became emperor. Disillusioned, bitter, unmollified by a chateau, a pension, a husband and a title, she died in 1865.

From pub to palace: the fragrant Miss Howard.

The period 1848 to 1851 demolished the orthodox liberal view that France and Britain were following converging paths. France had had a revolution, a civil war and a coup d'état, and then over the next two decades, Louis-Napoleon (who made himself Emperor Napoleon III in 1852) turned France into a modernizing dictatorship. Britain, in contrast, had survived 'the year of revolutions' without even the resignation of a minister. The Chartist and Irish campaigns of 1848 were soon forgotten or incorporated into the national narrative of continuity, consensus, moderation and reform. Britain, said an Austrian minister, was 'apart from the European Community'.[35] It was, in Tennyson's famous lines,

> A land of settled government,
> A land of just and old renown,
> Where freedom slowly broadens down
> From precedent to precedent.

This sense of apartness shaped British identity, and France again gave the fullest example of what Britain was apart from: 1830 had not after all been its 1688. The French, it seemed, were incapable of liberty. The British attained perhaps their highest-ever level of self-satisfaction. Schoolchildren would learn that they belonged to 'the greatest and most highly civilized people that the world ever saw . . . The modern era of European civilization receives its highest expression in the British isles . . . There are no people like the British.'[36] The French were mocked, or worse, pitied. This has been diagnosed as just the usual francophobia.[37] But things had changed. First, in contrast with the 1790s and 1800s, the old francophobic imagery – foppish mannerisms, skinniness, dandified appearance – had disappeared. In cartoons (some by French artists such as Gavarni, who worked for *Punch*), the French are no longer portrayed as a different genus from the English. Following the dictatorships of Cavaignac and Louis-Napoleon Bonaparte, the commonest symbols of Frenchness became army uniform and the fashionable military moustache and goatee. The French had formulated a concrete set of 'English' stereotypes since 1814, but the British no longer had a clear image of the modern French. Second, 'francophobic' British criticisms are indistinguishable from those expressed by French commentators themselves: British perceptions were influenced by the views of liberal and republican exiles, who had become pessimistic about their own nation.

EXILES: HUGO AND THE STORMY VOICES OF FRANCE

Victor in Drama, Victor in Romance,
Cloud-weaver of fantasmal hopes and fears,
French of the French, and Lord of human tears . . .
As yet unbroken, Stormy voice of France!
Who dost not love our England – so they say;
I know not – England, France, all men to be
Will make one people ere man's race be run.
ALFRED TENNYSON, 'To Victor Hugo'

The question now is whether these islands belong to us
or to Victor Hugo & Co.
LORD PALMERSTON, October 1855

In 1848 one French exile left England – Louis-Napoleon Bonaparte – and a stream flowed back. Louis-Philippe and his entourage. Guizot and other minis-

Victor Hugo on Jersey.

VICTOR HUGO, Par Carjat

ters. Left-wing refugees after June 1848. More left-wing politicians after a doomed uprising in May 1849. Then a sizeable and diverse influx after the coup d'état in December 1851, which included Catholic conservatives, liberals and republicans, and the protean Victor Hugo, who had been through several political reincarnations, but now found his vocation as arch-exile. They totalled about 4,500, some banished, most fleeing prison or penal colonies. Though Dover complained about the cost to its ratepayers, the British as a whole were proud to give refuge with no questions asked: from 1823 to the end of the century, not a single asylum-seeker was refused or expelled. This was bitterly resented by other governments, who suspected that the British and Palmerston, 'the most universally and cordially hated man in Europe', were encouraging subversion for their own machiavellian ends.[38]

Exile, poverty, inactivity and frustration do not generate affection for hosts, or for fellow exiles. Most exiles kept to themselves, uninterested in English life. The English were equally indifferent, for these were not allies in a common struggle. Most refugees gathered in the cheap grimy streets near the traditional

Hugo's thoughts in his island exile: the tidal wave of 'destiny'.

haunts of Soho and Leicester Square, where they frequented cafés, political
clubs, and Thomas Wyld's Reading Rooms. In March 1851 a republican banquet
had 600 participants. A policeman reported that meetings were 'a very curious
sight . . . the words Canaille, Voleur, Brigand, Coquin, Jean-foutre continually
used in speaking of each other'.[39] They were no less critical of their hosts. The
radical leader Ledru-Rollin caused offence by dashing off *La Décadence de
l'Angleterre*, gleefully predicting its inevitable collapse into mass famine. It was
the usual, if rather well-expressed, diatribe against 'the vulture alone in its
eyrie', its exploiting aristocracy, starving workers, hellish slums, suffering
colonies, universities sunk in 'pleasure and dissipation', and its lack of idealism,
organization and even grammar.[40] The Russian exile Alexander Herzen thought
that 'the Frenchman cannot forgive the English, in the first place, for not speaking
French; in the second, for not understanding him when he calls Charing Cross
Sharan-Kro, or Leicester Square, Lessesstair-Skooar. Then his stomach cannot
digest the English dinners . . . the whole *habitus*, all that is good and bad in the
Englishman is detestable to the Frenchman.' Hugo declared superbly that 'when
England wishes to converse with me, it will learn to speak French'.[41]

Assimilation, even if it were possible, would negate the integrity of exile.
Guizot declined a chair at Oxford. A leading socialist was sneered at as 'Louis
Blanc Esquire' for settling in too well, even having English books and furnishings. Hugo rejected the life of literary and social London, the receptions and
the country houses which his fame and his royalties would have opened. Not
even his sexual rapacity prevented his choice of an exile within exile, the closest

he could get to France, the Channel Islands (where he contented himself with maidservants and needy local women). He worked ingeniously at smuggling his book-length philippics *Napoléon le Petit* and *Les Châtiments* into France; they also had a considerable influence in Britain. He invented a new religion (still practised in Vietnam), and experimented with spiritualism (Napoleon I communicated his approval of Hugo's opposition to his nephew.) About 100 of the most militant exiles – 'hairy, hunch-backed and obtuse', according to Hugo's long-suffering lover Juliette Drouet[42] – gathered round him in Jersey, under the surveillance of the French vice-consul and the Royal Navy. But they had less legal protection than in England, and after one exile published rude remarks about Queen Victoria, several dozen were expelled, really as a sop to the French government, by now Britain's ally in the Crimean war. Hugo simply moved to Guernsey. Real exile, like that of his former hero Napoleon, had to be on a sea-girt rock – 'I shall gaze at the ocean.' Napoleon had had Longwood House; he had Hauteville House, both shrines to their masters' egos. Guernsey was a rejection of Victorian England as well as of Imperial France – especially when the former began to find virtues in the latter.

Hugo spent nearly twenty of his most superhumanly productive years in exile, and he became a worldwide celebrity, even more so than his English counterparts Dickens and Tennyson. He finished *Les Misérables*, the overflowing political and social saga of post-Napoleonic France, a huge popular success. He wrote vast quantities of poetry and visionary literature, and two novels, one set in the Channel Islands, the other in a fantasy Britain inhabited by characters such as Gwynplaine, Dea and Lord Linnaeus Clancharlie. Meanwhile, his son translated Shakespeare. Hugo, like most of the disillusioned French Left, abandoned nationalism, which had been hijacked by Napoleon III. France – 'that wretched fellow's whore' – had shown itself unworthy of its sacred mission to liberate mankind. As Lamartine grandly put it, 'too bad for the people'. Hugo turned to pacifism, campaigns against the death penalty, and dreams of a united Europe that would have to manage for the time being without French leadership, but which would eventually, and inevitably, have Paris as its capital – 'Before it has a people, Europe has a city.' Above all, he remained as the 'unbroken voice' of opposition to Napoleon III's dictatorship:

> If we're but a thousand, count me in,
> If only a hundred, there I'll be.
> If ten stand firm, I'll be the tenth
> And if there's only one, it will be me!

'Such a faithful ally', 1853–66

Napoleon broods for years over an Idea, and sooner or later tries to carry
it out; . . . before he became Emperor one of his fixed Ideas was to wipe
out Waterloo by the Humiliation of England . . . He hardly knows himself
how he may feel Six or Twelve Months Hence.

PALMERSTON, 1859[43]

Really it is too bad! No country, no human being would ever dream
of *disturbing* or *attacking* France; every one would be glad to see
her prosperous: but *she* must needs disturb every quarter of the Globe
and try to make mischief.

QUEEN VICTORIA, 1860[44]

Napoleon III was the most ambitious ruler France has had since his uncle,
Charles de Gaulle included. That he is not as famous as either is because
he failed disastrously, and his failure, unlike that of Waterloo, could not be
transformed into heroic myth. Domestically, he wished to 'end the revolution' by creating popular authoritarian government, buttressed by a
modernized economy. Like all his predecessors since Charles X, he wanted
to supersede the 'treaties of 1815', regain territories lost in Napoleon's defeat,
and make France the dominant power in a new European system based on
what he called 'the principle of nationalities' – broadly speaking, national
self-determination. This 'principle' would justify France's expansion to her
'natural frontiers', fragment her multinational enemies, Austria and Russia,
and create new nation-states allied to France, especially Poland and Italy. If
carried out it would inevitably bring France into confrontation with other
Great Powers, but if it worked it would restore French hegemony. Napoleon
III, who claimed, probably sincerely, to be carrying out the ideas of his uncle,
had learned one vital lesson from the St Helena pronouncements: 'all our
wars came from England' – though he reassuringly ascribed this to a regret-
table misunderstanding.[45] To change Europe he needed British acquiescence.
So, unlike Charles X or Louis-Philippe, he would champion causes popular
in France and Britain, offering to be Britain's ally. He was the least anglophobe of French nationalists. He had enjoyed his exile in London, and used
it to make friendly contacts. He admired British modernity, expressing none
of the fastidious distaste shown even by relatively anglophile intellectuals.
He is surely the only French ruler to have served a British monarch as a
special constable.

Opinions of the new emperor were divided in Britain as in France. Was
he the man of destiny who had saved France from anarchy, or the 'conspir-
ator . . . the walking lie', as Prince Albert put it,[46] who had cruelly destroyed

its liberties? Should British criticisms be moderated for the sake of good relations – should 'our free press cease to brawl', as the prolific and political poet Tennyson put it, so as not to 'sting the fiery Frenchman into war'? Was it true, as Napoleon had proclaimed, that 'the Empire means peace', or would a Bonaparte inevitably menace Britain? British confusion manifested itself early on. Palmerston's unauthorized expression of approval for the coup d'état in December 1851 got him the sack. The Foreign Office was unhappy at Bonaparte calling himself 'Napoleon' or 'the Third', not least because this was forbidden by the 1815 Treaty of Paris. British consuls in French ports were instructed to watch out for preparations to invade. Over the next two years, Britain hastily built up its navy to deter such a possibility, but ended up using those ships as France's ally in a war against Russia.

The Crimean War, remembered now on both sides of the Channel for a few vignettes – the Taking of the Malakoff, the Charge of the Light Brigade, the Lady with the Lamp – was the deadliest war fought anywhere between 1815 and 1914, costing some half a million lives, mainly Russian and Turkish. It shattered the European peace established in 1815, and, together with the 1848–9 revolutions, of which it was a consequence, ignited a century of conflict. Tsar Nicholas I, untouched by the revolutions, flexing his muscles, and hostile to the new Bonaparte, quarrelled with the French over the conflicting rights of Christian churches in Palestine. Behind the monkish squabbles stood two states whose ancient claims to 'protect' Christians were excuses to interfere in Ottoman politics. Nicholas recklessly used the quarrel to manufacture a crisis intended to destroy the Ottoman empire and redistribute its territories. No other state wanted this, and Britain especially wanted to prop up the Turks to keep European rivals away from its land route to India.

Napoleon III and his able advisers realized that the crisis could put France back at the centre of European affairs, whether they brokered a compromise or fought a war in alliance with Britain – this, according to the foreign minister Walewski (Napoleon I's illegitimate son) would be 'a gift inspired by Providence'.[47] A Russian attack on Turkey in 1853 brought the British and French navies into the Black Sea to protect Constantinople, and led to war. London and Paris decided to attack Russia's naval base at Sebastopol, in the Crimean peninsula, the source of the tsar's seaborne threat to Constantinople. An expedition duly landed in the Crimea in September 1854 and fought its way to Sebastopol – an epic commemorated in patriotic paintings, verse and street names on both sides of the Channel. Napoleon made a state visit to Britain, and the queen was delighted to find him 'as *unlike a Frenchman* as possible'. She returned the visit, making a pilgrimage with her son to Napoleon's tomb, a gesture which, she hoped, wiped out 'old enmities and rivalries'. Palmerston (prime minister from 1855) and Napoleon both fantasized about 'rolling up' Russian power, and the navies operated in the Baltic (bombarding Russian bases) as well as the Black Sea. But Sebastopol held out, and the Allies were forced into a winter siege, in which disease and cold killed far more men than bullets.

COMRADES IN ARMS

This was the first time French and British had fought as allies since the Dutch war of 1674. The elderly British commander Lord Raglan, once Wellington's dashing aide de camp who had lost an arm at Waterloo, occasionally referred absent-mindedly to the enemy as 'the French', as every textbook relates. Yet he got on well with them, and spoke the language fluently. Indeed, relations between the Allies at all levels were good. Wrote one British corporal, 'The French and ourselves got on capitally, particularly the Zouaves whom we found a very jolly set.' The British were impressed by the uniformed female *cantinières*, 'very ugly,

A decorative ribbon from the Crimean War, symbolizing the new alliance.

but pronounced by our men to be stunning'. Even a gaffe by the Duke of Cambridge, who without realizing it invited General Canrobert to review the troops on the anniversary of Waterloo (which Canrobert had also forgotten) was treated with good humour. The difference between the Allies was that the French were more professional. Canrobert said that seeing the British was like going back a century. French professionalism included grabbing the best billets and the best food, skills the British soldiers rather admired. British blunders – most notoriously the charge of the Light Brigade – seem to have evoked both sympathy and professional disapproval. General Bosquet's comment, 'C'est magnifique, mais ce n'est pas la guerre', remains famous; and another French general exclaimed 'I have seen many battles, but this is too much.' There was some British resentment that as their own numbers and morale dwindled through sickness the French took the leading role, and there were accusations of too much 'talk and bravado'. But at the culmination of the siege, the French took the key position, the Malakoff, whereas the British could not take their objective, the Redan – 'a shameful and disastrous failure' after which the French seem to have regarded the British as negligible.[48] The poor equipment and administration and inept leadership of the British army caused a political scandal, whereas the French army (despite even worse losses from disease) proved that it was once more the most effective in Europe.

The length and cost of the war caused alarm in France, especially when Napoleon announced that he would go and take command in person – something his advisers managed to prevent. When Sebastopol was finally taken in September 1855, the French were determined to make peace. The war transformed the standing of Napoleon III and France. It broke up the alliance of Britain, Russia, Austria and Prussia that had defeated the first Napoleon and kept the Bourbons and Louis-Philippe in a position of inferiority. The peace conference was held in Paris in 1856, a recognition of France's status. For the emperor, it was the first step towards his vision of a new Europe. He explained to his ministers that the war had been 'the revolution everyone expects', and he told the foreign secretary Lord Clarendon 'frankly' that his real objects had been 'Poland and Italy'. The Russians, who had refused to recognize him as a legitimate monarch, now depended on him to protect them from the consequences of defeat, and were delighted to find him treating them as long-lost friends. The British were furious: 'the Emperor and His Minister have behaved . . . ill'.[49] It worked. The Russians, weakened, humiliated and feeling betrayed by their former allies Austria and Britain, were willing to give Napoleon a free hand in western Europe. The conference was still in session at the Quai d'Orsay when in July 1858 the emperor slipped away to the spa at Plombières, not to take the waters, but secretly to meet

ATTEMPTED ASSASSINATION OF THE EMPEROR OF THE FRENCH. (See p. 9.)

Orsini's bomb attack outside the Opéra.

Camillo Benso di Cavour, prime minister of the Kingdom of Sardinia.*
Together they planned a war to eject the Austrians from Italy and create an
Italian confederation under French protection. In return France would obtain
the territories of Savoy and Nice, won and lost by Napoleon I.

Britain had played an unwitting part in Napoleon's Italian machinations.
On 14 January 1858 three Italian republican nationalists exiled in Britain,
led by Felice Orsini (the son of a survivor of Napoleon's retreat from
Moscow), threw bombs at the emperor's carriage as it arrived at the Paris
Opéra. They hoped that killing him would bring back a republic that would
intervene in Italy. He was unharmed, but 156 people had been injured, eight
of whom died. Orsini was guillotined, but was permitted to make a stirring public appeal to the emperor to free Italy: 'Prince, the roots of your
power cling to a revolutionary stem. Be strong enough to assure independence and liberty, they will make you invulnerable.' This Napoleon himself
fundamentally believed, and his narrow escape convinced him that he should
act – hence the meeting with Cavour. However, he and his ministers had
been angered and scared: had Napoleon been killed, France would have

* Despite its name, the Kingdom of Sardinia was ruled by the House of Savoy, and its main
territory and capital, Turin, were on the mainland, on both sides of the Alps, hence the
Kingdom was often known as Piedmont.

been thrust into turmoil. When it was realized that Orsini and his comrades had prepared their attempt in Britain, Bonapartists rounded on the old enemy.

BRUMAGEM BOMBS FOR BONAPARTE

In October 1857, a Birmingham metal-caster, Joseph Taylor, received an unusual order from a certain Thomas Allsop, whom he assumed had some connection with the army. The specification was for thin steel cases for six large grenades of a new design. Each was made of two hemispheres, the lower having several protruding detonators, the upper being segmented to produce 150 fragments. Allsop was a middle-class Chartist, the son of a Derbyshire landowner acquainted with the radical writers Cobbett and Hazlitt. A French refugee, Simon Bernard, bought mercury and nitric acid from several London pharmacists to make the highly unstable explosive fulminate of mercury. Orsini's housekeeper Eliza Cheney helped to dry it in front of her kitchen stove in Kentish Town. A prototype bomb was successfully tested in an empty quarry in Sheffield by George Holyoake, a Birmingham craftsman turned journalist, former Chartist parliamentary candidate, and supporter of the co-operative movement. The steel hemispheres were carried via Belgium as 'gas equipment', and filled in Paris. Although when thrown the bombs all exploded, one right under the emperor's carriage, they failed in their main purpose. Flying fragments caused many injuries, but the bombs' design may have made the fragments too small to penetrate the coachwork. None of the 'English connection' was ever caught.[50]

Whitehall was crimson with embarrassment – 'we are a nuisance to Europe', admitted Clarendon. Yet there was no question of handing over refugees: 'we might just as well ask Parliament to annex England to France'. Lord Cowley, ambassador in Paris, urged that it did not matter '*what* is done provided *something* is done'. This timeless political wisdom caused Palmerston to introduce a Conspiracy to Murder Bill, intended to convince the French that action was being taken while assuring the British that nothing had really changed. But, as one minister confided to his diary, 'John Bull has got his back up.' A leading Liberal condemned the government as 'abject, afraid of France, and bold only in the massacre of Chinese'. A protest rally was held in Hyde Park. The Bill failed in the Commons, and the government resigned. Most of Orsini's helpers escaped, but Simon Bernard was caught and in April 1858 tried at the Old Bailey for murder. The defence council turned it into a political trial, alleging that its purpose was to 'gratify a foreign potentate', whose throne was 'built upon the ruins of the liberty of a once free and still mighty people'. He urged the jury to stand up for the 'cause of freedom and civilization throughout Europe . . . though 600,000 French bayonets glitter in your sight'. They duly acquitted Bernard. The foreign secretary thought this 'a rascally demonstration, disgraceful to our country'.[51]

The French ambassador Persigny was threatening and the foreign minister Walewski demanded whether 'the right of asylum [ought] to permit such things? Is hospitality due to assassins?'[52] Several army regiments petitioned the emperor to let them 'get at these wild beasts even in the recesses of their lair'. Once again the prospect of a French invasion loomed, and there were even fears that India, in the throes of the Great Mutiny, might have to be abandoned to concentrate troops for home defence. Napoleon, however, was determined to prevent a breach, and three months later welcomed Victoria and Albert to the gala opening of the naval base at Cherbourg, begun under Louis XVI – an ambiguous compliment, as it would be the base for an invasion, 'a knife pointing directly at Britain's jugular'.[53]

In April 1859 Napoleon and Cavour began their war against Austria, France's main enemy on the Continent. Since 1815 Austria had been the dominant power in Italy, and its ejection was a dream of French policy. The violent counter-revolution of 1848–9, in which Austria had been the most ruthless agent, had made British public opinion anti-Austrian and no less pro-Italian. 'I side with those who are at war with Russia and Rome, with earthly and spiritual despotisms,' wrote one of Gladstone's friends, 'and who stand for the liberty of enslaved nations and consciences.' Giuseppe Garibaldi, the nationalist guerrilla, was a hero in Britain – perhaps the most popular foreign hero there has ever been. The British government's pleas for a negotiated compromise were ignored by everyone. Though it was highly suspicious of French 'piracy', it was certainly not going to help Austrian 'tyranny'.[54] So French troops could be ferried from Marseilles to Genoa without fear of interference from the Royal Navy. They duly defeated the Austrians in June 1859. The Kingdom of Sardinia expanded into the Kingdom of Italy. The British applauded and tried to take some credit. The new nation then ceded Savoy and Nice to France.

British opinion was thoroughly confused. Since the revolution, French patriots had demanded their 'natural frontiers' of sea, mountain, and river. Savoy and Nice gave them the Alps. But 'natural frontiers' also meant the Rhine, which implied absorbing parts of Germany, Luxembourg and that most sensitive of trouble-spots, Belgium. Did Napoleon intend to take these too? It seemed that the Bonapartes had not changed their spots. The launching in 1860 of the world's most powerful warship, the ironclad *Gloire*, made the British wooden battlefleet semi-obsolete. Gentlemanly espionage took place, including by Lord Clarence Paget, parliamentary secretary to the admiralty, who bluffed his way on to the *Gloire* and made measurements with his umbrella. The British responded with the even more powerful *Warrior*, the first all-iron battleship, and an expensive arms race began. Experts on both sides, professionally inclined to worst-case analysis, saw the other as planning aggression. Napoleon sent officers – ostensibly doing research for his book on Julius Caesar – to study landing places in England.[55] Both sides spent huge sums on coastal defences. Palmerston persuaded Parliament to double the military budget to fortify the south coast and the colonies – something that had been advocated and tinkered with ever since the Spanish marriages dispute. Now, at last, mighty structures of brick, stone and iron took shape to defend Portsmouth, Plymouth and the Thames estuary: in all, seventy-six forts and batteries were built in probably the largest such programme in British history. Others can still be seen as far from Cherbourg as Australia and New Zealand.

The queen feared a future of 'bloody wars and universal misery.'[56] So did Tennyson:

> Be not deaf to the sound that warns,
> Be not gull'd by a despot's plea!
> Are figs of thistles? Or grapes of thorns?
> How can a despot feel with the Free? [. . .]
> Form, be ready to do or die!
> Form in Freedom's name and the Queen's!
> True we have got – *such* a faithful ally
> That only the devil can tell what he means.

This poem, published in *The Times* (and confiscated in Paris), not only expressed a fear, it had also proposed a remedy: volunteer military units, unseen since the first Napoleon. Men flocked to join up. Patriotism and genuine fear mingled with the excitement of wearing a uniform and handling a rifle – volunteering was most popular in Scotland, where the invasion threat was least. The volunteers quickly drew in 100,000 men. Units were based on local communities and existing social networks: there were university units, factory units (the initiative often coming from the workers), the famous 'Artists' Rifles' and 'London Scottish', and also teetotallers, cricketers, freemasons, and some radical units dressed in Garibaldian red shirts. In short, the Volunteers were a social and political cross-section, and an undeniable manifestation of the unity that patriots were so proud of. As many as one man in twelve served at some time. They changed the face of Britain, by popularizing military-style beards. Many believed they would stand no chance against French regulars hardened in North Africa, the Crimea and

Italy, but they did provide 'the spectator sport of mid-Victorian Britain',[57] attracting crowds to their parades, balls, concerts, shooting matches and field-days, even if these also attracted some mockery – a gentle example being Mr Pooter's experience at the East Acton Rifle Brigade ball, in George and Weedon Grossmith's *Diary of a Nobody* (1892). The Volunteers continued until replaced in 1908 by the Territorial Army.

Yet Britain and France continued to act together. Their 1860 expedition against China remains notorious because, in retaliation for the torture and execution of captured diplomats and soldiers, they sacked and burnt the imperial summer palace, one of China's greatest cultural monuments. Booty turned up in salerooms and museums. Victor Hugo condemned the outrage – and bought some silk for his Guernsey salon. In Mexico, Britain, France and Spain sent ships in 1861 to force the Mexican government to honour its debts – though Palmerston (who had already dismissed Mexican requests to join the British empire) refused to join France in sending troops. Most seriously of all, the two countries teetered on the brink of intervening in the American Civil War. The French and British publics were divided over the rights and wrongs, but both countries depended on cotton imports from the slave-owning South. The British government hoped to keep a distance – 'They who in quarrels interpose, Will often get a bloody nose,' quipped Palmerston.[58] But the British faced unwonted problems arising from being a neutral (trading with and supplying armaments to both sides), and hence the victim, rather than the enforcer, of a blockade. There were heated exchanges between Washington and London. Napoleon had a political interest in involvement, as the Confederacy was offering to support his adventure in Mexico, which he was trying to turn into a quasi-colony under the cricket-playing Habsburg Archduke Maximilian. In the summer of 1862, with the American civil war seemingly deadlocked, Napoleon suggested joint mediation by France, Britain and Russia. But neither Britain nor Russia agreed. Soon afterwards, a temporary improvement in the military situation of the North, and more importantly Abraham Lincoln's belated proclamation of slave emancipation, made British intervention on behalf of the slave-owners unthinkable. Anglo-French mediation, backed by naval blockade-breaking, would have saved the Confederacy, with unpredictable long-term consequences. But Napoleon could do nothing without British support. Sudden European problems caused him to abandon Mexico and Maximilian, who was executed. The events of the 1850s and 60s showed how powerful a combination France and Britain might be, but also how uncertain and mistrustful their partnership was.

They did became economic allies, however, signing a commercial treaty in 1860, negotiated by the idealistic free traders Richard Cobden and Michel Chevalier. This was proposed by the British, and agreed by the emperor as a 'bone' to stop Britain 'growling' over the annexation of Savoy.[59] For Napoleon and his advisers it was also a bold step to cut working-class living costs and stimulate growth. The influence of former Saint-Simonians (an 1830s sect that combined socio-economic and religious utopianism), who included Chevalier, was strong under the Empire. They were keen on railways, canals (both Panama and Suez were planned by them), modernization and free trade. The treaty was popular among British industrialists and in the City. France's powerful silk and wine producers also approved, and their exports ensured that France had a trade surplus with Britain. But the treaty was highly unpopular with the French coal, metallurgical and cotton industries. Protests by employers and workers revived the hitherto weak opposition to Napoleon. Critics recalled the Eden Treaty of 1786, which had preceded the revolution. They argued that France was not like Britain and ought not to be: everyone knew that Britain was full of starving proletarians, and had to depend on imports for its food and raw materials. France should remain 'balanced', harmonious and if possible self-sufficient. The treaty remains controversial with economic historians, who perpetuate contemporary arguments: was free trade a gust of fresh air, doubling Franco-British trade, and blowing away economic cobwebs; or was it a doctrinaire experiment that damaged French agriculture and industry, and precipitated economic depression?

The Anglo-French treaty was the core of an embryonic European economic community, soon extended to the whole of western and central Europe, with free movement of population and certain rights of citizenship. Europe became for a time Britain's main trading outlet.[60] The French also sponsored a Latin Monetary Union, with Italy, Belgium, Switzerland and the Papal state, whose common currency lasted until the First World War. Yet cross-Channel relations remained tense and suspicious.

Tales of Two Cities

London may become Rome, but it will certainly never be Athens:
that destiny is reserved for Paris. In the former we find gold, power,
material progress to the highest degree . . . the useful and the comfortable,
yes; but the agreeable and the beautiful, no.
THEOPHILE GAUTIER, 1852[61]

Paris . . . is a wicked and detestable place, though wonderfully attractive.
CHARLES DICKENS[62]

Cities, multiplying their turbulent populations, overflowing their boundaries, stinking, smoking, germinating new diseases, vices and crimes, multiplying opportunities and dangers, dissolving old conventions and distinctions, producing prodigies of technology and wealth, became a dominating manifestation of the nineteenth century, its vanities and fears. The two cities par excellence were London and Paris, perpetually compared and contrasted, 'the two faces of civilization', which crystallized the differences and rivalries of their respective countries.[63] Writers and artists thrilled and alarmed the public with tales of their mysteries and dangers. Governments competed to penetrate the mysteries, control the dangers, tidy up the filth and put the cities on show.

The century's two greatest popular novelists, Charles Dickens and Victor Hugo, created haunting images of the two cities, most famously in *Oliver Twist* (1837–8) and *Les Misérables* (1862). Balzac, Stendhal and a host of lesser but popular writers shared the fascination and the sales. Hugo had begun with *Notre Dame de Paris* (1831), quickly translated, which took the medieval city as its protagonist. He was palely copied by W.H. Ainsworth, in *Old St Paul's* (1841). The pioneer of the contemporary urban romance was Pierce Egan, in the very successful *Life in London* (1821), with heroes Tom and Jerry. Eugène Sue, scapegrace dandy, member of the Jockey Club and brilliant populist, was commissioned to write something similar on Paris. His rambling *Mystères de Paris* (1842–3), combining sex-and-violence with sentimentality, promised 'episodes in the lives of barbarians as uncivilized as the savage tribes portrayed by Fenimore Cooper. But these barbarians are among us.' His poor but honest victims, spine-chilling criminals, heartless oppressors, a repentant prostitute and a philanthropic prince in disguise, drew a huge and demanding readership of all classes from the prime minister down. As the newspaper serial appeared, they corresponded with the author, demanded story lines, gave and asked advice, and eventually elected him to parliament as a socialist. Sue spawned an international literary craze. Paul Féval cheekily cashed in with *Mystères de Londres* (1844), without having set foot there, presenting London as 'that great whore expert in every vice, whose colossal corruption when one day exposed will horrify the world, and which will finally collapse, rotted like Sodom and Nineveh, under the crushing weight of its shame'.[64] But Sue's real counterpart was G.W.M. Reynolds, in *Mysteries of London* (1844–8). He also paralleled Sue's politics, becoming a leading Chartist and owner of the radical *Reynolds' News*. There were also many more-or-less factual investigations and revelations, most famously the memoirs of the Paris criminal-turned-detective Vidocq, the pessimistic Frégier's *Des Classes dangereuses* (1840), which identified the criminal poor as a threat to the State, and Henry Mayhew's more sympathetic *London Labour and the London Poor* (1851). Reporting of real crimes was popular in both cities.

This literary interchange between London and Paris created a picture of the nineteenth-century city that we still recognize. It is 'a most intricate maze of narrow streets and courts'[65] of incomprehensible behaviour and secret languages (the *argot* of Paris and the *cant* of London), of feral children and sinister criminals. 'There are in Paris horrible passages, labyrinths, ruins . . . Paris at night is fearsome . . . when the tribe of the underworld sets forth . . . In the hideous lairs which Paris hides away behind its palaces . . . there lurks a swarming and oozing population.'[66] This mysterious urban life takes place in a metaphorical and sometimes literal underworld (caverns and sewers), sometimes in desolate suburbs where the respectable never venture, sometimes in inner-city criminal strongholds. Dickens's Jacob's Island is matched by Hugo's Cour des Miracles; Saffron Hill by the Boulevard de l'Hôpital; the Artful Dodger by Gavroche. Paris has its stink, reminder of corruption; London has its fog, symbol of mystery.

Paris had one secret that London did not share: revolution. One of the many dramatic climaxes in *Les Misérables* is the barricade, during the abortive 1832 insurrection, from which the heroes escape through the ancient Paris sewers, 'the city's conscience'. Fear of revolution lies behind much of the writing on nineteenth-century Paris. But there is no great French novel about Paris during the revolution of 1789, too huge and too controversial a challenge: even Balzac and Hugo stayed silent. So the great Paris revolutionary novel is Dickens's *Tale of Two Cities* (1859), which fixed the revolution in the collective imagination of the English-speaking world, and thus created lasting ideas about the French.

Dickens's novel crystallized round his imaginative preoccupations – imprisonment, rebirth, renunciation, sacrifice – and its plot was borrowed from a forgotten melodrama. It reflected British ambivalence about the revolution, 'in favour of reforms and violent against violence'.[67] Yet the British were also fascinated by that violence, as shown by the success of Madame Tussaud's exhibition of revolutionary horrors. Dickens, a Tussaud enthusiast, was equally impressed by his friend Thomas Carlyle's lurid *French Revolution*, with its moralism, melodrama, sentimentality and spluttering rhetoric. Carlyle guided Dickens's research on the revolutionary period, which he did seriously – his French was good – and he was sensitive to criticism of inaccuracy. His caricature of the 'cringing and fawning' Old Regime was all cruel, foppish aristocrats, hungry Parisian workers and emaciated, clog-shod peasants – just like Hogarth and Gillray. The seminal event in the *Tale*, the killing of a child by a nobleman's carriage, recalls many eighteenth-century complaints about Paris streets. Dickens claimed 'full authenticity' for this episode, and insisted that noble privileges had led to 'frightful oppression of the peasant', whose lot, 'if anything be certain on earth . . . was intolerable'.[68] Hence, he shows the revolution as a terrible act of popular justice and revenge, but which corrupted those carrying it out. There are no French heroes in the *Tale*, only predators and victims. The English, on the other hand, though often absurd, represent kindness, humanity and self-sacrifice, and England, with its manifold faults, is a haven where people can lead 'peaceful, useful, prosperous and happy lives'. Even in Soho, the exiles' refuge, 'forest trees flourished, and wild flowers grew . . . country airs circulated with vigorous freedom'.[69] This idea of England as haven was given further popular expression in Baroness Orczy's *Scarlet Pimpernel* (1905). Dickens's hope for France was expressed in his hero's prophetic thoughts at the foot of the guillotine: that 'the evil of this time', caused jointly by the aristocrats and the revolutionaries – 'new oppressors who have risen on the destruction of the old' – would end by 'gradually making expiation for itself and wearing out'.[70]

A Tale of Two Cities was neither francophobic nor reactionary. Conservative French critics attacked it for condoning revolution. If characteristically English in its interpretation, it was not exclusively so. Most French people also rejected the Terror. 'Human blood has a terrible power against those who have spilt it,' wrote the republican historian Michelet. 'The Terrorists have done us immense and lasting harm. Were you to go into the last cottage in the farthest country of Europe, you would meet that memory and that curse.'[71] What changed France's own view was a long rehabilitation of the revolution by liberals and moderate republicans from the 1820s onwards, who repudiated the Terror and created an expurgated vision of the revolution as the messy birth of a better age. This is compatible with the Dickensian picture. But French republicans also exalted the revolutionaries as heroes, the revolution as the climax of modern history, and France as the vanguard of humanity. Their revolution is not just tragedy, as it was for Dickens, but mystical redemption: France 'owed it to the world . . . those laws, that blood and tears she gave to all, saying: Take, drink, this is my Blood'.[72] This version of world history fell on deaf ears across the Channel, where Progress had a different pedigree, and where the Dickensian view of the revolution as tragedy not triumph prevailed.

London, disparaged during the eighteenth century for its lack of dignified monuments, took up the challenge after Waterloo. The Prince Regent urged John Nash to outdo Paris. In the biggest single building plan ever carried out in London, he created Regent Street, Regents Park and Carlton House Terrace, remodelled St James's Park and Buckingham Palace, and planned Trafalgar Square. But a financial slump in 1825, the death of George IV, and a complete change in aesthetic taste, put an end to visions of stuccoed grandeur. Paris after Napoleon remained largely static, with its medieval street plan forming the swarming, picturesque, dirty and dangerous warren evoked by Hugo and Sue. The centre was becoming a vast slum, choked by people, traffic and refuse, and deserted by its richer inhabitants.

Both cities were manufacturing centres specializing in small-scale skilled production, though Paris had more heavy industry and far more bureaucrats, while London had more commerce and banking. Already the largest cities in Europe, both had to cope with accelerating growth. During the first half of the century, Paris doubled and London trebled its population, London reaching 1 million in 1811, and Paris in 1846. Both received a grim warning in 1832 when cholera, spread through drinking water, killed 19,000 people in Paris and 5,000 in London. London had begun, however haltingly, to make the herculean effort to keep itself relatively clean and healthy. Both cities were to have their epic conquests of sewage, but Paris lagged generations behind, with its open sewers, its streets 'rivers of black and putrid muck', its overflowing cesspits, and its notorious suburban mountain of refuse. Despite the condemnation of London by French (and many British) observers as a purgatory of filth, poverty and smog compared with the charms of Paris, Londoners had much more space, better hygiene, a higher standard of living, more children of whom a larger proportion went to school, and longer life expectancy. Despite accusations that London epitomized harsh class inequality, income was more evenly distributed there than in Paris, where more people lived on unearned income, and far more children worked.[73] A British artisan visiting Paris in the 1860s found 'the general domestic condition of the French *ouvrier* greatly inferior to that of the British workman'.[74]

The Great Exhibition of 1851, coming so soon after the devastating depression of the late 1840s and the upheavals of 1848–51, showed off Britain's self-confidence and London's primacy. The idea had come from a businessman, Henry Cole, who had got it from the 1849 exhibition held in Paris – one of the regular exhibitions of French goods. The Great Exhibition, however, was unprecedentedly international. The astounding glass and iron Crystal Palace, four times as long as St Paul's, was 'indescribably glorious', thought the queen. Few dissented, as 15,000 exhibitors from round the world displayed their wares to an average of 43,000 people every day for six months – the largest indoor crowds ever assembled. The French press urged readers to go to London and be 'dazzled'. French exhibitors and the French government regarded it as a Franco-English contest – no one else counted – which they felt they had won on grounds of quality. They were determined to outdo the original exhibition by their own version in Paris in 1855: 'The struggle is keen . . . France is incontestably ahead in all that concerns art, taste, finish, elegance, distinction . . . England is ahead in strength, power, the astonishing, the enormous, the useful.'[75] More broadly, French writers liked to claim Paris as the cultural capital of the world, while the British saw London as the centre of its political, moral and economic progress.

London, despite or because of its decentralized governance, was the more modern and economically successful city. Probably most French people did not admit this. One who did was Louis-Napoleon Bonaparte, and his view counted. He wanted to transform Paris, making it the hallmark of his rule. He began model workers' housing within months of being elected president, and the young architect Baltard was commissioned to design a huge covered market, inspired by the Crystal Palace – the famous Halles Centrales, begun in 1851. After his coup d'état Bonaparte had power to do what previous regimes had only dreamt of, and he found an effective agent in Georges Haussmann, prefect of the Seine department. London was their model. They conceived a Parisian 'Hyde Park' complete with Serpentine in the Bois de Boulogne, and planned small urban parks described by the franglais term *square*. Parisian versions of 'English gardens' were built in the new parks at Montsouris, the Buttes Chaumont, and Monceau (the neglected site of the Duc d'Orléans's 1770s extravaganza), with artificial lakes and mountains – though walking on the sparse *pelouses* was forbidden. Successful efforts were made to equal, and surpass, London's standards of policing, street lighting, traffic access, public transport, shopping, sanitary regulation, and water supply. At last, in the 1870s, Paris began a real sewerage system, and the 60,000 domestic cesspits faded into odoriferous memory. The 'métro' was, however, forty years behind the 'tube'.

Both cities demolished swathes of their past, grew in size and wealth, were hailed as the 'capital of the world' and denounced as the 'modern Babylon'. They scrutinized each other, and deliberately grew apart. London, loosely administered and market-driven, sprawled into its surrounding villages, so land, building and rents stayed cheap for a century, and even working-class families could have houses. Victorians hated being crowded into the city, which they saw as dirty and dangerous: they wanted space, freedom, family life and domestic privacy – in short, suburbia. The ideal was to express individuality through variety of styles, decorations and materials. Paris, hemmed in until the 1920s by a moat and ramparts, whose line still forms its administrative and psychological frontier, and ruled by a central authority, remained more compact and densely populated. Defence, prestige and internal security were its priorities. Its new style was disciplined, uniform, monumental and aggressively modern. Some compared it with London: 'Go to the Rue de la Paix, the Rue Castiglione, the Rue de Rivoli: it's a real piece of London on the banks of the Seine.'[76] Others thought of New York or San Francisco. New roads prised open the riot-prone slums and dispersed their inhabitants. The medieval Ile de la Cité was mostly razed and made into an official enclave. The Faubourg Saint-Antoine, hotbed of revolution, was outflanked by wide avenues. The intention was 'to assure wide, direct and multiple connections between the main parts of the capital and the military bases destined to protect them'.[77] One critic mocked that the aim was 'to promote the free circulation of ideas and of troops'.[78] Haussmann, less philanthropic than his master, concentrated more on the opulent west than the poorer east of the city. The outer districts, where working-class immigrants were piled, were neglected wastelands, 'the first big social ghettos in urban history'.[79] 'Families are crowded worse than in any Irish hovel,' wrote the London *Building News* in 1861, in 'houses built of lumps of plaster from demolitions . . . roofed with old tin trays'.[80] It is hard to know what sort of city Parisians wanted, but it was not that of Haussmann. Political opposition grew, which aggravated the problems, because Napoleon and Haussmann reacted by pushing factories and workers out into the *banlieue*. Only in the twentieth century were tentative experiments made to copy English 'garden suburbs' near Paris, but without affecting the character of the *banlieue* as a whole. The problem thus originated still plagues France 150 years later. Yet the achievements of two decades were stupendous, and came in the nick of time. London too lives with its Victorian legacy, its 'inner city' problems balancing Paris's blighted *banlieue*.

The changes in London and Paris attracted admiration and condemnation on both sides of the Channel as contrasting visions of modernity. Each was seen as the antithesis of the other. Critics saw London, four times the size of Paris and twice as populous, as a drab, featureless monster, whose dispersal of its residents into suburbs and separate houses destroyed community. 'London is not really a city,' wrote a French essayist in 1862, 'it is an agglomeration of boroughs, villages, countryside, plains, meadows, and gardens . . . It is not an entity.'[81] Paris, more compact and crowded, was more convivial – or, to English and some French critics, lacked domesticity and that untranslatable concept, privacy. Paris became more like Samuel Johnson's London, with its social life in public; whereas London democratized the salon, as middle-class families entertained at home. Although the two cities wrote another chapter in the great saga of Franco-British incompatibility, there was more to it than the usual prejudices. Attitudes towards the new Paris were aesthetic, political and ethical, not national. Critics of the Empire, French as much as British, saw it as the stultified expression of centralized dictatorship: 'we have only one street . . . under a multitude of names'.[82] Moralists deplored it as materialistic and corrupt. Taxpayers jibbed at the cost. Aesthetes discovered the treasures of the old city, fast disappearing into rubble: 'poor, brilliant, joyous, sublime, filthy and adorable Paris' was being replaced by 'a city without a past . . . the quintessence of dullness, pomposity and straight lines'.[83] Criticisms were shared by Left and Right, and could take many forms. French republicans condemned speculators' profiteering, lamented the economic and social costs and demanded urban self-government. British liberals pointed to the 'un-English' methods of Haussmann as an argument against over-regulation and expensive new building projects in London. British governments, on the other hand, were determined that new official buildings, notably the Foreign Office, the India Office and Somerset

House, as well as churches, law courts, museums, and the new Thames Embankment (rivalling the *quais* of the Seine), should keep pace with Paris and sustain London's pretensions to be the 'capital of the world'.[84]

Policing was also a cause of debate. Though both cities had a reputation for criminality, Paris was seen as more heavily policed -- even though the Second Empire police copied the British 'beat' system. Libertarians often commented unfavourably on the visibility of the French police, but it was accepted that they made Paris more orderly. The streets and theatres were safer, without fights and drunkenness; and prostitutes, under police regulation, were less intrusive than in London. This relative 'decency' of public places in Paris meant that bourgeois women could move around more freely. However, when regulation of prostitution, modelled on Parisian practice, was imposed in English garrison towns by successive Contagious Diseases Acts of the 1860s, this 'Napoleonic system' of 'legislating on behalf of vice and against women' was fought by feminist moralists.[85]

To other Victorians, the Paris that Carlyle condemned as 'a corrupt, abominable city . . . nothing but a brothel and a gambling hell' was a potent attraction – 'a huge university where [men] go to graduate in vice'.[86] Visits were promoted from 1855 through a series of six increasingly grandiose International Expositions over the next eighty years – more than any other city has ever staged. The Empire and the succeeding Republic deliberately set out to outdo the Great Exhibition and supplant London as the world's metropolis. For the first time, international tourism became the experience of hundreds of thousands, and Thomas Cook extended his operations to the Continent: 26,000 British tourists visited Paris in 1852, 40,000 in 1856, 60,000 in 1867. Much of the excitement lay in the imagination, for what seemed new and unique to Haussmann's Paris could often be found elsewhere, and reality often fell short of fantasy. The risqué new entertainments of the boulevards and *café-concerts*, for example, were often pale copies of London's music halls. The 'Sodom and Gomorrah' of Napoleon's court (which Queen Victoria feared had done 'frightful harm to English society'[87]) normally amounted to croquet and charades. But more important was the impression of newness, excitement and indeed alarm inspired by 'the American Babylon of the future', as the fastidious Goncourt brothers dubbed it.[88] A vogue for nostalgic books about 'vanishing Paris' was balanced by an equal vogue for futuristic fantasies. Paris and London, as it were, changed places: the quaint and traditional deliberately made itself the epitome of the new. In Baudelaire's famous lines,

> Old Paris is no more (alas! a city's form
> Changes more quickly than a mortal's heart).

This was Napoleon's intention – even though behind the new façades, with apt if unintended symbolism, Paris retained more ancient buildings than any other northern European metropolis. An economic boom after the lean years of the late 1840s, the reassertion of French military power, a dynamic regime relatively open to *nouveaux riches* and strenuously fashionable, and even a feeling in the 1860s – familiar to earlier French regimes – that they were 'dancing on a volcano' created a worldwide image of Paris as the quintessence of modernity. The images were fixed for later generations by artists and writers who set out to pin this florid butterfly. In their different ways Baudelaire, the Goncourts, Flaubert, Manet, Renoir, Caillebotte, Pissarro, Monet, Morisot, Degas, Zola, Toulouse-Lautrec, even Offenbach, set out to 'paint modern life', anonymous, venal and alluring – which largely meant Parisian life. The titillating notion of a can-can-dancing 'gay Paree', always to a large extent a creation of and for tourism, became from the 1860s onwards a central feature of British stereotypes of France.

ENGLISHNESS IN PARIS: THE DRESSMAKER AND THE WHORE

We are Englishing ourselves more and more. Women are beginning to wear
leather belts à *l'anglaise*, with steel trimmings . . . they have an Englishman,
the famous Worth, as their couturier; they buy plaids and tweeds.
Meanwhile, men are not being cured of their whiskers à *l'anglaise*, their
suits à *l'anglaise*, their bearing and jargon à *l'anglaise*. Those purveyors of
Parisian elegance who are not called Worth are called 'John's' or 'Peter's'.
Paris Amoureux, 1864[89]

Two celebrities of the new Paris were English. Charles Frederick Worth established *haute couture* as an international industry. He also, incidentally, universalized the slang term *chic*.[90] Cora Pearl was one of the most famous of Paris's few dozen luxury whores, the *grandes horizontales*.

Worth (1825–95), the son of a bankrupt Lincolnshire solicitor, was apprenticed to the fashionable Regent Street drapers Swan & Edgar. In 1845, he went to widen his experience in France, where the finest textiles came from, and worked for the leading Paris draper, Gagelin-Opigez. One of his jobs was showing customers shawls and cloaks, using a live model for whom he designed plain dresses to set off the merchandise. At customers' demand, Gagelin reluctantly agreed to sell such dresses, which were then shown at the Great Exhibition and the Paris exposition of 1855, where they won a medal. Worth opened his own shop in the Rue de la Paix, not then a fashionable shopping street, with a Swedish male partner also trained in London. Male dressmakers – and foreign to boot – were unheard of, and regarded as improper, owing to the physical intimacy established with their customers. Worth's breakthrough was due to two other foreigners, uninhibited by Parisian convention. He offered dresses at a very advantageous price to the unconventional Austrian ambassadress, Princess Metternich, who introduced him to her friend, the new Spanish-born Empress Eugenie, who liked his extravagant and colourful styles. This made Worth's name and fortune. The empress never wore the same dress twice, and the same expectation was imposed on all women at court: a week's stay at Compiègne required fifteen new dresses. 'Monsieur Vorss' became *de rigueur*, and his clothes feature in many portraits, including those by Renoir, Manet and Degas. How did he do it? His skills as a salesman (honed from the age of twelve) helped, and he developed them into a dictatorial caricature of the 'artistic genius': 'I use colour like Delacroix and I compose.'[91] He introduced English male tailoring techniques to achieve better fit and finish, and used sewing machines, a design studio, and 1,200 staff to speed production. He knew the textile trade, and had an excellent range of fabrics. Clothes became big business in Second Empire Paris: dresses for the 130 balls in the 1864 season cost some 29 million francs.[92] Worth charged unheard-of prices and made unprecedented profits. He also standardized the features of the modern fashion industry: seasonal collections, live mannequins, branding and franchising. Helped by the Paris expositions, he made fashion into a global industry, with large sales in Britain and America – something only a man could have done at that time. Generations of English couturiers followed (including Redfern, who in 1885 introduced the suit for women, Creed, and Molyneux) all further bringing masculine cut and materials and freer, slimmer sporting styles into French female fashion – a continuation of an old tradition (see above, page 90). Even Coco Chanel, epitome of Parisian *chic*, based her daring 1920s innovations on clothes borrowed from English lovers.[93] The 'arrival' of British designers in Parisian couture in the 1990s was the resumption of a long association.

'Cora Pearl', née Emma Crouch (1835–86), daughter of a bigamous musician, won comparable celebrity though inevitably less durable financial success. Educated at a convent in Boulogne, she became a prostitute in the 1850s and moved from London to Paris, where she quickly became famous for her ostentatious and spendthrift life financed by a succession of wealthy men-about-town, many of them members of the Jockey Club. Buying her was an initiation rite into a select yet raffish fraternity that included the emperor's cousin Prince Napoleon and allegedly the Prince of Wales. Her career languished in the 1870s owing to her age, a change in political atmosphere, and a scandal when a young heir she had bankrupted shot himself in her house. She became dependent on gifts from former lovers, and tried to make money from her memoirs. She had received vast sums, and spent them. Lavish entertaining, jewels, clothes, horses and carriages were a necessary professional expense, because public notoriety – above all the knowledge that only the very rich could afford her – was a more important part of her allure than beauty or, probably, sex. 'Women were luxuries for public consumption,' wrote Dumas the younger, 'like hounds, horses and carriages.'[94]

Worth and Pearl were English in occupations in which the islanders were not popularly believed to excel. Yet both flaunted and profited from their Englishness. Worth used only English sales assistants. High-class French prostitutes adopted ladylike public behaviour, but Pearl, 'the English style of courtesan', was famous for loud, 'un-French' manners, accent and appearance, including being one of the few women of her time to dye her hair blonde. Englishness enabled them to get away with and profit from unconventional behaviour, including aggressive entrepreneurialism. Pearl possibly benefited from the ingrained French belief in English kinkiness, and she was certainly advantaged by her horsey reputation among the Jockey Club set: 'riding like a jockey, wielding her crop with a swagger,' wrote a contemporary, 'she drank a lot . . . her bosom [was] marvellous.'[95]

The successes of Worth and Pearl show that anglomania was still going strong. They also show that the style and image of Paris had become cosmopolitan.

LONDON THROUGH FRENCH EYES

Gustave Doré, whose popularity in England led to a gallery devoted to his work being established in London, produced in the late 1860s some of the most famous images of the 'Dickensian' city, published in 1872 as *London, a Pilgrimage*. Unlike many French observers, Doré liked the life and bustle. He shows 'typical' scenes of work and leisure, including docks, slums, Hyde Park, the Boat Race, and the Derby. Yet his seemingly realistic images have a dreamlike quality: the sombre, foggy atmosphere; impossibly dense, but orderly and unthreatening crowds; rather beautiful but inanimate faces – all reflecting common French perceptions.

The 1870 war with Germany and the 1871 Paris Commune led several French artists to take refuge in Britain. Among them were Claude Monet, living in Kensington, and Camille Pissarro, who got married at Croydon registry office. 'Monet and I were very enthusiastic about the London landscapes. Monet worked in the parks, whilst I, living at Lower Norwood, at that time a charming suburb, studied the effects of mist, snow and springtime.'[96] They also studied Turner and Constable, with their 'open air' paintings of

Doré's British: an alien
but unthreatening
species.

Pissarro's Impressionist view.

Tissot: making London *chic*.

light and 'fugitive effects'. British and French historians long disagreed on whether this had a significant effect on their art. It now seems clear that if for Pissarro it was superficial, for Monet Turner became a life-long source of inspiration, visible in his paintings of the Thames and the Seine. One contemporary French critic even called him 'the French Turner'.[97]

Pissarro found no demand for his paintings, and grumbled that 'only when abroad does one feel how beautiful, great and hospitable France is, what a difference here, one meets only disdain, indifference, even rudeness . . . there is no art here, only business'. Ironically, his correspondent was simultaneously writing to tell him that 'Horror and terror are everywhere in Paris . . . my only desire is to get out . . . One would think that Paris had never had any artists.'[98] Pissarro was being rather unfair to London, but certainly contemporary French painting was not then highly considered in comparison with British or German. Jacques-Joseph – alias 'James' – Tissot, who left Paris because of the Commune, also discovered this. Yet after a few months Degas wrote to him enviously that 'they tell me you're making a lot of money. How much?' Tissot succeeded, according to a jealous compatriot, by being an 'ingenious exploiter of English stupidity'. His works were both admired and criticized for their Frenchness – that is, Second Empire Frenchness, flashy, modern, hard and shallow. His glossily *chic* paintings of English scenes and people – in 'Neo-French-English' style – were seen as verging on the improper, and making the London elite look vulgar and nouveau-riche, like Parisian 'swells' or 'French actresses', or else like French caricatures of Britishness, 'supercilious, 'disdainful, 'cold and antipathetic', with 'lanky faces and crane necks'. Many felt that Tissot was giving distasteful messages. Oscar Wilde found him 'deficient in feeling and depth', showing 'over-dressed, common-looking people'.[99]

Spectators of Disaster, 1870–71

[The English] are a terrible race, and I would not like my fatherland to be their enemy – or their friend.

JULES VALLES[100]

I fear the French are so fickle, corrupt & ignorant, so conceited and foolish that it is hopeless to think of their being sensibly governed . . . I fear they are incurable as a nation though so charming as individuals.

QUEEN VICTORIA[101]

France blundered into one of the worst years in its history – what Hugo called 'the terrible year' – in July 1870. Britain stood by and watched with mixed feelings. Britain and France, if united, were strong enough to deter any attack on Europe's power structure. But they were not united. British suspicions of Napoleon's intentions ensured that he was seen as the problem, not the solution. So London had done nothing effective to prevent Prussia from starting successful aggressive wars against Denmark in 1864 and against Austria and other German states in 1866.

Napoleon was playing with fire. He was under domestic pressure to show that he was still the master of European affairs. So in July 1870, the emperor and his ministers, in a dispute with Prussia over the Spanish throne, pushed the crisis to the point of war. French generals believed that they had the world's most effective army, as did cheering Parisian crowds chanting, 'To Berlin!' The chief minister of Prussia, Otto von Bismarck, believed that a war with France was inevitable before Germany could be united, so he goaded them into declaring it. He also leaked to *The Times* proof of Napoleon III's intrigues to annex Belgium, which confirmed London's worst suspicions.[102] British opinion thought the French were the aggressors as usual. Most sympathized with what they thought was the underdog – in Carlyle's famous letter to *The Times*, 'noble, patient, deep, pious and solid Germany'. The queen expressed the general view in characteristically emphatic prose: 'We must be neutral *as long as* we can, but *no one* here conceals their opinion as to the *extreme iniquity* of the *war*, and the *unjustifiable* conduct of the French!'[103]

War had become a spectator sport. The electric telegraph, the war artist and the photographer had brought the immediacy of the Crimea and the American civil war to the public. Battles a few hours from London were a thrilling prospect. The national dailies, and the *London Illustrated News*, had unrivalled abilities to bring back news and pictures fast. They had famous correspondents with both armies, who were on familiar terms with generals and statesmen, and there was no effective censorship. The French and German armies clashed on the frontier in August, and the British settled down to watch. The German armies, instead of being thrown back in disorder by the battle-hardened French, advanced with astonishing speed. Most of the French regular army was chased into the great fortress of Metz, and besieged. The rest of the army, and the emperor himself, were forced to capitulate at Sedan on 2 September. When the incredible news reached Paris, the imperial regime evaporated. Empress Eugenie, joined eventually by the emperor, became the fourth successive monarch to flee across the Channel.

The veteran statesman Adolphe Thiers came to London to plead for British assistance in securing moderate peace terms. The prime minister, William Ewart Gladstone, made it clear that France should make concessions. Its refusal to cede territory was 'out of proportion' to the military situation. He did not oppose annexations on grounds of British interest, but only disliked the 'transfer of human beings like chattels'; 'It would comfort me to find that the Alsatians were disposed to be German.'[104] The press tended to think that France deserved all it got, and that Thiers, the jingoist of 1840, was the ideal recipient of condign humiliation. The *Manchester Guardian* gloated that 'when he sues for peace . . . the vainglorious spirit of his country, which he personifies, has at last been sufficiently chastised'.[105] The *Pall Mall Gazette* mocked his pleas in a Tennysonian parody: 'Thiers, idle Thiers, I know not what you mean.' (The original, from *The Princess*, was 'Tears, idle tears, I know not what they mean . . .') France was, however, allowed to borrow in the City, and weapons were sold to the new Republic. Thiers summed up the British position acutely: 'the European balance, of which we speak to her endlessly, is not much changed for her . . . the sleepless nights that France used to cause her will now come from Prussia'.[106] An indignant Parisian wrote to a London friend that 'The influence of Britain in Europe is down; England is now a merchant's country, as America is.'[107] British residents in Paris were far from popular. The perception of the British as amused bystanders appears in a story by Guy de Maupassant, in which a duel between a bullying German officer and a peaceful French bourgeois is witnessed by two English tourists, 'close up to see better . . . full of joy and curiosity, ready to wager on either combatant'.[108]

Paris was surrounded on 19 September. The siege, an epic for France, became a gripping drama for Britain, and a lifetime's adventure for 4,000 British residents who had stayed until they were effectively trapped. They included Edwin Child, a jeweller's apprentice learning his craft in Paris, who volunteered for the National Guard, Richard Wallace, the wealthy heir of the Hertfords, Frederick Worth, Cora Pearl, clergymen, journalists, doctors and charity workers for the British Red Cross and the English Seed Fund Society.[109] The embassy and consulate departed, leaving about 1,000 British subjects dependent on the financial help of their wealthy compatriots, who set up a British Charitable Fund, chaired by Wallace. Supervised by Ellen and Annette Sparks, this provided money and modest weekly rations – 2oz of meat extract, 1lb of rice and 8–12lb of bread.[110] Many besieged Britons later published reminiscences, including the wealthy radical MP Henry Labouchère. All were fascinated by the contrast between the frivolous Paris of the 1860s, 'a modern Babylon, celebrated for its dolls and bonbons', with 'vice flaunting unrestrained about the streets'[111] and the fervently patriotic fortress-city of 1870 – a change from which moral lessons were drawn. Newspaper reports and memoirs emphasized the incongruities: epicures eating *salmis de rat*; dandies in uniform; placid bourgeois with rifles; fashionable actresses bandaging the wounded, the zoo elephants bought by the Boucherie Anglaise. The British tone was often sardonic, sometimes in reaction against the gales of bombast from republicans such as Victor Hugo, who had returned from exile. There was much head-shaking over the decadence supposedly caused by the Empire, and doubts

as to whether the French could muster genuine, as opposed to histrionic, patriotism: 'the Paris of the Empire and of Haussmann is a house of cards . . .
The war and the siege have knocked down the cards.'[112] Such attitudes
mirrored those of French upper-class milieux in which many journalists
moved, despising both the Empire and the Left.

The proclamation of the new German Empire in Louis XIV's Hall of
Mirrors at Versailles on 18 January 1871, followed ten days later by the
surrender of Paris without a death-or-glory battle, was a double humiliation
that confirmed many sceptics in their views of Parisian efficiency, courage
and moral fibre. Edwin Child

> Gave my resignation to the Captain, feeling heartily disgusted with
> the whole affair. 400,000 men capitulating . . . What an end of 20
> years uninterrupted prosperity, and what a lesson to a nation fond
> of flattery and calling itself the vanguard of civilisation . . . [After]
> a bloodless campaign . . . without hardly seeing the enemy . . . they
> talk about giving everyone a medal. Why I should be ashamed to
> wear it![113]

Yet as the war progressed, the British tone had changed. The French bully
had become the underdog. Wrote one British radical, 'Ab[ou]t the war I
think the Prussians were right at 1st but in its present phase my sympathies
are intensely & most painfully French.' The foreign secretary Lord Granville
wrote 'my heart bleeds for the misery of France – I lie in bed thinking whether

"CALL OFF THE DOGS!"

The French, at first blamed for the war, attracted increasing sympathy, even admiration.

there is nothing to be done'.[114] Many were moved by the gruelling struggle in the provinces, where newly raised French armies, badly equipped and barely trained, fought on despite repeated defeats. At least one British officer cadet joined them – Herbert Kitchener. The siege of Paris ceased to be a joke when real hunger, cold and disease began to kill its inhabitants. Women waited for hours outside food shops in long patient lines, called *les queues* – a new word for which there was 'no equivalent in English – happily!'[115] When the Germans, frustrated by Paris's refusal to surrender, began to bombard the city in January 1871, there were diplomatic protests and a small demonstration in Trafalgar Square. The change in sympathy is clear in *Punch*'s cartoons. The allegorical representations of France and of the Republic for the first time ever are unambiguously heroic and pathetic, while the Germans begin to appear as heartless barbarians, foreshadowing the 'Huns' of 1914–18.

The French surrender in January 1871 was welcomed in Britain. Fortnum & Mason and Crosse & Blackwell received orders for large hampers from ravenous Britons in Paris. The Lord Mayor of London's Relief Fund, with the help of the British government, sent in shiploads of supplies – 1,000 tons of flour, 450 tons of rice, 900 tons of biscuit, 360 tons of fish, 7,000 live animals and 4,000 tons of coal – and it provided grants to destitute peasants and workers to buy seed and tools. The mayor of Paris telegraphed that 'the citizens of Paris will never forget', and anti-British feeling subsided. Meanwhile, Richard Wallace had quietly given an estimated total of 2.5 million francs to relieve suffering in Paris.[116]

Paris and France faced further disaster. In March 1871, patriotic Parisian radicals rebelled against the newly elected national government led by Thiers, and full civil war broke out a fortnight later. The regular army, controlled by the government (which had retreated to Versailles) began a second siege of Paris, defended by an army of republican National Guards (some equipped with British Snider rifles supplied during the war) commanded by an elected Commune – a name taken from the revolutionary city government of the 1790s. British sympathy for the rebels was limited. Republicans, socialists, free-thinkers and Nonconformists were the most favourably inclined. Some, praising the Communards as 'thorough patriots and true republicans', organized a rally in Hyde Park in which 3–4,000 took part. *Reynolds' News* and the International Working Men's Association, directed from London by Karl Marx, gave support. George Holyoake (the tester of Orsini's bombs) compared the Communards to the Roundheads. The *Economist* admitted that the Commune was effectively a legal government, and the poet and critic Matthew Arnold wrote privately that 'all the seriousness, clear- mindedness and settled purpose is hitherto on the side of the Reds'.[117] Several British visitors (who were allowed to travel in and out) reported sympathetically that Paris was calm and normal. At least one young Englishman was

'The Commune or Death': a British vision of the Commune: a nightmarish world turned upside down.

conscripted into the National Guard, and wrote that 'I can never forget the kindness I met with from them.'[118] The Methodist Revd Gibson had some sympathy for their hatred of 'priestcraft', and Positivists explained Communard anti-clericalism on the grounds that 'the Romish priesthood' were 'active enemies of liberty and progress'. *The Times*, also anti-Catholic, gave credence to Communard tales of priestly crimes. But Protestants generally were revolted by acts of anti-Catholic violence, even if they thought that Catholicism was partly to blame for France's problems. Many British republicans and trade unionists distanced themselves from the 'Red Republicans'. The strait-laced Edwin Child thought that 'the words Liberty, Fraternity and Egalité mean obedience to our orders, pillage of all churches and fighting against your own brothers'. British newspapers were alarmed by the Commune's (largely rhetorical) resurrection of what *The Times* called 'the Terror according to the golden model of '93'. They dismissed Communard politics as 'childish' and 'theatrical', but were fascinated by women making speeches in political clubs and wearing uniform – a shocking,

FIRE AND SMOKE.

French-Communist. "ALLONS, MON AMI, LET US GO BURN OUR INCENSE ON THE ALTAR OF EQUALITY."
British Workman. "THANKS, MOSSOO, BUT I'D RATHER SMOKE MY 'BACCY ON THE HEARTH OF LIBERTY."

The decent British workman rejecting French extremism.

though titillating, proof of the boldness of Parisiennes. Hostility grew when the Commune arrested the archbishop of Paris and several priests as hostages. Many observers regarded the Commune as having been taken over by 'ruffians, thieves and assassins' manipulated by extremists. Child 'would string 'em up, the cutthroat vagabonds'.[119]

On 21 May 1871 the regular army broke through the city's fortifications and a nightmarish week of street fighting began. Huge fires were started, as acts of defence or defiance. Many of the greatest public buildings – including the Tuileries palace, the Hôtel de Ville, the Palais de Justice and the Palais Royal – were destroyed or severely damaged. The Louvre, Notre Dame and the Sainte-Chapelle had narrow escapes. The *Daily News* compared it to the simultaneous burning of 'the Tower of London, the Houses of Parliament, Buckingham Place, Windsor Castle, the National Gallery and the British Museum'.[120] The London Fire Brigade offered help. The British press, like the French, propagated the myth of women *pétroleuses* setting fire to buildings. The army shot thousands of actual or suspected rebel combatants and arsonists. The rebels replied by shooting some hostages, mainly policemen or priests, including the archbishop. It would be hard to exaggerate the sensation caused by 'a week of horrors, unparalleled in the History of the World' – tinged with occasional hints of grim satisfaction that 'Babylon' had been chastized. The British press harrowingly reported the army's atrocities – 'shooting, bayoneting, ripping up prisoners, women and children' – as well as those of the rebels. British journalists and press artists were probably the only people freely roaming the city (at least one came close to being executed by both sides) and they provided eye-witness reports and pictures. A *Daily News* reporter watched as prisoners were picked out to be shot: 'It was not a good thing on that day to be noticeably taller, dirtier, cleaner, older or uglier than one's neighbours.' *The Times* thundered that 'The French are filling up the darkest page in the book of their own or the world's history . . . The Versailles troops seem inclined to outdo the Communists in their lavishness of human blood.'[121] One of the last of thousands of prisoners to be shot was an English student named Marx (no relation).

The grim irony of these events was heavily underlined: 'the capital of civilization' was 'blazing to the skies', and in a 'France boasting of culture, Frenchmen [were] braining one another with the butt-ends of muskets'. The even-handed reporting of both sides' atrocities must have made many Britons feel, even more strongly than after 1848–51, that all parties in France were beyond the pale. France was 'a nation determined to be lost' in which 'all the wild passions of the human heart have been fused into one vast and indistinguishable conflagration'.[122] Again, how fortunate Britain was to be different! This, for *Punch*, was the 'French lesson'.

Ravaged Paris became a tourist attraction, while the city authorities hastened to show that Paris 'was herself again'. French governments always removed traces of civil conflict as soon as possible. Worth bought stones from the gutted Tuileries to make picturesque ruins in his suburban garden. Edwin Child wrote to his father a fortnight after the fighting ended that in six months 'we shall wonder where all the fires took place'. Revd Gibson was shocked that the city did not seem 'saddened by the disasters'.[123] Thomas Cook organized excursions to see the sights, and Parisians were annoyed by 'big herds of English, binoculars round their necks, guidebook to the ruins under their arms', 'feverishly taking notes . . . occasional gutteral exclamations revealing them to be from across the Channel'.[124] Tourists bought faked photographs of the dramas of the revolution, including the killings of the hostages. A fragment of sculpture from the demolished Vendôme Column was recovered by the French Embassy from a London saleroom. French observers vilified the 'English' tourists as gloating voyeurs; but they also contributed money to restore damaged buildings.[125] Some at least were clearly motivated by solidarity, not merely curiosity.

British visitors to the ruins of Paris caused resentment: here a Parisian urchin threatens 'mylord' that if he finds it so amusing the Parisians might go and do the same in England. Yet many of the 'mylords' gave generously to feed and rebuild the city.

— Mylord, faut pas vous gêner! si ça vous amuse, on peut aller faire ça chez vous.

EXILES: AFTER THE 'TERRIBLE YEAR'

There are only seven leagues of salt water between Calais and Dover – but between the English and French character there is an abyss.

JULES VALLES, exiled Communard[126]

Crossing the Channel in the opposite direction were 3–4,000 men, women and children fleeing the repression in which at least 12,000 people had been killed and 40,000 arrested. There was less sympathy than for past asylum-seekers: the world had been horrified by the Commune, grossly caricatured by conservative French propaganda. But this horror was partly counteracted by the brutality of the repression. The French government, eager to pin responsibility elsewhere, was trying to blame the disaster on an international conspiracy directed from London by the International Working Men's Association. Some conservatives denounced a Protestant–Masonic plot against France, initiated by the late Lord Palmerston and inherited by 'his pupil Gladstone', in which Bismarck and Karl Marx ('Bismarck's secretary') were all accomplices.[127] The French government put pressure on foreign governments to treat fleeing Communards as criminals and refuse asylum. The *Economist* responded that though England was 'disgusted with the horrible atrocities of the Commune's last acts', they were clearly political crimes, and not amenable to extradition. So as in the past: 'our government had no power whatever to prevent any of the Communist leaders from coming to England'.[128] England was the safest refuge, and many of the leaders came. The British authorities paid little attention, apart from asking Karl Marx for information and sending a police sergeant to attend a 'communist' meeting at a pub in Islington. He was swiftly thrown out with the promise to break his head if he came back: 'I did not return,' he reported with dignity, 'in order that no breach of the peace should take place.'[129]

Most refugees clustered as ever round Soho. A few hundred remained until an amnesty was given in 1880. Some settled for good. It was the usual wretched and poverty-stricken ordeal, spiced with recrimination, factionalism and accusations (sometimes justified) of spying for the police. Marx quarrelled with the Communards – though two of them married his daughters – and the International broke up. Positivists, who at first idealized the Communards, soon ended financial aid. So the refugees had to rely on themselves, and set up mutual aid societies, a school, political clubs, freemasons' lodges and a co-op, with expulsion for adultery, homosexuality or drunkenness.

More than fifty refugees set up businesses in London, using their skills in *articles de Paris*. A musical instrument maker employed fifteen other Communards in Camden Town; others set up a wallpaper business, others again the typically Parisian manufacture of artificial flowers. Several lost savings in a porcelain-painting venture. More successful was the Maison Bertaux, a patisserie in Greek Street, still flourishing in 2006. Pascal Grousset, the Commune's foreign minister, developed an interest in sport, which he was later to transfer to France. The sculptor Jules Dalou, despite not speaking the language, found that 'the English welcome us with open arms'.[130] He taught at the Royal College of Art and led a new Naturalist school in Britain, receiving many commissions, including for the royal chapel at Frogmore, before returning to Paris to create the huge statue of the Triumph of the Republic in the Place de la Nation. Even more extraordinary was the career of the revolutionary extremist Georges Pilotell, an artist who, fleeing a death sentence for murdering hostages, became a successful theatrical designer, memorably creating the costume for the 'super-aesthetical' poet Bunthorne in Gilbert and Sullivan's operetta *Patience*.[131] Life was harder for men of letters. Several struggled to make a living with a newspaper aimed at bringing Parisian arts and literature to a British readership. Another abortive scheme was a French cultural centre in Bloomsbury. Teaching was the eternal standby. General La Cécilia (who failed to get a chair in Sanskrit at University College, London), Colonel Brunel (notorious for burning down the Rue de Rivoli) and other leading Communards taught at Eton, Sandhurst, the military academy at Woolwich and the naval college at Dartmouth. Brunel taught at Dartmouth for more than thirty years, where his pupils may have included the future George V. The poets Paul Verlaine and Arthur Rimbaud – 'deux Gentlemen parisiens' – advertised 'LEÇONS de FRANÇAIS, en français – perfection, finesses' in the *Daily Telegraph*, and at least one student took them up at ten shillings a time. Rimbaud later got a job at a language school in Berkshire.[132]

Verlaine and Rimbaud had come to London to escape disapproval of their sexual relationship as well as possible police enquiries into their tenuous connections with the Commune, for which Verlaine had been a newspaper censor. Rimbaud was 'delighted and astonished' by what French visitors usually hated – the 'energy', the 'tough' but 'healthy' life, the fog ('imagine a setting sun seen through grey crêpe'), the drunkenness and the vice, which made Paris seem provincial.[133] They found a job writing French business letters for an American newspaper. Rimbaud spent much time in the Reading Room of the British Museum, published a poem in the *Gentleman's Magazine*, and wrote the greatest work of Franglais, *Illuminations*.

Rimbaud's excitement with London was not shared by the leading Communard journalist, Jules Vallès, who bemoaned the 'horrors of pale ale' and 'everyone' being drunk. His corrosive *La Rue à Londres* (1876) followed in the footsteps of Flora Tristan forty years earlier by savaging almost every aspect of English life, from boys whistling in the street to the colour of the buildings – and he added some that Tristan had overlooked, such as London's deplorable lack of facilities for illicit sex. English girls were 'shocking' in their willingness to pet on park benches, though the damp climate made them 'stupid' and 'frigid', incapable of real sensuality. Older English women, with 'horse lips', were lazy, drunken and after their early twenties unpalatable – they went off quickly, 'like game'. Besides, they showed a disgraceful lack of interest in exiled foreign writers. Worst of all were female 'eccentrics': campaigners against prostitution or cruelty to animals, explorers, mountaineers or evangelists – 'neither man nor woman'. He was appalled by the lack of class-consciousness of London workers, who dressed like everyone else, rather than in the costumes of their trade, and he was incensed by the patriotism of the poor. Indeed, patriotism was for Vallès the essential vice of the English, above all their abominable dislike of the French, which even caused them to drive perversely on the wrong side of the road. The conflict was fundamental: 'the furious fog that resents the sun . . . the duel between beer and wine!' He did, however, grudgingly allow that 'the black city' was free: although 'it never speaks ill of the queen [it] taught me, from a republican country, what liberty is'.[134]

A very different kind of refugee was Richard Wallace, who decided, given its narrow escape from bombardment and arson, to move the most valuable part of the vast Hertford art collection to London. Since the 1st Marquess of Hertford had been ambassador in 1763, successive marquesses and their illegitimate offspring had become the most prominent, wealthy, cultivated and dissolute Parisian–British family. Wallace now abandoned the boulevards to become a rather French-looking country squire, baronet and Tory MP, as popular for his munificence in Ireland and England as he had been in Paris. It is for his parting gift to the city, the drinking fountains he provided soon after the war (of which some fifty survive) that he is remembered there. He died in 1890, leaving everything to his widow, née Amélie Castelnau, whom he had met more than fifty years earlier as a nineteen-year-old selling perfume in a Paris shop. She subsequently bequeathed the world's finest collection of eighteenth-century French paintings, furniture, jewellery and porcelain to the British nation as the Wallace Collection – 'the greatest gift ever made by a private person to a state'.[135]

CHAPTER 9

Decadence and Regeneration

We must remember that progress is no invariable rule.

CHARLES DARWIN, *The Descent of Man*, 1871[1]

Pécuchet sees Humanity's future as dark: Modern man is diminished and becomes a machine. Final Anarchy of the human race. Impossibility of Peace. Barbarity due to excessive individualism, and the madness of Science . . . There will be no more ideal, religion, humanity. America will have conquered the earth . . . *Bouvard* sees Humanity's future as bright. Modern man is progressing . . . Balloons. Submarines . . . Evil will disappear as want disappears. Philosophy will be a religion. All people will be united . . . When the earth is exhausted, Humanity will move to the stars.

GUSTAVE FLAUBERT, *c.*1880[2]

Certainties were dissolving. Religion was questioned, but so was rationalism. Tradition had failed, but so had revolution. 'Progress' itself generated new and incomprehensible evils. All over Europe people detected the whiff of decay. Optimists hoped it would nourish regeneration. It certainly fed a flush of intellectual, political and artistic blossoms, some carnivorous. Conservatives demanded a return to faith and discipline. But strange faiths appeared that were new and far from disciplined. Some sought escape from politics into aesthetics ('art for art's sake') but others applied aesthetics to politics – one of the seeds of totalitarianism. Rationalists trusted in science, but science was not always rational. Reason itself proved its own limitations, and psychological theories stressed the importance of the unconscious. Flaubert's unfinished book, *Bouvard et Pécuchet*, was a bitter satire not only on the pretentions to wisdom of the semi-educated, but on the chaos of modern culture, in which everything had been said and the result was cacophony.

Intellectual alarms were linked with social and political upheavals: population growth, urbanization, economic change, migration, labour militancy, mass education, and pressure for increasing democratic rights, culminating in socialism and even violent anarchism. To many, the rise of what came to be called 'the masses' threatened social and political stability, and especially cultural standards, threatened by a 'vulgar' and 'philistine' commercial culture.

Scientists came up with theories endorsing and explaining the sense of foreboding. Darwin, and those claiming to apply his ideas to human societies, created 'a sense of permanent crisis',[3] in which the achievements of the last century were threatened from within. Urban life, industrial society, crowds and democracy seemed to be causing mankind to regress. A eugenics movement demanded limits on the reproduction of inferior human types. All over Europe, modernist intellectuals denounced the 'bourgeoisie' and the 'masses' with loathing, and sought 'avant garde' forms and 'aristocratic' values that would exclude them.

France's recent disasters aggravated its intellectual and moral turmoil. The defeat by Germany and the Commune crisis were taken as signs of decadence (the word itself was a novelty). Conservatives blamed the revolution for weakening religion, solidarity and hierarchy. Republicans blamed Catholicism for destroying virile patriotism. Liberals blamed excessive centralization of authority. Everyone blamed the Second Empire for its materialism, immorality, and above all for its defeat. France seemed sick: its falling birthrate and near stagnant population seemed unanswerable proof. Politicians and intellectuals proposed incompatible remedies which led to thirty years of bitter political disputes, seen as further proof of decadence. Paradoxically, as Frenchmen lamented their sliding status, France attained a worldwide cultural dominance, especially in the fine arts, that had not been seen since the days of Louis XIV.

Britain found its own reasons to worry about decadence. Its industrial revolution had created ugly cities that seemed hotbeds of new dangers, and caused intellectuals and the middle classes to yearn for authenticity, craft-made goods and rural retreat, even if only behind a suburban privet hedge. The economic dominance that had compensated for ugliness was slipping. At the Paris exhibition of 1867, British goods had won prizes in only ten of the ninety categories. France remained ahead in quality, and America and Germany were forging ahead in quantity. Religious revivalism, appealing to women and men of the numerous, prosperous, educated and respectable lower-middle and working classes, fuelled an obsessive concern with moral and social evils – especially concerning sex and drink – that earlier generations had regarded as normal or at least irremediable.

Purity campaigns were one reason why artists and writers, led by Walter Pater, Algernon Swinburne and later Oscar Wilde, were attracted to the exquisite *pourriture noble* across the Channel. By the end of the century Britain was showing other signs of decadence, such as a falling birthrate, strategic vulnerability, and the poor physical condition of many city-dwellers. A motley crusade of Christians, eugenicists, imperialists, radicals and feminists ran a range of vocal reform groups. Some intellectuals, most famously G.K. Chesterton, the half-French Hilaire Belloc, and later T.S. Eliot, were attracted by the drastic remedies against corrupt modernity being preached by French nationalists, most importantly Charles Maurras. He rediscovered Catholicism as a barrier against democracy and a source of fragrant distinction, showing that 'we are the bosses, the chic.'[4]

Germany's growing power changed the relationship between France and Britain. For two centuries, their concern had been with each other, as antagonists and as rival models of civilization. Everyone else had shared the fascination. But France was now in another tense relationship, which has lasted until the present day. Germany became for France (and others) a new model, combining authoritarian rule with modern efficiency. For Britain it became an economic rival whose success cast doubt on progressive British assumptions about free trade, free enterprise and an unobtrusive state. America and Russia, long seen as future superpowers, were stirring. Cultural inspiration was coming too from non-European societies. There were other vistas than that from Calais to Dover.

Nevertheless, the old fascination did not disappear. Though Germany's universities, industry, music and military science might dazzle, its political and social systems were too alien to exert much influence on France or Britain. When France adopted a republican constitution in 1875, its largely anglophile creators tried to make it as close as possible to a parliamentary monarchy, with a conservative upper house and a president with the right to be informed, to advise and to warn. Global competition led to a wave of imperial expansion that saw Britain and France again as rivals, as in the 1840s. Whether in search of difference or similarity, people still crossed the Channel to learn, and, as ever, to praise and to blame.

Into the Abysm

I was hardly a progressive or a humanitarian. Yet I had my illusions! And I
didn't expect to see the end of the world. Because that's what it is. We are
witnessing the end of the Latin world.

GUSTAVE FLAUBERT, 1871[5]

Authors – essayist, atheist, novelist, realist, rhymester, play your part,
Paint the mortal shame of nature with the living hues of Art.
Rip your brothers' vices open, strip your own foul passions bare;
Down with Reticence, down with Reverence – forward – naked – let them stare.
Feed the budding rose of boyhood with the drainings of your sewer;
Send the drain into the fountain, lest the stream should issue pure.
Set the maiden fancies wallowing in the troughs of Zolaism, –
Forward, forward, ay and backward, downward too into the abysm.

ALFRED TENNYSON, 1886[6]

French observers interpreted the disasters of 'the terrible year' within
pre-existing ideological frameworks, even if those frameworks had to
bend to accommodate them. The two most prominent intellectuals, Ernest
Renan and Hippolyte Taine, show this well. Renan, far from being an
anglophile, shared the usual stereotypes of the British as materialistic, practical, unintellectual and lacking idealism, but after 1870 he began to think
that France should try to obtain at least the benefits of these attributes. Taine
was a real anglophile, mainly through studying English literature: his visits
to England were few and short, and his spoken English poor. He explained
human societies as the products of race, geography and circumstance, and
this coloured his *Notes sur l'Angleterre* (1871), one of the most intelligent of
the travel-book genre, and which was soon published in English. Taine's
observations certainly featured the conventional tropes: fog; wet Sundays;
teeming London; speed and efficiency; high living standards alongside
extreme poverty; ugly, badly dressed women; brutal popular amusements
and drunkenness; the taste for facts rather than theory; snobbery; electoral
corruption; Oxbridge idleness and so on. His famous conclusion was that
'the English [were] stronger and the French happier'.[7] But his principal
lesson concerned the competence of the English ruling class: 'expressive,
decided faces, which bear, or have borne, the weight of responsibility, less
worn than in France, less quick with smiles and the tricks of politeness, but
[creating] a broad impression of respect . . . peers, MPs, landowners in their
manners and physiognomies show men used to authority and action'.[8] The
principal cause was education – 'no comparison better brings out the difference between the two peoples'.[9] English public schools, though he deplored

their brutality and intellectual narrowness, he thought freer and more natural: 'the children' – here comes another hoary simile – 'are like trees in an English garden, ours like the clipped, straight hedges of Versailles'. Their sports, though time-consuming, reminded him of the ancient Olympics – an idea that was soon to bear fruit in France. The boys' self-government, with teams, societies and prefects, was 'an apprenticeship for command and obedience'.[10] Taine later undertook a pessimistic six-volume historical panorama of France's plight, *Les Origines de la France contemporaine* (1878–94), which impartially blamed the Old Regime, the revolution and the Empire for France's decline, making a sustained implicit contrast with Britain. France, in short, was on a downhill path. Taine's arguments were seminal.

Writers and artists too were concerned with various notions of decadence. Common ground was rejection of the exuberant literary and political romanticism of the 1840s, now seen as absurd and empty, and equal disgust with the corrupt populism of the Second Empire, commonly compared with decadent imperial Rome. Many artists rejected a public role for art, seen as producing propagandist kitsch, and stressed its self-justification – *l'art pour l'art*. Some took this to involve a fastidious withdrawal into purely aesthetic values, introspection, social and intellectual elitism, and contempt for politics and convention. Baudelaire and Flaubert, both prosecuted for outraging public morality in the 1850s, were the heroes of this tendency. The 'Parnassian' poets, less controversially, espoused purely aesthetic concern with style and beauty. 'Realism' and 'Naturalism' – the anti-Romantic ambition to create objective, 'scientific' art – inspired the painting of Courbet and Manet, and the novels of the Goncourt brothers. After the defeat of 1870 and the fall of the Empire, Emile Zola and his followers, influenced by Taine and contemporary scientific theories of heredity, embarked on deliberately shocking exposures of the greed, lust, hypocrisy and savagery of degenerate French society. Poets such as the Symbolists Verlaine, Stéphane Mallarmé and Rimbaud sought new forms of poetic expression and self-exploration. A review, *Le Décadent*, defined its eponymous condition enticingly as 'refinement of appetites, of sensations, of taste, of luxury, of pleasures; neurosis, hysteria, hypnotism, morphinomania, scientific skulduggery, extreme schopenhauerism'.[11]

French self-flagellation and self-indulgence were equally absorbing spectacles for foreigners. British missionaries laboured to convert French workers to Protestantism – something that French liberals such as Renan approved of. France's missing out on the Reformation in the sixteenth century was widely seen as its first step towards decadence, whereas Protestantism, with its supposed fostering of the work ethic and intellectual liberty, was the road to modernity. Another mission was that of the charismatic Christian feminist Josephine Butler, who took her crusade against prostitution across the Channel: 'Two words from the mouth of a woman, speaking in the name of all women, and these two words are – We rebel!'[12] She and her many supporters were outraged by the Contagious Diseases Acts, which gave the police powers to declare women prostitutes and force them to submit to intimate medical examinations. This law was modelled on Continental practice, most fully developed in Paris, where the *police des moeurs* ('morality police') regimented prostitutes in closed brothels and prison-hospitals. Butler, who aimed to abolish prostitution, first targeted the laws and regulations by which the French and British states connived in the trade. Victor Hugo (doubtless a little guiltily, considering his personal penchants) wrote to her, 'The slavery of black women is abolished in America, but the slavery of white women continues in Europe.' The analogy with slavery was doubly appropriate because, after the destruction of slavery in the United States, the great abolitionist alliance was free to take up new moral causes. Butler found allies in France among those who, after the 'terrible year', wanted to regenerate French society. Support came from Protestants, feminists and liberals; also from Left-wingers who detested oppressive police authority. Like many abolitionists in Britain, they saw prostitition as a class issue: the sons of the rich defiling the daughters of the poor with the connivance of the State. More broadly, a great crusade for moral purity tried to desexualize culture, stressing the deadly dangers of venereal diseases and masturbation. This was often linked with eugenics, obsessed with the need for 'the regeneration of the race'. Sex, whether hetero, homo or auto, was regarded by doctors in both countries as a dangerous and debilitating activity, to be repressed as much as possible.

Yet moralistic head-shaking was not the most significant reaction to France. Writers and artists looked for inspiration to 'decadent' France, and particularly to Paris, to a degree unseen for a century, and this would continue until the disaster of 1940. We can suggest several contributory reasons. Paris still enjoyed the notorious glamour of the Empire, and the new Third Republic continued promoting it as the world's cultural centre, for example by the lavish Universal Exposition of 1889, which made the Eiffel Tower a universally recognized symbol of bold modernity. French was still the most widely spoken foreign language. Paris had good and inexpensive public and private art schools, most famously the Académie des Beaux Arts, major universities, state-sponsored exhibitions, and prestigious official cultural institutions such as the Académie Française. As the world's main tourist destination, it had plenty of hotels, restaurants, cafés, theatres – and brothels. It had a concentration of economic, political, social and cultural life unparalleled in any other city: only one-third of British intellectuals lived in London, whereas two-thirds of French intellectuals lived in Paris.[13] So there were many small reviews, and cafés and clubs in the Latin Quarter or bohemian Montmartre where writers and artists congregated, and could be admired and even approached. Leaders of the Irish literary world, including

Yeats and Synge, were particularly impressed, and wanted cafés to replace Dublin pubs.

The Third Republic was uniquely free. The influence of the Church shrank and censorship relaxed. Social barriers were relatively permeable – though intellectuals could rarely if ever be accepted in high society, as Proust (who tried hard) found. Personal freedom – artistic, intellectual and not least sexual – increased. As reformers battled against prostitution, painters and writers found it a fascinating subject. The cosmopolitan, noisy and undisciplined atmosphere of the famous Académie Julian, a private art school, was more exciting than the austere Slade School in London – it had, noted George Moore, a 'sense of sex'.[14] This comment presumably referred not mainly to the students – Parisian schools were predominantly, and in the case of Beaux Arts exclusively, male, unlike the largely female Slade – but to the nude models, which were a Paris speciality. The experience could be a shock: one Scottish woman student, at her first sight of naked men, 'shut myself in the lavatory and was sick'.[15] Finally, Paris was cheap, at least for British and Americans, who crowded the art schools: 'best brandy two francs a bottle and claret for a song, peaches and grapes enough for two pence and *Women* for *asking*'.[16] There were plenty of underpaid young women in the city's huge fashion trade ready to provide modelling, skivvying and sex – for of course, sexual liberation for men often meant sexual servitude for women. The dark side of Bohemia was syphilis – the nemesis for youthful transgressions that returned years later to destroy mind and body, and passed from one generation to the next. So it became the obsessive literary metaphor for degeneration.[17]

There were also purely cultural reasons for Paris's attractiveness. French 'decadence' and the cultural response to it seemed relevant to those intellectuals who condemned western society, and who tried to apply French artistic approaches in their own cultures. These might be the unsparing investigations of the Naturalists; or a search for the unspoilt exotic in warmer climates; or the aesthetic refinement epitomized by the effete Duc des Esseintes, hero of Joris-Karl Huysmans's novel *A Rebours* (1884) – published in English as *Against Nature*. Esseintes, last of an 'effeminate' aristocratic family, bored with orgies and 'the innate stupidity of women', gives a banquet to mourn his dead virility (all the dishes are black – caviar, truffles, black pudding, etc.). He then withdraws into a contrived world of exquisite sensation, a refuge from 'the waves of human mediocrity', with a pet cricket, a gold-plated tortoise, Turkish cigarettes, a machine for mixing exotic cocktails, and a library of 'decadent' Latin authors, where he is nourished by gourmet meals fed by enema. Esseintes became a hero for aesthetes. 'I have the same sickness,' proclaimed Oscar Wilde, who seems to have misunderstood Huysmans's irony.

In short, Parisian culture provided inspiration at every turn. Wilde, working on *Salome* but short of ideas despite the stimulus of Egyptian cigarettes laced with opium and copious draughts of absinthe, asked a violinist in a boulevard café to improvise some music suitable for 'a woman dancing with bare feet in the blood of a man she has craved for and slain'. He produced such 'wild and terrible music that those who were there stopped talking and looked at each other with blanched faces. Then I went back and finished Salome.' It could never have happened at the Crown in the Charing Cross Road, where Wilde and his friends, absinthe-less, had to make do with mulled port.[18]

British, Irish and American intellectuals – and not only intellectuals – flocked to Paris. The image of 'Bohemian' life in the Latin Quarter, popularized during the 1840s in short stories by the cynical Henri Murger, was sentimentalized in *Trilby* (1894), a hugely popular novel and play by the Anglo-French artist and writer George du Maurier. Bohemia (from the French for 'gipsy') promised a coming-of-age away from the constraints of home: drinking absinthe, perorating in cafés, fighting duels, sleeping with adoring *grisettes* – perhaps even learning to paint. Murger's French bohemians had been poor; their foreign emulators often were not. The Irish painter-turned-novelist George Moore, the heir to a large estate, led an elegant 'student' life in Paris in the 1870s, where studios and models were cheaper than in London, on £400 a year – six times a French schoolteacher's salary. His boastfully embroidered *Confessions of a Young Man* (1888) include wonderful pieces of self-parody, as in his description of his lodgings: 'The drawing-room was in cardinal red . . . looped up to give the appearance of a tent; a faun, in terra cotta, laughed in the red gloom, and there were Turkish couches and lamps . . . an altar, a Buddhist temple, a statue of Apollo and a bust of Shelley . . . a Persian cat and a python that made a monthly meal off guinea pigs.'[19] Cultural tourists flocked to the Latin Quarter, Montparnasse and Montmartre. They mixed mostly with other foreigners. At least one art school taught in English. Many models were foreign too, especially Italian immigrants, though the 'most famous model in Paris' was an English girl, Sarah Brown, who caused a scandal by appearing at the annual student Bal des Quat'z Arts as Cleopatra, wearing only gold gauze – and risking several days in gaol for 'outraging public morals'.[20] A remarkable feature of *Trilby* is that there are no major French characters. It is the story of three British art students, the Franco-British model Trilby O'Ferrall, and the sinister German-Jewish musician and hypnotist Svengali. Trilby herself – she of the soft felt hat – a statuesque Pre-Raphaelite beauty, is portrayed as more British than French, not least in her strapping physique. In the end she, like Murger's Mimi, has to die: a working girl (even the daughter of a disgraced Fellow of Trinity) has no future with a gentleman (even an artist).

A spell in Paris, and proclaimed affinity with French culture, was a mark of distinction: 'no other country has been so consistently used to help define British class differences'.[21] The belief that culture was being debased and provincialized in a Britain ruled by a vulgar bourgeoisie and increasingly dominated by a strident, semi-educated and prudish 'mass' was a central aspect of the 'decadence' of these years. Britain was 'philistine' (the word popularized by the francophile Matthew Arnold). French culture, and Parisian style, were escapes and weapons for those who could 'exult in beautiful English over the inferiority of English literature, English art, English music, English everything else'.[22] Oscar Wilde assured a French newspaper that 'To me there are only two languages in the world: French and Greek. Though I have English friends, I do not like the English in general. There is a great deal of hypocrisy in England that you in France very justly find fault with. The typical Briton is Tartuffe, seated in his shop behind the counter.'[23] British and American modernists in every genre established Parisian links: painters such as Sickert and Whistler (who set up an art school for English-speaking students); 'Naturalist' novelists and dramatists such as George Gissing and Arnold Bennett; and the overlapping 'aesthetic' and 'decadent' coteries – Walter Pater and his acolytes, Oscar Wilde and his friends, the Yellow Book group, the Café Royal set, the Rhymers' Club, and the New English Art Club. The Parisian connection was similarly cultivated in the early twentieth century by T.S. Eliot (influenced by the Symbolists and the extreme nationalist Action Française) and by the Bloomsbury group, who tried to emulate a fanciful notion of eighteenth-century French salon culture. In 1910, Roger Fry organized a sensational exhibition in London of what he named 'post-Impressionism'. 'On or about December 1910' wrote Virginia Woolf with an odd mixture of cosmopolitanism and insularity, 'human character changed'.[24]

Although artistic influence flowed strongly from France to Britain in these years, there were interesting counter-currents. Some French critics even deplored 'invasion' by British and 'Northern' culture, including the novels of George Eliot, dismissed as emotional and moralistic. While British modernism was marked by an 'aggressive internationalism, or even antinationalism',[25] in France, the dominant current was a reassertion of national identity, in a perennial conflict between French 'clarity', often associated with the sunny classical south, and British (or German and Scandinavian) obscurity, associated with the gloomy romantic north. But some French artists wanted to touch realities beyond the visible and the rational, and try new ways of expressing them. The old obsession with fog thus found new meanings, and its great artistic celebration in Monet's paintings of the Thames, viewed in 1899–1901 from St Thomas's Hospital and his room at the Savoy Hotel: 'I adore London' – except on Sundays – 'but what I love more than anything else is the fog . . . the beautiful effects I have observed on the Thames over a two-month period are scarcely to be believed . . . No country could be more extraordinary for a painter'.[26] Rimbaud and Mallarmé, both English teachers, were interested by the sounds of English words.

Mallarmé, who considered that English had retained the youthful vigour of old French, translated poems by Poe and Tennyson, wrote potboilers for learners of English (featuring phrases such as 'Knit my dog a pair of breeches and my cat a tail coat'), and invented a toy with a moveable tongue to help French children pronounce 'th'. His work in English influenced the development of both the lexicon and the syntax of his idiosyncratic French. Marcel Proust admired George Eliot and was influenced by the aesthetic ideas of John Ruskin, some of whose works he translated despite not knowing much English – but, he said, he knew Ruskin. The young sculptor Henri Gaudier spent his short career in London, where he came to earn a living, to avoid military service, and to escape petty persecution over his unusual platonic but emotional relationship with the older Zofia Brzeska.[27]

So obvious was the British presence in Paris that Huysmans's effete Duc des Esseintes finds that on a suitably rainy day he can make a virtual trip to London and be 'saturated with English life' without the bore of crossing the Channel. In the Rue de Rivoli he visits Galignani's English bookshop and a bar serving port, sherry, Palmer's biscuits, mince pies, and sandwiches 'hiding hot mustard plasters within their bland envelopes'. In an English tavern near the Gare Saint-Lazare he manages oxtail soup, haddock, roast beef, Stilton ('sweetness impregnated with bitterness') and rhubarb tart, washed down with three pints of beer ('a little musky cowshed taste'). Above all there are the English themselves, tweed-clad and smelling of wet dog, the men with 'pottery eyes, crimson complexions, thoughtful or arrogant expressions'; the 'robust' women stuffing themselves with steak pie, 'without male escorts, dining together, boys' faces, teeth as big as bats, apple cheeks, long hands and feet'.[28]

PILGRIMS OF PLEASURE: THE PRINCE OF WALES AND OSCAR WILDE

I want to make my life itself a work of art. I know the price of a fine verse, but also of a rose, of a vintage wine, of a colourful tie, of a delicate dish.
OSCAR WILDE, Paris, 1891[29]

See the twinkle in me eye?
Just come back from France, that's why
Do you like my make-up? Ain't it great?
It's the latest thing from Paris straight
And I'd like to go again
To Paris on the Seine
For Paris is a proper Pantomime

And if they'd only shift the Hackney Road and plant it over there
I'd like to live in Paris all the time!

MARIE LLOYD, 'The Coster Girl in Paris', 1912

The Prince was a regular visitor from the 1870s onwards, usually incognito to avoid state protocol, though there were still numerous courtesy visits and sometimes political meetings. Paris meant freedom to indulge in his favourite pastimes, including sex, food, gambling, the theatre, racing and socializing with old friends, mostly members of the French aristocracy, some whose ancestors had been 'anglomaniac' cronies of an earlier Prince of Wales in the 1780s. The Jockey Club provided congenial sport at Longchamps and Chantilly. The boulevard theatres provided nightly variety: his taste was more for the diverting than for earnest explorations of social problems – though the press reported that his liking for Sarah Bernhardt caused a ban on the rather daring *Dame aux Camélias* to be lifted, causing the author, Dumas the Younger, to thank him for his 'gracious protection'.[30] Gambling took place late at night, after the theatre, in private houses, some specializing in semi-professional gaming. Eating, of course, was amply provided for. The prince's favourite was appropriately the Café Anglais, for decades one of the best restaurants in Paris. His Paris life followed a routine: the Place Vendôme; the restaurants and theatres of the Boulevard a few hundred yards north; the houses of friends, in neighbouring quarters, and the racecourses in the suburbs. It was a strenuous round, rarely ending before the early hours. The Princess of Wales, if she was present, went to bed just after the theatre. His social life was fairly common knowledge: on one occasion in 1886 the police tore down posters advertising a publication entitled 'Les Amours du Prince de Galles'.

The police kept a close eye on his activities, both to ensure his safety (especially if there were Irish Fenian conspirators in town) and to monitor political and other contacts.[31] Some of his aristocratic friends were enemies of the Republic. More worryingly, a few of his meetings were with *republican* opponents of the government, most importantly Léon Gambetta. He first met Gambetta in 1878, probably through the mediation of his friend the aristocratic but republican General de Galliffet and the Radical MP Sir Charles Dilke. The intention seems to have been to help Gambetta, France's rising politician, to improve his standing as an international statesman, and to prepare a future Anglo-French rapprochment, including a trade agreement – Dilke advised that 'M. Gambetta is a free-trader and desires that which we desire.'[32] The prince, though keen to make a personal diplomatic contribution, was no loose cannon: the meeting was prepared in Whitehall and the embassy. With similar discretion, he adroitly avoided meeting the extreme nationalist General Boulanger, who came hopefully hanging round his hotel in the 1880s.

His gambling was something the French police were concerned about. It seems that the prince needed money, and winning in Paris was one way of getting it. But some of his gambling acquaintances had bad reputations, and there were complaints from French losers. Women were an equal concern. The police wanted to know all the prince's lovers, mainly to ensure that they were not royalist 'agents of influence'. They followed the women and ensured they had identified them, where necessary by questioning neighbours, servants and concierges. But the prince was careful: his mistresses, despite legend, were rarely if ever Parisian. Only on one occasion did the police report that he and some of his Jockey Club cronies were ogling the professionals on the boulevard. This was not only, presumably, because he had a taste, noted the police, for tall well-dressed blondes, but because of the need for discretion and reliability. The lover of the moment would arrive from London in advance, and took up residence usually at the Hôtel du Rhin, or piquantly the Balmoral, near his own *pied à terre*, the Hôtel Bristol in the Place Vendôme, where a suite was kept permanently. Taking his dog for a walk provided a discreet opportunity for assignations. The social-climbing Miss Jennie Chamberlain from Baltimore, chaperoned by her mother, took up residence in the Place Vendôme in 1884. She later married a Guards officer. Several aristocratic Russians were obligingly furnished by the diplomatic corps during the 1880s, for example Baroness Pilar von Pilchau, wife of a Russian military attaché in London, and Countess Buturlin, wife of the Warsaw chief of police and sister-in-law of another attaché. This did not guarantee complete discretion, however: the gossipy Goncourt reported a Russian woman as saying 'The Prince of Wales is exhausting: he doesn't just screw you, he eats you alive.'[33] On one occasion in 1888, the police became very concerned that he was seeing an unknown French-sounding 'Madame Hudrie', but investigation soon established that this was a Russian who had borrowed her chambermaid's surname.[34]

Wilde made a fairly triumphant visit to Paris in 1891, where he met the right people, paid court to the sociable Mallarmé, was rude to Proust, and made friends with the young André Gide. He enthralled some and bored others. Perhaps his laboured paradoxes were less amusing in strongly accented French, or perhaps the French were harder to amuse ('Cet Anglais est emmerdant,' thought the poet Jean Moréas).[35]

The prince and the poet seem not to have met in Paris, though such a meeting would have been possible, given that Edward asked to meet Oscar and spent an evening with him in 1881 in Chelsea, along with the actress Lillie Langtry, Oscar's friend and Edward's mistress. He had subsequently praised Oscar's plays, greatly to his pleasure – 'What a splendid country, where princes understand poets.'[36] Their Parisian paths might easily have crossed at the theatre or on the boulevards, or the more daring places where the prince and other tourists occasionally set foot: the Moulin Rouge and the famous artistic Chat Noir (where Erik Satie played the piano, and establishment figures mingled with the avant garde) or the rather notorious Latin Quarter Mabille dance hall, a traditional pick-up place for students and grisettes. Wilde too went slumming, visiting the Chateau Rouge dancehall at Montmartre, but he found it rather scary.

Victorianism fought back against decadence and 'Zolaism'. In March 1888 the crusading *Pall Mall Gazette* carried a racy interview with a French publisher entitled 'Why French novels sell'.[37] The answer was that 'the average aristocratic young lady in this country dotes on anything naughty . . . You English are fond of prattling about the purity of your literature, and yet English society is shrieking for Zola' – hence British sales of 200,000 copies of *Nana*, the story of a Parisian courtesan. In June, the *Channel*, Boulogne's English newspaper, reported that the stage version was drawing crowds to the local theatre – presumably including English tourists.[38] In August, the National Vigilance Association began a private prosecution of Henry Vizetelly, a leading London publisher of foreign literature, for selling slightly expurgated translations of three of Zola's punishing twenty-volume Rougon-Macquart cycle, *Nana*, *La Terre* and *Pot-Bouille* (thrillingly titled *Piping Hot!*) Vizetelly pleaded guilty to charges under the Obscene Publications Act after the blushing jury pleaded to have no more extracts read out – they balked at a scene where a little girl helps a bull mount a cow. Vizetelly was fined. But he soon brought out newly expurgated editions, was prosecuted again in 1889, and this time was given three months in Holloway Prison, the first publisher to be imprisoned for publishing works of recognized literary importance. The flood of 'foreign filth' was not to be staunched so easily. The following year the headmaster of Eton complained to the prime minister that boys were receiving parcels of porn from Paris. Eventually, the National Vigilance Association got their French ally, the redoubtable Senator Béranger, to prosecute the main international peddler, who turned out to be an Englishman named Charles Carrington.

Wilde too suffered when *Salome* (written in French) was banned in England for portraying biblical characters on stage. He indignantly proclaimed that 'I shall leave England to settle in France where I shall take out letters of naturalization. I will not consent to call myself a citizen of a country that shows such narrowness in artistic judgement.'[39]

Vizetelly and Zola could hardly have found themselves in more hostile circumstances than the 1880s. We have noted the political and moral unease in both Britain and France. In 1887, France was rocked by political corruption and the rise of the demagogic nationalism of General Boulanger, while London had the 'Bloody Sunday' riots. There had been militant cross-Channel campaigning against prostitution, child abuse, alcoholism (one of several newly classified social diseases) and cruelty to animals, and this reached a climax in the 1880s. In 1885, the brilliant political career of Sir Charles Dilke was ruined when a woman accused him of teaching her 'every form of French vice'.[40] The Cleveland Street scandal of 1889, involving enterprising telegraph boys making more than the regulation deliveries to gentlemen customers, made world headlines, and much scorn in France at English perversion. The *Pall Mall Gazette* and its editor William Stead, combining moralism with circulation, carried the notorious exposé of 'white slavery' in July 1885, 'The Maiden Tribute of Modern Babylon', in which Stead claimed that he had been able to buy a twelve-year-old girl. The outcry culminated in a rally of over 100,000 people in Hyde Park, including feminists, socialists, clergymen of all denominations, and trade unionists. It forced Parliament to repeal the Contagious Diseases Act and pass the Criminal Law Amendment Act, outlawing brothels and pimping, raising the age of consent to sixteen and (in an amendment proposed by the francophile radical MP Henry Labouchère) criminalizing homosexual acts. The National Vigilance Association, established during this campaign, was soon prosecuting rapists, paedophiles, homosexuals, pornographers and pimps. To crown it all, Vizetelly's prosecution coincided with the eight murders, mainly of prostitutes, by 'Jack the Ripper'. It is significant that the extracts from Zola stressed in Vizetelly's trial concerned predatory female sexuality, child sex, incest and a combination of these – the rape of a girl abetted by her sister – not least shocking because the victim derives pleasure from it. The campaigners saw Vizetelly's offence as aggravated by publishing the translations in cheap illustrated series called 'Sensational Novels' and 'Boulevard Novels', made accessible to young women and 'scattered broadcast among the lightly educated'. They believed cultural representations of sex stimulated the social evils they were fighting.

Petitions were produced calling for Vizetelly's release, signed by writers, artists, actors, and a few maverick MPs. Though they deplored his imprisonment and were alarmed by the threat to artistic freedom, their comments were embarrassed, often criticizing Zola's work. Zola did not help, saying that his books were not meant for a large readership, should not be read in translation, and that in France young women would not be allowed to read them.[41] The many critics of Zola – who included Gladstone – alleged that he and Vizetelly were no better than pornographers, motivated by profit. The whole affair led to timidity and sullen self-censorship among British authors, who realized more than ever that, unlike in France, 'Grocerdom is organized in conventicle and church and rancorously articulate.'[42] The struggle continued. A diplomatic incident was narrowly avoided when the government rescued twenty-two paintings of scenes from Rabelais by a French artist, which zealous purity crusaders were about to have destroyed. There were scandalized protests when Degas's *L'Absinthe* was exhibited in 1893.

DEPRAVITY AND CORRUPTION

Why should England be flooded with foreign filth, and our youth polluted by having the most revolting and hideous descriptions of French vice thrust upon

SANCTA SIMPLICITAS!

Mamma. "Don't stand idling there, Tommy! Why don't you read French sometimes! Look at dear Papa, he hasn't his time for Reading; but whenever he's got a spare moment or two, he takes a French Book out of his Pocket and reads it—just to keep up his French, you know!" [*Dear Papa is much tickled, but keeps his amusement to himself.*

Punch had little doubt why English gentlemen really read Zola.

their attention?
Pall Mall Gazette, 1 May 1889[43]

The intolerable Anglo-Saxon hypocrisy of these austere Englishmen . . .
would have the world believe that all the evils of their social system are
imported from us, and they seem to consider me the incarnation of all that
is worst in France.

EMILE ZOLA, 1888[44]

The Frenchness of Zola, Degas and others was, if not an offence in itself, at least prima facie evidence of turpitude. Being famous and dead could not save Balzac from the zeal of the Manchester branch of the NVA, which had 25,000 copies of his novels pulped. For several years, until ruthlessly expurgated, many French novels disappeared from circulation in Great Britain, and Zola remained banned in Ireland long after independence. But despite the fears of moralists for 'the budding rose of boyhood' and unleashed 'maiden fancies', the most popular French books among English readers appear to have been Alexandre Dumas's swashbuckling adventures, and histories of the Napoleonic period.[45]

The contrast between repressive (or decent) Britain and liberated (or corrupted) France was overdrawn for obvious polemical reasons. Many modern French artists were feted in Britain, in Establishment as well as dissident circles. Impressionism swept British art schools when the French art establishment still resisted it. French art was regularly exhibited in London, and all the British reviews reported in detail on Paris shows. Verlaine and Mallarmé were invited to speak in London, Cambridge and Oxford, and given more recognition than they had received in France – indeed, Christ Church had some difficulty in getting a happy Verlaine to vacate his rooms.[46] Auguste Rodin, who in France had 'never altogether escaped the whiff of scandal associated with "modern art"', was acclaimed in England as the heir of Michelangelo.[47] He was given an honorary degree by Oxford in 1907, and was so proud that he often wore his doctoral gown in Paris and wanted it placed on his coffin. King Edward VII visited his studio in 1908.[48] Edmond de Goncourt was assured by a female friend that on the London stage 'kissing, caressing and touching up went much further than one would dare in any French theatre'.[49] On the other hand, Wilde found himself ostracized by Parisian society after his 1895 prosecution – the left-wing Paris City Council had recently been pressing Parliament to outlaw homosexual acts. In rural France sexual conduct was closer to Galway than to Gomorrah, with young women treated with 'a degree of strictness of which English people have no conception'.[50] English women had much more freedom, and were suspected of unsettling their French sisters. As late as 1907, a school inspector criticized a teacher who 'scandalized' her provincial town by walking on her own: 'Having spent a long time in England [she] has adopted the free manners of English *misses*.'[51] Bourgeois French families did not allow their sons and daughters to study art in Paris – one reason why the schools were so dependent on British and American students. As for 'Zolaism', it was frowned on in France too. Zola himself escaped with having publication of his novels suspended in the late 1870s and failing twenty-four times to get into the French Academy. But during the 1880s seven 'Naturalist' authors, including Guy de Maupassant, were prosecuted for obscenity, and three were jailed. Zola was publicly repudiated by five of his disciples for *La Terre*, a book for which Vizetelly was prosecuted.[52] Finally, if Britain was prudish, it is not clear that it merited the traditional French reproach of greater hypocrisy. The greatest tribute paid by vice to virtue, to adopt the elegant French definition, was regulated prostitution, a nasty secret known to all but officially ignored.[53]

Despite the images of brutish French peasant life created by Zola, Maupassant and others, these years saw the first flirtation in the long

British love affair with rural France. Of course, thousands of British had spent time in provincial France from 1815 onwards. But most of the landscape was regarded as monotonous, with too many poplars and dull plains,[54] and the presence of French people had been an unavoidable necessity rather than a positive attraction. However, one aspect of the concern with decadence was repudiation of 'mass' urban industrial society and a search for the primitive and unspoilt. For an earlier generation, this could be done by fleeing to the Lake District, but by the last quarter of the century, with population growth, urban sprawl and mass education, urban society by the charabanc-load was catching up. France, whose population was barely increasing, had many 'unspoilt' regions, whose people seemed to embody values dead or moribund in Britain. Descriptions and novels appeared for readers interested not only in the comforts of Pau or Biarritz, or the glories of the Alps and Pyrenees, but in the natives and their ways in less-favoured regions. The pioneer rural colonist and writer on rural France was an art critic, P.G. Hamerton, who bought a house in the Rhône valley for 'beauty and convenience'. In *Around My House* (1876) he wrote in detail about peasant society as the bedrock of France, and stressed its cultural remoteness. Though his peasants are less cuddly than in popular twentieth-century descriptions, he and other writers began to assert their moral superiority over English farmers and labourers. A pioneer in another genre was Robert Louis Stevenson, in *Travels with a Donkey* (1879), an account of a walking holiday in the Cevennes highlands. Far from sentimental – the peasants are mainly unfriendly, and he takes a revolver to be on the safe side – the book was ahead of its time, thought, even by its author, to be an odd idea. It would need a generation of tourist penetration for the French countryside – still typified by squalor, linguistic incomprehension and bad food – to become visitor-friendly. Henry James's *A Little Tour in France* (1884) is still largely about buildings and history, with the people only intruding to disappoint expectations by being dirty, taciturn and eating disgusting food. But a stream of new perspectives began appearing, such as *A Year in Western France* (1877), *Life in a French Village* (1879), *Our Home in Aveyron* (1890) and even *The Romance of a French Parsonage* (1892). By the 1930s, writers such as Lady Fortescue, in *Perfume from Provence*, were creating the now familiar image of comfortable exoticism 'before the £ collapsed'. Her workmen were comical and 'Rabelaisian', her peasants 'perfectly maddening, entirely without initiative, and quite irresponsible, but most lovable', and sometimes 'very, very wise'.[55] The age of Elizabeth David, Peter Mayle and mass-conversions of farmhouses was beginning to dawn.

Regeneration: Power and Empire

We have to cure the very soul of France.
JULES SIMON, philosopher and politician, to French Academy, 1871[56]

In the North we have the rising of the future; in the South,
the crumbling of a decaying past.
EDMOND DUMOLINS, *Anglo-Saxon Superiority* (1898)[57]

As some intellectuals, artists and politicians were deploring or celebrating 'decadence', others – or sometimes the same ones – were trying to end it. Renan and Taine, despite their pessimism, had not despaired of France: they advocated profound political and educational reforms to cure the country's ills. Republicans, who took power at the end of the 1870s, intended to recreate a healthy, patriotic nation cleansed of the vices of Catholicism and Bonapartism. Catholics too, though despondent at the Republic's victory, and tempted to see France's fate as divine punishment, had not abandoned hope of redemption. Many people remained optimistic about the future, and the novels of Jules Verne or the opinions of Flaubert's M. Bouvard were closer to their views than the writings of Zola, Huysmans, Ibsen or Hardy. Optimism was not complacency: reformers agreed that France needed to be bolder, healthier, and better educated, even if they disagreed about the means.

Colonial expansion had been a remedy for French ills ever since the Restoration, and the argument changed little from Tocqueville to de Gaulle. France had to prove that it was still a great nation, and this was more urgent than ever at a time of defeat and decadence. As the republican leader Jules Ferry said in 1882, 'France would not easily be content to count for no more in the world than a big Belgium.' Imperialism would be a unifying national adventure, and would create a breed of intrepid soldiers and hardy colonists who would rejuvenate the flabby body politic. A great imperial population would supplement the flagging birthrate – one of the deepest concerns of late-nineteenth-century nationalists. The republican patriot Léon Gambetta declared that 'it is through expansion, through influencing the outside world, through the place that they occupy in the general life of humanity, that nations persist and last'. This was something that both Right and Left could support. For the Right, France was spreading Catholicism as well as its own influence through its widespread missionary activities. The Left set up the Alliance Française in 1883 as a secular missionary organization, 'to make our language known and loved' and hence contribute to 'the extension beyond the seas of the French race which is increasing too slowly on the Continent'.[58] Novelists such as Pierre Loti and Ernest Psichari lauded the invigorating effects of desert air and oriental sensuality; and Gauguin's friends paid for him to go and seek passion and inspiration among the dusky maidens of Tahiti. Even Rimbaud was toughened up trading coffee and guns in Abyssinia.

Not everyone thrilled to these visions. Voters feared war and expense. Investors sought safer profits. Some nationalists regarded imperialism as weakening France on the Continent, and they disdained colonies as an unworthy distraction from recapturing Alsace and Lorraine: 'I have lost two sisters and you offer me twenty servants,' cried the nationalist leader Paul Déroulède. Bismarck indeed encouraged French ambitions overseas for that very reason, and with the added bonus that it created rivalry with Britain. French colonial expansion relied on the minority enthusiasm of leading republican politicians, geographical societies, missionaries, the armed forces and a few economic interests. Their sights were set on North Africa and Indo-China. It proved possible to compromise with the British over the latter, and London raised fewer objections to the French declaration of a protectorate over Tunisia in 1881 than did critics inside France. Gambetta proclaimed that 'France has regained her rank as a great power.'

France and Britain did quarrel seriously over Egypt, a cause of periodic contention from 1798 to 1956. As in 1840, the French considered they had not merely interests but an affinity with Egypt, as if Napoleon's invasion had been a delicate compliment to an ancient civilization. They had invested money and effort in building up cultural, economic and political influence. This was crowned in 1869 by the opening of the Suez Canal, an idea of Napoleon and the Saint-Simonians, and built by Ferdinand de Lesseps, one of France's greatest (though finally ill-fated) economic adventurers. The canal was a strategic asset, above all for British communications with India. So when in 1875, the khedive of Egypt, short of money, sold his shares in the Suez Canal Company, they were snapped up by Disraeli's government. In 1881–2, nationalist riots in Egypt led to naval action and military intervention by Britain, which the French held back from, mainly because of domestic opposition. The British found themselves governing Egypt. French colonialists and – too late – French public opinion were outraged at the latest trick of perfidious Albion, depriving France of a great colonial prize. The British were even accused of bribing the Egyptians to pretend to revolt in order to provide a pretext for intervention. As during colonial friction in the 1840s, the French navy meditated on how to steal a march on the British. Plans for a Channel Tunnel, for which excavations had begun, were called into question.

THE TUNNEL: FALSE DAWN

The first Channel tunnel proposal came from a French engineer, Albert Mathieu, in 1802, during the Peace of Amiens. The idea never entirely went away. A

multitude of plans had been drawn up for bridges, tunnels, submerged tubes
and even a waterproof train driven by compressed air. New means of crossing
the Channel always guaranteed publicity. The first balloon crossing (by a Frenchman and an American) had happened as early as 1785. A submarine telegraph
cable had been laid in 1851, making Britain and France 'Siamese twins', according
to one enthusiast. An American, Paul Boyton, 'swam' across in April 1875, using
an inflatable suit, a paddle and a small sail, and smoking a cigar. The first true
Channel swim was the following August by a merchant navy captain, Matthew
Webb, sustained by beer, brandy and coffee. By this time, a tunnel had strong
supporters on both sides of the Channel, and they sponsored Channel swims as
publicity. Bills had been submitted to Parliament, and an Anglo–French commission in 1876 produced a draft treaty ready for ratification. Blithely confident

that the technical problems could be overcome by technology recently developed for digging under the Alps, a Submarine Continental Railway Company and a Société Française du Tunnel Sous-marin were set up. They started experimental tunnelling at Shakespeare Cliff, near Dover, and Sangatte, near Calais, using boring machines invented by a British colonel. By 1882, the British tunnel had progressed more than a mile, and politicians, journalists, soldiers and celebrities were taken for champagne and canapés under the sea. The companies expected the two tunnels to meet in four or five years. However, there were fears on both sides. If some in France suspected British designs on Calais, most fears, given the weakness of their army, were British, and strongest of all among military men. However many assurances were given that a tunnel could be fortified, mined, filled with poison gas or instantly flooded, they could not rule out the possibility of its being captured by an invading force. As cross-Channel relations suddenly turned sour, a parliamentary select committee found against the tunnel in 1883, and the Gladstone government agreed. Though the tunnel companies kept up the argument, and the House of Commons was told in April 1913 that a tunnel was still being considered, no government before 1914 was willing to reopen the question.[59] This surely prevented at least technical and financial disaster. Meanwhile, Louis Blériot had shown the shape of things to come and caused a sensation on both sides of the Channel by flying from near Sangatte to a golf course near Dover in the early hours of 25 July 1909.

Unfair though it might be, the British were undeniably the more successful imperialists, not only in Egypt or India, but by spawning new settler colonies, including the United States. Some in France emphasized the global power of *les Anglo-Saxons* – a concept that now entered the French political vocabulary.[60] 'The great peril, the great rivalry' was not now 'on the other side of the Rhine', but 'on the other side of the Channel [and] the Atlantic'.[61] French resentment was displayed when almost alone they resisted an American suggestion to agree a universal prime meridian, as this meant adopting the Greenwich Meridian; and in 1894 a young French anarchist killed himself trying to blow up the Greenwich Observatory.[62] Several influential commentators in the 1880s and 90s, mostly admiring liberals, asked brutally frank questions. What explains Anglo-Saxon superiority? What must France do to compete, and keep her place in the sun? A series of publications identified the 'political psychology of the English people' and the 'education of the middle and ruling classes' as their advantages.[63] Not all these diagnoses were new. Indeed, some went back not only to Taine, but to Tocqueville, and even Voltaire. But there was an important novelty. They looked less admiringly now at British parliamentary institutions, which after the 1884 Reform Act seemed little different from those of France. Instead, they focused on the men they considered the real rulers – civil servants, colonial administrators, and businessmen – and how they were produced.

The British education system, they argued, did not cram its victims with rote-learned classics and undigested theory as in France, but taught practical skills, encouraged intellectual freedom, and above all developed self-reliance, teamwork and character – precisely what a modern economic and a political elite of 'practical energetic men' required.[64] Taine had not gone quite so far a generation earlier. It had, after all, been commonplace for French and many British commentators to condemn British universities and schools for incompetence or worse; and it was generally accepted that, whatever their other failings, the French were well educated. Dr Arnold, the famous headmaster of Rugby, considered that France produced 'more advanced and enlarged minds' than England, and took his children on visits.[65] His son Matthew, one of the most influential of Victorian intellectuals, had in the 1860s praised 'the French Eton' – a provincial *lycée* – for the quality of education given to the middle classes, and had pressed for French-style reforms. It was he who enviously reported the famous story that the French minister of education could see from a chart on his wall what every schoolboy was doing at every minute of the day. But the defeat of 1870, commonly attributed to 'the Prussian schoolmaster', tarnished the prestige of French education and caused the republicans to look for models abroad. They studied English and Scottish educational legislation in creating that hallmark of Frenchness, the *école laïque*.[66] Critics now attacked the French classical tradition itself as sterile, and the Napoleonic *lycées* as stultifying 'barracks'. Moreover, they were doing something about it. The sociologist Edmond Demolins in 1899 founded the model Ecole des Roches in Normandy (still in existence as France's leading independent school), modelled on progressive English boarding-schools such as Bedales. More importantly, Emile Boutmy (with Taine as an adviser) had founded in 1871 the Ecole Libre des Sciences Politiques – soon famous as 'Sciences Po'. This was not modelled on any English institution – in fact the London School of Economics was copied from it – but it was a conscious attempt to create a new ruling class as practical-minded as the one its founders thought Britain, having escaped revolution and the Napoleonic state, already possessed. Within a generation Sciences Po was educating a high proportion of senior French civil servants, and it has done so ever since.

EDUCATION, EDUCATION, EDUCATION

Whatever the aspirations of reformers such as Arnold and Desmolins, educational ideas, habits and institutions in both countries have proved singularly impermeable to the influence of the other – the reason they are not treated at length in this book. But we must suggest briefly some of the effects educational difference (in turn connected with differences in religion, legal systems and intellectual traditions) has had for the broader relationship. To cut a very long story short, French education remains essentially 'classical': it hands down approved models of the right way of doing things, which are to be mastered and reproduced. This remains true from *école maternelle* to *grande école*. A bright young Oxford-trained British civil servant seconded in 2004 to the elite École Nationale d'Administration told us that 'if you haven't been sitting in front of a lecturer for four hours they don't think you've learnt anything'. The approved models include ideas, techniques and – a central feature – styles of ordering and presenting knowledge, usually the famous 'three-part plan' based on traditional principles of logic and rhetoric: thesis, antithesis and synthesis. This is often characterized as 'Cartesian', based on deductive reasoning – that is, the theory comes first, applications follow. British education is unsystematic, and it tends to aim at individual expression rather than correctness or mastery of a body of knowledge. Success requires at least an attempt at originality and 'lateral thinking', and mistakes and gaps in knowledge are tolerated. Thinking usually proceeds inductively, from facts to theory. The French tradition assumes that specialist training is required for professional activity at all levels, and the higher the level, the greater the specialization. The British is more sceptical of 'paper qualifications'; it regards non-intellectual qualities such as enthusiasm, teamwork and imagination as valuable, and values non-specialist education as giving potentially fresh insights. Both approaches, of course, have characteristic strengths and weaknesses. What is important from our point of view is that they still produce different styles of thought and expression, which are noticeable whenever the French and British come into contact. In politics, the French have complained for generations that the British refused to discuss hypotheses, but would only consider actual problems. Palmerston stated that 'it is not usual for England to enter into engagements with reference to cases which have not wholly arisen', and Granville a generation later echoed that British practice was to 'avoid prospective understandings to meet contingencies, which seldom occur in the way which has been anticipated'.[67] The British, as the French saw it, were incapable of thinking logically about future possibilities. In the 1920s André Tardieu, a future prime minister, deplored the 'repugnance of the Anglo-Saxon to the systematic constructions of the Latin mind'. An ambassador in the 1950s agreed: 'For an Englishman a proposition has no real existence.' Nothing had changed by 2003: a British diplomat found that 'the French are most comfortable when they can define a set of principles . . . The British shy away from principles.'[68] So the British have tended to dismiss general statements about future intentions as empty verbiage – something they at times had reason to regret. Margaret Thatcher, for example, admitted that in discussions about European integration 'we in the British delegation were inclined to dismiss such rhetoric as cloudy and unrealistic expectations which had no prospect of being implemented'.[69] In business relations, French interlocutors were often thought better prepared, with a clear agenda worked out in advance, but incapable of 'brainstorming' and unwilling to discuss and take on new ideas. Their practice was to define their position logically at the outset, and defend it. This was often seen by the British as arrogant and inflexible: 'the French don't listen, they stick to their positions, they mock your ideas.' But British 'open-mindedness' seemed to the French to be illogical, indecisive and time-wasting.[70] The difference is summed up by Graham Corbett, finance director of Eurotunnel: 'The French can only think in threes, the Brits without any structure at all; the French are more likely to keep you out of trouble, but the Brits will get you out of it once you're in it.'[71]

– Putting Colour into French Cheeks

I shall put colour into the cheeks of solitary and confined youth.
PIERRE DE COUBERTIN[72]

Imitate the English. The taste for struggle that the French have learnt on the sports field is showing itself boldly in seeking to conquer a bigger share of the globe.
GABRIEL BONVALOT, explorer[73]

It would seem to be infinitely more important for French boys to become aware of the poetry to be found in a whole afternoon spent playing with a ball, than in struggling to uncover . . . the poetry that may or may not reside in a given verse by Racine.
HENRY DE MONTHERLANT, writer[74]

One aspect of English culture and education that the French had long disdained now began to be singled out as a vital ingredient of Anglo-Saxon success: games. 'Boys who learned to command in games were learning to command in India,' concluded the headmaster of an elite Dominican school near Paris after visiting Eton.[75] The defeat of 1870 had made physical exercise a patriotic duty. Its first aim was military training, and its first manifestation was a vast gymnastics movement, copied from Germany. Collective gym fostered strength and coordination useful in military drill. For several decades it was immensely popular, especially in the patriotic north-east, and in 1900 was still the main single form of mass recreation. But gymnastics had limits. It did not foster the desired liberal qualities of voluntary cooperation, individual effort combined with imaginative teamwork, and fair play. What were called *les sports anglais* came in useful here: cycling, swimming, rowing, athletics, boxing, tennis, competitive skiing, and especially the team games football and rugby. Within a generation, what began as an aspect of educational reform and a means of countering national decadence revolutionized popular culture. Along with parliamentary government, it is France's most important import from Britain.

Before the 1860s, the French did not much play team games, sometimes called 'les petits jeux anglais'. Gratuitous outdoor exertion was not common. 'The word *sport*,' explained the mayor of Pau in 1842, 'is one of those English expressions that are impossible to translate into French.' One Paris news-paper in the 1890s believed that football required 'long flat mallets'.[76] The upper classes, and their emulators, continued hunting and racing. That one French prime minister had a Cambridge rowing blue is the exception and far from the rule. Fencing, and even duelling, expanded into the lower-middle classes late in the century. The lower classes had bull-baiting, bowls, cockfighting, shooting and so on, and these survived and expanded as leisure opportunities increased. English sports, involving violent physical contact, had long been despised as expressions of English brutality, mindlessness, and lack of social propriety. One of Béranger's most sarcastic anglophobe songs is 'Le Boxeur'. Early Parisian rugby players found physical contact and rolling in the mud distasteful, and placed less emphasis on the scrum and the tackle – arguably initiating the French national style.[77]

Games codified in British schools and universities in mid-century were soon being played in France by men working or holidaying. The regional pattern of French sport was shaped by social and economic contacts with Britain: the Channel ports, the Paris region, the south-west (tourism and wine) and the north (textiles and engineering) were the main areas of influ-ence. The first sports clubs in France were the Havre Athletic Club (1872) and in Paris the English Taylors' Club (1877). Old boys of Scottish Catholic schools were prominent in establishing soccer. These expatriates had no missionary aim of promoting sport in France or playing against Frenchmen. Rather, the initiative was taken by Parisian schoolboys. The famous Racing Club de France, the first native sports club, was set up by boys from four right-bank schools in 1882, and its rival Stade Français mainly by boys from the left-bank Lycée Saint-Louis. 'Racing', as it was called, was extremely 'aristocratic' and intellectual in its values and membership. At first they failed to get it quite right, sprinting round the Gare Saint-Lazare dressed as jockeys and taking bets. Others went in for acrobatics, and ran a highly exclusive private circus. But British-style orthodoxy soon prevailed, as expatriates joined in. British players took part in the first French national rugby cham-pionship in 1892. In 1893 Racing Club played Oxford, and introduced their visitors to the delights of the Moulin Rouge. In 1900 they hosted the athletics events of the second Olympic Games.[78]

The spread of sports owed much to enthusiastic individuals, who believed that they were fighting modern decadence. Their missionary zeal is shown by the prominence of Frenchmen in organizing international organizations – hence FIFA, not IFAF. The great apostle was a Sciences Po graduate, Baron Pierre de Coubertin. He was inspired by Taine's praise of English public schools, by reading *Tom Brown's Schooldays*, by the ideal of *le fair-play*, and by the wish to 'exalt the fatherland, the race, the flag'. In his twenties, during the 1880s, he used his social and political connections to lobby for the introduction of games. There was an early setback: in 1893 he brought a French crew to the Henley Regatta, and the Thames Rowing Club rammed them. Undeterred, in 1894 Coubertin set up the largest French sports federation, and the same year he founded the modern Olympic movement. His inspiration was the Much Wenlock Olympian Games, a festival of miscellaneous sporting contests enlivened by heraldic processions, award ceremonies and flags, which took place every year in a Shropshire village, and to which Coubertin had been a delighted visitor.[79] Other sporting pioneers were Georges de Saint-Clair, formerly French consul in Edinburgh, who wanted games to 'forge the man of action . . . who knows how to will, to dare, to undertake, organize, govern and be governed'.[80] Pascal Grousset, the former Communard exile, did not wish to leave sport to right-wingers and anglophiles, and in the late 1880s he tried to push French sport in a nationalist direction, as in the United States and Ireland, by developing native games. A doctor, Philippe Tissier, in 1888 founded the first non-Parisian sporting association, the Ligue Girondine de l'Education Physique in Bordeaux. All but Grousset were anglophiles, and their success at a time of relative anglophobia showed yet again that ill-feeling did not prevent fashionable emulation.

The pioneers made use of existing educational, religious and political networks. Tissier made rugby the sport of the south-west. Helped by the strong British presence at Bordeaux, Pau and Biarritz, he persuaded the republican education authorities to support rugby in state schools, not least to counter Church sponsorship of football. It is tempting to think that rugby has an affinity with the rugged masculine culture of the rural south – bull-fighting in the summer and scrums in the winter. It became an expression of fierce loyalties to city, to village, and to Basque, Béarnais and Provençal ethnicity. There is a chapel dedicated to Notre Dame du Rugby in a village in the Landes, with a stained glass window of the Madonna and Child holding a rugby ball and seemingly taking part in a celestial line-out. Today, the small Landes town of Saint Vincent de Tirosse, with seven clubs, can claim to be the capital of French rugby. By 1900, it had become the national game. In 1911, France won its first international, against Scotland. A new standard in fast, open play – the French style – was set by a former rowing club, Aviron Bayonnais, which dominated the game for years thanks to its Welsh fly-half and coach Owen Roe, who is commemorated by a stained-glass window in Biarritz's British church. This proudly Basque team popularized the regional beret – thus first establishing as fashionable for young men and women a hat often thought of by foreigners as universally French.

Boxing was another Anglo-Saxon import (the first Paris boxing hall in 1907 was named 'Wonderland' after its Whitechapel model), and it similarly became naturalized when Georges Carpentier beat 'Bombardier' Billy Wells for the world light-heavyweight championship in 1913. Boxing defied some stereotypes of Frenchness – 'All England had roared. A boxing Frenchman! It was the absurdest of paradoxes.' But other stereotypes were maintained: French commentators praised Charpentier for his skill, speed, courage and honour, in contrast to Anglo-Saxon brute force.[81] Soccer was small before the First World War, and at first almost entirely British. The first club, Standard Athletic, an anglophone enclave to this day, was founded by the employees of a British firm in Paris. The 1894 national championship was won by a team with ten British players. By 1914 there were only four fairly large clubs: Paris, Marseilles, Lille and Strasbourg. Popular interest was confined to the industrial north and the towns of the south-east.[82] The First World War was a watershed, owing to contacts with British soldiers and matches organized by the armies. Thereafter, the game expanded rapidly, though it remained less popular and less professionalized than in Britain or neighbouring Continental countries, and France was consequently unsuccessful in international competitions.

Cycling, athletics, team sports and boxing brought changes in social and cultural life, in dress and body shape, in gender relations, even in ideas. Yet as they were adopted, sports were transformed. Cycling is the best example. The first road races in the 1870s were dominated by upper-class British and French amateurs. But road racing was banned in Britain in 1896, and the sport declined. In France, it democratized as bicycles grew cheaper, and their manufacture became an important industry. Sponsoring races – both indoor and road – enabled manufacturers and new sporting newspapers to reach a growing market.[83] Cycle racing became France's first commercial spectator sport – and a highly exploitative and corrupt one. The Tour de France, its name recalling the traditional wanderings of the journeyman craftsman, and also the title of a best-selling patriotic children's book, became the first national sporting event. It was started in 1903 during the turbulent Dreyfus affair by the right-wing sporting paper *L'Auto* to scoop its political rivals. The race – a gruelling test of will and endurance on heavy gearless bicycles – became a celebration of France's unity in diversity, a lesson in history and geography, and an exciting taste of modernity for remote towns and villages on the route. People came 'out of the tavern' to cheer the riders 'as yesterday's crowds hailed the return of Napoleon's grizzled veterans from Spain and Austria.'[84]

Seen as a means of national regeneration, sport attracted intellectuals and artists. Sport expressed modernity, rebellion against tradition, and a new experience of the body. Avant-garde artists painted sporting subjects. Some of the most fashionable pre- and inter-war literary figures were enthusiasts, including the novelist Alain-Fournier, the writer and producer Jean Cocteau and the playwrights Jean Giraudoux and Henry de Montherlant. The poet Charles Péguy introduced football – played in the street – to his lycée at Orleans, and he took up rugby when he moved to Paris. Because of its nationalist and militarist associations – 'war is sport for real' – sport long remained a male activity, with women marginalized until well after the Second World War, except in tennis.

The First World War increased the appeal of sport, and superseded its upper-class anglophile origins. Political groups, and firms such as Peugeot and Michelin, took increasing interest. The southern mining town of Carmaux, with a history of violent labour relations, had two clubs, one Catholic and subsidized by the bosses, the other supported by the trade union. Such links intensified an already high level of violence on and off the pitch – knuckle-dusters were confiscated from the players in a schools soccer championship in 1905, and the France–Scotland rugby match in 1913 led to riots from which the English referee had to be rescued by the gendarmerie.[85] Uncontrollable violence in the 1920s led to the British, Dominions and Irish rugby unions breaking off relations. The French continued to play against Germany, Italy and Romania, whose authoritarian regimes took to rugby. But the game declined in France, and it was overtaken in popularity by football. Only under strong pressure from both governments did a British team agree to play France in January 1940 as a gesture of allied solidarity: it won 38–3.

The modern rise in popularity, quality and participation in French sport has very different foundations from the British system of plucky amateurism or commercial professionalism: namely, state support. Schoolteachers and soldiers had always played a part, but from the late 1930s, the central state increased its role. The left-wing Popular Front in 1936 began spending money on sports facilities, and this was greatly increased by the right-wing Vichy regime under its minister of sport, Jean Borotra, a Wimbledon champion. General de Gaulle took a personal interest in sports success in the 1960s. Effectively, sport was nationalized: the State took over the organization of major sporting events and the selection of national teams.[86] By the early twenty-first century, in Britain, there were ten civil servants involved in running sport; in France, 12,000. Sport, a predictable, rule-bound and repetitive activity, is one where bureaucracy can excel. As in the 1880s, national regeneration and prestige provide the motives for promoting both grass-roots participation through state-funded mass coaching (including skiing for schoolchildren and compulsory sport as part of the *baccalauréat* and university degree courses) and also advanced training facilities and financial support for international performers. In 2002, 83 per cent of the French between the ages of fifteen and seventy-five took part in some sporting activity, and 8 million in competitions.[87] This explains the success of French athletes in a range of sports, and the prominence of French-trained specialists in transforming the training, tactics, diet and discipline of professional British football teams – a piquant historical irony. If we consider the prominence of sport in French culture, the numbers participating in a wide variety of activities, and the high level of international achievement in a unique range of sports from rugby and football via tennis and athletics to skiing and ocean yachting, France could claim to be the world's most sporting nation. Britain, the sometime model, might just, on the same criteria, be thought a distant runner-up.

The one major British game the French do not play is cricket – their single rebellion against the Victorian sporting empire. There were attempts. The Standard Athletic Club had a ground just south of Paris, and in the 1900 Paris Olympics, France missed the only ever gold medal in cricket, losing to Devon County Wanderers. But from then to the present-day Fédération Française du Cricket, practically all players have been expatriates.[88] This absence should tell us something, but what? Did the Victorians mainly play their winter team games in France? Was there some socio-economic barrier? Unlike football, the urban sport par excellence, proper cricket needs sophisticated team organization, complex skills, a pitch, elaborate equipment, and leisure. Yet English children, like those in India, Pakistan and the Caribbean, play with bits of wood and stumps chalked on walls. Is there some uncrossable French cultural barrier, as has often been jokingly suggested? But rugby and boxing were far more alien practices. Cricket, on the contrary, would perfectly fit French self-images – subtlety, intelligence, dexterity, courage, elegance. Moreover, the cricketing ethos of sportsmanship, teamwork and self-control perfectly fitted the aspirations of anglophile educational reformers – *le fair-play* did indeed enter French vocabulary. The lone struggle of the batsman against overwhelming odds would have seemed admirable training for patriotic resistance to the Teutonic hordes. So let us regret the aristocratic Parisian batsmen and the terrifying Basque bowlers that never were. The sports historian Richard Holt suggests that cricket seemed insufficiently strenuous, even too plebeian for the likes of Coubertin, and too rooted in the pastoral idyll of the English village. The French equivalent of cricket is the Tour de France – a summer sport that is prolonged, tactical, unendurable for outsiders, and an excuse to sun-bathe.

Food and Civilization

Paris is the culinary centre of the world. All the great missionaries of good cookery have gone forth from it, and its cuisine was, is and ever will be the supreme expression of one of the great arts in the world.

The Gourmet's Guide to Europe (London, 1903)

If sport is Britain's great cultural export to France, the French have reciprocated with *la cuisine*. The British were 'always the primary audience for French food'.[89] There is the same conscious emulation; the same lamentation of one's own inferiority; and the same influence of fashion. There is even a connection with the fin-de-siècle obsession with decadence: for many cultural critics, the inferiority of English food was a symptom of aesthetic decline, proof of the rise of the philistine 'masses' and the horrors of urban life. As John Carey remarks, tinned food aroused particular ire among British intellectuals. The Bloomsbury critic Clive Bell lamented that there were 'but two or three restaurants in London where it is an unqualified pleasure to dine'.[90] French food, like its art and literature, was the cynosure of the cultivated Briton. However, the British have been less successful at internalizing (in all senses) French cuisine than the French with English sport. The history of French culinary influence in Britain is complex, and rather sad. The undoubted desire of the British social elite and their emulators to eat as well as the French has repeatedly turned to ashes in their mouths at home, and is a major cause of their pilgrimages, and even migrations, to rural France.

The restaurant, a Parisian development of the late-eighteenth century, was partly copied from London taverns – an aspect of contemporary anglomania. The first famous and successful example, opened at the Palais Royal in the 1780s by Beauvilliers, a former royal cook, was called La Grande Taverne de Londres. London at that time was a city where eating out was more established as a social activity than in Paris. This had been condemned as one of the barbarities of London life, where lodgings were inadequate for entertaining properly. The revolution boosted the Paris restaurant by abolishing remaining guild restrictions and creating new customers, including politicians and the new rich. What distinguished the restaurant from the tavern and the inn were its separate tables, relative privacy, and choice of dishes. There is some truth in the old story of cooks from the court and aristocratic houses opening restaurants, though they had done so before the revolution too.[91] Some came to London, notably Louis-Eustache Ude, formerly employed by Louis XVI, who cooked at Crockford's Club. Paradoxically, the revolution made the cooking of the court and the great nobility the basis of the new commercial *haute cuisine* – an aspect of the Old

Regime that France's new rulers did not repudiate. Some cooks became international celebrities, moving between private patrons, official households, and restaurants. The greatest was Antonin Carême, who cooked, among others, for Talleyrand, the Prince Regent, and the tsar. He laid down strict standards for *la haute cuisine*, a world away from domestic cooking, *la cuisine bourgeoise*. The summit of the style was artistically pretentious, lavishly expensive and visually impressive, with food being decoratively arranged and displayed on pedestals. On grand occasions there would be picturesque ruins carved from lard and Carême's particular speciality, miniature classical architecture in icing-sugar.

Throughout the nineteenth century this *haute cuisine*, hard on the purse and the arteries, became the speciality of the great Parisian restaurants, most of them neighbouring establishments at the Palais Royal and later on the boulevards – the Café Anglais, the Café de Paris, the Café Riche, the Maison Dorée, the Trois Frères Provençaux and (the only one that survives) the Grand Véfour. They created an autonomous form of inventive professional cooking, attracting customers by quality and constant innovation: *sauce béarnaise*, for example, comes from the boulevards, not the Pyrenees.[92] French *cuisine* was not, and is not, a single style, but a variety of styles to which skill and attention were applied by craftsmen in a cultural context in which food, like clothes and manners, was regarded as a badge of gentility. *Haute cuisine* became the epitome of elegance and excellence in food, and an important aspect of social prestige. Talleyrand used Carême's cooking as a diplomatic instrument, and the Paris Rothschilds used him as the 'principal attraction in this early phase of [their] social ascent', giving four grand dinners a week for the international aristocracy and diplomatic corps.[93] As Lady Morgan put it after one such occasion, this was 'an art form by which modern civilization is measured'.[94]

British tourists were an important part of restaurant clientèle. The 11th Duke of Hamilton even gave *haute cuisine* a martyr, when on 15 July 1863 he broke his neck falling down the stairs after a good dinner at the Maison Dorée. British lack of taste, some said, lowered standards – though these were defended by a superb waiter at the famous Voisin's, who one Christmas told a British customer asking for plum pudding that 'The House of Voisin does not serve, has never served, and will never serve plum pudding.'[95] French cooks, exclusively male, rigorously trained, organized, articulate and imperialistic, were in demand all over the world. One of the most famous, Alexis Soyer, chef of London's Reform Club, became a prominent Victorian dandy, entrepreneur and character, organizing soup kitchens for the poor in London and Ireland during the 1840s, and eventually working alongside Florence Nightingale in the Crimea to improve the nutrition of the troops. London became the principal annexe of *haute cuisine*. Yet London, in the mid nineteenth century, had practically no restaurants, with the exception of a few in Soho – smoky, noisy and alarmingly foreign – run by and for expatriates. London had, of course, many eating places, from pubs at one end of the spectrum to gentlemen's clubs at the other. The latter (notably Crockford's and the Reform) provided some of the best food in London, and fulfilled some of the functions of Paris restaurants, where it was similarly not customary for men to go with their wives. Unlike in London clubs, however, they could go with other women, and the private rooms of boulevard restaurants were famous for more than gastronomic pleasures. The other British shrines to *haute cuisine* were a few aristocratic houses, and one or two hotels. This difference between London and Paris (where in 1890 some 10,000 people worked in the restaurant trade) reflects Paris's unique importance as a tourist centre. It also reflects a difference already noted. London's development emphasized domestic comfort, space and privacy, with the growth of suburban houses – the ecology of that English phenomenon, the dinner party. Most Parisians lived in relatively small flats or furnished rooms, and dined and entertained in a range of eating-places, from the cheap to the hugely expensive. So Paris had a large, highly professional food trade, whereas most English professional cooks, poorly trained and badly paid, worked for families.

This had two consequences for British eating habits. First, the most prestigious food was French, and this is what the best cooks tried to produce – and many mediocre ones too. English 'country-house' cooking had been considered until the end of the eighteenth century equally prestigious and in some respects of better quality than the French. The last important English cookery books in this tradition date from the eighteenth century, such as Elizabeth Raffald's *The Experienced English Housekeeper* (1769).[96] Thereafter it was, in Stephen Mennell's term, 'decapitated',[97] with declining respect, and without well-trained professional cooks to set standards and innovate, as French restaurant chefs did through cookery books, lectures and the press. During the nineteenth century, a derivative, 'bastardized', pseudo-French style became common, in which the appearance of Frenchness was more important than the substance.[98] When between 1860 and 1880 large modern restaurants such as the Café Royal and the Criterion did open in London, this was what they offered, though without equalling the effort or skill of their Parisian models.

English native cookery survived in vestigial form in cheaper eating places, or was relegated to the home. But domestic cooking, often for upwardly mobile families with limited means, epitomized by Mrs Beeton's mid-century collection, began to emphasize economy, short-cuts, the basic and the safe. The economical use of leftovers became a major theme – one consequence of the prominence in English cooking of large roast joints.

British cooks suddenly reversed their eighteenth-century practice and began over-cooking meat and vegetables – whereas the French, under the older British influence, now did the opposite. The ostensible reason was hygiene, preached by the German chemist Justus von Liebig, but it may be that gentility was also at work: bloody meat and flavoursome vegetables were not quite 'nice'. So Britain ended up with the worst of both worlds: the prestige of French *haute cuisine* led to the neglect of native traditions, but only a tiny minority actually ate genuine French-style food, whose influence was always more aspirational than real. The middle-class French ambassador Paul Cambon was shocked by Queen Victoria's 'detestable' food at Windsor: 'in my household such a dinner would not have been tolerated'.[99] Less august British families were condemned to the rissoles-and-boiled-cabbage style of English cooking at home; and if they went out, to food 'cooked without care [and] given a French title because it was thought the diner would be conned into thinking it better'.[100] No wonder they tried to get it over with quickly and talk as little about it as possible. Not all of this, of course, can be explained as a perverse effect of French influence. Urbanization, the rise of convenience foods, imports, and the baleful effects of an incompetent and greedy catering trade also had a strong, early and lasting effect on British tastebuds.[*]

The great Georges Auguste Escoffier came to the rescue in 1890, and for a generation ran the kitchens of the Savoy Hotel and later the Carlton as the prototypes of modern, efficient cooking. He made London the headquarters of a new 'French' cuisine. One stunt was to prepare an 'epicurean dinner' at the Cecil Hotel, and have it simultaneously served to hundreds of diners in thirty-seven Continental cities.[101] Escoffier rewrote the rules of professional cooking, and standardized it worldwide. Traditional *haute cuisine* had become too staid, too expensive, too fattening, even too inedible. Escoffier simplified, rationalized and modernized it for an expanding international clientele, largely tourists in the big new seaside and city hotels. His *Guide Culinaire* (1903) became the bible of what was later called 'international hotel and restaurant cooking' – Sole Véronique and Pêche Melba are perhaps his most famous creations. Escoffier's fans (including the Prince of Wales) took little notice when he was sacked by the Savoy in 1898 for peculation gross beyond even the usual standards of the trade.[102] An artist, after all, had to be excused his foibles.

Escoffier's greatest innovation was to bring enriched versions of French provincial cooking into the professional repertoire. Previously, country food had been at best considered a dubious oddity. Paris's only important

---

[*] When first in France, RT remembers being asked by the mother of a French friend how the English made *crème anglaise*. She expected tips about vanilla pods and egg yolks; he had to admit to Bird's Custard Powder.

restaurant with regional connections, Les Trois Frères Provençaux, soon dropped nearly all its Mediterranean dishes. In Alexandre Dumas's exhaustive *Grand Dictionnaire de cuisine*, written in 1869, there is no mention of such subsequent staples as *cassoulet*, *boeuf bourguignon*, *coq au vin*, *poulet à la basquaise* or *choucroûte à l'alsacienne* – though there *is* plum pudding, 'very widespread in France in recent years'.[103]

The discovery of French country cooking was an important aspect of the discovery of rural France mentioned earlier. The British were pioneers. *The Gourmet's Guide to Europe* (1903), by Lieut. Col. Nathaniel Newnham-Davis, an early food journalist, and Algernon Bastard, provided one of the earliest surveys. Unlike Henry James, who twenty years earlier had pronounced *gras double* 'a light grey, glutinous, nauseating mess', the *Guide* found *tripes à la mode de Caen* 'a homely dish, but it is not to be despised'. Only Paris and the holiday regions on the coasts and in the Pyrenees were covered; the whole of inland France, even Lyon, France's second culinary city, was *terra incognita* to the authors and their readers. Caen was 'an oasis in the midst of the bad cookery of Western Normandy'. Roquefort, the cheese town, the authors confused with Rochefort, the seaport. They described *brandade* as 'codfish stew', and *confit* as 'a sort of goose stew, utterly unlike anything you have ever tasted before'. Relatively intrepid as the *Guide* was, it periodically warned its readers to steel themselves for exposure to garlic and other strong tastes and odours.[104]

Parisians only began to take an interest in provincial cooking in the 1920s and 30s, with the growth of motoring and the *Guide Michelin*. The upside-down caramelized apple tart accidentally invented near Orleans by the Demoiselles Tatin, for example, was discovered and publicized by the first encyclopedia of provincial food, *La France Gastronomique*, in the 1930s.[105] This made those maiden ladies immortal – even commemorated, in anaemic, reduced-cholesterol form, in the frozen-food sections of British supermarkets. The vogue for traditional peasant food arguably came to France as late as the 1970s.

Provincial cooking has been the aspect of French cuisine that has most influenced British eating habits – even if *cassoulet* might be thereby transformed into 'some pieces of old sausage warmed up with beans'. This is fitting, because provincial cuisine owed its development largely to tourism. Poverty meant that everyday French peasant food, as in England, was poor, monotonous and badly prepared; it often still is. Vegetable soup – the *soupe maigre* mocked by Gillray – was the main staple, thickened with stale bread. Good food was 'a costly luxury . . . an indulgence which is not for them.'[106] Only on special occasions were festive dishes prepared, and they were eaten somewhat more frequently by prosperous peasant farmers, artisans and the rural middle classes. These dishes were the main source of the provincial specialities discovered by tourists in the early twentieth century, provided in rural inns that smartened themselves into hotels and restaurants for the tourist trade, and eventually universalized by the Escoffier school. After the rigours of the Second World War, Patience Gray, Elizabeth David and their successors made the ability to cook like an idealized French grandmother an aspiration for smart metropolitan Englishwomen, hinting at hedonistic Mediterranean summers.

One British writer quipped that it was as if Paris society had gone mad for Lancashire hot-pot.[107] That this is funny shows how much had changed even since the mid nineteenth century, when French gourmets admitted to liking *le rosbif, le plumpouding* and other goodies. By the 1920s, not even British gourmets were interested. When the English Folk Cookery Association tried to collect and promote traditional British recipes, they were discouraged by professional caterers and British gastronomes, both equally francocentric. It is safe to bet that no folk recipes crossed the Channel from north to south. Probably the only major book by a Frenchman on English cooking, *La Cuisine anglaise*, was published in 1894 by Alfred Suzanne, who had spent his career cooking for the British nobility. His intention was not to introduce French eaters to the delights of steak and kidney pudding and spotted dick, but to instruct French chefs working in England on how to give their employers the occasional nursery-style treat – though Frenchified by the addition of 'refinement and the cachet of good taste'.[108]

Nevertheless it seems clear – though rarely remarked on – that British tastes, refined or not, transformed French eating habits, through fashion, through their effect on Parisian and later provincial restaurants catering to tourists, and through French cooks who spent time working in England. Beef, in the eighteenth century considered an English speciality, became 'sovereign' in nineteenth-century Parisian haute cuisine.[109] Carême served *rosbif à l'anglaise*, while French-sounding dishes such as *selle de mouton* and *faisans rôtis* served at the Reform Club[110] and on the Paris boulevards seem suspiciously English in substance. Underdone grilled and roasted meat, barbarously English in the eighteenth century, became naturalized. We have seen (see above, page 316) how steak arrived. The *tartine à l'anglaise*, the card-table snack of the Earl of Sandwich (gambler, lecher and able First Lord of the Admiralty), spread during the nineteenth century. French gourmets adapted these imports to their own tastes. Alexandre Dumas devised elaborate instruction for the proper preparation of sandwiches. Although he agreed with the English choice of the 'infinitely more tasty' rump for steaks ('it must be eaten in English taverns') over the French preference for insipid *aloyau* (fillet), he noted the poverty of English sauces, and suggested adorning *le bifteck* with truffles or crayfish butter. Dumas in 1869 described saddle of lamb *à l'anglaise* as 'much prized by those Parisian gourmets in whom our

217 years of war with England have not inspired an inveterate horror of all that comes from across the Channel'.[111] In the provinces, however, peasants 'had a profound feeling of disgust for mutton'.[112] But a century later, that English staple *gigot rôti* had become France's favourite dish among all ages, social groups and political tendencies – twice as popular as the quintessentially French *pot-au-feu*, and most popular of all among peasants. And whisky had become more popular than Armagnac or Calvados.*

Perhaps we might end by sagely recalling the vanity of human ambitions. The British Empire survives mainly in sport. French aspirations to universal cultural influence were only really achieved at the table. But now British football teams depend on Frenchmen, while London is hailed (though not by President Chirac) as the capital of world gastronomy. Worse still, French home cooks have resorted to Jamie Oliver's *Rock 'n roll cuisine* and Delia Smith's *La Cuisine facile d'aujourd'hui*.

On the Brink, 1898–1902

France in general is off its head . . . a standing danger and menace to Europe.
SIR EDMUND MONSON, British ambassador, February 1898[113]

England is the most domineering and violent of countries.
THÉOPHILE DELCASSÉ, foreign minister, April 1900[114]

Three simultaneous crises – the Fashoda incident, the Dreyfus affair and the Boer war – made Franco-British relations worse at the turn of the century than they had been for at least fifty years, with extremes of vituperation, and even, many feared, the danger of war. All three crises were connected to the pervading fear of decline. The two African episodes stemmed from the urgent desire of both France and Britain to consolidate their imperial power before challenges from newer rivals, Germany, Russia, Japan and America, became too great. The Dreyfus affair grew directly from French fears of both external and internal threat. The belief of one prominent French nationalist was that 'a gang of free-masons, Jews and foreigners are trying, by discrediting the army, to hand over our country to the English and the Germans'.[115] The British interpretation was that France was decadent indeed.

---

* Survey in the magazine *Cuisines et Vins de France*, September 1984. Gigot was most popular among Gaullists, and least among Communists. The preferred composite meal consisted of: oysters, smoked salmon, leg of lamb, Camembert (those epicurean Communists preferred Roquefort!) and strawberry charlotte. This is not a very traditional French meal, though somewhat less cosmopolitan than the British love of curry – which was, however, already established in the eighteenth century.

In 1894, Captain Alfred Dreyfus, one of the few Jewish officers in the French army, was found guilty by court martial of spying for Germany, and sentenced to degradation and life in solitary confinement on tiny Devil's Island, off French Guiana. British observers considered this treason a symptom of French rottenness, but had no inkling that Dreyfus was innocent or that France was on the verge of a profound crisis. This only began to emerge three years later, when the Dreyfus family (who had engaged a firm of London detectives) discovered that a disreputable swashbuckler with expensive tastes, Commandant Esterhazy, was the real traitor. The embassy in Paris soon informed London that Dreyfus was in fact innocent, and had suffered owing to a 'diabolical conspiracy' by the army, supported by a 'fanatical and anti-Semitic public'.[116] The affair only engaged British opinion, however, in January 1898, when Esterhazy was acquitted by court martial – a verdict of 'really surprising perversity', thought *The Times*. The Prince of Wales concluded that 'there is evidently some mystery wh[ich] the French govt do not wish should be made public'.[117] This was too generous a view: the only secrets being hidden were the prejudice and corruption of the general staff. As this became increasingly clear, British press comment grew more and more scathing, as the French government officially complained. The scandal broke when an intelligence officer was found to have forged the evidence incriminating Dreyfus, and committed suicide. Dreyfus, in bad health from his harsh treatment, was retried at Rennes by a new court martial in August and September 1899. So great was the interest that the queen asked the lord chief justice to attend and report to her. When Dreyfus was again found guilty there was a storm of protest, not only in Britain but across the world: Dreyfus, it has been said, became the most famous Frenchman since Napoleon.[118]

British reactions were heightened by knowledge that Dreyfus's persecutors were anglophobic nationalists, who accused Britain and Germany of funding the Dreyfusard campaign. The Fashoda incident in November 1898 seemed to show their bellicosity. A military coup in France (as attempted, though with farcical incompetence, in February 1899) would be dangerous for Britain, because, warned the ambassador, a nationalist regime would try 'to divert attention by a foreign quarrel from the contemplation of internal discord and disgrace'.[119] Queen Victoria was particularly indignant at the 'monstrous horrible sentence against the poor martyr Dreyfus', as she put it to the prime minister Lord Salisbury, and she repeated similar sentiments in an unciphered telegram to the Paris embassy, which, as she must have expected, was leaked to the press. She also cancelled her regular holiday in France – regarded by both governments (and the tourist trade) as an important token of good relations.[120] The queen's outrage was shared by most of her subjects. British tourists stayed away. Businesses considered boycotting

the 1900 Exposition. The British Association for the Advancement of Science was urged to cancel the forthcoming Franco-British congress at Boulogne. A French honeymoon couple were ordered out of their Lake District hotel. The French ambassador was bombarded with protests, and he demanded that the government should deploy 3,000 policemen to prevent the tricolour from being insulted at a mass rally at Hyde Park of some 50,000 people.

British Dreyfusards found their prejudices about French decadence confirmed. The persecution of Dreyfus, they thought, was the culmination of France's long history of cruelty and oppression. The rights of the individual were not respected by the State, the mob, or the press. French civilization, declared *Blackwood's Magazine* (October 1899), was 'a mere external skin, veneering a body corrupt, decaying and ready to perish'. Not all accepted this picture. The main exceptions seem to have been Catholics, who saw the Dreyfus affair as an indirect attack by the Left on the Church. They including the lord chief justice, Lord Russell of Killowen, a Dubliner whose report on the Rennes trial to the queen was markedly cool towards the 'mean-looking' Dreyfus.[121] The other main group that did not share the nation's Dreyfusard fervour were anti-semitic socialists, who, caught between their detestation of 'reactionists', the 'rascally Jew press', 'self-righteous Pharisees' in Britain, and 'our ultra-German royal family', got 'heartily sick of the Dreyfus case'. Besides, the British, starting a war in South Africa as 'the hirelings of a ravenous horde of Jewish diamond thieves', had no right to preach.[122] Overall, the agitation over Dreyfus served to confirm the widespread view, not only in Britain, that France was unstable and degenerate. However, in June 1899 a moderately Dreyfusard 'government of republican defence' took office, including radicals, a socialist, and republicans such as the Prince of Wales's crony General de Galliffet. It was greeted with relief as being composed of 'honest and upright men' and friends of Britain – practically synonymous concepts. They pardoned Dreyfus, who was subsequently exonerated.

At the height of the Dreyfus crisis, on 10 July 1898, eight French and 120 Senegalese soldiers raised the tricolour over the ruined fort of Fashoda, on the Sudanese upper Nile, after a testing two-year journey from French West Africa. For even such a small party to travel through central Africa, a huge effort had been required, above all by thousands of porters and paddlers, 'any man or women we could find', often requisitioned by force, who manhandled equipment and supplies. These included 100,000 rounds of ammunition, 16 tons of coloured beads, 70,000 metres of coloured cloth, 10 tons of rice, 5 tons of corned beef, 1 ton of coffee (though only 50 kilos of tea), a mechanical piano, 1,300 litres of claret, 50 bottles of Pernod absinthe, brandy, champagne and a very unsuitable little steamboat, which often had to be dismantled and dragged through the bush, sometimes at a rate of only 300 yards per day. Yet they reached their objective, despite mosquitoes, crocodiles, angry hippopotami and understandably fearful natives ('It was no use even shooting or hanging those that were caught . . . Sometimes the whole population would flee, in which case I would set fire to one or two huts. This generally brought everyone back . . . It is the only way to get anything from these brutes').[123]

The plans of the expedition were undefined, other than to annoy the British in Egypt – it was 'a deliberate attempt on the part of responsible authorities across the Channel to oppose us'.[124] The Sudan, originally governed by Egypt, had since 1882 been in the hands of an Islamic 'Mahdi', who had expelled the Egyptians and killed their governor, the British General Gordon, in 1885. In 1898, an Anglo-Egyptian army under General Kitchener was defeating the Mahdist forces and bringing the Sudan under Anglo-Egyptian control. French nationalists had not forgiven the original occupation of Egypt, and the British now had the gall to use it as a base for further expansion. Marchand's expedition was a rash attempt to block this move by establishing a presence and trying to win support among the Mahdists, or local inhabitants, or independent Abyssinia. Fanciful plans had long been floated for building dams on the upper Nile that could hold Egypt to ransom and force the British to make concessions – though given the difficulty of moving even the mechanical piano to the Nile, building dams would have been an interesting challenge. In brief, the French hoped to stir up enough trouble to force the calling of an international conference on the future of Egypt, and hence shake Britain's grip on the country. Three weeks after Marchand reached Fashoda, Kitchener's army of 26,000 men crushed the Mahdist army on 2 September 1898 at Omdurman. The French press applauded this as a victory for civilization. But on 18 September Kitchener arrived in person at Fashoda with five gunboats, a company of the Cameron Highlanders, and two battalions of Sudanese. 'Our poor Froggies are virtually our prisoners, they cannot budge a step,' noted one officer.[125] Kitchener's instructions were to remove them by persuasion.

Oscar Wilde observed that life imitates art, and the confrontation between Kitchener and Marchand was a Franco-British pantomime. Observers with binoculars saw Marchand gesticulating, and Kitchener being phlegmatic. Kitchener gave him a whisky and soda: 'one of the greatest sacrifices I ever made for my country was to drink that horrible smoky alcohol'. When Kitchener returned the visit, Marchand's men were in new uniforms carefully carried across Africa. Toasts were drunk in sweet, warm champagne. Kitchener noticed that the French had planted a garden – 'Flowers at Fashoda! Oh these Frenchmen!' Kitchener warned Marchand's officers that France was too occupied with other matters to give them support, and to prove it left copies of French newspapers giving details of the Dreyfus affair, which the French expedition knew nothing about: 'an hour after we opened the French newspapers [we] were trembling and weeping.'[126]

In both countries, news of the distant confrontation provoked self-righteous emotion. Neither side wanted war, but for a time both took the possibility seriously. The French hoped that the British would offer a deal. Instead, they strengthened their Mediterranean fleet. The French, fearing a Copenhagen-style surprise attack to destroy their fragile navy, agreed to withdraw Marchand unconditionally. He pluckily insisted on marching out through Abyssinia rather than steaming comfortably down the Nile in British gunboats. Fortunately, the soldiers on the spot generally got on well. Kitchener spoke French, having served as a volunteer in the French army in 1871. As Marchand left, the British presented him with a captured Mahdist flag and played the 'Marseillaise'.

Marchand returned home a hero, and French politicians claimed a moral victory. Winston Churchill agreed: 'Happy the nation that can produce such men. Dark though her fortunes, and vexed though her politics may be, while France can find soldiers like Marchand . . . her citizens need not despair.' Many French politicians realized their narrow escape: 'We have behaved like madmen in Africa,' exclaimed the President. Colonial enthusiasts realized that their policy of confrontation with Britain had failed, and they became early advocates of an *entente*. Yet bitterness at the humiliation remained, as Charles de Gaulle, then eight years old, later recalled: 'Nothing saddened me more profoundly than our weaknesses and our mistakes, as revealed to my childhood gaze . . . : the surrender of Fashoda, the Dreyfus case, social conflicts, religious strife.'[127]

EXILES: OSCAR WILDE AND EMILE ZOLA

Oscar Wilde entered Pentonville prison in 1895 within a month of Alfred Dreyfus's arrival on Devil's Island. Wilde's ordeal, beginning with his imprudent libel case against the Marquess of Queensberry in 1894 for calling him a 'somdomite' [sic], led to his prosecution for sex with teenage rent-boys. He had refused to flee to France, as people in scrapes traditionally did. His fate was widely reported there, and relished by anglophobes. 'What joy to see your nose out of joint, Old England,' wrote the fashionable writer Willy. The sordid details, declared the *Echo de Paris*, 'would never be made public in any French court' – anyway, such things did not happen in France. Members of Edmond de Goncourt's literary circle speculated that English sexual proclivities were 'engendered by Anglo-Saxon furniture, and the increase in pederasty brought about by Liberty fabrics'; or perhaps the problem was that English women were made skinny and 'mannish' by sport. Whatever the explanation, coming from 'perfidious Albion' the scandal was 'particularly pleasant to French ears', thought *La Lanterne*, and 'the whiff of this filth is for us the perfume of vengeance', proving that the decadent English 'have more urgent need of purification than us'. It also provided a weapon in literary feuds. *Le Figaro* began to publish the names of Wilde's Paris acquaintances. The poet Catulle Mendès denied friendship with Wilde, 'whose talent I respect very little', and fought a duel with a journalist who suggested otherwise. Wilde's sentence of two years' hard labour was hypocritical as well as barbarous, said the French, because much of English high society shared Wilde's sexual preferences: 'London is closer to Sodom than Cairo or Naples.' So 'the disgust I feel for the aesthete I also feel for those who have condemned him', wrote Mendès. The *Echo de Paris* stigmatized England for the 'frightful brutality . . . of its gaols and labour camps . . . We are rather more generous and kind in our country of France', where Wilde would find defenders. One of them exclaimed 'With what joy should I see Pentonville in flames . . . on behalf of all of us pagan artists and writers.' However, if indignation with England was strong, sympathy for Wilde was limited. Many leading writers, including Zola, declined to sign a petition for clemency. The avant-garde theatre director Lugné-Poë did however put on *Salomé* during Wilde's imprisonment. On his release in 1897 he crossed the Channel, staying first near Dieppe, where he organized a party for the diamond jubilee of Queen Victoria. But he was ordered out of a restaurant and threatened with expulsion by the sub-prefect, and so moved to the more anonymous world of Paris.[128]

Emile Zola was as notorious a writer as Wilde. He published his famous open letter, *J'accuse*, on 13 January 1898, two days after the Rennes court-martial, and a month before Wilde sought refuge in Paris. His letter accused the army, ministers and the clergy of conniving in the punishment of an innocent man. He was prosecuted for insulting the army, and, amid riots and threats, sentenced to a year's imprisonment – a reminder that the freedom to write about sex did not extend as far in politics. The British ambassador reported that 'there are many people who declare that his acquittal would produce a revolution or at least a Jewish massacre'.[129] Zola fled to England. His reputation for quasi-pornography meant that many suspected his motives: he was accused of using the agitation to revive his flagging career. Yet sympathy for Dreyfus was so overwhelming that public attitudes changed. *The Times* soon hailed Zola as a new Voltaire. Rather than allowing himself to be fêted or taking part in Dreyfusard protests, he kept his movements secret to avoid being officially served notice of his conviction and sentence. He lived mainly in a rented house in Weybridge, protected by his faithful publisher Vizetelly. As well as using a grammar book to plough through accounts of *l'Affaire* in the *Telegraph* and the *Standard*, he kept busy cycling through the lanes, and writing another novel, *La Fécondité*.[130]

Wilde also lived quietly in Paris, where he spent most of the remaining months of his life. It was a miserable time. Parisian society was shocked by open homosexuality, and decadence was no longer so fashionable: they 'licked my conqueror's boots only ten years ago' but 'everyone cuts me now'. One who did seek his company was Commandant Esterhazy. This bizarre encounter inspired some of Wilde's silliest pronouncements. 'The innocent must always suffer . . . it is their *métier*,' he reassured Esterhazy. 'The interesting thing surely is to be guilty and wear as a halo the seduction of sin.'[131] At times he was reduced to cadging drinks and asking near strangers for money in the street. He was kept going by the generosity of the owner of the then humble Left Bank Hôtel d'Alsace, in the Rue des Beaux-Arts, where he died of meningitis in November 1900.

The Boer war, which began in 1899, offered the French an opportunity for a dazzling political and moral revenge over their British rivals. Britain had sought to bring the two Boer republics, the Orange Free State and the Transvaal, to heel. The reason was not overweening imperial arrogance, but fear. London believed that the Pretoria government, rich with gold from the Rand ('the Boers have arms and ammunition enough to shoot down all the armies of Europe'), was aiming to destroy British predominance in southern Africa, with French and German support. This would not only threaten the vital Cape sea-route to Asia, but show the world that Britain was no longer the dominant power. Imperialists, led by the colonial secretary Joseph Chamberlain, believed that this was their last opportunity to check Britain's decline by creating an imperial confederation strong enough to withstand the growing power of Russia, Germany and the United States – any of whom might ally with the eternal mischief-maker, France. 'What is now at stake is the position of Great Britain in South Africa, and with it the estimate of our power and influence in our colonies and throughout the world.'[132]

Sympathy for the Boers' resistance, joy at their early successes, disappointment at their setbacks, and outrage at British treatment of women and children (of whom thousands died in 'concentration camps') was worldwide. The exceptions were Africans and their sympathizers, who hoped that a British victory would protect them against the Boers, and who played a major part in their eventual defeat. In France, admiration for the Boers' self-proclaimed 'struggle against the new world tyranny of Capitalism'[133] united nationalists who detested the British and the Jews; socialists who detested imperialism and capitalism; conservatives who admired a patriarchal white race of peasant-farmers; and republicans who respected self-determination. Ladies wore slouch hats *à la Boer*. The military cadets at Saint-Cyr christened their 1900 cohort 'Transvaal'. At the 1900 Paris Exposition, one of the most popular exhibits was a Boer farmhouse. Hardly any Frenchman doubted that the war was due to 'the insatiable appetites of the City gold merchants'.[134] This fitted the old belief that 'only financial interest counts for an Englishman'. The French had the rest of Europe on their side, and a chance to harm those who had humiliated them in Egypt and Fashoda and insulted them over the Dreyfus affair: 'That tricolour flag pulled down at Fashoda and torn up in London has been carried to Pretoria by French volunteers.'[135]

Those volunteers (including a prince of the deposed French royal family, and a descendant of Charette, the Chouan leader of the 1790s) went to join a picturesque International Legion some 1,600 strong, among them Russians, Germans, Dutch, Irish, Van Gogh's brother, the Pope's nephew and Graf von Zeppelin. They were commanded by a French officer, Colonel the Comte de Villebois-Mareuil. *L'Evénement* wrote, 'Like Lafayette [he showed] that

France was the protector of the weak, and that no one asked in vain for the help of its sword and shield.'[136] People who take extreme positions on faraway issues of which they know little are generally motivated by matters closer to home. So it was with Villebois-Mareuil. The son of an old military family, he was a ferocious anti-Dreyfusard and a co-founder of the nationalist Action Française. Disgust over the Dreyfus affair caused him to resign his commission and offer his services to the Boers. This, he hoped, would in some degree vindicate the honour of France and its army. 'France,' he declared, 'is treated with contempt by other nations . . . decadence and cosmopolitan customs witness the end of a nation's genius.'[137] He appeared to be a stereotypical French hero: his admiring cousin, the playwright Edmond Rostand, may have used him, with his bristling imperial whiskers and taste for grandiloquent proclamations, as a model for his *Cyrano de Bergerac* (1897). Yet there were unexpected sides to him. He was known as an anglophile, spoke good English, had his clothes made in London, and had an English governess for his daughter. He knew Oscar Wilde and the Prince of Wales, and was a friend of the writer J.E.C. Bodley, whose important book on France he had begun translating, and at whose Biarritz house he was entertained just before leaving for Africa.

The exploits of Villebois-Mareuil and the International Legion were brief. He was determined to prove the Legion's worth to the sceptical Boers, who found the European volunteers rather a nuisance. So he led 600 men on a reckless raid in April 1900, ignoring information about superior enemy forces. Lord Methuen and a force of imperial yeomanry surrounded them. Dug in on a *kopje*, Villebois-Mareuil refused to surrender, and when the British finally charged he managed to shoot Sergeant Patrick Campbell (husband of the famous actress) before himself being killed. This futile little fiasco, far from causing mockery or outrage against what might now be considered 'illegal combatants' – who were expecting to be shot – produced a lavish display of chivalrousness. At Villebois-Mareuil's funeral ('too sad for words' wrote Methuen) the Legion's second-in-command, another French nobleman, the Comte de Bréda, declared that 'we are prisoners of an army which is the bravest of the brave'. Methuen paid for the headstone, and wrote expressing 'my sympathy and the sympathy of my comrades' to Villebois-Mareuil's daughter: 'we all regret the death of an accomplished and gallant soldier but he preferred death to becoming a prisoner'. The Frenchman's horse was brought back to England as a cherished trophy, and now has its own memorial plaque on a Buckinghamshire village green. The French volunteers were relieved to find that their captors were 'young people of very good family, and nearly all of them members of Oxford University'. One English major 'treats us with great kindness and speaks French very well, having studied at the Lycée Sainte-Barbe'. Many were released, including Bréda. Those less lucky ended up following in Napoleon's footsteps to St Helena.[138] In France, Villebois-Mareuil became a hero. In 1971 his body was ceremoniously reburied in the Boer national cemetery, in the presence of a French government envoy – one of the last gestures of European solidarity with Afrikaner nationalism.

During these eventful years the British and French came close to being enemies, and were, as we shall see, very ready to imagine themselves as such. But however sharp the verbal exchanges, personal relations even at points of confrontation seem lacking in bitterness and real hatred. On both sides, resentment in some circles was balanced by admiration in others. Perhaps so much cultural and personal contact created a wish for better relations. There were substantial economic ties. There were political affinities as Europe's most democratic and liberal Great Powers. Certainly, a sense was growing that in some contexts, Britain and France ought to be on the same side.

IMAGINING THE ENEMY

Invasion scares and fictions about war were nothing new, but the 1890s and 1900s were the heyday of war fantasy novels in England and France. The leading practitioners were the Anglo–French fantasist and amateur spy William Le Queux, and the nationalist French officer Captain Emile Driant. Serialized in new mass-circulation papers such as Alfred Harmsworth's *Daily Mail*, they reached huge readerships, and were also adapted for the stage. One of Le Queux's books was translated into twenty-seven languages and sold a million copies. Harmsworth insisted on accounts of bloody battles in as many places as possible to attract local readers. Hull, Birmingham, Glasgow, Eastbourne, London and many others were fictitiously bombarded and invaded, with street names and buildings tediously listed, and actual local Volunteer units and their commanders being heroically massacred in print. The alarmist tone of British writing was not accidental. In an international system now divided into alliances, Britain stood alone. 'We are an object of envy and greed to all the other Powers,' lamented the secretary of state for India in 1901.[139] Pessimists imagined Britain as one day 'a crippled island under the heel of a despotic military government, a tributary state of less consequence than Bulgaria, and a people crushed, ruined and enslaved'.[140]

If English books were nightmares of vulnerability, French books were fantasies of revenge. In the very successful *Plus d'Angleterre* (1887) – *Down with England* in its translated edition – a war over Egypt ends with France depriving Britain of its colonies and confiscating the Elgin marbles.[141] Driant, writing as 'Capitaine Danrit', produced several popular novels describing war against England, culminating in the three-volume *La Guerre fatale:*

France–Angleterre (1902–3). This 'inevitable war' was against British world economic domination. Its hero, Henri d'Argonne, is a predestined anglophobe, being of Breton descent and engaged to a red-haired Irish beauty, Maud Carthy (based on Maud Gonne, an extreme Irish nationalist familiar in French pro-Boer and anti-semitic circles). Driant drew on familiar themes: Britain is 'Carthage' exploiting the world, but is far weaker than it appears. The French land at Deal and take London, where they are welcomed by downtrodden English workers. They blow up the 'Waterloo Column', distribute the Empire to more deserving nations, free Ireland, and levy a 10 billion franc indemnity. To perpetuate British subjection, they make them build a Channel tunnel, garrisoned by French soldiers. Although Driant began to write about war with Germany from 1906 onwards, and was said to have retracted his anglophobia, as late as 1908 a new edition of *La Guerre fatale* claimed that anglophobia had 'spread throughout the mass of the [French] population, despite official pressure and the trickery of the entente cordiale'.

Though these fictions were shocking and gory, and necessarily show foreign governments as scheming and ruthless, they did not generally go in for stimulating visceral national hatred. Even Le Queux's French master spy, Gaston La Touche, though a 'fiendish' and 'pitiless' villain, is also 'easy-going, devil-may-care', possessing 'iron nerve and muscles that rendered him practically invulnerable in a tussle' and full of 'droll stories which convulsed his companions with laughter'.[142] Tracy, another popular author, refers to 'the splendid spirit of the French soldier'.[143] There is little heavy caricaturing of the enemy, as was to be common in twentieth-century war fiction, and no lingering over atrocities. The French army is shown as efficient, gallant and patriotic, though often gratifyingly ready to admit British superiority. When a doughty Cockney cyclist is captured by Zouaves and threatened with shooting as a spy, his defiant cry that 'La Hongletaire est la première nation de la monde' [*sic*] has the French muttering 'Sacré bleu, c'est vrai!' and releasing him with a hearty handshake.[144]

The most significant feature of these stories is that they signalled a change of enemies. In 1890s publications, the French and their Russian allies are always the invaders. Hordes of Cossacks and Zouaves come sailing from the Baltic or charging through a Channel tunnel. The United States and Italy are usually cast as friendly or neutral, and Australians, Canadians and the Indian army – even sometimes Germany – figure as last-minute saviours. In one story a surprise attack by France and Russia is triggered by the signature of an Anglo-German alliance. In the 1900s, the line-up changed, owing to fears about German naval expansion. In the best written work of the genre, Erskine Childers's sensational success *The Riddle of the Sands* (1903), the German navy plots a surprise invasion one misty morning from the soggy coast of Frisia. This was plausible enough for the Admiralty to investigate.

It found the danger illusory – as had the Germans themselves, who had drafted an experimental invasion plan in 1896. The importance of Childers's book and others that followed lay in reiterating that Germany was now the danger, and hence that France and Britain were potential allies. Their French counterparts did the same, eventually even fire-breathing anglophobes such as 'Capitaine Danrit'.

These stories were absurd, but not wholly absurd. The sudden outbreak of war in 1914 due to a Balkan assassination, Germany's surprise attack through Belgium, naval bombardment of Hull and Lowestoft, and the sinking by submarines of British cruisers in the Channel would have seemed very familiar to keen readers of Le Queux or Danrit. Moreover, the apocalyptic dénouement of these stories, ending with absolute victory followed by universal peace and happiness, foreshadows the idea of a great war to end wars.

Back from the Brink:
Towards a New *Entente Cordiale*, 1902–4

Let us admit it fairly, as a business people should,
We have had no end of a lesson: it will do us no end of good.
RUDYARD KIPLING

This policy . . . has brought conflict with England, the main customer
for our agriculture, commerce and industry, and not only with England,
but with . . . the whole British empire, those young states . . . whose
giant strides we have been too ignorant even to suspect.
PAUL D'ESTOURNELLES, republican deputy[145]

I fear . . . that anything like a hearty good will between the two nations
will not be possible.
LORD SALISBURY, prime minister[146]

The Boer war was finally won in May 1902, a victory for the Empire and even for 'Splendid Isolation'. Solidarity with Australia, New Zealand and Canada had been strengthened. The main strategic and political object – British control of the Cape – had been preserved, and it was to last through two world wars. A compromise with the Boer leadership, creating an autonomous Union of South Africa, even won their alliance. The long-term losers were the Africans, though Whitehall, genuinely concerned to circumscribe Boer oppression, retained Swaziland, Bechuanaland and Basutoland outside the Union as protectorates.[147] The war had been far longer, bloodier and costlier than expected. Seen from Whitehall, an empire scattered round the globe was vulnerable, and the cost of defending it potentially crushing. Yet seen from Paris, St Petersburg and Berlin, it was formidable. The French had even feared a pre-emptive British attack on their navy or colonies, and the war minister warned that the British army in South Africa might follow up its victory by invading Madagascar.[148] However popular the Boer cause, no country thought of taking on the Royal Navy. At most, there were circumspect diplomatic soundings to see what other countries might be thinking. The French foreign minister from 1898 to 1905, Théophile Delcassé, was as cautious as the rest.

Consequently, it is difficult to know precisely when he and other French decision-makers decided that a change of policy towards Britain would be advantageous. He had told the British ambassador that he hoped for a *rapprochement* between Britain, France and Russia, and the ambassador reported that 'I really do believe the little man is honest in saying this.'[149] The French bluff had been called at Fashoda, and France's ally Russia refused to support its colonial adventures. During the Boer war, cooperation with Germany and Russia had aborted when the Germans insisted that France should explicitly endorse the 1871 loss of Alsace-Lorraine. If Russia and Germany would not back France's colonial tussles with Britain, the alternative was to make a bargain with Britain itself. Immediately after Fashoda the French colonial lobby, hitherto a hotbed of anglophobia, had begun urging an Anglo-French agreement. Politicians began to speak about an 'entente cordiale', even if at first to dismiss the idea. The bait was Morocco, attractive because colonialists imagined it as the cornerstone of a North African empire whose closeness to France made it less dependent on seapower. Almost 'part of France itself', it could become a French Australia, with eventually 'fifteen to twenty million of our compatriots'.[150]

The British knew that 'splendid isolation', without treaty ties to any of the Great Powers, was increasingly risky and expensive. Russia, whose strength was over-estimated by everyone, seemed by far the most dangerous antagonist. It was expansionist in the Middle East, central Asia and China; industrializing rapidly; and 'compared to our empire . . . invulnerable. [There is] no part of her territory where we can hit her.'[151] Germany seemed the obvious counterweight. Apart from racial and religious affinities, which at the time all thought important, its land power complemented British sea power. Approaches were made in the 1890s, but came to nothing. The Kaiser was erratic, the German public was anglophobic, and then, in 1900, Germany began expanding its navy, which, the First Lord warned the Cabinet in 1902, 'was being carefully built up from the point of view of a war with us'.[152] That left France as a possible partner, but in the aftermath of the Dreyfus crisis, it was regarded as politically unstable and militarily weak – as well as being devoted to Russia and fundamentally anglophobic. As the twentieth century began, there was little to suggest that Britain and France were on the verge of a new and historic relationship. The prime minister Lord Salisbury hoped at best for 'a mutual temper of apathetic tolerance'.[153]

To lighten their strategic burden, Salisbury's government did not seek a partnership with any European state, but rather worked to improve their relations with the United States and signed a treaty with Japan in 1902. This was to encourage the Japanese to stand up to Russian expansionism in north China. It proved to be the catalyst in Franco-British relations, because Japan wanted Britain to prevent France from aiding Russia in case of war. Neither Whitehall nor the Quai d'Orsay wished to find themselves fighting in the Channel because of Russo-Japanese conflicts over Manchuria or Korea. This, in A.J.P. Taylor's view, made an agreement between Britain and France 'inevitable'.[154]

It was not, however, politically easy, given the ill feeling in both countries. 'We must not forget,' the embassy in London reminded Delcassé, 'the anti-English prejudices of a notable part of French opinion.'[155] King Edward VII took a personal initiative, with the lukewarm acquiescence of the government, by making in May 1903 the most important royal visit in modern history. It was doubly important because the French wrongly believed that the king 'personally directs the foreign policy of Great Britain'.[156] Paradoxically, foreign policy was much more decided by a small inner circle in the Republic than in the monarchy. Little is known about the king's inner thoughts, though it is assumed that affection for France – he had referred in a speech to the *entente cordiale* as early as 1878[157] – combined with suspicion of his nephew the Kaiser caused him to want a rapprochment. It was a bold strategy, as a visit unsuccessful in terms of popular reaction would make diplomatic agreement more difficult. There were assassination attempts on visiting heads of state in 1900 and 1905. Insulting cartoons of Victoria and Edward had already caused irritation. The effect if the king were jeered, or worse, in the streets of Paris would be grave. The visit has gone into legend as a watershed, with the king's astute charm and flattery winning over a hostile people in a few days. The reality is a little more complex.

'VIVE NOTRE BON EDOUARD!'

He comes to us as a conqueror,
But only to conquer the prettiest girls
So come on ladies, stand in line.
It's among us that he spent his youth
And he's the only king who agrees
That this is the realm of liberty.
It's here he thinks his kingdom is
Let's cheer this Rabelaisian king,
For that will make Emperor William squirm
And give a boost to Parisian business.
Song, 1903[158]

The royal plan was to spend several days in Paris at the end of a European tour, and to invite President Loubet to make a return visit. The main danger came from anglophobe, pro-Boer and anti-semitic nationalists, who were strongest in Paris and had a record of violence, including a public assault on Loubet himself. When the visit of 'the king of the hereditary enemies of the French' was announced, *La Patrie* headlined 'Down with Fashoda! Down with the murderers of the Boers!' Many wished to shout pro-Boer slogans and hang out Transvaal flags on the royal route. However, the principal nationalist leader, the quixotic Paul Déroulède, was – unusually – an anglophile. He had always put the recovery of Alsace-Lorraine ahead of colonial expansion, and saw that an agreement with Britain would strengthen France against Germany. His Ligue des Patriotes threatened to expel any member guilty of anglophobic agitation, for that amounted to 'going over to the enemy' – Germany. His followers grumbled but obeyed, and subsequently support for the *entente cordiale* became official Ligue policy.[159] Moreover, upper-class nationalists, often royalists, whose political anglophobia clashed with their social anglophilia, were unlikely to insult a monarch or spoil an occasion in which they played a prominent part. So shouts of 'Vive les Boers' or 'Vive Fashoda' rarely assailed royal ears – and when they did, Delcassé pretended they were enthusiastic cheers.

The other popular force, the socialists, were less dangerous, even though the king was arriving on May Day, a time of violent demonstrations. He later joked that 'it will interest him to see a Revolution'.[160] In fact, the socialists and trade unions were relatively anglophile, seeing Britain as a model of high wages, social legislation, and limited working hours. Although some socialist leaders deplored the 'sheer stupidity of the masses neglecting their interests,

One of the many satirical postcards confiscated by the French police before Edward VII's visit, and which have barely seen the light of day since. His reputation as a *bon viveur* was widespread.

preferring to watch a king go by', most welcomed the visit as a token of international peace and proof that republican France was not 'ruined and humiliated in the eyes of other powers', as claimed by right-wing propaganda.[161] In the old revolutionary Faubourg Saint-Antoine Edward was more cheered than in Paris's elegant west end.

Hosts and guest were equally out to please. At the Elysée the king was served (not, one imagines, his favourites) *crème Windsor*, oxtail soup, *œufs à la Richmond, selle de mouton à l'anglaise* and *pudding à la Windsor*. The Quai d'Orsay achieved true cross-Channel commensality with a luncheon of *jambon d'York truffé champenoise*. The king played effectively on his reputation as a Parisian *homme du monde*. He went racing with his Jockey Club friends (the horse *John Bull* won – surely not a fix?). At the theatre he spoke to an actress he had known in London, complimenting her on 'all the grace and *esprit* of France'. At the Elysée he spoke 'charmingly' of his 'childhood memories' of Paris and of his many later visits to a city where one meets 'all that is intelligent and beautiful'. These words were reported in the press, contributing to his image as a true lover of France and 'le roi parisien'. He charmed and flattered his audiences in French, speaking without notes, and repeatedly stressed his personal wish for good relations.

It was politically desirable to have cheering crowds, and they duly appeared, shouting 'Vive notre bon Edouard!' and 'Vive notre roi!' mixed undogmatically with 'Vive la République!' The throng was strengthened by British tourists. Business interests greatly favoured better relations, Britain being France's biggest customer. Commerce contributed to the festive atmosphere. Part of the lavish street decoration was provided by the many British shops, and there was an advertising campaign for English goods. New fashions were launched, for example a coat called 'Le King Edward'; and street vendors peddled handkerchiefs printed with the programme of the visit, walking sticks carved with the king's head, and countless trinkets and postcards. Café owners were keen to encourage the jollifications, and make money out of the authorities' permission for dancing in the streets.

President Loubet made an immediate return visit, which was less charismatic but also successful. According to the ambassador Paul Cambon 'that coldness, that reserve that normally characterizes the English had momentarily disappeared', and the president was given a popular ovation.[162] He met the 'French colony' in London, some of whom told him they were 'children of political exiles' who had lived in 'this great country' for half a century. A ticklish problem was overcome by permitting him and Delcassé to appear at court 'in Trousers instead of "Tights"' – too embarrassing for heirs of the *sans-culottes*.[163] The king made a point of drinking a toast to Loubet from 'the goblet given to me by the city of Paris', and Nelly Melba sang songs by Bizet, Gounod and Reynaldo Hahn. Edward decided that as Loubet was a farmer, he would present him with a pedigree shorthorn bull and a heifer from Windsor – apparently much appreciated.[164] Loubet's down-to-earth image was well received by the British press. They liked, as Cambon summed it up, his 'love of simplicity, calm good sense, hard work, spotless private life, and preference for the solid over the superficial and brilliant'.[165] In short, the English liked Loubet for what they thought were his un-French qualities, just as the French liked Edward for his un-English ones – cross-Channel reconciliation in homeopathic doses.

The visits injected cordiality into a *rapprochement* that might otherwise have amounted to no more than mean-minded haggling. A veteran French diplomat, Vicomte d'Harcourt, wrote privately that the king had 'blown away the dark clouds', and he expressed his 'joy' that the years of 'misunderstandings and prejudices' had ended.[166] Cheering crowds and expressions of friendship, reiterated in the press, produced a world-wide response, especially in the colonies where friction had been greatest. The Australian government sent a goodwill message to its French neighbour, New Caledonia. In Singapore, 400 French marines were allowed to sight-see, and were spontaneously cheered as a British military band played the 'Marseillaise'. In Madagascar, recently bracing itself for an attack by the Royal Navy, the officers of HMS *Fox* were lavishly entertained by the French garrison.[167]

Edward VII visited France regularly throughout his life, where he was always treated as the personification of the *entente*. Herbert Asquith, uniquely in

British history, was formally made prime minister at Biarritz in April 1908 – an event commemorated by a plaque in the lobby of the Hôtel du Palais. The king spent most of his last months by the sea there, also visiting Pau and the Pyrenees. He returned to England only ten days before he died in May 1910.

The haggling could now begin. 'In a word,' said Cambon at the start of negotiations, 'we give you Egypt in exchange for Morocco.'[168] That was always the essential, but the negotiations were a long unravelling of two centuries of bickering. Britain, notes A.J.P. Taylor, had won, and was happy to give 'a sporting victor's cheer . . . for a gallant loser'.[169] Harcourt pleaded for 'a few sops to our pride'.[170] One of the knottiest problems – French cod-fishing privileges at Newfoundland – had been an issue at every negotiation since the Treaty of Utrecht. The difficulty was that the Newfoundland government was putting pressure on the foreign secretary, Lord Lansdowne, while representatives of Breton fishing ports – led by M. Surcouf, presumably a descendant of the famous Saint-Malo privateer who had been a thorn in Britain's side under Napoleon – were putting pressure on M. Delcassé. After nine months of tough negotiations, Cambon and Lansdowne shook hands on a deal by which France recognized British occupation of Egypt, Britain promised to aid a French protectorate over ramshackle Morocco, and there was give-and-take on the details. Lansdowne, the 5th marquess, must surely have reflected on his hereditary fitness for his role: the 1st marquess (previously Lord Shelburne) had signed the Treaty of Versailles ending the American war in 1783, and had welcomed the French revolution. Subsequent Lansdownes were also descended – unofficially – from Talleyrand. The formal agreement, christened the *entente cordiale* long before it was concluded, was signed on 8 April 1904.

It was far from clear that it was the historic watershed that many hoped. For Whitehall, its purpose was to stave off conflict, not create amity. The need for this agreement, and the similar deal in 1907 with Russia, France's ally, was because they were the two countries with whom there were most difficulties. By resolving them, Britain confirmed its detachment from European alliances, defended by a naval superiority stronger than before the Boer War. Moreover, the cheering crowds – dismissed by cynics as displaying emotion to order – cannot obscure the deep ambivalence that the French and British felt about each other.

PART II: CONCLUSIONS AND
DISAGREEMENTS

After a century of war had come a century of peace between France and Britain, which, given their history, was no mean achievement. It also gives us less cause to disagree. Yet there were at least half a dozen occasions when war was seriously expected, and even expensively prepared for on both sides. That it did not happen was owing to more than just good luck or good sense. There was after Waterloo rarely if ever a credible prospect of French Continental hegemony. The expansionary policy of Napoleon III seemed the nearest to a threat – though in fact he was determined never to make an enemy of Britain. So most disputes, from the July Monarchy to the Third Republic, were colonial. Tahiti, Egypt or Fashoda could cause strong emotions, but they were never important enough to motivate a major conflict. Besides, wars only break out when both sides think they can win. The French no longer did. The Royal Navy made Britain invulnerable, and the only time the British worried was when something happened to make them doubt that, as for example when the French launched the steam-powered ironclad *La Gloire* in 1860. But British naval power could meet any challenge, while its economic strength and eventually even its population outdistanced that of France.

Peace gave opportunities for trade, investment, tourism and cultural exchange. As in the eighteenth century, they were amply taken, but now they affected a far greater proportion of the two populations, and extended into more areas of life. In economic development, literature, ideas, politics, fashion, art, sport and even food, both countries gave (or sold) so much to each other that they permeated each other's material and cultural lives. If Paris was, as is often said, 'the capital of the nineteenth century' in fashion and amusement, London was the capital of the world in finance and politics. Both remained very interested in each other, and many distinguished writers wrote thoughtful analyses. From the Hebrides to the Pyrenees, increasing numbers came to look, learn and enjoy. For all that, nineteenth-century relations often leave a sour taste: the bickering, sneering and overweening self-glorification on both sides soon ceases to be amusing, whether it comes from pompous British conservatives or envious French republicans. That the bluster often betrayed unease hardly makes it less tedious.

Does it matter? The Pritchard affair, the Spanish marriages, the prudery of the anti-Zolaists, the jingoism over Fashoda and so on could simply be taken as burlesque. Yet there is a serious side. France and Britain were the two most powerful constitutional states. Idealists wanted them to form an alliance to defend and promote liberal values in Europe: together, they might have calmed the political conflicts of the mid-century decades in Spain, Italy and Central Europe. Had they restrained their rivalry in colonial matters, it would have benefited non-European peoples. All in all, a more stable world, extending into the twentieth century, might have been within the reach of genuine Franco-British cooperation. So their failure was a serious one.

RT: France was unfortunately not a reliable partner in a project to stabilize and liberalize Europe or the wider world. A recent study concludes that 'liberal solidarity played no discernible role' in French foreign policy.[1] It was constantly trying to overturn the 1815 treaties. French historians are now recognizing the virulence of French nationalism, which even idealists such as Guizot were obliged to genuflect to. Outside Europe, France, whatever the nature of its regime, was grabbing at anything within reach, from Mexico to Indochina. Liberalism and republicanism both encouraged a rapacious imperialism based on the claim to possess a unique global 'civilizing mission'. Perhaps, with hindsight, Britain should have tried harder to restrain Prussian expansion in the 1860s. But given the instability in Europe that Napoleon III had deliberately created, it is hard to see what it could have done. And there is no reason why Britain should – even if it could – have intervened in 1870 to save Napoleon III and strengthen him for further adventurism. That was no way to prevent future disasters.

IT: The real roots of the problem were Britain's growing detachment – diplomatic and psychological – from Europe, combined with an invincible suspicion of France. We have seen how the genuine desire of the July Monarchy for an *entente cordiale* was repeatedly rebuffed by jingoists like Palmerston, who nourished absurd fears about France's eternal enmity, even covering the South Coast with huge fortresses. This culminated in a myopic lack of interest in European affairs in the 1860s, including near indifference to France's fate in 1870–71. As French politicians warned, this was against Britain's own interests, as it permitted Bismarck's Prussia to set up an illiberal and potentially aggressive German Reich, with terrible consequences for France, Britain and the world. Britain only woke up to this when it was too late.

INTERLUDE: PERCEPTIONS

ENGLISHMEN: All rich
ENGLISHWOMEN: Be amazed that they have such pretty children.
GUSTAVE FLAUBERT, 'Dictionary of Commonplaces'[1]

Victorian England was vaguely convinced that nineteenth century France
had too good a time; that Frenchmen laughed too much and cooked too
well . . . More serious still, Victorian England suspected that the French
put more into, and got more out of, sex than the English. Victorian
England had not the vaguest idea of how this was done, but was sure that
the advantage was not fair, and quite sure that it was not nice!
SIR ROBERT VANSITTART, diplomat[2]

Franco–British perceptions – or, as the French thought of them, Franco–
English – developed by repetition and accretion. Many clichés were old:
snails, garlic and frogs' legs were proverbial in Hogarth's time; as were French
pronouncements on English weather, women and taciturnity. The stock of
images was adapted and added to, but rarely invented or abandoned: thus
le milord anglais of the eighteenth century evolves into *le gentleman anglais*
of the twentieth. They were embodied in phrases, allusions, songs, books,
events, legends and pictures, and held together by a history and a logic not
necessarily grasped by the perceivers. People – not least writers and politicians – often believe they are thinking or saying something original when
their minds are sliding down deep ruts of convention.

Mutual stereotypes were largely accepted on both sides. It is impossible
to class as 'English' or 'French' statements such as 'The English like tradition', 'The French are politically unstable', 'The English are eccentric', 'The
French are frivolous', or indeed 'English food is dreadful' or 'French women
are attractive'. There were exceptions: the British never accepted that they
were perfidious or the French that they were effeminate. But a wide range
of negative and positive views were accepted on *both* sides of the Channel.
Many French 'anglophobe' views were accepted in England (e.g. 'We English
are philistines'), and many British 'francophobe' views were shared in France
(e.g. 'We French are vain'). At the same time, as we have already emphasized, there was always in both countries a strong, if often ambivalent,
admiration for the qualities of the other: from Voltaire to Clemenceau, and
from Lord Chesterfield to Winston Churchill ('Those British are so orderly';
'Those French are so cultured').

Many beliefs about Frenchness and Britishness can be interpreted either
in praise or in blame: 'philia' and 'phobia' are often two sides of the same
currency. For example, British economic success could be seen as 'enterprise'

or as 'greed'. French courtesy could be described as 'charming' or as 'affected'. French taste could be praised as 'elegant' or criticized as 'foppish'. British 'phlegm' could be admired as 'calmness' or condemned as 'coldness'. And so on. When 'philes' and 'phobes' disagreed, it was rarely that they contested the reality of certain characteristics – by denying that the French had taste, for example, or that the English were phlegmatic. This agreement about each other, combined with fluid ambivalence, made possible a close but unstable relationship. It made transition between positive and negative feelings easy without the need for any reassessment. As at the time of the *entente cordiale*, sullen hostility changed rapidly to effusions of friendship. It also gave an illusory sense of mutual understanding. 'This is typical of the British/French' has always been a more common refrain than 'Perhaps we have misunderstood the French/British.'

National stereotypes are based on observation, if usually at second or third hand. It would to some extent be possible, and even mildly interesting, to gauge the accuracy of some of them. (Was it as foggy in London as French writers suggest? No. Was inequality of living standards greater in London than Paris? No. Did British tourists wear tweeds? Often. Did the French eat better than the British? It depends who. Was French sexuality less repressed? Yes and no.[3]) But more important than accuracy is interpretation – joining the dots to make a picture. Perceptions were selective (only certain things were seen as significant), partial (whole swathes of the other society were never seen or registered) and archaic (based on events and literature from earlier generations). Here, books (and later newspapers, films and television) have always been crucial. Voltaire, Byron, Dickens, Dumas, Thackeray, Taine, Verne and Conan Doyle had huge and lasting influence. So, in the twentieth century, did André Maurois, Agatha Christie, Ian Fleming, Georges Simenon – and perhaps Peter Mayle and Julian Barnes. Once it was accepted that certain characteristics were 'British' or 'French', this affected what people saw and felt. Commandant Marchand's dislike of Kitchener's whisky (see above, page 429) was not because it was *bad* whisky, but because it tasted of Britain – rather as Irish whiskey reminded Des Esseintes of an unpleasant trip to the dentist. Parisian fashions were elegant, not because of their intrinsic qualities, but because they were Parisian.

French perceptions of Britain – even before the revolution – have been influenced by internal French politics: extreme Right and Left have tended to anglophobia, centrists to anglophilia. But English perceptions of France have rarely been determined by politics (since the 1790s there has been little British interest in French politics, and usually complete indifference). Instead, British attitudes have been cultural, social and moral. The overall balance of 'favourable' and 'unfavourable' feelings is influenced by the relative success, wealth and power of the two countries.[4] A sense of inferiority produces stronger feelings, both of admiration and of resentment. Hence, dramatic changes in relative power have been watersheds in modifying perceptions.

Even when relations have been bitter, commentators in France and Britain have recognized the other as in some ways a model, for example the British in government and administration, the French in culture. This was as true in the twentieth century as it had been during the eighteenth. British intellectuals praised, envied and went to live among their French *confrères*. French social reformers referred to British achievements in health, social security, wages and housing. Such cross-Channel references were handy weapons against opponents at home, whether British 'philistines' being exhorted to show as much regard for culture as the French, or French republicans being urged to show 'solicitude for our workers at least equal to that shown by the English monarchy'.[5] Even if grudgingly, most agreed that both were nations and cultures of historic importance, with special roles in the world, notoriously described as the *mission civilisatrice* and the 'White man's burden'.

The 'languages' of Englishness and Frenchness were comprehensible to a large audience: the frequency and consistency with which stereotypes appear show that they were widely understood. Let us try to explore their origins, meanings and logic.

Origins: Race, Land, Climate

Ideas about why Britain and France were different went back at least to the seventeenth century, and were updated by nineteenth-century theories about climate, race and history. 'As is the nest, so is the bird', as Michelet put it. The British nest was a sea-girt rock, inhospitable, wet, foggy, northern, and cut off. The French still tell a joke about British insularity, supposedly based on a British newspaper headline: 'Fog in the Channel: Continent isolated.' France was the Continent, comfortable, sunny, and central, a sort of European 'Middle Kingdom' commonly described as complete within itself: 'France is a beautiful garden. Its provinces are like flowers of all kinds . . . which together make our beloved Fatherland the finest country and the most pleasant to live in.'[6] Moreover, the bedrock of France came to be seen in the later nineteenth century as the peasantry: this was reflected in British cartoons showing France as a peasant girl rather than as a soldier. As racial theories grew in importance, it was accepted that the British were essentially Germanic, with ancient liberties inherited from the Teutonic tribes. The French were seen as predominantly Celtic and Latin – 'Gallo-Roman'. The essential France was seen as Mediterranean, although most of its population undeniably lived in the cool damp north. As Latins they were supposedly civilized and socially stable, while the Celtic element was discerned more in social egalitarianism, cultural freedom and general bloody-mindedness than in political liberty – it was commonly said that they liked authority. The leading critic Paul Bourget pronounced in 1891 that 'there is between an Anglo-Saxon and a Gallo-Roman a mutual incomprehensibility, an invincible diversity of mentality and feeling'.[7]

Religion, Immorality and Perfidy

The contrast of Protestantism and Catholicism always seemed significant. Until the late nineteenth century, Protestantism was seen as the basis of freedom and individualism, while Catholicism meant authority and hierarchy. This idea was brought up to date at the end of the century by the influential nationalist Charles Maurras, who praised Catholicism as the pillar of national unity and classical culture, France's unique inheritance. He blamed the French revolution on Luther and ultimately on Abraham – spreaders of individualism and revolt. Protestantism was also seen as joyless and repressive, and this view became prominent as parts of France became more openly irreligious during the late nineteenth century. Then, France seemed more 'free-thinking', more 'pagan', and more frankly hedonistic than puritanical, repressed and hence hypocritical Britain. The old label 'perfidious Albion' – originally a reproach for its infidelity to Rome – came to signify the gulf (as perceived by the French) between the Victorian show of piety and the reality of vice, both in politics and in private life. Just as in the eighteenth century, Catholic monks were a symbol of despotism and Frenchness, by the late nineteenth the Protestant *pasteur* symbolized Britishness, foisting bigotry, cotton frocks and capitalism on free and happy natives, after having imposed inspissated gloom at home. 'The Protestant missionary is always a pure businessman,' the Senate was told in 1895.[8]

The British tended to agree with at least part of this analysis: that is, they criticized (and sometimes admired) the French for flagrant libertinism. France, particularly Paris, became in British eyes (though, of course, not only theirs) the epitome of sexual licence. This had not been so before 1850. It is in part a consequence of anti-Bonapartist criticism of Second Empire Paris as the corrupt 'New Babylon' (combining political oppression and moral decadence), followed by the cultural and moral libertarianism of the Third Republic. A disillusioned Matthew Arnold thundered in the 1880s against French worship of 'the great goddess Lubricity'. 'French' came to be used in colloquial English to mean sexually explicit.

Nature versus Civilization

Another basic contrast was the idea, inherited from the eighteenth century, that Britain stood for nature, and France for civilization (see above, page 100). This continued to be applied to culture, social conventions, and even politics. The 'rough practicality' of the British, as one early twentieth-century French writer put it, produced a feeling of difference that was 'in our bones.'[9] The British valued 'facts', the French, 'theory'; the British favoured domesticity, the French, sociability; the British had 'humour', the French, 'wit'; the British 'ate', the French 'dined'; the British valued the 'practical', the French the 'elegant', and so on. Visual imagery expressed variations on this theme. The British were 'bulldogs'; the French (in British imagery), 'poodles', decorative, unnatural and impractical. Hyppolite Taine analysed the symbolism of John Bull, significant because it was the image chosen by the English themselves, and hence the 'essence of national character'. He was a 'bulldog', a 'cattle dealer', having 'a few limited ideas', yet 'sensible', 'energetic', 'good-humoured', 'honest', 'determined' – characteristics that made a man successful and 'if not likeable, at least useful'.[10]

There is hardly an area of life to which the distinction between nature and civilization, and its range of vocabulary and imagery, were not applied. We might think of art and literature (British 'genius' versus French 'taste'), with Shakespeare still the touchstone. Thus Matthew Arnold, though a francophile, decided that French drama could never attain the level of Shakespeare because of the 'incurable artificiality' of Alexandrine verse.[11] French classicists argued the very opposite: blank verse could not produce the highest poetry because it was too much like natural speech. French critics could not accept Dickens as a great novelist because, typically English in his exuberance and spontaneity, he was unsophisticated, vulgar, prudish and sentimental. Education, the matrix of culture, became one of the most thoroughly debated areas of difference. English schools were said to be modelled on the 'natural' institutions of home and family, and hence to encourage individual development. French schools were modelled on the 'artificial' regulated environments of the regiment or the convent. The schools themselves – which often did broadly conform to the stereotypes, as in the 800-page regulations of Ursuline convent schools – and the debates about them did much to confirm and perpetuate contrasting views of the two nations.[12] Were the French cultured and clever, or just conformist and superficial, having 'dabbled in everything and being able to write and speak about everything'? The English, 'practical and energetic', were not 'mere scholars'.[13] But were they mere philistines, 'polished barbarians'?

Masculinity and Feminity

Related to the nature/civilization contrast was the significance ascribed to the role, character and treatment of women. In societies run by men, women were objects of devotion, luxury commodities, the bearers of higher values and the epitome of civilization. The supposed differences between French and British women are endlessly reiterated both seriously and satirically as symbols of difference – and, no doubt, as an effective way of delivering insults. French (particularly Parisian) women were accepted on both sides of the Channel as embodying the best and worst of French civilization: elegance, wit, sociability, charm and sophistication; but also superficiality, luxury, fickleness, immorality. British women were characterized as sincere, modest, religious, serious-minded and independent; and conversely, as naïve, prudish, unsociable, inelegant, indecorous and masculine.

The importance of women as symbols of civilization explains the virulence of French attacks on British women, found not only in anglophobe propaganda but in serious analyses too. Though part of this may be associated with women's changing roles, it long predates the rise of feminism and the suffragettes. Since the eighteenth century, the ugliness and lack of sartorial taste of English women were reiterated themes. Teeth become an amazingly insistent *leitmotif*. Even the beautiful Trilby has 'big British teeth'. The scholarly Taine noted British women's 'protruding carnivorous jaws'[14] – or, in the phrase still current, *les dents qui courent après le bifteck*. These featured in satirical drawings of Britannia, and were still present in caricatures of Elizabeth II and Margaret Thatcher a century later. Scarcely less common are other masculine characteristics such as large hands and especially feet. This is explicit in one cartoon (below, page 451), whose caption explains that 'the body of the English woman is serious, without those frivolous and indecent attractions which are the sad lot of the French woman'.[15]

British women were unfeminine because Britishness was masculine. Conversely, Frenchness was feminine. This distinction was commonplace as early as the eighteenth century. 'For better or worse France has been and remains a feminine nation: not effeminate or cowardly, but containing within herself a preponderance of the virtues and vices of woman, from mother to courtisan.'[16] Symbols were often gendered, most obviously in John Bull and Marianne. Symbols of France become not merely allegorically female, but alluringly feminine, compared with frigid Britannia or butch Germania. Characteristic British activities were seen as masculine – whether heavy industry or sport (in which women's participation was a sign of 'mannishness'). Many characteristically French activities, most obviously cooking and the manufacture of fashion goods, had feminine connotations. In the greatest nineteenth-century industry, textile manufacture, France exported woollens

English women are a favourite target: the sexless and big-footed nude; and the two ugly tourists absurdly worrying about Frenchmen's advances.

and silks for women to Britain; Britain exported wool for men's clothing to France. Male fashions were predominantly British; female fashions were overwhelmingly French. Characteristics ascribed to French men – most obviously foppishness – were seen as effeminate. This was accentuated by the increasing disparity of power between the two states during the nineteenth century – painfully underlined by the failing French birthrate, seen on both sides of the Channel as proof of flagging national virility. French unhappiness with such ideas can perhaps be seen in common assertions of English sexual inadequacy or aberration, far from extinct in present-day French folklore, especially concerning the Royal Family, the symbol of the nation.[17] Homosexuality was declared a British speciality, and it was a common theme of French literature that British heterosexual relations were repressed, hypocritical and bizarre – in contrast with the vigorous orthodoxy of the French.

Materialism, Exploitation and Greed

Linked with both the Protestant/Catholic and the nature/civilization contrasts is the French idea (shared by others) of the British state as a materialistic conspiracy aiming at economic domination. The historic mission of France was to lead world resistance against the power of English gold. The

'Carthage' or 'nation of shopkeepers' theme, powerful before 1815 as we have seen, was adopted by the mid-nineteenth-century French Left, and inherited by late-nineteenth and twentieth-century nationalists. As early as the 1830s it was linked with anti-semitism and anti-Americanism, which was largely a reinterpretation of familiar Anglophobic ideas. One of Capitaine Danrit's English villains gives the game away in 1902:

> The Fatherland, the flag! These are prejudices from another age . . .
> But today, with our civilization, we have means of transport and
> communication that link the most distant nations together . . . today
> the word border has no sense! There is now only one human race
> seeking the greatest well-being possible through the application
> of science. And what is the universal key to this well-being?
> It's money! . . . Because France opposes all these new ideas despite
> all our propaganda . . . France is doomed!'[18]

Even writers and politicians less rabid than Danrit took it for granted that the British state, using the power of the navy and (a later bugbear) the Intelligence Service, was merely an agent of the City. Anything Britain did that might appear disinterested was merely hypocritical cover for economic self-interest. France – whether royal, imperial or republican – was the opposite, pursuing an altruistic mission to civilize and liberate. In the words of one of the most widely used school textbooks, 'A noble country like France does not think only of making money.'[19] That these perceptions are still going strong was shown in French reactions to the award in July 2005 of the 2012 Olympic Games to London rather than Paris, which commentators and politicians blamed on British cheating, international capitalism, Anglo-Saxon solidarity, and even the Intelligence Service.[20]

During the nineteenth century British visual images of France became both less visceral and less vivid, whereas in France the opposite is true. This doubtless reflects the changed balance of power, jealousy and fear, as well as Victorian inhibitions. Unlike in Hogarth, Gillray or Rowlandson, with their preening fops and famished peasants, there is little that is essentially 'French' or inherently hostile in mid or late-nineteenth-century British imagery, which in order to identify nationality often falls back on uniforms or other conventional symbols. The most common French types are the soldier (especially the exotic colonial Zouave) and, after 1871, the pretty female in republican Phrygian bonnet and/or peasant clogs. Though there were hostile portrayals of French revolutionaries in 1848 and 1871, they are far tamer than the equivalents by Gillray or indeed by contemporary French artists. French satirists, in contrast, developed a range of pungent British types comparable in verve and vitriol to Gillray's Frenchmen, and even now instantly recognizable. They are evidently drawn from observation of British tourists, who are then caricatured and systematized to fit anglophobe beliefs, teaching the French public how to interpret what they saw. Tweeds become a symbol: 'the regulation check suit . . . of the middle-class Englishman when travelling on the Continent' and sometimes a 'cricket cap, with the peak turned the wrong way round'.[21] As in the eighteenth century, casual sports clothes were seen as an affront to French elegance and decorum. But what to many seemed uncouth and insolent could equally be admired – a perfect example of the ambivalence of stereotypes. Demolins was so impressed to meet a tweedy English headmaster who made him think of 'a pioneer, a squatter of the far west' that he described him in detail: 'tall, spare, muscular . . . grey tweed jacket . . . knickerbockers, thick woollen stockings folded under the knees, big strong boots . . . a Tam o'Shanter cap'. He was the antithesis of the musty French schoolmaster in 'long, dark frock-coat' and 'an extraordinary amount of dignity'.[22] This encapsulated the contrast of two cultures as clearly as in the days of Rousseau – the new, vigorous and 'natural' versus the stale, conventional and 'civilized'.

The climax of French hostility was the period of Fashoda, the Boer war and the visit of Edward VII. The most outspoken publications were nationalist or anarchist. Two important themes, illustrated here,[23] are the cruelty and rapacity of perfidious Albion; and the sheer nastiness of the English as people, especially when they come to France.

Willette's 1899 panorama shows perfidious Albion in procession: dandified soldiers (including an alluringly mini-kilted Scot), vapid Salvation Army

Tralala, tralala, voilà les Anglais . . .

bigots (doubly disturbing, because outraging feminine decorum, but in the name of conservative morality) juxtaposed with child prostitutes; a grim parson peddling bibles, gunpowder and samples, a brutal John Bull with rifle in hand and money-bag under arm, plague in their wake, Boers dangling from telegraph poles, and a flag whose battle-honours go from Joan of Arc via Napoleon to the Transvaal.

The typical Englishman: '*Un monsieur qui gêne les autres chez lui, mais qui ne se gêne pas chez les autres.*'

The untranslatable caption means that he makes visitors feel awkward at his house, but makes himself too much at home at theirs: the uncouth, vacuous male, hairy, unkempt, and above all too relaxed, insultingly careless of proper behaviour and manners – an old French theme. A popular novel published in 1908 asserted that 'everywhere the Englishman goes he is detested for his disdainful haughtiness, his total lack of tact and manners. Excessively polite in his own country, he believes that when he's abroad he does not have to bother and makes himself at home with an impertinent disregard for others.'[24]

— La loge du Président de la Répioublique, please ?

'*La loge du Président de la Répioublique*, please': the contrast between the civilized French and the ugly and absurd English, badly dressed in tweed travelling clothes, speaking bad French and demanding privileged treatment, is another favourite theme. A popular music hall song concerned an Englishman at the Opéra who refused to remove his hat from a Frenchman's seat.

— Une seule chambre pour Monsieur et Madame ?
— Nô... deux chambres... avec communiquécheun...

'Separate rooms with a communicating door': hypocrisy and a hint of sexual oddity involving a (for once) pretty but typically vacuous and naïve English girl – the type defined by Taine as 'simple *babies* [sic], wax dolls with glass eyes empty of any idea'.[25]

Mock advertisements for British goods typifying hypocrisy: the 'hermetic salvation shirt' for Protestant clergy; the abortion pills for Salvation Army women; and telegram boys 'for all needs' – a reference to the notorious Cleveland Street scandal fourteen years earlier.

PART III: SURVIVAL

French and British fought side by side for survival in the two most destructive wars in history. After terrible trials and sufferings, they twice emerged victorious, and at the moments of triumph paid each other generous and heartfelt tribute. But they did not understand each other. Nor did they establish trust and durable affection, either at the level of governments or – exceptions notwithstanding – among the generality of their citizens. Even in the best of circumstances, alliance is a potential source of resentment, as partners pursue differing aims, and seek to shift some of the burden of suffering. The First World War was no exception. The absence of Franco-British solidarity during the inter-war decades fatally dashed the hopes of both peoples – and of the world – that they had fought 'a war to end war'. The different fates of the two during the Second World War, even if both were finally victors, planted further seeds of mistrust, and created divergent national myths.

CHAPTER 10

The War to End Wars

The argument that there is no written bond binding us to France is strictly
correct. There is no contractual obligation. But the *entente* has been made,
strengthened, put to the test and celebrated in a manner justifying the
belief that a moral bond was being forged. The whole policy of the *entente*
has no meaning if it does not signify that in a just quarrel England would
stand by her friends . . . Our duty and our interest will be seen to lie in
standing by France in her hour of need. France has not sought the quarrel.
It has been forced upon her.

Foreign Office memorandum, July 1914

From *Entente* to Alliance, 1904–14

France . . . is a country and a nation whose ideas, whose ambitions, whose
ideals we can understand and know the *limits* of . . . There is no fear now
or sentimentality on either side . . . France has become bourgeois . . .
sensible, prudent, *cautious* in her old age.

GEORGE SAUNDERS, foreign correspondent.[1]

The Entente is not an alliance. For purposes of ultimate emergencies it
may be found to have no substance at all.

EYRE CROWE, foreign office, 1911[2]

During the early years of the twentieth century, the British, whether
they admired or disapproved, were no longer afraid of France, but
they worried about Russia and were beginning to be alarmed by Germany.
The French rarely felt particular affection for Britain, but regarded the
entente cordiale as a potential source of security in the face of a Germany
they regarded not only as a historic enemy, but as a reviving menace. The
entente was not evidence of a more intimate relationship, however. If there
were two European countries that had long regarded themselves as having
affinities, they were Britain and Germany. They were huge trading partners. Liberals admired German earnestness and efficiency; the Left envied
the massive organization of its Social Democrats and trade unions; and
intellectuals admired its universities. German cavalry officers came to hunt
with the Pytchley and the Quorn. German students won Rhodes schol-
arships to Oxford, whereas French students hardly ever attended British
universities. Admiral von Tirpitz, architect of Germany's naval challenge,
sent his daughters to Cheltenham Ladies' College.[3] It would be hard to
identify such spontaneous links between the French and the British,
except, as we have noted, in the artistic and literary worlds. There was
often a cultural and social divide between French and British diplomats
and politicians. Few French politicians (with the notable exception of
Georges Clemenceau) visited Britain. Organized expressions of friendship tried to bridge the gap. Most famous then, though since forgotten,
was the Franco-British Exhibition of Science, Arts and Industries – popularly known as the 'Franco' – held in London at the specially constructed
'White City' in 1908.[4] There were many other official gestures of goodwill, including the statues of Queen Victoria at Nice and Biarritz, and of
Edward VII at Cannes and in Paris.

There was no certainty that Britain would be an ally of France in any

European war. In both countries there were influential voices resisting entente euphoria. A.J. Balfour, prime minister when the *entente* was signed, had no idea 'what may be expected for the Anglo–French understanding and would be ready to make an agreement with Germany tomorrow'.[5] France's eyelashes fluttered only at Russia, a virile protector kept happy with large amounts of cash. But Britain's relations with Russia were chilly. The Admiralty and the Indian government considered that Russia and France were still the main long-term global threat. In both Paris and London, some feared that excessive concessions were being made and, more ominously, that the other might drag them into an undesired conflict with Germany.

What transformed the situation were the actions of Berlin, so unpredictable and confused that even now it is impossible to interpret them with certainty. Germany in the 1900s was building a short-range battle fleet, which had no purpose other than to threaten British home security. In March 1905, Germany interfered with the Anglo–French deal to let France take over Morocco. The reason was to show the world, and particularly France, that no deals could be made without German consent, at Germany's price, and thus to show that the *entente* was worthless. The French government panicked. Delcassé, architect of the *entente*, was forced out of office in June 1905. As with most German diplomatic initiatives in these years, the outcome was the opposite of that intended: Britain drew closer to its arch-rival, Russia. 'An entente between Russia, France and ourselves,' wrote Sir Edward Grey, the Liberal foreign secretary from 1905, 'would be absolutely secure. If it is necessary to check Germany it could then be done.' In April 1906 he began the negotiations that led to the Anglo–Russian *entente* of August 1907. Still, in colonial matters, Britain and France, as well as Britain and Russia, continued to cause each other suspicion and annoyance down to 1914.

When Germany made a second attempt to exert pressure over Morocco in 1911, it sent a gunboat, *Panther*, to Agadir to 'protect' German residents. (One was sent specially to be protected.) This annoyed the British, who regarded the sending of gunboats as their prerogative. The chancellor of the exchequer, David Lloyd George, made a vehement though vague speech at the Mansion House that in effect threatened war with Germany. No one wanted a war over Morocco, any more than they had over South Africa, but it was a sign that European diplomacy was becoming rougher. Governments and peoples began to think that a major war was possible, and even to plan for one. Britain recognized, and perhaps exaggerated, German ambitions. Many Germans did regard Britain as arrogant, oppressive and corrupt (as, indeed, did many French). But anglophobe fantasies about a struggle for global dominance were very far from Berlin's actual foreign policy, which was incoherent and blustering rather than megalomaniac.

The Kaiser as stage villain brings France and Britain together. France is now habitually represented as a pretty peasant girl.

Lloyd George's speech was significant because he was a leading radical, a former 'pro-Boer'. Yet despite his strong words, the Liberals, who came into office in 1905, were more pacific, less pro-French, more pro-German and more anti-Russian than their Tory predecessors. Most Liberals wanted appeasement of Germany and refused any commitment to France. Grey's foreign policy therefore had to be ambiguous, even duplicitous. Grey, the scion of an old Whig dynasty, was an introspective bird-watcher whose mild manners concealed a surprising ruthlessness. He had to square what he thought necessary for national security with what the Liberal Party and their Labour allies would swallow – broadly speaking, nothing threatening, unethical, or pro-Russian. Unlike his Tory predecessors Lansdowne and Salisbury, Grey did not speak French. Paul Cambon (ambassador since 1898 but never at home in London) did not speak English. They conversed by articulating very slowly in their respective languages. Not surprisingly, subtle nuances of British policy – perfidy and hypocrisy as the French were tempted to see it – were lost in the process. But the real misunderstanding was not linguistic, but political: the combination of Grey's ambiguity, secrecy, and sometimes high-minded duplicity, with Cambon's stubbornly logical wishful thinking. For Cambon, a Franco-British alliance was desirable, it followed rationally from earlier agreements, and hence it must be deemed to exist, whatever the Liberal government and its followers in Westminster might think. Secret meetings began between British and French generals to discuss how – were it ever necessary – a British army might be sent to France. Friendly contacts were encouraged at a lower level. General Henry Wilson, the War Office's director of operations, a fervently francophile Ulsterman, spent his holidays cycling round spying out the land. He even left a small map showing his planned movements of British troops as a sort of votive offering at a French war memorial on one of the 1870 battlefields.[6] An agreement was reached by which the Royal Navy concentrated in home waters, to face the German battle fleet, while the French navy concentrated in the Mediterranean. In November 1912, Grey and Cambon exchanged letters setting out their understanding of what the two countries agreed to do if there were a threat of war. The British insisted on wording that denied any obligation. Whereas the French wanted to say that the two countries 'will immediately deliberate on the means for acting together', the British would only agree to 'discuss with the other *whether* [to] act together . . . and *if so* what measures they would be prepared to take'.[7] This enabled Grey and Asquith to assure Parliament that Britain was bound by no commitment. The French assumed that Britain would in practice support them if they were the victims of German aggression. Grey hoped that public opinion would indeed demand intervention in such a case. But a senior foreign office official still thought in April 1914 that 'should war break out on the Continent the likelihood of our dispatching any expeditionary force is extremely remote.'[8]

In July 1914, the disaster came. It began in the Balkans with a shady dispute between Serbia, Austria-Hungary and Russia – just the kind of conflict Liberals, and the Liberal press, were least inclined to get involved in. 'We care as little for Belgrade,' declared the *Manchester Guardian*, 'as Belgrade for Manchester.'[9] Grey detected a feeling in Britain that France was only being dragged in because it 'had the misfortune to be involved in a Russian quarrel'. Asquith struggled privately with the contradictions of his own policy, writing in his diary on 2 August that 'We have no obligation of any kind either to France or Russia to give them military or naval help . . . We must not forget the ties created by our long-standing and intimate friendship with France.'[10]

On 1 August Germany declared war on France, having long before decided that in case of war with Russia, France must be eliminated first. Asquith, Grey and some other Liberals, notably Winston Churchill, most Tories, and many diplomats and soldiers, believed that Britain had a national interest and a moral obligation to prevent France from being crushed. Grey wrote later that 'Germany . . . would then have been supreme over all the Continent of Europe and Asia Minor', which would mean 'the isolation of Britain, the hatred of her by both those who had feared and those who had wished for her intervention; and ultimately that Germany would wield the whole power of the Continent'.[11] Churchill argued that British intervention would be decisive without being too burdensome, as a limited military presence would have a strong moral, political and even strategic effect, while the main effort would fall to the Royal Navy. So 'the presence or absence of the British army . . . will very probably decide the fate of France'; yet 'the naval war will be cheap'. Grey even argued that Britain would be practically as much affected by staying out of the war as by going in.[12]

The government was threatened with collapse: Asquith and Grey would resign if the Cabinet refused to aid France; at least three and perhaps five members would resign if it agreed to do so. Liberal back-bench opinion was strongly anti-war.[13] Had the government fallen, a Coalition including Tory ministers would have favoured intervention, but there would certainly have been serious division within Britain, a delay in acting, and tension with France. While the Cabinet thrashed about – 'It was decided not to decide,' said one of the anti-war ministers[14] – Grey played desperately for time, telling the Germans they should not count on British neutrality, and the French that they should not count on British support. Cambon, going through 'the darkest moments of my life', asked bitterly 'whether the word "honour" should be struck out of the English vocabulary'.[15] His counterpart in Paris, Sir Francis Bertie, felt 'sick and ashamed . . . Here today it is "Vive l'Angleterre", tomorrow it may be "Perfide Albion".'[16] He began to prepare the embassy for a mob attack.

The dilemma was ended by Germany's invasion of neutral Belgium on 2 August, in order to outflank France's frontier defences and take her army in the rear. Britain was committed to defending Belgian neutrality by the Treaty of London (1839), an expression of one of the oldest principles of British foreign policy: the need to keep a potential enemy (in the past, of course, France) away from the ports of the Low Countries, springboards for invading England. The defence of Belgium provided both a pretext and a genuine reason for joining the war. As far as the Cabinet was concerned, however, it might not have been a sufficient reason had the view not been gaining ground that Britain had a vital interest in standing by France. Wavering ministers, such as Lloyd George, knew that resigning would simply bring in a Liberal–Tory coalition that would intervene anyway. As far as the public was concerned, Belgium's fate showed that the war was just – an impression confirmed by savage German atrocities against civilians.

Controversy has persisted ever since. Hardly had fighting begun than it was argued that if Britain had been open and definite either that it would, or would not, join a war, then either the Germans, or the Franco-Russian allies, would have drawn back. Historians now agree that the other governments made their decisions irrespective of British action or inaction. Both Berlin and Paris believed that the British army was too weak to affect a conflict that most expected to be decided quickly. The French (far more committed to Russia than to Britain) wanted political, financial and naval support, but regarded the presence of British troops in France as symbolic. When in 1909 General Wilson had asked his friend General Foch what would be the smallest force that could be helpful in case of war, he replied 'One single private soldier, and we would take good care that he was killed.'[17]

A second, weightier, argument concerns the broader consequences of the war: no political goal seems worth the stupendous suffering and destruction of 1914–18, which dealt a permanent blow to Europe, weakened Britain, and created the conditions for later catastrophe. Nearly a century later, we are likely to feel that the war was not worth fighting, that its objects were at best ephemeral, and that it was futile and frivolous in its archaic values of national prestige and honour. This was not, of course, the view of most participants. On all sides people were convinced not only that they were defending their countries against aggression, but that they were fighting for universal values. The view quickly formed in France and Britain that they were defending justice, democracy and civilization against the violence of 'militarism', and hence were fighting '*la dernière des guerres*', as the poet Charles Péguy put it; or in H.G. Wells's famous phrase, 'a war to end war'. Ideas have changed: yet even now it is impossible to imagine that democratic states would not oppose by force an act of aggression such as that carried out by Germany in 1914.

In 1914 few, if any, realized how horrific industrial war would be. It is arguable that a quick German victory – assuming this to have been the outcome if Britain had refused to help France – would have been less disastrous than the Allies' pyrrhic victory after four years of carnage. Such a judgement requires hindsight: but can we be sure what hindsight shows? Interventionists feared that German victory would mean not peace, but further aggression against Britain and the Empire, probably with French and Russian connivance, forcing Britain into a fatal war resulting in ruin and loss of independence. We might find this melodramatic. But it is no more convincing to go to the extreme of optimism, and assume that British neutrality and German victory would have meant lasting peace, leaving Britain and its empire intact, and merely creating a forerunner of the European Union under enlightened German hegemony.[18] It is impossible to know what the effects of a complete German victory would have been on the victors or the vanquished. It would undoubtedly not have advanced or even preserved liberal and democratic government in Europe. It is reasonable to imagine Germany, Russia, Austria and France all under authoritarian regimes, and large populations in the Low Countries, northern France and eastern Europe annexed against their will to the victor states. Nor would colonial peoples have benefited from being fought over and parcelled out.

Grey's fear that a triumphant Germany would not be content with primacy in Europe, but would have regarded Britain as its next target, was, and remains, plausible.

The British and the Defence of France, 1914

We . . . fight beside our gallant allies in France and Belgium in no war of
arrogance, but to uphold our national honour, independence and freedom.
We have violated no neutrality, nor have we been false to any treaties . . .
Having then this trust in the righteousness of our cause, pride in the glory
of our military traditions, and belief in the efficiency of our army, we go
forward together to do or die for GOD – KING – AND COUNTRY.

SIR JOHN FRENCH, Order of the Day[19]

Britain entered the war on 4 August without a plan of campaign. It was decided at the last minute to send the British Expeditionary Force (originally designed for service in India against Russia) – an enterprise that two days earlier Asquith had said was 'out of the question'.[20] There seemed to be no other options. The navy's schemes to land troops on the German coast, reminiscent of the good old days of Pitt the Elder, were scotched by the army. The BEF arrived in France with remarkable dispatch. Using 1,800 special trains, 240 requisitioned ships, 165,000 horses, London buses, and delivery vans (some proclaiming HP Sauce to be 'the World's Appetiser') – 'immense convoys' recalled one Frenchman, 'loaded with bacon, tea and marmalade' – it was in place in France only sixteen days after the war began.[21] Some of its units wore pith helmets, as if for colonial service, and the inhabitants of Boulogne were thrilled that the first troops ashore were Highlanders with kilts and bagpipes. The modern khaki uniforms of most of the army reminded some of golfing clothes. Regimental bands played the 'Marseillaise', and soldiers threw coins to chidren. The French responded with generous quantities of drink, and even, so eager rumour had it, with patriotic sexual favours. One soldier recalled that 'It was good to be an Englishman that day; good to feel that Englishmen then in France could now look Frenchmen squarely in the face.'[22]

The BEF is often said to have been the finest army Britain has ever had. It was certainly the finest with which Britain has ever begun a war. Lessons from South Africa had been learned: the infantry had been taught to shoot accurately and fast; the cavalry could fight on horseback or on foot. Morale was high: 'our motto was, "We'll do it. What is it?"'[23] But it was small. Containing nearly all the regular troops in the United Kingdom supplemented by reservists (60 per cent of the total), it mustered some 110,000 men at the outset, of whom 75,000 were combat troops. But there were 1.7

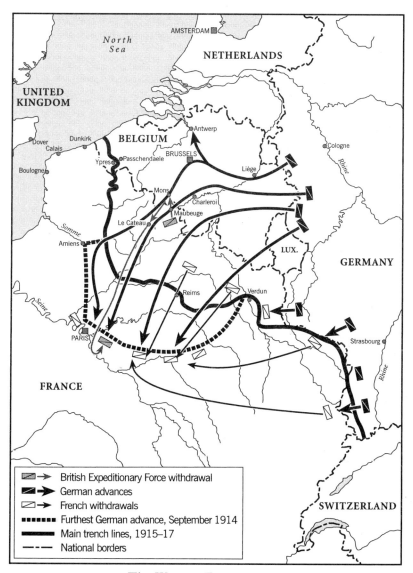

The Western Front 1914–17

Legend:

- British Expeditionary Force withdrawal
- German advances
- French withdrawals
- Furthest German advance, September 1914
- Main trench lines, 1915–17
- National borders

million Germans and 2 million French. The new secretary of state for war, Field-Marshal Lord Kitchener, instructed the BEF's commander, Field-Marshal Sir John French, that he could expect few reinforcements and so must avoid heavy casualties. Even so, it was estimated that 75 per cent of the force would be killed, wounded or captured in six months of fighting.[24] This proved an under-estimate.

Neither the British nor the French had much idea of each other's intentions. The latter, commanded by General Joseph Joffre, had not been sure whether the British – called *l'armée W* – would turn up at all, and if so how many there would be. So there were no plans for what the BEF might do. As earlier agreed, they assembled to the left of the French army, round the antique fortress of Maubeuge, near the Belgian border. As neighbours they had a French cavalry corps, patrolling the open spaces beyond the armies' flanks, and some elderly French territorials. They relied on French planning, and had no fall-back position in case things went wrong.[25] This must have seemed a remote danger, as the main fighting was expected to be 150 miles to the east on the German frontier.

It had long been supposed, even by popular novelists, that the Germans would send forces into Belgium, but the French high command maintained that it would only be a feint. By mid-August, the most perceptive – including Kitchener – deduced that it was much more. It was in fact the spearhead of the notorious Schlieffen Plan, intended to knock the French out by aiming the decisive blow through central Belgium and north-western France, reaching Paris, and taking the main French army from behind. This plan – if it worked – was supposed to finish the war in the west in weeks, permitting Germany and Austria to turn their main forces against Russia.

No one had planned that the five British divisions, barely arrived, would be directly in the path of this German right hook: thirty-four divisions totalling 580,000 men. The Belgians had decided to fight, and appealed for Allied aid. The BEF and French forces advanced into Belgium, hoping to stem the German advance, which they still greatly underestimated. Some young British officers realized the truth as night fell:

The evening was still and wonderfully peaceful . . . A dog was barking at some sheep. A girl was singing as she walked down the lane behind us . . . Then, without a moment's warning, with a suddenness that made us start . . . we saw the whole horizon burst into flames . . . A chill of horror came over us . . . we felt as if some horrible Thing, utterly merciless, were advancing to grip us.[26]

The BEF dug in near the industrial town of Mons. The hurrying Germans, unaware that they were there, crashed into them on 23 August, the first

British battle in western Europe since Waterloo, thirty miles away. British rifle fire, so intense that the Germans thought that they were facing automatic weapons, inflicted 5–10,000 casualties on the massed columns. Yet the BEF, outnumbered three to one, and with the French on their right in sudden retreat, had to fall back, fighting another delaying action, again outnumbered, at Le Cateau on the 26th. This time they lost more heavily, and were forced into a rapid retreat of 100 miles in ten days, slogging through sweltering heat along roads clogged with vehicles and refugees, and harried by German cavalry. Part of this disarray was due to their commander, Sir John French, a dashing cavalry leader in South Africa out of his depth in France. Mistrust and misunderstanding between the new Allies almost caused disaster. Sir John had been unnerved by the sudden retreat of the French army on his right, commanded incompetently and with arrogant disregard for the British by General Lanrezac. The situation was aggravated by the inability of the senior commanders on either side to speak each other's language, hence great responsibility fell on junior liaison officers, such as the bilingual Lt Edward Spears, son of a cosmopolitan Franco-Irish family, born and largely brought up in France. There were cultural barriers more mysterious than language: when a British officer was arrested by the French as a suspected spy, his captors wanted him to undress to provide 'some proof that you are English'. It was unclear exactly what they were hoping to see.[27]

French's object became to save his BEF from the danger of annihilation, irrespective of what his ally might do. For a time he wanted to make a dash for the coast, almost anticipating the events of 1940. By early September he was near Paris, demanding to pull out of the fighting for two weeks' rest and refit – a crazy idea as the war reached a crisis. Asquith wrote, 'We all think this quite wrong because he would . . . give our allies hereafter some pretext for saying that, at the pinch, the English had deserted them.'[28] Kitchener hastened to Paris to tell him to fight on. Sir John's panic was in a sense understandable, as the French seemed to be in serious trouble, and many British units had been in practically ceaseless retreat, averaging three hours' rest per night. Up to 20,000 men had been killed, wounded, captured, or left behind.[29] One Dragoon Guards trooper recalled that horses and men fell asleep on the march: 'I fell off my horse more than once . . . Pain could be endured, food scrounged, but the desire for rest was never-ending.'[30] Fortunately, the pursuing Germans were in no better condition, with their lorries mostly broken down, their horses dying, and their men exhausted.

By 5 September, the German armies were in a rough line along the River Marne, east of Paris, with their nearest units only some twenty miles from the city walls. Joffre had been pulling divisions from the east to stem this advance, ordering that anyone showing weakness should be shot, and sacking incompetent generals. These included Lanrezac, replaced by the dashing Franchet d'Esperay, soon known to the admiring BEF as Desperate Frankie. Joffre came to plead with French to join in a great counter-offensive: 'Monsieur le Maréchal, c'est la France qui vous supplie.' Sir John struggled to reply in French, then burst out, 'Damn it, I can't explain. Tell him that all that men can do our fellows will do.'[31] The BEF found themselves by chance opposite a wide gap between the German 1st and 2nd Armies, held only by a screen of cavalry. In the words of an unimpressed French historian, 'Despite Joffre's pleas and their crushing numerical superiority, the British attacked with great diffidence, exploiting none of their local successes.'[32] The BEF did indeed remain cautious, but rarely was the 'miracle of the Marne' marked by rapid or decisive action: all the armies were too exhausted. The real miracle was that the German high command decided it had lost, and from 9 to 14 September pulled back thirty miles to the River Aisne. This marked the failure of the German plan to knock out France quickly, though it had cost the French 385,000 casualties in five weeks of fighting.[33]

British historians have usually emphasized the key role of the BEF. Having slowed the German advance at Mons and Le Cateau, they were in just the right place to turn the tide at the Marne. This view confirmed the arguments of those who had pressed for intervention when war broke out: if the BEF had not been there, or even if it had arrived a few days later, Germany would have conquered France, and the history of the world would have been different. French historians, however, rarely acknowledge any such debt. In their view, the French army stopped the German invasion, with the BEF playing a negligible part. It is far from clear that it was the BEF that decisively delayed the German spearhead, which, because of exhaustion, lack of supplies, and the diversion of troops to other fronts, was grinding to a halt anyway. The 'miracle of the Marne' was a vast operation involving over a million men on a 100-mile front. The British did little fighting, suffering only 1,701 casualties compared with French losses of 80,000. The BEF was important more for what the Germans feared it might do than for what it actually did: they had decided that if the British crossed the Marne – which they did on 9 September – they would retreat.[34] Hence, the BEF did contribute to the sudden German loss of confidence that was the main outcome of the battle.

The rest of 1914 saw the two sides still striving for rapid victory by manoeuvring to outflank each other to the north-west. The BEF was redeployed on the left of the Allied line, close to its supply ports. In October and November French, British, Indians and Belgians fought a long and bloody battle in defence of the Belgian town of Ypres – the first of four ever bloodier battles over its ruins. From then on, the lines were fixed. The old

BEF had largely been wiped out, having lost 90,000 men killed, wounded or captured, two-thirds of them at Ypres. Many of its regiments were down to 100 men; the 2nd Highland Light Infantry had only thirty of some 600 who had been mobilized at Aldershot three months earlier. By the end of 1914, the French had lost 995,000 men, killed, wounded and prisoners, and the Germans 800,000. These were the deadliest months of the whole war — the clash of armies in the open was far more lethal than the worst battles in the trenches.[*35]

The year had not, as most experts had expected, ended in a knockout. The French army and government were too strong and resilient to succumb to the Schlieffen Plan. The war would become a harrowing test of endurance, blood and treasure that Germany was never likely to win. Kitchener had realized early on that it would be a long struggle, and that Britain would have to raise a mass army for the first time. He warned the French that Britain had practically no more troops, for 'to send untrained men into the fighting line was little short of murder'. Consequently, 'no very important supply of British effectives could be looked for until the late spring of 1915 and . . . the British army would only reach full strength . . . during the Summer of 1917'.[36] For the time being, the French would have to bear the brunt of the slaughter.

The Germans were occupying the coalfields, iron mines and industrial cities of northern France. So the French built new factories in Paris, Lyons and Toulouse; perfumeries turned to making explosives; dozens of hydro-electric power stations were built in mountain valleys. French arms factories would in time supply the Serbs, the Russians and finally the Americans with artillery, machine guns and eventually aircraft and tanks.[37] But all this depended on British money, coal, steel and ships, for Germany had seized 75 per cent of French coal production and 63 per cent of its steel. The French government had expected to pay for a short war with their large gold reserves, but as early as April 1915, 1.5 billion francs of British credit was needed to finance purchases in the USA, Canada and Britain — the first of many loans. From August 1916, France became dependent on British subsidies, without which it could not have fought on. This recalled every war since 1688: Britain financing Continental allies to prevent the hegemony of a hostile power. In modern conditions, unprecedented control of both economies was necessary. The Allies set up a joint purchasing authority, so that they would not bid up world prices against each other in commodities such as wheat and sugar. As the war went on, economic symbiosis increased. British and American imports were vital for arms production. France's normal overland

---

[*] In men killed, the French army lost approximately 60,000 per month in 1914; 30,000 in 1915; 21,000 in 1916; 14,000 in 1917; 22,000 in 1918.

trade with her Continental neighbours had halted, so exports to Britain were needed to maintain civilian employment and plug the trade deficit. By 1917, over 60 per cent of French GNP was being swallowed up by the war – comparable with the effort of the USSR during the Second World War.[38]

Wrangling over money, with the French suspecting the British of profiting from the war, and the British annoyed that the French wanted to preserve gold reserves while spending British subsidies, caused lasting resentment. Most imports and exports had to be carried in British ships, for which there was increasing demand, and this effectively brought the French economy under British supervision. The British government requisitioned all ships and restricted the import of non-essentials into Britain (which included the luxury goods so crucial to the French economy) to clear shipping capacity for food and raw materials. It insisted that the French should do the same if they wanted the use of British ships. In September 1916, British consuls reported that 200 merchant ships were daily lying idle in French ports, and the British government began withdrawing ships from French service. This slowed coal and steel imports and arms production. There were accusations of 'misuse' of British ships, and angry press comment in both countries. The French government agreed to speed up loading and unloading by freeing up more rail traffic, which meant restrictions on civilian travel and on home leave for the troops. The British and French economies came under joint official control, with inter-allied authorities for purchase and allocation of goods. The aim was that all allied citizens should carry a comparable economic burden. By November 1917, the British and French effectively pooled their economic resources. They also created a single body for buying supplies from the USA. The French trade minister, Etienne Clémentel, hoped that after the war ended, this joint trading system would continue, as a barrier against German economic dominance. Jean Monnet, his English-speaking assistant, revived these ideas during the Second World War.

French ministers knew that controls were necessary, but it was politically useful to blame unpopular restrictions on British pressure. The ambassador, Bertie, warned that 'there is an inclination . . . to think that we are making use of France against Germany for our own sole benefit'. British trade unionists came over to try to convince French socialists that Britain was not fighting for profit, and delegations of schoolteachers also went. The historian H.A.L. Fisher, who had studied in France, was sent on an official mission in 1916. He was worried by what he perceived as unawareness of British efforts, and even 'actual depreciation of the part which England was playing in the war', especially after the battle of Verdun, which left a sense of grievance in France. Yet Whitehall disliked the idea of propaganda, and little was done to put the British case in France. The ambassador noted in his diary that many French believed that Britain was being 'enriched by the war which we consequently wish to protract, and the longer it lasts, the more certain we are to get into our hands . . . all the commerce of the world'.[39] 'Carthage' was alive and well.

Les Tommy and the French

Après la guerre finie
Soldat anglais parti
Once the war is done,
English soldier gone.
Song

As the BEF disembarked in August 1914, the mayor of Boulogne called for 'an enthusiastic and brotherly welcome' to 'the valiant British troops'. Fearing that the welcome might be more than brotherly, Kitchener warned of 'temptations, both in wine and women. You must entirely resist both . . . and while treating all women with perfect courtesy you should avoid any intimacy.'[40] Rarely can a field-marshal's instructions have been so energetically breached.

By summer 1917 there were over 2 million 'British' (including Indian and Dominion) troops in France – the peak. During the course of the war, over 5 million served in France – the most intense and numerous direct contacts that have ever occurred between the two nations, and the biggest single experience of 'abroad' ever undergone by British men. Remarkably, this has been little studied[41] – a proof of how inward-looking and selective memory of the Great War became, with each nation wrapped up in its own trauma. What we can say is therefore both impressionistic and somewhat speculative.

The limitations imposed by circumstance partly explain why this experience has been so little remembered (compared, for example, with the American presence in Britain during the Second World War), and also why it left ambivalent feelings. The contact was geographically restricted. The war from 1915 was largely static, and political, practical, and strategic motives kept the BEF mainly confined to the three north-western departments – Pas de Calais, Nord and Somme – bisected by the trench lines. This region had a history of economic contacts with the North of England's textile industries. Lille was France's main centre for studying English. Roubaix had its second oldest football club, set up by English textile engineers.[42] British military presence became massive and visible. In many areas there were more British than French. There were British buses, roadsigns, posters and goods in the shops. Place names were informally anglicized: Monchy Breton to 'Monkey Britain', for example, and Auchonvillers to 'Ocean Villas'. Military needs kept soldiers moving: from the devastated battle zone, emptied of civilians, to inhabited rest areas in the rear, where the closest soldier–civilian contacts took place, and via transit depots and bases (notably Amiens, Rouen, Le Havre and Etaples) to and from Britain. Most of France did not see *les Tommy*, while those regions that did mainly saw them on the move. Personal contact was therefore fleeting. Moreover, the military authorities and welfare bodies worked to limit contacts with civilians, keeping the troops 'out of mischief' through sport, concerts, training, canteens, libraries and hostels.[43] Only non-combat troops – a large number – at the depots and lines of communication, including administrators, storekeepers, medical staff and military police, had lasting contacts with French civilians.

The war also imposed socio-economic constraints. Life in northern France had been shattered, creating broken families, loss of livelihoods and destitution. Many people had fled or been evacuated; others had arrived as refugees from Belgium and occupied northern France, ruled by the Germans with a very heavy hand. If the BEF was a manifestation of war, and itself an instrument of devastation, it was also a source of income: British, compared with French soldiers, had plenty of money, and Dominion troops even more. Routine contacts soldiers had with civilians once the euphoric welcome of August 1914 had passed were wholly or partly commercial: with the owners and staff of *estaminets* (the northern name for bars), peasants selling food and illicit alcohol, householders providing billets, and women offering sex. Reported one cynical French official in 1917, 'the English are loved in propor- tion to the money they leave'.[44] There were cultural differences between a largely rural society and a mostly urban army, whose men often found local conditions primitive: 'The farmer and his wife curmudgeons, everything filthy; we slept in our "flea bags" in preference to the dirty, filthy bed in the room.'[45] At least one regular battalion wore shorts, as if still in India, and 'The men treat the French civilians just like "niggers", kick them about, talk army Hindustani to them.'[46] Many French households found the compulsory billeting of large numbers of often noisy and demanding troops a disruptive burden: 'No one in the area is master of his own house.'[47]

Language difficulties were overcome by the rapid acquisition of pidgin English and French (*il n'y a plus* and *ça ne fait rien*, for example, becoming *napoo* and *san fairy ann*). 'Och, it's easy,' explained a Scottish soldier, 'I just ask the wifie for twa iffs an she gives me three eggs.' A French waitress was equally fluent: 'Messieurs, when you 'ave finis, 'op it.' But letter-writing was difficult, and hence the maintenance of relationships once men had been moved. Nevertheless, one French postal censor was shocked in 1916 at the number of women writing to British soldiers after their units had left, 'as if engaged'. The Irish war artist William Orpen thought that by 1917 'nearly every French girl could speak some English, and great was their anger if one could not understand them'.[48]

What we know of this long, abnormal and often intense relationship comes from letters (monitored by the authorities, and often self-censored for the folks at home), diaries, later memoirs and works of literature. It also comes from the records of military authorities concerned with order and discipline – something bound to skew our vision by giving prominence to theft, vandalism, drunkenness and prostitution. Theft and vandalism came in many forms. Hungry and thirsty soldiers retreating after Mons helped themselves to apples from the orchards, and to anything else they could find. In the battle zone, abandoned and semi-abandoned houses and farms were sources of firewood and building materials. Fires were started to keep warm, and these often spread. It was little consolation to locals that the Germans were worse, and the French no better. 'Scrounging' was a developed art, and it took place on a huge scale. Anything removable – potatoes, coal, straw, chickens, eggs, milk, wood – was likely to be removed. To the frustration of the military police, this was winked at by regimental officers. We might wonder why the former bothered, but they were responding to complaints from local people and mayors, which greatly increased from 1916. The British were convinced that the French were exaggerating losses as they knew the army would pay. Worse was the impact of official military activity. Horses were pastured in the fields, which were also trampled in exercises. Fodder was requisitioned and barns occupied, disrupting farming activity. Land was taken over for everything from football pitches to airfields.[49]

Drink fuelled the Franco-British relationship. One of the few booming industries close to the front line was its manufacture and supply, drawing on established practices of home brewing and distilling. In some villages, every second house turned into an *estaminet*, also supplying food. 'The estaminets with their cheap wine and feeds of eggs and chips were paradise to us.'[50] If there was wrangling over prices, and no doubt difficulty with unruly soldiers, there must also have been much complicity between soldiers and civilians to hoodwink the military authorities. One young officer, Robert Graves, was disgusted by the whole situation:

I find it very difficult to like the French here . . . I have not met a single case of the hospitality that one meets among the peasants of other countries [though] we are fighting for their dirty little lives. They suck enormous quantities of money out of us too . . . Every private soldier gets his five-franc note (nearly four shillings) every ten days, and spends it at once on eggs, coffee and beer in the local *estaminets*; the prices are ridiculous and the stuff bad . . . the other day I saw barrels of already thin beer being watered from the canal with a hose-pipe.[51]

He was surprised that 'there were so few clashes between the British and the local French – who returned our loathing and were convinced that, when the war ended, we would stay and hold the Channel ports'. If this was an extreme view – coloured by Graves's rather priggish fastidiousness – the ancient fear of post-war occupation was voiced even in French government circles. President Poincaré was uneasy at being invited to lunch by George V, who was visiting his troops – he felt that he should have been the host on French soil.[52] At a less exalted level, ordinary people simply got tired of the overwhelming presence of so many foreign men.

'BENE AND HOT'

A picturesque example of how France could leave traces on British behaviour was the taste acquired by troops from Lancashire for the sweet liqueur Benedictine, especially mixed with hot water – 'Bene and hot' – creating something resembling warm cough mixture. After the war, the habit flourished, and Lancashire became a centre of Benedictine drinking. Nearly a century later, the Burnley Miners' Club remains the world's largest single consumer of Benedictine.

William Orpen, 'Dieppe': British troops acquiring a taste for Benedictine.

'LE FOOT'

We know little of whether the British presence produced durable effects on French life, except in one important area: football. The ubiquitous British habit of starting kick-abouts at any spare moment, as well as organized tournaments whenever circumstances permitted, amazed both the French and the Germans. The common practice of kicking balls into no man's land as a 'kick-off' for attacks was considered by the Germans as shockingly unmilitary. The French 'could not understand the reason why the English spent so much of their life on football . . . instead of practising warfare'.[53] Eventually the French 5th Army set up sports teams, and there were inter-Allied matches. French inexperience was evident, 'the French players never being able to control the ball sufficiently to bring it near to the goal mouth . . . [They] were fast enough and would no doubt make good footballers if they had more practice with British teams.'[54] This wartime experience began the take-off of football as a mass sport all over France.

Villages in the rest areas, where soldiers normally spent four days out of twelve, provided a haven where they could get clean, sleep, eat and for a time forget the war. In contrast with the trenches – 'devastation, desolation and khaki' – it seemed a rural idyll: 'the ground was everywhere carpeted with anemones and cowslips . . . in the heart of the forest, it was impossible to catch a sound of the outside world'; 'How much we owe to that peaceful little village fourteen miles behind the lines for restoring us all to sanity and our customary high spirits.' As well as communing with nature, human contact with civilians, especially women, was a crucial part of relaxation: 'one gets dreadfully tired of eternally seeing people in trousers, and those khaki!'[55] Billeting in houses and farms allowed relationships, resembling domestic life, to form – and billeting allowances (1 franc per day for officers, 50 centimes for NCOs, 5 centimes for private soldiers) kept many French families going. Soldiers were very appreciative of kindness: one sick man, who was nursed by his hosts, said that 'they could not have done more for me had I been their most loved relation'.[56]

The local French communities had become predominantly female, as most men between the ages of eighteen and fifty had been mobilized and were away fighting outside the British zone. If this could create a maternal atmosphere for young soldiers in *estaminets* and billets, it also meant a very erotic one. Pre-war stereotypes created fantasies, not only of Paris as 'a sort of gigantic brothel where women wore nothing but georgette underwear and extra long silk stockings', but in general of 'a different system of taboos about sex'. This expectation could rather comically lead to disappointment, with 'the poorer

British expectations about the French led to absurd misunderstandings.

THE FRENCH GIRL.
AS IMAGINED   AS SHE IS.
AT HOME.

classes' being found 'rather repellent',[57] and to huge misunderstanding, when highly unusual wartime sexual behaviour – sternly disapproved of in France – was interpreted by the British as 'typically French'.

Contemporaries reiterated that war created special conditions: the absence of normal social controls, the need for affection and intimacy on the part of frightened and traumatized men (including boys who 'did not want to die virgins'[58]), pressure from comrades to prove virility, boredom, ready money, the effects of drink and – among the privileged behind the lines – ample opportunity. Among civilians, the absence of male breadwinners, homelessness, the need to bring up children amid food shortages and spiralling prices, especially during the severe winter of 1916–17, the inadequacy of government aid, and the harsh official requisitioning policy of farm produce, all created an impoverished female population. This was the context for relationships running from patriotic infatuation on the French side and boyish fantasy on the British – one soldier was content 'just to sit and look . . . without speaking' at the daughter of the family where he was billeted[59] – via flirtation and touching, to romantic passion, and commercial or semi-commercial sex. Some peasant families adopted a practical attitude that would not have surprised readers of Maupassant, and in some cases at least must have combined pleasure with business: 'the farm was run by a widow and her three daughters all good looking. The sergeant slept in the farmhouse and after two days I found out that my two mates had fixed up with two of the daughters to sleep with them leaving the youngest one for me. I was indeed sorry when we were moved.'[60] Relationships such as these, and the wholly commercial ones near base camps, ports and railway stations, led to an epidemic (highest among the Australians) of venereal diseases, 'a grave danger to the troops' fighting ability, especially for the officer'.[61] About

55,000 British soldiers – about one in thirty – needed hospital treatment during 1917 alone.[62] Exhortation and punishment having a predictably limited effect, the army eventually turned to regulated brothels on the French pattern – displaying a blue light for officers, red for other ranks – in spite of criticism in Britain. It was estimated that 50–60,000 women were working as prostitutes for British soldiers. Those found to be infectious were liable to internment in Rouen.

French soldiers were naturally resentful of *les Anglais*, who had more money and were regarded as more smartly uniformed – hence punningly nicknamed *les sanglés*, 'the tightly fitted'. Fear of infidelity among women at home was obsessive in all the armies, and for most of the war the main suspect seducers for the French (apart from the detested *embusqués*, the shirkers) were the British. Characters in one famous war novel complain of 'More women arrested at the English camp. And not whores, you can be sure: married women . . . What a blow for their husbands, when they find out . . . they should have their heads shaved.'[63] It was considered 'shameful' for married women to be seen with British soldiers, and indignant neighbours sometimes had offenders arrested as prostitutes. There was a report that one married woman, learning that her husband was arriving on leave, claimed that she had been raped. A visiting British politician was worried by 'the attitude of our junior officers . . . towards French women, the light way they treat them in public'.[64] French feminists were shocked to discover an 'almost pornographic' soldiers' phrase-book entitled 'Five Minutes Conversation with Young Ladies'. Starting with 'Voulez-vous accepter l'apéritif?' and 'Pouvez-vous dîner avec moi?' it progressed briskly to 'Permettez-moi de vous baiser la main – de vous embrasser' and 'Où habitez-vous?' and the wistful but frank observation that 'Notre bonheur sera de courte durée.' The book was denounced not only as an insult to France, but as a blow against Anglo–Saxon women who expected their men to be returned 'morally and physically pure'.[65]

For all these reasons, wartime contacts did not create unalloyed affection. Alongside British memories of cheering crowds and hospitable peasants were others of rapacity, promiscuity and dirt. If the French were grateful to their British defenders, they often felt that they were behaving like conquerors. The massive British presence, if it created friendships and a few marriages, also gave rise to mutual dislike – even 'loathing' according to Robert Graves – on both sides. Fortunately, the BEF was 'one of the best-mannered armies in history'.[66] French relations with the notoriously indisciplined Australians and the late-arriving Americans were worse, culminating in serious Franco-American brawls in Paris, and a 'horribly violent' Inter-Allied rugby final between France and the USA in 1919 (France won).[67] Nevertheless, the arrival of the Americans put the British in the shade. The reasons seem plain: the warmly welcomed arrival of the BEF in 1914 had not brought

William Orpen,
'Changing billets':
Troops billeted on
French civilians often
formed intense if short-
lived relationships.

rapid victory, but the arrival of the American Expeditionary Force in 1918 promised to do just that.

No precise balance sheet of memories is possible, but two points are worth noting. First, the memory of the British presence was positive enough to make it a rallying point for resistance against the new German occupation in 1940, and to add extra warmth to the welcome given to the British in northern France in 1944. On the other hand, the number of Franco–British marriages seems to have been quite small – only fifty-one in Calais during the whole war, for example.[68] Richard Cobb mentions a sprinkling of ex-Tommies who settled in northern France, often making advantageous marriages with the daughters of shopkeepers or *estaminet* owners, and speaking 'an odd blend of English and *chtimi*' (the dialect of the industrial north).[69] Nevertheless, the war did not create numerous cross-Channel family bonds.

Some French civilians had far more dangerous, and sometimes tragic, contact with the British. It began early and accidentally, as soldiers left behind in the 1914 retreat were found and helped by French families, including children, sometimes after weeks of hiding in the woods. It was widely believed that the Germans were killing and even torturing captured soldiers – all too plausible, given the atrocities in Belgium. As the months passed, it did indeed become the case that isolated soldiers were liable to be shot as spies, and civilians helping them risked death or forced labour, and the burning of their houses. In one incident, eleven British soldiers hiding in a mill were captured and shot, along with their French protectors. Some took part in more-or-less informal escape networks; others simply sheltered British troops in their own houses. The most nightmarish case was that of Trooper Fowler, of the 11th Hussars, who was found in January 1915 wandering dazed, filthy and starving in the woods near Le Cateau. He was hidden by a peasant family, the Belmont-Goberts, in a cupboard in their kitchen, which was crowded with billeted German soldiers. In the cupboard he stayed until 1918, air and food reaching him through a gap in the wood, only emerging when the Germans were away. Despite the strain on the physical and mental health of Fowler and his hosts, they all managed to survive the war. Less lucky was a corporal from the same regiment hidden in the same village, who was caught in September 1915 and shot, his hostess being sentenced to twenty years' hard labour in Germany. There were several similar cases.[70]

The best known, thanks to recent investigation by Ben Macintyre, is that of Private Robert Digby, of the Hampshires, who with several comrades was sheltered from September 1914 onwards by the people of Villeret, a village twenty miles south-west of Le Cateau.[71] Several families became directly involved, pooling their meagre rations and providing hiding places from the Germans billeted in the village. Many neighbours knew what was going on, because the soldiers attempted to pass as locals – not too difficult where German soldiers were concerned, but transparent to real Picards. Digby, sheltered by the Dessennes, a family of peasants cum tobacco smugglers, fell in love with twenty-year-old Claire, and they had a daughter, Ellen/Hélène, born in November 1915. Whether through jealousy, village feuding, or simply fear at increasingly ferocious German threats against abettors of British 'spies', Digby and three comrades were betrayed and shot publicly in the village in May 1916. He wrote 'the last letter of my life' to 'darling Claire': 'Farewell, and never forget Robert, who dies happy and satisfied for France and for my own country . . . Embrace my baby girl and later, when she is grown, tell her the truth about her father.'[72]

When the Germans retreated the following year to the Hindenburg Line, they systematically razed Villeret and hundreds of other villages in a vast swathe of desolation. People returned after the armistice, destitute. During the 1920s, some received medals and financial compensation from the British government and public for their help to British soldiers. The poverty-stricken Madame Belmont-Gobert was decorated and paid back-dated mess fees (tuppence a day) for the years that Trooper Fowler had spent in her cottage;

and the 11th Hussars raised further money for her – and acquired the cupboard itself for the regimental museum.[73]

The other way for French civilians to become dangerously involved with the British was through espionage or resistance behind the German lines. Women led important networks, helped by their greater ability to move around in occupied France and Belgium. Louise Thuliez, a schoolteacher from Lille, began travelling round 'like a determined terrier', contacting lost soldiers, finding them hiding places, and then guiding them through Belgium to Holland. Princesse Marie de Croÿ (who was half British) joined in, offering her château north of Le Cateau, which had become a military hospital, as a hiding place, and providing clothes, food, money and forged papers. Networks also provided military information to the Allies (for example, by counting troop trains) and distributed resistance literature. There were several such networks, but they had no experience in security, nor did the soldiers they helped. Marie de Croÿ was compromised by a letter of thanks sent to her from Britain by a grateful escaper. Another, Eugène Jacquet, a Lille wine merchant, was shot and his large network destroyed partly on the evidence of a diary left behind by an escaping British airman.[74] Such organizations were quickly penetrated and their organizers arrested. An important contact in Belgium was Edith Cavell, the principal of a nursing school in Brussels. She agreed to shelter escapers brought in groups by Louise Thuliez and subsequently shepherded to the Dutch frontier by teams of couriers (some of them peacetime smugglers). More professional resistance activity was undertaken by Louise de Bettignies, a young English-trained governess from Lille, who was recruited by British intelligence when she arrived in Folkestone as a refugee in 1914. Using Catholic connections, she built up a network of 200 agents, gathering material on the German army and maintaining contact by wireless and carrier pigeon. She was regarded as 'an utterly trustworthy and reliable individual who was a masterly judge of character and drove her agents hard'. In 1915 the chief of the imperial general staff wrote of her that 'neither asking nor accepting any reward, she organized and directed an extensive and most efficient service of intelligence . . . sending complete records of troops movements for many months past'.[75]

In August 1915 Edith Cavell was arrested, possibly because neither she nor escaping soldiers paid much attention to security. For reasons unclear, she admitted everything, including the names and activities of other members of the network.[76] She and a male associate were executed in October. She was hailed as a martyr, frequently referred to in France as a new Joan of Arc – a real sign of reconciliation, considering that Joan had long been a symbol of anglophobia. Thuliez, de Croÿ and others received long prison sentences, but were released in 1918. Louise de Bettignies was caught in November

1915, but she managed to swallow a report she was carrying and gave no information. Chastened by the international outcry over Cavell's shooting, the Germans commuted her death sentence to hard labour, but she continued to resist in prison, and harsh treatment contributed to her death in September 1918. A memorial was erected in Lille, and her name was used to inspire resistance in 1940, though subsequently she, and other resisters – 600 women were in German prisons by the end of the war – have faded from popular memory, overshadowed by the Resistance of the Second World War.[77]

Stalemate and Slaughter, 1915–17

In the most literal sense . . . we are defending England in France.
'A Paper by the General Staff on the Future Conduct of the War' (1915)[78]

It does not appear to me that the gain of two or three more kilometres of ground is of much consequence . . . Our object rather seems to be to kill as many Germans as possible at the least loss to ourselves.
British general[79]

Whatever you do, you lose a lot of men.
French general[80]

How should the war be fought? How could it be won? The assumptions of most experts that for military, economic and political reasons a modern war could only last a few months had been confounded. One conclusion, that of 'westerners', was that the decisive struggle was the Western Front, where the British and French must defeat the German armies. This view required Britain to commit its maximum force as soon as possible, preferably by adopting conscription. Numbers and firepower would bleed the enemy to death, at the necessary cost of the blood of one's own soldiers. Those who balked at this prospect sought other strategies: naval blockade to strangle German trade, and if necessary starve its people; or the opening of new eastern fronts in the Balkans or the Turkish empire. 'Easterners' hoped to force Germany to disperse its forces to aid its allies. They also wanted to prop up the Russians, who had suffered heavy defeats, but whose manpower might eventually bring victory. This required acceptance of a long war and a defensive strategy on the Western Front. It also meant that new British forces would be diverted to other theatres, and so the French army would bear the brunt in the west. This had both moral and political implications. The French (and the Russians) would have to do most of the dying for the time being. The British army, when it reached maximum strength in 1917, could be expected to play the decisive role in winning the war, giving the British government a predominant voice in the peace.

This strategic dilemma was not a Franco-British divide. Some French politicians, mistrusting their own generals, were receptive to 'eastern' enterprises; most British generals were or became 'westerners'; and all British politicians and generals knew that their own security demanded that France should not be defeated, or seek peace. But in practice, the debate did turn on whether Britain would agree to French demands to send more and more men to France, and take over far more of the trench line. This grew to 450 miles long, but the British at most held only a quarter of it – admittedly, including highly contested areas that had to be strongly manned. But how strongly? Should not the British take over more? This constant tussle meant that relations between the British and French governments, and between British and French headquarters, were often strained, and at times neared breaking point: 'in each other's eyes at least, the French expected too much too soon, while the British did too little too late'.[81] Inevitably there were suspicions of bad faith. 'While we knew that we were "playing the game" loyally and unselfishly by our allies,' noted a senior BEF staff officer blandly, 'the idea of "Perfide Albion" is by no means dead in France and probably our allies did not place implicit confidence in the honesty of our policy and diplomacy.'[82]

As the two Allies were, though side by side, fighting independently, it was difficult to resolve differences and make joint decisions. Two sovereign governments controlled two independent armies, took their own decisions, and kept their secrets. Cooperation was decided by negotiation at ministerial and military conferences. There was no joint strategic authority or unified command. Much depended on personal contact and confidence among ministers and generals who came and went. Traditional Franco-British prejudices aggravated by linguistic incomprehension were always a factor. It did not seem to help much that Sir John French was an enthusiastic collector of Napoleonic memorabilia or that his successor Sir Douglas Haig had communicated with Napoleon at spiritualist seances. The British found the French demanding, secretive, emotional, talkative and bad-mannered. The French found the British amateurish, slow, timid, uncooperative and uncommunicative. The mercurial Sir John French wrote in his diary that 'the conversation was of the usual kind when I am confronted with the French Generals. It is very difficult to describe; but they appear to throw all logical argument to the winds when their own ideas are in the least degree opposed. They become absolutely *mulish*.' Haig at least took French lessons, and apparently became reasonably fluent – in so far as such a notoriously inarticulate man could. He liked Joffre ('not clever, but reliable') and although 'they are funny fellows the French Generals . . . I think I can work with them'. Yet we should not exaggerate the effects of personal and national friction. Both sides knew that they had to get on, and relations somewhat improved after the bad start in 1914. 'The great thing to remember in dealing with them,' advised the chief of the imperial general staff, 'is that they are Frenchmen and not Englishmen, and do not and never will look at things the way we look at them. I suppose that they think that we are queer people.'[83]

In 1915, the 'easterners' had their chance. The French suggested an expedition to Salonika to aid the Serbs. The British, particularly Kitchener and Churchill, preferred a seaborne attack on Constantinople – 'the one imaginative strategic idea of the war on the Allied side'.[84] The potential gains from a relatively small effort seemed dazzling compared with the bloody stalemate in France: to knock Germany's new ally Turkey out of the war, relieve Russia from Turkish advances in the Caucasus, have a warm-water route through the Black Sea to supply Russia with munitions, and so keep its huge potential strength harnessed to the Allied cause. Other benefits might be to bring Italy and some Balkan states into the war on the Allied side. But was this too optimistic? Even if the plan had worked and the fleet reached Constantinople, would the Turkish government have tamely surrendered? Arguably, the whole strategy was unrealistic.[85]

The French were willing, as the British would provide most of the forces and take most of the risk. On 18 March 1915, an Anglo-French fleet under the British Admiral de Robeck, including sixteen mostly obsolescent battleships, attempted to force the narrow straits to Istanbul. They were nearly successful, but mines, hard to sweep under fire from shore, sank several ships, including three battleships, and – perhaps with victory in their grasp – they drew back. Troops would have to clear the land defences. On 25 April, 200 ships landed British troops, French colonial troops, and the Australian and New Zealand Army Corps (ANZAC) at the tip of the narrow Gallipoli peninsula. They mostly took the Turks by surprise, and their best chance was to break through before they could rally. But the Anzacs were fought to a standstill within sight of the goal. Thereafter, they could not advance against increasing Turkish resistance. In August, a second landing of 20,000 British and Gurkhas again came within yards of breaking through. The peculiar horrors of the campaign included the cramped area of fighting; lack of shelter from artillery fire; heat; thirst; and epidemics. A French Zouave captain wrote:

Diseases snake through the trenches under the burning sun . . .
in the air, in the food, in the stinking water, in the irritating whine
of mosquitoes, the alarming buzzing of huge flies, the countless
tormenting bites of fleas and lice . . . as millions of fragments
of metal tear the unbreathable air . . . We eat our bread kneeling
on the ground. And our air is made of dust and iron.[86]

The casualties were large: probably over 250,000 Turks were killed and 46,000 of the Allies (21,000 British, 15,000 French and 10,000 Anzacs). A casualty of a different kind was Winston Churchill, who resigned from the Cabinet and went to fight in the trenches. It was decided to end the campaign, and the troops were efficiently evacuated, without loss of life, in December and January. The French-led Salonika expedition was also a failure, though a less bloody one. The problem of supplying Russia was partly alleviated by building a railway from the northern port of Murmansk – which would prove a lifeline in the Second World War.

Both sides intended to force a decision in 1916. The result would be a series of battles of industrialized destruction which left permanent scars on the societies, cultures and memories of all the participants. At a general staff conference at Chantilly on 6 December 1915, France, Britain (which adopted conscription early in 1916), Russia and Italy had agreed to launch 'a simultaneous combined offensive with the maximum of troops possible on their respective fronts'.[87] This would force the Germans to fight everywhere at once, 'wear out' – i.e. kill – their reserves, overwhelm them and bring victory. After much polite negotiation – in which Joffre was reluctant to 'force my choice of the theatre of operations upon our Allies', while Haig was eager to 'do everything possible' to fall in with his plans[88] – it was decided that the main effort would involve both the French and British attacking astride the River Somme in June 1916, to coincide with Russian and Italian offensives.

The Germans also had a plan to finish the war. General von Falkenhayn intended to pre-empt the Allied attack, rather than waiting for the moment 'when the balance of numbers will deprive Germany of all remaining hope'. He, like many German nationalists, saw Britain as the 'arch enemy' holding the *entente* together, just as it had led the alliance against Napoleon. British strategists feared a German surprise attack to seize the Channel ports and invade England while the BEF was stuck in Flanders mud. But Falkenhayn ruled out invasion as unfeasible, and considered the British army too strongly entrenched to attack directly. Instead, he decided to destroy the French army, and so deprive Britain of its Continental auxiliary:

> The strain on France has reached breaking point – though it is
> certainly borne with the most remarkable devotion. If we succeed
> in opening the eyes of her people to the fact that in a military sense
> they have nothing more to hope for, that breaking point would
> be reached and England's best sword knocked out of her hand.

The French army was too strong to be defeated conventionally, so Falkenhayn decided to force it to fight in unfavourable circumstances. This would be done by attacking a place so significant it would force the French 'to throw in every man they have. If they do so the forces of France will bleed to death.' If the French did not take the poisoned bait and retreated, 'the effect on French morale will be enormous'.[89] Moreover, the plight of the French would force the inexperienced British to attack to help them, thus suffering huge casualties too. The chosen killing-ground for Operation *Gericht* – 'Judgement' – was the exposed fortress town of Verdun. Judgement Day came on 21 February 1916. 'Capitaine Danrit' (the nationalist writer Emile Driant), who was holding a forward position, had written to a friend the previous day, 'To foresee "the war of tomorrow" was not difficult: it was bound to come. To predict this attack on Verdun . . . was more daring. We're about to have it.'[90] He was among the first to be killed. For four months the Germans struggled forward, with men on both sides lost in a chaos of devastation that all found hard to describe. 'Imagine, if you can, a storm, a tempest, growing steadily worse, *in which the rain consists entirely of cobblestones, in which the hail is made up entirely of masonry blocks.*' No one has managed to compute exactly the human cost – 'I realize that I'm walking on corpses, from the way the soil gives under my feet, and feels slippery and soft' – but both sides suffered casualties of over 300,000.[91]

Haig, in response to Joffre's pleas, reluctantly took over part of the French line. Kitchener's new army was scarcely ready to attack, and Haig was unwilling to have his men killed in place of Frenchmen. He did not want to be diverted from the Somme offensive planned for June, which he was unwilling to bring forward except in case of 'an emergency to save the French from disaster, and Paris perhaps from capture'.[92] So for three months the French had to bear the brunt of the Verdun offensive themselves. This had a lasting effect on French perceptions of the British, and in many soldiers' letters there were complaints at British inaction. One wrote that the British were 'holding on to their beautiful army for after the war'.[93] The idea that the British were willing to 'fight to the last Frenchman' was sufficiently widespread to be used as German propaganda not only during this war, but in the 1930s and 1940s too.

Verdun became, and in French memory remains, the Calvary of their nation, the supreme ordeal of will and endurance, the turning point of the First World War, and its deepest horror. The battle continued because for both the French and the Germans Verdun became a symbol of victory or defeat: the more soldiers died, the more important it became to persevere. Its dominance in the French imagination is an important reason why they remember the First World War as a French, rather than an Allied, effort – even though the Germans attacked Verdun as a blow against Britain.

For the British, the equivalent national memory is of the Somme, 'the ghostly twin of Verdun'.[94] The general staff hoped the offensive might land the decisive blow. For the first time the British army would take the lead – increasingly so as the French haemorrhaged at Verdun, and were obliged greatly to reduce their share in the offensive. President Poincaré feared that 'the English will say they have saved France; the victory will be an English victory; the peace will be an English peace'.[95] But there was no victory. On 1 July 1916, nineteen British and three French divisions attacked simultaneously. The French made reasonable advances, as did some of the British formations, mainly those benefiting from French heavy artillery support. But the British suffered 57,000 casualties, of whom 19,000 were killed, out of the 100,000 men who advanced – the worst losses ever suffered by the British army in a single day, and as many as the French lost at Leipzig (1813), the bloodiest battle of the Napoleonic wars. Advancing reinforcements heard a sound like 'wet fingers screeching across an enormous plate of glass' – the screams of thousands of wounded men.[96] A British officer advancing over the same ground weeks later found bodies of men wounded that day, who had 'crawled into shell holes, wrapped their waterproof sheets round them, taken out their bibles and died'.[97] The carnage on 1 July – a subject that still arouses passionate controversy – was due to an over-estimate of the effects of the huge artillery bombardment of 1.7 million shells, which it was wrongly believed would have smashed the German defences. The French attack suffered less, and the failure of British commanders to profit from greater French experience may have been a consequence of imperfect inter-Allied relations.

Though the memory of horror and waste is common to Verdun and the Somme, there is a great difference. Verdun, the indomitable defence of French soil, could have meaning. The Somme, a failed attack on muddy foreign fields, became a crowning symbol of futility – even though a central image of that futility, that of untrained British troops advancing in lines against machine guns, was a later myth. Haig later pleaded that he had undertaken and pursued the offensive to take the pressure off the French at Verdun. This question too still causes controversy.[98] The campaign had been planned before the Germans attacked Verdun as part of a joint Allied strategy. It was not brought forward, but was launched on the original schedule, albeit with far less French involvement. While helping the French became a significant aim, it was neither the principal nor the original motive, and cannot be regarded as the reason for the heavy British losses. It was the Russians, not the British, who came to the aid of Verdun by attacking early. Meticulously planned by General Alexei Brusilov, theirs was the only Allied success, shattering the Austrian army and advancing some sixty miles on a broad front, forcing the Germans to transfer forces from the Western and Italian fronts. Yet in the ghastly logic of the war of attrition, the Somme did have major consequences. The Germans found the British army far more formidable than expected, and they too suffered grievously, even more than at Verdun. Though the British lost roughly twice as many lives as the Germans, they had not collapsed, and the Germans could not mount the decisive counter-attack they had planned. Far from winning the war, the Germans were only just holding on. The British, despite their losses, were now the leading Allied power.[99]

France and Britain determined to try again in 1917, while the new democratic Russian republic, in power since March, was still fighting on the Eastern Front. The new prime ministers David Lloyd George and Aristide Briand, horrified by the carnage and mistrusting their generals, wanted a different solution. 'They looked for a new man with promise,' observes William Philpott. 'They found a man who made promises.'[100] This was General Robert Nivelle, who had a British mother and spoke excellent English. This should have been an advantage, but it contributed to disaster. Nivelle was clever, optimistic and persuasive. He convinced Lloyd George to support his plan for winning the war at a stroke, through a coordinated Franco-British attack. French ministers dubiously acquiesced. The sceptical Haig was placed by Lloyd George under Nivelle's direction. The latter believed that he had discovered 'the formula' for a rapid breakthrough without huge losses: overwhelming and carefully coordinated artillery fire, followed by rapid advance by concentrated masses of infantry. This was something like what Brusilov had done the previous year. But Nivelle was no Brusilov, and the Germans were not the Austrians. The Germans had decided to remain on the defensive in the west, while finishing off the Russians, decimated by Brusilov's costly victory. So in March 1917, taking the Allies by surprise, they abandoned their positions opposite the British and withdrew thirty miles to the Hindenburg Line. The abandoned area was thoroughly devastated: buildings were blown up, trees cut down, wells poisoned, ruins booby-trapped. The new line was shorter, and required fewer troops. It meant that the planned British attacks in support of Nivelle's offensive had lost much of their point. Yet Nivelle went ahead, and the French attacked on 16 April, focusing on the Chemin des Dames on the heights north of the River Aisne. The result was carnage comparable with that of the British at the Somme: 130,000 soldiers were killed or wounded in five days. The attack was called off, and Nivelle sacked. The government and high command were in crisis. French soldiers had had enough, and there were mutinies involving about 40,000 men in half the army's divisions.

These were strange mutinies, however. There were riots, a good deal of speech-making and vandalism, and some men, doubtless inspired by events in Russia as well as their own history, shouted 'Vive la Révolution!' But there was little violence, and few men deserted to the enemy or abandoned forward positions. They had gone on strike against futile slaughter. The response was also moderate. Though a few officers ordered summary executions, most – led by the new chief of the general staff, the phlegmatic General

Pétain – took steps to rally the men. They promised no more useless attacks, and better food, rest and leave. Though over 3,000 men were found guilty of mutiny, and 499 sentenced to death, only twenty-seven were executed.[101] The Germans never realized how vulnerable the French army was during the summer of 1917. Had they done so, they might have won the war. Arguably – though it is an argument found more among British than French writers – the French army remained largely passive until the final battles in 1918. Pétain decided to 'wait for the Americans and the tanks'.

Instead of following Pétain's defensive strategy, Haig decided that he could break through from Ypres. An important reason was to force the Germans away from the coast, and capture their submarine bases, for the submarine campaign, aimed at starving Britain, was inflicting its highest-ever level of sinkings. Haig accepted optimistic intelligence reports, based on intricate but unreliable estimates of German casualties. These indicated that the Germans were close to collapse, and that a final effort could break them.[102] The result was the third battle of Ypres, remembered as Passchendaele, which began in July 1917. To the grimly familiar pattern – early advances followed by immobility and mutual slaughter – was added the ordeal of mud, stirred up by shells and unseasonably heavy rain: 'the ground is churned up to a depth of ten feet and is the consistency of porridge'.[103] Thousands of men were lost in the quagmire. The British, Australians and Canadians lost over 250,000 men, as did the Germans. It was suggested, as after the Somme, that the battle had been necessary to take the strain from the demoralized French, but the real reason was Haig's conviction that the British could strike a blow to hasten the end of the war.

All schemes for forcing a decision, at Gallipoli, Verdun, the Somme, and Ypres, turned into struggles of attrition: while the attacking side, usually the Allies, inevitably lost heavily, so did the defenders, as they were forced to move reinforcements forward under earth-shattering shellfire. The British called it 'wearing-out', the French 'usure'. But every army was wearing itself out as much as it wore out the enemy: every one approached breaking point, and some broke. The Brusilov offensive crippled the Austrian army, which began to dissolve with desertions and mass surrenders; but the Russians themselves lost a million men, and this contributed to revolution. The French, mangled by Verdun and then by Nivelle's futile offensive, mutinied in April 1917. The Italian army disintegrated in October 1917. The British and German armies fought on, racked by the horrors of the Somme and Ypres. The British came briefly in sight of collapse in the face of the last German onslaught in March–April 1918, and the Germans effectively did collapse from August 1918 onwards.

The Germans had always been pessimistic about a long war. In manpower and production, the Central Powers were outweighed by the Allies. Austria and Turkey required German troops to prop them up. The bloodbath on the Western Front was eviscerating their army. An equally decisive struggle was taking place at sea. The Royal Navy throttled German maritime trade, and put pressure on neutrals. British money and credit sustained the Allied effort, and (as Napoleon had found) could outbid its enemy in the few neutral markets the Royal Navy did not control. Germany's industry was short of raw materials, and its population was increasingly hungry. The average daily calorie intake fell from 3,400 to 1,000, and the civilian deathrate increased by 37 per cent. The German surface fleet – one of the causes of the conflict – could not shake British control even of the North Sea, and after the battle of Jutland (May 1916) it stayed in port. Submarines seemed to offer the means of starving Britain as Britain was starving Germany. But the German navy's plans were absurdly optimistic. In 1915 it had only twenty-seven U-boats, which managed to sink only twenty-one of 5,000 ships travelling to and from Britain. Its declaration of unrestricted submarine warfare in February 1915, sinking on sight all ships in European waters, was politically disastrous, especially when the liner *Lusitania* was sunk in May 1915. The United States – already a vital source of war materials for the Allies – was brought closer to war. During 1917, the Germans pinned their last hopes on another U-boat campaign. The navy calculated that by sinking 600,000 tons of shipping per month for six months they could force Britain to surrender by 1 August 1917. But though sinkings reached a frightening level in the spring of 1917, and Britain adopted mild rationing, the German sums were disastrously wrong, and Britain was never in danger of defeat.[104] The main result of their campaign was to make American entry into the war inevitable.

In every country, there were calls for peace negotiations, mostly from left-wing, humanitarian or religious voices. The American president, Woodrow Wilson, announced 'Fourteen Points' for a peace based on compromise and self-determination. But compromise had become impossible: all had sacrificed so much that governments and peoples alike wanted victory, and both sides thought it was possible. A report on British army morale in December 1917, based on monitoring soldiers' letters, concluded that 'War weariness there is, and an almost universal longing for peace but there is a strong current of feeling that only one kind of peace is possible and that the time is not yet come.'[105] Similar comments could have been made of every army, except the Russian and part of the Austrian. The Allies were fighting a war to destroy 'militarism', and this required not only victory, but dismantling the structures in Germany and Austria that sustained military power. Germany – now effectively under a military dictatorship run by the stolid Marshal Hindenburg and the brilliant, ruthless and unstable General Ludendorff – needed victory to maintain Germany's status as a great power and stave off revolution at home.

The Road to Pyrrhic Victory, 1918

Many of us are now tired. To those I would say that victory will belong to
the side that holds out the longest . . . there is no course open to us but
to fight it out. Every position must be held to the last man: there must be
no retirement. With our backs to the wall and believing in the justice of
our cause each one of us must fight to the end. The safety of our Homes
and the Freedom of mankind alike depend on the conduct of each one of
us at this critical moment.

FIELD-MARSHAL HAIG, 'Order of the Day', 11 April 1918

The Germans knew that their last chance of victory was during the first
half of 1918. Lenin's Bolsheviks, who seized power in Russia in
November 1917, abandoned the struggle and ceded huge territories to
Germany, providing vital resources for war and releasing German troops for
use in the West. The United States had declared war in April 1917, but
would not have a significant army in Europe for many months. Ludendorff
returned to the logic of the Schlieffen Plan: destroy the most dangerous
opponent first. This was now the British army. On 11 November 1917, it
was decided to launch 'an annihilating blow', in the form of a series of
massive surprise attacks. It was Germany's final gamble.

The first blow was struck on 21 March 1918 on the old Somme battlefield. 'Operation Michael' began with an intense bombardment by 6,600 guns
and 3,500 mortars, followed by an attack led by storm troops armed with
flame-throwers and machine guns, and cloaked by fog. The brunt of the
attack was borne by the British 5th Army, thinly spread, under-gunned and,
having recently taken over part of the French line, with incomplete defences.
The British expected an attack further north, to threaten the Channel. Instead,
the Germans had hit at their weakest point, where they linked up with the
French. As in 1914, the Germans nearly split the Allies apart. There was
confusion and panic, with large numbers of men surrendering, and a disor-
derly retreat marked by looting and drunkenness – 'the Boche could not do
worse', wrote one Frenchwoman. The civilian population were suddenly
exposed to another German invasion, and many had to leave everything and
flee. Many felt let down by the British, and the prefect of the Nord department reported that the BEF had 'earned the hostility of the population'. An
Australian soldier was shot dead by the owner of a house he was looting.[106]
Communication and command collapsed in places, and rumours of German
breakthroughs increased the panic. 'The whole truth cannot of course be
told,' commented the British official historian later.[107] Was this at last the
breaking point, the delayed consequence of the Somme and Passchendaele?
It was the closest the British came to the sort of débâcle the Russians, Austrians

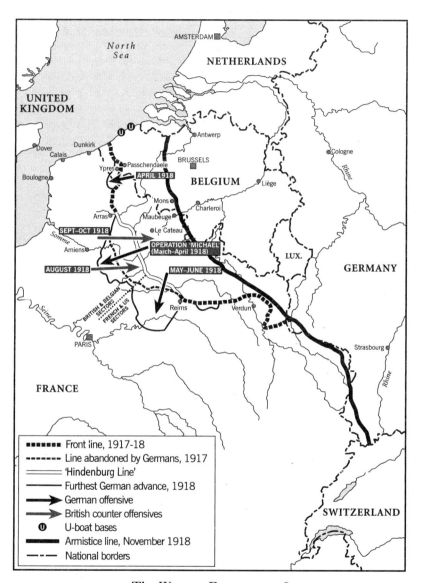

The Western Front 1917–18

and Italians had suffered: 'we had to make a hasty retreat with all our worldly possessions – every road out of the village was crowded with rushing traffic – lorries, limbers . . . wagons, great caterpillar tractors with immense guns behind them, all were dashing along in an uninterrupted stream'.[108] The Kaiser was jubilant: 'if an English delegation comes to sue for peace it must kneel before the German standard for it was a question here of a victory of monarchy over democracy.'[109] One hard-bitten French infantry officer was entirely unsympathetic (and entirely unjust[110]):

> the English gave way . . . It was our troops, yet again, who saved
> the situation . . . the inhabitants are glad to see the French again.
> They have no confidence in the English any more . . . on the
> first day, regiments – at Amiens – threw down their weapons
> and fled with the civilians. It is said that they have lost 70,000 men
> and 1,100 guns . . . People have nothing but praise for the
> Canadians, Australians and Indians – it was they who stopped the
> enemy advance . . . [the English] were arriving panic-stricken,
> having fled fifteen kilometres, shouting 'Run for it' . . . everyone
> says the same: the English are hopeless, it's the Scots, the
> Australians, and Canadians who do all the work.[111]

The postal censors reported 'since the beginning of the German offensive . . . a marked animosity toward British troops'.[112]

Things were not really so bad for the BEF. Although 21,000 prisoners had been taken on 21 March – one of the biggest totals in British history – this was largely because of surprise, overwhelming odds and faulty positioning. The men streaming rearwards or wandering about lost were often support troops or non-combatants. According to the military police, combat troops on the road 'were chiefly those who were genuinely lost and anxious to rejoin their units.' If the morale of 5th Army really had collapsed, the Germans would probably have won the war.[113] Although they smashed a wide gap forty miles deep through the British line, and advanced towards the communications centre of Amiens, from the beginning they were failing to reach their planned objectives.

The British appealed to the French for help. But General Pétain was reluctant to send too many of his reserves in what seemed a lost cause. He was expecting an attack himself and was determined to defend Paris, which on 23 March was shelled by huge German guns sixty-five miles away. He told Clemenceau that the British army was defeated and would be forced to surrender, and that the French might be too.[114] His pessimism, and mistrust of the British, would reappear fatefully in 1940. Nevertheless, within a few days French divisions did arrive to plug the gap between the two armies.

The crisis brought about what had for years been ineffectively discussed: unity of command. General Ferdinand Foch was appointed supreme Allied commander. He was the only conceivable generalissimo – especially given Lloyd George's loathing of Haig. A man of intellectual and personal authority, Foch had been involved in Anglo-French coordination since before 1914, and was already the military adviser to the inter-governmental Supreme War Council.

On 9 April Ludendorff launched his second offensive against the BEF further north – 'Operation Georgette', threatening the Channel ports, the Allies' carotid artery for supplies and for American manpower. British and Germans were now both flagging. Haig issued his famous Order of the Day calling for a fight to the last. Foch, in the British view, was miserly with French reinforcements, but the BEF managed to halt the German advance. One unexpected obstacle were lavish British supply dumps, at which German troops, subsisting on ersatz bread and turnips, stopped to 'gorge themselves on food and liquor.'[115] They were disheartened to discover, despite the vaunted submarine campaign, how much better supplied the Allies were than they themselves and their families at home. Ludendorff then launched his third offensive, on 27 May, this time against the French and Americans along the Aisne, who were also thrown back. The Germans crossed the Marne, as far as they had got in 1914. This was more than Ludendorff wanted, for he had intended the attack here to be only diversionary, to keep the Franco-Americans occupied while he launched a final decisive blow against the British in Flanders. This he was forced to postpone, when the French counter-attacked on the Marne in July, supported by American, British and Italian troops.

Instead of Ludendorff attacking the British, they attacked him. On 8 August, the Germans were completely surprised by an offensive east of Amiens by 450 British tanks leading Canadian and Australian infantry. They pushed foward eight miles, the longest one-day advance of the whole war. Ludendorff later called this 'the black day of the German army . . . [It] put the decline of [our] fighting power beyond all doubt [and] opened the eyes of the staff on both sides.'[116] Not only had they been surprised by an undetected concentration of British forces, and overwhelmed by new technologies of war, but many soldiers had given up. Germany's leaders realized that they could no longer win. But they did believe they could hold on.

General Foch, although associated with the lethal policy of all-out attack in 1914, had, like other Allied generals, rethought his views. These he demonstrated to the surprised British foreign secretary A.J. Balfour with 'violent pugilistic gestures first with his fists and then with his feet'.[117] He wanted a succession of rapid blows all along the German line, using superiority of guns, tanks and aircraft. The aim was not to make a breakthrough – so often shown to be impossible – but to force the enemy into a general retreat. His order was 'Tout le monde à la bataille!' The tired French and keen but inexperienced Americans struck in the Argonne on 12 September. Everyone had been waiting for the Americans to arrive in large numbers. When they did, reactions were mixed. Wrote one French soldier in August 1918: 'everywhere is invaded by Americans, who get everything they want. But you can't blame them because they've really got down to work, and where they've fought they haven't been like the cowardly English, they've given the Boches a good thrashing.'[118] In the occupied areas, reactions to the British were different. The BEF at last had the satisfaction – after the bitter experiences of the March retreat – of being feted as liberators. 'The people are so crushed by Jerry's persistant [sic] cruelty, and every little kindness that we can show them, is too much for them, and the tears roll down their cheeks.' When Scottish troops liberated Lille – with a pipe band described as 'funny but nice' – they were mobbed by the welcoming crowd and covered in flowers. In the industrial town of Avesnes, liberated by an English patrol, people 'laughed and wept at the same time, everyone shook hands in a kind of wild delirium. Only those who lived though those unforgettable moments can really understand.'[119]

The biggest and most decisive campaign of the war was fought in the autumn of 1918, principally between the British and the Germans. For the first time since 1914 the former proved markedly superior in skill, tactics, leadership, ideas, organization and equipment. The Germans were dug into their strongest-ever defensive position, the Hindenburg Line, six layers deep. General Rawlinson's 4th Army assaulted it at the end of September. The main defence line ran along the deep Saint-Quentin canal, impassable to tanks and fortified with masses of barbed wire and machine-gun emplacements. Only in one place, where the canal ran through a tunnel, did attack seem conceivable, but the carefully prepared assault by the Australian Corps and two fresh but inexperienced American divisions was thrown back in confusion. The 46th (North Midland) Division launched an alternative attack where both sides had assumed it was impossible: across the canal itself. On 29 September, aided by painstaking intelligence, minute planning, successful concealment, and scientifically precise artillery fire, they stormed across equipped with life-jackets and rafts from Channel ferries, at a cost of only 150 casualties. The North Staffordshires seized the vital Riqueval bridge, bayoneting a German sapper as he lit the demolition fuse. This amazing feat proved that the BEF could now pierce the strongest defences the Germans could construct, defended by their best troops. They 'had not only broken the Hindenburg Line, they had broken the will of the German Army and the German leadership'.[120] From then on, the Germans retreated along the whole front, and the Central Powers began to collapse. The cost in lives was terrible, as warfare in the open brought casualties again to 1914 levels. The BEF suffered 260,000 casualties at the highest daily rate of the whole war. But the result was decisive. The French, Americans and Belgians combined took 193,000 prisoners during the culminating four months of combat; the British and Imperial forces, less than half their number, took 200,000.[121] Yet few on the Allied side thought the end was imminent. The British expected to be fighting until 1920. But after the loss of the Hindenburg Line the German High Command feared total military collapse and anarchy at home. So on 5 October, hoping to divide their enemies, they asked President Wilson for an armistice. French and British politicians and generals were willing to agree, rather than demanding unconditional surrender. They feared that if the war continued American power would increase and their own diminish, thus weakening their ability to influence the peace terms.[122] On 11 November, fighting stopped. The BEF – now 1,859,000 men, half of them teenagers – halted just north of Mons, where it had begun in 1914:

We marched back fifteen miles . . . A blanket of fog covered the countryside. At eleven o'clock we slung on our packs and tramped along the muddy pavé. The band played but there was very little singing . . . we were very old, very tired, and now very wise.[123]

Remembrance

The war had created new cross-Channel ties. There had been much sympathy for French sufferings in the war-ravaged north. Winifred Stephens's *Book of France* (1915) was part of a campaign to raise relief funds. After the war, devastated towns and villages were adopted by towns in Britain, the Dominions and the United States, which raised funds and gave direct help. For example, Newcastle adopted Arras; Sheffield, Bapaume; Llandudno, Mametz; Birmingham, Albert – often places where local regiments had fought. Visits to the war zone by the bereaved, and by former soldiers and their families, began soon after the armistice. Michelin published a guidebook. The British were the first to come in large numbers. The British Legion organized a visit of 15,000 people to Ypres in 1928.[124] Memorials were built to the 600,000 men who had been killed in France. Some had only just been completed when the next war began. People came to remember their own nation's sacrifices, and mourn their personal losses. British emotions focused on Flanders and Picardy, with pilgrimages to British military cemeteries. The French had their own tragic shrine far to the east at Verdun.

Perhaps such divergence happens after every war. Yet this seems an extreme case. Part of the explanation is the way the war had been fought. General Robertson had written in 1915, 'I believe [the French] are as good allies as any country could have. I merely wish to emphasize the great diffi-culty there has been and always will be in operations conducted by allied armies. It is only natural.'[125] Anglo–American relations in the Second World War probably benefited from the fact that the two Allies fought mostly in separate theatres, except towards the victorious conclusion. The Western Front from 1914 to 1918, in contrast, was particularly unfavourable to promoting inter-Allied affection. This is not only because of the appalling and inglorious conditions. The British and French although in proximity fought largely separate wars, less as comrades in arms than as wary and sometimes jealous neighbours. When they did fight close together, in Gallipoli, they maintained, says one French historian, 'a strong feeling of solidarity'.[126] But on the Western Front they were largely confined to helping each other out in crises, inevitably a cause of tension. The British resented taking over French trenches because they found them badly built and filthy – a lingering folk memory. Some Frenchmen, as we have seen, came to despise British – particularly English – soldiers as slow, incompetent and even cowardly. Their letters suggest that much of the time they had little awareness of the British presence.[127] The exploits of the BEF in finally forcing the Germans out of France in August–October 1918 were largely overlooked amid the general Allied advance, in which each ally cheered on its own. French historians today regard the turning point as the French attack on the Marne, not the British attack at Amiens, Ludendorff's 'black day'. On the other hand, the hasty British retreat in March – which must have been seen by many French soldiers as putting them back where they started in 1914 – was not forgotten. Captain Charles de Gaulle ended the war convinced of the 'insolence and uselessness of allied officers' and 'overwhelmed by general feelings of xenophobia'. Captain Robert Graves, returning to Oxford, found among undergraduates back from the trenches an 'anti-French feeling . . . amounting almost to an obsession'.[128]

Many memoirs, histories and novels simply ignored the existence of the ally; many still do. Those that did not conveyed a mixture of messages. Rudyard Kipling and John Buchan praised the French, and emphasized the dour endurance of their tough peasant soldiers. André Maurois, a writer who had served as a liaison officer with the BEF, produced a widely read series of novels featuring 'Colonel Bramble' and his friends, a supposedly affectionate portrayal of the British as pathologically eccentric, cold and alien. Two other liaison officers, Spears and Huguet, wrote personal accounts arguing respectively for the importance and the insignificance of the BEF's part in the war, which Huguet thought reflected the insular, mercenary and treacherous nature of the British race. Official memorials and ceremonies, of course, gave thanks to the Allies. In France in particular, they still do: ninetieth anniversary remembrance ceremonies of the battle of the Marne in 2004 paid generous tribute to the BEF. But the victory did not lead to trust and cordiality between France and Britain in the post-war years. For that to happen, 'the war to end war' would have had to be followed by a confident agreement on maintaining peace. It was not. Revulsion from the slaughter, yearning for reconciliation with the former enemy, and fear that the bloodshed had been futile inevitably devalued the wartime alliance.

CHAPTER 11

Losing the Peace

Yes, we have won the war, and not without difficulty; but now we are going to have to win the peace, and that will perhaps be even more difficult.

GEORGES CLEMENCEAU, 1918[1]

This is not a peace, it is an armistice for twenty years.

MARSHAL FOCH[2]

The greatest failure in our common history was to have lost the opportunity to consolidate peace after the costly victory of 1918. This was not solely, or even primarily, a Franco-British responsibility. Germany, without doubt, was the chief culprit. The United States was to blame for its culpable irresponsibility. The Soviet Union, Japan and Italy dripped poison. But a firm and trusting Franco-British partnership would have been the best hope of preventing another, even more devastating, war. It was the world's tragedy that firmness and trust were qualities they could not summon up. This is a story not of wickedness, but of fear and selfishness, individual and collective.

Paris and Versailles, 1918–19: A Tragedy of Disappointment

What I seem to see – with all my heart I hope that I am wrong –
is a tragedy of disappointment.
WOODROW WILSON, 1918[3]

I beg you to understand my state of mind, just as I am trying to understand yours. America is far away and protected by the ocean. England could not be reached by Napoleon himself. You are sheltered, both of you; we are not.
GEORGES CLEMENCEAU, 1919[4]

I find [the French] full of intrigue and chicanery of all kinds, without any idea of playing the game.
MAURICE HANKEY, secretary to the conference, 1919[5]

The peace conference, on French insistence, was convened in Paris. Delegations from the now numerous Allied states,[*] journalists and not a few political voyeurs flocked to the city. The mixture of politics and pleasure reminded many of Vienna in 1814. The Foreign Office thoughtfully commissioned a history of British diplomacy in that period by Charles Webster, in case it provided useful insights. It is a valuable work. Not many read it. Yet there were similarities between 1814 and 1918. The 'Big Three', President Woodrow Wilson, and prime ministers David Lloyd George and Georges Clemenceau, frequently closeted together in secret, and all speaking English, exercised personal power not very different from that of Lord Castlereagh, Tsar Alexander and Prince Metternich. They ignored advisers, colleagues, and parliaments, left piles of expert reports unread, and excluded journalists.

[*] Technically, the United States was not an Ally, but an 'Associated State'.

While they did not, of course, share the manners and assumptions of a cosmopolitan aristocracy like their predecessors in Vienna, they did establish close personal relationships. They also attempted to balance altruism and national interest in order to create a durable peace. But unlike those predecessors, they did have to pay occasional attention to electorates – a diplomatic difficulty, but also a useful diplomatic lever.

A thoughtful reader of Webster's history, while approving Castlereagh's dictum that the aim was 'not to collect trophies but to bring back the world to peaceful habits', would have realized that there was a geopolitical problem not present in 1815. Then it was clear that France had lost, and that the Allies, whose armies were in Paris, had a common interest in preventing the re-emergence of a French threat. They also had ample power to do so. The French had few illusions, and the restored Bourbons had an interest in cooperating with the Allies, who consequently allowed Talleyrand to join in the negotiations. Even after Napoleon's Hundred Days, the Allies were confident enough to treat France quite generously – not that the French thought so. But in 1918, it was not clear that Germany had really been defeated. It had suffered negligible material damage. Its armies were on foreign soil, and even the most belligerent soldiers, such as Foch, feared invading the German heartland. Only small border areas were occupied by the Allies, whose war-weary armies were being demobilized. It was Germany's relative strength, not its weakness, which necessitated its exclusion from the negotiations. How to deal with that strength was the most difficult and divisive problem for the victors. They failed to solve it.

Large delegations installed themselves in Paris in some style. Lloyd George was lent a large flat by a wealthy Englishwoman, where he installed himself with his mistress and secretary Frances Stevenson, his teenage daughter Megan, and his assistant Philip Kerr. The British Empire delegation was based at the Hôtel Majestic. This became a little bit of England near the Arc de Triomphe, as the French staff (to prevent spying) were replaced by Britons. The food was therefore that of 'a respectable railway hotel', and the house rules reminded some of school. Free drinks were provided for the Dominion and Indian delegates, but the British had to buy their own. Once settled in, the delegates and their staffs put on concerts and had plenty of parties (Augustus John, the bohemian official artist, spent more time partying than painting, and his colleague, William Orpen, designed posters for the concerts). The Saturday night dances became so popular that the authorities thought of stopping them. One elderly diplomat found the nurses and typists like 'nymphs'. They knew all the latest dances, and Foch was astonished that 'the British have such sad faces and such cheerful bottoms'. Lord Balfour, the foreign secretary, was taken out to a nightclub for the first time in his life by an American socialite, Elsa Maxwell – 'the most delightful and degrading evening I have ever spent'. The leading statesmen, however, worked hard and with few distractions. Clemenceau, aged seventy-eight, led a monk-like existence, going to bed at nine o'clock after a supper of bread and milk; Wilson, aged sixty-three, was usually asleep by ten. Lloyd George, a vigorous fifty-six, 'as free from care as a schoolboy on holiday', had rather more fun, going out to cafés and restaurants to observe the Parisians, and leading sing-songs round the piano in his flat.[6]

The 'Big Three' did not like each other. Wilson, as all soon realized, was amply endowed with the defects of idealism: priggishness, vanity and arrogance. Clemenceau, nicknamed 'the Tiger', struck Lloyd George as 'a disagreeable and rather bad-tempered old savage'. He had risen in the carnivorous world of French politics, beginning on the extreme Left in opposition to Napoleon III, and thrusting himself to the fore from the 1880s onwards as a wrecker of governments, and then in power as a breaker of strikes. One of his many enemies said he was feared for three things: his

Clemenceau's genuine anglophilia had years before given rise to nationalist accusations that he was in British pay – in this 1893 cartoon he juggles bags of sterling.

Le Petit Journal

SUPPLÉMENT ILLUSTRÉ

CLÉMENCEAU
Le pas du commandité

sword, his pistol and his tongue. Age had not mellowed him. He had come to power in the dark days of 1917, when he had snuffed out defeatism by means of the prison cell and the firing squad. Many thought he dominated the Conference, as he chaired its sessions. But he knew that France was the smallest of the Big Three, and was more moderate than critics or admirers believed. Clemenceau regretted that Lloyd George – an archetype of the modern professional politician, clever, hard-working, duplicitous and shallow – was not 'an English gentleman'. He found him devious, opportunistic and rude – 'You are the very baddest boy' he exclaimed after one shouting match, and is said to have challenged him to a duel.[7] Yet they knew that they had to get on, and to a remarkable extent they did. But the personal clashes aggravated the divergences of national interest. They made it more difficult to understand and sympathize with genuine differences of view.

CLEMENCEAU, A DISILLUSIONED ANGLOPHILE

England is the disillusion of my life.

GEORGES CLEMENCEAU

The man who epitomized French intransigence in British eyes was the greatest anglophile to dominate France since Guizot, and probably the last. This was not only a matter of fashion – English clothes, English dogs, furniture from Maples, attendance at Ascot, the habit of shaking hands – but also of ideas, friendships and tastes. As a young man he met John Stuart Mill, one of whose books he translated, and he formed lasting associations with prominent English radicals, liberals, and socialists. He said in 1917 that he had read 'every substantial book published in the English language in the past twenty years',[8] which is more than Lloyd George could have claimed. He had also lived in New York, and had married (unhappily) an American. His closest cross-Channel relations were with British disciples of Positivism – the progressive French philosophy-cum-sect – who were francophile, democratic, anti-imperialist and anti-German. He formed a lasting friendship with the unusual Maxse family – 'ma famille anglaise' – who somehow managed to combine Positivism, journalism, and interest in French culture with successful careers in the armed forces. In their circle were francophile intellectuals including Matthew Arnold and George Meredith and radical politicians such as Joseph Chamberlain and John Morley. These English connections led to damaging attacks on Clemenceau in the 1890s, when he was accused of being in English pay: nationalists heckled his speeches with shouts of 'Aoh yes!'

As prime minister from 1906 to 1909, Clemenceau worked to turn the *entente* into an alliance. Secret military talks began and he ordered the army to tear up its war plans against Britain. In 1910 he toured the frontier with Sir John French, and in 1911 even joined the British National Service League, campaigning for conscription. During the war, his friendship with General Ivor Maxse, one of the ablest British corps commanders, facilitated a cordial association with the British army; and perhaps helped decide him to back Foch's decision to reinforce the British in the crisis of spring 1918. These very contacts developed in Clemenceau a healthy mistrust of the British political establishment, and especially for centrist politicians such as Lloyd George. But, as we shall see, he was not mistrustful enough.

Clemenceau came to England in 1921 to collect an honorary doctorate from Oxford, and visited Parliament at Lloyd George's invitation. Unmollified, Clemenceau asked him why he had become an 'enemy of France', to which he replied 'was it not always our traditional policy?'[9] Clemenceau was not 'English' enough to realize this was a rather awkward joke, and he took it as a 'cynical' admission by the man he regarded as the embodiment of perfidious Albion – or perhaps perfidious Wales. But he still regarded the Franco-British relationship as essential. The British, however, did not.

The Conference found itself dealing with all the problems of the world, especially those arising from the collapse of the Russian, Austrian and Turkish empires. But its biggest problem was what to do about Germany. German politicians claimed that they had asked for an armistice on the understanding that a peace settlement would follow Woodrow Wilson's announcement of 'no annexations, no contributions, no punitive damages'. The notion peddled by many Anglo-Saxons that France had insisted on harshness in contrast with their own enlightened generosity was self-serving propaganda. All agreed that Germany must be punished and restrained. None were ready to be generous until their own interests had been met. The British had got what they wanted: Germany was deprived of its navy and colonies, and Belgian independence restored. They also insisted on financial reparations, and secured a good share. Yet there were differences of principle too. Wilson and the Americans – and their many British admirers – wanted a new world order based on self-determination, and they believed that their cherished League of Nations would solve all problems. Lloyd George, aiming at reconciliation with Germany, opposed territorial changes that would cause lasting resentment, as the annexation of Alsace-Lorraine in 1871 had done in France. Rather to their surprise, the British and Americans found themselves taking similar views. Clemenceau and the French were sceptical about the League of Nations, Anglo-Saxon promises, and German reconciliation. Unlike their Allies, they did not think that a change to a republic removed the potential German threat. They would have

The Rhineland 1919–1936 – Deterring Germany: possession of the Rhineland threatened the vital Ruhr and offered a possible link with France's ally Czechoslovakia, 150 miles away.

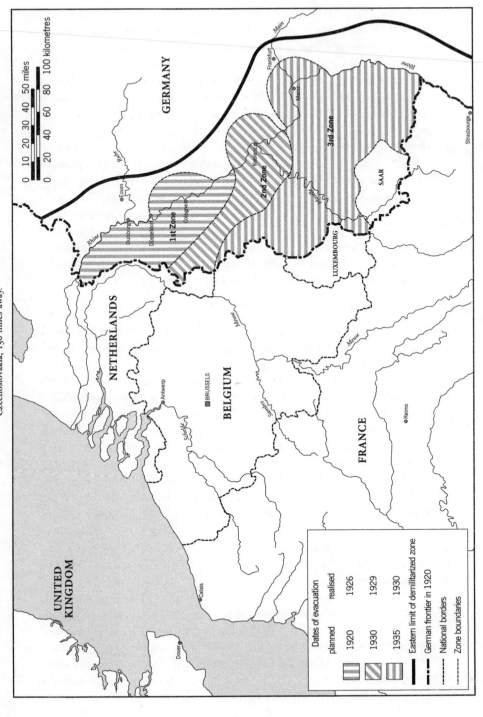

GERMANY

Main

Frankfurt

Mainz

3rd Zone

Rhine

Strasbourge

Koblenz

2nd Zone

SAAR

Essen

Ruhr

Duisburg

Düsseldorf

Cologne

1st Zone

Moselle

Rhine

LUXEMBOURG

NETHERLANDS

Meuse

Meuse

Antwerp

Scheldt

BRUSSELS

BELGIUM

Scheldt

Reims

FRANCE

UNITED
KINGDOM

Calais

Dover

0 10 20 30 40 50 miles
0 20 40 60 80 100 kilometres

Dates of evacuation

planned   realised

1920   1926

1930   1929

1935   1930

Eastern limit of demilitarized zone

German frontier in 1920

National borders

Zone boundaries

liked to break up the Reich, and failing that wanted concrete territorial, strategic, economic and treaty guarantees against renewed attack. They focused on issues that Louis XV would have found familiar: creating a strong Poland, and controlling the Rhine, the 'natural frontier' between France and Germany. Marshal Joffre wrote that 'the frontier of 1815 was a frontier for the defeated, and is no longer suitable for the victors of the Great War'.[10]

A compromise was reached over Polish borders. The Rhine was far more difficult, because the French regarded it as essential to their security. Controlling its crossings would protect France and make Germany vulnerable. Combined with disarmament, it made future German aggression unthinkable. Annexation of German territory was ruled out by America and Britain. The French demanded instead to turn the Rhineland into a separate state under French influence, and to garrison troops on the west bank and in bridgeheads on the German side, at Cologne, Koblenz and Mainz (considered by Napoleon to be the strategic key to central Europe). The French also wanted the Saarland, mainly because of its coalfields. The Anglo-Saxons would agree only to limited occupation and subsequent demilitarization of the Rhineland, and temporary occupation of the Saar.

This confrontation nearly wrecked the conference, amid much bad temper and threats to walk out. In March 1919, Lloyd George dramatically offered a permanent British guarantee to France against German aggression, and Wilson agreed to do the same. Lloyd George backed this up with an offer to build a Channel tunnel to speed up British reinforcements in case of a future German attack. This broke the deadlock: the French agreed to drop their insistence on a separate Rhineland state. Clemenceau, a realist who regarded Allied solidarity as France's only real security, was delighted: 'What a stroke of fortune for France!' But he hid his feelings, and demanded military occupation of the Rhineland for up to fifteen years, with reoccupation if Germany misbehaved. This annoyed the Anglo-Saxons, but they agreed. Balfour thought that 'no manipulation of the Rhine frontier is going to make France anything more than a second-rate Power', so the French ought to work for a stable international system, rather than treating it with 'ill concealed derision'.[11] But Clemenceau seemed to have got what he really wanted.

The other great issue was 'reparations' – a politically correct neologism. The payments levied on Germany became, and perhaps have remained, the most criticized part of the treaty, dismissed as squalid and irrational, and blamed for destabilizing Germany, distorting the world economy, bringing Hitler to power and contributing to a second war. Yet in 1919 all accepted reparations in principle as just, necessary and a deterrent to future aggressors. In the words of the Allies' blunt official statement, 'Somebody must suffer the consequences of the war. Is it to be Germany or only the peoples she has wronged?'[12] Germany had suffered less cost and damage than most of the victors. It had pillaged conquered territories, shifting most of the northern French textile industry lock, stock and barrel to Germany. It had deliberately wreaked destruction on France and Belgium in the closing months of the war, and even during the armistice negotiations. It seemed just that Germany should help to 'repair' the damage, especially as economic and financial health determined military strength. All countries had run up huge debts, to their own citizens through war bonds, and to Britain and America. Britain and France had been the largest per capita spenders. France's national debt has been estimated as equal to 94 per cent of its national wealth. Britain had itself spent £7 billion – equal to forty years of pre-war public spending. It had also been the biggest lender, advancing £1.6 billion to the Allies, principally Russia. It had lent £416 million to France, which in turn had lent to Russia and smaller Allies. Britain had also borrowed over £800 million from the USA, largely to lend on to less credit-worthy countries.[13]

If Germany, potentially Europe's strongest economy, did not pay, then the burden would fall on the French, British or American taxpayers – above all the British. The Americans, who posed as disinterested, vehemently rejected every suggestion of cancelling or writing down inter-Allied debts. The British would not simultaneously pay their debts to America while cancelling their loans to France and Italy, though they did repeatedly seek all-round cancellation. No French government dared to impose taxation and unemployment on its people while letting Germany off scot-free. The only acceptable solution seemed to be to extract as much as possible from Germany and divide it among the Allies according to their costs – which led to unseemly haggling, as well as German lamentation. A liability clause was inserted into the peace treaty – subsequently notorious as the 'war guilt clause', though it made no mention of guilt – to provide a legal foundation. The amount finally demanded was £6.6 billion to be paid over thirty-six years. But this was a notional figure, less than half being considered actually recoverable.[14]

German delegates had taken no part in negotiations. On 7 May 1919 they were summoned to receive the text of the Treaty of Versailles in what turned into a bitter scene, in which the chief German delegate refused to accept responsibility for the war – 'a lie' – and falsely accused the Allies of killing 'hundreds of thousands' of German civilians 'with cold deliberation' by continuing the blockade after the armistice.[15] The Germans were given two weeks to make written comments, and these, when they came, practically rejected the whole treaty. It seemed possible that they would refuse to sign, in which case the Allies would face having to invade and administer a Germany in chaos. Lloyd George and the British Empire delegation were the first to get cold feet. The South African General Jan Smuts

PEACE AND FUTURE CANNON FODDER

OLD CLASS

PEACE TREATY

The Tiger: "Curious! I seem to hear a child weeping!"

This astonishingly perceptive cartoon parallels Marshal Foch's prediction that the peace was only a twenty-year truce, but Dyson's explanation is quite different – he blames Clemenceau for ignoring the future.

POUR UN RENSEIGNEMENT

19 mars 1919

— Je viens leur demander si, oui ou non, je suis vainqueur.

A crippled French soldier comes to the conference chamber to ask the politicians 'whether I'm a victor, yes or no'. It was not an easy question to answer.

was 'grieved beyond words' and said that he might not sign a treaty 'full of menace for the future of Europe'. The Cabinet was unanimously critical, most on practical, some on moral grounds. Youthful officials were outraged: 'this bloody bullying peace is the last flicker of the old tradition . . . we young people will build again'.[16] They began lobbying to weaken the terms concerning Poland, reparations and the Rhineland. At the Hôtel Majestic on 30 May they set up an Institute of International Affairs to express their disquiet. The Archbishop of Canterbury voiced unease. Lloyd George began to back-track.

The corollary of a desire to mollify the Germans was to blame the French for being vindictive. 'There is far too much of the French demands in the settlement,' Smuts told the Delegation. 'They seem completely defective in all sense of justice, fair-play or generosity,' thought an influential Foreign Office official. 'They bargain like Jews and generally are Jews.' Winston Churchill declared that 'the hatred of the French for the Germans was something more than human'.[17] Thus, hopeful idealism at the end of the war began the 'appeasement' current that quickly dominated official British policy, and made enforcement of the Treaty of Versailles unfeasible. As a first step, the British insisted on allowing Upper Silesia to remain part of Germany rather than joining the despised French satellite, Poland ('Kaffirs', to Smuts).[18] Otherwise, an impatient Wilson refused modifications. Preparations were made to invade Germany, so the Germans gave in. The French arranged a grand signing ceremony in the Hall of Mirrors, where the German Empire had been proclaimed in 1871 as German armies completed their conquest of France. Some thought this was poor taste. British officers saluted the German delegates – the only ones who did.

THE POLITICAL CONSEQUENCES
OF MR KEYNES

If we take the view that . . . our recent enemies . . . are children of
the devil, that year by year Germany must be kept impoverished and
her children starved and crippled, and that she must be ringed round
with enemies; then . . . heaven help us all.

JOHN MAYNARD KEYNES[19]

We must be sweet
And tactful and discreet
And when they've suffered defeat

We mustn't let
Them feel upset
Or ever get
The feeling that we're cross with them or hate them
Our future policy must be to reinstate them.
NOEL COWARD, 'Don't let's be beastly to the Germans'[20]

In June 1919, in the tense days when the treaty hung in the balance, J.M. Keynes, a Cambridge don and principal Treasury adviser at the conference, resigned, concluding that 'hope could no longer be entertained of substantial modification in the draft Terms'. Smuts urged him to write an accessible critical account of the conference. *The Economic Consequences of the Peace* duly appeared in December. It quickly sold over 100,000 copies, becoming a bestseller in Britain and America, and it was translated into eleven languages. In the opinion of one French critic, no book since Burke's *Reflexions on the French Revolution* had wielded 'such a widespread and immediate influence . . . over the destinies of Europe'.[21] More than any single work, it discredited the Versailles settlement, and its assertions became the commonplaces of progressive opinion for generations. It also fed British hostility to France.

Part of its impact was due to Keynes's position as an insider, expressing views widely shared among British and American officials. Much was due to his authority as a recognized expert on the difficult and opaque subject of reparations. But much came from the vehemence of his opinions expressed in thumping prose. Paris had been a 'morbid . . . treacherous . . . morass', a 'nightmare'. Wilson, a 'blind and deaf Don Quixote', had been hoodwinked by sophisters and hypocrites, especially the crafty Lloyd George and the cynical Clemenceau. In the background were 'hard-faced men who look as if they had done very well out of the war'. The treaty was motivated by 'imbecile greed . . . prejudice and deception . . . one of the most outrageous acts of a cruel victor in civilized history'. Its imposition of fraudulent and impossible reparations 'reduced Germany to servitude'. He endorsed the protest of the chief German delegate: 'Those who sign this treaty will sign the death sentence of millions of German men, women and children.'[22]

If the victims were the Germans, the villains were the French, to whom Keynes had already during the war shown a lack of sympathy.[23] Though he claimed to understand Clemenceau's fears, nevertheless he presented him as a wizened misanthrope, blind to the new dawn:

dry in soul and empty of hope . . . he had one illusion – France; and
one disillusion, mankind . . . His philosophy, therefore, had no place
for 'sentimentality' in international relations [and had] a
consequent scepticism of all that class of doctrine which the League

of Nations stands for . . . He sees the issue in terms of France and Germany, not of humanity and of European civilization struggling towards a new order.[24]

Keynes accused the French of 'shamelessly exaggerating' the extent of physical damage through 'ill-judged greed', and told them rhetorically that 'my arguments are not seriously disputed, outside France', where politicians 'blind their eyes and muffle their ears'. He later condemned France as a 'Shylock', 'whining' for its 'pound of flesh', and he accused it of following 'a definite and scarcely concealed plan [to dominate] the whole of Europe'.[25]

That pound of flesh, of course, meant reparations, and Keynes's main thrust was the impossibility as well as the iniquity of the sums imposed through 'revenge' and 'greed'. This was a travesty of the truth. Modern economic historians mostly agree that the reparations were reasonable, and within Germany's capacities. Keynes made himself the invaluable accomplice of a calculated propaganda effort by the new German republic to undermine the treaty. His personal motives were guilt as a liberal intellectual involved in running a war, sharpened by his crush on an 'exquisitely clean' Hamburg banker named Karl Melchior.[26] But biographical details explain little, for Keynes had written what many were saying: his very vocabulary can be found in the letters and diaries of British Empire and American delegates in Paris.

Why were Keynes's arguments welcomed by the liberal elites in Britain, America and even France? The young Kingsley Martin, later editor of the *New Statesman*, then a Cambridge undergraduate attending Keynes's lectures, found it 'wonderful for us to have a high authority saying with inside knowledge of the Treaty what we felt emotionally'.[27] This emotion sprang from the idealism which had been used to justify the war, from revulsion against the horrors of the trenches, and from the late flood of optimism evoked by Woodrow Wilson's 'Fourteen Points'. War-weary people were horrified at any suggestion that the sacrifices of the war to end war might be thrown away in what Keynes condemned as 'a peace to end peace'. Future reconciliation could be guaranteed if the victors were generous, guided by 'our moral and emotional reaction to the future of international relations'.[28] Idealists wanted to believe, in Balfour's words, 'that Germany was repentant, that her soul had undergone a conversion and that she was now absolutely a different nation'.[29] Besides, encouraged by German and Soviet propaganda, many insisted that Germany had not been 'guilty' of starting the war: the fault lay with the tsar, or Poincaré, or Grey, or imperialism, or capitalism.

So all were guilty. And France, not Germany, was the danger now: France would be blamed in Britain for inter-war tensions. Keynes was right to see Clemenceau as his opposite. Few wanted to listen to Clemenceau's grim message that 'we must have a great deal of vigilance . . . Yes, this treaty will bring us burdens, troubles, miseries, difficulties, and that will continue for long years.'[30] It was another slightly disillusioned anglophile Frenchman, Etienne Mantoux, who wrote the most heart-felt refutation of Keynes's thesis, *The Carthaginian Peace, or The Economic Consequences of Mr Keynes* (1946). The son of the professor of French at London University who had acted as official interpreter at the Paris conference, Mantoux had been partly brought up in England. His argument was that Keynes had weakened Allied solidarity and encouraged appeasement of Germany, which had paved the way for Hitler and another war. He completed his book in 1944, while serving in the Free French air force. 'It was to the coming generation that Mr Keynes dedicated his book twenty-five years ago. This is an answer which comes from that generation.' He was killed ten days before the war ended.

Wilson and Lloyd George left France immediately after the treaty was signed. Wilson had to persuade the United States Senate to ratify the treaties and join the League of Nations. In the debate his opponents extensively quoted or paraphrased Keynes in their attacks on the treaty. The Senate refused to ratify the Treaty of Versailles, membership of the League, or the treaty guaranteeing French security. Americans withdrew with relief from European affairs. Thus ended the one fleeting moment in world history when the United States held uncontested moral leadership.

Lloyd George had no such problems with the House of Commons, which in 1919, without a division, accepted the Anglo-French Treaty (Defence of France) Act, unprecedented in peacetime. He could have maintained the alliance even without the Americans – and without the Dominions, who also cried off – but he chose not to. He had slipped into the draft treaty a provision that it would come into force 'only when [the American treaty] is ratified', and when this had been read out to Clemenceau it had apparently not registered. Lloyd George had probably made up his mind to trick the French, knowing that the American guarantee was unlikely to materialize.[31] He may have made the decision when Clemenceau, having agreed to give up the idea of separating the Rhineland from Germany, insisted instead on military occupation – this too a piece of duplicity, as the French intended to use every pretext to stay as long as possible, and use the time to work secretly for Rhenish separation. The British, including Lloyd George, did not realize that France's ability to balance German power unaided could only be temporary.[32] Their *chargé d'affaires* in Paris warned that if the French held the Rhine, they 'would have Germany at their mercy for all time; and then as sure as winter follows summer they, feeling themselves absolute masters of the Continent, will turn round on us'. This fear was shared by the foreign secretary, Lord

Curzon, who said that France might become 'the military monarch' of Europe. If this was an absurd exaggeration, it was given credence by French sabre rattling. At an imposing military ceremony in 1919, the revolutionary General Hoche was reburied in the Rhineland to symbolize reconquest: 'Here,' proclaimed a French general, 'France feels again that she is *la Grande Nation*.' So neither side was innocent; but the British were more efficiently perfidious. 'I trusted Lloyd George,' admitted Clemenceau, 'and he got away from me.'[33]

Estrangement, 1919–25

The Latin mind was more logical than ours and was always inclined to press arguments . . . to their logical conclusions. It was our nature to shun these logical conclusions.
AUSTEN CHAMBERLAIN, foreign secretary, 1926[34]

It is childish to make long-range policy with people who dislike hypotheses and live only for the present.
PAUL CAMBON, ambassador in London, 1898–1920[35]

Lloyd George's nullification of the defence treaty began a parting of the ways between Britain and France. Paris had considered the British guarantee more important than the nebulous American commitment. As a senior French diplomat put it, 'We cannot remain at peace in Europe if we are not in agreement with England.'[36] As much as the League of Nations, that guarantee was a pillar of the peace settlement. Without it, the French might have refused to make crucial concessions over the Rhineland. French politicians and public felt cheated by Britain. Deprived of both the strategic and political guarantees of their security, they fell back on trying rigorously to enforce the Treaty of Versailles, and established close military ties with Poland and Czechoslovakia. This worsened their relations with both Britain and Germany.

The Middle East, a source of Franco-British rivalry since Napoleon, was the occasion of more ill-feeling. The British, in their struggle against the Turks, had made potentially conflicting promises: to Zionists, to T.E. Lawrence's Arabs, and not least to the French, in the Sykes–Picot agreement of 1916. The eccentric diplomat Sir Mark Sykes (who privately considered French colonists 'incapable of commanding respect, they are not sahibs, they have no gentlemen') had agreed to French control of the Syrian coast. The British now wanted to water down the deal, arguing that the French had done little of the fighting against the Turks. This incensed the French, who considered that the diversion of large British forces to the Middle

East had left them to do disproportionate fighting on the Western Front. In reality, a deal, including over oil, was not difficult to reach – indeed, it would have been in the interests of both countries to involve themselves as little as possible in the region, as they soon began to realize – but prestige was at stake. The British thought it impertinent of the French to interfere in an area that should not concern them. The French were determined to show that they were not a British satellite. The very triviality of some of the issues made the quarrels all the more venomous. 'The notes that are coming in from the French government,' reported the British ambassador in 1919, 'could hardly be worse if we were enemies instead of allies.'[37] During the early 1920s, British intelligence constantly uncovered French 'dirty work' in the Levant. 'The French were considered cads. They did not . . . play cricket.' After one confrontation with his counterpart Raymond Poincaré in 1922, the British foreign secretary Lord Curzon staggered out of the room in tears repeating, 'I can't bear that horrid little man. I can't bear him.'[38] Colonial exhibitions had been planned to take place simultaneously in London and Paris as a gesture of imperial cooperation; the French postponed theirs.

Money was the root of much evil and resentment. The Americans insisted on repayment of loans, convinced that they had done more than enough to help Europe. The French believed that they should repay nothing, as they had contributed disproportionately in blood: how could their Allies charge extortionate prices for the imported uniforms in which French soldiers had died? The British kept pressing for a general writing down of debts and reparations, but were unwilling to be the only ones paying. The Germans sought every excuse not to pay. The French authorities tried to use the unstable world financial situation to amass a hoard of sterling and gold, and rival London as Europe's financial centre. This created a chill between the Bank of England and the Banque de France, and caused the governor of the former, Montagu Norman, to add the French to his list of dislikes (Catholics, Jews, chartered accountants and Scotsmen).[39] Money meant power. The British were annoyed, and even alarmed, that the French, while pleading their inability to pay interest on their debts, were spending more money on arms. France was the world's largest military power by far, following the demobilization of the British and Americans and the disarmament of the Germans: it still had 900,000 soldiers in July 1920, and the world's largest air force. Further spending, especially on bombers, caused concern in London. Although few thought the 'world calamity' of an Anglo-French war likely, Britain felt obliged to spend more on air defence just in case.[40]

In January 1923, after warnings to Germany, and despite British and American disapproval, 70,000 French troops occupied the Ruhr basin, which furnished 85 per cent of Germany's coal and 80 per cent of its steel. Many

French soldiers hated the Germans, and were glad of the opportunity to avenge what German troops had done in France. There were complaints of looting, vandalism, casual violence and rape, though it seems that French commanders made efforts to maintain discipline. There was a shrill German propaganda campaign against French brutality, which stressed the presence of African and Arab soldiers, a racial insult and a menace to Aryan women.[41] (Recent research suggests that sexual relations were generally consenting, and even long-term; resulting mixed-race children were later to be victims of the Nazis.) Though British public opinion had also been anti-German during the war, it had fewer personal causes for lasting resentment, and now some were receptive to German propaganda. A leading Labour MP, Philip Snowden, attacked the Ruhr occupation as 'an old and vicious policy', aggravated by its use of 'barbarians . . . with tremendous sexual instincts'. The French socialist party also condemned their government's action.[42]

Poincaré at first defied criticism. The Germans began strikes, 'passive resistance' and sabotage, partly spontaneous, partly organized by Berlin. The currency collapsed – a bus ticket soon cost 150 million marks. The French proclaimed martial law, shot some saboteurs, and eventually expelled 150,000 'trouble-makers' from the occupied zone, including civil servants and policemen. The Germans had to abandon resistance and make at least some reparations payments. Berlin had been given a serious fright by the economic chaos and ensuing political unrest – including a failed nationalist coup in Munich involving one Adolf Hitler. The occupation cost the French more than it secured in reparations, and it also precipitated a devastating run on the franc, which lost 48 per cent of its value. For many it confirmed the already common view that France had become dangerously aggressive. Balfour thought them 'impossible' and 'insane', 'afraid of being swallowed up by the tiger . . . yet they spend all their time poking it'.[43] The Americans and the British, briefly under a Labour government that sympathized with the Germans, called for compromise. This produced the Dawes Plan, meant to be a final agreed settlement of reparations. The bill was reduced, and provisions for enforcement dropped. In all, Germany paid only about £1 billion over thirteen years, less than one-third of it in cash.[44] But the Weimar Republic was further weakened, and nationalist propaganda given a plausible grievance.

The Dawes Plan was followed up by a treaty concluded at Locarno between Britain, France, Germany and Italy. It admitted Germany to the League of Nations and jointly guaranteed Germany's western – though not eastern – borders. The signatories renounced military aggression. The new Tory foreign secretary, the comparatively francophile Austen Chamberlain, waxed lyrical: 'I rub my eyes and wonder whether I am dreaming when the French Foreign Minister invites the German Foreign Minister and me to celebrate my wife's birthday, and incidentally talk business, by a cruise on the Lake in a launch called *Orange Blossom*, habitually used by wedding parties.'[45] The treaty was formally signed in London on 1 December 1925, and for the occasion the delighted Foreign Office redecorated its grandest rooms, still called the Locarno Suite.

Behind the euphoria, France's single-handed attempt to enforce the Versailles treaty had been defeated. Faced with German resistance, the Anglo-Saxons compromised. This had 'an enormous psychological impact' on the French.[46] There were few regrets in Whitehall. Churchill, chancellor of the exchequer, voiced a common opinion when he argued that Britain should keep out of European disputes and concentrate on the Empire. France would have to make 'sweeping' concessions to the Germans, who could flex their muscles in eastern Europe, a matter of no concern to Britain. The Locarno frontier guarantee was considered the end of a problem, rather than the beginning of a military commitment, and British defence spending was further cut. The French evacuated the Ruhr, and soon afterwards the remaining Allied troops left the Rhineland. The French government made a virtue of necessity, and led by foreign minister Aristide Briand briefly won plaudits by advocating Franco-German reconciliation and European federation. When he spoke of French and German mothers no longer having to worry about the future of their children, cynical diplomats wept. He himself was dry-eyed: 'I make the foreign policy of our birth rate.'[47] The discordant notes came from Berlin, where even the Dawes Plan was denounced. Communists and Nazis attacked it as an imposition by capitalists and Jews. The German government was working to re-establish Germany as the dominant power in Europe, including by illegal rearmament. Locarno wound up the vestigial organization for monitoring German disarmament: foreign politicians preferred to turn a blind eye.

Only five years after their victory, the French and British regarded each other with mistrust, dislike and incomprehension. What the French took for British machiavellianism was mostly wishful idealism. What the British took for French militarism was a fearful sense of vulnerability. The responsibility for this misunderstanding was shared. French politicians, led by 'the Tiger' Clemenceau and his unbending successor Poincaré, were not good at making friends or influencing public opinion. Perhaps their post-war flexing of military and financial muscle was ill-judged. The misjudgements north of the Channel were vastly greater: over-estimating French strength, and absurdly suspecting a battered and worried France – a victor scared of the vanquished – of aiming to resurrect Napoleonic hegemony. Some of this can be put down to the strength of old prejudices on both sides. *Les Anglais* could never be other than mercenary and hypocritical; the French were necessarily posturing and vainglorious. But the real problem was their conflicting assessment of Germany. The French did not trust the Germans. They saw no reason, as Clemenceau said, to apologize for their victory. This was unsporting of them, but alas, they were right. Only a penalty-free peace treaty, which would have left Germany dominant in Europe and its neighbours weak and impoverished, would have been enough to avoid resentment. Even that would have been no guarantee of future peace: it was not Hitler who invented *Lebensraum*. German nationalism, even before the emergence of the Nazis, was strong, and it had never accepted the outcome of the war. Allied concessions failed to mollify it. But British opinion – at least among the political elite, probably less among the public at large – believed that a democratic Germany must be conciliated and strengthened. A confidant of Lloyd George noted in his diary:

> The official British point of view is that the German nation were not responsible for the war, that the Junkers have been ejected, that the German government should be supported, that German industries should be revived, and that, generally, the Germans should not be regarded with suspicion.[48]

A leading British historian has recently concluded that 'international stability would have been better protected if the Anglo-Saxons had accepted more of the French demands'.[49] Instead, France's policy of deterrence, based on occupation of the Rhineland, was opposed. The disarmament provisions of the treaty were tacitly abandoned. So in the long run, security in Europe would depend on German self-restraint. This was accepted in Whitehall and Westminster, except perhaps in the armed forces. Austen Chamberlain did not think Germany could possibly be a threat before 1960. The old enemies Poincaré and Clemenceau were at one in their foreboding. Peace, the former observed, 'rests upon the good faith of Germany . . . not only of the present government in Berlin, but of all those governments that will follow it'. Clemenceau saw another German attack as inevitable – 'in six months, in a year, in five years, in ten years, when they like, as they like'.[50]

THE TUNNEL: BOWING TO PROVIDENCE

Providence has made us an island – I think for a great purpose in the
history of Europe and of the world.
MAURICE HANKEY, cabinet secretary, November 1919[51]

Early in 1914, a Channel tunnel was again discussed by the Committee of Imperial Defence. It concluded that 'if our troops were to become engaged in a European war fighting alongside the French the more tunnels we possess the better, if on the other hand no such operations are in contemplation then we want no tunnels at all.' Only if Britain and France were such close allies that 'in the event of war they could be regarded as one nation' would the project be desirable.[52] The French set up a committee to study the project in 1918, and they decided that it would be strategically and economically beneficial. In 1919 Lloyd George, as we have seen, dangled the prospect of a tunnel to persuade the French to give up their plans for the Rhineland: it would so speed up British deployment that, unlike in 1914, the Allies would be able to protect France's northern industrial areas, and so make the Rhineland defensive zone less vital. A House of Commons Channel Tunnel Committee obtained indications of support from 310 MPs for what they asserted would be a highly profitable project. The French proposed a joint study. But Whitehall then had second thoughts. To build a tunnel, said the army, would bind Britain firmly to the defence of France and Belgium, and because Russia was no longer an ally this would demand 'nothing short of our maximum effort'. Otherwise a tunnel would be a danger: 'for an offensive war on the Continent we want the Tunnel, but

By the interwar period, the Tunnel had become a joke

for a defensive war in England we do not.' If this was the case, thought Austen Chamberlain, it made the tunnel 'the master of our military and political future', and hence undesirable.[53] Besides, it would be expensive: the estimate was £60 million. Hankey, who wrote the Cabinet minutes, delayed a decision. The Foreign Office reminded everyone that 'until a century ago France was England's historic and natural enemy, and that real friendship between the inhabitants of the two countries has always been very difficult'. The damning conclusion was that 'our relations with France never have been, are not, and probably never will be, sufficiently stable and friendly to justify the construction of a Channel tunnel'.[54]

Mixed Feelings, 1919–39

Nothing can alter the fundamental fact that we are not liked in France, and never will be.

Foreign Office memorandum, 1920[55]

No more wars for me at any price! Except against the French. If there's ever a war with them I'll go like a shot.

EDMUND BLUNDEN, war poet[56]

The war affected every aspect of life. It forced itself into thoughts and memories; it changed culture, behaviour, beliefs, loyalties, ideologies, fears and hopes. Yet revulsion from its horrors also created a desire to return to normal, and to recover what seemed to have been the pillars of pre-war society. Relations between the French and the British fitted this pattern. Alongside new circumstances stemming from the war, we also see ideas and habits that continued seemingly unaltered.

British intellectuals soon reconnected with Paris's pre-war avant-garde: 'The war has not killed the movement,' wrote the Bloomsbury critic Clive Bell. In 1919 young Osbert Sitwell, just out of the army, organized the first exhibition of French painting in London since 1914. The show featured the leaders of Parisian modernism – Matisse, Picasso, Derain, Vlaminck and Modigliani. As tradition required, it was controversial, with six weeks of press debate provoked by 'the fury of the philistines', some of whom had not forgotten the polemics of the 1880s.[57] Things were changing within the art establishment, which for years had been dithering about introducing modern French art into Britain's national collections. Still in 1914, one elderly trustee of the National Gallery protested that he would 'as soon expect to hear of a Mormon service . . . in St Paul's Cathedral as to see an exhibition of . . . modern French Art-rebels in the sacred precincts of Trafalgar Square.' But thanks largely to the generosity and enthusiasm of the textile magnate Samuel

Courtauld, change came rapidly, and during the 1920s the National Gallery and the Tate both acquired stunning Impressionist and post-Impressionist works.[58] Paris still retained its status as the Mecca of art. This primacy was vigorously asserted by the French, who were aware of its national and political value – though Proust felt embarrassed at 'assuming that role ourselves'.[59]

But a younger generation – from Christopher Isherwood to P.G. Wodehouse – were looking elsewhere for stimulation: Berlin, Moscow, Vienna, Rome, even New York and Hollywood. Paris was no longer the only foreign city offering liberation and a good exchange rate. Moreover, probably for the first time, Anglo-Saxon tourists met open hostility and even crowd violence in Paris, with occasional attacks on tourist buses.[60] This seems to have been a mixture of economic resentment and a feeling that the former Allies were betraying France's interests. Tourists at least brought money. People who went to work in France felt that 'we . . . are not really welcomed, but are merely tolerated'.[61] Britain had long been a source of new entertainments for the French, but it was eclipsed by the impact of the United States, accelerated by the presence of American troops. American influence on fashionable culture was unmistakable. Jazz hit Paris in the 1920s, and Britain offered nothing as sexy as Josephine Baker. The American impact aroused some opposition. George Duhamel, famous for his anti-war novels, called on 'us Westerners' to root out everything American 'from our houses, our clothes, our souls'.[62] The career of Maurice Chevalier illustrates the shift of fashion from London to New York and Hollywood.

FROM ENGLISHMAN IN PARIS TO FRENCHMAN IN HOLLYWOOD

The young Maurice Chevalier, born in 1888, had begun as a comic singer before the war. Wounded and captured, he learned English in a POW camp from British fellow-prisoners, and joined them in putting on concerts – his introduction to British show-business. He worked in London after the armistice and adopted an English performing style, with dinner jacket or striped blazer, bow tie, and boater – trademarks throughout his long career. He incorporated British elements into his off-stage persona, notably a highly publicized keenness on sport, and so created a modern image of French masculinity: 'He is elegant . . . he is a sportsman, he is casual. He belongs to the times of the automobile, boxing and rugby . . . we thank him for so well representing us.'[63] But American influence counted increasingly in what became a mid-Atlantic style, combining Anglo-Saxon sheen with a traditional Parisian content of risqué working-class cheekiness and seductive charm. He went to America in 1928, and earned more money than any contemporary

French performer, remaking himself as an archetypal Frenchman for the English-speaking world (with a carefully preserved French accent) rather than as an English-style performer in France.

In Britain, for the first time since the Second Empire – perhaps since the revolution – progressive opinion became francophobic. As the playwright and diplomat Jean Giraudoux lamented, 'in five years from a country which represented the liberty of the world we have become a personification of reaction'.[64] In different ways, this attitude extended across the political spectrum, from pacifists such as the Labour leader George Lansbury, who wanted Britain to disarm and give up its empire, to Tory imperialists such as Churchill who wanted to abandon European entanglements. Support for appeasement of Germany was strongest among Liberal and Labour sympathizers. These views were idealistic, generous, and decent, at least towards Germany. They were also self-righteous, self-deluding – and inevitably anti-French. If the Germans were doing their best to be good citizens, any trouble must logically be the fault of those 'impossible people' the French.[65]

On both sides of the Channel, polemicists searched for historical parallels and explanatory stereotypes. Both sides referred learnedly to the Napoleonic wars. According to H.N. Brailsford, a leading Labour journalist, 'France has recovered the military predominance she enjoyed under the first Napoleon', and he warned of 'the persistent military tradition of this most nationalist of peoples'. The aggressive attitude of the Labour chancellor, Philip Snowden, led him to be threatened with a duel by his French counterpart and compared with Joan of Arc's executioners by the French press (his wife explained it was only his Yorkshire manner). Widely read attacks on Britain appeared in France, which sufficiently upset Whitehall for official complaints to be made.[66] Nationalists and the Left denounced the sins of the City of London. In the most notorious attack, published in 1935, the prominent journalist Henri Béraud asked whether 'England must be reduced to slavery'. His gist would have been familiar in the 1890s or even the 1790s: 'John Bull has only one policy, that of its bankers and its merchants.' Britain foments global discord to gain power and profit, sending shiploads of 'Messrs Vickers' toys, the gentlemen of the Intelligence Service, the yapping cargo of big-footed ladies and insipid male virgins from Oxford' to govern the Empire. Béraud lacked the space 'to recall every notorious example of the violence, perfidy, implacable selfishness and disloyalty that sully its national history'. Its habitual victims were the Irish, the Boers, the Indians, the Arabs (in a particularly dastardly trick, it was encouraging them to resist beneficent French rule), Europeans as a whole ('les nègres commencent à Calais'), and above all the French. 'The Englishman has always been both our hereditary enemy and the enemy of Europe.' During the war, the English 'fought *with* us' but 'not *for* us'. Now they were siding with the Germans, even gratuitously insulting France by signing a naval agreement with Germany on the anniversary of Waterloo. 'I hate this people, for myself and for my ancestors, by instinct': they were deliberately 'sabotaging our victory'.[67] A new villain had appeared: the 'infernal' Intelligence Service, which in several popular books became the symbol of British global power and an explanation for the world's mysterious problems. In a sensational 1926 exposé Robert Boucard revealed its secret headquarters at 10 Downing Street – 'a building with an imposing façade and impeccable sobriety of line – English puritanism in all its splendour'. The Intelligence Service had kept the war going so that the City could profit from clandestine trade with Germany.[68] Such widely-sold works must have had an effect. A shocked embassy official reported in October 1935 that a newsreel showing the Prince of Wales had been hissed in Paris. Armed police were stationed outside the embassy.[69]

Cross-Channel hostility was not universal. There were pro-French voices in Whitehall and Westminster – some of them recent converts – who began in the mid-1930s to press for closer relations and a firmer line towards Germany. These 'pro-Frog boys' (as that political Bertie Wooster, the Tory MP and diarist 'Chips' Channon, called them) included Sir Robert Vansittart, permanent under-secretary at the Foreign Office, Sir Edward Spears, chairman of the Great Britain–France Association, and their patron, Winston Churchill. At the Quai d'Orsay, and more widely in France, persistent voices emphasized that partnership with Britain was indispensable. Advocates included the urbane Philippe Berthelot, Vansittart's opposite number at the Quai d'Orsay, and his entourage of diplomat-intellectuals, including his eventual successor, Alexis Léger (alias the poet Saint-Jean Perse). There were small-scale educational and local initiatives, and polite contact through elite pressure-groups (such as the Club Interallié). The Great Britain–France Association combined something of both, holding annual dinners to which ministers were invited, and local branches organizing talks and social events. On the British side, the government was slow to take an interest in propaganda, considering it un-British. Hence, the British Institute in Paris, set up in 1926, received a subsidy of £2–3,000, compared with the Institut Français in Kensington, which received £200,000. The British Council only opened a Paris office in 1939. Academic contacts, never vigorous, dwindled in the 1920s, despite gestures such as the establishment of the Foch Professorship of French History at London University. Before 1914, some 200 French students annually attended courses at British universities; by 1926, there was only one.[70]

In the late 1930s, when cordiality became frighteningly urgent, efforts were made in both countries to bring public feeling into line with strategic necessity. Artistic events were organized. In 1937 Sir Thomas Beecham and the LPO performed Elgar, Delius and Berlioz in Paris. The Cambridge University Madrigal Society followed. In 1938, an exhibition of British paintings was held at the Louvre. In July there was a successful royal visit. An *Ode à l'Angleterre* was run up, paying tribute to 'English soldiers lying beneath white crosses', and *Le Figaro* helpfully printed a phonetic version of 'Godd saive zhe Kingg'. A huge monument to Britannia was unveiled where the first BEF units had disembarked in 1914 at Boulogne, not far from where Napoleon had failed to embark in 1805. (It was blown up by the Germans two years later.) President Lebrun visited London in March 1939 in what Channon dismissed as 'Frog week' (though he enjoyed wearing court dress – 'my Lord Fauntleroy velvet number'). In July, the 150th anniversary of the revolution, the Grenadier Guards marched down the Champs Elysées. The intention was to stress the democracies' shared cultural, historical and political heritage. This was the avowed aim of the Cannes Film Festival, set up in 1939 to rival Mussolini's Venice festival. The French cultural attaché asked for Alexander Korda's patriotic spectacular *The Four Feathers* to be shown there instead of at Venice. This story of a British officer who abandons the army because he is afraid of war, but recovers to become a hero, must have resonated with many in the circumstances. So did Marcel L'Herbier's lavish *Entente Cordiale* (1939). This romanticized history, scripted by André Maurois, gave a flattering portrait of Edward VII, 'the greatest of diplomats' and stressed the historical necessity of Anglo-French partnership for peace and victory. It gently celebrated cross-Channel stereotypes with a love triangle between the pretty but pallid daughter of an English diplomat ('I'd prefer her to marry an Englishman – less fun but more durable') and two dashing French brothers, one a soldier from the Fashoda expedition, the other a journalist on a rabid anglophobe newspaper – 'A Frenchman, a dancer, and a journalist – that's all we need!' There was a lot of ground to be made up, however, before cross-Channel love broke out *en masse*, and as before 1914, it would need a German matchmaker all could agree to hate.

Towards the Dark Gulf, 1929–39

There was no sense in rushing into alliance and making Germany feel that
she was being threatened.

JAMES RAMSAY MACDONALD, prime minister, 1933[71]

It's high time the French were 'told where to get off' . . . It's time we
ceased being tied to their leading strings, and a rare lot of people in this
country think so too.

Assistant secretary to the Committee of Imperial Defence, March 1936[72]

Who in France would have imagined in 1930 that in less than 10 years this
great democratic nation would have become a second-rate power shorn of
its influence in central Europe and dependent on a stubborn and
demanding ally for its own security?

HENRY MORGENTHAU, US treasury secretary, September 1938[73]

Optimists could be fairly content as the 1920s reached their end. Churchill
told an audience in Montreal that 'the outlook for peace has never been
better for fifty years'.[74] The legacy of the war seemed to have been liquidated by a combination of coercion, pay-offs and exhaustion.[75] Germany
was borrowing from the United States, partly to pay much-reduced reparations, but also to increase public spending at home. Britain had returned to
the gold standard at the pre-war parity of sterling to the dollar, to demonstrate that things were back to normal and that London was still the world's
financial market-place. The United States was enjoying an investment boom.
France had stabilized the franc at a quarter of its pre-war rate against sterling. Thanks to this undervaluation France was exporting vigorously, and
turning its foreign earnings into gold, in part to increase its clout against
what the governor of the Banque de France called 'the imperialism of the
Bank of England'.[76] The financial system, however, was fragile; and over
much of Europe political systems were equally so. In October 1929 the New
York stock market crashed. Individuals and businesses were ruined. Banks
failed. America stopped lending. All countries sought to protect themselves
by cutting domestic spending and costs, and reducing imports. World trade
collapsed. Millions lost their jobs. The causes of the crash and its aftermath
still engage economic historians. Many at the time thought the cause was
obvious: France. The British Treasury thought that 'the monetary policy
pursued by the French was largely responsible for the world crisis'.[77] Its
cheap currency and accumulation of gold had undermined the international
financial system, forced other countries to take deflationary measures, and
thus widened and deepened the slump. France itself, meanwhile, was

relatively immune from the consequences. This analysis held some truth, though there were more profound causes.

Every country felt the political shock. Resentful voters turned to extremist parties, which drew on the experience of the war to advocate state action, discipline, and violence. In July 1932, the most extreme of the German nationalist parties, Hitler's National Socialists, doubled their 1928 vote to 37.4 per cent of the total, and the following January were brought into a coalition government. They seized the opportunity to establish a one-party dictatorship. Their supporters wanted them to bring down unemployment – which broadly speaking they did. They also planned to speed up and radicalize the policy pursued by all their predecessors: destroying what was left of the Versailles settlement, on which they blamed Germany's economic disasters, and thus nullifying the outcome of the war.

This frightening development did not alter British and French policies. Many made the same assumption as Hitler's erstwhile coalition partners: that he could not really mean his own rhetoric, and that the realities of being in power would sober him up – or he would be overthrown. The logic of appeasement was confirmed: it was because Germany had been treated 'harshly' that this nationalist backlash had occurred, and therefore it had to be calmed by moderate and just concessions. As the *Manchester Guardian* saw it, 'the Nazi revolution' was an outcome of 'brooding over the wrongs of Germany'. This was blamed largely on the French: 'Had there been no Tardieu,' thought the prime minister MacDonald, referring to France's recent hard-line prime minister, 'there would have been no Chancellor Hitler.'[78]

Furthermore, the danger of *not* appeasing Germany had suddenly increased. British and French intelligence reports tended to underestimate German ambitions, and overestimate German force – the perfect recipe for concession. In both countries, any response was inhibited both by cost and by vehement public opposition to any hint of military confrontation. In Britain the Labour party condemned it as 'the merest scaremongering . . . to suggest that more millions of money needed to be spent on armaments'. Churchill hoped that Hitler could be contained by a mixture of deterrence and concession, and that a strong Britain could 'stand aside' from European conflicts: 'I hope and trust that the French will look after their own safety, and that we shall be permitted to live our life in our island . . . we have to be strong enough to defend our neutrality.'[79] In France, now also belatedly stuck in economic depression, the arguments were similar. French politicians and diplomats who were sceptical of appeasement had no option but to wait and hope that British and French voters would come to support a stronger policy before it was too late.

In the meantime, France's policy rested on two foundations. Having lost the Rhineland, it had built an elaborate and expensive system of fortifications, the Maginot Line – modernized Vauban. It consolidated links with other potential targets of Germany, most crucially Poland and Czechoslovakia. It was unclear whether these states were militarily viable. Mussolini's Italy was another matter, however, for it shared with France an interest in preventing Germany from absorbing Austria. An alliance with Italy would transform France's strategic position. Mussolini was planning to conquer the independent African monarchy, Abyssinia. The French government, and less willingly the British, were prepared to acquiesce as the price of Italian support in Europe. Prime minister Pierre Laval and foreign secretary Sir Samuel Hoare agreed a secret compromise in December 1935 to give part of Abyssinia to Italy. This was leaked to the press, and it caused an outcry in Britain: here was a plot to connive in blatant aggression and undermine the League of Nations. Hoare resigned. Britain supported economic sanctions imposed on Italy by the League, and also sent a fleet into the Mediterranean. France was forced to follow Britain. The main effect of the sanctions was to end the prospect – perhaps illusory – of a Franco-Italian alliance. French nationalists were apoplectic. Perfidious Albion had deprived France of defences on the Rhine and was now wrecking its best alternative chance of security. The idealism of the British public was thus interpreted as Whitehall cynicism.

That year did see Whitehall cynicism, however. Britain wanted to avoid an arms race with Hitler, and offered bilateral arms limitation agreements. But this meant accepting German rearmament, despite its being illegal under the Versailles treaty. France was not even consulted. Britain began a five-year rearmament programme, but its purpose was not to resist Hitler. Early advocates of rearmament, notably Churchill, wanted a bigger navy and air force to make Britain strong enough to avoid European quarrels and safeguard the Empire. It was hoped that the RAF would provide a means of deterrence that would be relatively cheap in money and manpower. The army was not a priority. The term 'British Expeditionary Force', redolent of 1914, was taboo. The most Whitehall would envisage was a token 'Field Force' of two divisions.

Franco-British disarray encouraged Hitler in his first gamble: the illegal remilitarization of the Rhineland in March 1936. This began as the most tentative dipping of the jackboot toe. The German army was unready for a war, so a mere 3,000 troops advanced into the zone, with orders to withdraw immediately if the French reacted. This was the point at which, legend has it – a legend encouraged by Hitler himself – the Nazi adventure could have been snuffed out: the Führer would have been humiliated, and the army might have overthrown him. In fact the risk was small. Even Churchill hoped for a 'peaceful and friendly solution'.[80] For idealistic appeasers, the Rhineland issue was a hangover from the 'unjust' Versailles treaty and a symbol of

French 'militarism'. MacDonald hoped that Hitler's bold action had taught the French a 'severe lesson'. Snowden muttered that the 'damned French are at their old game of dragging this country behind them in the policy of encircling Germany'.[81] Nothing could have been further from the truth. London did not have to restrain Paris from military action, because there was no appetite for it. The commanders of the army, still seen abroad as dangerously powerful, informed their government that they had no rapid reaction force to evict the Germans, whose strength they vastly overestimated.[82]

The pattern for the next three years was of usually relieved French acquiescence in British appeasement. The French historian François Bédarida described this as France being on the leading-strings of its 'English governess' – an influential idea in French accounts. British historians reply that French politicians used Britain as an excuse for their own unwillingness to act. This is clearly shown in Spain, where a nationalist military rebellion against the left-wing government began in July 1936. Spain became an ideological and political battleground for Europe, especially when Italy and Germany gave aid to the nationalists. Spain was governed by an anti-fascist 'Popular Front' coalition of republicans, socialists and Communists, and so, since June 1936, was France, under the socialist Léon Blum. The Blum government, especially certain of its ministers, wanted to help the Spanish republicans. So did the whole of the European Left. In

Rejection of war was even stronger in France than in Britain, and came from both sides of the political spectrum. Conservatives feared that only the Communists would benefit. Here John Bull and Marianne squabble with Mussolini and Franco while Hitler looks on. Stalin gloats in the background.

contrast, the British government, and most of the public except groups on the Left, had little sympathy for either side. They wanted to prevent the war from spreading and remain on reasonable terms with whoever won. At the time, and in many accounts since, Britain was shown as preventing the French government from helping the republicans. In fact, it was the Blum government that proposed a policy of non-intervention and encouraged London to take the lead in ineffective measures to enforce it. Blum knew that open French aid to the Republic would destroy his coalition and cause civil unrest in France, so while permitting token arms deliveries, he was relieved to have Britain as an excuse for neutrality. The Quai d'Orsay thought this saved the French government.[83] French nationalists identified strongly with Mussolini and the Spanish General Franco, and now supported appeasement. French foreign policy became far more ideologically divisive than before. Nevertheless, Blum took the brave step in September 1936 of beginning substantial French rearmament, though its cost forced him to suspend social reforms, disappointing his own supporters.

Rearmament in France and Britain was not undertaken with resolve or confidence. All feared new Sommes and Verduns, of which many politicians had personal experience. All feared the economic and political effects of rearmament. All feared gas and biological weapons. The nervous lay awake at night listening for air-raid sirens. The British, warned by the new prime minister Stanley Baldwin that 'the bomber would always get through', were convinced that for the first time in history the Channel gave no protection. The philosopher Bertrand Russell predicted in 1936 that 'London . . . will be one vast raving bedlam, the hospitals will be stormed, traffic will cease, the homeless will shriek for help . . . the government . . . will be swept away by an avalanche of terror'. One French expert stated that in an hour 100 bombers could cover Paris with a sheet of poison gas twenty metres thick. The commander of the Paris fire brigade gave lectures warning that fifty incendiary bombs could reduce the city to ashes, and the only hope was flight. It was seriously suggested that Parisians should be rehoused in tower blocks with armoured roofs, to raise them above the gas sheet.[84] These were not the fears of lunatics: the British Committee of Imperial Defence expected half a million casualties in the first weeks of war, and planning for them was the first step towards what became the National Health Service.

In France especially, there was a dull apprehension that all effort was hopeless: Germany was continuously increasing its superiority in both manpower and production. The French population, stagnant for half a century, actually decreased in the 1930s as a delayed consequence of 1914–18. Pacifism among veterans and the peasantry (who were conscious of providing most soldiers, and many of whom turned to Communism as a result) was based on the conviction that France could not stand another war. One farmers' newspaper wrote in 1938 that 'another bloodbath would mean the destruction of our peasantry, and without peasants what would be left of France? A victory would be almost as devastating as a defeat.'[85]

The high point of anti-war fervour in Britain had come when the Nazis, who came to power in January 1933, first revived the spectre of war. There were highly publicized events such as the Oxford Union's 'King and Country' debate in February 1933[*] and the Peace Ballot in 1934–5. This, organized by the League of Nations Union, was signed by over 11 million people. It stressed disarmament, support for the League, and prevention of aggression by economic sanctions. In France, much of the Left shared the quasi-religious attachment to the League of Nations of their British comrades, and also their condemnation of the treaty of Versailles, their suspicion of 'imperialist' military alliances, and their idealistic desire to appease Germany. French schoolteachers' leaders saw themselves as working for 'moral disarmament' by teaching hatred of war.[86] George Lansbury, leader of the Labour Party, and Paul Faure, secretary-general of the socialist SFIO, were both pacifists. But the Left began to change as fascist power increased. Lansbury was brutally attacked by the trade unionist Ernest Bevin at the 1935 party conference for 'hawking his conscience round . . . asking to be told what to do with it' – a scene that reduced Virginia Woolf to tears. The French Communist Party, responding to Moscow's sudden alarm at the fascist threat, supported Blum's rearmament. Abyssinia, and even more Spain, encouraged the shift. The Labour Party began slowly to turn away from the blanket rejection of rearmament dear to its intellectuals and party workers, and in 1937 it gave cautious support to the Conservatives' programme. Yet the great majority of French and British people believed that appeasement could defuse conflict. 'Even Hitler,' wrote Blum, 'cannot be thought to have such absurd and mad intentions.' Lansbury went to meet Hitler, and wrote enthusiastically of the latter's desire for peace – he was, after all, 'a total abstainer, non-smoker [and] vegetarian'.[87] Because they had rejected the germanophobic propaganda of 1914–18, well-meaning progressives refused to see Hitler's Germany as truly evil. Like the generals, they were preparing for the last war.

Even soldiers, sailors, and diplomats who were professionally hardened to the prospect of war were haunted by insoluble strategic problems. The French were now potentially threatened by Italy and Spain as well as by Germany and Japan, and accepted that their richest colony, Indochina, was indefensible. The British expected to face war from the Hebrides to Hong Kong, which would mean the end of Britain as a world power. They refused

---

[*] A motion was passed in the prestigious student debating society that 'This House will not fight for King and Country' – widely interpreted as evidence of pacifism among the youthful elite.

to join the French in any serious planning, because the latter would 'flaunt' it and this would annoy Germany. Rearmament, all hoped, would lead eventually to negotiated disarmament, not to war. To make sure, the Foreign Office laboured to 'embarrass and weaken' Blum, regarding him as too close to the Czechs.[88]

In March 1938 a Nazi coup was engineered in Vienna, and Hitler was invited to incorporate Austria into the Reich. The Versailles treaty had forbidden this, but legality had become irrelevant. Self-determination backed by tanks prevailed. Churchill now sounded a clear warning: 'I have watched this island descending, incontinently, fecklessly, the stairway which leads to a dark gulf.' He began to contact like-minded people in France. But public opinion still supported appeasement, 'the most noble term in the diplomatic vocabulary'.[89] As Neville Chamberlain, prime minister from May 1937, put it, 'we are all members of the human race . . . There *must* be something in common between us, if only we can find it, and perhaps by our very aloofness from the rest of Europe we may have some special part to play as conciliator.'[90]

Czechoslovakia, the last true democracy east of Switzerland, was now largely an enclave in Germany, and the obvious next target. The Treaty of Versailles, mainly to give the new state defensible frontiers, had incorporated within it the largely German-speaking Sudetenland, whose ethnic nationalists had been a pernicious nuisance since Habsburg days. Hitler promised to rescue them from Czech domination. Czechoslovakia, like Poland, was a French protégé, one of the states that Paris had hoped might collectively balance German power. However, this strategy had withered. The Czechs had a well-equipped army of thirty-five divisions which was prepared to fight. But Italy's alignment with Germany and Hitler's occupation of the Rhineland meant that France could give no rapid help. Whitehall had always deplored France's east-European alliances as a provocation to Germany, and was dead against war for 'a country which we can neither get at nor spell', and which was widely regarded as one of the Versailles treaty's mistakes. Both French and British intelligence grossly overestimated the German army and airforce, which the British believed could cause 50,000 civilian casualties in Britain within twenty-four hours.[91]

It seemed absurd even to think of fighting a world war – in which Japan and Italy were expected to join – in order, as a left-wing French trade unionist put it, 'to force three million Germans to remain within the Czechoslovakian border'.[92] The right-wing journalist Henri Béraud agreed: 'Why die for the Sudetenland?' Frightened people began to leave Paris – including the family of the air minister. London and Paris were resigned to German economic and political dominance of much of central and eastern Europe, if only the Germans would, however crudely, play by the rules. The Foreign Office view was that 'as long as Hitler could *pretend* he was incorporating Germans in the Reich we could *pretend* that he had a case'.[93] London and Paris separately concluded that the Czechs must allow the Sudeten Germans to go their own way, and the Czech government reluctantly acquiesced. But Hitler wanted to take by force what was being offered peacefully. Chamberlain, believing a German attack imminent, disconcerted Hitler by inviting himself to Berchtesgaden on 15 September 1938 to tell him in effect that he could have the Sudetenland in return for a four-power guarantee of the new borders. The *Daily Herald*, the popular Labour paper, declared that he had 'the sympathy of opinion everywhere, irrespective of Party'. Léon Blum admitted in his party paper *Le Populaire* that he was 'torn between cowardly relief and shame' – a feeling widely shared on both sides of the Channel. One of his party comrades replied defiantly that 'we are scared, and that's a good thing'.[94] On 22 September, Chamberlain met Hitler again at Bad Godesberg, on the Rhine, to seal the bargain, but found to his surprise and anger that Hitler was now tearing away the fig-leaves of international diplomacy by claiming more territory and threatening an immediate invasion. Chamberlain returned to London, and the Cabinet rejected the German demand. In both Britain and France, public opinion was divided and volatile.

The French prime minister Edouard Daladier, a stubborn southern radical known as 'the Vaucluse bull', made the agonizing decision that it was 'better to fight and die than accept such a humiliation'.[95] He came to London on 25 September and told Chamberlain that France would resist the destruction of Czechoslovakia. He warned eloquently of Hitler's ambitions, far more dangerous than those of Napoleon – 'awful rubbish', thought the Foreign Office.[96] The French armed forces began partial mobilization. London warned Berlin that Britain would join in. But Chamberlain made clear to the French – while trying not to 'offend France beyond what was absolutely necessary' – that there was little Britain could do on the Continent.[97] The British ambassador, friendly with Daladier's pro-appeasement opponents, insisted that the French really wanted peace.

The leaders addressed their peoples. Hitler gave one of his frightening rants to a baying Nazi audience at the Berlin Sportpalast. Daladier stoutly told the French nation that they could not buy peace at the price of national dishonour, which would 'open the door to future disasters'. Chamberlain made his notorious and characteristically disheartening broadcast lamenting the 'nightmare' of war over 'a far away country of which we know nothing'. This the French found 'a perfect example of appeasement policy.'[98] With war seeming inevitable, Mussolini proposed an immediate conference to reach a peaceful settlement.

'Munich', where the conference met on 29 September, was to became part of the political vocabulary of the western world, a byword for myopia, betrayal and cowardice, and one of the most discredited episodes in Franco-British history. At the time, it seemed the only chance of saving the world from war. People cheered, from the benches of the House of Commons to the streets of Munich, where they threw flowers and shouted 'Heil Chamberlain!' Even Churchill – now the leading critic of appeasement – wished him well. Daladier had tried to telephone Chamberlain before they left for Bavaria, but he was unobtainable. When the delegations arrived at their Munich hotels, the French tried again to contact the British, but without success. There was no consultation at all. Chamberlain and Daladier did not meet before the conference opened in the flashy new Führer Building. The former seemed aloof, and Daladier began to fear having 'fallen into a trap'.[99] The meeting began with a blustering attack on the Czechs by Hitler, to which Daladier replied angrily, saying that if Hitler planned to destroy Czechoslovakia, it was a crime that he would not connive in, and he would return to Paris. Mussolini calmed things down by producing a 'compromise' plan (which the Germans had given him) and the delegations went to study it over lunch. Again, there was no consultation between the French and the British. The accounts given by the two sides diverge. The French believed that Daladier, who was trying to take a strong line, was being deliberately isolated and abandoned by Chamberlain, bent on appeasement: 'I was on my own, Chamberlain did not help me at all.' But Chamberlain claimed that the French delegation was 'passive' and 'demoralized', and Daladier so timid and unsure of himself that he gave up on them.[100] The likely explanation is that the British had in general lost confidence in French political leaders, and in particular believed that Daladier was not supported by his own Cabinet – a view pushed by the Paris embassy. Consequently, Chamberlain kept the real negotiations in his own hands, leaving Daladier in the dark. The 'Italian' plan was accepted, with a few minor concessions by Germany – notably that the takeover of the Sudetenland should take place in stages under international supervision.

Chamberlain asked for a private meeting with Hitler, where he produced a declaration of 'the desire of our two peoples never to go to war with one another again' and promising 'consultation' and 'efforts to remove possible sources of differences . . . to ensure the peace of Europe'. He and Hitler signed. Daladier only learned of this after he had returned to Paris, and could not but think that it cast doubt on British commitment to France. Hitler was angry at having been tricked, as he saw it, into negotiations that deprived him of the prestige of a military victory – 'that fellow Chamberlain has spoiled my entry into Prague'.[101] He was secretly ashamed of his loss of nerve, and was determined next time to engineer the war he desired. Ironically, his popularity and prestige benefited anyway, for he had gained the Sudetenland despite the pessimism of many of his military and diplomatic entourage, and without the war the German people feared. An insubstantial army plot to remove him in case of war was cancelled. Thereafter he acted without constraint: 'Our enemies are small worms. I saw them in Munich.'[102]

Chamberlain and Daladier won plaudits, for a time. In France, socialist pacifists proclaimed a 'Victory of the democracies', in which there were 'no corpses, no wooden crosses, no widows, no orphans. The age of Napoleons, of heroes, of Joans of Arc is over.'[103] Chamberlain was 'the most popular man in the world', receiving 40,000 mainly congratulatory letters and hundreds of presents. Blackpool football club offered to build twelve houses for ex-servicemen in his honour. The French right-wing intellectual Charles Maurras – who had been proposed for a Nobel Peace Prize by sympathetic academics in fourteen countries – announced that he would prefer the prize to go to Chamberlain.[104] Many a French town acquired its 'Rue Chamberlain', and a new dance, 'Le Chamberlain' (involving an umbrella), appeared in Paris. The newspaper *Paris-Soir* started a subscription to buy him a trout stream so that he could indulge his hobby in France. In Fleet Street, only the *Daily Telegraph* was strongly critical. So, at the other end of the political spectrum, were some left-wing anti-fascists. Chamberlain was convinced that he had won a success. Daladier, who returned to France visibly down-hearted, was not. Both had been met on their return by cheering crowds. Chamberlain responded, waving his friendship declaration and speaking of 'peace for our time'. Daladier's terse remark was 'people are mad' – or, in Jean-Paul Sartre's account, simply 'Les cons!'

This difference between Chamberlain and Daladier was the culmination of the disagreement between British and French attitudes since 1919. Daladier had at least as profound a hatred of war as Chamberlain – he had been seriously wounded in the trenches. Both knew the horrors war would bring, and how distant were the prospects of victory. It would be too simple to say that Chamberlain believed Hitler and Daladier did not, but it was the case that Chamberlain was still willing to hope that Hitler could be induced to behave rationally and with some regard to international proprieties. That had been the basis of appeasement since 1919: that Germany had a set of reasonable grievances that could be resolved, and the causes of hostility removed. But Daladier realized that Hitler was using grievances arising from the Versailles treaty as pretexts for unlimited expansion, and concluded that as France would be forced to fight, it should fight without further loss of self-respect, international credibility, and allies. But without British support, that was impossible. There is still debate over whether the real aim at Munich was to gain time to prepare for an inevitable war. It does not seem that such a calculation existed on the French side, where the government was bitterly divided. On the British side, the aim was not to prepare for future conflict, but to win time to build up an air force that could deter one – even if this meant having an army incapable of fighting on the Continent and a navy too weak to face up to Japan. The only people planning to use the respite to prepare for war were the Germans: 'Now it's a matter of rearm, rearm, rearm.'[105]

Although Munich was and is a powerful symbol, it was not the ideal occasion for forcing a confrontation with Germany. It is surprising that the French, and even the British, contemplated going to war at all. The transfer of Sudetenland, arguably an act of self-determination, had already been accepted, so the dispute was over means, not ends – a French trade-union declaration denounced it as merely 'procedure, ego or prestige'.[106] Such an issue would not rally appeasers in France, Britain and the Dominions, let alone America. Hitler, convinced he could win, would not have accepted humiliation by backing down, so France, Britain and Czechoslovakia would really have had to fight. It remains a matter of debate whether the chances of defeating Germany were greater in 1938 than in 1939 or 1940. All knew that they could do little or nothing to help the encircled Czechs, who, the French army reckoned, might hold out for a month. One could argue that September 1938 was either too late or too early to go to war with Germany. Too late because the Rhineland, the jumping-off point for invasion, had been lost, and the French army had been run down. Though still numerically impressive, it was not trained or equipped to invade Germany. Too early, because appeasement had not yet been discredited: Hitler proclaimed repeatedly that Sudetenland was his last territorial claim in Europe, and many wanted to believe him. Also too early because British and French rearmament had only just begun. The French air force thought it would be wiped out in two weeks, and the RAF was barely emerging from post-1918 hibernation. They were better armed by 1940. So were the Germans.

Yet if Hitler had persisted in forcing a war, if Chamberlain had not leapt at negotiations, if Daladier had had his way and resisted concessions, and if the Franco-British could have girded themselves up to invade – a steep mountain of ifs – so weak was the German army and so incapable of sustaining a simultaneous war on two fronts that it is just imaginable that Hitler would have been defeated or overthrown, and the world spared its looming catastrophe.

The leading critic of the Munich agreement was Churchill: 'do not suppose that this is the end . . . This is only the first sip, the first foretaste of a bitter cup.' (An unknown French colonel, Charles de Gaulle, wrote similarly to his wife: 'We shall drink the cup to its dregs.'[107]) Churchill called for a Franco-British alliance as the core of a 'grand alliance' to contain Hitler. Public opinion in both Britain and France was now moving in the direction of Churchill and his French friends such as the centre-right politican Paul Reynaud. But appeasement was not dead. There remained strong grass-roots pacifism on the French Left: 'The most onerous concessions are better than the most victorious war.'[108] The extreme Right was virulently anti-war, sniffing out a plot in Moscow to provoke war in the west to destroy France and bring about a Communist revolution. Britain was less ideologically divided. Much of the press – notably *The Times* – continued to favour appeasement, though it was probably lagging behind public opinion. Some Welsh miners even demonstrated against Munich. But despite Bevin and the TUC, many in the Labour and Liberal parties still criticized arms spending and opposed – the Labour leader Clement Attlee 'shaking with rage' – the first steps towards conscription in April 1939.[109]

Events soon confirmed Churchill's grim predictions. *Kristallnacht*, the first mass violence against Jews in Germany, took place on 9 November 1938. 'I must say Hitler never helps, and always makes Chamberlain's task more difficult,' grumbled Channon.[110] Opinion polls showed that most people no longer believed Hitler's statement that he had no further territorial ambitions in Europe. In France, 70 per cent thought that further German demands should be resisted. The subscription for Chamberlain's trout stream raised only £1,500. On 13 March 1939, the German army occupied Prague, violating the Munich agreement. A Gallup poll showed 87 per cent in Britain now favoured an alliance of Britain, France and Russia, though 55 per cent still trusted Chamberlain.[111]

Sensational intelligence reports arrived that Germany was planning surprise attacks on Holland and even Britain. This was false information, leaked by conservative anti-Nazi elements in Germany in the hope of goading the West into action. They succeeded in creating high excitement and galvanizing Whitehall. Far from panicking, the British were strangely confident as their rearmament programme accelerated: 'We have at last got on top of the dictators,' wrote Chamberlain in February.[112] He surprised Parliament with a sudden public pledge of support to France – 'Really Chamberlain is an astonishing and perplexing old boy,' noted one MP.[113] Joint military planning at last began. The British government now adopted French political and military strategy wholesale – years too late. Offers of support were showered on France's allies in Eastern Europe, especially Romania (important for its oil) and Poland. Poland was the crux, as the Nazis had begun to repeat their Sudetenland tactic, using as a pretext for aggression Danzig and the corridor through German territory connecting Poland with the sea. On 31 March 1939 Chamberlain told the Commons that Britain and France would aid Poland if its independence were endangered.[114] It was not, however, that he had decided to pick up Hitler's gauntlet and face an inevitable war. Ministers and officials in London and Paris aimed to avert war by combining deterrence (through rearmament and alliances) and appeasement (offering Hitler African colonies and economic inducements).

Deterrence was also the purpose of the unenthusiastic Franco-British attempt in August 1939 to negotiate an alliance with the Soviet Union, even now a controversial issue. It was not clear – and is still not – what the duplicitous and paranoid Stalin really wanted, and whether he would or could provide effective aid in case of war. Moreover, neither Poland nor Romania wanted the Red Army on their soil. Negotiations stagnated. On 23 August, Stalin astonished most of the world by concluding a non-aggression pact with Germany instead. This is probably what he had intended all along: negotiations with France and Britain were bargaining counters to get a good deal from Hitler, while promoting a destructive war among the 'imperialist' states. The Soviet Union began to sell huge amounts of food and raw materials to Germany. This set the seal on Hitler's war.

It arrived with chilling predictability. Hitler increased pressure over Danzig. This time there was no Munich: Hitler wanted his war, and Daladier and Chamberlain were less willing to offer concessions. Hitler had exhausted appeasement, by showing that both its idealism and its expediency were illusions. A right-wing French newspaper asked sarcastically, 'Die for Danzig?' But opinion polls showed that 76 per cent of the French people were ready to risk precisely that.[115] There was little of the emotion of the Munich crisis, only twelve months before. 'I suppose it is like getting married,' reflected Channon. 'The second time it is impossible to work up the same excitement.'[116] The French and British governments renewed their guarantees to Poland – whose military strength, for no obvious reason, they exaggerated – and their peoples resigned themselves to war. Their last hope was that Hitler might be bluffing.

Appeasement, broadly speaking, had been a British choice, and a French necessity. 'Anglo-Saxon' opinion had always been far more sanguine about building a new world order based on the League of Nations, which they assumed Germany would willingly join, once its reasonable grievances had been met. As the Foreign Office put it, 'from the earliest years following the war, it was our policy to eliminate those parts of the Peace Settlement which, as practical people, we knew to be untenable and indefensible'.[117] The arrival of Hitler made no difference: Whitehall did not grasp what Nazi foreign policy was really aiming at – unlimited conquest. The failure of appeasement was not only a failure of British diplomacy, but also of British understanding of Europe – in a sense, of British understanding of human nature. The pessimistic predictions of Foch, Poincaré and Clemenceau were confirmed: Europe had not had peace, but only a truce, during which France had grown weaker. The supposedly theoretically minded French had been sceptical and hard-headed; the supposedly practical and empirical British – veering crazily between fear of French power and disdain for French weakness – had been governed by utopianism and wishful thinking.

Could the war have been prevented? Churchill in his memoirs and later historians have concluded that the only chance would have been by a strong alliance between France and Britain. The only problem with this analysis is that no one in Britain, including Churchill, wanted it until it was far too late. So, as Lord Halifax, the foreign secretary, summed it up, the French thought that 'war has come upon them again owing to our having taken the teeth out of the Versailles settlement, and having ever since shown a sentimental spinelessness in dealing with Germany'.[118]

Whitehall and Paris even failed to act together when the Germans attacked Poland on 1 September. Mussolini tried to repeat the Munich trick by proposing another conference. An angry House of Commons forced the flustered Chamberlain to ignore him and send an ultimatum to Germany at nine o'clock on 3 September. The French, however, in the person of their foreign minister Georges Bonnet, wanted to delay, which caused increasingly heated exchanges between the Allies. France finally declared war six hours after Britain.

CHAPTER 12

Finest Hours, Darkest Years

Upon this battle depends the survival of Christian civilization. Upon it
depends our own British life . . . Hitler knows that he will have to break us
in this island or lose the war. If we can stand up to him, all Europe may be
free and the life of the world may move forward into broad, sunlit uplands.
But if we fail, then the whole world . . . will sink into the abyss of a new
dark age . . . Let us therefore brace ourselves to our duties, and so bear
ourselves that, if the British Empire and its Commonwealth last for a
thousand years, men will still say: 'This was their finest hour.'

WINSTON CHURCHILL in the House of Commons, 18 June 1940

Is the last word said? Must hope disappear? Is defeat final? No! . . . For
France is not alone! She is not alone! She is not alone! She has a vast
empire behind her. She can make common cause with the British empire,
which commands the seas and is continuing the struggle . . . This war has
not been decided by the battle of France. This war is a world war . . . The
fate of the world is at stake . . . Whatever happens, the flame of French
resistance must not and shall not be quenched.

CHARLES DE GAULLE on the BBC, 18 June 1940

On 18 June 1940 the two nations' destinies intersected. The two dominating figures of their modern histories summoned both to a common struggle not just for themselves, but for humanity – a grand role which patriots had often claimed for them, though never with such good reason. The next five years would draw them closer than ever before, but also create differences of emotion and memory that would mark them for the rest of the century and beyond.

The 'Phoney War', September 1939–May 1940

He [Daladier] fully expected to be betrayed by the British and added
that this was the customary fate of allies of the British.
Comment by EDOUARD DALADIER, prime minister, January 1939[1]

The English have . . . such confidence in the French army that they
are tempted to consider their military support as a gesture of solidarity
rather than a vital necessity.
French ambassador, October 1939[2]

As Chamberlain broadcast the news that Britain was again at war, air-raid sirens sounded over London. But no bombs fell. The French army's fear that bombing might disrupt their mobilization – the reason they had delayed France's declaration of war – was similarly unfounded. The barracks filled; the Maginot Line was manned; the RAF improvised bases in France; the British army crossed the Channel undisturbed and returned to places familiar to the older men. One general, at a Franco-British wreath-laying at the war memorial at Lens, remembered over twenty years earlier giving orders 'to shell this self-same square'.[3] The 'phoney war', the 'drôle de guerre', had begun. French and British governments and commanders were convinced that they could do nothing to save the Poles. The French army had promised Warsaw it would launch an offensive on the seventeenth day of mobilization. It took the form of a token attack on the Saar, cynically exaggerated in the press. Two-thirds of the German army were in Poland. On the Western Front, Germany was defended by middle-aged reservists with three days' ammunition and no air cover. The Allies had a superiority of three to one in men, five to one in artillery, and all the German tanks were in the east. But the Allies had no intention of attacking, or of bombing German factories in the Ruhr, for fear of retaliation against France. The Poles were abandoned to conduct a hopeless defence, which lasted a month. German commanders could not believe their luck.[4]

The Allies did nothing because they feared repeating the carnage of the last war. Both sides had used that experience to build scientifically planned defensive systems, the 'Siegfried Line' and the Maginot Line, elaborate crystallizations of the lessons learnt in 1916–18. The Germans were manufacturing barbed wire and shells more than aircraft and tanks. The Allies planned a modern, relatively bloodless version of the previous war. Then, Germany had been worn down by superior resources and the strangling blockade. The Allies' main fear since 1936 had been of an immediate German knockout blow from the air. This had not happened, so it was possible to believe, as Chamberlain proclaimed, that Hitler had missed the bus. Both British and French appeared confident, and tended to over-estimate each other's strength.[5] The plan was that this strength would increase as the British army swelled with conscripts, the forces of the two Empires rallied, and rearmament programmes, adopted in the nick of time, reached completion in 1940–41. German strength would decline as the blockade deprived it of vital food and raw materials, and domestic opinion turned against Hitler. Germany would then be defeated in 1943 or 1944, unless, as optimists predicted, Hitler were overthrown earlier. It was a great relief that Italy and Japan had not immediately entered the war. Perhaps in time, the United States would again join the coalition.

However, the French suddenly developed doubts about this optimistic vision, owing to the collapse of the eastern front, to political divisions at home, and to realization that French industry was failing to meet arms production targets.[6] They began to fear that a long war might actually favour Germany, and desperately sought some way of winning quickly. Their two main ideas were to help the Finns, who were resisting attack from Hitler's Soviet ally, and to bomb Russian oilfields. Alliance with Finland might permit them to cut off Swedish iron-ore exports, 40 per cent of Germany's needs, and bombing Baku would reduce the flow of Russian oil to Germany. Daladier derided the British, who were dubious, as 'all old men'. This French strategy was dangerously unrealistic, and risked bringing the USSR into the war as Hitler's ally. But the Germans moved first. In April 1940, they invaded Denmark and Norway with the connivance of the Russians and the Swedes. An Allied expedition to help the Norwegians failed, though it did cripple the German surface navy. Daladier and Chamberlain resigned, and were replaced by Paul Reynaud and Winston Churchill.

The British Expeditionary Force – more correctly, the Field Force – was, as in 1914, the junior partner, roughly one-tenth the size of the French army. The British acquiesced in French leadership, acknowledging that French commanders, under the quietly cerebral General Gamelin, were professionally pre-eminent. They certainly treated their British counterparts with some condescension: 'it is for us to give them moral support, to organize the strategy of the campaign, and to provide the necessary planning and inspiration'.[7] The astonishing dependence of the British is shown by a diary entry as late as 17 December by General Ironside, chief of the imperial general staff: 'So far I have failed to get out of Gamelin his idea as to a possible offensive. Perhaps it is probable that he has none.'[8] The BEF's original four divisions rose to nine divisions and an armoured brigade by May 1940. Unlike in 1914 it was placed, if rather ambiguously, under French command. It was more than the token two divisions promised in 1938, but was far from what the French had hoped for. They had wanted the British to compensate for their small numbers by creating a mechanized and armoured striking force in case of another Schlieffen Plan. But British rearmament had concentrated on the RAF, to build a deterrent bomber force and fighters for home defence. This had required money and industrial capacity, to the neglect of the army.

The BEF embodied twenty years of collective British reluctance to contemplate involvement in another European war. It was small, abysmally trained, and poorly equipped. It even lacked modern maps of France. The regulars had until recently been on imperial police duties in Palestine and India. The territorials were still amateurs. The BEF was admittedly the only fully mechanized army, with plenty of lorries – the German army had bought up many of their discarded horses. But they were lamentably short of artillery, had few usable radios and their 'main defect', as the commander-in-chief Lord Gort unanswerably observed, was 'the absence of a tank with a gun'.[9] The French hoped that the RAF would be used to provide compensating air power, both to defend French cities and to support the armies. But the British had their sights fixed on the strategic air war of the future, defending British cities and bombing German ones. They sent a modest force of Hurricanes and reconnaissance aircraft for the BEF, and an Advanced Air Striking Force (ten squadrons of obsolescent short-range light bombers and six squadrons of fighters) to eastern France to bomb neighbouring areas of Germany when the time came. The limits of British air support would become 'the single greatest irritant' between the Allies and a rankling French reproach.[10]

The French army had belatedly started to modernize its equipment, and there is ample evidence of its difficulties. Powerful interests long defended the proven methods of 1914–18. Mechanization, for example, threatened those French farmers who produced horses, mules and fodder. A strong parliamentary lobby protested when Daladier began to replace animals with lorries. Nevertheless, the Popular Front and its successors had forced through a rearmament programme, and by 1940 the French had a bigger tank force than the Germans, and with better tanks. But they were handicapped by the experience of 1914–18. Their commanders had perfected defensive tactics founded on sophisticated theory and mathematics: 'all is foreseen and prepared'. They believed a strategic breakthrough to be impossible. This pseudo-science was inward-looking and reluctant to consider other possibilities. One bizarre symptom was the dislike expressed by military writers for 'barbarous' *franglais* neologisms such as *le tank, la motorisation* and *la mécanisation* – 'Must we continue to take from the English all the horrors of their language?'[11] Defensive doctrine had been powerfully endorsed by Marshal Pétain, the dominant inter-war military figure, whose cautiousness had founded his success and popularity in 1917: defence meant sparing soldiers' lives. Defensiveness had taken literally concrete form in the Maginot Line, which reminded several visitors of a fleet of sunken battleships. One British general was suitably impressed when shown round – 'a masterpiece in its way' – but he wondered whether the money would not have been better spent on tanks and aircraft, and he worried that if the 'fence' were brought down, 'French fighting spirit [would] be brought crumbling down with it.'[12] The Maginot Line did not impose passivity, however: it freed France's best infantry and armoured units for an advance into Belgium and Holland. The French were even keen on sending expeditions far afield, from Finland to Salonika. Yet old assumptions lingered. Though they were hastily creating new mobile armoured divisions, two-thirds of their tanks were still, as in 1918, dispersed in small groups, communicating by flag, not radio, to support the infantry. As one French general later put it, they had a thousand groups of three tanks; the Germans had three groups of a thousand tanks.

During the coldest winter of the century, the Allies waited. The king, the prime minister, and Gracie Fields visited British units. Senior officers attended lunches with French authorities, and one found having to eat oysters 'a very high test of "l'entente cordiale"'. A French visitor was struck by the characteristic English smell of cigarettes and bacon.[13] RAF pilots shared goodwill binges with their French counterparts, interspersed with the occasional inconclusive dogfight. The army trained for defence and built pillboxes. Major-General Montgomery advised his men about venereal disease in such 'obscene' terms ('any soldier who is in need of horizontal refreshment would be well advised to ask a policeman for a suitable address') that the army's Anglican and Catholic chaplains almost got him sacked. The great French historian Marc Bloch, brought from Cambridge to serve as a liaison officer with the BEF, had mixed feelings about the British regulars. 'The soldier immortalized by Kipling knows how to obey and how to fight . . . But he is, by nature, a looter and a lecher . . . vices which the French peasant finds it hard to forgive when both are satisfied to the detriment of his farmyard and his daughters.' Moreover, he noted that the Englishman, though 'kindly and good-natured' at home, tended when abroad to 'confuse his European hosts with "natives"' – a boorishness aggravated by 'natural shyness'. There was annoyance that British soldiers were paid vastly more than the French. British officers – so memoirs suggest – were over-keen to

The BEF settles in for a long war. By some accounts, the BEF were leading a very quiet life. The Revd Thomas Tiplady reported with satisfaction in the *Methodist Recorder* that 'I saw no British soldier under the influence of drink. The army keeps itself to itself . . . It was very rarely indeed that I saw an officer or soldier with a lady, and when I did the circumstances would not have justified me in attributing evil to the association.'[15]

discover whether their French comrades were 'gentlemen'. They must frequently have been disappointed. Sometimes up to 40 per cent of officers in infantry regiments were schoolteachers, many of them socialists.[14]

The commander of II Corps, General Alan Brooke, a French speaker brought up in Pau and educated at the local French school, 'could not help wondering whether the French are still a firm enough nation to again take their part in seeing this war through'. Although he found them welcoming, their 'slovenliness, dirtiness and inefficiency are, I think, worse than ever'. Many of their defences were 'to all intents and purposes non-existent'. The soldiers had 'a very amateur appearance', and Gamelin looked 'old and tired'. Brooke was no less scathing about his own men, largely untrained, and his superior, Lord Gort, VC, who had the 'brain . . . of a glorified boy scout'.[16] On the surface, confidence reigned. Churchill was impressed by the French army when he visited in October. Ironside was delighted in March 1940 to find French officers and soldiers 'working like beavers, and very intelligent', not, like the British, distracted by square-bashing which 'smothered the intelligence of our men'.[17] The French had limited confidence in the BEF.

Gamelin believed that '1914–18 has shown that one must always keep large French forces alongside the . . . British. Whenever these were removed, they had to be rushed back in times of crisis.' He redeployed the strongest element of France's strategic reserve, the 7th Army, on to the BEF's left, to counter a possible German advance into Holland, and to discourage any British rush for the ports.[18] This was to prove a disastrous move.

The French government and public had a number of grievances, most stemming from the realization that France, with millions of men in the army, was far more affected by the war than Britain. Some worried that the British, 'with their bishops and their socialists', would again let them down at peace negotiations. To bolster the alliance, schemes for 'ever closer union' in economic and political matters, and even for an 'Anglo-French Federation' were floated in Paris and Whitehall. Ideas were suggested for strengthening Franco-British solidarity at grass-roots level: mutual playing of national anthems in cinemas, special postage stamps, tactfully edited history text-books, compulsory language lessons, and French cookery demonstrations in British schools.

In both countries, some urged that the war should be stopped and a deal done with Hitler or preferably a more rational Nazi leader. There was still a pro-appeasement current composed of pacifists, the anti-imperialist Left, the revolution-fearing Right, and all those whose terror of Armageddon induced wishful thinking, or just non-thinking, among them establishment figures, celebrities and intellectuals. In Britain, these included Lloyd George, George Bernard Shaw, a clutch of bishops, the Peace Pledge Union with the vocal feminist Vera Brittain, Bloomsbury aesthetes, show-business celebrities such as John Gielgud, eccentric pro-fascists, socialist academics such as G.D.H. Cole, and a solid number of MPs and peers of all parties, notably the mostly Labour 'Parliamentary Peace Aims Group', which even made contact with the Germans. In France, opposition was far more dangerous. The Communist Party, powerful among the trade unions, campaigned against the war and was banned. Some pro fascists took a similar line, though many had been called up and subsequently fought. More dangerous were those who campaigned from inside the establishment, including pro-appeasement politicians such as former prime minister Pierre Laval, and the foreign minister Georges Bonnet, for the moment in favour of prosecuting the war, but pessimistic as to its outcome. When things went disastrously wrong, such people would make many converts. For the moment, they were a minority, as mass support for pacifism collapsed. For most people, appeasement had failed and war was necessary to stop Hitler. There was one Franco-British divergence, however, which echoed pre-war views. Polls showed that the French thought they were fighting the Germans. The British overwhelmingly thought they were fighting Hitler, not the German nation as a whole.[19]

Hitler returned the compliment by regarding Britain as his main enemy. His plan was for a thrust into Holland and Belgium to secure airfields and ports for bombing and eventually invading England. The Allies captured a copy of this plan, and decided to counter it by a rapid advance through Belgium. But the inaction of France and Britain when Hitler had remilitarized the Rhineland had scared the Belgians into declaring neutrality. They feared that complicity with the Allies might bring on a German attack, and so refused to allow joint planning. They had their own modern frontier fortifications, and were confident of holding out until help arrived. So the French and British armies would have to leave their carefully constructed trenches to improvise a hasty defence on unknown Belgian ground. Having to move fast, they would send their best-equipped mobile divisions. Brooke worried that if this went wrong 'not only would we lose the whole of Belgium but probably the war as well.'[20]

The Real Disaster, May–June 1940

Greenwood [a Labour member of the Cabinet] was inclined to say 'these bloody gallant Allies'. I told him that we had depended upon the French Army. That we had made no Army, and that therefore it was not right to say 'these bloody Allies'. It was for them to say that of us.
GENERAL SIR EDMUND IRONSIDE, chief of the imperial general staff,
17 May 1940[21]

You, the English, were done for [in March 1918]. But I sent forty divisions to rescue you. Today it's we who are smashed to pieces. Where are your forty divisions?
MARSHAL PETAIN to WINSTON CHURCHILL, 11 June 1940[22]

On 10 May, the day Churchill took office, the Germans launched their long-awaited invasion of Holland, Luxembourg and Belgium. The Dutch retreated, and the Belgians failed to hold their border fortresses. Allied bombers failed to destroy the Rhine bridges at Maastricht. All thirty-two RAF planes engaged were damaged or destroyed. Ground support operations were suspended: the Advanced Air Striking Force had lost half its aircraft in forty-eight hours. The French and British armies hastened north to hold a line in central Belgium and south-west Holland. The first tank battles in history took place, and the French won them: near Breda, they destroyed 100 German tanks with a loss of five of their own.[23]

However, to their original plan, which the Allies knew about, the Germans had made an ambitious and risky addition. As well as invading the Low

Countries, they would launch a nearly simultaneous attack further south through the wooded hills of the Ardennes. Reaching the River Meuse at Sedan, a weakly defended sector, they would break through to cut off the Allied forces in Belgium and end the war at a blow. This plan was a result not of confidence but of desperation: it seemed the only possibility of avoiding a long unwinnable replay of the First World War, which the Germans feared as much as the French did. The chief of the general staff concluded that 'Even if the operation had only a 10 per cent chance of success, I would stick to it. Only this operation will lead to the destruction of the opponent.' In case it failed, Hitler ordered continuing preparations for a long war.[24]

Success depended on surprise and concealment. Moving tanks and vehicles through the Ardennes was slow and dangerous, for they would have to stick to the roads, and the packed queues of vehicles would be vulnerable to air attack. It is often said that French commanders believed that the Ardennes were impassable. In fact, Gamelin had earlier expected an attack there. But the French did overestimate the time it would take an attacker to get through that terrain. They expected to have time to bring up reinforcements if necessary. The Allies were misled by their capture of the original German plan – the most disastrous intelligence success in history. Their intelligence services failed to detect the other build-up in the southern Rhineland. The air forces, committed further north, did not attack the world's biggest-ever traffic jam, created by 134,000 German soldiers, 1,200 tanks and thousands of other vehicles. Nor did the French army rush in reinforcements to destroy them as they trickled out of the forests. It took four days, until 14 May, for the Allies to realize that this was not merely a diversion. By then, the Germans had reached Sedan (the site of their crushing victory in 1870), and on 13 May had crossed the Meuse. Most French troops in that sector were second-line reserves, with no effective anti-tank or anti-aircraft weapons. Taken by surprise, they were subjected without air support to the heaviest air bombardment so far in history: 'it goes on and on and on . . . Not a French or British plane to be seen. Where the hell are they?'[25] Whole units eventually broke. At last, on 14 May, the Allied air forces intervened, trying to bomb the Sedan bridges, on which, said the French commander General Billotte, hung victory or defeat. Attacking in small groups, the obsolescent light-bombers failed: bridges are difficult targets, and the bombs were too small. If they flew high, they were shot down by fighters; if low, they were shot down by ground fire. Some French officers accused the British of not pressing home their attacks, though forty of their seventy-one bombers were shot down – the highest casualty rate ever suffered by the RAF. The French air force lost 30 per cent of all its aircrew in a month – a higher proportion of casualties than the army had

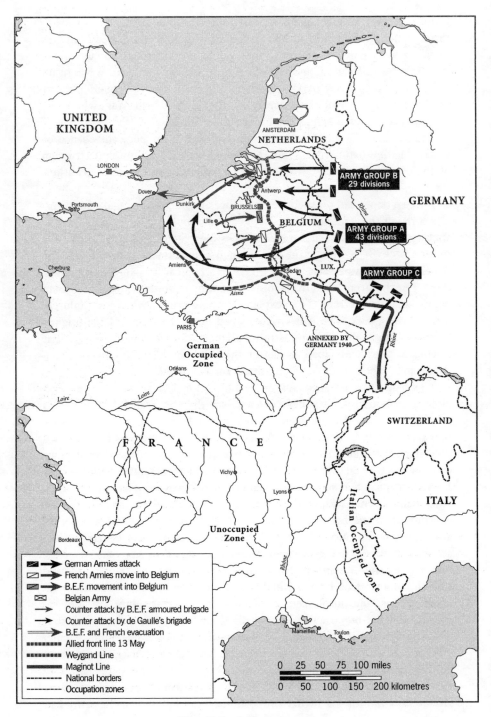

The Fall of France, 1940

'Well, Poilu, my friend'
German propaganda
played on the plausible
belief that the British
were happy to rely on
the French to bear the
brunt of the fighting – a
belief inherited from the
First World War

suffered during the whole of 1918 – and it reported that in two weeks it would have no more fighter aircraft.[26]

The news of the Sedan breakthrough caused incredulity and panic at headquarters. 'French officers were in tears . . . at having to admit the shame they felt in acknowledging the appalling fact that the French had walked out of their forward positions without any attempt at genuine resistance.'[27] Resistance did continue south of Sedan. A German officer wrote later of a Moroccan cavalry brigade, half of whom were killed, that 'I have fought against many enemies in both wars . . . Seldom has anyone fought as outstandingly.'[28] They were protecting the northern flank of the Maginot Line, assumed to be the target. But the Germans moved not south, or south-west towards Paris, but west at full speed where there was nothing in their path. This exceeded the original plan: it was carried out by General Guderian in defiance of orders, and in consequence he was temporarily sacked.[29]

Reynaud telephoned Churchill on 14 May to break the news and ask for ten more squadrons of fighters to counter the dive-bombers. A British army liaison officer with the RAF thought that '500 fighters could have saved

Sedan' by chasing away the Stukas, and that 'lack of fighter support is in my opinion the only justified grouse that the French have against us'. In London, General Ironside, furious with the 'wretched' airmen, thought the same, and considered that 'this battle may be decisive of the whole war and it is impossible to neglect a call such as this from the French'. But the RAF was determined not to send major reinforcements. Bomber Command deluded itself that it could win the war once it was allowed to bomb the Ruhr. Fighter Command considered itself indispensable to Britain's survival and insisted that a minimum of thirty-six squadrons should be kept at home. The RAF based in France had lost roughly half its combat aircraft in ten days, including 195 Hurricanes – a quarter of all Britain's modern fighters – and with negligible impact on the German advance. Most of the Hurricanes, under repair or without fuel, were abandoned in the retreat. As one pilot put it, 'here we were with all our beautiful little aeroplanes, but no bloody troops, no bloody equipment, no bloody petrol'.[30] At that rate, in two weeks there would not be a single Hurricane left anywhere. Without fighter opposition, the Luftwaffe would be able to bomb industry by day, cripple the navy, and cover an invasion. Air Marshal Sir Hugh Dowding put the issue starkly: 'If the Home Defence Force is drained away in desperate attempts to remedy the situation in France, defeat in France will involve the final, complete and irremediable defeat of this country.' Reynaud's plea for ten more squadrons was refused, but it was agreed to commit four.[31]

By 15 May, seven German armoured Panzer divisions were on the loose. Reynaud rang Churchill at 7.30 a.m., announcing in English and 'evidently under stress' that 'We have been defeated . . . we have lost the battle.' Churchill hoped he was exaggerating, and offered to fly over to 'have a talk'. But he also told him that 'whatever the French might do, we should continue the fight – if necessary alone'. Arriving in Paris the next afternoon, he was told that the Germans were expected within days. At the Quai d'Orsay, where he met the French government and high command, clouds of smoke were rising from bonfires of official documents. In the dramatic account in Churchill's memoirs, Gamelin described the situation, and when Churchill asked about the strategic reserve he replied 'None.'[32] The best reserve formations, it may be recalled, had been rushed into Holland partly owing to French doubts about the BEF. Churchill's account – 'a superbly artful passage' – went down in history as effectively 'the obituary of the Third Republic', bereft of ideas and determination. In fact, Reynaud was far from accepting defeat, and the discussion was less 'melodramatic' than Churchill's description.[33] Nevertheless, the British did face a recurring and insoluble dilemma: how to bolster French morale and resistance, which seemed essential to any chance of victory, and yet prepare for the possibility of having to fight on alone. The first object required whole-hearted commitment; the second, the preservation of both the BEF and the RAF. Their first gesture demonstrates the contradiction. They now agreed to the earlier French request to engage ten new squadrons of fighters, but kept them based in Kent; while squadrons already in France soon began to withdraw. Churchill also ordered preliminary planning for a possible evacuation of the BEF.[34] Late that night, wreathed in cigar smoke, he tried to 'revive the spirits' of French ministers by promising that Britain would fight on whatever happened, and would bomb German towns and burn their crops and forests. The effect on at least one French minister of this 'apocalyptic vision' was counter-productive: Churchill 'saw himself in the heart of Canada directing, over an England razed to the ground by high-explosive bombs and over a France whose ruins were already cold, the air war of the New World against the Old'.[35] This was not an attractive vision, and a growing number of French politicians and soldiers began to think that they must 'get France out of the ordeal she is undergoing so as to allow her, even if defeated in the field, to rise again'.[36]

The Germans were nervously aware that their advancing Panzers were vulnerable to a simultaneous attack from the north and the south, which would cut them off as they were trying to cut off the Allies. Hitler was close to a nervous breakdown, and ordered his forces to slow down.[37] The French, now under General Weygand, wanted the BEF, as yet less involved in the fighting, to take the lead by attacking from the north. But the British were now fighting the Germans in Belgium, making an about-turn dangerous, if not impossible. They were running short of food and fuel, and had ammunition for only one battle. Gort, increasingly doubting the ability of the French to fight back, concluded that evacuation was the only way to save his army. But London insisted on an attack to join up with Weygand and isolate the German spearhead. Ironside, a large and forceful man, came over to ginger up both Gort and the French. He thought he had managed by losing his temper and shaking the demoralized French General Billotte – notionally in charge of the BEF – 'by the button of his tunic'. Any galvanizing effect was short-lived. The best the BEF managed was on 21 May near Arras, when their single armoured brigade – two battalions of the Royal Tank Regiment, backed by two territorial battalions of the Durham Light Infantry – gave General Rommel's Panzer division a fright by tearing into its supply columns, and slaughtering some poorly trained SS infantry. But it lost most of its tanks and withdrew. Gort had earmarked two divisions to join up with the promised French attack from the south, but on 25 May he redeployed them to meet growing German pressure from the north-east – without consulting the French and against orders from London. This decision was blamed by many Frenchmen, not only anglophobes, for losing the last chance to turn the tide. But were Weygand's forces really going to attack? Gort believed not.

The Allies, trained for static warfare, slow to react, confused, sometimes panicky, their communications and supply lines disrupted, and without effective leadership, never acted fast enough or with enough coordination to stop the German rush. Large parts of their armies, deprived of information and orders, with hundreds of tanks and aircraft out of fuel and ammunition, began to disintegrate. 'This is like some ridiculous nightmare,' wrote a British officer in his diary. 'The BEF is cut off. Our communications have gone . . . I have told myself again and again that the German threat could not be sustained. Against all the rules of warfare it has been sustained. The Germans have taken every risk – criminally foolish risks – and they have got away with it.' Ironside thought the French generals were 'in a state of complete depression. No plan, no thought of a plan. Ready to be slaughtered . . . *Très fatigués* and nothing doing.'[38] Gort insisted on retreating on Dunkirk. The BEF carried out a skilful fighting withdrawal, but hampered their allies by blowing up bridges with abandon and destroying the Lille telephone exchange, which deprived the French First Army of most of its communications.[39]

This was the lowest point for the British. The BEF seemed trapped at Dunkirk. Voices inside and outside the government urged peace, and muttered criticisms of Churchill. On 28 May he insisted to his colleagues that successful resistance was still possible, while nothing could be hoped for from Hitler. 'If this long island story of ours is to end at last, let it end only when each one of us lies choking in his own blood.'[40]

DUNKIRK AND THE FRENCH, 26 MAY–4 JUNE

General Alexander: All that could be saved has been saved.
Capitaine de La Pérouse: No, General. There remains honour.
Dunkirk, 31 May, 4.30 p.m.[41]

England's day has passed. No matter what happens now, she will lose her empire . . . She will not gain a foothold in Europe again. She left it forever when she re-embarked at Dunkirk . . . Everything that doesn't end up by being Russian will be American . . . the British empire will become an American empire.
PERRE LAVAL, Vichy prime minister, August 1940[42]

Dunkirk is, for the British, the most moving epic in their history. An outnumbered and seemingly doomed army is brought home from under the enemy's nose to fight another day; by the quiet courage and spontaneous ingenuity of ordinary people, sailing off in fishing boats, yachts and pleasure steamers not to conquer, but to face bombs and shells unarmed in a mission of mercy. It

Dunkirk is portrayed in this Vichy poster as a betrayal: British troops leave, and force the French to stay behind

has profound meaning for an island people wary of continental dangers. But for many French, it seemed typically British in a different way: 'They can't resist the call of the harbours,' jeered Weygand. 'Already in March 1918 they wanted to embark.'[43] Dunkirk meant being abandoned by the British to face defeat alone.

The British began to think about leaving a week after the German attack began. As in 1914, they mistrusted their allies, and feared being overwhelmed if the French and the Belgians gave way. As early as 18 May, preliminary planning began for evacuation through Dunkirk. This was a desperate extremity, for it was thought impossible for more than a small number of men to escape. By the 23rd, General Brooke thought that 'nothing but a miracle can save the BEF . . . We are . . . beginning to be short of ammunition, supplies still all right for three days but after that scanty.'[44] The Germans had reached the coast, cutting communications with Calais and Boulogne. But on 24 May, Hitler, still highly nervous, ordered the Panzers to halt. The French agreed to a retreat towards Dunkirk. But the two Allies had different intentions. The British wanted to embark, and on 26 May Churchill gave the order. The French, however, wanted to establish a strong Franco–British bridgehead, supplied by sea, to threaten the German rear if they turned their forces south against the French heartland. This was a way to buy time – but at a price that Britain could not accept, namely the probable sacrifice of their whole army, and heavy naval and airforce casualties, leaving Britain exposed to invasion. Though the French must have realized that the BEF might leave – as had nearly happened in 1914 and 1918 – the British kept their intentions secret until 27 May. This caused anger and misunderstanding at all levels. The French commanding general threatened to stop the evacuation by force. French soldiers, intending to fight on, were incensed when British troops preparing evacuation destroyed weapons and equipment. The French were left defending more and more of the Dunkirk perimeter as the British left. As Marc Bloch noted, French soldiers 'would have needed a superhuman dose of charity not to feel bitter as they saw ship after ship drawing away from the shore, carrying their foreign companions in arms to safety'.[45] By 29 May, 72,000 British had already left, but only 655 French. Some French who tried to board ships were turned away, sometimes by force – but many of these were stragglers or deserters regarded as not deserving embarkation when places were so short that the wounded had to be left behind.

Gort, before being ordered back to England, had promised that elements of three British divisions would help to defend the town, but on 31 May, in a tense and bitter scene, General Harold Alexander told the French commander Admiral Abrial that the BEF was pulling out as fast as possible. 'So you are admitting that the French army alone will cover the embarkation of the English army, while the English army will give no help to the French army in covering its own withdrawal', French officers protested. 'Your decision . . . dishonours England.'[46] Paris was equally indignant, and Churchill gave orders that British and French must leave 'bras-dessus bras-dessous' – arm in arm. He promised that the BEF would help hold the perimeter, and some did for a time. But the War Office and commanders on the spot disagreed with Churchill. It was more-over hard for men to stay put when there was a chance of going home, and many units melted away, eventually leaving the French unsupported. Fortunately, French troops fighting from house to house in Lille held seven German divisions away from Dunkirk for four vital days until 1 June. Then the French 12th infantry division, supported by local reservists, was 'deliber-ately sacrificed' to hold the approaches to Dunkirk.[47] The Germans, tired and short of ammunition, were ordered by Hitler, in a panic at the risks being taken, not to press home their attack. Men and tanks were needed to move south and complete the conquest of France. Hitler did not believe the BEF could all escape – neither, after all, had the French or the British themselves.

By the evening of 31 May, there were only 50,000 British troops still in Dunkirk, and 200,000 French. Some places on ships were now being reserved for French troops. From 1 June onwards, as the BEF had mostly gone, the effort was directed to taking off as many French as possible. French navy ships and French and Belgian civilian craft joined in, taking off about 30–40,000 men. On 3 June, the Royal Navy sank blockships to render the harbour useless to the Germans, which had it worked would have trapped the remaining French inside. But another 30,000 French troops were taken off that night. When the rearguard finally left their combat positions the last ships had gone. A British naval officer compared them to the Spartans at Thermopylae. A German officer put it less elegantly: 'Tommies gone and you here; you crazy.'[48]

French troops reaching England were greeted by 'ham and cheese sandwiches handed through the windows by girls in multi-coloured dresses . . . the faint, sweet smell of cigarettes showered on us . . . the acid taste of lemonade and the flat taste of tea with too much milk . . . groups of cheering children at level-crossings . . . "How genuinely kind they are!" said my companions.' They had only a dazed view of 'the cosy green of lawns; a landscape made up of parks, cathedral spires, hedges' as they were rushed across to Plymouth and sent back to Cherbourg to rejoin the fight after only a few hours in England.[49]

Dunkirk surrendered on 4 June. About 40,000 French troops were captured. But 186,000 British (mainly between 29 May and 1 June) and 125,000 French and other Allied troops (mainly between 1 and 4 June) had been rescued – vastly more than anyone had thought possible.[50] Although Churchill reminded the House of Commons that wars are not won by evacuations, defeat was certainly avoided by this one. It dealt, concludes a German military historian, 'a fatal blow to German strategy.'[51] Without the intrepid professionalism of the Royal Navy, the bravery of civilian boat crews, and the tenacity of the French troops holding off the Germans, the BEF could not have lived to fight another day. Admiral Abrial was invited to Buckingham Palace on 5 June to receive the personal thanks of the king. Perhaps it was some consolation. But the French ambassador was bitterly disappointed that Churchill said so little in the House of Commons about the courage of the French army. The epic boosted British confidence, and enabled Churchill on 4 June to make his defiant promise – perhaps inspired by a famous speech by Clemenceau that he knew well – that 'We shall fight on the beaches, we shall fight on the landing-grounds, we shall fight in the fields and in the streets, we shall fight in the hills; we shall never surrender.'*

Across the Channel, anglophobia sprouted, and Dunkirk provided material for anti-British propaganda. Was there genuine cause for reproach? Some French commanders accused the British of deceiving them over their evacuation plans and leaving French troops behind. It was not so simple. Only during the night of 28 May did the French army order its troops to embark,

---

* Clemenceau had said 'We shall fight before Paris, we shall fight in Paris, we shall fight behind Paris.' Churchill had quoted this speech to Pétain a few days before his own.

and the French navy delayed its participation until the 29th. The French were then slow to realize how little time was left, and failed to tell the Royal Navy how many men they had to be taken off. Some French soldiers anyway decided to stay put.

The French government at first considered two options for continuing the war: to withdraw the army to Brittany and Normandy, in sea contact with Britain, or to retreat at once to North Africa. Weygand, however, insisted on another course: a last-ditch defence of a line across northern France, along the Somme and the Aisne, the killing fields of 1914–18. If this failed, it would leave little option but an armistice, as Weygand knew. But France and Britain had signed an agreement on 28 March not to make peace without the consent of the other. Reynaud had gone to London on 26 May to hint at either a joint request for an armistice, or British consent to a French request. The British refused, and urged the French to keep fighting.

Both sides began to shuffle responsibility for defeat on to the other. 'Many people now blamed the whole horrible fiasco on the English High Command, or on some rumoured counter-order of Churchill, which had marred Weygand's last attempt to get through.'[52] Weygand accused the BEF of a 'refusal to fight'.[53] The British could reply that French commanders talked of fighting on although they had no realistic plans and perhaps no real belief in their chances – they had begun thinking of an armistice as early as 16 May – and they had no right to demand the sacrifice of Britain's army and air force in a lost cause. Leaving aside emotional recriminations, the two governments had increasingly different aims: the British, to provide for the defence of their islands and continue the war; the French, to prolong resistance with a view to gaining reasonable peace terms. A growing number in the French government, army and public believed that France must now look after itself.

The French army fought on, having already lost a quarter of its strength. A young officer wrote stoically on 7 June, in words that Churchill would certainly have approved, 'I am waiting to be thrown on to the red-hot anvil with my peasants from the French countryside, men of little faith but prepared to die in vain.' British liaison officers and the Germans reported rising French morale and strengthening resistance, as they fought to hold the Somme and the Aisne. This was the great battle of 1940, largely forgotten in France, and never heard of in England. The German casualty rate doubled after 3 June. The 10th Panzer Division lost two-thirds of its tanks between 5 and 7 June near Amiens. Every anti-tank gun of the 17th Infantry Regiment on average destroyed five German tanks before being knocked out. A regiment of foreign volunteers fought to the end, the last survivors killing themselves to avoid falling into German hands. A French tank officer wrote to his wife:

> We've taken a heck of a pasting, and there's hardly anyone left, but those still here have fantastic morale . . . we no longer think about the awful nightmare we've been through. That's typical of the French soldier; if you could only know the happiness of going into a scrap with chaps like these . . . My wound is completely healed. I don't know if I've been mentioned in dispatches, by the way, but I don't give a damn. You do what you have to do without thought of reward.[54]

In factories and shipyards too the effort stepped up. Despite invasion and bombing, arms production leapt in May and June. In the biggest northern tank factory, workers loaded unfinished tanks on to trains under German bombs. Much of this eventually benefited the Wehrmacht, amply supplied with French tanks and aircraft for its 1941 attack on Russia. The French were demanding that the whole RAF should be committed to the battle, as the French air force was now outnumbered three to one in front-line aircraft. But the RAF had lost 959 aircraft and 435 pilots in two months. Its ground attacks had been entirely ineffective: by day, the bombers were shot down, and by night they could not see their targets. Over 400 Hurricanes and Spitfires had been lost in France, and there were only 331 modern fighters left. Increased production could replace the aircraft, but not the men. There was therefore no reason to think that the RAF could save France, but the chiefs of staff officially advised the government that only air power could prevent a German invasion of England. They resisted reinforcing the three squadrons still based in France, although English-based aircraft did make sorties over western France.[55] On 7 and 9 June the Panzers began to pierce the overstretched front, and on the 12th Weygand ordered a general retreat. The Germans marched into Paris two days later.

A growing French belief that they were making disproportionate sacrifices while the British held back was corroding the alliance. Weygand and Pétain (the most popular man in France and now deputy prime minister) were incensed at British 'selfishness', which they blamed for their inability to stop the German advance. There were angry scenes, with Weygand 'literally yelling' about British backsliding.[56] Pétain told the American ambassador that Britain would 'fight to the last Frenchman and then seek a compromise peace', and he said to Paul Baudoin, war cabinet secretary, that 'England has got us into this position. It is our duty not to put up with it but to get out of it.'[57] Weygand was determined to preserve the honour of the army (and his own) by forcing the politicians to ask for an armistice.

Most of the government wanted to fight on, but their resolve was steadily eroded. Having evacuated Paris on 10 June, ministers and officials were scattered among various Loire châteaux, where communication was hampered by rustic shortage of telephones, and where 'motors were . . . as important and rare as horses on the battlefield of Bosworth'.[58] Reynaud was increasingly beleaguered, including by his ubiquitous and interfering mistress, the defeatist Comtesse de Portes, whose appearance in red pyjamas reminded Edward Spears that 'I had not seen red trousers on French legs since 1914'. This situation confirmed censorious British stereotypes of the French. Churchill had sent Spears, the young liaison officer of 1914, now stouter, a general and a Tory MP, as his personal representative. Although a leading member of the 'pro-Frog boys', he knew France too well to be a starry-eyed francophile, and he and Churchill soon began to regard their beloved ally as a hopeless case.

Churchill was determined to prolong French resistance, eventually from North Africa. Both countries were bound by their March agreement not to seek a separate peace. For the French, it was a matter of honour, and also of not antagonizing the British empire and America. On 13 June, the last meeting between Churchill and the French took place at Tours, where the British rather alarmingly found no one awaiting them at the airport, no French government, and no lunch. When they found the appointed venue, Churchill insisted that the fight must go on: Britain would accept no terms, and could not agree to France considering terms either. Reynaud replied tartly that he was sure that Great Britain would not give way 'until she had known sufferings equal to those now endured by the French people'. Churchill argued that the United States would soon be an ally. Meanwhile, France must fight on, as it had nothing to hope for from Hitler. The army, if overwhelmed, should wage a 'gigantic' guerrilla war. The government should withdraw to North Africa if necessary. The French must accept that British self-defence came first, because 'if Germany failed to destroy England . . . then the whole hateful edifice of Nazism would topple over', and France could share in an eventual Anglo-Saxon victory.[59] The gamble the French faced was whether to commit their future to a seemingly punch-drunk Britain, or to bargain for a place within a German-dominated Europe. Reynaud still preferred the former. He told his colleagues that Hitler was not the Kaiser, he was Genghis Khan. The newly promoted Brigadier-General Charles de Gaulle, junior defence minister, was sent to London to organize shipping to North Africa. But the balance of opinion within the government was shifting.

Meanwhile, the last British forces were leaving. Reinforcements, including units from Dunkirk, had been sent back to Normandy to form a second BEF. The 51st (Highland) Division, the only formation really to have taken part in the fighting, was trapped in the Norman port of Saint-Valéry-en-Caux and surrendered on 12 June. The rest were ordered on 14 June to re-embark. Their commander was 'anxious not to remain in this country an hour longer than necessary'.[60] Soon after, the last RAF aircraft flew home. Large quantities of war material were again abandoned. Unserviceable planes and other equipment were destroyed – all except one staff car, given to a friendly café proprietor.

On 16 June 1940 was seen arguably 'the most dramatic and confusing sequence of events perhaps ever recorded in the history of either nation'.[61] The French government asked for British consent to an exploration of armistice terms. The first British reply, as before, was that France should fight on, with a government in exile in England or North Africa. Second thoughts were that this was a lost cause, and that the best was to limit the damage. London informed the French at midday that they could make enquiries about peace terms, but only on condition that the French fleet sailed at once for Britain. There then arrived a telephone call from de Gaulle in London conveying the astounding offer of a political union between France and Britain, creating a single war cabinet, dual citizenship, unified military command, and financial partnership. De Gaulle even suggested that Reynaud might lead the joint government.

'NO LONGER TWO NATIONS': 16 JUNE 1940

It was a myth, made up like other myths by Jean Monnet.
Neither Churchill nor I had the least illusion.
CHARLES DE GAULLE[62]

This proposal 'that France and Great Britain shall no longer be two nations, but one Franco-British Union' could figure on any list of great might-have-beens of history. The idea was suggested to Churchill following a meeting on 14 June between Sir Robert Vansittart, his francophile chief diplomatic adviser, his private secretary Major Morton, and René Pleven and Jean Monnet, both of the French economic mission in London, who drafted a Declaration of Union together. Monnet's later career as 'father of Europe' gives extra spice to an idea often regarded as essentially his. It stemmed from Monnet's work during the First World War and earlier proposals for economic union. The idea had other sources. Professor Arnold Toynbee, director of the Royal Institute of International Affairs, had suggested it late in 1939. The left-wing intellectuals Hugh Dalton and Philip Noel-Baker wanted France and Britain to form the nucleus of a post-war European Union and the 'hard core of a new world order'. A French senator had proposed union in March 1940. The idea was being discussed by several committees, notably that chaired by the definitely non-francophile Lord Hankey, and language about Anglo-French union became current in Whitehall. The Franco-British declaration of 28 March had already proclaimed 'community of action in all spheres'.

Churchill's reaction to the June proposal was sceptical, but he was impressed by the support shown in his cabinet and by French representatives in London, and especially by the 'unwonted enthusiasm' displayed by the phlegmatic de Gaulle. It may have been de Gaulle's fighting spirit that made Churchill think that it was worth trying something spectacular to keep France in the war. However, there is less to this British plunge into Europe than meets the eye. Hankey was 'shocked' by 'these half-baked ideas' to 'merge our nationhood . . . our most precious possession', especially as he blamed France, 'our evil genius from the time of the Peace Conference', for the war and the defeats. But he was reassured by Chamberlain, now Lord President of the Council, and by the foreign secretary, Lord Halifax, who both stated that the Union was a wartime measure only. French ministers reacted even more cynically. Most assumed it was a symptom of collapse rather than of resolve, a ruse to implicate France further in Britain's inevitable defeat. Pétain said grimly that it was an invitation to marry a corpse. Hélène de Portes urged Reynaud not to imitate Isabelle of Bavaria – the French queen who in 1420 had disinherited her son in favour of Henry V of England. The French suspected that the real British motive was to control their fleet and colonies, and ingrained anglophobia ascribed this to calculating selfishness, rather than to determination to fight to the finish. The Union proposal was contemptuously dismissed by the council of ministers that evening. There were sour comments about not wishing to become subjects of His Britannic Majesty and make France a dominion of the British empire. Reynaud thereupon resigned, and was succeeded by his deputy, Pétain. Only a week after it was formally proposed, Halifax wrote that, to widespread relief, the idea was 'completely dead'. Yet the brusqueness of the French rejection had a significant impact on British attitudes. No offer was made again for such close alliance or post-war association, and no promises were made about the future, other than basic restoration of independence. Halifax predicted that after the war the *entente cordiale* would be replaced by a special relationship between Britain and the United States.[63]

Much has been written on the rights and wrongs of these events, and the complex motives of their protagonists. What must be remembered is the vertiginous crisis assailing France. The army was beginning to disintegrate. The enemy advance was unstoppable. Between 6 and 8 million refugees were flooding south from the war zone. The government was being chased across France, from Paris via Tours to Bordeaux, without parliament and the usual levers of power. There was public pressure for peace, and threats of rioting in Bordeaux. The pressure to find a way out was agonizing, and the moderates buckled.

Those who pushed themselves to the fore were inclined to believe on ideological grounds that the war had been a terrible mistake and that defeat was preordained. Pétain, an admirer of General Franco, had a sentimental view of himself as the paternal saviour of France, as at Verdun. He utterly rejected the view that the government should go abroad, abandoning the nation to its fate and scrambling on board the sinking British ship: France would be left to the mercies not only of the Germans but also of their Communist allies. How anyway, asked Weygand, could a republic go into exile? Pétain's first act on 17 June was to broadcast to the nation that 'with a heavy heart, I tell you today that the fighting must cease'. That evening, he requested an armistice.

Pétain's ambiguous broadcast – for there was not yet an armistice – cut the ground from under those still fighting. German soldiers waving white flags encouraged the belief that the war was over. Only then were there mass surrenders: nearly two-thirds of all French prisoners of war were captured after Pétain's broadcast, as over a million soldiers began to lay down their arms. Civilian officials tried to stop the fighting, especially after the new interior minister ordered that no towns should be defended. Yet some soldiers fought on regardless. The Loire bridges were held until 20 June: alongside aristocratic cadets of the Saumur cavalry school fought ordinary students doing their reserve-officer training and an infantry battalion notorious for Left-wing militancy. Among those who fought most determinedly were colonial troops from Africa, up to 3,000 of whom were subsequently murdered by the Germans – in part belated revenge for the Ruhr occupation in 1923.[64] In total, the French had lost over 50,000 killed; the BEF, 13,000; the Germans over 27,000.[65]

Churchill and the British realized France's plight, and sympathized – but not to the extent of acquiescing in a total French surrender. Churchill appealed by radio to the French people over their new government's head, and his Cabinet agreed, 'not without argument', to let 'a French general' speak on the BBC at 10 p.m. on 18 June. This was de Gaulle's 'Appeal to the French People', the most famous broadcast in French history, though few heard it live and it was not even recorded. He called on them to reject Pétain's policy and join him in continuing the struggle alongside Britain.[66] His global conception of the war – 'France is not alone!' – in contrast with the Eurocentric view of Pétain and Weygand, was exactly Churchill's.

The immediate British concern was not to risk the French navy falling into German hands. London repeatedly insisted that it must sail to Britain or the USA as an absolute precondition of British consent to the French government's seeking peace. But the French – even those sympathetic to the alliance – saw the navy as a vital safeguard of their empire against Italian attack, and as strengthening their future bargaining position with Hitler. Those unsympathetic to the alliance thought that the half-heartedness of British military and air support removed any right for London to make conditions. To let the fleet go to Britain would anger the Germans, and wreck any chance of favourable terms. Besides, Britain would soon surrender. The French were unanimous that the British should accept assurances that they would not allow the fleet to be used against them. Hitler showed unwonted subtlety in offering Pétain's government a 'golden bridge': to leave an unoccupied zone in southern France, and to allow France its government and administration, an army of 100,000 men and continuing possession of its colonies and navy. Like the British, he was thinking of the future.

London redoubled its pressure because the armistice terms of 21 June, while declaring that Germany 'had no intention' of using the French fleet, required it to be disarmed 'under German or Italian control'. Semantics aggravated the dispute: *contrôle* meant supervision; *control* implied possession. If the French navy had been added to the German and the Italian, the Royal Navy would have been outnumbered in capital ships. The Mediterranean would have been lost, and Atlantic convoys would have been in greater danger from surface ships than they ever were from submarines. Churchill fulminated that Britain would not forgive such a betrayal 'for a thousand years'.[67] France would face blockade and bombing, and would suffer serious post-war punishment. The two governments practically broke off relations during the last week in June.

MERS-EL-KÉBIR

The wrenching break came on 3 July. 'Operation Catapult' aimed to seize or otherwise neutralize the French fleet. Ships in British ports – 200 in all – were boarded, with little resistance, and seized (along with 7,000 barrels of wine).[68] Those in Alexandria, after tense negotiations, agreed to disarm themselves. A battle-cruiser at Dakar was torpedoed. The nub was the core of the main Atlantic fleet, which had sailed to Mers-el-Kébir, the naval base of Oran, in north-western Algeria. Here were half the navy's biggest ships – two modern battle-cruisers and two older battleships – plus destroyers and a seaplane carrier. Admiral Sir James Somerville arrived on 3 July with a force including a battle-cruiser, two battleships and an aircraft carrier. He presented a polite ultimatum: Admiral Marcel Gensoul could rejoin his 'comrades up to now' and fight the Germans; he could sail with reduced crews either to a British port, to the French West Indies or to the United States; or he could scuttle his ships. Otherwise, 'whatever force may be necessary' would be used. The Admiralty expected that the French would scuttle. Gensoul considered that honour and duty forbade acceptance of the ultimatum. (He also felt insulted that it had been brought by a mere captain, a French-speaking former naval attaché.) He thought the British were bluffing, and played for time so that reinforcements could arrive. But Churchill was not bluffing. The Admiralty warned Somerville that French reinforcements were on the way, and reluctantly he told Gensoul that he must accept the ultimatum or be sunk. Gensoul's position was poignant. Unusually for a French naval officer, he was an English-speaking anglophile Protestant, and his wife was distantly related to the Duke of Wellington. He admired the Royal Navy, and the summit of his career had been commanding a mixed squadron of French and British ships. Although he had prepared for action, he had convinced himself that his British comrades would never open fire. After eleven hours' stand-off, they did, and within ten minutes fired 144 fifteen-inch shells which sank or disabled a battle-cruiser and two battleships. The French lost 1,297 men killed and 351 wounded – their worst naval losses of the war.[69] Two British sailors were slightly injured. In seventeen days the two countries had gone from discussing an Indissoluble Union to armed conflict.

What the French remember as 'Mers-el-Kébir', almost forgotten in Britain, remains a raw nerve, and the subject of a steady stream of writing. French naval officers today are taught it as a case study in the problems of command. Most take the view that Gensoul was right.[70] Few Frenchmen have ever regarded the British attack as justified: the French government and navy had promised that the ships would not be used against Britain, and they would have kept their word. French naval officers sent a letter to Admiral Somerville expressing their 'disgust' that 'the glorious White Ensign had been sullied with the indelible stain of murder'.[71] Hitler was pleased. De Gaulle was described as either 'exasperated' or 'shattered', and he momentarily considered leaving for Canada. But a few days later he appeared 'objective', and made a speech which, while expressing pain at the 'odious tragedy', recognized that destroying the ships was better than surrendering them.[72] Hindsight is ambiguous. When the Germans occupied southern France in 1942, the French warships at Toulon were indeed scuttled. On the other hand, those at Bizerta were handed over. In 1940, the British were not sure they could trust Pétain's government; even less sure that they could trust some unknown future regime; and quite sure that they could not trust the Germans. The Americans were 'very apprehensive', and President Roosevelt said that if there were only one chance in ten that the Germans might get the fleet, it was a risk Britain must not run. For a week, other options were explored – even the idea of offering to buy the fleet for up to £100 million.[73] The Admiralty, and at first the Cabinet, were willing to trust the French navy. They thought it unlikely that the Germans could find crews for the ships even if they obtained them. British naval officers involved were extremely reluctant to attack their former comrades. But Churchill, backed by the Chiefs of Staff, finally insisted on ruthless action. By his own account, he realized that as well as removing a mortal danger, it would prove that Britain truly meant to fight on, as when the French revolution guillotined Louis XVI. 'I thought of Danton in 1793: "The coalesced Kings threaten us, and we hurl at their feet as a gage of battle the head of a King."'[74]

France's defeat was seen by many in Britain, and by others across the world, as a failure of determination, leadership and national cohesion. This continues to colour perceptions: critics of French policy decades later are quick to sniff out the spirit of 1940. British soldiers, politicians and journalists formed this view early through contacts with French politicians and generals. It was not simply a resurgence of traditional francophobia. It was a view shared by disillusioned francophiles, such as Churchill, Spears and Ironside, who concluded bluntly that 'the French [were] not fighting and not even trying to fight'.[75] This reversed the staple francophobe view, particularly marked since 1919, that the French were aggressive and militaristic: now they were seen as a nation of effete capitulators. 'They are too much attached to their mistresses, and their soup, and their little properties,' wrote Dalton, the new Labour minister of economic warfare. 'We see before our eyes nothing less than the liquification of France.'[76] A similar judgement was propagated by the French themselves, particularly by Pétain and his millions of admirers. He blamed defeat not only on weak allies, but on national vices. He dourly pronounced that since 1918 'the spirit of pleasure has overcome the spirit of sacrifice'. Pre-war leaders, notably Blum and Daladier, were blamed for defeat and put on trial. A rump parliament voted full powers to Pétain, and a new capital was set up at the spa town of Vichy. An authoritarian 'National Revolution' set out to regenerate the country by combating democracy and individualism, rooting out Jews, freemasons and foreigners, restoring religious authority, imposing traditional values – in short, liquidating the inheritance of 1789.

If defeat in 1940 were proof of national 'decadence', it would apply not only to France (and other countries that were defeated), but to Britain too. Its contribution to the Alliance was shamefully feeble. As in France, 'guilty men' blamed for Britain's weakness were publicly vilified. Ironically, in both countries, those blamed included those who had begun rearmament against widespread opposition. If the French government failed to give united leadership, this was not unique in Europe. Had Britain been successfully invaded, Lloyd George or the Duke of Windsor might have played the role of a Pétain.

France's defeat in 1940 was not, in fact, due to some general moral failure. The people faced up to war in a way not dissimilar from 1914, and soldiers continued fighting until Marshal Pétain, a man they trusted, told them to stop. Defeat was due to strategic mistakes and political decisions. Ever since 1940 it has been common to criticize the French for trying to refight the last war. In a sense they (and the British) did. But so did the Germans. The difference is that the latter – however nervous they were about their chances – did it successfully, having developed the tactics and technology pioneered by both sides in 1918: ground infiltration, tanks and aircraft. The breakthrough in 1940 achieved what the Schlieffen plan had failed to do: smash the French army, take Paris, and throw the BEF into the sea. French and British politicians and generals had not prepared adequately for war because they had hoped never to fight one: their goal had been deterrence, not victory. They aimed to limit the war and to keep it at a distance, rather than undergo a repetition of the carnage of 1914–18. The defeat of France at least avoided that ordeal, and also the danger that the Allies might have reverted to the French plan for bombing Russian oilfields, thus creating a Nazi–Soviet alliance of incalculable danger. Then came the 1940 equivalent of the 'Miracle of the Marne' – the Battle of Britain. Hitler's inability to defeat or cajole Britain spurred him into his long-term fantasy, a genocidal attack on Russia in 1941. Japan widened the conflict, which forced the United States to fight. Britain and France would emerge as victors largely owing to the carnage of the Eastern Front and the resources of America. As the French historian Robert Frank has pointed out, the original logic of the Phoney War still applied in the West: the Allies waited until 1944 to launch an offensive, when they had built up massive forces and German capacity had been eroded.[77]

The British and French did respond differently to the catastrophe of 1940, however, and this was not only a matter of geography. The defeatist, even treasonable, behaviour of key French politicians was a blatant continuation of the factional conflicts of the 1930s. Britain did have greater political cohesion in the face of disaster – though as Reynaud observed, it was a far less overwhelming disaster. The American historian John Lukacs, in a generous yet acute assessment, identifies an 'obtuse' British bravery that refused to recognize the extent of the danger. He quotes George Orwell: 'You have all the time the sensation of kicking against an impenetrable wall of stupidity. But of course at times their stupidity has stood them in good stead.' Lukacs emphasizes the difference in historical experience: 'The English, who had not been conquered by an invader for nearly one thousand years, knew in their bones that their defeat would mean a kind of death for England, that its effect would not be temporary. The French, on the other hand, knew in their heads . . . the memory of national defeats together with the memory of their national recoveries.'[78] A Foreign Office memorandum put the British view bluntly: 'either the German Reich or this country has got to go under, and not only under, but right under'.[79] The alternative visions were respectively incarnated in the bellicose Churchill, offering 'blood, toil, tears and sweat', and the lacrymose Pétain, promising to 'attenuate the disaster'.

Great though these differences were, Britain's resistance owed much not only to the width of the Channel, to the heroic 'Few', and to German failures, but also to the unsung sacrifices of French soldiers. France's defeat, on the other hand, owed much to pre-war British appeasement, which not only made Britain a feeble ally, but had a profound effect on France's diplomacy, strategy and confidence. If Dunkirk was not the callous desertion that many Frenchmen felt, it was nevertheless the consequence of a policy of deliberate estrangement from France pursued from 1918 to 1939. Britain had the long war it had always expected, and its people lived 'their finest hour'. But France, the only major power unprotected by sea or distance from Germany, had succumbed, as Foch, Clemenceau and Poincaré had long before predicted, and it faced its darkest years.

Churchill and de Gaulle

My mission seemed to me, all of a sudden, clear and terrible. At this
moment, the worst in her history, it was for me to assume the burden
of France.

CHARLES DE GAULLE[80]

I knew he was no friend of England. But I always recognized in him
the spirit and conception which, across the pages of history, the word
'France' would ever proclaim. I understood and admired, while I resented,
his arrogant demeanour . . . The Germans had conquered his country.
He had no real foothold anywhere. Never mind; he defied all.

WINSTON CHURCHILL[81]

Mr Churchill and I agreed modestly in drawing from the events which had
smashed the West this commonplace but final conclusion: when all is said
and done, Great Britain is an island; France, the cape of a continent;
America, another world.

CHARLES DE GAULLE[82]

The strained interconnectedness of French and British history is embodied in the stormy intimacy between the men each nation regards as its greatest historic figure. Both were writers as well as men of action, and by the power of their words breathed life into stricken nations. Both drew on history, theatre, poetry and patriotism. Both mastered the drama of public oratory, not yet emasculated by the cosiness of the airwaves. To defeat the apocalyptic future imagined by Hitler and Mussolini, they conjured up the past, with images of continuity, destiny, and romance. 'The emotional side of me tends to imagine France, like the princess in the fairy tales . . . as dedicated to an exalted and exceptional destiny.' 'We must regard the next week or so as [ranking] with the days when the Spanish Armada was approaching the Channel, and Drake was finishing his game of bowls; or when Nelson stood between us and Napoleon's Grand Army . . . but what is happening now is . . . of far more consequence to the life and future of the world.'[83]

What gave them both the confidence to speak for nations facing disaster? Both had dreamt of themselves from childhood as men of destiny. Both said so. On 10 May, when called to power, Churchill felt 'as if I were walking with destiny, and that all my past life had been but a preparation for this hour'. On 18 June, as de Gaulle made his broadcast, and 'the irrevocable words flew out upon their way, I felt within myself a life coming to an end . . . I was entering upon adventure, like a man thrown by destiny outside all terms of reference.'[84] These pretensions evoked exasperation and mistrust, as well as loyalty and adulation. Churchill, conscious of his descent from the Duke of Marlborough, a leading politician for a generation, whose return to office had been increasingly called for since 1938, and who held the power and prestige of legitimate office, was eminently placed to command exceptional authority. De Gaulle, the son of a schoolmaster from Lille, an unknown middle-ranking army officer, never part of the establishment, and a rebel against his country's saviour, could only rise, like Napoleon, in the wake of a cataclysm. What gave him the magnificent effrontery to 'assume the burden of France', with neither royal blood like Louis XIV, nor divine inspiration like Joan of Arc, with both of whom he was mockingly and admiringly compared? As a Catholic, a republican, and a soldier he combined three powerful but often conflicting elements of French identity, and so was potentially able to rally broad support. As a writer in uniform (like Napoleon) he drew inspiration from French high culture, and from earlier patriotic intellectual exiles in England, men he admired and quoted, René de Chateaubriand and Victor Hugo.

Both Churchill and de Gaulle gained moral strength from being proved right. Churchill had famously opposed disarmament and appeasement – even if not as early or as bluntly as later (partly self-composed) history suggested. 'My warnings over the last six years . . . were now so terribly vindicated that no one could gainsay me.' De Gaulle, naturally prickly and insubordinate, had criticized the conservatism of the high command, advocated a modern, mechanized army, and predicted that without it the Germans would 'advance from the Ardennes to Bayonne in three weeks'.[85] He had been opposed by the military establishment, led by Pétain. When the latter blamed France's defeat on deep-seated national ills, de Gaulle could retort that the real cause was the blindness of men like Pétain. Both Churchill and de Gaulle realized that they were engaged in a long world war. This was a reality easier to grasp in the islands than on the 'cape of a continent': Weygand had said to de Gaulle on 8 June, 'As for the world, when I've been beaten here, England won't wait a week before negotiating.' That de Gaulle did not believe it testifies to his vision.

As soon as he was made a junior minister, de Gaulle called in the press. Already, said one witness, he was preparing France's 'resurrection myth', with himself as messiah.[86] But his epiphany depended on others – above all, Churchill. They met early on 9 June – what one French historian calls 'the meeting of the century'.[87] A veteran Gaullist has summarized their relationship as 'instant attraction, followed by a passionate engagement, a hasty wedding and a stormy marriage, to end in an old couple forever linked by history'.[88] De Gaulle's escape from Bordeaux was arranged by Spears, who on 17 June literally pulled him on to a British plane. The following day, he was allowed to make his historic broadcast in reply to Pétain's message thirty hours earlier.

The Foreign Office grumbled that Churchill was enlisting 'every crank in the world'.[89] He seemed too little known to lead national resistance. The intention was to rally weightier figures and leave de Gaulle only military command of French forces in Britain. Men who were better qualified – Reynaud, or Blum – did not, or could not, arrive. Georges Mandel, Clemenceau's tough and dauntless former acolyte, an admired friend of Churchill, would have been the British choice. Fatally, he hesitated: he was a Jew, and knew that anti-semites would accuse him of running away. Then it was too late. He was arrested to prevent him leaving for England, imprisoned, and murdered by French fascists.

Churchill was a life-long francophile. His time in France added up to nearly four years, beginning with childhood visits to Paris. Admiration for French military glories, 'a mixture of Péguy and the Napoleonic',[90] dated from his attendance at army manoeuvres in 1907. In the trenches in 1916 he wore a French helmet. He admired Clemenceau. He shared the usual Edwardian pleasure in French sights, tastes and sunshine, and regularly wintered on the Riviera. His first post-war holiday in July 1945 was near Biarritz. He enjoyed speaking 'strange and at times incomprehensible' French. 'He speaks remarkably well but understands very little.' He played this up as part of his John Bull persona: 'If I spoke perfect French, they wouldn't like it very much.'[91] In the late 1930s he and the 'pro-Frog boys' had developed political friendships with like-minded opponents of appeasement, including Reynaud and Mandel. Yet this represented a change of tack, not consistent prescience. A few years earlier, he had urged leaving France to 'stew in her own juice', and preferred a trilateral agreement including Germany rather than an alliance with France alone.[92] He had shared the general desire in the 1920s to conciliate Germany and avoid European commitments, and was unorthodox only in his impatience with disarmament and insistence on appeasement from a position of strength. His famous exclamation in 1933 – 'Thank God for the French army!' – was not a call for an alliance, but support for French containment of Germany while Britain 'stood aside'. This was complete fantasy. Only in 1938 did he urge treating 'the defensive needs of the two countries as if they were one.'[93]

De Gaulle had no comparably romantic feeling for Britain. He was brought up in a patriotic atmosphere as resentful of 'England' as of Germany: he recalled Fashoda as a childhood tragedy, and admired the nationalist writings of Maurice Barrès and Charles Péguy praising the French soil, Catholicism, Joan of Arc and Napoleon. His history of the French army omits Waterloo. Suspicion of the British – 'that oligarchy that Napoleon mocked' – was second nature in these circles, and he retained it. His ideas about English national character were conventional: the action at Mers-el-Kébir he considered 'one of those dark bursts by which the repressed instinct of this people sometimes smashes all barriers'.[94] He knew little English literature, except some Shakespeare and Kipling in translation; spoke little English, unwillingly; and had never been to Britain before 1940. He disparaged the British military contribution in the First World War, and saw the 1940 disaster as largely Britain's fault.[95] After 1940, he depended on Churchill for status and every means of action, from office space and money to troops, weapons and above all communication with France. 'He had never pretended to like the English. But coming to them as a beggar, with his country's wretchedness branded on his forehead and in his heart, was unbearable.'[96] An acquaintance recalled that 'He was often biting, scathing, in his criticism of England and the English . . . just as much or more so than France.'[97] This came naturally, but he also calculated that aggressiveness was the right way of dealing with the British: 'you have to bang the table,' he told his subordinates, 'they back down.'[98] Whether this was always the best way seems doubtful: it helped to exclude de Gaulle from Allied liberation of the French empire. But it made sense to a man who viewed *les Anglais* as cold, ruthless and duplicitous. He thought that 'a few hundred lords, big businessmen and bankers exercised real power' in 1940.[99] Closeted at his headquarters, surrounded by his French entourage, and cut off within his carapace of prejudice, he thus failed to perceive one of the most momentous acts of genuinely popular resistance in history. One thinks of the Duke of

Dorset's attempt to head off the French revolution with a cricket match.

Churchill and de Gaulle are often taken to exemplify the characteristics of their respective nations. In fact, they did much to change those perceptions: across Europe, the stiff, umbrella-carrying Chamberlain and the dapper Reynaud were considered national archetypes. Churchill and de Gaulle each embodied many supposed characteristics of the other nation. The tall Frenchman, cold, laconic, mordant, prudish, monoglot and arrogant, could have stepped from the pages of *Colonel Bramble*. The chubby Englishman, ebullient, emotional, artistic, hedonistic and eloquent, would have been more at home with Cyrano. Perhaps this partly explains why they were so much appreciated in each other's country.

Bearing the Cross of Lorraine

Our two ancient peoples, our two great peoples, remain linked together. They will both succumb or else they will win together.
CHARLES DE GAULLE, 23 June 1940[100]

The general stereotype of the French . . . is of a voluble, excessively excitable, often slightly bearded and somewhat lecherous personality.
Mass-Observation, 'Public opinion about the French', 1939–41[101]

Sometimes we can see France shining like a mirage at the end of a London street.
ANDRE LABARTHE, exiled journalist[102]

Personally I feel happier now that we have no more allies to be polite to & to pamper.
KING GEORGE VI, 27 June 1940

The king spoke for many. In Britain, as in France, the disaster was blamed on the failings of the ally. In Britain, this fed determination to fight, in Churchill's words, 'if necessary for years, if necessary alone'. The historian G.M. Trevelyan, Master of Trinity College, Cambridge, ordered champagne for the high table on 18 June, proclaiming 'I know we will win this war.' The Canadian historian Talbot Imlay argues that the suspension of the war on the Continent in 1940 was indeed 'the best of all available alternatives' for Britain and the world, for it made eventual victory possible.[103]

In France, on the contrary, the sense of isolation justified acceptance of defeat. Anglophobia was an active element of this acceptance. It comforted amour-propre to have a scapegoat. It drew on ancient and familiar themes. Not least, much of it was justified. The most ideological variety, bringing the old 'Carthage' idea up to date with an injection of anti-semitism, saw Britain as the core of global capitalism. 'The British,' said one French general, 'represent those things that almost destroyed us: democratic-masonic politics and Judeo-Saxon finance. They represent the past, nothing constructive.' This appealed to reactionary intellectuals such as Charles Maurras and to fascists eager to ingratiate themselves with the winning side. Old-fashioned authoritarians had not forgotten historic grievances – Joan of Arc was conscripted by Vichy propaganda – and they acquired a set of new ones, especially Dunkirk and Mers-el-Kébir. Some wanted Britain to be defeated, both to salve their own pride and to improve France's relative international position. Such views were shrilly reiterated by newspapers, books, cartoons, newsreels, films and radio programmes both in the German occupied zone and in the 'free zone'. Bombing of London gave rise to gleeful reports of panic and starvation. Later, British bombing of France provided a new anglophobe theme.

Anglophobic propaganda had limited, and decreasing, effects, once the Luftwaffe lost the Battle of Britain and the Wehrmacht failed to invade England. In the unoccupied zone, French newspapers continued to print British communiqués alongside, and even before, German ones. Official anglophobic statements were printed, but were rarely backed up by editorial comment. This was noticed by British observers: 'Reserve regarding "collaboration", and reticence and respect regarding Britain and her effort, are the attitudes to be read between the lines.'[104] Many people combined loyalty to Marshal Pétain with goodwill towards Britain. They imagined that he was secretly cooperating with London and hoodwinking the Germans. Others were torn between their anger with the British and their detestation of the Germans. It was thus summed up by someone pro-British enough to write a letter to the BBC:

> the immense majority of people, despite the hatred the cowardly attack on Mers el Kébir has inspired, despite everything, wants to see England victorious. If the French gain nothing from this victory, because of the ferocious egotism of Albion, they know nonetheless that they have everything to lose if Hitler wins.[105]

The Vichy regime took the opposite view, and gambled on a German victory. Pétain was prudent in public, but outspoken in private: 'England [was] the source of all evils that had befallen France.' As early as 1936 he had told the Italian ambassador that 'England has always been France's most implacable enemy', and he hoped for an alliance of France, Italy and Germany

Joan of Arc, Napoleon and Fashoda feature in this poster combining historic grievances with fears for the future.

to ensure 'a more equitable distribution of British colonies [to] provide wealth and work for all'.[106] Pierre Laval, prime minister in 1940–41 and 1942–4, believed that whatever happened overseas Germany would dominate the Continent, and that France must seek junior partnership by 'collaboration'. Admiral Darlan, commander of the navy and briefly prime minister in 1941–2, wanted a German victory over Britain to prevent France from being 'the principal victim of this war of nerves and famine', suffering unemployment, poverty, revolution and the breakaway of its colonies.[107] He hoped to use the colonies and the navy to make France a key partner in a global struggle between the Continent and the Anglo-Saxons, and eventually a leading power in a future German-led European federation.

It took a long time for people in France, including many in the Resistance, to realize that Vichy's leaders were truly working for Germany. Some never realized it. Pétain was revered as the humane defender of Verdun and as one of the patriarchs the French turn to in adversity. 'Are you more French than he?' ran one slogan. He was a formidable obstacle for those trying to continue resistance. Vichy did maintain ambivalent contacts with the Allies. The British were sceptical, having decided early on that 'the Marshal and his friends are too old, or too crooked, to clean up France or anything else'.[108] They were willing to retain indirect contacts in the hope that some elements in Vichy or the Empire might change sides. But the Americans subsequently remained wedded to the idea of a rapprochement with Vichy despite the evidence, thus enraging de Gaulle and damaging post-war relations.

Churchill recognized de Gaulle officially on 28 June 1940 as 'leader of all the Free French'. This was vital, but it laid him open to accusations of being a British puppet. Pétain's authority and the ambient Anglophobia blighted de Gaulle's efforts to rally support. Mers-el-Kébir came at the worst moment. A French naval officer in England wrote that 'there is no longer any question of joining those with French blood on their hands. Only adventurers and fools are staying in England. Between our two navies, if not our two countries, there will be the same tenacious hatred as after Trafalgar . . . and that for a century!' Of 11,500 French sailors in England, only 882 joined de Gaulle and 700 the Royal Navy (whose pay was three times the French); the rest went home. Some airmen joined the RAF, and fought in the Battle of Britain. Among the military, de Gaulle rallied some 2,000 men by July 1940. Sailors and soldiers were loosely interned – loosely enough for at least one to meet an English girl at a dancehall and marry her. Spartan conditions in the early days increased French sentiments of being hard done by, which pro-Pétain officers encouraged. Those who did join de Gaulle were not only adventurous but junior and often rather unusual, none more so than the aristocratic monk turned naval officer, Thierry d'Argenlieu. This gave the Free French a reputation for extremism and eccentricity. De Gaulle was no more successful among permanent French residents in London, of whom there were about 10,000: only 300 volunteered.[109] Civilian refugees, like those in uniform, mostly wanted to get home.

The little that was known about de Gaulle – that he was a regular soldier of conservative views and authoritarian temperament – put many off. Admittedly, had he been a politician, he might have put off even more. Spears, now Churchill's representative with the Free French, put it rather well: he 'compelled admiration while rejecting sympathy.'[110] A less polite description would have been that he was cold, rude and arrogant: he had an extraordinary capacity for alienating wellwishers. Leading French personalities in London, whether for political or prudential reasons, refused to join him. The authors André Maurois (famous from his writings on Britain), Jacques Maritain and George Bernanos left for north or south America, as did the former ambassador in London Charles Corbin. The poet-diplomat Alexis Léger and the businessman-cum-bureaucrat Jean Monnet went to preach against de Gaulle in Washington, with damaging results. Even politicians, academics and journalists who decided to stick it out in London were not all eager to rush to the Gaullist banner. Some preferred independent activity or direct involvement with the British, and were to play vital roles within the BBC and the Special Operations Executive. The most influential exile paper, *La France Libre*, run by the left-wing scientist André Labarthe, kept its distance from de Gaulle.

Amid the many exiles making 'our London . . . the metropolis of the banished',[111] the Free French formed a visible and distinct community. In the early days, the French colony offered clothes, money and hospitality. De Gaulle was given 4 Carlton Gardens, the site of Lord Palmerston's house overlooking the Mall, as his headquarters. (His statue there today looks unfortunately like someone asking for a tip.) He lodged at the Connaught Hotel, joining his family in the suburbs at weekends. Free French troops were camped at Olympia and the White City (built for the Anglo–French exhibition of 1908), before being relocated to various army bases, where they were 'impressed by the comfort of the barracks'.[112] Civilians found cheap accommodation in Kensington, some occupying rooms at the French Institute, or in Soho, traditional quarter for French exiles. They colonized pubs, clubs and restaurants including Chez Céleste and Chez Rose (frequented by Free French sailors and Soho hookers). The Petit Club Français, in the Astors' house in St James's Square, became one of wartime London's smartest and raciest nightspots. The British government were active in promoting the Free French image. The king and queen visited them. Churchill invited de Gaulle to Chequers, and Mrs Churchill took flowers to his office. The government, to the general's annoyance, paid for a professional public relations campaign ensuring laudatory press coverage of de Gaulle the man of destiny and 'the flood of recruits' joining him: 'The flag of Joan of Arc floats over England.' On 14 July 1940, the Free French paraded down Whitehall, and on the 21st, French aircrews played a symbolic role in a bombing raid on the Ruhr. A Mass-Observation survey in September 1940 showed that de Gaulle was the most popular foreign personality. French military personnel in England after Dunkirk had aroused public criticism because of their eagerness to accept the armistice and their indisciplined behaviour, but once they had gone home, the Free French volunteers were more popular, and were constantly invited to stay with English families.[113] One young French woman soldier recalled having her restaurant bill paid by anonymous English well-wishers; and 'How often in the street the British shouted "Vive la France" when I was wearing my uniform!'[114] Friendship societies held collections, French choirs gave concerts, and numerous sporting fixtures were arranged. Better still, 'the English girls were receptive to [our] advances'.[115] De Gaulle himself recalled 'the generous kindness which the English people everywhere showed'. When he was sentenced to death and had his property confiscated by Vichy, quantities of gifts were sent to his office.[116]

Official relations soured in the autumn of 1940. Churchill got de Gaulle to agree to a Franco-British expedition to Dakar, the French West African naval base strategically placed on the route to the Cape. At Dakar were the modern battleship *Richelieu* and the Belgian and Polish gold reserves. De Gaulle believed he could persuade the garrison to join him, but a sizeable British naval force went along in case. However, most French colonial administrators were pro-Vichy and anti-British, and those at Dakar were no exception. The operation became a fiasco, with several hasty changes of plan and some bad luck ending in an abortive landing and a long exchange of shells in which several British ships were seriously damaged. De Gaulle was devastated at being implicated in a failed British attack on French forces, which scuppered his hopes of rallying the Empire and seemed to confirm Vichy propaganda about British designs on French colonies. Some thought he contemplated suicide. Spears denied this, but found him more remote and difficult. He certainly considered abandoning his whole mission. Churchill and the British had been badly humiliated at a critical time: 'to the world at large it seemed a glaring example of miscalculation, confusion, timidity and muddle'.[117] Churchill defended de Gaulle publicly in the House of Commons, but both sides blamed each other. Free French intelligence had been too optimistic about the attitude of the garrison. When things went wrong the British thought the Free French reluctant to fight against their compatriots. They also blamed the French for gross lapses of security: there had been public toasts 'A Dakar!' and de Gaulle had openly bought tropical kit at Simpsons in Piccadilly. Vichy never got wind of this, but belief that the Free French talked too much caused the British to consider them a permanent security risk, with major consequences. De Gaulle (nicknamed 'Cheer-Up Charlie') tried harder to assert political independence of his ally, and in a way that maximized ill feeling. Some in Whitehall looked for other Frenchmen to deal with: 'the number of occasions when British officials withdrew their support after making contact with Carlton Gardens is truly astonishing'.[118] Clashes of personality and of cultural styles aside, it became increasingly clear that the priorities of de Gaulle and the British conflicted. The former aimed to take over in the Empire and eventually France, in order to rebuild France as an independent power. The latter – like the Americans later – subordinated French politics to winning the war, and were prepared to use any means or persons to that end.

British policy towards France was formulated by several competing bureaucracies: the Foreign Office, the Secret Intelligence Service, the Political Warfare Executive, the Special Operations Executive, and the BBC. There were three fundamental problems, all connected. First, how to treat Vichy and Pétain. Second, how to treat de Gaulle. Third, how to respond to the French Resistance. Pétain remained popular, as all realized. German intelligence reported in May 1941 that 'For 90 out of 100 Frenchmen the Marshal represents France and is beyond criticism. Even in working class circles he is considered as entirely decent and as the nation's guide.'[119] As late as 1944 Pétain was cheered by huge crowds in Paris. Direct attacks on him might be counter-productive in propaganda terms, and might also hamper efforts to win over patriots in France and the Empire. Some Vichy officials and soldiers were already working secretly for the Allies, which made that hope seductive.

Second problem: how to treat de Gaulle. The Gaullist view – now broadly accepted in France – is that the British, by prejudice and by toadying to the Americans, treated de Gaulle disgracefully, fearing his proud independence. The reality is more complex. Much of the opposition to de Gaulle originated with French politicians, journalists and broadcasters in London and figures in Washington such as Monnet and Léger, who helped to turn Roosevelt against him. They feared that he had reactionary if not fascist views and dictatorial ambitions. Moreover, de Gaulle seemed to be a failure by 1941–2. He was not attracting support beyond 'sand-blown colonials, a few soldiers, and the most rigidly Teutophobic readers of Action Française'.[120] He had not won over the Empire. He produced few constructive political or social ideas. He seemed more concerned with accumulating power than with fighting the Germans: again, this was the impression of some French patriots as well as London and Washington, and it was partly true. British pressure aimed to induce de Gaulle to broaden his political support, which might – some hoped – loosen his control of the Free French. In July 1941 he had to agree to a French National Committee. The true architect of the new Free French structure came from inside France. A young former prefect, Jean Moulin, arrived in London via Lisbon in October 1941 and presented himself as the spokesman of several important resistance organizations, largely unknown to London. He impressed the British, and persuaded de Gaulle, whom he regarded as a useful figurehead and an essential link with the British, to sanction a broad organization encompassing the Resistance movements, the Free French in London, and other sympathetic politicians. This would carry on a more aggressive campaign inside France, 'organize the French people for a nation-wide uprising at the appropriate time',[121] and not least show the world that de Gaulle was recognized as leader inside France. Until then, the general had shown little interest in clandestine activity. Moulin went back to create a federated national Resistance movement, which in time increased de Gaulle's leverage with the Anglo-Saxons.[122]

De Gaulle persisted with his claim to be an 'Ally of the Allies', with the right to pursue independent policies. This attitude, which seemed to his supporters (and his subsequent admirers) the height of courageous patriotism, was to his critics arrogant and irresponsible. De Gaulle at his best or worst can be seen over the Levant, where his 1940 rescuer Spears became his main antagonist. In May 1941, with the Middle East and its oil threatened by Rommel, a British and Free French force invaded French-ruled Syria and Lebanon, to prevent Vichy offering air bases to the Luftwaffe, and there was quite serious fighting against Vichy forces. The British, needing to conciliate Arab opinion, wanted independence for the two territories. De Gaulle convinced himself that this was a British plot against France, and he reacted violently. This worked, and the British – who hated scenes, as their representative admitted – largely gave in. But the bickering continued beyond all reason throughout and even after the war. All this dangerously damaged de Gaulle's relations with the British, on whom he depended. But he had decided that his most effective tactic was intransigence. It had its costs, not least in confirming the suspicions of the Americans. De Gaulle and his troops were excluded from future colonial expeditions, and not informed when the British occupied the French colony of Madagascar in May 1942, or when an American and British force landed in Morocco in November. This led to the greatest threat to de Gaulle's position, as the Americans persisted in trying to have him replaced with a more pliable, and less anti-Vichy, figure, such as General Giraud, General Weygand, or even Admiral Darlan.

Late in 1942, the crisis broke. One of the worst moments was a coldly venomous face-to-face row between Churchill and de Gaulle on 30 September at Downing Street. Churchill told him that 'I cannot look upon you as a comrade or a friend . . . Instead of making war on Germany you have made war on England and you have been the chief obstacle to an effective collaboration with Great Britain and the United States.' De Gaulle responded with laconic insolence.[123] Churchill was determined not to quarrel with Roosevelt over de Gaulle, and allowed the Americans to prod him into a violently anti-Gaullist position. But this American policy of wooing Vichy was not well received in Whitehall, including by Churchill's Cabinet colleagues. The Foreign Office warned that it risked creating a semi-fascist oligarchy in North Africa and civil war in France. As the war was supposedly being fought for democracy and progress, this would send a disastrous message all across occupied Europe. A deal with Vichy would also amount to an American takeover of policy towards France. Cadogan, permanent under-secretary at the foreign office, promised himself a 'God-Almighty show down' with the Americans.[124] Although 'Charles of Arc' caused gibbering irritation in Whitehall, he also retained support – partly because it would have been embarrassing to disavow the monster they had created, and partly because he was the only man who could unite the kaleidoscope of Resistance activity. Churchill was persuaded by his Cabinet to be more emollient, and he urged de Gaulle to be calm and wait for the Americans to realize their error.[125] The American secretary of state, Cordell Hull, complained that the British were 'behind' de Gaulle 'with money, the aid of their radio stations, and through other methods'.[126] American policy was sent sprawling by the German occupation of the whole of France in November 1942 (which ended the vestiges of Vichy's independence), by stubborn British support for de Gaulle, and by the general's own astuteness. Admiral Darlan, Washington's strongest candidate for French leadership, was assassinated in Algiers in December 1942 by a young Frenchman with SOE connections whose full contacts were never discovered as he was immediately executed. So de Gaulle remained the only credible leader of Fighting France, although Roosevelt continued to suggest silly schemes for getting rid of him. De Gaulle's belief in Anglo-Saxon perfidy was confirmed. He told Monnet that after the war France might turn to Germany or Russia to resist their dominance.[127]

The third problem of British policy was: what was French resistance for? The BBC succeeded brilliantly in creating a dissident atmosphere in France and countering anglophobia. Optimists in London hoped that influencing French public opinion might force a change of policy in Vichy. For many French patriots, the dissident atmosphere was an end in itself: they were fighting for self-respect.[128] But some British and French policy-makers feared, on the contrary, that making the French feel better about themselves was doing nothing to liberate France or help the struggling Allies.[129] Some wanted an aggressively anti-Vichy Resistance movement aimed at military action – setting France ablaze, as Churchill had wanted. On the other hand, sporadic and premature acts, such as derailing trains or killing lone Germans, simply invited massive reprisals – a strategy many regarded as immoral as well as counter-productive. The Allied chief of staffs, for their part, wanted a disciplined military resistance that could act under orders to support an invasion, but this was still far off. For de Gaulle and his entourage, the real purpose of the Resistance was not military – an aspect he as a regular soldier never took seriously. It was a way for France to reassert its independence by participating in its own liberation. It was also a means for taking over power from Vichy. To this end the Gaullists laboured to bring all resistance activity under their control. This caused doubts in French as well as Allied circles, not least because of Free French incompetence in security matters.

The consequence of all these dilemmas was a fluctuating set of British policies that one might regard as timid, or as subtly balanced, or perhaps just as the inevitably incoherent product of differing aims and rival organizations. To avoid violent criticism of Pétain, while criticizing acts of his government and encouraging defections. To avoid encouraging aimless violence, yet without condemning it. To build up military units, but keep them on the leash until the right moment. To try to influence and control de Gaulle, without disavowing him. Broadly speaking, the British – Cabinet, officialdom, and public – always backed de Gaulle, even against the Americans and at times against Churchill. When they realized that, however eccentric, he was not a crackpot, his larger-than-life manner began to win grudging admiration.[130] The foreign secretary, Anthony Eden, a devoted francophile, played a vital part in mollifying American hostility and Churchillian exasperation. But the British did nevertheless restrain de Gaulle, especially by limiting Free French access to the airwaves and censoring broadcasts. Also, they insisted on operating separate and independent intelligence and Resistance organizations within France.

Feeding the Flame

The anglophiles are those who want 'our English friends' to win; the anglophobes are those who want 'those English swine' to win.
French comment[131]

How was it possible to fight when France had been defeated and Britain ejected from the Continent? One way was strategic bombing, which turned out to need hugely greater efforts than pre-war air forces had imagined. Another way – which Churchill favoured – was to 'set Europe ablaze' by encouraging resistance in the occupied countries. But this too would require long and costly preparation, not least because the British had no intelligence networks in France.

Spontaneous resistance in France began at once. Early acts were associated with pro-British sentiments, especially in northern areas with memories of an earlier British liberation, and again experiencing German military rule. As the police reported, 'the people of the Nord now await a new 1918 . . . their hope of salvation is England'.[132] Rebuttals of Vichy anglophobia often referred back to the earlier war. One underground newspaper referred to 'the great voice' of the British dead of 1914–18 'who contradict, Pétain, your criticisms of today'. Some acts were symbolic or commemorative, and however small created a sense of resistance. Armistice Day saw collective gatherings at war cemeteries, the placing of wreaths on British graves, and the distribution of leaflets: 'Have confidence, the English will rescue us, and France will be France again.' British army songs were sung in the presence of German soldiers. People wore red roses on the king's birthday. At the beginning of 1941, the BBC launched the 'V for Victory' campaign, and so many Vs appeared on walls that the Germans tried to stop the sale of chalk. Flowers were laid in Lille at the memorial of Louise de Bettignies. The

Germans replied with other symbolic acts, such as blowing up certain First World War monuments, most spectacularly the new 'Britannia' at Boulogne.

Other activities built on experiences of the earlier war, for example helping escaping British soldiers and airmen, now in a long trip across France to Spain. The Comtesse de Milleville (née Mary Lindell), an admirer of Edith Cavell, organized escape routes, travelling France in her red-cross uniform bearing British decorations won in 1914–18. In time, elaborate escape networks, of which women were the mainstay, involved couriers, forgers, doctors, Pyrenean smugglers, and suppliers of food, clothes and safe-houses. There was even an 'exotic dancer' – subsequently decorated by the British government – whose private performances helped to maintain the morale of escapers waiting in hiding.[133] All were risking not only their own lives, but those of their families and friends. This created intense and personal Franco-British links, as escapers had to entrust themselves implicitly to their rescuers – doctors, housewives, farmers, students, railwaymen, teachers, even a Scottish missionary. One Australian airman reckoned that twenty families had aided his escape. Many of the helpers were very young, though one of the most successful was the elderly Mademoiselle Françoise Dissart (with her cat Mifouf), who sheltered escapers in her flat in Toulouse near Gestapo headquarters – she used their lunch hour to ferry her charges in and out. Although there are many picaresque stories, the activity was deadly dangerous. Though Mary de Milleville carried scissors to snip off mous-taches, fit young men speaking no French often looked exactly what they were: one officer disguised in workman's clothes still looked 'as if he had just come out of the Guards depot at Pirbright'. The need to accept unknown escapees made the organizations vulnerable to penetration by German agents and traitors. The worst of these was a fatally plausible British conman, Harold Cole, a petty criminal who deserted from the BEF, worked for the Germans, infiltrated and betrayed the famous 'Pat O'Leary' escape line, and was eventually killed in a gun battle with French police in 1946. Moreover, as in 1914–18, servicemen were sometimes careless. One group was caught, and their female courier tortured and sent to a concentration camp, because an RAF man lit a cigarette. Mary de Milleville had 'one rule for Englishmen . . . NO GIRLS . . . once they meet a pretty girl everything goes to hell'. But there was at least one marriage.[134] Air force morale benefited from the crews' realization that if shot down they had a good chance of being rescued, but word spread unofficially of where to go and whom to contact, multiplying the dangers for the organizers. In one café that became known, RAF men in uniform walked in openly asking for help. Late in 1941, a successful escaper gave a close friend contact details of families who had helped him. The friend was shot down and killed, the addresses were found on his body, and the families were executed. Devoted amateur organizers received limited help from London, and were left operating too long for safety. Hence, one of the biggest lines, which saved 600 airmen, at its peak involved 250 helpers; but it lost 100 people killed or sent to camps. In all, 5–6,000 allied airmen were aided. Some 12,000 people were part of organized escape lines, in addition to those who helped spontaneously. Thousands suffered torture, concentration camps or death.[135]

Intelligence gathering, vital to a Britain threatened with invasion and attacks on its shipping, also began spontaneously as people sought to pass on things they saw near their homes or learned at work. A right-wing patriot set up a large network which penetrated the Vichy intelligence service and sent information to MI6. Post-office workers tapped the main German telephone cables, and for months sent a stream of information to Vichy, where a senior officer passed it on to MI6. Several groups formed in western France, whose naval ports – built for earlier wars against Britain – were strategically vital in the gruelling Battle of the Atlantic as bases for German surface ships and submarines. One network, the largely Catholic Confrérie Notre-Dame, sent information about the German fleet, and contributed to the successful hunting of the battleship *Bismarck* in 1941. Detailed plans of Hitler's Atlantic Wall coastal defences were delivered to London before they were even built.[136]

Intelligence of a less spectacular kind came from published sources.[137] Churchill complained in August 1940 of the paucity of information even from the unoccupied zone: 'We seem to be as much cut off from these territories as from Germany.'[138] In time, however, France can never have been so closely scrutinized. And never can the French people, through the BBC and a mass of print, have been so exposed to British influences. Total mobilization for war provided unprecedented resources. The Royal Institute of International Affairs set up a Foreign Research and Press Service in September 1939, for a time based at Balliol College, Oxford, and in 1943 this became part of the new Foreign Office Research Department. Its French Section (eventually led by the Cambridge historian J.P.T. Bury) had 150 people monitoring and interpreting French radio broadcasts and newspapers, as well as confidential information from agents. Letters leaving France were read. They even received official reports on French public opinion from friendly sources in Vichy. Material was brought out by agents. Even newspapers used as wrapping paper were recovered and analysed. From the earliest days, masses of clandestine material – from handwritten leaflets to increasingly sophisticated newspapers – was produced in one of the earliest forms of resistance. Late in 1941, an agent brought a suitcase full of these underground publications, the biggest arrival so far. From 1942, the Free French systematically copied and circulated every sample they obtained. Legal French newspapers were bought and dispatched by the British embassies in Lisbon and Stockholm.

The information thus gleaned had many uses. Highly detailed fortnightly reports on conditions, public opinion and political changes in France were circulated to more than twenty government departments. There were important conclusions for policy. It was realized that anglophobia was limited, and that anti-British propaganda was ineffective. It became clear that Pétain was personally very popular, and so hostile propaganda was directed at his entourage, not him. By 1943 it was clear that de Gaulle had become the accepted leader of the whole Resistance movement. Fresh and detailed information made British propaganda material convincing. For the secret services, it was vital to make sure that new agents were familiar with details that might catch them out: 'Did we want to know what the bicycle tax was? . . . some obscure provincial newspaper . . . used to wrap up a refugee's smuggled bottle of wine, might provide us with a clue.'[139]

Knowledge of conditions in France also helped a sustained effort to give the British a favourable image of the French. There were many newspaper articles and BBC programmes on the Free French and the Resistance. On 14 July 1943, there was a BBC French Night. That October, a Resistance exhibition, sponsored by the Free French and the British government, was mounted in London. A show of Impressionist paintings was held at the National Gallery. A Franco-British friendship week included a competition for schoolchildren to paint their ideas of France, which produced charming paintings of picturesque villages, women in folk costumes, and Joan of Arc being welcomed by John Bull and Britannia. Such events, and essays by leading French and British writers on the *entente cordiale*, were reflected back to France in broadcasts and French-language papers as evidence of British friendship.

'At the beginning', wrote one French socialist, 'the BBC was everything.'[140] It countered the attacks of the official media, and created links between Britain and the French people that have never been equalled. A foreign journalist in France reported 'a veritable pandemonium of British radios pouring news through balconies, windows and patios'. German intelligence reported in February 1941 that 'the majority of the population continue to believe in an eventual British victory'. Young people, the Germans realized, were speaking English in private – 'with a dreadful accent, it is true'. Vichy's own radio propagandists, though far from ineffective, admitted by late 1943 that they were losing the contest. A secret Vichy report (which someone sent to the BBC) complained that 'every household is imbibing ever-increasing doses'. Admitting defeat, the authorities first forbade listening and then vainly ordered the confiscation of wireless sets.[141] The BBC's success rested on a talented French team. They were new to broadcasting, tending rather to have experience of journalism, show business or the arts. They became household names – though several of those names were false. 'Pierre Bourdan' was Pierre Maillaud, a journalist. 'Jacques

Duchesne' was Michel Saint-Denis, a theatre producer, who had served as a liaison officer with the BEF and been evacuated from Dunkirk. Jean Oberlé was an artist. Pierre Dac was a nightclub comedian, twice imprisoned while trying to reach London, who specialized in writing satirical words to popular songs. As stressed by the title of its most popular programmes, 'Ici la France' and 'Les Français parlent aux Français', the service had to be authentically French, not British propaganda. 'The very soul of French wit has fled to London,' wrote one listener. As well as providing reliable news, talks and discussions, it featured satire, catchy slogans, and jingles – the most famous (sung to 'La Cucaracha') being 'Radio Paris ment, Radio Paris ment, Radio Paris est allemand.'* Radio Paris was France's biggest radio station. A Spanish newspaper reported hearing their songs hummed across France. They cleverly kept in touch with their audience. Amazingly, listeners kept writing in: letters from the unoccupied zone arrived by the hundred, and even people in the occupied zone managed to get letters through. One wrote that his 'greatest pleasure is listening to English broadcasts, the only ones that give me the truth and are not under the Boche jackboot'. A French postal censor sent on the letter to the BBC with the comment, 'All my best wishes to you who have the courage to fight for liberty.'[142] The BBC had its own French intelligence department. Letters were carefully analysed and people arriving from France were interviewed. Many letters were acknowledged over the air, thus encouraging a feeling of involvement and encouraging yet more correspondence. Letters also provided valuable intelligence information, which was regularly circulated to government departments and to the Free French.

The broadcasts were backed up with vast quantities of printed material produced by the Political Warfare Executive. This was grudgingly carried by the RAF, who only liked dropping things that exploded. A bomber carried up to 24,000 leaflets, and over 500 titles were produced in French, as was an illustrated magazine, *Accord*. They carried justifications of British policy, circulated detailed war news from around the world as well as from inside France (including resistance activity and German exactions) and gave advice ('Look after your radios'). The regular *Courrier de l'Air* carried BBC wavelengths as well as news, photographs, features, and cartoons.[143] Literary reviews aimed to show that the intellectual elite was not collaborating with the Germans, and carried pieces by leading writers including T. S. Eliot and Georges Bernanos. There was a book of satirical radio songs mocking Vichy and the Germans, delivered by 'your friends in the RAF', as well as the 'Song of the Partisans', which became the anthem of resistance. Newspapers were also produced in English to represent the French view to the outside world. The first, *La France Libre*, began in November 1940. Clandestine

* 'Radio Paris lies, Radio Paris is German.'

Part of the mass of propaganda dropped by 'your friends of the RAF', here containing new satirical words written to popular songs broadcast by the BBC.

newspapers from inside France were republished, including extracts in translation. One of their great themes, of course, was the closeness of Franco-British friendship. They underlined changes in Britain, to show that the war was aimed not only at defeating Germany, but at creating a better world. The Beveridge Report was important here and attracted wide attention. An underground Catholic newspaper remarked that Britain no longer fitted 'the familiar images of Colonel Bramble': 'Mr Churchill presents . . . the traditional face of John Bull. But how his compatriots have changed!'[144]

Resistance of a more active kind was the domain of SOE, the Special Operations Executive.[145] France was its most important theatre of operations, and eventually it had five sections there (including an escape section and one working with Polish immigrants) and another in Algeria. It had huge influence on the French resistance, controlling all radio and air communications, providing all weapons and explosives, and committing 1,200 British, French and Polish agents on the ground. Its two most important sections were F and RF. F Section was the original French section, set up in October 1940, recruited from French-speaking British subjects and French volunteers. RF Section was set up in May 1941 to provide backing for the Free French: its agents were nearly all French, and its operations were in practice directed by de Gaulle's intelligence service, the Bureau Central de Renseignements et d'Action, BCRA.

Both BCRA and SOE had started from scratch. De Gaulle's intelligence chief, André Dewavrin, 'Colonel Passy', was a very young army officer with no intelligence training: de Gaulle was not interested in subversion and did not expect it to be an important job.[146] Also a beginner was Colonel Maurice Buckmaster, longest-serving head of F Section, who had been in the motor trade in France. Many recruits were drawn from similar Anglo-French business circles. The most famous British member of RF Section, its intrepid second-in-command F.F. Yeo-Thomas, had been educated and spent much of his life in France, and worked in the Paris fashion business – an unlikely occupation for a man who had volunteered to fight for the Poles against the Bolsheviks in 1920 and escaped execution by strangling his guard. Most of RF Section were French citizens, and came from a wide range of backgrounds. Their most successful sabotage team, trained in Britain, consisted of a fireman, a chauffeur, a garage mechanic and a student. They destroyed a strategic canal system, wrecked a tank factory and killed eleven Gestapo officers (during the appropriately named Operation RATWEEK). F Section agents were mostly British subjects, and the need to speak French well enough to pass as French – or at least Belgian or Swiss – meant that they were typically drawn from Franco-British families and international business circles. In background they ranged 'from pimps to princesses'. About 500 were sent to France, of whom over 100 were killed. They were usually recruited by recommendation: SOE tried to avoid those keen to volunteer for the wrong reasons, especially the 'neurotic or crossed in love'.[147] Some were the products of the First World War, being children of British soldiers. Motives were and are difficult to assess, but Franco-British patriotism, a taste for adventure, and personal animus against the enemy made an effective combination. Violette Szabo, for example, born in Paris in 1921, the daughter of a British army boxing champion and a French dressmaker from the Somme, married a Free French officer who was killed at El Alamein. When recruited she was working at the perfume counter of the Bon Marché store in Brixton. The discreet recruitment networks could sometimes cause surprises: F Section agent Francis Cammaerts, a Cambridge-educated Belgian, was taken aback to be asked casually by his old college tutor when he was going back to France.[148] They also recruited in the field: F Section included two French police inspectors. Women were important in SOE, which employed about 3,000 women and 10,000 men in all. F Section's intelligence officer and its 'hub' was the highly competent Vera Atkins, born in Bucharest to parents of Ukrainian Jewish origin, and educated in Switzerland and Paris. In France, women attracted less suspicion as couriers and radio operators, and fifty were sent, of whom a quarter never returned. One courier, Pearl Witherington, ended up commanding 3,000 men in central France. Some, especially those who met tragic deaths, became famous after the war, notably Violette Szabo and Noor Inayat Khan, a direct descendant of Tipu Sultan.[149]

Communications were crucial to organized resistance, and they were controlled by the British. At first they relied on conventional means, often age-old and similar to those used against the Bourbons and Napoleon, for example fishing boats and smuggling routes over the Pyrenees. Small flotillas of boats operated from Cornwall and Gibraltar. One convenient Breton cove had already been used during the French revolutionary wars.[150] Eventually the RAF became the main means of contact, dropping agents, weapons and equipment by parachute. Here too they had to learn by trial and error: once a team landed on the roof of a police station, and once inside a POW camp. From 1941, small Lysander aircraft dropped and picked up from improvised landing fields. Despite the risk, for resisters this could be a thrilling, even somewhat festive, occasion. The British tried to instil discipline: 'There must be no family parties on the field. If the pilot sees a crowd he may not land . . . Anybody . . . approaching the aircraft from the right is liable to be shot by the pilot.' Radios were essential, but they were the greatest source of vulnerability. They were big – the equivalent of a heavy suitcase – and the Germans developed efficient detection techniques. Moreover, they were sometimes able to use captured radios to set traps.

De Gaulle resented SOE, and especially F Section, as a challenge to his (and France's) sovereignty, and his views seem to have been coloured by a paranoid view of the 'Intelligence Service' popularized in inter-war anglo-phobic writings. He and Dewavrin believed that they were being starved of resources to favour British operations – in fact, resources were simply short – and they were often exasperatingly unreasonable: 'for God's sake send that mad Joan of Arc to inspect his troops in Central Africa', was one SOE plea.[151] The British refused to place all underground operations in Free French hands. They were unwilling to make de Gaulle the only leader of French resistance, and insisted on the opportunity to work with non-Gaullist groups. There were also operational considerations. The Gaullist priority was political: to create a large, obedient, national movement. The British priority was in two senses non-political. They did not want to get involved in domestic intrigues 'to secure the post-war establishment . . . of any partic-ular form of government or of any particular persons as government'.[152] They did want to maximize demolitions, sabotage and guerrilla warfare. These differing priorities led to fundamentally different ways of operating. The Gaullists wanted to set up central controlling institutions, most famously the Conseil National de la Résistance (CNR), and recruit large numbers. F Section wanted small units, well trained, decentralized, and unknown to each other, and in all it set up 100 separate 'circuits', as SOE called them. The former model was very dangerous; the latter, comparatively secure. This did not persuade de Gaulle or Dewavrin: 'as Frenchmen we could not accept the British argument, however logical . . . What counted above all for us was to create a national entity of Resistance . . . to prove to the world that

France as a whole was gradually resuming its place in the war alongside its allies.'[153] The British thought the French were negligent about security; the French thought the British were obsessive. Both had security disasters, inherent in the nature of their activity. But French disasters were aggravated both by their centralizing objectives and by failures in elementary precautions, which meant that all their radio communications with France were liable to be read by the enemy: a major reason for British mistrust. Eventually a young SOE cryptographer went round to show the French on a blackboard how easy it was to break their code.[154] Contemporaries thought that this cavalier attitude was 'typically French'; but it can perhaps be explained by the lack of training of senior figures, and by a paradoxical pitfall: operating on home ground created a dangerous feeling of safety. At times, both the Gaullists and the British government froze cooperation, but generally relations between junior officers were far better than between their masters. Agents and resisters in the field were often blissfully unaware of any divergence at all. For them, 'London' meant a united force, the source of weapons, radios, technical training and money, and the symbol of a wider and prestigious national movement.

These were grim and testing years. There is some evidence that French public opinion criticized the British – 'good sailors but bad soldiers' – for postponing an invasion of Europe. It is true that Churchill and his advisers feared a premature invasion, and a repeat of the carnage of 1914–18. There were also enormous practical problems. But this perception in France contributed to a waning of British prestige and the growing admiration for America and Russia, seen in the later stages of the war and afterwards. Opinion surveys in Britain showed a similar decline in friendly feelings towards the French.[155]

Liberation, 1943–4

It's we who are breaking the bars of our brothers' prisons,
With hatred at our heels, and hunger and misery to goad us.
There are countries where people lie in warm beds dreaming,
But here, can't you see, we're marching, we're killing, we're dying.
'Song of the Partisans', JOSEPH KESSEL and MAURICE DRUON, written in the Savile
Club, London, May 1943, and dropped over France by the RAF

Without the organization, communications, material, training and leadership
which SOE supplied . . . 'resistance' would have been of no military value.
Secret report to combined Allied chiefs of staff, 18 July 1945[156]

Public support for Vichy had been waning since 1940, as Germany failed to defeat Britain and the benefits of 'collaboration' failed to materialize. Dramatic changes came in 1941 and 1942. Russia was invaded, bringing the French Communist Party into the patriotic cause. The United States entered the war, which seemed, as in 1917, to guarantee eventual German defeat. Violent resistance began on 19 August 1941 with the killing by a Communist of a German naval officer in the Barbès métro station in Paris. Churchill, pressed to do something to help the Russians, endorsed such acts, and the British decided to arm the Communists, who developed a large and diverse movement. Vichy's desire to 'collaborate' led to mass round-ups of Jews – a generally unpopular measure – and the deportation of many thousands to death camps; and then in September 1942 to the Service du Travail Obligatoire, the conscription of workers to go to Germany. This hated 'STO' forced young Frenchmen and their families either to defy the government or to risk a grim future in Germany – a dilemma emphasized by the BBC. Thousands of young men evaded STO by hiding out in the central forests, the eastern mountains and the *maquis*, the Mediterranean scrub that gave mass resistance its name. Allied landings in Morocco caused the Germans to invade the unoccupied zone in November 1942, ending the only benefit of the armistice. The numbers participating in resistance swelled. But so did the involvement of Frenchmen in its repression, especially through the quasi-fascist Milice. There began a vicious semi-clandestine civil war.

Jean Moulin succeeded in setting up the Conseil National de la Résistance (CNR) in May 1943 to provide unified leadership. De Gaulle and 'London' were a potent attraction, and the separate Resistance networks, with some reservations, fell in with Moulin's plans. As Michael Stenton puts it, 'if de Gaulle had never been invented, Moulin might not have unified the Resistance'. This had major political consequences for postwar France. But almost at once, on 21 June 1943, Moulin and seven other resistance leaders were caught when meeting near Lyon. Moulin died under torture. This is the murkiest and most emotive episode in Resistance history, with persistent allegations that Moulin was betrayed. Whatever the truth, the Gaullist ambition to centralize, combined with undeniable laxity in security, invited disaster. General Delestraint, commander of the 'secret army' set up on de Gaulle's orders, had already been arrested when he forgot the password of a safe house in Paris where he was to stay, and booked into a neighbouring hotel in his own name. He was later killed in Dachau. In September, one of de Gaulle's aides de camp was caught, and in his Paris flat were found four months of decoded dispatches and the names of fourteen proposed members of the CNR.[157] The Gaullist national hierarchy was thus short-lived. When later reconstituted it had little contact with the grass-roots resisters. Essentially political, it devoted its attention to planning post-war administration. The combat side of the Resistance instead adopted the decentralized British model. There would be no nationwide uprising, but hundreds of small military operations. These activities depended largely on SOE, which provided weapons, equipment, and wads of cash to feed the *maquis* without alienating local farmers. This did not change the political outcome, as de Gaulle was backed by London and Moscow, and now grudgingly accepted by Washington. Whatever he did, he would be the titular leader of French resistance and would benefit from its struggle. He poised himself to take power as soon as liberation began.[158]

In 1943 and early 1944, the Resistance was organized for war. This was a slow process, as trained men and women had to be dropped to give military instruction, and stockpiles of weapons, explosives and ammunition built up. The RAF was never keen on dropping sten-guns on French fields when it could be dropping bombs on German cities. Moreover, the winter weather in 1943–4 imposed delays, and the Germans captured many arms dumps. Nevertheless, thanks to Churchill's backing, SOE by the end had dispatched 10,000 tons of stores, including nearly 200,000 sten-guns and 800,000 hand-grenades.[159] The plan was to launch a campaign of sabotage and disruption when the Allied armies landed on D-Day, and to continue it as they fought their way out of the bridgehead. Military leadership on the ground was reinforced by 2,000 SAS men (including two French SAS regiments), by ninety-three 'Jedburgh' teams composed of three agents (one British, one American, and one French) including a radio operator, and by lone agents. One such was André Hue, a twenty-one-year-old Franco-Welshman, who after involvement in intelligence gathering and escape lines had been brought out and given SOE training. With a British army commission, he was parachuted back in June 1944 to organize contacts with the *maquis* in Brittany. He then arranged arms drops and the arrival of French SAS units, which led to a general uprising in Brittany, slowing the movement of German forces and greatly facilitating the American push south out of Normandy.[160] Thus, in the nick of time, Anglo-French disagreements were resolved on the ground. After D-Day, the various organizations in London merged as the État-Major des Forces Françaises de l'Intérieur (EMFFI), a chaotic hybrid nominally commanded by de Gaulle's General Koenig.

D-Day saw another spat between de Gaulle and Churchill. That an invasion was imminent was well known. But the date and the place were top secret, and elaborate subterfuge persuaded the Germans that it would take place near Calais. In April 1944 the British suspended diplomatic privileges and insisted on decoding and censoring all messages leaving Britain. The French regarded this as an insulting imposition, despite their history of security failures. De Gaulle, in Algiers, was not told the D-Day plans. Churchill asked him to fly to England, and near Portsmouth on 5 June told him personally that the invasion of France was about to begin. Practically none of de Gaulle's troops were taking part. Churchill – who had insisted against the opposition of the Americans and his own chiefs of staff on informing de Gaulle before the invasion began – intended this as a conciliatory gesture. He greeted de Gaulle literally with open arms. Accounts differ as to whether de Gaulle was angry at being kept in the dark. He was certainly outraged when Churchill, trying as usual to mediate between his two awkward allies, urged him to go and see Roosevelt and reach an agreement over the administration of liberated France. This was anathema to de Gaulle, who responded with his characteristic icy anger that he would not present himself to Roosevelt as a 'candidate' to govern France: 'The French government exists. I have nothing to ask, in this sphere, of the United States of America or of Great Britain.' He refused to dine with Churchill and left him feeling 'chilled'. Things got worse when de Gaulle refused to make a BBC broadcast to France or give permission for French liaison officers to go to Normandy. 'I knew he would be a pest,' wrote General Brooke, 'and recommended strongly that he should be left in Africa, but Anthony Eden would insist on bringing him over!' A senior Foreign Office official wrote in exasperation, 'It's a girl's school. Roosevelt, PM and . . . de Gaulle – all behave like girls approaching the age of puberty.'[161] Several intermediaries, most importantly Eden, tried to calm things down, but sniping continued. To Churchill's annoyance, much of the Cabinet, Parliament and Fleet Street supported de Gaulle. De Gaulle's suspicions about Anglo-Saxon conspiracy were further strengthened. His account of an exchange with Churchill remains famous in France as the summation of Albion's sempiternal attitude: 'Each time we must choose between Europe and the open sea, we shall always choose the open sea. Each time I must choose between you and Roosevelt, I shall always choose Roosevelt.'[162]

Despite this ringing declaration, Britain, which had always considered the restoration of France as a great power to be one of its principal war aims, insisted, through the mouths of Churchill and Eden, that France should be treated as one of the victor powers, with a zone of occupation in Germany. This was condescendingly agreed at the Yalta conference in February 1945 by Roosevelt and Stalin, who were willing to humour what they saw as their British ally's strange indulgence.

A company of the 2nd Oxfordshire and Buckinghamshire Light Infantry were the first Allied soldiers to set foot in France in the early hours of 6 June 1944, followed shortly afterwards by other British and American airborne troops, and then the huge American, British and Canadian seaborne landings. The Germans never seriously threatened the bridgeheads, but they did block the advance inland. This led to heavy aerial and naval bombardments, which devastated tracts of Normandy and killed several thousand

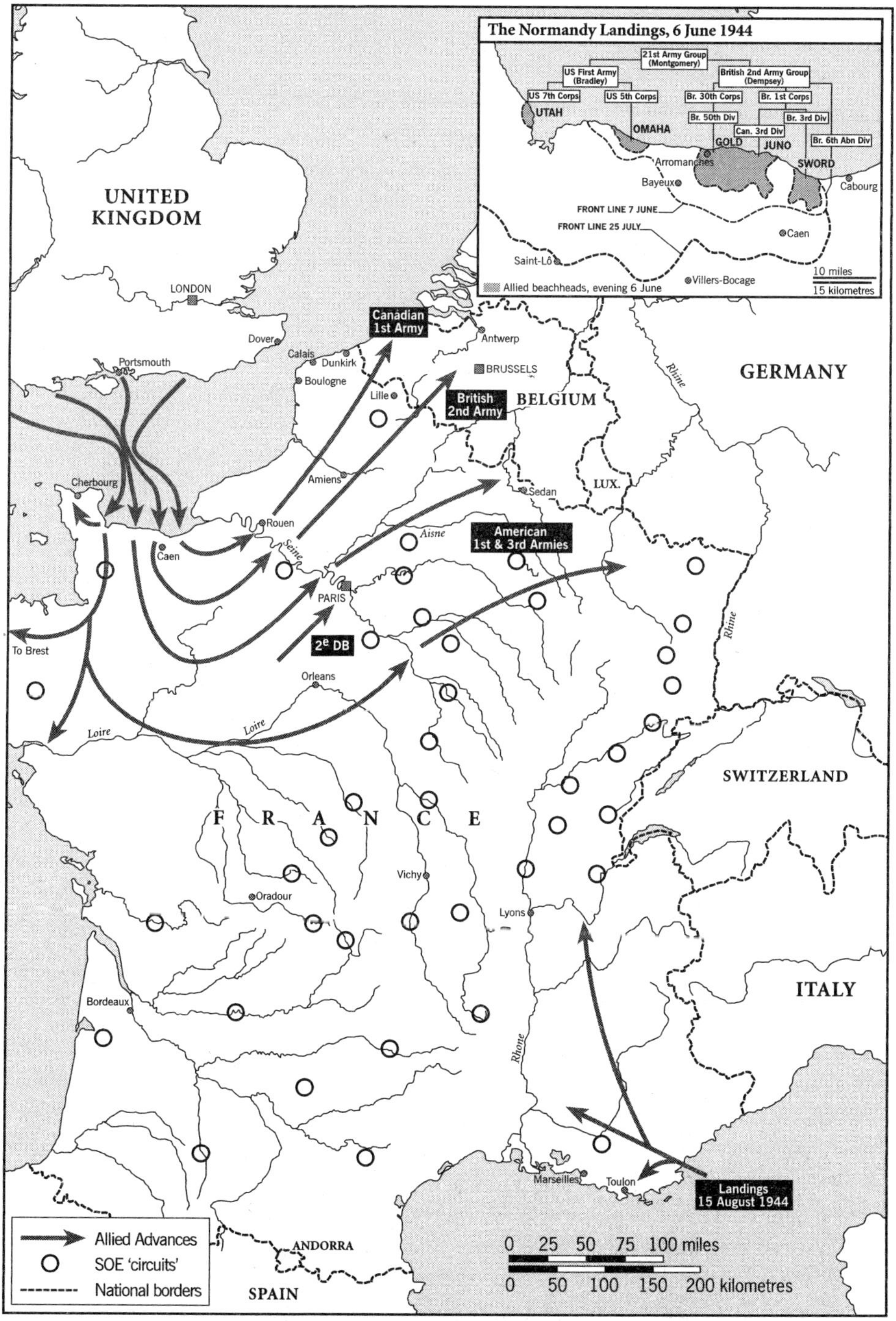
The Normandy Landings, 6 June 1944
21st Army Group (Montgomery)
US First Army (Bradley)
British 2nd Army Group (Dempsey)
US 7th Corps
US 5th Corps
Br. 30th Corps
Br. 1st Corps
Br. 50th Div
Br. 3rd Div
Can. 3rd Div
Br. 6th Abn Div
UTAH
OMAHA
GOLD
JUNO
SWORD
Arromanches
Bayeux
Cabourg
FRONT LINE 7 JUNE
FRONT LINE 25 JULY
Caen
Saint-Lô
Villers-Bocage
Allied beachheads, evening 6 June
10 miles
15 kilometres
UNITED KINGDOM
LONDON
Portsmouth
Dover
Calais
Dunkirk
Boulogne
Canadian 1st Army
Antwerp
BRUSSELS
BELGIUM
British 2nd Army
Lille
GERMANY
Rhine
Amiens
Sedan
LUX.
Cherbourg
Rouen
Caen
Seine
Aisne
American 1st & 3rd Armies
PARIS
2e DB
To Brest
Orleans
Loire
SWITZERLAND
F R A N C E
Vichy
Oradour
Lyons
ITALY
Bordeaux
Rhone
Marseilles
Toulon
Landings 15 August 1944
Allied Advances
SOE 'circuits'
National borders
ANDORRA
SPAIN
0 25 50 75 100 miles
0 50 100 150 200 kilometres

The Liberation of France, 1944

French civilians. The town of Caen, wrote one British soldier, was left 'a waste of brick and stone, like a field of corn that has been ploughed. The people gazed at us without emotion of any kind; one could hardly look them in the face, knowing who had done this.'[163] There followed a ten-week battle of attrition between the British (supported by Canadians and Poles) and the main German forces, including seven of their ten armoured divisions, which cost some 65,000 British casualties – a proportion similar to that at Passchendaele in 1917. This helped the Americans to break out further south. The Germans clung to the defensive landscape of *bocage* banks and hedges – a problem the British had last met in 1758 (see above, page 134). Though the Germans underwent shattering air attacks, it took until the last week in August to destroy, capture or throw them back.

All over France, D-Day brought the Resistance its finest hour. Its job was to hamper and delay the movement of German reinforcements to the beach-heads. Tens of thousands of *maquisards* had been called into action on 5 June by the BBC's famous coded messages. They were now reasonably well provided with small arms, explosives, training, leaders and radios. That night, there were 950 attacks on the railway system. The telephone network was also disrupted, forcing the Germans to use radio, to which the Allies could listen. The most celebrated joint operation was that which delayed an SS armoured division ordered from Toulouse to Normandy. F Section agents blew up its fuel dumps. An attempt to move by rail was blocked by numerous demolitions. Having collected more fuel, it tried again by road, but was harried by several SOE circuits. What should have been a three-day journey took two weeks – twice as long as its journey from the Russian front.[164] Its most notorious reprisal was the massacre of the inhabitants of Oradour-sur-Glane. Another tragedy was taking place in eastern France, on the Vercors plateau, where a large *maquis* unit tried to stand and fight against much larger numbers of German troops supported by tanks and aircraft, and was massacred. These were not isolated atrocities: the Germans and their French collaborators commonly tortured, mutilated and killed prisoners, hostages and local people. By causing disruption and chaos, the Resistance made a substantial contribution in the vital period round D-Day. The mainly Franco-American landings in Provence on 15 August were given indispensable assistance by the Royal Navy, the RAF and British-led resistance groups which helped to clear their rapid progress north. France was finally ablaze.

Participation by the Resistance and by French regular troops in the Liberation was of great significance for national self-respect and for de Gaulle. It helped him to assume the position he had always claimed as France's legitimate ruler. He insisted that General Leclerc's 2nd armoured division – trained in Britain and partly drawn from French units of the British 8th Army – should race 'towards the Eiffel Tower', where the 'national insurrection' had begun on 19 August. His purpose was to forestall German reprisals, to show that the capital was not the passive recipient of Anglo-Saxon liberation – and to ensure that Gaullists took charge. Leclerc arrived on the 25th, followed swiftly by de Gaulle himself. In a famous speech at the Hôtel de Ville he declared that 'Paris [had been] liberated by itself, liberated by its people with the help of the armies of France, with the support and the help of the whole of France, of France that is fighting, of France alone'.[165] Untroubled by magnanimity, wherever de Gaulle met a British SOE officer, his response was, 'You have no place here,' followed by an order to leave the country. Lieutenant-Colonel Starr, who commanded much of Gascony, answered back bluntly, and the row ended with de Gaulle shaking his hand and saying 'they told me . . . you were fearless and knew how to say *merde*'. Nevertheless, F Section 'packed its bags and slipped out as gracefully as it could'.[166] One young agent, Peter Maroger, son of a Franco-British family, decided to go and join in the liberation of Paris, where he was killed.[167] No British units shared in the glory. According to the journalist and intelligence officer Malcolm Muggeridge, 'The Americans had insisted that, because of [Mers] El Kebir, not to mention the Battle of Trafalgar . . . the British were unpopular among the French and should as far as possible be kept out of sight.' But he and some colleagues made their way to Paris, and happily profited from the 'rarity value' of the British uniform, which ensured 'friendly smiles, embraces, bed-fellows even, as and when required, as well as limitless hospitality'. Some young Guards officers, among them Peter Carrington (later to be foreign secretary), bluffed their way in for a break at the Ritz.[168]

Meanwhile, the British army was moving north. The terrible battle for Normandy – 'dust, slit trenches, bulldozers and dead cows' – was followed by rapid movement through cheering crowds along the familiar roads through Picardy and Flanders, via Amiens, Arras and Lille, to the Channel ports and into Belgium. It was one of the speediest advances in military history, meeting only sporadic resistance: 'on the whole . . . more tiring than dangerous'.[169] Franco-British contacts, for good or ill, were therefore fleeting. The British authorities had been worried that the troops might be unruly. One officer had warned that 'We, with memories of our fathers going to Paris to misbehave themselves, look upon the French as a light-moralled, rather lecherous race, not hospitable but grasping . . . They judge us on our late Victorian reputation for prudery . . . Both couldn't be more wrong.' An instruction booklet had been issued exhorting the men not to eat or drink too much – the French disliked British drunkenness – and to avoid arguments about 1940. It also urged dropping 'any ideas about French women based on stories of Montmartre and nude cabaret shows . . . Like us, the French are on the whole a conventional people.' For most soldiers, such problems barely arose.

One officer of the 6th Airborne Division wrote, 'I have few opportunities of meeting any French people. A pity: I should have liked to have learned so much more about them.'[170] Sergeant Richard Cobb (later an illustrious historian of France) had no such complaint. His job was producing a news-sheet in French, which permitted fraternization with a picturesque variety of people, including a Norman schoolmistress 'so blond that she looked as though she had come down in direct descent from the Vikings. She had taken a liking to me (this was reciprocated) and used to cook me steaks, which we ate out in the vegetable garden . . . I used to think that I was perhaps the luckiest soldier in the British army.'[171]

Resentments among the leaders, politically motivated snubs and differ-ences of policy did not dispel the euphoria of liberation, despite the destruc-tion and death caused by the fighting and bombing. The scenes of joy and revenge marked the memories of all who witnessed them, and, as newsreel images, would enter the collective memory of generations yet unborn. Cobb, passing through the textile town of Roubaix, found 'enormous friendliness': many houses displayed photographs of British soldiers billeted there in 1918. The new ambassador, Duff Cooper, thought that 'Never have the English been so popular in France . . . and the most popular of all of them is the Prime Minister . . . The general public have not the slightest idea that [he and de Gaulle] are anything but the firmest of friends.' On 11 November 1944, Churchill came to Paris, and, wrote de Gaulle, 'Paris cheered with all its heart.' Cooper thought it 'greater than anything I have ever known'. The two leaders descended the Champs Elysées together, there was a march-past of French and British troops, and Churchill laid a wreath at the statue of his hero Clemenceau. The band played a jaunty march Churchill knew well, 'Père la Victoire'. It had been written in praise of Clemenceau, father of an earlier victory, but today, said de Gaulle in English, 'For you!' Churchill, weeping 'buckets', told de Gaulle 'I felt as if I were watching a resurrec-tion.'[172] A large equestrian statue of Edward VII, 'promoter of the entente cordiale', saved from destruction and somehow hidden for two years by employees of the Société Génerale bank, was replaced on its plinth as a gesture of 'sincere gratitude and profound friendship'. Showing less grati-tude, the French rugby team thrashed the British army 21 to 9.[173]

The *entente* was at last truly *cordiale*. The bitterness of the inter-war years and the trauma of 1940 gave way to shared joy and triumph. The anglophobe tradition was discredited with the Vichy regime that had espoused it, and only fragments lingered. The French patriotic saga was suffused with British images: Churchill, the BBC, de Gaulle in London, the RAF, parachute drops to the *maquis*, and D-Day. For the British, the indomitable figure of de Gaulle was part of their 'finest hour'; and the heroism and suffering of men, women and children in the Resistance – a vision of what Britain might have under-

The struggles of each side became part of the national story of the other.

gone – blotted out the shared failings of 1940. These powerful impressions, celebrated in speeches, films, oral traditions, public ceremonies, history books, children's comics and novels, even when memory dims, add something to that stock of images through which one nation perceives another, familiar enough to become even the subject of affectionate comedy. The most popular French film ever made – seen by 17 million people – is Gérard Oury's slapstick *La Grande Vadrouille* (1966), the story of three British airmen rescued by a Paris house-painter and an orchestral conductor. It is practically unknown in Britain. Watching it now, it is striking that the British characters are amiable but remote, disruptive creatures from another planet. The really close relationship is between the French and the Germans.

Over the years there has been what Robert Frank calls 'meaningful amnesia'. Opinion polls have shown that the French, irrespective of age, sex and class, now attribute a negligible role in France's liberation to the British – seen as far less important than the Americans, the *maquis*, the Free French, or the Russians. Remarks made in September 2005 by the French foreign minister, Philippe Douste–Blazy, were widely interpreted as showing that he thought that Britain too had been defeated and occupied. Frank suggests that for the French to recognize the true British contribution would be too painful a reminder of 'the different destinies of the two countries.'[174] The British are no more generous: who remembers the French soldiers who died defending Dunkirk? The year 2004 combined the sixtieth anniversary of D-Day and the centenary of the *entente cordiale*. On both sides, ceremonies great and small proclaimed friendship and recalled what the two countries had survived together. Yet an opinion poll showed that among the words the French most commonly chose to describe the British were 'isolated', 'insular', and 'selfish'. The British, though somewhat less negative, commonly described the French as 'untrustworthy' or 'treacherous', and nearly one in three considered them 'cowardly'[175] – doubtless a distorted echo of 1940. How sad that when our two peoples want to feel proud of themselves they need to slight each other.

PART III: CONCLUSIONS AND DISAGREEMENTS

In so far as millions of deaths, impoverishment and political decline permit celebration, we can celebrate our shared victories in 1918 and 1945: the consequences of defeat are too appalling to contemplate. Common struggles brought the French and British people closer together than they have ever been, and rightly so. The fundamental causes of war in 1914 are still hard to grasp, yet it seems unlikely that France and Britain, even if their relationship had been closer, could have prevented it. By the standards of the time, and even those of our time, they could hardly keep out once war began. Their culpable failure, it seems to us, begins after 1918, and the arguments are as plain now as then.

Between the Wars

RT: Much of Europe was ravaged by war, and it needed cooperation and reconstruction. Germany was inherently too powerful to be restrained for ever by force, and surely the idealists were right that the only hope was a new democratic order based on self-determination and international co-operation, with the League of Nations as the symbol and forum. There was a hunger all over Europe for reconciliation and an end to the old systems of rivalry and power politics. One can understand French fears, but the fact is that they did poison the atmosphere and probably weaken democratic forces in Germany, not only by their demands at Versailles, but even more by covert territorial ambitions in the Rhineland, by sabre-rattling, by actual use of force in 1923, and by setting up alliances with eastern European states that proved effective only in giving a pretext for German rearmament and a subject for Hitler's rhetoric.

IT: This is naïve. It is clear that relying on permanent German good will was not a guarantee of peace. A reasonable deterrent – alliances, the garrisoning of the Rhineland, and firm prevention of illegal rearmament – would not have been oppressive, and could even have strengthened German democracy by showing that there was no future in aggression. This worked after 1945. The problem was not French ambition, but self-indulgent British idealism combined with idiotic francophobia and a strong dash of duplicity. Franco-British solidarity was the indispensable core of a peaceful system, but the British slid out of the guarantee they had given at the peace conference. Their deplorable failure of vision and responsibility, whether under

Liberal, Labour or Conservative leaders, culminated at Munich. The British – even the most clear-sighted of them – saw the error of their ways much too late, and bear a heavy responsibility for subsequent disaster.

The Second World War

The defeat of 1940 was truly shared, and with the worst will in the world we can find no reason to quarrel substantially. If France exposed its political sores, Britain demonstrated its military irrelevance. The former has been reproached to France ever since; the latter has been effaced by the Battle of Britain. But the fact is that they let each other down, and neither has entirely forgotten it. Victory in 1945 was as complete as it was moral. It had none of the shadows of 1918, and it largely – though not completely – effaced the trauma of 1940. Yet alliances rarely lead to affection: they create too much friction.

RT: I hesitate to criticize France's national hero, and I admit to admiring his grand gesture of defiance in 1940; but thereafter de Gaulle was a pernicious nuisance. Why does a democratic republic need a Man of Destiny? Denmark, Norway, Holland, and Belgium somehow managed to resist, be liberated and rebuild their post-war societies without one. Not only did he 'assume' the burden of France, he also 'assumed' the credit for what was being done by a large number of brave people quite independently of him. What did de Gaulle actually do, apart from fostering a myth that subsequently gave much satisfaction to nationalists? Surely his inflated reputation is due for a critical re-evaluation? But that is more a Franco-French than a Franco-British issue. As far as our mutual relations are concerned, could he not have made a more responsible and positive contribution to an Allied war effort that was trying to save millions of lives and liberate Europe? Would not a small sacrifice of his own ambition and even of national dignity have been a more genuine cause for patriotic pride than his sullen and paranoid intransigence?

IT: In fact France did need a 'man of destiny', because it was one of Europe's two largest democracies and was facing unprecedented dangers and temptations – to betray its democratic traditions and collaborate with Nazi Germany. De Gaulle had to persuade a demoralized nation to refuse what seemed inevitable defeat and prepare its own liberation. Did not Britain also need a 'man of destiny' when it was facing defeat in 1940, even though unlike France all its symbols of nationhood, principally the monarchy and Parliament, were intact? The main cause of de Gaulle's intransigence was the mistreatment that he and the Free French received. Admittedly this was primarily due to perverse American insistence on maintaining ties with a dishonest and discredited Vichy regime. But Churchill connived, and went against his own francophile instincts to pander to an ungrateful Roosevelt – a template for the 'special relationship' to come! De Gaulle was right to insist on French sovereignty and his equal status as an ally. He showed great determination and dignity in impossible circumstances, and thus preserved France's self-respect, which was of huge value for the country's long-term post-war recovery – and, indeed, for the long-term future of a Europe that wanted to be more than a mere dependency of the super-powers.

The experiences of the war from 1940 to 1944 left a different imprint on each country. On Britain, a durable sense of pride and unity, perhaps combined with a tendency to complacency and self-delusion. On France, a mixture of pride and shame amounting to a chip on its collective shoulder; festering internal divisions; but also a willingness to change its ways. This difference would have long-term consequences for Franco–British relations. But let us end on a positive note. The two nations together had survived the greatest danger in their history, and had helped to save the world from what Churchill rightly called a new Dark Age. Genuinely shared effort, involving hundreds of thousands of men, women and children, created mutual affection and respect. It has not been entirely forgotten. Whatever their disagreements, France and Britain lived the greatest moments of their modern history together.

INTERLUDE: THE FRENCH
AND SHAKESPEARE:
The Other French Revolution

Racine inspires me with an emotion that Shakespeare never gives me –
the emotion that comes from perfection.
ANDRE GIDE, novelist and translator of Shakespeare[1]

I'm not saying it's a bad thing, I'm not saying it's a good thing that
Shakespeare played integrally should succeed integrally in front of
a French public . . . I'm saying that when this happens – if it happens –
the French race will have changed absolutely.
EMILE FAGUET, cultural historian, 1904[2]

'The slow and chequered conversion of France to Shakespeare,' writes John
Pemble, 'was the other French Revolution.'[3] In the early twentieth century,
he was enrolled in the avant-garde, alongside Ibsen and Strindberg. The first
complete performance in French of *King Lear* took place in 1904, with the
experimental director Antoine as Lear, and the first complete performance
anywhere of *Troilus and Cressida* was given at the Paris Odéon in 1912. Yet
for much of the twentieth century, Shakespeare in France remained an exotic
spectacle, with large casts and lavish staging. Just as two centuries earlier,
his work was regarded as embodying the gulf separating French and English
cultures, intellects, and even races. Now he was seen as embodying the foggy
'north' versus the sunlit 'south', infidelity against faith, the 'Teuton' against
the 'Latin'. For many nationalist, Catholic and neo-classical writers of the
1920s and 30s, the gulf must have seemed even wider than in Voltaire's day
between a 'theatre of bestiality . . . instinct . . . and blood' and 'a theatre of
exquisite ideas, of refined sentiments'.[4] But the successive catastrophes
of the twentieth century made the classical perfectionism of orderly plots,
strict versification, 'refined' language, and happy endings seem relics of a
vanished age. As the Existentialist writer Albert Camus put it, there was
now no hope of a promised land. Shakespearean tragedy finally entered
French consciousness. His bleak universe, in which 'as flies to wanton boys
are we to the gods; they kill us for their sport', had become, in the words
of the Catholic novelist François Mauriac, 'terribly present' to 'survivors
struggling on the surface of a Europe three-quarters destroyed, in this glacial
May of 1945'.[5] Shakespearean themes and language appeared in the works
of leading modern writers such as Camus, Jean Anouilh, Samuel Beckett
and Louis Aragon. Shakespeare could now be presented for the first time,

not as a colourful archaic spectacle, but unadorned, in starkly simple productions. Twenty of his plays were performed between 1940 and 1960, many for the first time in France. The old idea that Shakespeare was quintessentially English, and had to be adapted to a quite separate French sensibility by being made tidier, more logical and more poetic, evaporated. This was the revolution in which the French 'rejected syntax and structures and happy endings, and opened their minds and their stage to the unruly pulse of Shakespeare's hours and years'.[6] An entirely new French translation, with the full English text in parallel, began to appear in 2002[7] – a sign both of the acceptance of Shakespeare into the French theatre and of a more general ability to read English. The French habitually refer to English, with a characteristic mix of envy and irony, as *la langue de Shakespeare*. For two centuries, since Voltaire's time, there has been a complete translation into French on average every twenty years – one for each generation. As Shakespeare's English becomes remote from native speakers, 'each new translation is a resurrection'.[8] In that sense, the language of Shakespeare is also French.

PART IV: REVIVAL

[The English] are a worn-out people. They need to regenerate themselves.

CHARLES DE GAULLE, 1964[1]

For half a century we have been obsessed by a doubt: are we still a
great people?

EDOUARD BALLADUR, French prime minister, 1994[2]

The Second World War and the Cold War ended three centuries of European
internal wars and imperial domination. Elites and peoples willingly replaced
nationalist passions with a 'Venusian' devotion to peace, prosperity and cooperation, extended to most of the Continent after the collapse of the Soviet
Union. There were two important exceptions: France and Britain did not
forsake Mars, or readily acquiesce in their reduced role. They continued to
claim exceptional rights – even virtues – and accept corresponding duties.
The fear of national decline marked the outlook of their politicians and
peoples. In Britain it was often expressed as sour self-denigration; in France
as blustering self-affirmation. The desire to arrest decline helped to push
through undeniable changes. France after de Gaulle's return to power in 1958
and Britain after the Thatcher years of the 1980s could no longer be considered economically, socially or politically moribund, as both had been before.
They converged with each other in wealth, power and population, and yet
they followed different paths to revival. Both still claimed prominent roles
both outside and inside Europe, whose leadership they regularly disputed.
This shared outlook at times revived the *entente cordiale*, and periodically over
sixty years there have been calls for partnership. Yet their ambitions have
more often caused rivalry than solidarity. Each, it can safely be predicted,
will continue to find the other a necessary help and a perpetual hindrance,
fluctuating between profuse expressions of friendship and traditional abuse.

CHAPTER 13

Losing Empires, Seeking Roles

The tragedy of it all is that we agree with de Gaulle on almost everything.
We like the political Europe (union des patries . . .) that de Gaulle likes.
We are anti-federalists; so is he. We are pragmatists in our economic
planning; so is he . . . but his pride, his inherited hatred of England . . .
above all his intense 'vanity' for France – she must dominate – make him
half welcome, half repel us, with a strange 'love–hate' complex.

HAROLD MACMILLAN, 29 November 1961[1]

Our greatest hereditary enemy was not Germany, it was England. From the
Hundred Years War to Fashoda, she hardly ceased to struggle against us . . .
She wants to stop us succeeding with the Common Market. True, she was our
ally during two world wars, but she is not naturally inclined to wish us well.

CHARLES DE GAULLE, 27 June 1962[2]

The fall from power of Churchill in July 1945 and of de Gaulle in January 1946 showed that their electorates wanted the fruits of peace harvested quickly. Yet successive governments in both countries were far from accepting diminished ambitions. They were eager to renew and deepen a partnership that could enable them jointly to lead and defend Europe against possible Soviet aggression and the risks either of American withdrawal or of American hegemony. As we shall see, genuine differences of view over relations with Germany, the United States, and the Arab world broke up their partnership. This hastened the decline of their power outside Europe, and began a still continuing struggle to shape Europe in their own image.

European Visions, 1945–55

To proceed as the French suggest, namely by making advance commitments
and hoping that the details will look after themselves, is likely to lead to
acute disappointment.
Foreign Office dispatch, 1950[3]

It is commonly believed in Britain that a great post-war opportunity was somewhere lost: that its leaders, chasing outdated imperial glories or the illusion of a special relationship with America, refused the proffered leadership of Europe, and lost the chance of controlling the formative period of 'European construction'. In the words of Tony Blair, 'British politicians surveying Europe then, in those almost unrecognizable days of powdered egg and Empire, failed the test . . . clutching at irrelevant assumptions and forgotten shibboleths.'[4] Some of those taking this view believe that the aim should have been to lead the inevitable march to European unity; others, to head it off in a different direction. This is myth. Britain's policy-makers were neither blind nor indifferent to what was happening. Britain did have ambitious aims for European leadership. But, as Alan Milward states bluntly, 'Europe was not asking to be led.' The notion that Britain could have taken the helm 'is shot through with nationalistic assumptions . . . as great as and more misguided than' those underlying its world-power pretensions.[5]

The bluff trade-union veteran Ernest Bevin, Labour foreign secretary from 1945 to 1950, wanted a 'Western Union', centred on a Franco-British partnership, taking in the Benelux countries, Scandinavia and a democratic Germany, and having links with British, French and Belgian African colonies and independent Commonwealth countries. This, he believed, would make a unit economically and militarily strong enough to act as an equal with the United States, and resist the Soviet threat. Bevin wanted American protection against the Red Army, but only to 'gain time' until 'the countries of

Western Europe would be independent both of the US and the Soviet Union'. He hoped in four or five years to have the Americans 'eating out of our hands'.[6] French politicians, and particularly the socialist Léon Blum (who had survived a German concentration camp), broadly accepted this view, and were willing to follow British leadership. Blum negotiated the first step, the Franco-British Treaty of Dunkirk (1947) – he and Bevin chose the place to show the rebirth of the old alliance. De Gaulle, out of power, opposed it. The Treaty of Brussels (1948) brought in the Benelux countries, and also promised 'harmonization' in economic matters, and common social and cultural policies. Anglo-French leadership of an ambitious and outward-looking Europe seemed to be emerging. Bevin looked forward to a common market and a common currency, and believed that 'we've made the union of England and France'.[7] But there were formidable counter-currents.

Cross-Channel economic interests had diverged. Since the eighteenth century, the two economies had been complementary: France had bought British coal and machinery; Britain had bought agricultural products and luxury goods. Britain had been France's biggest export market. The Wall Street Crash, the panicky protectionism of the 1930s, and then the war had reduced and then stopped exchanges. Peace did not restore the old relationship. The two economies proved impossible to coordinate, as the austerity policy followed by the Labour government, aimed at controlling inflation, contradicted the French policy of export-led modernization. Two events, now forgotten, signalled a parting of the ways. In the disastrous winter of 1947, as blizzards paralysed transport and industry, financial crisis threatened and trouble erupted in the Balkans and Palestine, Europe ran short of coal, which supplied over 80 per cent of primary energy needs. Britain thereupon suspended coal deliveries to France, causing an acute economic crisis. This was 'almost as important as the psychological break of 1940'.[8] It drove the first steps towards integration of the Continent's coal supplies, as British coal was replaced by German. Two years later, in 1949, Britain devalued sterling without warning France, hitting French exports. Germany took Britain's place as France's main trading partner. Moreover, while British purchases remained largely traditional (fashion goods, wines, spirits) German purchases (cars, chemicals, electrical goods) helped the rapid modernization that was beginning to transform France.

A fundamental political divide was also appearing: what Robert Frank has called 'the German obsession of the French and the American obsession of the British'.[9] For the French, Germany, though necessary economically, remained potentially an enemy and a threat – a deep conviction built on three wars and three invasions in eighty years. They refused any suggestion that Germany might become an ally. In 1945 de Gaulle had wanted (echoing 1918) the detachment of the Ruhr and Rhineland from Germany, and control of Rhineland coal to enable France to replace Germany as Europe's leading steel producer, thus blocking future German rearmament. But the British and Americans regarded Russia as the greater threat. They decided to maintain Germany's western frontier and restore its economy as the motor for European recovery. They intended that a new democratic West Germany should in time be recruited as an ally. They promised guarantees for French security, but the French, recalling the 1920s, considered Anglo-Saxon promises insufficient: America might again withdraw its forces from Europe, in which case Britain would do so too. The French had to find another way of controlling Germany, and this has always remained the basis of their European policy.

The Soviet takeover of Czechoslovakia and pressure in Scandinavia and Germany caused a crisis, leading to the Berlin blockade and airlift in 1948–9. When British and French military staffs met to make contingency plans in case of a Soviet attack, they could only debate whether they should immediately withdraw on Dunkirk or stage a longer retreat to the Pyrenees.[10] Bevin's idea of an independent Europe dimmed. Both London and Paris concluded that American protection was indispensable for the foreseeable future. Bevin came to see Britain's role less as a partner with France than as the 'pivot' or bridge between Europe and America. The North Atlantic Treaty, of which France was the main proponent, was signed in April 1949, to last in the first instance for ten years. But the treaty contained a provision for Germany to join when suitable. The French, with deep misgivings, had been forced to accept the 'Anglo-Saxon' view of European security.

Their persisting fears of German military revival and of possible Anglo-Saxon abandonment increased their desire to tighten their grip on Germany. Supranational European control – an idea familiar since Aristide Briand's hard-headed attempt at rapprochement in the 1920s – provided an answer. Thus French fears – with hindsight groundless – were to be decisive for European integration. There had since the 1920s been many voices – including the high-minded, the eccentric, and the calculating – urging European unity. The French philosopher Julien Benda wrote in 1933 that 'Europe will not be the fruit of a mere economic or even political transformation, it will only truly exist if it adopts a system of moral and aesthetic values'.[11] In Britain too there were enthusiastic federalists, some of the pioneers, at first sight surprisingly, being visionary imperialists too. Christian anti-modernists such as the writers G.K. Chesterton, T.S. Eliot and C.S Lewis yearned for 'a super-national state made up of units like Wessex and Picardy'.[12] At a less elevated level, there had been a steel cartel and a campaign for a customs union. The war had given a strong impetus to such ideas on both the right and the left. Nazi espousal of the 'European' theme had not discredited it, but for some had further proved that the era of independent states was over. For the chairman of the Fabian Society, G.D.H. Cole, 'better be ruled by Stalin than by a pack of half-hearted and half-witted social democrats . . . who still believe in the "independence" of their separate obsolete national states'.[13] Shared disaster between 1929 and 1945 created a desire to overcome past enmities and build anew. Memory of the economic failures of the 1930s and experience of wartime economic controls made the post-war years the heyday of centralization and planning. Not only 'the man in Whitehall', but also the men in Paris, Bonn, Moscow and Luxembourg really did seem to know best. The Cold War and decolonization seemed to be creating trading blocs, regional federations and supranational organizations. The leading Labour intellectual Harold Laski predicted in 1944 that 'the age of the nation state is over . . . economically, it is the Continent that counts: America, Russia, later China and India, eventually Africa . . . the true lesson of this war is that we shall federate the Continent or suffocate'.

In time, most of these visions faded: including pan-Africanism, pan-Arabism, the European Defence Community (a 1950s scheme for European armed forces controlled by a European quasi-government), and the European Political Community (1952). Others survived. For those that did, idealism had little influence compared with diplomatic and economic necessities. But the visionary aspect of European integration did give lustre to often rather sordid bargaining, and ensured an enthusiastic following that prosaic economic organizations such as the European Coal and Steel Community could hardly have inspired unadorned. A foundation myth built up, by which pragmatic and rather haphazard initiatives were interpreted in retrospect as a predestined march towards unity. The main importance of this belief was that it favoured expanding membership, and this would inevitably transform the institutions set up in the unrepeatable circumstances of the 1950s.[14]

In Britain and France there was both popular and political resistance to federalism. Both countries possessed strong traditions of representative self-government, had recently defended national independence, retained imperial or Commonwealth links, and shared a simple suspicion of interfering foreigners. Moreover, in Britain, integration had against it overwhelming economic interests. So London persistently pushed for open, inter-governmental organizations, such as the Organization for European Economic Cooperation, the Council of Europe, and the Western European Union, and away from supranational or federal institutions. But the French were less confident about remaining outside the current. Paris fluctuated between close alliance with Britain and a more integrationist strategy with Continental partners. Old fears tipped the balance. A degree of integration would prevent France being left alone (as in the 1920s) to control Germany, and might induce Germany to surrender key elements of its sovereignty. Some politicians and officials (especially those with regionalist, Catholic and trade-union backgrounds) were eager for supranational apolitical bodies. Jean Monnet believed that only a strong and unaccountable executive could take fast and decisive action. The Schuman Plan (drafted by Monnet and put forward by the French foreign minister Robert Schuman in 1950) provided for a 'high authority' of neutral experts to control the coal and steel industries of Germany, France and the Benelux countries. A council of ministers, a court, and an assembly were added to provide some legitimacy and idealism – 'illusions and dreams', as one French minister put it to Bevin. This initiative, less grandiose than Bevin's visions of world power, still required 'tough and even brutal' negotiations. The Americans applied strong pressure to conclude. Of all the governments involved, the United States was by far the keenest on supranationalism, because it wanted a cooperative and effective economic and Cold War partner in matters that seemed too important to subject to shaky European democracy.[15] Europeans, if less enthusiastic, could also see attractions: 'to the French [it was] a flag of convenience, to the Italians it was preferable (by definition) to government by Rome, to the Germans a welcome escape route, and to the Benelux nations a better choice than being dominated by powerful neighbours'.[16] To politicians, a supranational authority offered a way of passing on unpopular decisions (closing coal mines) and expensive burdens (subsidizing agriculture). The Treaty of Paris (April 1951) set up the European Coal and Steel Community, with an explicit commitment to eventual political unity.

That Attlee's Labour government did not join is often taken as a historic failure to participate in European integration at the outset, and so to be the origin of the interminable dilemma over 'Europe' that has marked British foreign and domestic politics for more than half a century. Moreover, it enabled France to take political leadership inside Europe, which, in an unprecedented triumph of single-minded determination, it retained for at least four decades. In taking this bold step, Schuman and Monnet acted with American backing. Five days after Bevin had told the American secretary of state Dean Acheson that Britain would not take on 'obligations' in Europe that restricted its interests elsewhere, Acheson urged Schuman to assume 'leadership of Europe on these problems' for France.[17] Bevin was angry at what seemed a Franco-American plot. The British were suspicious of supranational institutions – 'a Pandora's box full of Trojan horses', in Bevin's attributed phrase. Labour's sweeping policy of nationalization, especially of coal and steel, meant that government and unions were unwilling to hand over recently acquired control to an unaccountable body in Luxembourg – the meaning of the home secretary Herbert Morrison's famous pronouncement that 'the Durham miners won't wear it'.[18]

The British position was genuinely difficult. Since the 1930s, its trade had moved outside Europe, to the United States and especially to the Empire and Commonwealth, aided by sterling payments and preferential tariffs. Britain imported cheap food and exported manufactured goods. In 1950, Europe, though a reviving market, took only 10 per cent of British exports, while the Commonwealth and colonies took over 50 per cent. Australia was as economically important to Britain as 'the Six' (members of the Coal and Steel Community) combined, and New Zealand more important than Germany. This was clearly abnormal – the proximity and size of Continental markets would naturally attract trade if markets were freer, and Commonwealth countries would also diversify their trade. It would be damaging for Britain in the long run to be shut out of a European trading bloc if one formed, but it would be devastating to lose Commonwealth trade. Moreover, Europe seemed at the time too vulnerable to Soviet aggression and Communist subversion for it to be chosen deliberately as the pillar of the British economy. Such doubts were not only a British phenomenon: the Belgian foreign minister (and later 'father of Europe') Paul-Henri Spaak seriously considered whether Belgium and Holland should apply to join the Commonwealth.[19] An open 'one-world' trading system was the constant British aspiration. The worst outcome would be isolation between a protectionist Europe and an inward-looking America. As well as being economically disastrous, it would reduce Britain's influence and prestige, always crucial for Whitehall: Britain might lose at every table – powerless in Europe, fading in the Commonwealth, discounted in Washington.

In the mid-50s, France and Britain were on parallel courses. They wished to follow independent military policies. They had worldwide interests. Both wished to maintain an imperial role. In European matters, both opposed federalism. They were suspicious when in 1955 Holland and Belgium pressed for a committee, chaired by Spaak, to study further steps to European integration. The French representative on the Spaak committee assured his British colleague that France would only accept further integration on one condition: 'that the United Kingdom was also taking part or in some way closely associated . . . if the United Kingdom seemed to disassociate itself . . . France would make no move'. The Paris embassy was sure the French parliament would take a similar stand. So the British representative withdrew from the committee, confident, as a foreign office official put it, that 'the dragging of French feet will stop the Six from forging ahead'.[20] Britain's strategy – to be 'associated' with Europe economically, while maintaining global connections – thus depended on French support. Imperial crises seemed to make that support more solid than ever.

Imperial Debacle, 1956

The war had left Britain and France with new reasons for wanting to maintain imperial roles. Both wished to bolster their status. Both needed colonial trade and resources. Both aimed to resist Communism. So both were willing to some extent to cooperate, even though both at times found the other's presence an exasperating nuisance. Yet their strategies were different. The Empire had been the pillar of Free France. De Gaulle had made Algiers his capital in 1943; colonial troops had helped liberate Paris; and France's damaged prestige made the retention of imperial power a keenly felt obligation. Britain, in contrast, was aware of the strategic and financial burdens of imperial defence. There were also long-standing ideological differences. The Republican tradition saw French imperialism as emancipation, freeing benighted peoples as 1789 had freed French peasants. This involved their accepting French values and culture. Abandonment of this 'civilizing mission' would be a defeat not only for France as a power, but for French ideas of progress. Their remedy for discontent was not decolonization, but a modernized imperial structure. The Brazzaville Conference, called by de Gaulle in 1944, had declared that 'the aims of the civilizing mission . . . exclude any idea of autonomy and any possibility of evolving outside the French empire'. Demands for independence were condemned as reactionary. British imperialism, even at its most missionary, had never been so ambitious. It had aimed to modernize, to maintain peace; to secure communications and trade; and to recruit when necessary collaborative local rulers. But it had rarely sought to supplant local cultures, or absorb territories and peoples into a Greater Britain. It had not seriously attempted to prevent self-government in settler colonies. So the idea of a freely associated Commonwealth as the natural culmination of empire was broadly accepted. On a cynical viewing, this offered a dignified way of abandoning empire when it became unprofitable, unpopular or impossible to maintain. Geography and practicality were also, of course, important. The size of India meant that the most diehard imperialist realized that it could not be held by force. This was not obviously the case with Indochina. For reasons of proximity, it was easier to imagine Algeria as part of France than Kenya as part of Britain. Consequently, especially under a Labour government, Britain was willing to accept a gradual process of decolonization. France, even under socialist governments, was not.

The first post-Liberation tussle between London and Paris was once again over Syria and Lebanon, while the war in Europe and Asia was still raging. De Gaulle accused the British in highly intemperate terms of trying to push the French out of an area where they claimed special privileges. The Levant was an unfortunate sign of things to come. French determination to regain authority in Indo-China and North Africa conflicted with the expectations of local nationalists that the defeat of 1940 had been the beginning of the end of French rule. It was no coincidence that the first major outbreak of violence in Algeria took place amid celebrations of VE Day, 8 May 1945. Although the British helped to re-establish the French empire in 1944–5 (for example, by shipping French forces to Syria and Indochina), they became increasingly opposed to what became full-scale colonial wars in both Indochina and Algeria. French determination – increasingly backed by the Americans – to keep on fighting in Indochina rather than negotiating a settlement seemed to London hopeless and destabilizing for the whole region, especially for economically precious Malaya, where the British were successfully defeating a Communist revolt thanks in part to the promise of independence. The final Indochina disaster, predicted by the British, came when a large French force was killed or captured at Dien Bien Phu in May 1954. This led to negotiations, in which the British prime minister, Anthony Eden, brokered a settlement at Geneva in July. Algeria was another matter. It was for the French what India, Ireland, Australia and Southern Rhodesia combined had been for the British: the jewel in their imperial crown; a source of bitter internal dissent; their largest colony of settlement; and the home of an insubordinate settler population. Moreover, it provided them with oil, gas and space for atomic weapons testing.

The Algerian revolt, which became more violent and more widespread from 1955 onwards, had serious consequences for Franco–British relations. The British thought the French too intransigent. Their conduct was damaging Western, especially British, relations with the Arab world, where Britain was trying to maintain hegemony by supporting client states – something the French resented and criticized. Eden, francophile though he was, exasperatedly declared that the French were 'our enemies in the Middle East', especially because of France's support for Israel, which the British regarded as destabilizing, and which risked involving Britain in a war against Israel in defence of its protégé Jordan. Britain refused to supply helicopters for use in Algeria, and would not allow its anti-insurgency specialist General Templer to give advice on what he had learned in Malaya. But the main impact of Algeria on Franco–British relations was that it led indirectly to the most dramatic event in the twilight of the two empires, the Suez crisis.

Colonel Gamal Abdel-Nasser, the popular Egyptian dictator, caused France and Britain to shelve their differences. His ambition was to destroy Western – which principally meant British – power in the Middle East. He was also encouraging the Algerian revolt against the French, by means of arms (some British-made), training and political support. In July 1956, he ordered the nationalization of the Suez Canal, run by an international company largely owned by the British and French. In addition to its practical consequences, this was a challenge to London and Paris, a calculated blow against their prestige in the Arab world. So France and Britain had a common enemy.

They also had prime ministers, the Conservative Anthony Eden and the socialist Guy Mollet, who for the first time in 100 years were fluent and willing speakers of each other's languages, and both wanted to strengthen their alliance. Mollet was a former English teacher from a traditionally anglophile Protestant background. Eden was a true and life-long francophile. He enjoyed French literature, and had a collection of paintings that included works by Corot, Monet, Degas, Cézanne and Braque. During the war, he had defended de Gaulle against the Americans and Churchill, and the recognition given to France after the war, including a permanent seat on the UN Security Council, owed more to him than to any other individual.[21] Eden admired his French colleagues, several of whom had Resistance backgrounds. Of Mollet, he said 'I have never enjoyed more completely loyal understanding with any man.'[22] Sadly, this increased the dangers: the usual cross-Channel suspicion might have inspired greater prudence.

Historical bugles blew in both capitals, as governments imagined themselves facing another Munich, with Nasser as Hitler – the first time that 'Munich' became a rhetorical standby. Though the stakes were high, both sides greatly exaggerated them. The French believed that the Algerian revolt, following the humiliating defeat in Indochina, threatened France's self-respect, status and internal stability, but that without Nasser's help and encouragement the revolt could be defeated. Otherwise, they assured the Americans, the whole of Africa would be lost to Communism.[23] The British believed that their dominance of the Middle East was at stake, and with it their supply of cheap oil paid for in sterling. Whitehall estimated that if oil had to be bought in dollars, it would cost the economy another $500–700 million annually, and cause economic collapse. British gold reserves would disappear, the sterling area would disintegrate, and they would be unable to pay for their armed forces – 'a country that cannot provide for its own defence is finished'.[24]

On 10 September 1956 Mollet came to London and revived the 1940 idea of a Franco-British Union, with France (and perhaps Belgium, Holland and Norway) joining the Commonwealth trading system. Eden was keen to respond, despite resistance in Whitehall. No other European states had ever twice considered voluntary political union. This demonstrated the desire of the French Left to maintain a special relationship with Britain. Few remember this approach, which at best is regarded as simply bizarre. But had the Suez adventure ended differently, at least a symbolic link might have been created between the two countries at a turning point in European history. France and Britain would necessarily have taken a common position over the Common Market negotiations that a few months later would materialize in the Treaty of Rome. In short, Britain's relationship with the Continent over the next half century was to be decided on the banks of the Seine – and the Nile.

While Whitehall wrung its collective hands over Egypt, the Quai d'Orsay came up with a bold plan: an invasion to remove Nasser. They offered to place their armed forces under British command. This was not a sign of confidence in superior British leadership – far from it – but a means to tie them into joint action. A problem for the British, though apparently not for the French, was that Nasser had the legal right to nationalize the canal. The Law Officers advised that 'we are on an extremely bad wicket'.[25] Fortunately, the Lord Chancellor thought of a way round the UN Charter. But there was a danger that Nasser might offer concessions. The French again had the answer: their Israeli friends would attack Egypt, and the Franco–British expedition could go in to keep the two sides apart and safeguard the canal – and replace Nasser with someone more amenable. Eden nervously sent two officials for a secret meeting with the French and Israelis in a private house outside Paris, and was distressed when they came back with an agreement on paper – he had wanted nothing written down. The intervention force gathered with painful slowness. Its commander, a New Zealander, worried that the French 'are doing a lot covertly' to help the Israelis. Eden warned Mollet – in what the French must surely have regarded as a prize example of English hypocrisy – that such acts would 'harm . . . our role as peacemakers'.[26] Throughout these transparent cloak-and-dagger preparations, the Americans warned repeatedly against the use of force. Eden assumed that they would acquiesce in a fait accompli.

In October 1956, Israeli forces crossed the border. The Egyptian air force was destroyed on the ground. On 5 November, the Allies reached Port Said. The Russians made threats, which were not taken very seriously. The Almighty Dollar was another matter. Sterling was being sold, and the Bank of England was losing its gold and dollar reserves. They were too small to cope. In October 1956, they stood at $2.24 billion. As $2 billion was regarded as the minimum, the Bank had a cushion of only $244 million, and $50 million was lost during the first two days of the Suez operation. Simple arithmetic showed that a sterling crisis – indeed a possible run on the currency, the collapse of the Sterling Area, and the ruin of Britain's commercial position – was only days away unless the Americans provided credit in dollars. It had been supposed that they would, as in the past. But genuinely angered at being both ignored and deceived, President Eisenhower said that 'he did not see much value in an unworthy and unreliable ally and that the necessity to support them might not be as great as they believed'.[27] To maintain and increase the viability of sterling, it had been made partly convertible into dollars as recently as February 1955. It was this that made

The Suez crisis led to petrol shortages in both France and Britain

Britain vulnerable to American pressure that France – whose currency was not convertible – could defy. The chancellor of the exchequer, Harold Macmillan, told the Cabinet that they faced an imminent sterling crisis. Washington's condition for a loan was an immediate ceasefire and a rapid withdrawal of Anglo-French forces. A British diplomat in Washington wrote, 'they seem determined to treat us as naughty boys who have got to be taught that they cannot go off and act on their own without asking Nanny's permission first'.[28] Eden telephoned Mollet at 4 p.m. on 6 November. In the same room happened to be his foreign minister Christian Pineau and the West German chancellor Konrad Adenauer. Eden told them that the British were frightened of a run on sterling, and that Eisenhower was insisting on a ceasefire within twelve hours. Mollet urged him to play for time, while the troops advanced. Eden answered that it was too late: he had already agreed without consulting the French. Pineau 'guessed Mollet's feelings . . . for a convinced partisan of the Franco–British alliance, abandonment in such conditions was a bitter blow'.[29] Adenauer commented that it would be wise to accept defeat: 'Europe,' he added 'will be your revenge.'

The Suez episode had proliferating consequences for Britain, France and their mutual relationship. For Britain, it threatened a general unravelling of an interconnected world outlook based on partnership with the United States, leadership of the Commonwealth, the international role of sterling, hegemony in the Middle East, and *entente* with France permitting influence in Europe. But America had been hostile. The Commonwealth had been divided and impotent. Sterling had been the Achilles heel. Hegemony in the Middle East crumbled, with the hostility of Egypt, a nationalist revolution in Iraq, and increasing regional instability. The alliance with France proved insufficient. Not least, the British political class, including the ruling Conservative party, had been divided over Suez: the will to maintain a world role at all costs was not there, as Eden's successor Harold Macmillan soon showed. The political climate was for rapid decolonization and a renunciation of pretensions to world power. Commonwealth relations were rebuilt, but their meaning had changed: they could no longer be considered an instrument of power; indeed, some would see them as a source of weakness.

The consequences for France were far greater: it was 'never the same again' after Suez.[30] Like Britain, it had to face the limits of its power. If Britain had been brought to heel by Eisenhower, a mere phone call from Eden had done the same to France. Once again, timorous Albion had let France down. It lost its remaining position in the Middle East, including cultural institutions built up over 150 years in Egypt, and which had formed the basis of a cultural affinity between the old Egyptian ruling class and France. But in contrast with British contrition, French reaction to the humiliation was unforgiving and determined. The month after Suez, plutonium was ordered for a French nuclear weapons programme. It was decided to win the Algerian war whatever the cost. Mollet decided to send conscripts, and eventually 400,000 French soldiers served there. Ruthless methods were adopted by an army no longer willing to allow politicians to accept defeat as they had done in Indochina and Suez. The eventual outcome was a military revolt and the return to power of General de Gaulle in May 1958 as the man to save Algeria and prevent civil war. But de Gaulle, like Eden's successor Macmillan, saw that imperialism was no longer worth the effort, and by 1962 he withdrew from Algeria. He would concentrate instead on transforming France and its relations with Europe and the world.

Suez required the British and the French to reassess their relations with each other, with America, and with Europe. London and Washington hastily patched up their rift. Though British anti-Americanism was for a time intense, there was a realization in Westminster that Eden had been reckless and the Americans arguably right. A British defence review in 1957 concluded that 'in a limited war in the Mediterranean or in the Far East the UK would only act in cooperation with the US'.[31] The French felt their exclusion from this rapprochement, and resentment of Anglo-Saxon separateness was naturally confirmed. A Foreign Office official said – fortunately not to a Frenchman – that Britain's alliance with France was like a frustrated suitor going to a whorehouse: 'The United States was the woman she loved and France the brothel.'[32] For the British, Suez proved that *only* America could be the buttress of their security, power and interests. For the

French, Suez proved that America could *never* be that buttress. This necessarily involved diverging interpretations of 'Europe'.

Both Britain and France needed Europe as an economic and political prop to their shrinking world power. Britain wanted a broad European-centred free-trading system. Mollet, taking up Adenauer's suggestion of a European 'revenge', resolved France's disagreements with Germany in the weeks after Suez, and now accepted a more supranational structure. So the Treaty of Rome was signed in March 1957 setting up a European Economic Community committed to 'ever closer union'. France could hope to lead it, compensating for the humiliation of Suez. The Suez debacle thus caused 'the two ancient nation-states [to go] their separate ways . . . there was no more talk of Anglo-French union. With much trepidation, France took its road into the Common Market without Britain.'[33]

European Revenge, 1958–79

I want her naked.
CHARLES DE GAULLE[34]

He talks of Europe and means France.
HAROLD MACMILLAN, November 1961[35]

It is often said that, under the shock of Suez, both Britain and France had to choose between a diminished but sensible role within an integrating Europe, or a vain attempt to cling to the vestiges of vanished power. Those who discern such a choice invariably see France as having taken the virtuous path. Yet the analysis is misleading in implying that for France a 'European' policy meant carpet-slippered retirement, as it did for Germany and Italy. For France 'Europe' was not a substitute for a global role, but a means of exercising it; not a means of sharing sovereignty, but of augmenting power. So Paris accelerated its nuclear arms programme, juggled European markets and funds to consolidate its neo-colonial influence in Africa (reminiscent of Ernest Bevin's earlier dreams), and amplified its voice in world affairs. Britain too saw involvement in Europe not as a renunciation, but as necessary to maintain its influence in Washington and the Commonwealth. This very similarity of ambition made rivalry inevitable. De Gaulle, thought Macmillan, only wanted one cock on the dunghill.

The years after Suez saw a fundamental shift in Franco–British relations: for the first time since the 1860s – perhaps since 1812 – France had the upper hand. This was to last for over thirty years. Before Suez, French governments would rarely contemplate a major step inside or outside Europe without British support, and the British took this for granted. Things unmistakably changed with the return of de Gaulle, through a combination of political self-confidence and relative economic performance. It drew on broader perceptions, within the political classes, the media and the public, of where the two countries were going. France could hardly have ended the 1950s in a worse crisis, amid the atrocities of the Algerian war, with military revolt and a settler uprising threatening a collapse of the State. De Gaulle returned to power in May 1958 in a polite coup d'état after twelve years in the political wilderness. He quelled the army and prepared to leave Algeria. This made him a target for assassination by partisans of 'French Algeria', but he survived to give the country firm if relatively unaccountable government. Britain, on the contrary, seemed to slide into decadence and accelerating decline, marked by political scandal, raucous mockery of its rulers, social unrest, and recurrent economic and financial crises on a scale unseen for more than a century. Though Macmillan won the 1959 elections with the slogan 'You've never had it so good', Britain soon became the 'sick man of Europe'. *La maladie anglaise* caused much head-shaking and some *Schadenfreude*. Both French strength and British weakness were perhaps exaggerated. But for a whole generation, pessimism reigned in Whitehall and Westminster. The waning of Britain's overseas power begun by the collapse of influence in the Middle East, accelerating economic decline, and the apparent unravelling of its social and cultural cohesion – all seemingly out of control – led to a panicky loss of self-confidence among the elites.

Economic performance was the bedrock of domestic politics and international power. The generation after 1945 saw a level of economic and social change in France – dubbed 'the Thirty Glorious Years' – that enabled it to surmount chronic domestic political conflicts and recover from bloody and humiliating colonial wars. France was transformed from a fragile and somewhat archaic economy with a large peasant sector and a flagging birthrate into an industrial power that by the 1960s compared in technique and productivity with the world's best. The Caravelle airliner (though with Rolls-Royce engines), the Renault Dauphine, Mirage fighters, the Tour Montparnasse and nuclear power symbolized a new France, strong as well as chic. The *bébé boom* suddenly increased the population at a rate unknown for over a century. These transformations were believed to owe much to state planning by the brainy technocrats of Jean Monnet's Commissariat-Général du Plan, to growing European economic integration, and to a change in collective mentality arising from the war – a rejection of old habits and a shared determination to change. This gave muscle to de Gaulle's revived international assertiveness. It put France ahead of Britain not only in wealth, but in perceived international influence. This provoked an upsurge in francophobia balanced by grudging admiration. For Britain did not experience economic transformation. It did not have a comparable agricultural sector to develop. But there were perhaps cultural and political reasons too. It is often observed that defeat was a necessary condition for an 'economic miracle' in the 1950s, and that France had been sufficiently defeated to make a break with the past. Britain, proud of its wartime achievements in economic and social as well as military domains, and thirsting to enjoy the rewards of victory, was not under such pressure to change: old industries, old methods, old markets and old attitudes survived, and for a time prospered. Only from the late 1950s, and especially from the late 1960s, did it seem that things were going wrong. But it was far from clear how, if at all, they could be put right.

Attempts had been made from the beginning to negotiate associate status with 'the Six'. No British government could be attracted by a protectionist Continental system that would curtail its trade with the Commonwealth and North America. The economic effects would have been devastating, and anyway it would have been politically impossible. British governments from 1945 persistently advocated worldwide reduction of trade barriers. This would have permitted trade with the Continent without closing off that with the rest of the world. The Treaty of Rome – with its tariff wall, protectionist agricultural policy, and goal of economic and monetary union – contradicted these aims, unless it could be modified or circumvented. Britain's answer was a Free Trade Area. Within this, the Six could pursue economic and political integration through their new Common Market, while permitting other European and Commonwealth countries to trade with them. This was not a vain or foolish idea: it would have been more favourable to Third World economic development and to long-term European growth.[36] The great obstacle was agriculture, which in all countries was subsidized, regulated and politically powerful. French (also Italian and Danish) farmers did not want to compete in European markets with Commonwealth imports. So the British suggested leaving agriculture out of their free trade system. But that removed the attraction for Continental farmers – free access to the British food market, Europe's largest importer. There were other political obstacles. Free trade was anathema to federalists, for it would undermine the regulatory and protectionist function that was the sinew of political integration. Nevertheless, the proposed Free Trade Area had a good chance of being accepted. It offered political and economic benefits, not least to German exporters, who wanted Britain in a European trading system. Ludwig Erhard, the powerful German finance minister and architect of the 'economic miracle', was a strong supporter of the Free Trade Area.[37] The British thought that Germany, and in particular Erhard, would have a decisive influence. Practical problems, it seemed, could be resolved by negotiation. Macmillan, the first foreign leader to visit de Gaulle in June 1958, tried to convince him that Britain's European plan was necessary for security in the face of the Soviet menace.

De Gaulle, however, feared that the British were trying to take over European leadership.[38] A free trade area would damage French agriculture. Above all, it would tend to loosen the economic and political influence France intended to exercise over Germany, always its principal policy objective. In November 1958, the negotiations – 'vain tractations'[39] – were abruptly stopped by de Gaulle, who feared they would succeed. This was the first and most damaging of his three vetoes. It confirmed France's cutting loose from Britain occasioned by the Suez crisis. De Gaulle had made sure that Chancellor Adenauer, who regarded the Paris–Bonn relationship as indispensable, would follow his lead, and Erhard was overruled.[40] This required political nerve in Paris, for it was based – like all Gaullist and post-Gaullist policy – not on confidence in French power, but on 'weakness and sometimes desperation'.[41] The French wanted to stem what they saw as their relative economic, political and military decline while there was time. De Gaulle, strongly anti-federalist, would probably have refused to sign the Treaty of Rome had he been in power at the time, but once in power he accepted it. French industry, and above all agriculture, needed a privileged European market, not a free-for-all with New Zealand butter and Canadian wheat. This was guaranteed just over three years after de Gaulle's veto, in 1962, when the Common Agricultural Policy (CAP) was signed. France's international priority was partnership with Germany within an integrated (though non-federal) European system – an alternative which in various forms it had flirted with since the 1920s, if not since the 1860s. For the moment, de Gaulle could treat Bonn with condescension, and even arrogance. But the French knew that they had only a limited time to enmesh Germany in a European net. Britain could not be allowed to fray the strands with proposals for a free trade area: *zone de libre-échange* became dirty words.

De Gaulle's veto led Britain to set up the European Free Trade Association in 1959, with Sweden, Denmark, Norway, Iceland, Finland, Switzerland, Austria, Ireland and Portugal. This worked efficiently, cheaply, and amicably – it has recently been proposed as a model for a decentralized and non-bureaucratic European union. Had it not been for the CAP, and French determination, EFTA and the EEC would probably have merged fairly quickly to form a wider free trade area, such as now exists between the EC and the remaining EFTA members, Switzerland, Norway and Iceland.[42] But EFTA was too small to provide the diplomatic clout craved by Whitehall. Besides, Washington disliked it as a distraction from their aim of an integrated Europe – a very important consideration for Macmillan. The Americans put heavy pressure on London to apply to accede to the Treaty of Rome. The government duly did. 'It is only full membership, with the possibility of controlling and dominating Europe,' wrote an optimistic official, 'that is really attractive.' Whitehall still assumed that it could make

'Europe' accommodate its non-European political and economic links, at least during a long transitional period. 'The question is,' wrote the foreign secretary Selwyn Lloyd, 'how to live with the Common Market economically and turn its political effects into channels harmless to us.'

The ambition to use Common Market membership to bolster Britain's influence in Washington and the Commonwealth as their 'bridge' to Europe remained central. Otherwise, thought the Foreign Office, 'at the best, we should remain a minor power in an alliance dominated by the United States, at the worst we should sit hopelessly in the middle while the two power blocs drifted gradually apart'. The Foreign Office was more interested in influence than in sovereignty, an issue that the cabinet now considered for the first time. Some fears were expressed of 'the ghosts of Louis XIV and Napoleon'. The Lord Chancellor pointed out that the Treaty of Rome 'would go far beyond the most extensive delegation of powers . . . that we have ever experienced.' But Edward Heath, the minister leading negotiations, declared that only in specific commercial policies was sovereignty affected. Federalism was not in the treaty, he said, and anyway it would recede once Britain joined. 'We could certainly make it clear in parliament and elsewhere that we had no intention of agreeing to a federation.'[43] It suited most of those involved to deny or play down the dynamic nature of the treaty's commitment to ever closer union, to dismiss it as quaint foreign rhetoric, or to assume that once inside Britain could prevent it. This is a wonderful example of the ingrained British tendency, complained of by the French at least since Napoleon, to ignore what agreements actually said in favour of what British common sense assumed they ought to mean. As Alan Milward puts it, there was a general agreement in Britain to accept something that was not on offer,[44] and particularly not on offer from de Gaulle. Concluded one historically minded official, 'Let us hope that Pitt will have the last word: we will save England by our exertions and Europe by our example.'[45]

De Gaulle understood the British position perfectly: it was, after all, similar to his own – to use Europe as a pedestal for national power. In sinking the Free Trade Area, he had blocked the persistent British ambition to combine 'European' and global connections. The long transitional period the British wanted for entry, de Gaulle suspected, was another stratagem with the same purpose, and would wreck the pristine Community. Often recalling Churchill's declaration that Britain would always choose 'the open sea' over Europe, he wanted to force Britain to make the choice: Europe *or*, not Europe *and*.[46] This is a choice the British – like the French themselves – have obstinately resisted. Macmillan tried to change de Gaulle's mind by offering to help him acquire nuclear weapons, and to persuade Washington to allow France at least nominal partnership with the Anglo-Saxons in running NATO. But this would have restored France to its previous role as

AFTER THE BALL WAS OVER ...

Macmillan's attempts to woo de Gaulle encountered little *entente* and less cordiality.

Britain's junior partner in an alliance dominated by the 'Anglo–Saxons' (a term that de Gaulle made current in French political vocabulary). This might have tempted de Gaulle's predecessors. It was anathema to de Gaulle, even if – which is doubtful – he thought that Britain could deliver.[47]

Meetings took place at the presidential chateau at Rambouillet and at Macmillan's house at Birch Grove in Sussex. These were picturesque occasions. The Macmillans' cook refused to find room in her fridge for de Gaulle's blood (for transfusion in case of another assassination attempt): 'It's full of haddock.' Many pheasants were shot by Macmillan in spite of police dogs disturbing the coverts. At Rambouillet, things were much grander, with beaters and loaders in uniform, which reminded Macmillan of Edwardian England – except that he was charged for his cartridges. De Gaulle limited his participation to standing by and commenting when his guest missed. But despite the slight personal thaw, the political climate remained frozen. Macmillan found that de Gaulle 'does not apparently listen to argument . . . He merely repeats over and over again what he has said before . . . based on intuition, not ratiocination.' De Gaulle told his ministers that he had offered 'the poor man' no encouragement: he had felt like quoting Edith Piaf's song: 'Ne pleurez pas, milord!'[48]

Between 1961 and 1963, British negotiations to enter the Common Market ground laboriously on. At some meetings the French foreign minister Maurice Couve de Murville ostentatiously occupied himself by reading, entering the discussion only to refuse every British amendment. After one late-night session, the Luxembourg foreign minister collapsed from exhaustion. Heath reported that 'The French are opposing us by every means, fair and foul. They are absolutely ruthless. For some reason they terrify the Six – by their intellectual superiority, spiritual arrogance, and shameful disregard of truth and honour.'[49] The perennial problems were Commonwealth imports, notably Indian textiles and Australasian food. Diplomats, led by the indefatigable Heath, employed endless ingenuity to square circles concerning sugar, bananas, lamb and tinned pineapple. The British found the Continentals more protectionist and 'parochial' than they had hoped – 'shrinking into Europe', as Alan Milward puts it – and indifferent to the needs of the rest of the world, to which Britain was necessarily more sensitive. Yet British ministers and officials, haunted by fear of decline and isolation, saw no alternative to jettisoning most of their Commonwealth links and becoming 'as parochial as the European Community'.[50] Their fear was put into blunt words in December 1962 by the former American secretary of state Dean Acheson ('a conceited ass' – Macmillan):

> Great Britain has lost an empire, and has not yet found a role. The
> attempt to play a separate power role . . . apart from Europe . . .
> based on a 'Special Relationship' with the United States [or] being
> head of a 'Commonwealth' which has no . . . unity or strength . . .
> this role is about played out.

Commonwealth trade fell sharply as businesses and governments prepared for British concessions to the Six. The danger for the French was that the negotiations might therefore succeed – though it is possible that even if they had the British government would have split and Parliament and public opinion would have found the terms unacceptable. De Gaulle spared the British that painful dilemma.

His famous televised press conference on 14 January 1963 – the first anniversary of his success in securing the Common Agricultural Policy – took everyone by surprise, including his own ministers. He was a master of the regal style, a philosopher-king disposing of respectfully prearranged questions before a large invited audience in the gilded salons of the Elysée. When the subject of Britain and Europe came up, he delivered his grand judgement:

> England is an island, sea-going, bound up, by its trade, its markets,
> its food supplies, with the most varied and often the most distant

countries . . . The entry of Great Britain first, and then of those other states will completely change the whole set of established adjustments, agreements, compensations and rules . . . We would have to think of building another Common Market [with] all the problems of economic relationships with a host of other countries . . . The cohesion of all these very numerous, very diverse members would not last long, and in the end there would emerge a colossal Atlantic community under American dependence and direction . . . This is not at all the truly European construction that France has wanted and still wants. It is possible that one day England will manage to transform herself sufficiently to take part in the European Community, without restriction or reservation and in preference to anything else, and in that case . . . France will raise no obstacle.[51]

This admirably trenchant statement – underlined a fortnight later by the Elysée Treaty between France and Germany – summarizes what de Gaulle really thought. He had already told Macmillan so privately in November 1961, when he had said that Britain's 'great escort' of global connections would disrupt the complicated arrangements negotiated with such difficulty between the six neighbours. The British had been told that though the Gaullists regarded Monnet's supranational ideas as 'wholly impracticable and very dangerous', they equally rejected a 'Western worldwide free trade area' or anything that diluted the vision of a white, Christian, non-American 'European Europe'.[52] Though Macmillan had assured him that Britain was ready to jettison the Commonwealth, embrace the CAP, and cooperate over European nuclear defence, de Gaulle did not believe that nations – 'incomparable, inalterable' – could so easily change their spots. Eight hundred years of European history, he reflected, revolved round Britain's struggles with the Continent. He expressed doubts to Macmillan that Britain would really agree to 'shut itself up' in Europe at such cost to its wider interests.[53] Some inter preters have emphasized his undoubted detestation of American hegemony, for which Britain acted as a 'trojan horse' – Macmillan and President Kennedy talked this over and agreed that de Gaulle had 'gone crazy', which rather confirmed his point.[54] The 'special relationship' had recently been prolonged by the Nassau agreement to sell Polaris missiles to Britain – Britain, declared de Gaulle, had 'sold its birthright for a mess of polaris'.[55] Britain's hankering after global trade threatened the Common Agricultural Policy, so important to France economically and to the Gaullists electorally. All these considerations were 'inextricably mixed'[56] for a man who combined romantic ideas of national destinies with a shrewd grasp of present political realities.

In any case, his analysis stands as the historic definition of the matters at stake, which have remained the fundamental issue of European politics ever since – in Brussels jargon, 'deepening' versus 'widening'. He realized that the British wanted 'a Europe without boundaries', which he saw as 'an American Europe', which would 'lose its soul'.[57] He doubtless also enjoyed avenging ancient and modern slights by the 'Anglo-Saxons', of which he was bitterly mindful in private. Occasionally he let it show. When Paul Reynaud, the prime minister of 1940, criticized him for isolating France and 'flouting the Entente Cordiale', he replied with a scribbled note 'to be forwarded to Agincourt or Waterloo'. Macmillan thought that 'if Hitler had danced in London we'd have had no trouble with de Gaulle' – a perception that was rather confirmed by some of the general's own pronouncements.[58] But his deepest reason for excluding Britain – apart from an instinctive presumption of Anglo-French rivalry – was his pessimistic belief that the traditional, enclosed, francocentric Europe he and other idealists envisioned would be shattered by an irruption of Anglo-Saxon disorder. 'We are the last Europeans of the Europe that was Christendom . . . It is no longer a question of whether France will make Europe, but rather of understanding that France may die if Europe dies.'[59]

Like Groucho Marx, the British placed ever more value on the club that blackballed them. Harold Wilson, Labour prime minister from 1964, began by expressing no interest in what was now called the European Economic Community (EEC), and his party was committed to developing Commonwealth links. But within two years, he was contemplating a new application, as long as it could be 'the right sort of Europe . . . outward looking and not autarkic' – in other words, not damaging to Commonwealth trade and not anti-American.[60] Wilson's motivation, like that of Macmillan, was essentially diplomatic. The Foreign Office tirelessly reiterated the dangers of isolation and loss of influence. Financial constraints undermined military commitments 'east of Suez', seeming to leave Europe as the only forum for Britain to play an international role, and thus justify its privileged position in Washington. Indeed, Wilson told the American President Johnson that Britain could not afford both an 'east of Suez' role and membership of the EEC, given that both would be expensive. Wilson hoped that Britain would be able to act as the bridge between Europe, America and indeed the Commonwealth and the United Nations. Otherwise, de Gaulle, with the Germans in tow, seemed capable of wrecking the Atlantic alliance and leaving soft, rich Europe open to Soviet penetration. Some ministers, especially those on the right of the Labour Party such as Douglas Jay, worried about loss of sovereignty. The orthodox response was that in practice problems would not arise, and that any notional loss of sovereignty would be outweighed by gains in that intangible essence, 'influence'. In bizarre contrast with these grandiose visions of a renewed global role was the depressing spectacle of chronic economic and financial weakness. The failure of successive economic planning policies made the EEC seem a necessary crutch for the sick man of Europe, too feeble and incompetent to manage its own domestic affairs. Wilson mused that Britain was like a faded beauty, and Europe a go-ahead young man with good prospects. If not a love match, it could be Britain's last chance for a comfortable settlement. But could it afford the dowry?

Britain had long been ready to join 'the right sort of Europe'. But what about the wrong sort of Europe – that is, the 'Europe' that actually existed, vigilantly guarded by Charles de Gaulle? Like their predecessors and successors, Wilson and his colleagues convinced themselves that once inside they would steer Europe in a British direction: 'if we can't dominate that lot,' said Wilson, 'there's not much to be said for us.' De Gaulle, oddly enough, tended to agree, suspecting the smaller states of being potential British satellites. But he need not have worried: the British had no ideas, little real confidence, and no plan to wrest control from the French. Their hope was to form a dominating partnership with Paris once de Gaulle had gone – a departure devoutly wished.

Meanwhile, they were willing to sweeten the future *entente* with joint projects for the aircraft Concorde, Jaguar and Airbus. The French were eager to take up these offers and learn from British expertise – de Gaulle was annoyed that France could not make successful jet engines. But he had no intention of making concessions over Europe, or indeed over NATO or competing interests in Africa. In October 1966, Wilson made a new application without specifying prior conditions, to make it more embarrassing for de Gaulle to veto. If he did veto none the less, the application would be left on the table until he left office – 'returning the ball . . . into the General's twenty-five' – for it was plain that de Gaulle himself was the only insurmountable obstacle to British accession.

Wilson cherished some hope of winning de Gaulle over, and was encouraged by his private secretary Michael Palliser, an extremely europhile Foreign Office man who happened to be the son-in-law of the European 'founding father' Paul-Henri Spaak. Palliser's plan was to 'appeal to [de Gaulle's] sense of history and his monumental vanity. He has no doubt that he is the greatest Frenchman since Napoleon . . . To be fair, he is probably right, and wants to go down in history accordingly.' Wilson's argument was that only within a Europe including Britain could France be truly great. However, de Gaulle easily outmatched the British in disdain. He said he would 'perhaps receive' Wilson but not 'converse' with him: 'he's light-headed, banging about like a bug in a drum'.[61] He conceded to Wilson that he was inclined to believe that Britain did now *aspire* to 'become a European country.'[62] But it had not happened yet.

De Gaulle was in a difficult position, as George Brown, the foreign secretary, marshalled support for Britain's entry among the other Five. At first Paris tried to persuade the British to drop their application. As they persisted, de Gaulle used their economic weakness to justify another veto at a press conference on 16 May 1967. The Foreign Office thought he used language of 'quite exceptional bitterness, hostility and scorn'.[63] Britain, he said, was economically incapable of bearing the obligations of membership, and its premature desire for accession was driven by desperation – 'her national personality [was] now at stake'. British entry would disrupt the Community. His other objection was familiar: Britain wanted a mere free trade area that would undermine the Community. The British consoled themselves that France's relations with the Five had been damaged, and believed that time was on their side.

On this point they were right, as de Gaulle seems to have realized. He even told Wilson that he feared that a 'European Europe' might one day be submerged by an Atlantic community – an admission of pessimism that encouraged the British.[64] At virtually every European Council meeting 'relentless' pressure was put on the French. Yet only after the students of Nanterre and the Sorbonne had dented the general's majestic prestige in the riots of May 1968 and hastened his retirement was the drawbridge to British membership of the EEC lowered, and the principle of progressive enlargement decisively endorsed. The British, now under Edward Heath's Conservative government, seized their opportunity with undisguised avidity. Belief that membership at any price was the only cure for Britain's diplomatic, economic and political ills was now the orthodoxy in most official circles: Britain was 'the sinking *Titanic*', and 'Europe' the lifeboat.[65] Ironically, the lifeboat was soon to spring a leak itself.

Heath had made his reputation as the dogged negotiator of the first application. To succeed now would ensure his place in history. Sir Roy Denman, an adviser to both Wilson and Heath, has argued that Wilson and the Labour party would not have pushed through the negotiations, and that Heath took what might have been Britain's last opportunity to join.[66] Heath assured President Georges Pompidou that Britain was ready to 'give priority to [Europe] over their other interests in the world'. Sir Con O'Neill, former ambassador to Brussels, was appointed the chief official negotiator, and the main strategist of Britain's entry. His views were plain: the EEC was about power. 'None of its policies was essential to us; many of them were objectionable.' But outside, Britain would decline into 'a greater Sweden'[67] – something Whitehall regarded as a fate worse than death. O'Neill sympathized with the view expressed by the ultra-europhile Tory backbencher Sir Anthony Meyer: 'it would be in the interests of this country to join the EEC whatever the terms'. Though the terms were tough – 'we would of course have had a much easier passage but for the French' – the British team managed, in O'Neill's words, to 'swallow the lot'. They accepted a Common Fisheries Policy, making all coastal fishing waters a common resource – a *fait accompli* hastily arranged by the existing members. (Norway refused it and stayed out.) They agreed to a disproportionate financial contribution through the CAP as the price of concessions over New Zealand food imports. But O'Neill felt 'rather complacent' about Britain's future ability to influence the Community: the fisheries policy would be moderated, he thought, and the costs of the CAP 'would tend to diminish'.[68] Britain (with Ireland and Denmark) formally entered the EEC on 1 January 1973. When Labour returned to power in 1974, they announced the intention of renegotiating a settlement they condemned as unfavourable, and putting the result to a referendum. Their renegotiation had no significant outcome, but it was represented as a victory. The referendum voted to stay in by 67 per cent of those voting, but only 40 per cent of the electorate as a whole.

This hardly demonstrated popular rapture: Britain had been constrained by fear of isolation and economic decline to join a French-dominated Community structurally unfavourable to its economic interests. Its rulers' principal motive had been to bolster diplomatic influence; but for public consumption economic benefits were stressed. Politicians and diplomats concealed – perhaps from themselves – the commitments to further integration clearly spelt out in the treaties, dismissed as mere rhetoric. Their outlook combined a highly pessimistic reading of Britain's economic and social condition with a strangely optimistic belief in their own ability to lead their new partners. Their motives were sincere and patriotic. But it was the despairing patriotism of an elite that had lost confidence in its country, had little faith in its ability to arrest its decline, and could only see salvation as climbing into someone else's 'lifeboat'. The ambivalence of the process stored up political trouble for the future.

Moreover, the sea suddenly grew stormy. Beginning in 1973, Middle East oil crises added to Britain's woes, and also ended both France's 'thirty glorious years' and West Germany's 'economic miracle'. Thus ended the halcyon period of post-war European growth and integration, based on a unique combination of post-war reconstruction and economic modernization. The CAP greatly raised food prices in Britain. The introduction of VAT further raised consumer prices. In the words of a recent American historian, this amounted to 'the maximum adverse impact on every single citizen of the United Kingdom'.[69] Attempts to control the situation were at best ineffective, and at worst damaging, as governments tried feebly to imitate French economic planning and German corporatism, but without the concentrated power of the Fifth Republic or the 'social partnership' of Germany. Heath, Wilson and James Callaghan were defeated in turn by a deadly combination of economic stagnation and inflation, which reached levels rarely seen in a developed county. The cost of public borrowing rose faster in 1974 than in 1797, when Pitt was forced to abandon gold. Efforts to restrain state spending and limit wage inflation led to strikes and public disorder unknown since the 1920s, or even the 1830s. Britain was in no position to attempt its vaunted leadership of Europe. The Franco-German relationship, begun by de Gaulle and Adenauer, was consolidated by Valéry Giscard d'Estaing and Helmut Schmidt, who barely concealed their contempt for Anglo-Saxon failures. The ambassador in Paris, Sir Nicholas Henderson, noted that Giscard considered that 'the age-long competitive struggle between France and the UK was over for good, with France the victor'. Henderson seems to have agreed, reporting mournfully in a dispatch that was leaked to the press in June 1979, that 'our decline in relation to our European partners has been so marked that today we are not only no longer a world power, but we are not in the first rank even as a European one'.[70]

HIGHER, FASTER, DEARER: THE CONCORDE COMPLEX

Plans for a supersonic airliner began separately in Britain and France in the 1950s.[71] The pace was set by Britain. The motives were political as much as commercial: to foster world-class technology and lubricate entry into the Common Market. The French were less enthusiastic, but allowed themselves to be wooed. In November 1962 a treaty was signed. A highly complex joint administration was created, which needed repeated reorganization as French and British manufacturers began learning to work together. Macmillan had insisted on a non-cancellation clause to stop the French backing out: it was to work the other way, preventing Labour from cancelling the project in the late 1960s and 70s as costs exploded. Anthony Wedgwood Benn, the boyishly enthusiastic minister for technology, stressed its importance for jobs. He also settled a long dispute over the name: Concord or Concorde, the latter supposedly insisted on by de Gaulle himself. Benn accepted the E, he said, for Excellence, Europe and Entente Cordiale – though it seemed to concede French claims that the aircraft was predominantly theirs. When the United States dropped its plans for a supersonic airliner, the project, employing 30,000 people, seemed vindicated. A Russian rival, rumoured to have been copied from stolen plans, crashed at a Paris air show. In May 1971, President Pompidou made an inaugural flight in Concorde 001, while the Queen flew to Toulouse in 002. But the loud supersonic boom caused the United States to ban overland flights in 1973: American airlines cancelled their orders, and the rest of the world followed. The simultaneous leap in world oil prices, as well as straining both countries' budgets, made Concorde ever more expensive to fly. After much debate, the two governments agreed to persevere: prestige was at stake. But only sixteen aircraft were ever built – one tenth of original expectations. The taxpayers met the development and production costs, so that British Airways and Air France could afford them. Concorde was a remarkable technical success, and won much affection, even among those who could not afford its fares, as a patriotic symbol and an elegant piece of flying sculpture.

There was a pattern here, repeated in other joint projects over the last half-century: the political and diplomatic motivation, the complexity of control, the difficulty of backing out, the importance of prestige, and the consolation that someone else was paying part of the bill.

Satisfactions of Grandeur and Pleasures of Decline

France cannot be France without grandeur.
CHARLES DE GAULLE

Sexual intercourse began
In nineteen sixty-three
Between the end of the Chatterley ban
And the Beatles' first L.P.
PHILIP LARKIN, 'Annus mirabilis' (1974)

On 21 December 1958, General de Gaulle was elected first president of the new Fifth Republic, a system designed in his image. In February 1960, France exploded its first atom bomb in the Sahara. That same year, for the first time for several centuries, French GDP per head overtook that of Britain. De Gaulle set out to make France again a great power and the leader of Europe. He intended to stand up to the 'Anglo-Saxons', insist on equality of status, and act as a spokesman for non-aligned nations. All this was possible because of de Gaulle's prestige, both as a war leader and – because the former had not been enough to allow him to get his way in 1946 – as the saviour of France from disaster. The Fifth Republic was intended to lead, rather than follow, the whims of a turbulent people de Gaulle regarded with affectionate contempt. He was a republican and a democrat – his admirers say fundamentally and sincerely so. But it was a different kind of democracy from that which he had criticized and blamed for French weakness between the wars and since 1945. The Third and Fourth republics had been parliamentary systems, with governments accountable to Parliament and frequently overturned. De Gaulle's system was, as the main draughtsman of its constitution put it, a 'republican monarchy'.[72] The parties and Parliament had their powers curtailed. Economic modernization was pushed ahead, with state assistance and direction, and non-political experts were appointed to high office. Directly accountable to the people, not Parliament, and with a long term of office, the president would reign and rule. Though much criticized at first (François Mitterrand called it a 'permanent coup d'état') and never wholly popular during de Gaulle's tenure of power, the system did win a broad measure of acceptance, which became all the firmer once de Gaulle himself had left office.

Without these political changes, and an underpinning of economic dynamism, it is unthinkable that de Gaulle could have played such a powerful role in Europe and outside. This, if with less panache, has been the policy of his successors ever since: power in and through Europe based on partnership with Germany; a patriotic emphasis on France's special role in the world, especially in its former colonies; independent military power; and vocal opposition to 'Anglo-Saxon' domination. It is a heritage that no subsequent leader can disavow. Given the previous forty years of history – of political division, economic fragility, and unstable leadership – this was an incredible renaissance for France. The country most put in the shade was Britain, its future seemingly at the disposal of the French president. Britain, it seemed, was in irreversible decline and was becoming ungovernable.

Decline could be fun, however, and grandeur rather burdensome. The post-war years – and especially the 1960s and 70s, when the 'baby-boom' generation reached puberty – saw profound cultural changes throughout the Western world, associated with increased incomes, educational opportunities and leisure. In Britain, which had previously been unusually stable, unusually secure, and perhaps unusually deferential, these changes were felt with particular acuteness. Conscription was abolished in 1960, while universities multiplied. The humiliations and failures of the ruling elite were liberating for their subjects. The traditional British taste for parody and the absurd was politicized, and 'satire' became a characteristic form of expression in television, radio and newspapers. Taboos were gleefully broken. The failed prosecution of Penguin Books in 1960 for publishing D.H. Lawrence's 1928 novel *Lady Chatterley's Lover*, and the Profumo scandal in 1963 (when the Tory minister of war had to resign following involvement with a prostitute), made authority seem both hypocritical and absurd – and media coverage provided children with an early form of sex education. Theatre censorship was abolished in 1969. The rusting away of old industries and the patriarchal working-class communities they had created caused searing hardship and long-term demoralization, but also pushed a new generation into other ways of living.

It is no coincidence that London replaced Paris as the cultural centre of Europe, and England became, for the first time for nearly two centuries, the epitome of cultural modernity. If decline meant liberation, Gaullist grandeur meant state power in the media and patronage in the arts culminating in a 'culture state' that combined conformity, bureaucratic control and a touch of nepotism. Certain areas of French cultural life, combining impressive intellectualism with fashionable chic, enjoyed international prestige, not least among British intellectuals. The experimental French cinema was the universal reference. Philosophical plays and novels, the Annales school of history, and reinterpretations of German philosophy applied to literature and the humanities attained unparalleled influence in anglophone university departments. But in mass youth culture, especially that associated with music, clothes and morals, London and Liverpool – that exotic imagined city – had a global impact, in comparison with a Paris where fashion and entertainment were elegantly middle-aged and middle-class. This is too well known to need elaboration. Of interest from our perspective are changing French perceptions of Britain. If the bowler hat, the crown, the kilt and the teacup (and, according to the humorist Pierre Daninos, the cat o'nine tails and the schoolgirl in black stockings) represented Britishness in French imaginations, they were now joined by long hair, miniskirts, 'yé yé', films, television programmes, fashion designers and, later, by skinheads, punks, football hooligans and rap artists.

There was, however, commercial and intellectual resistance at first. In the early 1960s, France had its own highly popular Americanized entertainers, such as Johnny Hallyday (né Jean-Philippe Smet) and Eddie Mitchell. The Beatles, already world-famous, were little noticed on their first French tour in 1964, almost ignored by state television, and dismissed by *France-Soir* as 'outdated'. When in 1965–6, the Rolling Stones and the Beatles nevertheless began to arouse youthful emotions in France, critics deplored the phenomenon as unhealthy commercial exploitation. But for the first time, masses of French adolescents began to flock across the Channel. Brigitte Bardot sang that 'le diable est anglais' and lived in Carnaby Street. In theatre, television and cinema too, the mid-60s saw an influx of British works, from Shakespeare to James Bond.[73]

If, as Larkin declared, sexual intercourse in Britain began in 1963, this was soon discovered by the French. It was an unexpected find. British sexual incompetence was, and is, an ingrained belief among the French, a foil to their own self-proclaimed virtuosity. Pierre Daninos's best-seller, *Les Carnets du Major Thompson* (1954) joked that 'if Englishmen had found a way to make babies without involving women, they would be the happiest people on earth . . . Frenchmen are the gastronomes of love; Englishmen merely do it.'[74] But 'merely doing it' was not to be despised by adolescents in a France that was (and to some degree still is) a relatively controlled, conventional and domesticated society. The student revolt of May 1968 started at Nanterre university, legend has it, when a request that boys and girls should be allowed in each others' rooms was rebuffed by the education minister with the injunction to 'cool off' in the new swimming-pool. The realization that girls from non-Catholic and non-'Latin' societies might actually be accessible was intoxicating. English girls had long had a reputation for being independent and eccentric, but the 'Swinging Sixties' images of miniskirts, flowers and free love added a new dimension. French boys hoped that their national reputation for charm and romance would pay dividends where girls were easy and condoms were available from vending machines.[75] The highly popular 1975 film *A nous, les petites Anglaises* – 'Come here, English girls' – gave expression to these fantasies and added a phrase to the language. The film was the story of two French schoolboys sent to England to learn the language, but whose main occupation was what the title suggested.

JE T'AIME, MOI NON PLUS

The most notorious Franco-British cultural product of the 1960s was the record 'Je t'aime, moi non plus', a duet whose whispered endearments and ecstatic sighs thrilled and shocked both countries, just when 'May '68' had made Paris the co-capital of the youth revolution. Boosted by being banned by the BBC, forbidden by French radio before 11 pm, and denounced by the Vatican, it reached Number 2 in the British pop charts in 1969 before being withdrawn. The female part had originally been recorded in Paris by Brigitte Bardot, the global symbol of French sensuality, but her entourage vetoed it as too sexy. Her replacement for a new recording at London's Marble Arch studio was a young English actress, Jane Birkin, who would go on to marry her co-artist, Serge Gainsbourg, the writer of the song. There could hardly be a greater contrast with the pouting, pneumatic Bardot. Birkin was the gawky, slightly toothy Home Counties daughter of a naval officer, with an angelic face, a strong English accent ('je t'ayme, oh wee') and a choirboy voice – just what the French thought *les petites Anglaises* should be. Her cherubic vocalizing gave the record more than a hint of perversity – for the French knew that if the British were not much good at straight sex, kinkiness was their forté. Gainsbourg seemed the quintessence of Left Bank Frenchness, cynical, moody, intellectual, drunken and reeking of Gauloises. After his death, he was compared with other outragers of tradition, Rabelais, Baudelaire and Rimbaud. Yet he had a hidden side – no less typically 'French' – that was shy, conventional and even prudish. Like General de Gaulle, he would never be seen naked. Unlike the general, he was an anglophile, much impressed by 'Swinging London'. His stage name showed his admiration for the painter Gainsborough. He preferred working in London, bought his clothes in the

In one form at least cross-Channel relations blossomed: Gainsbourg and Birkin looking sultry.

King's Road, and wrote songs that included scraps of English or Franglais. There was more to this than merely latching on to the fashion for English pop. 'He loved Tommy Cooper, Morecambe and Wise . . . and London taxis,' recalled Birkin. 'It would have meant so much to him if a major British artist – like his idols the Stones – had covered just one of his songs. But it never happened.' She, however, had a successful film and stage career epitomizing the English *ingénue*, for which she was awarded the OBE in 2001. She reflected that 'If I'd stayed in England I'd have ended up just being someone's wife, and I often think how nice it would be to have a cottage in Kent and someone to pour me a glass of sherry in the evening. But I think the life we have reflects who we are, and that just wasn't for me.'[76]

As in the eighteenth and nineteenth centuries, there are careers to be made in representing one nation to the other in a way that confirms their expectations. Birkin, like the English roses Charlotte Rampling and more recently Kristin Scott-Thomas, did so in straight acting. More conscious self-caricatures (following in the footsteps of Maurice Chevalier, who worried he was losing his French accent) were Sacha Diestel, more recently Antoine de Caunes, and even footballers such as Eric Cantona. It is intriguing that

British cultural icons in France have all been women, and their French counterparts in Britain all men.

If British women were less commonly imagined now as frumpish prudes, British men – despite Mick Jagger and James Bond – did not enhance their reputation in all quarters. France's first woman prime minister (in 1991), Edith Cresson – an upper-class Protestant who spoke excellent English, thanks to her nanny – was so cross at not being ogled in the streets of London ('all girls notice it') that she complained that 'the Anglo-Saxons are not interested in women as women . . . It is a problem of upbringing and I consider it a sort of disease.' She later explained that she knew this because her brothers had been to public schools – an experience 'from which it is difficult to recover'.[77]

CHAPTER 14

Ever Closer Disunion

Since the 1970s, France and Britain have grown to resemble each other more than any other two large states. For the first time, their wealth, populations, military power and external influence reached almost identical levels. International comparisons and league-tables showed astonishing similarities. Never before had so many French and British people visited, worked in or lived in each other's country, appraised each other's qualities, or understood so much of each other's languages. The French even managed to laugh at British humour. Their leaders often proclaimed the existence of, or at least the aspiration to, a special relationship. But – and how many 'buts' there are! – politicians, commentators and ordinary citizens espoused conflicting views about politics, society and economic life. Rarely since the first Napoleon had they embodied such clear differences, or tried to remake Europe in their own contrasting images.

A French or British Europe? Napoleon versus Adam Smith

It was clear to me from the start that there were two competing visions of Europe.
MARGARET THATCHER[1]

At one end of the range of concepts are those states that favour institutional or indeed political projects designed to ensure the qualitative leaps dear to the hearts of all staunch Europeans, including, I am bound to say, myself. At the other are all those who, whether out of realism or for ideological reasons hold to a purely libertarian vision of Europe.
JACQUES DELORS, 1986[2]

Twenty-two years ago, in Paris, I was a barman . . . There was a common pot, where they told me you had to put all the tips. After two months, I found out I was the only one doing it! That was my first lesson in applied socialism!
TONY BLAIR to the Assemblée Nationale, 24 March 1998

The European Community in which Britain was floundering in the 1970s was largely a French creation, its institutions and methods modelled on France. This was not due to some vision of the 'founding fathers', whose acts were largely pragmatic and only some of whom, notably Monnet and Schuman, were French. It was rather because of the tenacious pursuit of national objectives by generations of French politicians and officials. Germany, often expected to emerge as the real leader of Europe, did not do so, handicapped politically before 1989, economically since, and perhaps psychologically always. So 'Europe' could be made a lever for French ambitions: to control Germany and rival America; to serve France's dynamic, changing but vulnerable economy; and to protect the identity of a 'European Europe', in which French language and culture took pride of place.

As de Gaulle had warned, Britain could not help but be the serpent in this Eden. Its governments, irrespective of party, pressed for a comparatively liberal and Atlanticist view of Europe. They supported expansion of its membership – suspected by the French, rightly, to be a strategy to subvert the system. But British governments found it much harder to lead the Community than the optimists of the Macmillan and Wilson eras had expected. This was partly because of entrenched French opposition, which readily used 'European' rhetoric against Britain, but also because of Britain's economic weakness and and its leaders' lack of confidence and of clear ideas. British politicians, accused of nostalgia for lost glories and xenophobic anti-Europeanism, usually lost the rhetorical battles, even if they had some success in modifying the reality. European rhetoric was genuinely more congenial to French than British ears, for it could be presented as the fulfilment of France's national destiny as the European pioneer. French 'Europeanism' could be traced back to Victor Hugo in the mid nineteenth century (see above, page 355), to Napoleon's jackbooted integration, to the 'armed missionaries' of the revolution, and to the gentler 'republic of letters' of the Enlightenment. So, at least, French federalists liked to see it.[3]

The political, economic and psychological benefits that France obtained from leadership of Europe – and even more those it hoped to obtain – tended to calm fears about sovereignty and accountability in a country traditionally highly sensitive to such matters. Yet French governments – and citizens, when they were asked – have been suspicious of genuine federalism, which would take power away from them: as one French social scientist put it nicely, French politicians wanted 'a strong Europe with weak institutions'.[4] The 'empty chair' crisis in 1965–6, when de Gaulle boycotted Community business, halted supranationalist trends for twenty years. A hybrid structure of governance, one part embryonic federation, two parts association of states, was sealed by an agreement in Paris between Georges Pompidou and Edward Heath in 1971 to create a European Council. This body was as opaque and unaccountable as the Congress of Vienna, with methods that would have been familiar to Castlereagh and Talleyrand – the reason why politicians and diplomats liked it. It embodied control of the Community by its states – de Gaulle's 'Europe des patries' – not by federal institutions such as the Commission and the Parliament. On this point, Britain and France – and a large part of their peoples – agreed. President Valéry Giscard d'Estaing later stated that 'the entry of Great Britain made the federal idea, which had been dominant until then, impossible'. But that was not the crux of the problem. As Giscard put it, 'we have to choose between a structured system and an amorphous space [*un espace mou*]'.[5]

This choice was the heart of the Franco-British difference: should Europe evolve towards the British model of economic freedom with a minimum of central control (the 'amorphous space'), or the French model of an economically and socially regulated Europe (the 'structured system'). To speak of 'British' and 'French' models is of course a simplification, for the debate crosses national boundaries. But only a slight simplification. Britain and France most of the time advocated and practised different economic, social and diplomatic strategies, and their publics showed a high level of consensus concerning them. This difference from the beginning focused on the Common Agricultural Policy (CAP), which for decades demonstrated the contrast between French and British conceptions of Europe, of economics, of social policy, of relations with the outside world, and even of national identity. The British, long accustomed to a small agricultural sector and cheap imported food, dismissed the CAP as a patently unfair and expensive absurdity. The French saw it as the Community's great achievement, creating solidarity across national borders, and protecting against merciless commercial pressures a precious way of life that epitomized Frenchness. At stake were not merely rational economic advantages, but a tissue of customs, sentiments and beliefs that had ancient roots and could rouse feelings little amenable to argument or explanation.

From the 1980s onwards, Britain and France diverged dramatically. Margaret Thatcher on one hand, and François Mitterrand and Jacques Delors on the other, pursued bold, and utterly opposite, solutions to the economic stagnation that had persisted since the early 1970s. These ideologically driven governments broke from the relative consensus of the previous generation, and extended their efforts from the domestic to the European and international arenas. From then onwards, the existence of French and British 'models' for Europe became unmistakable.

Britain's road to Damascus came fairly soon after it joined the EEC. Financial crisis brought intervention by the International Monetary Fund and 'third-world treatment'. The prime minister, James Callaghan, admitted in 1976 that 'the cosy world we were told would go on for ever . . . is gone'.

An attempt to limit pay rises caused widespread public-sector strikes in the 'winter of discontent', 1978–9. This brought to power a Conservative government under Margaret Thatcher in May 1979, with the stated conviction – shared by a sufficient number of the public – that drastic and radically different action had to be taken to reverse economic decline. The economic liberalization she forced through – rejection of state interventionism; the curbing of trade unions; sharp disinflation; and privatization of state-owned industries – was bitterly divisive. Uncompetitive industries collapsed and unemployment doubled. In 1981, with Britain in crisis, France took the very opposite path. François Mitterrand was elected as the first socialist president of the Fifth Republic. As euphoric crowds waved red roses, he and his finance minister Jacques Delors began a crash programme of 'socialism in one country', reminiscent of the Popular Front in 1936. This was the last full-blooded left-wing economic experiment anywhere in the world. Dozens of banks and industries were nationalized, bringing a quarter of industrial workers into state employment. A thirty-nine hour week was decreed, and the minimum wage substantially raised.

The outcomes were as different as the measures. By 1982–3, inflation in Britain was falling and productivity rising. Though undetectable at the time, 1985 was the watershed: before then, the British economy performed consistently worse than those of France and Germany; afterwards, it performed consistently better than they did.[6] In France, the Mitterrand–Delors experiment caused surges in inflation and imports. Yet the economy remained sluggish and unemployment actually increased. The franc had to be devalued twice, and the IMF and the West German government threatened to withdraw support. Delors imposed austerity to control inflation. In 1983 France pegged its economic policy to that of Germany – the end of its economic autonomy, and a strong reason to try to 'Europeanize' Germany's financial power. Mitterrand and Delors concluded that they had failed because France had been too small. What was needed was action on a bigger, European scale, so that politicians could master economic forces: 'Only Europe,' declared Mitterrand, 'allows politics to restore its power.'[7]

Mitterrand's desire to assert politics over economics recalls a point already made: that the French have never been convinced by the ideas of Adam Smith (see above, page 65). Free trade has never been a popular political and moral crusade, as in nineteenth-century Britain. Significant French liberal economists over the last two centuries can easily be counted on the fingers. Right- and left-wing politicians have agreed in deploring 'untamed liberalism' and exalting a benign State as champion of the general good. Small businessmen and farmers, armed with votes as early as 1848, and willing to use the barricade as well as the ballot-box, have long practice in forcing politicians to pay heed to their wishes, which have usually included protection against 'unfair' competition. Politicians have been correspondingly aware of the electoral benefits of having favours to distribute. The economic role of the State grew in France as elsewhere between the 1930s and the 1990s, and indeed it grew more than in most countries. This greatly increased the political weight of beneficiaries of the public payroll (57 per cent of the population) and many more who shared in a complex system of rights and privileges in employment and benefits.[8] A uniquely homogenous elite, with at its apex the *énarques* (graduates of 'ENA', the Ecole Nationale d'Administration, founded in 1945, smaller than the smallest Oxbridge college) dominated politics, the civil service and business. By 1997, ENA had produced two of the three previous presidents, six of the eight previous prime ministers, and the leaders of the three main political parties.[9] All this added up to a durable cross-party consensus in favour of economic and social protection, state intervention, mandarin values, and 'Europe' – what is often called *la pensée unique*. Thatcherite liberalization challenged and affronted it, and made very few French converts.

FRANCE AND THE FALKLANDS WAR

We wanted to affirm our solidarity with Great Britain, which . . .
had been the victim of aggression against both its national interests
and its national pride.
FRANÇOIS MITTERRAND[10]

In so many ways Mitterrand and the French were our greatest allies.
JOHN NOTT, secretary of state for defence.[11]

Argentina invaded the Falkland Islands on 2 April 1982 – the first time those lonely territories had ignited a crisis since 1770 (see above, page 159). Mitterrand phoned Thatcher the following day to pledge support, overruling his foreign minister, Claude Cheysson, who wanted to side with Argentina on 'anti-colonialist' grounds. Mitterrand declared that 'we are the allies of the English, not of Argentina', and to do otherwise would be politically 'catastrophic'. Moreover, France had island colonies of its own. The trickiest complication was that France had sold arms to Argentina, including Mirage and Super-Étendard aircraft and a small number of Exocet anti-ship missiles, of which five were operational. These missiles were a serious threat to the British taskforce: one of them was to sink the destroyer *Sheffield*. The Argentinians had ordered fifty more Exocets, but the French halted shipments. They also found excuses to delay deliveries to Peru, in case they reached Argentina. The French did not withdraw technicians who were in Argentina putting weapons into service; but they gave the British complete technical information about Argentinian military capacities, including how to deal with Exocets. The French air force flew a Mirage and a Super-Étendard over to East Anglia so that RAF pilots could get to know their capacities. The latter were relieved to discover that in dogfights they were no match for Harriers.[12]

Politically, Mitterrand maintained a 'middle position', supporting Britain against aggression, but urging negotiations over the islands. This placed France closer to Britain than most European countries except Norway. In some ways they were more consistently supportive than the vacillating United States, though of course less so than most of the Commonwealth. Within the EC, the French supported economic sanctions against Argentina, against Irish and Italian opposition. But they could not resist taking advantage of British vulnerability to overrule them on the Community budget and the CAP – 'European solidarity ought not to be one way', said a French MEP. For the first time since de Gaulle had introduced a national veto into European deliberations, that of Britain was overriden.[13] In the UN, the French abstained (rather than voting with Britain) in a ceasefire resolution in June. Yet in the view of the historian Philip Bell, French assistance went further than self-interest; and for once the 'Atlantic triangle' of Britain, the USA and France worked.[14]

Thatcher was personally grateful to Mitterrand. The French, however, were aggrieved that the British did not repay the favour when the French secret services blew up a Greenpeace ship, *Rainbow Warrior*, in Auckland harbour in 1985 – 'They shouldn't have dragged us through the mud,' thought Cheysson.[15]

Mitterrand and Thatcher had a strange relationship. Mitterrand regarded her as a 'petty-bourgeois ideologue' and she thought his economic ideas 'barmy'. But he was a ladies' man, despite or because of a certain reptilian quality, and thought he could influence her by 'turning on the charm' with the elaborate courtesy the British consider typically French. His notorious remark (repeated in varying forms) that she had 'the eyes of Caligula/Stalin and the mouth/legs of Messalina/Marilyn Monroe' may have reflected genuine appreciation of the 'sole woman among all these men, the flower brightening their austere labours', as well as French imperviousness to political correctness.[16] She, in some ways a francophile in the usual British manner – she relished the lavish cuisine and collected the menus – enjoyed all this and rather liked him. She also remembered with gratitude his support during the Falklands War. This did not, of course, prevent antagonism over the disproportionate British contribution to the Community budget, a consequence of the CAP, which made it the only net payer. Both tried to outwit the other over figures: Thatcher, more attentive to small print than the princely Mitterrand, who was presiding over the European Council, secured a substantial rebate in 1983, and provoking a presidential outburst about 'perfidie, mascarade, malhonnêteté'.[17] Relations were not improved when, during a visit by Mitterrand to London in 1984, a French security man tested Scotland Yard by planting plastic explosive in the French embassy – a trick by which the British were not amused.

At first, Britain and France had pursued their respective liberal and socialist experiments in isolation. 'Europe', which during the 1970s had been dormant, brought them face to face. Thatcher's economic successes had an impact throughout Europe and beyond. So did Mitterrand's failures. The British gained the confidence and opportunity to press for European liberalization. This was their old refrain, but now pushed as an ideology and a programme further than previous governments would have wanted or even conceived. And it now chimed with changing ideas and practices in Europe and elsewhere in the world. A Whitehall paper, 'Europe – the Future' (1984) was the precursor of the 1986 Single European Act (SEA) creating a Single Market 'without internal frontiers in which the free movement of goods, peoples, services, and capital is assured'. This was the first general liberalizing measure since the Common Market had been created, and 'Mrs Thatcher's baby'.[18] It was pushed through by her appointee to the Brussels Commission, Lord Cockfield, a former Trade and Industry minister. His plan was accepted 'without much opposition' by the Commission.[19] The SEA set up the 'European Union' and held out the prospect of a genuine European market by gradually removing more than 300 non-tariff barriers to trade, including in public contracts, state aids, financial regulations, agreements in restraint of trade, and discriminatory standards. The major recent history of European integration describes this as 'perhaps the greatest single contribution ever made to the construction of Europe', and – only slightly tongue in cheek – hails Margaret Thatcher as the 'founding mother of the new Europe'.[20]

Internal liberalization of the Community 'complemented, reinforced, and furthered the worldwide trend' towards freer trade.[21] The Single Market plan gave impetus to the international trade negotiations of the Uruguay Round of 1986–94, which began to abolish industrial tariffs and liberalize services and investment. A more powerful World Trade Organization was created to pursue these aims. A start was made on agricultural reforms, although the CAP (and comparable American and Japanese agricultural protection) survived to scandalize both liberals and Third World lobbyists. Numerous bilateral trade agreements were concluded over the next decade between the EC and other states, though the EC trade commissioner Leon Brittan's proposal for a treaty with the USA creating a 'New Transatlantic Market' was firmly squashed by the French in 1998. All EC countries increased their trade outside the Community.

The Single Market project potentially changed the Community's *raison d'être* and the role of the Commission. As Ernest Bevin might have said, this Trojan horse was full of Pandora's boxes. The key principle of 'mutual recognition' by member states of each other's standards (if an article was suitable for sale in one country, it was suitable for sale in all) meant that Brussels would not be needed to negotiate and formulate complex 'harmonization'. Liberalization threatened to make EC institutions increasingly redundant, as both its internal barriers and external boundaries were dismantled. In a speech at The Hague in May 1992 Thatcher said that a free-trade Europe 'does not need a Commission in its present form'. A Thatcherite EC would inevitably evolve into the *zone de libre-échange* the French had always abhorred. Like Marx's classless state, 'Europe' would wither away.[22]

This prospect – for many of those who realized the implications – was anathema. Liberal enthusiasts who regarded the free market as an unalloyed good were never a majority, or not for long, even in Britain. Many people – including some of Thatcher's own supporters – considered it a necessary evil. Many others considered it an evil *tout court*. Jacques Delors, who in 1985 went from being Mitterrand's ill-starred finance minister to president of the European Commission, took a more moderate view: economic change was inevitable, but it had to be directed and firmly regulated.

Delors and Thatcher had wary mutual respect. They were similar in their interest in ideas, attention to detail and driving ambition. Their discussions, recalled Delors politely, were 'always fascinating'.[23] They contrasted with their cautious, pragmatic, indolent colleagues, led by Mitterrand and the German chancellor Helmut Kohl. Born the same year, Thatcher and Delors were perfect embodiments of two cultures. She was a Protestant individualist, a daughter of the nation of shopkeepers (Grantham branch), an inheritor of Nonconformist values of work and self-reliance, and an alumna of the hard school of Westminster politics. He was a Catholic paternalist, by birth and career part of the financial bureaucracy, an activist in a white-collar Christian trade union, whose entry into politics had been as a back-room adviser until translated to the ivory tower of the European parliament. He was a sincere disciple of Personalism, a Christian 'Third Way' philosophy fashionable in the 1930s to 50s, which rejected both capitalism and totalitarian mass politics as inhuman, and aspired to create social and economic systems based on human creativity and solidarity, not on liberal individualism and competition. Some Personalists advocated dismantling the nation state through regionalism and non-partisan (i.e. unelected) federal institutions. The collapse of his and Mitterrand's strategy in the early 1980s did not convert them to liberalism. Rather, it convinced them that France must accept greater European integration than hitherto contemplated. They realized, in the dictum of intelligent French conservatives facing revolution, that everything had to be changed so that everything could remain the same.

Delors's appointment as president of the previously inactive Commission was his last chance to create a 'European model of society' that would be 'France . . . partly Germanized and writ large'.[24] It would have to be economically successful enough to preserve the social benefits conferred by postwar Christian democracy and socialism – in Delors's own words, 'to be a hope, a model and a shelter in a world turned upside down by globalization'.[25] This was an attractive message, including in Britain, where it converted Labour and the trade unions from their traditional anti-Europeanism. In short, while Thatcher saw 'Europe' as a step towards globalization, Delors gave it a new purpose: as a haven from Thatcherism.

Delors's audacious strategy was to use Thatcher's Single Market as an opportunity to lead Europe simultaneously in the opposite direction. He argued that the Single Market, because it removed existing national controls, required the Commission's powers to be extended into the environmental, social, monetary and regional fields. He repeatedly insisted that both the Single Market and enlargement of the Community had to be preceded by greater political integration and an extension ('deepening') of the Commission's regulating authority. This was made possibly by part three of the Single European Act (SEA), accepted reluctantly by Thatcher, which extended the 'competencies' of the Commission. Although this was presented as functional and economic, in fact it was ideological and political – to create, in Delors's own words, an 'organized space' rather than a 'free trade zone'.[26] A considerable economic price, in terms of slow growth and unemployment, was worth paying to this end, and particularly in preparing for monetary union, conceived as a federalizing measure. Delors did not underestimate the danger Thatcherite liberalism posed to his 'European Model'. He believed that he had only a limited time to counter it.

Delors's 'frantic state building'[27] proceeded by increasing the economic, regulatory and political powers of the Commission, and 'elevating his own position', wrote an admirer, 'well beyond what the Commission's institutional configuration formally allowed'.[28] He packed the Commission with French officials led by *énarques* Pascal Lamy and François Lamoureux. New 'structural', 'regional' and 'research and development' funds were means of winning allies in politics and business, especially in major recipient countries such as Ireland and Greece, whose finances were transformed by a tidal wave of cash. All politicians bribe people with their own money; but Delors had the irresistible advantage of being able to bribe them with other people's money, and make them feel virtuous for pocketing it. The inevitable result was waste, corruption, and the permanent installation in Brussels of an international army of lobbyists. The Commission became what one highly pro-European British official called 'Tammany Hall with a French accent.'[29] The Delors strategy was christened the 'Russian doll' method by Lamoureux: 'inside it is another one, which leads you to another . . . until it is too late to turn back'. According to an insider, 'the trick was putting together complex packages which . . . could appeal to differing member state interests'. An important aspect of this was to find 'proposals that played enough to British neoliberalism to lower the British guard against the further pooling of sovereignty down the line'.[30]

The 'Russian doll' strategy created an integrationist momentum. It was difficult to resist, especially when the only weighty opponent was the increasingly isolated Thatcher, who rejected integration as economically damaging and politically unacceptable. Delors's activity brought down on him the opprobrium of parts of the British press, almost equalled by later French denunciation of the mild-mannered British trade commissioner Leon Britten, demonized as a Thatcherite Genghis Khan. Admittedly, the populist francophobia of the tabloid *Sun* (whose headline 'Up Yours, Delors' won notoriety) bore little resemblance to the silky intellectual anglophobia of *Le Monde* or the *Nouvel Observateur*. Apart from support from within France, Delors had the weighty advantage of an alliance with Helmut Kohl. Germany's 'Rhenish capitalism', stable, consensual, with high levels of social welfare, and yet internationally competitive, had influenced Delors. Problems caused by rigidity and high costs had begun to appear in the 1970s, but the picture was still impressive. Moreover, the problems, so hard to remedy, were an argument for protecting the system against 'unfair' competition by extending German-style social policy throughout the Community. The end of the Cold War and the increasing prospects of German reunification made Kohl eager to win allies and reassure his partners, especially the French, that Germany was a 'good European'. Delors responded by astutely welcoming German reunification while Mitterrand and Thatcher clumsily urged delay. So a Kohl–Delors alliance solidified. Mitterrand, once reunification had happened, decided that further European integration was 'the only response to the problem that confronts us',[31] by tying a more powerful Germany into tighter economic and political structures.

Delors's Commission was a nimble political player, not weighed down by accountability to electors or responsibility for consequences. It was a dream factory, whose job was 'to create and promote plausible scenarios'.[32] It could select popular causes, such as environmental protection, regional aid, health and safety and workers' rights, enshrined in the Social Charter (1989). This incidentally aimed to isolate the British, make Thatcher 'domestically vulnerable', and pave the way for later British U-turns.[33] Thatcher was increasingly unpopular at home, as shown in election results in the later 1980s, and weakened by the open dissension of powerful colleagues, notably the foreign secretary Geoffrey Howe and the chancellor of the exchequer Nigel Lawson. Both wanted to compromise with Delors's strategy, and thought Thatcher's stubborn resistance doomed.

THATCHER AND THE REVOLUTION, 1989

In July 1989, Mitterrand presided over a huge political carnival in Paris to celebrate the bicentenary of 1789: the revolutionary tiger was now a cuddly toy. Western leaders met for a summit, and many other world politicians were invited. Thatcher gave Mitterrand a first edition of *A Tale of Two Cities*, one of the formative books of her youth.[34] *Le Monde* ran interviews inviting visitors to pay tribute to the revolution and France's unique historic role. Many played the game, producing some rather burlesque results: for example, the Austrian Kurt Waldheim (later exposed as a war criminal) praised the Declaration of the Rights of Man. *Le Monde* kept Thatcher for the climax, on 13 July. In reply to a teasing question – had human rights begun with the French revolution? – she referred briefly to Judeo-Christian tradition, Magna Carta, the Bill of Rights and the Glorious Revolution. This was hardly new to the French: the great liberal François Guizot had taught in the 1820s that 'everyone knew' the importance of Magna Carta. Other interviewees had made similar points. Daniel Cohn-Bendit – the 1968 student leader 'Danny the Red' – had even mentioned Magna Carta. But *Le Monde* gave a front-page headline and a cartoon to Thatcher. Who was provoking whom? For her many critics it was Thatcher, commonly presented as an aggressive, insular

Le Monde's view of Margaret Thatcher's refusal of the revolution's Phrygian bonnet. Just visible are her protruding teeth – symbol of British womanhood.

francophobe. Christopher Hill, a veteran left-wing historian, summoned her to 'apologize to the people of France'.

Thatcher fell from power in November 1990, brought down by a Conservative Party rebellion initiated by the party's most Europhile wing. Yet the Thatcherite implications of the Single Market legislation remained. Delors knew this, and 'sometimes doubted that [European] unification would happen in the way he wished'.[35] But he was an 'active pessimist' – a Personalist term meaning that you should persist even if you expect to fail. There was an inescapable tension between furthering liberalization through the Single Market and the World Trade Organization while simultaneously extending social protections which, however popular, increased costs and rigidities. The danger was to make 'Europe' a mechanism for shifting investment and jobs elsewhere. No less serious was rising disquiet among the citizens of the member countries. The much discussed 'democratic deficit' was inherent in Monnet's blueprint for supranational management by apolitical experts. It was acceptable as long as their activities were narrowly defined and largely invisible. The more Thatcher and Delors brought 'Europe' into everyday life – respectively by removing old protections and imposing new restrictions – the more the deficit became glaring. The Single Market threatened vested interests while the 'Russian dolls' method of integration meant, in Delors's own words, 'drawing up the marriage contract before asking the couple ['Europe' and its peoples] if they wanted to wed'.[36] His solution was to press ahead before opposition grew too strong – his aim, he said, was a federation by 2000 – and to create popular consent afterwards, on the pattern of nineteenth-century nation-building: 'We have made Europe, now we must make Europeans'.[37] What Delors termed cultural management – semi-official lobbies, subsidized cultural activities, youth groups, prizes, 400 endowed professorships, 1,700 teaching projects, edifying schoolbooks, films and videos – would inculcate pride in being European and an acceptance that 'ever closer union' was the goal of history.

The Maastricht Treaty on European Union (February 1992) formally tied Delors's programme of 'economic and monetary union' to the Single Market. The gamble almost failed. The Danes voted in a referendum against ratification. Mitterrand too called a referendum, expecting a convincing Yes to counteract the Danish No. The French government's appeal to the voters was couched in traditionally patriotic terms: 'France at the head of Europe' magnified the power of 'sovereign France', and provided protection for its social system, economy and culture against the outside world.[38] As one slogan put it, 'Napoleon would have voted Yes.' But the French electorate, as prone to grumbling as the Grande Armée, followed its politicians on 20 September

1992 by the narrowest of margins: 51 to 49 per cent. Broadly, the Yes vote, urged by all the mainstream parties, was urban and middle class; the No, that of workers and farmers, angered by attempts to liberalize the CAP.

Mitterrand, in an election broadcast to reassure his voters, had stated (wrongly) on 3 September that the planned European Central Bank would be subject to political control, implying a more relaxed monetary policy. At this, the international currency markets 'freaked out', argues the historian John Gillingham, and began a series of speculative assaults on the already creaking Exchange Rate Mechanism, which coordinated the values of EC currencies. The speculators forced devaluations in Finland, Sweden, Italy and Spain. The climax came when sterling was forced out of the system on 'Black Wednesday' (16 September 1992), four days before the French referendum.[39] Thus, a political ploy by Mitterrand struck a heavy blow to John Major's Conservative government – being 'at the heart of Europe' with a vengeance. But the humiliation proved beneficial to the British economy which, for once without the burden of an overvalued currency, performed buoyantly. Britain, for a mixture of political and economic reasons, subsequently stayed outside the single currency, the Euro, introduced between 1999 and 2002 – the crowning achievement of French strategy to Europeanize the financial power of Germany and to create an economic and political system capable of standing up to America in the global economy.

Both Thatcher and Delors had left office with the painful conviction that the other had won. But the tug-of-war between the British and French models continued unabated. British politicians liked to repeat that they were 'winning the argument in Europe', but they were certainly not doing so in France. The disagreement was as stark as ever: faced with the tide of global competition, should one plunge into the surf or shore up the dykes? French governments clung to the CAP and in 1998 the employment minister Martine Aubry (Delors's daughter) introduced a compulsory thirty-five hour week. Despite EU injunctions to apply competition policy and open their market, French governments continued to direct and protect industries whether formally by State shareholdings and grants, or informally by pressures and favours. They reiterated demands that this 'industrial policy' should be adopted officially by Europe, and repeatedly condemned Single Market competition as irrational and destructive. Colossally expensive failures of 'national champions' were shrugged off. The losses to the taxpayer caused by one such champion, the bank Crédit Lyonnais, were reckoned to be the equivalent of a month's holiday for every French family. The burning down of its Paris headquarters cut short potentially embarrassing enquiries. Other financial black holes over the years were Air France (saved by Delors personally), the computer manufacturer Bull, the conglomerate Vivendi and the technology group Alstom. Such collapses engendered recrimination and a string of prosecutions of buccaneering industrialists previously lauded as heroes – and even of a few greedy politicians. Yet the principle of such a policy was rarely contested, and the British alternative of non-intervention, as followed by Thatcher and her successors, seemed to entail reckless sacrifice of the industrial base of the economy in favour of fragile service industries – not a tempting prospect. So the French treasury continued to make huge grants and preferential loans, in defiance of Single Market competition policy. Public utilities such as Electricité de France and France-Télécom, protected at home from foreign purchase or competition, were able to buy up utilities in other European countries, particularly in deregulated Britain. Despite these efforts, France lagged economically. Traditional industries languished: the last French coalmine closed in April 2004. The Stability and Growth Pact, the guarantor of the Euro, made things worse by its deflationary effect. It was openly broken by France and Germany after 2003, and in 2005 they forced its abandonment. The British Treasury were pleased, because it showed that they had been right to stay outside the Euro. The French were pleased, because it showed that they had the power to break or change the rules. Only the smaller states were not pleased, because the demise of Jean Monnet's vision of the rule of law and regulation by neutral experts exposed their weakness.

Evidence of French economic decline, especially in comparison with Britain, became a subject of lively debate in the 2000s. But there were few calls for British-style liberalization, seen as destructive, harsh and politically suicidal. A generation of readers of progressive newspapers such as *Le Monde*, *Libération* and *Le Nouvel Observateur*, and the many French admirers of radical British film-makers such as Ken Loach, shuddered at the Dickensian horrors of the new Britain, with its armies of beggars and its bumptious millionaires. France and Europe had to be spared its successes no less than its failures. Events strengthened this repulsion. The 'mad cow' crisis of the 1990s and fears of the spread of BSE to humans led the French government to impose a ban on British beef imports, which was maintained with public support until 2002, three years after the EU lifted its own embargo. Here was an unmissable opportunity to trumpet the superiority of French agriculture and the value of the CAP. French visitors to England refused to touch anything associated with meat; children were forbidden to eat sweets that might contain gelatine. Newspapers sniffed out a secret organization smuggling the deadly beef into France with the aid of the British army, while the perfidious Tony Blair exported animal feed to France that was banned in Britain.[40] The directors of a chain of restaurants were imprisoned for serving British steaks. When the ban was finally lifted, not surprisingly imports did not revive. In 2001 came the foot and mouth epidemic in Britain, with mass slaughter and burning of animal carcasses shown repeatedly on television. 'The medieval glow of funeral pyres' was condign retribution for 'twenty years of ultraliberalism'.[41] The lesson was reiterated that the British model was a public danger compared with the wise interventionism of the French model. Controversial and highly publicized business decisions such as the closing down of all Marks and Spencer stores in France and the 'delocalization' of Hoover from Burgundy to Scotland provided further proof of the menace. Articles appeared with headlines such as 'England: total crisis' and 'The illusions of ultraliberalism'.[42] No one talked about 'Carthage' – classical education was as moribund as in Britain – but the idea of the 'nation of shopkeepers' was not far away. The Sangatte refugee camp (finally closed under British pressure in November 2002), from which non-European migrants stowed away on Channel Tunnel trains to England, encapsulated the difference. The French, relieved yet somewhat offended that asylum-seekers were so eager to leave France, blamed Britain's deregulated system: no identity cards, lax policing, and a 'grey' economy of menial jobs. The British were being punished where they had sinned.

So the 'French' and 'British' models continued in sharp opposition. It was not negligence that made France one of the most recalcitrant countries (Britain was one of the quickest) in applying Brussels directives. In 2004, the supposedly liberal finance minister Nicolas Sarkozy laboured to prevent the bankrupt Alstom from being taken over by 'foreigners' – the German firm Siemens. The EU Single Market commissioner, Frits Bolkestein, exclaimed in exasperation that 'I cannot help feeling that I am in a time warp. I have to pinch myself to make sure that I am not back in the 1960s, 1970s or 1980s . . . To listen to recent statements by French and German politicians, you would think the [single market] strategy had never existed.' He criticized them for favouring their own companies, while aiming to handicap new EU members by forcing up their costs.[43] Trade between EU members had stagnated. 'Anti-dumping' measures (against allegedly unfair competition) and other non-tariff barriers were estimated in 2004 as equivalent to a 40 per cent import tariff on manufactured goods from outside the Union, rising to 60 per cent for 'hi-tech' products. The CAP, despite reforms, kept Europe's food prices 50–60 per cent above world levels. Two decades after the Single European Act, only 16 per cent of member states' own purchases fully applied Single Market rules, and tight restrictions remained on trade in services – Britain's strongest suit.[44] Hence, its chronic trade deficit with the rest of the EU, above all with France. Bolkestein's modest plan to begin to apply the Single Market to some services caused an outcry in France, and was squashed by Chirac, with German support, in March 2005. Some British trade unionists wanted Britain to imitate French protectionism. The chancellor, Gordon Brown, retorted that 'the old integrationist project . . . the vision of a trade bloc Europe, is fatally undermined'.

Significantly, these comments were made in a speech on 'Britishness'.[45] But Delors's former assistant François Lamoureux, still a senior official in Brussels, proudly declared that 'Europe today . . . is not a liberal Europe. It is extremely regulated [to preserve] a certain social model.'[46] As in the days of Thatcher and Delors, Europe was heading simultaneously in opposite directions.

The commitment to enlarge the EU in 2004 – most popular in Britain and least in France[47] – brought the perennial differences to a head. Bringing in much of eastern Europe would make the CAP and Delorean subsidies unaffordable. Moreover, the new states were disinclined to follow the French model. As the British thought they were coasting to victory, the French took pre-emptive action. Disagreement with the Anglo-Saxons over Iraq had revitalized the 'Franco-German couple'. In October 2002, without consulting other governments, Chirac persuaded the German chancellor Schröder to agree to preserve the CAP for its existing beneficiaries, keep its budget rising, withhold structural funds from new EU members, and curtail the rights of their citizens to work in Western Europe – in short, to preserve the 'French model' by excluding new members from full participation. He later boasted to the French electorate that '80 per cent of aid to French farmers comes from Europe. We were the only ones who wanted it. How did we manage it? By an understanding with our German friends.'[48] This French coup caused an angry exchange between Blair and Chirac. It was a costly victory for France, whose single-minded defence of its own interests, its bending or defiance of EU rules, and its overt lack of sympathy for the new member states meant that any idea of France as leader of the new Europe had evaporated. Whereas de Gaulle had wanted Europe to be a 'lever' for French power, it had become in French eyes principally a barrier against change. Although claiming to be the 'dynamo of Europe', the 'Franco-German couple' had really become its brake, as the two sick men of Europe struggled to prevent an enlarged community from running away from them.

A Convention on the Future of Europe, appointed in February 2002 to suggest ways of bringing the EU closer to its citizens, instead set out to 'deepen' it by drafting a Constitution before the accession of the new members. Britain urged simpler and more flexible rules, and its foreign secretary Jack Straw urged that the Constitution should be 'just a few lines'.[49] But the Convention, chaired by the former French president Valéry Giscard d'Estaing, produced several hundred pages. EU leaders met in Brussels in June 2004 to approve the draft constitution and choose a new Commission, an unprecedently difficult task. Differences were aggravated by recrimination over the war in Iraq, which exploded into European politics.

At least one neutral observer supposed that the Blair government must only be pretending to support a dying federalism in order to maintain British influence in Brussels and Washington until the French model inevitably gave up the ghost.[50] If so, it was a convincing performance. Blair tried to push the bloated Giscard Constitution through Parliament as a mere 'tidying up exercise'. But he surrendered to political and media pressure in April 2004, and conceded a referendum. The French government, scarcely concealing its annoyance, felt obliged to do the same. Thus a match was applied to the combustible material that had been accumulating since the days of Thatcher and Delors. Opinion polls left little doubt that the British electorate would vote No. *Le Monde*, always suspicious of cross-Channel machinations, feared that Blair would lose the referendum, 'drag the constitution down with him' and thus 'deserve the thanks of perfidious Albion'.[51] The British government scheduled their referendum as late as possible, in 2006. This left the possibility that some other country – perhaps Poland – would save them by voting No first. Or, if all the other members voted Yes, they would be able to deploy the usual desperate argument that Britain dared not 'miss the European train' and face isolation.

Was the Constitution the last chance to fix the 'French model' into law before the new member countries could have a say? Would it have been the means of finally imposing the 'British model' on a reluctant France? Or was it an exercise in equivocation that would have generated years of political and legal wrangling? We shall never know. But the debate in Britain and France showed how wide the cross-Channel divide had grown. In Britain, critics attacked the EU for interfering too much. In France, they condemned it for not interfering enough.

So Near and Yet So Far

Always when we left, with peeling noses and regret, we promised ourselves that one day we would live here. We had talked about it during the long grey winters and the damp green summers . . . And now, somewhat to our surprise, we had done it. We had committed ourselves. We had bought a house, taken French lessons, said our goodbyes, shipped over our two dogs, and become foreigners.

PETER MAYLE, *A Year in Provence*, 1989

Based in the UK, you have more of the feeling that you're part of the global economy. France seems to do business at a slower pace. The culture of entrepreneurship, although it has developed a lot recently, is certainly less developed in France than the UK.

French businessman in London, 2000[52]

> The English hate the French. Who reciprocate . . . A purée of prejudice
> on a bed of inherited loathing. The French consider the English to be
> arrogant islanders, eating boiled lamb with mint, and not knowing how to
> be seductive. The English consider us talkative, arrogant, dirty, smelling
> of sweat and garlic, flighty, cheating and corrupt . . . The English love
> France, but not the French.
>
> *Le Point*, 30 July 1999

The 1990s saw the beginning of an unprecedented cross-Channel migration. The explosion of tourism is part of the story: in 2000, 11.9 million Britons – one in five! – spent on average a week in France, and 3 million French a long weekend in Britain.[53] But residence, not tourism, is the real novelty. By the end of 2002 some 74,000 adult Britons held *cartes de séjour* giving them the right to work in France, an increase of a quarter in ten years. The total figure for residents was higher, including dependants, pensioners, and above all intermittent residents. Here is an unprecedented phenomenon: official French figures estimated that 600,000 houses were owned by Britons.[54] This equated roughly to one for every thirty British families. The traditional holiday areas of the Midi remained the favourites. But the West saw a new influx (with a rise of 120 per cent in Brittany), as did rural areas of the South, such as Languedoc and Gascony. The biggest increase of all was in newer, cheaper regions such as Poitou-Charente (170 per cent).[55] Some less sunny regions, however close and even picturesque, such as Nord-Pas-de-Calais, Lorraine and Champagne-Ardennes, saw declines. Cheap flights, cheap car ferries and high-speed trains made distance less of a factor.

The arrival of the French in Britain from the 1990s onwards is more striking still in both quantity and novelty: for the first time ever, there were more French in Britain than British in France. French consulates registered 91,500 French citizens resident – an increase of 250 per cent in ten years. The real number, however, was estimated to be around 300,000, with probably about two-thirds in the London area. Over the same period, the number of British residents in Paris fell by nearly a quarter, as businesses escaped French labour regulations by concentrating in London. Britain in a few years hugely outdistanced Germany and Belgium, long the main European destinations of French migrants, and equalled or overtook the United States. London suddenly became the world's eighth-largest French city. The French in Britain, unlike those in other countries, were varied in status and much younger, most in their twenties.[56]

These movements renewed a very old difference, manifest since the eighteenth century. 'No Frenchman ever goes to England for pleasure, he never lives there by choice, and thinks only of coming back as soon as possible' has long been a familiar refrain.[57] This was no more strictly true than its corollary that the English *only* went to France for pleasure – there were

1.5 million British business trips to France in 2000 compared with 1 million French business trips to Britain[58] – but it was broadly true. Most French came to Britain to make money; most British went to France to spend it: at least 5 billion euros a year, a significant boost to the rural economy. The prosperous middle-aged British families who bought property in Languedoc in many ways resembled their forbears who had settled not far away in Pau. The relative cheapness of France has for centuries permitted a genteel lifestyle, with a pleasant climate, sparsely inhabited countryside, and gastronomic pleasure.

Similarly, the young French men and women prominent in the restaurants, bars, football teams and offices of what French newspapers called 'the European Eldorado' were not so different from the wig-makers, dancing masters, maids, waiters and cooks who had preceded them over three centuries. French craftsmen have always been better trained in certain luxury occupations. London had long been a magnet, but the boom of the 1990s multiplied its attractiveness. In 2003, for example, one-third of the graduates of the Lyon business school went to work in the City – more than went to Paris. The modern equivalent of the dancing master is perhaps the football manager: Arsène Wenger, after a mediocre playing career in France, went to Paris to learn scientific sports management and to a Cambridge language school to learn English. 'The professor' had a transforming impact on English football in the 1990s by applying professional rigour to the training of Arsenal, which he made one of the world's best teams.

Unemployment in 2004 was twice as high in France as Britain, and youth unemployment, estimated at 26 per cent (double in ethnic ghettos) was the highest in Europe.[59] Those who did find a job were subject to seniority in promotion, still important in French firms. Those seeking work, or trying to change careers, sought opportunities in England, often intending to stay for a few months or a few years, obtain experience, and improve their English. Nowhere else in Europe or America offered this. L'Express's business supplement Réussir published an eighty-four-page special in 1999 giving advice on studying in England, finding a job and setting up a business: 'Here, when you're young, you can start from scratch'; 'For the English, only results count; the school you come from doesn't matter and careers are less political.' French firms large and small set up British operations, or even moved there: by 2004 there were 1,700 French companies employing 330,000 people. Lower taxation and less regulation were powerful attractions. In Britain, it took two days and £200 to set up a business; in France, thirty-five times as much and forty times as long.[60] There was a brain-drain of entrepreneurs in new industries, such as Philippe Foriel-Destezet, creator of the world's leading personnel services company, and Marc Lassus, 'the dot of French dotcom, the Fifth Republic's answer to Bill Gates'.[61] The French 'Silicon Valley' was the

Thames Estuary. Seven of the 2004 French national football team were employed by English clubs, whose pay rates, under British taxation, gave them on average five times as much cash as at home. The departure from Paris to London of the 'supermodel' Laetitia Casta in 2000 ruffled patriotic feathers because she had modelled for the official statue of Marianne, the symbol of the Republic that adorns every town hall. No less a personage than a former minister of the interior, Jean-Pierre Chevènement, warned darkly that not only would she find London rents higher than in Paris, and the Tube less good than the Métro, but 'if she gets sick, which I hope she won't, the healthcare in a British hospital will be far short of French hospitals'.

As Chevènement predicted, many French Londoners did find the Great Wen hard going. *L'Express* told its readers they would be amazed by the tolerance for eccentricity, the amount of beer drunk, the respect given to customers, the informality of work relationships, and the ease of finding a job.[62] Not very different, in fact, from what was being said in the 1750s. Most intended to stay for a fairly short time, so the level of integration with the natives or even with each other was limited. A monthly magazine, *Ici Londres* – an ironic echo of the 1940s – carried lists of French shops, dentists, doctors, clairvoyants, lonely hearts, and groups for playing *belote*. Families unwilling to rely on British state or private schools had to brave the living costs of the West End to be close enough to the Lycée Charles de Gaulle in South Kensington. This replaced Soho as the nearest thing to a French colony. The nearby embassy and consulate, the cultural institute and the *lycée* spawned cafés and bookshops, and streets adorned by elaborately casual teenagers who could have come straight from the Boulevard Saint-Michel. Fulham boasted a French pub. Provincial towns acquired their smaller French colonies. But all in all their presence attracted little notice. Institutionally, it was barely visible outside London: the single French *lycée* might be compared with thirty in Spain; the two consulates with Britain's five in France; the two French churches with eight British churches and thirty chaplaincies.[63] This no doubt reflects the suddenness of the French influx, and probably a tacit admission that to establish a noteworthy official cultural presence in Britain would be too costly in money and effort.

As young French people went to share in the excitement and profits of the 'British model', older British people and their families sought the security and comfort of the 'French model'. The high-speed trains, well-kept motorways, small provincial airports, plethoric medical care, and subsidized cultural events gave pleasure unalloyed by thoughts of the tax bill they entailed. Even British Conservatives expressed admiration for French hospitals and state schools. Rural France was the recipient of a unique devotion going well beyond considerations of price, convenience and weather, and which, as we have seen (see above, page 406), dates back to the nineteenth century. Now, however, there was a rush to buy property, whereas earlier generations had rented. Cashing in the huge increase in house values in Britain enabled them to buy and renovate properties ranging from *châteaux* to *chaumières* abandoned as the rural population dwindled. *French Property News* circulated lists of desirable residences. Owning a corner of France, and making it a second or even a first home, came to embody the Arcadian dream close to British hearts, but unobtainable at home at a reasonable cost. Those buying houses in France gave their reasons as 'lifestyle', a 'slower pace of life', a 'traditional rustic' atmosphere. One estimate is that half the buyers were retired, a quarter came for holidays, and a quarter – and growing – came to seek a new, less 'stressful', career.[64]

Becoming foreigners, as Mayle puts it, could be a rebirth, shedding old identities. But rebirth is testing, particularly when the midwife is a French notary, mayor or tax inspector. Most sold up within the first two years; thereafter, they tended to stay.[65] Television programmes followed the adventures and misadventures of intrepid purchasers of overgrown vineyards, run-down caravan sites and ramshackle hovels without plumbing. Expatriate estate agents, advisers, architects, builders, landscape gardeners and troubleshooters multiplied to service them. Books on how to manage in France were published. Magazines such as *France* ('Your passport to France and the French way of life') encouraged potential settlers with tourism features, basic information ('Petit déjeuner, as the French refer to break-fast'), tips on house-hunting, avoiding mosquitoes, or learning French fast, and weightier advice on French tax law. The prevailing tone was one of enthusiastic goodwill towards a society depicted as a quaint but benevolent Ruritania: 'Can you imagine a law whereby parents have to name their offspring from a government list? Incredible, but it was statutory in France until 1981.'[66] There were more than 100 British clubs and societies, including the Dordogne Ladies Club, established in the mid 1980s (which organized shopping trips to Bordeaux and a Christmas bazaar), the Dordogne Old Gentlemen, branches of the British Legion, and a number of cricket teams.

This might recall the expatriate exclusiveness of the Pau Hunt or the English Club. One French newspaper indeed complained of 'colonials', and pointed out that Christopher Patten, the last governor of Hong Kong, had exchanged the Peak for the Brussels Commission and a house near Albi. But modern British settlers, unlike their forerunners, yearned to be accepted by the locals. This was an important part of the appeal for enchanted admirers of Peter Mayle. A study of Basse Normandie found not only that all wanted to be part of the community, but that most thought they already were. In a few cases, this is undoubted: there have been British-born mayors, municipal councillors, and a parish priest. On the whole, though, Normans considered British participation to be 'very superficial'; their knowledge of the economy, culture and politics 'elementary'; and their competence in French 'very limited'. Not all Normans were flattered to be regarded as picturesque natives of a rural backwater. There was little hostility towards the newcomers (though a few still considered them 'the hereditary enemy'), but not much enthusiasm either, except for those in poor rural areas who benefited economically. The friendliest elements were the young, the middle-class, and those who spoke English. Some criticized the British for being mean, keeping to themselves, and spending all their time renovating their houses. They also suffered some guilt by association with 'booze-cruisers' and football hooligans, being suspected of a penchant for drunkenness and violence. Worst of all, they might raise property prices beyond local reach – by 35 per cent between 2000 and 2002 in Aquitaine. Old-established francophiles deplored the arrival of ignorant newcomers: 'One foreign family in the village in enough.' Peter Mayle raised hackles among his neighbours by attracting coachloads of tourists. In Chamonix – 'an English suburb for all but tax purposes' – 10 per cent of the population was British. The French joked uneasily that in Charente there was now one Englishman per village, but in Dordogne, there was only one Frenchman per village. A politician warned that 'when 80 per cent of the population of Dordogne is English then it will not quite be Dordogne'.[67] As far as we know, no equivalent fear has yet been expressed about the fate of South Kensington.

THE TUNNEL: BREAKTHROUGH

During the Second World War, the old tunnel workings at Sangatte had been blown up by the Germans, while from Shakespeare Cliff the British had kept a wary ear open for possible secret digging. Revival of the tunnel idea in 1954 – the fiftieth anniversary of the *entente cordiale* – had other historical echoes. The suggestion was made by Paul Leroy-Beaulieu, an administrator of the still surviving 1874 tunnel company and the grandson of Michel Chevalier, the French negotiator of the free trade treaty of 1860 (see above, page 364).[68] In 1956 the Suez Canal company, having lost its canal, joined the project. With Britain's attempt to join the Common Market, the idea took on new significance. It was briefly discussed by Macmillan and de Gaulle, and de Gaulle's 'Non' did not kill the project. The real problem was money: the British Treasury and the French finance ministry were hostile. But the promoters kept promoting, and after Britain finally entered the EEC, a tunnel seemed an important symbol of the new era. In 1973, a treaty and convention were signed, ninety years after the first works had been suspended. However, the costs were daunting, and no one wanted an 'underground Concorde'. The project was suspended again in 1975, with 1,000 yards of tunnel dug. At least one prominent French politician took this as proof of Britain's 'weak taste for Europe'.[69] It was Margaret Thatcher who revived the project at her first summit with Mitterrand, on condition that it was paid for by private capital. A report in 1982 readopted the 1970s plan for a bored railway tunnel, rather than one made of prefabricated segments, a bridge or some combination. Banks and small shareholders – largely French – were tempted, to their subsequent chagrin, by low cost estimates and wildly optimistic traffic forecasts. The Tunnel was opened by the Queen and President Mitterrand on 6 May 1994. He remarked that French travellers would have leisure to admire the Kent countryside, owing to the modest speed of the trains in England. At last, after 138 projects over 192 years, British coyness had been overcome.

The British and French thus came into contact with each other more often, longer, and for more reasons than ever before. Both wanted certain things from the other, and tended to ignore the rest. No doubt there were exceptions. There must have been young French entrepreneurs who frequented the Tate galleries, sampled country pubs, and went walking in the Cairngorms. Equally, there were doubtless British home-owners in Provence who followed the political reports in *Le Monde*, read the latest French novels, and became experts on local history. But was there that urgent interest in each other's life and culture that gripped so many in the eighteenth or nineteenth centuries?

One test is the exchange of books.[70] The French published far more English books in translation, and imported far more in the original, than the British did French books. Is this one more proof of philistine British insularity and cultivated French cosmopolitanism? Not quite. French imports were fairly narrow in range. Most were children's books, language textbooks, or non-fiction best-sellers such as *Le Livre Guinness des Records*. Some of the more popular British authors – the novelist and essayist Julian Barnes ('the incorrigible francophile' – *L'Express*); the historian Theodore Zeldin, and indeed Peter Mayle – were those who wrote admiringly about France. If the French translated more contemporary English fiction, the British continued to buy large numbers of nineteenth-century French novels. The British also imported more serious non-fiction works than did the French, a sign of their more outward-looking academic world. Some, such as Emmanuel Le Roy Ladurie's *Montaillou*, even became best-sellers. Philosophical and critical works, by Foucault, Derrida, Lacan, Barthes, Bourdieu, Braudel and others, had huge influence in Anglo-Saxon academia. The French showed no comparable interest in any anglophone intellectual, however eminent.

Popularity, in both books and films, often reflected established expectations.[71] P.D. James and Ruth Rendell (one of whose novels was filmed with authentic creepiness by France's master of suspense, Claude Chabrol, as *La Cérémonie*) owed some of their success to a genre which the French considered quintessentially English – the murder mystery. A similar comment could be made about some successful French authors in Britain, such as Michel Houellebecq – porn, philosophy and provocation had long been considered quintessentially French. Eroticism was also the subject of Catherine Breillat's *Romance* (1999), which changed film censorship in Britain by being the first mainstream film showing unsimulated sex and being given an '18' certificate: the British Board of Film Censors explained that it was 'very French'.[72] Critics agreed: it displayed 'the venerable French tradition of philosophy in the boudoir', cutting 'straight to the heart of sex in a way that Bridget Jones would never understand'.

Among younger age-groups, there were signs of a less stereotyped interest, perhaps reflecting the mutual attraction of London and Paris. There was a large market for light-hearted and/or highly romanticized depictions of the cities, hence the success of writers such as Nick Hornby and Helen Fielding, and of films such as *Amélie* or *Notting Hill*. In music Daft Punk (two Frenchmen) were highly fashionable in the 1990s, and objects of intense study in the British musical press. The most startling cultural phenomenon of the turn of the century, however, was an international craze for British-inspired books and films intended mainly for children – *Harry Potter* and *The Lord of the Rings*. In 2000, the four best-selling works of fiction in France were all 'Arri Pottair' novels, of which 7 million copies were sold in four years. It is impossible to imagine even a fraction of the same audience being interested by any book or film set in the real Britain, whether contemporary or historical.

Both countries had a voracious appetite for South American, Indian, African and American films and novels – often the same ones. The French (leaving aside Harry Potter!) bought more German, Italian, Belgian and American novels than British. With a few exceptions, contemporary French novelists had limited sales in Britain, and only a few serious weeklies carried occasional reviews of untranslated French works. One British publisher blamed French writers for being inward-looking, complacent and provincial.[73] So however one qualifies the picture, the general French and British publics in the 2000s showed a far shallower interest in each other's contemporary cultures than at key moments in the past. Yet this was a time of unprecedented personal contacts between the two peoples. Was it simply that familiarity bred indifference?

Both nations tended to value in each other echoes of a more prestigious past, rather than a prosaic present. These inchoate but ingrained feelings emerged in advertising images, consumer goods and opinion polls. Advertisements for British and pseudo-British products in French magazines emphasized refinement, aristocracy, exclusivity, tradition, even, occasionally, eccentricity – all old themes. (A famous Paris department store's 2005 display of a fashion line startlingly called 'Essex Girls' is perhaps the exception to the rule.) Jaguar and Rover cars were sold for their leather seats and wooden trimming more than their mechanics. The imagery was 'English', even when it featured tartan.[74] The French upper classes still liked having English nannies, and some drawled in what could seem a slightly English intonation. The Paris shop Old England, for generations owned by the same (French) family, supplied expensive tweeds and mackintoshes to *bon chic bon genre* Parisians: its ideal was 'something with history and a rustic element'. The style of expensive casualness was predominantly masculine, as it had been for over two centuries; and – as during all that time – its peak of elegance was when worn by French women.

Advertising for French goods in Britain was similarly conventional: the old themes of *chic* and sexy. A widely shown series of television advertisements for Renault cars in the 1990s featured a pert, quintessentially Left Bank 'Nicole' (played by a Czech actress), her raffishly sophisticated 'Papa', his mistress, his mother, and the family chauffeur – a sort of miniature Pagnol story oddly redolent of the 1950s. This is perhaps why more recent advertising for cars attempted first to be more openly erotic and then steadily less 'French'. There seemed to be a general trend away from emphasis on French or British *images de marque*, which may reflect strained cross-Channel relations. An exception is Stella Artois beer, brewed in Britain and marketed through comical 'Jean de Florette' rusticity. Where Frenchness signified modernity, it was in female fashions and cosmetics. French masculine images (except the occasional macho footballer) apparently did not appeal to British male consumers. This may echo the gendering of national stereotypes that appeared in the late nineteenth century (see above, page 450).

Opinion surveys gave bizarre insights into what the mixture of nostalgia, current affairs and memory boiled down to. Fairly searching studies in the 1990s and for the centenary of the *entente cordiale* in 2004 showed much continuity and some change.[75] Ancient stereotypes were alive and well. The British associated the French with elegance, refinement, culture, talkativeness, gastronomy, seductiveness and arrogance. The French associated the British with humour, eccentricity, insularity, coldness, principle, egotism, drunkenness, tradition and snobbery, and thought that 'five o'clock tea' was a universal British custom. These notions would have been familiar to Dr Johnson and Abbé Le Blanc, and to Flora Tristan and William Makepeace Thackeray. They are deeply rooted in literature, memory and language. Reality was often bent to fit them: hence the durable popularity of the puerile comedian Benny Hill in France, regarded as a brilliantly surrealist manifestation of British humour, or the belief in Britain that French footballers talk philosophy. A small proportion of each nation continued to think the other smelly and repulsive, though in fact both had improved their personal hygiene beyond recognition. Yet there were also changes. The British admired the once ignored French countryside – a constant theme of weekend supplements – while the French, who once universally praised the British landscape, no longer noticed it. Nor did the French any longer admire the British political system. Many British continued to judge the French 'cowardly' (something that would never have occurred to Marlborough or Wellington, who would rather have seen reckless courage as a French characteristic). Some once universal clichés seemed to be fading. The French less commonly described the British as 'perfidious' or 'hypocritical': indeed, they regarded their strongest characteristic as 'sticking to their principles' – not seen as an unalloyed virtue. Nor were the British any longer regarded as *sportifs*. Both nations still regarded each other as independent, selfish, proud and arrogant – very old complaints arising from irritation that the others 'can be so proud of their country to the extent of failing to perceive the paragon across the Channel'.[76] Yet contrary to a widespread view influenced by the (usually jocular) francophobia of their tabloid press, the British appear to like, admire and trust the French considerably more than the French do them.[77]

If these notions of the other were ingrained, they were based on only the skimpiest knowledge of geography, history, culture or politics. Frequent coverage in each other's press – tourist spreads, advice on what to see in Paris and London, book and film reviews, and frequent articles on fashion – left little definite impression. Only London and Paris, with Big Ben, the Eiffel Tower, the Louvre pyramid and the Arc de Triomphe, struck immediate chords, along with Oxford and Cambridge. The millions who travelled in the 2000s seemed to pick up little general knowledge. In history, only the great upheavals were recalled: the British knew about the French revolution, and many French remembered Waterloo, but otherwise the Second World War was the only shared event that left a deep mark, with de Gaulle and Churchill bestriding the common memory. Among politicians, only the incumbent French president and British prime minister were known across the Channel, along with Margaret Thatcher. Apart from the royal family, always prominent in French consciousness, few British contemporaries were recognized. Knowledge of each other's culture was just as sketchy. The French knew about Shakespeare, and the British, the Impressionists. Contemporary culture left little or no trace. For the British in the 1990s, Simone de Beauvoir and Jean-Paul Sartre were still the intellectuals to conjure with, and the most famous Frenchwomen were Edith Piaf (thirty years after her death) and Brigitte Bardot – the only French actress engraved in British memories nearly forty years after *Et Dieu créa la femme*.[78] In most cultural perceptions, there seemed to be a long time-lag. Almost every British broadcast item on France was accompanied by the accordion music popular in the 1950s. Music (not however that of Purcell, Elgar, or Britten) was the aspect of British culture that the French in 2004 said they admired most, though the names they recalled were from a generation or two earlier – the Beatles and the Sex Pistols. Though 80 per cent of the British expressed admiration for French art, culture and creativity, the only contemporary names those polled in 2004 recognized were those of footballers – and, for a highly knowledgeable 1 per cent, the burly actor Gérard Depardieu. Six out of ten could name no living French person at all.[79] In short, the British rather like France for what they think it was; the French rather dislike Britain for what they think it is.

As always, each country offered the other a mirror in which to examine itself. For a generation after 1960, the British saw in a successful and assertive France a measure of their own decline. When from the 1980s that decline, at least economically, was reversed, they saw in French 'lifestyle' – from *trains à grande vitesse* to lunches of *extrême lenteur* – a reminder of the cost of their own revival in terms of spending cuts and workaholism. This was a message that many in France were eager to listen to, as it confirmed their determination to defend the 'French model' both at home and in Europe. But dissenting voices increased, and in the 2000s bookshops were piled with tracts asserting that France was now in decline. Some even pointed to Britain as the example that a French revival would have to follow.

LANGUAGE: VOTING WITH YOUR TONGUE

Recall the quip of Charles V: one speaks Spanish to God, French to men, Italian to women, and German to horses . . . He doesn't envisage that one should speak the Goddams' idiom to anyone   even horses!
CHARLES DE GAULLE[80]*

There is an interdependence between the economic power of a nation and the radiation of its culture . . . this is why the spread of French culture in the world must be ceaselessly reinforced and extended.
VALÉRY GISCARD D'ESTAING[81]

No country has been more sensitive about language than France. A concern to preserve the new international status of French emerged as early as the

---

* 'Goddams' – *les Godons* – is an old French nickname for the English, derived from their frequent swearing.

eighteenth century. It has always been a political as well as a cultural issue, because French has been both a means and a sign of influence. As material power declined, its language, values and culture still ensured France a unique prestige. The State strove to maintain this: in 2000 there were 85,000 *agents culturels* working abroad, and considerable efforts were made to consolidate La Francophonie, roughly a linguistic counterpart of the Commonwealth. The reduction of the international use of French explained much of France's pessimism towards the outside world. Public bodies such as the French Academy or the Ministry of Culture were concerned with one enemy: English. French borrowings from other languages caused little disturbance. No one insists on calling a *pizza* a 'flan aux fromages' or a *corrida* a 'concours tauromachique'. In contrast, thanks to the Haut Comité de la Langue Française, software is officially *le logiciel* and email *le courrier électronique*. The Toubon Law of 1994 (introduced by the minister of culture Jacques Toubon) required the exclusive use of French words in all official contexts, including conferences and lectures supported from public funds. 'The use of a language is not innocent,' explained the minister. 'It becomes . . . an instrument of domination.'[82] French and European regulations – promoted by Paris – aimed to protect French commercial culture from American competition, for example by limiting the amount of American pop music that could be broadcast. Fashionable French performers, presumably seeing a gap in the market, started recording in English – and some British critics felt that they had the advantage of being able to sing lyrics such as 'mmm baby, I feel right' with greater conviction. The French authorities also maintained many regulatory and technical barriers in telecommunications and broadcasting systems, in dubbing and subtitling. 'Europe' had long been seen as the strongest bulwark against what Toubon (nicknamed 'Allgood' by his irreverent compatriots) called 'Anglo-merchant culture'.[83] English was banned from the European Commission's press room until 1995. But European integration in fact became one of the greatest vectors for English. After the 2004 enlargement, the Commission was largely anglophone – despite the French government's offering sybaritic French lessons to new Commissioners in a château near Avignon. Some British and French officials think that this linguistic shift must subtly change how Brussels thinks, though the repellent jargon appropriately nicknamed 'le Bad English' suggests that its cogitations will remain less than limpid. Even the French finance ministry began to use English internally, when discussing documents destined for Brussels, where all economic and financial reports were drafted in English. A self-appointed watchdog, the Académie de la Carpette Anglaise (Academy of the English Doormat), gave an annual 'civic indignity' award (the 'English Doormat') to 'deserters' among the national elite who 'collaborated' in the spread of English. More significant than the existence of this eccentric body was the telling range of those it stigmatized, who included the president of the European Central Bank; the Brussels mandarin Pascal Lamy; the head of Presses Universitaires de France (for publishing a management textbook in English); and the boss of Christian Dior, for marketing beauty products with 'anglomaniac' names. But even the Académie's own webpage advertised immersion language courses in London and an English-language dating agency in Paris. Campaigning to prevent the use of English seemed ever more blimpish, not least when in March 2006 Chirac walked out of a European Council meeting 'profoundly shocked' to hear a Frenchman speak English.

The great change took place at the grass-roots: the French learned English, or, as some prefer it, American. Only a generation ago, educated French people rarely spoke English, and read only a little. Those who regarded themselves as knowing English were rarely fluent. Leading academics published major works without reference to anything published in English. In the 2000s, it became rare to find any fairly educated person who did not understand some English, and reasonable fluency was common. The 2004 Thélot Report on educational reform urged more teaching of English at primary school (winning its author an 'English Doormat'). Since the 1960s, a period at a language school in Britain had become a rite of passage for many French adolescents. Cradles of the French elite such as 'Sciences Po' and 'HEC'[84] began teaching whole courses in English. European integration in higher education proved a further vehicle for anglicization, as student exchanges created a large influx of students to Britain – 50,000 full-time undergraduates in 2004 – not balanced in the other direction. Visionary French europhiles aimed to redress the balance by requiring compulsory study in *two* countries for all Europe's university students.

Inevitably, the British bothered less and less to learn other languages, though they remained the world's main foreign learners of French.[85] Anglo-Saxons could travel and do business in English, a convenience they paid for by monoglot cultural impoverishment. The French could no longer regard their language as the world's principal cultural medium – a status it had, in fact, held quite briefly. But they were compensated by the stimulus of having to learn another language, and this, to a society that had traditionally been rather inward-looking and stay-at-home, was of incalculable long-term importance. The alternative would have been increasing marginalization: to reverse the old joke, 'Fog in Paris, world isolated.'

Size Matters

Countries constantly compare themselves with their neighbours, but few do so with the compulsive concern of France and Britain. Commentators and politicians in both countries constantly proclaim themselves 'the world's fourth-largest economy', after the United States, Japan and Germany.[*]

---

[*] In purchasing power, however, they are joint seventh – behind China, India . . . and Italy!

BRITAIN - FRANCE: WHO HAS THE BIGGEST SUBSIDIES?

French commentators talk confidently about being the world's 'third military power', or even its only 'world' power apart from the United States. If British voices rarely make such a claim, few would concede primacy to France. Opinion polls regularly show that each country regards itself as considerably more important than the other.

For the first time in their histories, the two countries are keeping neck and neck. Their populations are, despite France's much larger territory, now practically identical. On broad measures of economic, social and cultural development, little separates them, despite their trumpeted differences of approach to education and health care. In intriguingly miscellaneous areas of life – age of first sexual intercourse (the French reported losing their virginity on average a month earlier), sporting achievement, artistic activity, even cigarette-smoking and murder rates – they are similar or identical. Some striking differences, as in road deaths, may be narrowing. Alcohol consumption too is converging, as the French cut down and the British binge. The Corruption Index does show a difference, with Britain still considered the world's cleanest large state: here France shows alarming signs of deterioration.

Where the Franco-British comparison engenders controversy is when it affects real and perceived power: that is, in economic performance and military force. The two economies are comparable. Both are leading traders in both 'visibles' (goods) and 'invisibles' (money and services). Each has

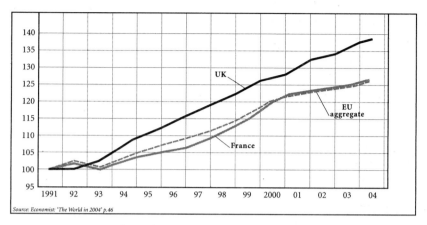

Growth Rates (real GDP: 1991=100)

Source: Economist: 'The World in 2004' p.46

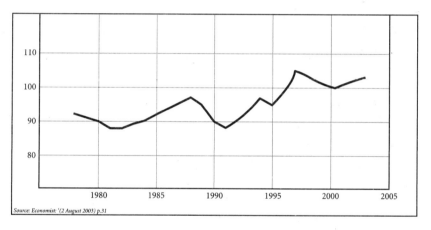

Source: Economist: '(2 August 2003) p.31

Wealth (British GDP per person as a percentage of French GDP per person)

characteristic advantages: for example for Britain the City of London (helping to make it the world's second exporter of services), and for France tourism (two-thirds of its earnings from services). The two economies have become so similar in size that patriotic statisticians disagree as to which is larger, and small fluctuations in the values of the pound or the euro can be sufficient to make one appear wealthier than the other. Yet the trends are clear. In the post-war period, French growth was markedly higher, and in 1960 France's GDP per head overtook Britain's. From the 1980s the trend reversed. British growth-rates overhauled those of France from the early 1990s. Its wealth per capita overtook that of France in the mid-1990s, making the British for the time being the richest of Europe's large nations.

THE NON-IDENTICAL TWINS[86]

	France	Britain
Population	60.4 m	60.5 m
Density (per sq km)	108	244
GDP	$1,911 bn	$1,927 bn
GDP per head	$28,600	$30,200
GDP growth, %	1.7	3
Inflation, %	1.6	1.5
Total labour force	27.2 m	30.2 m
Unemployment, %	9.8	4.8
Annual hours worked	1,500	1,750
National debt as % of GDP (and OECD ranking)	50.9 (10th)	40.4 (16th)
Government spending (% of GDP)	53.5	40.7
Trade as % of world exports (and ranking)	5.18 (6th)	6.74 (4th)
Invisible trade as % of world exports	5.61 (5th)	10.91 (2nd)
Trade balance (2003–4)	$4.6 bn surplus	$88.4 bn deficit
Main trading partner	Germany	USA
Cross-Channel exports[87]	perfume, plastic, rubber, paper, cars, furniture, fashion products	chemicals, metal goods, machinery, electricals, men's and sports clothes
Productivity in manufacturing (% increase, 2000–02)[88]	13.7	11.3
Direct incoming foreign investment 1994–2003	$351.6 bn	$463.1
European ranking (2004)[89]	2nd	1st
Competitiveness (2004 world ranking)[90]	27th	11th
Human Development Index	92.8	92.8
Nobel prizes	44	88

	France	Britain
Universities ranked in world top 25[91]	0	4
Corruption (10=clean)	6.3	8.7
Health spending as % of GNP	9.7	7.7
Life expectancy	79 years	78.2 years
Av. age of first sexual intercourse (1998)[92]	16.6	16.7
Prison population	63,000	73,000
Murders (1999)[93]	953	927
Road deaths (1996)[94]	8,080	3,598
Smoking (annual cigarettes per capita, and European ranking)	1,303 (13th)	1,106 (14th)
Alcohol (annual per capita)	11 litres	8 litres
Book sales (annual)	$2.5 bn (7th)	$4.3 bn (4th)
Foreign aid (annual)	$4.2 bn	$4.6 bn
Olympic gold medals (1896–2004)	200	197
Rank in Eurovision song contest (2005)	23rd	22nd

French commentators pointed to their superior productivity per worker, and their regular (though declining) trade surpluses – bigger with Britain than with any other country. This showed the strength of the French economy in certain areas (e.g. cars, luxury goods, tourism, food processing), higher investment, and a somewhat better trained workforce. This view minimized British strength (notably in financial services, the only sector potentially able to benefit, rather than suffer, from the economic renaissance of China and India). It also overlooked the disadvantages for France. High productivity was the consequence of a highly regulated labour market with uniquely heavy payroll taxes, which made firms install machines rather than employ workers. Many refused to expand if it meant taking on more staff. Most incoming foreign investment therefore went into the high-productivity industrial sector, creating few new jobs. The consequence was chronic unemployment and under-used capacity. The facts of higher British growth and lower unemployment impinged on French public awareness – by 2005 it was something 'everyone knows'.[95] In the simplest terms, in Britain the State took less, more people had jobs and they worked longer hours. In France, the State and public sector were unusually big, unemployment unusually high, and those with jobs worked less. It was, of course, possible to prefer one model to the other, as cross-Channel migration demonstrated. Though the Labour government followed a less market-oriented policy than the Tories, the difference between Blair and Thatcher was still less than that between Blair and Chirac. By some criteria, Britain in the early 2000s was economically more like the United States or Japan than like France. In some ways this divergence was widening, confirming Britain as the least 'European' of the EU economies. The share of Britain's trade with the United States had been rising since the 1990s, while that with the EU had been falling. Gordon Brown observed that 80 per cent of Britain's potential trade lay outside the EU. Continental investment in Britain for a time collapsed after 2002, while that of the United States forged ahead, making Britain by far the biggest destination for American capital, bigger than the whole of Asia, and the largest European recipient (with France second) of foreign investment. Britain was Europe's biggest foreign investor by far, and it invested twice as much outside as inside the EU.[96]

But it was not clear how long the economic divergence between Britain and France would continue. Tony Blair assured the European Parliament in 2005 that it was a 'caricature' that Britain was 'in the grip of some extreme Anglo-Saxon market philosophy': he had 'increased investment in our public services more than any other European country'.[97] Britain was indeed converging with the euro zone in levels of taxation, public borrowing, and public sector employment and spending, which rose 64 per cent in eight years. Incoming foreign investment, for years far ahead of France, temporarily fell far below ($14.6 bn in 2003 compared with $45.3 bn to France) and the longer-term trend was unclear.[98] In 2005, British economic growth slowed abruptly to its lowest since 1993, and some forecast that French growth would overtake it in 2006 for the first time in two decades.[99] While Britain moved towards France, France seemed ready to move towards Britain and – more importantly – many commentators began to recognize publicly that 'Europe' could not shut out the rest of the world, and especially the growing economic power of Asia. An official report admitted 'the limits of our model', and declared that France must slash the 'stifling' level of public spending, slim the public sector, reduce public debt and become less 'afraid' of the outside world.[100] To evade the 'French model' of legal employment protection, private-sector employers were increasing the number of part-time workers and short-term contracts. To plug the gap in state revenues, in 2005 privatization of gas, motorways and electricity accelerated. It therefore seemed possible that France and Britain were set to change economic places once again. Yet foreign investors remained sceptical that France would really change,[101] and the sudden political storm in 2005 over the EU Constitution demonstrated how deep and strong public hostility to economic liberalism remained, especially, of course, in the public sector.

Europe's Warrior Nations

France must continue to behave as a great power precisely because she no longer is one.

CHARLES DE GAULLE

In recent years, Britain has punched above her weight in the world. We intend to keep it that way.

DOUGLAS HURD, foreign secretary, 1992

Our two nations understand power. They are not afraid of it; they are not ashamed of it either. Each wants to remain a force for progress in the world

TONY BLAIR to the Assemblée Nationale, 1998

The dividing line . . . is between those who have a neutralist, pacifist or hedonistic vision of Europe and an idealistic vision of international relations, and the others who are aware that the world is still governed by balances of power . . . France and Britain should be on the same side on this point.

HUBERT VEDRINE, former foreign minister, 2004

Britain wants to punch above its weight in the world. So does France. Or at least, their politicians and diplomats do. It is an unusual and risky ambition. Most countries prefer to punch below their weight. Most European countries are happy not to punch at all. This has been described as the contrast between Europe's 'Venus' and America's 'Mars'.[102] Britain and France, however, are Europe's surviving Martians. Both emphasize their armed forces as a symbol of national identity and international influence. They are the only European states regularly willing and able to use military force far from home. It has cost them a vast amount of treasure and a steady trickle of blood, with substantial effects on their economic and political lives. The British believe more than any other European nation that war is sometimes justified. The French want to make the EU a military power.[103] This proclivity both divides and unites them.

French commentators, following de Gaulle, stress France's unique independence, equipped with its own conventional and nuclear arms. As de Gaulle put it, 'let us drink from our own cup: it may be smaller but at least it's ours'. In fact, France's nuclear deterrent always relied on NATO early-warning systems and other technical cooperation to make it viable.[104] The British, in contrast, were often discounted by the French as dependent on, and hence mere auxiliaries of, the United States. French politicians have therefore claimed to be the only genuine European great power, and hence the leader and protector of Europe. This argument has never been accepted outside France. Tireless efforts to promote independent European military force have borne little fruit, and in practice require the cooperation of the pro-NATO British. French independence has been costly, not only in money. French armed forces could not acquire the best equipment – unless it happened to be French. France also paid a diplomatic price for independence, such as the unpopularity of nuclear testing in the Pacific Ocean. In intelligence matters, being outside the 'Anglo-Saxon' system handicapped it. With the exception of small expeditions in Africa, it lacked the ships and aircraft to transport major forces. Moreover, its Europe-focused armed forces were based until 2002 on short-service conscription, with a small volunteer element outweighed by large, poorly trained, poorly equipped and inflexible conscript forces. They were incapable of operating at the highest professional and technological level, either alone or in conjunction with the Anglo-Saxons. All in all, its military independence has been more symbolic than real.

Two conflicts revealed the differences between British and French capacities. In the Falklands War in 1982, Britain dispatched a self-sufficient task force a long distance, and, despite risks, defeated Argentina near its home ground. France could not have attempted the equivalent. The First Gulf War in 1991 showed up the weakness of its army. A small light mobile force had to be scratched together by pulling professional soldiers out of their normal units, and it could play only a symbolic role well away from the main American-British force. Notional independence was nullified by actual impotence. So the French revolutionized their armed forces. The nuclear deterrent was cut back, and conscription was phased out between 1996 and 2002, abandoning the cherished republican principle of a citizen soldiery. For the first time in its history, France decided to copy the British army.

The long Balkan tragedy from 1991 to 1999 was the bloodiest episode in European history after 1945, costing certainly tens of thousands, and possibly hundreds of thousands of lives. For Britain and France, the break-up of Yugoslavia was a test of their capacity and ambition to be the military leaders and guardians of Europe. The United States had no wish to be involved, and the European states had no wish to involve it. The crisis was proclaimed as 'the Hour of Europe'. France and Britain took charge. The French had clear ambitions. In the view of the British foreign secretary Douglas Hurd – relatively francophile but none the less suspicious – their aims were for 'France and French policy to shine'; for 'a big European army in Yugoslavia and an Anglo-French protectorate'; and – as always – to promote a European military power independent of the United States. For the British government, after the removal of Margaret Thatcher, going along with the French was an opportunity to demonstrate its new position 'at the heart of Europe'. 'Defence in Europe is not an opt-out subject for us – like the Social Chapter,' declared Hurd. 'Working with the French is an important aspect.'[105] Britain and France directed European policy, and must bear responsibility for its outcome. They stubbornly misread the crisis, and their unwillingness to allow other approaches dragged out the agony.[106]

Unfortunately for the peoples of disintegrating Yugoslavia, neither London nor Paris was willing or able to back its political pretensions with corresponding military force. Neither were they willing to let the situation resolve itself – which would have been a brutal but logical alternative. Instead, a succession of British and French generals and semi-retired, mainly British, politicians (including Lords Carrington and Owen) went out to try to run the affairs of the Balkans. Both British and French liked to justify their involvement in international affairs by claiming great experience in such matters, inherited from imperial days. This time it led them astray. An erroneous consensus developed on three points. First, that this was an incomprehensible 'tribal' conflict based on ancient hatreds, in which all sides were equally blameworthy. Second, that it would prove a 'quagmire' (analogies with Vietnam and Northern Ireland were common) which would absorb hundreds of thousands of soldiers and cause enormous casualties. Third, that the Serbs were indomitable and practically invincible (here it was common to make fallacious references to the Second World War). The conclusions drawn from these assumptions were that the proper attitude of outsiders was to refuse to take sides, to avoid military involvement except in a humanitarian role, and to press for a compromise that would necessarily favour a Greater Serbia. A UN arms embargo favoured the Serbs, who were already well-armed. These views were the height of 'realism', showing a refusal to be 'simplistic'; and critics were met with angry and contemptuous dismissal.

But the analysis was wrong. The crisis, far from being lost in the mists of Balkan history, was caused by the aggressiveness of the ex-Communist Serbian regime of Slobodan Milosevic, first against Croatia, and subsequently against Bosnia and Kosovo. Events would show that he could be defeated with relative ease and expedition. British and French politicians and soldiers developed an odd rapport with the Serbs. For the French, not least President Mitterrand, this was based on a confused sense that they had been allies during both World Wars, and that they had to be conciliated. The British agreed. It was repeatedly stated that vast German forces had been unable to defeat the Serbs between 1941 and 1944. While those in office in Paris and London bore the primary responsibility, their highly pessimistic view was overwhelmingly supported by British and French politicians of all parties, and by soldiers and experts, whether official, academic or journalistic. The intelligentsia of both countries showed excessive confidence in their own judgement, in which lack of real knowledge was eked out with inaccurate and misapplied historical and political analogies. A few genuine experts who knew from their own experience that the received wisdom was a distortion were ignored.[107]

The Anglo-French consensus was disastrous. It prolonged the conflict and unintentionally encouraged Serb aggression, accompanied by organized rape, massacre and 'ethnic cleansing'. Yet the policy was persisted in even when it was clearly not working, and London and Paris went to great lengths to defend their policy when the Clinton administration in Washington began reluctantly to advocate a policy of 'lift and strike' – lifting the arms embargo to Bosnia, and launching air strikes against Serb military targets. Hurd wrote in his diary that 'Our prudent stance looks feeble and inhumane. Yet I cannot think that air strikes would settle anything much and a ground operation to deal with snipers etc would be interminable.'[108] Conservative ministers derided internal critics such as Thatcher, and the French socialist ministers ignored left-wing advocates of 'humanitarian intervention'. Those running policy in both countries could not contemplate a change that would condemn their earlier stance. Moreover, the British and French, having finally agreed to commit a few troops for humanitarian purposes, found that these became in effect hostages against further military action. The secretary-general of the French charity Médecins sans Frontières condemned the situation as a 'shameful farce'.[109]

During the course of the Balkan imbroglio, an even greater disaster occurred in Africa: the Rwanda genocide of 1994. Both the British and French, as the main former colonial powers, had a feckless record of semi-involvement in African affairs. The French had since the 1960s pursued a neo-colonial policy in west and central Africa, run by a small inner circle reporting to the president. In pursuit of commercial advantages, strategic bases and prestige, there had been few scruples over methods, and corruption was rife. Paris had propped up several regimes with money, arms and troops, and received favours in return. One of these was the Hutu ethnic government of Rwanda, especially as it was francophone whereas the Tutsi opposition was regarded in Paris as 'anglophone' and too close to the Anglo-Saxons. In April 1994, the Hutu authorities ignited a genocidal attack on the Tutsi minority in which 800,000 people were slaughtered. The French were slow to react, and then continued to play politics under the cover of the United Nations, 'protecting the génocidaires and permanently destabilizing the region'.[110] The British, bogged down in the Balkans, looked the other way. No other country took an interest until it was too late.

By late 1994, Britain's Balkan policy was 'falling to bits around us'[111] and Whitehall was increasingly condemned for preventing action. Dénouement came in 1995. Continued Serb shelling of the Bosnian capital Sarajevo caused a new British commander to order air strikes against Serb ammunition dumps, the first such action of the war: one of his French predecessors had been sacked for urging it. The Serbs responded by seizing UN soldiers –

including thirty British – as hostages. In July 1995, Serbian troops overran the 'safe haven' of Srebrenice, and slaughtered several thousand Bosnian men and boys. Although a small Dutch force had been the nominal protectors, the ultimate failure was an Anglo-French one. The new French president, Jacques Chirac, broke ranks with the British, and agreed to American demands for serious military intervention. London, alarmed at the prospect of a Franco-American agreement excluding them, hastened to agree, and a small Franco-British Rapid Reaction Force, created some months earlier, was dispatched. The crucial element in the new strategy was American air power, however, supporting counter-attacks by Croatian and Bosnian forces. The Serbs, belying earlier predictions, retreated rapidly, and a compromise agreement was signed at Dayton, Ohio. Many observed that this could have been done years earlier. As well as devastating former Yugoslavia, the war had damaged Anglo-American relations. The British were criticized for stubborn timidity. Americans referred to Suez and the 1930s. Thatcher is said to have compared Hurd with Chamberlain, and Chirac similarly condemned previous Anglo-French policy towards the Serbs as 'like Chamberlain and Daladier'.[112] Some American politicians openly questioned the value of the 'special relationship' and of NATO as a whole.

Under military and political pressure, the French and British drew together. In Hurd's view, 'Bosnia brought service cooperation between the British and the French to a new postwar high.'[113] In 1993 and 1994, steps were taken towards air force and nuclear deterrence coordination. The 1997–2002 French defence programme spoke of a 'privileged partnership' with Britain, and the new Blair government signed a military agreement in 1998 at Saint-Malo which led to a European Rapid Reaction Force being set up in 2000 round a Franco-British core. The signatories, as always, did not agree on what they were aiming at. The British foreign secretary stated that 'collective defence is not the job of the European Union [but] remains the job of NATO'. The French foreign minister said that the aim was to 'go beyond' NATO, but Chirac agreed to 'put a little bit of NATO in it' as a concession to London.[114]

BANGS AND BUCKS

French conventional and nuclear forces were still considerably larger than the British in the early 2000s, though the trend was convergent as the former ended conscription. In spending terms Britain, France and Japan were almost identical, outdistanced only by America – hugely – and, according to some measures, by China, slightly. This, given Japan's essentially defensive stance, and the immobility and technical limitations of Chinese, Russian and Indian forces, made Britain and France the world's most effective second-rank militarily powers.[115] Both had taken a 'peace dividend' by slashing spending in the 1990s, along with the rest of Europe. But they were the only European states to increase defence budgets modestly from 2003, and they were accounting for two-thirds of total European spending on military hardware. France's effective military power was hampered by its policy of independence, including a sizeable, expensive and obsolescent nuclear deterrent. It was also handicapped by the hybrid nature of its forces, until conscription was finally phased out. Conversion to all-professional forces and modernization of equipment required money and time: full completion was planned for 2015. Much French material was out of commission or inferior – for example the Leclerc tank, the Mirage fighter without night vision, and warships capable only of patrolling. Post Cold War requirements – coercion of 'rogue states', operations against elusive terrorist networks, and peace-keeping in failing states – needed trained personnel, able to react rapidly and deploy widely, using expensive detection and communications equipment, and armed with precision weapons. Crucially, Britain had spent considerably more on equipment, research and development for its smaller professional forces. Its willingness to buy weapons and equipment abroad increased their effectiveness. The Royal Navy had a greater capacity than the French navy to project force at a distance.

MILITARY FORCE[116]

(world ranking in brackets)	*France*	*Britain*
Defence spending (2003)[117]	$35 bn (4th)	$37.1 bn (3rd)
as % of GDP	2.5	2.4
Defence personnel		
(incl. civilians)	428,000	304,000
Soldiers (2004)	134,000	113,000
Sailors and marines (2004)	42,866	40,880
Aviation (2004)	60,990	53,390
Expenditure on		
equipment (2003)	$7.2 bn	$8.7 bn
Expenditure per		
soldier (1999)	$92,400 (15th)	$167,000 (3rd)
Ships (2003)		
Aircraft/helicopter carriers	2	3
Major surface ships	23	31
Submarines	10	15
Nuclear warheads	348 (4th)	185 (5th or 6th)
Aircraft (combat)	329	324
Armoured fighting vehicles	754	1,026

Both countries maintained arms manufacturing as a foundation of national security and an important source of foreign earnings and diplomatic leverage. Both have wasted vast sums on individual and joint projects – arguably inevitable where diplomatic criteria outweigh military and economic ones, and doubly so if ambitions exceed capacities. It would be hard to decide whether to give the booby prize to France's accident-prone nuclear aircraft carrier, the *Charles de Gaulle*, or to Britain's share in the fabulously expensive Eurofighter. In a triumph of hope over experience, in June 2004 the two countries agreed on joint construction of up to three largely identical aircraft carriers. The main contrast, however – which reflected a basic Franco-British ideological difference – is that the British government fostered international competition in its arms supply, and the British arms industry was genuinely more independent of government and active in both inter-European and trans-Atlantic links. The French government retained very close relations with its arms manufacturers, bought major weapons only from them, and was not involved with America. To buttress the relationship, by 2004 arms companies owned some 70 per cent of the French press.[118] France pressed for joint European military projects, including for spy satellites and telecommunications, and aimed at a European military aerospace industry. Cynics might suspect that the goal was a sort of military Common Agricultural Policy, with France as the main beneficiary and Britain the main contributor. As an arms manufacturer and exporter, despite a notoriously unscrupulous sales policy, it had usually been far less important than Britain. However, a 50 per cent fall in British arms exports in the early 2000s, and a surge in French sales – many of them at below the cost of manufacture – to the Middle East, Taiwan, India and Pakistan, made it the world's third largest supplier. Britain (which mainly supplied Commonwealth countries) fell to sixth place.[119]

Although British and French military power appeared on paper to be broadly in balance, the defence minister, Michèle Alliot-Marie, appointed in 2002, was 'shocked' to be told that in equipment and deployability all three armed forces remained 'significantly below the British'.[120] A leading American defence expert told *Le Monde* that Britain was the world's second most powerful country 'in influence and world role', and Germany the third.[121] France was determined at least to catch up with Britain, which would otherwise dominate any European defence organization, and it officially announced a 'special partnership' with Britain. All would depend on how much each country was willing and able to spend. Both faced similar dilemmas. State spending, borrowing and taxation had reached levels considered politically dangerous and economically damaging. Both had budgets heavily committed to welfare and to a growing civilian public sector. Both had pensions crises looming. But both wanted to be able to operate independently or as leaders of a European coalition. The British wanted to stay technologically advanced enough to operate alongside the United States, the French, to lead Europe as a counterweight to the United States. This meant heavy expenditure on technology – including continuing bills for past mistakes – at the expense of manpower. France substantially pushed up its defence spending, breaking the European Union Stability and Growth Pact in the process; it demanded first that defence spending should not be counted, and then simply ignored the pact. In July 2004 Britain – whose state finances had swung in five years from a large budget surplus to a large deficit – managed a nominal increase in defence spending, but accompanied by large cuts in manpower, regiments, tanks, ships and aircraft. Yet people, not just gadgets, were needed for peacekeeping and to meet increasing overseas commitments. Financial logic – despite political differences – pushed the two countries towards cooperation where their interests overlapped. The French, for example, largely abandoned their military protectorate over francophone Africa in favour of coordinating 'spheres of influence' with Britain; and despite the quarrel over Iraq, the joint aircraft carrier project was in theory to begin in 2006–7.

Did all this show that both countries were indeed punching above their weight? Exasperated by the Iraq disaster, one left-wing commentator raged that Britain spent 'more than all Europe except France on defence we can't afford [like] distressed gentlefolk keeping up appearances, making ourselves ridiculous and obnoxious to our real equals, the Europeans . . . isolated from Europe, reviled in most of the world, still posturing absurdly . . . we must give up punching at any weight, beyond peacekeeping contributions to UN and European forces'.[122] Some right-wing commentators agreed with the conclusion, if not the sentiment. Yet France and Britain were among the world's richest states, with wide interests and obligations. For them to play a part in world affairs – however particular policies might be judged – was in no way anachronistic or ridiculous. Arguably, they were punching *below* their weight – or, to drop the boxing metaphor, were unwilling to pay the price of their pretensions. They were spending far less than the USA (or indeed Greece) as a proportion of GNP, and little more than Norway. If the American effort was some indication of the cost of international ambitions, it indicated that Britain and France would need to increase defence spending by a third – unthinkable in either country. British and French politicians often justified a special role for themselves less by the facts of wealth and power than by claiming a superior wisdom that 'new' powers could not match. The experiences of the 1990s and 2000s amply showed that wisdom was as rare a commodity in London and Paris as elsewhere. Was this an argument for them to give up the 'posturing' and mind their own business? That would mean leaving the United States the sole actor on the world stage. If the two countries were serious about not wanting this, they would somehow have to pay the cost. To claim responsibility without power risked doing more harm than good, to themselves and to others.

Jacques Chirac was elected president in 1995, and Tony Blair became prime minister in May 1997. Ironically, given later events, the former was unusually Atlanticist, and the latter, enthusiastically 'European'. Both embarked on new and ambitious foreign policies. Chirac began a short period of nuclear-weapons testing in the Pacific, and announced greater involvement in NATO. The French, encouraged by the British, had begun attending NATO summits in 1995 for the first time in thirty years, but they intended it to be on their own terms: 'the extent to which we participate in the alliance will reflect the degree to which it changes'.[123] Their aims were to be treated as equal to the British, and to develop an autonomous European means of action within the NATO system. Chirac proposed, and then imprudently announced in September 1996, that a European officer (i.e. a Frenchman) would take over command of the southern sector of NATO from an American. When the Americans demurred, Chirac was seriously embarrassed, and developed a serious grudge.[124] Blair's policy was intended to be more principled, assertive, and effective than that of his Conservative predecessors, and both restore Britain's relations with the United States and place it at the centre of European affairs. This led to an unparalleled frequency of military action: five times in six years.[125] Though Blair has claimed the legacy of Gladstone, he is really the heir of Palmerston, with a similar combination of idealism and bombast: 'I am a British patriot,' he proclaimed in 1997. 'Britain in my vision is not Britain turning its back on the world – narrow, shy, uncertain . . . We are a leader of nations or nothing.'[126] But he arguably lacked Palmerston's hard headedness, and he certainly lacked Palmerston's power.

The new government, buoyed up by popularity at home and the interest they aroused abroad, defined a new 'ethical', even 'post-modern', strategy not tied to traditional concepts of national interest or national sovereignty. The aim was to do good and to feel good. The first act was participation in a US-led bombing campaign in Iraq in November 1998. The second, in 1999, was in the Balkans, following more Serb aggression in Kosovo. A meeting with the Serbian leader Milosevic at Rambouillet, jointly chaired by the French and British foreign ministers Hubert Védrine and Robin Cook, failed to stop the violence. Blair urged first a bombing campaign against the Serbs, and then pressed for ground troops, promising if necessary the largest British military expedition since 1945. Eventually, NATO forces, led by

Britain and France, and Russian troops, occupied Kosovo to impose peace. The process was far from bloodless, it outraged the pacifist Left, it precipitated a vast refugee crisis, and it left a violent and unstable aftermath. Yet it was generally regarded as the lesser evil, and a success for the new doctrine of 'humanitarian intervention', formulated by the French Left, taken up by Blair and supported by most of the Labour party. The United Nations had not given its approval, but the sanction of NATO, the EU, and majority opinion was taken to give sufficient justification to what Blair thought was the first-ever 'progressive' war. France and Britain were in unison. The main Balkan troublemaker, Milosevic, was overthrown.

Hubris beckoned. Failures in the 1990s had been due to timidity: on this, Downing Street and the White House agreed. The diplomatic and military experts, always pointing out difficulties, had been in charge when catastrophe struck Bosnia and Rwanda. Blair, a man previously uninterested in foreign affairs, had enrolled both Europe and America in his Balkan policy. Boldness and new ideas had worked. Those who had advocated the use of force against Milosevic would advocate it against Saddam Hussein; those who had opposed it in Bosnia would oppose it in Iraq.

The destruction of the Twin Towers in New York on 11 September 2001, it has often been said, changed the world. But it did not change everything. The Iraq problem predated it. The nature of that problem seemed clear. Saddam Hussein, the Iraqi dictator, had used chemical weapons. He had attacked his neighbours. He had developed long-range artillery and missiles, and there was plausible evidence that he still intended to make or buy chemical, biological or nuclear 'weapons of mass destruction' – the soon notorious 'WMDs'. His main preoccupation was his old enemy Iran, itself aiming at WMDs. Victory over Iran would have made him the dominant figure in the Islamic world, with potential control of a large part of the world's oil. Since the invasion of Kuwait and defeat in 1991, Iraq had been sporadically subject to UN economic sanctions and inspections to forestall rearmament. This policy was more effective than anyone realized, and more than Saddam dared to admit: he no longer had WMDs.

Saddam's priority was to end UN sanctions and controls. He made various secret offers of rapprochement with the United States, which were ignored. Nevertheless, controls were breaking down. One reason was because of the appalling suffering they caused the Iraqi population – aggravated by Saddam for propaganda purposes. The other was the reluctance of any countries but the United States and Britain to enforce them. The UN Oil for Food programme (1995) – ostensibly to allow necessities to be imported to relieve the people's sufferings – gave Saddam a means of buying political and economic friends. Russia and France were the largest recipients of secret payments and of trade.[127] Here the role of France – and Russia, China and others – became important and controversial, if not sinister. At best, it showed a desire to engage with and influence Saddam. At worst, it was corrupt and reckless. The Iraqis believed, somewhat simplistically, that France's interest was purely mercenary, especially concerning oil. They thought that greasing palms in Paris would give access to Chirac.[128] Why they should think so is plain: the financing of political parties was one of the murkiest aspects of French life, and the source of widespread and contagious corruption at home and abroad. But French motives went deeper, and were linked with their great-power ambition.

The origins of their policy lay in the 1920s, when Iraqi oil formed part of the spoils of the First World War. To assert influence in the Middle East in rivalry with the 'Anglo-Saxons' was a later obsession of de Gaulle, and to grab a share of world markets in the strategic areas of nuclear power, arms sales and oil was a continuing preoccupation of his successors. In 1972, the young second-in-command of the Baathist regime, Saddam Hussein, was invited to the Elysée Palace, where he assured his host that he had 'chosen France' – which had the inestimable advantage of not being Britain, Russia or America. France began selling arms, and its oil company Total secured privileges. Jacques Chirac's first venture into foreign affairs, as a youthful prime minister, was establishing personal contact with Saddam. In 1975, he invited him to visit French nuclear installations, treating him to a weekend tête-à-tête in Provence and a gala reception at Versailles. Chirac announced that France was aiding Iraq to acquire two reactors and 600 French-trained technicians. Saddam told an Arab newspaper that this was 'the first step towards the production of an Arab atomic bomb'.[129] The Israelis – France's earlier protégés – put a stop to that by bombing the first unfinished reactor on 7 June 1981. Iraq's attack on Iran that year increased the demand for French arms – which Arab governments urged Paris to supply. France (like the USSR) was happy to oblige. Iraq had become France's second most important source of oil, while its war helped keep the French arms industry afloat: 14 billion francs of exports in 1981, 13 billion in 1982. Iraq soon owed so much money, as the finance minister Jacques Delors pointed out, that France had to help it win. France's most modern aircraft were delivered, some taken from its own navy. The defence minister stated that 'Iraqi security is an imperative of French national defence'.[130] The oil company Elf – a factotum of the French government, and later the focus of a string of corruption prosecutions in the 2000s – made itself at home in Baghdad.

The First Gulf War caused a chill. Mitterrand and his ministers tried literally until the last hours to persuade Saddam to withdraw peacefully from Kuwait, but then felt obliged to take part in the UN-sanctioned Coalition campaign, although the defence minister, Jean-Pierre Chevènement, resigned in protest. French politicians, the oil and arms industries and other business interests restored relations in the 1990s, anticipating the end of UN sanctions. From the late 1990s, French firms were angling to supply aircraft, military vehicles and other armaments. In 1997, the French, Russians and Chinese pressed for the end of sanctions and of UN weapons inspections. Saddam duly began to block inspections, and the inspectors were withdrawn. This was dangerous, as it encouraged the Americans and British to fear the worst. In 1998 – over French and German opposition – they launched air strikes on supposed weapons development sites. France successfully brokered a compromise, but withdrew from enforcing controls. During 2000–2001 the French and Russian governments – whom Saddam played off against each other – pressed the UN to declare that Iraq had disarmed, to end weapons inspections, and to lift sanctions. French businessmen went to negotiate reconstruction and oil contracts. Lobby groups and 'solidarity' committees in Paris were encouraged with 'copious amounts of oil money'.[131] Remaining sanctions were increasingly ignored by many countries, prominent among them France, which bought oil, sold agricultural produce and arms, and signed public works contracts – already worth 1.6 billion euros in 2001. The Iraqi foreign minister observed that Paris was adhering to the letter of sanctions but not the spirit.[132] All had an eye on big future profits. Their greed made the situation dangerously unstable.

No one knew whether Saddam Hussein had disarmed and abandoned his military ambitions. If he had, normalization of relations would be possible and perhaps beneficial, if – a big if – Saddam was thereby induced to behave better towards his own people and his neighbours. If not, the end of sanctions would let him off the leash to use Iraq's oil wealth to perpetuate domestic oppression, resume a WMD programme and prepare further aggression. Blair was alarmed by 'scary' intelligence reports on Iraqi weapons. He was eager to do something to ward off future danger, and discussed the problem with President Clinton. As early as November 1997 Blair said privately that Saddam was 'very close to some appalling weapons of mass destruction. I don't understand why the French and the others don't understand this.'[133] His perplexity was comprehensible: the French, like the other powers and the UN experts, assumed that Saddam still had weapons and plans for more, and they expected that weapons inspections would find evidence. Unless some new means of containment could be found, a war to remove him – especially in the aftermath of the 11 September attack on New York, which heightened American desire for pre-emptive action against 'rogue states' – was likely. The only hope of peaceful containment would have been a united front of the Western powers to intimidate Saddam, in which France, as Saddam's best friend in the West, would have been pivotal. Blair hoped that the French would broker 'a face-saving way out'. But

Saddam was told by his intelligence service in May 2002 that a prominent French politician had assured them that France would use its position on the UN Security Council veto any military attack.[134] If this encouraged Iraqi over-confidence, it was fatal, because the Americans were already willing to go to war.

The 'special relationship' had never been so special as during 2001–3. Churchill had never had – and would never have accepted – such absorption into Roosevelt's government, nor Thatcher into Reagan's. Blair, for domestic and diplomatic reasons, persuaded the sceptical George W. Bush to use the United Nations procedure against Saddam Hussein, and promised that he would 'deliver' European support. It seems likely that in return he pledged to fight alongside the Americans if necessary – an outcome that suited his own inclinations and reading of events.[135] He seems to have made this decision privately during the spring or summer of 2002 – perhaps, piquantly, in France in August while communing with nature in the Pyrenees.[136] In a reversion to seventeenth-century government, British state policy was made by Blair and his small entourage in an inextricable tangle of vision, audacity, deceit and incompetence. Their intimate contact with Washington surpassed that of Charles II with Versailles – though with no known equivalent of the Duchess of Portsmouth. The Cabinet was supine, content with occasional 'unscripted' briefings.[137] Its Defence and Overseas Policy Committee and its Intelligence Committee never met. The Foreign Office was bypassed, and legal advice given short shrift. Constitutional government had effectively been suspended by a prime minister convinced that the road to heaven was paved with good intentions. Hence the amateurish use of 'sexed up' intelligence information, the elementary errors of fact, and the frenetic and futile efforts to 'deliver' Europe and the UN by a handful of excited and rather ignorant courtiers in Downing Street. Preoccupied with selling rather than questioning policy, they were constantly surprised by events, and misunderstood the views of other states, above all the French.

The growing crisis revived the jaded 'Franco–German couple', as German public opinion was increasingly hostile to American policy. One insider commented that for the first time, Franco–German relations passed from wary politeness to real cordiality. Chancellor Schröder was glad to follow Chirac's lead – a situation from which the French were eager to profit. This had repercussions on EU politics. A Franco–German agreement to preserve the CAP was sprung on the British at the Brussels EU summit on 24 October 2002 (see above, page 652). Blair denounced the deal as illegitimate and a blow to Third World farmers. Chirac – who had earlier lectured Blair on what his son 'little Leo' might one day think about what Daddy had done in the war – was livid. Perhaps grown used to the deferential treatment accorded to Fifth Republic presidents, he buttonholed Blair, ticked him off for being 'bad-mannered' (*mal élevé*) and cancelled the annual Franco-British summit. This was a priceless moment for those who recalled his famous laddish interjection during a Thatcher tirade in 1987.* A British witness saw them like 'lads looking for a brawl outside a pub on a Friday night.'[138] Personal relations between the two men, originally quite friendly, became increasingly antagonistic.

Far less has been – and doubtless far less will be – disclosed about goings on at the Elysée and the Quai d'Orsay than those in Downing Street. Any French government was certain to try to rein in American action, and preserve its long-cultivated status as friend of the Arabs. This was not only to preserve its sleazy and profitable economic foothold, and ensure payment of huge Iraqi debts. French politicians are highly sensitive to their Mediterranean position on the 'fault line' between Europe and the Arab world,[139] and to the number and feelings of their own Muslim citizens. Whether Chirac, known to be a headstrong character, and his foreign minister Dominique Galouzeau de Villepin, a decorative, aristocratic-sounding career diplomat with political ambitions and Napoleonic nostalgia, had a long-term plan for handling Saddam is unclear. It seems unlikely, however, that they planned an outright confrontation with the Anglo-Saxons. The French intelligence services were cooperating with their allies as usual, and Paris was putting pressure on Baghdad to give way.[140] Paris agreed to Resolution 1441 (8 November 2002) imposing stringent demands on Iraq, but denied that this automatically sanctioned war if the demands were not met. French policy was to use its contacts in Iraq and other Arab countries to persuade Iraq to accept more extensive weapons inspections. Presumably this was intended to save the Iraqi regime or at least protect France's influence in the Arab world. Yet from September 2002 to January 2003, the French – unlike the Germans – said that they would if necessary take part in military action, as they had done in the first Gulf War. However, this was only to happen if Saddam resisted weapons inspections, and if the UN Security Council approved an invasion. In January 2003, the Americans and British began sending troops to the Persian Gulf. On 7 January, Chirac told the French armed forces to prepare to participate.[141] But Saddam, rather than resisting UN demands, was allowing weapons inspectors to search for evidence of WMDs, and playing for time. Paris in effect supported him by calling for delay while the inspectors pursued their 'long and difficult work'. But the Anglo-Saxons could not keep armies in the Gulf indefinitely. They would inevitably use them unless Saddam capitulated by allowing ever more stringent inspections, which would mean the

---

*One version is 'Est-ce qu'elle veut mes couilles?' ('Does she want my balls?') An alternative, more idiomatic and untranslatable, is 'Ça m'en touche une sans faire bouger l'autre.' See *L'Express* (14 November 2002), and *Le Monde* (4–5 April 2004).

end of his prestige and probably of his power. Rapidly and publicly, the French and Anglo–American positions diverged.

The Franco–British relationship failed to provide a transatlantic bridge, the idea cherished by British politicians from Bevin to Blair. Cross-Channel diplomacy was barely operating. Influencing public opinion became more important than inter-governmental good manners, let alone serious consultation. Opinion in France and elsewhere so detested American policy that Chirac and Villepin must have been simultaneously tempted and impelled to give it voice. This was an opportunity for Chirac, reelected in 2002 in demeaning circumstances – some of his supporters using the slogan 'better a crook than a fascist'* – to become a true national leader. For Villepin, a romantic nationalist obsessed with reviving French grandeur,[142] it was a chance to proclaim opposition to superpower arrogance as in the glory days of de Gaulle.

British and French policy spectacularly collided in January 2003. On the 20th, Villepin, to widespread applause, announced at the UN that 'nothing today justifies military action' – indicating that France might use its UN veto. There ensued a trial of Franco–British diplomatic strength inside and outside Europe, watched with some bemusement by the Americans. The French and German parliaments held a ceremonial joint meeting at Versailles. On 30 January a public letter of support for American policy over Iraq from Blair and seven, and eventually fifteen, European prime ministers, was drawn up without French (or indeed British) diplomats being informed. One French commentator described the declaration, which spoke on behalf of 'Europe', as being 'written on English dictation'.[143] Perfidious Albion, thought the French, had deliberately and publicly split Europe to please the Americans – just what de Gaulle had always feared. Moreover, Blair had enlisted new and candidate EU states in defiance of Franco–German leadership. The abrasive American defence secretary Donald Rumsfeld declared gleefully that France, Germany and their supporters were merely 'old Europe'. Chirac reacted with characteristic unsubtlety, telling 'infantile' new EU members that they would shut up if they knew what was good for them. This underlined France's barely concealed desire for a 'two-tier' Europe.

Either Blair or Chirac faced humiliation. On 20 February, the French privately urged the Americans to drop the idea of a UN resolution to authorize an invasion, and act without one, so as to avoid an open split in the Security Council.[144] This indicates that Chirac was trying to avoid a final confrontation. The Americans suggested that Britain might prefer to keep its troops out of the invasion of Iraq, which would remove the need to return

---

*The French electoral system combined with the collapse of the Socialist Party made the ageing right-wing demagogue Jean-Marie Le Pen the only other candidate, which forced the Left to vote for Chirac.

to the Security Council. But Blair insisted on full British participation and hence on a new Security Council resolution. He needed this for domestic reasons, as Labour MPs grew unwontedly restive and protesting crowds filled the streets. Demonstrators in London sang the 'Marseillaise' and the embassy received a flood of letters praising French policy – an espousal of French leadership unseen in Britain since the 1790s. In France, public opinion was overwhelmingly against a war, and some observers think that only at this late stage did French policy become fixed.[145] After a short meeting with Chirac at Le Touquet on 2 March, Blair seems to have convinced himself that he could win the French over, and the British were foolish enough to hint publicly that Chirac was about to give in.[146] The *Guardian* (2 March) thought that the French were 'almost certainly willing . . . to wage war on Iraq and to play their part in post-Saddam reconstruction'.

The British soon realized that this was an illusion. The two foreign ministers swapped honeyed insults at the UN, Straw addressing Villepin with forced matiness as 'Dominique'. French and British ministers chased each other round the world trying to drum up votes in the Security Council. 'Francophonie' and Commonwealth contacts were mobilized. Robert Mugabe, the Zimbabwean dictator, was welcomed to Paris as a gesture to Africa – an act the British regarded as shameless. Blair angrily concluded that Chirac was out to wreck his position in Europe and even bring him down. Chirac might well have harboured similar suspicions. On 10 March the latter blundered. In a broadcast interview, he said that 'whatever the circumstances' France would vote against – that is veto – the Anglo–American UN resolution 'because there are no grounds for waging war in order to . . . disarm Iraq'. Whitehall seized on this, with what the French considered typical perfidy, as a way of escaping a UN vote. If the French were going to veto a resolution, said the British, then the process was nullified – an argument the attorney-general privately dismissed as lacking any basis in law.[147] The French and their supporters claimed that the British argument was a pretext: Britain would have lost the vote anyway. In that case, why did Chirac promise to veto? Blair described Chirac's position as 'foolish' and 'irresponsible'. Straw called it 'the Napoleon route – and remember who won'. The French ambassador was greeted by a jubilant Straw waving *Le Monde* and saying 'It's such a gift, we won't stop there.' Villepin complained of 'comments unworthy of a country which is both a friend and a European partner'.[148]

Euphoria created by the quick victory over the Iraqi army in April 2003 was soon overshadowed by darkening disillusion. The political damage done by false and exaggerated intelligence concerning WMDs – surely the most important peacetime failure since 1939 (see above, page 536) – and by a range of errors, follies and unintended consequences, including domestic

A British view of a raddled Marianne wooing Saddam Hussein.

terrorism in Britain, was immense. Press comment in both countries recalled the great phobias of the past, stressing Chirac's dishonesty and Blair's sycophancy, with suggestions too that the latter had gone mad, descending into religious mania, 'New Age lunacy' and 'off the peg mysticism'.[149] The attacks went beyond the politicians to the nations themselves.

But 'Anglo-Saxon' reverses did not mean French victory. An optimistic French socialist at first declared that the anti-war protests had meant that 'a new nation was born in the streets – the European nation'. But an influential critic discerned the 'collapse' of France's whole postwar strategy.[150] The Coalition's subsequent difficulties spared France the 'diplomatic Agincourt' it seemed to face when Saddam was overthrown. Nevertheless, Paris's loss of authority in Europe and impotence to influence world events was flagrant. Its call for a European summit to create a new defence organization – a gauntlet thrown down to the British – rallied only the Germans, the Belgians and the Luxemburgers. Countries such as Poland and Portugal that had supported the Anglo-Saxons might well have regretted their involvement, but they did not forgive Chirac's arrogance or forget his weakness: token forces from half a dozen European countries served for a time under British command in southern Iraq. Blair immediately, and Bush reluctantly, tried to shore up the swaying Atlantic bridge by approaches to Paris

French public opinion, here expressed by the country's most popular cartoonist, had no doubt that Blair was lying.

and Berlin, with little or no response. Both sides continued to insist that they were in the right. Bush's re-election in November 2004 was an undoubted setback for Paris, where it had been hoped his defeat would bring in a more amenable administration. France (and Germany) refused to take part in peacekeeping and reconstruction in Iraq: the French agreed to contribute one officer! This enabled them to take a high moral tone, and in any case outraged public opinion would not have allowed involvement. But it perpetuated the split between 'old Europe' and 'new Europe', under-lined the isolation of Paris and Berlin, and deprived them of a voice in Middle Eastern politics at a crucial time. The idea of a Franco-German political union (reminiscent of the abortive Franco-British unions of 1940 and 1956) was floated in November 2003. As the French prime minister Jean-Pierre Raffarin put it, 'If the Europe of 25 fails, what is left for France? Just the Franco-German rapprochement.'[151] This would once have been sensational. Now, hardly anyone took any notice. There was unprecedented difficulty in forming and then approving a new European Commission in 2004. Its dominance by 'free-marketeers and Atlanticists' (according to *Le Figaro*) led by José Manuel Barroso, one of the signatories of the notorious January open letter, caused gnashing of teeth in Paris, and a mounting realization that 'Europe' was slipping away from them.

The crisis once again underlined the remoteness of a genuine European defence and foreign policy, even if it were possible to create an institutional façade. The French knew that they needed the involvement of Britain, Europe's leading military power, if such a policy was to be credible. Though a French diplomat repeated the usual line about Britain having to choose – 'Either they are with us, united in Europe where they should be, or they are destined to become . . . something like an American state' – behind the scenes they feared that the British would 'lose interest' in a defence partnership amid the post-Iraq recriminations.[152]

Forty years earlier, Dean Acheson had dismissed as 'played out' Britain's role based on the 'special relationship' and the Commonwealth. After the Iraq invasion its prime minister was hailed by some commentators as the 'real vice-president' of the United States (ironically, a proverbially powerless office), and he was regarded across America as a combination of Winston Churchill and Nelson Mandela. Britain was part of a coalition with Australia which also drew in a large group of European states. When Acheson spoke, Britain, choosing a European future, had withdrawn from 'east of Suez'. Now it had most of its front-line forces in Iraq. France, nearly forty years after the fall of de Gaulle, had opposed the Anglo-Saxons more vehemently than the General had ever done. History's fundamental lesson is that the future will always surprise us. But it also teaches that our reactions to its surprises are shaped by habits of thought and sentiment that are very durable. So, despite frenetic negotiations and the appearance of uncertainty and suspense, Blair and Chirac ended up predictably playing Churchill and de Gaulle in miniature. Long-established assumptions about national interest, and instinctive sympathies and prejudices, were strong among the publics of both countries, as well as among politicans and diplomats. Neither government had much freedom of action: the grooves were too well worn. France's cherished ambition of opposing Anglo-Saxon dominance of NATO had been taken further than ever. But the object of that policy – a strong, French-led Europe standing up to America – evaporated. Britain's equally cherished policy of being a transatlantic bridge had proved highly dangerous in terms of domestic policy, and incompatible with Blair's previous ambition to join with France and Germany in leading the EU. Perhaps a historic compromise between London and Paris was overdue.

DESPERATE TO BE FRIENDS: CELEBRATING THE *ENTENTE CORDIALE*, 1904–2004

Irony was heaped on irony when, amid the bitterest row for a generation, both countries gamely set out to commemorate the centenary of the *entente cordiale*. The nineteenth-century philosopher Ernest Renan famously declared that national solidarity required a willingness to forget unhelpful history. International solidarity required no less. Academics (including ourselves) participated in numerous conferences and produced papers and books. Cross-Channel businesses provided modest subsidies for celebrations. Parties were held. Programmes were broadcast. Supplements were printed. The Queen, following her father and great-grandfather, set out to charm the French public in April, the centenary of the signing. The French, staunch republicans and avid royal-watchers, responded. The royal visit probably explains why the *entente* gave rise to more and deeper discussion in France than Britain. The Grenadier Guards marched down the Champs Elysées on 14 July, making the point that British and French, despite fallings out, were Europe's warriors: 'Our military relationship has . . . brought our two countries together.'[153] The French radio, nervous of hostile demonstrations, falsely explained that the Guards were merely for show, not combat troops like those in Iraq. Chirac's return visit in November made less of a stir, though his being treated to a command performance of a musical version of *Les Misérables* in the Waterloo Chamber at Windsor caused some French journalists to suspect a mysteriously subtle insult.

In both countries, there was a praiseworthy desire to be nice, and, as the historian Philip Bell has put it, to present the relationship as they would like it to be. The French press conjured up the sort of England they liked, in which eccentricity, cups of tea and fictional detectives were prominent. At grass-roots level there were dozens of touchingly odd celebrations, which showed how extensive personal contacts had become: the Warwick Chapter of the Commanderie du Taste Saumur held a banquet; Chester had a rally of vintage French cars and a commemoration of the 1918 armistice; a tram in Sarajevo was painted red white and blue.[154] But despite personal bonhomie, opinion polls showed that political feelings had been affected by Iraq. Only 9 per cent of the French expressed 'great trust' in the 'pro-American' British, compared with 28 per cent who greatly trusted the Germans. Only the Americans and the Russians were trusted less. The British trusted the Americans far more than they trusted the French. A more extensive study of French public attitudes showed that the 'English' aroused the strongest and least favourable reactions of all European peoples. A free word-association test produced 'conceited', 'snobbish', 'rude', 'haughty', 'cold', 'selfish', 'arrogant', 'hypocritical' and 'unpleasant'; though there apparently survived a small minority of traditional anglophiles who thought of 'pragmatic', 'elegant', 'funny', 'courteous', 'gentlemanly', 'nice', 'tolerant', etc. There was wide agreement that the English were very different: 'insular', 'monarchist', 'anti-European', and 'independent'.[155]

It is common in both countries to express pained surprise over the persistence of ill feeling, though the causes are ever more plain. More surprising is their equally deep-seated desire to be friends. It is hard to think of any other two countries that so strenuously demonstrate cordiality, with the possible exception of France and Germany. This of course is a clue: lavish expressions of affection are intended to exorcize hostility. But as the jollifications of the Warwick Chapter of the Commanderie du Taste (and many like them) demonstrate, the British and French also find each other intriguing, amusing, and even agreeable, as they have for centuries. And they are much more like each other than they suppose – more than the British are like the Americans or the French are like the Germans. If we were to take a word-association test ourselves on Franco-British similarities, we would come up with 'cynical', 'irreverent', 'stoical', 'bloody-minded', 'individualistic', 'tolerant' – and of course 'self-righteous'.

2005: Déjà Vu All Over Again

Hegel says somewhere that all great personalities and events in world history reappear in one fashion or another. He forgot to add: the first time as tragedy, the second as farce.

KARL MARX

The 'Anglo-Saxon model' . . . is based on social inequalities accepted by the British but which would seem intolerable here . . . One cannot expect a people that made a revolution, guillotined its king and hung aristocrats on lamp-posts to have the same conception of social relations as a monarchy where one of the chambers of parliament is composed exclusively of lords.

Le Monde, 5–6 June 2005

I am a passionate pro-European . . . I believe in Europe as a political project. I believe in Europe with a strong and caring social dimension. I would never accept a Europe that was simply an economic market . . . But tell me: what type of social model is it that has 20 million unemployed?

TONY BLAIR to European Parliament, 23 June 2005

Blair is a worse version of Thatcher. Just as arrogant but selfish too.

JACQUES CHIRAC, June 2005[156]

On 29 May 2005, the French people rejected the European Constitution, scorning their government, shattering all the mainstream political parties, and leaving the country politically rudderless. The referendum campaign and its aftermath – including a No vote in Holland a few days later – made the half-century struggle between France and Britain again explicitly the focus of European politics, as in the time of de Gaulle. Indeed, as a perceptive French journalist pointed out, the 'No' of 2005 fundamentally resembled de Gaulle's 'No' to British entry in 1963 – both expressed 'persistent suspicion' of the consequences for France of Britain's links with the wider world.[157]

The French vote was by far the most important event in Franco-British history for nearly half a century. It nullified the strategy followed by the British governing elite since the 1960s: to clamber on board the departing European train with as much good grace as they could muster. Blair had long proclaimed his mission to ensure that Britain would never be 'isolated or left behind', and he had committed himself to joining the Euro and adopting the constitution. The French vote enabled him to drop the British referendum, saving him from terminal humiliation – opinion polls indicated over 70 per cent 'No'. He adroitly seized the chance to redefine what it meant to be pro-European. An admiring opponent commented that it was 'just the same as what many of us have always meant by Eurosceptic'.[158] So ended for the time being the British divide over 'Europe'. Blair was restored to a position of authority at home, and became, above all in French eyes, the dominating figure in Europe. With astounding good fortune, he was due to take over as chairman of the G8 group and as president of the European Council. Meanwhile, as if to underline his resurgence, the largest peacetime assembly of warships in history met at Portsmouth to celebrate the bicentenary of Trafalgar. Even the award of the 2012 Olympic Games to London on 5 July was interpreted by the French as a triumph for Blair's irresistible magnetism, as a defeat for French ideals of non-commercialism and *le fair-play*, as proof of the power of 'the Anglo-Saxons', and as another alarming symptom of France's waning global influence. The customary cross-Channel exchange of media insults was cut short by the tragedy of the London terrorist bombings on 7 July. A few months earlier, such an event would have shaken Blair's position, but now it silenced criticism.

In retrospect, the French No vote seems predictable: they had almost voted No to the Maastricht treaty in 1992, had always been suspicious of true federalism ('One does not impose on our country that which does not please us'[159]), and had been growing disenchanted with an expanding and liberalizing 'Europe'. It had been easy enough to expect that 'as cherished traditions of domestic and foreign policy collide, the question of whether present European policy is compatible with informed democratic consent may soon have to be faced'.[160] Yet if predictable, the vote was not predicted. Opinion polls indicating opposition to the Constitution were discounted. It seemed unthinkable that the French would really resist the customary appeals to national pride as historic leaders of Europe and national fear of being isolated in an unfriendly world. Giscard proclaimed that the Constitution would make the EU 'a political power that will talk on equal terms to the greatest powers on our planet'.[161] This quasi-nationalist ambition was the strongest argument for the French public. In the bluntest terms, 'to say No to the European constitution is to say Yes to Bush'. But economic fears were overtaking political hopes. The French socialists had gained in the 2004 European elections by campaigning 'against a liberal Europe'. Almost everyone, not least previously pro-European Catholics, strongly opposed the accession of Turkey (supported by Britain), which if it happened would mark the end of de Gaulle's 'European Europe' and create 'a multicultural space, elastic and without identity'.[162] France raised a unilateral barrier against eventual Turkish entry by changing its own constitution to forbid further EU enlargement unless sanctioned by a special French referendum. Attacks in Brussels and Strasbourg on the British budget rebate, on Britain's opt-out from rules on maximum working hours, and on the Bolkestein directive to introduce a single market in services (see above, page 651) showed that French politicians shared public disquiet. But the publicity given to these disputes in France increased the feeling that 'Europe' was going wrong.[163] Even French federalists who supported the constitution as a step towards 'a European republic' criticized it as 'not social enough, not federalist enough, not democratic enough, too complex, too liberal' and giving too much to 'the English'.[164]

The crux was summed up by Dominique de Villepin, soon to be prime minister: 'We do not want a liberal Europe – which would signify the victory of the British vision of Europe as a mere market.'[165] Supporters of the Constitution insisted that it would prevent this disaster. Jacques Chirac, in his televised attempt to rally the public to vote Yes, insisted that the Constitution would prevent 'an Anglo-Saxon, Atlanticist Europe'. When a journalist remarked on the lower level of unemployment in Britain, he replied that this was due to 'methods and social rules . . . that would not be accepted or acceptable to us'. In private, he put it more bluntly: 'Over the years the English have wrecked their agriculture and then their industry. Now they only survive due to property inflation, financial speculation and their oil and gas.'[166]

Having barely given a thought to the pros and cons of Europeanism for years, the French now surpassed the British in suspiciousness, and began scrutinizing the Constitution's small print with an attention and sense of civic responsibility that few political cultures could match. The document's virtuosic ambiguity challenged their much-vaunted 'Cartesianism'. On one hand, it contained the familiar Delorean elements of a 'social market economy' and new 'competences' for the Commission, including new powers to regulate public services. On the other hand, its Articles 1.3 and 1.4 would make 'an internal market where competition is free and fair (*non faussée*)' and 'free circulation of persons, services, goods and capital' part of Europe's basic law. Opponents seized on these words. Glossed in the light of the Bolkestein directive, they threatened an influx of foreign workers – whether Polish plumbers or British bankers – who would not be subject to French labour laws, and hence would be able to undercut French workers. This became the central theme of the campaign, as headlines leaked the contents of a suppressed government study warning that 200,000 jobs in services might be lost.[167] Supporters of the Constitution pointed out that the offending phrases had been in all the past European treaties. In vain: much of the French electorate, at least by implication, now rejected the very basis of the original Common Market.

The vote gave a 55 per cent No. Exit polls showed that fear of unemployment was the key. Only sixteen of France's 100 departments – the most affluent and the most Catholic parts of the country – voted Yes, though usually narrowly. Enthusiastic Europeanism was confined to the wealthiest suburbs and quarters of Paris and to the Pacific and Caribbean territories. In mainland France, the only socio-economic groups that voted Yes were big business, the liberal professions, academics and the retired. Young voters and the traditional Left voted emphatically No. What shifted the balance from a tiny Yes in 1992 to a substantial No in 2005 was defection among the numerous public-sector middle class such as teachers, nurses, social workers and civil servants,[168] and consequently, of part of the Socialist Party, their political representative. This group favoured the political vision of 'ever closer union', but only on condition that it would protect *le service public* and hence their jobs against 'ultraliberal' competition.

The shock to the French political and intellectual establishment was profound. This was far more than simply a rebellion against the politicians in power, whose expressed opposition to the 'British vision of Europe' was the same as that of the electorate. It was the voters' verdict that those politicians – despite their insistence that the Constitution reflected French ideals and traditions – were failing to ensure that Europe remained the bulwark of France. An entire vision of history and of the future, and of France's place in it, was thereby called into question. Perhaps after all, mused one commentator, 'the tide of history in Europe' was running towards 'the desires of Albion'.[169] The chancellor of the exchequer, Gordon Brown, emphatically agreed:

the assumptions that became rooted in the very idea of European integration were that a single market and single currency would lead to tax harmonization, a federal fiscal policy, and something akin to a federal state. But by its very nature globalization changes all this . . . Identities have remained rooted in the nation state . . . the old assumptions about federalism do not match the realities of our time.[170]

The French flatteringly over-estimated Whitehall's foresight, assuming that somehow the British had planned this all along. Blair was hailed, bitterly and sometimes admiringly, as the new 'strong man of Europe'.

Chirac's first public statement after the referendum took up the challenge: 'I shall act . . . in defence of our national interests . . . resolutely respecting the French model, which is not an Anglo-Saxon type model.'[171] His reported private reaction was typically blunt: 'that conceited prat Blair . . . is only too happy with the No vote. You'd think he gets off on it. He wants to use the British presidency to grab the limelight . . . I won't put up with his English arrogance.'[172] Chirac's gambit was familiar, and expected in both London and Paris: to attack the British rebate secured by Margaret Thatcher, and thus embarrass Blair at home and isolate him in Europe as his presidency began. The British response was equally obvious: to attack the Common Agricultural Policy, what Chirac called 'their *idée fixe*'. Worryingly for the French, their special relationship with Germany seemed in doubt, as Blair's new enthusiasm for 'modernizing' the EU was said to be shared by the German opposition leader Angela Merkel, soon to be the German chancellor.

The sinking of the Constitution marked a kind of velvet revolution in the EU. By exploding the last of the Enlightenment grand narratives,[173] according to which ever closer union was historically predestined for Europe and hence beyond democratic choice, it had shaken every certainty. The strategy of European leadership followed unwaveringly and brilliantly by France's governing elite for half a century had, concluded *Le Monde*, met its Waterloo, marking 'a formidable victory of Great Britain over France and its idea of Europe':

Never has Albion seemed so perfidious and so lucky . . . For the French electors have, by their vote, satisfied two long-cherished English hopes: they have dealt a blow, perhaps a fatal one, to the project of political union; and they have driven a wedge into the Franco-German alliance.[174]

Blair, previously assumed to be nearing a disappointing end to his career, had stumbled to victory. The French people gave him the chance to make his mark on history. His arresting mixture of statesmanship and showmanship linked him with other charismatic British leaders at crucial moments of rivalry with France – Pitt the Elder, Palmerston, Lloyd George, Macmillan. He suddenly had thrust upon him the greatest opportunity of any British politician since Bevin to shape the future of the Continent.

But as Bevin had found, Europe was hard to shape. Six months later, as the British presidency ended in December 2005, little had been discussed about the future of Europe, and nothing decided. Paris's spoiling tactics, implacably pursued, had been effective against a British government that seemingly had no idea what to do beyond exhortation. The British ambassador explained in *Le Monde* (4 January 2006) that Britain had delayed putting forward any precise suggestions in case they aroused opposition. French commentators realized with open relief that there was to be no European revolution, and that even British aspirations to reform the budget were insubstantial. On the headline-catching symbolic issues, the CAP actually increased its share of EU spending, while Britain gave up part of its budgetary rebate, in direct contravention of Blair's declaration to the European Parliament. Chirac proclaimed in his 2006 New Year broadcast that France would continue to lead Europe towards a more 'political', 'social', protectionist and interventionist future. His message was diffused in all twenty-four languages. But even the French press doubted that anyone was listening. France had won a short-term tactical victory, but had shown again that it was incapable of any positive initiative in European politics.

So French and British visions remained as contradictory as ever, and their resolution was postponed indefinitely. However, the one significant act of the British presidency had the potential to force a decision: the beginning of formal negotiations for the admission of Turkey to the EU. Turkish membership, bitterly resisted by many in France and elsewhere, could finally destroy the aim of an 'ever closer union', and so dilute the EU into that '*vaste zone de libre-échange*' feared by de Gaulle. Or it could, on the other hand, divide the Continent into the 'inner' and 'outer' circles that French policy favoured. The European 'Great Game' is still to be played out.

PART IV: CONCLUSIONS AND DISAGREEMENTS

Our story over the last sixty years has been surprising, even encouraging. In 1945, a damaged France and an exhausted Britain shivered in the post-war chill. Decline stared them in the face: loss of empire, loss of reputation, loss of wealth, loss of cohesion, loss of confidence – 'Lo, all our pomp of yesterday is one with Nineveh and Tyre.' Yet, as Adam Smith once said, there is a great deal of ruin in a nation. They revived. That both countries would be the most assertive, ambitious and articulate members of a peaceful and undivided Europe, would overtake Russia in usable military power, and be among the half-dozen richest countries in the world, would have seemed fantastic. Whether they have used their new lease of life wisely is another question. Yet although they shared both the problem of decline and the conscious desire to resist it, they rarely showed much solidarity. They have followed very different paths, both internationally and domestically. They have a recent history of rivalry hard to match by any other pair of allies – and it shows no sign of abating.

IT: The core problem has long been obvious: the malaise of a Britain unable to accept its true position in the world, that is, as a country in the heart of Europe. This is the source of Britain's difficulty with France and its other neighbours, of damaging foreign entanglements, and of domestic political divisions. Like France, it should have realized from the 1950s that it could find a new role – and a means of resisting decline – by throwing itself wholeheartedly into the construction of Europe: a task of truly historic importance. Had it seized the opportunity in the 1950s of being one of the early leaders of Europe, its position in the world and its economic and social solidity would be less uncertain. As Tony Blair put it, 'We said it wouldn't happen. Then we said it wouldn't work. Then we said we didn't need it. But it did happen. And Britain was left behind.'[1] It adopted two demeaning and self-defeating positions: trailing behind the United States and trailing behind Europe – taken for granted by the former, and a burden to the latter. In particular, had it built up a European partnership with France, owing to similarly rooted traditions of representative government, national identity, and engagement with the outside world, it could have helped to make the European Union both more democratic internally and more effective externally. Britain turned its back to the future, and one consequence of that is the crisis Europe is now facing.

RT: This is a very romantic – and in some ways of course a very French – view. It assumes that nations and Continents have destinies, and that history follows preordained paths. But there are no paths to the future: we have to blaze the trail as we go. Even if, for the sake of argument, one accepted the 'destiny' idea, one might conclude that Britain had a different destiny from that espoused by France. Britain seems set on an 'ever closer union' with the world – de Gaulle's *grand large*. One might even conclude that Europe is likely to choose that destiny too, eventually, and that here British influence has been and will be important. That is what de Gaulle feared and resisted. It is by no means clear today, as it seemed in the 1970s, that British governments in the 1950s were wrong in staying outside the early Common Market, which would have devastated their world trade and made subsequent economic revival harder. Indeed, from an economic point of view the EFTA strategy of creating a purely trading relationship with the EEC would probably have been more beneficial. But Britain's motives were always political more than economic. It pursued traditional policies: to prevent the domination of the Continent by a single (in this case collective) power, and to press for freer trade – in effect, to prevent a new 'Continental System'. In that sense, it has been fairly successful – the events of 2005 even suggest very successful. One might regard this as purblind, or clear-sighted, or just lucky. But these are matters for legitimate political choice: there is no 'Future' to which 'History' ordains us to conform.

PICKING UP THE THREADS

We have tried to tell the story of the relationship between the French and British over more than three centuries. We believe that this relationship is unique in the modern world, not only for its duration and the breadth of its cultural, economic and political ramifications, but also for its global consequences. By all these measures it is more important than any other relationship France or Britain has had – with Germany, for example, or America. We would go further and say that it has been heavier with consequences than any other relationship between two countries in modern times. It is scarcely possible to imagine what each might have been like without the other. Their political systems, their economic characteristics, the size and composition of their diverse populations, their ideas and national sentiments have all been profoundly altered and shaped by mutual contact since the 1680s. Rudyard Kipling rightly said that the task of each had been 'to mould the other's fate as he wrought his own.' Asia, Africa and the Americas were also deeply affected by their struggles.

When we began this book, we were far from sure that this really was a single story. Would it turn out merely to be a succession of episodes linked only by geography and whatever narrative coherence we could contrive? Could there really be meaningful threads stretching from the Sun King to Tony Blair? A French historian has recently observed that 'even though after Waterloo there was never again armed conflict between the two countries, in a way the struggle is still being pursued today'.[1] Could he be right, or is this an illusion sustained by political propaganda, the press, and a surfeit of history books? Many commentators – not least French anglophiles and British francophiles genuinely distressed by the 'frog-bashing' of the tabloids – do consider 'the struggle' an illusion, which should be dispelled by argument, positive reporting and goodwill. Until recently, it was commonplace to claim that it was only a British, or English, obsession – silly xenophobia which the French regarded with lofty indifference.[2]

At first sight, it might seem plausible that present-day friction is merely a lingering echo of a violent past. Repeated conflicts created a feeling of underlying difference, even of hereditary enmity, and so contributed to that over-used concept, 'identity'. In the mid nineteenth century, the great historian Michelet wrote that 'the struggle against England has done France a very great service by confirming and clarifying her sense of nationhood. Through coming together against the enemy the provinces discovered that they were a single people. It is by seeing the English close to that they felt they were French.'[3] From the mid eighteenth century, and particularly during the revolutionary and Napoleonic wars, Britain – or *l'Angleterre* – came to be seen as the arch enemy, representing not only a rival power, but a contrary set of values: commercial, unstable, and individualistic. Britain was 'Carthage' challenging Rome, and like Carthage, it had to be destroyed. A similar phenomenon has been identified in Britain. Linda Colley believes that the United Kingdom, and British identity (as opposed to the separate identities of the island nations), were products of the eighteenth-century conflicts with France. Hence to be, or feel, British involved feeling anti-French.

But there is a counterbalancing Franco–British story, which is not about conflict, but about mutual fascination, amusement, admiration, exchange and imitation. Ideas, art, fashion, sport, food, and literature, backed by tourism, job-seeking and residence, have caused such intermingling over three centuries that it is often difficult to see at first sight what began as British and what began as French. There are long continuities, reflected in some remarkably durable stereotypes, many of which were accepted on both sides. The French tended (tend?) to see Britain as culturally detached, eccentric, unpolished, and therefore the origin of the new and unusual – often amusing, always disturbing. The British saw (see?) the French as highly civilized, the hallmark of sophisticated taste and manners, whether in dress, food or art. More British have always come to France to admire, experience, and enjoy. The French have been happy to accept this tribute without reciprocating it. Rather, they have learned and imported things from Britain, and travel there has generally been for practical and limited purposes – often to earn money. Counter-intuitively, the prevailing cultural current has been from north to south – at least in the sense that novelty came from England, even if it was transformed (like cycle-racing, rugby, beefsteak, Monet's fogs or Coco Chanel's suits) into things quintessentially French. The consequence is that few countries have such intermingled cultures. Amusingly, they like to think of each other as opposites.

If the Franco–British conflict, however formative, in reality ended in 1815, it must follow that whatever survives consists only of fading myths, trans-mitted by stories, books, pictures, and what the French call 'places of memory', such as Napoleon's tomb in the Invalides and Nelson's Column in Trafalgar Square, both dating from the 1840s. Many enjoy the Napoleonic novels of Patrick Rambaud or Patrick O'Brian, but the old chauvinistic tradi-tions, occasionally resuscitated by unscrupulous politicians and journalists, remain only in a few dark corners. Linda Colley's prediction was that without the Protestant militancy, the imperial rivalry, and the superior prosperity that underpinned the eighteenth-century conflict with France, Britishness, and the British state, had no purpose, and logically would dissolve into both smaller and larger entities, such as Scotland and Europe. The same argument could be applied to France, abandoning 'Jacobin' centralization (a war-making system) in favour both of the rediscovery of Corsica, Brittany, Occitanie and so on, and of integration into Europe.[4] Yet both Britain and

France are old nations (and unions of nations), old in their unity as well as in their diversity. Reports of their demise seem exaggerated.[5]

Should one connecting theme of our story, therefore, be the transformation from eighteenth-century enmity to twenty-first-century friendship, and from aggressive patriotism to pacific cosmopolitanism? Yes, at one level – though the process has never been straightforward. Love and hate were always excitingly simultaneous, rather than alternating – we form what the French call *un couple infernal*. Intellectual and cultural relations were never more intense than during the merciless struggles of the 'second hundred years war'. Even in wartime, French intellectuals tried to think like the English; the British gentry tried to behave like the French; and anglomaniacs and Macaronis vied in fashionable imitation. After 1789, British radicals and French conservatives found themselves supporting the enemy. In the nineteenth century, the open conflict was finished, and although both sides loved sneering at the other, French politicians and British artists looked across the Channel with fervent admiration. In the twentieth century, the two countries were allies, but rarely friends, and both looked elsewhere for novelty and cultural stimulation. But in times of deadly danger the two peoples experienced a closeness rarely paralleled in history. During the First World War, hundreds of thousands of British men lived and died in France. During the Second, London became the capital of Free France. French soldiers, sailors and airmen fought to defend Britain. British men and women, in uniform or in secret, risked their lives to liberate France. Finally, the twenty-first century, despite incorrigible sourness, produced a historic surprise: more than ever before, crowds of people swarmed across the Channel to seek a new life in the country of the other.

But there are obvious problems if we want our story to be simply that of fading national rivalry and growing friendship. Why, after two centuries of peace, *entente* and alliance, do British and French governments follow policies over fundamental issues that conflict not merely occasionally, but predictably and systematically? Their citizens continue to feel and express considerably less affection towards each other than towards most other nations. Well-meaning commentators often blame the London tabloids. But despite the non-existence of a French *Soleil* or *Courrier Quotidien* the French are cooler towards the British than the British are to them. Just as two centuries ago, Britain is seen as a challenge to French values.

It is important to understand this Franco-British difference, and not dismiss it as mere prejudice. To paraphrase Leon Trotsky, you may ignore history, but history doesn't ignore you. The beginning was Britain's enrolment into the Continental struggle against Louis XIV. This developed into a conflict primarily between France and Britain, because Britain, through naval power, trade and finance, could increasingly mobilize world resources for European contests. The crucial time was between 1750 and 1815. Both states were forced into a conscious struggle for predominance, to control the connections between Europe and the outside world. France, bigger, stronger, and combining land and sea power, seemed better placed than Britain to dominate the globe. Had it been able to knock Britain out – for example in one of its repeated attempts to invade – there is every reason to think that it could have become the global power. But it failed to land the decisive blow. Even its victory in 1783, though it created the United States of America, did not reduce Britain to impotence. The effort bankrupted the Bourbon monarchy and led to the revolution. The open warfare resumed in 1792 and culminated in Napoleon's fatal effort to control the sea by conquering the land. France's defeat meant that she 'missed her rendezvous with the ocean' (see above, page 148), while Britain kept 'Neptune's trident, the sceptre of the world'.

The consequences for both countries were, and still are, momentous. In the nineteenth century Britain followed a commercial, imperial, globalizing path, its economy specializing in mass production, exporting manufactured goods and capital throughout the world, increasingly importing its food from distant producers, dependent on income from services and investments, and pressing endlessly to open up new markets. Its population boomed, and migrated to every continent, becoming 'an association of insular and emigrant peoples'.[6] France lost its eighteenth-century colonial trade, and its coastal regions declined. Wealth creation now took place in the north and east, not the west and south. France still nursed global ambitions. Like Britain, it believed it had the right, and duty, to create an empire and pursue a 'civilizing mission' in the world. Its parliament was told in 1846 to prepare 'for a time unknown when, on the great battlefield of the sea, we shall have to contest the influence' of Britain. But that 'time unknown' never came, and the French even stopped thinking about the world as a whole: there were no influential French writers on geopolitics, as there were British, German and American. France focused on Europe and the Mediterranean. It tried to absorb its main colonies into the metropolis, making Frenchness the universal model. Yet one leading politician complained that the only thing about their empire that interested the French people was the belly dance; and many of the white settlers in Algeria came from Italy and Spain. Its colonial trade and investment remained marginal. It could not compete with Britain as a maritime power or as an industrial mass producer. Instead, its livelihood came from perfecting traditional industries and methods, and selling high-quality goods in Europe. Britain, Germany and Russia were its main economic partners. Most of its governments, supported by popular opinion, protected the domestic economy against external competition, preferring social stability to economic dynamism. There was an extraordinary slowing down, most strikingly in population. France remained a society of small towns and villages, with a large population of land-owning peasants, and many small businesses. Few people moved far, and few went overseas. This constituted much of its charm for the urban British: it was unspoilt, quaint, cheap, seemingly less obsessed with making money, and it preserved traditional cultural values.

The above descriptions, allowing for general technological change, apply as well to the 1930s as to the 1830s. But meanwhile there had been a new, though connected, development. In the briefest terms, the end of France's maritime conflict with Britain, and the consequent redirection of its main ambitions towards becoming again the leading power on the Continent, led to successive wars with Russia, Austria and Prussia, ending in 1871 with Prussia's defeat of France and creation of a new German Reich. Britain, occupied with its global interests, stood aside. But by the beginning of the twentieth century, Germany seemed to be following France's earlier path, aiming at Continental predominance as a means to world power. For France first and then Britain, Germany became the national enemy. This brought France and a hesitant Britain together as allies in 1914 and 1939, with Britain, as 200 years earlier, at the centre of successful coalitions against the Continental threat. But how different the outcome was.

Undoubtedly the Second World War ended an era. Britain and France were diminished. Western Europe was no longer the world's hub. The Cold War meant the forty-year hegemony of the two Superpowers. Colonies were liberated, or liberated themselves, and the 1956 Suez crisis gave both France and Britain a painful lesson in reality. At the same time, Britain, France and their neighbours underwent a period of rapid economic, social and cultural change. For France in particular, the Thirty Glorious Years from 1945 to 1975 were a transformation.

Yet the eighteenth- and nineteenth-century orientations not only persisted after 1945, they were reinforced. France's political and economic attention was more than ever focused on the Continent. Though it fought harder than Britain to keep fragments of empire, and to invent post-imperial networks, the loss of its biggest colonies was soon shrugged off. Its trade was with its neighbours. It also had to ensure that no German threat revived. Hence its participation in supranational plans to regulate and protect Western Europe. As in the nineteenth century, its economy and political system seemed fragile, and so modernization proceeded, as in the past, under the direction and protection of the State, aiming to manage change and maximize security and stability. It succeeded: the State acquired unprecedented economic, fiscal, and social powers, and created a complex system of rights and privileges in which most people had a stake. Britain's position was quite different. Its governments still worked consistently to reduce world trade barriers and maintain global contacts. The huge importance of Commonwealth and

American trade, and of the City of London, meant that this was not mere nostalgia. World competitiveness, rather than adaptation to a regional trade bloc, was always accepted in Britain as imperative. Its systems of state welfare and state economic intervention aimed to cope with misfortune rather than create felicity. Membership of the EEC, which in the 1970s seemed a complete change of direction, proved only a bend in the road: by 2005, less than half of British trade was with its European neighbours, and the proportion had been falling since the early 1990s. This was broadly the same as in 1900, or indeed 1800. But two-thirds of France's trade was European – also about the same as in the 1900s.[7]

Long-accumulated differences have a profound effect: they have been summed up as constituting an 'eccentric' (British) and a 'concentric' (French) type of society; while anthropological studies have suggested that French behaviour in economic life is more hierarchical, cautious, and 'feminine', and British behaviour more egalitarian, risk taking, and 'masculine'.[8] These differences can partly be explained by the long-established importance of commerce and finance in British life, and of agriculture and small business in French. There are also ancient differences of view concerning the legitimacy of individual compared with general rights. As noted earlier, Adam Smith has never convinced the French. So when France and Britain applied starkly opposite remedies to their economic decline in the 1980s – the former, trying to resist world economic pressures, the latter, to embrace them – they were reaffirming the divergent courses set during their eighteenth- and nineteenth-century rivalry. People crossed the Channel in ever greater numbers seeking what they could not find at home – proof not of increasing similarity, but of continuing difference.

In politics, divergence was most visible in attitudes towards Europe and America. France had enjoyed some success in turning European integration into a vehicle for its own security, interests, ambitions and even fantasies. There grew up a powerful political consensus that the solution to all difficulties was (in Mitterrand's slogan) 'Always more Europe'. It was a conception of Europe – as can be seen from endless articles and books on European history, ideas and politics – from which Britain was explicitly or implicitly omitted. France's attitude to the United States, the new Carthage, grew out of traditional anglophobia, as habitual French use of the term 'Anglo-Saxon' shows.[9] It was not mere whimsy that some in France saw 'Europe' as a vindication of Napoleonic ambition: the Continent united under French leadership against *le grand large*. Patriotic Frenchmen were even willing to merge France itself into this new creation that carried its genes. Hence the real trauma, culminating in the 2005 referendum, when they began to suspect that Europe might not after all be their offspring. Underlying the political disagreements with Washington or

London, there is a fundamental pessimism about the perceived decline of French language, culture and values.

British attitudes to 'Europe' are the counterpart of French attitudes to 'America', and are equally rooted in the eighteenth-century divergence. Unlike in France, there could be no idea in Britain that integration into Europe was the fulfilment of its historic destiny. On the contrary, it was seen as the crestfallen abandonment of a unique world role, and a penitent acceptance of reduced status. This for many was its political and emotional attraction: commitment to Europe meant rejection of a detested imperial past – 'cutting Queen Victoria's umbilical cord'.[10] But such rejection was not universally approved. Nor, of course, could the British welcome Europe as a defence against the 'Anglo-Saxon' world, from which EEC membership meant partial separation. So from the beginning of European integration, British governments laboured to 'bridge' the two worlds – or, as many French see it, to act as a Trojan horse for the chaotic and philistine forces of globalization. De Gaulle saw this very well: he called Britain 'insulaire', but realized that this meant not isolated, but connected.

Britain – with what de Gaulle called its 'great convoy' of overseas partners – was a global entity trying to be European. France was a European entity trying to be global. Politicians in both countries hoped that Europe would provide a post-imperial pedestal for enhanced international status. That they both, alone in modern western Europe, retained the aspiration and to some extent the capacity to play an overseas political role backed by armed force was a significant element in drawing them towards 'Europe' and, warily, towards each other. Their strategies, however, remain different. Britain, through closeness to America, tries to be more than it seems. France, through proclaiming its independence, tries to seem more than it is – as de Gaulle put it, behaving like a Great Power precisely because it no longer is one. Britain's position seems to the French to be subservient; France's, to the British, to be posturing. Their attitudes towards European defence and foreign policy manifest this difference. The irony, of course, is that cherished ambitions could be served if they acted together, but they could only act together by giving up cherished ambitions.

Events inside and outside Europe in the 1980s and 90s gave French and British ambitions new urgency. Economic globalization, competition from other continents, the end of the Cold War, German unification and the dissolution of the Soviet empire woke the European Community from torpor. Britain, its economic potency amazingly revived, was the main supporter of the Single Market, and it consistently supported the accession of new member states. France pressed for political and monetary union. Europe was pulled simultaneously in opposite directions which were officially stated to be complementary: towards liberalization and eastern enlargement (potentially the '*vaste zone de libre-échange*' detested by de Gaulle) and towards economic and political integration (potentially the 'superstate' denounced by Thatcher). Squaring this circle became the EU's task, and the resulting 2004 Constitution made some decisions inescapable by forcing referendums on embarrassed governments. Few expected that it would be the French who in 2005 halted integration for the foreseeable future by saying No to a constitution that they feared embodied a 'British vision of Europe'.

French anglophiles long urged Britain to embrace a European destiny – in other words, to become more like France. It may be that Britain will encourage France to widen its horizon again to *le grand large* – not least by learning English. The threads of our story – of which Voltaire and Shakespeare are as much a part as Marlborough or Napoleon – would thus be neatly connected. At least until history's next surprise.

Notes

Abbreviations used in notes

AN Archives Nationales, Paris
AGR Archives Générales du Royaume, Brussels
AP Annales Parlementaires (published record of parliamentary debates)
APP Archives de la Préfecture de Police, Paris
BL British Library
MAE Ministère des Affaires Etrangères, Paris
MD series 'Mémoirés et Documents'
MDA series 'Mémoires et Documents: Angleterre'
MDF series 'Mémoires et Documents: France'
ODNB Oxford Dictionary of National Biography (2004)
OHBE Oxford History of the British Empire 3 vols. (1998)
PRO Public Record Office (National Archives), London
FO Foreign Office series
RA Royal Archives, Windsor Castle
SIPRI Stockholm International Peace Research Institute

Introduction (pp. 1–3)

1 Semmel (2004), p. 9.

PART I: Struggle (p. 5)

1 Scott (2000), p. 7.

1: Britain Joins Europe
(pp. 7–54)

1 Scott (2000), p. 461.

2 Hoppit (2000), p. 5.
3 Wolf (1968), p. 89.
4 Churchill (2002), vol. 2, p. 228.
5 Wolf (1968), p. 182.
6 Bennett (1997), p. 363.
7 Petitfils (1995), p. 330.
8 Scott (2000), p. 170.
9 Pincus (1995), p. 346.
10 Levillain (2004), p. 108.
11 Scott (2000), p. 65.
12 Petitfils (1995), p. 485.
13 Hoppit (2000), pp. 17–18.
14 Morrill (1991), pp. 79–81.
15 Israel (1991), p. 10.

16 Pincus (1995), p. 352.
17 Bély (1992), p. 283.
18 Israel (1991), p. 105.
19 ibid., p. 120.
20 ibid., p. 109; Troost (2005), p. 193.
21 Report by French agent Usson de Bonrepaus, 6 September 1688 [n.s.], in AN: AE B1 758. We owe this reference, and that in footnote 25, to Charles-Edouard Levillain.
22 Wolf (1968), p. 649.
23 Cénat (2005), pp. 104–5; Rose (1999), p. 115; see also Miller (1978), pp. 190–92.
24 Speck (2002), p. 70; Troost (2005) pp. 192–3.
25 Report of Sancey to governor-general, 3 September 1688 [n.s.] AGR T 100/409 fo 53.
26 Israel (1991), p. 108; Rodger (2004), p. 151.
27 Scott (2000), p. 217.
28 Israel (1991), p. 32.
29 Jackson (2005), p. 568.
30 Beddard (1991), p. 242.
31 Hoppit (2000), p. 33.
32 Morrill (1991), p. 98.
33 Rose (1999), p. 105.
34 Childs (1996), p. 210.
35 Lenman (1992), p. 23.
36 Rose (1999), p. 218.
37 An English officer, in Kishlansky (1996), p. 295.
38 For details, see Murtagh, in Caldicott et al. (1987).
39 Padfield (2000), ch. 6.
40 Wolf (1968), p. 459.
41 Lynn (1999), pp. 215–16; Rodger (2004), p. 147.
42 Cullen (2000).
43 Gwynn (1985), p. 68.
44 Rose (1999), p. 112.
45 Scott (2000), p. 474.
46 Padfield (2000), pp. 144–50; Rodger (2004), p. 150.
47 Dickson (1967), p. 28.
48 Wolf (1968), p. 487.
49 Petitfils (1995), p. 512.
50 Wolf (1968), p. 487.
51 Baxter (1966), p. 379.
52 Wolf (1966), p. 511.
53 Baxter (1966), p. 388.
54 Bély (1992), p. 397.
55 Voltaire (1966), vol. 1, p. 251.
56 ibid., p. 239.
57 Churchill (2002), p. 15.
58 McKay and Scott (1983), p. 138.
59 ibid., p. 149.
60 Bartlett and Jeffery (1996), p. 299.
61 Lenman (1992), p. 84.
62 MAE MDA, vol. 52, fos 38–9.
63 Black (2000), p. 89.
64 Antoine (1989), p. 357.
65 Lenman (1992), p. 14 – a lucid and pithy summary.
66 MAE MDA, vol. 53, fo 24.
67 ibid., vol. 77, fo 98.
68 ibid., vol. 78, fos 73–4 (dated 12 June 1745).
69 Dates are given according to the 'old style' Julian calendar, used in Britain until 1751, eleven days behind the 'new style' Gregorian calendar used in France.
70 Roberts (2002), p. 112.
71 For numbers and social composition, see McLynn (1998), pp. 18–28.
72 The arguments are summarized in a paper (September 1745) drawn up by the Duc de Noailles, the king's closest adviser and a leading sceptic. MAE MDA, vol. 52, fos 38–49.
73 Black (2000b), p. 84.
74 Lenman (1992), p. 107.
75 Bongie (1977), p. 12.
76 McLynn (1998), p. 80.
77 31 December to 3 January 'new style'. McLynn (1981), pp. 154–5.
78 Bongie (1977), p. 15.
79 Roberts (2002), p. 144.
80 Black (2000b), p. 183.
81 Roberts (2002), p. 168.
82 McLynn (1981), p. 235.
83 Dziembowski (1998), pp. 81–2, 464.
84 Interim report of the Life in the UK Advisory Group.
85 Brecher (1998), p. 9.
86 Fumaroli (2001), p. 53.
87 Black (1987), p. 3
88 Scott (2000), p. 487.
89 Black (1998), p. 126.
90 Ferguson (2001), p. 49.

91 See Bowen (1998), pp. 18–22.
92 A criticism of the cost of operations in the Seven Years War, quoted by Chesterfield (1932), vol. 2, p. 387.
93 Winch and O'Brien (2002), p. 263.
94 Capie in Prados de la Escosura (2004), p. 216.
95 J.R. Jones, in Hoffman and Norberg (1994), p. 89; Brewer (1990), pp. 90–91.
96 Martin Daunton in Winch and O'Brien (2002), p. 319.
97 Brewer (1990), p. 79; Lindert (2004), pp. 46–7.
98 O'Brien in *OHBE*, vol. 2, p. 66.
99 Dickson (1967), p. 51.
100 North and Weingast (1989), p. 824.
101 Middleton (1985), p. 153.
102 On John Law, see Lüthy (1959), vol. 1; and on the South Sea Bubble, Hoppit (2002) and Dickson (1967), ch. 5.
103 Dickson (1967), p. 198.
104 Neal, in Prados de la Escosura (2004), p. 185.
105 Dziembowski (1998), p. 265.
106 Lüthy (1959), vol. 1, p. 290. See also Crouzet (1999), pp. 105–19.
107 See summary by Bonney (1999), ch. 4.
108 Hoffman and Norberg (1994), p. 258.
109 ibid., pp. 273–4.
110 Antoine (1989), p. 493.
111 Jones (2002b); Lüthy (1959), vol. 2, p. 324; Chaussinand-Nogaret (1993).
112 Lüthy (1959), vol. 1, p. 415; vol. 2, pp. 468–521.
113 See Sonenscher (1997), pp. 64–103, 267–325
114 Kwass (2000), p. 255.

2: Thinking, Pleasing, Seeing (pp. 55–111)

1. Gunny (1979), p. 21.
2. Chesterfield (1932), vol. 1, p. 130.
3. Courtney (1975), p. 273.
4. Fumaroli (2001), p. 53.
5. Alexander Murdoch, in Fitzpatrick et al. (2004), p. 104.
6. Grente and Moureau (1995), p. 61. On eighteenth-century culture generally, see Pomeau (1991), Roche (1993), Brewer (1997), Ferrone and Roche (1999), Fumaroli (2001), Porter (2000), Blanning (2002), Fitzpatrick et al. (2004).
7 Mornet (1910), p. 460.
8 For statistics, Sahlins (2004), pp. 159, 172.
9 Jones (2002), p. 180.
10 Girard d'Albisson (1969), p. 65.
11 Kölving and Mervaud (1997), vol. 1, p. 80.
12 Acomb (1950), p. 27.
13 Dziembowski (1998), p. 355.
14 Pomeau (1979), p. 12.
15 ibid., p. 12.
16 Rousseau (1979), pp. 25, 32, 40.
17 Pomeau (1979), p. 11. See also Mervaud (1992) and Buruma (2000).
18 Fumaroli (2001), p. 22.
19 Fougeret de Montbrun (1757), p. 8.
20 Grieder (1985), p. 4.
21 Much of what follows in based on Shackleton (1961).
22 Courtney (1975), pp. 275–6. See also Dedieu (1909).
23 Sylvana Tomaselli, unpublished lecture quoted by kind permission of the author.
24 ibid.
25 Shackleton (1961), p. 301.
26 Courtney (1975), pp. 286–7.
27 Jones (2002), p. 173.
28 Ross (1995), p. 219. See also Mossner (1980).
29 Ross (1995), p. 217.
30 Smith (1991), vol. 1, p. 13; vol. 2, p. 180. See the subtle discussion in Rothschild (2001).
31 Nicolet (1982), pp. 479–80. On Smith's early reception in France, see Whatmore (2000).
32 Jean-Pierre Langellier, in *Le Monde* (7 June 2005).
33 Le Blanc (1751), p. 50.
34 Chesterfield (1932), vol. 1, pp. 329–30.
35 Andrews (1783), p. 266.
36 This section owes much to Black (1999).
37 Newman (1997), p. 43; Roche (2001), pp. 15–17.

38 From Garrick's play *Bon Ton*, 1775, in Eagles (2000), p. 49.

39 Tyson and Guppy (1932), p. 149.

40 Eagles (2000), p. 109.

41 La Combe (1784), p. 50.

42 McCarthy (1985), p. 150.

43 Grieder (1985), p. 40.

44 Grosley (1770), vol. 1, pp. 23, 85.

45 Mornet (1910), p. 460.

46 Le Blanc (1751), p. 16.

47 Dziembowski (1998), p. 23.

48 *Gentleman's Guide* (n.d.), pp. 5, 39.

49 Thicknesse (1766), pp. 9, 44–5, 105; Gosse (1952).

50 Du Bocage (1770), vol. 1, pp. 1–2.

51 Smollett (1999), p. 4.

52 Grosley (1770), vol. 1, p. 19.

53 Walpole (1904), p. 421.

54 Black (1992), p. 98.

55 Pasquet (1920), p. 835.

56 Black (1992), p. 18.

57 ibid., pp. 185–6.

58 *A Five Weeks' Tour to Paris, Versailles, Marli &c* (1754), p. 15; *Gentleman's Guide*, p. 88.

59 Black (1992), p. 196.

60 Pasquet (1920), pp. 847–8.

61 Grosley (1770), vol. 1, p. 79.

62 Donald (1996), p. 121.

63 Grieder (1985), p. 109.

64 Chesterfield (1932), vol. 2, p. 87.

65 Thicknesse (1766), p. 9.

66 Dziembowski (1998), pp. 207–11.

67 Taylor (1985), p. 43; Harvey (2004), p. 140; Holmes (2001), p. 104.

68 Mennell (1985), p. 138.

69 La Combe (1784), p. 14.

70 Pasquet (1920), pp. 838–9.

71 *Five Weeks' Tour* (1754), p. 25.

72 Chesterfield (1932), vol. 1, p. 103.

73 Radisich (1995), p. 411.

74 Chesterfield (1932), vol. 2, p. 198.

75 Tyson and Guppy (1932), pp. 103, 146, 232.

76 Klein (1997), pp. 362–82.

77 Taylor (2001), pp. 17, 41.

78 McIntyre (2000), p. 369.

79 Cranston (1997), pp. 164–71; Uglow (2002), p. 182.

80 Tyson and Guppy (1932), p. 7.

81 Chesterfield (1932), vol. 2, p. 100.

82 Black (1992), p. 60.

83 Chesterfield (1932), vol. 2, p. 106.

84 Black (1992), p. 206.

85 Harris (1998), pp. 225–30, 434–45, and *passim*.

86 Patterson (1960), p. 33; Harris (1998), pp. 249, 313, 600.

87 Harris (1998), pp. 441, 546–7, 550–51, 560.

88 La Rochefoucauld (1933), *passim*; Crouzet (1999), p. 115; Harris (1998), p. 547. See also Scarfe (1995), and Bombelles (1989), an officer and diplomat who came to sniff the air after the American war.

89 See Rothschild (2002), pp. 46–59.

90 Grieder (1985), p. 17.

91 Eagles (2000), pp. 63–5.

92 Grosley (1770), p. 165.

93 Grente and Moureau (1995), p. 62.

94 Mornet (1910), p. 461; Pemble (2005), pp. 77–8; on Sade, see Schama (1989), p. 391.

95 Porter (2000), p. 286.

96 Grieder (1985), pp. 74–5, 151–62.

97 Walpole (1904), pp. 422, 523.

98 Saint-Girons (1998).

99 ibid.

100 Plaisant and Parreaux (1977), p. 289.

101 Newman (1997), p. 125.

102 Girardin (1777), pp. 34–5.

103 Dulaure, *Nouvelle Description des Environs de Paris* (Paris 1786), in Taylor (2001), p. 99.

104 *George IV and the Arts of France* (1966), p. 5.

105 *The Lady's Magazine*, Nov. 1787, in Ribeiro (1983), p. 116.

106 Chesterfield (1932), vol. 1, p. 330.

107 Grieder (1985), pp. 10, 25; Acomb (1950), p. 15.

108 Steele (1998), p. 32.

109 Buck (1979), p. 44; and see Sheriff, in Bermingham and Brewer (1997), pp. 473–5.

110 Boucher (1996), p. 299.

111 Steele (1998), p. 34.

112 Grieder (1985), p. 16.

113 Britsch (1926), pp. 376–8. See also Ward (1982).

114 Whether she was secretly the child of Genlis and Chartres, and the foundling story was an elaborate cover, still divides specialists. The 2004 *ODNB* (though not the 1884 *DNB*) thinks she was; recent French biographers of the d'Orléans – Lever (1996) and Antonetti (1994) – say emphatically not.

115 Mercier (1928), p. 135.

116 Rothschild (2002), p. 40.

117 Grieder (1985), pp. 20–21.

118 Mercier (1928), p. 74.

119 Newman (1997), p. 38. See also Rauser (2004).

120 Watkin (1984), p. 116.

121 Chesterfield (1932), vol. 1, p. 163.

122 Gury (1999), p. 1047.

123 Walpole (1904), p. 417.

124 Scott (1990), p. 52.

125 Clark (2000), p. 260.

126 Blanning (2002), p. 415.

127 Grieder (1985), p. 110.

128 McIntyre (1999), pp. 244–5; Dziembowski (1998), p. 55. See also Hedgecock (1911).

129 Foote (1783), vol. 1, *The Englishman in Paris*, pp. 13–14; *The Englishman Returned from Paris*, p. 22.

130 J.C. Villiers, *A Tour through part of France* (1789), in Maxwell (1932), p. 144.

131 Reddy (2001), p. 151.

132 Villiers (1789), in Maxwell (1932), p. 359.

133 Smollett (1981), p. 53.

134 *Gentleman's Guide* (n.d), p. 33.

135 Black (1992), p. 196.

136 Garrick (1939), p. 10.

137 Shoemaker (2002), pp. 525–45.

138 Mennell (1985), p. 309.

139 John Andrews, *An Account of the Character and Manners of the French; with occasional Observations on the English* (London, 1770), in Donald (1996), p. 86.

140 Cardwell (2004), 78f.

141 Clairembault-Maurepas (1882), vol. 10, p. 23.

142 Mercier (1928), pp. 74–5.

143 La Rochefoucauld (1933), pp. 57–8.

144 Tyson and Guppy (1932), p. 99.

145 Mercier (1933), p. 213.

146 Fumaroli (2001), p. 190.

147 Fumaroli (2001), p. 181.

148 Chesterfield (1932), vol. 2, pp. 105, 146; Rousseau (1969), pp. 245, 515.

149 Chesterfield (1932), vol. 2, pp. 105, 145; Rousseau (1969), p. 391.

150 Uglow (2002), pp. 185–8, 190–91.

151 Monaco (1974), p. 4.

152 Le Tourneur, 1776 preface, in Genuist (1971), p. 20.

153 Pappas (1997), p. 69.

154 Monaco (1974), p. 9.

155 ibid., p. 73; Pappas (1997), p. 67.

156 Voltaire (1785), vol. 61, pp. 350–76.

157 Genuist (1971), p. 198.

158 Williams (1979), p. 321.

159 Pemble (2005), pp. 95–8.

3: The Sceptre of the World (pp. 112–53)

1 MAE MDA, vol. 52, fo 108.

2 Corbett (1907), vol. 1, p. 189.

3 MAE MDA, vol. 55, fo 74.

4 Crouzet (1999), p. 106.

5 Patrick O'Brien, in *OHBE*, vol. 2, p. 54; Crouzet (1999), p. 300.

6 Duffy (1987), pp. 385, 371.

7 For an excellent summary, see Bruce Lenman, in *OHBE*, vol. 2, pp. 151–68.

8 Black (1998), p. 181.

9 Bayly (2004), part I; see also Alavi (2002), esp. ch. 4.

10 Pluchon (1996), vol. 1, p. 246. On the general issues, see Scott (1992), Black (1998 and 2000), Brecher (1998) and the magisterial surveys by Bayly (2004) and Marshall (2005).

11 Duffy (1987), p. 6.

12 Duffy (1987), pp. 7, 12; Prados de la Escosura (2004), pp. 41–3.

13 Duffy (1987), p. 385.

14 Thomas (1997), p. 249; Duffy (1987), pp. 12–13.

15 Deerr (1949), vol. 1, pp. 240, 293.

16 Thomas (1997), p. 300.

17 ibid., pp. 303–4, 340.

18 MAE MDA, vol. 52, fo 234.

19 Das (1992), p. 7.
20 See Subramanian (1999), Manning (1996).
21 Llewelyn-Jones (1992).
22 Vigié (1993), p. 504.
23 Pluchon (1996), vol. 1, p. 191.
24 P.J. Marshall, in *OHBE*, vol. 2, p. 501.
25 Vigié (1993), p. 8.
26 Brecher (1998), pp. 18–19.
27 Anderson (2000), p. 29; Meyer, Tarrade and Rey-Goldzeiguer (1991), vol. 1, p. 146.
28 Anderson (2000), pp. 35–40.
29 MAE MDA, vol. 52, fos. 104–10.
30 Brecher (1998), p. 11.
31 MAE MDA, vol. 52, fo 109.
32 Brecher (1998), p. 60.
33 MAE MDA, vol. 52, fos 103–4.
34 Dziembowski (1998), p. 216.
35 Anderson (2000), p. 17; Meyer, Tarrade and Rey-Goldzeiguer (1991), vol. 1, pp. 145–9.
36 Bell (2001), p. 86.
37 Dziembowski (1998), p. 81.
38 Dull (2005), p. 31.
39 'Mémoire sur les partis à prendre dans les circonstances présentes' (Aug. 1755), MAE MDA, vol. 52, fo 134.
40 Béranger and Meyer (1993), p. 278; Vergé-Franceschi (1996), pp. 122, 221; Meyer, Tarrade and Rey-Goldzeiguer (1991), vol. 1, p. 148.
41 Pocock (1999), vol. 1, p. 94.
42 Lenman (2001), p. 136.
43 Béranger and Meyer (1993), pp. 210–11; Pluchon (1996), vol. 1, p. 166. See also Plank (2001).
44 Dziembowski (1998), p. 81, Bell (2001), p. 87.
45 Dziembowski (1998), p. 85.
46 Ambassadorial instructions, quoted by Chaussinand-Nogaret (1998), p. 63.
47 Pluchon (1996), p. 248.
48 Anderson (2000), ch. 19.
49 Woodbridge (1995), p. 94.
50 Dziembowski (1998), pp. 100–101.
51 Middleton (1985), p. 41.
52 Voltaire (1992), p. 68.
53 Rodger (2004), p. 272; Rodger (1988), pp. 266–7.
54 Cardwell (2004), p. 78.

55 Colley (1992), pp. 87–98; Wilson (1995), pp. 185–93.
56 Van Kley (1984), pp 36, 39–40.
57 Woodbridge (1995), p. 48.
58 Van Kley (1984), p. 145.
59 Instructions to envoy to Prussia, quoted in Middleton (1985), p. 27.
60 Woodbridge (1995).
61 Dziembowski (1998), pp. 122–30.
62 Kwass (2000), pp. 156–92.
63 Van Kley (1984), p. 39.
64 Dziembowski (1998), pp. 499–504.
65 Walpole (1904), pp. 430–31.
66 Peters (1980), p. 104.
67 Earl Waldegrave, in Peters (1998), p. 73.
68 Peters (1998), p. 83.
69 Chaussinand-Nogaret (1998), p. 216.
70 ibid., p. 132.
71 ibid., p. 15.
72 Peters (1998), p. 246.
73 Chaussinand-Nogaret (1998), p. 129.
74 ibid.
75 Béranger and Mayer (1993), p. 243.
76 Lacour-Gayet (1902), p. 295; Dull (2005), p. 61.
77 Lacour-Gayet (1902), p. 307.
78 ibid., p. 312.
79 Waddington (1899), vol. 3, p. 346.
80 ibid., p. 348.
81 Lacour-Gayet (1902), p. 316.
82 Waddington (1899), vol. 3, p. 353.
83 Letter of 2 October 1758, in Lacour-Gayet (1902), p. 316.
84 Brumwell (2002), p. 51; Kennett (1967), p. xiv.
85 Middleton (1985), p. 116.
86 McIntyre (1999), p. 291.
87 Walpole (1904), p. 260.
88 Brumwell (2002), p. 271.
89 Anderson (2000), p. 375. See also Rogers (2004), pp. 239–59.
90 Kennett (1967), p. 57.
91 The profit from engraved reproductions totalled a huge £15,000 by 1790. Blanning (2002), p. 300.
92 Dull (2005), p. 161.
93 McLynn (2005), p. 370.
94 Padfield (2000), p. 212.
95 Lacour-Gayet (1902), p. 342.
96 Middleton (1985), p. 177.

97 Vincent (1993), p. 231.
98 Blanning (1977).
99 Black (1998), pp. 181–2; see also Middleton (1985), pp. 22, 183, 188, 208–21; Peters (1998), p. 116.
100 Dull (2005), pp. 199, 241.
101 MAE MD, Indes Orientales 1755–1797, vol. 13, 'Observations sur l'article 10 des préliminaires de paix', March 1763.
102 Robert Allen, in Prados de la Escosura (2004), p. 15.
103 Stanley Engerman, ibid., p. 280. See also Javier Esteban, ibid., pp. 59–60; and Jacob M. Price, OHBE, vol. 2, p. 99.
104 Anderson (2000), p. 507.
105. Glyn Williams, in OHBE, vol. 2, pp. 555–6.
106 Salmond (2003), p. 31.
107 ibid., p. 53.
108 Landes (2000), pp. 165, 176.
109 Robson (2004), p. 68.
110 Ormesson and Thomas (2002), p. 206.
111 Richard Drayton, in OHBE, vol. 2, p. 246; Whiteman (2003), pp. 28–41.
112 Chaunu (1982), p. 262.
113 Girardet (1986), pp. 158–61.
114 Genuist (1971), p. 16.
115 Boswell (1992), p. 188. The eighty Frenchmen 'beat' by Johnson were the members of the French Academy, authors of the official French dictionary.
116 Béranger and Meyer (1993), p. 73.
117 Crystal (2004), p. 433.
118 Statistics in Ferrone and Roche (1999), pp. 297–8.
119 Mercier (1928), p. 158.
120 Grosley (1772), vol. 1, p. 93; Semmel (2004), p. xiii.
121 Bellaigue (2003), p. 64.
122 Plaisant (1976), pp. 197, 211.
123 Grieder (1985), p. 29.
124 Bernard Saurin, L'Anglomane ou l'orpheline léguée (1772), in Répertoire (1818), vol. 7, p. 246.
125 Hardman and Price (1998), p. 89.
126 'Appeal to all the nations of Europe' (1761), in Voltaire (1785), vol. 61, p. 368.

127 Cohen (1999), pp. 448–59.
128. Newman (1997), p. 114; Lancashire (2005), p. 33.
129 Rivarol (1998), pp. 8, 32, 36, 42, 46–51, 68–70, 76–86, 90–91.
130 Fumaroli (2001), p. 19.
131 Ostler (2005), p. 519.

4: The Revenger's Tragedy (pp. 154–92)

1 Dziembowski (1998), p. 206.
2 ibid., p. 264.
3 ibid., p. 7.
4 Choiseul (1881), p. 172.
5 ibid., pp. 178, 253.
6 Conlin (2005), pp. 1251–88.
7 Dziembowski (1998), p. 283.
8 Farge (1994), p. 172.
9 L'Année littéraire, 1766, in Acomb (1950), p. 61.
10 Goudar, L'Espion chinois, in Acomb (1950), p. 61.
11 Choiseul (1881), p. 178.
12 Chaussinand-Nogaret (1998), p. 252.
13 'Mémoire sur l'Angleterre', MAE MDA, vol. 52, fo 180.
14 Abarca (1970), p. 325; Patterson (1960), pp. 32–4.
15 Conlin (2005).
16 Belloy (1765), preface.
17 ibid., pp. 55–6. Interestingly, the copy in the Cambridge University Library was presented by Belloy to David Garrick in April 1765.
18 Choiseul (1881), pp. 252, 254. See also Scott (1990), pp. 74–9, 140–54.
19 Dull (2005), p. 248.
20 'Mémoire' (1777), MAE MDA, vol. 52, fo 230.
21 Sorel (1969), p. 382.
22 Anderson (2000), p. 605.
23 Unpublished paper by Kirk Swinehart, which we are grateful for permission to cite, in anticipation of his forthcoming book, Molly's War. See also Mintz (1999).
24 Holton (1999).
25 Conway (2000), p. 145.

26 Wilson (1995), p. 240.
27 Murphy (1982), p. 235.
28 Turgot (1913), vol. 5, pp. 405–6.
29 Poirier (1999), p. 315.
30 To Louis XVI, 1776, in Poirier (1999), p. 310.
31 Murphy (1982), p. 400.
32 Patterson (1960), p. 227.
33 Hardman and Price (1998), p. 237.
34 Poirier (1999), p. 309.
35 ibid., p. 304; Conlin (2005).
36 Poirier, p. 305.
37 ibid., p. 313.
38 Dull (1985), p. 62.
39 Vergé-Franceschi (1996), p. 154.
40 Clairambault-Maurepas (1882), vol. 10, p. 155.
41 Hardman and Price (1998), p. 48.
42 Murphy (1982), p. 260.
43 MAE MDA, vol. 52, fo 233.
44 Dull (1985), p. 99.
45 Acomb (1950), pp. 76–7.
46 Clairambault-Maurepas (1892), vol. 10, p. 155.
47 Schama (1989), p. 49.
48 Schama (1989), p. 25.
49 Kennett (1977), p. 51.
50 Rodger (2004), p. 335.
51 Conway (2000), pp. 321–2.
52 Patterson (1960), p. 42.
53 'Mémoire sur l'Angleterre' (1773), in MAE MDA, vol. 52, fos 180–223.
54 Lacour-Gayet (1905), pp. 252–3.
55 Patterson (1960), p. 154.
56 Chateaubriand (1973), p. 55.
57 Foreman (1999), pp. 64–5.
58 Conway (2000), p. 89.
59 Patterson (1960), pp. 112, 117.
60 Manceron (1979), pp. 148, 155.
61 Conway (2000), pp. 22, 198–9.
62 Lacour-Gayet (1905), p. 232.
63 ibid., pp. 256, 274; Manceron (1979), p. 175.
64 Murphy (1982), p. 279.
65 Manceron (1979), p. 181.
66 Vergé-Franceschi (1996), p. 148; Murphy (1982), p. 245; Béranger and Meyer (1993), p. 316; Kennedy (1976), p. 111.
67 Bamford (1956), p. 210.
68 Dull (1985), p. 110 (totals for 1781).
69 Mackesy (1964), p. 382.
70 Blanning (2002), p. 339.
71 Rogers (1998), p. 152.
72 Clairambault-Maurepas (1882), vol. 11, p. 16.
73 Schama (1989), p. 47.
74 ibid., p. 44.
75 Moore (1994), p. 137. See also Schama (2005).
76 Ferling (2003), p. 224.
77 Dull (1985), pp. 109–10.
78 Kennett (1977), pp. 30, 52; Mackesy (1964), p. 350.
79 Kennett (1977), p. 56.
80 Mackesy (1964), p. 384; Hardman (1995), pp. 54–62.
81 Mackesy (1964), p. 385.
82 Kennett (1977), p. 91.
83 Grainger (2005), p. 176.
84 Mackesy (1964), p. 424.
85 Kennett (1977), p. 121; Harvey (2001), pp. 410–11.
86 Kennett (1977), p. 156.
87 Mayo (1938), pp. 213–14.
88 Manceron (1979), p. 514.
89 Mackesy (1964), p. 435.
90 Dull (1985), p. 120.
91 Kennett (1977), p. 160.
92 Dull (1985), p. 153.
93 Conway (2000), p. 202.
94 Mintz (1999), p. 173. See also Scott (1990), pp. 324–31.
95 Hulot (1994); Rodger (2004), p. 357.
96 Bruce Lenman, in *OHBE*, vol. 2, p. 166.
97 Mackesy (1964), pp. 383–4.
98 Wilson (1995), p. 435.
99 Béranger and Meyer (1993), p. 316.
100 Lüthy (1959), vol. 2, p. 592.
101 Esteban, in Prados de la Escosura (2004), p. 53.
102 Acomb (1950), p. 86.
103 Jarrett (1973), p. 34.
104 Statistics: Prados de la Escosura (2004); Hoffman and Norberg (1994); Murphy (1982), pp. 398–9; Conway (2000), pp. 236, 316, 352; Bowen (1998), pp. 19–20.
105 Whiteman (2003), pp. 22, 23 (our translation).
106 Browning (1909), vol. 1, p. 99.

107 Whiteman (2003), p. 29; Price (1995), p. 67.
108 Browning (1909), vol. 1, p. 134.
109 Talleyrand, quoted in Jones (2002), p. 343.
110 Hardman (1995), p. 153.
111 ibid., p. 244.
112 Ozanam (1969), p. 169.
113 Murphy (1998), pp. 73-7.
114 Chaussinand-Nogaret (1993), pp 9, 112–13.
115 Jones (2002), p. 382.
116 Egret (1977), p. 22.
117 Schama (1989), p. 267.
118 Whiteman (2003), pp. 37–9, 54; Price (1995b), pp. 895, 903.
119 Blanning (2002), p. 422.
120 Whiteman (2003), p. 63. See also Murphy (1998), pp. 94–5; Price (1995b), p. 904.
121 Blanning (2002), p. 421.
122 Hardman and Price (1998), p. 105.
123 Hopkin (2005), p. 1130.
124 Jarrett (1973), pp. 274–5.
125 Browning (1909), vol. 1, p. 148.
126 ibid., vol. 2, p. 243.
127 ibid., vol. 2, p. 259.
128 Black (2000), p. 267.
129 Samuel Boddington.
130 Godechot (1956), vol. 1, pp. 66–7; see also Wahnich (1997), pp. 282–3.
131 Browning (1909), vol. 2, p. 251.
132 Hampson (1998), p. 16; Jarrett (1973), p. 275.
133 Acomb (1950), p. 121.
134 Hammersley (2004); Acomb (1950), p. 121.
135 Baker (1990), pp. 277–8.
136 Jarrett (1973), p. 286.
137 Goulstone and Swanton (1989), p. 18.

5: Ideas and Bayonets
(pp. 193–237)

1 Second 'Letter on a Regicide Peace', Macleod (1998), p. 13.
2 'French Revolution: as it appeared to enthusiasts at its commencement' (1809).
3 Ehrman (2004), vol. 2, p. 4.
4 Hampson (1998), p. 47; Jarrett (1973), p. 279; Mori (2000), p. 188; Barker (2001), pp. 68–73.
5 Andrews (2003), pp. 6, 31, 33; Macleod (1998), p. 154.
6. Watson (1977), p. 49; Ehrman (2004), vol. 2, p. 47.
7 Garrett (1975), p. 131; Bentley (2001), pp. 186, 196; Andrews (2003), pp. 95–104; McCalman (1998).
8 Burke (2001), pp. 63–5.
9 Paine (1989), p. 59.
10 Beales (2005), p. 418.
11 Macleod (1998), p. 12.
12 AP, vol. 91, p. 38.
13 O'Gorman (1967), p. 66.
14 Burke (2001), p. 62. See also Welsh (1995).
15 Mehta (1999), p. 158.
16 Burke (2001), p. 291.
17 ibid., p. 328.
18 ibid., pp. 328, 339. See also Pocock (1985), p. 208.
19 Claeys (2000), p. 41.
20 Paine (1989), p. 141.
21 Ehrman (2004), vol. 2, p. 80.
22 Paine (1989), pp. 86, 120.
23 Rapport (2000), p. 691.
24 Frank O'Gorman, in Dickinson (1989), p. 29.
25 Dickinson (1985), p. 11–12.
26 The best analysis is Rose (1960).
27 Andrews (2003), p. 35.
28 Monod (1989), p. 194.
29 Garrett (1975), p. 139.
30 Ehrman (2004), vol. 2, p. 226.
31 Dickinson (1989), pp. 36, 103.
32 Christie (1984), p. 93.
33 Rothschild (2001), p. 233.
34 Hampson (1998), p. 137.
35 Linton (2001), p. 213.
36 Speech to National Convention, 17 Pluviôse Year II (5 February 1794), Robespierre (1967), vol. 10, pp. 352, 353, 357, 358, 359.
37 Rose (1911), p. 32.
38 Blanning (1986), p. 111.
39 Speech of 29 December 1791, Hardman (1999), p. 141.
40 Speaker in National Assembly, October 1791, Blanning (1986), p. 108

– the best general analysis of the coming of war, as Ehrman (2004) is of the British perspective.

41 Blanning (1986), p. 133, and Duffy, in Dickinson (1989), p. 128.
42 Blanning (1986), p. 134.
43 Ehrman (2004), vol. 2, p. 205; Blanning (1986), p. 139.
44 Lefebvre (1962), p. 264.
45 ibid., pp. 274–6.
46 Blanning (1986), p. 149.
47 Ehrman (2004), vol. 2, p. 239.
48 Pitt (n.d.), pp. 32–3.
49 Lefebvre (1962), p. 280.
50 Furet (1992), p. 104.
51 Guiomar (2004).
52 Hampson (1998), p. 94.
53 Ehrman (2004), vol. 2, p. 237.
54 Bertaud (1988), p. 120.
55 Wawro (2000), p. 3.
56 Lord Auckland, in Macleod (1998), p. 39.
57 Macleod (1998) gives an excellent summary of public opinion. See also Cookson (1997), and on poor relief, Lindert (2004), p. 47.
58 'Aperçu [sic] d'un plan de politique au dehors', MAE MDF, vol. 651, fo 155. See also Rothschild (2002), Wahnich (1997) and Guiomar (2004).
59 Hampson (1998), p. 117.
60 Hammersley (2005).
61 'Situation politique de la République française . . . avril 1793', MAE MDF, vol. 561, fo 33.
62 Speech to Convention, 17 November 1793, Hampson (1998), p. 130.
63 'Aperçu', MAE MDF, vol. 651, fo 155.
64 MAE MDF, vol. 651, 'Situation politique', fos 27–8, 37.
65 ibid., fo 35.
66 'Aperçu', ibid., fo 155; 'Diplomatie de la République française', ibid., fo 239.
67 Hampson (1998), p. 133.
68 Report of the Committee of Public Safety, 7 prairial, Year II [26 May 1794] AP, vol. 91, pp. 32–41.
69 Hampson (1998), p. 142; Wahnich (1997), p. 239.
70 Alger (1898), p. 673.

71 Carpenter (1999), p. 155.
72 Alger (1898), p. 673.
73 Rapport (2000), chs. 3 and 4.
74 Weiner (1960), pp. 59, 65–6.
75 ibid., p. 43.
76 Carpenter (1999), p. 54.
77 Chateaubriand (1973), p. 404.
78 Carpenter (1999), p. 111.
79 ibid., pp. 166 and 155.
80 Chateaubriand (1973), p. 404.
81 Macleod (1998), p. 19.
82 Pitt (n.d), p. 287.
83 Marianne Elliott, in Dickinson (1989), p. 83. See also Elliott (1982) passim.
84 Gough and Dickson (1990), p. 60.
85 Kevin Whelan, in Wilson (2004), pp. 222–3.
86 Bartlett and Jeffery (1996), p. 260.
87 Smyth (2000), p. 8.
88 Mitchell (1965), p. 20.
89 Mori (1997), p. 700, 704–5; Thrasher (1970), pp. 284–326.
90 Martin (1987), pp. 197–8, 230, 316; Forrest (2002), pp. 29, 160–61.
91 Gabory (1989), p. 1193.
92 ibid., p. 1230.
93 Jones (1950), p. 119; Quinault (1999), pp. 618–41.
94 Rodger (2004), pp. 442–53; Wells (1986), pp. 79–109.
95 Bartlett and Jeffery (1996), p. 270.
96 Simms (2003b), pp. 592, 595.
97 Tom Bartlett, in Smyth (2000), p. 78.
98 Martin (1987), pp. 315–16.
99 Smyth (2000), p. 16.
100 Eliott, in Dickinson (1989), p. 101.
101 Pitt (n.d.), p. 430.
102 Schama (1989), p. 207; Blanning (1983), pp. 318–20; Blanning (1996), pp. 160–63.
103 Mackesy (1984), p. 12.
104 ibid., pp. 37–8.
105 Sorel (1969), p. 362.
106 Bluche (1980), p. 24.
107 George Canning, quoted in Mackesy (1984), p. 43.
108 ibid., pp. 124–5, 132.
109 ibid., pp. 206–7.
110 ibid., p. 209.
111 Pitt (n.d.), pp. 430–33 (3 November 1801).

112 Emsley (1979), p. 96; Semmel (2004), pp. 26–9; Macleod (1998), p. 109.

113 Browning (1887), p. 12.

114 Grainger (2004), pp. 61–5, 93–9, 131–5; Keane (1995), pp. 441, 455, 493; Morieux (2006); Pilbeam (2003), pp. 65–6.

115 Haskell (1976), p. 27.

116 Buchanan (1824), vol. 1 *passim*; see also Reitlinger (1961), vol. 1, ch. 1; Ormesson and Thomas (2002), pp. 255–6.

117 Bourguet (2002), p. 102. See also Jasanoff (2005).

118 St Clair (1967), p. 58, from which the following section is derived.

119 ibid., pp. 96, 110.

6: Changing the Face of the World (pp. 238–93)

1 Furet (1992), p. 254.

2 Evans (1999), p. 74.

3 Herold (1955), p. 276.

4 Englund (2004), p. 279.

5 William Doyle, in *TLS* (6 March 1998), p. 15.

6 The best modern biography is Englund (2004). Indispensable for the international context is Schroeder (1994).

7 Sorel (1969), p. 343. See also Bluche (1980) and Martin (2000).

8 Grainger (2004), p. 8.

9 Dwyer (2002), p. 137.

10 Letter to brother, June 1793, Herold (1955), p. 67.

11 Conversation, 1805, in ibid., p. 243. On Napoleonic Europe, see Broers (2001).

12 The best military study is Chandler (1966).

13 Schroeder (1994), p. 446.

14 Herold (1955), p. 276.

15 Regenbogen (1998), p. 16.

16 Lovie and Palluel-Guillard (1972), p. 46.

17 Crouzet (1999), pp. 242–3.

18 Englund (2004), p. 254.

19 Schroeder (1994), p. 233.

20 Grainger (2004), p. 153.

21 Burrows (2000), pp. 114–26.

22 Grainger (2004), p. 173.

23 Semmel (2004), p. 30; Browning (1887), pp. 116–17; Grainger (2004), pp. 153, 159–60, 168.

24 Browning (1887), p. 116.

25 ibid., pp. 135–6, 263; Grainger (2004), p. 175.

26 Schroeder (1994), p. 229. See also Englund (2004), p. 262; Grainger (2004), pp. 191, 211.

27 Emsley (1979), p. 94.

28 Schroeder (1994), p. 230.

29 Regenbogen (1998), p. 115.

30 Ehrman (2004), vol. 3, p. 808.

31 Emsley (1979), p. 99.

32 Battesti (2004), *passim*; Humbert and Ponsonnet (2004), pp. 110–19; Rodger (2004), pp. 529–30.

33 Battesti (2004), p. 38.

34 To Villeneuve, 14 April; to Decrès, 20 June 1805. Napoleon (1858), vol. 10, pp. 398, 676.

35 Regenbogen (1998), p. 114.

36 We are grateful to Commodore John Harris, RN (retd), for his advice on this point.

37 Marshal Bernadotte, in Battesti (2004), p. 53.

38 Herold (1955), p. 192; Chandler (1966), p. 322.

39 Battesti (2004), p. 53.

40 Herold (1955), p. 191.

41 Colley (1992), p. 306; Emsley (1979), p. 112; Semmel (2004), pp. 39–40.

42 Cookson (1997), p. 66. See also Gee (2003).

43 Esdaile (1995), pp. 144–5.

44 Cookson (1997), pp. 95–6.

45 New words to a song by Purcell, which had long been one of several national anthems. Klingberg and Hustvedt (1944), p. 73

46 'Fellow Citizens . . . A Shopkeeper' [June 1803], in Klingberg and Hustvedt (1944), p. 193. See also Semmel (2004), ch. 2.

47 Guiffan (2004), p. 100; Bertaud (2004), pp. 60–66; Battesti (2004), p. 75.

48 Colley (1992), p. 306.

49 For details, see Cookson (1997), Longmate (2001), McLynn (1987), Gee (2003).

50 Napoleon (1858), vol. 11, pp. 51–2.

51 Battesti (2004), pp. 180, 182–3, 187, 192.

52 Napoleon (1858), vol. 11, p. 142.

53 Saunders (1997), pp. 80–89

54 Sorel (1969), p. 367. For a superb biography of Pitt, see Ehrman (2004).

55 Rev. Sydney Smith, Ehrman (2004), vol. 3, pp. 847–8.

56 Longmate (2001), pp. 291–2.

57 Rodger (2004), p. 536.

58 4 August 1805, Napoleon (1858), vol. 11, p. 71.

59 Blanning (1996), p. 196.

60 Mackesy (1984), p. 13.

61 Lewis (1960), pp. 346–9; Béranger and Meyer (1993), pp. 282–3.

62 Rodger (2004), p. lxv.

63 Vergé-Franceschi (1996), p. 307.

64 Stone (1994), p. 10.

65 Rodger (1986), p. 343.

66 Daniel Baugh, in Prados de la Escosura (2004), p. 253.

67 Battesti (2004), p. 333.

68 Rodger (1986), p. 11.

69 Béranger and Meyer (1993), p. 387.

70 Albion (2000), p. 93.

71 Béranger and Meyer (1993), p. 313.

72 Bamford (1956), p. 208.

73 Albion (2000), p. 67.

74 Rodger (1986), pp. 83–4.

75 Rodger (2004), p. 345, and ch. 27 *passim*.

76 Dull (2005), p. 114; Bowen (1998), p. 17; Albion (2000), p. 86.

77 Kennedy (1976), p. 109.

78 Rodger (1986); Haudrère (1997), p. 81; Béranger and Meyer (1993), p. 332; Brioist (1997), p. 36.

79 Dull (2005), p. 113; Morriss (2000), p. 197.

80 Jean Meyer, in Johnson, Crouzet and Bédarida (1980), p. 150.

81 Vergé-Franceschi (1996), p. 132.

82 Antier (1991), pp. 244–5.

83 Rodger (1986), pp. 13, 208–9; and see Macdonald (2004), *passim*.

84 Rodger (1986), p. 136.

85 Meyer and Acerra (1994), p. 162.

86 Humbert and Ponsonnet (2004), pp. 128–9; Lewis (1960), pp. 361–70; Padfield (1973), p. 133.

87 We thank the military historian Dennis Showalter for this judgement.

88 Charlton (1966), p. 140.

89 He was quoting what must have been a well-known remark by the Prince de Condé. Guéry (1991) remarks that in fact 'a Paris night' produced only a few dozen babies.

90 Quimby (1957); Charlton (1966), pp. 136–43; Nosworthy (1995), pp. 103–16.

91 Guiomar (2004), p. 13.

92 Lynn (1989).

93 Blanning (1983), p. 106; Blanning (2003), p. 55; Esdaile (1995), p. 100.

94 Guéry (1991), pp. 299–300.

95 Tulard (1977), p. 208.

96 Duffy (1987), pp. 8–9, 379.

97 Anstey (1975), pp. 407–8.

98 The Lord Chancellor, in Colley (1992), p. 358.

99 Ferguson (1998), p. 91; Ferguson (2001), pp. 47–50.

100 Sherwig (1969), pp. 338, 350.

101 Tulard (1977), p. 206.

102 Schroeder (1994), p. 330.

103 Tulard (1977), p. 211.

104 The French economist J.-B. Say, in ibid., p. 375.

105 Rowe (2003), p. 201.

106 Sherwig (1969), pp. 328–9, 342, 354–5; Ferguson (1998), pp. 94–7; Esteban (2001), pp. 58–61; Rowe (2003), p. 216.

107 Sherwig (1969), p. xiv.

108 Sherwig (1969), pp. 4, 11, 350.

109 Webster (1921), pp. 1, 393.

110 Mitchell and Deane (1962), pp. 8–10, 388, 402–3.

111 Sherwig (1969), p. 344.

112 Estimates in Lewis (1962) and Bowen (1998), p. 41.

113 Jones (1950), pp. 125–6; Harvey (1981), p. 84.

114 Lewis (1962), pp. 231–6.

115 Charlton (1966), p. 597.

116 Esdaile (2002), p. 87.
117 Letter from Napoleon to Tsar Alexander, February 1808, Herold (1955), p. 196.
118 Guéry (1991), p. 301.
119 George Canning, 1807, in Schroeder (1994), p. 330.
120 Harvey (1981), p. 48.
121 Marshal Soult, in Gotteri (1991), p. 245.
122 Esdaile (2002), p. 153.
123 Gates (2002), p. 36.
124 Wheatley (1997), p. 24.
125 Blakiston (1829), vol. 2, pp. 300ff.
126 See e.g. Esdaile (2002), p. 206; Holmes (2001), pp. 373–6; Wheatley (1997), p. 33.
127 Wheatley (1997), p. 12.
128 Gates (2002), p. 219.
129 Esdaile (2002), p. 331.
130 Englund (2004), p. 517.
131 Muir (2001), pp. 208–9.
132 Michael Duffy, in Dickinson (1989), p. 137; Charlton (1966), pp. 834, 852–3.
133. Schroeder (1994), p. 448; Englund (2004), p. 383.
134 Schroeder (1994), p. 504 – a magisterial analysis.
135 Esdaile (2002), p. 456.
136 To Metternich, in Ellis (1997), p. 100.
137 Migliorini and Quatre Vieux (2002), pp. 199–201; Duloum (1970), pp. 106–7; Gotteri (1991), pp. 466–7.
138 Wheatley (1997), pp 30–31.
139 Blakiston (1829), vol. 2, p. 338.
140 Mansel (1981), pp. 166–7.
141 Gotteri (1991), p. 467.
142 Weiner (1960), p. 195; Mansel (1981), p. 168; Emsley (1979), p. 167; Semmel (2004), p. 148; Wheatley (1997), p. 54.
143 Wheatley (1997), pp. 45, 46, 48, 50.
144 Information kindly provided by Mr Jack Douay, MBE, secretary of the Bordeaux branch of the British Legion.
145 Kennedy (1976), p. 123.
146 Semmel (2004), p. 164.
147 Hugo (1967), vol. 1, pp. 377–8.
148 Schroeder (1994), pp. 551–3.
149 Colley (1992), p. 191.
150 From a patriotic song of 1797 by Thomas Dibdin.
151 Largeaud (2000), vol. 2, p. 610.
152 Hugo (1967), vol. 1, pp. 373–4. The dread word was omitted by his English translator.
153 Largeaud (2000), vol. 1, pp. 255–6, vol. 2, 555–6.
154 Largeaud (2000), vol. 2, pp. 595–6.

PART I: Conclusions and Disagreements (pp. 294–302)

1 Guéry (1991), p. 301; Bertaud (1998), pp. 69–70; Esdaile (1995), pp. 300–301; Bowen (1998), pp. 16–17; Charle (1991), p. 16.
2 Meyer and Bromley, in Johnson, Bédarida and Crouzet (1980); and see Crouzet (1996), and Scott (1992).
3 See especially the pioneering and scholarly Dziembowski (1998) and the brilliant simplification by Colley (1992). Greenfeld (1992), Bell (2001) and Blanning (2002) are thought-provoking. Eagles (2000) balances Colley by emphasizing francophilia. Langford (2000) and Newman (1987) are useful but often unconvincing. For penetrating scepticism, see Clark (2000).
4 Furet (1992), p. 103.
5 Bertaud, Forrest and Jourdan (2004), p. 16.
6 Crouzet (1996), pp. 435–6.
7 ibid., p. 433.
8 Fumaroli (2001), pp. 45, 53.
9 Porter (2000), p. 3; Blanning (2002), pp. 385–7, 417.
10 Furet (1992), p. 130.
11 Villepin (2002), p. 583; Roberts (2001), p. 298.
12 Herold (1955), p. 243.
13 Schroeder (1994), p. 395
14 Las Cases (1968), vol. 2, p. 1208
15 Crouzet (1996), p. 450.

Interlude: The View from St Helena
(pp. 303–6)

1 Ellis (1997), p. 196.
2 See Semmel (2004).
3 Herold (1955), p. xxxvii. See also Petiteau (1999), pp. 244–52.
4 Roberts (2001), p. 29; Herold (1955), p. 255; Las Cases (1968), vol. 1. p. 445.
5 Thiers (1972), p. 680.
6 Petiteau (1999), pp. 391–5.
7 Englund (2004), pp. 456–67.
8 Villepin (2002), pp. 572–3, 592–4.

PART II: Coexistence (p. 307)

1 Bodley (1898), vol. 1, pp. 59–61.

7: Plucking the Fruits of Peace (pp. 309–38)

1 Chateaubriand (1947), vol. 4, book 5, p. 15.
2 Guizot (1854), p. 310 (13th lecture).
3 Rosanvallon (1994), pp. 7–8.
4 Poumiès de La Siboutie (1911), p. 171.
5 Browne (1905), p. 122.
6 Léribault (1994), p. 7.
7 Browne (1905), p. 22.
8 Beal and Cornforth (1992).
9 Martin-Fugier (1990), p. 151.
10 Browne (1905), p. 67.
11 Hantraye (2005), pp. 19–20.
12 Longford (1969), vol. 2, pp. 16, 26, 42.
13 Hazareesingh (2004), p. 64.
14 Wheeler (1951), pp. 176–7.
15 Boigne (1971), vol. 1, p. 348.
16 Mansel (2001), pp. 92–6.
17 Antonetti (1994), p. 523.
18 Mansel (2001), pp. 58–9.
19 Darriulat (2001), p. 144.
20 Browne (1905), p. 84.
21 Duloum (1970), p. 136.
22 Hickman (2000), pp. 121, 123.
23 Dumas (2000), p. 142. The origin of chips is uncertain.
24 'Le bifteck et les frites', in Barthes (1957).

25 Léribault (1994), p. 59.
26 ibid., p. 60.
27 Browne (1905), p. 105; Mansel (2001), p. 47; Fierro (1996), p. 1177.
28 Martin-Fugier (1990), pp. 332–40. See also Guillaume (1992), vol. 3, pp. 511–12.
29 Tucoo-Chala (1999), p. 26.
30 Duloum (1970), p. 120.
31 Tucoo-Chala (1999), p. 57.
32 Duloum (1970), p. 136.
33 Pyrénées Magazine (Juillet–Août 2004), p. 7.
34 Noon (2003), p. 13.
35 Boigne (1971), vol. 1, p. 373.
36 Gury (1999), pp. 591, 608, 617, 622.
37 Guizot (1850), p. 1.
38 ibid.
39 Arnold Scheffer, in Noon (2003), p. 21.
40 William Shakespeare, published 1864, in Hugo (1937), p. 195.
41 Berlioz, in Cairns (1989), p. 228.
42 ibid.
43 Hugo (1937), p. 250.
44 Hugo (1922), pp. 19, 20, 25, 32, 50.
45 ibid., pp. 714, 719, 726, 15, 20.
46 Pemble (2005), pp. 105–6.
47 Hugo (1937), p. 195.
48 Robb (1997), p. 337.
49 Gury (1999), p. 1079.
50 ibid., p. 939.
51 Asselain (1984), vol. 1, p. 136.
52 Katznelson and Zolberg (1986), p. 116; Rougerie (1971), p. 13.
53 Walton (1992), pp. 222–3.
54 Crouzet (1996), p. 448. This 100 million was later a fantasy of de Gaulle.
55 Landes (1969), pp. 288, 149.
56 Gury (1999), p. 82.
57 ibid., p. 111.
58 ibid., p. 92.
59 Gerbod (1995), pp. 26–7, 29–30.
60 Gury (1999), p. 111.
61 Gerbod (1995), pp. 32–3.
62 Darriulat (2001), p. 104.
63 Custine, in Gury (1999), p. 1051.
64 Hugo (1972), p. 294.
65 Gury (1999), p. 81.
66 ibid., pp. 788, 1021.
67 Pilbeam (1991), pp. 6–7.

68 Darriulat (2001), p. 53.
69 ibid., p. 58.
70 Beach (1964), p. 133.
71 Antonetti (1994), p. 356.
72 Guizot (1971), p. 356; Bullen (1974), p. 4.
73 Considérant (1840), p. 8; *L'Atelier* (socialist workers' paper), May 1842.
74 Michelet (1946), p. 240.
75 Tudesq (1964), vol. 1, pp. 486–7.
76 Antonetti (1994), p. 816.
77 Guizot (1971), p. 344.
78 Bury and Tombs (1986), p. 67.
79 ibid., p. 72.
80 *AP* (1840–41), vol. 3, p. 195.
81 Letter to J.S. Mill, 6 February 1843, in Lawlor (1959), p. 90.
82 Knapp (2001), p. 98.
83 Bourne (1982), p. 613.

8: The War That Never Was (pp. 339–89)

1 Longmate (2001), p. 307.
2 Lawlor (1959), p. 74.
3 Antonetti (1994), p. 858.
4 ibid., p. 897.
5 Charles II and James II had of course been there as exiles.
6 Antonetti (1994), p. 858.
7 Hugo (1972), p. 292.
8 Guizot (1884), p. 227.
9 Bullen (1974), p. 38.
10 Saville (1987), p. 53.
11 Johnson (1963), p. 203.
12 Guizot (1884), p. 244.
13 Antonetti (1994), p. 821.
14 Johnson (1963), p. 308.
15 Knapp (2001), p. 100.
16 Letter of 4 November 1846, in Guizot (1884), pp. 244–5.
17 Pitts (2005).
18 Hamilton (1989), pp. 18–21.
19 Taylor (2000), pp. 146–80.
20 Antonetti (1994), pp. 904, 906.
21 Grenville (1976), p. 24.
22 ibid., p. 22.
23 Tudesq (1964), vol. 1, p. 546.
24 Jennings (1973), p. 48.
25 Saville (1987), p. 77.

26 Thompson (1984), p. 318.
27 26 February 1848, in Bullen (1974), p. 330.
28 Lamartine (1870), p. 277.
29 Jennings (1973), p. 50.
30 Lamartine (1870), pp. 278–85.
31 Jennings (1973), p. 19.
32 Saville (1987), p. 89.
33 Taylor (2000), pp. 173–5.
34 Saville (1987), p. 131.
35 Porter (1979), p. 64.
36 Constable Educational Series, 1860, in Baudemont (1980), p. 157.
37 See the valuable survey by Bensimon (2000).
38 Porter (1979), p. 56.
39 ibid., pp. 27–8.
40 Ledru-Rollin (1850).
41 Porter (1979), pp. 23–4; Robb (1997), p. 324.
42 Robb (1997), p. 330.
43 Beales (1961), p. 120.
44 Newsome (1998), p. 110.
45 Bonaparte (1839), pp. 143, 145.
46 Parry (2001), p. 152.
47 Goldfrank (1994), p. 178
48 Hibbert (1961), pp. 17, 18, 28, 45, 147, 274, 298–9.
49 Echard (1983), pp. 51, 63.
50 Packe (1957).
51 Porter (1979), pp. 192–4.
52 ibid., pp. 173–4.
53 Hamilton (1993), p. 84.
54 Beales (1961), pp. 20, 55.
55 Hamilton (1993), pp. 83–9, 275, 280, 285.
56 Beales (1961), p. 142.
57 Cunningham (1975), p. 70 and *passim*.
58 McPherson (1988), p. 384.
59 Lord Clarendon, in Beales (1961), p. 139.
60 Marsh (1999).
61 Marchand (1993), p. 156.
62 Delattre (1927), p. 170.
63 Jules Vallès, in Bernard (2001), p. 229.
64 Gibson (1999), p. 47. Our translation.
65 *Oliver Twist* (1994), p. 103.
66 Jules Janin, in Chevalier (1973), p. 67.
67 Ben-Israel (1968), p. 278.
68 Dickens (1965), vol. 9, pp. 258–9.
69 *A Tale of Two Cities* (1993), p. 95.

70 ibid., p. 403.
71 Furet (1992), p. 374.
72 Jules Michelet (1847), in Talmon (1960), p. 252.
73 Lees (1973).
74 Olsen (1986), p. 181.
75 Hancock (2003), p. 259.
76 ibid., p. 229.
77 Gaillard (1977), p. 38.
78 Veuillot (1867), p. v.
79 Marchand (1993), pp. 156–7.
80 Olsen (1986), p. 181.
81 Hancock (2003), p. 60.
82 Bernard (2001), p. 184.
83 Edmond About, in Fournier (2005), p. 45; Veuillot (1867), pp. vii, x.
84 Bremner (2005).
85 Hancock (2003), pp. 158–9, 182–3; Parry (2001), pp. 166–7.
86 Helen Taylor (daughter of J. S. Mill), in Watt (1999), p. 11.
87 Parry (2001), p. 166.
88 Christiansen (1994), p. 94.
89 Gibson (1995), p. 211.
90 Marly (1980), p. 209.
91 Simon (1995), p. 128.
92 Marly (1980), p. 52.
93 J.-D. Franoux, in Bonnaud (2004), pp. 175–80. See also Charles-Roux (2005).
94 Rounding (2003), p. 234.
95 Rounding (2003), p. 237. See also ODNB (2004).
96 Brettell and Lloyd (1980), p. 117.
97 Lochnan (2004), pp. 22, 33, 40–49, 181, 183.
98 Adler (2003), p. 8; Frankiss (2004), p. 472; Tillier (2004), p. 82.
99 Tillier (2004), p. 189; Wentworth (1984), pp. 88, 95–8, 122, 139.
100 Vallès (1951), p. 184.
101 Pakula (1996), p. 278.
102 Millman (1965), pp. 114–22, 199–207.
103 Pakula (1996), p. 271. See also Varouxakis (2002), pp. 152–63.
104 Ramm (1952), vol. 1, pp. 124, 135, 137.
105 Raymond (1921), p. 228.
106 Bury and Tombs (1986), p. 186.
107 Horne (1965), p. 165.
108 'Un Duel' (1883), in Maupassant (1984), pp. 192–8.

109 Watt (1999), pp. 3–4.
110 Horne (1965), pp. 170–71.
111 Watt (1999), p. 10.
112 ibid., p. 13.
113 Horne (1965), pp. 241–2.
114 ibid., p. 163; Millman (1965), p. 216.
115 Horne (1965), p. 182.
116 Blount (1902), pp. 218–19; Horne (1965), pp. 167, 249.
117 Watt (1999), pp. 19, 26; Lenoir (2002), p. 55.
118 Macmillan's Magazine, vol. 24 (May–October 1871), p. 386.
119 Watt (1999), pp. 14, 15, 29.
120 Lenoir (2001), p. 185.
121 ibid., pp. 189, 194.
122 Watt (1999), pp. 37, 39, 40.
123 Horne (1965), pp. 421–2.
124 Contemporary quotations, in La Commune photographiée (2000), p. 7. See also Fournier (2005), pp. 384–92.
125 We are grateful to Professor Florence Bourillon for this information.
126 Vallès (1951), p. 247.
127 Roberts (1973), pp. 15, 41.
128 Lenoir (2001), pp. 199–200.
129 Andrew (1986), p. 17.
130 Tillier (2004), p. 188.
131 Information kindly supplied by Pilotelle's grandson, Mr A. E. Bohannan.
132 Martinez (1981), vol. 1, pp. 138–46, vol. 2, 340–74; Delfau (1971), pp. 70, 354; Horne (1965), p. 425; Robb (2000), pp. 208–9.
133 Robb (2000), pp. 184, 194.
134 Vallès (1951), pp. 2, 3, 7, 90–91, 164–8, 174–7, 184–5, 223, 250.
135 Mallet (1979), p. xviii. It remains freely open to the public in their house in Manchester Square, once the French embassy.

9: Decadence and Regeneration (pp. 390–442)

1 Pick (1989), p. 19.
2 Bouvard et Pécuchet (1991), pp. 411–12.
3 Burrow (2000), p. 95.
4 Belloc, in Carey (1992), p. 82.

5 Swart (1964), p. 124.

6 'Locksley Hall, Sixty Years After'.

7 Taine (12th edition, 1903), p. 394.

8 ibid., p. 26.

9 ibid., p. 135.

10 ibid., p. 139.

11 Pick (1989), pp. 41–2.

12 Bristow (1977), p. 82.

13 Charle (2001), pp. 185–6.

14 Moore (1972), p. 57.

15 Reynolds (2000), p. 333.

16 Moore's valet, 1873, in Moore (1972), p. 235.

17 Corbin (1978), part III.

18 Ellmann (1988), p. 324; Rothenstein (1931), vol. 1, p. 238.

19 Moore (1972), p. 75.

20 Rothenstein (1931), vol. 1, p. 129; Weber (1986), p. 10.

21 Crossley and Small (1988), p. 7.

22 Du Maurier (1995), p. 165.

23 Ellmann (1988), p. 352.

24 *Mr Bennett and Mrs Brown* (1924).

25 Collini (1993), p. 369.

26 Lochnan (2004), pp. 52, 180, 181.

27 Sieburth (2005), p. 4; Aubert (2004), p. 117.

28 Huysmans (2001), pp. 237–48.

29 Ellmann (1988), p. 329.

30 *L'Eclair* (23 January 1901).

31 The accuracy of the reports in the French police file on the Prince, *APP* Ba 1064, seems to be confirmed, though of course discreetly, by his appointments diaries at Windsor, RA VIC/EVIID passim.

32 RA VIC/Add C7/1/21, February 1881: Dilke to Knollys. See also Bury (1982), pp. 196–7.

33 Goncourt (1956), vol. 3, p. 625.

34 APP Ba 1064. We are grateful to Hubertus Jahn for verification concerning the Russians.

35 'This Englishman's a bore.' Ellmann (1988), p. 328.

36 ibid., p. 360.

37 Much of this section is based, with the author's kind permission, on Caie (2002).

38 *The Channel/Le Détroit: A Weekly Résumé of Fact, Gossip and Fiction* (25 June 1881). BL (Colindale) F Misc 2213.

39 Ellmann (1988), p. 352.

40 Gibson (1999), p. 46.

41 Caie (2002), pp. 59–60.

42 Frank Harris, in Bristow (1977), p. 202.

43 Caie (2002), p. 24.

44 ibid., p. 15.

45 Campos (1965), pp. 242–5.

46 Rothenstein (1931), vol. 1, p. 151.

47 Whiteley (2004), pp. 17–18.

48 RA VIC/EVIID/1908.

49 Goncourt (1956), vol. 3, p. 1142.

50 Hamerton (1876), p. 365.

51 Weber (1986), p. 263.

52 Leroy and Bertrand-Sabiani (1998), p. 168; Leclerc (1991), pp. 387–421.

53 Corbin (1978), pp. 460–64.

54 Marandon (1967), pp. 155–7.

55 Fortescue (1992), pp. 1, 59.

56 Digeon (1959), p. 79.

57 Demolins (1898), p. 93.

58 Andrew and Kanya-Forstner (1981), p. 27.

59 Navailles (1987).

60 Pitt (2000).

61 Demolins (1898), p. 104.

62 Galison (2004), pp. 144–51, 159.

63 Edmond Demolins, *A quoi tient la supériorité des Anglo-Saxons?* (1897); Emile Boutmy, *Essai d'une psychologie politique du peuple anglais au XIXe siècle* (1901); Max Leclerc, *L'Education des classes moyennes et dirigeantes en Angleterre* (1894).

64 Demolins (1898), p. 51.

65 Varouxakis (2002), p. 47.

66 Bauberot and Mathieu (2002), p. 22–3.

67 Millman (1965), p. 207.

68 MacMillan (2001), p. 63; Bell (1996), p. 50; Cogan (2003), p. 123.

69 Thatcher (1993), p. 552.

70 Cogan (2003), ch. 4; Clodong and Lamarque (2005), pp. 3–7; Chassaigne and Dockrill (2002), p. 159. We are grateful to Victoria Argyle for her comments.

71 Mayne et al. (2004), p. 263.

72 Weber (1991), p. 208.

73 Quoted by Dick Holt in his Sir Derek Birley Memorial Lecture, April 2003.
74 Dine (2001), p. 61.
75 Holt lecture, 2003.
76 Tucoo-Chala (1999), pp. 56, 177; Weber (1986), p. 220.
77 Dine (2001), p. 33.
78 Guillaume (1992), vol. 3, pp. 513–16; Dine (2001), pp. 25–7; Weber (1986), p. 221.
79 Buruma (2000), pp. 173–5.
80 Guillaume (1992), vol. 3, p. 515; Weber (1991), p. 205.
81 Holt (1981), pp. 143–4; Holt (1998), p. 291.
82 Holt (1981), p. 66; Weber (1986), p. 222; Lanfranchi and Wahl (1998), pp. 322–3.
83 Vigarello (1997), p. 472.
84 ibid., pp. 470, 471, 477.
85 Dine (2001), pp. 63, 80–82.
86 Dine (1998), p. 305.
87 Le Monde (2 August 2004).
88 Holt lecture, 2003. See also Labouchere et al. (1969), pp. 83–5.
89 Trubek (2000), p. 42.
90 Carey (1992), p. 80.
91 Spang (2000), p. 140.
92 Pitte (1991), p. 167; Aron (1973).
93 Ferguson (1998), p. 208.
94 ibid., p. 209.
95 Newnham-Davis and Bastard (1903), p. 11.
96 Spencer (2002), p. 229–30.
97 Mennell (1985).
98 Spencer (2002).
99 Andrew (1968), p. 113.
100 Spencer (2002), p. 299.
101 Pitte (1991), p. 175.
102 Taylor (2003), pp. 147–56.
103 Dumas (2000); see also Aron (1973), pp. 181–3.
104 James (1984), p. 112; Newnham-Davis and Bastard (1903), pp. 44, 49, 55, 69–70.
105 Pitte (1991), pp. 178ff.
106 Hamerton (1876), p. 243. For modern confirmation of this summary, see Weber (1976), ch. 9.
107 Mennell (1985), p. 329.
108 ibid., p. 176.
109 Aron (1973), p. 125.
110 Trubek (2000), p. 46.
111 Dumas (2000), p. 88.
112 Hamerton (1876), p. 245.
113 Tombs (1998), p. 500.
114 Brisson (2001), p. 9.
115 ibid., p. 32.
116 PRO FO 27 3320 696 (19 November 1897) and 698 (23 November).
117 RA VIC/Add A 4/48 (25 January 1898).
118 On British reactions, see Cornick (1996) and Tombs (1998).
119 PRO FO 27 3459 382 ('Secret'), 14 August 1899.
120 Victoria (1930), vol. 3, p. 386; RA VIC/Add U 32/16 September 1899.
121 The original is in RA VIC/J 91/61; and see O'Brien (1901), pp. 314–25.
122 See e.g. socialist papers Justice (20 May and 16 September 1899) and Clarion (23 September).
123 Edwards (1898), p. 371
124 Edwards (1898), p. 362.
125 Smith (2001), p. 105.
126 ibid., pp. 110, 112.
127 Gaulle (1998), p. 4.
128 Langlade (1994), pp. 111, 115, 117, 119, 125, 128, 136, 137; Goncourt (1956), vol. 3, pp. 1118, 1136–7, 1216; Ellmann (1988), pp. 453, 466.
129 PRO FO 27 3393 100 (20 February 1898).
130 Vizetelly (1904), pp. 467–80.
131 Ellmann (1988), pp. 530, 540.
132 Wilson (2001), pp. 14, 22.
133 Iain R. Smith, in Lowry (2000), p. 26.
134 Speech in French parliament, Brisson (2001), p. 28.
135 Vaïsse (2004), p. 30.
136 Macnab (1975), p. 235.
137 ibid., p. 53.
138 ibid., passim.
139 Wilson (2001), p. 160.
140 Tracy (1998), pp. 2, 13.
141 Clarke (1992), pp. 53–4.
142 Andrew (1986), p. 35.
143 Tracy (1998), p. 80.
144 ibid., p. 271.
145 Brisson (2001), p. 97.
146 Andrew (1968), p. 116.

147 Hyam and Henshaw (2003), pp. 98–9.
148 Andrew (1968), p. 114.
149 ibid., p. 91.
150 ibid., p. 106.
151 First Lord of the Admiralty, Lord Selborne, in Wilson (2001), p. 161.
152 Kennedy (1976), p. 215.
153 Andrew (1968), p. 116.
154 Taylor (1971), p. 404.
155 MAE Papiers Delcassé: Angleterre II, vol. 14 (15 March 1903).
156 A senior French diplomat, in Andrew (1968), p. 195.
157 Cutting from *Morning Post* (7 May 1878), in *RA*.
158 APP Ba 1064.
159 APP Ba 112: daily reports to prefect of police (April–May 1903); see also Joly (1998), pp. 331–2.
160 RA PS/GV/Visits/France/1914/12; and X32/306.
161 APP Ba 112 (2 and 3 May 1903).
162 Cambon to Delcassé, 31 July 1903, MAE Grande-Bretagne (nouvelle série), vol. 14, fo 136.
163 Bodleian Library, Monson Papers, MS Eng. Hist. c. 595, fos 108–9.
164 RA PP/EVII/B2164.
165 MAE Grande-Bretagne (nouvelle série), vol. 14, fo 137.
166 RA VIC/W 44/49 (our translation from French original).
167 MAE Grande-Bretagne (nouvelle série), vol. 14.
168 Andrew and Vallet (2004), p. 23
169 Taylor (1971), p. 413
170 RA VIC/W 44/49.

PART II Conclusions and Disagreements (pp. 443–4)

1. Rendall (2004), p. 599.

Interlude: Perceptions (pp. 445–56)

1 'Dictionnaire des Idées reçues', in *Bouvard and Pécuchet*.
2 John Keiger, in Mayne et al. (2004), p. 4.
3 For example, there was less illegitimacy in France, a more rural, hence controlled, society. On the other hand, French married couples generally had fewer children, but married earlier and had them sooner, and then practised contraception; British couples married later and spaced children out, probably by less-frequent sex. (We are grateful to Simon Szreter for this information.)
4 See discussion by Crouzet (1999).
5 Brisson (2001), p. 11.
6 School book, in Maingueneau (1979), p. 273.
7 Pemble (2005), p. 58.
8 Brisson (2001), p. 58.
9 Pemble (2005), p. 58.
10 Taine (1903), pp. 277–8.
11 Arnold (1960), vol. 9, p. 71.
12 Bellaigue (2003), p. 35.
13 Demolins (1898), p. 12, 51.
14 Taine (1903), p. 25.
15 *Le Rire* (23 November 1899).
16 *Fortnightly Review*, 1888, in Marandon (1967), p. 230.
17 Roudaut (2004), p. 230; Gibson (1999), pp. 51–2.
18 *La Guerre fatale: France-Angleterre* (1902–3), in Cornick (2004b).
19 Maingueneau (1979), p. 61.
20 *Le Canard Enchaîné* (13 July 2005), pp. 1, 8.
21 Tracy (1896), p. 7; Du Maurier (1998), p. 79.
22 Demolins (1898), p. 52.
23 *L'Assiette au Beurre*: 'Les Anglais chez nous' (3 January 1903).
24 Cornick (2004b).
25 Taine (1903), p. 25.

10: The War to End Wars (pp. 459–99)

1 Morris (1984), p. 52.
2 Hinsley (1977), p. 324.
3 Richard Cobb, in Evans and von Strandmann (1990).
4 Martyn Cornick, in Mayne et al. (2004), pp. 17–19.

5 Andrew and Vallet (2004), p. 23.
6 Terraine (1972), p. xix.
7 Taylor (1971), p. 480. Taylor's italics.
8 Sir Arthur Nicholson, in Wilson (1996), p. 90.
9 Steiner (1977), p. 223.
10 Andrew and Vallet (2004), p. 30.
11 Ferguson (1998b), p. xxxix.
12 Wilson (1995), p. 177.
13 Bernstein (1986), p. 193; Steiner (1977), pp. 223, 231–3.
14 Wilson (1995), p. 189.
15 Keiger (1983), p. 116, 162.
16 Andrew and Vallet (2004), p. 31.
17 John Keiger in Mayne et al. (2004), p. 8.
18 e.g. Ferguson (1998b), pp. 460–62.
19 Macdonald (1989), p. 76.
20 Philpott (1996), pp. 7–8.
21 Strachan (2001), vol. 1, p. 206; Keegan (1998), p. 83; Macdonald (1989), p. 73; Lyautey (1940), p. 8.
22 Terraine (1972), pp. 7–8.
23 ibid., p. 4.
24 Strachan (2001), vol. 1, p. 200.
25 Philpott (1996), pp. 4–6.
26 Spears (1999), p. 106.
27 Macintyre (2001), p. 20.
28 Philpott (1996), p. 26.
29 Macintyre (2001), p. 12.
30 Keegan (1998), p. 118.
31 Spears (1999), pp. 417–18.
32 Isselin (1965), p. 192.
33 Strachan (2001), vol. 1, p. 278.
34 Stevenson (2004), p. 59.
35 Strachan (2001), vol. 1, p. 278; Farrar-Hockley (1970), p. 190; Herwig (1997), p. 119; J.-J. Arzalier, in Jauffret (1997), p. 400.
36 Neillands (1999), p. 133.
37 Greenhalgh (2005), p. 610.
38 Godfrey (1987); Serman and Bertaud (1998), p. 728; Horn (2002), p. 141.
39 Horn (2002), p. 118; Ogg (1947), p. 58.
40 Terraine (1972), pp. 7–8.
41 The recent pioneering work of Kenneth Craig Gibson marks a welcome change.
42 Cobb (1983), p. 45.
43 Fuller (1990), passim.
44 Gibson (2003), p. 180.
45 Holmes (2004), p. 354.
46 Graves (1960), p. 107.
47 Gibson (2003), p. 183.
48 Gibson (2001), p. 574, and (2003), p. 161; Orpen (1921), p. 57.
49 See Gibson (1998), (2001), (2003) and (2003b) passim.
50 Gibson (1998), p. 53.
51 Graves (1960), p. 140.
52 Bell (1996), p. 99.
53 Fuller (1990), p. 135.
54 The Outpost (trench newspaper), May 1917, in Fuller (1990), p. 136.
55 Orpen (1921), p. 41; John Glubb, in Keegan (1998), p. 336; Gibson (2001), pp. 545, 541.
56 Gibson (1998), p. 53.
57 Lewis (1936), p. 74; soldiers' memoirs, in Gibson (2001), pp. 537, 539.
58 Graves (1960), p. 195.
59 Gibson (2001), p. 540.
60 ibid., p. 546.
61 Official report, in ibid., p. 569.
62 Rousseau (2003), p. 313.
63 Dorgelès, 'Les Croix de bois', in Rousseau (2003), p. 193.
64 Gibson (2001), pp. 560–61.
65 Grayzel (1999), pp. 126–7.
66 Gibson (2001), p. 564.
67 Dine (2001), p. 63.
68 Gibson (2001), pp. 573–7; Bell (1996), p. 99.
69 Cobb (1983), p. 46.
70 Spears (1999), pp. 519–24; McPhail (1999), pp. 27–30.
71 Macintyre (2001).
72 ibid., p. 191.
73 Spears (1999), pp. 523–4.
74 McPhail (1999), pp. 117–23.
75 Occleshaw (1989), p. 244; McPhail (1999), p. 153.
76 Hoehling (1958), pp. 88–91.
77 Darrow (2000), pp. 277–84.
78 Philpott (1996), p. 83.
79 Sir Henry Rawlinson, in Travers (1990), p. 135.
80 General Charles Mangin, in Sheffield (2001), p. xxii.
81 Philpott (1996), p. 94.

82 ibid., p. 94.
83 ibid., pp. 98, 103, 115.
84 Marder (1974), p. 1.
85 Stevenson (2004), p. 118.
86 Jauffret (1997), pp. 361–2.
87 Conference conclusion, Philpott (1996), p. 112.
88 ibid., p. 115.
89 Foley (2005), pp. 187–92; Herwig (1997), pp. 180–88; Ousby (2002), pp. 39–40; Keegan (1998), pp. 299–300.
90 Ousby (2002), p. 49.
91 ibid., pp. 65–6, 245.
92 Philpott (1996), p. 121, 124.
93 Gibson (1998), p. 63.
94 Ousby (2002), p. 231.
95 Horn (2002), p. 128.
96 Macdonald (1983), p. 65.
97 Keegan (1998), p. 318.
98 See Greenhalgh (1999); Philpott (2002); Prior and Wilson (2005), pp. 47–50.
99 Foley (2005); Prior and Wilson (2005).
100 William Philpott, in Mayne et al. (2004), p. 58.
101 Serman and Bertaud (1998), pp. 764–6. More were executed for other offences.
102 Travers (1990), p. 208; Occleshaw (1989) pp. 336–9.
103 Keegan (1998), p. 388.
104 Herwig (1997), pp. 287, 295–6, 312–25.
105 Occleshaw (1989), p. 372.
106 Gibson (1998), pp. 216–17.
107 Travers (1990), pp. 221 231.
108 Sheffield (2001), pp. 226–7.
109 Herwig (1997), p. 406.
110 On the relative fighting quality of English troops, see Holmes (2004), pp. 180–81.
111 Desagneaux (1975), pp. 56–8.
112 Gibson (1998), p. 217.
113 Sheffield (2001), p. 232.
114 Griffiths (1970), p. 71.
115 Herwig (1997), p. 410.
116 Ludendorff (n.d.), vol. 2, pp. 680, 684.
117 William Philpott, in Mayne et al. (2004), p. 60.
118 Jauffret (1997), p. 378.

119 Gibson (1998), p. 220; McPhail (1999), pp. 192, 199.
120 Hughes (1999), p. 56.
121 Statistics (1922), p. 757.
122 Stevenson (2004), pp. 476–81.
123 Holmes (2004), p. 614.
124 Becker et al. (1994), pp. 413–14, 419–24.
125 Philpott (1996), p. 161.
126 Jauffret (1997), p. 363.
127 Bell (1996), p. 96.
128 Adamthwaite (1995), p. 79; Graves (1960), p. 240.

11: Losing the Peace
(pp. 500–538)

1 MacMillan (2001), p. 39.
2 Churchill (1948), vol. 1, p. 7.
3 Mantoux (1946), p. 3.
4 Adamthwaite (1995), p. 40.
5 MacMillan (2001), p. 39.
6 ibid., pp. 53–4, 156–8; Lentin (2001), p. 4.
7 MacMillan (2001), pp. 43, 447.
8 Hanks (2002), p. 56. See also Hanks, in Mayne et al. (2004).
9 Watson (1974), p 388.
10 Guiomar (2004), p. 281.
11 Lentin (2001), pp. 50–54; MacMillan (2001), p. 205.
12 'Reply of the Allies and Associated Powers', 16 June 1919, Mantoux (1946), p. 94.
13 Turner (1998), pp. 4–5; Marks (1998), p. 360; Horn (2002), pp 120–24, 183.
14 Shuker (1976), p. 14.
15 Marks (1998), p. 351.
16. Harold Nicolson, in Lentin (2001), p. 74.
17 Lentin (2001), pp. 73–7; MacMillan (2001), p. 479.
18 Lentin (2001), p. 81.
19 Keynes (1971), pp. 169–70.
20 Coward (2002), p. 271.
21 Mantoux (1946), p. 6.
22 Keynes (1971), pp. 2, 26–8, 32, 90, 91, 92, 146.
23 Horn (2002), p. 119.
24 Keynes (1971), pp. 20–23.

25 Preface to French edition of Keynes, in Mantoux (1946), pp. 22–3.
26 Skidelsky (1983) vol. 2, p. xvii.
27 ibid., p. 4.
28 Keynes (1971), p. 170. See comments by Martel (1998), pp. 627–36.
29 Lentin (2001), p. 81.
30 Watson (1974), p. 361.
31 Lentin (2000), pp. 106–8.
32 Steiner (2005), p. 605.
33 Lentin (2001), pp. 60, 64; Guiomar (2004), p. 282.
34 Adamthwaite (1995), p. 74.
35 Keiger (1998), p. 41.
36 Adamthwaite (1995), p. 75.
37 MacMillan (2001), p. 404.
38 Alexander and Philpott (1998), p. 56; Andrew (1986), p. 296.
39 Turner (1998), p. 241.
40 ibid., p. 20.
41 Fischer (2003), *passim*; Cabanes (2003), pp. 86–95, 234–9; Kleine-Ahlbrandt (1995), p. 117.
42 Shuker (1976), p. 380; Jackson (2003), p. 67; Gombin (1970), pp. 49–50.
43 Shuker (1976), p. 388.
44 Cash and goods to the value of 21.5 billion gold marks. Marks (1998), p. 367.
45 Bell (1996), p. 150.
46 Shuker (1976), p. 392
47 Jackson (2003), p. 215; Steiner (2005), pp. 615–19.
48 George Riddell, in Lentin (2001), p. 65.
49 Stevenson (1998), p. 24.
50 Shuker (1976), pp. 388, 393.
51 Bell (1996), p. 157.
52 Wilson (1994).
53 Wilson (1994), pp. 86, 89, 90.
54 Bell (1996), pp. 158–9.
55 ibid., p. 159.
56 Graves (1960), p. 240.
57 Sitwell (1949), pp. 151–2, 331.
58 House (1994), pp. 11–21.
59 Adamthwaite (1995), p. 78.
60 ibid., p. 79.
61 Chalon (2002), p. 13.
62 Rioux and Sirinelli (1998), p. 162.
63 Rearick (1997), p. 80.
64 Adamthwaite (1995), p. 77.
65 Balfour, in Shuker (1976), p. 388.

66 Bell (1996), p. 161; Adamthwaite (1995), p. 129; Cornick (1993), pp. 3–17.
67 Béraud (1935), pp. 6, 7, 8, 11, 13, 17, 19.
68 Boucard (1926), pp. 17, 264–5, 269.
69 Cornick (1993), p. 12.
70 Chalon (2002), *passim*, on which by kind permission of the author this section is largely based.
71 Bell (1996), p. 175.
72 Col. H.R. Pownall, in Dockrill (2002), p. 95.
73 Adamthwaite (1995), p. 140.
74 Parker (2000), p. 14. For a general analysis of British policy, see Reynolds (1991).
75 Maier (1975), p. 579.
76 Keiger (1997), pp. 327–31; Frank (1994), p. 161.
77 Thomas (1996), p. 10.
78 Bell (1996), p. 178.
79 To House of Commons, 14 March 1933, in Carlton (2004), p. 170.
80 Parker (2000), p. 87. See Kershaw (1998), vol. 1, pp. 582–9.
81 Adamthwaite (1995), p. 203.
82 Doise and Vaïsse (1987), pp. 303–4.
83 Thomas (1996), p. 69.
84. Dutton (2001), p. 170; Mysyrowicz (1973), pp. 185, 195–7, 320; Weber (1995), p. 239.
85 Mysyrowicz (1973), p. 337.
86 Siegel (2004), *passim*.
87 Lacouture (1977), p. 251; Lansbury (1938), pp. 127–45. See also Shepherd (2002), pp. 325–7; Gombin (1970), p. 122.
88 Dockrill (2002), pp. 97–8; Dutton (2001), p. 164.
89 Thompson (1971), p. 27.
90 Mangold (2001), p. 147.
91 Bell (1996), p. 212; Stone (2000), p. 193.
92 Siegel (2004), p. 200.
93 Mangold (2001), p. 56.
94 Crémieux-Brilhac (1990), vol. 1, pp. 94–5.
95 Réau (1993), p. 268.
96 Sir Alexander Cadogan, permanent under-secretary, Cadogan (1971), pp. 72–3.

97 Dockrill (2002), p. 99.
98 Réau (1990), pp. 273–4.
99 ibid., p. 277.
100 ibid., pp. 278–9.
101 Kershaw (1998), vol. 2, p. 164.
102 ibid., vol. 2, 123.
103 Crémieux-Brilhac (1990), vol 1, p. 95.
104 Weber (1962), pp. 394, 426.
105 Hermann Goering, in Kershaw (1998), vol. 2, p. 122.
106 Siegel (2004), p. 200.
107 Lacouture (1990), vol. 1, p. 154.
108 *Bulletin Socialiste* (September 1938), in Gombin (1970), p. 246.
109 Channon (1967), p. 194; Dutton (2001), p. 132.
110 Channon (1967), p. 177.
111 Frank (1994), p. 88; Jackson (2003), p. 149; Parker (2000), p. 223.
112 Watt (2001), pp. 99–108, 164.
113 Nicolson (1980), p. 145.
114 Watt (2001), p. 185.
115 Adamthwaite (1995), p. 221.
116 Channon (1967), p. 209.
117 Memorandum, 1935, in Dutton (2001), p. 201.
118 November 1939, in Gates (1981), p. 61.

12: Finest Hours, Darkest Years (pp. 539–96)

1 Conversation with American ambassador, in Jackson (2003), p. 70.
2 May (2000), p. 306.
3 Alanbrooke (2001), p. 43.
4 Crémieux-Brilhac (1990), vol. 2, pp. 400–401; Jersak (2000), pp. 566–7.
5 See Alexander and Philpott (1998), pp. 72–6.
6 This is the argument of Imlay (2003).
7 Gamelin, in Bloch (1949), p. 74n.
8 Ironside (1962), p. 172. See also Alexander and Philpott (1998).
9 Harman (1980), p. 70.
10 Gates (1981), p. 74.
11 Mysyrowicz (1973), pp. 43, 49, 155–6.
12 Alanbrooke (2001), pp. 26, 37.
13 ibid., p. 7; Lyautey (1940), p. 14.

14 Bloch (1949), pp. 69–70; Johnson (1972), p. 145; Crémieux-Brilhac (1990), vol. 2, p. 508.
15 Barsley (1946), p. 3.
16 Alanbrooke (2001), pp. 4, 7–8, 13, 18, 20, 35.
17 Johnson (1972), p. 145; Ironside (1962), pp. 231–2.
18 Letter of 6 February 1940, in Rocolle (1990), vol. 1, pp. 282–3.
19 Jackson (2003), pp. 201–6; Gates (1981), pp. 21–5; Crémieux-Brilhac (1990), vol. 1, p. 61; Frank (1994), p. 251.
20 Alanbrooke (2001), p. 18.
21 Ironside (1962), p. 313.
22 Gaulle (1998), p. 65.
23 May (2000), pp. 402–4.
24 Jersak (2000), p. 568.
25 Jackson (2003), p. 164.
26 *Diary* (1941), p. 13; Rocolle (1990), vol. 2, pp. 83–5; Richards (1974), p. 120; Crémieux-Brilhac (1990), vol. 2, pp. 657–9.
27 *Diary* (1941), p. 10.
28 May (2000), p. 432.
29 Jersak (2000), p. 568.
30 Richey (1980), p. 106. See also Richards (1974), pp. 125–7.
31 *Diary* (1941), p. 18; Ironside (1962), p. 307; Gates (1981), pp. 74–9, 125.
32 Churchill (1948), vol. 2, pp. 38–9, 42; Gates (1981), p. 124.
33 Reynolds (2004), pp. 166–7.
34 Churchill (1948), vol. 2, pp. 41–2; Gates (1981), pp. 77 9.
35 Churchill (1948), vol. 2, p. 46; Réau (1993), p. 425; Gates (1981), pp. 125–6.
36 Paul Baudoin, in Gates (1981), p. 134.
37 Jersak (2000), p. 568.
38 *Diary* (1941), p. 26; Ironside (1962), p. 321.
39 Bloch (1949), p. 75.
40 Dalton (1986), pp. 27–8.
41 Rocolle (1990), vol. 2, p. 224.
42 Lukacs (1976), p. 407.
43 Spears (1954), vol. 2, p. 24.
44 Alanbrooke (2001), pp. 67–8.
45 Bloch (1949), p. 71.
46 Rocolle (1990), vol. 2, p. 224.

47 Crémieux-Brilhac (1990), vol. 2, pp. 631–2.
48 Harman (1990), p. 228.
49 Bloch (1949), pp. 20–21.
50 Numbers from Harman (1990), *passim*. There are differing estimates, depending mainly on whether one includes the mainly British non-combatants evacuated earlier.
51 Magenheimer (1998), p. 25.
52 Clare Booth Luce, in Gates (1981), p. 133.
53 Spears (1954), vol. 2, p. 24.
54 Crémieux-Brilhac (1990), vol. 2, p. 641.
55 Crémieux-Brilhac (1990), vol. 2, pp. 337–45, 668; Gates (1981), pp. 118–19, 161; Richards (1974), p. 150.
56 Spears (1954), vol. 2, p. 76.
57 Lukacs (1976), p. 406.
58 Spears (1954), vol. 2, p. 188.
59 Churchill (1948), vol. 2, pp. 159–60; Gates (1981), pp. 191–2.
60 Alanbrooke (2002), p. 84.
61 Gates (1981), p. 219.
62 Lacouture (1990), vol. 1, p. 202.
63 Johnson (1972), p. 154; Dalton (1940), p. 154; Mayne et al. (2004), pp. 99–100; Gates (1981), pp. 227–33, 517–18; Delpla (2000), pp. 515–16; Frank (1994), pp. 260–61. For the full text, Churchill (1948), vol. 2, pp. 183–4.
64 Crémieux-Brilhac (1990), vol. 2, pp. 696–8; Jackson (2003), p. 179; Scheck (2005), pp. 325–44.
65 Jackson (2003), pp. 179–80; Horne (1979), p. 650.
66 Full text in English, Gaulle (1998), pp. 83–4.
67 Delpla (2000), p. 505.
68 Atkin (2003), p. 98.
69 Lasterle (2000), pp. 71–91; Marder (1974), ch. 5; Brown (2004).
70 We are grateful to Jean de Préneuf, of the Service Historique de la Marine, for this information.
71 Marder (1974), p. 277.
72 Lacouture (1984), vol. 1, p. 402.
73 Marder (1974), p. 222; Bell (1974), pp. 142–3.
74 Churchill (1948), vol. 2, p. 206; Gates (1981), pp. 258–61, 352–68, 555–63.

75 Ironside (1962), p. 355 (6 June 1940).
76 Dalton (1986), p. 48.
77 Frank (1994), pp. 91–3. See also Imlay (2003), p. 363.
78 Lukacs (1976), pp. 417–19.
79 Robert Vansittart, 6 September 1940, in Jersak (2000), p. 578.
80 Gaulle (1998), p. 88.
81 Churchill (1989), p. 646.
82 Gaulle (1998), p. 104.
83 ibid., p. 3; Churchill (1948), vol. 2, p. 291.
84 Churchill (1948), vol. 1, pp. 526–7; Gaulle (1998), p. 84.
85 Lacouture (1990), vol. 1, p. 154.
86 ibid., vol. 1, p. 191.
87 Delpla (2000), p. 450.
88 Maurice Druon, in Mayne et al. (2004), p. 102.
89 Stenton (2000), p. 123.
90 Roy Jenkins, in Mayne et al. (2004), p. 93.
91 Cooper (1953), p. 341; Briggs (1970), vol. 3, p. 230.
92 Adamthwaite (1995), p. 120.
93 Parker (2000), pp. 31–4, 43, 157.
94 Gaulle (1998), p. 92.
95 Kersaudy (1981), pp. 34–5.
96 Lady Spears, in Lacouture (1990), vol. 1, p. 265.
97 Egremont (1997), p. 203.
98 Crémieux-Brilhac (1996), p. 161.
99 Larcan (2003), p. 490.
100 Crémieux-Brilhac (1996), p. 65.
101 Atkin (2003), p. 66.
102 Roderick Kedward, in Mayne et al. (2004), p. 132.
103 Imlay (2003), p. 16.
104 'The French Press since the Armistice,' Foreign Research and Press Service, 20 January 1941. Cambridge University Library Official Publications Room.
105 Cornick (2000), p. 80.
106 Lukacs (1976), p. 408; Cornick (2000), p. 69.
107 Frank (1993), p. 315.
108 Foreign Office minute, 6 July 1940, Stenton (2000), p. 127.
109 Crémieux-Brilhac (1996), pp. 87–8, 91–2; Atkin (2003), p. 84.

110 Egremont (1997), p. 209.

111 Jean Oberlé in *Le Populaire*, 4–5 November 1944.

112 Letter to the authors from Jacques Herry, who, aged eighteen, sailed to Falmouth in a fishing boat to volunteer.

113 Atkin (2003), pp. 158, 259.

114 Torrès (2000), pp. 182, 220.

115 Letter from Jacques Herry.

116 Crémieux-Brilhac (1996), pp. 72–5; Gaulle (1998), p. 102.

117 Churchill (1948), vol. 2, p. 437.

118 Atkin (2003), pp. 257–8.

119 Stenton (2000), p. 163.

120 ibid., p. 173.

121 De Gaulle to Major Morton, October 1941, in Young de la Marck (2003), p. 26.

122 Stenton (2000), p. 198; Crémieux-Brilhac (1996), p. 305.

123 Lacouture (1990), vol. 1, p. 368; Crémieux-Brilhac (1996), p. 414.

124 Cadogan (1971), p. 494.

125 Lacouture (1990), vol. 1, p. 404.

126 Stenton (2000), p. 219.

127 Jackson (2003), p. 241.

128 Frank (1995), p. 471.

129 Stenton (2000), p. 170.

130 ibid., p. 181.

131 Frank (1994), p. 256.

132 Police report, November 1940, kindly communicated to us by Professor Annette Becker.

133 Ottis (2001), p. 45.

134 ibid., pp. 41, 160.

135 Neave (1969), *passim*; Foot (2004), pp. 87–94; Ottis (2001), pp. 22, 44–6.

136 Roderick Kedward, in Mayne et al. (2004), pp. 124–5; Foot (1978), pp. 239–45.

137 See Tombs (2002).

138 Cornick (1994), p. 319.

139 Buckmaster (1952), pp. 67–8.

140 Briggs (1970), vol. 3, p. 251.

141 ibid., p. 255; *Pariser Zeitung*, in Foreign Research and Press Service report, 18 May 1942; Stenton (2000), p. 161; Cornick (2000), p. 77.

142 Cornick (1994), p. 322.

143 Noblett (1996), p. 23; see also 'A Complete Index of Allied Airborne Leaflets and Magazines', Cambridge University Library Official Publications Room.

144 *Témoignage Chrétien*, 23 February 1945.

145 Works on the Resistance and its London links are legion. For concise summaries, see Foot (1978), and Kedward, in Mayne et al. (2004). The standard French works are Crémieux-Brilhac (1975), and (1996). On SOE, the main work remains Foot, first published in 1966, now in a new edition (2004). See also the recently published official 'secret history' by Mackenzie (2000).

146 Young de la Marck (2003), p. 22.

147 Foot (2004), pp. 41–58, 222, 322.

148 'A useful racket', *TLS* (27 April 2001).

149 Foot, entries on Szabo and Atkins in *ODNB* (2004); Binney (2002), *passim*.

150 Foot (1978), p. 39.

151 Mackenzie (2000), p. 289.

152 Foreign Office policy statement, 1942, Mackenzie (2000), p. 265.

153 Passy (1947), vol. 2, p. 167.

154 Marks (1999), pp. 390–96.

155 Frank (1994), pp. 258–9, 270.

156 Foot (2004), p. 388.

157 ibid., p. 217.

158 Young de la Marck (2003); Buton (2004), pp. 85–6, 93–5; Crémieux-Brilhac (1996), pp. 778–82

159 Foot (2004), pp 421–4.

160 See his recently published memoir, Hue (2004).

161 Alanbrooke (2001), p. 554; Kersaudy, (1981), p. 346.

162 Gaulle (1998), p. 557. The official British record is less poetic, see Kersaudy (1981), p. 343.

163 Keegan (1983), p. 188.

164 Foot (2004), pp. 386–7.

165 Lacouture (1990), vol. 1, p. 575.

166 Mackenzie (2000), pp. 584, 598.

167 Castetbon (2004), p. 168.

168 Muggeridge (1973), vol. 2, pp. 210–15; Carrington (1988), pp. 53–5.

169 Carrington (1988), p. 57.

170 *Instructions 1944* (2005); Footit (2004), pp. 24–6, 45, 63.
171 Cobb (1998), p. 28.
172 Kersaudy (1981), p. 369; Cooper (1953), p. 341; Gaulle (1998), p. 723; Nicolson (1967), p. 412.
173 *Résistance*, 5 September 1944 and 2 January 1945.
174 Frank (1994), p. 244.
175 *Libération*, 5 April 2004.

Interlude: The French and Shakespeare (pp. 600–601)

1 Pemble (2005), p.133.
2 ibid., p. 119.
3 ibid., p. 141.
4 Léon Daudet, in ibid., p. 63.
5 Pemble (2005), p. 155.
6 ibid., p. 163.
7 Morse (2002), pp. 4–5.
8 ibid.; Pemble (2005), pp. 69, 92.

PART IV: Revival (p. 603)

1 Peyrefitte (1994), vol. 2, p. 311.
2 Thody (1995), pp. 27–8.

13: Losing Empires, Seeking Roles (pp. 605–36)

1 Diary entry, Horne (1988), vol. 2, p. 319.
2 Peyrefitte (1994), vol. 1, pp. 153–4.
3 Mangold (2001), p. 55.
4 Speech to European Research Institute, Birmingham, 23 November 2001.
5 Milward (2002), p. 3.
6 Greenwood (2000), p. 259.
7 Cooper (1953), p. 377.
8 Frank (1994), p. 271.
9 ibid., p. 260.
10 John Young, in Sharp and Stone (2000), p. 268.
11 Réau (2001), pp. 77–8.
12 Passerini (1999), p. 218.
13 Cole (1941), pp. 102–3.

14 See the brilliant summary by Judt (1997), and for detail Milward (1992) and (2002).
15 Gillingham (2003), pp. 25, 27, 496.
16 Gillingham (2003), p. 27. See also Greenwood (2000), and Milward (1992), chs. 3, 5 and 6.
17 Milward (2002), p. 44.
18 ibid., p. 71.
19 Milward (1992), p. 210.
20 Milward (2002), pp. 200, 203.
21 David Dutton, in Mayne et al. (2004), pp. 136–8.
22 Milward (2002), p. 258.
23 Vaïsse (1989), p. 137.
24 Permanent Under-Secretary of Foreign Office, in Kyle (1989), p. 123; Kunz (1989), p. 220.
25 Kyle (1989), p. 114.
26 ibid., p. 128.
27 Kunz (1989), p. 225.
28 Kunz (1989), 228.
29 Pineau (1976), p. 177.
30 Vaïsse (1989), p. 335.
31 Kyle (1989), p. 130.
32 Fry (1989), p. 312.
33 Milward (2002), p. 260.
34 ibid., p. 475.
35 Diary entry, Horne (1988), vol. 2, p. 319.
36 Milward (2002), pp. 306–8.
37 Mierzejewski (2004), pp. 158–9.
38 Milward (2002), p. 288.
39 Gaulle (1970), pp. 196, 204.
40 Schaad (2002), pp. 70–77.
41 Milward (2002), p. 291.
42 Gillingham (2003), pp. 37, 76.
43 Milward (2002), pp. 317–18, 330, 345, 348, 444–8.
44 ibid., p. 60.
45 ibid., p. 327.
46 Gaulle (1970), p. 236; Peyrefitte (1994), vol. 1, pp. 368, 370–71.
47 Lacouture (1990), vol. 2, pp. 355–7. A careful analysis of de Gaulle's position is in Milward (2002), pp. 463–83. His popularization of the term 'Anglo-Saxon' was pointed out by Colin Jones in an unpublished paper given in 2005 at CRASSH, Cambridge.
48 Horne (1988), vol. 2, pp. 314–19,

429–32; Lacouture (1990), vol. 2, p. 357.

49 Horne (1988), vol. 2, p. 428.

50 Milward (2002), pp. 416–20.

51 Full text, Lacouture (1984), vol. 3, p. 337.

52 Milward (2002), pp. 474–5; Gaulle (1970), pp. 185, 186, 215; Peyrefitte (1994), vol. 1, p. 61; see also Horne (1988), vol. 2, pp. 314–19.

53 Gaulle (1970), pp. 203, 236; Peyrefitte (1994), vol. 1, p. 63.

54 Horne (1988), vol. 2, p. 446; Peyrefitte (1994), vol. 1, p. 348.

55 Peyrefitte (1994), vol. 1, p. 348.

56 ibid., p. 303.

57 ibid., p. 367.

58 Horne (1988), vol. 2, p. 319; and see Peyrefitte (1994), vol. 1, pp. 62–3.

59 Larcan (2003), p. 670.

60 Wilson in 1965, in Parr. We are most grateful to Dr Helen Parr for kindly allowing us a preview of her book *Britain's Policy towards the European Community: Harold Wilson and Britain's World Role, 1964–1967* (London: Routledge, 2005) on which this section, including quotations not otherwise attributed, is based.

61 Vion (2002), p. 219.

62 British record of January 1967 talks, in Parr (2005).

63 O'Neill (2000), p. 11.

64 In Parr (2005).

65 Denman (1996), p. 233.

66 ibid., pp. 231–2.

67 O'Neill (2000), p. 355; dispatch 1964, in Parr (2005).

68 O'Neill (2000), pp. 39, 40, 355, 358–9.

69 Bernstein (2004), p. 243.

70 Henderson (1987), p. 143.

71 Bonnaud (2004), pp. 220–21.

72 Michel Debré, in Gildea (1994), p. 82.

73 Lemonnier (2004), pp. 196–202.

74 Daninos (1954), pp. 91, 97.

75 Lemonnier (2004), p. 214.

76 Interview in *Daily Telegraph* (10 May 2003); and see Simmons (2001), and *Le Monde* (19 July 2005), p. 16.

77 Vion (2002), p. 273.

14: Ever Closer Disunion (pp. 637–96)

1 Thatcher (1993), p. 536.

2 Gillingham (2003), p. 240.

3 For a semi-official reiteration of these themes, see 'Building a Political Europe' (2004), a report commissioned by the European Commission from a committee chaired by a former French finance minister, Dominique Strauss-Kahn, pp. 31–5.

4 Anne Marie Le Gloannec, in Gillingham (2003), p. 343.

5 *L'Express* (17 May 2004), p. 34.

6 Card and Freeman (2002), pp. 20, 70.

7 Gillingham (2003), p. 143.

8 Smith (2004), ch. 2.

9 Keiger (2001), p. 27.

10 Freedman (2005), vol. 2, p. 531.

11 Nott (2002), p. 305.

12 Favier and Martin-Rolland (1990), vol. 1, pp. 382–5; Nott (2002), p. 305; Freedman (2005), vol. 2, pp. 71, 281.

13 Edwards (1984), p. 307.

14 Bell (1997), p. 249.

15 Favier and Martin-Rolland (1990), vol. 1, p. 385.

16 ibid., p. 364, quoting former ministers Claude Cheysson and Michel Jobert.

17 ibid., p. 370.

18 Gillingham (2003), p. 231; Reynolds (1991), p. 267; James (2003), pp. 368–9.

19 Delors (2004), p. 255.

20 Gillingham (2003), p. 136, 146.

21 ibid., pp. 307, 310–11.

22 See e.g. Thatcher (1993), pp. 548–9, 553.

23 Delors (2004), p. 237.

24 Gillingham (2003), p. 160.

25 Interview in *Le Nouvel Observateur* (20–26 March 1997), p. 26.

26 Speech in Stockholm, 1988, in Ross (1995), p. 43.

27 Gillingham (2003), p. 261. See also Shore (2000), *passim*.

28 Ross (1995), p. 36.

29 Denman (1996), p. 281.

30 Ross (1995), pp. 34, 229.
31 Quoted in an unpublished paper by John Keiger, cited by kind permission of the author.
32 Ross (1995), p. 29.
33 ibid., p. 45.
34 Campbell (2000), vol. 2, p. 619.
35 Interview in *Le Nouvel Observateur* (20–26 March 1997), p. 25.
36 *Le Monde* (30 October 1994); Ross (1995), pp. 232–4.
37 Strauss-Kahn (2004). See also Shore (2000), pp. 21–9, 58–61.
38 'Lettre de Matignon', July 1992.
39 Details in Gillingham (2003), pp. 288–9.
40 See e.g. *Le Canard Enchaîné* (9 July 1997), *Le Monde* (29 November 2000).
41 *Le Monde diplomatique* (April 2001), p. 1.
42 See e.g. *Le Nouvel Observateur* (7–13 June 2001).
43 *Financial Times* (14 June 2004), p. 19.
44 Frits Bolkestein, paper given at ELDR seminar at European Parliament, 8 January 2004; Patrick Minford, unpublished lecture, June 2004, cited by kind permission of the author.
45 British Council lecture, July 2004.
46 Interview in *Le Monde* (5 April 2005), p. 16.
47 A poll showed that 40 per cent in Britain supported enlargement, only 26 per cent in France – the lowest in Europe. Gillingham (2003), p. 416.
48 Broadcast 'débat avec les jeunes', 14 April 2004.
49 *The Economist* (10 July 2004).
50 Gillingham (2003), p. 403.
51 'Tony Blair, l'européen?', *Le Monde* (30 April 2004), p. 16.
52 *The Spectator* (19 August 2000), p. 13.
53 Bell (2004), p. 246.
54 We are grateful to Senator Joëlle Garriaud-Maylam for this figure.
55 Garriaud-Maylam, in Mayne et al. (2004), p. 271.
56 ibid., pp. 271–2; *L'Express* (14 October 1999), pp. 34–8 and (31 January 2002), pp. 126–8; *Le Monde* (21 May 1997).
57 Lemoinne (1867), vol. 2, p. 1053.
58 Bell (2004), p. 246.
59 Bavarez (2003), pp. 46, 82–3; Smith (2004), pp. 178–9.
60 Kremer (2004), p. 87.
61 *The Spectator* (19 August 2000), pp. 12–13.
62 *L'Express* (31 January 2002), p. 127.
63 Garriaud-Maylam, in Mayne et al. (2004), p. 273.
64 *Le Point* (30 July 1999).
65 We are grateful to the châtelain of Moncla, John O'Beirne Ranelagh, for some of these insights, and for general comments on this chapter.
66 *France* (May–June 2003).
67 *Le Point* (30 July 1999), pp. 46–8; Aldridge (1992), pp. 98–100; *L'Express* (19 July 2004); Roudaut (2004), p. 247; Gillian Tindall, in Mayne et al. (2004), p. 276; *The Spectator* (16 October 2004), p. 57.
68 Bonnaud (2004), p. 218. See also Navailles (1987).
69 Bonnaud (2004), p. 239.
70 See Ardagh, Crouzet and Delouch (1996).
71 Special thanks to Simon Prince for his guidance in this section.
72 *Guardian* (8 October 1999).
73 Evans (2004), pp. 42–5.
74 Sadler (1992), pp. 67–79.
75 Campos (1992) and (1999); *Libération/Guardian*, 5 April 2004 – a telephone poll of 1,005 people.
76 Campos (1999), p. 42.
77 *Libération/Guardian* poll, 5 April 2004.
78 Campos (1999), pp. 50–52.
79 *Libération/Guardian* poll, 5 April 2004.
80 Vion (2002), p. 219.
81 Keiger (2001), p. 21.
82 Keiger (2001), p. 224; see also Thody (1995), *passim*.
83 Thody (1995), p. 63.
84 The Institut des Sciences Politiques and the École des Hautes Études Commerciales.
85 *The Economist* (25 October 1997), p. 68.
86 Figures for 2003 unless otherwise stated. Sources unless otherwise

stated: *OECD in Figures* (2004);
OECD Main Economic Indicators
(2004); *The Economist* (19 June 2004);
Pocket World in Figures 2004
(Economist and Profile Books, 2003);
The World in 2004 (London:
Economist, 2003); OECD International Direct Investment Database.
87 Categories in which each country has
an export surplus with the other.
Isabelle Lescent-Giles, in Bonnaud
(2004), pp. 248–9.
88 US Dept of Labor: Bureau of Labor
Statistics.
89 *Le Monde* (30 June 2005), p. 17.
90 World Economic Forum ranking.
91 Shanghai Jiao Tong University study,
2004.
92 *L'Express* (3 January 2002), p. 53.
93 UK Home Office Crime Statistics.
94 International Road Federation
Statistics.
95 *Le Monde* (3 January 2005), p. 1.
96 Sources: A.T. Kearney (report on
foreign direct investment, October
2004); HM Treasury paper 'UK and
EU Trade', pp. 21–3; G. Brown,
Mansion House speech, 22 June 2005.
97 Speech of 23 June 2005.
98 OECD International Direct
Investment Database.
99 *The Economist* (9 July 2005), pp. 12–13,
25; *The World in 2006* (The
Economist, 2005), pp. 106–8.
100 Letter from finance minister Nicholas
Sarkozy to Michel Camdessus
(honorary governor of the Banque de
France) and Camdessus report 'Vers
une nouvelle croissance pour la
France', 19 October 2004.
101 Report by Ernst and Young, in *Le
Monde* (30 June 2005), p. 17.
102 Kagan (2004).
103 Transatlantic Trends 2004 (German
Marshall Fund), pp. 8, 18.
104 Keiger (2001), p. 76.
105 Simms (2003), p. 111.
106 See Simms (2003), on which much of
this section is based.
107 Simms (2003), pp. 264–6.
108 August 1992, Hurd (2003), p. 455.
109 Simms (2003), p. 35.
110 Dallaire (2004), p. 515.
111 Hurd (2003), p. 471.
112 Simms (2003), pp. 50, 325.
113 ibid., p. 111.
114 Robin Cook to Foreign Affairs Select
Committee, 21 November 2000;
Cogan (2003), p. 143.
115 For a concise summary, see
Stockholm International Peace
Research Institute [SIPRI] *Yearbook*
(2004), pp. 322–3.
116 Sources: *SIPRI Yearbooks*, 2003 and
2004; Ministry of Defence/Ministère
de la Défense nationale, 'Une com-
mémoration statistique de l'entente
cordiale' (2004); *Jane's World Armies*
(2003); *Jane's World Air Forces* (2004).
117 In US dollars, at constant 2000 prices
and market exchange rate.
118 *The Economist* (7 August 2004), p. 36.
119 *SIPRI Yearbook* (2004), pp. 456–7.
120 *Jane's World Armies*, issue 14,
December 2003, p. 264.
121 Zbigniev Brzezinski, in *Le Monde* (15
July 2004), p. 2.
122 Polly Toynbee, *Guardian* (16 July
2004), p. 27.
123 Simms (2003), pp. 111, 113.
124 Keiger (2005); Cogan (2003).
125 Kampfner (2003), p. ix.
126 21 April 1997, in Kampfner (2003),
p. 3.
127 *Comprehensive Report of the Special
Adviser to the DCI on Iraq's WMD*
(2004), p. 31.
128 ibid., p. 56.
129 *L'Express* (13 February 2003), p. 85.
130 ibid., p. 88.
131 Styan (2004), p. 377.
132 *Comprehensive Report*, p. 111; Styan
(2004), p. 378.
133 Ashdown (2001), p. 127.
134 ibid., p. 163; *Comprehensive Report*,
p. 56.
135 Kampfner (2003); Stothard (2003),
p. 13.
136 We owe this suggestion to John
Ranelagh, presently preparing a
biography of Blair. See also Hoggett
(2005), p. 418.

137 Butler (2004) para. 610
138 Kampfner (2003), p. 245.
139 Keiger (2001), p. 221.
140 Kampfner (2003), p. 204; Styan (2004), p. 381.
141 Cogan (2003), p. 206.
142 See review of Villepin's book on Napoleon by Bell (2003).
143 Bavarez (2003), p. 57.
144 Cogan (2003), pp. 209–10.
145 Styan (2004), p. 384.
146 Naughtie (2005), p. 143; Kampfner (2003), p. 267.
147 Lord Goldsmith's secret advice to the prime minister, 7 March 2003, para. 31.
148 Kampfner (2003), pp. 286–8; Stothard (2003), pp. 14, 28, 41–2; Roudaut (2004), p. 39.
149 e.g. 'Blair est-il fou?' *Marianne* (24–30 July 2004), pp. 34–5.
150 Bavarez (2003), pp. 43, 61.
151 *Sunday Times* (23 November 2003), p. 25.
152 *Sunday Times* (23 November 2003), p. 25; *Jane's World Armies*, issue 14, December 2003, p. 262.
153 Geoff Hoon, defence secretary, in *Daily Telegraph* (15 July 2004), p. 3.
154 Part of a wealth of information on Franco-British celebrations kindly sent to us by Patrice Porcheron of the Mairie de Paris.
155 Clodong and Lamarque (2005), pp. 17–19.
156 Private remarks reported in *Le Canard Enchaîné* (15 June 2005), p. 2.
157 Jean-Pierre Langellier, in *Le Monde* (7 June 2005).
158 Peter Oborne, in *The Spectator* (25 June 2005).
159 A French diplomat, in Cogan (2003), p. 89.
160 R. Tombs, in *TLS* (19 January 1996), p. 7.
161 *The Economist* (25 September 2004).
162 *Le Figaro* (25 March 2005), p. 11.
163 Poll and commentary in *L'Express* (14 March 2005), p. 43; *Le Canard Enchaîné* (23 March 2005), p. 1.
164 *Le Monde* (21 July 2004), p. 14.

165 *L'Homme Européen* (Paris, Plon, 2005), in *TLS* (3 June 2005), p. 24.
166 *Le Canard Enchaîné* (15 June 2005), p. 2.
167 *Le Monde* (20 April 2005), p. 1.
168 Goux and Maurin (2005), pp. 16–17.
169 J.-P. Langellier, in *Le Monde* (7 June 2005).
170 Speech at the Mansion House, 22 June 2005.
171 'Déclaration aux Français', 31 May 2005.
172 *Le Canard Enchaîné* (15 June 2005), p. 2.
173 Shore (2000), p. 207.
174 *Le Monde* (6 June 2005).

PART IV: Conclusions and Disagreements (pp. 697–8)

1 Speech of 23 November 2001.

Picking Up the Threads (pp. 699–706)

1 Guiomar (2004), p. 21.
2 e.g. Young (1998); Roudaut (2004).
3 Bell (1996), p. 1.
4 In both countries, there has been an enormous volume of academic and journalistic cogitation on these perceived crises of national identity. In Britain, the predominant line has been to endorse and welcome the decline of Britishness. In France it has been to regret and attempt to revive Frenchness. In both countries, much of this writing has been oddly introspective, as if identities develop in isolation from the outside world. An egregious example is Nora (1984). For a powerful antidote, see Pocock (2005).
5 For a magisterial account of these, and other aspects of Europe's recent history, see Judt (2005).
6 Pocock (2005), p. 21.
7 HM Treasury, 'UK and EU trade' (2004), pp. 17–18, 23; *The World in 2006* (The Economist, 2005), p. 34;

Mitchell and Deane (1962), pp. 311, 316–22; French government paper 'France in the World' (10 January 2005).

8 Kremer (2004); Lescent–Giles, in

Bonnaud (2004), pp. 255–9.

9 See the important study by Roger (2002).

10 Anthony Wedgwood Benn, in Reynolds (1991), p. 232.

Bibliography of works cited

Where possible, accessible modern editions are given

Abarca, Ramón E. (1970), 'Classical Diplomacy and Bourbon "Revanche" Strategy, 1763–1770', *Review of Politics* 32, pp. 313–37.

Acomb, Frances (1950), *Anglophobia in France 1763–1789*, Duke, NC, Duke University Press.

Adamthwaite, Anthony (1995), *Grandeur and Misery: France's Bid for Power in Europe 1914–1940*, London, Arnold.

Adler, Kathleen (2003), *Pissarro in London*, London, National Gallery.

Alanbrooke, Field Marshal Lord (2001), *War Diaries 1939–1945*, eds. Alex Danchev and Daniel Todman, London, Phoenix.

Alavi, Seema, ed. (2002), *The Eighteenth Century in India*, New Delhi, Oxford University Press.

Albion, Robert Greenhalgh (2000), *Forests and Sea Power*, Annapolis, US Naval Institute.

Aldridge, E.-M. (1992), 'Le retour de Guillaume le Conquérant', *Franco-British Studies*, 14, pp. 97–101.

Alexander, Martin S. (1992), *The Republic in Danger: General Maurice Gamelin and the Politics of French Defence, 1933–40*, Cambridge, Cambridge University Press.

Alexander, Martin S., and Philpott, William J. (1998), 'The entente cordiale and the next war: Anglo-French views on future military cooperation, 1928–1939', *Intelligence and National Security*, 13, pp. 53–84.

Alger, J. G. (1898), 'The British Colony in Paris, 1792–1793', *English Historical Review*, 13, pp. 672–94.

Allen, Robert C. (2004), 'Britain's economic ascendancy in a European context', in L. Prados de la Escosura, ed., *Exceptionalism and Industrialisation*.

Anderson, Fred (2000), *Crucible of War: The Seven Years' War and the Fate of Empire in British North America. 1754–1766*, London, Faber and Faber.

Andrew, Christopher (1968), *Théophile Delcassé and the Making of the Entente Cordiale*, London, Macmillan.

Andrew, Christopher (1986), *Her Majesty's Secret Service: The Making of the British Intelligence Community*, New York, Viking.

Andrew, Christopher, and Kanya-Forstner, A. S. (1981), *France Overseas*, London, Thames and Hudson.

Andrew, Christopher, and Vallet, Paul (2004), 'The German threat', in Richard Mayne et al., eds., *Cross Channel Currents*.

Andrews, John (1783), *Remarks on the French and English Ladies in a series of letters interspersed with various anecdotes and additional matter, arising from the subject*, London, Longman & Robinson.

Andrews, Stuart (2003), *Unitarian Radicalism: Political Rhetoric, 1770–1814*, London, Palgrave.

Anstey, Roger (1975), *The Atlantic Slave Trade and British Abolition, 1760–1810*, London, Macmillan.

Antier, Jean-Jacques (1991), *L'amiral de Grasse, héros de l'indépendance américaine*, Rennes, Ouest-France.

Antoine, Michel (1989), *Louis XV*, Paris, Fayard.

Antonetti, Guy (1994), *Louis-Philippe*, Paris, Fayard.

Ardagh, John, Crouzet, F., and Delouch, F. (1996), 'Situation du livre', *Franco-British Studies*, 22, pp. 1–37.

Arnold, Matthew (1960), *Complete Prose Works*, ed. R. H. Super, 11 vols., Ann Arbor, University of Michigan Press.

Aron, Jean-Paul (1973), *Le Mangeur du XIXe siècle*, Paris, Robert Laffont.

Arzalier, Jean-Jacques (1997), 'Dénombrer les pertes: les difficultés françaises d'adaptation à la Grande Guerre', in Jean-Charles Jauffret, ed., *Les Armes et la Toge*.

Ashdown, Paddy (2001), *The Ashdown Diaries: vol. 2, 1997–1999*, London, Allen Lane.

Asselain, Jean-Charles (1984), *Histoire Economique de la France*, 2 vols., Paris, Seuil.

Atkin, Nicholas (2003), *The Forgotten French: Exiles in the British Isles, 1940–44*, Manchester, Manchester University Press.

Aubert, Natalie (2004), 'L'esthétique des brumes: 1904, Proust traducteur de Ruskin', *Franco-British Studies*, 35, pp. 107–19.

Baker, Keith M. (1990), *Inventing the French Revolution: Essays on French Political Culture in the Eighteenth Century*, Cambridge, Cambridge University Press.

Bamford, P. W. (1956), *Forests and French Sea Power, 1660–1789*, Toronto, Toronto University Press.

Barker, Juliet (2001), *Wordsworth: A Life*, London, Penguin.

Barnouw, Jeffrey (1997), 'The contribution of English to Voltaire's Enlightenment', in Ulla Kölving and Christian Mervaud, eds., *Voltaire et ses combats*, vol. 1.

Barsley, Michael, ed. (1946), *This England*, London, New Statesman.

Barthes, Roland (1957), *Mythologies*, Paris, Seuil.

Bartlett, Thomas, and Jeffery, Keith, eds. (1996), *A Military History of Ireland*, Cambridge, Cambridge University Press.

Battesti, Michèle (2004), *Trafalgar: les aléas de la stratégie navale de Napoléon*, Paris, Napoléon 1er Editions.

Bauberot, Jean, and Mathieu, Séverine (2002), *Religion, modernité et culture au Royaume-Uni et en France, 1800–1914*, Paris, Seuil.

Baudemont, Suzanne (1980), *L'Histoire et la légende dans l'Ecole élémentaire victorienne, 1862–1901*, Paris, Klincksieck.

Baugh, Daniel A. (2004), 'Naval power: what gave the British navy superiority?', in L. Prados de la Escosura, ed., *Exceptionalism and Industrialisation*.

Bavarez, Nicholas (2003), *La France qui tombe*, Paris, Perrin.

Baxter, Stephen B. (1966), *William III and the Defense of European Liberty 1650–1702*, New York, Harcourt, Brace & World Inc.

Bayly, Christopher A. (2004), *The Birth of the Modern World, 1780–1914*, Oxford, Blackwell.

Beach, Vincent W. (1964), 'The Polignac ministry: a revaluation', *University of Colorado Studies: series in history 3*.

Beal, Mary, and Cornforth, John (1992), *British Embassy, Paris: the house and its works of art*, London, Government Art Collection.

Beales, Derek (1961), *England and Italy 1859–60*, London, Thomas Nelson.

Beales, Derek (2005), 'Edmund Burke and the monasteries of France', *Historical Journal*, 48, pp. 415–36.

Becker, Jean-Jacques, et al., eds. (1990), *Les sociétés européennes et la guerre de 1914–1918*, Nanterre, Publications de l'Université.

Becker, Jean-Jacques, et al., eds. (1994), *Guerre et cultures, 1914–18*, Paris, A. Colin.

Beddard, Robert, ed. (1991), *The Revolutions of 1688*, Oxford, Clarendon Press.

Bell, David A. (2001), *The Cult of the Nation in France*, Cambridge, Mass., Harvard University Press.

Bell, David A. (2003), 'The Napoleon complex: Dominique de Villepin's idea of glory', *The New Republic*, 14 April 2003.

Bell, P.M.H. (1974), *A Certain Eventuality: Britain and the Fall of France*, Farnborough, Saxon House.

Bell, Philip M. (1995), 'Some French diplomats and the British, c. 1940–1955: aperçus and idées reçues', *Franco-British Studies*, pp. 43–51.

Bell, P.M.H. (1996), *France and Britain, 1900–1940: Entente and Estrangement*, London, Longman.

Bell, P.M.H. (1997), *France and Britain, 1940–1994: The Long Separation*, London, Longman.

Bell, P.M.H. (2004), 'The narrowing Channel?' in Richard Mayne et al., eds., *Cross Channel Currents*.

Bellaigue, Christina de (2003), 'A comparative study of boarding-schools for girls in England and France, c. 1810–1867', Cambridge University PhD.

Belloy, Pierre (1765), *Le Siège de Calais: tragédie dédiée au Roi*, Paris, Duchesne.

Bély, Lucien (1992), *Les relations internationales en Europe, XVIIe – XVIIIe siècles*, Paris, Presses Universitaires de France.

Ben-Israel, Hedva (1968), *English Historians on the French Revolution*, Cambridge, Cambridge University Press.

Bennett, Martyn (1997), *The Civil Wars in Britain and Ireland, 1638–1651*, Oxford, Blackwell.

Bensimon, Fabrice (2000), *Les Britanniques face à la révolution française de 1848*, Paris, Harmattan.

Bentley, G.E. (2001), *Stranger from Paradise: A Biography of William Blake*, New Haven and London, Yale University Press.

Béranger, Jean, and Meyer, Jean (1993), *La France dans le monde au XVIIIe siècle*, Paris, Sedes.

Béraud, Henri (1935), *Faut-il réduire l'Angleterre à l'esclavage?*, Paris, Editions de France.

Bermingham, Ann, and Brewer, John, eds. (1997), *The Consumption of Culture 1600–1800: Image, Object, Text*, London, Routledge.

Bernard, Jean-Pierre A. (2001), *Les Deux Paris: les représentations de Paris dans la seconde moitié du XIXe siècle*, Seyssel, Champ Vallon.

Bernstein, George L. (1986), *Liberalism and Liberal Politics in Edwardian England*, Boston and London, Allen & Unwin.

Bernstein, George L. (2004), *The Myth of Decline: The Rise of Britain since 1944*, London, Pimlico.

Bertaud, Jean-Paul (1988), *The Army of the French Revolution: From Citizen-Soldiers to Instrument of Power*, Princeton, Princeton University Press.

Bertaud, Jean-Paul (1998), *Guerre et Société en France de Louis XIV à Napoléon 1er*, Paris, Armand Colin.

Bertaud, Jean-Paul (2004), 'Le regard des Français sur les Anglais', in Jean-Paul Bertaud, Alan Forrest and Annie Jourdan, eds., *Napoléon, le monde et les Anglais: Guerre des mots et des images*, Paris, Editions Autrement.

Binney, Marcus (2003), *The Women Who Lived for Danger*, London, Coronet.

Black, Jeremy (1987), 'Fit For a King', *History Today*, 37 (4 April), p.3

Black, Jeremy (1998), *America or Europe? British Foreign Policy, 1739–63*, London, UCL Press.

Black, Jeremy (1999), *The British Abroad: The Grand Tour in the Eighteenth Century*, London, Sandpiper.

Black, Jeremy (2000), *A System of Ambition: British Foreign Policy 1660–1793*, Stroud, Sutton.

Black, Jeremy (2000b), *Culloden and the '45*, Stroud, Sutton.

[Blakiston, John] (1829), *Twelve Years' Military Adventures in Three Quarters of the Globe*, 2 vols., London, Henry Colburn.

Blanning, T.C.W. (1977), '"That horrid electorate" or "ma patrie germanique"? George III, Hanover, and the *Fürstenbund* of 1785', *Historical Journal*, 20, pp. 311–44.

Blanning, T.C.W. (1983), *The French Revolution in Germany: Occupation and Resistance in the Rhineland 1792–1802*, Oxford, Clarendon Press.

Blanning, T.C.W. (1986), *Origins of the French Revolutionary Wars*, London and New York, Longman.

Blanning, T.C.W. (1996), *The French Revolutionary Wars 1787–1802*, London, Arnold.

Blanning, T.C.W. (2002), *The Culture of Power and the Power of Culture: Old Regime Europe 1660–1789*, Oxford, Oxford University Press.

Blanning, T.C.W. (2003), 'The Bonapartes and Germany', in Peter Baehr and Melvin Richter, eds., *Dictatorship in History and Theory: Bonapartism, Caesarism, and Totalitarianism*, Washington, Cambridge University Press.

Bloch, Marc (1949), *Strange Defeat*, London, Oxford University Press.

Blount, Edward (1902), *Memoirs of Sir Edward Blount*, ed. S. J. Reid, London, Longman.

Bluche, Frédéric (1980), *Le Bonapartisme: aux origines de la droite révolutionnaire*, Paris, Nouvelles Editions Latines.

Bluche, Frédéric (1990), *Louis XIV*, Oxford, Basil Blackwell.

Bodley, J.E.C. (1898), *France*, 2 vols., London, Macmillan.

Boigne, Comtesse de (1971), *Mémoires de la Comtesse de Boigne, née d'Osmond*, ed. Jean-Claude Berchet, 2 vols, Paris, Mercure de France.

Bombelles, Marc de (1989), *Journal du voyage en Grande-Bretagne et en Irlande, 1784*, trans. and ed. Jacques Gury, Oxford, Voltaire Foundation.

Bonaparte, Napoléon-Louis (1839), *Des Idées Napoléoniennes*, London, Colburn.

Bongie, Laurence L. (1977), 'Voltaire's English high treason and a manifesto for bonnie prince Charles', *Studies in Voltaire and the Eighteenth Century*, 171, pp. 7–29.

Bonnaud, Laurent, ed. (2004), *France-Angleterre: un siècle d'entente cordiale 1904–2004*, Paris, Harmattan.

Bonney, Richard, ed. (1999), *The Rise of the Fiscal State in Europe, c. 1200–1815*, Oxford, Oxford University Press.

Boswell, James (1992), *The Life of Samuel Johnson*, London, Everyman.

Boucard, Robert (1926), *Les Dessous de l'espionnage anglais*, Paris, Henri Etienne.

Boucher, François (1996), *A History of Costume in the West*, London, Thames & Hudson.

Bourguet, M.-N. (2002), 'Science and memory: the stakes of the expedition to Egypt 1798–1801', in Howard G. Brown and Judith A. Miller, eds., *Taking Liberties: Problems of a New Order from the French Revolution to Napoleon*, Manchester, Manchester University Press.

Bourne, Kenneth (1982), *Palmerston, The Early Years 1784–1841*, London, Allen Lane.

Bowen, H. V. (1998), *War and British Society, 1688–1815*, Cambridge, Cambridge University Press.

Boyce, Robert, ed. (1998), *French Foreign Policy and Defence Policy, 1918–1940: The Decline and Fall of a Great Power*, London, Routledge.

Brecher, Frank W. (1998), *Losing a Continent: France's North American Policy, 1753–1763*, Westport, Conn., and London, Greenwood Press.

Bremner, G. Alex (2005), 'Nation and empire in the government architecture of mid-Victorian London: the Foreign and India Office reconsidered', *Historical Journal*, 48, pp. 703–42.

Brettell, Richard R. and Lloyd, Christopher (1980), *The Drawings of Camille Pissarro in the Ashmolean Museum*, Oxford, Clarendon Press.

Brewer, John (1990), *The Sinews of Power: War, Money and the English State, 1688–1783*, Cambridge, Mass., Harvard University Press.

Brewer, John (1997), *The Pleasures of the Imagination: English Culture in the Eighteenth Century*, London, HarperCollins.

Briggs, Asa (1970), *The History of Broadcasting in the United Kingdom*, vol. 3, *The War of Words*, Oxford, Oxford University Press.

Brioist, Pascal (1997), *Espaces Maritimes au XVIIIe Siècle*, Paris, Atalante.

Brisson, Max (2001), *1900: quand les Français détestaient les Anglais*, Biarritz, Atlantica.

Bristow, Edward J. (1977), *Vice and Vigilance: Purity Movements in Britain since 1700*, Dublin, Gill & Macmillan.

Britsch, Amédée, ed. (1926), *Lettres de L.-P.-J. d'Orléans, duc de Chartres à N. Parker Forth*, Paris, Société d'Histoire Diplomatique.

Broers, Michael (1996), *Europe Under Napoleon 1799–1815*, London, Arnold.

Broers, Michael (2001), 'Napoleon, Charlemagne and Lotharingia: acculturation and the boundaries of Napoleonic Europe', *Historical Journal*, 44, pp. 135–54.

Brown, David (2004), *The Road to Oran: Anglo-French Naval Relations, September 1939–July 1940*, London, Frank Cass.

Browne, Mary (1905), *Diary of a Girl in France in 1821*, London, John Murray.

Browning, Oscar, ed. (1887), *England and Napoleon in 1803, being the dispatches of Lord Whitworth and others*, London, Longman.

Browning, Oscar, ed. (1909), *Despatches from Paris 1784–1790*, 2 vols., London, Camden Society.

Brumwell, Stephen (2002), *Redcoats: The British Soldier and War in the Americas, 1755–1763*, Cambridge, Cambridge University Press.

Buchanan, William (1824), *Memoirs of Painting with a Chronological History of the Importation of Pictures of the Great Masters into England since the French Revolution*, 2 vols., London, Ackermann.

Buck, Anne (1979), *Dress in Eighteenth-Century England*, London, Batsford.

Buckmaster, Maurice (1952), *Specially Employed*, London, Blatchworth.

Bullen, Roger (1974), *Palmerston, Guizot and the Collapse of the Entente Cordiale*, London, Athlone.

Burke, Edmund (2001), *Reflections on the Revolution in France*, ed. J.C.D. Clark, Stanford, Stanford University Press.

Burrow, J. W. (1983), *A Liberal Descent*, Cambridge, Cambridge University Press.

Burrow, John (2000), *The Crisis of Reason: European Thought, 1848–1914* New Haven and London, Yale University Press.

Burrows, Simon (2000), *French Exile Journalism and European Politics, 1792–1814*, London, Royal Historical Society.

Buruma, Ian (2000), *Voltaire's Coconuts, or Anglomania in Europe*, London, Phoenix.

Bury, J.P.T. (1982), *Gambetta's Final Years: 'The Era of Difficulties', 1877–1882*, London, Longman.

Bury, J.P.T., and Tombs, R.P. (1986), *Thiers 1797–1877: A Political Life*, London, Allen & Unwin.

Butler of Brockwell, Robin, Lord (2004), *Review of Intelligence on Weapons of Mass Destruction: Report of a Committee of Privy Counsellors*, House of Commons paper 898.

Buton, Philippe (2004), *La Joie douloureuse: la Libération de la France*, Brussels, Complexe.

Cabanes, Bruno (2003), *La Victoire endeuillée: la sortie de guerre des soldats français, 1918–1920*, Paris, Seuil.

Cadogan, Alexander (1971), *The Diaries of Sir Alexander Cadogan, O.M., 1938–1945*, ed. David Dilks, London, Cassell.

Caie, Katy (2002), 'The Prosecution of Henry Vizetelly: A Study of Attitudes to French Morals and Literature', Cambridge University MPhil.

Cairns, David (1989), *Berlioz: The Making of an Artist*, London, André Deutsch.

Caldicott, C.E.J., Gough, H., and Pittion, J.-P., eds. (1987), *The Huguenots and Ireland: anatomy of an emigration*, Dun Laoghaire, Glendale Press.

Campbell, John (2000), *Margaret Thatcher*, 2 vols., London, Jonathan Cape.

Campos, Christophe (1965), *The View of France: From Arnold to Bloomsbury*, London, Oxford University Press.

Campos Christophe (1992), 'La Grand-Bretagne et les Anglais', *Franco-British Studies*, 14, pp. 53–66.

Campos Christophe (1999), 'English stereotypes of the French', *Franco-British Studies*, 27, pp. 39–54.

Card, David, and Freeman, Richard B. (2002), 'What have two decades of British economic reform delivered?', Washington DC, National Bureau of Economic Research, Working Paper 8801.

Cardwell, M. John (2004), *Arts and Arms: Literature, Politics and Patriotism during the Seven Years War*, Manchester, Manchester University Press.

Carey, John (1992), *The Intellectuals and the Masses: Pride and Prejudice among the Literary Intelligentsia, 1880–1939*, London, Faber and Faber.

Carlton, David (2004), 'Churchill and the two "evil empires"', in David Cannadine and Ronald Quinault (eds.), *Winston Churchill in the Twenty-First Century*, Cambridge, Cambridge University Press.

Carpenter, Kirsty (1999), *Refugees of the French Revolution: Emigrés in London, 1789–1802*, London, Macmillan.

Carrington, Charles (1970), *Rudyard Kipling: His Life and Work*, Harmondsworth, Penguin.

Carrington, Peter, Lord (1988), *Reflect on Things Past*, London, Collins.

Castetbon, Philippe (2004), *Ici est tombé: paroles sur la Libération de Paris*, Paris, Tirésias.

Cénat, Jean-Philippe (2005), 'Le ravage du Palatinat: politique de destruction, stratégie de cabinet et propagande au début de la guerre de la Ligue d'Augsbourg', *Revue Historique*, 307, pp. 97–132.

Chalon, Philippe A.S. (2002), 'The setting up of the Anglo-French "cultural front" and its manifestations in the French public sphere (1938–1940)', Cambridge University MPhil.

Chandler, David G. (1966), *The Campaigns of Napoleon*, London, Weidenfeld & Nicolson.

Channon, Henry (1967), *Chips: The Diaries of Sir Henry Channon*, ed. Robert Rhodes James, London, Weidenfeld & Nicolson.

Charle, Christophe (1991), *Histoire sociale de la France au XIXe siècle*, Paris, Seuil.

Charle, Christophe (2001), *Les intellectuels en Europe au XIXe siècle*, Paris, Seuil.

Charles-Roux, Edmonde (2005), *The World of Coco Chanel: Friends, Fashion, Fame*, London, Thames & Hudson.

Chassaigne, Philippe, and Dockrill, Michael, eds. (2002), *Anglo-French Relations, 1898–1998: From Fashoda to Jospin*, London, Palgrave.

Chateaubriand, René de (1973), *Mémoires d'Outre-Tombe*, Paris, Livre de Poche.

Chaunu, Pierre (1982), *La France: histoire de la sensibilité des Français à la France*, Paris, Robert Laffont.

Chaussinand-Nogaret, Guy (1993), *Gens de finance au XVIIIe siècle*, Paris, Seuil.

Chaussinand-Nogaret, Guy (1998), *Choiseul (1719–1785): Naissance de la gauche*, Paris, Perrin.

Chesterfield, Earl of (1932), *Letters of the Earl of Chesterfield to his Son*, ed. Charles Strachey, London, Methuen.

Chevalier, Louis (1973), *Labouring Classes and Dangerous Classes in Paris during the First Half of the Nineteenth Century*, London, Routledge & Kegan Paul.

Childs, John (1996), 'The Williamite war, 1689–1691', in Bartlett, Thomas, and Jeffery, Keith, eds., *A Military History of Ireland*, Cambridge, Cambridge University Press.

Choiseul, Duc de (1881), 'Mémoire de M. de Choiseul remis au roi en 1765', *Journal des Savants*, pp. 171–84, 250–57.

Christiansen, Rupert (1994), *Tales of the New Babylon*, London, Sinclair-Stevenson.

Christie, Ian R. (1984), *Stress and Stability in Late Eighteenth-Century Britain: Reflections on the British Avoidance of Revolution*, Oxford, Clarendon Press.

Churchill, Winston Spencer (1948), *The Second World War*, 6 vols., London, Cassell.

Churchill, Winston Spencer (2002), *Marlborough, His Life and Times*, 2 vols., Chicago, University of Chicago Press.

Claeys, Gregory (2000), 'The Reflections refracted: the critical reception of Burke's Reflections on the Revolution in France during the early 1790s', in John C. Whale, ed., *Edmund Burke's Reflections on the Revolution in France: New Interdisciplinary Essays*, Manchester, Manchester University Press.

Clairambault-Maurepas (1882), *Chansonnier historique du XVIIIe siècle*, ed. Emile Raumé, 10 vols., Paris, Quentin.

Clark, J.C.D. (2000), 'Protestantism, nationalism, and national identity, 1660–1832', *Historical Journal*, 43, pp. 249–76.

Clarke, I.F. (1992), *Voices Prophesying War: Future Wars 1763–3749*, Oxford, Oxford University Press.

Clodong, Olivier, and Lamarque, J.-M. (2005), *Pourquoi les Français sont les moins fréquentables de la planète*, Paris, Eyrolles.

Cobb, Richard (1983), *French and Germans, Germans and French*, Hanover and London, Brandeis University Press.

Cobb, Richard (1998), *Paris and Elsewhere: Selected Writings*, ed. David Gilmour, London, John Murray.

Cogan, Charles (2003), *French Negotiating Behaviour: Dealing with La Grande Nation*, Washington DC, US Institute of Peace Press.

Cohen, Michèle (1999), 'Manliness, effeminacy and the French: gender and the construction of national character in eighteenth-century England', in Tim Hitchcock and Michèle Cohen, eds., *English Masculinities, 1660–1800*, London, Longman.

Cole, G.D.H. (1941), *Europe, Russia and the Future*, London, Gollancz.

Colley, Linda (1992), *Britons: Forging the Nation 1707–1837*, New Haven and London, Yale University Press.

Collini, Stefan (1993), *Public Moralists*, Oxford, Clarendon Press.

Commune photographiée, La (2000), Paris, Editions de la Réunion des Musées Nationaux.

Conlin, Jonathan (2005), 'Wilkes, the Chevalier d'Eon and "the dregs of liberty": An Anglo-French perspective on ministerial despotism, 1762–1771', *English Historical Review*, 120, pp. 1251–88.

Considérant, Victor (1840), *De la politique générale*, Paris, La Phalange.

Conway, Stephen (2000), *The British Isles and the War of American Independence*, Oxford, Oxford University Press.

Cookson, J.E. (1997), *The British Armed Nation 1793–1815*, Oxford, Clarendon Press.

Cooper, Duff (1953), *Old Men Forget: The Autobiography of Duff Cooper*, London, Hart-Davis.

Corbett, Graham (2004), 'The Tunnel', in Mayne et al., eds., *Cross Channel Currents*.

Corbett, Julian S. (1907), *England in the Seven Years War*, London, Longmans, Green, 1907.

Corbin, Alain (1978), *Les filles de noce*, Paris, Aubier.

Cornick, Martyn (1993), '*Faut-il réduire l'Angleterre en esclavage?* French anglophobia in 1935', *Franco-British Studies*, special number (January 1993), pp. 3–17.

Cornick, Martyn (1994), 'The BBC and the propaganda war against occupied France: the work of Emile Delavenay and the European Intelligence Department', *French History*, 8, pp. 316–54.

Cornick, Martyn (1996), 'The Impact of the Dreyfus Affair in late-Victorian Britain', *Franco-British Studies*, 22, pp. 57–82.

Cornick, Martyn (1999), The Dreyfus Affair – another year, another centenary. British Opinion and the Rennes Verdict, September 1899', *Modern and Contemporary France*, 7, pp. 499–508.

Cornick, Martyn (2000), 'Fighting myth with reality: the fall of France, Anglophobia and the BBC', in Valerie Holman and Debra Kelly, eds., *France at War in the Twentieth Century: Propaganda, Myth and Metaphor*, New York and Oxford, Berghahn.

Cornick, Martyn (2004), 'The White City, 1908', in Mayne et al., eds., *Cross Channel Currents*.

Cornick, Martyn (2004b), 'Colonel Driant and his "Inevitable War" [*La Guerre fatale*] against Britain', paper given at the conference *Refocusing on Europe? International Relations from the Entente Cordiale to the First World War* at Salford University, March 2004.

Courtney, C.P. (1975), *Montesquieu and Burke*, Westport, Conn., Greenwood Press.

Coward, Noël (2002), *The Lyrics*, London, Methuen.

Crane, Ronald S. (1922), 'The diffusion of Voltaire's writings in England', *Modern Philology*, 20, pp. 260–71.

Cranston, Maurice (1997), *The Solitary Self: Jean-Jacques Rousseau in Exile and Adversity*, London, Allen Lane.

Crémieux-Brilhac, Jean-Louis (1975), *Ici Londres, 1940–1944: les voix de la liberté*, 5 vols, Paris, La Documentation Française.

Crémieux-Brilhac, Jean-Louis (1990), *Les Français de l'an 40*, 2 vols., Paris, Gallimard.

Crémieux-Brilhac, Jean-Louis (1996), *La France libre: du 18 juin à la Libération*, Paris, Gallimard.

Crossley, Ceri, and Small, Ian, eds. (1988), *Studies in Anglo-French Cultural Relations: Imagining France*, London, Macmillan.

Crouzet, François (1996), 'The second hundred years war: some reflections', *French History*, 10, pp. 432–50.

Crouzet, François (1999), *De la supériorité de l'Angleterre sur la France: l'économique et l'imaginaire, XVIIe-XXe siècles*, Paris, Perrin.

Cruickshanks, Eveline (2000), *The Glorious Revolution*, London, Macmillan.

Crystal, David (2004), *The Stories of English*, London, Penguin.

Cullen, Fintan (2000), 'Radicals and reactionaries: portraits of the 1790s in Ireland', in Jim Smyth, *Revolution, Counter-Revolution and Union: Ireland in the 1790s*, Cambridge, Cambridge University Press.

Cullen, L.M. (2000), *The Irish Brandy Houses of Eighteenth Century France*, Dublin, Lilliput Press.

Cunningham, Hugh (1975), *The Volunteer Force: A Social and Political History, 1859–1908*, London, Croom Helm.

Dallaire, Roméo (2004), *Shake Hands with the Devil: The Failure of Humanity in Rwanda*, London, Arrow Books.

Dalton, Hugh (1940), *Hitler's War, Before and After*, Harmondsworth, Penguin.

Dalton, Hugh (1986), *The Second World War Diary of Hugh Dalton, 1940–45*, ed. Ben Pimlott, London, Jonathan Cape.

Daninos, Pierre (1954), *Les Carnets du major W. Marmaduke Thompson*, Paris, Hachette.

Darriulat, Philippe (2001), *Les Patriotes: la gauche républicaine et la nation, 1830–1870*, Paris, Seuil.

Darrow, Margaret H. (2000), *French Women and the First World War: War Stories of the Home Front*, Oxford, Berg.

Das, Sudipta (1992), *Myths and Realities of French Imperialism in India, 1763–1783*, New York, Peter Lang.

Dedieu, Joseph (1909), *Montesquieu et la tradition politique anglaise en France: les sources anglaises de l'Esprit des lois*, Paris, J. Gabalda.

Deerr, Noël (1949), *History of Sugar*, London, Chapman & Hall.

Delattre, Floris (1927), *Dickens et la France: Etude d'une interraction littéraire anglo-française*, Paris, Librairie universitaire J. Gamber.

Delfau, Gérard (1971), *Jules Vallès: l'exil à Londres*, Paris, Bordas.

Delors, Jacques (2004), *Mémoires*, Paris, Plon.

Delpla, François (2000), *Churchill et les Français: six hommes dans la tourmente, septembre 1939-juin 1940*, Paris, Plon.

Demolins, Edmond (1898), *Anglo-Saxon Superiority: To What Is It Due?*, London, Leadenhall Press.

Denman, Roy (1996), *Missed Chances*, London, Indigo.

Desagneaux, Henri (1975), *A French Soldier's War Diary 1914–1918*, Morley, Elmsfield Press.

Diary (1941), *The Diary of a Staff Officer (Air Intelligence Liaison Officer) at Advanced Headquarters North BAAF 1940*, London, Methuen.

Dickens, Charles (1965), *The Letters of Charles Dickens*, ed. Madeline House et al., 12 vols., Oxford, Clarendon Press.

Dickens, Charles (1993), *A Tale of Two Cities*, London, Everyman.

Dickens, Charles (1994), *Oliver Twist*, London, Penguin.

Dickinson, H.T. (1985), *British Radicalism and the French Revolution, 1789–1815*, Oxford, Blackwell.

Dickinson, H.T., ed. (1989), *Britain and the French Revolution, 1789–1815*, London, Macmillan.

Dickson, P.M.G. (1967), *The Financial Revolution in England: A Study of the Development of Public Credit, 1688–1756*, London, Macmillan.

Digeon, Claude (1959), *La Crise allemande de la pensée française (1870–1914)*, Paris, Presses Universitaires de France.

Dine, Philip (2001), *French Rugby Football: A Cultural History*, Oxford, Berg.

Dockrill, Michael (2002), 'British official perceptions of France and the French', in Philippe Chassaigne and Michael Dockrill, eds., *Anglo-French Relations, 1898–1998*, London, Palgrave.

Doise, Jean, and Vaïsse, Maurice (1987), *Diplomatie et outil militaire 1871–1969*, Paris, Imprimerie nationale.

Donald, Diana (1996), *The Age of Caricature: Satirical Prints in the Reign of George III*, New Haven and London, Yale University Press.

Drayton, Richard (1998), 'Knowledge and empire', in *OHBE*, vol. 2.

Druon, Maurice (2004), 'Franco-British Union: a personal view', in Richard Mayne et al., eds., *Cross Channel Currents*.

Du Bocage, M.-A., (1770), *Letters concerning England, Holland and Italy: By the celebrated Madam du Bocage*, 2 vols., London, E. and C. Dilly.

Duffy, Michael (1987), *Soldiers, Sugar and Seapower: The British Expeditions to the West Indies and the War against Revolutionary France*, Oxford, Clarendon Press.

Dull, Jonathan R. (1985), *A Diplomatic History of the American Revolution*, New Haven and London, Yale University Press.

Dull, Jonathan R. (2005), *The French Navy and the Seven Years War*, Lincoln, Nebr., and London, University of Nebraska Press.

Duloum, Joseph (1970), *Les Anglais dans les Pyrénées et les débuts du tourisme pyrénéen, 1739–1896*, Lourdes, Les Amis du Musée Pyrénéen.

Dumas, Alexandre (2000), *Grand Dictionnaire de Cuisine*, Paris, Phébus.

Du Maurier, George (1995), *Trilby*, Oxford, Oxford University Press.

Dutton, David (2001), *Neville Chamberlain*, London, Arnold.

Dutton, David (2004), 'A Francophile', in Richard Mayne et al., eds., *Cross Channel Currents*.

Dwyer, P. G. (2002), 'From Corsican nationalist to French revolutionary', *French History*, 16, pp. 132–52.

Dziembowski, Edmond (1998), *Un nouveau patriotisme français, 1750–1770: La France face à la puissance anglaise à l'époque de la guerre de Sept Ans*, Oxford, Voltaire Foundation.

Eagles, Robin (2000), *Francophilia in English Society 1748–1815*, London, Macmillan.

Echard, William E. (1983), *Napoleon III and the Concert of Europe*, Baton Rouge, Louisiana State University Press.

Edwards, F.A. (1898), 'The French on the Nile', *The Fortnightly Review*, 63, pp. 362–77.

Edwards, Geoffrey (1984), 'Europe and the Falkland Islands crisis,' *Journal of Common Market Studies*, 22, pp. 295–313.

Egremont, Max (1997), *Under Two Flags: The Life of Major-General Sir Edward Spears*, London, Phoenix.

Egret, Jean (1977), *The French Pre-Revolution, 1787–1788*, Chicago and London, University of Chicago Press.

Ehrman, John (2004), *The Younger Pitt*, 3 vols., London, Constable.

Elliot, Marianne (1982), *Partners in Revolution: The United Irishmen and France*, New Haven and London, Yale University Press.

Ellis, Geoffrey (1997), *Napoleon*, London and New York, Longman.

Ellmann, Richard (1988), *Oscar Wilde*, Harmondsworth, Penguin.

Emsley, Clive (1979), *British Society and the French Wars 1793–1815*, London, Macmillan.

Engerman, Stanley L. (2004), 'Institutional change and British supremacy, 1650–1850: some reflections', in L. Prados de la Escosura, *Exceptionalism and Industrialisation*.

Englund, Steven (2004), *Napoleon: A Political Life*, New York, Scribner.

Esdaile, Charles (1995), *The Wars of Napoleon*, London, Longman.

Esdaile, Charles (2002), *The Peninsular War: A New History*, London, Allen Lane.

Esteban, Javier C. (2001), 'The British balance of payments, 1772–1820: India transfers and war finance', *Economic History Review*, 54, pp. 58–86.

Esteban, Javier C. (2004), 'Comparative patterns of colonial trade: Britain and its rivals', in L. Prados de la Escosura, *Exceptionalism and Industrialisation*.

Evans, Eric J. (1999), *William Pitt the Younger*, London, Routledge.

Evans, Julian (2004), 'Europe's lost stories', *Prospect* (July 2004), pp. 40–45.

Evans, R.J.W. and Pogge von Strandmann, Hartmut, eds. (1990) *The Coming of the First World War*, Oxford, Clarendon Press.

Farge, Arlette (1994), *Subversive Words: Public Opinion in Eighteenth-Century France*, Cambridge, Polity Press.

Farrar-Hockley, Anthony (1970), *Ypres 1914: The Death of an Army*, London, Pan.

Favier, Pierre, and Martin-Rolland, Michel (1990), *La Décennie Mitterrand*, 4 vols., Paris, Seuil.

Ferguson, Niall (1998), *The World's Banker: The History of the House of Rothschild*, London, Weidenfeld & Nicolson.

Ferguson, Niall (1998b), *The Pity of War*, Harmondsworth, Allen Lane.

Ferguson, Niall (2001), *The Cash Nexus: Money and Power in the Modern World, 1700–2000*, Harmondsworth, Allen Lane.

Ferling, John (2003), *A Leap in the Dark: the struggle to create the American Republic*, Oxford, Oxford University Press.

Ferrone, Vincenzo, and Roche, Daniel, eds. (1999), *Le Monde des Lumières*, Paris, Fayard.

Fierro, Alfred (1996), *Histoire et Dictionnaire de Paris*, Paris, Robert Laffont.

Fischer, Conan (2003), *The Ruhr Crisis, 1923–1924*, Oxford, Oxford University Press.

Fitzpatrick, Martin, Jones, Peter, Knellwolf, Christa, and McCalman, Iain, eds. (2004), *The Enlightenment World*, London, Routledge.

A Five Weeks' Tour to Paris, Versailles, Marli &c (1754), London.

Flaubert, Gustave (1991), *Bouvard et Pécuchet*, Paris, Gallimard.

Foley, Robert T. (2005), *German Strategy and the Path to Verdun: Erich von Falkenhayn and the Development of Attrition, 1870–1916*, Cambridge, Cambridge University Press.

Foot, M.R.D. (1978), *Resistance*, London, Paladin.

Foot, M.R.D. (2004), *SOE in France: An Account of the Work of the British Special Operations Executive in France, 1940–1944*, London, Frank Cass.

Foote, Samuel (1783?), *The Dramatic Works of Samuel Foote, Esq.*, 4 vols., London, Rivington, Lowndes.

Footitt, Hilary (2004), *War and Liberation in France: Living with the Liberators*, London, Palgrave.

Foreman, Amanda (1999), *Georgiana Duchess of Devonshire*, London, HarperCollins.

Forrest, Alan (2002), 'La patrie en danger', in Daniel Moran and Arthur Waldron, eds., *The People in Arms: Military Myth and National Mobilization since the French Revolution*, Cambridge, Cambridge University Press.

Fortescue, Winifred (1992), *Perfume from Provence*, London, Black Swan.

Fougeret de Montbrun, Louis Charles (1757), *Préservatif contre l'anglomanie*, Minorca.

Fournier, Eric (2005), 'Paris en ruines (1851–1882): entre flânerie et apocalypse, regards, acteurs, pratiques', Paris, Université de Paris I, thèse de doctorat.

Frank, Robert (1993), 'Pétain, Laval, Darlan', in Jean-Pierre Azéma and François Bédarida, eds., *La France des années noires*, vol. I, Paris, Seuil.

Frank, Robert (1994), *La hantise du déclin: Le rang de la France en Europe, 1920–1960: Finances, défense et identité nationale*, Paris, Belin.

Frank, Robert (1995) 'Résistance et résistants dans la stratégie des Britanniques et Américains', in L. Douzou et al., eds., *La Résistance et les Français: villes, centres et logiques de décision, Bulletin de l'Institut d'Histoire du Temps Présent*, supplement no. 61, pp. 471–83.

Frankiss, Charles C. (2004), 'Camille Pissarro, Théodore Duret and Jules Berthel in London in 1871', *Burlington Magazine*, pp. 470–502.

Freedman, Laurence (2005), *The Official History of the Falklands Campaign*, 2 vols., London, Frank Cass.

Fry, Michael G. (1989), 'Canada, the North Atlantic Triangle, and the United Nations', in Wm Roger Louis and Roger Owen, eds., *Suez 1956*.

Fuller, J.G. (1990), *Troop Morale and Popular Culture in the British and Dominion Armies, 1914–1918*, Oxford, Clarendon Press.

Fumaroli, Marc (2001), *Quand L'Europe parlait français*, Paris, Editions de Fallois.

Furet, François (1992), *Revolutionary France, 1770–1880*, Oxford, Blackwell.

Gabory, Emile (1989), *Les guerres de Vendée*, Paris, Robert Laffont.

Gaillard, Jeanne (1977), *Paris, la Ville*, Paris, Honoré Champion.

Galison, Peter (2004), *Einstein's Clocks, Poincaré's Maps: Empires of Time*, London, Sceptre.

Garrett, Clarke (1975), *Respectable Folly: Millenarians and the French Revolution in France and England*, Baltimore and London, Johns Hopkins University Press.

Garriaud-Maylam, Joëlle (2004), 'The French in Britain', in Richard Mayne et al., eds., *Cross Channel Currents*.

Garrick, David (1939), *The Journal of David Garrick: Describing His Visit to France and Italy in 1763*, ed. George Winchester Stone, New York, Modern Language Association of America.

Gates, David (2002), *The Spanish Ulcer: A History of the Peninsular War*, London, Pimlico.

Gates, Eleanor M. (1981), *End of the Affair: The Collapse of the Anglo-French Alliance, 1939–40*, London, Allen & Unwin.

Gaulle, Charles de (1970), *Mémoires d'espoir*, 2 vols., Paris, Plon.

Gaulle, Charles de (1998), *The Complete War Memoirs of Charles de Gaulle*, New York, Carroll & Graf.

Gault, Henri, and Millau, Christian (1970), *Guide Gourmand de la France*, Paris, Hachette.

Gee, Austin (2003), *The British Volunteer Movement, 1794–1815*, Oxford, Clarendon Press.

The Gentleman's Guide in his Tour through France wrote by an officer in the Royal Navy, n.d [c. 1760], Bristol and London.

Genuist, André (1971), *Le Théâtre de Shakespeare dans l'œuvre de Pierre Le Tourneur, 1776–1783*, Paris, Didier.

George IV and the Arts of France (1966), London, Queen's Gallery.

Gerbod, Paul (1995), *Les Voyageurs français à la découverte des îles britanniques du XVIIIe siècle à nos jours*, Paris, Harmattan.

Gibson, Kenneth Craig (1998), 'Relations between the British army and the Civilian Populations on the Western Front, 1914–18', PhD dissertation, Leeds University.

Gibson, Kenneth Craig (2000), '"My chief source of worry": an assistant provost marshal's view of relations between the 2nd Canadian division and local inhabitants on the Western Front', *War in History*, 7, pp. 413–41.

Gibson, Kenneth Craig (2001), 'Sex and soldiering in France and Flanders: the British Expeditionary Force along the Western Front, 1914–1919', *International History Review*, 23, pp. 535–79.

Gibson, Kenneth Craig (2003), 'Through French eyes: the British Expeditionary Force and the records of the French postal censor, 1916–18', *History Workshop Journal*, 55, pp. 177–88.

Gibson, Kenneth Craig (2003b), 'The British army, French farmers and the war on the Western Front, 1914–18', *Past & Present*, 180, pp. 175–239.

Gibson, Robert (1995), *Best of Enemies: Anglo-French Relations since the Norman Conquest*, London, Sinclair-Stevenson.

Gibson, Robert (1999), 'All done by mirrors: the French and English in each other's fiction', in James Dolamore, ed., *Making Connections: Essays in French Culture and Society in Honour of Philip Thody*, Bern, Peter Lang.

Gildea, Robert (1994), *The Past in French History*, New Haven and London, Yale University Press.

Gillingham, John (2003), *European Integration 1950–2003*, Cambridge, Cambridge University Press.

Gilmour, David (2002), *The Long Recessional: The Imperial Life of Rudyard Kipling*, London, John Murray.

Gilmour, Ian (1992), *Riot, Risings and Revolution*, London, Pimlico.

Girard, Louis (1986), *Napoléon III*, Paris, Fayard.

Girard d'Albisson, Nelly (1969), *Un précurseur de Montesquieu: Rapin-Thoyras, premier historien français des institutions anglaises*, Paris, Klincksieck.

Girardet, Raoul (1986), *Mythes et Mythologies Politiques*, Paris, Seuil.

Girardin, René Louis de (1777), *De la Composition des Paysages sur le Terrain, ou des moyens d'embellir les campagnes autour des Habitations en joignant l'agréable à l'utile*, Paris.

Godechot, Jacques (1956), *La Grande Nation*, 2 vols., Paris, Aubier.

Godfrey, John F. (1987), *Capitalism at War: Industrial Policy and Bureaucracy in France, 1914–1918*, Leamington Spa, Berg.

Goldfrank, David M. (1994), *The Origins of the Crimean War*, Harlow, Longman.

Gombin, Richard (1970), *Les socialistes et la guerre: la SFIO et la politique étrangère française entre les deux guerres mondiales*, Paris, Mouton.

Goncourt, Edmond and Jules de (1956), *Journal: Mémoires de la vie littéraire*, ed. Robert Ricatte, 3 vols., Paris, Robert Laffont.

Gosse, Philip (1952), *Dr Viper, the Querulous Life of Philip Thicknesse*, London, Cassell.

Gotteri, Nicole (1991), *Soult: Maréchal d'Empire et homme d'Etat*, Besançon, Editions la Manufacture.

Gough, Hugh and Dickson, David, eds., (1990), *Ireland and the French Revolution*, Dublin, Irish Academic Press.

Goulstone, John, and Swanton, Michael (1989), 'Carry on Cricket: the Duke of Dorset's 1789 Tour', *History Today*, 39 (8 August), p. 18.

Goux, Dominique, and Maurin, Eric (2005), '1992–2005: comment le oui s'est décomposé', *Le Monde* (2 June 2005), pp. 16–17.

Grainger, John D. (2004), *The Amiens Truce*, Woodbridge, Boydell Press.

Grainger, John D. (2005), *The Battle of Yorktown 1781: A Reassessment*, Woodbridge, Boydell Press.

Graves, Robert (1960), *Goodbye to All That*, London, Penguin.

Grayzel, Susan R. (1999), *Women's Identities at War: Gender, Motherhood, and Politics in Britain and France during the First World War*, Chapel Hill and London, University of North Carolina Press.

Greenfeld, Liah (1992), *Nationalism: Five Roads to Modernity*, Cambridge, Mass., Harvard University Press.

Greenhalgh, Elizabeth (1999), 'Why the British were on the Somme in 1916', *War in History*, 6, pp. 147–73.

Greenhalgh, Elizabeth (2005), 'Writing about France's Great War', *Journal of Contemporary History*, 40, pp. 601–12.

Greenwood, Sean (2000), 'The most important of the western nations', in Sharp, Alan, and Stone, Glyn, eds., *Anglo-French Relations in the Twentieth Century*, London, Routledge.

Grente, Georges, and Moureau, François, eds. (1995), *Dictionnaire des Lettres françaises: le XVIIIe siècle*, Paris, Fayard.

Grenville, J.A.S. (1976), *Europe Reshaped 1848–1878*, London, Fontana.

Grieder, Josephine (1985), *Anglomania in France, 1740–1789: Fact, Fiction, and Political Discourse*, Geneva and Paris, Librairie Droz.

Griffiths, Richard (1970), *Marshal Pétain*, London, Constable.

Grosley, Pierre-Jean (1770), *Londres*, 3 vols., Neuchâtel, Société Typographique.

Guéry Alain (1991), 'Les comptes de la mort vague après la guerre: pertes de guerre et conjoncture du phénomène guerre', *Histoire et Mesure*, 6, pp. 289–314.

Guiffan, Jean (2004), *Histoire de l'anglophobie en France: de Jeanne d'Arc à la vache folle*, Rennes, Terre de Brume.

Guillaume, Pierre (1992), 'L'hygiène et le corps', in J.-F. Sirinelli, ed., *Histoire des droites en France, vol. 3, Sensibilités*, Paris, Gallimard.

Guiomar, Jean-Yves (2004), *L'Invention de la guerre totale, XVIIIe-XXe siècles*, Paris, Le Félin.

Guizot, François (1850), *On the Causes of the Success of the English Revolution of 1640–1688*, London, John Murray.

Guizot, François (1854), *Histoire de la Civilisation en Europe*, Paris, Didier.

Guizot, François (1884), *Lettres de M. Guizot*, Paris, Hachette.

Guizot, François (1971), *Mémoires pour servir à l'histoire de mon temps*, Paris, Robert Laffont.

Gunny, Ahmad (1979), *Voltaire and English Literature: a Study of English Literary Influences on Voltaire*, Oxford, Voltaire Foundation.

Gury, Jacques (1999), *Le voyage outre-Manche: Anthologie de voyageurs français de Voltaire à Mac Orlan*, Paris, Robert Laffont.

Gwynn, Robin D. (1985), *Huguenot Heritage: The History and Contribution of the Huguenots in Britain*, London, Routledge.

Hamerton, Philip Gilbert (1876), *Round My House: Notes of Rural Life in France in Peace and War*, London, Seeley, Jackson & Halliday.

Hamilton, C.I. (1989), 'The diplomatic and naval effects of the Prince de Joinville's *Note sur l'état des forces navales de la France* of 1844', *Historical Journal*, 32, pp. 675–87.

Hamilton, C.I. (1993), *Anglo-French Naval Rivalry 1840–1870*, Oxford, Clarendon Press.

Hammersley, Rachel (2004), 'English republicanism in revolutionary France: the case of the Cordelier Club', *Journal of British Studies*, 43, pp. 464–481.

Hammersley, Rachel (2005), 'Jean-Paul Marat's *The Chains of Slavery* in Britain and France, 1774–1833', *Historical Journal*, 48, pp. 641–60.

Hampson, Norman (1998), *The Perfidy of Albion: French Perceptions of England during the French Revolution*, London, Macmillan.

Hancock, Claire (2003), *Paris et Londres au XIXe siècle: représentations dans les guides et récits de voyage*, Paris, CNRS Editions.

Hanks, Robert K. (2002), 'Georges Clemenceau and the English', *Historical Journal*, 45, pp. 53–77.

Hantraye, Jacques (2005), *Les Cosaques aux Champs-Elysées: l'occupation de la France après la chute de Napoléon*, Paris, Belin.

Hardman, John (1993), *Louis XVI*, New Haven, Yale University Press.

Hardman, John (1995), *French Politics, 1774–1789: From the Accession of Louis XVI to the Fall of the Bastille*. London, Longman.

Hardman, John, and Price, Munro, eds., (1998), *Louis XVI and the Comte de Vergennes*, Oxford, Voltaire Foundation.

Harman, Nicholas (1980), *Dunkirk: The Necessary Myth*, London, Hodder and Stoughton.

Harris, J.R. (1998), *Industrial Espionage and Technology Transfer: Britain and France in the Eighteenth Century*, Aldershot, Ashgate.

Harvey, A.D. (1981), *English Literature and the Great War with France*, London, Nold.

Harvey, Karen (2004), *Reading Sex in the Eighteenth Century: Bodies and Gender in English Erotic Culture*, Cambridge, Cambridge University Press.

Harvey, Robert (2001), *A Few Bloody Noses: the American War of Independence*, London, John Murray.

Haskell, Francis (1976), *Rediscoveries in Art: Some Aspects of Taste, Fashion and Collecting in England and France*, London, Phaidon.

Haudrère, Philippe (1997), *Le Grand Commerce Maritime au XVIIe Siècle*, Paris, Sedes.

Hawkes, Jean, ed. (1982), *The London Journal of Flora Tristan*, London, Virago.

Hazareesingh, Sudhir (2004), *The Legend of Napoleon*, London, Granta.

Hedgcock, Frank A. (1911), *David Garrick and his French Friends*, London, Stanley Paul.

Henderson, Nicholas (1987), *Channels and Tunnels: Reflections on Britain and Abroad*, London, Weidenfeld & Nicholson.

Herold, J. Christopher, ed. (1955), *The Mind of Napoleon: A Selection from His Written and Spoken Words*, New York, Columbia University Press.

Herwig, Holger H. (1997), *The First World War: Germany and Austria-Hungary 1914–1918*, London, Arnold.

Hibbert, Christopher (1961), *The Destruction of Lord Raglan; A Tragedy of the Crimean War. 1854–55*, London, Longman.

Hickman, Katie (2000), *Daughters of Britannia: The Lives and Times of Diplomatic Wives*, London, Flamingo

Hinsley, F.H., ed. (1977), *British Foreign Policy under Sir Edward Grey*, Cambridge, Cambridge University Press.

Hoehling, Adolphe A. (1958), *Edith Cavell*, London, Cassell.

Hoffman, Philip T., and Norberg, Kathryn, eds. (1994), *Fiscal Crises, Liberty and Representative Government, 1450–1789*, Stanford, Stanford University Press.

Hoggett, Paul (2005), 'Iraq: Blair's mission impossible', *British Journal of Politics and International Relations*, 7, pp. 418–28.

Holmes, Richard (2001), *Redcoat: The British Soldier in the Age of Horse and Musket*, London, HarperCollins.

Holmes, Richard (2004), *Tommy: The British Soldier on the Western Front, 1914–1918*, London, HarperCollins.

Holt, Richard (1981), *Sport and Society in Modern France*, London, Macmillan.

Holt, Richard (1998), 'Sport, the French and the Third Republic', *Modern and Contemporary France*, 6, pp. 289–300.

Holton, Woody (1999), *Forced Founders: Indians, Debtors, Slaves and the Making of the American Revolution in Virginia*, Chapel Hill, University of North Carolina Press.

Hopkin, David (2005), 'The French army, 1624–1914: from the king's to the people's', *Historical Journal*, 48, pp. 1125–37.

Hoppit, Julian (2000), *A Land of Liberty? England 1689–1727*, Oxford, Clarendon Press.

Hoppit, Julian (2002), 'The myths of the South Sea Bubble', *Transactions of the Royal Historical Society*, 12, pp. 141–65.

Horn, Martin (2002), *Britain, France and the Financing of the First World War*, Montreal, McGill-Queen's University Press.

Horne, Alistair (1965), *The Fall of Paris: The Siege and the Commune 1870–71*, London, Macmillan.

Horne, Alistair (1979), *To Lose a Battle: France 1940*, Harmondsworth, Penguin.

Horne, Alistair (1988), *Macmillan: The Official Biography*, 2 vols., London, Macmillan.

House, John, ed. (1994), *Impressionism for England: Samuel Courtauld as Patron and Collector*, London, Yale University Press.

Hue, André, and Southby-Tailyour, Ewen (2004), *The Next Moon: The Remarkable True Story of a British Agent behind the Lines in Wartime France*, London, Penguin.

Hughes, Jackson (1999), 'The battle for the Hindenburg Line', *War and Society*, 17, pp. 41–57.

Hugo, Victor (1922), *Hernani*, in *Oeuvres Complètes: théâtre*, vol. 1, Paris, Albin Michel.

Hugo, Victor (1937), *William Shakespeare*, in *Oeuvres Complètes: philosophie*, vol. 2, Paris, Albin Michel.

Hugo, Victor (1967), *Les Misérables*, 3 vols., Paris, Garnier-Flammarion.

Hugo, Victor (1972), *Choses vues: souvenirs, journaux, cahiers 1830–1846*, ed. H. Juin, Paris, Gallimard.

Hulot, Frédéric (1994), *Suffren: L'Amiral Satan*, Paris, Pygmalion.

Humbert, Jean-Marcel, and Ponsonnet, Bruno, eds. (2004), *Napoléon et la mer: un rêve d'empire*, Paris, Seuil.

Hurd, Douglas (2003), *Memoirs*, London, Little, Brown.

Huysmans, J.-K. (2001), *A rebours*, Paris, Gallimard.

Hyam, Ronald and Henshaw, Peter (2003), *The Lion and the Springbok: Britain and South Africa since the Boer War*, Cambridge, Cambridge University Press.

Imlay, Talbot C. (2003), *Facing the Second World War: Strategy, Politics and Economics in Britain and France, 1938–1940*, Oxford, Oxford University Press.

Instructions for British Servicemen in France 1944 (2005), Oxford, Bodleian Library.

Ironside, Edmund (1962), *The Ironside Diaries*, ed. R. Macleod and D. Kelly, London, Constable.

Israel, Jonathan I., ed. (1991), *The Anglo-Dutch Moment: Essays on the Glorious Revolution and Its World Impact*, Cambridge, Cambridge University Press.

Isselin, Henri (1965), *The Battle of the Marne*, London, Elek.

Jackson, Clare (2005), '"The rage of parliaments": the House of Commons, 1690–1715'. *Historical Journal*, 48, pp. 567–87.

Jackson, Julian (2003), *The Fall of France: The Nazi Invasion of 1940*, Oxford, Oxford University Press.

James, Harold (2003), *Europe Reborn: A History, 1914–2000*, Harlow, Pearson Longman.

James, Henry (1984), *A Little Tour in France*, Oxford, Oxford University Press.

Jarrett, Derek (1973), *The Begetters of Revolution: England's Involvement with France, 1759–1789*, London, Longman.

Jasanoff, Maya (2005), *Edge of Empire: Conquest and Collecting on the Eastern Frontiers of the British Empire*, London, Fourth Estate.

Jauffret, Jean-Charles, ed., (1997), *Les Armes et la Toge*, Montpellier, Université Paul Valéry.

Jennings, Lawrence C. (1973), *France and Europe in 1848*, Oxford, Clarendon Press.

Jersak, Tobias (2000), 'Blitzkrieg revisited: a new look at Nazi war and extermination planning', *Historical Journal*, 43, pp. 565–82.

Johnson, Douglas (1963), *Guizot: Aspects of French History, 1787–1874*, London, Routledge & Kegan Paul.

Johnson, Douglas (1972), 'Britain and France in 1940', *Transactions of the Royal Historical Society, 5th Series*, 22, pp. 141–57.

Johnson, Douglas, Crouzet, François, and Bédanda, François (1980), *Britain and France: Ten Centuries*, Folkestone, Dawson.

Johnson, Jo (2003), 'French Farce', *The Spectator* (28 June 2003), pp. 22–3.

Joly, Bertrand (1998), *Déroulède: l'inventeur du nationalisme français*, Paris, Perrin.

Jones, Colin (2002), *The Great Nation: France from Louis XV to Napoleon 1715–99*, London, Penguin.

Jones, Colin (2002b), *Madame de Pompadour: Images of a Mistress*, London, National Gallery.

Jones, E.H. Stuart (1950), *The Last Invasion of Britain*, Cardiff, University of Wales Press.

Judt, Tony (1997), *A Grand Illusion: An Essay on Europe*, London, Penguin.

Judt, Tony (2005), *Postwar: A History of Europe since 1945*, London, William Heinemann.

Kagan, Robert (2004), *Of Paradise and Power: America and Europe in the New World Order*, London, Vintage.

Kampfner, John (2003), *Blair's Wars*, London, Simon & Schuster.

Katznelson, Ira, and Zolberg, A.R., eds. (1986), *Working-Class Formation: Nineteenth-Century Patterns in Western Europe and the United States*, Princeton, Princeton University Press.

Keane, John (1995), *Tom Paine: A Political Life*, London, Bloomsbury.

Kedward, H. Roderick (2004), 'Britain and the French Resistance', in Mayne, Richard, et al., eds., *Cross Channel Currents*.

Keegan, John (1983), *Six Armies in Normandy: From D-Day to the Liberation of Paris*, London, Penguin.

Keegan, John (1998), *The First World War*, London, Hutchinson.

Keiger, John F.V. (1983), *France and the Origins of the First World War*, London, Macmillan.

Keiger, John F.V. (1997), *Raymond Poincaré*, Cambridge, Cambridge University Press.

Keiger, John F.V. (1998), 'Perfidious Albion: French perceptions of Britain as an ally after the First World War', *Intelligence and National Security*, 13, pp. 37–52.

Keiger, John F.V. (2001), *France and the World since 1870*, London, Arnold.

Keiger, John F.V. (2004), 'How the Entente Cordiale began', in Mayne, Richard, et al., eds., *Cross Channel Currents*.

Keiger, John F.V. (2005), 'Foreign and defence policy', in Alistair Cole et al., eds, *Developments in French Politics 3*, London, Palgrave.

Kennedy, Paul M. (1976), *The Rise and Fall of British Naval Mastery*, London, Allen Lane.

Kennett, Lee (1967), *The French Armies in the Seven Years War: A Study in Military Organization and Administration*, Durham, NC, Duke University Press.

Kennett, Lee (1977), *The French Forces in America, 1780–1783*, Westport, Conn., and London, Greenwood Press.

Kersaudy, François (1981), *Churchill and de Gaulle*, London, Collins.

Kershaw, Ian (1998), *Hitler* 2 vols., London, Penguin.

Keynes, John Maynard (1971), *The Collected Writings of J.M. Keynes*, 10 vols., London, Macmillan.

Kishlansky, Mark (1996), *A Monarchy Transformed: Britain 1603–1714*, London, Penguin.

Klaits, Joseph (1976), *Printed Propaganda under Louis XIV*, Princeton, Princeton University Press.

Klein, Lawrence E. (1997), 'Politeness for plebes: consumption and social identity in early eighteenth-century England', in Ann Bermingham and John Brewer, eds., *The Consumption of Culture 1600–1800*.

Kleine-Ahlbrandt, William Laird (1995), *The Burden of Victory*, Lanham, Md, University Press of America.

Klingberg, Frank J., and Hustvedt, Sigurd B. (1944), *The Warning Drum: The British Home Front Faces Napoleon: Broadsides of 1803*, Berkeley and Los Angeles, University of California Press.

Knapp, J.M. (2001), *Behind the Diplomatic Curtain: Adolphe de Bourqueney and French Foreign Policy, 1816–1869*, Akron, Ohio, University of Akron Press.

Kölving, Ulla, and Mervaud, Christiane, eds. (1997), *Voltaire et ses combats*, 2 vols., Oxford, Voltaire Foundation.

Kremer, Thomas (2004), *The Missing Heart of Europe*, Totnes, June Press.

Kunz, Diane B. (1989), 'The importance of having money: the economic diplomacy of the Suez crisis', in Louis and Owen, *Suez 1956*.

Kwass, Michael (2000). *Privilege and the politics of taxation in eighteenth-century France: liberté, égalité, fiscalité*, Cambridge, Cambridge University Press.

Kyle, Keith (1989) 'Britain and the crisis, 1955–56' in Louis and Owen, *Suez 1956*.

Labouchere, P.C.G., et al. (1969), *The Story of Continental Cricket*, London, Hutchinson.

La Combe, M. (1784), *Observations sur Londres et ses environs avec un précis de la constitution de l'Angleterre et de sa décadence (La vérité offense les méchans et les sots)*, Londres, Société typographique.

Lacour-Gayet, Georges (1902), *La marine militaire de la France sous le règne de Louis XV*, Paris, H. Champion.

Lacour-Gayet, Georges (1905), *La marine militaire de la France sous le règne de Louis XVI*, Paris, H. Champion.

Lacouture, Jean (1977), *Léon Blum*, Paris, Seuil.

Lacouture, Jean (1984), *De Gaulle*, 3 vols., Paris, Seuil.

Lacouture, Jean (1990), *De Gaulle*, 2 vols. London, HarperCollins.

Lamartine, Alphonse de (1870), *History of the French Revolution of 1848*, London, Bell & Daldy.

Lancashire, Ian (2005), 'Dictionaries and power from Palgrave to Johnson', in Lynch, Jack, and McDermott, Anne, eds., *Anniversary Essays on Johnson's Dictionary*, Cambridge, Cambridge University Press.

Landes, David S. (1969), *The Unbound Prometheus*, Cambridge, Cambridge University Press.

Landes, David S. (2000), *Revolution in Time*, London, Viking.

Lanfranchi, Pierre, and Wahl, Alfred (1998), 'La professionnalisation du football en France (1920–1939)', *Modern and Contemporary France*, 6, pp. 313–26.

Langford, Paul (2000), *Englishness Identified: Manners and Character, 1650–1850*, Oxford, Oxford University Press.

Langlade, Jacques de (1994), *La mésentente cordiale: Wilde – Dreyfus*, Paris, Julliard.

Lansbury, George (1938), *My Quest for Peace*, London, Michael Joseph.

Larcan, Alain (2003), *De Gaulle inventaire: la culture, l'esprit, la foi*, Paris, Bartillat.

Largeaud, J.-M. (2000), 'Waterloo dans la mémoire des Français (1815–1914)', 3 vols., doctoral thesis, Université Lumière Lyon II.

La Rochefoucauld, François de (1933), *A Frenchman in England, 1784: being the Mélanges sur l'Angleterre of François de La Rochefoucauld*, ed. Jean Marchand, Cambridge, Cambridge University Press.

Las Cases, Emmanuel de (1968), *Mémorial de Sainte-Hélène*, 2 vols., Paris, Seuil.

Lasterle, Philippe (2000), 'Marcel Gensoul (1880–1973), un amiral dans la tourmente', *Revue Historique des Armées*, 219, pp. 71–91.

Lawlor, Mary (1959), *Alexis de Tocqueville in the Chamber of Deputies: His Views on Foreign and Colonial Policy*, Washington, Catholic University of America Press.

Le Blanc, Jean-Bernard (1751), *Lettres de Monsieur l'Abbé Le Blanc, historiographe des bastiments du Roi*, Amsterdam.

Le Blanc, Jean-Bernard (1745), *Lettres d'un François*, The Hague, J. Neaulme.

Leclerc, Yvan (1991), *Crimes écrits: la littérature en procès au XIXe siècle*, Paris, Plon.

Ledru-Rollin, Alexandre Auguste (1850), *The Decline of England*, 2 vols., London, E. Churton.

Lees, Lynn (1973), 'Metropolitan types: London and Paris compared', in H.J. Dyos and Michael Wolff, *The Victorian City: Images and Realities*, vol. 1, London, Routledge.

Lefebvre, Georges (1962), *The French Revolution from Its Origins to 1793*, London, Routledge & Kegan Paul.

Lemoinne, John (1867), 'La colonie anglaise', in *Paris Guide par les principaux érivains et artistes de la France*, 2 vols., Paris, Lacroix, Verboeckhoven.

Lemonnier, Bertrand (2004), 'La culture pop britannique dans la France des années 60, entre rejet et fascination', in Laurent Bonnaud, ed., *France–Angleterre: un siècle d'entente cordiale*.

Lenman, Bruce (1992), *The Jacobite Cause*, Edinburgh, Chambers.

Lenman, Bruce (1998), 'Colonial wars and imperial instability, 1688–1793', in *OHBE*, vol. 1.

Lenman, Bruce (2001), *Britain's Colonial Wars 1688–1783*, Harlow, Longman.

Lenoir, Marion (2002), 'Regards croisés: la représentation des nations dans la caricature, Allemagne, France, Royaume-Uni, 1870–1914', *maîtrise* dissertation, Université de Bourgogne.

Lentin, Anthony (2000), 'Lloyd George, Clemenceau and the elusive Anglo-French guarantee treaty, 1919: a disastrous episode?' in Alan Sharp and Glyn Stone, eds., *Anglo-French Relations in the Twentieth Century: Rivalry and Cooperation*, London, Routledge.

Lentin, Anthony (2001), *Lloyd George and the Lost Peace: From Versailles to Hitler*, London, Palgrave.

Léribault, Christophe (1994), *Les Anglais à Paris au 19ᵉ siècle*, Paris, Editions des Musées de la Ville de Paris.

Leroy, Géraldi, and Bertrand-Sabiani, Julie (1998), *La vie littéraire à la Belle Epoque*, Paris, Presses Universitaires de France.

Lever, Evelyne (1996), *Philippe Egalité*, Paris, Fayard.

Levillain, Charles-Edouard (2004), 'Ruled Britannia? Le problème de l'influence française en Grande-Bretagne dans la seconde moitié du XVIIe siècle', in Laurent Bonnaud, ed., *France–Angleterre: un siècle d'entente cordiale*.

Lewis, Cecil (1936), *Sagittarius Rising*, London, Davies.

Lewis, Michael (1960), *A Social History of the Navy 1793–1815*, London, Allen & Unwin.

Lewis, Michael (1962), *Napoleon and His British Captives*, London, Allen & Unwin.

Lindert, Peter H. (2004), *Growing Public: Social Spending and Economic Growth since the Eighteenth Century*, Cambridge, Cambridge University Press.

Linton, Marisa (2001), *The Politics of Virtue in Enlightenment France*, London, Palgrave.

Llewellyn-Jones, Rosie (1992), *A Very Ingenious Man: Claude Martin in Early Colonial India*, Oxford, Oxford University Press.

Lochnan, Katharine, ed. (2004), *Turner, Whistler, Monet*, London, Tate Publishing.

Longford, Elizabeth (1969), *Wellington*, 2 vols., London, Weidenfeld & Nicolson.

Longmate, Norman (2001), *Island Fortress: The Defence of Great Britain 1603–1945*, London, Pimlico.

Louis, Wm Roger, and Owen., R., eds. (1989), *Suez 1956: The Crisis and Its Consequences*, Oxford, Clarendon.

Lovie, J., and Palluel-Guillard, A. (1972), *L'Episode napoléonien*, Paris, Seuil.

Lowry, Donal, ed. (2000), *The South African War Reappraised*, Manchester, Manchester Univeristy Press.

Lucas, William (1754), *A Five Weeks' Tour to Paris, Versailles, Marli &c.*, London, T. Waller.

Ludendorff, Erich von (n.d.), *My War Memoirs*, 2 vols., London, Hutchinson.

Lukacs, John (1976), *The Last European War, September 1939–December 1941*, London, Routledge.

Lüthy, Herbert (1959), *La Banque protestante en France de la révocation de l'Edit de Nantes à la Révolution*, 2 vols., Paris, SEVPEN.

Lyautey, Pierre (1940), *Soldats et marins britanniques*, Paris, Plon.

Lynn, John A. (1989), 'Toward an army of honor: the moral evolution of the French army, 1789–1815', *French Historical Studies*, 16, pp. 152–73.

Lynn, John A. (1999), *The Wars of Louis XIV 1667–1714*, London and New York, Longman.

Macdonald, Janet (2004), *Feeding Nelson's Navy: The True Story of Food at Sea in the Georgian Era*, London, Chatham.

Macdonald, Lyn (1983), *Somme*, London, Michael Joseph.

Macdonald, Lyn (1989), *1914*, London, Penguin.

Macintyre, Ben (2001), *A Foreign Field: A True Story of Love and Betrayal in the Great War*, London, HarperCollins.

Mackenzie, William (2000), *The Secret History of SOE*, London, St Ermin's Press.

Mackesy, Piers (1964), *The War for America, 1775–1783*, London, Longman.

Mackesy, Piers (1984), *War without Victory: The Downfall of Pitt, 1799–1802*, Oxford, Clarendon Press.

Mackesy, Piers (1989), 'Strategic problems of the British war effort', in Dickinson, *Britain and the French Revolution*.

Macleod, Emma Vincent (1998), *A War of Ideas: British Attitudes to the Wars against Revolutionary France, 1792–1802*, Aldershot, Ashgate.

MacMillan, Margaret (2001), *Peacemakers: The Paris Conference of 1919 and Its Attempt to End War*, London, John Murray.

Macnab, Roy (1975), *The French Colonel: Villebois-Mareuil and the Boers, 1899–1900*, Oxford, Oxford University Press.

Magenheimer, Heinz (1998), *Hitler's War: German Military Strategy, 1940–1945*, London, Arms and Armour.

Maier, Charles B. (1975), *Recasting Bourgeois Europe: Stabilization in France, Germany and Italy in the Decade after the First World War*, Princeton, Princeton University Press

Maingueneau, Dominique (1979), *Les livres d'école de la République, 1870–1914*, Paris, Sycomore.

Mallett, Donald (1979), *The Greatest Collector: Lord Hertford and the Founding of the Wallace Collection*, London, Macmillan.

Manceron, Claude (1977), *The Men of Liberty*, London, Eyre Methuen.

Manceron, Claude (1979), *The Wind from America, 1778–1781*, London, Eyre Methuen.

Mangold, Peter (2001), *Success and Failure in British Foreign Policy: Evaluating the Record, 1900–2000*, London, Palgrave.

Manning, Catherine (1996), *Fortunes à Faire: The French in Asian Trade, 1719–48*, Aldershot, Variorium.

Mansel, Philip (1981), *Louis XVIII*, London, Blond & Briggs.

Mansel, Philip (2001), *Paris between Empires, 1814–1852*, London, John Murray.

Mantoux, Etienne (1946), *The Carthaginian Peace, or The Economic Consequences of Mr Keynes*, Oxford, Oxford University Press.

Marandon, Sylvaine (1967), *L'Image de la France dans l'Angleterre Victorienne*, Paris, Armand Colin.

Marchand, Bernard (1993), *Paris, Histoire d'une ville (XIXe–XXe siècle)*, Paris, Seuil.

Marder, Arthur J. (1974), *From the Dardanelles to Oran: Studies of the Royal Navy in War and Peace*, Oxford, Oxford University Press.

Marks, Leo (1999), *Between Silk and Cyanide: A Codemaker's War, 1941–1945*, London, HarperCollins.

Marks, Sally (1998), 'Smoke and mirrors: in smoke-filled rooms and the Galerie des Glaces', in Manfred F. Boemeke et al., *The Treaty of Versailles: A Reassessment after 75 Years*, Cambridge, Cambridge University Press.

Marly, Diana De (1980), *Worth: Father of Haute Couture*, London, Elm Tree Books.

Marsh, Peter T. (1999), *Bargaining on Europe: Britain and the First Common Market, 1860–1982*, New Haven and London, Yale University Press.

Marshall, P.J. (2005), *The Making and Unmaking of Empires: Britain, India and America c. 1750–1783*, Oxford, Oxford University Press.

Martel, Gordon (1998), 'A Comment', in Manfred Boemeke et al., *The Treaty of Versailles: A Reassessment after 75 Years*, Cambridge, Cambridge University Press.

Martin, Andy (2000), *Napoleon the Novelist*, Cambridge, Polity.

Martin, Jean-Clément (1987), *La Vendée et la France*, Paris, Seuil.

Martin-Fugier, Anne (1990), *La Vie élégante, ou la formation du Tout-Paris, 1815–1848*, Paris, Fayard.

Martinez, Paul (1981), 'Paris Communard refugees in Britain, 1871–1880', 2 vols., University of Sheffield PhD.

Maupassant, Guy de (1984), *Boule de Suif*, Paris, Albin Michel.

Maxwell, Constantia (1932), *The English Traveller in France, 1698–1815*, London, Routledge.

May, Ernest R. (2000), *Strange Victory: Hitler's Conquest of France*, London, I.B. Tauris.

Mayne, Richard et al., eds. (2004), *Cross Channel Currents: 100 Years of the Entente Cordiale*, London, Routledge.

Mayo, Katherine (1938), *General Washington's Dilemma*, London, Jonathan Cape.

McCalman, Iain (1998), *Radical Underworld: Prophets, Revolutionaries, and Pornographers in London, 1795–1840*, Oxford, Clarendon Press.

McCarthy, William (1985), *Hester Thrale Piozzi: Portrait of a Literary Woman*, Chapel Hill NC, University of North Carolina Press.

McIntyre, Ian (2000), *Garrick*, London, Penguin.

McKay, Derek, and Scott, H.M. (1983), *The Rise of the Great Powers 1648–1815*, London and New York, Longman.

McLynn, Frank (1981), *France and the Jacobite Rising of 1745*, Edinburgh, Edinburgh University Press.

McLynn, Frank (1987), *Invasion from the Armada to Hitler, 1588–1945*, London, Routledge.

McLynn, Frank (1997), *Napoleon: a biography* London, Jonathan Cape.

McLynn, Frank (1998), *The Jacobite Army in England 1745*, Edinburgh, John Donald.

McLynn, Frank (2005), *1759: The Year Britain Became Master of the World*, London, Pimlico.

McPhail, Helen (1999), *The Long Silence: Civilian Life under the German Occupation of Northern France, 1914–1918*, London, I.B. Tauris.

McPherson, James M. (1988), *Battle Cry of Freedom*, New York, Ballantine.

Mehta, Uday Singh (1999), *Liberalism and Empire: A Study in Nineteenth-Century British Liberal Thought*, Chicago, University of Chicago Press.

Mennell, Stephen (1985), *All Manners of Food: Eating and Taste in England and France from the Middle Ages to the Present*, Oxford, Blackwell.

Mercier, Louis Sébastien (1928), *The Picture of Paris before and after the Revolution*, London, Routledge.

Mercier, Louis Sébastien (1933), *The Waiting City, Paris 1782–88*, London, Harrap.

Mervaud, Christiane (1992), 'Des relations de voyage au mythe anglais des Lettres philosophiques', *Studies on Voltaire and the Eighteenth Century*, 296, pp. 1–15.

Meyer, Jean, and Acerra, Martine (1994), *Histoire de la Marine Française*, Rennes, Editions Ouest-France.

Meyer, Jean, Tarrade, Jean, and Rey-Goldzeiguer, Annie (1991), *Histoire de la France coloniale vol. 1 La conquête*, Paris, Armand Colin.

Michelet, Jules (1946), *Le Peuple*, Paris, Calmann-Lévy.

Middleton, Richard (1985), *The Bells of Victory: The Pitt-Newcastle Ministry and the Conduct of the Seven Years' War, 1757–1762*, Cambridge, Cambridge University Press.

Mierzejewski, Alfred C. (2004), *Ludwig Erhard: A Biography*, Chapel Hill, NC, and London, University of North Carolina Press.

Migliorini, Pierre, and Quatre Vieux, Jean (2002), *Batailles de Napoléon dans le Sud-Ouest*, Biarritz, Atlantica.

Miller, John (1978), *James II, a Study in Kingship*, Hove, Wayland.

Millman, Richard (1965), *British Foreign Policy and the Coming of the Franco-Prussian War*, Oxford, Clarendon Press.

Milward, Alan S. (1992), *The European Rescue of the Nation-State*, London, Routledge.

Milward, Alan S. (2002), *The UK and the European Community, vol. 1, The Rise and Fall of a National Strategy, 1945–1963*, London, Frank Cass.

Mintz, Max M. (1999), *Seeds of Empire: the American Revolutionary Conquest of the Iroquois*, New York and London, New York University Press.

Mitchell, B.R. and Deane, Phyllis (1962), *Abstract of British Historical Statistics*, Cambridge, Cambridge University Press.

Mitchell, Harvey (1965), *The Underground War against Revolutionary France: The Missions of William Wickham, 1794–1800*, Oxford, Clarendon Press.

Monaco, Maria (1974), *Shakespeare on the French Stage in the Eighteenth Century*, Paris, Didier.

Monod, Paul Kléber (1993), *Jacobitism and the English People, 1688–1788*, Cambridge, Cambridge University Press.

Moore, Christopher (1994), *The Loyalists: Revolution, Exile, Settlement*, Toronto. McClelland & Stewart.

Moore, George (1972), *Confessions of a Young Man*, ed. Susan Dick, Montreal, McGill-Queens University Press.

Mori, Jennifer (1997), 'The British government and the Bourbon restoration: the occupation of Toulon, 1793', *Historical Journal*, 40, pp. 699–720.

Mori, Jennifer (2000), *Britain in the Age of the French Revolution 1785–1820*, London, Longman.

Morieux, Renaud (2006), '"An inundation from our shores": travelling across the Channel around the Peace of Amiens', in Mark Philip, ed., *Resisting Napoleon: The British Response to the Threat of Invasion, 1797–1815*, Aldershot, Ashgate.

Mornet, Daniel (1910), 'Les enseignements des bibliothèques privées, 1750–1780', *Revue d'Histoire Littéraire de la France*, pp. 458–62.

Mornet, Daniel (1967), *Les Origines Intellectuelles de la Révolution Française 1715–1787*, Paris, Librairie Armand Colin.

Morrill, John (1991), 'The sensible revolution', in Jonathan Israel, ed., *The Anglo-Dutch Moment*.

Morris, A.J.A. (1984), *The Scaremongers*, London, Routledge & Kegan Paul.

Morriss, R. (2000), 'British Maritime Supremacy in 1800: Causes and Consequences', *Napoleonic Review*, 1–2, pp. 193–201.

Morse, Ruth (2002), 'I will tell thee in French: Pléiade's parallel-text Shakespeare', *Times Literary Supplement* (9 August. 2002), pp. 4–5.

Mossner, E.C. (1980), *The Life of David Hume*, Oxford, Clarendon Press.

Muggeridge, Malcolm (1973), *Chronicles of Wasted Time*, 2 vols., London, Collins.

Muir, Rory (2001), *Salamanca 1812*, New Haven and London, Yale University Press.

Murphy, Orville T. (1982), *Charles Gravier, Comte de Vergennes: French Diplomacy in the Age of Revolution, 1719–1787*, Albany, State University of New York Press.

Murphy, Orville T. (1998), *The Diplomatic Retreat of France and Public Opinion on the Eve of the French Revolution, 1783–1789*, Washington, Catholic University of America Press.

Mysyrowicz, Ladislas (1973), *Autopsie d'une défaite: origines de l'effondrement militaire français de 1940*, Lausanne, L'Age d'Homme.

Napoleon (1858–69), *Correspondance de Napoléon Ier*, 32 vols., Paris, Imprimerie Impériale.

Naughtie, James (2005), *The Accidental American: Tony Blair and the Presidency*, London, Pan.

Navailles, Jean-Pierre (1987), *Le Tunnel sous la Manche: deux siècles pour sauter le pas, 1802–1987*, Seyssel, Champ Vallon.

Neave, Airey (1969), *Saturday at MI9: A History of Underground Escape Lines in North-West Europe in 1940–5*, London, Hodder & Stoughton.

Neillands, Robin (1999), *The Great War Generals on the Western Front 1914–18*, London, Robinson.

Newman, Gerald (1997), *The Rise of English Nationalism: A Cultural History, 1740–1830*, London, Macmillan.

Newnham-Davis, Lieut.-Col. N., and Bastard, Algernon (1903), *The Gourmet's Guide to Europe*, London, Grant Richards.

Newsome, David (1998), *The Victorian World Picture: Perceptions and Introspections in an Age of Change*, London, Fontana.

Nicolet, Claude (1982), *L'Idée républicaine en France (1789–1924)*, Paris, Gallimard.

Nicolson, Harold (1980), *Diaries and Letters 1930–1964*, ed. S. Olsen, London, Collins.

Noblett, W.A. (1996), `Propaganda from World War II', *Bulletin of the Friends of Cambridge University Library*, no. 17, pp. 22–5.

Noon, Patrick, ed. (2003), *Constable to Delacroix: British Art and the French Romantics*, London, Tate Publishing.

Nora, Pierre, ed. (1984), *Les Lieux de mémoire*, 3 vols., Paris, Gallimard.

North, Douglas C., and Weingast, Barry R. (1989), 'Constitutions and commitment: the evolution of institutions governing public choice in seventeenth-century England', *Journal of Economic History*, 49, pp. 803–32.

Nosworthy, Brent (1995), *Battle Tactics of Napoleon and His Enemies*, London, Constable.

Nott, John (2002), *Here Today, Gone Tomorrow: Recollections of an Errant Politician*, London, Pimlico.

Ó Ciardha, Eamonn (2002), *Ireland and the Jacobite Cause, 1685–1766*, Dublin, Four Courts Press.

O'Brien, R. Barry (1901), *The Life of Lord Russell of Killowen*, London, Smith, Elder.

O'Gorman, F. (1967), *The Whig Party and the French Revolution*, London, Macmillan.

O'Neill, Con (2000), *Britain's Entry into the European Community: Report by Sir Con O'Neill on the Negotiations of 1970–1972*, ed. D. Hannay, London, Frank Cass.

Occleshaw, Michael (1989), *Armour against Fate: British Military Intelligence in the First World War*, London, Columbus Books.

Ogg, David (1947), *Herbert Fisher, 1865–1940: A Short Biography*, London, Arnold.

Olsen, Donald J. (1976), *The Growth of Victorian London*, London, Batsford.

Olsen, Donald J. (1986), *The City as a Work of Art: London, Paris, Vienna*, New Haven and London, Yale University Press.

Ormesson, François d', and Thomas, Jean-Pierre (2002), *Jean-Joseph de Laborde: Banquier de Louis XV, mécène des Lumières*, Paris, Perrin.

Orpen, William (1921), *An Onlooker in France, 1917–1919*, London, Williams & Norgate.

Ostler, N. (2005), *Empires of the Word: A Language History of the World*, London, HarperCollins.

Ottis, S. G. (2001), *Silent Heroes: Downed Airmen and the French Underground*, University Press of Kentucky.

Ousby, Ian (2002), *The Road to Verdun: France, Nationalism and the First World War*, London, Jonathan Cape.

Ozanam, Denise (1969), *Claude Baudard de Sainte-James*, Genève, Librairie Droz.

Packe, Michael (1957), *The Bombs of Orsini*, London, Smith, Elder.

Padfield, Peter (1973), *Guns at Sea*, London, Hugh Evelyn.

Padfield, Peter (2000), *Maritime Supremacy and the Opening of the Western Mind*, London, Pimlico.

Paine, Thomas (1989), *Political Writings*, ed. Bruce Kuklick, Cambridge, Cambridge University Press.

Pakula, Hannah (1996), *An Uncommon Woman: The Empress Frederick*, London, Phoenix Giant.

Pappas, John (1997), 'La campagne de Voltaire contre Shakespeare', in Ulla Kölving and Christian Mervaud, eds., *Voltaire et ses combats*, vol. 1.

Parker, R.A.C. (2000), *Churchill and Appeasement*, London, Macmillan.

Parr, Helen (2005), *British Policy towards the European Community: Harold Wilson and Britain's World Role, 1964–67*, London, Routledge.

Parry, Jonathan P. (2001), 'The impact of Napoleon III on British politics, 1851–1880', *Transactions of the Royal Historical Society*, 11, pp. 147–75.

Pasquet, D. (1920), 'La découverte de l'Angleterre par les Français au XVIIIe siècle', *Revue de Paris* (15 Dec. 1920).

Passerini, Louisa (1999), *Europe in Love, Love in Europe: Imagination and Politics in Britain between the Wars*, London, I.B. Tauris.

Passy, Colonel [André Dewavrin] (1947), *Souvenirs*, vols. 1 and 2, Monte Carlo, R. Solar; vol. 3, Paris, Plon.

Patterson, A. Temple (1960), *The Other Armada: The Franco-Spanish Attempt to Invade Britain in 1779*, Manchester, Manchester University Press.

Pemble, John (2005), *Shakespeare Goes to Paris: How the Bard Conquered France*, London, Hambledon & London.

Perrod, Pierre Antoine (1976), *L'Affaire Lally-Tolendal: une erreur judiciaire au XVIIIe siècle*, Paris, Klincksieck.

Peters, Marie (1980), *Pitt and Popularity*, Oxford, Clarendon.

Peters, Marie (1998), *The Elder Pitt*, London, Addison Wesley Longman.

Petiteau, Natalie (1999), *Napoléon de la Mythologie à l'Histoire*, Paris, Seuil.

Petitfils, Jean-Christian (1995), *Louis XIV*, Paris, Perrin.

Peyrefitte, Alain (1994), *C'Etait de Gaulle*, 2 vols., Paris, Fayard.

Philpott, William (1996), *Anglo-French Relations and Strategy on the Western Front, 1914–18*, London, Macmillan.

Philpott, William (2002), 'Why the British were really on the Somme: a reply to Elizabeth Greenhalgh', *War in History*, 9, pp. 446–71.

Pick, Daniel (1989), *Faces of Degeneration: A European Disorder, c. 1848–c.1918*, Cambridge, Cambridge University Press.

Pilbeam, Pamela (1991), *The 1830 Revolution in France*, London, Macmillan.

Pilbeam, Pamela (2003), *Madame Tussaud and the History of Waxworks*, London and New York, Hambledon & London.

Pincus, Steven (1995), 'From butterboxes to wooden shoes: the shift in English popular sentiment from anti-Dutch to anti-French in the 1670s', *Historical Journal*, 38, pp. 333–61.

Pineau, Christian (1976), *1956: Suez*, Paris, Robert Laffont.

Pitt, Alan (1998), 'The irrationalist liberalism of Hippolyte Taine', *Historical Journal*, 41, pp. 1035–53.

Pitt, Alan (2000), 'A changing Anglo-Saxon myth: its development and function in French political thought, 1860–1914', *French History*, 14, pp. 150–73.

Pitt, William (n.d.), *Orations on the French War, to the Peace of Amiens*, London, J.M. Dent.

Pitte, Jean-Robert (1991), *Gastronomie française: histoire et géographie d'une passion*, Paris, Fayard.

Pitts, Jennifer (2005), *A Turn to Empire: The Rise of Liberal Imperialism in Britain and France*, Princeton, Princeton University Press.

Plaisant, Michel (1976), *L'Excentricité en Grande-Bretagne au 18e siècle*, Lille, Publications de l'Université de Lille III.

Plaisant, Michel, and Parreaux, André, eds. (1977), *Jardins et Paysages: Le Style Anglais*, 2 vols., Lille, Publications de l'Université de Lille III.

Plank, Geoffrey (2001), *An Unsettled Conquest: The British Campaign against the Peoples of Acadia*, Philadelphia, University of Pennsylvania Press.

Pluchon, Pierre (1996), *Histoire de la Colonisation Française: des origines à la Restauration*, Paris, Fayard.

Pocock, J.G.A. (1985), *Virtue, Commerce, and History: Essays on Political Thought and History*, Cambridge, Cambridge University Press, 1985.

Pocock, J.G.A. (1999), *Barbarism and Religion* vol. 1, *The Enlightenments of Edward Gibbon, 1737–1764*, Cambridge, Cambridge University Press.

Pocock, J.G.A. (2005), *The Discovery of Islands: Essays in British History*, Cambridge, Cambridge University Press.

Poirier, Jean-Pierre (1999), *Turgot: laissez-faire et progrès social*, Paris, Perrin.

Pomeau, René (1979), 'Les Lettres Philosophiques: le projet de Voltaire', in *Voltaire and the English: Studies on Voltaire and the Eighteenth Century*, no. 179, Oxford, Voltaire Foundation.

Pomeau, René (1991), *L'Europe des Lumières: Cosmopolitisme et unité européenne au XVIIIe siècle*, Paris, Stock.

Porter, Bernard (1979), *The Refugee Question in Mid-Victorian Politics*, Cambridge, Cambridge University Press.

Porter, Roy (2000), *Enlightenment: Britain and the Creation of the Modern World*, London, Allen Lane.

Poumiès de La Siboutie, François Louis (1911), *Recollections of a Parisian Doctor under Six Sovereigns, Two Revolutions, and a Republic (1789–1863)* London, John Murray.

Prados de la Escosura, Leandro, ed. (2004), *Exceptionalism and Industrialisation: Britain and Its European Rivals, 1688–1815*, Cambridge, Cambridge University Press.

Price, Munro (1995), *Preserving the Monarchy: The Comte de Vergennes, 1774–1787*, Cambridge, Cambridge University Press.

Price, Munro (1995b), 'The Dutch affair and the fall of the ancien régime, 1784–1787', *Historical Journal*, 38, pp. 875–905.

Prior, Robin and Wilson, Trevor (2005), *The Somme*, London, Yale University Press.

Quimby, Robert S. (1957), *The Background of Napoleonic Warfare: The Theory of Military Tactics in Eighteenth-Century France*, New York, Columbia University Press.

Quinault, Roland (1999), 'The French invasion of Pembrokeshire in 1797: a bicentennial assessment', *Welsh History Review*, 19, pp. 618–41.

Radisich, Paula Rea (1997), '"La chose publique." Hubert Robert's decorations for the "petit salon" at Méréville', in Ann Bermingham and John Brewer, eds., *The Consumption of Culture 1600–1800*.

Ramm, Agatha, ed. (1952), *The Political Correspondence of Mr Gladstone and Lord Granville, 1868–1876*, London, Royal Historical Society.

Rapport, Michael (2000), *Nationality and Citizenship in Revolutionary France: The Treatment of Foreigners, 1789–1799*, Oxford, Clarendon Press.

Rauser, Amelia (2004), 'Hair, authenticity and the self-made Macaroni', *Eighteenth-Century Studies*, 38, pp. 101–17.

Raymond, Dora N. (1921), *British Policy and Opinion during the Franco-Prussian War*, New York, Columbia University Press.

Rearick, Charles (1997), *The French in Love and War: Popular Culture in the Era of the World Wars*, New Haven and London, Yale University Press.

Réau, Elisabeth du (1993), *Edouard Daladier 1884–1970*, Paris, Fayard.

Réau, Elisabeth du (2001), *L'Idée d'Europe au XXe siècle*, Brussels, Complexe.

Reddy, William M. (2001), *The Navigation of Feeling: A Framework of the History of Emotions*, Cambridge, Cambridge University Press.

Regenbogen, Lucian (1998), *Napoléon a dit*, Paris, Les Belles Lettres.

Reitlinger, Gerald (1961), *The Economics of Taste*, 2 vols., London, Barne & Rockliff.

Rendall, Matthew (2004), '"The Sparta and the Athens of our Age at Daggers Drawn": Politics, Perceptions, and Peace', *International Politics*, 41, pp. 582–604.

Répertoire (1818), *Répertoire générale du théâtre français*, 67 vols., Paris, Petitot.

Reynolds, David (1991), *Britannia Overruled: British Policy and World Power in the Twentieth Century*, London, Longman.

Reynolds, David (2004), *In Command of History: Churchill Fighting and Writing the Second World War*, London, Allen Lane.

Reynolds, Siân (2000), `Running away to Paris: expatriate women artists of the 1900 generation, from Scotland and points south', *Women's History Review*, 9, pp. 327–44.

Ribeiro, Aileen (1983), *A Visual History of Costume: The Eighteenth Century*, London, Batsford.

Richards, Denis (1974), *Royal Air Force, 1939–1945, vol. 1: The Fight at Odds*, London, HMSO.

Richey, Paul (1980), *Fighter Pilot: A Personal Record of the Campaign in France, 1939–1940*, London, Jane's Publishing Co.

Rioux, Jean-Pierre, and Sirinelli, Jean-François (1998), *Histoire culturelle de la France, vol. 4, Le Temps des masses*, Paris, Seuil.

Rivarol, Antoine (1998), *L'Universalité de la langue française*, ed. Jean Dutourd, Paris, Arléa.

Robb, Graham (1997), *Victor Hugo*, London, Picador.

Robb, Graham (2000), *Rimbaud*, London, Picador.

Roberts, Andrew (2001), *Napoleon and Wellington*, London, Phoenix Press.

Roberts, J.M. (1973), 'The Paris Commune from the Right', *English Historical Review*, supplement 6.

Roberts, John L. (2002), *The Jacobite Wars: Scotland and the Military Campaigns of 1715 and 1745*, Edinburgh, Polygon.

Robespierre, Maximilien (1967), *Oeuvres de Maximilien Robespierre*, Bouloiseau, Marc, and Soboul, Albert, eds., 10 vols., Nancy, Société des Etudes Robespierristes.

Robson, John, ed., (2004), *The Captain Cook Encyclopedia*, London, Chatham.

Roche, Daniel (1993), *La France des Lumières*, Paris, Fayard.

Roche, Daniel, ed. (2001), *Almanach parisien: en faveur des étrangers et des personnes curieuses*, Saint-Etienne, Publications de l'Université de Saint-Etienne.

Rocolle, Pierre (1990), *La guerre de 1940*, 2 vols., Paris, Armand Colin.

Rodger, N.A.M. (1988), *The Wooden World*, London, Fontana.

Rodger, N.A.M. (2004), *The Command of the Ocean*, London, Allen Lane.

Roger, Philippe (2002), *L'Ennemi américain: généalogie de l'antiaméricanisme français*, Paris, Seuil.

Rogers, Nicholas (1998), *Crowds, Culture and Politics in Georgian Britain*, Oxford, Clarendon Press.

Rogers, Nicholas (2004), 'Brave Wolfe: the making of a hero', in Kathleen Wilson, ed., *A New Imperial History: Culture, Identity and Modernity in Britain and the Empire, 1660–1840*, Cambridge, Cambridge University Press.

Rosanvallon, Pierre (1985), *Le moment Guizot*, Paris, Gallimard.

Rosanvallon, Pierre (1994), *La Monarchie Impossible*, Paris, Fayard.

Rose, Craig (1999), *England in the 1690s: Revolution, Religion and War*, Oxford, Blackwell.

Rose, John Holland (1911), *Life of William Pitt*, 2 vols., London, G. Bell

Rose, R. B. (1960), 'The Priestley riots of 1791', *Past and Present*, 18, pp. 68–88.

Ross, George (1995), *Jacques Delors and European Integration*, Cambridge, Polity Press.

Ross, Ian Simpson (1995), *The Life of Adam Smith*, Oxford, Clarendon Press.

Rothenstein, William (1931), *Men and Memories, 1872–1900*, 3 vols., London, Faber and Faber.

Rothschild, Emma (2001), *Economic Sentiments: Adam Smith, Condorcet, and the Enlightenment*, Cambridge, Mass., Harvard University Press.

Rothschild, Emma (2002), 'The English Kopf', in Donald Winch and Patrick K. O'Brien, eds., *The Political Economy of British Historical Experience, 1688–1914*, Oxford, Oxford University Press.

Roudaut, Christian (2004), *L'Entente glaciale: Français–Anglais, les raisons de la discorde*, Paris, Alban.

Rougerie, Jacques (1971), *Paris libre 1871*, Paris, Seuil.

Rounding, Virginia (2003), *Grandes Horizontales: The Lives and Legends of Four Nineteenth-Century Courtesans*, London, Bloomsbury.

Rousseau, A.M. (1979), `Naissance d'un livre et d'un texte', in *Voltaire and the English, Studies on Voltaire and the Eighteenth Century*, no. 179, Oxford, Voltaire Foundation.

Rousseau, Frédéric (2003), *La Guerre censurée*, Paris, Seuil.

Rousseau, Jean-Jacques (1969), *Emile, ou de l'Education*, in *Œuvres Complètes*, eds. B. Gagelin and M. Raymond, Paris, Pléiade.

Rowe, Michael (2003), *From Reich to State: The Rhineland in the Revolutionary Age*, Cambridge, Cambridge University Press.

Sadler, M. (1992), 'Classy customers: the image of the British in French magazine advertising, 1991–2', *Franco-British Studies*, 14, pp. 67–79.

Sahlins, Peter (2004), *Unnaturally French: Foreign Citizens in the Old Regime and After*, Ithaca and London, Cornell University Press.

St Clair, William (1967), *Lord Elgin and the Marbles*, Oxford, Oxford University Press.

Saint-Girons, Baldine (1998), 'Le sublime de Burke et son influence dans l'architecture et l'art des jardins', *Canadian Aesthetics Journal/Revue canadienne d'esthétique*, 2.

Salmond, Anne (2003), *The Trial of the Cannibal Dog: The Remarkable Story of Captain Cook's Encounters in the South Seas*, New Haven and London, Yale University Press.

Sanderson, Claire (2003), *L'impossible alliance? France, Grande-Bretagne et défense de l'Europe (1945–1958)*, Paris, Sorbonne.

Sareil, Jean (1969), *Les Tencin: histoire d'une famille au dix-huitième siècle*, Geneva, Droz.

Sargent, T.J. and Velde, F.R. (1995), 'Macroeconomic Features of the French Revolution', *Journal of Political Economy*, 103, pp. 474–518.

Saunders, Andrew (1997), *Channel Defences*, London, Batsford.

Saville, John (1987), *1848: The British State and the Chartist Movement*, Cambridge, Cambridge University Press.

Scarfe, Norman (1995), *Innocent Espionage: The La Rochefoucauld Brothers' Tour of England in 1785*, Woodbridge, Boydell Press.

Schaad, Martin P. C. (2002), 'Bonn between London and Paris', in Jeremy Noakes et al., eds., *Britain and Germany in Europe 1949–1990*, Oxford, Oxford University Press.

Schama, Simon (1989), *Citizens: A Chronicle of the French Revolution*, London, Viking.

Schama, Simon (2005), *Rough Crossings: Britain, the Slaves and the American Revolution*, London, BBC Books.

Scheck, Raffael (2005), '"They are just savages": German massacres of Black soldiers in the French army in 1940', *Journal of Modern History*, 77, pp. 325–44.

Schom, Alan (1987), *Emile Zola: A Bourgeois Rebel*, London, Macdonald.

Schroeder, Paul W. (1994), *The Transformation of European Politics 1763–1848*, Oxford, Clarendon Press.

Scott, H.M. (1990), *British Foreign Policy in the Age of the American Revolution*, Oxford, Clarendon Press.

Scott, H.M. (1992), 'The second "hundred years war", 1689–1815', *Historical Journal*, 35, pp. 443–469.

Scott, Jonathan (2000), *England's Troubles: Seventeenth-Century English Political Instability in European Context*, Cambridge, Cambridge University Press.

Semmel, Stuart (2004), *Napoleon and the British*, New Haven and London, Yale University Press.

Serman, William, and Bertaud, Jean-Paul (1998), *Nouvelle Histoire Militaire de la France 1789–1919*, Paris, Fayard.

Shackleton, Robert (1961), *Montesquieu: A Critical Biography*, Oxford, Oxford University Press.

Sharp, Alan, and Stone, Glyn, eds. (2000), *Anglo-French Relations in the Twentieth Century*, London, Routledge.

Shawcross, William (2003), *Allies: The United States, Britain, Europe and the War in Iraq*, London, Atlantic Books.

Sheffield, Gary (2001), *Forgotten Victory*, London, Review.

Shepherd, John (2002), *George Lansbury: At the Heart of Old Labour*, Oxford University Press.

Sheriff, Mary D. (1997), 'The immodesty of her sex. Elisabeth Vigée-Lebrun and the Salon of 1783', in A. Bermingham and J. Brewer, eds., *The Consumption of Culture 1600–1800*.

Sherwig, John M. (1969), *Guineas and Gunpowder: British Foreign Aid in the Wars with France, 1793–1815*, Cambridge, Mass., Harvard University Press.

Shoemaker, Robert B. (2002), 'The taming of the duel: masculinity, honour and ritual violence in London, 1660–1800', *Historical Journal*, 45, pp. 525–45.

Shore, Cris (2000), *Building Europe: The Cultural Politics of European Integration*, London, Routledge.

Shuker, Stephen A. (1976), *The End of French Predominance in Europe*, Chapel Hill, NC, University of North Carolina Press.

Sieburth, Richard (2005), 'Over to the words: translations from the English and other shimmering Mallarmé', *Times Literary Supplement* (14 Jan. 2005), pp. 3–4.

Siegel, Mona L. (2004), *The Moral Disarmament of France: Education, Pacifism, and Patriotism, 1914–1940*, Cambridge, Cambridge University Press.

Simmons, Sylvie (2001), *Serge Gainsbourg: A Fistful of Gitanes*, London, Helter Skelter.

Simms, Brendan (2003), *Unfinest Hour: Britain and the Destruction of Bosnia*, London, Penguin.

Simms, Brendan (2003b) 'Continental analogies with 1798: revolution or counter-revolution?', in Thomas Bartlett, David Dickson, Daire Keogh and Kevin Whelan, eds., *1798: A Bicentenary Perspective*, Dublin, Four Courts Press.

Simon, Marie (1995), *Mode et peinture: le Second Empire et l'impressionnisme*, Paris, Hazan.

Sirinelli, Jean-François, ed. (1992), *Histoire des droites en France*, 3 vols., Paris, Gallimard.

Sitwell, Osbert (1949), *Laughter in the Next Room: An Autobiography*, London, Macmillan.

Skidelsky, Robert (1983), *John Maynard Keynes: A Biography*, 3 vols., London, Macmillan.

Smith, Adam (1991), *The Wealth of Nations*, 2 vols., London, Everyman.

Smith, Hillas (2001), *The Unknown Frenchman, the Story of Marchand and Fashoda*, Lewes, Book Guild.

Smith, Timothy B. (2004), *France in Crisis: Welfare, Inequality and Globalization since 1980*, Cambridge, Cambridge University Press.

Smollett, Tobias (1999), *Travels through France and Italy*, Oxford, Oxford University Press

Smyth, Jim, ed. (2000), *Revolution, Counter-Revolution and Union: Ireland in the 1790s*, Cambridge, Cambridge University Press.

Sonenscher, Michael (1997), 'The nation's debt and the birth of the modern republic: the French fiscal deficit and the politics of the revolution of 1789', *History of Political Thought*, 18, pp. 64–103 and 266–325.

Sorel, Albert (1969), *Europe and the French Revolution: The Political Traditions of the Old Regime*, ed. and trans. A. Cobban and J.W. Hunt, London, Collins.

Spang, Rebecca L. (2000), *The Invention of the Restaurant: Paris and Modern Gastronomic Culture*, Cambridge, Mass.., Harvard University Press.

Spears, Edward (1954), *Assignment to Catastrophe*, 2 vols., London, William Heinemann.

Spears, Edward (1999), *Liaison 1914*, London, Cassell.

Speck, W. A. (2002), *James II*, London, Longman.

Spencer, Colin (2002), *British Food: An Extraordinary Thousand Years of History*, London, Grub Street Publishing.

Spiers, Edward M., ed. (1998), *Sudan: The Reconquest Reappraised*, London, Frank Cass.

Statistics (1922), *Statistics of the Military Effort of the British Empire during the Great War, 1914–1920*, London, HMSO.

Steele, Valerie (1998), *Paris Fashion: A Cultural History*, Oxford, Berg.

Steiner, Zara S. (1977), *Britain and the Origins of the First World War*, London, Macmillan.

Steiner, Zara S. (2005), *The Lights That Failed: European International History 1919–1933*, Oxford, Oxford University Press.

Stenton, Michael (2000), *Radio London and Resistance in Occupied Europe: British Political Warfare 1939–1943*, Oxford, Oxford University Press.

Stevenson, David (1998), 'France at the Paris peace conference: addressing the dilemmas of security', in Robert Boyce, ed., *French Foreign and Defence Policy: The Decline and Fall of a Great Power*, London, Routledge.

Stevenson, David (2004), *1914–1918: The History of the First World War*, London, Allen Lane.

Stone, Glyn (2000), 'From entente to alliance: Anglo-French relations, 1935–1939', in Sharp, Alan, and Stone, Glyn, eds., *Anglo-French Relations in the Twentieth Century*, London, Routledge.

Stone, Lawrence, ed. (1994), *An Imperial State at War: Britain from 1689 to 1815*, London, Routledge.

Stothard, Peter (2003), *30 Days: A Month at the Heart of Blair's War*, London, HarperCollins.

Strachan, Hew (2001), *The First World War: vol 1: To Arms*, Oxford, Oxford University Press.

Strauss-Kahn, Dominique (2004), *Oui! Lettre ouverte aux enfants d'Europe*, Paris, Grasset.

Styan, David (2004), 'Jacques Chirac's "non": France, Iraq and the United Nations, 1991–2003', *Modern and Contemporary France*, 12, pp. 371–85.

Subramanian, Lakshmi, ed. (1999), *The French East India Company and the Trade of the Indian Ocean: A Collection of Essays by Indrana Ray*, Calcutta, Munshiram Manoharlal.

Swart, Koenraad W. (1964), *The Sense of Decadence in Nineteenth-Century France*, The Hague, Martinus Nijhoff.

Taine, Hippolyte (1903), *Notes sur l'Angleterre*, 12th edn, Paris, Hachette.

Talmon, Jacob L. (1960), *Political Messianism: The Romantic Phase*, New York, Frederick A. Praeger.

Taylor, A.J.P. (1971), *The Struggle for Mastery in Europe, 1848–1918*, Oxford, Oxford University Press.

Taylor, Derek (2003), *Ritzy: British Hotels, 1837–1987*, London, Milman Press.

Taylor, James Stephen (1985), *James Hanway, Founder of the Marine Society: Charity and Policy in Eighteenth-Century England*, London, Scolar.

Taylor, Miles (2000), 'The 1848 revolutions and the British empire', *Past and Present*, 166, pp. 146–80.

Taylor, Patricia (2001), *Thomas Blaikie (1751–1838): The 'Capability' Brown of France*, East Linton, Tuckwell Press.

Terraine, John (1972), *Mons, the Retreat to Victory*, London, Pan.

Thatcher, Margaret (1993), *The Downing Street Years*, London, HarperCollins.

Thicknesse, Philip (1766), *Observations on the customs and manners of the French nation: in a series of letters, in which that nation is vindicated from the misrepresentations of some late writers*, London, Robert Davis.

Thiers, Adolphe (1972), *Histoire du Consulat et de l'Empire*, Paris, Robert Laffont.

Thody, Philip (1995), *Le Franglais: Forbidden English, Forbidden American: Law, Politics and Language in Contemporary France*, London, Athlone Press.

Thomas, Hugh (1997), *The Slave Trade: The History of the Atlantic Slave Trade, 1440–1870*, London, Picador.

Thomas, Martin (1996), *Britain, France and Appeasement*, Oxford, Berg.

Thomas, Martin (1997), 'From Dien Bien Phu to Evian: Anglo-French imperial relations', in Sharp, Alan, and Stone, Glyn, eds. (2000), *Anglo-French Relations in the Twentieth Century*, London, Routledge.

Thompson, Dorothy (1984), *The Chartists*, New York, Pantheon.

Thompson, Neville (1971), *The Anti-Appeasers: Conservative Opposition to Appeasement in the 1930s*, Oxford, Clarendon Press.

Thrasher, Peter Adam (1970), *Pasquale Paoli: An Enlightened Hero, 1725–1807*, London, Constable.

Tillier, Bertrand (2004), *La Commune de Paris, révolution sans images?*, Seyssel, Champ Vallon.

Tombs, Isabelle (2002), 'Scrutinizing France: collecting and using newspaper intelligence during World War II', *Intelligence and National Security*, 17, pp. 105–26.

Tombs, Robert (1998), 'Lesser breeds without the law: the British establishment and the Dreyfus affair, 1894–1899', *Historical Journal*, 41, pp. 495–510.

Torrès, Tereska (2000), *Une Française libre: Journal, 1939–1945*, Paris, Phébus.

Tracy, Louis (1998), *The Final War*, ed. G. Locke, London, Routledge.

Travers, Tim (1990), *The Killing Ground*, London, Unwin Hyman.

Troost, Wout (2005), *William III, the Stadholder-King: A Political Biography*, Aldershot, Ashgate.

Trubek, Amy B. (2000), *Haute Cuisine: How the French Invented the Culinary Profession*, Philadelphia, University of Pennsylvania Press.

Tucoo-Chala, Pierre (1999), *Pau, ville Anglaise*, Pau, Librairie des Pyrénées & de Gascogne.

Tudesq, André-Jean (1964), *Les Grands Notables en France*, 2 vols., Paris, Presses Universitaires de France.

Tulard, Jean (1977), *Napoléon: ou, Le mythe du sauveur*, Paris, Fayard.

Turgot, Anne Robert Jacques (1913), *Oeuvres de Turgot et documents le concernant*, ed. Gustave Schelle, 5 vols., Paris, Alcan.

Turner, Arthur (1998), *The Cost of War: British Policy on French War Debts, 1918–1932*, Brighton, Sussex Academic Press.

Tyson, Moses, and Guppy, Henry, eds. (1932), *The French Journals of Mrs Thrale and Doctor Johnson*, Manchester University Press.

Uglow, Jenny (2002), *The Lunar Men: The Friends Who Made the Future, 1730–1810*, London, Faber and Faber.

Vaïsse, Maurice (1989), 'Post-Suez France', in W.R. Louis and R. Owen, *Suez 1956*.

Vaïsse, Maurice, ed. (2004), *L'Entente cordiale de Fachoda à la Grande Guerre: dans les archives du Quai d'Orsay*, Brussels, Complexe.

Vallès, Jules (1951), *La Rue à Londres*, ed. L. Scheler, Paris, Editeurs français réunis.

Van Kley, Dale K. (1984), *The Damiens Affair and the Unravelling of the Ancien Régime, 1750–1770*, Princeton, Princeton University Press.

Varouxakis, Georgios (2002), *Victorian Political Thought on France and the French*, London, Palgrave.

Vergé-Franceschi, Michel (1996), *La Marine Française au XVIIIe Siècle*, Paris, Sedes.

Veuillot, Louis (1867), *Les Odeurs de Paris*, Paris, Balitout.

Victoria, Queen (1930), *The Letters of Queen Victoria, 3rd series: a selection from her majesty's correspondence and journal between the years 1886 and 1901*, 3 vols., London: Murray.

Vigarello, Georges (1997), 'The Tour de France', in Pierre Nora, ed., *Realms of Memory: The Construction of the French Past, vol. 2, Traditions*, New York, Columbia University Press.

Vigié, Marc (1993), *Dupleix*, Paris, Fayard.

Villepin, Dominique de (2002), *Les Cent-Jours ou l'esprit de sacrifice*, Paris, Perrin.

Vincent, Rose, ed. (1993), *Pondichéry, 1674–1761: l'échec d'un rêve d'empire*, Paris, Autrement.

Vion, Marc (2002), *Perfide Albion! Douce Angleterre?*, Saint-Cyr-sur-Loire, Alan Sutton.

Vizetelly, Ernest Alfred (1904), *Emile Zola, Novelist and Reformer: An Account of His Life and Work*, London, Bodley Head.

Voltaire, François-Marie Arouet de (1785), *Du théâtre anglais (Appel à toutes les nations d'Europe)* in vol. 61, *Oeuvres Complètes de Voltaire*, 92 vols., Kehl, Société littéraire-typographique.

Voltaire, François-Marie Arouet de (1946), *Lettres philosophiques*, ed. F.A. Taylor, Oxford, Blackwell.

Voltaire, François-Marie Arouet de (1966), *Siècle de Louis XIV*, 2 vols., Paris, Flammarion.

Voltaire, François-Marie Arouet de (1992), *Candide and Other Stories*, trans. R. Pearson, London, Everyman.

Waddington, Richard (1899), *La guerre de sept ans: histoire diplomatique et militaire*, 5 vols., Paris, Firmin-Didot.

Wahnich, Sophie (1997), *L'impossible citoyen: l'étranger dans le discours de la Révolution française*, Paris, Albin Michel.

Walpole, Horace (1904), *Letters of Horace Walpole*, trans. C.B. Lucas, London, Newnes.

Walton, Whitney (1992), *France at the Crystal Palace: Bourgeois Taste and Artisan Manufacture in the Nineteenth Century*, Berkeley, University of California Press.

Ward, Marion (1982), *Forth*, Chichester, Phillimore.

Watkin, David (1984), *The Royal Interiors of Regency England*, London, Dent.

Watson, D.R. (1974), *Georges Clemenceau*, London, Eyre Methuen.

Watson, George (1976), 'The revolutionary youth of Wordsworth and Coleridge', *Critical Quarterly*, 18, pp. 49–65.

Watt, Donald Cameron (2001), *How War Came*, London, Pimlico.

Watt, Katie (1999), 'Contemporary British Perceptions of the Paris Commune, 1871', Cambridge, historical tripos part II dissertation.

Wawro, Geoffrey (2000), *Warfare and Society in Europe, 1792–1914*, London, Routledge.

Weber, Eugen (1962), *Action Française: Royalism and Reaction in Twentieth-Century France*, Stanford, Stanford University Press.

Weber, Eugen (1976), *Peasants into Frenchmen: The Modernization of Rural France, 1870–1914*. London, Chatto & Windus.

Weber, Eugen (1986), *France Fin de Siècle*, Cambridge, Mass., and London, Harvard University Press.

Weber, Eugen (1991), *My France: Politics, Culture, Myth*, Cambridge, Mass., Harvard University Press.

Weber, Eugen (1995), *The Hollow Years: France in the 1930s*, London, Sinclair Stevenson.

Weber, Jacques (2002), *Les Relations entre la France et l'Inde de 1673 à nos jours*, Paris, Les Indes Savantes.

Webster, C.K. (1921), *British Diplomacy, 1813–1815*, London, G. Bell.

Webster, Paul (2001), *Fachoda*, Paris, Félin.

Weinburg, Gerhard L. (1994), *A World at Arms: A Global History of World War II*, Cambridge, Cambridge University Press.

Weiner, Margery (1960), *The French Exiles, 1789–1815*, London, John Murray.

Wells, Roger (1986), *Insurrection: The British Experience 1795–1803*, Gloucester, Alan Sutton.

Welsh, Jennifer M. (1995), *Edmund Burke and International Relations: The Commonwealth of Europe and the Crusade against the French Revolution*, London, Macmillan.

Wentworth, Michael (1984), *James Tissot*, Oxford, Clarendon Press.

Whatmore, Richard (2000), *Republicanism and the French Revolution: An Intellectual History of Jean-Baptiste Say's Political Economy*, Oxford, Oxford University Press.

Wheatley, Edmund (1997), *The Wheatley Diary*, Gloucester, Windrush Press.

Wheeler (1951), *The Letters of Private Wheeler*, London, Michael Joseph.

Whiteley, John (2004), 'Auguste Rodin in Oxford', *The Ashmolean Magazine*, summer 2004.

Whiteman, Jeremy J. (2003), *Reform, Revolution and French Global Policy, 1787–1791*, Aldershot, Ashgate.

Williams, David (1979), 'Voltaire's war with England: the Appeal to Europe, 1760–1764', in *Voltaire and the English, Studies on Voltaire and the Eighteenth Century*, no. 179, Oxford, Voltaire Foundation.

Wilson, Kathleen (1995), *The Sense of the People: Politics, Culture and Imperialisms in England, 1715–1785*, Cambridge, Cambridge University Press.

Wilson, Kathleen, ed. (2004), *New Imperial History: Culture, Identity and Modernity in Britain and the Empire, 1660–1840*, Cambridge, Cambridge University Press.

Wilson, Keith M. (1994), *Channel Tunnel Visions, 1850–1945: Dreams and Nightmares*, London, Hambledon Press.

Wilson, Keith M. ed. (1995), *Decisions for War, 1914*, London, UCL Press.

Wilson, Keith M. (1996), 'Henry Wilson and the Channel Tunnel before and after the Great War: an example of policy and strategy going hand in hand', *Franco-British Studies*, 22, pp. 83–91.

Wilson, Keith M., ed. (2001), *The International Importance of the Boer War*, Chesham, Acumen.

Winch, Donald, and O'Brien, Patrick K., eds. (2002), *The Political Economy of British Historical Experience, 1688–1914*, Oxford, Oxford University Press.

Wolf, John B. (1968), *Louis XIV*, London, Gollancz.

Woodbridge, John D. (1995), *Revolt in Prerevolutionary France: The Prince de Conti's Conspiracy against Louis XV, 1755–1757*, Baltimore, Johns Hopkins University Press.

Woolf, Virginia (1924), *Mr Bennett and Mrs Brown*, London, L. and V. Woolf.

Young, Hugo (1998), *This Blessed Plot: Britain and Europe from Churchill to Blair*, London, Macmillan.

Young, Robert J. (1986), *France and the Origins of the Second World War*, London, Macmillan.

Young de la Marck, David de (2003) 'De Gaulle, Colonel Passy and British intelligence, 1940–42', *Intelligence and National Security*, 18, pp. 21–40.

Index

Navy, French: in eighteenth century 10, 17, 23, 26, 112, 133, 157–8, 242, costs 260, failures to invade 141–2, 170–71, 251, problems of command 257, 262, technical lag 259–60, timber shortages 259; in 1940 562ff; in twenty-first century 675ff

Navy, Spanish 156, 170–71, 242

Necker, Jacques 51, 174, 187

negotiating styles 243, 342, 412–13, 462, 622; de Gaulle's 569, 623

Nelson, Horatio 81, 229, 231, 251, 253, 263, 297

Newcastle, Duke of 48, 118, 136

Newton, Isaac 55, 58–9

Nile, battle of the 229, 263, 341

Noailles, Marshal Maurice de 36, 42, 111, 119, 708 n. 72

North, Lord 174, 177–8, 180

Orange, principality of 14–15

Orléans, dukes of: Philippe (Regent) 32, 50; Louis Philippe Joseph ('Philippe Egalité') 95–6, 186–7, 212; sale of art collection 234. See also Chartres, Louis Philippe Joseph, Duc de; Louis-Philippe, King

Orpen, William 474, 480, 502

Oxford 76, 78, 215, 330, 414; drunken orgies 69; 1848 revolution celebrated 347; lost causes 40; male virgins 522; students rationed 230; welcomes Verlaine, Rodin 405; would not fight for king and country 530

Paine, Thomas 195ff, 208, 215, 233

Palais Royal 78, 95, 317

Palmerston, Viscount xxv, 79, 333–4, 337, 339–40, 343, 346ff, 353, 356–7, 361, 444

Pamela, Lady Fitzgerald (née Sims) 93, 711 n.114

Paris 73, 75ff, 316–17, 366ff, 399, 443; besieged (1870) 380–81; bohemia 395, 397; the boulevard 317–18, 400, 420–21; civil war (1871) 382ff; compared with London 73, 370–71; cultural centre 395ff; liberation (1944) 592–3; modernization of 370ff; 'vice' in 372, 380

Pâris family 52

parlements 129, 132, 135, 186

Parthenon 17, 235ff

Pau 318ff

Pearl, Cora 373–4, 380

Pétain, Marshal Philippe 490, 494, 543, 546, 557, 578; anglophobia 571; and 1940 defeat 560–61, 564ff; popularity 572

philosophes 86, 128, 132

physiocrats 64, 161

Pissarro, Camille 375–6

Pitt, William, the elder 129ff, 134, 136, 145, 160, 296

Pitt, William, the younger 132, 180, 183, 185–6, 194, 205, 622; in France 81; view of French Revolution 199–200; war 208, 220, 227–8; support for peace 230–31; Napoleonic wars 237, 244; plans for Europe 253, 274; death 253; assessment as war leader 253–4

Poincaré, Raymond 476, 488, 515ff, 537

Pompadour, Marquise de 44, 52, 64, 128, 131, 144, 157–8

Price, Richard 188, 194, 196ff

Priestley, Joseph 188, 194–5, 202; riots 201, 297,

Prior, Matthew xxv, 31–2

prisoners of war 261, 274ff

Pritchard, Rev. George 341ff

Proust, Marcel 396, 399, 401, 520

Prussia 123, 125. See also Germany

Pyrenees 79, 319

Quebec, siege of 138–9, 149

Quiberon Bay, battle of 141; landing 215, 221–2

RAF (Royal Air Force) 527, 535, 542, 546–7, 549ff, 557, 583–4, 589, 592; escapers 580–81; in twenty-first century 675ff

Raglan, Lord 285, 358

Rapin, Paul de 56, 58,

religious conflict 12ff, 18, 21, 31, 37, 98, 127–8, 171–2, 295–6; decline of 76, 99

reparations, after First World War 507–8, 510, 512–13, 515–16

Resistance: in First World War 482–3; in Second World War 576ff, combat 589ff, contacts with Britain 585ff, politics 588. *See also* SOE

restaurants 76, 232, 400; origins 419; in Paris 419–20; in London 421

revolutions: 'Glorious' (1688) 18, 20ff, 25, 26, 42–3, 198; French Revolution (1789) 51, 107, 162, 171, beginnings of 185ff, attitudes towards England 189–90, British responses to 188–9, 193ff, 208, 297–8, values of 297; French Revolution (1830) 334; 1848 Revolutions 345ff

Reynaud, Paul 535, 626, 541, 549–50, 558

Rhineland: after First World War 506–7, 510, 517–18, 531, 535, 597; remilitarization of 527–8; after Second World War 607–8

Richardson, Samuel 5ff; *Paméla* 85, 94

Richelieu, Marshal Duc de 39ff, 123

Rimbaud, Arthur 388, 394, 398–9, 408

Rivarol, Antoine 152

Robespierre, Maximilien 190, 194, 202, 205, 212ff, 217, 233, 297, 299

Rochambeau, Comte de 173ff, 186, 206

Rodney, Adm. George 175, 178

Romanticism, British influences 320ff

Rousseau, Jean-Jacques 64, 85–6, 88, 94, 106–7, 453; in England 79ff; *Julie* 86–7; *Emile* 105–6

rugby 415–16, 417, 479, 594

Rwanda 674, 680

Saints, battle of the 178, 263

Salisbury, 3rd Marquess of 426, 436, 438, 462

salons 77, 103, 107

Scotland 1, 11, 20ff, 31, 36ff, 320–21; union with England 31. *See also* 'Forty-Five' rebellion

Shakespeare, William 59, 86–7, 108–10, 149, 600–601, 662; and Romantics 321ff; translations of 110, 324, 355, 601; untutored genius 108, 110, 449; violence in 70, 104, 109, 600

Shelburne, Earl of 161, 178ff. *See also* Lansdowne, 1st Marquess of

Shenstone, William 87–8

Sidney, Algernon 7

slave trade 32, 50, 115, 261; abolition of 269, 298, 337

slaves in American War of Independence 173

Smith, Adam 64–5, 79, 150, 181; French responses to 65, 704

Smollett, Tobias 70–71, 86, 99, 104

SOE (Special Operations Executive) 575, 584ff, 589, 592; agents 585

Somme, battle of the 29, 486ff

South Sea Company 50

Spain 2, 10, 27–8, 32, 44, 167, 342ff

Spears, Edward 469, 498, 523, 558

Spectator, The 55, 58

sport 104, 319, 394, 416ff, 425; British influence in 414ff; national regeneration and prestige 412ff, 417–18. *See also* football; rugby; cricket; horse racing

Stair, 2nd Earl of 37, 49

Sterne, Laurence 79, 99

Stuarts 8, 10, 11, 25, 27–8, 32, 36–7, 138, 222

Suez crisis 613ff; consequences 617–18

sugar 114ff, 143, 178, 228, 261, 268–9; beet sugar 271

Swift, Jonathan 55–6, 58, 68

Taine, Hippolyte 393, 407, 410–11, 415, 456

Talleyrand, Charles Maurice de 202–3, 238, 240, 252, 273, 297, 333–4, 420, 502, 639

taxation: British 47ff, 126, 160, 171, 345, income tax 269; French 51, 53, 129, 161

Tencin, Claudine de 32, 77

Tennyson, Alfred 351–2, 357, 363, 393, 399

Thatcher, Margaret 450, 603, 637, 639ff, 649–50, 659, 662, 670, 674–5, 706

Thicknesse, Philip 70, 72, 74

Thiers, Adolphe 303–4, 333, 335, 337, 379–80, 382

Thrale, Hester 67, 72, 76, 78, 105

Three Kingdoms 2, 5, 8, 10, 25, 42

Tissot, Jacques-Joseph (James) 376–7

Tocqueville, Alexis de 333, 336, 340, 344, 407, 410

Tories 20, 26–7, 32, 131, 462

Toulon, occupation of (1793) 220

trade: in eighteenth and nineteenth centuries, competition for 112, 114,

136, 144, 154, 180–81, 261, 268, mutual 184, during Napoleonic wars 270ff; in twentieth and twenty-first centuries 611, 620, 624, 643–4, 651, 666ff, 670, 704. *See also* sugar

Trafalgar, battle of 253, 255–6, 263, 593; bicentenary 692

travel and tourism 66–82, 103, 310, 319–20, 329ff, 372, 385–6, 397, 521, 662; costs 71–2, 329. *See also* migration

travel writings 67ff, 103

treaties: Rijswijk (1697) 27–8; Utrecht (1713) 32, 37, 50, 55, 149, 442; Aix-la-Chapelle (1748) 42–3, 117; Versailles (1756) 123; Paris (1763) 144, 154; Versailles (1783) 179–80; 'Eden Treaty' (1786) 184; Amiens (1802) 231–2, 241, 243, 274, 408; Chaumont (1814) 310; 'treaties of 1815', 348, 444; London (1839) 333, 464; commercial treaty (1860) 364–5; Versailles (1919) 508ff, 517; Locarno (1925) 516–17; Dunkirk (1947) 607; Brussels (1948) 607; North Atlantic (1949) 608; Paris (1951) 610; Rome (1957) 615, 618, 620ff; Single European Act (1986) 643–4, 651; Maastricht (1992) 648, 692

Tristan, Flora 331–2, 334, 388
Turgot, Anne-Robert 64, 161–2, 181
Turner, J.M.W. 233, 252, 305, 322, 375ff
Tussaud, Madame 233
twinning of towns 497

umbrellas 75, 96
United States of America 364, 599; abandons world leadership 510; in Second World War 577–8, 588, 590ff, 595, 599; postwar relations with Britain 606ff, 610–11, 615ff, 624, 626, 674–5, 683ff

Vallès, Jules 378, 386, 388
Vauban, Marshal de 10, 14, 24, 28
Vendée rebellion 219, 221–2, 224, 230, 298
Verdun, battle of 472, 487–8
Vergennes, Comte de 161ff, 167, 173ff, 177–8, 181–2
Verlaine, Paul 388, 394, 405
Versailles 8, 77, 90, 99
Victoria, Queen 337, 340–41, 343, 346, 355ff, 363, 378–9, 426, 438, 460; 'detestable' food 422

Villebois-Mareuil, Col. 432–3
Villeneuve, Adm. Pierre de 247, 251–2, 255, 257
Villepin, Dominique de 304–5, 684–5, 693
Vizetelly, Henry 402ff, 431
Voltaire, François-Marie Arouet de 29–30, 39ff, 54, 56ff, 62, 66, 69, 126, 128–9, 133, 135, 410; British visitors 79; and English language 149ff; and Shakespeare 59, 108ff, 323; *Candide* 58–9, 68, 117, 125; *Letters concerning the English Nation* 58ff

Waldegrave, Earl 37, 61
Wales, Edward Prince of 400ff, 422, 426, 433. *See also* Edward VII
Wales, George Prince of (Prince Regent) 96, 187, 199, 368
Wallace, Richard 380, 382, 388–9; Wallace Collection 159, 234, 389
Walpole, Horace 57, 77, 80, 87, 98, 130–31, 136, 151
Walpole, Robert 33, 50
Walsh, Anthony 38–9, 42
wars: Thirty Years War 8; Nine Years War 25, 27; Spanish Succession 25, 28; Jenkins's Ear 33; Austrian Succession 33, 37, 118; Seven Years War 51,79, 95, 99, 109, 119ff, 264, preparations and outbreak 120ff, political repercussions 127ff, 132–3, 154, 160–61, in North America 136–7, 142, in India 137, 142, consequences 143ff; American War of Independence 93, 95, 148, 160ff, French planning for 155, French intervention 164–5, 167, 173ff, peace negotiations 178–9, costs 171ff, 182–3, 266, consequences 172, 180–81, 186–7; French Revolutionary Wars 205ff, 227–8, involvement of Britain 208, 210, total war and terror 209–10, 265, civil wars 217–26, French victory 231–2, 241; Napoleonic Wars: outbreak 244–5, geopolitics of 266–7, economic warfare 268–74, 301, cost 274, in Peninsula 278–82, atrocities 279–80, 28, invasion of Russia 282, fall of France 284–5; Crimean War 355, 357ff, 420; Franco-Prussian 379ff, sympathy for France 381–2; Boer War 425, 432ff,